International
Encyclopedia of the
SOCIAL
SCIENCES

International Encyclopedia of the SOCIAL SCIENCES

DAVID L. SILLS EDITOR

VOLUME 15

The Macmillan Company & The Free Press

International
Encyclopedia of the
SOCIAL
SCIENCES

S

[CONTINUED]

SOCIOLOGY

The articles under this heading provide a broad introduction to the discipline of sociology: the history of sociology as an academic field; the major strands of thought that have contributed to the current body of theory; and an account of various early attempts in England and on the Continent to provide systematic quantitative knowledge about human society. All the major subfields of sociology are represented in the encyclopedia; for a list of articles relevant to sociology, consult the classified list of articles in the index volume.

I
THE FIELD

A commonly accepted definition of sociology as a special science is that it is the study of social aggregates and groups in their institutional organization, of institutions and their organization, and of the causes and consequences of changes in institutions and social organization. The major units of sociological inquiry are social systems and their subsystems; social institutions and social structure; and social aggregates, relationships, groups, and organizations.

Sociological units. The most inclusive sociological unit is the *social system*, which is constituted by the interaction of a plurality of actors whose relations to each other are mutually oriented by institutions. A *society* is an empirical social system that is territorially organized, with its members recruited by sexual reproduction within it, and that persists beyond the life-span of any individual member by socializing new members into its institutions. Any social system has subsystems that are partial systems functionally related to it, such as human ecological systems and kinship, legal, educational, and ideological or religious subsystems.

Social institutions are general patterns of norms that define behavior in social relationships. Institutions define how people ought to behave and legitimate the sanctions applied to behavior. Contract is a good example of a social institution: as an institution, it consists of quite general norms that regulate entry into and the consequences of contractual agreements; it prescribes neither who shall enter into such agreements nor—within certain institutionally defined limits—what the agreements shall contain. Finally, *social structure*, or *social morphology*, is the integration and stabilization of social interaction through an organization of statuses and roles, such as age, sex, or class.

Sociologists are primarily interested in human beings as they appear in *social interaction*, i.e., as actors taking account of one another in their behavior. The major systems or units of interaction that interest sociologists are *social groups*, such as the family or peer group; *social relationships*, such as social roles and dyadic relationships; and *social organizations*, from such formal or bureaucratic organizations as governments, corporations, and school systems to such territorial organizations as communities or to the schools, factories, churches, etc., that are components of communities. Although sociologists are principally concerned with human beings in social interaction, they are also concerned with *social aggregates*, or *populations*, in their institutional organization.

Sociologists are interested in the analytical prop-

1

erties of these sociological units and treat the relationships among them as problematic. Thus, they are interested in such properties of the processes of institutionalization as legitimation, consensus, and stratification. They concern themselves with elements of social relationships, such as power and dominance, or elements of interaction, such as coercion and reciprocity. They investigate the properties and processes of groups or organizations, such as their capacity to take collective action toward goals, as in the sanctioning of deviant behavior or the allocation of organizational resources.

Types of sociological theory. The theories of sociology make problematic the relationships among the analytical properties of the units. The character of the theory in each case defines the problematics. For example, ecological theory in sociology is concerned primarily with the causal interconnections in the human ecological complex: technological accumulation at an accelerated rate, exploitation of the environment, demographic transition, and organizational revolution (Duncan 1961; Duncan & Schnore 1959). A macrosociological theory, such as that of Talcott Parsons, originally made problematic how various value and motivational orientations of actors are institutionalized and organized as social systems (1951; 1938–1953). In later elaborations of his theory Parsons has focused more on the internal dynamics of social systems, though he has largely neglected to make external relationships problematic (1960; 1966).

The writings of early sociologists either consisted largely in speculation or were grand philosophical achievements of a synthetic sort that did not lend themselves to the development of a body of knowledge which was cumulative and also met the canons of science. Over time, most sociologists have come to use what Robert K. Merton (1949) called theories of the middle range. These are theories that include a limited number of interrelated concepts from which one may derive hypotheses that can be investigated through empirical research. An example from Merton's own writings is that of reference group theory ([1949] 1957, chapter 8).

Schools of sociology. The history of sociology discloses several major strategies for dealing with its theoretical and methodological problems. To a degree these strategies represent schools within sociology, but the lines are by no means firmly drawn. Human ecologists and demographers are concerned with problems that involve the investigation of social aggregates. They are particularly interested in the morphological or structural characteristics of these aggregates, such as age, sex, race, education, and income. Another school, often characterized as formal sociology, is associated particularly with the work of Georg Simmel and of phenomenologists such as Alfred Vierkandt; more recently, it has included some investigators of small groups. The emphasis in formal sociology is on studying societal forms, particularly forms of interaction or association, such as dyadic relationships. Formal sociology focuses on the "essence" of phenomena in which form is a principle of individuation and organization. The primary goal of this type of sociology is description of human groups and processes in social relationships. A third school is characterized as historical–interpretative sociology; its emphasis is as macroscopic as that of formal sociology is microscopic. Attempts are made to describe the general features of the history of man, to delineate the different spheres of the historical world, and to understand ideas as the expression of historical periods or events. The major works of Max Weber and the German historical school, particularly Weber's methodological writings, have served as a model for contemporary historical sociology (Aron 1935). However, most writing in contemporary sociology focuses on relational properties among persons as social actors (an emphasis characteristic of much work in social psychology) or on the relationship among properties of institutions and organizations in societies or social systems (an emphasis that practically defines the field of social organization).

Sociology and the other social sciences

The relationship of sociology to the other social or behavioral sciences is much debated. Is sociology, as Comte would have had it, the queen of the social sciences—a general social science of societies? Or is it a more specialized social science, one that systematizes problems that can be defined as sociological, as distinct from economic, psychological, or cultural?

The most systematic modern attempt to resolve this question is found in the writings of Parsons (1938–1953; 1951; 1960; 1966). In Parsons' view, sociological theory is an aspect of the theory of social systems and sociology is thereby defined as a special social science. Sociology is concerned "... *with the phenomena of the institutionalization of patterns of value-orientation in the social system,* with the conditions of that institutionalization, and of changes in the patterns, with conditions of conformity with and deviance from a set of such patterns and with motivational processes in so far as they are involved in all of these" (1951, p. 552).

The other major theory of social systems, according to Parsons, is that of economics; it is "... concerned with the phenomena of rational decision-making and the consequences of these decisions within an institutionalized system of exchange relationships" (*ibid.*, p. 550). Within this framework, political science is viewed as a synthetic rather than a special social science, constructed as it is around a restricted set of variables concerned with political power rather than around a scientifically distinctive analytical scheme.

Parsons, furthermore, has defined the theory of the social system as but one of three analytical sciences of action, the other two being the theory of personality and the theory of culture. The theory of cultural systems is the particular province of anthropology, and that of personality systems is generic to psychology [*see* SYSTEMS ANALYSIS, *article on* SOCIAL SYSTEMS; *see also* Parsons & Shils 1951; Parsons 1951, chapter 12].

Sociologists work on problems that are related to the subject matter of other disciplines, both humanistic and scientific. For the most part, however, these problems fall within fields that are part of sociology, and they are dealt with from a sociological perspective. Thus, although problems of knowledge are indeed treated by the sociology of knowledge, and although the sociology of knowledge is in an important sense a branch of epistemology, it has not developed as an interstitial field between sociology and philosophy. The same may be said of such fields as historical sociology and sociolinguistics, as they have so far been developed within sociology.

Historically, some disciplines did emerge as interstitial to their parent disciplines. The most notable cases in the history of sociology are human ecology (or human geography, as it is called in some countries), demography, and social psychology. Social psychology, a subfield of both psychology and sociology, is concerned primarily with personalities and motivational processes as they relate to the institutional organization of societies. Demography and human ecology are somewhat different, perhaps not qualifying fully as interstitial disciplines. Human ecology broadly conceived as an aspect of ecosystem theory is interstitial to the environmental and social sciences. The development of a theory of the ecosystem, however, is in a rudimentary state; for that reason much of the work in human ecology is carried on within the separate environmental and social sciences rather than in any border discipline. Work in demography is carried on largely by sociologists and economists, though more recently biomedical scientists have joined them in a synthetic field that is becoming known as population studies.

The fields of sociology

There is no altogether rational division of sociology into fields of inquiry that are both derived from a general sociological theory and susceptible to relatively independent investigation and formulation as separate bodies of knowledge. Lacking a commonly accepted sociological theory that would permit such rational division of sociology, sociologists have developed fields of interest around the major units of sociological inquiry described above and around certain social problems, such as juvenile delinquency, that have come to constitute fields through being viewed in a sociological perspective.

Comte's division of sociology into "social statics" and "social dynamics" dominated much of the writing of Herbert Spencer and Lester F. Ward (see especially Ward 1883, volume 1). With the emergence of sociology as an academic discipline, there was a tendency, particularly in American sociology, to classify it in a more detailed fashion into subject-matter fields as a means of organizing the curriculum. At the same time, leading scholars —particularly when, like Durkheim, they served as editors of major journals—felt called upon to divide sociology into "fields" in which a sociological perspective was applicable.

The 1902 volume of *L'année sociologique* presented such a scholarly classification, by Durkheim and his editorial colleagues, of publications in sociology. They subdivided sociology into the fields of general sociology, religious sociology, juridical and moral sociology, criminal sociology and moral statistics, economic sociology, social morphology, and a miscellaneous group including aesthetic sociology, technology, language, and war. The editors noted that the *Zeitschrift für Socialwissenschaft,* the *Rivista italiana di sociologia,* and the *Vierteljahrschrift für wissenschaftliche Philosophie und Soziologie* utilized some other categories. In the *Zeitschrift,* for instance, one finds mass and individual psychology, medicine and hygiene, social history and social jurisprudence, and social philosophy and social ethics. The *Rivista* included politics, social psychology, and demography, while the *Vierteljahrschrift* included psychology and the science of language, aesthetics, and education. Quite clearly, by 1902 sociologists had identified most of what were to become the major fields of scholarly interest in sociology during the next five decades.

These fields of sociology were not given anywhere near equal attention in every country, nor did sociologists in any country give more than token attention to some of these fields until quite recently. Interesting and important contrasts developed among the countries in the attention given to various fields. Some fields that developed quite early in the European countries were given only token attention in the United States until World War II, after which they developed quite rapidly. Among the more important of these were political sociology, the sociology of law, and the sociology of religion. Among the fields that still receive only occasional attention in American sociology, as contrasted with the attention given them in some European countries, are the sociology of the creative and performing arts, of sport, and of language. Apart from shaping the development of the sociology of science, American sociologists have done little work in the sociology of knowledge.

American developments before 1940. The rather late development in American sociology of some of the fields listed above is the result of a variety of factors, two of which stand out as particularly important. First, American universities separate sociology more sharply from some other academic disciplines than do European universities. This is particularly notable in the case of law, which in the United States is taught in professional schools quite separate from the faculties of philosophy, the sciences, and the humanities. Indeed, prior to 1940, American sociologists had little contact with professional schools other than those of social work and education. Furthermore, in their drive toward status as scientific disciplines, all of the social sciences in American universities were increasingly divorced from the humanistic disciplines and the arts. Even today this is true, so that American sociologists undertake little work on the sociology of the creative or performing arts [*see, however,* CREATIVITY, *article on* SOCIAL ASPECTS; FINE ARTS, *article on* THE RECRUITMENT AND SOCIALIZATION OF ARTISTS]. Since history, more often than not, is defined as a humanistic discipline, American sociology has been ahistorical. No doubt the fact that many American sociologists took the natural science model of investigation as a desideratum also led to the separation of sociology from both history and the humanities, including philosophy.

A second major factor accounting for the failure of American sociology to develop some of the problems of concern to European sociologists has been the deliberate neglect of problems of value—of how values are institutionalized and how they are organized in American or other societies. While there were exceptions, such as the studies of immigrant groups by W. I. Thomas and Florian Znaniecki (1918–1920), American sociologists generally took values for granted and were inclined to make values problematic only in the limited sense that they believed a truly scientific sociology had to be "value-free." Furthermore, they did not generally think of values as amenable to empirical investigation except when they took the form of personal attitudes or opinions. Comparative studies of values in belief systems such as the ideological, religious,

and legal systems were therefore unlikely to be investigated.

To be sure, American sociologists gradually began to investigate problems in some of these fields, but largely through other generic interests in sociology, such as occupations and professions or the social organization of work, rather than through an interest in comparative institutions or systems. Thus, the sociology of law began largely with studies of lawyers; the sociology of medicine, with studies of doctors and the social organization of doctor–patient relationships in hospitals; and the sociology of the arts through studies of musicians and writers.

American sociology, however, was almost alone in its attempts to develop research methodology as a special field. Although few of the major techniques for gathering and analyzing data were invented by American sociologists, these techniques were readily accepted as part of the sociological curriculum and their use became a criterion—sometimes mistakenly applied—for evaluating the state of "the science." Recently, American sociologists have rather self-consciously developed the field of mathematical sociology, noteworthy more for its attempts to formalize models of behavior or organization by mathematical means than for its theoretical or substantive contributions to sociology.

Although in European countries human geography continued to develop, it grew primarily outside of sociology [*see* GEOGRAPHY]. American sociologists, however, developed human ecology, which has much in common with human geography. The only comparable development in Europe was that of social morphology in France, under Durkheim and his disciple Maurice Halbwachs.

Up to 1940 American sociology appeared to contain a substantial number of fields of inquiry in addition to sociological theory and methods of research. One cluster included community study, with human ecology, rural sociology, and urban sociology as major divisions. Another was that of social problems, with race relations, poverty and dependency, and juvenile delinquency being important specialties. Social psychiatry emerged as a special field with a strong interest in mental health; now it arouses considerably less interest and is regarded as a part of social psychology. Demography and the family were the other major areas of interest during the period before 1940. Sociology curricula also included courses that covered rather broad interests—the main courses of this kind were social institutions, social organization, and social change; after 1945 the subject matter of these courses was integrated with new special fields.

Fields in modern American sociology. The development of fields of interest in sociology may be viewed as a problem in the sociology of knowledge. While problem finding in sociology undoubtedly is a result of the growth of theory and method, it also is subject to social determinants within the society (Merton [1949] 1957, pp. ix–xxiv). The problems of the immigrant in American society, and more recently of the Negro minority, undoubtedly influenced the development of the field of race and ethnic relations within American sociology more than did the theory of culture contact or intergroup relations. Similarly, the strong interest in ideology within European political sociology and the dominance of Marxist sociology in the east European countries and the Soviet Union are intimately connected with changes in the political systems of those countries. The importance of historical conditions and events in determining the fields and problems of sociology undoubtedly has been far greater than any influence from the cumulative development of the science. The resources available in any society for the investigation of given problem areas naturally affect the relative growth of specialties in any science, but these resources are allocated according to the historical significance of the problem areas.

The number of special areas of inquiry in American sociology has grown so large that a typical program of the American Sociological Association includes papers in some forty areas. The National Register of Scientific and Technical Personnel in the United States lists 53 specialties within sociology. But these specialties are usually grouped into a much smaller number of broad fields of inquiry. The emerging organization of the discipline can be described as follows: (1) sociological theory and methodology; (2) social organization, including comparative institutions, comparative social organization, and comparative social structure (or, as it is sometimes called, social morphology); (3) social groups. Demography, human ecology, and social psychology continue as major interstitial disciplines with strong programs in academic departments of sociology or as joint programs with the departments of other sciences. There remains a strong interest in what now is generally called applied sociology, including social planning and social problems.

Specialties within sociology are increasingly likely to derive their core problems from sociological theory (Faris 1964; March 1965). There is also less separation between theory and methodology. More and more, sociologists who work either in the interstitial fields or in applied sociology define the problematics of their specialties in terms of generic problems of sociological interest (Lazarsfeld et al. 1967). The work of sociologists today in criminology, for example, no longer covers the entire field. Rather, it focuses on the sociology of crime: problems of interaction between victims and offenders, socialization into delinquent and criminal behavior, sanctions and the formal organization of sanctioning systems, and the differential social risks of and opportunities for crime that are structured into social systems. Within social psychology, sociologists have turned their interests to the more generic problems of role socialization—the relationship of social structure and organization to personality and of social institutions to personality systems—and to explanations of conformity and deviant behavior. Human ecologists are giving major attention to organized communal networks, to the division of labor and its stratification, and to the growth and organization of technology. Within demography, sociologists have turned increasingly to the questions of how social institutions and social structure help to determine the basic processes of fertility, mortality, and morbidity, as well as the secondary processes of migration and the structural differentiation of the labor force. Both formal and comparative demography are growing as areas of specialization.

Within these major divisions of sociology, the fields of comparative institutions and comparative social organization have not yet been subdivided into distinct analytical areas. Some analytical organization is apparent; it derives either from an interest in some major analytical properties of the units of social organization or of institutions, or from an interest in some set of problems in institutions and institutional organization. Interest in social change, for instance, may be reflected in the study of collective behavior and social movements or in the study of the social and economic development of the new nations. Specialization in social stratification or occupations and professions derives from the more generic interest in social structure or morphology. Formal or bureaucratic organization has emerged as a specialty in comparative social organization.

The formidable task of mastering the literature on institutions and their organization, together with the social organization of academic inquiry and training, has led to a whole series of fields of specialization focusing on particular institutions and their organization into subsystems of societies. Among the more prominent of such special fields are economy and society, political sociology, industrial sociology, and the sociology of education, of religion, of medicine, of law, of leisure and sport, and of science. Set somewhat apart is the sociology of knowledge, with its strong roots in epistemology as well as in sociology.

There is growing interest as well in certain synthetic areas that may emerge as interstitial disciplines. Among these are sociolinguistics, the sociology of culture (as in the study of popular culture), and the field of mass communication and public opinion. Applied sociology includes the traditional areas of criminology and juvenile delinquency, and areas of more recent origin, such as mental health, social gerontology, and poverty and dependency. Following a period during which there was a shift from an emphasis on social reform, there has arisen a growing interest in empirical research related to the problems and policies of formal organizations. Accordingly, research undertaken with practical applications in view can now be found in almost all major fields of sociology (Gouldner & Miller 1965).

The origins of sociology as a science

Sociology as a more or less systematic body of knowledge emerged late among the scientific disciplines. The major problems in sociological theory —broadly conceived—recur in the writings of learned men of all periods. They relate to the nature of man as it is influenced by group behavior and by the social order in general. But it was not until late in the nineteenth century that attempts were made to organize the problematics of sociology into a science, either in the general sense of a science of society as a system with its own principles of organization and change or in the more specific sense of a systematic attempt to describe and explain how values and norms enter into social organization, how institutions are organized in societies, or how societies and their organized subsystems change.

The emergence of sociology among the sciences is itself treated as problematic within sociology or, more precisely, as a problem in the sociology of knowledge. The preconditions for its emergence can be traced both to currents of thought that began with the Enlightenment and to social changes in the nineteenth century that generated both social problems and reform movements. These developments placed the nature of societies and their change in a problematic light.

In his concise account of the history of sociology in the *Encyclopaedia of the Social Sciences*, R. M. MacIver stated: "The rise of sociology comes with the perception that no one order of social phenomena is adequate to comprehend, directly or indirectly, the manifold activities, processes and trends

of society, a perception which itself was advanced by the increasing range and complexity of social relationships which began with the era of modern civilization" (1934, p. 235). Thus, the rise of sociology as a distinct discipline did not parallel in any exact sense its rise as a scientific discipline, which depended not only on the recognition that societies are systems with their own principles of organization and change but also upon the application of scientific method and techniques of investigation that are appropriate, if not unique, to the empirical study of societies.

Both of these concerns were stated in a general way by Comte in his *Cours de philosophie positive* (1830–1842) and his *Système de politique positive* (1851–1854). Yet Comte was more the godfather than the progenitor of sociology, providing only its name and, in positivism, a philosophy that helped shape the discipline as a science. In fact, Comte's conception of sociology as both a general and a special social science and his definition of its problematics are now primarily of historical interest. His major concern was with the political and practical reorganization of society conceived of as the totality of human experience and thought. He believed more in the evolution of the human mind than in the evolution of societal forms and processes. He therefore sought to advocate rather than to prove that the application of what he called positivistic methods would establish that the evolution of the human mind follows definite laws.

Sociology emerged as a special discipline among the social sciences toward the end of the nineteenth century. To attribute its rise to a particular historical circumstance or to the writings of a particular man is somewhat arbitrary. Nonetheless, one can argue strongly that sociology as a special science of society had its origins in France, and that the sociologist who contributed the most to its emergence was Émile Durkheim.

The tradition of social research. Charting the rise of sociology as a special social science discipline in the nineteenth century, we find that two major traditions of scholarship coalesced in Durkheim's work. One of these was a tradition of empirical research; the other, the development of abstract conceptions of society.

There were two major elements in the tradition of empirical social research. The first of these to emerge was the collection and quantification of social data that were relevant to matters of the state —an early beginning of the policy sciences [see CENSUS; GOVERNMENT STATISTICS; VITAL STATISTICS]. The second, though it did not eschew quantification, was more concerned with the observation of social life and the development of techniques for gathering as well as analyzing social data (Lazarsfeld 1961).

The tradition of quantification in social research originated with the English "political arithmeticians," notably John Graunt and William Petty, and with the development in Belgium and France of *statistique morale*. The object of political arithmetic, as its name implies, was to obtain descriptive statistics for use in public policy and administration. However, the rise of insurance systems and other commercial activities may have led to other than political needs for this kind of quantification (Lazarsfeld 1961, p. 279). Description of local and state populations was among the first statistical tasks to be undertaken systematically, so that the tradition of political arithmetic in England seems more directly linked to the development of modern demography than of sociology as a special science.

The second major development in the early history of quantification, namely, *statistique morale*, is usually attributed to the Belgian, Adolphe Quetelet. But while Quetelet gained a larger audience than any other man associated with *statistique morale*, claims that he was the first in the field can be disputed. The concept of *statistique morale* and much statistical work not only on crime but also on suicide, illegitimacy, and similar phenomena appear in the work of André de Guerry de Champneuf, director of the Department of Criminal Justice in the French Ministry of Justice from 1821 to 1835 (see Guerry 1833). Work along the same lines was done also by Jean Baptiste Fourier and André de Chabrol de Crousol; they contributed statistical studies during the period from 1821 to 1829 to the *Recherches statistiques sur la ville de Paris et le département de la Seine* (see Seine . . . 1821–1860). At the same time, the French physician Parent-Duchâtelet undertook research on public health that led to a series of publications of the same kind, the most famous being his study of prostitution (1834), which stands as one of the early contributions to human ecology as well as to moral statistics [see SOCIOLOGY, *article on* THE EARLY HISTORY OF SOCIAL RESEARCH].

But even if we abandon the attempt to settle claims to priority, we must conclude from the available evidence that early in the nineteenth century considerably more empirical work in *statistique morale* was under way in France than in Belgium. The attention this work attracted did much to acquaint all learned Frenchmen with quantitative empirical research into social facts. Parent-Duchâtelet, for example, was inspired to do ingenious work in collecting and analyzing data on the recruitment and social origins of Paris prostitutes. As a result of these early French developments, Durkheim was perhaps more familiar with the tradition of quantitative research represented by *statistique morale* than with the achievements of political arithmetic.

A second major branch of empirical research that clearly originated in France is that associated with the work of Frédéric Le Play. Though obviously interested in quantification, Le Play invented new techniques for both gathering and analyzing nonquantitative data. While Le Play is perhaps best known for his emphasis on the empirical observation of contemporary social life, particularly his studies of family budgets, he was much concerned with the development of social indicators and with the problems of classification that arise in the analysis of social data (Lazarsfeld 1961).

Despite Le Play's great originality, his work had no direct impact on the development of sociology as a special science in France. The main reason for this appears to lie in the fact that Le Play was as much linked with his own reform movement, which espoused a conservative view of society, as he was with social research. His followers founded a journal with the promising name of *Science sociale*, but they eventually divided into two camps, one clearly reformist and one identified more with Le Play's method. [*See the biography of* LE PLAY.] Durkheim meanwhile gained the dominant position in French sociology, in part perhaps because he was an influential member of the rising group of French intellectuals that had won in the Dreyfus affair.

The tradition of sociological theory. The other main tradition before Durkheim was that of sociological thought and, more specifically, the development of abstract conceptions of society, some of them very elaborate. Here I would list geographical determinists such as Friedrich Ratzel and H. T. Buckle, social Darwinists such as Herbert Spencer and W. G. Sumner, and organismic theorists such as A. Schaeffle, P. Lillienfeld, René Worms, and J. Novicow. Other outstanding figures, such as Engels and Marx, were more closely identified during their lifetimes with socialist doctrines or economic theories than with the development of sociology as such. Marx's influence in shaping sociological theory came after his death and consisted mainly in having presented Max Weber with a set of sociological problems, but also in the development of a Marxist sociology that has pursued a largely independent course [see MARXIST SOCIOLOGY].

Almost all of these early writers failed either to differentiate sociology as a special science of society or to make its scientific status problematic. Even though by the close of the nineteenth century most sociologists were writing essays arguing the case for sociology as a special science of society, it remained for Durkheim to state and document that case effectively by merging and making problematic the scientific elements in the two traditions I have mentioned.

Durkheim and scientific sociology. Many sociologists view Durkheim as having established scientific sociology through his quantitative empirical research on suicide, in which he approached suicide rates as sociological rather than as psychological phenomena. But it could as easily be argued that he established scientific sociology by his historical and nonquantitative research, for example, in his writings on religion. For Durkheim, method, not quantification, was the central issue. He sought both the theoretical problems that are fundamental to a study of human social organization and the method that is indispensable to such a study. Sociology, for Durkheim, was the study of *"social* facts," and it should not be forgotten that his first major work after completing his French and Latin theses was *The Rules of Sociological Method* [1895; *for a discussion of Durkheim's conception of social facts, see the biography of* DURKHEIM]. In his introduction to this work Durkheim made it explicit that he considered his predecessors as having failed to advance "beyond the vague generalities on the nature of societies, on the relations between the social and the biological realms, and on the general march of progress" ([1895] 1958, p. lix). Indeed, he went on to say:

Sociologists have been content, therefore, to compare the merits of deduction and induction and to make a superficial inquiry into the most ·general means and methods at the command of the sociological investigators. But the precautions to be taken in the observation of facts, the manner in which the principal problems should be formulated, the direction research should take, the specific methods of work which may enable it to reach its conclusions—all these remained completely undetermined. (*ibid.*, pp. lix–lx)

Whether Durkheim ever succeeded in making a case for sociology as a special science (let alone as the special synthesizing social science that he considered it to be) is, on the evidence of his essays about sociology and the social sciences, a debatable matter. Furthermore, he was clearly dissatisfied with his own attempts—so prominent among the contents of *L'année sociologique*—to classify the subject matter of the field. Yet he never gave up these attempts, whether they consisted in delineating sociology as the study of social morphology or, as they did later, in the analysis of society in terms

of shared systems of moral rules and values. As a result, his writings established the major problematics of modern sociology in both a theoretical and a methodological sense.

The study of social facts, Durkheim concluded, requires the genetic, or comparative, method. "Comparative sociology is not a particular branch of sociology; it is sociology itself, in so far as it ceases to be purely descriptive and aspires to account for facts" (*ibid.*, p. 139). What he did not foresee was that the debate on method was far from settled; not only would the old controversies continue but they would take new forms. Before long, sociologists would engage in often bitter controversy over the empirical methods most appropriate for sociological use, the status of sociology as a science, and the role of quantification in sociological research. The battle lines were soon drawn as polemical positions.

Early empirical studies

Before considering the whole controversy over sociological method, it may be helpful to review briefly the history of quantitative social research in various countries as it relates to the development of sociology. Though there is no comprehensive historical study of quantitative social research, either generally or relating specifically to sociology, a number of accounts have dealt with its rise and development in particular countries.

Germany. Oberschall (1965) has carefully documented that there was much empirical social research in Germany from 1848 to 1914, but that it lacked continuity and failed to become institutionalized either in the universities or even in such organizations as the Verein für Socialpolitik. Thus, quantitative research, despite attempts by Max Weber and other sociologists in the twentieth century, did not become part and parcel of the development of sociology in Germany. Oberschall adduced several arguments to account for this failure. He found the root cause in the German intellectual heritage: the prevalence of historicism and the legacy of idealist philosophy, which favored an intuitive and phenomenological approach to social phenomena. German sociology also did not succeed in developing a tradition of quantitative social research, partly because it was never institutionalized as a discipline and partly because academic sociologists such as Tönnies and Weber failed to overcome the hostile value climate of the university, the apathy of their colleagues, and lack of resources to further their attempts to establish empirical research as part of the university curriculum. Perhaps they failed also because their own attempts at such research were counted as failures, while their theoretical and historical studies were recognized as achievements.

France. The strong quantitative traditions of French demography and of the Le Play school have been reviewed by Lazarsfeld (1961). But the social reform elements in the Le Play school separated it in the long run from sociology as a special discipline, and the disciples of Le Play were rather more inclined to criticize their master than to develop his investigatory method and techniques. Nor did the Le Playists and their journal *Science sociale* ever become identified in any total sense with the French university system. This, too, must have contributed to the demise of the Le Play school.

It is not clear why Durkheim's quantitative work did not have more of an influence on the development of French sociology, since, apart from demographic studies, there was little in French sociology that was quantitative until the years after World War II. Even now, there is no dominant group in France that emphasizes quantification in sociology. There are several explanations, none entirely satisfactory. It is true that Durkheim did little important quantitative work during the years when the future French sociologists were being trained. But during this same period Maurice Halbwachs published a quantitative study of suicide that was more elegant, from a statistical point of view, than Durkheim's, and François Simiand branched into econometrics. However, the rapid development of ethnological research in French sociology and anthropology served to stifle the growth of a quantitative tradition.

England. The case of quantitative social research in England is somewhat different. Quantitative work of the kind associated since the late nineteenth century with Charles Booth and Seebohm Rowntree has continued to be done up to the present time, and has slowly but surely evolved into a tradition of social research, particularly through the development of the social survey. Beatrice and Sidney Webb, partly through the early association of Beatrice Webb with Charles Booth, assiduously fostered social research in England as a basis for public policy. During the early 1930s the Webbs wrote a text on methods of social research (1932) that emphasized quantitative as well as observational techniques of social investigation. The work of English statisticians in sampling affected social research in England before it had a similar impact in the United States. Social investigation in England nevertheless developed primarily outside the universities and quite independently of sociology. Indeed, a few government departments and private foundations accounted for nearly all of the empirical social research in England after 1930. Except

at the London School of Economics, where, through the influence of the Webbs, academic sociology fostered some quantitative social research, there was virtually no quantitative sociological research of any sort in British universities until the 1950s.

The United States.   It would have been difficult to foretell, at the end of the nineteenth century, that quantitative sociology was to have its greatest development in the United States. Indeed, it is not entirely clear even today why this should have been the case. The preconditions for such a development were not altogether favorable. Despite early attention to censuses of the population and to public accounting systems, both of which generated a plethora of statistics, there was perhaps less emphasis on empirical social research in the United States when sociology first gained academic status than there was during the same period in England, France, Germany, or Italy. Such early sociologists as Lester F. Ward, who came from a natural science background, showed little concern for empirical research. Others, such as Sumner, were primarily interested in making general cultural or historical comparisons after the manner of Spencer. Although Cooley's doctoral dissertation was a major empirical investigation of transportation, he was soon distinguished more for the art of introspection and reflective observation than for empirical research.

During this period, however, some statistical studies appeared under the auspices of academic sociology. The students of Franklin H. Giddings at Columbia University were introduced to statistics in their training. One of the early sociological dissertations at Columbia University was a statistical study by Adna F. Weber (1899) of the growth of cities in the world during the nineteenth century. The first volume of the *American Journal of Sociology* included an article on population statistics by Walter Willcox. It was only the first of a long series of articles in this area.

But more important than any single publication to the development of empirical sociology in the United States was the growing acceptance of academic sociology in the universities. Higher degrees necessitated the writing of both master's theses and doctoral dissertations. In sociology, these theses and dissertations soon became a reservoir of empirical research on contemporary social life. The studies carried out in fulfillment of degree requirements were not necessarily quantitative, nor did they at first usually involve quantitative analysis. Nevertheless, they were empirical in the broad sense that they involved original investigation of some aspect of social life. Although attempts usually were made to ground them in some general theory of social life, they tended to build more on the literature of previous investigations, generating a genuine tradition of empirical research, albeit one that did not result in the orderly accumulation of a body of scientific knowledge. Many of these early empirical studies were closely tied to movements for social reform and social progress in American society, and they did not conform to any model of comparative research. More often than not, they dealt with but a single case—a community, an organization, a social movement.

The debate over sociology as a science

As sociology evolved in the United States, there developed an almost obsessive concern with its status as a science. There were those who would make it one and those who argued it could not be one. Polemics on each side may have been equally heated, but it was a somewhat unequal contest because the "scientific" group vindicated its position by fostering a strongly empirical tradition that increasingly succeeded in quantifying social data and inventing techniques of investigation. Their opponents, on the other hand, had little to offer but timeworn appeals to philosophical and historical tradition.

To be sure, American sociologists were not alone in this argument, but the lines were more sharply drawn in the United States, partly because it had more sociologists than any other country and partly because these sociologists were engaging in more and more empirical investigation. At times it began to seem almost as if it were more important to argue in favor of systematic empirical investigation than to use it in one's own work. Thus, the distinguished Italian sociologist Vilfredo Pareto in his *Trattato di sociologia generale* (1916) argued persuasively for the development of a sociology that eschewed all value judgments and relied instead on the logico-experimental method. Yet Pareto's discussion of "residues" and "derivations" as motivations in action, like his famous theory of the circulation of elites, rests primarily on social data of an illustrative and anecdotal nature.

From the 1920s on, debates among American sociologists about the appropriate methodology, methods, and techniques for sociological investigation began to overshadow controversies about the state of sociological theory. There soon developed a polarization of positions and of persons. On one side the principal spokesmen were the European-trained sociologists P. A. Sorokin and Florian Znaniecki. On the other were the American-trained sociologists whose principal spokesmen

were George Lundberg and Stuart Dodd, with support from W. F. Ogburn (who was less vocal, though a prolific author of quantitative studies) and his student Samuel A. Stouffer.

Sorokin and Znaniecki maintained that the social sciences are cultural sciences. Sociocultural phenomena are fundamentally different from physiochemical or biological phenomena, Sorokin argued, in that they have three major components: (1) immaterial, spaceless, and timeless meanings; (2) material objects that objectify the meanings; (3) human beings who bear, use, and operate these meanings with the help of material objects (Sorokin 1943, p. 4). The cause-and-effect models of the traditional sciences do not apply to sociocultural phenomena, he maintained, because the members of a sociocultural class are bound together by cultural meanings, not by their intrinsic properties. Hence, the sociocultural sciences require a special methodology, that of logico-meaningful causality, or the "integralist method" (*ibid.*, chapter 2). Znaniecki argued (1934, chapter 6) that the cultural sciences differ from other sciences because of the "humanistic coefficient," an infusion with culturally defined values and meanings. The appropriate method of sociology, he maintained, is analytic induction. [*See the biographies of* LUNDBERG; OGBURN; *and* STOUFFER *for discussion of their methodological positions.*]

This period also saw debate among sociologists concerning some of the classic philosophical issues. Were social concepts nominal or real? Did sociology eliminate free will by adopting social determinism? Were sociologists guilty of solipsism or of an irresponsible cultural relativism? Though many sociologists never comfortably resolved these issues, in practice their position was not unlike that of Ogburn. A minority, however, advanced arguments based on phenomenology and on the concept of *verstehen* [*see* VERSTEHEN *and the biographies of* HUSSERL; SCHUTZ].

The line that separated the major positions in the controversy over sociological method reflected not so much the issue of whether or not social data should be quantified as the choice of logical bases for determining cause-and-effect relationships among sociological variables. In the view of such critics as Sorokin, MacIver, and Robert S. Lynd, the quantitative school with its espousal of statistics (particularly methods of correlation) and of laboratory or natural experiments followed, in the view of its critics, the logic of J. S. Mill. And, in the opinion of these critics, the application of Mill's logic to social phenomena was an error. Thus Sorokin was not averse to the quantification of social data but to the logic implicit in certain models of quantitative analysis. To a substantial degree, MacIver raised similar doubts, maintaining that social causation, in contrast with physical and biological causation, involves the "socio-psychological nexus" (1942, chapter 14). The "quantifiers," as they came to be called, were attacked on other grounds, such as that they were testing simple tautological hypotheses or engaging in research on problems that were trivial in their implications for sociological theory. Lynd's *Knowledge for What?* (1939) is an outraged cry against these and other tendencies in American social science during the 1920s and 1930s.

Sociology since World War II

From 1945 on, the battleground shifted somewhat to arguments about the nature of operationism in sociology and the criteria for selecting analytical models in social investigation. These controversies never became as polemical as those of the prewar period. The entry of mathematical sociology on the scene, while met with skepticism by many sociologists, is hardly controversial within the discipline as a whole. Indeed, many sociologists today speak of interaction effects, for instance, in a statistical as well as a theoretical sense.

Perhaps the most important deterrent to controversy during this period was the decreasing separation between sociological theory and methodology. This was due in part to the monumental efforts of Parsons to bring sociological theory to bear upon sociological inquiry. Whether or not they accepted Parsons' theories, sociologists became more aware of how important theory was to their own investigations. Merton became the principal spokesman for the integration of sociological theory and empirical investigation. The new spokesmen for quantification in sociology, such as Paul F. Lazarsfeld and Louis Guttman, worked toward a closer integration of models of quantitative analysis with sociological theory. Above all, however, empirical research in sociology matured, so that an increasing number of studies derived more directly from problems in sociological theory than from immediate practical interests, and were far more sophisticated in their technical execution than the older studies had been. Certain major empirical investigations that addressed themselves to problems in sociological theory likewise exerted considerable influence in the immediate postwar period, much as the studies of Thomas and Znaniecki and those of the Chicago school under E. W. Burgess and Robert Park had done in the 1920s. The two-volume *The American Soldier* (Stouffer et al. 1949), the

culmination of several years' research by social scientists of the Research Branch of the United States Army, undoubtedly stands as a major model for its time of how sociological theory could be integrated with empirical quantitative investigation and analysis. In similar fashion the Indianapolis studies of social and psychological factors in human fertility, under P. K. Whelpton and Clyde Kiser (1943–1954), reoriented investigation in demography. Another very influential work of the period was *The Authoritarian Personality* (Adorno et al. 1950), which, with other major studies of prejudice, signaled a shift in social psychology to empirical study of the relationship between personality and social structure, an area that had been neglected after the work of Thomas and Znaniecki. Although subsequently these studies were subjected to some negative reassessment, they undoubtedly were very influential in shaping the investigations of postwar American sociologists.

Lack of receptivity to Marxism. Throughout the 1930s and 1940s Marxism and other socialist doctrines were a major influence on European sociology. The historical materialism of Marx may even have hindered the development of an empirical sociology in Europe during this period. Why was Marx less influential in the United States? To be sure, American sociology bore the marks of acquaintance with the problems of Marxian sociology. But even the writings of Ogburn, Lynd, and, later, of C. Wright Mills, which perhaps owed a greater intellectual debt to the writings of Marx than did those of most sociologists, were not Marxian sociology; and the influence of Weber and Durkheim on the development of American sociology continued to be far greater than that of Marx.

There are a number of reasons why a Marxian sociology never developed in the United States. It could readily be argued that the ideological and political climate of the United States was hostile to such a development; certainly, Marxism never received the encouragement in the United States that fostered its growth in other countries. But that would hardly explain the lack of receptivity to Marxism among those members of the sociological profession in America who considered themselves intellectuals. Perhaps, as Mills suggested, the social origins of American sociologists precluded such interests. Yet many American sociologists of Mills's generation became thoroughly acquainted with Marx and Marxist ideas in their youth. Perhaps more to the point is the fact that most American sociologists since the early 1920s have been more highly committed to an empirical sociology than to and ideological or theoretical position. They agree that some of the major problems of sociology are to be found in Marx—but only some, since for them a science of sociology is one in which theory can be tested because it supplies problems that are open to empirical investigation. Within this context, Marxian sociology and the whole tradition of historical materialism seems to them somehow old-fashioned.

The rise of scientific sociology. Has sociology, then, arrived at the status of a special science? Sociologists might assert that this is in itself a problem requiring sociological investigation. But there are bases for arguing that it has indeed achieved that status in American society. Moreover, it seems reasonably clear that, at least in some areas of sociology, knowledge gained through scientific investigation is cumulative (Berelson & Steiner 1964). Likewise, it is apparent that the decline in polemics about the respective importance of sociological theory and methodology has made it possible to integrate them more closely.

Furthermore, American sociologists and social psychologists in the postwar period have successfully developed research institutes that facilitate research training and scholarly investigation. The Bureau of Applied Social Research at Columbia University, the Institute for Social Research at the University of Michigan, with its Survey Research Center and Research Center for Group Dynamics, and the National Opinion Research Center at the University of Chicago have all grown into major centers of sociological research and have served as models for the development of smaller centers at other universities. Although the cost of doing research has increased sharply, the availability of research grants has enabled the sociologist to carry on his work as scientist [see RESEARCH AND DEVELOPMENT, *article on* FINANCING SOCIAL RESEARCH].

By 1960 most graduate students in sociology in American universities were receiving financial support comparable to that for students in the traditional sciences. Sociology, after a brief period of waiting, became a program division in the National Science Foundation and before long was admitted to the Behavioral Sciences Division of the National Research Council [see BEHAVIORAL SCIENCES]. By 1967, though membership in the prestigious National Academy of Sciences still awaited American sociologists, all other barriers to full professional status had been scaled.

The interpenetration of sociology with psychology in the area that has come to be known as social psychology has certainly affected the development of American sociology as a science. At the same time, psychology has so shaped American sociology

that the latter's methods of investigation are adapted to the study of individual actors rather than of the organizational context in which their acts take place. The other major models for quantification have come from demography and statistics. They, too, have shaped the character of sociology, since they are more easily applied to the study of social aggregates than to that of the relationships among properties of organizations. Research investigations in the fields of comparative institutions and social organization, therefore, often display less technical sophistication than those in the interstitial fields of demography and social psychology. The core of sociology, which is social institutions and their organization, is only now developing its own methods of investigation (March 1965).

Sociology as an academic discipline

Formal university instruction in sociology leading to a doctorate was offered first in the United States. Only slowly did sociology develop as a distinct discipline within the universities of other countries. In no country other than the United States has provision been made for formal instruction in sociology in academic departments or faculties throughout the system of higher education. Furthermore, only in the United States has formal instruction in sociology spread to precollege curricula.

To be sure, in the nineteenth century, universities outside the United States harbored instruction in sociology either through the system, once common in the universities of continental Europe, of permitting lectures by independent private scholars, or, on occasion, by creating a chair in sociology for a distinguished scholar. More often, however, a professor in economics, history, law, political economy, or philosophy offered instruction in "sociology"—though not usually by that name. Georg Simmel's only professorial appointment (which he was granted after 15 years as a *Privatdozent*) was in philosophy; those of Max Weber and Pareto, in economics. Durkheim was among the few Europeans in the nineteenth century to attain academic title as a sociologist; he was a professor of sociology and education at the University of Paris.

The United States. The first recorded instance of formal instruction in a course called sociology within the United States occurred in 1876 at Yale University, where William Graham Sumner offered such a course. However, until his death in 1910 Sumner was identified at Yale as a professor of political and social science. Luther L. Bernard (1909; 1945), Albion W. Small (1916), and Jessie Bernard (1929), in their discussions of sociological instruction in the United States, give accounts of the early courses in sociology and the beginning of academic departments. The period from 1889 to 1892 brought formal instruction in sociology to 18 colleges and universities in the United States (*ibid.*, chart 1). But it remained for the University of Chicago, when it opened in 1893, to establish the first academic department in the United States with work leading to the doctorate in sociology.

At the outset, instruction in sociology was more often established in joint departments than in departments devoted entirely to sociology. By far the most common alliance was made with economics, with history a distant second. Where sociology was not entitled to independent or joint departmental status, it was usually taught in departments of economics, history, philosophy, political science, or general departments of social sciences.

Despite the fact that the first department of sociology at the University of Chicago was a joint department of sociology and anthropology, anthropology was not generally linked with sociology in this early period. Actually, sociology in the United States gradually added anthropology to its offerings, so that by the 1920s there were a substantial number of departments of sociology and anthropology. By 1965, however, most of these academic partnerships had been dissolved as anthropology achieved status as a separate academic discipline.

By 1910 most colleges and universities in the United States were offering courses in sociology (Bernard 1945, p. 535). The actual establishment of separate departments of sociology occurred at a much slower rate. By 1960 most American universities and colleges had a department of sociology, although only 70 of them were offering a doctorate in sociology. The number of higher-degree programs in sociology in the United States, however, is probably greater than that in all other countries combined.

Two very important conditions appear to have led to the establishment of sociology as an academic discipline in the United States to a greater extent than in any other country. First, sociology in the United States was oriented toward pragmatic as well as theoretical and philosophical interests. Although the alliances formed between sociologists and social reformers were sometimes uneasy, there remained an overriding concern in American sociology with developing an empirical science based on research into social problems. The early issues of the *American Journal of Sociology*, in contrast with those of *L'année sociologique*, were as much devoted to applied sociology as to theoretical or scientific sociology.

A second major factor undoubtedly was the rapid growth of mass public education in the United States following the Civil War. With the rapid expansion of the universities, beginning in 1897, there undoubtedly was less pressure on university administrations to restrict professorships to established disciplines and on professors to compete for students, of whom there were many. Indeed, while there was some antagonism from the other social sciences in American, as in European, universities, the organization of American universities into largely autonomous departments made it possible for these departments to add instruction in sociology to their other offerings.

Equally important may have been the administrative organization of American universities. There is abundant evidence that the separation of administration from direct faculty control in the American university has facilitated the introduction of new subject matter, including sociology, into the curriculum. It may be significant, too, that during the period up to 1900 at least seven American university presidents were themselves the first to offer formal course work in sociology at their universities.

Another factor that may have been significant in the development of American sociology was a consequence of its institutionalization within the universities. This was the use, from quite an early date, of textbooks in sociology as the mainstay of college courses in the subject. The earliest of these textbooks was *An Introduction to the Study of Society*, by Small and Vincent of the department of sociology at the University of Chicago (1894). This was followed in 1896 by Franklin H. Giddings' *Principles of Sociology*. These and other such works influenced the training of large numbers of undergraduate students in sociology and helped to recruit some of them for graduate training in the field. The textbook is indeed a hallmark of undergraduate education in the United States. In the case of sociology, despite the seeming diversity in approaches of authors, textbooks represent an important element in standardizing the discipline.

American sociologists have carefully documented the development of academic sociology and its growth as a science and a profession. Among the major surveys are those by Small (1916), Wirth (1948), Odum (1951), Lundberg and others (1929), Ross (1945), Bernard and Bernard (1943), and Shils (1947). There is no single work that chronicles the rise and development of sociology as an academic discipline in other parts of the world, although *Twentieth Century Sociology* (Gurvitch & Moore 1945) and *Contemporary Sociology* (Rouček 1958) provide brief overviews of the origins and development of sociology in the major countries.

Other countries. The progress of instruction in sociology was not uniform in continental Europe, England, Russia, the Orient, or Latin America. From time to time chairs or positions were added at various universities, but up to World War II the largest concentrations of appointments in academic sociology were in the United States and Germany.

England. Despite the spectacular success attained by Herbert Spencer in popularizing sociology not only in England but also in the United States, where he was a best seller (Hofstadter 1944, chapter 2), and despite the monumental research achievements of Booth and Mayhew and the pioneering comparative analyses of Hobhouse and his associates (1915), academic sociology developed very slowly in England. Perhaps one of the major reasons for this was the successful establishment of social anthropology in the British universities, especially through the work of A. R. Radcliffe-Brown and Bronislaw Malinowski, the former defining the field as "comparative sociology" (MacRae [1948–1961] 1961, pp. 22–24).

The American sociologist Edward Shils (1960), in trying to account for the failure of sociology to establish itself in British universities during the first half of the twentieth century, has argued that the principal reason was the refusal of the British academic elite to raise questions about contemporary life in England. This elite, based in Oxford and Cambridge, is self-sustaining and exclusive; since its existence is founded on privilege and class prejudice, it actively discourages a sociology which would make for critical investigation of the society that nurtures it. British social anthropologists, on the other hand, had no such inhibitions about studying the "primitive" inhabitants of British colonial territories.

France. Although the precursors of sociology— Montesquieu and the Encyclopedists, the godfather of sociology Comte, and many of its early distinguished practitioners, such as Alfred Espinas and Frédéric Le Play—were French intellectuals, sociology was long distrusted in French academic circles. It remained for Durkheim to gain university status for sociology, first through a lectureship created for him at the University of Bordeaux in 1887 and then at the Sorbonne, to which he was called in 1902. Henri Peyre has suggested that the resistance to sociology in French academic circles was so intense that it probably accounts for the dogmatic fervor in Durkheim's writings (foreword in Durkheim [1892–1918] 1960, p. ix).

As in Britain—and, to a degree, in the United States during the first two decades of this century— academic sociology in France was closely associated with anthropology. In the United States, sociology dominated this partnership; in France, as in England, the reverse was true, and academic sociology evolved more slowly as a result. Nonetheless, Durkheim and his followers succeeded in establishing the academic credentials of certain sociological fields, the main ones of which were the sociology of education, of religion, of law, and of the economy (Gurvitch & Moore 1945). Although historical and philosophical sociology spread in this way among the several faculties of French universities, quantitative sociology has remained centered largely outside the universities in a number of institutes (most of which are, however, part of the French system of higher education). On the whole, therefore, there is a breach between the sociology of the academy and that of the institutes.

Germany. Sociology in Germany lacked from the outset the public recognition and support it had gained in England and the United States through being associated with the name of Spencer. While sociology early became the concern of scholars who were established in chairs at major German universities, it remained a humanistic rather than a scientific discipline, and never gained widespread support even among the humanists (König 1958, pp. 779–781).

Yet it was Germany, more than any other country, that in the nineteenth and twentieth centuries produced sociological writers who exercised a major influence on modern sociological theory—Marx, Tönnies, Simmel, Max Weber, and Karl Mannheim. The academic connections of this group of scholars with German universities were tenuous, however, for various reasons. Marx was an itinerant intellectual whose political views made it advisable for him to live in exile most of his life; Simmel held a regular professorship in philosophy at the University of Berlin only late in life, possibly because, like Marx, he was Jewish; Weber taught at Heidelberg only sporadically, largely because of illness; Mannheim became a refugee from Nazism and ended his career at the London School of Economics. Of this distinguished group, only Tönnies spent his entire academic career at a German university, in his case the University of Kiel. Although sociologists could be found in most German universities before 1933, they were as likely to hold chairs in political economy or philosophy as in sociology. No strong center of sociological inquiry emerged within the German university system because both the university traditions and organization and the nature of sociological inquiry among German sociologists tended to restrict academic sociology to a small circle composed of a professor and his assistants.

Undoubtedly the development of academic sociology in Germany suffered more from upheavals within the society than it did in other European nations. By 1933 most German universities were offering lectures and degree courses in sociology, so that a substantial number of young German sociologists had been trained by that time; almost all of them, however, fled within a few years of the rise of the Nazi government. Among those who had been major sociologists in Germany in the 1920s, only Leopold von Wiese remained in a German university throughout the Nazi period. He appears in no way to have cooperated with the Nazi regime.

Within 10 years of the defeat of the Nazi government, sociology re-established itself in the major universities of West Germany. The chairs were usually offered to sociologists who had fled during the Nazi period and who lacked strong training in quantitative sociology. With few exceptions, they have fitted rather comfortably into the philosophical and historical traditions of German sociology.

Israel. Among the smaller nations of the world, nowhere does sociology flourish as it does in Israel. Its growth is virtually simultaneous with the growth of the state of Israel. One of those towering intellects who transcend disciplinary boundaries, Martin Buber, established and headed the department of sociology at the Hebrew University [*see the biography of* BUBER].

Buber's leading student, Shmuel N. Eisenstadt, has developed a tradition of both theoretical studies and empirical research at the Hebrew University [*see* SOCIAL INSTITUTIONS]. There also is a strong school of applied sociology in Israel [*see* REFUGEES, *article on* ADJUSTMENT AND ASSIMILATION]. The American-trained sociologist Louis Guttman is an influential member of the Israel Institute of Applied Social Research in Jerusalem. Most Israeli sociologists have close ties with government officials and leaders; sociological investigation often is linked to policy decisions. No doubt some of this close alliance between sociology and social policy in Israel is due to the small size of the country, so that intellectuals in the universities are more closely linked to their government. But Hebrew traditions contribute to the relationship.

Russia. Sociology emerged as an academic discipline in Russia with the founding of a department of social sciences at Moscow that included a chair of sociology. The department was abolished in 1924 (Kozlova & Cheboksarov 1956). Despite some empirical research by younger Russian sociologists, sociology up to this point was largely based in philosophy and history and soon became Marxist sociology. It should be noted that sociology throughout the Soviet period of Russian history has been under the direct control of the ideological branch

of the Communist party. Soviet sociology defined as Marxist sociology has been widely taught both within and outside the universities, though until recently without special academic or faculty recognition (see Fischer 1964; Simirenko 1966). Up to 1966, at least, most sociologists in the Soviet Union taught and did research within faculties of philosophy and institutes (Fischer 1966, p. 127).

Japan. Sociology entered the curriculum of the Tokyo Imperial University almost as early as it entered that of any American university. Ernest Fenollosa, an American philosopher, came to the Tokyo Imperial University in 1878 and offered lectures in *shakaigaku* (sociology) based on the work of Herbert Spencer. A chair of sociology was established at Tokyo Imperial University in 1893 (Odaka 1950). Prior to World War II, the principal centers of academic sociology in Japan were at Tokyo and Kyoto, each of which represented a school of sociological thought. The Tokyo school was regarded as more empirical than that of Kyoto, which was regarded as formal and phenomenological (*ibid.*, p. 404).

India. The relatively late arrival of sociology in the universities of India perhaps reflects the essentially philosophical orientation of Indian intellectuals, who were generally unreceptive to the idea of an empirical sociology. Also, there was resistance from the university system to the establishment of such a sociology; this resistance was inevitably exacerbated by the universities' civil service structure.

Sociology was not introduced as a course in an Indian university until 1917, when it was offered in the economics department at Calcutta University. Even today Calcutta University, with nearly 100,000 students (including those in affiliated departments), does not have an independent department of sociology (Clinard & Elder 1965, p. 582). Bombay University established the first Indian department of sociology in 1919. Almost all doctoral work in sociology in 1965 was concentrated at the universities of Bombay, Delhi, Agra, Baroda, and Lucknow, with neither Calcutta nor Madras universities offering such programs. Most Indian universities still lack honors courses leading to a sociology degree.

Central and South America. The political structure and climate of the Central and South American republics and their universities have hindered the development of sociology as an academic discipline. Nonetheless, today chairs in sociology are to be found in nearly all these republics—in faculties of law, philosophy, or social sciences and on occasion in schools of sociology. Though the division is by no means clear-cut, the countries of the

Atlantic have been more likely to develop an academic sociology based on European, particularly Hispanic, traditions and writings, while those of the Pacific have developed a more empirical sociological tradition (Bastide 1945). Since 1945 most of the larger republics have had at least one major institute devoted primarily to sociological research. The greatest range of academic programs representing the different fields of sociology has been offered in the universities of Brazil and Mexico, although Argentina, which has the largest number of universities, experienced a sociological renaissance during the period between the Perón and the Ongania regimes.

Eastern Europe. The development of sociology in the eastern European nations was closely linked to their political independence. While there were sociologists within eastern European universities prior to 1920, there was no recognition of sociology as an academic discipline. The growth of sociology within the universities was slow until World War II, with only Poland and Hungary developing major centers of sociology; since World War II, Poland especially has produced a number of distinguished theorists and, particularly at Warsaw, empirical research in the sociology of law. In the postwar period, sociology in the east European countries was dominated until quite recently by conservative Marxist sociology, though the influence of French and American sociology was already evident in the 1960s.

Southern Europe. Among the countries of southern Europe, only Italy could claim before World War II that a sociological tradition existed in its universities. However, Italian sociology did not emerge with separate departmental status, usually being confined to faculties of law, philosophy, or economics. As in Germany, the rise of fascism created a climate that was inhospitable to academic sociology as it evolved in other countries.

Scandinavia. Despite their small size, the Scandinavian countries have witnessed probably the most rapid growth of sociology in the period since World War II. Except in Finland, there was little academic sociology in these countries before that time. Even today, however, because of the relatively small scale of Scandinavian higher education, most sociologists hold posts outside the universities. Scandinavian sociology has historical roots in demography and tends to favor a positivistic, quantitative approach to social phenomena, often linked with a deep interest in social policy and legislation.

Reasons for the growth of sociology. Even a brief overview of the rise and development of sociology makes apparent that its rise and growth as

an intellectual and an academic discipline depends upon social and political conditions in nation-states. This is perhaps especially true of academic sociology, which has, for the most part, experienced its greatest growth in the systems of mass public higher education that are found in modern industrial democracies. Academic sociology undoubtedly suffered most in countries where totalitarian governments regarded it as dangerous on ideological grounds, since most sociologists with university appointments were either compelled to resign or found it prudent to do so (many of them, of course, became refugees). This was particularly true for Germany from 1934 to 1946, the period of National Socialism; for the Soviet Union since 1924; for Japan during much of its history; and for the eastern European countries since the late 1930s. The two world wars also greatly affected the training of young sociologists and the careers of established ones in countries that were either occupied or under siege (probably the most distinguished sociologist to become a direct victim of these upheavals was Halbwachs, who died in Buchenwald in 1945).

In all countries, however, it was the structure of the system of higher education and of the universities that undoubtedly played the most important role in developing academic sociology. There was strong resistance from the traditional faculties to the entrance of sociology and to any claims that it might be a science. Since in almost all countries appointments to the faculty were closely controlled by the faculties themselves, not by a separate administration, the development of academic sociology encountered considerable resistance in all but the American universities.

Furthermore, in most countries higher education was designed for an elite, not the masses, and the system did not have the resources to develop sociology on a substantial scale. Indeed, it must be admitted that a major factor in the establishment of academic sociology, particularly as a science, has been the character of the financial resources that could be allocated to it for empirical research. Such resources historically have come to universities primarily through private foundations and government subsidies or grants. In countries such as England and the United States, the private foundation played an important role in the early development of sociology as an empirical science, but in recent years the role of government in supporting research has become even more important, irrespective of country. Thus sociology has become dependent upon the state for its growth as a research enterprise. In the countries where sociology has increasingly gained state support for research, it has grown most rapidly as a research discipline. The growth of sociology as an intellectual discipline reflects the same resource base. Rural sociology and the sociology of social problems, among other fields, grew under the impetus of the availability of financial resources for research, particularly state resources [see RURAL SOCIETY; SOCIAL PROBLEMS].

It should be clear that all the aforementioned conditions for the growth of sociology as an academic discipline and an empirical science were most easily satisfied within the context of American society. These conditions—free inquiry both within and without the university, mass public education, a loosely organized, decentralized university system, and large resources for the financial support of research—therefore appear essential to the rise and rapid development of sociology in the ways already mentioned. Sociology is among the sciences that may become dangerous to the state and to society; the growth of such sciences as academic disciplines is therefore intimately bound up with the state of society.

Professional training of sociologists

The sociologists of the late nineteenth and twentieth centuries were largely scholars who had been trained in branches of knowledge other than sociology. In the German, French, and American universities they were generally products of the faculties of law, economics, political economy, and philosophy. With the establishment of academic departments or chairs of sociology in the universities, the training of sociologists gradually fell to scholars or professionals who had been trained in sociology. Yet for much of its history the sociological profession has judged applicants for academic appointment or certification as sociologists less by the kind of academic training they have received than by the sociological character of their writings or research.

In no country has the professionalization of sociology moved as far as in the United States. Although the American Sociological Association still admits to membership persons who do not hold a degree in sociology, fellows or active (that is, voting) members with few exceptions must hold the PH.D. degree in sociology.

American universities have provided the best opportunities for the rapid growth of sociology as a profession, since they are structured around academic departments that provide doctoral training. By the mid-1960s there were some seventy universities in the United States offering graduate work in sociology leading to the doctoral degree,

with an annual output of over 260 such degrees. However, the distribution of PH.D.'s in sociology by university is highly concentrated: three universities granted about a quarter, 9 almost half, and 23 some four-fifths of all doctoral degrees conferred in sociology in the United States during the decade 1950–1960 (Sibley 1963, chapter 4).

The largest single concentration of professionally trained sociologists in 1967 was in the United States, though the numbers in all the continental European countries and in England, India, Japan, and Latin America had grown substantially since 1950. Indeed, by 1960 almost every new nation had a few sociologists. Almost two thousand sociologists assembled in 1966 at the Sixth World Congress of Sociology of the International Sociological Association, with no country accounting for more than one-tenth of those in attendance.

The United States provides the most detailed information on its professional sociologists, though it is difficult to estimate their total members because of hidden variation in the definition of "sociologist." There were an estimated three thousand holders of doctor's degrees in sociology in the United States in 1966. In 1964, 2,703 sociologists were registered in the National Science Foundation Register of Scientific and Technical Personnel (Hopper 1966, p. 71). Active members and fellows (a majority of whom hold the doctorate in sociology) in the American Sociological Association numbered 3,626 in 1965.

Sociologists in the United States, in contrast with those in many other countries of the world, are employed primarily in colleges and universities. Of those in the National Register in 1964, 77 per cent were so employed (Hopper 1966, table 4).

The employment of sociologists outside universities is relatively recent in the United States, so that American sociology has been the sociology of the academician rather than the sociology of the administrator or reformer. In the 1960s university employment still carries far greater prestige for American sociologists than does any other form of employment, but there are indications that, as the total number of sociologists increases, this may gradually cease to be true. No comparable statistics are available about the employment of sociologists in countries other than the United States. It appears, however, that, except in Canada, a substantially smaller proportion of them are employed in universities. Moreover, a growing proportion of the employment of all sociologists in England, Europe, the United States, and the Soviet Union is accounted for by the civil service and by research institutes.

The extent to which sociologists are employed professionally outside of universities depends to a great extent on the development of the applied fields of sociology—for example, on whether there are sociologically trained criminologists, welfare administrators, and social planners. Unlike psychologists, sociologists have not organized their professional training around specialized clinical training programs. Within the United States, in fact, the difference in the size of the professional associations of psychologists and sociologists can nearly all be accounted for by the large number of clinical psychologists in the American Psychological Association.

Sociology in both England and the United States was long associated with the profession of social work. By 1940, however, most large sociology departments in the United States had ceased to provide any training preparatory for social work. Though there were still a few doctoral programs in "sociology and social work" at leading American universities in the late 1960s, generally speaking, there was no longer a close link between professional sociologists and professional social workers.

The growth of sociology as a scientific discipline has led, in fact, to less curricular emphasis on areas that formerly were classified as "applied" sociology. Within the United States the decline in emphasis on training applied sociologists can be attributed in large part to professional efforts to establish the status of sociology as a science, but it is also due in part to the fact that other disciplines, such as social work, now train their own practitioners.

All of this should not be allowed to obscure the fact that sociologists in most countries are deeply involved with the problems confronting their societies. But here their roles are primarily those of scientific investigator and policy scientists [see POLICY SCIENCES]. Increasingly, too, sociology has developed subfields of specialization, such as medical sociology and the sociology of education, that are related to practice in other professions.

Professional associations and journals

The recognition that sociologists gradually gained within the universities of their own countries did not necessarily rescue sociology from the insularity in which it found itself. All too often the early academic sociologists wrote quite unaware of the work of important sociologists within as well as outside their own countries. Though Durkheim went to Germany for a period, he does not seem to have encountered Simmel. The pioneer American sociologist Lester F. Ward produced much of his early work unaware even of the existence of major scholars in sociology in his own country. The truth seems to be that while most of the early sociologists belonged to learned societies or intellectual circles within their own countries, their diverse scholarly origins often gave them little contact with one another. Following the model of other scholars and scientists, however, sociologists established their own learned or scientific societies, some with overtones of professionalism.

In a U.S. education report of 1900 on the Social Economy Section of the Paris Exposition of 1900, Ward wrote of sociology and its development in somewhat prophetic terms, though that was not his intent:

All the countries of the civilised world are contributing to the sociological movement, but the activity is greater in some than in others. It is perhaps least in England. In Germany, it has a distinctive character, with a tendency to evade the name of sociology. . . . In the United States this activity is most intense and very real and earnest. But there can be no doubt that it is in France, which was also the cradle of the science, that sociology has taken the firmest hold upon the thinking classes, and it is there that we find the largest annual output, whether we confine ourselves to the literature or include in our enumeration the practical applications of Sociology in the form of institutions, such as the Musée Social, for carrying on lines of operation calculated to educate and enlighten the people in social matters. ([1900] 1901, p. 1454)

American and French sociologists were the first to develop learned societies and journals of sociology. They were also among those who early and consistently worked toward establishing the status of sociology as a scientific discipline and a profession. These events did not all occur at the same period. Overall, however, American sociologists moved more rapidly than their counterparts in other countries in shaping sociology as a distinct discipline, so that, within little more than sixty years of its formal inauguration, it had an established place not only within the universities but within almost all organized parts of American society.

No doubt the rapid increase in the number of sociologists in the United States made these developments more feasible there. Yet it is clear that even in the early days, when the American Sociological Society had fewer than one hundred members, American sociologists took the initiative in developing means for scholarly communication and association in their discipline. In 1895, at the University of Chicago, Small established the second sociological journal in the entire world: the *American Journal of Sociology*. Small's initial editorial statement promised that "a large number of American scholars, with many representative European sociologists, will also try to express their best thoughts upon discoverable principles of societary relationships . . ." (1895, p. 13). Small not only invited original papers from an advisory board of European sociologists and their colleagues, but himself translated portions of their published writings, to avoid, as he put it, the development of a provincial science.

Small later reported that there were many who tried to dissuade him from publishing even the first issue, on the ground that there was not enough sociological writing to fill such a journal (1916, p. 786). Nonetheless, the first issue appeared in July 1895, even though there were not at that time enough articles to fill a second issue in September. In response to Small's pleas, Ward and Ross submitted papers; the second issue appeared on time and, with an occasional translation from the writings of European sociologists but relying mainly on American contributors, Small soon established the *American Journal of Sociology* as a success.

The first sociological society in the world was the Institut International de Sociologie. It formally came into being with the meeting of its first congress in Paris, in October 1894. Beginning in 1895, the Institut published the *Annales de l'Institut International de Sociologie*, under the editorship of René Worms. The world's first journal of sociology, the *Revue internationale de sociologie*, had appeared in 1893 under the same editorship.

The Institut International de Sociologie was an international association of sociologists that held congresses until 1960. Following World War II, there were objections to the fascist sympathies of some of the members and officers of the Institut, and to the circumstances under which the organization had continued to function during World War II in countries subject to the Axis powers. Not long after the founding of UNESCO, a number of sociologists, including Morris Ginsberg of England, Georges Gurvitch and Georges Davy of France, and Louis Wirth of the United States, persuaded that body to call a constituent congress to found a new international organization of sociologists. Meeting in Oslo in 1948, with 24 delegates from 21 countries, the International Sociological Association (ISA) was organized, with Louis Wirth as its first president. The First World Congress of Sociology of the ISA was held in Zurich in 1949, with 124 delegates from 30 countries. By 1966, the Sixth World Congress of Sociology, at Évian, France, was attended by almost two thousand sociologists from all countries of the world where there are academic appointments in sociology, other than mainland China.

French sociologists have failed so far to establish a viable national association of their own. Nonetheless, the moving spirits in the founding of the first international organization of sociologists were French; the oldest of all sociological journals, the *Revue internationale de sociologie*, is a French publication; it was a distinguished French sociologist, Émile Durkheim, who in 1898 established *L'année sociologique* as a journal that for years represented all that was newest and most authoritative in the field. During the 1950s, French sociologists were influential in establishing the multilingual *Archives européennes de sociologie; European Journal of Sociology*. In 1946, French demographers established *Population*, a journal that soon gained international attention in the field of population studies.

The second sociological society to be formed anywhere was the Sociological Society of London, organized at a general meeting in November 1903, with James Bryce as its first president. British sociologists did not develop a national organization until 1951, when the British Sociological Association was founded. Its membership in 1961 was more than five hundred (MacRae [1948–1961] 1961, p. 25). Also in 1951 appeared the first number of the *British Journal of Sociology*, but neither it nor the *Sociological Review* published by the Sociological Society of London has received the international attention given the more specialized British sociological journals, *Population Studies* and the *British Journal of Delinquency*.

In December 1905, about one hundred American sociologists gathered in Baltimore to consider their dissatisfaction with the American Historical, Economic, and Political Science associations, since none of these cognate societies gave sociologists who were members much opportunity to present their work at annual sessions. They concluded the meeting by forming the American Sociological Society (now the American Sociological Association). The first meeting of the society was held in 1906, in connection with the meetings of the cognate societies. Ward was elected its first president and Sumner and Giddings were vice-presidents. The *American Journal of Sociology* became the official organ of this new society, whose officers were advisory editors. In 1936, the society severed its relationship with the *Journal* and established the *American Sociological Review* as its official journal. In the interim two other sociological journals had made their appearance: *Social Forces* at the University of North Carolina under the editorship of

Howard Odum, and *Sociology and Social Research* at the University of Southern California under Emory S. Bogardus.

During the 1930s the rural sociologists severed their ties with the American Sociological Society, on the ground that it was neglecting their special interests, and formed the Rural Sociology Society, with *Rural Sociology* as their official journal. Those sociologists interested in social problems did likewise in the 1950s, founding the Society for the Study of Social Problems and an official journal, *Social Problems*. In part to forestall further fragmentation, the American Sociological Association has since approved specialized sections within it. Three additional official journals have been added, representing sectional interests: J. L. Moreno's journal *Sociometry* was acquired by the association and is now devoted solely to papers in social psychology; more recently, the association also acquired the *Journal of Educational Sociology*, retitled the *Journal of the Sociology of Education*, and the *Journal of Health and Human Behavior*, retitled the *Journal of Health and Social Behavior*.

As the American Sociological Society grew, it developed in consciousness of itself as a professional association as well as a learned society. The official journal carried news of job changes and opportunities and gradually came to include an employment bulletin. Also, discussions of the problems of professionalization appeared within its covers. By the early 1950s the society had almost four thousand members (including associate and student members) and found it necessary to create the post of executive secretary, and by the early 1960s, it had a national office in Washington, D.C., headed by a sociologist. During 1966 it developed a special journal, the *American Sociologist*, devoted to professional matters.

The expansion of sociology in the United States included the expansion of regional, state, and even local sociological societies. Some of these established their own sociological journals or took over journals already in existence. Many American sociologists hold membership in both a regional body and the national body of sociologists. The American Sociological Association, in the course of its growth, has become a body of professionals as well as of scholars. No other national sociological association has moved so far in recognizing both professional and scholarly interests; associations of sociologists outside the United States usually limit themselves to sponsoring annual or biennial meetings devoted almost entirely to scholarly interests, and in general follow the model of the traditional scholarly or learned society rather than the more professionalized American model.

Under the leadership of Weber and his contemporaries, German sociologists founded the Deutsche Gesellschaft für Soziologie. The association was disbanded with the exodus of sociologists upon the accession to power of the National Socialist party in 1933; its last convention, which was its seventh, had been held in Berlin in 1930. Leopold von Wiese, professor of sociology at Cologne, was its president at the time of its demise and served as its first president when it was revived in 1946. It continues as the major learned society of German sociologists. There are no official journals of the association.

The major sociological journal in Germany for much of the period before 1930 was the *Archiv für Sozialwissenschaft und Sozialpolitik*. Max Weber served for a time as editor, and practically all of his sociological writings were first published in the *Archiv*. From 1921 to 1934 the *Kölner Vierteljahrshefte für Soziologie* was published under the editorship of von Wiese. This journal came forth under his editorship again in 1948 as the *Kölner Zeitschrift für Soziologie und Sozialpsychologie*; René König assumed the editorship in the early 1950s, a position that he still held in 1967.

Soviet sociology remained without any organization of sociologists until the mid-1950s, when the Soviet Sociological Association was founded. However, the first national meeting of Soviet sociologists did not take place until February 1965 (Fischer 1966, p. 128). In the same year the first Soviet sociology series, *Sotsialnye issledovaniia* ("Social Research"), appeared (see Akademiia Nauk ... 1965). The number of Soviet sociologists is difficult to estimate, though about six hundred of them took part in the 1965 meeting.

In 1924 a nationwide sociological society was formed in Japan, with the establishment of the Shakai-Gaku (Sociological Society). Up to 1943 the official publications of the society were the *Shakaigaku zasshi* ("Journal of Sociology") and *Nempō seijigaku* ("Annual of the Japan Sociological Society"). At the close of World War II, these two publications were combined under the title *Shakaigaku kenkyū* ("Sociological Research").

The prewar membership of the Japan Sociological Society numbered around seven hundred. Because of the rapid growth of academic sociology in the postwar period, its numbers are now greater, though it is difficult to ascertain how many hold higher degrees in sociology.

There is some difficulty in estimating the number of sociologists in India. The total membership of the Indian Sociological Society in 1963 was only 268, of whom Clinard and Elder (1965, p. 582) estimate 16 per cent were foreigners. While the civil service and other institutes may employ sociologists who are not affiliated with the professional society, the total number of Indian sociologists undoubtedly is very small—in fact, there may be fewer sociologists per head of population in India than in almost any of the other nations with an established university system.

The principal Indian sociological journal is the *Sociological Bulletin,* founded in 1952 as the official publication of the Bombay Sociological Society. Sociological writing in India appears also in the *International Journal of Comparative Sociology,* published in Dharwar.

Universities in the Scandinavian countries, except for those in Finland and Denmark, gave almost no formal recognition to academic sociology before 1946. Though the scale of sociology still is small in any country of Scandinavia, there is considerable interaction among sociologists from the several countries. By 1956, they had established their own journal, entitled *Acta sociologica.* Most articles in this journal are published in English, though an occasional article appears in French or German.

One of the early journals to include the word "sociology" in its title was the *Rivista di sociologia,* which appeared in Italy in 1897. But Italian sociology, although it has produced a few distinguished figures in the twentieth century, has hardly succeeded in advancing its standing since the days of Pareto (who lived in Switzerland).

Without a doubt, the founding of sociology journals was an important factor in the early development of academic and scientific sociology. The early sociology journals were often outlets for the publications of a "school" of sociology or for those of the editor and his students. Thus *L'année sociologique* was clearly Durkheim's journal; Worms dominated the *Revue internationale de sociologie;* for a time Weber shaped the *Archiv für Sozialwissenschaft und Sozialpolitik;* Odum and his students used *Social Forces* to foster regional sociology; and Moreno developed a school in *Sociometry.* Even the *American Journal of Sociology* and *Sociological Papers,* which at the outset were open to submission of papers from any sociologist, were influenced respectively by the personalities and interests of Albion Small and Victor Branford. While a particular school or group of individuals, or occasionally a leading figure, still plays a role in founding or editing a sociology journal, most such journals today, whether general or specialized, are more universalistic in their standards.

ALBERT J. REISS, JR.

BIBLIOGRAPHY

ADORNO, THEODOR W. et al. 1950 *The Authoritarian Personality.* American Jewish Committee, Social Studies Series, No. 3. New York: Harper.

AHMAD, IMITAZ 1965 Note on Sociology in India. *American Sociologist* 1:244–247.

AKADEMIIA NAUK SSSR, INSTITUT FILOSOFII 1965 *Sotsialnye issledovaniia.* Moscow: Nauka.

AMERICAN SOCIOLOGICAL SOCIETY (1959) 1962 *Sociology Today: Problems and Prospects.* Edited by Robert K. Merton et al. New York: Basic Books.

ARON, RAYMOND (1935) 1957 *German Sociology.* Glencoe, Ill.: Free Press. → First published in French.

BASTIDE, ROGER 1945 Sociology in Latin America. Pages 615–637 in Georges Gurvitch and Wilbert E. Moore (editors), *Twentieth Century Sociology.* New York: Philosophical Library.

BECKER, HOWARD; and BOSKOFF, ALVIN (editors) 1957 *Modern Sociological Theory in Continuity and Change.* New York: Dryden.

BERELSON, BERNARD; and STEINER, GARY A. 1964 *Human Behavior: An Inventory of Scientific Findings.* New York: Harcourt.

BERNARD, JESSIE 1929 The History and Prospects of Sociology in the United States. Pages 1–71 in George A. Lundberg, Read Bain, and Nels Anderson (editors), *Trends in American Sociology.* New York: Harper.

BERNARD, L. L. 1909 The Teaching of Sociology in the United States. *American Journal of Sociology* 15:164–213.

BERNARD, L. L. 1945 The Teaching of Sociology in the United States in the Last Fifty Years. *American Journal of Sociology* 50:534–548.

BERNARD, L. L.; and BERNARD, JESSIE 1943 *Origins of American Sociology: The Social Science Movement in the United States.* New York: Crowell.

BOOTH, CHARLES et al. (1889–1891) 1902–1903 *Life and Labour of the People in London.* 17 vols. London: Macmillan.

BOTTOMORE, T. B. 1962 Sociology in India. *British Journal of Sociology* 13:98–106.

BOWLEY, ARTHUR LYON 1915 *The Nature and Purpose of the Measurement of Social Phenomena.* London: King.

BRYSON, GLADYS 1945 *Man and Society: The Scottish Inquiry of the Eighteenth Century.* Princeton Univ. Press.

BUKHARIN, NIKOLAI I. (1921) 1965 *Historical Materialism: A System of Sociology.* Translated from the 3d Russian edition. New York: Russell. → First published as *Teoriia istoricheskogo materializma.*

CHABROL DE CROUSOL, ANDRÉ J. C. 1818 *Sur les événemens de Lyon, au mois de juin 1817.* Paris: Égron.

CLINARD, MARSHALL B.; and ELDER, JOSEPH W. 1965 Sociology in India: A Study in the Sociology of Knowledge. *American Sociological Review* 30:581–587.

COMTE, AUGUSTE (1830–1842) 1877 *Cours de philosophie positive.* 4th ed. 6 vols. Paris: Baillière.

COMTE, AUGUSTE (1851–1854) 1875–1877 *System of Positive Polity.* 4 vols. London: Longmans. → First published in French.

DUNCAN, OTIS DUDLEY 1961 From Social System to Ecosystem. *Sociological Inquiry* 31:140–149.

DUNCAN, OTIS DUDLEY; and SCHNORE, LEO F. 1959 Cultural, Behavioral, and Ecological Perspectives in the Study of Social Organization. *American Journal of Sociology* 65:132–146. → A "comment" by Peter H. Rossi and a "rejoinder" by Otis Dudley Duncan and Leo F. Schnore appear on pages 146–153.

DURKHEIM, ÉMILE (1892–1918) 1960 *Montesquieu and Rousseau: Forerunners of Sociology.* Ann Arbor: Univ. of Michigan Press. → Part 1 is a translation of Durkheim's thesis *Quid Secundatus politicae scientiae in-*

stituendae contulerit (1892); Part 2 was first published in Volume 25 of *Revue de métaphysique et de morale.*

DURKHEIM, ÉMILE (1895) 1958 *The Rules of Sociological Method.* 8th ed. Edited by George E. G. Catlin. Glencoe, Ill.: Free Press. → First published as *Les règles de la méthode sociologique.*

FARIS, ROBERT E. L. (editor) 1964 *Handbook of Modern Sociology.* Chicago: Rand McNally.

FISCHER, GEORGE 1964 *Science and Politics: The New Sociology in the Soviet Union.* Cornell Research Papers in International Studies, No. 1. Ithaca, N.Y.: Cornell Univ., Center for International Studies.

FISCHER, GEORGE 1966 Current Soviet Work in Sociology: A Note in the Sociology of Knowledge. *American Sociologist* 1:127–132.

GIDDINGS, FRANKLIN H. (1896) 1911 *The Principles of Sociology: An Analysis of the Phenomena of Association and of Social Organization.* New York: Macmillan.

GOULDNER, ALVIN W.; and MILLER, SEYMOUR M. 1965 *Applied Sociology: Opportunities and Problems.* New York: Free Press.

GUERRY, ANDRÉ M. 1833 *Essai sur la statistique morale de la France.* Paris: Crochard.

GURVITCH, GEORGES; and MOORE, WILBERT E. (editors) 1945 *Twentieth Century Sociology.* New York: Philosophical Library.

HOBHOUSE, LEONARD T.; WHEELER, GERALD C.; and GINSBERG, MORRIS (1915) 1965 *The Material Culture and Social Institutions of the Simpler Peoples: An Essay in Correlation.* London: Routledge.

HOFSTADTER, RICHARD 1944 *Social Darwinism in American Thought, 1860–1915.* Philadelphia: Univ. of Pennsylvania Press.

HOPPER, JANICE A. 1966 Sociologists in the National Register of Scientific and Technical Personnel. *American Sociologist* 1:71–78.

KÖNIG, RENÉ 1958 Germany. Pages 779–806 in Joseph S. Rouček (editor), *Contemporary Sociology.* New York: Philosophical Library.

KOZLOVA, K. I.; and CHEBOKSAROV, N. N. 1956 The Social Sciences in the U.S.S.R. *Soviet Survey: A Journal of Soviet and East European Studies* No. 10:1–19.

LAZARSFELD, PAUL F. 1961 Notes on the History of Quantification in Sociology: Trends, Sources and Problems. *Isis* 52, part 2:277–333. → Reprinted in the same year on pages 147–203 in Harry Woolf (editor), *Quantification: A History of the Meaning of Measurement in the Natural and Social Sciences.* Indianapolis, Ind.: Bobbs-Merrill.

LAZARSFELD, PAUL F.; SEWELL, WILLIAM H.; and WILENSKY, HAROLD L. (editors) 1967 *The Uses of Sociology.* New York: Basic Books.

LUNDBERG, GEORGE A.; BAIN, READ; and ANDERSON, NELS (editors) 1929 *Trends in American Sociology.* New York: Harper.

LYND, ROBERT S. 1939 *Knowledge for What? The Place of Social Science in American Culture.* Princeton Univ. Press.

MACIVER, ROBERT M. 1934 Sociology. Volume 14, pages 232–246 in *Encyclopaedia of the Social Sciences.* New York: Macmillan.

MACIVER, ROBERT M. 1942 *Social Causation.* Boston: Ginn. → A paperback edition was published in 1964 by Harper.

MACRAE, DONALD G. (1948–1961) 1961 *Ideology and Society: Papers in Sociology and Politics.* New York: Free Press.

MANNHEIM, KARL (1923–1929) 1952 *Essays on the Sociology of Knowledge.* Edited by Paul Kecskemeti. New York: Oxford Univ. Press.

MANNHEIM, KARL (1929–1931) 1954 *Ideology and Utopia: An Introduction to the Sociology of Knowledge.* New York: Harcourt; London: Routledge. → A paperback edition was published in 1955 by Harcourt. Part 1 is an introduction to this edition. Parts 2–4 are a translation of *Ideologie und Utopie* (1929); Part 5 is a translation of the article "Wissenssoziologie" (1931).

MANNHEIM, KARL (1935) 1940 *Man and Society in an Age of Reconstruction: Studies in Modern Social Structure.* New York: Harcourt. → First published as *Mensch und Gesellschaft im Zeitalter des Umbaus.*

MANNHEIM, KARL 1950 *Freedom, Power, and Democratic Planning.* New York: Oxford Univ. Press. → Published posthumously.

MARCH, JAMES G. (editor) 1965 *Handbook of Organizations.* Chicago: Rand McNally.

MAYHEW, HENRY (1851) 1861 *London Labour and the London Poor.* London: Griffin.

MAYHEW, HENRY; and BINNY, JOHN 1862 *The Criminal Prisons of London and Scenes of Prison Life.* London: Griffin.

MERTON, ROBERT K. (1949) 1957 *Social Theory and Social Structure.* Rev. & enl. ed. Glencoe, Ill.: Free Press.

MOSER, CLAUS A. 1958 *Survey Methods in Social Investigation.* New York: Macmillan.

OBERSCHALL, ANTHONY R. 1965 *Empirical Social Research in Germany, 1848–1914.* Paris and The Hague: Mouton; New York: Humanities.

ODAKA, KUNIO 1950 Japanese Sociology: Past and Present. *Social Forces* 28:400–409.

ODUM, HOWARD W. 1951 *American Sociology: The Story of Sociology in the United States Through 1950.* New York: Longmans.

PARENT-DUCHÂTELET, ALEXANDRE J. B. (1834) 1857 *On Prostitution in the City of Paris.* 3d ed. 2 vols. London: Burgess. → First published in French.

PARETO, VILFREDO (1916) 1963 *The Mind and Society: A Treatise on General Sociology.* 4 vols. New York: Dover. → First published as *Trattato di sociologia generale.* Volume 1: *Non-logical Conduct.* Volume 2: *Theory of Residues.* Volume 3: *Theory of Derivations.* Volume 4: *The General Form of Society.*

PARSONS, TALCOTT (1938–1953) 1963 *Essays in Sociological Theory.* Rev. ed. New York: Free Press. → A paperback edition was published in 1964.

PARSONS, TALCOTT 1951 *The Social System.* Glencoe, Ill.: Free Press.

PARSONS, TALCOTT 1960 *Structure and Process in Modern Societies.* Glencoe, Ill.: Free Press.

PARSONS, TALCOTT 1966 *Societies: Evolutionary and Comparative Perspectives.* Englewood Cliffs, N.J.: Prentice-Hall.

PARSONS, TALCOTT; and SHILS, EDWARD (editors) 1951 *Toward a General Theory of Action.* Cambridge, Mass.: Harvard Univ. Press. → A paperback edition was published in 1962 by Harper.

POPPER, KARL R. 1957 *The Poverty of Historicism.* Boston: Beacon.

ROSS, EDWARD A. 1945 Fifty Years of Sociology in the United States. *American Journal of Sociology* 50:489–501.

ROUČEK, JOSEPH S. 1958 *Contemporary Sociology.* New York: Philosophical Library.

SAKSENA, R. N. (editor) 1961 *Sociology, Social Research, and Social Problems in India.* New York: Asia Publishing.

SEINE (DEPT.) 1821–1860 *Recherches statistiques sur la ville de Paris et le département de la Seine.* 6 vols. Paris: Imprimerie Royale.

SHILS, EDWARD 1947 The Present Situation in American Sociology. *Pilot Papers* 2, no. 2:8–36.

SHILS, EDWARD 1960 On the Eve. *Twentieth Century* 167:445–459.

SHILS, EDWARD (1961) 1965 The Calling of Sociology. Pages 1405–1448 in Talcott Parsons et al. (editors), *Theories of Society: Foundations of Modern Sociological Theory.* New York: Free Press.

SIBLEY, ELBRIDGE 1963 *The Education of Sociologists in the United States.* New York: Russell Sage Foundation.

SIMIRENKO, ALEX 1966 *Soviet Sociology.* Chicago: Quadrangle Books.

SMALL, ALBION W. 1895 The Era of Sociology. *American Journal of Sociology* 1:1–15.

SMALL, ALBION W. 1916 Fifty Years of Sociology in the United States (1865–1915). *American Journal of Sociology* 21:721–864.

SMALL, ALBION W.; and VINCENT, GEORGE E. 1894 *An Introduction to the Study of Society.* New York: American Book.

SOROKIN, PITIRIM A. (1943) 1964 *Sociocultural Causality, Space, Time: A Study of Referential Principles of Sociology and Social Science.* New York: Russell.

STOUFFER, SAMUEL A. et al. 1949 *The American Soldier.* Studies in Social Psychology in World War II, Vols. 1 and 2. Princeton Univ. Press. → Volume 1: *Adjustment During Army Life.* Volume 2: *Combat and Its Aftermath.*

THOMAS, WILLIAM I.; and ZNANIECKI, FLORIAN (1918–1920) 1958 *The Polish Peasant in Europe and America.* 2d ed. 2 vols. New York: Dover.

WARD, LESTER F. (1883) 1926 *Dynamic Sociology: Or Applied Social Science, as Based Upon Statical Sociology and the Less Complex Sciences.* 2d ed. 2 vols. New York: Appleton.

WARD, LESTER F. (1900) 1901 Sociology at the Paris Exposition of 1900. U.S. Congress, *House Documents* 56th Congress, 2d session, Document No. 5, 41:1451–1593.

WEBB, SIDNEY; and WEBB, BEATRICE 1932 *Methods of Social Study.* London and New York: Longmans.

WEBER, ADNA F. (1899) 1963 *The Growth of Cities in the Nineteenth Century: A Study in Statistics.* Ithaca, N.Y.: Cornell Univ. Press.

WHELPTON, P. K.; and KISER, CLYDE V. 1943–1954 *Social and Psychological Factors Affecting Fertility.* Vols. 1–4. New York: Milbank Memorial Fund. → Commonly called the Indianapolis Study.

WIRTH, LOUIS 1948 American Sociology, 1915–1947. Pages 273–281 in American Journal of Sociology, *Index to Volumes I–LII, 1895–1947.* Univ. of Chicago Press.

ZNANIECKI, FLORIAN 1934 *The Method of Sociology.* New York: Farrar & Rinehart.

ZNANIECKI, FLORIAN 1951 *Cultural Sciences.* Urbana: Univ. of Illinois Press.

II

THE DEVELOPMENT OF SOCIOLOGICAL THOUGHT

Modern sociological thought and theory, as distinct from the purely contemplative or philosophical analysis of society, emerged in the late eighteenth and early nineteenth centuries as a result of several major changes in the perception of social order.

One such change was a growing emphasis in social and political thought on the task of differentiating the civil from the political order. Civil society came to be seen as a distinct, autonomous entity no longer subsumed under the political or even the "natural" order but tending, rather (especially in later theoretical formulations), to subsume the political order as only one of its several constituent institutional spheres. The main representative of this change in emphasis was perhaps Rousseau; at any rate, his approach to social contract and his definition of the general will can be regarded in this light. The names of Lorenz von Stein, Tocqueville, and, in a different way, Marx were most closely related to the first phase of this trend, which was later to be developed in a more systematic and detailed way, in conjunction with other developments, by all of the major figures of sociological thought in the later nineteenth and early twentieth centuries—Spencer, Pareto, Durkheim, Max Weber, and later Karl Mannheim.

The second major starting point of modern sociological inquiry was rooted in what may be called the "dialectical dissociation" between the transcendental order, on the one hand, and the sociopolitical and individual orders, on the other. It was gradually realized that the religious and moral attitudes of individuals can vary greatly, with a corresponding range of possible commitment to the transcendental and moral realms. It also became clear that religion and morality are only one determinant of individual behavior and that they, like other determinants of human behavior, develop to a large extent within social settings. Individual variations in behavior could not, therefore, be explained in terms of purely individual differences.

Further, there was a growing awareness of the improbability that any single institutional arrangement could fully epitomize *the* best moral order or, indeed, represent any transcendental order at all adequately. It therefore became obvious that different types of social or political regimes could not be compared or ranked according to the faithfulness with which they embodied this or that transcendental ideal.

The major representatives of these views, at least in the early stage of their development, were, of course, Hobbes, Rousseau, and (to a lesser extent) Locke. It was they who, by posing the question of the very possibility of social order, by not assuming that it was "naturally" ordained, opened up this question in modern terms, even if their specific answers were still very much tied to the older conceptions and perceptions. Even more crucial here was the later contribution of the Scottish moralists—Ferguson, Millar, and above all Adam Smith.

The third starting point of modern sociological thought was an increasing recognition of the great variety of different types of social order and of their internal changeability. History itself—the temporal dimension of human experience—was admitted to be the locus of change and variability, if not (as in some of the cases to be discussed later) their sole determinant.

The recognition of the variety of types of political order goes back, of course, at least to Aristotle, as does the search for the relation between this variety and the different types of civic attitude and moral posture that characterize the behavior of individuals. In these two respects modern sociological thought is very much in the Aristotelian tradition; however, it goes beyond this tradition in its incorporation of the first and second starting points described above. Thus, it departs from Aristotle, first, by refusing to identify the social with the political order (and, hence, by stressing the greater variety of their possible interrelations) and, second, by stressing the variety of the interrelations between moral or religious attitudes and types of social order. In this respect, as Shils has pointed out: "Sociology has partially closed the gap left by Aristotle between the *Ethics* and the *Politics*" (1961*a*, p. 1419). Third, and probably most important, it attempts to allow or account for temporal development as one major mechanism in the change and variability of social orders.

A fourth starting point of modern sociological theory was the importance given to environmental factors as influencing or even determining social order in general, and the variety of the types of such order in particular. Here the first major modern figures were Montesquieu and some of the Scottish moralists, especially Ferguson and Millar, then the various ethnologists and anthropologists such as Tylor, and later the members of the various evolutionary schools of the nineteenth century. The most recent important offshoot of this tradition is the large number of comparative studies made in the 1940s.

Out of these various approaches to the problem of social order there emerged a great many new intellectual trends, some of them taking the form of ideologies, others of social philosophies or theories of history. There were also more specifically sociological theories; these last, while very closely related to the others, nevertheless developed, even if intermittently and haltingly, their own characteristic set of problems. These can perhaps be formulated in the most general way as the search for the conditions and mechanisms of the continuity, disruption, and change of social order in general, and of the variety of different types of such order in particular.

Sociology and social order

The sociological approach recognized four basic focuses or components of social order: the individual, with his personal goals and interests; various social groups, such as organizations and institutions; the sphere of cultural symbols and creations; and the environmental forces within which all these components develop and which impinge on them. The sociological attitude toward the problem was characterized by its very lack of interest in searching for "natural" preconditions of social order or for any one specific type of society or polity as epitomizing the best model of moral or social order. Instead, the major focus of inquiry was shifted to analysis of the actual conditions and mechanisms of social order and its constituent components in continuity and change, both in general and with regard to different types of social order.

Precisely because of this concern with the conditions and mechanisms of social order, the problems of social disorder, disorganization, and change have become central focuses of sociological theory. The existence of social disorder, the ubiquity of internal conflicts, and the demise of sociopolitical systems have of course long been recognized as facts of life in any society; Plato and Aristotle, for instance, were deeply influenced by the turmoil of Greek political life in the fourth century B.C. But it was Hobbes who first treated social disorder as the starting point for analysis of the possibility of social order. Since Hobbes, there has evolved a characteristically sociological viewpoint in which social disorder is seen not as prior to and, hence, different from social order, but as constituting a special constellation of elements which, in a different combination, constitute the core of social order itself. Hence, an index of advances in sociological thought and analysis can very often be found in the extent to which the phenomena of social disorder are analyzed in the same terms and concepts as those of social order. This type of analysis deepens understanding of the conditions and mechanisms of continuity and change. Moreover, it focuses attention on the transformative propensities of social systems and sees such propensities as not determined by "external" or "random" events but, rather, as an important aspect of the phenomenon of social order. In other words, the sociological approach to social systems assumes that at least some elements of the mechanisms of social disorganization, change, and transformation can be found in all societies, while others are distributed among them in some predictable pattern.

Some basic dilemmas. Analysis of the processes of social continuity, change, and transformation has often faltered on two major stumbling blocks. One is the search for or belief in the conflictless society—an interest closely related to the ideological genesis of sociological theory. While this interest can very often lead to analysis of the patterns of conflict and disorganization in any given society, it has often tended to minimize the general applications of the insights so gained. On the other hand, many thinkers of the so-called "functional" or "structural–functional" schools have often been criticized on the grounds that they focus on the mechanisms of social order and neglect the problems of social change, although the result of this very emphasis of theirs has often been to dramatize the inevitability of disorder, even when this was not their intention.

Similarly, the search for some general and comparative analysis of social order, disorganization, and change can also very easily become wayward or blocked because of stress on the ultimateness and unbridgeability of the dichotomy between general laws or regularities and the uniqueness of specific social, cultural, and historical events. Here again, while many such analyses of various social situations as unique events can often greatly help in the development of insights about the "dynamics" of each such situation, yet these insights can easily be lost, or at least minimized, because their implicit general assumptions have not been made explicit. On the other hand, more generalized studies that do not attempt to deal with the explanation of unique constellations of different societal situations have tended to issue in empirically vacuous typologies of a scope so broad as to be self-defeating (Parsons 1965).

The progress of sociological thought has depended to no small degree on breaking through these barriers—and the breaks have often been only partial ones. Thus, for instance, the great novelty and strength of Marx's analysis lay not only in his recognition of the ubiquity of conflict but also, and perhaps mainly, in the possible relation between conflict and social change. The weakness of his analysis was in his assumption of the temporality of this conflict in the "class" society and of its disappearance in the supposedly "classless" future. Hence, he concentrated on those aspects of the conflict which he believed would lead to the con-

flictless society. By contrast, Simmel was content to analyze conflict as it presented itself in any type of social situation, although his view was limited by his focus on the purely "formal" aspects of social interaction.

But the two major analytical breakthroughs in this area were made by Durkheim and Weber, each of whom concentrated on the analysis of social disorganization as a possible key to deeper understanding of social order in general, and each of whom brought a systematically comparative perspective to his analysis. Durkheim's preoccupation with anomie was the counterpoint of his preoccupation with social integration, especially on the level of "organic solidarity." Similarly, Weber never ceased to be impressed by the confrontation between the institution-building and institution-destroying propensities of charisma in various societal settings.

Sociological analysis

The shift to a specifically sociological frame of reference not only involved a transition to more specific and concrete questions but also opened up the possibility of empirical investigation of various hypotheses about the conditions and mechanisms of social order. Continuous combination of these two approaches provided a base for the development of scientific sociological thought and theory.

The very formulation of propositions about social order has, of course, always necessitated the elaboration of what may be called the phenomenology of the basic components of social order. The latter include the orientations and activities of individuals; the characteristics and composition of groups, collectivities, institutional spheres, and major cultural objects; and the various environmental factors impinging on social life. The sociological approach is distinguished from pure contemplation or speculation by the fact that it subjects phenomenological analysis of these phenomena to empirical test. Accordingly, sociological conceptions of the basic elements of social order, as well as assumptions about the varying types and mechanisms of concrete interrelations among these elements, can be and have to be continually revised. Thus, the extension of sociological inquiry was a very important step in the development of the critical approach to the basic phenomena of human and social existence, and provided a potential focus for its continuous extension and growth (Shils 1961a; Parsons 1965).

Sociological analysis obviously is only one of the several streams in this tradition of critical appraisal of social life (Gellner 1965). But it is a very crucial component of the tradition not only because of its ability—even if a very limited one— to provide some testable knowledge about society, but also because its continual reappraisal of basic concepts helps to keep the spirit of social criticism alive in a world full of orthodoxies.

Four starting points of sociology

Each of the four basic components of social order outlined above offers a natural starting point for sociological analysis, and each has been somewhat differently emphasized by the major figures in the history of sociological thought. To recapitulate: these components are the individual, with his personality, goals, aspirations, and orientations; the various "autonomous" characteristics of social structure, such as groups and institutions; the nature and organization of the basic products of cultural activity (the realms of symbolic creativity); and environmental and biological factors.

These various starting points of sociological thought were very closely related to some of the major philosophical traditions from the eighteenth century onward, especially to the utilitarian and the idealist schools (Parsons 1965). But with the passage of time they loosened this connection and acquired some autonomy in the form of their own specific approaches, problems, and concepts. This makes it possible to treat the history of each starting point individually.

The individual. The attempts to explain the conditions, mechanisms, and varieties of social order from the vantage point of the individual can be broadly subdivided into two major subtypes. The first is the explanation of social order in terms of individual drives, habits, or goals. These explanations have ranged from simple ones stated in terms of instincts, drives, or the vulgar versions of psychoanalysis, through sophisticated explanations of social order in terms of generalized goals— whether they are those of power, love, or some "deeper" personality variables connected with various basic mechanisms of learning and cognition.

A very important variant of this approach, best exemplified by the work of Pareto, was the explanation of conditions and mechanisms of social order in terms of the distribution of various types of attitudes and personalities within a society, and of their pressures on institutional structure and its changes.

The second major variant of this approach has been in terms of the exigencies and structure of the social interaction derived from individuals' pursuit of their respective goals. We find this em-

phasis in the work of the formal school of sociology, especially that of Simmel and, to a smaller extent, von Wiese; it was also an important element in the "interactionist" approach of some of the older American sociologists, notably Ross. The analyses of Homans and Coleman, and some of the various applications to social life of game theory and of economic theory (see, for example, Friedman 1962; Downes 1957), are further developments in this tradition.

Social groups and institutions. Explanations of the conditions and mechanisms of social order in terms of some aspect of social groups and institutions ("societal" explanations) have been even more variegated in details and specifications than explanations in terms of individual goals. Broadly speaking, societal explanations can be divided into two major types. One type has emphasized the contents of social interaction, its goals or its rootedness in the basic needs of social groups and systems. This approach has usually tended to emphasize the analysis of institutional spheres, their internal organizational and structural characteristics or dynamics, and, possibly, their interrelations. It is this type of sociological explanation that has produced probably the greatest number of sociological works, both descriptive and analytical (see Sorokin 1928).

The second major type of societal explanation has been in terms of what have often been called the formal aspects of social life—a conception very close to, but not fully identical with, the structure of interindividual interaction. Three principal variants of this second major type can be discerned. One of them distinguishes between different types of social interaction according to the "quality" of the mutual or common social commitment which binds the members together; it is best represented by Tönnies' classic distinction between *Gemeinschaft* and *Gesellschaft*, which was later taken up by students of primary groups.

The second variant deals mainly with the types and vicissitudes of interaction between individuals within different group structures, ranging from the two-person group, or "dyad," up to the greater complexities of interaction in larger groups. Here we may cite the work of Simmel and the many subsequent studies of interpersonal relations and perceptions, from small groups to game theory.

The third variant, closely related to Simmel's but different in its emphasis and analytical orientation, has been mostly developed by Vierkandt and von Wiese; it emphasizes what may be called the elementary formal forces or characteristics of social interaction, such as distance and cooperation.

The cultural sphere.   Social order has also been explained in terms of major cultural forces or products. This approach is much more than a variant of the kind of institutional analysis that emphasizes, for instance, the importance of religious institutions; rather, it attempts to explain social order by positing autonomous, immanent laws in the sphere of cultural creativity. Social order and its variations are seen as manifestations of a "world spirit" consisting in the totality of human culture and its immanent laws, or in any one of the major spheres of cultural creativity—be it religion, art, or language—and its laws. Apart from the great idealist tradition of the nineteenth century, this approach can be seen best in the works of those anthropologists who have defined types of social order in terms of patterns or styles of culture (see, for instance, Benedict 1934; Kroeber 1901–1951). Perhaps the most interesting recent derivatives of this approach are certain developments in linguistics and some of their applications to the explanation of social phenomena, especially the work of Lévi-Strauss (1958).

The environment.   Of the environmental theories, the most important (if we discount simplicist biological approaches, such as racism) were the geographic–ecological approaches, starting with the simpler forms of geographical determinism. A fructifying influence here was institutional economics, as well as economic determinism in general. The environmental approach has come to full flower in the more sophisticated ecological theories that conceive social order in terms of ecosystem (Duncan 1964).

Three types of sociological explanation

From each of the four starting points of explanation of the conditions of social order there have developed, in the history of sociology, three major types of explanation. We may call them, first, the "simplicist" and/or "discrete" type; second, the "closed-system" type; and third, the "open-system" type.

The discrete approach.   Discrete explanations present the activities of individuals, as well as various social and cultural arrangements, in terms of discrete, relatively disconnected traits, which are seen as coalescing in a rather haphazard way. This type of explanation may very often, although certainly not always or necessarily, be connected with what may be called a simplicist or deterministic explanation, i.e., one that attempts to explain the bases and variations of social order in terms of nonsocial, "external" forces, whether biological, ecological, or geographical.

But the analytically discrete approach to social phenomena has not been limited to such simplicist, deterministic explanations. Indeed, it has gone far beyond them, encompassing many diverse approaches and lasting as a tradition of research long after simplicist explanations were given up. This is true of many types of social survey, as well as certain areas of attitude research.

The discrete approach usually developed some emphasis on generalizations or on general laws; at the very least, it included a search for regularities or patterns of individual and group behavior. But the connections that were assumed to exist between different elements of social order often were not conceived in terms of any system. Thus, the hypotheses built upon these supposed connections often were easily shattered; often, too, they degenerated into mere commonplaces, or into vague, purely classificatory typologies. The best that the discrete approach could offer by way of general explanation was to emphasize the uniqueness of this or that correlation between variables whose deeper connections were left obscure. It is also among exponents of the discrete approach that sociological "provincialism"—concentration on parochial problems, to the neglect of broader historical and comparative implications—has most tended to flourish, although, needless to say, it has also characterized many of the other approaches.

The closed-system approach.   The breakthrough from the discrete to the closed-system approach has been associated historically with a growing perception of the personal, social, and cultural orders, together with the surrounding environmental forces, as systems of interrelated components. These systems are held to have at least some autonomous mechanisms of self-maintenance, and possibly mechanisms to insure change as well. But in this approach the notion that any component of social order has systemic qualities is combined with the assumption that each such component is self-sufficient—i.e., closed to the others, as far as social causation is concerned. Moreover, few of the thinkers in this tradition were able to resist the temptation to explain all the salient aspects of social order in terms of the "laws" or dynamics of one particular component, such as the economic system.

A special type of closed-system approach can be found in those authors who explain the variety and change of types of social order in terms of certain inherent global tendencies, mostly of a historical nature, which are seen as both autonomous and inevitable. It is thus that laws of social dynamics have been formulated in terms of general evolutionary theory (Comte, Spencer, and Hobhouse), Hegelian dialectic as applied to economic institutions (Marx), or certain immanent characteristics of culture and of the human spirit (Croce). Whatever the particular theory, it was within the closed-system approach that the idealist tradition of the uniqueness of social and cultural entities could most easily flourish.

The open-system approach. The open-system theorists began by recognizing that although the closed-system theorists had been right in positing certain constituents of social order, they were wrong in assuming that any one element was invariably more important than all the others. In other words, the open-system approach conceived of the elements of social order and their interrelations as variables rather than known quantities. Thus the way was opened to a far greater flexibility in empirical generalization, as well as to the possibility of bridging the gap between historical generalization, on the one hand, and the irreducible uniqueness of specific historical events, on the other.

The breakdown of closed-system theories

Progress from the discrete to the closed-system approach and from that to the open-system approach was not only a natural outcome of the internal dialectics of the various schools of contemplative sociological thought. The advancement of sociological knowledge depended first of all on the success with which concepts describing the basic constituents of social order could be operationalized—i.e., defined in terms of actual observation and analysis. In other words, operationalization entailed the definition of these concepts in ways which could make them constituent elements of testable hypotheses about the conditions of social order—hypotheses which could be examined, however haltingly or inadequately, through some kind of empirical observation or research and which could help in the systematic accumulation of knowledge.

But an increase in the mere volume of empirical research was not in itself a sufficient condition for the progress of systematic sociological analysis (see Merton [1949] 1957). Much empirical observation, especially when it formed part of a critical appraisal of social problems, added very little to the analytic techniques available to sociologists. The least fruitful types of research were those which were based—implicitly or explicitly—on the discrete approach to social phenomena and which minimized the systemic properties of the basic phenomena or components of social order.

Such research often made use of grandiose but shallow typologies.

It was mainly insofar as research became closely related to the closed-system and, later, to the open-system approaches that its impetus to analytical and theoretical progress, and to the deepening of the understanding of conditions of social order, became very great. Indeed, considerable progress could often be made within the closed-system approach alone, because of the very fact that all the components of social order, as well as many of their subdivisions, do indeed exhibit some closed-system characteristics. But the most crucial breakthrough in the history of sociological thought and inquiry was from the closed-system to the open-system approach. The basic analytical step in this breakthrough consisted not so much in the direct testing of the "rightness" or "wrongness" of the concepts that defined the basic components of social order, but in critical re-examination of two basic assumptions which could be found, either explicitly or implicitly, in almost all closed-system approaches. The first of these was that there exist fixed relations between the basic variables that constitute the components of any closed system. Thus, in classical Marxism, for instance, there was an assumption of fixed relations between the means of production, the relations of production, class interests, and the prevailing ideology. This did very often give rise to the elaboration of broad typologies of societies (or of cultural or personality systems) which were often seen not only as of heuristic but also as of explanatory and even predictive value. The second assumption was that the laws or relations characteristic of one "basic" component of social order (whatever this might be in a particular theory) also regulated all the other components, so that the latter were not autonomous and could not shape the variability of the "basic" component.

Because of these assumptions each of the closed-system approaches faltered when it came to explain those aspects of social order in which the other components became interrelated independently of the presumably "basic" component; still less could they explain how or why the "basic" component was influenced by the others. Thus, the purely individualistic approach could not account for the way in which variations in systems of cultural symbols and of social organization do in fact influence the individual's commitment to transcendental value orientations and to collective goals. This was because the individualistic approach took individual goals and commitments as given, using them as the basic starting point for the explanation of individual behavior, and so accounting for the conditions of social order. Thus the features of individual behavior that were caused by collective influences, such as cultural tradition or social organization, could not be systematically treated.

The different sociological or culturological explanations could not, on the other hand, explain how the variability of individual social behavior is influenced not only by its own internal systemic properties but also by its interaction with other spheres, whether social or symbolic. Nor did they show how individual goals can greatly influence the variation of concrete social, institutional, and organizational settings and the crystallization of symbolic realms. Such explanations also overlooked the way in which the great variability of individual orientations to symbols on different levels of social organization can influence the crystallization of different types of social and cultural spheres, their continuity, and their change. Similarly, sociological closed-system approches emphasizing one institutional sphere could not explain the possible autonomy of other institutional spheres, their internal variability and changeability, and their possible influence on the component of order presumed to be "basic."

Of special importance in this context is the confrontation between the purely societal or sociological and the purely culturological closed-system approaches. The purely culturological systems, whether they are the older idealist approach represented by Croce, the newer culture pattern approach of Benedict and others, or such contemporary derivatives of pure linguistics as the work of Lévi-Strauss, are faced with the problem of explaining the social order. Neither the concrete exigencies of organized social life—the organizations and mechanisms through which social order is maintained or shaped—nor the problems and tendencies of the social organizational sphere in general can be explained wholly in terms of principles deduced from some a priori conception of the symbolic sphere. Still less can the culturological approach account for the way in which social organization may greatly influence the form actually taken by any given symbolic order, or the way in which it finds acceptance and is able to function.

The weakness that becomes apparent in the purely sociological approaches when they are confronted with the culturological ones, and vice versa, closely resembles the rift that developed within sociology itself between what may be called the "formal" and the "institutional" approaches. The purely formal approach could not fully explain how the organizational exigencies of social life are shaped by variation in the social content of institutional goals or of such basic societal resources as money, power, and prestige. Purely institutional analyses, on the other hand, cannot explain how different basic orientations to social interaction and to primordial attachments and collective commitments can vary autonomously within organizational and institutional settings, and can even influence the form that these settings take.

The "environmental" closed-system approach in sociology faced problems even more difficult than those faced by almost all the other major approaches. The more sophisticated environmental approaches, while admitting that there were some institutional or organizational mechanisms through which the initial impact of the environment on society was mediated, could not fully explain the extent to which the nature of this impact was determined not only by a society's level of technology but also by its symbolic spheres. Thus these approaches overlooked the extent to which the symbolic sphere constitutes a basic part of that environment on which a society expends its technological resources and an individual his mental energy.

Most of the other closed-system approaches, whether individualistic, societal, or culturological, tended to ignore the possibility that there might be autonomous demographic, biological, and ecological forces that impinged on the institutional structure. At most they paid some general lip service to the basic importance of such forces, but only rarely did they attempt to analyze the mechanisms through which the forces made themselves felt.

But perhaps the most crucial area in which almost all the closed-system approaches faltered was the comparative explanation of social order and the dynamics of social change. With regard to the mode and direction of change in systems of social order, some closed-system approaches tended to ignore them on the grounds that they were not amenable to any systemic explanation, but had to be accounted for in terms of the uniqueness of particular historical or ethnographic situations. Other such approaches subsumed all the various types of societies, regardless of how they had developed, under "laws" derived from various dialectical or dynamic models of the historical process. Very often this was accompanied by a utopian search for the ultimate conflictless society and, for the most part, by neglect of the way in which the different spheres of social order could vary internally. The possibility that such variability might influence the developmental tendencies of all spheres of social order was also overlooked; it does not seem to have occurred to the closed-system theorists that there might not be any single over-riding developmental trend, or that the existence of a multiplicity of possible avenues of change might allow a certain openness of historical choice (for further discussion, see Gellner 1965).

Similarly, most such closed-system theorists did not deal fully or systematically with the processes of social disorder, disorganization, and anomie, nor did they fully explore the positive contributions of these processes to social change and transformation. Social disorder was usually seen by them as deviance from the fixed relation between the subcomponents of the sphere, whatever it might be, that they took as "basic." Because of this, these various approaches usually could not analyze the way in which different types of social systems differed in their potential for internal change as well as in the conditions and processes through which change took place.

From assumptions to problems for research

The opening up of closed systems has come about through the recognition not only that the basic component of any system is itself subject to variation but also that the phenomena belonging to spheres not regarded as basic are independent components of social order.

This breakthrough involved much more than a general, vague admission of "interdependence" or "interconnection" between the different components of social order; such an admission could easily be found on the level of the "discrete" analytical approach. Rather, it involved attempts at formulating such interconnections in mutual systemic terms, in order to show how each such element of social order, while constituting a system of sorts, also constitutes a basic systemic component or referent of the other elements.

On the substantive level, this meant that analysis of the internal systemic influence and continuous feedback of these other elements was henceforth to be a crucial focus of sociological analysis. On the methodological level, it meant that the existence of some such systemic interrelation was accepted not merely as a working assumption but as a hypothesis to be tested by actual research and analysis. Earlier assumptions about the existence of fixed relations between the subcomponents of the social system now became problems to be investigated; the grandiose typological schemes that had pretended to explain so much fell into disuse.

Only a few illustrations of the crucial importance of this breakthrough in the history of sociological thought can be given here. One such illustration can be found in the work of G. H. Mead, whose importance lies in his conception of the "social"

as one constituent element in personality which, while present in all personalities, may yet systematically vary among them according to both personality structure and social conditions.

Another instructive illustration can be found in the field of so-called formal sociology. If we compare the classificatory schema of Vierkandt or von Wiese with that of Tönnies in terms of their usefulness in opening up new lines of thought and inquiry, it is quite clear that the influence of Tönnies has been far more fruitful. The reason for this lies in the fact that although Tönnies tended to view *Gesellschaft* and *Gemeinschaft* as concepts describing total structural–societal entities as well as stages of historical development, yet these same "totalistic" concepts could be transformed into the more processual ones of *Vergemeinschaftung* and *Vergesellschaftung*, as was done by Max Weber. In this way they came to designate certain basic types of individual orientation and commitment to society and social relations. The usefulness of these concepts lies in the way in which, while always having some social structural implications, they do not exclude consideration of other aspects or elements of social life, such as goals and institutional contents. In other words, while originally closed-system concepts, they can be adapted for use with the open-system approach. In this way they have given rise to the whole gamut of primary group research and, more recently, to redefinition of the nature of attachment to primordial relations and symbols (Shils 1957).

The case of Marxism (the classic Marxist system, not the popularized version of it) offers a good example of the breakup of a sophisticated closed system. In this system, the interrelations between its basic components—"relations of production," class struggle, and historical change—were treated as constants, and the other components of social order, such as individual goals and cultural symbols, were subsumed under them. The breakthrough from this system—as effected, for instance, by Weber—was achieved not by negation of the concepts but, rather, by giving up the assumption of the existence of a fixed relation between them either over time or at any one time. Thus the relations were transformed from assumptions into problems for research.

It was only after this transformation had taken place that the concepts themselves became subject to revision and that new questions were formulated about the mechanisms and conditions of the relations between them. In this way, a newer, deeper perception of the basic phenomenology of social order was developed, and the task of sociology itself was greatly clarified. From this point of view

Weber's comparative analysis of religion in general and his thesis of the Protestant ethic in particular are of special importance. The significance of the latter lies not so much in its general recognition of the role of nonmaterial, cultural factors but, rather, in its attempt to formulate with some degree of precision the mechanisms through which such factors can enter into institutional change. Whatever the correctness of the details of Weber's thesis, we have here an attempt to explain a whole process of sociocultural transformation through a change in the type of relations between personal and collective identities, on the one hand, and between these identities and various institutional and organizational activities, on the other. This alone represents a decisive advance in the history of sociological thought.

A similar analysis could be undertaken to demonstrate the historical importance of the theory of action, as developed by Parsons and others. Here, too, concepts like individual interests, norms and values, symbols, groups and institutions, which had existed separately in closed systems, were related to one another. In this way Parsons and his followers have been able to stress the basic structural cores of these concepts, their continuous systemic interconnections, the potential variability of these interconnections, and, finally, the importance of investigating the mechanisms through which such interconnections may be maintained.

Some problems of open-system analysis

The breakthrough to the open-system approach put sociological theory in an excellent position from which to advance, but did not insure that it woud do so. This was because sociological theory had yet to solve many of the methodological problems inherent in systems analysis.

Systems that were open, in the sense that they recognized the interrelations that existed between the basic components of social order in the basic systems, could as yet concentrate methodologically on only one of these components (Gluckman 1965). Thus, it was often assumed that fixed relations existed between the basic components of such systems. In this way, emphasis was placed upon the supposed possibility of generalizing from the analysis of unique situations. From this it can be seen that the critical advance which took place when the assumption of fixed relations between components of social order was abandoned was not confined to the transition from closed to open systems, but was also to be found in some of the more sophisticated open-system approaches.

The social-anthropological model. One very instructive example of a sophisticated open-system approach is British social anthropology (see Eisenstadt 1961). As is well known, most social-anthropological studies combine the analysis of social behavior, institutional norms, groups, and societies in one basic model, and then attempt to show how these aspects of social order are always very closely interrelated. Indeed, it is because they contribute both to each other and to the society as a whole that they are often said to have "functions" and to stand in "functional relations" to each other.

The maintenance of such interrelations cannot, of course, be conceived of without assuming the operation of certain societal mechanisms. The social-anthropological model of society therefore made provision for several such mechanisms and contained, if only implicitly, several additional assumptions about their nature. The first such mechanism was the interaction of the same people or groups in different situations, an interaction that made their mutual commitments in one situation or group greatly influence their behavior in others. The second was the relation between "culture" (or, rather, values) and ritual symbols, on the one hand, and social relations, on the other. The third was the continuous interrelation, in most groups and situations in primitive societies, between different types of social activities. Ritual, jural, contractual, and political activities were seen as interwoven in most of the situations and groups encountered in these primitive societies. These three mechanisms have been found by the social anthropologists to be operative—even if in varying degrees—in most parts of the primitive societies studied by them. Presumably, the same mechanisms also insure close interrelations between the major aspects of social order in these societies.

This model of the social system, which has greatly contributed to the development of systematic anthropology and which still guides much of the work done by anthropologists, faced several crucial problems when it was applied to the analysis of so-called complex societies, whether historical or modern. Studies of such societies have indeed shown that there exist specific areas in which some of the mechanisms emphasized in this model do in fact shape the patterns of interrelations between individual behavior, social norms, and group activities. However, all these studies have also faced problems that cannot be dealt with within the limits of this model. Among these problems are, first, the ways in which behavior is regulated in situations in which individuals can choose between different roles and groups and in which various contradictory and discrete institutional forces impinge on the individuals participating in these groups. Second, this model could not explain the ways in which many patterns of behavior and activities of individuals are not entirely tied to concrete groups or embedded in them but are dispersed between various discrete and seemingly unconnected situations. Third, the model did not explain how new patterns of behavior, new groups, and new situations are continuously emerging, crystallizing, and impinging on different individuals and making different, often conflicting, demands on them. Fourth, the model did not explain the ways in which different types of social activities—contractual, juridical, political, ritual, and so on—are organized in different "orders" within a society, and how all these orders impinge on and regulate various situations, groups, and patterns of behavior within the society. Fifth, the model did not explain how, if at all, many conflicts between different groups in complex society are regulated or can be said simply to contribute to the continuous integration of the ongoing society. In the more complex societies it was, of course, even more difficult to delineate the exact nature of each function that such groups perform in relation to the basic institutions.

But this inability of the social-anthropological model to explain these various problems did not necessarily mean the over-all rejection of its concepts and approach. It did, however, necessitate giving up the assumption of relatively fixed relations between the different components of social order—norms, individual behavior, "functional" contributions to society, and the various societal mechanisms specified above. Instead, these fixed relations were transformed from assumptions into problems for research. Once this happened, it entailed, on the empirical side, limiting the application of the social-anthropological model to select parts or aspects of complex societies. On the analytical side, it entailed searching for the conditions under which various types of relations between these diverse aspects of social order are indeed maintained, for the mechanisms that maintain these relations, and for new mechanisms (and adequate concepts) with reference to which the problems of social order in more complex societies could more adequately be explained.

Analysis of roles and institutions. Another illustration of this kind of analytical development may be taken from the way in which the concepts of role and of institutions have evolved in recent years. For a time, roles were designated as the basic units of social behavior of individuals. Indeed, it was one of the major contributions of the structural–functional school to emphasize the great importance and the dynamic quality of roles as per-

haps the most important meeting points between individual behavior and societal functions. But this concept of role was usually treated as a unified one, representing a functionally indivisible unit. Recent analysis, however, has shown that roles have several components, such as their goals, their norms, and their relations to other roles (Goode 1960). Although certain role components do in fact tend to go together, they may also vary independently and should be studied from this viewpoint. The variations are not, of course, infinite. But each of these components is often subject to independent influences, and thus may constitute a focus of change, affecting the role as a whole in different ways and to varying degrees. Hence, the concept of role should not be taken to mean a pattern of behavior or be treated as a normative definition of behavior that is given—i.e., fixed in the institutional structure of society so that the individual must adjust himself to it through the process of socialization and through interaction with other people. Rather, the very formation of any specific role—the articulation of its goals and the crystallization of its various components—is an outcome of various social forces or mechanisms that create, out of the potential of various contents, demands, and institutional and personal needs existing in the given society, the actual specific crystallizations of the different role components. Consequently, different components of any role can profitably be studied with an eye to the degree to which each of them has become institutionalized. Comparisons between role components can then be made in this respect.

Similarly, the crystallization of different roles may, in turn, influence the development of a society's institutional structure. In all societies, even the most stable ones, roles are continually crystallizing and being created. Even if, in some cases, the basic definition of a role is more or less constant over long periods of time, the relative emphasis on its different components will vary according to the different situations and forces that impinge on it. Thus the role map of a given society, instead of being treated as if it were completely fixed and given, has to be perceived as being continuously recrystallized.

Similarly, as this approach implies, the performance of roles should not be viewed as a static process in which individuals either assume or do not assume certain attributes in order to realize certain types of fixed expectations and norms set by "society." Rather, it should be conceived of as a differentiated process, in which the individual's aspirations interplay with his perceptions in a variety of situations and emphasize different aspects of normatively regulated behavior in each of them. Indeed, it is precisely the encounter between individuals and supposedly given roles that often creates the possibility of role innovation (Eisenstadt et al. 1963).

A similar and closely related analysis can be applied to the concept of institutions. Here, the crucial transition was from defining institutions as given, fixed entities to viewing them as focuses of processes of institutionalization [see SOCIAL INSTITUTIONS, *article on* THE CONCEPT].

An analysis of some of the more recent criticisms of the structural–functional school, especially with regard to its supposed neglect of problems of change, will show that most of these criticisms—insofar as they are not couched in purely ideological terms or concerned with purely ideological problems—are not directed against the concepts developed in this approach or against the assumption of the crucial importance of systemic interrelations between the basic components of social order. Rather, they are directed against the alleged assumption of certain *constant* interrelations between such components as ultimate values, consensus, and roles [see FUNCTIONAL ANALYSIS, *article on* VARIETIES OF FUNCTIONAL ANALYSIS; SOCIAL STRUCTURE, *article on* SOCIAL STRUCTURAL ANALYSIS].

Substantive developments

The principal substantive development attendant on the major conceptual breakthroughs—whether from closed-system to open-system approaches or from less to more sophisticated versions of the latter—has always been a growing awareness that the conditions and mechanisms of social order depend on the dynamics of interaction among its major components. This development has entailed, first, a continuous shift of emphasis to the processes of role formation and institutionalization as meeting points between the major components of social order. Second, it has involved more intensive analysis of the mechanisms through which interaction between the social and cultural subsystems takes place. Third, it has highlighted the connections between the processes of social disorganization and anomie, and the processes of institution building and transformation of personality.

Nor did these conceptual breakthroughs entail ceasing to emphasize the systemic qualities of the different components of social order. On the contrary, even greater stress was placed upon the fact that each such component has certain basic "needs," or structural prerequisites, as well as special mechanisms through which these prerequisites are maintained or changed. It was also realized that relations between the components are not purely random and may not vary indiscriminately. All of these insights were essentially legacies from the closed-system approach.

The special contributions of the open-system approach was that it exposed the great variety of systemic components and subcomponents of social order, each with its basic systemic problems and its openness to penetration by any of the other components and subcomponents. But the fact that it was open to penetration in this way did not imply that different types of social institutions, organizations, or cultural systems could covary without limit. Rather, it suggested a shift in the focus of analysis to such problems as the extent to which any given type of family system sets limits to the development of other types of social institutions, personality types, or symbolic systems. Thus there developed a more generalized concern with the mechanisms through which such relations between different subsystems are maintained or transformed [see SOCIAL INSTITUTIONS, *article on* COMPARATIVE STUDY]. Such breakthroughs made possible the testing of various hypotheses at any given level of conceptual formulation. They also led to the redefinition and what may be called the decomposition of the basic concepts of sociological inquiry. The result has been a continuous increase in sophistication concerning the basic phenomena of social order and the different ways in which they are related to each other.

These same developments have made it easier to overcome the dilemma posed by the apparent irreconcilability of the analysis of general trends with that of unique events. Thus it has become obvious to practitioners of the open-system approach that it is not necessary to deny the uniqueness of many structures or the worthwhileness of the application of sociological analysis to the study of concrete single cases. Rather, such analysis has come to be seen as complementary to and dependent on analysis of general systemic tendencies. In fact, it appears that insofar as the characteristics unique to any type of social order can be analyzed in broad comparative terms, the possibility of understanding these characteristics is maximized [see *also* SOCIAL INSTITUTIONS, *article on* COMPARATIVE STUDY; *for an opposing viewpoint, see* HISTORY, *article on* THE PHILOSOPHY OF HISTORY].

Sociological theory and analysis today

Sociological theory, considered as a body of examinable, potentially testable propositions capable of shedding light on the nature of social order in all its variety and complexity, has reached its present state mainly through the rather intermittent analytical breakthroughs outlined above. The uneven progress of the different schools of sociology in the past indicates that the future development of sociological theory, in which the past forms only a chapter, will be equally checkered and unpredictable.

Progress in the accumulation of systematic knowledge has, of course, always been influenced by many diverse factors. The specific rates of progress of the different branches of sociological research have greatly depended on various external factors. Among these should be listed diverse ideological impetuses, the development of public interest in selected fields, certain types of institutional development involving the academic community (for instance, the growth of relations between academic and semiacademic research institutions), and the differential availability of research funds. In addition, the development of research methodology has played a large part in determining the amount of attention given to particular lines of research. This has been especially true of many microsociological studies.

The picture that sociological knowledge presents today is very uneven, not only in the relative development of different areas of research but also in the degree to which each of these areas is oriented toward the basic problems that first provided the impetus of sociological thought. The strongest developments in sociological thought and research have been in those fields that use as their point of departure some basic component of social order itself. Such points of departure can be found in the manifold studies of individual behavior, attitudes, and personality dynamics; in descriptive accounts of regularities in social behavior and group structure; and in typological studies of collectivities. They also underlie some studies of social institutions and a few studies of the major types of cultural and symbolic subsystems. Within each of these fields there has developed not only a body of concrete and systematic studies about the diverse phenomena encompassed by the field but also a continually, if intermittently, growing perception of how intricate are the systemic properties of these phenomena, and how varied their interrelations. Even their possible orientation to other components of social order began to be considered.

Admittedly, these developments did not affect all fields to the same extent. Thus, within the psychological, or "individualistic," framework the most important instances of such development are the studies of socialization, culture and personality, and, to some extent, those of communication and reference group behavior. Within the field of organizational and group structure the greatest advances are in the analysis of different types of organization in their relationship to broader institutional structure. Other advances took place in the study of primary groups—their location in institutional structure and their role in personality development—and in studies of the relation between individual interaction and the emergence of group structure (Thibaut & Kelley 1959; Coleman 1964). Within the field of institutional analysis, the most successful analyses of internal systemic properties are to be found in family and kinship studies, at least for those societies where kinship relations are dominant. For more complex societies such studies have been less successful in analyzing the relations between the kinship system and other institutional spheres.

Economic structure has, on the whole, been more extensively studied at the macrosocietal level and in connection with the microanalysis of economic organizations. The relation of economic structure to patterns of economic behavior has been comparatively neglected. In political analysis, the two major types of empirical studies—those of the macroanalysis of political structure, on the one hand, and of political behavior and socialization, on the other—have both been intensively pursued, but, until recently, in different directions. In the field of social stratification, the separateness of these two directions of research has been even more pronounced. Analyses of prestige and of the power system, as well as of broad developmental trends in the distribution of prestige and power, have only lately begun to be connected with studies of individual perception of status position and group membership, and with studies of how various processes of exchange influence crystallization of the broader institutional structure. Even in areas that, like communication or reference group behavior, have been natural connecting points between these two directions of research, understanding of what the existing empirical studies imply about the processes of institutionalization has only just begun [see SOCIAL INSTITUTIONS, *article on* THE CONCEPT].

Perhaps the weakest connections between the different types of studies are to be found in the area of cultural symbols. Here most anthropological and philosophical approaches have proceeded in isolation from other disciplines and have been relatively unaware of the part played by the exigencies of systemic organization in the crystallization of the symbolic fields. Similarly, study of the full implications of the interrelation between the symbolic realms and individual orientation is, apart from the existing "culture and personality" studies, in only a rudimentary stage. This weakness in the sociological analysis of the cultural realm can also be seen in the neglect of various crucial aspects of individual cultural orientation. For instance, the study of the different orientations of individuals to primordial images, and of the interweaving of these images with varied organizational settings, is in its infancy (Shils 1957). Other basic categories of interrelation between the symbolic realm and individual orientations—as, for instance, the category of play or that of orientation to a temporal system—have only begun to be systematically explored in terms of their implications for social order [see TIME; see also Caillois 1958].

Two other weak or neglected areas in the present state of sociological knowledge should also be mentioned. One is the analysis of change in social systems—the mechanisms of transition from one type of society to another, and the transformative capacities of societies and groups. The other such area has been the one that lies between demography, population genetics, and ecology, on the one hand, and institutional and cultural analysis, on the other. While all these disciplines have made great strides within their own spheres, their interconnection with the processes of institutionalization has as yet received very little systematic examination, although claims have often been made on behalf of the independence of this area of analysis. We therefore know relatively little about the mechanisms through which this interconnection is effected.

But in spite of all the unevenness in the development of the various areas of sociological research, a growing analytical convergence of these areas has lately been discerned. The major analytical traditions that have been guiding this convergence are (1) structural–functional analysis, from Pareto, Durkheim, and Weber to such contemporary figures as Parsons, Shils, and Merton; (2) game theory and exchange theory; (3) philosophical and anthropological study of symbolism. It is in areas affected by these trends that the major advances and breakthroughs can be discerned. One such breakthrough is taking place through a convergence of structuralist anthropology and certain basic trends in social psychology. Here the possibility of a systemic rapprochement between the structural analysis of symbolic values (Lévi-Strauss 1958),

the analysis of how universal concepts such as space and physical causation are acquired by young children (Piaget 1950), and the new sociolinguistic analysis (Bernstein 1965; Gumperz & Hymes 1964) is a most significant development.

Also important is Shils's treatment of the concepts of center and charisma (1961b; 1965). By showing that charismatic quality refers to the ability to order various dimensions of human experience, that it evinces a tendency to become closely interwoven with the center of society, and that the need for such ordering can be found distributed in varying degrees among different individuals and different organizations, Shils has added a new dimension to our conception of the interrelation between cultural, social, and personality systems. He has also helped to distinguish between the universal prerequisites for the functioning of any society or system of social organization and those dimensions of symbolic meaning which enable a society to create for itself new and more complex systemic orientations.

Similar exploration of the connection of the historical dimension of social change with the systemic propensities of societies to internal change and transformation has resulted from the increase in comparative studies and in studies of social change and modernization. Work of this kind may eventually enable sociologists to go beyond generalities and undertake more systematic analysis of the transformative and degenerative properties of social systems. Such studies may also contribute to the understanding of an even more problematic and difficult area, interest in which has been reviving—the combination of studies of human development with environmental analysis. The focal point of this interest has been the problem of evolution. Here the difficulties facing social scientists are even greater. Indeed, they have only just begun to explore the interaction of different kinds of environments, institutions, and cultural symbols, and to accumulate systematic data on the building up of the biological potential of human populations. But even this beginning seems to be significant.

SHMUEL N. EISENSTADT

[Directly related are the entries EVOLUTION; INTERACTION; ROLE; SOCIAL INSTITUTIONS; SOCIAL STRUCTURE; SOCIETY. Other relevant material may be found in ANTHROPOLOGY, article on SOCIAL ANTHROPOLOGY; CHARISMA; ECOLOGY, article on HUMAN ECOLOGY; ECONOMY AND SOCIETY; FUNCTIONAL ANALYSIS; HISTORY; LINGUISTICS; REFERENCE GROUPS; SOCIAL CONTROL; and in the biographies of ARISTOTLE; BENEDICT; COMTE; CROCE; DURK-

HEIM; FERGUSON; HOBBES; HOBHOUSE; LOCKE; MANNHEIM; MARX; MEAD; MILLAR; MONTESQUIEU; PARETO; PLATO; ROSS; ROUSSEAU; SIMMEL; SMITH, ADAM; SPENCER; STEIN; TOCQUEVILLE; TÖNNIES; TYLOR; WEBER, MAX; WIESE.]

BIBLIOGRAPHY

BENEDICT, RUTH (1934) 1959 *Patterns of Culture.* 2d ed. Boston: Houghton Mifflin. → A paperback edition was published in 1961.

BERNSTEIN, BASIL 1965 A Socio-linguistic Approach to Social Learning. Pages 144–168 in *Penguin Survey of the Social Sciences.* Edited by Julius Gould. Baltimore: Penguin.

CAILLOIS, ROGER (1958) 1961 *Man, Play and Games.* New York: Free Press. → First published as *Les jeux et les hommes.*

COLEMAN, JAMES S. 1964 Collective Decisions. *Sociological Inquiry* 34:166–181.

DOWNS, ANTHONY 1957 *An Economic Theory of Democracy.* New York: Harper.

DUNCAN, OTIS DUDLEY (1964) 1966 Social Organization and the Ecosystem. Pages 36–82 in Robert E. L. Faris (editor), *Handbook of Modern Sociology.* Chicago: Rand McNally.

EISENSTADT, SHMUEL N. 1961 Anthropological Studies of Complex Societies. *Current Anthropology* 2:201–222.

EISENSTADT, SHMUEL N.; WEINTRAUB, DOV; and TOREN, NINA 1963 Analysis of Processes of Role-change: A Proposed Conceptual Framework. Unpublished manuscript, Hebrew Univ., Department of Sociology.

FRIEDMAN, MILTON 1962 *Capitalism and Freedom.* Univ. of Chicago Press.

GELLNER, ERNST 1965 *Thought and Change.* Univ. of Chicago Press.

GLUCKMANN, MAX (editor) 1965 *Closed Systems and Open Minds: The Limits of Naivety in Social Anthropology.* Chicago: Aldine.

GOODE, WILLIAM J. 1960 A Theory of Role Strain. *American Sociological Review* 25:483–496.

GUMPERZ, JOHN J.; and HYMES, DELL H. (editors) 1964 The Ethnography of Communication. *American Anthropologist* New Series 66, no. 6, part 2.

KROEBER, A. L. (1901–1951) 1952 *The Nature of Culture.* Univ. of Chicago Press.

LÉVI-STRAUSS, CLAUDE (1958) 1963 *Structural Anthropology.* New York: Basic Books. → First published in French. See especially the chapters on myth and religion, pages 167–245.

MERTON, ROBERT K. (1949) 1957 *Social Theory and Social Structure.* Rev. & enl. ed. Glencoe, Ill.: Free Press.

PARSONS, TALCOTT 1965 Unity and Diversity in the Modern Intellectual Disciplines: The Role of the Social Sciences. *Dædalus* 94:39–65.

PARSONS, TALCOTT et al. (editors) (1961) 1965 *Theories of Society: Foundations of Modern Sociological Theory.* New York: Free Press.

PIAGET, JEAN 1950 *Introduction à l'épistémologie génétique.* 3 vols. Paris: Presses Universitaires de France.

SHILS, EDWARD 1957 Primordial, Personal, Sacred and Civil Ties. *British Journal of Sociology* 8, no. 2:130–145.

SHILS, EDWARD (1961a) 1965 [Epilogue] The Calling of Sociology. Pages 1405–1448 in Talcott Parsons et al.

(editors), *Theories of Society: Foundations of Modern Sociological Theory.* New York: Free Press.

SHILS, EDWARD 1961b Centre and Periphery. Pages 117–130 in *The Logic of Personal Knowledge: Essays Presented to Michael Polanyi.* London: Routledge; New York: Free Press.

SHILS, EDWARD 1965 Charisma, Order and Status. *American Sociological Review* 30:199–213.

SOROKIN, PITIRIM A. 1928 *Contemporary Sociological Theories.* New York: Harper. → A paperback edition was published in 1964 as *Contemporary Sociological Theories Through the First Quarter of the Twentieth Century.*

THIBAUT, JOHN W.; and KELLEY, HAROLD H. 1959 *The Social Psychology of Groups.* New York: Wiley.

III

THE EARLY HISTORY OF SOCIAL RESEARCH

Beginings of research in England

The idea that social topics could be subjected to quantitative analysis first acquired prominence in England in the latter half of the seventeenth century. The influence of Francis Bacon had already created a favorable intellectual climate; now a political motive was added by the growing currency of the notions that good government should be based on precise information and that population was a primary source of national power and wealth. Moreover, the rise of the life insurance business and the general expansion of commerce and trade called for a rational and calculable foundation in statistical fact. Curiosity and fear also played a part in the interest in vital statistics: people wanted to know how many had died in the Great Plague of 1665 and other epidemics and what effect this would have on population growth. Finally, the size of London, compared with that of Paris and Amsterdam, became a matter for English national pride, and there was a demand for statistics illustrating the city's growth.

Political arithmetic. The English political arithmeticians, as they called themselves, never formed an organized school. Single individuals of varied backgrounds pursued political arithmetic as an avocation. They were compelled to work with existing administrative records, which were incomplete, of varying quality, and scattered in parishes all over the country. John Graunt, a London draper who lived from 1620 to 1674, was the first, in his *Natural and Political Observations Made Upon the Bills of Mortality* (1662), to make a systematic analysis of the London parish records on christenings and deaths. In order to assess the validity and completeness of the bills of mortality, he described in great detail how they were recorded and assembled. Graunt drew attention to the fact that the mortality rate was higher in London than in the rest of the country; he estimated, by several independent methods, the total population of the city; he noted the rapid recovery of the London population after the Great Plague; and he estimated the extent of migration into the city. Graunt's friend William Petty, who lived from 1623 to 1687, coined the term "political arithmetic"; he was in turn seaman, physician, professor of anatomy, inventor, and land surveyor in Ireland, as well as being one of the founders of the Royal Society. During the period 1671–1676 he wrote *The Political Anatomy of Ireland*, which was based on his personal observations and experiences and in which he formulated a general theory of government founded on concrete empirical knowledge. Edmund Halley, the astronomer, published the first life tables (1693), based on mortality records of the city of Breslau in Silesia, which had been forwarded to the Royal Society by a number of intermediaries (including Leibniz). Their advantage over Graunt's London bills was that the age of death was recorded. Assuming a stable population and a constant rate of birth, Halley calculated the chances of surviving to any given age. The actuarial techniques needed for life insurance were thereafter slowly perfected, calculations being based on the information accumulated by the insurance companies.

Political arithmetic also had a hand in reshaping the descriptive "state-of-the-kingdom" literature: numerical data were added to geographical, biographical, and historical descriptions. Gregory King, who lived from 1648 to 1712, in his "Natural and Political Observations and Conclusions Upon the State and Condition of England" (1696), divided the entire population into 24 strata, from lords spiritual and temporal to vagrants, and estimated not only the total number of families but also the average family income and the share of the total national wealth that each family enjoyed.

The rise of demography.   Demography as a science grew out of political arithmetic. The notion became accepted that regularities in human events, similar to the laws of natural science, existed; initially, these regularities were taken to be a demonstration of divine order and benevolence, but progressively the concept of regularity was secularized. In his "Argument for Divine Providence" (1710), based on the observed number of christenings of infants of each sex in London from 1629 to 1710, John Arbuthnott argued, from the exact balance that he found maintained between the numbers of males and females, that polygamy was contrary to the law of nature and justice. Noting

that in every year the number of male births slightly exceeded that of female births, he showed, by analogy with a fair-coin-tossing experiment, that in a large number of binomial trials both an extreme unbalance in the sex ratio and an even split between the sexes were very improbable events. The Reverend William Derham's *Physico-theology: Or, a Demonstration of the Being and Attributes of God From His Works of Creation* (1713), another demographic classic, ran through 13 English editions and one each in French, German, and Swedish.

Interaction of English and Continental work. The works of Derham and the other English political arithmeticians were a major influence upon the physician–pastor Johann Peter Süssmilch, whose *Die göttliche Ordnung in den Veränderungen des menschlichen Geschlechts* (1741) was the most complete demographic compendium of the time. In Süssmilch's work, in particular in the second, enlarged edition of *Die göttliche Ordnung*, published in 1761, the field of demography was clearly defined for the first time. Süssmilch systematically introduced the concepts of fertility, mortality, and nuptiality (marriage rates) and assessed their effects upon population size.

Süssmilch in turn provided much information and inspiration for Thomas Malthus when the latter wrote his influential *Essay on Population* (1798), in which the notion of an inexorable law of population growth was linked with the problems of pauperism and food supply. But in the absence of censuses, demography and vital statistics in England remained on a shaky empirical foundation. At the end of the eighteenth century the most sophisticated analytic and empirical work on population was being carried on in France. Indeed, by that date the promise of political arithmetic as a major instrument of government and as a foundation for an empirical social science had not been fulfilled. The new school of political economists, in particular Adam Smith, was highly skeptical of the methods and data of the political arithmeticians, as well as of their protectionist and state-interventionist economic policies. In over-all terms, political arithmetic split into a number of specialized branches and did not join the mainstream of thought on social theory and on social problems.

Beginnings of social research in France

The social research conducted in France at the time when political arithmetic was flourishing in England contrasted with it in three respects: because of monarchical centralization, most inquiries were conceived and carried out by the administration; the results were kept secret; and the data related to the kingdom as a whole.

Colbert's inquiries. The search for qualitative or numerical information on French society far antedates Colbert (who was controller general of finances from 1661 until his death in 1683), but it was he who was largely responsible for systematizing the previously scattered efforts in this field. The general inquiries that he instituted consisted of descriptions of the territorial units governed by intendants. Two trial runs (one in Alsace in 1657, the other throughout Alsace, Lorraine, and Trois-Évêchés in 1663) preceded the 1664 inquiry. A uniform circular (Esmonin 1956) asked the intendants for information about the existing maps of the district, ecclesiastical matters (especially the "credit and influence" of the bishops), the military government and the nobility, the administration of justice, and the condition of the district's finances and economic life.

The first special inquiry ordered by Colbert was one into manufactures, in 1665. He also concerned himself with inquiries into the state of the population: in 1667 he issued an ordinance on the keeping of parish registers, and three years later, under the influence of Graunt, he instituted publication of yearly data on births, marriages, and deaths.

Vauban's inquiries. Sébastien le Prestre, marquis de Vauban, undertook several far-reaching inquiries, with the aid of the military authorities. Vauban was commissioner general of fortifications from 1677 until he was forced to retire in disgrace thirty years later. He set out to describe territorial units: his papers contain the *Agenda pour faire l'instruction du dénombrement des peuples et la description des provinces* (possibly dating from 1685), as well as 24 memoirs describing provinces, *élections*, or cities, including the celebrated "Description de l'élection de Vezelay," written in 1686. In his *Méthode générale et facile pour faire le dénombrement des peuples*, written in 1686 (see 1707), Vauban recommended taking the census by counting individuals rather than households. And indeed, between 1682 and 1701 a number of censuses were taken in the manner that Vauban recommended. In subsequent censuses, however, the administration returned to the old method. [*For Vauban's other inquiries, see* LEISURE.]

The Grande Enquête. An impressive series of 32 memoirs, describing each of the administrative districts of France, was begun in 1697. The survey was made by the intendants, at the instigation of the duke of Beauvilliers, governor of Louis XIV's grandson, the duke of Burgundy. Known as the Grande Enquête, it was compiled for the purpose of demonstrating to the duke of Burgundy the undesirable consequences of Louis XIV's policy of war and excessive taxation (Esmonin 1954; 1956). Each memoir was based on a questionnaire sent to one of the district intendants and included a description of the territory and of "the nature of the peoples," a census of the population, the number and reputation of the clergy and nobles, and the answers to 15 questions on the district's economic life. Many copies were made for high dignitaries; the intendants also made use of the original memoir for various publications (Gille 1964). It is estimated that about 900 manuscripts relate to this vast inquiry, which served as a guide for the intendants until a new one was directed by Bertin in 1762. *L'état de la France*, by Henri de Boulainvilliers (1727), sheds light on the contents of the Grande Enquête and contains some savage criticisms.

Research in France in the later eighteenth century

Administrative inquiries were resumed in 1724, shortly after the death of the regent and the end of the financial crisis into which the collapse of "Law's system" in 1720 had plunged the country. With a few exceptions these inquiries were nationwide. However, the general descriptions favored by Colbert and his followers now tended to be replaced by the study of specific problems, such as manufactures, public administration, beggary, and wages. In 1730 Orry, a worthy successor to Colbert, instituted a general economic inquiry, and in 1745 another of his inquiries, on the "resources of the people" and on militia recruiting, led to a census (authentic according to Dainville 1952; fictitious according to Gille 1964). In addition, the intendants were instructed to spread rumors concerning increases in town dues and the raising of a militia and then to make conscientious reports (which have survived) of the citizens' reactions. Great pains were taken to make the answers comparable and to involve in the inquiry scholars from outside the government. A member of the French Academy was entrusted with drawing up the final document.

Scholars and learned societies. About 1750 the French government yielded its place as the leading exponent of social research to learned societies and private individuals, who were to dominate the field until 1804, when Napoleon, then first consul, had himself proclaimed emperor.

At the same time that political arithmetic was

losing its impetus in England, it began to take hold in France, where its exponents confined themselves to population studies, thereby avoiding criticisms such as Diderot made of Petty (see "Arithmétique politique," 1751). The advances made in the calculus of probabilities during this period led Deparcieux to draw up a mortality table, published in 1746 in his *Essai sur les probabilités de la durée de la vie humaine*. Buffon made use of these data in the second volume of his *Histoire naturelle*, published in 1749.

More original studies tried to measure the population on the basis of the number of births given by the parish registers. Between 1762 and 1770 the abbé Expilly, with the help of a huge number of subscribers and correspondents who answered his questionnaires, published his *Dictionnaire géographique, historique et politique des Gaules et de la France* (see Esmonin 1957). From 1764 on, he ceased basing his estimate of the total population on the number of hearths. Instead, he had the parish registers examined for the years 1690–1701 and 1752–1763, drawing up lists of names of the inhabitants of each parish in order to establish the population size on the basis of the number of births. The results for 9,000 parishes, published in 1766, showed that contrary to current opinion the population had increased. The population was estimated by Expilly at 22 million for the entire kingdom. The same method was employed in the *Recherches sur la population des généralités d'Auvergne, de Lyon, de Rouen et de quelques provinces et villes du royaume*, a work published in 1766 under the name of Messance, receiver of taxes for the district of Saint-Étienne (the actual author may have been La Michodière, intendant of Lyons). The author of this work made use of variable coefficients in order to estimate the number of inhabitant–birth ratio in each area (the highest such coefficient used by Expilly was 25); he, too, concluded that the population had increased and estimated it at 23,909,400.

These efforts were crowned by the *Recherches et considérations sur la population de la France* written in 1774 and published in 1778 under the name of Moheau, secretary of Montyon, the former intendant of Auvergne, who was undoubtedly the real author (Chevalier 1948; Esmonin 1958). Montyon compared the various research methods and came to the conclusion that the firmest foundation was that offered by study of the parish registers and of the number of births. By these means he estimated the population to be 23,687,409. His great originality lies in his analysis of the distribution of the population (by age groups and sex, by civil status, and by marital condition) and of the natural and social factors affecting fertility.

Research undertaken by the Academy. During the latter half of the eighteenth century the French Academy of Sciences was responsible for the development of social research in two areas. The first was the application of the calculus of probabilities to quantitative social data. In this connection, there was a controversy in 1760/1761 between d'Alembert and Bernoulli on the statistical measurement of vaccination, and Laplace wrote a memorandum in 1778 on the ratio in Paris of the sexes at birth, and another in 1786 on births, marriages, and deaths; Condorcet (1785) used the calculus of probabilities to study jury verdicts and election results (see Rosen 1955; Westergaard 1932).

The second area was that of the technical problems on which the government frequently consulted the Academy. Thus, in 1762 Deparcieux prepared a report for the government on the supply of drinking water to Paris, and in 1764 one on floods. In 1785 the new statutes of the Academy, thanks to Lavoisier and Condorcet, included the specification that an agricultural section should be set up. In the same year Calonne, the controller general, formed an agricultural commission, of which Lavoisier was a member; and the Academy appointed a committee for reforming the Hôtel-Dieu.

Lavoisier's labors on behalf of Calonne's commission supplied material for the publication, in 1791, of *Résultats d'un ouvrage intitulé: De la richesse territoriale du royaume de France* (this work actually appeared under the auspices of the Taxation Committee of the Constituent Assembly). Lavoisier obtained an estimate of cereal production by combining data on the size of the population (derived from Messance and Montyon) with data on consumption. From the population, he passed to the number of plows, to a "hypothetical census" of livestock, and to the area of land under cultivation. He advocated the centralization of official statistics and their publication.

The committee for reforming the Hôtel-Dieu (comprising Bailly, Lavoisier, Laplace, and Tenon) engaged in a vast inquiry, from 1785 to 1789, on the organization of hospitals in France and in Europe. The official conclusions, based on documents, questionnaires, and direct observation, were presented in three reports by Bailly (1790). In addition, Tenon (1788) published a detailed description of how Parisian hospitals were organized and went on to examine their deficiencies and to propose steps toward a more rational organization. Early in 1790 Cabanis published his *Observations sur les hôpitaux*, in which he proposed more radical measures than those proposed by the commissioners of the Academy. A new generation had appeared, the generation of the ideologues.

The ideologues and the Institut. Social research began again after the fall of Robespierre. In 1795 the Convention set up the Institut National des Sciences et des Arts, intended to replace the academies, which had been suppressed in 1793. The Institut included a "second class," devoted to the moral and political sciences, the official doctrine of which was the ideology laid down by Destutt de Tracy and Cabanis. This doctrine, with its stress on the analysis of language and of signs and its notion of a perceptible relationship between the moral and the physical, influenced empirical social research in ethnography and hygiene and also affected government administration.

In ethnography the outstanding figure was Volney, first a physician and then an Orientalist and traveler, who gave an exact description and systematic analysis of Middle Eastern society in his *Voyage en Égypte et en Syrie*, published in 1787. Taking his inspiration from a questionnaire compiled in 1762 by the German Orientalist Michaelis and from the instructions to representatives of the Ministry of the Interior, he addressed his *Questions de statistique à l'usage des voyageurs* (1795) to diplomatic agents (Gaulmier 1951). Other ethnographic activity included the foundation, in 1800, of the Société des Observateurs de l'Homme in Paris. Two years later the Institut organized a scientific expedition to New Holland, for which Gérando wrote *Considérations sur les diverses méthodes à suivre dans l'observation des peuples sauvages*, published in 1801.

The reform of medical education ordered by the Convention in 1794, under the influence of Cabanis, Pinel, and Bichat—ideologues all three—put great emphasis on hygiene and forensic medicine (Rosen 1946; 1958; Foucault 1963). Hygiene was seen as linked up with welfare work and philanthropy (Cabanis 1803). The minister of the interior under the Directory, François de Neufchâteau, a physiocrat and ideologue, had translations made of a collection of English and German works on "humanitarian establishments." In 1802 the Conseil de Salubrité de la Seine was established. It was used as a model by industrial cities after 1815. In it the physician appeared as a social inquirer and reformer. The hygienist movement continued to develop in the period of industrialization, when it attained its apogee (the complete works of Cabanis were published in the early 1820s). Gérando's career is an illustration of the movement's con-

tinuity; he was general secretary of the Ministry of the Interior under the Empire and published *Le visiteur du pauvre* in 1820 and *De la bienfaisance publique* in 1839.

Other research in continental Europe

In other continental European states in the eighteenth century, census-type information was occasionally assembled for the government by individuals appointed specifically for that purpose. No permanent machinery for collecting and tabulating the information existed, and no standardized methods were used. It is therefore not surprising that the results were generally incomplete and unreliable.

The aim of these surveys was, for the most part, to obtain information useful for taxation and military planning—information that was naturally intended to be kept secret. In Austria, Belgium, and several other countries, occasional enumerations of the population, dwellings, livestock and other aspects of agriculture, commerce, industry, and the army were undertaken, usually only for a given region or city. In Denmark population enumerations took place in 1769 and in 1787. In Sweden, by the law of 1686, parish registers had to be kept of the number of births and deaths and of migration, as well as a list of parish members. The size of the population was of particular concern because of a suspected population decline in the early eighteenth century. In 1748 provision was made for the regular deposit and analysis of these records at a central location. The parish clergy completed the local enumeration for their parishes on standardized forms and forwarded them through the church bureaucracy. The summary for 1749, prepared by Per Wargentin, is probably the oldest national census report. Additional data were published in 1761 by the Swedish Academy of Science. Much of this information, however, remained unanalyzed, even though, unlike French work in this area, the Swedish census was made public.

In the numerous German kingdoms, principalities, and free cities of the seventeenth century, civic reconstruction became the major concern after the devastation of the Thirty Years' War. As a result, a need was felt for systematic information about countries and states. The term "statistics" derives from the activities designed to fulfill this need. Originally, "statistics" meant a mixture of geography, history, law, political science, and public administration. Hermann Conring, who died in 1681, was a professor at Brunswick who developed a set of categories for the purpose of characterizing the state. He was especially concerned with interstate comparisons. He was explicit about his method, classified his sources, and gave criteria for evaluating their reliability. By the early eighteenth century his system was being widely taught at German universities to future civil servants. The later academic school of "statistics," whose outstanding representatives were Achenwall, Schlözer, and Nieman, centered in Göttingen and further perfected Conring's system. In the early nineteenth century these descriptive statisticians were challenged by the "table statisticians," who used the increasingly available quantitative data to make numerous cross-classifications.

At this time, too, a number of statistical associations were formed in Germany, and several states created statistical agencies. After lengthy and bitter polemics, the older statistical tradition slowly underwent a three-way division of labor. The academic discipline of political science and public administration (*Staatswissenschaften*) continued the descriptive tradition. Political economy (*Volkswirtschaftslehre*) became established in the universities and combined the historical and descriptive with the newer, quantitative methods. Finally, statisticians monopolized the statistical agencies and census bureaus.

Research in nineteenth-century Britain

British decennial censuses were started in 1801, under the direction of John Rickman. The first three concentrated on the enumeration of inhabitants, families, and dwellings. The clergy filled returns for each parish, and the quality of the returns left much to be desired. The 1831 census was the first to probe for occupation. It gained added importance because precise demographic data were needed for parliamentary reform. This new information was quickly incorporated into such works as Patrick Colquhoun's *Treatise on the Wealth, Power, and Resources of the British Empire* (1814), William Playfair's *Statistical Breviary* (1801), and John R. McCulloch's *Descriptive and Statistical Account of the British Empire* (1837). They were the equivalents of today's statistical abstracts, yearbooks, who's whos, and information almanacs.

Rural surveys. The latter part of the eighteenth century was the period of the agricultural revolution in Britain. Novel techniques of social research were brought to bear upon the pressing rural problems of the day. Arthur Young, who lived until 1820, carried out social investigations of rural areas. Unlike the extensive travel literature that focused merely on the peculiar customs of rural folk, Young's works described the actual way of life of the rural areas and assessed their agricultural resources with a view to improving cultivation and husbandry. Young's extensive travel accounts covered the rural scene in England, France, and Ireland (1771*a*; 1771*b*; 1780; 1793).

It remained for the Scotsman John Sinclair to introduce quantitative techniques into rural surveys. Sinclair was a wealthy landowner, scientific farmer, traveler, member of Parliament, and writer on many topics. He was familiar with the German statistical tradition, and when in 1755 a private population census of Scotland was carried out through the agency of the Scottish clergy, he conceived work along the same lines but far more ambitious. This work eventually became a monumental social statistical inquiry so broad that it took over seven years to complete. It was published in 21 volumes, between 1791 and 1799, as *The Statistical Account of Scotland*. Sinclair defined statistics as "an inquiry into the state of a country for the purpose of ascertaining the quantum of happiness enjoyed by its inhabitants and the means of its future improvement" (1791–1799, vol. 20, p. xiv). In several appendixes, contained in the last volume, he gave a clear account of his methodology and techniques. He enlisted the cooperation of the Scottish clergy, from whom he eventually obtained parish accounts for each of the 881 parishes of Scotland. The heart of the inquiry was a questionnaire schedule with over a hundred separate questions. In later stages he also used a shorter form, which merely required the respondents to fill numbers into tables. In the appendixes, he reprinted the 23 follow-up letters which over the years he had sent to nonrespondents, in which he alternately begged, cajoled, argued, and threatened. In the end he was forced to send several "statistical missionaries" to complete certain parish returns. He presented a table of the number of returned schedules by date. He urged the ministers to send him all manner of information and the results of their own studies, in addition to replying to his inquiry. The questionnaire itself is divided into several parts. The first 40 questions deal with the geography, geology, and natural history of the parish. Questions 41 to 100 deal with the population: age, sex, occupation, religion, estate and profession (nobility, gentry, clergy, attorneys, etc.), births, deaths, suicides, murders, and number of unemployed, paupers, habitual drunkards, etc. Questions 101 to 116 deal with agricultural produce, husbandry, and minerals; a series of miscellaneous items at the end inquires into wages, prices, history of the parish, character of the people, patterns of land tenure, and comparisons of present conditions in the parish with earlier periods.

Sinclair had a thoroughly modern attitude toward quantification. When he made inquiries about the character of the parish population, he asked whether the people were fond of military life and wanted to know the number of enlistments in recent years. When he asked, "Are people disposed to humane and generous actions," he wanted to know whether they "protect and relieve the ship-wrecked, etc." The quality of the returns varied widely; understandably, there were major difficulties in analyzing, summarizing, and publishing them. Sinclair employed several paid assistants to compile county tabulations from the parish returns, but a definitive quantitative exploitation of the data was not published until 1825, after Sinclair had retired from public life. In the end, *The Statistical Account of Scotland* was a collection of the parish accounts, with a few county summary tabulations by Sinclair and his assistants.

Sinclair's *Statistical Account*, however, was a useful precedent for a census and demonstrated that one could be made. He tried to induce European governments to establish a decennial census, and his efforts certainly contributed to the adoption of the census by many nations in the first half of the nineteenth century. His two-volume summary was translated into French. However, his method of choosing the parish as the reporting unit and the clergy as reporting agents was even then outdated, since the parish, as a unit of local government and administration, had already largely broken down under the impact of the industrial revolution and the growth of cities. Later social investigators of industrial and urban problems had to devise a different approach, the house-to-house survey, which Charles Booth was still using at the end of the century.

Research on problems of industrialization. In order to understand the extraordinary outpouring of social research in the period from 1780 to 1840 in Britain, it must be remembered that this was a time of great efforts aimed at reforming outdated social institutions, including the poor laws, the educational system, local government, public health institutions, and Parliament itself. Independent authorities, commissions, and improvement associations were set up and were staffed by lawyers, businessmen, ministers, educators, physicians, and other civic leaders. Many of these reformers doubled as social researchers. Thus, social policy, social research, reform, and legislation formed a part of a single, broad effort. Many physicians were engaged in reform activities and social investigations, for two reasons at least. First, they were daily reminded, through their contacts with working-class patients and the poor, of the magnitude of the problem, as far as health, diet, poverty, and unsanitary living conditions were concerned. Second, the miasmatic theory of the origin and spread of diseases, which was then prevalent, gave their reforming outlook a justification from the point of view of medical science.

The most frequent pattern of action, involving social policy, social research, reform, and legislation, was as follows. First, a social evil was recognized by an individual or a small group, who often initiated research into the topic. Second, as a result of this initiative, other studies and local experiments and improvements were undertaken by larger, more organized groups. Third, these efforts stirred up and molded public opinion, attracted government attention, and finally led to government action in the form of boards of inquiry and royal commissions, which, when successful, led in turn to legislation attempting to correct the evil. Finally, legislation provided for inspection systems and other institutionalized means of controlling the implementation of social change.

Of the numerous reformer–investigators, perhap the most outstanding were Howard, Eden, Kay-Shuttleworth, and Chadwick. John Howard, a country squire, became a tireless researcher into prison conditions and an advocate of prison reform. By his own account, he traveled over 42,000 miles, all over Great Britain and Europe, during his investigations. In *State of the Prisons* (1777) and *An Account of the Principal Lazarettos in Europe* (1789), he described in detail the conditions within hundreds of prisons and prison hospitals: how the prisoners passed the time; what they were given for food; what illnesses and discomforts they suffered; the manner of prison administration; the number of prisoners, by sex and crime category, in every English prison; and so on. His books were filled with comparisons of the treatment of criminals in different countries and with suggestions for improvements. Thanks to his efforts and those of his backers, more humane treatment was introduced in many prisons.

Sir Frederick Morton Eden was a businessman. The inflation of 1794–1795 was the immediate cause of his empirical investigation into the number and conditions of the poor. He visited many parishes and carried on a voluminous correspondence with the local clergy. The fruit of his efforts, the three-volume *State of the Poor*, was published in 1797. Most of the work is taken up by parochial reports, which contain information, some of it in numerical detail, on the size of the population, the number of houses that paid taxes, the principal manufactures, the typical wages in the principal occupations, the rent of farms, the prices of foods, the friendly societies and their membership, the number of poor, and detailed description of conditions of the parish workhouses, among other things. He also presented 43 detailed family budgets of laborers, weavers, miners, masons, and other workers. He used a paid investigator for much of this detailed work, an innovation later adopted by the statistical societies. He based his recommendation for reform of the poor-law system on his findings. His budgetary studies and detailed empirical method represent an innovation in social research which was later developed further by Le Play and his school.

The physician James Phillips Kay-Shuttleworth was an active sanitary reformer, one of the founders of the Manchester Statistical Society, and, later, assistant poor-law commissioner. His early surveys were published as *The Moral and Physical Condition of the Working Classes Employed in the Cotton Manufacture in Manchester* (1832). These set a model for the more comprehensive surveys undertaken by the statistical societies. After 1840 he devoted his energies to introducing and developing a national system of education.

Edwin Chadwick was a civil servant who was active on parliamentary and other commissions throughout his life. More than any other person he was responsible for the *Report on the Sanitary Condition of the Labouring Population of Gt. Britain*, published in 1842, which eventually led to the Public Health Act of 1848 and the establishment of the Central Board of Health. The report set a precedent for subsequent administrative and parliamentary investigations into social problems.

In the 1830s a large number of local statistical societies were founded by citizens active in social reform. The two oldest and most active, those of Manchester and London, have survived to the present day. In addition, a statistical section of the British Association for the Advancement of Science was founded in 1833, at the insistence of Babbage, Malthus, and Quetelet.

The aim of these statistical societies was social improvement based on matter-of-fact, quantitative inquiries into problems of society. The societies organized committees of inquiry to carry out research into the health, living conditions, education, religious practices, and working conditions of the lower classes. The surveys were often large undertakings that took several months and many hundreds of pounds to complete. Paid agents were sent to hold door-to-door interviews based on a prepared schedule of questions. Results were tabulated centrally and presented at the annual meetings of the British Association or of the societies themselves and often appeared in such publications as the *Journal of the Royal Statistical Society*. Dozens of such surveys were completed, some making use of quite sophisticated multivariate cross-tabulations. Other studies were based on existing institutional records.

Decline of research related to social problems. However, toward the end of the 1840s a decline in social research set in. The major aims of the researcher-reformers were increasingly fulfilled as Parliament passed the Factory Acts and numerous other bills and measures; the economic conditions of the working people noticeably improved, and their political activities collapsed with the defeat of Chartism. Few original surveys were undertaken, and the methodology of those that were undertaken was inferior. Many of the local statistical societies themselves passed out of existence. In Manchester a large number of the original founding members became increasingly absorbed in civic and political activity. In the London Statistical Society, interest shifted to public health, vital statistics, the health of troops, mortality in the colonies, the duration of life in different occupations, etc., for which secondary analysis of published statistics sufficed. There was generally a lack of interest in methodology, whether in questions of study design, techniques of data collection, or analysis. For a time the National Association for the Promotion of Social Science, founded in 1857, rallied individuals concerned with the empirical investigation of labor relations, education, and social problems. But increasingly it was social Darwinism which shaped the intellectual life of Britain. The separation of the social research organizations from any academic context accounts in part for the lack of institutionalization of social research in Britain in the mid-century period. Absence of continuity in recruiting interested researchers, of continuous improvement in the methods of research, of a tradition oriented beyond the short-range goals of social betterment, and of regular financial backing—these were some of the disadvantages that this lack of institutionalization entailed.

The discovery of evolution, the advances in the biological sciences, and the increasing acceptance of race and heredity as fundamental categories in social analysis produced a shift in the intellectual climate. Whereas earlier researchers linked crime with indigence and lack of education, the newer outlook searched for evidence of hereditary degeneracy and other physical and psychological impairments. The lower classes, the destitute, criminals, and other unfortunate groups were often considered an inferior species of humanity. Social policy to ease their condition was viewed by many with alarm because it would prevent the fittest from being the only ones to survive and would thus slowly degenerate the stock of the entire nation. The same sort of educated, middle-class or upper-middle-class individual with a scientific turn of mind who in the 1830s and 1840s might have joined the statistical societies and conducted door-to-door parish surveys of the working people later in the century became a member of anthropological, ethnographic, and eugenics societies and spent his time in the study of primitive cultures or modern genealogies, making hundreds of cranial and other physical measurements in endless efforts at classification and typology. The burden of proof devolved upon the environmentalists.

Booth and the study of the poor. Starting in the 1880s there took place a revival in the scientific study of the poor, which culminated in the monumental social investigations of Charles Booth. Booth came from a wealthy family of Liverpool shipowners. His object was to show one-half of London how the other half lived, more particularly, "the numerical relation which poverty, misery, and depravity bear to regular earnings, and to describe the general condition under which each class lives" (1889–1891, vol. 1, p. 6). Gathering around him such researchers as Beatrice Potter Webb and Octavia Hill and other social workers and social economists, Booth started work in 1886 on what was to become the *Life and Labour of the People in London*, published from 1889 to 1891 in many volumes and several editions. London at the time already had four million inhabitants. Booth at first collected available information from the census and from the four hundred school-attendance officers, who kept records on every poor family. These records were cross-checked with information available to the police, sanitary inspectors, friendly societies, and the numerous charitable organizations and agencies dealing with a wage-earning clientele. Later, Booth followed up these data with participant observation of particular streets and households, and for a time he was himself a lodger with various workingmen's families.

Booth divided the families of London into eight classes, according to the amount and regularity of their earnings and, for the well-to-do, the number of their domestic servants. In his analysis he proceeded to characterize each city block according to the predominant class of the families in it. Assigning a color to each of the eight classes, he prepared colored maps of the entire city. He proceeded to describe, district by district, street by street, the style of life, the problems, and the prospects of the families living in them, including their religious practices, their recreation, and the use made by them of public houses and of the voluntary organizations to be found in their district. He devoted several volumes to description of the wages and working conditions in the trades of the city. The end result was the most detailed and large-scale social description ever achieved, which stirred up the contemporary social conscience and eventually led to the Old Age Pension Act of 1908, a legal minimum wage in the "sweated" trades, state provision for the sick and the disabled, and the start of unemployment insurance.

Booth's work inspired urban surveys by other investigators, who perfected his techniques. The most notable of these was B. Seebohm Rowntree, whose *Poverty: A Study of Town Life*, published in 1901, dealt with one city, and Arthur L. Bowley and A. R. Burnett-Hurst, whose *Livelihood and Poverty*, published in 1915, was a multicity study, the first in which sampling was used systematically in place of a complete enumeration. Booth's analysis of the causes of poverty left much to be desired, as contemporary statistical critics pointed out. One of these, G. Udny Yule, using Booth's data, subjected social data for the first time to multiple-regression and correlation techniques (1899). However, the systematic application of the statistical techniques developed by Galton, Edgeworth, Pearson, and Yule had to wait until the twentieth century, when these techniques entered social research by way of the biological, agricultural, and psychological sciences [see STATISTICS, *article on* THE HISTORY OF STATISTICAL METHOD].

Research in nineteenth-century France

The creation in 1800/1801 of the *Statistique de la République* (Gille 1964, pp. 121–147) and the suppression in 1803 of the second class of the Institut gave the lead once more to governmental inquiries. Until 1806 there prevailed great enthusiasm for statistics, sustained by the *Annales de statistique*, published from 1802 to 1804, and the Société de Statistique, which lasted from 1803 to 1806. The Bureau de Statistique published statistical memoirs by the various *départements*; these memoirs were based on the general inquiry ordered in 1801 by Chaptal, then minister of the interior (Pigeire 1932), and by Duquesnoy. The questions asked of the prefects relate to the location, condition, and movement of the population in 1789 and 1801; the "state of the citizens" and the changes therein from 1789 to 1801 for six categories; the religious and lay ways of life, habits, and customs; and finally, the changes of agriculture and industry since 1789. Many errors were discovered, leading to cessation of publication and reorganization of the Bureau de Statistique in 1806. However, works based on the data collected continued to appear until about 1810. The Bureau also received regular reports from the prefects and undertook such special inquiries as the so-called census of 1801, which was conducted by the *maires* (Reinhard 1961), and an estimate of the population carried out in 1802 with the collaboration of Laplace and described in his *Théorie analytique des probabilités* (published in 1812). After 1806 the Bureau was in charge of Coquebert de Monbret, who was interested in inquiries on special subjects: an industrial and an agricultural inquiry in 1806, and the next year an inquiry into what was described as the means of support, kind of occupation, and various religions of more than sixteen social categories. A second census of the population was carried out in 1806.

The idea of a general inquiry was picked up again in 1810. A questionnaire containing 334 items was sent to the prefects, and a general estimate of the population was made in the following year. But the failure of the general inquiry led to a return to special inquiries (for instance, into industry and communications), which taken together form the *Exposé de la situation de l'Empire, présenté au corps législatif dans sa séance du 25 février 1813* by Jean-Pierre Montalivet, minister of the interior. The Bureau de Statistique had already been abolished, in September 1812, and from that time on the collection of industrial and agricultural statistics was a government prerogative.

Research on problems of industrialization. The importance given to social research by the various revolutionary governments explains the initial distrust of such studies on the part of the monarchy, which had been restored in 1815. However, urbanization and industrialization were accompanied by social problems, which were played up in parliamentary debates and in the press, and a number of institutions were created in order to study these problems.

The philanthropic movement continued under the Restoration, with the Société Royale pour l'Amélioration des Prisons and, outside Paris, the Société Industrielle de Mulhouse. Villermé's early classic of penology, *Des prisons, telles qu'elles sont, et telles qu'elles devraient être,* appeared in 1820. Public health research founded on observation and quantification increased (see Ackerknecht 1948). The force of the movement resulted in the establish-

ment of the Académie Royale de Médecine (1820), the Conseil Supérieur de Santé (1822), the creation of health councils (*conseils de salubrité*) in the provinces between 1822 and 1830, and the founding in 1829 of the *Annales d'hygiène publique et de médecine légale,* which affirmed the role of the physician as investigator and social reformer.

Statistical research had been resumed with the census of Paris ordered in 1817 by the prefect Chabrol and published in the six volumes of *Recherches statistiques sur la ville de Paris et le département de la Seine* (see Seine 1821–1860). These volumes contained data not only on the population but also on goods consumed, levels of wealth, causes of death, suicide, etc. There also appeared the *Compte général de l'administration de la justice criminelle* (see France, Ministère de la Justice), which classified the types of crimes, as well as the criminals, and the *Comptes présentés au roi sur le recrutement de l'armée,* in which the conscripts' degree of education was made public (see France, Ministère de la Guerre). Publication of this information made possible the rise of "moral statistics," a field in which one of the earliest achievements was a study of crime and education by Balbi and Guerry (1829).

The July revolution of 1830 promoted social research in two ways. The reinstatement in 1832 of the second class of the Institut, under the title Académie des Sciences Morales et Politiques, enabled public health workers and statisticians to undertake their own research, since the new academy sponsored prize competitions. Two winners of these competitions were Frégier's *Des classes dangereuses de la population dans les grandes villes,* published in 1840, and Buret's *De la misère des classes laborieuses en Angleterre et en France,* published the same year. In 1832 there was created the Statistique Générale de la France, which began its publications in 1834 and in 1836 carried out the first trustworthy census of the whole of France in 15 years and which provided scholars with extensive and solid data.

Social research was also stimulated by the labor question, to which Villeneuve-Bargemont had drawn attention in 1828 with his unpublished *Rapport sur le département du Nord* (see Beautot 1939–1943) and which could no longer be ignored after the insurrections of 1831 and 1834. There were an increasing number of inquiries and books devoted to the working classes (Rigaudias 1936). In 1834 the Académie des Sciences Morales directed Benoiston de Chateauneuf and Villermé to find out as precisely as possible the physical and moral condition of the working classes. Villermé's researches, conducted in the mill towns from 1835 to 1840, were published in 1840 as *Tableau de l'état physique et moral des ouvriers employés dans les manufactures de coton, de laine et de soie.*

Guerry's "statistique morale." Guerry, an attorney born in Tours, took an interest in the official statistics on crime. In his *Essai sur la statistique morale de la France* (1833) he studied the relationship of two social variables, the crime rate and the level of education. He came up against two methodological problems: the absence of any measure of statistical correlation, and the difficulty of using collective measures, such as the crime rates or average level of education for a whole county, to explore questions of individual behavior, such as whether the better educated commit more or fewer crimes than the less well educated. Having established, over a six-year period, that the crime rate tended to remain stable—a fact he attributed to the systematic and constant nature of the causal forces at work—Guerry tried to compare the ecological distribution of criminality with that of education, ranking the 85 *départements* of France by their crime rate, on the one hand, and their level of literacy, on the other, and then looking to see whether a county at the extreme of one of these two distributions had the same position on the other. Since the counties ranked at the extremes of the distribution for education were not the same counties that were at the extremes of the distribution for crimes against the *person* but were the same counties as those at the extremes of the distribution for crimes against *property*, Guerry was led to conclude that there was no negative correlation between education and criminality and that the intervening variable might be level of industrialization. [*For other research by Guerry, see* SUICIDE, *article on* SOCIAL ASPECTS.]

Parent-Duchâtelet and prostitution. Parent-Duchâtelet, a member of the group that had founded the *Annales d'hygiène*, was responsible for two important works: *Hygiène publique* (1836), which brought together the 30 reports drawn up since 1825 for the Conseil de Salubrité de la Seine, and a two-volume work entitled *On Prostitution in the City of Paris* (1834), one of the best inquiries of the period in this field. The origins of this inquiry were both philanthropic and administrative. A philanthropist friend of the author's, eager to help prostitutes by publishing the truth about them, discovered that they lived in a world apart (what would nowadays be called a subculture) and that the first thing that had to be done was to get to know them. The municipality, which had succeeded in curbing prostitution and as a result was receiving requests for information from abroad, wanted an "evaluation" of what it had done [*see* EVALUATION RESEARCH]. In his research Parent-Duchâtelet combined the use of documents, such as police files; personal observation in the field and interviews (something unusual in the France of that period, when researchers, including Villermé, obtained their information indirectly, through observer reports); and statistical method (he compiled about 150 tables). He tried to determine the number of prostitutes and how the total varied over time; the prostitutes' regional and social origins; their physiological and social characteristics; their attitudes toward institutions such as marriage and religion; the reasons that had led them to a life of prostitution; and ways in which they left it. The study ended with an acknowledgment of the inevitability of prostitution and set forth arguments for the moral and material necessity of caring for prostitutes (a matter debated at the time) and of providing institutions designed to receive repentant prostitutes. Parent-Duchâtelet appended a draft law for checking the offenses against public decency that were caused by prostitution. In its scientific neutrality on a problem laden with moral taboos, as well as the use of direct observation and interviews, his whole approach was astonishingly modern.

Villermé's study of textile workers. Born in Paris in 1782, Villermé was 52 years old when he began his great inquiry into the conditions of textile workers. He spent six years observing workers in the most important centers of textile manufacturing. His two-volume report is the crowning work of a career that began in 1819 and was devoted to both hygiene and statistics. Between 1819 and 1834 Villermé published more than forty articles, in seven different journals (Guérard 1864). Some of these articles are simply collections of observations on problems of hygiene or other social problems; they reveal Villermé's skill in observation, which he had developed while serving as a surgeon in the Napoleonic armies from 1802 to 1814 and while studying to become a physician (he received his medical degree in 1818). Beginning in 1822 he became interested chiefly in the mortality statistics of Paris and of France, especially as they were related to income: he wrote several papers showing that the mortality rate of the poor was much higher than that of the well-to-do (Vedrenne-Villeneuve 1961).

In his study of the textile workers, Villermé used both statistical data and his own qualitative observations. He found some statistics in the annual reports of the *départements*, but for the most part he collected them himself. The statistics dealt with the number of workers (difficult to establish in the absence of a census by occupation, which did not exist in France until 1851); the average rate of pay for different kinds of workers (the data were provided by owners and foremen); the length of the working day; demographic information (births, marriages, number of children, number of illegitimate births); and the budgets of working families. Villermé's own observations concerned the cleanliness of the workshops and of the workers' dwellings, and he took note of the workers' clothing and diet and various aspects of their behavior (for example, the amount of alcoholism and prostitution).

Both when he used statistics and when he used qualitative observations, Villermé made use of indicators, without designating them as such. Thus, he took a high number of illegitimate births to be a reliable index of the disruption of customs, and he interpreted qualitative indices such as being paid monthly (rather than by the day or week), having wine with Sunday dinner, using window curtains, or owning an umbrella as signs of affluence.

Like Guerry in his *Statistique morale*, Villermé ran into two difficulties in his interpretation of statistical data: first, the lack of a measure of correlation; second and more important, the ecological character of the data, which described predominantly working-class neighborhoods but not the workers themselves. These handicaps made it necessary for him to perform statistical calculations that were often very interesting, for example, when he demonstrated that at Amiens more than 70 per cent of working-class conscripts were rejected by the army for reasons of health, as against 50 per cent of nonworking-class conscripts (1840, vol. 1, pp. 311–317).

In the first volume of his work, Villermé brought together all his facts, arranging them in almost the same way for every industrial area he studied, a procedure that enabled him to present a systematic description. The second volume, which he presented in 1837 to the Académie des Sciences Morales, covers most of the same categories in an analytical way.

Villermé's inquiry is methodologically less highly developed than that of Parent-Duchâtelet. He did not interview workers, with the exception of the silk workers of Lyon; he used only informants. But Villermé's subject was far more controversial. At the end of his careful description, he maintained that the lot of the workers had slightly improved, a conclusion that was attacked in socialist circles, especially by Buret. At the same time, Villermé's facts about wages and budgets dramatically revealed the inadequacy of the workers' resources and their miserable living conditions, and his denunciation of the employing of very young children in factories made him the target of attacks by orthodox liberals and supporters of the established order. The controversy about Villermé has continued into recent times: Rigaudias (1936) accepted without question the position taken by Buret, while Fourastié (1951) applauded the precision of Villermé's descriptive and statistical information and the solidity of his conclusions.

The facts about child labor collected by Villermé were discussed and criticized in England, in the debates of May and June 1839 in both the House of Lords and the House of Commons, and they played a part in the enactment of the law regulating child labor that was passed on March 22, 1841.

Inquiry into agricultural and industrial labor. The National Assembly that was elected after the fall of Louis xviii decided in May 1848 to undertake an inquiry into the state of agricultural and industrial labor. The inquiry took up the same subjects that Guerry, Villermé, and Buret had dealt with. Completed by the end of 1850, it was the last large-scale official inquiry that sought to study major problems in France as a whole. After 1852 the government authorized either statistical surveys of the whole country or detailed studies of limited problems. As for studies by individuals, these were hereafter generally monographs; the work of Le Play illustrates this development [*see the biography of* LE PLAY].

The inquiry by the National Assembly precipitated a lively ideological debate concerning social research (Rigaudias 1936). Between 1840 and 1848 the socialists had repeatedly and vainly demanded an official inquiry into working-class conditions (Ledru-Rollin's Workers' Petition was rejected by the Chamber of Deputies in 1845); but now, with Louis Blanc as their spokesman, the socialists demanded the establishment of a ministry of labor. Moderates and conservatives, on the other hand, opposed such a ministry, favoring instead an inquiry of the kind they had earlier rejected. Social research based on the observation of facts became identified with moderate and conservative bourgeois ideology and was therefore rejected by the various strains of socialist thought. Open socialist opposition to such research continued until the time of Durkheim and his school.

The questionnaire used by the inquiry contained 29 questions about major problems in each district, the general state of industry, the economic and social condition of the industrial workers, and the general state of agriculture. Answers were to be supplied by district commissions, presided over by the justice of the peace of the district and composed of one employer and one worker for each industrial specialty. The carrying out of the inquiry was hampered by the imprecision of the questionnaire (stressed in Gille 1964), and by doubts, shared by the government and the workers, as to its usefulness. (In the opinion of Rigaudias, the workers' lack of confidence constituted the essential obstacle.) Although responses were received from 76 per cent of the districts—a high rate of response—the Assembly ordered, after a brief debate, that the questionnaires be placed in the files of the Ministry of Industry and Commerce, with no provision for publication of the results.

Even to the present day, only a small part of the results of the inquiry of 1848 has been published by historians (Gossez 1904; Kahan-Rabecq 1934/ 1935; 1939; Vincienne & Courtois 1958). There are gaps in the documents in the Archives Nationales: missing are the materials on 22 *départements*, on almost all the large industrial centers, and on all the large industrial cities except Marseilles. Investigations, made in the archives of the *départements*, of the working of the commissions (Vidalenc 1948; Agulhon 1958; Guillaume 1962; all of these are cited in Gille 1964, p. 216) show that the answers to the questionnaire reflected the point of view of the leading citizens of the towns—sometimes, indeed, simply those of the presiding justice of the peace.

The failure of the great inquiry of 1848 served as a justification for the abandonment of national social inquiries conducted by representatives of the government. It also led to the breach between socialism and empirical social research. The publication in 1855 of Frédéric Le Play's *Ouvriers européens* marked the beginning of a new kind of research and was the most important event in the history of social research during the Second Empire. Like the hygienists earlier, especially Villermé, Le Play used direct observation and the monographic method. He was more like the traditionalists and the socialists (and unlike the hygienists) in basing a scheme for the global reorganization of society on his "method of observation," yet he differed from the socialists in striving for the restoration of traditional principles, rather than for a new social order.

Finally, it may be noted that Le Play, like all social philosophers and researchers before him, remained outside the university system. Only with the generation of Tarde and Durkheim and the establishment of the Office (later Ministry) of Labor, endorsed by the parliamentary socialists, was there a reconciliation of empirical social research with socialist thought and with the university system.

Research in nineteenth-century Germany

Unlike social research in Britain, which was mainly the work of private individuals and voluntary associations, the bulk of German social research in the nineteenth century was carried out by academic scholars and professional organizations. At that time the German universities constituted the most advanced system of higher education in the world. The historical school of economics, which rejected the views of the British political economists, contributed most to social research and to the gradual emergence of sociology as a distinct discipline. These economists sympathized with the underprivileged and firmly believed that research would contribute to a progressive social policy and the solution of social problems.

In the 1860s and 1870s, as a result of Quetelet's influence, moral statistics and demography became important areas of research in Germany. Ernst Engel, who was to become the head of the Prussian and German statistical bureaus, made use of both Le Play's and Quetelet's budget data and methodology to demonstrate his "law." Engel's law stated that regardless of the total size of the family budget, there exists the same priority of needs, as measured by the total amounts spent on certain types of expenditures and that, furthermore, the poorer a family, the larger will be the proportion of its budget spent on food alone. M. W. Drobisch, G. F. Knapp, Adolf Wagner, Johannes Conrad, Wilhelm Lexis, Alexander von Oettingen and others subjected statistical data on crime, suicide, marriage, jury convictions, conscripts' characteristics, and other economic and social data to analytic scrutiny in their varied attempts to establish empirical constancies in social life. Unfortunately, these attempts were involved with the prolonged and sterile debate on free will and determinism that Quetelet's ideas had provoked. However, more and more areas of social life were gradually made the object of quantitative study: occupations and social mobility, higher education, voting, the circulation figures of newspapers, the clientele of public libraries, the composition of military and political elites, and many others. At best, important monographs on single topics were completed. At worst, voluminous compilations of statistics with no theoretical underpinning were endlessly gathered and offered as proof that a new social science discipline had come into existence.

Tönnies and his sociographic method. Ferdinand Tönnies throughout his life fought against the narrow conception of empirical sociology as the mere compilation of facts. To this he opposed his own notion of "sociography," in which systematic observation, case studies, and other qualitative methods were included, together with statistical description. The goal of sociography was to arrive at empirical laws by the method of induction, applied to systematically collected information. Sociography was to be one of the three branches of sociology, equal in importance to theory. Tönnies himself had studied statistics with Engel, who impressed upon him the importance of Quetelet's accomplishments. Starting in 1895, and continuing for the rest of his life, he published intensive statistical monographs on land tenure and agrarian social structure, demography, crime, suicide, and voting. Most of the studies dealt with his home state of Schleswig-Holstein. Tönnies developed a measure of association and a method for the analysis of correlation between time series. In later life he repeatedly called for the creation of sociographic observatories, where specialists of many disciplines, together with members of the liberal professions and educated laymen, would collaborate in studying the facts of social life, especially those considered of moral significance. However, many of Tönnies' methods were not free from error, and he was unable to arouse the enthusiasm of his colleagues for sociographic observatories or sociography.

Research concerning the agrarian problem. After the unification of Germany in 1871, the agrarian problem received a great deal of attention; rural poverty and ignorance were prevalent, and there was a gradual displacement of native German peasants by Polish wage workers, especially in East Prussia. Many peasants emigrated; under the impact of the capitalist methods of agricultural production, introduced by the *Junker* with the help of protective tariffs, others were gradually reduced to the level of a rural proletariat. Everywhere the earlier, paternalistic type of labor relations was disappearing. The first large-scale survey of agricultural laborers to concern itself with these problems was undertaken in 1874–1875, on behalf of the Congress of German Landowners, by Theodor von der Goltz.

The Verein für Sozialpolitik, founded in 1872, conducted, among other nationwide surveys, two on agricultural laborers, one on usury in rural areas, and one on cottage industry. The Verein was part professional association, part pressure group, and part research organization. At its conventions the implications of survey findings were debated with an eye to influencing social policy and legis-

lation; further surveys were planned by an executive committee that enlisted the cooperation of key professors, who in turn brought their students into the survey. Max Weber's first empirical work was done under the auspices of the Verein (Weber 1892).

In the Verein surveys a schedule of questions was usually drawn up by topic. Questionnaires on such topics as land tenure, production, wages, living conditions, composition of the work force, and the extent of theft and drunkenness were then answered by landowners, ministers, doctors, notaries, teachers, members of agricultural societies, and other informed persons. The weaknesses of this methodology were that it assumed accurate knowledge on the part of the informants, that the questions were imprecisely put and were grouped in a haphazard fashion, that low response rates were achieved, and that the returns were only imperfectly exploited. In short, perfection of the techniques of survey research did not concern the Verein members; only Gottlieb Schnapper-Arndt (1888) subjected their methodology to a sharp critique. He had previously published *Fünf Dorfgemeinden auf dem Hohen Taunus* (1883), a very detailed field study of rural life, based on several months of painstaking participant observation and explicitly indebted to Le Play. Unfortunately, Schnapper-Arndt's impact upon his contemporaries remained minimal.

Religious organizations, such as the Evangelical-Social Congress, also conducted rural surveys. Their main interest was understandably in the morals, religion, and literacy of the rural population, and they sought the information primarily from ministers.

Studies of industrial workers. With the retirement of Bismarck and the repeal in 1890 of the laws banning socialist political activity, the working-class question began to receive much attention. Repeated socialist successes at the polls alarmed the German middle and upper classes. Increasing international competition and trade union demands for shorter working hours brought up the issue of productivity and the ability of German industry to compete against Britain in world markets.

In 1890 a young theology student named Paul Göhre, later a Social Democratic deputy in the Reichstag, decided to find out what he hoped would be the whole truth about the working classes. He spent three months working in a factory, pretending to be an apprentice and sharing in every way, both on and off the job, the daily life of the work force. Every night he wrote down his experiences of the day in the form of field notes, which he later published (Göhre 1891). His book was a remarkable document of the social structure on the factory floor and of the life styles, aspirations, and religious conceptions of the workers, and it received widespread recognition from the academic and general public alike. Göhre and Max Weber teamed up a year later as research directors for a study of agricultural laborers under the auspices of the aforementioned Evangelical-Social Congress. Göhre later edited a series of workers' autobiographies.

Adolf Levenstein, a self-educated worker, undertook, from 1907 to 1911, what is probably the first large-scale attitude and opinion survey on record. He sent out 8,000 questionnaires to miners, steelworkers, and textile workers, using a snowball procedure which started with his many friends. He achieved a 63 per cent rate of return, which is remarkably high. The questionnaire itself, despite technical shortcomings, explored the workers' attitudes on many of the important issues of the day —their material and political hopes and wishes, and their aspirations, religious beliefs, political activities, recreational and cultural pursuits, satisfaction or boredom with their work, and drinking habits, in addition to the standard information on social background and wages. Levenstein at first refused to make the findings public, but was persuaded by Weber and others to code and tabulate the answers, which eventually appeared in book form (Levenstein 1912). In many ways Levenstein followed Weber's advice (1909) on how to analyze an attitude survey, which foreshadowed some present-day procedures.

Weber himself at this time was the principal moving force behind the Verein für Socialpolitik survey of industrial workers. This was planned as a large-scale attempt to determine the occupational careers, social origins, and style of life of the workers; some of the data were to be obtained directly from the workers themselves. Weber also intended to test a number of hypotheses about worker productivity. In particular he wanted to find out to what extent the laboratory methods of experimental psychophysics might be adapted to field experiments and surveys in a factory setting. In preparation for these tasks, he spent a whole summer observing the workers in a textile mill and analyzing their production figures. At the same time, he drew up a plan of procedure for the Verein researchers and wrote an explanation of the theoretical and methodological underpinning of the entire undertaking. The survey came to an unhappy end when the vast majority of the workers refused to cooperate in the study. Nevertheless, Weber's preparatory conceptual and statistical studies were acclaimed at the time as pathbreaking; they were indeed highly sophisticated, although they reflected the then current psychophysical approach to worker productivity. Weber's own attitude toward the often tedious tasks involved in social research is evident in his famous address, "Science as a Vocation," in which he said, "No sociologist . . . should think himself too good, even in his old age, to make tens of thousands of quite trivial computations in his head and perhaps for months at a time" ([1919] 1946, p. 135). Weber's own plans for encouraging social research in Germany remained unfulfilled. However, it is clear from the works reviewed in this article that there was no lack of historical precedents for his stress on the collection and analysis of empirical social data. Rewriting of the history of sociology to take full account of these precedents is a task that is long overdue.

BERNARD LÉCUYER AND
ANTHONY R. OBERSCHALL

[*See also the biographies of* BOOTH; CONDORCET; DURKHEIM; GRAUNT; KING; LAPLACE; LE PLAY; PETTY; QUETELET; SÜSSMILCH; TÖNNIES; WEBB, SIDNEY AND BEATRICE; WEBER, MAX.]

BIBLIOGRAPHY

ACKERKNECHT, E. H. 1948 Hygiene in France, 1815–1848. *Bulletin of the History of Medicine* 22:117–155.

AGULHON, MAURICE 1958 L'enquête du Comité du Travail de l'Assemblée Constituante (1848): Étude critique de son exécution dans deux départements du Midi. *Annales du Midi* 70:73–85.

Annales d'hygiène publique et de médecine légale. → Published from 1829 to 1950. From 1923 called *Annales d'hygiène publique, industrielle et sociale.*

Annales de statistique. → Published from 1802 to 1804. Superseded by *Archives statistiques de la France.*

ARBUTHNOTT, JOHN 1710 An Argument for Divine Providence, Taken From the Constant Regularity Observ'd in the Births of Both Sexes. Royal Society of London, *Philosophical Transactions* 27:186–190.

Arithmétique politique. 1751 Volume 1, pages 678–680 in *Encyclopédie, ou, Dictionnaire raisonné des sciences, des arts et des métiers.* Edited by Denis Diderot. Paris: Briasson.

BAILLY, JEAN S. 1790 *Discours et mémoires.* Volume 2. Paris: de Bure.

BALBI, ADRIANO; and GUERRY, ANDRÉ M. 1829 *Statistique comparée de l'état de l'instruction et du nombre des crimes dans les divers arrondissements des académies et des cours royales de France.* Paris: Renouard.

BEAUTOT, ÉMILE 1939–1943 Le département du Nord sous la Restauration: Rapport du préfet Villeneuve-Bargemont en 1828. *Revue du Nord* 25:243–277; 26:21–45.

BOOTH, CHARLES et al. (1889–1891) 1902–1903 *Life and Labour of the People in London.* 17 vols. London: Macmillan.

BOULAINVILLIERS, HENRI DE (1727) 1752 *L'état de la France.* 2 vols. London: Wood & Palmer. → Written in 1711; published posthumously.

BOWLEY, ARTHUR L.; and BURNETT-HURST, A. R.   1915   *Livelihood and Poverty: A Study in the Economic Conditions of Working-class Households in Northampton, Warrington, Stanley and Reading.* London: Bell.

BUFFON, GEORGES-L.   1749   *Histoire naturelle générale et particulière avec la description du cabinet du roy.* Volume 2: Histoire naturelle de l'homme. Paris: Imprimerie Royale.

BURET, EUGÈNE   1840   *De la misère des classes laborieuses en Angleterre et en France.* 2 vols. Paris: Paulin.

CABANIS, PIERRE JEAN G.   1790   *Observations sur les hôpitaux.* Paris: Imprimerie Nationale.

CABANIS, PIERRE JEAN G.   (1803) 1956   Quelques principes et quelques vues sur les secours publics. Volume 2, pages 1–63 in Pierre Jean G. Cabanis, *Oeuvres philosophiques.* Paris: Presses Universitaires de France.

CHEVALIER, LOUIS   1948   Préface à Moheau. *Population* 3:211–232.

COLQUHOUN, PATRICK   1814   *A Treatise on the Wealth, Power, and Resources of the British Empire.* London: Mawman.

CONDORCET   1785   *Essai sur l'application de l'analyse à la probabilité des décisions rendues à la pluralité des voix.* Paris: Imprimerie Royale.

DAINVILLE, FRANÇOIS DE   1952   Un dénombrement inédit au XVIIIᵉ siècle: L'enquête du contrôleur général Orry—1745. *Population* 7:49–68.

DEPARCIEUX, ANTOINE   1746   *Essai sur les probabilités de la durée de la vie humaine.* Paris: Guérin & Delatour. → A supplement entitled *Addition à l'essai . . .* was published in 1760.

DERHAM, WILLIAM   (1713) 1742   *Physico-theology: Or, a Demonstration of the Being and Attributes of God, From His Works of Creation.* 10th ed. London: Innys.

Dictionnaire géographique, historique et politique des Gaules et de la France. Edited by Jean-J. Expilly. 6 vols. 1762–1770 Paris: Desaint & Saillant.

EDEN, FREDERICK M.   (1797) 1928   *The State of the Poor.* 3 vols. London: Routledge.

ESMONIN, EDMOND   1954   Quelques données inédites sur Vauban et les premiers recensements de population. *Population* 9:507–512.

ESMONIN, EDMOND   1956   Les mémoires des intendants pour l'instruction du duc de Bourgogne (étude critique). Société d'Histoire Moderne, Paris, *Bulletin* 55:12–21.

ESMONIN, EDMOND   1957   L'abbé Expilly et ses travaux de statistique. *Revue d'histoire moderne et contemporaine* 4:241–280.

ESMONIN, EDMOND   1958   Montyon, véritable auteur des *Recherches et considérations sur la population* de Moheau. *Population* 13:269–283.

FOUCAULT, MICHEL   1963   *Naissance de la clinique: Une archéologie du regard médical.* Paris: Presses Universitaires de France.

FOURASTIÉ, JEAN   (1951) 1960   *The Causes of Wealth.* Glencoe, Ill.: Free Press. → First published in French.

FRANCE, MINISTÈRE DE LA GUERRE   *Comptes présentés au roi sur le recrutement de l'armée.* → Published from 1819 to 1908. Until 1837 published as *Comptes présentés en exécution de la loi du 10 mars 1818 sur le recrutement de l'armée.*

FRANCE, MINISTÈRE DE LA JUSTICE   *Compte général de l'administration de la justice criminelle en France et en Algérie.* → Published from 1827 to 1907; includes Algeria from 1853.

FRÉGIER, H. A.   1840   *Des classes dangereuses de la population dans les grandes villes, et des moyens de les rendre meilleures.* 2 vols. Paris: Baillière.

GAULMIER, JEAN   1951   *L'idéologue Volney (1757–1820): Contribution à l'histoire de l'orientalisme en France.* Beirut: Presses de l'Imprimerie Catholique.

GÉRANDO, JOSEPH-MARIE DE   1801   *Considérations sur les diverses méthodes à suivre dans l'observation des peuples sauvages.* Paris: Société des Observateurs de l'Homme.

GÉRANDO, JOSEPH-MARIE DE   (1820) 1837   *Le visiteur du pauvre.* 4th ed. Paris: Colas.

GÉRANDO, JOSEPH-MARIE DE   1839   *De la bienfaisance publique.* 4 vols. Paris: Renouard.

GILLE, BERTRAND   1964   *Les sources statistiques de l'histoire de France, des enquêtes du XVIIᵉ siècle à 1870.* Paris, École Pratique des Hautes Études, Centre de Recherches d'Histoire et de Philologie, Publications, Section IV, Série V: Hautes études médiévales et modernes, No. 1. Geneva: Droz; Paris: Minard.

GÖHRE, PAUL   1891   *Drei Monate Fabrikarbeiter und Handwerksbursche.* Leipzig: Grünow.

GOSSEZ, A. M.   1904   *Le département du Nord sous la Deuxième République (1848–1852): Étude économique et politique.* Lille (France): Leleu.

GRAUNT, JOHN   (1662) 1939   *Natural and Political Observations Made Upon the Bills of Mortality.* Edited and with an introduction by Walter F. Willcox. Baltimore: Johns Hopkins Press.

GREAT BRITAIN, POOR LAW COMMISSIONERS   (1842) 1965   *Report on the Sanitary Condition of the Labouring Population of Gt. Britain,* by Edwin Chadwick. Edinburgh Univ. Press.

GUÉRARD, ALPHONSE   1864   Notice sur M. Villermé. *Annales d'hygiène publique et de médecine légale* Second Series 21:162–177.

GUERRY, ANDRÉ M.   1833   *Essai sur la statistique morale de la France.* Paris: Crochard.

GUILLAUME, P.   1962   Département de la Loire. Pages 429–450 in Congrès des Sociétés Savantes de Paris et des Départements, 86ᵉ, *Actes.* Paris: Imprimerie Nationale.

HALLEY, EDMUND   1693   An Estimate of the Degrees of the Mortality of Mankind, Drawn From Curious Tables of the Births and Funerals at the City of Breslaw. . . . Royal Society of London, *Philosophical Transactions* 17:596–610.

HOWARD, JOHN   (1777) 1929   *State of the Prisons.* New York: Dutton. → First published as *State of Prisons in England and Wales.*

HOWARD, JOHN   (1789) 1791   *An Account of the Principal Lazarettos in Europe.* . . . 2d ed. London: Johnson.

KAHAN-RABECQ, MARIE M.   1934/1935   Les réponses hâvraises à l'enquête sur le travail industriel et agricole en 1848. *La Révolution de 1848* 31:95–113.

KAHAN-RABECQ, MARIE M.   1939   *L'Alsace économique et sociale sous le règne de Louis-Philippe.* Volume 2: Réponses du département du Haut-Rhin à l'enquête faite en 1848. Paris: Presses Modernes.

KAY-SHUTTLEWORTH, JAMES PHILLIPS   1832   *The Moral and Physical Condition of the Working Classes Employed in the Cotton Manufacture in Manchester.* London: Ridgway.

KING, GREGORY   (1696) 1936   Natural and Political Observations and Conclusions Upon the State and Condition of England. Pages 12–56 in *Two Tracts by*

Gregory King. Edited by George E. Barnett. Baltimore: Johns Hopkins Press. → The manuscript of 1696 was first published in 1802, in George Chalmers' *Estimate of the Comparative Strength of Great-Britain.*

LAPLACE, PIERRE SIMON DE   (1812) 1820   *Théorie analytique des probabilités.* 3d ed., rev. Paris: Courcier. → This work also published as Volume 7 of *Oeuvres de Laplace.*

LAVOISIER, ANTOINE L.   (1791) 1819   *Résultats d'un ouvrage intitulé: De la richesse territoriale du royaume de France.* Paris: Huzard. → Published in 1791 by order of the National Assembly.

LEVENSTEIN, ADOLF   1912   *Die Arbeiterfrage mit besonderer Berücksichtigung der sozialpsychologischen Seite des modernen Grossbetriebes und der psychophysischen Einwirkungen auf die Arbeiter.* Munich: Reinhardt.

McCULLOCH, JOHN R.   (1837) 1854   *A Descriptive and Statistical Account of the British Empire.* 4th ed., rev. 2 vols. London: Longmans. → First published as *A Statistical Account of the British Empire.*

MALTHUS, THOMAS R.   (1798) 1958   *An Essay on Population.* 2 vols. New York: Dutton. → First published as *An Essay on the Principle of Population.* A paperback edition was published in 1963 by Irwin.

MESSANCE, RECEVEUR DES TAILLES DE L'ÉLECTION DE ST-ÉTIENNE   1766   *Recherches sur la population des généralités d'Auvergne, de Lyon, de Rouen et de quelques provinces et villes du royaume . . . .* Paris: Durand.

MOHEAU, M.   (1778) 1912   *Recherches et considérations sur la population de la France, 1778.* Paris: Geuthner. → Written in 1774.

MONTALIVET, JEAN-PIERRE   1813   *Exposé de la situation de l'Empire, présenté au corps législatif dans sa séance du 25 février 1813.* Paris: Imprimerie Impériale.

PARENT-DUCHÂTELET, ALEXANDRE J. B.   (1834) 1857   *On Prostitution in the City of Paris.* 3d ed. 2 vols. London: Burgess. → First published in French.

PARENT-DUCHÂTELET, ALEXANDRE J. B.   1836   *Hygiène publique, ou Mémoires sur les questions les plus importantes de l'hygiène appliquée aux professions et aux travaux d'utilité publique.* 2 vols. Paris: Baillière.

PETTY, WILLIAM   (1671–1676) 1963   The Political Anatomy of Ireland. Volume I, pages 121–231 in William Petty, *The Economic Writings. . . .* New York: Kelley. → Written between 1671 and 1676; first published posthumously, in 1691.

PIGEIRE, JEAN   1932   *La vie et l'oeuvre de Chaptal, 1756–1832.* Paris: Domat-Montchrestien.

PLAYFAIR, WILLIAM   1801   *The Statistical Breviary.* London: Wallis.

REINHARD, MARCEL   1961   *Étude de la population pendant la Révolution et l'Empire.* Gap (France): Jean.

RIGAUDIAS, HILDE (WEISS)   1936   *Les enquêtes ouvrières en France entre 1830 et 1848.* Paris: Alcan.

ROSEN, GEORGE   1946   The Philosophy of Ideology and the Emergence of Modern Medicine in France. *Bulletin of the History of Medicine* 20:328–339.

ROSEN, GEORGE   1955   Problems in the Application of Statistical Analysis to Questions of Health: 1700–1800. *Bulletin of the History of Medicine* 29:27–45.

ROSEN, GEORGE   1958   *A History of Public Health.* New York: MD Publications.

ROWNTREE, B. SEEBOHM   (1901) 1922   *Poverty: A Study of Town Life.* New ed. London and New York: Longmans.

SCHNAPPER-ARNDT, GOTTLIEB   1883   *Fünf Dorfgemeinden auf dem Hohen Taunus.* Leipzig: Duncker & Humblot.

SCHNAPPER-ARNDT, GOTTLIEB   1888   *Zur Methodologie sozialer Enquêten.* Frankfurt am Main (Germany): Auffarth.

SEINE (DEPT.)   1821–1860   *Recherches statistiques sur la ville de Paris et le département de la Seine.* 6 vols. Paris: Imprimerie Royale.

SINCLAIR, JOHN   1791–1799   *The Statistical Account of Scotland: Drawn Up From the Communications of the Ministers of the Different Parishes.* 21 vols. Edinburgh: Creech.

SÜSSMILCH, JOHANN PETER   (1741) 1788   *Die göttliche Ordnung in den Veränderungen des menschlichen Geschlechts, aus der Geburt, dem Tode und der Fortpflanzung.* 3 vols. Berlin: Verlag der Buchhandlung der Realschule.

TENON, JACQUES RENÉ   1788   *Mémoires sur les hôpitaux de Paris.* Paris: Royez.

VAUBAN, SÉBASTIEN LE PRESTRE DE   (1707) 1943   *Projet d'une dîme royale.* Paris: Guillaumin. → The papers "Méthode générale . . . ," and "Description de l'élection de Vezelay," were written in 1686 and later incorporated as part 2, chapter 10 of the above volume. An English translation was published in 1708 as *A Project for a Royal Tythe, or General Tax.*

VEDRENNE-VILLENEUVE, EDMONDE   1961   L'inégalité sociale devant la mort dans la première moitié du XIXᵉ siècle. *Population* 16:665–699.

VIDALENC, JEAN   1948   Les résultats de l'enquête sur le travail prescrite par l'Assemblée Constituante dans le département de l'Eure. Pages 325–341 in Congrès Historique du Centenaire de la Révolution de 1848, *Actes.* Paris: Presses Universitaires de France.

VILLENEUVE-BARGEMONT, ALBAN   1837   Études spéciales sur le département du Nord. Pages 216–227 in Alban Villeneuve-Bargemont, *Économie politique chrétienne: Ou recherches sur la nature et les causes de paupérisme en France et en Europe.* Brussels: Meline, Cans. → Written in 1828.

VILLERMÉ, LOUIS R.   1820   *Des prisons, telles qu'elles sont, et telles qu'elles devraient être.* Paris: Méquignon-Marvis.

VILLERMÉ, LOUIS R.   1840   *Tableau de l'état physique et moral des ouvriers employés dans les manufactures de coton, de laine et de soie.* 2 vols. Paris: Renouard.

VINCIENNE, MONIQUE; and COURTOIS, HÉLÈNE   1958   Notes sur la situation religieuse en France en 1848, d'après l'enquête cantonale ordonnée par le Comité du Travail. *Archives de sociologie des religions* 6:104–118.

VOLNEY, CONSTANTIN   (1787) 1959   *Voyage en Égypte et en Syrie.* Paris: Mouton. → An English edition was published in 1798 by Tiebout.

VOLNEY, CONSTANTIN   1795   *Questions de statistique à l'usage des voyageurs.* Paris: Courcier.

WEBER, MAX   1892   *Die Verhältnisse der Landarbeiter im ostelbischen Deutschland.* Verein für Socialpolitik, Schriften, Vol. 55. Leipzig: Duncker & Humblot.

WEBER, MAX   1909   Zur Methodik sozialpsychologischer Enquêten und ihrer Bearbeitung. *Archiv für Sozialwissenschaft und Sozialpolitik* 29:949–958.

WEBER, MAX   (1919) 1946   Science as a Vocation. Pages 129–156 in Max Weber, *From Max Weber: Essays in Sociology.* Translated and edited by H. H. Gerth and C. W. Mills. New York: Oxford Univ. Press. → First published as "Wissenschaft als Beruf."

Westergaard, Harald 1932 *Contributions to the History of Statistics.* London: King.

Young, Arthur 1771a *The Farmer's Tour Through the East of England, Being the Register of a Journey Through Various Counties of This Kingdom, to Enquire Into the State of Agriculture, &c.* 4 vols. London: Printed for W. Strahan.

Young, Arthur 1771b *A Six Months Tour Through the North of England.* 4 vols. London: Printed for W. Strahan.

Young, Arthur 1780 *A Tour in Ireland: With General Observations on the Present State of That Kingdom.* 2 vols. Dublin: Printed for G. Bonham. → Volume 1 was printed by Whitestone, Sleater [etc.]. Volume 2 was printed by J. Williams.

Young, Arthur (1793) 1950 *Travels in France During the Years 1787, 1788 & 1789.* Edited by Constantia Maxwell. Cambridge Univ. Press. → First published in two volumes, as *Travels During the Years 1787, 1788, 1789, Undertaken More Particularly With a View of Ascertaining the Cultivation, Wealth, Resources and National Prosperity of the Kingdom of France.*

Yule, G. Udny 1899 An Investigation Into the Causes of Changes in Pauperism in England, Chiefly During the Last Two Intercensal Decades. Part 1. *Journal of the Royal Statistical Society* 62:249–286.

SOCIOLOGY OF KNOWLEDGE
See Knowledge, sociology of.

SOCIOMETRY

The term "sociometry" has several meanings, but historically the closest association is with the work of J. L. Moreno, particularly his analysis of interpersonal relations in *Who Shall Survive?* (1934). Sociometry is traditionally identified with the analysis of data collected by means of the *sociometric test*—a type of questionnaire in which, roughly speaking, each member of a group is asked with which members he would most like to carry out some activity. The sociometric test was developed by Moreno and his associates, who made brilliant use of it in their own research.

In the early 1940s a number of pronouncements were made on what the meaning of the word "sociometry" should be, and Moreno himself (1943) urged that the meaning should not be restricted to the instruments he had developed. Although his sentiment and that of others was that "sociometry" should refer generally to the measurement of social phenomena, the fact is that the instruments developed by Moreno are still the almost universal reference point for the term.

Data collection. The form of the sociometric question and the setting in which data are collected permit a great variety of alternatives. The question must indicate to the subjects the setting or scope of choice. Thus, if the setting is a classroom it is appropriate to phrase the question accordingly ("With which students in the classroom would you like to discuss this problem?"). Otherwise, the subjects might choose such persons as the teacher, friends or relatives outside the classroom, or even experts whom they do not know personally. The planned activity (in this case, a classroom discussion) should also be clearly defined, so that the subjects know for what purpose the choice is made. This procedure may be contrasted with *ratings*, by means of which a person attributes characteristics to others but does not have to decide whether he wishes to associate with any of them.

In the "applied" use of the sociometric technique, say by the classroom teacher, the choice of criteria may be related to practical objectives. On the one hand, the teacher may wish to restructure the group subsequently on the assumption that more effective work can be carried out by children when they themselves have selected their co-workers. On the other hand, the purpose of the teacher may run just counter to this type of restructuring, and the objective might be to force more interaction with persons one might ordinarily avoid. In the early days of sociometry, the experimenters, possibly because of the therapeutic concerns of Moreno and his associates, often felt obliged to restructure the group regardless of the circumstances. But with the more general use of the technique, this implication has disappeared. In fact, sociometric questions are often phrased hypothetically ("Assuming there could be another meeting of this group, with which persons would you most want to participate?"). There is no indication that a hypothetical phrasing of the question is less useful than one that implies actual restructuring of the group, but there is a continued mandate for relevance in the phrasing of the question.

As in any research procedure, the use of the sociometric question requires attention to the general abilities of the subjects; to take an obvious example, children who cannot yet read or write will have to be interviewed. Under such circumstances the social setting for asking the questions must ensure privacy and confidentiality, and the interviewer should make sure that the child is not intimidated by, or made fearful of, the situation; otherwise, the validity of the responses may be affected. Collecting data through the sociometric question, however, is intrinsically a simple procedure and should be adaptable to most situations. Variations range from the use of a single question asking for a simple listing of choices on one criterion to a battery of questions in which ordered choices and rejections are requested on many criteria.

Questionnaire construction. In utilizing sociometric questions, the form in which the data are collected determines the types of results that can be obtained. For example, the number of choices requested may be limited or unlimited. If the choices are unlimited, the total number of choices made in the group may be compared for different groups of the same size or for the same group on different occasions; if the choices are limited, however, comparisons based on the total number of choices are meaningless, since the total number of choices is determined by the instructions. But the total number of choices in a group has the advantage of being a relatively simple score to understand, and it has associations with *group cohesiveness* and *morale*. For instance, Goodacre (1951) found that a high rate of choosing within the group was associated with a high standard of group effectiveness; reduced to the simplest interpretation, it appears that if members of the group consider each other good for the operation of the group, the group is likely to be successful. While this may not seem a profound finding on the surface, it is at present virtually the only dependable association with group effectiveness beyond the predictions that successful groups will continue to be successful and that groups composed of persons with high demonstrated ability will be successful.

Permitting an unlimited number of choices is required if *networks* of social relationships are to be traced. Obviously, a clique structure involving ten people cannot effectively be found in a larger group if only three choices are permitted to each person. Since Moreno was originally concerned with the analysis of group structure at this level, the procedure traditionally recommended has been the use of unlimited choices. However, many alternative procedures have been suggested, including the following: a limited specific number of choices; a limited number of ordered choices; an ordered ranking of the entire group; paired comparisons within the group; estimates of the amount of time one wants to spend with others; guessing who has a particular characteristic or reputation; and rating each person within the group for particular characteristics. Of course, the possibility of negative choices (rejections) and the use of multiple criteria increase the number of alternative choices.

Sociometric description

The patterns of expressed choices can be represented graphically in the *sociogram*, which involves the use of some geometric figure to indicate each person (for example, a circle with a name in it) and connecting lines or arrows showing the direction of the choices. Although the use of sociograms in early studies was haphazard, a number of empirically based and theoretically important concepts were derived from them by Moreno and others.

The simplest concept is that of the *unchosen*, who may be viewed as the person socially isolated by others. In the early tradition, the *isolate* is the person who makes no choices and receives none; in this sense he is totally apart from the group. However, in common use, "isolate" has had the same meaning as "unchosen." The term "underchosen" is also found in the literature, but it tends to be less desirable, as it implies some expected level of being chosen. The *rejected* person, of course, can be distinguished only when the sociometric test has requested rejections ("With whom would you like to do this activity *least*?") as well as choices. Rejection of one person by another implicitly involves active dislike, while ignoring a person or not choosing him could indicate merely a lack of sufficient contact for the development of a crystallized attitude. When both positive and negative forms of the question are used in larger groups, however, persons who are unchosen when the positive-choice form of the sociometric question is used tend to be the ones who are rejected in the negative form of the question, and vice versa.

The highly chosen person has been viewed as being in a desirable position. The term "overchosen" was commonly encountered in the early sociometric literature but is no longer widely used. The concept of the *sociometric star* has had some appeal; the image evoked by the concept is one of the highly chosen persons surrounded by persons who are less chosen than the "star." The *popular leader* is a similar concept, and being highly chosen is most frequently associated with some notion of leadership. Popularity (being highly chosen) and leadership are not synonymous, however, and the distinction has been clearly indicated in the literature (Criswell & Jennings 1951). While the popular person may be the leader, there may be other persons with whom power resides, and the *power figure*—that is, the person chosen by others who are in key positions—may not be a popular person at all. The distinction between popularity and leadership arises most clearly in the sociometric literature in consideration of the content of sociometric questions. Helen H. Jennings (1947) has discussed the difference between *sociogroup* and *psychegroup*, distinguished according to whether the basis of choice lies in the task area or the social area. When the task-oriented (sociogroup) question is used, the highly chosen person is likely to be the leader; on the other hand, when the socially oriented (psychegroup) question is used, the highly chosen person is likely to be the popular or personally attractive person.

The concepts mentioned thus far, while related to the structure of relationships, refer to particular persons or types of persons within the structure. But even in the earliest sociometric studies, a great deal of attention was paid to networks of relationships. Part of the attraction was that arrangements or relationships between persons were easily named; for example, *mutual pair* and *mutual rejection* are obvious concepts. The description of relationships between persons becomes most intricate in the area that has come to be called *relational analysis*, which commonly involves both the calculation of all possible choices and rejections in a given situation and some attempt at predicting how the actual choices and rejections will be distributed (see, for instance, Tagiuri 1952). The study of even more complex arrangements of relationships has led to the use of more complex names for them. Geometric names, such as "triangle" and "quadrangle," have proved to have only limited applicability; more important theoretically have been looser configurations such as "chains" and "rings," which enter into the analysis of clique structure.

The sociogram—problems and proposals. The sociogram was ubiquitous in the early development of sociometric techniques, but although important concepts were associated with such diagrams, they were frequently used for display rather than for analytic purposes. When the person constructing the diagram had a specific implicit hypothesis, the diagrams could be dramatic. For example, the absence of choices across sex lines in elementary classroom groups would appear dramatic if the symbols for all the boys were located on one end of the page and those for the girls on the other. Similarly, if racial or ethnic groups were segregated in sections of the paper, the relative absence of connecting lines between these groups could be seen easily, in contrast to the many connecting lines *within* them. Analysis of clique structure, on the other hand, or the location of complex choice networks, can be almost impossible to represent in the form of a sociogram.

Alternative proposals for construction of sociograms have been numerous. Some techniques, such as the "target" sociogram (Northway 1940), emphasize *choice status*, indicated by concentric circles with the most chosen person as the center-

most circle and patterns of relationships shown in the usual way with arrows. This alternative has not been used extensively, nor have the other techniques that emphasize the choice status of the person. Another such method (Powell 1951) suggests the use of symbols of different sizes, with large symbols, for example, meaning a large number of choices received by the person; yet another method (Proctor & Loomis 1951) makes use of physical distance between points on the sociogram to represent the "choice distance" between persons (mutual pairs, very close; mutual rejections, very distant). Still more complex descriptive devices, such as multidimensional diagrams (Chapin 1950), are also used, but the fact is that the analytic utility of sociograms appears to be small. Their descriptive utility, however, has remained, and the trend in this direction has been toward the simplification of diagrams, the procedure of minimizing crossing lines being common (Borgatta 1951).

Sociometric analysis

Analytic techniques, as contrasted with descriptive techniques, have stressed both the development of meaningful indexes of choice and the need for systematic analysis of the total choice matrix. Indexes are usually developed with a view to applying particular concepts, and it should be recognized that even such arbitrary classifications as "unchosen" and "highly chosen" are already indexes of the simple concept of sociometric choice. But indexes in sociometry usually represent more complex classifications and are often directed toward making different sets of data comparable. For example, an index may take into account the number of persons choosing, so that groups of different sizes are made comparable. Many problems arise in the construction of indexes, however, and the literature abounds with cautions that the attempt to "take something into account" in an index may not only fail but may also involve even more serious problems than those the researcher is trying to alleviate.

Matrix techniques. Beginning with the work of Moreno and Jennings (1938), considerable attention has been given to the question of the statistical significance of findings. Earlier approaches to this problem (see, for instance, Bronfenbrenner 1943) are now generally regarded as impractical, but the discussion they provoked has resulted in emphasis on the *models* underlying choices in a group. In order to make sociometric data more amenable to statistical manipulation, Forsyth and Katz (1946) proposed that the cumbersome device of the sociogram be replaced by a matrix of $N \times N$ dimension (where N is the number of people in the group);

choices or rejections could then be indicated clearly by marking the appropriate cell in the matrix with a plus or minus sign—so that, for instance, a plus in the tenth column of the fifth row would record that the fifth person had chosen the tenth.

In their original study, Forsyth and Katz attached special importance to choices recorded near the main diagonal of the matrix (the diagonal itself, of course, indicated self-choices); they also paid some attention to clusters of mutual choices and to adjacent clusters that had some members in common. A sophisticated variation of this procedure by Beum and Brundage (1950) was subsequently generalized for efficient computer analysis (Borgatta & Stolz 1963).

Both of the techniques just described depend essentially on the notion of rearranging the data as already given in the $N \times N$ matrix. In contrast, the matrix multiplication approach suggested by Leon Festinger (1949) has emphasized the identification of more formally defined structures. Subsequent work of this kind has been particularly directed toward naming and detecting ever more complex patterns of relationships (see, for instance, Luce 1950; Katz 1953; Harary & Ross 1957). This is a definite advance from the earlier sociometric studies, which were concerned mainly with patterns of mutual choice.

Other approaches to analysis of the matrix of choices have made use of graph theory (Harary & Norman 1953; Ramanujacharyulu 1964) and factor analysis (MacRae 1960); factor analysis is related to the rearrangement techniques noted above, so that the two approaches complement each other. There is also a technique based on cluster analysis (Bock & Husain 1950) that has aroused favorable comment (Ragsdale 1965).

Interest in the development of these analytic procedures reached a peak in the early 1950s; since then, the number of studies published has fallen off but seems likely to maintain a steady level. Nevertheless, there have been few applications of these procedures, possibly because they call for types of data that are not readily accessible in many adult social situations.

Reliability and validity. Although some research has been done on the question of the reliability and validity of sociometric procedures, it has received little attention in recent years. One early review (Mouton et al. 1955) indicated some of the limitations of sociometric procedures from the point of view of the stability of measures. Among other problems, the stability of the measuring instrument is confounded with the stability of persons and social structures. Validity is especially difficult to assess in sociometry, since the sociometric indexes are so often seen as the criteria to be predicted. Intrinsically, sociometric information represents the objective depicting of the situation on the basis of the most relevant judges—those with whom one participates. Thus, there has been some tendency to emphasize the prediction of sociometric status on the basis of other characteristics rather than to use sociometric status to predict other variables.

Applications of sociometry

Sociometric procedures have been incorporated into many different types of studies. For example, in small group research one of the common types of information collected in post-meeting questionnaires is the set of sociometric ratings on criteria relevant to the group participation. On this score, it should be emphasized that sociometric procedures as classically defined have tended to merge with more general procedures for obtaining peer ratings and rankings. The structure of self rankings and peer rankings has been systematically explored by various researchers, with some convergence on the types of content involved and some crystallization of information about the stability of measures (Borgatta 1964). Content corresponding to that initially identified by Jennings (1947) with task and with social concerns has continued to be central, but other concepts have also been found to recur in analyses.

Sociometric procedures have also been important to the development of several other research areas. For example, study of the impact of group structure on the characteristics of its members or on group consequences, such as efficiency of task completion or morale of the group, has made necessary a more formal development of notions of communication networks. An extensive review of this research literature (Glanzer & Glaser 1961) has suggested the limitations of such approaches and has placed them in their historical context.

Sociometric techniques remain pervasive in the social sciences, having relevance to personality research, small group research, analysis of networks of communication and group structures, and to special topics such as the reputational study of social status in the community and the study of segregation patterns.

EDGAR F. BORGATTA

[*See also* COHESION, SOCIAL; GROUPS, *articles on* THE STUDY OF GROUPS, GROUP FORMATION, *and* ROLE STRUCTURE. *Other relevant material may be found in* CLUSTERING; FACTOR ANALYSIS; GRAPHIC PRESENTATION; SEGREGATION.]

BIBLIOGRAPHY

BEUM, CORLIN O.; and BRUNDAGE, EVERETT G.   1950   A Method for Analyzing the Sociomatrix. *Sociometry* 13:141–145.

BOCK, R. DARRELL; and HUSAIN, SURAYA Z.   1950   An Adaptation of Holzinger's B-coefficients for the Analysis of Sociometric Data. *Sociometry* 13:146–153.

BORGATTA, EDGAR F.   1951   A Diagnostic Note on the Construction of Sociograms and Action Diagrams. *Group Psychotherapy* 3:300–308.

BORGATTA, EDGAR F.   1964   The Structure of Personality Characteristics. *Behavioral Science* 9:8–17.

BORGATTA, EDGAR F.; and STOLZ, WALTER   1963   A Note on a Computer Program for Rearrangement of Matrices. *Sociometry* 26:391–392.

BRONFENBRENNER, URIE   1943   A Constant Frame of Reference for Sociometric Research. *Sociometry* 6:363–397.

CHAPIN, F. STUART   1950   Sociometric Stars as Isolates. *American Journal of Sociology* 56:263–267.

CRISWELL, JOAN H.; and JENNINGS, HELEN H.   1951   A Critique of Chapin's "Sociometric Stars as Isolates." *American Journal of Sociology* 57:260–264.

FESTINGER, LEON   1949   The Analysis of Sociograms Using Matrix Algebra. *Human Relations* 2:153–158.

FORSYTH, ELAINE; and KATZ, LEO   1946   A Matrix Approach to the Analysis of Sociometric Data: Preliminary Report. *Sociometry* 9:340–347.

GLANZER, MURRAY; and GLASER, ROBERT   1961   Techniques for the Study of Group Structure and Behavior: 2. Empirical Studies of the Effects of Structure in Small Groups. *Psychological Bulletin* 58:1–27.

GOODACRE, DANIEL M.   1951   The Use of a Sociometric Test as a Predictor of Combat Unit Effectiveness. *Sociometry* 14:148–152.

HARARY, FRANK; and NORMAN, ROBERT Z.   1953   *Graph Theory as a Mathematical Model in Social Science*. Research Center for Group Dynamics, Publication No. 2. Ann Arbor: Univ. of Michigan, Institute for Social Research.

HARARY, FRANK; and ROSS, IAN C.   1957   A Procedure for Clique Detection Using the Group Matrix. *Sociometry* 20:205–215.

JENNINGS, HELEN H.   1947   Sociometric Differentiation of the Psychegroup and the Sociogroup. *Sociometry* 10:71–79.

KATZ, LEO   1953   A New Status Index Derived From Sociometric Analysis. *Psychometrika* 18:39–43.

LINDZEY, GARDNER; and BORGATTA, EDGAR F.   1954   Sociometric Measurement. Volume 1, pages 405–448 in Gardner Lindzey (editor), *Handbook of Social Psychology*. Cambridge, Mass.: Addison-Wesley.

LUCE, R. DUNCAN   1950   Connectivity and Generalized Cliques in Sociometric Group Structure. *Psychometrika* 15:169–190.

LUCE, R. DUNCAN; and PERRY, ALBERT D.   1949   A Method of Matrix Analysis of Group Structure. *Psychometrika* 14:95–116.

MACRAE, DUNCAN JR.   1960   Direct Factor Analysis of Sociometric Data. *Sociometry* 23:360–371.

MORENO, JACOB L.   (1934) 1953   *Who Shall Survive? Foundations of Sociometry, Group Psychotherapy and Sociodrama*. Rev. & enl. ed. Beacon, N.Y.: Beacon House.

MORENO, JACOB L.   1943   Sociometry and the Cultural Order. *Sociometry* 6:299–344.

MORENO, JACOB L.; and JENNINGS, HELEN H.   1938   Statistics of Social Configurations. *Sociometry* 1:342–374.

MORENO, JACOB L. et al. (editors)   1960   *The Sociometry Reader*. Glencoe, Ill.: Free Press.

MOUTON, JANE S.; BLAKE, ROBERT R.; and FRUCHTER, BENJAMIN   1955   The Reliability of Sociometric Measures. *Sociometry* 18:7–48.

NORTHWAY, MARY L.   1940   A Method for Depicting Social Relationships Obtained by Sociometric Testing. *Sociometry* 3:144–150.

POWELL, REED M.   1951   A Comparative Social Class Analysis of San Juan Sur, and Attiro, Costa Rica. *Sociometry* 14:182–202.

PROCTOR, CHARLES H.; and LOOMIS, CHARLES P.   1951   Analysis of Sociometric Data. Part 2, pages 561–585 in *Research Methods in Social Relations, With Especial Reference to Prejudice*, by Marie Jahoda, Morton Deutsch, and Stuart W. Cook. New York: Dryden.

RAGSDALE, R. G.   1965   Evaluation of Sociometric Measures Using Stochastically Generated Data. Ph.D. dissertation, Univ. of Wisconsin.

RAMANUJACHARYULU, C.   1964   Analysis of Preferential Experiments. *Psychometrika* 29:257–261.

ROSS, IAN C.; and HARARY, FRANK   1952   On the Determination of Redundancies in Sociometric Chains. *Psychometrika* 17:195–208.

TAGIURI, RENATO   1952   Relational Analysis: An Extension of Sociometric Method With Emphasis Upon Social Perception. *Sociometry* 15:91–104.

SOMBART, WERNER

Werner Sombart, economist, was born in 1863 in Ermsleben, Germany, and died in 1941 in Berlin. His father, Anton Ludwig Sombart, was a landowner, industrial entrepreneur, a National Liberal member of the Prussian diet and of the Reichstag, and one of the charter members of the Verein für Sozialpolitik. As the son of a well-to-do and cultured member of the middle class, Sombart was able to study law at the universities of Pisa and Berlin and economics, history, and philosophy in Berlin and Rome. His studies in Berlin included the seminars of Gustav Schmoller and Adolph Wagner, the leading economists of the German historical school and prominent *Katheder*-socialists. He received his PH.D. from the University of Berlin in 1888, with a dissertation entitled "Über Pacht- und Lohnverhältnisse in der römischen Campagna."

In 1888 his father's influence enabled Sombart to obtain the position of syndic with the Bremen chamber of commerce. Two years later, he went as associate professor of political economy to the University of Breslau; in 1906 he became a full professor at the *Handelshochschule* in Berlin and in 1918 he was appointed to the University of Berlin as a full professor.

It is difficult to describe Sombart's *Weltan-*

schauung—his political views, social theories, and religious attitudes—because all aspects of his thought underwent repeated changes. In several instances, he approached a social or economic problem initially from the point of view of a Marxist and gradually moved toward a far more conservative position.

When in 1894 the third volume of Marx's *Capital* appeared, Sombart acclaimed its publication as an intellectual event and himself published a study of the Marxist system (1894) that was in turn praised by Engels. Two years later Sombart published a pamphlet that consisted of a series of lectures on socialism and social movements in the nineteenth century (1896), written from the point of view of an advanced advocate of reform. This pamphlet went through ten successively enlarged editions and was translated into 24 languages; the tenth edition, which appeared in 1924 and consists of two volumes (about 1,000 pages), is violently antisocialist, in general, and violently anti-Marxist, in particular. Three years after these wild diatribes of 1924 against Marx and Marxism, Sombart explained in the preface to the third volume of *Der moderne Kapitalismus* (see below) that this later work constitutes for the most part "nothing but a continuation and in a certain sense a completion of the work of Marx"—a claim that was rejected by representatives of all shades of socialist and social-democratic opinion (see [1902] 1924–1927).

Sombart's views on social classes were also unstable. In 1903 he published *Die deutsche Volkswirtschaft im 19. Jahrhundert*, which was revised and brought up to date seven times during his lifetime. In this historical exposition of great erudition, Sombart tried to describe the emergence of the various classes in German society. This was a subject that was to interest him for many years: he returned again and again to his studies of the character and function of classes, undaunted by the fact that his conclusions kept changing. In the belief that he was following Marx, Sombart began by defining classes partly on the basis of their formal position in the economy—for example, Junkers and small peasants were located in the same class because both are representatives of "the original owner-economy" (*urwüchsige Eigenwirtschaft*), and partly on the basis of their members' aims—for example, the proletariat was characterized as a class because of its "tendency towards socialization and democratization" (1897, p. 7). Finally, however, he came to the conclusion that Marx's approach to the problem of classes led nowhere and that, in fact,

it was not Marx's illness and death that had prevented him from completing the last chapter of *Capital*, which dealt with this problem, but the inadequacy of his theory. One of Sombart's later conclusions was that classes are a phenomenon peculiar to the "economic age," which he identified with "our epoch" (1934, p. 23).

Sombart's best-known work is on the subject of capitalism. *Der moderne Kapitalismus* (1902) deals with the history, the structure, and "the philosophy of the spirit" of capitalism. To a certain extent the work was influenced by Marx, by Max Weber, by Wilhelm Dilthey, and by Eduard Bernstein. It is an exciting and challenging book; valid facts and unreliable information stand side by side, and *liaisons dangereuses* between the most varied ideas demand critical attention.

The subtitle of *Der moderne Kapitalismus* shows how broadly it was conceived: *Historisch–systematische Darstellung des gesamteuropäischen Wirtschaftslebens von seinen Anfängen bis zur Gegenwart*. The first book deals with the transition from feudal society to capitalism, and the last book treats conditions in the twentieth century. The development of capitalism is divided into three stages: early capitalism (*Frühkapitalismus*), ending before the industrial revolution; high capitalism (*Hochkapitalismus*), beginning about 1760; and finally, late capitalism (*Spätkapitalismus*), beginning with World War I (discussed only briefly). The moving force during the first stage of capitalism was "a small number of enterprising businessmen, emerging from all groups of the population: noblemen, adventurers, merchants, and artisans" ([1902] 1924–1927, vol. 3, part 1, p. 11). In the second stage, the capitalist entrepreneur was in command and was "the sole organizer of the economic process." The third stage of capitalism is, according to Sombart, not a stage of decay; on the contrary, Sombart asserts that this stage represents capitalism in its "prime" (*die besten Jahre des Mannes*), even though economic motives are in his opinion no longer paramount, having been replaced by "the principle of agreement."

In connection with his magnum opus, Sombart published a number of special studies, among them *The Jews and Modern Capitalism* (1911), *The Quintessence of Capitalism* (1913a), and *Studien zur Entwicklungsgeschichte des modernen Kapitalismus* (1913b). In these studies his interpretations of capitalism still tended to be idealistic, although they did not exclude materialist conceptions, and, in *Luxus und Kapitalismus* (1913b, vol. 1), he even found explanations in the area of the erotic for the emergence and development of capitalism.

After the advent to power of National Socialism, many of Sombart's theories changed, in order that he might present "a unified view of the various social problems of the time from the point of view of the national socialist way of thinking" (1934, preface). One of the theories that Sombart clearly had to change was that of the role of the Jews in economic history. Nevertheless, official National Socialism never accepted Sombart as its interpreter, although it recognized him as a sufficiently close follower to permit him to print three pamphlets that essentially reproduced parts of *A New Social Philosophy* (1934).

If the number of editions and translations of his books were an index, Sombart would appear to have been one of the most successful German economists. But he had few disciples and no "school," just as he himself had never, for any length of time, belonged to any "school." Sombart was read all over the world but received little recognition in the way of academic or state honors. He was one of the most colorful (and chameleonlike) and interesting academic personalities that Germany produced in the decades from the 1890s to the 1930s.

JÜRGEN KUCZYNSKI

[*For the historical context of Sombart's work, see* CAPITALISM; ECONOMIC THOUGHT, *article on* SOCIALIST THOUGHT; MARXISM; MARXIST SOCIOLOGY; *and the biographies of* BERNSTEIN; DILTHEY; MARX; SCHMOLLER; WAGNER; WEBER, MAX.]

WORKS BY SOMBART

1888   Über Pacht- und Lohnverhältnisse in der römischen Campagna. Dissertation, University of Berlin.

1894   Zur Kritik des ökonomischen Systems von Karl Marx. *Archiv für soziale Gesetzgebung und Statistik* 7:555–594.

(1896) 1909   *Socialism and the Social Movement.* London: Dent; New York: Dutton. → First published as *Sozialismus und soziale Bewegung im 19. Jahrhundert.* Title later changed to *Sozialismus und soziale Bewegung.* The 10th edition was published in 1924 as *Der proletarische Socialismus* ("*Marxismus*").

1897   Ideale der Sozialpolitik. *Archiv für soziale Gesetzgebung und Statistik* 10:1–48.

(1902) 1924–1927   *Der moderne Kapitalismus: Historisch-systematische Darstellung des gesamteuropäischen Wirtschaftslebens von seinen Anfängen bis zur Gegenwart.* 2d ed., 3 vols. Munich and Leipzig: Duncker & Humblot. → Volume 1: *Die vorkapitalistische Wirtschaft.* Volume 2: *Das europäische Wirtschaftsleben im Zeitalter des Frühkapitalismus.* Volume 3: *Das Wirtschaftsleben im Zeitalter des Hochkapitalismus.*

(1903) 1927   *Die deutsche Volkswirtschaft im 19. Jahrhundert und im Anfang des 20. Jahrhunderts: Eine Einführung in die Nationalökonomie.* 7th ed. Berlin: Bondi.

(1911) 1913   *The Jews and Modern Capitalism.* London: T. F. Unwin. → First published as *Die Juden und das Wirtschaftsleben.* A paperback edition was published in 1962 by Collier.

(1913a) 1915   *The Quintessence of Capitalism: A Study of the History and Psychology of the Modern Business Man.* Translated and edited by M. Epstein. New York: Dutton. → First published as *Der Bourgeois: Zur Geistesgeschichte des modernen Wirtschaftsmenschen.*

1913b   *Studien zur Entwicklungsgeschichte des modernen Kapitalismus.* Munich: Duncker & Humblot. → Volume 1: *Luxus und Kapitalismus.* Volume 2: *Krieg und Kapitalismus.* Volume 1 was translated into English as a report on Project number 465–97–3–81 under the auspices of the Works Progress Administration and the Department of Social Science, Columbia University.

1930   Capitalism. Volume 3, pages 195–208 in *Encyclopaedia of the Social Sciences.* New York: Macmillan.

(1934) 1937   *A New Social Philosophy.* Translated and edited by Karl F. Geiser. Princeton Univ. Press; Oxford Univ. Press. → First published as *Deutscher Sozialismus.*

SUPPLEMENTARY BIBLIOGRAPHY

BRENTANO, LUJO   1916   *Die Anfänge des modernen Kapitalismus.* Munich: Akademie der Wissenschaften.

COMMONS, JOHN R.; and PERLMAN, SELIG   1929   [A book review of] *Der moderne Kapitalismus. American Economic Review* 19:78–88.

CROSSER, PAUL K.   1941   Werner Sombart's Philosophy of National-Socialism. *Journal of Social Philosophy* 6:263–270.

ENGEL, WERNER   1933   *Max Webers und Werner Sombarts Lehre von den Wirtschaftsgesetzen.* Berlin: Collignon.

Festgabe für Werner Sombart. Schmollers' Jahrbuch, Vol. 56, no. 6.   1932   Berlin: Duncker & Humblot.

KRAUSE, WERNER   1962   *Werner Sombarts Weg vom Kathedersozialismus zum Faschismus.* Berlin: Rülten & Loening.

KUCZYNSKI, JÜRGEN   1926   *Zurück zu Marx!* Leipzig: Hirschfeld.

MITCHELL, WESLEY C.   1929   Sombart's Hochkapitalismus. *Quarterly Journal of Economics* 43:303–323.

NUSSBAUM, FREDERICK   1933   *A History of the Economic Institutions of Modern Europe: An Introduction to Der moderne Kapitalismus of Werner Sombart.* New York: Crofts.

PLOTNIK, MORTIN J.   1937   *Werner Sombart and His Type of Economics.* New York: Eco Press.

POLLOCK, FREDERICK   1926   *Sombarts "Widerlegung" des Marxismus.* Leipzig: Hirschfeld.

SUTTON, F. X.   1948   The Social and Economic Philosophy of Werner Sombart: The Sociology of Capitalism. Pages 316–331 in Harry E. Barnes (editor), *An Introduction to the History of Sociology.* Univ. of Chicago Press.

SORCERY

See MAGIC.

SOREL, GEORGES

Georges Sorel, French political thinker, was born in Cherbourg in 1847 and died in Boulogne-sur-Seine, near Paris, in 1922. A graduate of the École Polytechnique, he was a successful engineer in the government department of Ponts et Chaussées until 1892. He then retired to the suburbs of Paris and for the next thirty years lived modestly, taking no active part in politics. He devoted himself exclusively to writing on a great variety of subjects: religion, history, economics, ethics, and political theory. The bulk of this work, lacking in system and varying in quality, remains hidden in the volumes of many French and Italian periodicals.

Sorel's education as an engineer gave rise to his lasting concern with problems of technology and the philosophy of science. In such works as *D'Aristote à Marx* (1894a), *Les préoccupations métaphysiques des physiciens modernes* (1907), and *De l'utilité du pragmatisme* (1921), he adhered to a relativistic and pluralist conception of scientific truth, but was by no means antirationalist. Science to him meant the harnessing of nature by industrial technology, and he often cited Vico's dictum: "Man knows only what he makes."

Sorel was brought up as a Jansenist, and although he had no personal religious faith, he always retained from Jansenism the sense of original sin, the idea that greatness must be painfully and precariously earned, and the notion that there is a natural trend toward corruption. This is the background for his constant opposition to the optimistic belief in progress that characterized the philosophy of the Enlightenment, expressed principally in *Les illusions du progrès* (1908a).

Sorel's first political views were those of a liberal conservative in the tradition of Tocqueville, Taine, and Renan; *Le procès de Socrate* (1889) was written in this spirit. However, his discovery of Proudhon, whose moral aspirations fascinated him, and then his discovery of Marx around 1893—as well as the feeling that bourgeois values were in a state of crisis—brought him ever closer to socialism.

After a period of qualified support of Marxism, which included very active involvement with two journals, first, in 1894, *L'ère nouvelle* and then, from 1895 to 1897, *Devenir social*, Sorel became increasingly critical and revisionist with respect to the then dominant militant interpretation, as shown in *Saggi di critica del marxismo* (1903) and "The Decomposition of Marxism" (1908c). These commentaries on Marxism, which had more influence in Italy and Germany than in France, may

well be the most original and permanent portion of Sorel's work. They manifest strong opposition to the schematic, deterministic, and dogmatic conceptions of Kautsky and, in line with the views of Bernstein, they stress the voluntarist and ethical aspects of the doctrine.

Both Sorel and the French poet Charles Péguy, fervent supporters of Dreyfus from 1897 on, were badly disappointed and even embittered by the way the socialist and radical politicians of the *bloc républicain* exploited the Dreyfus affair. The man whom both Sorel and Péguy unjustly blamed for this degeneration of the "mystique" into "politics" was Jean Jaurès. Thereafter Sorel's thought became more radical: he shifted from right-wing Marxist revisionism, of social-democratic inspiration, to left-wing revisionism. He became an enthusiast of revolutionary syndicalism, a movement with a strong tinge of anarchism, committed to the spontaneity of the struggle of the working class and to its independence from any party leadership. Between 1905 and 1908 he wrote primarily for the *Mouvement socialiste*, the organ of the movement, and his two best known works, *Reflections on Violence* (1908b) and *Les illusions du progrès* (1908a), first appeared there.

Reflections on Violence is the work of Sorel's which aroused by far the greatest response. This book is chiefly a philosophical commentary on revolutionary syndicalism, a commentary strongly inspired by Bergson's thought. In it Sorel developed the notions of "myth" and "violence." The model for a myth was the syndicalist vision of the general strike, which he interpreted as a moral commitment based on nonrational beliefs, as contrasted with a "utopia" which is constructed, however arbitrarily, on discursive reason. He also pointed out the creative role played by a kind of violence that appears above all in the class struggle and that constitutes a state of mind, a moral rejection of any concessions. He was careful to distinguish this violence from "force," the mere exercise of the state's power of coercion, and he never tired of denouncing the abuse of such force, especially as it occurred in the Jacobin reign of terror.

In Sorel's last years, his thought was uncertain and bitter. Disappointed by revolutionary syndicalism, he hoped, not without embarrassment and hesitation, to find a new source of energy in certain monarchist and nationalistic trends; then, disappointed yet again by World War I—which appeared to be the consequence of these same trends—he became enthusiastic about the Bolshevik Revolution (1919), chiefly because he believed it was a lost cause.

Sorel is often erroneously said to have played an ideological role in the advent of the modern dictatorships. His influence on Lenin, who quoted him only once and with complete contempt, was nil. He always denounced anything that might give socialist action a Jacobin or Blanquist cast, anything that might subject it to the authoritarian rule of a party and *a fortiori* to that of a man. Mussolini did frequently claim ideological descent from Sorel, but to do so he had to interpret the theory of the myth as an apologetic for the blind unleashing of passions and the theory of violence as a justification for brutality; these interpretations are far removed from Sorel's intentions. For all Sorel's shifts and uncertainties, he was always a passionate defender of liberty and an enemy of arbitrary government.

GEORGES GORIELY

[*For the historical context of Sorel's work, see* ANARCHISM; SOCIALISM; SYNDICALISM; *and the biographies of* PROUDHON; BERNSTEIN; KAUTSKY; MARX.]

WORKS BY SOREL

1889 *Le procès de Socrate: Examen critique des thèses socratiques.* Paris: Alcan.

(1894a) 1935 *D'Aristote à Marx (L'ancienne et la nouvelle métaphysique).* Paris: Rivière. → A series of articles originally published in *L'ère nouvelle* as "L'ancienne et la nouvelle métaphysique."

(1894b) 1925 *La ruine du monde antique: Conception matérialiste de l'histoire.* 2d ed. Paris: Rivière. → A series of articles originally published in *L'ère nouvelle* as "La fin du paganisme."

1899 *L'éthique du socialisme. Revue de métaphysique et de morale* 7:280–301.

1903 *Saggi di critica del marxismo.* Milan: Sandron.

1907 *Les préoccupations métaphysiques des physiciens modernes.* Paris: Cahiers de la Quinzaine.

(1908a) 1947 *Les illusions du progrès.* 5th ed. Paris: Rivière.

(1908b) 1950 *Reflections on Violence.* Translated by T. E. Hulme and J. Roth, with an introduction by Edward Shils. Glencoe, Ill.: Free Press. → First published in French as *Réflexions sur la violence*. A paperback edition was published in 1961 by Collier.

(1908c) 1961 *The Decomposition of Marxism.* Pages 207–254 in Irving Louis Horowitz, *Radicalism and the Revolt Against Reason: The Social Theories of Georges Sorel*. New York: Humanities Press. → First published as *La décomposition du marxisme.*

1909 *La religion d'aujourd'hui. Revue de métaphysique et de morale* 17:240–273, 413–447.

(1911) 1922 *Introduction à l'économie moderne.* 2d ed., rev. & enl. Paris: Rivière.

(1919) 1950 Appendix 3: In Defense of Lenin. Pages 303–311 in Georges Sorel, *Reflections on Violence*. Glencoe, Ill.: Free Press. → First published as an appendix, "Plaidoyer pour Lénine," in the 1919 edition.

1921 *De l'utilité du pragmatisme.* Paris: Rivière.

SUPPLEMENTARY BIBLIOGRAPHY

ANDREU, PIERRE 1953 *Notre maître, M. Sorel.* Paris: Grasset.

DELESALLE, PAUL 1939 Bibliographie sorelienne. *International Review of Social History* 4:463–487.

Devenir social: Revue internationale d'économie, d'histoire et de philosophie. → Published from 1895 to 1898.

FREUND, MICHAEL 1932 *Georges Sorel: Der revolutionäre Konservatismus.* Frankfurt am Main: Klostermann.

GORIELY, GEORGES 1962 *Le pluralisme dramatique de Georges Sorel.* Paris: Rivière → A bibliography appears on pages 225–238.

HOROWITZ, IRVING LOUIS 1961 *Radicalism and the Revolt Against Reason: The Social Theories of Georges Sorel.* London: Routledge; New York: Humanities.

HUMPHREY, RICHARD D. 1951 *Georges Sorel, Prophet Without Honor: A Study in Anti-intellectualism.* Harvard Historical Studies, Vol. 59. Cambridge, Mass.: Harvard Univ. Press.

Mouvement socialiste: Revue de critique sociale, littéraire et artistique. → Published from 1899 to 1914.

PIROU, GAËTAN 1927 *Georges Sorel: 1847–1922.* Paris: Rivière.

SOROKIN, PITIRIM A.

Pitirim Alexandrovich Sorokin was born in humble circumstances in the rural north of Russia in 1889. A prodigious zeal for work, combined with enormous erudition, has led him to write more than thirty volumes, many of which—for example, *Social and Cultural Dynamics* (1937–1941), *Social Mobility* (1927–1941), and *Contemporary Sociological Theories* (1928)—have become classics. His writings cover practically all fields of sociology, including the sociology of knowledge, the sociology of art, political sociology, social stratification, methodology, and theory. He was elected president of the International Institute of Sociology in 1936 and president of the American Sociological Association in 1964, and has received many other honors. His career may be broadly divided into two periods: the one before 1922, when he was banished from the Soviet Union for his opposition to the Bolshevik regime, and the one since then, which he has spent in the United States.

Sorokin attended the Psycho-Neurological Institute and the University of St. Petersburg; there he was influenced by De Roberty, Kovalevsky, Bekhterev, Petrajitzky, Rostovtzeff, and Pavlov. With a broad foundation in philosophy, psychology, ethics, history, and law, he came to sociology by way of criminology and soon rose in the Russian academic ranks.

In his student days Sorokin was politically active in the revolutionary circles of the noncommunist left; he participated in the Russian Revolution, was a member of the Constituent Assembly, secretary to Prime Minister Kerensky, and editor of the newspaper *Volia naroda*. The experiences of the revolution led Sorokin to make a radical break with the

optimistic view of one-directional, material progress. Since he has been in the United States, his
major sociological concerns have revolved around
the processes of social organization, disorganization, and reorganization, within a panoramic view
of history that stresses periodic fluctuations as the
heart of social change.

Analysis of sociocultural systems. Sorokin's
major sociological presupposition is that of social
realism, postulating the existence of a supra-
organic, supraindividual sociocultural reality. This
reality is objectified in material and other "vehicles," but it cannot be reduced to the physical, since
sociocultural phenomena are integrated in cohesive
fashion by their meaning structure. Sorokin has
designated his sociological and philosophical conceptions as "integralist." A comprehensive exposition may be found in his *Society, Culture, and Personality* (1947). Total reality is a manifold infinite
which transcends any single perspective; it encompasses the truth of the senses, of the rational intellect, and of suprarational, hyperconscious faith,
intuition, or insight. All three modes of cognition
must be utilized in the sociological endeavor to
systematically study sociocultural phenomena.

These sociocultural phenomena are not randomly
distributed but form coherent aggregates. Although
there is no meaningful integration of all the sociocultural items that coexist in a particular setting,
sociological analysis can reveal a hierarchy of levels
of integration. The highest level of integration of
sociocultural meanings and values is reflected in
major social institutions. All such high-level sociocultural systems (those whose scope transcends
particular societies) are existentially organized
around fundamental premises concerning the nature of reality and the principal methods of apprehending it. The range of major alternatives is
limited: reality is felt to be directly given by the
senses ("sensate") or disclosed in a supersensory
way ("ideational"), or else it is considered an organic and dialectic combination of the foregoing
possibilities ("idealistic"). Correspondingly, there
are three irreducible forms of truth: sensory,
spiritual, and rational. At various periods of history
the possible basic premises are in various phases
of development, and in any well-defined period of
history the five principal cultural systems (law,
art, philosophy, science, and religion) of a complex society exhibit a demonstrable strain toward
consistency in their expression of reality.

Cultural integration, for Sorokin, is by no means
a static condition. He considers social reality to be
an ever-changing process but one with recurring
uniformities. Moreover, the process within sociocultural systems is a dialectical one, for the very
accentuation and predominance of one fundamental *Weltanschauung*, or basic perception of
reality, leads to its exhaustion and eventual replacement by one of the two alternative *Weltanschauung-
en*. This dialectic is at the heart of Sorokin's
"principle of limits," which underscores the
rhythmic periodicity of sociocultural phenomena.
A correlative proposition is the "principle of immanent change," which locates the major causes of
change *within* a sociocultural system rather than
in external forces. Another source of change is the
necessarily incomplete state of integration; the malintegration of complex parts is one of the sources
of the ever-unfolding change of a system of organization.

Sorokin has asserted that the maximal development of a sociocultural system emerges only after
centuries. The process of transition of a super-
system from one dominant *Weltanschauung* to another (comparable to the change in direction of a
pendulum's swing) involves the radical transformation of social institutions and normative patterns
of interaction. Sorokin located three major types
of such patterns along a solidarity–antagonism
continuum: familistic, contractual, and compulsory. The collapse of one integrative base and the
emergence of an alternative dominant ethos are
attended by prolonged periods of social crisis, wars,
and other man-made disasters. Sorokin diagnosed
the Russian Revolution and World War I as symptoms of vast upheavals in the sociocultural system
of Western society, and as early as the 1920s he
forecast further social calamities; his prophecies
were borne out by the depression of the 1930s and
World War II.

At a time when the problem of social change
and social disruption at the societal level was receiving minimal attention, Sorokin, in such systematic and comprehensive works as *The Sociology
of Revolution* (1925) and *Man and Society in
Calamity* (1942), was formulating theories of sociocultural change and conducting investigations
of the impact of disaster and revolution on interpersonal behavior. One of his important generalizations in this area is the "principle of polarization,"
which holds that in the majority of actors the
normal tendency to moral indifference in everyday,
routine intersubjective behavior becomes intensified
in periods of severe crisis (revolutions, disasters);
the majority then seek only hedonistic, self-oriented
gratification, while a significant minority become
oriented to altruistic, religious, pietistic, and

otherworldly activity. When the social upheaval is over, this bimodal, or polarized, distribution of behavior reverts to the earlier, "normal" distribution.

At the end of World War II, Sorokin did not believe that the West had emerged from its phase of immanent crisis into a period of harmonious international development. Since then he has remained an alert critic of what he considers to be the major trends of modern society, including the concentration of power in irresponsible hands and the anarchization of sexual norms, both typical of the waning phase of sensate systems. He believes that Western Europe's rich sensate culture has passed its peak of creativity, and he has concentrated his research since World War II on modes of behavior that, in his view, are antithetical to late-sensate values: the forms and techniques of love and altruism, their distribution and social correlates. A knowledge of these is vital if sociology is to prepare for the likely aftermath of the sensate epoch. In a sense, Sorokin's work in "amitology" represents a return to the legacy of nineteenth-century Continental sociology, which saw its purpose partly in providing remedies for the dissolution of society. Thus, Sorokin appears as a successor to Comte because of his interest in consensus, to Durkheim because of his interest in solidarity, and to Kropotkin because of his interest in mutual aid.

Use of quantitative data. Although Sorokin has occasionally been seen as a theorist who is opposed to quantitative analysis, he has always used quantitative documentation for his theoretical interpretations. Moreover, before World War II he was a pioneer in the empirical study of small groups and in other aspects of "experimental sociology." At the same time, he has adamantly opposed both quantification and formalization per se of sociocultural phenomena, and his book *Fads and Foibles in Modern Sociology* (1956a) is a comprehensive methodological critique of contemporary research procedures.

His own early work, *Social Mobility*, codifies and interprets a vast array of data showing that social mobility is a basic feature of present Western societies, although rates of mobility and systems of stratification have varied in different periods of history. His work conceptualizes social mobility broadly; it suggests types and channels of social mobility, analyzes both the structural and functional aspects of mobility (including dysfunctional features), and relates the general phenomenon of mobility to its complement, social stratification.

Career and influence. Sorokin has been active not only as a writer but also as a teacher and a promoter of sociology as a discipline. At the University of St. Petersburg he was the first professor of sociology. After leaving Russia, he taught at the University of Minnesota from 1924 to 1930. There he was instrumental in training many of America's major rural sociologists, among them C. A. Anderson, T. Lynn Smith, O. D. Duncan (the elder), and Conrad Taeuber. In 1930 he established at Harvard a new department of sociology, which soon attracted such able students as R. K. Merton, K. Davis, C. Loomis, and J. W. Riley, Jr. In making Harvard one of the major centers of general sociology, Sorokin never sought to develop a school of his own, but his provocative teaching encouraged a sense of breadth, independence, and integrity in Harvard's sociology graduates.

During the period between the end of World War II and the 1960s, Sorokin's work was relatively neglected by American sociologists. Yet his seminal studies are gradually being rediscovered; sociologists are coming to appreciate his systematic approach to the study of social change and especially his recognition of the role of wars and revolutions in such change.

The scope and quality of Sorokin's contributions to sociology merit a place for him in the annals of the social sciences, among those who have been ahead of their contemporaries in understanding the existential problems of their age and who have, at the same time, endeavored to make their knowledge both rigorously scientific and socially responsible.

EDWARD A. TIRYAKIAN

[*For the historical context of Sorokin's work, see* INTEGRATION, *article on* SOCIAL INTEGRATION; SOCIOLOGY, *article on* THE DEVELOPMENT OF SOCIOLOGICAL THOUGHT; TYPOLOGIES. *For various discussions of the subsequent development of Sorokin's ideas, see* CREATIVITY, *article on* SOCIAL ASPECTS; INTEGRATION, *article on* CULTURAL INTEGRATION; SOCIAL CHANGE; STRATIFICATION, SOCIAL.]

WORKS BY SOROKIN

1925 *The Sociology of Revolution.* Philadelphia: Lippincott.

(1927–1941) 1959 *Social and Cultural Mobility.* Glencoe, Ill.: Free Press. → Contains *Social Mobility* (1927) and Volume 4, Chapter 5, of *Social and Cultural Dynamics* (1941).

1928 *Contemporary Sociological Theories.* New York: Harper. → A paperback edition was published in 1964 as *Contemporary Sociological Theories Through the First Quarter of the Twentieth Century.*

1929 SOROKIN, PITIRIM; and ZIMMERMAN, CARLE C. *Principles of Rural–Urban Sociology.* New York: Holt.

(1930–1932) 1965 SOROKIN, PITIRIM A.; ZIMMERMAN, CARLE C.; and GALPIN, CHARLES J. (editors) *A Sys-*

tematic Source Book in Rural Sociology. 3 vols. New York: Russell.

(1937–1941) 1962 *Social and Cultural Dynamics.* 4 vols. Englewood Cliffs, N.J.: Bedminster Press. → Volume 1: *Fluctuation of Forms of Art.* Volume 2: *Fluctuation of Systems of Truth, Ethics, and Law.* Volume 3: *Fluctuation of Social Relationships, War, and Revolution.* Volume 4: *Basic Problems, Principles, and Methods.*

1939 SOROKIN, PITIRIM A.; and BERGER, CLARENCE Q. *Time-budgets of Human Behavior.* Harvard Sociological Studies, Vol. 2. Cambridge, Mass.: Harvard Univ. Press.

1942 *Man and Society in Calamity: The Effects of War, Revolution, Famine, Pestilence Upon Human Mind, Behavior, Social Organization and Cultural Life.* New York: Dutton.

(1943) 1964 *Sociocultural Causality, Space, Time: A Study of Referential Principles of Sociology and Social Science.* New York: Russell.

(1947) 1962 *Society, Culture, and Personality; Their Structure and Dynamics: A System of General Sociology.* New York: Cooper.

1950a *Altruistic Love: A Study of American "Good Neighbors" and Christian Saints.* Boston: Beacon.

(1950b) 1963 *Modern Historical and Social Philosophies.* New York: Dover. → First published as *Social Philosophies of an Age of Crisis.*

1954 *The Ways and Power of Love.* Boston: Beacon.

1956a *Fads and Foibles in Modern Sociology and Related Sciences.* Chicago: Regnery.

1956b *The American Sex Revolution.* Boston: Sargent.

1957 *Integralism Is My Philosophy.* Pages 180–189 in Whit Burnett (editor), *This Is My Philosophy: Twenty of the World's Outstanding Thinkers Reveal the Deepest Meanings They Have Found in Life.* New York: Harper.

1959 SOROKIN, PITIRIM A.; and LUNDEN, WALTER A. *Power and Morality: Who Shall Guard the Guardians?* Boston: Sargent.

1963 *A Long Journey: The Autobiography of Pitirim A. Sorokin.* New Haven, Conn.: College and University Press.

1966 *Sociological Theories of Today.* London and New York: Harper.

SUPPLEMENTARY BIBLIOGRAPHY

ALLEN, PHILIP J. (editor) 1963 *Pitirim A. Sorokin in Review.* Durham, N.C.: Duke Univ. Press. → Contains an introductory chapter by Sorokin and a series of essays on Sorokin's contributions to various fields. Includes a bibliography.

COWELL, FRANK R. 1952 *History, Civilization, and Culture: An Introduction to the Historical and Social Philosophy of Pitirim A. Sorokin.* Boston: Beacon. → The best introduction to Sorokin's philosophy of history.

LOOMIS, CHARLES P.; LOOMIS, ZONA K.; and BRADFORD, REED M. (1961) 1965 *Pitirim A. Sorokin as Historical and Systemic Analyst.* Pages 442–497 in Charles P. Loomis and Zona K. Loomis, *Modern Social Theories: Selected American Writers.* 2d ed. Princeton, N.J.: Van Nostrand. → A bibliography of Sorokin's works appears on pages 769–776.

MAQUET, JACQUES J. P. (1949) 1951 *The Sociology of Knowledge, Its Structure and Its Relation to the Philosophy of Knowledge: A Critical Analysis of the Systems of Karl Mannheim and Pitirim A. Sorokin.* Translated by John F. Locke. Boston: Beacon. → First published in French.

TIRYAKIAN, EDWARD A. (editor) 1963 *Sociological Theory, Values, and Sociocultural Change: Essays in Honor of Pitirim A. Sorokin.* New York: Free Press. → Includes a bibliography of Sorokin's works.

SOUTH AMERICAN SOCIETY

The southern continent of the Western Hemisphere is divided into 11 republics and two European possessions. This article focuses on the nine Spanish-speaking countries which encompass 58 per cent of the continental area and half of its total population of 165 million. It does not discuss the Portuguese-speaking country of Brazil, the English-speaking republic of Guyana (formerly British Guiana), or the two remaining colonies, French Guiana and Surinam (Dutch Guiana).

The Spanish-speaking countries of South America share common institutional features that inhere in cross-national configurations of law, administration, religion, and status assignment, all having historical roots in the ideals and orientations of postmedieval Spain (Haring 1947; Morse 1964). Spanish South America merits attention as a distinctive social order whose properties are illuminated by comparison with other regional cultures or complex civilizations. There are at least six major contexts for such comparisons: values and beliefs (Mackay 1932; Gillin 1955; Fillol 1961; Graña 1962–1963; Zea 1949; Dore 1964; Lipset 1967); intergroup relations, including stratification (Tannenbaum 1947; Beals 1953; Elkins 1959; Council on Foreign Relations 1960; Whiteford 1960; Horowitz 1966); agrarian structures (McBride 1933; Simpson 1929; Bagú 1952); demographic patterns and urbanization (Seminar on Urbanization Problems . . . 1961; Davis 1964; Morse 1965); political and educational institutions (Kling 1956; Lipset 1959; Hagen 1962; Ben-David & Collins 1966; Ribeiro 1967); and economic growth in relation to the international system of markets and trade (United Nations 1950; Baran 1957; Hirschman 1958; Rosenstein-Rodan 1961). In all of these contexts, South America stands as a special variant of western European civilization. To classify these nations as "underdeveloped" or as "transitional societies" is to ignore their distinctive qualities and to oversimplify the description of an extremely complex sector of the contemporary world. Therefore, any attempt to examine these complexities within a single conceptual framework necessarily involves selective judgments by the observer; in this article, the emphasis is on the relationships between culture, institutions, and social change.

Despite the presence of crosscutting institutional features, the Spanish South American countries manifest conspicuous differences in a number of dimensions (Wagley & Harris 1955; Vekemans & Segundo 1963). The southern cone countries—Argentina, Chile, and Uruguay—are the most modernized in regard to level of living, size of the middle class, birth rates, strength of industry, and composition of the labor force. Peru, Bolivia, and Ecuador—the Andean republics—share common extremes in terrain and climate and are distinguished socially by their large Indian populations. Despite planned acculturation programs, these indigenous groups remain largely isolated from the values and influences of the modern urban centers. Paraguay has a good climate and rich soil; its population includes the Guarani Indians, whose language constitutes a distinctive contribution to South American culture. The northern countries of Venezuela and Colombia have mixed populations containing both Indians and Negroes. Venezuela has experienced a remarkable economic growth largely because of a major oil boom. Her population is growing and urbanizing rapidly and is centered largely in Caracas. Colombia, a major coffee producer for the world market, is a nation developed around a series of inland valleys and multiple urban centers, each with a distinctive history and self-image.

Yearly per capita incomes vary from $648 in Venezuela to $99 in Bolivia. Illiteracy rates for those over 15 years of age range from about 70 per cent in Bolivia to less than 14 per cent in Argentina. Health facilities also vary widely: the ratio of doctors to total population in Bolivia is one to 3,900, while in Argentina it is one to 660 (the U.S. rate is one to 780; Russett et al. 1964). These differences generally correlate with differences in other features of the society, such as power distribution, rate of economic growth, the nature of the class system, and demographic composition. (See Table 1.)

Caution must be exercised in drawing inferences about institutional change from these aggregate data. Statistical patterns do not provide reliable indicators of basic structural developments; consequently, the frequent use of economic factors as primary explanatory variables is rapidly being superseded by investigations of historical configurations (Morse 1964), social structure (Lipset 1967; Bonilla 1967; Horowitz 1967; Landsberger 1967), religion (Vallier 1967), and patterns of identity and motivation (Hagen 1962).

Spanish South America constitutes one of the last world areas in which traditional European–Christian values are undergoing the evolutionary changes which attend industrialization and secularization. Uruguay and Argentina have moved through an initial secular–industrial phase and seem to be on a developmental plateau. Though hindered by demographic dislocations and problems of economic development, Chile and Venezuela have been progressively institutionalizing stable political systems, thus developing bases for setting and implementing collective priorities. Bolivia, Peru, and Colombia are handicapped by deep ethnic cleavages between their large Indian populations and their Spanish and mestizo elites, but they are working toward more coherent integrative and distributive structures, which will aid in sustaining economic growth. Finally, Paraguay and Ecuador

Table 1 — Indicators of economic and political development in Spanish South America

	GNP per capita (in dollars)	Per cent urban[a]	Per cent literate[b]	University students per 100,000 population	Inhabitants per physician	Radios per 1,000 population	Per cent voting[c]	Percentage of population in military[d]
Bolivia	99	19.4	32.1	166	3,900	72.7	51.4	0.47
Paraguay	114	15.2	65.8	188	1,800	60.8	29.1	0.96
Peru	179	13.9	47.5	253	2,100	77.9	39.2	0.24
Ecuador	189	17.8	55.7	193	2,600	40.6	28.4	0.69
Colombia	263	22.4	62.0	296	2,400	139.5	40.2	0.27
Chile	379	46.3	80.1	257	1,700	130.2	37.4	1.06
Uruguay	478	—	80.9	541	870	286.0	58.3	0.45
Argentina	490	48.3	86.4	827	660	175.0	61.8	0.81
Venezuela	648	47.2	52.2	355	1,300	186.0	83.8	0.49

a. Percentage of population in cities of over 20,000 population.

b. Percentage of population aged 15 and over.

c. Votes in national election as a percentage of voting-age population.

d. Percentage of population aged 15–64 in the armed forces.

Source: Adapted from Russett et al. 1964, table B.2, pp. 294–297.

are in the introductory stages of awareness and aspiration for change; they have realized that the world is moving past them.

One of the major emerging links between South America's Roman Catholic-based values and its political development is Christian democracy. Christian Democratic parties now hold national prominence in Chile and Venezuela and to some extent in Argentina and Peru. Although Christian Democratic parties are explicitly nonconfessional, they frame their ideologies and programs of social reform in relation to Christian principles. Moreover, many of the key party leaders earlier held positions in church-sponsored lay organizations, such as Catholic Action. The Christian Democratic parties represent an important line of political differentiation and development in South America, since they hold a potential for aligning social change with Christian ideas, yet are independent of the church.

The rise of Christian Democratic movements in South America is only one of the more recent distinctive political developments of the past forty years. *Aprismo* in Peru, *Peronismo* in Argentina, Acción Democrática in Venezuela, and the Movimiento Nacional Revolucionario in Bolivia, although based on radically different ideologies and political strategies, share broad features, including goals of social justice, the incorporation of marginal status groups into national life, and economic growth based on autonomy from international controls. Except for *Aprismo*, all of these movements have gained national governmental power. Each in turn has encountered difficulties in resolving the problems inherent in pursuing social justice and economic growth simultaneously on a short-run basis. These difficulties have usually provoked one of three outcomes: a dilution of the program for change in order to retain the support of key economic groups; the internal fragmentation of party leadership and an accompanying loss of momentum; or a more decided emphasis on radical change, which in turn stimulates the interference of the military.

In the international arena, the Spanish South American countries manifest three major orientations. Their cultural, literary, and intellectual life is closely linked with that of France and Spain. Economically, they are most heavily involved with the United States. On the political and philosophical levels, they have been heavily influenced by doctrines and theories which emerged from the Enlightenment and such nineteenth-century thought systems as positivism, economic liberalism, and evolutionary theory (Zea 1949). However, since World War II, and especially since 1960, they have shifted their international orientations more toward the developing countries of the "third world" (Horowitz 1966).

The most distinctive demographic characteristic of South America is its rate of natural increase, which is the highest in the world. It has reached an annual average of 2.7 per cent and is expected to go higher. The rapid adoption of modern health practices, which has reduced mortality, and traditional attitudes against contraception have placed these countries—with the exception of Argentina, Bolivia, and Uruguay—in a high growth phase, despite high infant mortality rates.

As a whole, the population is relatively young, and a large proportion of it is underfed and afflicted with respiratory and intestinal diseases. No one who is familiar with the health, housing, and educational needs of South America's poor can fail to grasp the human implications of rapid population expansion.

The ecological configuration of South America is marked chiefly by a low ratio of people to land. The United States, which is considerably below the world average, has approximately 53 persons per square mile. In South America the highest densities are found in Ecuador, Uruguay, and Colombia, which have 45, 37, and 34 persons per square mile, respectively. Argentina has 20 persons per square mile, and Bolivia has only 8. Yet these low densities can be misleading, for the dominant South American settlement pattern is that of an immense urban concentration, with a sparsely settled hinterland dotted with towns and small cities. Buenos Aires, for instance, contains more than 40 per cent of Argentina's total urban population and over 30 per cent of the national population (*Statistical Abstract of Latin America* 1966). Because these "primate" cities are not functionally integrated or specialized along lines of commerce, industry, or finance, major portions of their populations live in marginal settlements characterized by poverty, isolation, and social disorganization (Morse 1965). There is heavy migration from the rural areas to the cities, a process which crowds even more masses of the unskilled, unemployed, homeless, and hungry into areas already deficient in economic growth, transportation, housing, and public services of all kinds.

The role of the Roman Catholic church

The Roman Catholic church arrived in South America with the conquistadors and subsequently served as one of Spain's major instruments for bringing the indigenous population under supervisory control (Mecham 1934). Thus, the church stressed territorial coverage rather than pastoral development and was itself subject to secular control. The crown's various prerogatives over church functioning placed religious leaders in a frustrating position, for secular priorities determined the principles guiding religious operations. On the other hand, the church was protected by the crown from religious competition through special institutions, such as the Holy Office of the Inquisition, which were designed to maintain the Catholic monopoly (De Egaña 1966). The result of this combination of subordination and protection was a decentralized, uncoordinated, and spiritually weak church. The South American Roman Catholic church evolved as a series of relatively isolated ecclesiastical units, each of which was strongly linked to the superstructure of the colonial enterprise. Its activities and allocation of resources were not governed by a shared set of religious objectives and universal norms, and the clergy, internally divided and oriented to secular elites, found it impossible to generate and maintain a stable position of moral authority. In short, they failed to create and institutionalize a religio–moral foundation for the growth of value consensus; instead, a decisive and enduring tie between secular political power and the central religious institution was established (Vallier 1967).

During the seventeenth century a deep cleavage developed between the official Roman Catholic church and the Catholic religion as it was practiced by the common people, and this gap between the ecclesia and individual spiritual needs became institutionalized. Although the church continued to be based in the cathedrals and chapels, Catholicism became grounded in extrasacramental contexts: in the family, in brotherhoods, in communal cults, and along informal lines in the everyday world. The populace's religious interests came to be focused on, and satisfied through, ad hoc practices, private devotions, and participation in festive, Catholic-toned social activities. The priest and his sacramental authority became peripheral to the religious life of large numbers of the people.

The achievement of influence and social control by the Roman Catholic church in South America has thus emerged not from its functioning as a system of pastoral activity but rather from the support its leaders have given to secular powers and from their multiple involvements in education, charity, and administration. Moreover, during the first century of political independence in South America, the church became firmly identified with the conservative factions, and its principal survival strategy until well into the twentieth century was to depend upon these groups for status, financial aid, and influence. However, as many of the national churches gained, or were forced into, political autonomy over the last fifty years, religious elites have been forced to reconsider these alignments; in the more progressive churches, especially in Chile and Brazil, church elites have begun to support and implement social reforms as a new strategy for exerting influence.

The institutionalized status of Roman Catholicism in South American culture as contrasted with the church's inability to generate an overarching moral basis for social values and consensus illuminates two important and chronic patterns of South American political life: its instability and the important role of the military.

The political process in complex, changing societies requires the presence of an underlying substratum of what Émile Durkheim referred to as moral norms; at the same time, these need to be relatively differentiated from the polity. The routine give-and-take of politics depends, for its stability, on a framework of meanings and orientations capable of providing legitimacy for political discipline and centers of power at the national level. The cultural base of these societies lacks this integrative, legitimizing property against which political conflicts can be worked out and energies can be linked to collective tasks bearing on the attainment of national objectives. The political process, comprising short-run, power-oriented contests, is not an effective mechanism when each political encounter between the claimants triggers a death struggle over ultimate ends and basic values.

From this perspective the chronic intervention of the military can be seen as providing a temporary, intermittent substitute for the broader moral consensus that does not exist. The military brings a combination of naked, authoritarian strength and "moral" protection to bear on various political situations. While the military's political involvements and interventions are the result of many factors (Lieuwen 1960; Johnson 1964; Horowitz 1967)—the class origins of the officers, their monopoly over the use of force, and pressures from civilian politicians—the relationship can be viewed in terms of functional hypotheses. For example, one hypothesis is that the military in South America sometimes functions as a kind of religious system and that the church frequently functions as a political system. If the church had developed as an extrapolitical symbol of religious values and an agency of moral authority, there would be less periodic intervention of the military authority.

Although Spanish South America is Roman Catholic, the current status of the church in these countries is ambiguous. More than 90 per cent of the population are baptized in the church, yet less than 25 per cent receive the sacraments regularly (Pin 1963, pp. 11–18). There is a shortage of priests: in Ecuador, Paraguay, and Peru the average is one priest for approximately 5,000 baptized church members (Pérez Ramírez & Wust 1961, p. 141). This figure does not take into account the geographical distribution of the priests or their parishioners. In a slum of Santiago one priest may be responsible for 7,000 families within a two-mile radius, while in the rural mountainous area of the Altiplano, another priest may be charged with only 2,500 people, but they are scattered over more than 100 square miles. The shortage of priests, combined with the weak pastoral tradition of the church, has only served to strengthen the folk nature of religion—the *ad hoc*, extrasacramental nature of participation (Houtart & Pin 1965, pp. 177–199).

Moreover, the rapid growth of indigenous religious movements, especially Protestant Pentecostalism, represents a generic break in the traditionally Roman Catholic traditions of value orientations, political participation, and membership forms (Willems 1964). The Pentecostal sects combine authoritarian doctrines, expressive modes of worship, lay leadership, and a radical conception of otherworldly salvation; their congregations are built around social fellowship and religious solidarity. Since their membership is drawn from the lower-status urban groups, a population among which Catholic commitment is very low, Pentecostalism represents the first serious religious competition to the Roman Catholic church in South America.

As to the future role of the church in South American institutional life, there are four major possibilities. It may continue to decrease in importance as the traditional oligarchies with which it has been associated lose their power positions; as secularism and social pluralism increase, the church may become a locus for only marginal loyalties, increasingly peripheral to major institutional patterns.

Three other views of the future of the church assign it a role of continuing importance. Two such views see the church as a negative factor in institutional change. On the cultural level, Catholic beliefs and their accompanying value orientations are seen as having encapsulated the total cultural system, anchoring it to an otherworldly perspective. This framework prevents adequate differentiation of the technical, the rational, and the scientific spheres from vertical sacred authority and supernatural sanctions (Vekemans 1964; Fals Borda 1965). Some type of disengagement from tradition is thus seen as a prerequisite for socioeconomic development.

On the political level, the church may continue in its role as a powerful pressure group that is predisposed to intervene on the side of the forces of traditionalism and conservatism (Blanksten 1959). Either on their own, or in coalition with the rural aristocracy and the military, church elites would define their role as being the defenders of cultural values against communism and other leftist forces and the preservers of Catholic tradition against such threatening modernisms as the liberalization of divorce laws, family-planning education, and the restriction of church property holdings. This type of church intervention has occurred during the Perón era in Argentina and during military regimes in Venezuela, Ecuador, and Peru.

In recent years some evidence has appeared to suggest that the church may play yet another role, a positive one, in institutional change processes. Progressive groups within the South American churches have begun to support social change by fusing Christian principles with the concept of social revolution. These progressives gain legitimation from European Catholic sources: Jacques Maritain, Emmanuel Mounier, the social encyclicals of Leo XIII, Pius XI, and John XXIII. The norms set by Vatican II and the power shifts reflected in these principles give increased support to the progressive factions and their desire for social and religious reforms. However, one of the basic deterrents to the possibility of a positive role for the church in social change lies in the conflicts and divisions to be found among the progressives themselves; they disagree over priorities, procedures, and relations with the secular left (Vallier 1967).

Properties of the normative order

Spanish South American society rests on, and operates through, a distinctive normative order. Although this order can be characterized in various ways, its principal elements flow from a dominant world view that posits a relatively immutable universe of an extraempirical order (Graña 1962–1963). This view is paralleled by an equally important pattern: an accommodative and somewhat passive posture toward the concrete events and conditions that make up everyday physical and social environments. The universe operates within a set of coordinates that possess eternal and ontological status and thus are not susceptible to reorganization. The expected course of action is that of temporizing and accommodating within this fixed system on a short-run and often *ad hoc* basis. It is a mistake, however, to translate this complex into oversimplified descriptive categories such as "traditional" or "sacred." While both characterizations are, with qualifications, justified, these terms are too broad; a sacred world view can contain a variety of religious orientations (Weber 1922).

Because of this base, the normative system supports and encourages extraordinary patience, various forms of ritual behavior, and a distinctive tendency to pursue personal goals (or those of one's group) through patterned reciprocities and political arrangements. The last-mentioned quality gives behavior, over time, a quality of inconsistency and unpredictability. Less attention is given to the future than to the present and past. This focus is in part a product of the assumption or cultural premise that the higher-order laws that rule destinies are unknowable and, even if knowable, are unalterable. The energies of South Americans are thus husbanded for handling the present and short-run problems, not disciplined toward the achievement of long-range collective goals.

The action orientation produced by this normative base is a distinctive mixture of the religious and political modes. In this context, "religion" does not refer to a specific experiential ideal or confessional content but rather to a basic predisposition to project the search for meaning onto a set of powers who can be petitioned on behalf of particular problems or needs, if certain ritual obligations—devotion, loyalty, and homage—are met. But these powers are not seen as entities that can be involved in any broad cooperative undertaking. The religious orientation thus stimulates the patterning of behavior around specific points of obligation and activity; its product is ritual action.

The second mode of action, the political, derives from the necessity to reach short-term goals within a heavily structured and static situation. Social structure is seen as a condition of the environment, to be either worked through, manipulated, or challenged by threat or actual force. This view predisposes South Americans to utilize power plays or discreet and indirect forms of problem solving, the former being a means of joining the established powers and the latter a means of accommodating or evading them. There are two critical instrumental resources in action situations: full knowledge of the ways in which the system is structured and awareness of the networks of reciprocal obligations that can be activated to assist in the solution of a problem. Thus, innovation in

Spanish South America takes place within these spheres of political action. Each problem stimulates responses, including temporary alliances, formal accommodative compliance, the activation of political networks, and if the foregoing resources fail, a recourse to myths and evasion (Alba 1961).

Three features of the colonial period stimulated and strengthened these normative postures: (1) the bountiful and easily accessible geological and agricultural wealth led to an ethic of "gathering" rather than one of rational production; (2) the colonies functioned as suppliers to the crown, and social life was therefore organized around a dependency on higher orders and specific instructions rather than around the development of autonomous models of problem solving; and (3) the distance between ruler and subject, supposedly mediated by functional authority structures, was complicated by a detailed system of codes and statutes that was often unsuited to the concrete situation and thus stimulated circumvention (Sarfatti 1966).

In short, the Spanish-American enterprise was not innovative, independent in orientation, or focused on problem solving, but rather it was dependent and oriented toward Spain via vertical structures. The Spanish-American inhabitants related to each other in terms of fixed status groups whose memberships were determined by a formal superstructure. Problem solving consisted mainly in the settlement of conflicting claims over jurisdiction or the distribution of privileges. The common focus was on the advantages or disadvantages to be derived from those in authority.

The foundation for a societal community was never laid, and when historical circumstances resulted in the formal creation of nations, there were no solid normative bases for nation building. The functional exigencies of a society—integration, distribution of power, socialization in common values, and a rational division of labor—were undertaken in the newly delineated territories by structures that were suited only to a role as appendages of a wider social system.

Institutional patterns

A special configuration of institutions resulted from the attempt to build a national society out of institutions grounded in the colonial enterprise. The chief characteristic of these institutions is "segmental association," the vertical and spatial disjunctive patterning of social units. There are strong boundaries and corresponding cleavages between any one segment and the rest of the system;

strong dimensions of internal solidarity pervade the segments. People, resources, and loyalties adhere to the various demarcated units, and the width of the vertical or horizontal cleavage between units varies from place to place. In Peru, for instance, class distinctions vary according to geographic location, ranging from a simple tripartite hierarchical division in the Sierra to complex divisions into levels and sublevels in the coastal areas that are based primarily on birth, wealth, and ethnic criteria. In Argentina three broad axes determine the pattern of segmentation: industrialists versus rural aristocracy, workers versus middle class, and Creoles versus immigrants and their descendants. Integration in South America is thus more an internal property of the various segments than an aspect of relationships between units.

Segmentalism can be expressed in a number of familiar categories: localism (geographically based clusters), patrimonial enclaves such as the hacienda complex, and elitism based on birth, wealth, and a characteristic privatism or distance that restrains open social relationships. The means for moving from one segment to another, whether for assistance in problem solving or for status purposes, are the personal-relationship networks based on blood ties, friendship, or obligations resulting from past favors. These are the same networks that operate to facilitate political problem solving.

Segmentalism restricts the process of structural differentiation in Spanish-American societies, since each social unit tends to be a microcosm which attempts to be self-sufficient and autonomous. The shift from segmental solidarity to over-all social integration has not occurred. Thus, whenever these social segments begin to polarize, especially in the direction of open conflict, the military intervenes to impose an artificial and temporary integration. Argentina is especially susceptible to this type of polarization and intervention, as are Bolivia and Peru.

Within the context of this institutional segmentalism, the second major characteristic of the normative order, "hierarchy," takes on added significance. Hierarchy, or a distinctive set of superordinate–subordinate relationships, is an institutional feature of all authority systems, but in South America it is a generalized form pervading social life. Two types of this generalized form are paternalism and authoritarianism; the former is characteristic of an economic or administrative complex that has become an enclave; the latter generally arises when a national problem requires control of all the segments and a dictatorship emerges.

The third institutional configuration is international symbiosis, the recurring tendency of social segments to forge links with extranational systems. It is utilized as one means of achieving competitive status vis-à-vis other segments and authoritarian potentialities and thus deflects loyalties away from the nation.

This type of symbiosis developed during the colonial period and prevailed after the colonial ties of dependency were formally severed. Thus, in the early independence period many of the provincial settlements and groups were unwilling to commit themselves to the republican elites, favoring instead their own direct ties with the government in Spain. During the nineteenth century, intellectual ties with Europe and economic ties with the wealthier industrial nations reinforced these symbiotic tendencies. During the twentieth century, however, the patterns have changed somewhat. The older pattern of industrial relations has been partly replaced by foreign economic ties and various forms of financial dependency provided through contracts of international assistance, grants, or loans. The intellectual and artistic ties have merged into a worldwide system of academic relations, although the older landowning groups still retain their traditional cultural ties with centers of style and expression in western Europe.

Institutionalized adjustments. Within these broad features, several distinctive patterns merit special attention: the reliance on ideology as an element of action, the politicization of nongovernmental units, the adoption of extralegal solutions to problem solving, and the institutionalization of informal systems of influence. These four characteristics tend to merge and overlap in many concrete situations.

Ideology and action. In South America, ideology is highly functional because of the weakness of common values. In order for a group to have a basis for action, it must develop an ideology linking its immediate interests to a wider set of meaning and values (Hirschman 1961). It is not possible simply to set goals and then act on them. So long as the process of change is not self-generating, it must be advanced by ideas that can persuade, that give meaning and direction. Ideology performs this function and also allows verbal conflict to take the place of more concrete forms of battle. It thus bridges the gap between immediate goals and a wider sense of direction and identity, legitimating action in situations where the ground rules are not clear. In short, ideology is an integral element of action in South America because it serves to create a common basis of action where an underlying normative order is weak and extreme segmentalism prevails.

Politicization of the social structure. In South American societies the political mode dominates all social processes, including the economic. Such societies are said to be highly politicized because power contests and the attempts to consolidate power involve nongovernmental and nonpolitical units. Organizations and groups that are in no way linked with the electoral machinery, the legislative assemblies, or party organizations are either deliberately co-opted for political capital or are drawn into the political arena in attempting to further their own interests.

For example, the trade unions in those countries that have developed an economic base for worker consciousness (Chile, Peru, Argentina, Uruguay, and Venezuela) are highly politicized (Alexander 1965, pp. 13–24; Poblete Troncoso & Burnett 1960). They arose under the influence of radical ideologies, such as anarchism, syndicalism, and socialism, and as a result have defined a new function for the type of government that they desire. They are not simply interested in a redistributive scheme (as are the major labor groups in North America) but demand, in addition, that the whole structure of society be changed and that the traditional monopolizers of power be dislodged.

As previously noted, the hierarchy of the Roman Catholic church is also highly involved in politics. It has slowly been trying to extricate itself from the political arena, although this process of autonomization has proceeded to an appreciable extent only in Uruguay, Chile, and Venezuela.

Extralegal solution of problems. South American individuals and groups tend to rely on *ad hoc*, extemporaneous methods of reaching their goals. This pattern is a special illustration of the patterns of accommodation and evasion. Various types of creative solutions are utilized in order to accomplish one's ends; whether one makes use of personal connections, pay-offs, or obligatory ties depends on the situation in question. But an overall disregard of administrative regularities has existed since colonial days.

Informal systems of influence. In South American countries concrete units, whether labor unions, political parties, or church units, have tended to carry out multiple functions, many of which are executed as a result of short-term pressures rather than on the basis of long-range goals or priorities. Much of the ferment in the South American countries derives from the attempt on the part of these organizations to extricate themselves from their traditional anchorages and systems of diffuse control. Labor unions, for example, want to be able to use politicians rather than being used by them. The institutionalization of informal systems of influence handicaps many groups by exhausting their resources on multiple projects rather than letting them exercise their capacities on formally decided long-range goals.

The problem of change

The central theme in contemporary South America is social change, with the problems of economic and social development as the focus. These issues have polarized the major power groups and engendered deep controversies as to the type, rate, and means of change.

In the economic sphere there are at least four major areas of controversy: (1) the problem of inflation, its causes, and the different means of control proposed by the "monetarists" and the "structuralists" (Massad 1964, p. 222); (2) the extent and effects of these countries' unfavorable trade balance in the international market and how it can be corrected (United Nations 1950; Viner 1952); (3) the role of the government in investment and general entrepreneurial activity, including the degree to which national planning is necessary and fruitful (Hirschman 1958); and (4) the strategy of economic development, whether through a "big push" and balanced planning or through imbalances and carefully initiated inducements (Rosenstein-Rodan 1961). Recently attention has moved to fiscal reforms, economic integration, and the agricultural sphere, particularly the relationship of land-reform measures to productivity (Carroll 1961), the problems created by disguised unemployment and the inefficient allocation of labor, and the appropriateness and feasibility of large-scale commercial farms (Santiago de Chile 1960).

On the political level, problems of productivity, welfare, and capital create questions concerning the distribution of power that, in turn, merge with ideological doctrines. Those in favor of rapid change may be divided into three groups. Two are evolutionary: one champions the liberal, capitalistic model with limited governmental intervention, and the other focuses on planned growth and strong state controls backed up by an indigenous ideology. President Frei in Chile and his Christian Democrats represent the most recent expression of the second position. The third strategy is that of a full revolution, capable of bringing about radical breaks in the economic bases of power and a valid participative base for all citizens. Both the Mexican and Cuban models are taken as reference points.

The chronic patterns of economic stagnation, demographic pressures, and political impotency have stimulated a series of vicious circles. Diagnoses and prescriptive cures have multiplied. Early positions favoring additional capital and technical assistance have been gradually replaced by political formulas and sociocultural programs, including increased attention to basic education, leadership training, and cooperative programs in credit, housing, and agriculture. These efforts to instigate change are paralleled by theoretical ventures that attempt to isolate the structural and ideological bases of South America's many problems (Medina Echavarría 1963).

Current hypotheses and research on social change are focused on the role of the middle classes in political development—both its positive (Johnson 1958) and negative (Nun 1965) aspects; the functions of nationalism for socioeconomic growth (Silvert 1963); ways of transforming traditional values and structures by means other than revolution (Hirschman 1958; 1963; Lipset 1967); the degree to which labor constitutes a revolutionary stratum (Landsberger 1967); and the conditions for the emergence of an entrepreneurial elite (Hagen 1962; Lipset 1967). Studies of social change involving sophisticated concepts and measures are largely absent. The extent of change is grossly exaggerated. Economic growth or rates of urbanization have no sociological meaning unless placed in the context of income distribution, changes in occupational opportunities, and investment in social facilities and services (Bonilla 1964). It is thus necessary to distinguish between legislative reforms, aggregate trends, and structural or relational changes. Although major legislative programs have been passed into law—for example, land reforms, tax provisions, and labor statutes—only minor changes have occurred in behavior and the control over resources. Changes in certain rates, such as that of rural–urban migration, are typically cited as indicators of change, yet they seldom involve positive structural changes. Though the size of the urban labor force continues to increase, the proportion involved in industrial pursuits remains stable, implying that most of the growth is in the tertiary, or service, occupations. Consequently, those who see rapid change in South America fail to show that there have been relational or basic structural changes between occupational structures and social mobility, between political parties and labor unions, between the church and the political system, or between the landowners and key financial institutions, such as the banks.

There are, however, some significant emerging trends. Changes in the relations between the Latin American countries deserve special recognition. Although Bolívar, el Libertador, envisioned a continental form of union during the era of independence, this ideal has lain fallow until recently. Through the mechanism of the Latin American Free Trade Association and its quasi-political and ideological corollaries, the theme of Latin American integration has brought elites of these countries into new lines of cooperation and consensus (Haas & Schmitter 1965). Formulated in part as an attempt to gain collective power vis-à-vis established centers of foreign control, this movement toward continental integration has helped draw together intellectual and middle-class groups from various countries (Dell 1966). For the first time in a century and a half, these nations are turning away from extracontinental ideas and elites to their own resources.

Another structural change has been the formation of technical–political complexes. Small elite groups in many South American countries have been created to deal with the problems of translating formal models and empirical data into national policies, regional programs, and simulation models dealing with production, use of public facilities, migrations, and labor-force distributions. These sociologists, economists, administrative experts, and information specialists are aiding in the rationalization of decision making and goal–resource combinations.

By virtue of their esoteric knowledge and trained capacity for manipulating data and concepts, these groups have tended to amass a considerable amount of technically based power. Moreover, they are integrated with other elites along international lines and thus possess generalized knowledge of the world situation on the basis of which they can develop programs, set priorities, and legitimate their plans.

The trend in South America toward increased governmental participation in economic development and the broad process of social change suggest that the emphasis on applied science at the national level will continue to increase and, in turn, so will the importance of the technical–political complex.

The emergence of the social sciences in South America also warrants special attention for its relevance to the problems of change and reconstruction. The role of science in South America shares some of the broader legitimacy of the whole intellectual tradition, and thus its influence on educational philosophy and curriculums is very large. Within the Roman Catholic educational system, the impact may have even greater significance, for the fusion of the priestly and scientific roles implies a double transformation. First, social science tends to eclipse some of the metaphysical and theological emphases as problems of society, law, and motivation are examined empirically. Second, the priest as economist or sociologist symbolizes a new role for the church in its relationship to social change. The fuller institutionalization of social science in the major Catholic universities in South America will continue to be a major source of leverage for modernizing the church and thus accelerating its positive role in social change (Vallier 1967).

The emergence of social science as a major component of the developmental effort in South America is of even more importance than its rise to eminence within the intellectual tradition. Many of the outstanding ideological spokesmen for change and even revolution are social scientists who are committed to changing the social system and yet maintain the highest professional respect from their colleagues at home and abroad. Such social scientists occupy key positions in the many agencies and organizations that carry out consultation, planning, research, and programming for South American development.

The traditional "intellectual," unable to connect thought with action, is rapidly disappearing. No doubt persons so inclined will tend increasingly to turn to more specifically literary pursuits, since they have been shown to be unable to handle analyses of social structure and of the norms governing the new rationalities and necessary responsibilities.

The new social scientists must be careful not to approach their tasks from either an exclusively practical or an exclusively ideological point of view, or they will damage the long-range plans for development. As the new social scientists are legitimated as part of the new developmental ethos, they will need to undertake sustained, objective empirical research and the corresponding theoretical work necessary to inform such research. If they fuse ideology with social science, so that only problems relevant to the revolution are worth investigating, the social sciences could easily become mechanisms of politics rather than bases for examining and understanding the world. For the first time, the intellectual has become an agent of change, but he must be aware that the danger exists that he will lose a perspective of disinterested inquiry.

The course of scholarship

South American societies are neither new nations nor unambiguously underdeveloped, and they failed to gain an immediate place in postwar thinking about change, modernization, and evolution. Despite a lively and competent tradition of work on Spanish South America by historians and anthropologists, the area remained relatively neglected. Four successive events helped to turn the tide: the fall of Perón in 1955, the gains of the far left in Chile's elections of 1958, the Cuban revolution of 1959, and the initiation of the Alliance for Progress in 1961. In a few years the continent has become a major new area of scholarly work (Seminar on Latin American Studies ... 1964). It is not surprising that political and economic topics dominate these new efforts. This emphasis carries its own limitations and ideological corollaries. Themes that would appear to be central to the study of complex societies—kinship, occupations, voluntary associations, child-training and educational institutions, as well as deviance, court procedures, and religion —remain peripheral. Theoretical problems of long-standing importance, including the question of limits on the range of structural variations, the Durkheimian problem of structural differentiation and integration, role strains, status sets, and informal modes of social control, are seldom mentioned (Vallier 1965). Although the international dimension is being considered and conceptualized to some degree, the major emphasis is on the country as the unit of analysis. Even when the focus is comparative in intent, the boundaries of the society are taken as cutoff points. Given the central role of extranational and international patterns in contemporary South America, the key analytical unit is either intersocietal or interlevel relationships. Both Kling (1956) and Baran (1957) make this intersystem perspective central, and Raúl Prebisch has played a particularly important role in increasing the visibility of this dimension (United Nations 1950). South America's close ties with the United States, the strength of cultural orientations toward certain features of western Europe, the growing links between Roman Catholicism as a world church and the South American episcopate, and the move toward continental integration all suggest the importance of focusing research on these wider units.

Despite imbalances, major gains are being made in conceptualization and research procedures. Cross-national comparisons and regional configurations based on aggregated data provide a series of illuminating correlations, for example, between indices of communication and political development and between economic growth and democracy (Cutright 1963; Lipset 1959; Russett et al. 1964). There is a decided move away from static descriptions of governmental structures and labor organizations to the formulation of dynamic models centered on a limited number of variables (Germani & Silvert 1961; Di Tella 1965; Payne 1965). Other advances are made through the reduction of complex substantive fields into analytically based typologies (Wolf 1955). One of the most illuminating research directions involves the study of change sequences in terms of institutional relationships, feed-back paths, and the multiple ways in which growth and development may be generated through carefully planned inducements (Hirschman 1958; 1963).

Decisions about scholarly priorities and the choice of research sites and methods are complicated by wider political issues. The vast amounts of socially based tensions and human misery pose significant moral dilemmas for the social scientist. Many of the South American scholars are caught by force of circumstances in everyday politics: the universities are highly politicized and often the object of political sanctions. The increase in contacts between social scientists from South America and the United States has brought the politico–ideological corollaries of research into sharp focus. Disagreements emerge over the choice of problems, the criteria for valid data, and the logic of inference. Various attempts to develop a more harmonious basis of cooperation and exchange include collaborative projects, a wider distribution of research funds, and greater stress on proper training prior to field work.

The current significance of South America is manifold. It is one of the world's most important political battlegrounds, as was demonstrated by the events subsequent to the Cuban revolution. Numerically it is the largest stronghold of the Roman Catholic church, and consequently it is one of the major arenas for the initiation of religious reform and mobilization. South American societies have become test laboratories for new economic policies, community development programs, aid arrangements, public health innovation, and educational experimentation. In the social sciences, South America offers one of the most important new areas for longitudinal and comparative studies, for its republics share many important cultural and institutional features yet have a great diversity in specific details and structural development which allows the comparative study of parallels, divergences, and deviant cases.

In addition, South America presents many important theoretical and practical challenges in the area of social change. The previously described characteristics of segmentalism, international symbiosis, and hierarchical arrangement, combined with the lack of an environmental-mastery set, have impeded its development.

Future development will involve at least two major changes in this institutional context. The first is the formation of differentiated, more specialized adaptive and integrative units, superseding the more traditional, multifunctional units and thus providing more flexibility and concentration of resources. The second change involves the redirection and utilization of human resources; they must be dislodged from their traditional bases of solidarity and loyalty by extensive alteration of the very institutions that locked the individual into the traditional matrix: the family, the educational and religious system, the political mode.

The crux of the South American problem of change lies in the realm of culture. The key question, which has not yet been directly attacked, is how this great cultural system in its search for certainty, grandeur, and recognition through intellectual and aesthetic means is to be transformed into a mundane, secular, rational social system. Upon this issue depend all others. There is no doubt that the single most important line of change in South America is the rationalization of the political economy, yet this cannot occur without the existence of a wider basis of legitimation, a cultural system of meanings that can generate, fuse, and legitimate the necessary processes of rationalization.

IVAN A. VALLIER AND VIVIAN VALLIER

[See also CAUDILLISMO; LATIN AMERICAN POLITICAL MOVEMENTS. Related material may be found in CARIBBEAN SOCIETY; MIDDLE AMERICAN SOCIETY; PEASANTRY; SOCIETAL ANALYSIS.]

BIBLIOGRAPHY

ALBA, VICTOR 1961 The Latin American Style and the New Social Forces. Pages 43–51 in Albert O. Hirschman (editor), Latin American Issues: Essays and Comments. New York: Twentieth Century Fund.
ALEXANDER, ROBERT J. 1965 Organized Labor in Latin America. New York: Free Press.
ALONSO, ISIDORO 1964 La iglesia en América Latina: Estructuras eclesiásticas. Fribourg (Switzerland): Oficina Internacional de Investigaciones Sociales de FERES.
AMERICAN ACADEMY OF POLITICAL AND SOCIAL SCIENCE 1965 Latin America Tomorrow. Edited by James C.

Charlesworth. Annals, Vol. 360. Philadelphia: The Academy.

BAGÚ, SERGIO 1952 *Estructura social de la colonia: Ensayo de historia comparada de América Latina*. Buenos Aires: Ateneo.

BARAN, PAUL 1957 *The Political Economy of Growth*. New York: Monthly Review Press.

BARRACLOUGH, SOLON L.; and DOMIKE, ARTHUR L. 1966 Agrarian Structure in Seven Latin American Countries. *Land Economics* 42:391–424.

BEALS, RALPH L. 1953 Social Stratification in Latin America. *American Journal of Sociology* 58:327–339.

BEN-DAVID, JOSEPH; and COLLINS, RANDALL 1966 A Comparative Study of Academic Freedom and Student Politics. *Comparative Education Review* 10:220–249.

BLANKSTEN, GEORGE J. 1959 Political Groups in Latin America. *American Political Science Review* 53:106–127.

BONILLA, FRANK 1964 The Urban Worker. Pages 186–205 in John J. Johnson (editor), *Continuity and Change in Latin America*. Stanford Univ. Press.

BONILLA, FRANK 1967 Cultural Elites. Pages 233–255 in Seymour M. Lipset and Aldo Solari (editors), *Elites in Latin America*. New York: Oxford Univ. Press.

CARROLL, THOMAS F. 1961 The Land Reform Issue in Latin America. Pages 161–201 in Albert O. Hirschman (editor), *Latin American Issues: Essays and Comments*. New York: Twentieth Century Fund.

COUNCIL ON FOREIGN RELATIONS 1960 *Social Change in Latin America Today: Its Implications for United States Policy*, by Richard N. Adams et al. New York: Harper. → A paperback edition was published in 1961.

CUTRIGHT, PHILLIPS 1963 National Political Development: Measurement and Analysis. *American Sociological Review* 28:253–264.

DAVIS, KINGSLEY 1964 The Place of Latin America in World Demographic History. *Milbank Memorial Fund Quarterly* 42:19–47.

DE EGAÑA, ANTONIO 1966 *Historia de la iglesia en la América Española: Desde el descubrimiento hasta comienzos del siglo XIX; Hemisferio sur*. Madrid: Biblioteca de Autores Cristianos.

DELL, SIDNEY 1966 *A Latin American Common Market?* Oxford Univ. Press.

DI TELLA, TORCUATO S. 1965 Ideologías monolíticas en sistemas politicos pluripartidistas: El caso latinoamericano. Pages 272–284 in Torcuato S. Di Tella et al., *Argentina, sociedad de masas*. Buenos Aires: Editorial Universitaria de Buenos Aires.

DORE, R. P. 1964 Latin America and Japan Compared. Pages 227–249 in John J. Johnson (editor), *Continuity and Change in Latin America*. Stanford Univ. Press.

ELKINS, STANLEY M. (1959) 1963 *Slavery: A Problem in American Institutional and Intellectual Life*. New York: Universal Library.

FALS BORDA, ORLANDO 1965 Violence and the Break-up of Tradition in Colombia. Pages 188–205 in London Conference on Obstacles to Change in Latin America, *Obstacles to Change in Latin America*. Edited by Claudio Véliz. Oxford Univ. Press.

FILLOL, TOMÁS ROBERTO (1961) 1963 *Social Factors in Economic Development: The Argentine Case*. Cambridge, Mass.: M.I.T. Press.

GERMANI, GINO; and SILVERT, K. H. 1961 Politics, Social Structure and Military Intervention in Latin America. *Archives européennes de sociologie* 2:62–81.

GILLIN, JOHN P. 1955 Ethos Components in Modern Latin American Culture. *American Anthropologist* New Series 57:488–500.

GILLIN, JOHN P. 1960 The Middle Segments and Their Values. Pages 28–47 in Council on Foreign Relations, *Social Change in Latin America Today: Its Implications for United States Policy*, by Richard N. Adams et al. New York: Harper.

GRAÑA, CÉSAR 1962–1963 Cultural Nationalism: The Idea of Historical Destiny in Spanish America. *Social Research* 29:395–418; 30:37–52.

HAAS, ERNST B.; and SCHMITTER, PHILLIPE C. 1965 *The Politics of Economics in Latin American Regionalism*. Univ. of Denver (Colo.).

HAGEN, EVERETT E. (1962) 1964 *On the Theory of Social Change: How Economic Growth Begins*. London: Tavistock.

HARING, CLARENCE H. 1947 *The Spanish Empire in America*. New York: Oxford Univ. Press.

HENRIQUEZ UREÑA, PEDRO 1966 *A Concise History of Latin American Culture*. New York: Praeger.

HIRSCHMAN, ALBERT O. 1958 *The Strategy of Economic Development*. Yale Studies in Economics, No. 10. New Haven: Yale Univ. Press.

HIRSCHMAN, ALBERT O. 1961 Ideologies of Economic Development in Latin America. Pages 3–42 in Albert O. Hirschman (editor), *Latin American Issues: Essays and Comments*. New York: Twentieth Century Fund.

HIRSCHMAN, ALBERT O. 1963 *Journeys Toward Progress: Studies of Economic Policy-making in Latin America*. New York: Twentieth Century Fund.

HOROWITZ, IRVING LOUIS 1966 *Three Worlds of Development: The Theory and Practice of International Stratification*. New York: Oxford Univ. Press.

HOROWITZ, IRVING LOUIS 1967 The Military Elites. Pages 146–189 in Seymour M. Lipset and Aldo Solari (editors), *Elites in Latin America*. New York: Oxford Univ. Press.

HOUTART, FRANCOIS; and PIN, ÉMILE 1965 *The Church and the Latin American Revolution*. New York: Sheed & Ward. → Also published in French in the same year.

JOHNSON, JOHN J. (1958) 1965 *Political Change in Latin America: The Emergence of the Middle Sectors*. Stanford Studies in History, Economics, and Political Science, Vol. 15. Stanford Univ. Press.

JOHNSON, JOHN J. 1964 *The Military and Society in Latin America*. Stanford Univ. Press.

KANTOR, HARRY 1953 *The Ideology and Program of the Peruvian Aprista Movement*. University of California Publications in Political Science, Vol. 4, no. 1. Berkeley: Univ. of California Press.

KLING, MERLE 1956 Towards a Theory of Power and Political Instability in Latin America. *Western Political Quarterly* 9:21–35.

LANDSBERGER, HENRY A. 1967 The Labor Elite: Is It Revolutionary? Pages 256–300 in Seymour M. Lipset and Aldo Solari (editors), *Elites in Latin America*. New York: Oxford Univ. Press.

LIEUWEN, EDWIN (1960) 1961 *Arms and Politics in Latin America*. Rev. ed. Published for the Council on Foreign Relations. New York: Praeger.

LIPSET, SEYMOUR M. 1959 Some Social Requisites of Democracy: Economic Development and Political Legitimacy. *American Political Science Review* 53:69–105.

LIPSET, SEYMOUR M. 1966 University Students and Politics in Underdeveloped Countries. *Comparative Education Review* 10:132–162.

LIPSET, SEYMOUR M. 1967 Values, Education, and Entrepreneurship. Pages 3–60 in Seymour M. Lipset and Aldo Solari (editors), *Elites in Latin America.* New York: Oxford Univ. Press.

McALISTER, LYLE N. 1964 The Military. Pages 136–160 in John J. Johnson (editor), *Continuity and Change in Latin America.* Stanford Univ. Press.

McBRIDE, GEORGE M. 1933 Land Tenure: Latin America. Volume 9, pages 118–122 in *Encyclopaedia of the Social Sciences.* New York: Macmillan.

MACKAY, JOHN A. (1932) 1933 *The Other Spanish Christ: A Study in the Spiritual History of Spain and South America.* New York: Macmillan.

MASSAD, CARLOS 1964 Economic Research in Latin America. Pages 214–242 in Seminar on Latin American Studies in the United States, Stanford, Calif., 1963, *Social Science Research on Latin America: Report and Papers.* Edited by Charles Wagley. New York: Columbia Univ. Press.

MECHAM, J. LLOYD (1934) 1966 *Church and State in Latin America: A History of Politico–Ecclesiastical Relations.* Rev. ed. Chapel Hill: Univ. of North Carolina Press.

MEDINA ECHAVARRÍA, JOSÉ 1963 A Sociologist's View. Volume 2, pages 13–137 in Expert Working Group on Social Aspects of Economic Development in Latin America, Meeting, Mexico City, 1960, *Social Aspects of Economic Development in Latin America.* Edited by José Medina Echavarría and Benjamin Higgins. Paris: UNESCO.

MORSE, RICHARD M. 1964 The Heritage of Latin America. Pages 123–177 in Louis Hartz et al., *The Founding of New Societies.* New York: Harcourt.

MORSE, RICHARD M. 1965 Recent Research on Latin American Urbanization: A Selective Survey With Commentary. *Latin American Research Review* 1, no. 1:35–74.

NUN, JOSÉ 1965 A Latin American Phenomenon: The Middle Class Military Coup. Pages 55–99 in *Trends in Social Science Research in Latin American Studies: A Conference Report.* Berkeley: Univ. of California, Institute of International Studies.

PAYNE, JAMES L. 1965 *Labor and Politics in Peru: The System of Political Bargaining.* New Haven: Yale Univ. Press.

PÉREZ RAMÍREZ, GUSTAVO; and WUST, ISAAC 1961 *La iglesia en Colombia: Estructuras eclesiásticas.* Bogotá: Oficina Internacional de Investigaciones Sociales de FERES.

PIN, ÉMILE 1963 *Elementos para una sociología del catolicismo latino-americano.* Fribourg (Switzerland): Oficina Internacional de Investigaciones Sociales de FERES.

POBLETE TRONCOSO, MOISÉS; and BURNETT, BEN G. 1960 *The Rise of the Latin American Labor Movement.* New York: Bookman.

RIBEIRO, DARCY 1967 Universities and Social Development. Pages 343–381 in Seymour M. Lipset and Aldo Solari (editors), *Elites in Latin America.* New York: Oxford Univ. Press.

ROSENSTEIN-RODAN, PAUL N. 1961 Notes on the Theory of the "Big Push." Pages 57–67 in International Economic Association, *Economic Development for Latin America: Proceedings of a Conference Held by the International Economic Association.* New York: St. Martins. → Includes comments on pages 67–78.

RUSSETT, BRUCE M. et al. 1964 *World Handbook of Political and Social Indicators.* New Haven: Yale Univ. Press.

SANTIAGO DE CHILE, UNIVERSIDAD CATÓLICA, CENTRO DE INVESTIGACIONES ECONÓMICAS 1960 *La intensidad del uso de la tierra en relación con el tamaño de los predios en el valle central de Chile.* Santiago: Universidad Católica de Chile.

SARFATTI, MAGALI 1966 *Spanish Bureaucratic-patrimonialism in America.* Berkeley: Univ. of California, Institute of International Studies.

SEMINAR ON LATIN AMERICAN STUDIES IN THE UNITED STATES, STANFORD, CALIF., *1963* 1964 *Social Science Research on Latin America: Report and Papers.* Edited by Charles Wagley. New York: Columbia Univ. Press.

SEMINAR ON URBANIZATION PROBLEMS IN LATIN AMERICA, SANTIAGO DE CHILE, *1959* 1961 *Urbanization in Latin America: Proceedings.* Edited by Philip M. Hauser. New York: International Documents Service.

SILVERT, K. H. 1963 The Costs of Anti-nationalism: Argentina. Pages 347–372 in American Universities Field Staff, *Expectant Peoples: Nationalism and Development.* Edited by K. H. Silvert. New York: Random House.

SIMPSON, LESLEY B. (1929) 1966 *The Encomienda in New Spain: The Beginning of Spanish Mexico.* Rev. & enl. ed. with added appendix. Berkeley: Univ. of California Press.

Statistical Abstract of Latin America. → Published since 1960 by the Center of Latin American Studies of the University of California. See especially the 1966 volume.

TANNENBAUM, FRANK 1947 *Slave and Citizen: The Negro in the Americas.* New York: Knopf. → A paperback edition was published in 1963 by Random House.

UNITED NATIONS, ECONOMIC AND SOCIAL COUNCIL, ECONOMIC COMMISSION FOR LATIN AMERICA 1950 *The Economic Development of Latin America and Its Principal Problems.* Lake Success, N.Y.: United Nations, Department of Economic Affairs.

VALLIER, IVAN 1965 Recent Theories of Development. Pages 6–28 in *Trends in Social Science Research in Latin American Studies.* Berkeley: Univ. of California, Institute of International Studies.

VALLIER, IVAN 1967 Religious Elites: Differentiations and Developments in Roman Catholicism. Pages 190–232 in Seymour M. Lipset and Aldo Solari (editors), *Elites in Latin America.* New York: Oxford Univ. Press.

VEKEMANS, ROGER E. 1964 Economic Development, Social Change, and Cultural Mutation in Latin America. Pages 129–142 in William V. D'Antonio and Frederick B. Pike (editors), *Religion, Revolution and Reform: New Forces for Change in Latin America.* New York: Praeger.

VEKEMANS, ROGER E.; and SEGUNDO, J. L. 1963 Essay of a Socio-economic Typology of the Latin American Countries. Volume 1, pages 67–93 in Expert Working Group on Social Aspects of Economic Development in Latin America, Meeting, Mexico City, 1960, *Social Aspects of Economic Development in Latin America.* Edited by Egbert de Vries and José Medina Echavarría. Paris: UNESCO.

VINER, JACOB (1952) 1953 *International Trade and Economic Development: Lectures at the National University of Brazil.* Oxford: Clarendon.

WAGLEY, CHARLES; and HARRIS, MARVIN 1955 A Typology of Latin American Subcultures. *American Anthropologist* New Series 57:428–451.

WEBER, MAX (1922) 1963 *The Sociology of Religion.* Boston: Beacon. → First published in German. A paperback edition was published in 1964.

WHITEFORD, ANDREW H. (1960) 1964 *Two Cities of Latin America: A Comparative Description of Social Classes.* Garden City, N.Y.: Doubleday.

WILLEMS, EMILIO 1964 Protestantism and Culture Change in Brazil and Chile. Pages 91–108 in William V. D'Antonio and Frederick B. Pike (editors), *Religion, Revolution, and Reform: New Forces for Change in Latin America.* New York: Praeger.

WOLF, ERIC 1955 Types of Latin American Peasantry: A Preliminary Discussion. *American Anthropologist* New Series 57:452–471.

ZEA, LEOPOLDO (1949) 1963 *The Latin-American Mind.* Norman: Univ. of Oklahoma Press. → First published as *Dos etapas del pensamiento en Hispanoamérica.*

SOUTH AND SOUTHEAST ASIAN SOCIETY
See under ASIAN SOCIETY.

SOVEREIGNTY

The concept of "sovereignty" implies a theory of politics which claims that in every system of government there must be some absolute power of final decision exercised by some person or body recognized both as competent to decide and as able to enforce the decision. This person or body is called the sovereign. The simplest form of the theory is the common assertion that "the state is sovereign," which is usually a tautology, just as the expression "sovereign state" can be a pleonasm. For the concept of "the state" came into use at about the same time as the concept of sovereignty, and it served the same purpose and had substantially the same meaning. Both concepts provided secular symbols to replace the decayed religious basis for authority.

The theory of sovereignty purports to state an essential condition for political order. Political theory has perpetually oscillated between stressing one or the other of the two primal functions of government—survival and betterment. Sovereignty sees the world in the light of survival alone and is most appropriate as a theory when the world of settled expectations seems urgently threatened. The phenomenon and the concept of sovereignty are best understood historically since they originated as an expression of the search for a purely secular basis for authority amid the new state organizations in Europe of the sixteenth and seventeenth centuries.

Like all political theories, the theory of sovereignty has both a prescriptive and a descriptive element. It has been argued that different statesmen and philosophers just happened to emphasize one *or* the other of these elements; but one could also say that these are only differences of degree and that the theory necessarily claims both that

sovereignty exists *and* that it is relevant to some favored purpose. For example, Blackstone asserted (1765–1769) that there is and must be in every state a supreme, irresistible, absolute, and uncontrolled authority, in which the *jura summa imperii*, or the right of sovereignty, resides. This supreme authority is by the constitution of Great Britain vested in King, Lords, and Commons. The claim has both an empirical and a logical character— "there is and must be in every. . . ." Plainly, Blackstone's claim was not an induction from widespread observation or the fruit of the application of comparative method; it was meant to be common sense, perhaps a "self-evident" truth, or rather something necessarily involved in the concept of the state. As an empirical proposition, it was obviously false. Jeremy Bentham devoted much of his *Fragment on Government* (1776) to exposing and ridiculing this claim. He asked whether Blackstone thought that the Swiss and the Germans had never known real government. Many states did not and do not possess such a unity, clarity, and effectiveness of command. Plainly, Blackstone thought that all governments *ought* to possess some clear sovereign power. The theory is much more plausible as a prescriptive proposition than as a descriptive one: States that lack sovereignty commonly find themselves in difficulties, both in defending themselves and in resolving internal conflicts.

By 1775 the former British colonists in North America had come not merely to regard the assertion of parliamentary sovereignty as tyranny but to equate the concept itself with tyranny. "Only the laws are sovereign," said John Adams of the new Massachusetts constitution—a remark, which if taken literally, states an impossibility almost as obvious as the famous republican boast of "a government of laws and not of men"; if rule by one sovereign was impossible or undesirable, so was rule by laws alone. Sovereignty to the American Whigs was not the minimum condition of any civilized order; it was the threat of intervention against an existing, traditional order. The theory of federalism was put forward to contradict that of sovereignty. For "federalism" was not just the name given to the peculiar arrangements by which 13 allegedly sovereign states associated themselves for certain specific or general purposes; it was also a theory of government (as the authors of Paper 39 in *The Federalist* argued at the time, and as Harold Laski did later in *Studies in the Problem of Sovereignty* [1917]). And even in Britain there were those who argued that Parliament itself was bound by the "fundamental laws of the constitution." This might seem implausible, but Lord Chatham, the elder Pitt, could argue that the

Stamp Act was, quite simply, unconstitutional. He said that Parliament held sovereign power only over those who were represented by it—giving rise to the most telling slogan of the so-called American Revolution: "Taxation without representation is tyranny."

Yet, on the other hand, it could be argued that the basic truth of the theory of sovereignty was demonstrated even amid the federalism and pluralism of the United States constitution of 1787. For after doing nearly everything possible to ensure that the president was both checked and balanced, the founding fathers nevertheless made the president the commander-in-chief of the armed forces and specifically gave him unlimited power to enforce the existing laws. The granting of the military power might appear to be due to exceptional circumstances—although a certain simplicity was revealed in thinking that the fear of war was exceptional; but the power to enforce the laws was no more and no less than what Hobbes meant in his famous epigram: "Covenants without the sword are vain."

These two functions of government, the defense of the realm and the enforcement of law and order, show that there is at least a germ of truth in even the most extreme formulation of the theory of sovereignty. All the wiser opponents of the extreme view of sovereignty did, in fact, see the difficulty. Fortescue, for instance, described England in the mid-fifteenth century as *regimen politicum et regale* ([1714] 1885, p. 119)—*politicum* in that the king could only declare what the law was after consulting with his peers, but also *regale* in that he was absolute in the task of enforcing the laws, punishing offenders, and defending the realm. Bracton in his *De legibus et consuetudinibus Angliae* (1569) had made a similar point almost two centuries before: There was a sphere of absolute royal prerogative, the *gubernaculum*, but there was also a sphere of absolute legal restraint, the *jurisdictio*—the king's duty was simply to declare and enforce the laws, and if he presumed to make new laws, the courts or Parliament could declare such acts illegal (see McIlwain 1940). The great debate of the Renaissance and early modern period was between those who said that "the first business of a government is to govern" (and justified this by the theory of sovereignty) and those who said either that "all government rests on consent" (and tried to justify this by theories of pluralism or of individualism) or that all government is "under natural law" and man should not attempt to change it. Although it is clear that this debate is now exhausted, the theory of sovereignty in a full sense did fulfill a particular political need in the particular circumstances of Europe in the sixteenth and seventeenth centuries. Before Bodin the use of the concept of sovereignty is an anachronism, although a depressingly common one. It was unknown to the Roman tradition of politics. Even the most famous and extreme formulation of imperial authority, in the *Institutes* of Justinian, does not contain a conception of sovereignty as understood by Bodin, Hobbes, Austin, or Jellinek. *Sed et quod principi placuit, legis habet vigorem*—"what pleases the Prince has the force of law"—is immediately qualified by *cum populus ei et in eum omne suum imperium et potestatem concessit*—"for the people make over to him their whole power and authority" (*Institutiones*, book 1, tit. 2, sec. 6). As a descriptive theory, this is plainly false. The people of Rome never did any such thing, nor were they ever in a position to do so. But the prescriptive argument is more substantial; it reminded even the heirs of Augustus Caesar that it was politically necessary for them to govern according to at least a myth of popularity, because even their power rested upon the consent of subjects who potentially had the power to overthrow the government.

The concept of sovereignty was also unknown to medieval Christendom. Disputes between popes and emperors often can be restated in terms of sovereignty; but if the two sides had understood this term, they would have had no dispute over it. As Christians, both recognized that some things were Caesar's and others, God's. The emperor held sovereign power over those things secular and the pope was sovereign over those things deemed to be divine. But to admit divided sovereignty is to make the concept almost meaningless. The papal–imperial controversies were not about sovereignty but about political predominance. Medieval political thought was inherently both constitutional and hierarchical. The rights and duties of kings were proper matters of dispute, but all agreed that they were bound by law—indeed, by different types of law: eternal, divine, natural, and positive law. Kings might claim to have the sole right to declare what the positive law was, but they could not claim to create it. The idea of creating new law by statute was an idea new to the Renaissance. To claim that the king was above the law would previously have been a kind of blasphemy; and to claim that "law" meant only what the king or sovereign body in fact enforced would have appeared a trivial cynicism.

Bodin. The theory of sovereignty that emerged from Bodin's *Six Bookes of a Commonweale* (1576) was a practical response to tension between the claims of church and state. He wrote as France was tearing itself to pieces in wars of religion. His patron, François, duc d'Alençon, was the official leader of the party of the *politiques*, who held that the state was primarily concerned with the maintenance of order and not with the establishment of true religion; therefore they sought, like the supporters of the "new monarchies" elsewhere in Europe, to strengthen the crown against both the nobility and the church. Like Hobbes, Bodin saw civil war as the worst of all evils; he defined sovereignty so as to leave no possible room for any right of resistance (in an age when both Protestant and Roman Catholic theologians took turns, as circumstances varied, in producing learned justifications of tyrannicide). "It is clear that the principal mark of sovereign majesty . . . is the right to impose laws generally on all subjects regardless of their consent. . . . If he is to govern the state well, a sovereign prince must be above the law . . ." (1576, p. 32 in the 1955 edition). Thus, the essence of sovereignty was the power to command, and commands must proceed from a single will. Since law was simply the command of the sovereign, obligation could not be conditional upon the *justice* of the command, but followed simply from its authenticity. "Open, in the King's name!" was to be enough. Bodin thought he had found in the existence of this principle of sovereignty a universal recipe for political stability.

This formulation had obvious descriptive and prescriptive advantages over that of medieval political thought. But Bodin was careful to make reasonably clear that his sovereign is not absolute and that, like Aristotle's monarch, he is not to be confused with a tyrant. He is bound by the natural law and the laws declared by God. For instance, "God has declared explicitly in His Law that it is not just to take, or even to covet, the goods of another. Those who defend such opinions are even more dangerous than those who act on them. They show the lion his claws, and arm princes under a cover of just claims" (*ibid.*, p. 35). He drew a curious distinction between *law*, which is a command by the sovereign, and *right*, which is a matter of equity and litigation, somehow apart from the sovereign. The founder of the theory of sovereignty was either too realistic descriptively or not ruthless enough prescriptively to make his sovereign completely secure. But he did make power the distinguishing mark of the ruler, rather than justice or the judicial function. He did not say, however, as did Hobbes, that there is no right or wrong until the sovereign makes laws creating such distinctions.

Hobbes. In *Leviathan*, Hobbes made the sovereign both morally and politically absolute. He attacked the whole Aristotelian tradition of moral philosophy and stated that "this private measure

of good is a doctrine, not only vain, but also pernicious to the public state" (1651, p. 372 in 1914 edition). Only law creates the distinction of right and wrong, and law is the creation of the sovereign. The fundamental law of nature is self-preservation; only sovereign power can prevent men from destroying each other; and the only sovereign power to be obeyed is an effective one—obligation ceases at the moment when a sovereign power ceases to be able to protect the lives of his subjects. Here is a ruthlessly rational view of sovereignty. There is no room for loyalty in the world of Hobbes. Most theories of political obligation had pictured sacrifice for the true monarch as the height of glory, but for Hobbes such terms as "sacrifice," "true monarch," and "glory" (or "honor") were metaphysical nonsense and, indeed, "baited hooks." He is astonishingly modern. He even speaks up for tyranny, saying that "the name of Tyranny signifieth nothing more, nor less, than the name of Sovereignty. . . . I think the toleration of a professed hatred of Tyranny is a Toleration of hatred to Commonwealth in generall" (*ibid.*, p. 388). Nothing is worse than the lack of sovereign power, that is, the state of nature; or the belief that power can be divided: "If there had not first been an opinion received of the greatest part of England, that these Powers were divided between the King and the Lords, and the House of Commons, the people had never been divided and fallen into this Civill Warre" (*ibid.*, p. 95).

Both Hobbes and Bodin were preoccupied with the problem of civil war; their theories are appropriate to states of emergency. And in Hobbes's theory, too, although the sovereign is absolute, he is bound by the laws of nature. These are no longer moral matters: the law of self-preservation dictates that no one can be expected to take his own life. Therefore, although a man may be commanded as a soldier, he may properly purchase a substitute; and as for men who run away in battle, "when they do it not out of treachery, but fear, they are not esteemed to do it unjustly, but dishonorably!" (*ibid.*, p. 115). Thus, the germ of the nineteenth-century bourgeois is planted in a work that otherwise might seem to be a throwback to Renaissance tyranny. Sovereignty is once again passionately advocated—and yet limited.

Machiavelli. A negative question may throw some light on this paradox: Why did not Machiavelli, of all men, develop a doctrine of sovereignty? In one sense he did, implicitly, throughout *The Prince*. Then in *The Discourses* he said: "Those republics that cannot against impending danger take refuge under a dictator or some such authority will in serious emergencies always be ruined"

(*Chief Works . . .*, vol. 1, p. 269). But by "republic" he meant a type of government in which there is a citizen body representative at least of the main social forces. Clearly, he thought, as did Aristotle, that this type of government is both the best and in the long run the most stable. But he realized that it is not always possible. And he was concerned not with a legalistic question but with the realistic question of the different needs during emergencies and under normal conditions. States that are threatened by external aggression or by severe internal conflict or that are in the process of being founded need princely (or sovereign) rule; those that have solved these difficulties need to spread power to ensure their stability through time, that is, to politicize themselves.

Machiavelli is perhaps more realistic than either Bodin or Hobbes in recognizing two archetypal situations, with different needs: normal politics (peace), which is republican, and states of emergency (war), which are dictatorial. This can be seen in the doctrine of "constitutional dictatorship" in the Roman Republic (see Rossiter 1948) and in later times in the assumption of emergency powers by Lincoln in the American Civil War and by Churchill in World War II. "Is there, in all republics," asked Lincoln in 1861, "this inherent and fatal weakness? Must a government, of necessity, be too strong for the liberties of its people, or too weak to maintain its own existence?" (*Speeches . . .*, p. 176). If sovereignty is taken as a potentiality to be realized in what are recognized as times of emergency, and not as a day-to-day activity, then there is no contradiction between the theory of sovereign power and the theory of representative consent. The same way of resolving the problem of sovereignty is implied in Rousseau's famous aphorism that however strong a man is, he is never strong enough to remain master always unless he transform his might into right and obedience into duty.

There is a long history of the intricate and largely futile attempts to reconcile the theory of sovereignty with that of consent (see Merriam 1900). The problem has seemed at once more urgent and intractable since the political consequences of the industrial revolution have made it clear that strong governments can thrive only with the active participation of the masses—whether in the manner of totalitarianism or of political democracy. The almost meaningless rhetoric of "sovereignty of the people" long held sway both in the United States and in France. In the United States it disguised the actual location of the exercise of central power; in France it long helped to prevent its exercise at all; and in both cases it strengthened what both Alexis de Tocqueville and John Stuart Mill called "the tyranny of public opinion."

The attempt to define a "sovereignty of Parliament" has nonetheless some considerable historical and philosophical interest. For it can be truly said that Britain lost any chance of conciliation with her North American colonies because of this dogma. To most men in Whitehall and Westminster, it seemed part of tradition, nature, and logic; to men in Boston, New York, and Williamsburg it seemed a specific threat. Even the promise not to exercise it for reasons of political prudence, such as Burke proposed, could not pacify the colonists when even Burke and the Rockingham Whigs, let alone the king's government, insisted on the retention of the theory as a necessary ultimate sanction. Burke himself had drafted the Declaratory Act of 1766, perhaps the high-water mark of the theory of sovereignty and certainly one of the strangest acts ever to appear in the statute book, for it added nothing to the law but only stated what was already clearly the case: that the power of Parliament was unlimited in law. But on both sides the question was, after all, not what could Parliament do but what was it likely to do, having in mind precedents and, still more, the traditions and habits of the people it had to govern. No wonder many so-called purely practical men appeared grossly doctrinaire on the point of sovereignty; and no wonder that many others felt torn between constitutional authority and sovereign power. A perplexed member of Parliament said during the debate on the repeal of the Stamp Act in 1766 that "two opinions, both equally true, (though carrying with them a seeming contradiction in this particular) were set before us. The one, that in all free countries no one can be taxed but by himself, or representative. The other, that there never was any country, since the Creation, where there was not somewhere lodged, for the superintendency of the whole, one supreme legislative authority, controlling, directing, and governing the whole" (Great Britain, Parliament 1813, vol. 16, cols. 108–109). "Seeming contradiction" was right. But for generations English lawyers stubbornly treated the doctrine of parliamentary sovereignty as if it were a political doctrine and not simply a legal doctrine.

Austin. Closely following Jeremy Bentham, John Austin argued that if a determinate human superior not in habit of obedience to a like superior receive habitual obedience from the bulk of a given society, that determinate superior is sovereign in that society, and the society (including the superior) is a society political and independent (1863, vol. 1, p. 227 in 1873 edition). And to Austin that sovereign in Britain was, of course, Parliament as a whole. But Parliament as a whole is an extremely legalistic concept, as is immediately apparent when the question is asked: Who receives habitual obedience in Parliament? Can we now say that the prime minister is sovereign? Yes, but then we must add, more explicitly than Hobbes, "while the going is good." In a word, such power is political and cannot be defined in legalistic terms. For political power to exist at all there must be the potentiality of sovereign power, but a sovereign power constantly exercised appears to be invariably self-defeating.

Austin assumed, like Blackstone before him and A. V. Dicey afterward, that in every government there is a clear place where such absolute power resides. This is plainly false. The example of federal constitutions alone refutes it.

It may be true that federal systems are prone to run into difficulties in times of emergency when they cannot, or cannot readily, summon and assert sovereign power; but it is equally true that the British system does not normally use it. What the concept of the "sovereignty of Parliament" does explain is that there are no possible *legal* limitations on the sovereignty of Parliament. But this is a very formal matter. What is interesting is not what could be done but what is likely to be done politically. It is not telling much to say that no court or other body can challenge an act of Parliament or a proceeding in Parliament. This led A. V. Dicey to distinguish between "legal" sovereignty, exercised by the Queen-in-Parliament, and "political" sovereignty, exercised by the electorate. The one is what is possible; the other, what is likely. But this distinction is not as helpful as it seems. For plainly Parliament as well as the electorate plays a role in political influence; and everybody (including members of Parliament) forms part of an electorate, which is itself only to be defined in legal terms. The real distinction is between what people may do in legal and in political capacities; but this does not correspond to any precise distinction between institutions like Parliament and the electorate. They are, in fact, linked indissolubly by the political processes of party.

The concept of sovereignty is thus best reserved for the conditional assertion that all governments may face conditions of emergency in which normal constitutional rules have to be set aside if the state is to survive. The theory of sovereignty according to Bodin, Hobbes, and the English positivist lawyers can be given a meaning only as a contradiction to those normal political conditions in which it is recognized—and acted upon—that power is divided and that the business of government is creative conciliation. But this contradiction is at times necessary: it lies in events and not in theory. It has appeared more relevant to some epochs than to others—which accounts for the time of its emergence and its peculiar setting in civil wars. Sovereignty is relevant to emergency situations, as the potentiality of maintaining order in face of clear and present danger, and the justification of emergency powers by which all regimes must find a capacity for decisive, centralized, and, for a time, unquestioned action if a state is to survive. Politics, as Voltaire said of liberty, has no relevance to a city in a state of siege. The practical difficulties of deciding when a state of emergency exists are always great and open to abuse—but they are practical and procedural difficulties; they do not destroy the real distinction between the time of sovereignty and the time of politics.

BERNARD CRICK

[*See also* AUTHORITY; CONSTITUTIONS AND CONSTITUTIONALISM; CRISIS GOVERNMENT; GENERAL WILL; GOVERNMENT; INTERNATIONAL POLITICS; MONARCHY; POLITICAL THEORY; RESPONSIBILITY; STATE; *and the biographies of* AUSTIN; BODIN; DICEY; HOBBES; MACHIAVELLI; ROUSSEAU.]

BIBLIOGRAPHY

AUSTIN, JOHN (1832–1863) 1954 *The Province of Jurisprudence Determined* and *The Uses of the Study of Jurisprudence.* London: Weidenfeld & Nicolson; New York: Noonday. → Two books reprinted in one volume.

AUSTIN, JOHN (1863) 1911 *Lectures on Jurisprudence: Or the Philosophy of Positive Law.* 5th ed. 2 vols. London: Murray.

BENTHAM, JEREMY (1776) 1951 *A Fragment on Government.* Edited by F. C. Montague. Oxford: Clarendon.

BLACKSTONE, WILLIAM (1765–1769) 1922 *Commentaries on the Laws of England.* 4 books in 2 vols. Edited by William Draper Lewis. Philadelphia: Bisel.

BODIN, JEAN (1576) 1962 *The Six Bookes of a Commonweale.* Edited by Kenneth D. McRae. Cambridge, Mass.: Harvard Univ. Press. → A facsimile reprint of the English translation of 1606, corrected and supplemented in the light of a new comparison with the French and Latin texts.

BRACTON, HENRI DE (1569) 1915–1942 *Bracton De legibus et consuetudinibus Angliae.* 2 vols. New Haven: Yale Univ. Press. → Published posthumously.

DICEY, ALBERT V. (1885) 1961 *Introduction to the Study of the Law of the Constitution.* 10th ed. With an Introduction by E. C. S. Wade. London: Macmillan; New York: St. Martins. → First published as *Lectures Introductory to the Study of the Law of the Constitution.*

EMERSON, RUPERT 1928 *State and Sovereignty in Modern Germany.* New Haven: Yale Univ. Press.

FORTESCUE, JOHN (1714) 1885 *The Governance of England: Otherwise Called the Difference Between an Absolute and a Limited Monarchy.* Rev. ed. Oxford:

Clarendon. → Published posthumously. First published as *The Difference Between an Absolute and a Limited Monarchy.*

GREAT BRITAIN, PARLIAMENT 1813 *The Parliamentary Debates.* Volume 16: A.D. 1765–1771. London: Hansard.

HAMILTON, ALEXANDER; MADISON, JAMES; and JAY, JOHN (1787–1788) 1961 *The Federalist.* Edited with introduction and notes by Jacob E. Cooke. Middletown, Conn.: Wesleyan Univ. Press.

HOBBES, THOMAS (1651) 1958 *Leviathan.* With an Introduction by Herbert W. Schneider. New York: Liberal Arts.

JOUVENEL, BERTRAND DE (1955) 1957 *Sovereignty: An Inquiry Into the Political Good.* Univ. of Chicago Press. → First published as *De la souveraineté: À la recherche du bien politique.*

LASKI, HAROLD J. 1917 *Studies in the Problem of Sovereignty.* New Haven: Yale Univ. Press.

LINCOLN, ABRAHAM *Speeches and Letters of Abraham Lincoln, 1832–1865.* Edited by Merwin Roe. London: Dent, 1919.

MACHIAVELLI, NICCOLÒ *Chief Works and Others.* 3 vols. Durham, N.C.: Duke Univ. Press, 1965.

McILWAIN, CHARLES H. (1940) 1947 *Constitutionalism: Ancient and Modern.* Rev. ed. Ithaca, N.Y.: Cornell Univ. Press. → A paperback edition was published in 1958.

MARSHALL, GEOFFREY 1957 *Parliamentary Sovereignty and the Commonwealth.* Oxford: Clarendon.

MEINECKE, FRIEDRICH (1924) 1962 *Machiavellism: The Doctrine of Raison d'État and Its Place in Modern History.* New York: Praeger. → First published as *Die Idee der Staatsräson in der neueren Geschichte.* A paperback edition was published in 1965.

MERRIAM, CHARLES E. 1900 *History of the Theory of Sovereignty Since Rousseau.* New York: Columbia Univ. Press.

REES, W. J. 1956 *The Theory of Sovereignty Restated.* Pages 56–82 in Peter Laslett (editor), *Philosophy, Politics and Society: A Collection.* Oxford: Blackwell.

ROSSITER, CLINTON L. 1948 *Constitutional Dictatorship: Crisis Government in the Modern Democracies.* Princeton Univ. Press. → A paperback edition was published in 1963 by Harcourt.

SPACE, OUTER

I

POLITICAL AND LEGAL ASPECTS

The fame of the first achievements in outer space in the 1950s and the high cost of space programs have encouraged a general belief that a new and radically different area of human activity has opened up. Yet the scientific principles of space flight were known, even though much new technology was required; communication to and from spacecraft differ more in degree than in kind from communication between other terminals; and the uses of spacecraft as aids to navigation and weather forecasting are extensions of familiar activities. Even the military uses of space, in their best-known applications (missiles, observation), seem to show no qualitative difference from similar activities conducted closer to earth. What distinguishes space activity is a combination of factors: the historic grip of space flight on man's imagination, the widespread though premature anxieties over military threat, and the need felt in the Soviet Union and the United States to concentrate national space activities on the space race. The one intrinsically unique aspect of space activity—the possibility of contact with extraterrestrial life, and especially with sentient or intelligent beings—has not yet had important political or legal effects. (See, however, the discussion of "contamination" below.)

After the dawn of space flight (October 4, 1957, Sputnik I) common opinion often held incompatible beliefs: one, that there was a deep and lasting rivalry between the Soviet Union and the United States in space technology; two, that space activity so transcended earthly divisions that international political competition was inconceivable. This antinomy in politics was matched by one in law: legal scholars often doubted that man-made law could apply to events in outer space but also insisted that treaties should be made drawing up a detailed code to govern space activities.

The political antinomy came from a figurative flight to utopia, which wistfully attempted to exclude human politics from the previously unsoiled depths of the universe. The legal antinomy rested on an underestimation of the flexibility and reach of existing law, on the assumption that international lawmaking could achieve results for which the international political climate was not ready, and on exaggeration of the importance of explicit formal agreement. After several years of partial accomplishment and growing familiarity, these contradictions faded.

As the political and legal issues raised by the advent of space flight came into clearer view, the official positions developed by states and (with varying fidelity) espoused by scholars and other citizens fell into several categories marked off by three different principles of cleavage.

The first cleavage separated states along the lines of the cold war: the two leading adversaries in the cold war were also the two space powers, whose allies, friends, and clients rejoiced in their principals' respective achievements and tended to agree with their respective contentions on international registration, satellite reconnaissance, the orbiting of nuclear devices, and so forth.

The second cleavage separated the two major space powers from all other states. As launchers, they had a common interest in minimizing the legal problem raised by "overflight" or in obtaining general acknowledgment of a permissive rule. As retrievers, they had a common interest in maintaining a claim to the recovery and return of "their" objects accidentally fallen from space onto the territory of third states or elsewhere. As trackers of spacecraft, they wished to obtain the cooperation of third states, allies as well as the nonaligned. As potential defendants, they wished to keep some limits on the extent or criteria of liability for damage caused by space activities. These common interests sometimes produced tacit agreement, or at least parallel unilateral action, during the bitterest days of the cold war.

The third cleavage, less conspicuous but important in the background, divided jurists according to the propensities of their legal systems and training. Those in the Anglo–American tradition tended to be suspicious of comprehensive codes and to celebrate the virtues of step-by-step experience in the new field of space law. Those trained in Continental legal systems usually assigned more importance to theoretical harmony and to systematic completeness.

Political problems

While the major concern was the threat to national security posed by space flight, attention also focused on the possibilities for international operation, control, regulation, and inspection, and serious consideration was given to the prestige and influence gained by space prowess. Some smaller political problems, not treated here, were raised by economic aspects of space activity and by the use of space for communications.

Some of the political and legal debates in the late 1950s over space flight resembled the discussions that had been held in the first decade of the century about the status and control of aircraft. The most significant differences were due to the intervening historical developments—two world wars, nuclear weapons, increased interdependence of nations, more comprehensive and rapid communication, denser international organization, and the somewhat greater general awareness of political opportunities and difficulties.

The military threat. Weapons of mass destruction were considered the chief space danger to national security (the "drop threat"). Although well-known tests of long-range ballistic missiles had preceded the launching of artificial earth satellites, the apparent separateness of space activity seemed to create an important distinction between the limitation or control of earth-based delivery systems and future bombs in orbit or missiles from the moon. Wide but not universal international agreement was reached on different aspects of the drop threat: in 1963 the agreement to ban nuclear tests included a provision against nuclear weapons test explosions or other nuclear explosions in outer space, and in the same year Resolution 1884 (XVIII) of the United Nations General Assembly expressed the unanimous opposition of the member states to the stationing in orbit of weapons of mass destruction. The placing of weapons on the moon or other celestial bodies was also abjured to the extent that a resolution of the General Assembly has a binding effect.

On several occasions some nonlaunching states, supported at first by the Soviet Union, sought to obtain international agreement restricting space to "peaceful uses." Such a restriction, if put into effect, might have differed from a ban on weapons by prohibiting certain "nonweapons" military uses of space, in particular, the use of satellites for photographic or other observation of the earth. Opponents of the restriction refused to concede the equation of "peaceful" and "nonmilitary" and pointed out that if "peaceful" could be taken to mean "nonaggressive," the task of characterization of any particular space activity would be as difficult as the notorious problem of characterizing aggression. They also contended that, in the absence of agreement on effective inspection of space payloads and effective data monitoring, an international prohibition would tend to restrain the most conscientious party or the party with the loosest security controls while leaving violators unchecked. The issue lost current political importance in 1963–1964, when, for reasons not yet fully clear, Soviet representatives ceased to press the point in the United Nations. In 1966, the treaty drafts submitted to the UN Committee on the Peaceful Uses of Outer Space by both the United States and the Soviet Union provided that celestial bodies should be used for peaceful purposes only; the U.S. draft would have protected the use of military personnel, facilities, or equipment for scientific research or other peaceful purposes. The final text of the treaty, opened for signatures on January 27, 1967, accorded with the U.S. draft as to military personnel but protected equipment and facilities only when necessary for peaceful exploration.

International cooperation. Some suggestions were put forward in the late 1950s by private citizens and by officials in a few smaller states for international ownership, launching, guidance, or comprehensive regulation of space flight. These suggestions gained fewer adherents and less prominence than had attended the unsuccessful Acheson–Lilienthal–Baruch proposals, made ten years before, for international control of atomic energy. In the current international atmosphere neither of the two states having launch capability would relinquish its power to an international body, even if such a body, equipped with the necessary strength and skill, could be created.

The participation of some nonlaunching states in space activity was necessary for technical purposes and was thought politically desirable. The United States, and to a far smaller extent the Soviet Union, concluded agreements with third states for the use of their territories (and sometimes of facilities and manpower) to track the flight of space vehicles and spacecraft. The United States, followed to a negligible extent by the Soviet Union, arranged to launch, in U.S. vehicles, payloads prepared by scientists and engineers of other states. Some technical training was given to, and some technical assistance was received from, experts from nonlaunching states; again the United States played the leading role.

An international system of limited registration of flight plans and payloads was put into effect under indirect supervision of the United Nations through a voluntary registry maintained by the secretary general. Two overlapping groups of European states formed organizations for cooperative space activity (European Launcher Development Organization, which includes Australia, and European Space Research Organization); they made slow progress against financial and technical difficulties, somewhat increased by political uncertainty in European international relations. Finally, the process of debate carried on in the organs of the UN General Assembly, concerned with space activities from time to time, served as a relatively informal and unorganized means of information, explanation, justification, exhortation, and pressure.

Prestige and influence. The spectacular immediate political effect of the opening of the space age was a gain of prestige for the Soviet Union, immeasurable but generally conceded. The positions were asymmetrical: the United States would not have gained as much had Vanguard preceded Sputnik. In some quarters of international public opinion the Soviet "first" was taken for general technological superiority, or even for scientific superiority, over the United States; remoter inferences were often suggested, and occasionally drawn, in favor of the Soviet social, economic, and political system. As time passed, the effect of this type of political gain receded.

Soviet publicists actively exploited the Soviet lead in propulsion development, calling attention to the connection between satellite launching capability and missile thrust, between earth-to-space guidance of satellites and missile command and control, and between retrieval of satellite capsules and targeting of delivery systems. Space propaganda served as an adjunct to nuclear diplomacy. The United States countered with its conspicuous shift of substantial appropriations to space research and development, its organizational decisions, and the conscientious openness of much (not all) of its space activities.

For several years the Soviet space launches followed an augmented course in which each of the publicized launches was reported as an advance over the last. After 1964 the ostensible frequency of such "topping" launches thinned out; it was not clear whether policy had changed or success had proved more elusive. Space prowess could still be called into political use, however; thus, in 1966, as a mark of special attention and respect, President de Gaulle of France was allowed to watch a Soviet space launching.

Legal problems

For descriptive purposes only, some of the problems of what came in 1958–1960 to be known as space law can be artificially separated from their political context, function, and purpose.

The legal question that deserved logical priority, in the opinions of some European and Latin American scholars, was the question whether human law, by its nature, could reach beyond its terrestrial origin. Within a few years this question was either answered in the affirmative or passed over as affording little guidance to those who sought to cope with current and foreseeable problems of space activity. Encounter with new forms of sentient or intelligent life would, it was acknowledged, revive the question in a different form.

A smaller version of this threshold question was whether international law applied of its own force to outer-space activities. Opinion coalesced, holding that international law was relevant where applicable; but this position was necessarily weakened by general doubts about the procedural efficacy of international law to the extent that it could be regarded as a body of rules. State officials dealing with the problem, even indirectly, spoke as if they did not regard international law as irrelevant to space activities, and in the United Nations explicit links between existing international law and the permissibility of space activities received early acknowledgment.

Exclusive sovereignty. The most urgent legal problem in space flight was resolved, at least for the time being, by tacit but widespread agreement. The question was whether overflights at very high altitudes were an impermissible infringement of the exclusive sovereignty of an unconsenting underlying state. Two roughly analogous precedents pointed in different directions. (The Antarctic Treaty of 1959, where previous territorial claims were suspended, represented a somewhat different legal situation.) In the law of the sea, centuries of accommodation had produced a complex of principles, of which the most important was that, beyond internal waters and the territorial sea, the high seas were accessible to all. In air law, after some controversy at the beginning of the twentieth century, a regime of giving nearly absolute air-space sovereignty to underlying states had evolved.

Space flight promised to present many of the same problems of security that had contributed to the establishment of exclusive sovereignty in air space; yet no state protested space overflights officially, and both scholarly and diplomatic opinion developed in the direction of favoring free access. The absence of protest was due in part to the reported peaceable character of early satellite payloads, and it may have owed something to the nearly world-wide enthusiasm for space exploits. What was decisive, however, in precluding the extension of air-space sovereignty was the awareness of certain physical facts: first, that at very high altitudes the notional cone of hypothetical "national" space would sweep over vast and changing regions with the earth's rotation and movement in orbit; second, that the "drop threat" from space weapons would not necessarily come from directly above a state's territory until the threatening object had descended to fairly low altitudes; third, that the defensive measures that a threatened state might take against a threat from space might, therefore, have to be applied at a point not directly above that state's territory.

Although the time during which unprotested space flights occurred was rather short, and the number of instances perhaps too small for the development of a principle of customary international law, freedom of access was proposed in early discussions in the UN and was accepted by Resolution 1962 (XVIII), December 13, 1963, which also declared that celestial bodies were not subject to exclusive appropriation by any state.

Altitude boundary. To many observers, freedom of access in outer space could not be harmonized with a continuing regime of air-space sovereignty unless an altitude boundary were fixed between air space and outer space. Several such boundaries were unofficially suggested. Writers sympathetic to space activities or particularly alert to the interests of launching states tended to favor a lower boundary than did others. Many of the suggestions, framed in candid recognition of the arbitrary character of any demarcation, set boundaries at a round number (20, 50, 100, 200) of miles or kilometers of altitude. One popular figure, 50 miles, would put the boundary well below the perigee of most orbiting satellites. A few proposals, based on physical determinants of orbital and escape velocity, would produce a family of curves of altitude boundaries dependent on physical variables (temperature, metallurgical characteristics, velocity, etc.).

Those who took another approach, loosely termed "functional," wanted to abandon the effort to arrive at an altitude boundary, on the ground that distinctions so drawn were irrelevant to the objectives underlying the regime of prohibition or permission. They recommended a consideration of the functions performed by spacecraft, with a generally permissive rule qualified by exceptions based on particular activities. Discussion of the relative merit of the two main approaches tended to lead to larger questions, also unsolved, of international registration, inspection, and regulation.

Particular issues. Through Resolution 2130 (XX) in 1965 the UN General Assembly urged the Committee on the Peaceful Uses of Outer Space "to continue with determination" the drafting of agreements on assistance to and return of astronauts and space vehicles and on liability for damage caused by objects launched into outer space. Both major launching powers had proposed provisions for possible international agreements on these subjects.

The major points of controversy over the duty to assist astronauts and to return astronauts and space vehicles were related to apprehensions of military activity. At one point a Soviet draft would have excluded the duty to return a space vehicle on which equipment for the gathering of intelligence data had been found; Soviet drafts were also less exigent with regard to the duty to return astronauts, unless their landing on another state's territory or on the high seas should have resulted from accident, distress, or emergency. Draftsmen may have had to balance the national interest in being a space power with the national interest in maintaining secrecy. Minor problems concerned the applicability of duties and rights to astronauts, vehicles, and equipment launched by associations of states or by private entities.

UN Resolution 1962 (XVIII) of December 1963 provided that each launching state and each state from whose territory a space object was launched should be liable for damage done to foreign states or their citizens. The resolution did not specify whether liability should be strict or imposed only in the event of fault; whether indirect consequences were to be compensated; whether liability should be unlimited in amount or limited to some predetermined maximum; or whether contributory negligence would be a defense. Rival drafts submitted to UN committees (by Hungary and the United States) took up some of these details. The possibility of agreement on substantive principles was overshadowed by the likelihood that at least some states would not agree in advance to submit disputes to third-party adjudication.

The scientific communities gave early warning to governments that space activities might inadvertently threaten harm to beings other than the astronauts—to other human space users, to extraterrestrial life, if any, and even (by back-contamination) to life on earth. They also wished to protect for future research the environment of the moon and other celestial bodies. The two large launching states announced from time to time that they were taking precautions to protect the extraterrestrial environment. Agreement on an international standard, to be internationally enforced, was rendered difficult by the fear that arguments against allegedly harmful space activities might be used in an effort to block other states from carrying on activities to which the real objection was based on other motives.

LEON LIPSON

[*Other relevant material may be found in* INTERNATIONAL LAW; INTERNATIONAL LEGISLATION; INTERNATIONAL ORGANIZATION; INTERNATIONAL POLITICS.]

BIBLIOGRAPHY

AMERICAN BAR FOUNDATION   (1960) 1961   *Report to the National Aeronautics and Space Administration on the Law of Outer Space.* Chicago: The Foundation. → Prepared by Leon Lipson and Nicholas deB. Katzenbach.

CHRISTOL, CARL Q.   1966   *The International Law of Outer Space.* Washington: Government Printing Office.

COOPER, JOHN C.   1947   *The Right to Fly.* New York: Holt.

HALEY, ANDREW G.   1963   *Space Law and Government.* New York: Appleton.

JENKS, C. WILFRED   1958   *The Common Law of Mankind.* New York: Praeger.

JESSUP, PHILIP C.; and TAUBENFELD, HOWARD J.   1959   *Controls for Outer Space and the Antarctic Analogy.* New York: Columbia Univ. Press.

McDOUGAL, MYRES S.; LASSWELL, HAROLD D.; and VLASIO, IVAN A.   1963   *Law and Public Order in Space.* New Haven: Yale Univ. Press.

U.S. LIBRARY OF CONGRESS, LEGISLATIVE REFERENCE SERVICE   1961   *Legal Problems of Space Exploration: A Symposium . . . .* Prepared by Eilene Galloway. 87th Congress, 1st Session. Senate Document No. 26. Washington: Government Printing Office.

U.S. LIBRARY OF CONGRESS, LEGISLATIVE REFERENCE SERVICE   1965   *International Cooperation and Organization for Outer Space: Staff Report.* 89th Congress, 1st Session. Senate Document No. 56. Washington: Government Printing Office.

II
SOCIAL AND PSYCHOLOGICAL ASPECTS

There are few topics in the social sciences without implications for space activities—from the behavior of human nerve fibers exposed to radiation to social systems exposed to ideological competition. Thus, we shall limit this article to research on space activities, as such, that are under way, contemplated, or needed and to those impacts and implications that are, or are expected to be, uniquely related to space activities that have been given special emphasis by them. Under psychological aspects we shall review studies pertinent to astronaut behavior; under social aspects we shall consider various implications of space activities for people and society.

Psychological aspects

Information about psychological challenges for man in space derives from both ground-based studies and actual experiences in space. Neither source of information is presently adequate for estimating the psychological challenges that may face men on flights now expected to be technologically feasible in the next two decades or so. Men have actually been exposed to space for only relatively short periods, but flights are anticipated that will last months, perhaps more than a year. Also, most long flights will have crews of more than one man. But so far, there is limited experience with multiperson crews closely confined in stressful circumstances while deeply dependent on one another. From exposure to the real space environment we have learned little to make us confident about the effects, over long time periods, of isolation, group performance under stress and close confinement, weightlessness, etc. Historical evidence from other unusual environments is suggestive, but these environments appear to differ importantly from the combination of circumstances expected to define the astronauts' situation.

Ground-based simulation studies are inherently seriously limited in their predictive utility: the subjects know they are on earth, that the experiment will be terminated at their wish, and that they can never be deliberately threatened with death or even serious physical or psychological damage. Moreover, the utility of present research is limited to some extent by the caution of space program sponsors regarding the publication of data or the undertaking of research that might complicate political or public support assumed to depend on the validity of optimistic assertions about the abilities of man in space or that might give support to those pressing for greater emphasis on unmanned space research. This is not to assert that simulated space environment studies have demonstrated overwhelming human inadequacies or that most of the studies that are reported are inferior in quality. But it is recognized within the small fraternity of researchers working on these matters that not all studies are done that ought to be, not all the results are released as quickly as scientific canons require, and not all publicized studies are as definitive or successful as public relations officers claim.

Nevertheless, present studies merit review for what they reveal about both our knowledge and our ignorance and because, while they do not tell us much about what man may not withstand psychologically, they do give us important information about what he *can* do in this strange and difficult environment. First, we shall review psychological aspects of the manned space experiments and then those ground-based studies not outmoded by actual astronaut experiences.

Space studies. The study of animals played an important part in the preliminary stages of the manned space flight program and will probably do so in more advanced stages, especially when it is time to learn the psychophysiological effects of prolonged exposure to space radiation, such as that occurring in the Van Allen belts.

Chimpanzee training and performance. One chimpanzee carried out a discrete avoidance procedure superimposed on a schedule requiring continuous avoidance behavior while riding a 136.2-nautical mile-high ballistic trajectory; the other performed a five-component, multiple-operant conditioning schedule while orbiting the earth twice. In addition to demonstrating that men would be able to perform in the capsule environment, the data demonstrated that both behavioral and physiological measures must be made in order to evaluate completely space flight performance (Rohles et al. 1963). Perhaps more important in the long run, the success of the total and continuous environ-

ment control technique used to program the activities of the chimps provided the design for the 152-day human encapsulation experiment described below. [*See* LEARNING, *articles on* INSTRUMENTAL LEARNING *and* AVOIDANCE LEARNING.]

Astronaut selection and performance. The experiences of American and Soviet astronauts, the criteria for their selection, and the methods of training seem to have been rather similar, with the exception of the Russians' use of conditioned response methodology described below (U.S. Manned Spacecraft Center 1963, pp. 171–198; Volynkin et al. 1962). However, unless otherwise specified, what follows refers to the initial American program, about which there is more detailed information.

Both nations decided that, lacking foreknowledge of required performance characteristics, prospective astronauts should have proven themselves to be highly successful in activities that seemed to have exposed them to not unrelated stresses and performance requirements, for example, piloting high performance jet aircraft.

The psychological study of the first American astronauts was divided into three phases: (1) interviews and tests assessing personality factors possibly relevant to later stress responses, (2) repeated application of tests before and after particular training events and during more relaxed control situations, and (3) intensive evaluation before and after suborbital and orbital flights (Korchin & Ruff 1964).

Psychiatric interviews, psychological tests, and observations of behavior, lasting 30 hours, were made during the screening stress experiments. Out of 55 candidates the 32 chosen for the final phase of the selection program were rated on a 10-point scale in each of 17 psychological categories. They were tested on 13 different measures of motivation and personality and 12 measures of intellectual functions and special aptitudes. Psychological data were also obtained from 6 stress tests: an uncomfortable pressure suit at simulated 65,000-foot altitude, extreme isolation, a complex behavior simulator, acceleration, noise and vibration, and heat.

Tests and interviews revealed that the candidates were comfortable, mature, and well-integrated individuals. Scores on reality testing, adaptability, and drive were particularly high. There was little evidence of unresolved conflicts sufficiently serious to interfere with expected functions. Suggestions of overt anxiety were rare. Defenses were effective, tending to be obsessive–compulsive. Most were direct, action-oriented individuals who spent little time introspecting. Unconscious feelings of inadequacy in sexual or other areas appeared to be no more or less common than in other occupational groups. Only 2 of the 32 finalists had lived in large cities before entering college. Twenty were either only or eldest children. (Of the 7 astronauts, 4 were named "Junior.") Reasons for volunteering for the space program were a combination of professionalism, love of adventure, and anticipated career benefits. The mean full-scale Wechsler Adult Intelligence Scale (WAIS) IQ was 133. Reactions to physiological stresses correlated positively with the psychiatric evaluations. Candidates who ranked highest on psychological variables tended to do best in acceleration, noise and vibration, heat, and pressure chamber runs. Their stress tolerance levels were among the highest of the hundreds previously subjected to these procedures (Korchin & Ruff 1964).

The astronauts themselves showed strong needs for achievement and mastery. They responded to stress with renewed effort and improved performance. Being passed over for the first flight was the hardest problem to cope with for most of them. In most cases, immediate preflight anxiety appeared more related to concern that the flights be a success than to fear of injury or death. Confidence that their past experience and intensive training prepared them for any emergency accounted for much of their ability to control anticipatory anxiety. Preflight to postflight changes in performance were rather small but larger than those produced during training. Compared to the preflight state, after the flights they tended to be somewhat less energetic and clear-thinking and somewhat more anxious; but they were more warmly related to people—according to their estimate of themselves on a four-point scale of adjectives (Ruff & Korchin 1964).

Analysis of the data in the light of actual astronaut performance seems to indicate the following: (1) Excellent health is requisite, but physiological stress tolerance, especially to acceleration and heat, can be somewhat de-emphasized. (2) Because he is involved in a complex organization and in complex technical activities, the astronaut needs technical knowledge and administrative and executive skills. (3) The astronaut's role as hero, the related loss of preflight and postflight privacy, and the tense atmosphere when preparing for the flight necessitate considerable social competence. (4) Knowledge of the resources men will use for handling problems seems more useful than knowledge of the problems themselves for predicting how men will tolerate a stressful mission. (5) None of the

aptitude, intelligence, or personality variables assessed seems importantly related to performance. Individual differences among the astronauts were not reflected in differences of performance. Since the flights were all successful, the number small, and the men very carefully preselected, even before the final screening, and then intensively trained in specific skills for three and a half years, this is not surprising. [See Engineering psychology; Industrial relations, *article on* industrial and business psychology; Psychology, *article on* applied psychology.]

It remains to be seen whether variations in these personality variables, operating in other astronauts and expressed in future administrative and space environments, will correlate significantly with performance.

Russian astronauts. It appears that the basis for final selection of the Russian astronauts was similar to the American procedures. It was important to identify those candidates with the most superior memories, the greatest presence of mind, the best ability to shift their attention from one concern to another, and the greatest capacity to develop finely coordinated movements ("Pervyi pol'et cheloveka v kosmicheskoe prostranstvo" 1961).

The important difference in training methods was the extensive use by the Russians of conditioned response methodology to elicit in their astronauts behavior corresponding to that displayed during exposure to training stresses and to build appropriate conditioned responses to them. The same techniques were used to elicit behavior characteristic of previous stressful situations and to inhibit this behavior if it was inappropriate for the space mission or to reinforce it if it was not (Gorbov 1962). The Russians now feel that inadequate training of their cosmonauts' vestibular apparatus was the chief shortcoming of early Soviet space flights. Present training programs are rectifying this. [See Learning, *especially the article on* classical conditioning.]

The Russians continuously telemetered 12 measures of biological and psychological states, including electroencephalogram (EEG), electrocardiogram (EKG), electromyogram (EMG), electro-oculargram (EOG), and dermogalvanic response (DGR). They found no significant variations between these measures and data collected in simulated environments during preflight training (Gorbov 1962). The Americans telemetered psychobiological data on bipolar EKG, blood pressure, temperature, and respiration. These provided no special psychological insights (U.S. Manned Space-craft Center 1963, pp. 309–326).

Laboratory studies—isolation. Concern over human performance under lengthy confinement in cramped quarters and with limited sensory stimulation has led to studies in environments reproducing some of the expected circumstances. These studies usually last from a few days to 30 days and use single subjects and two-man to four-man crews; they indicate that operator reliability can be maintained if there is a regular work–rest schedule and a reasonable amount of activity. Subjects' morale and motivation have remained unexpectedly high. However, postsimulation studies have demonstrated that during each multiman-crew experiment previously innocuous mannerisms become irritating. Hostility was acknowledged during debriefings and was reported in diaries but not during the simulated missions. Hostility was overtly expressed toward personnel outside the "space chamber": as time went on subjects grew to feel that those outside were giving inadequate support. Hostility toward those outside the cabin also gradually built up during the 7-day simulated flights involving single subjects. During the 30-day simulations, subjects experienced various aberrations in different degrees, all of which reduced operator proficiency (Simons et al. 1963; U.S. School of Aerospace Medicine 1960; 1961).

The longest time covered by a known encapsulation experiment was 152 days. A single subject lived in a programmed environment. Chains of behaviors were arranged so that weak, unreliable, or unreinforcing behaviors associated with necessary tasks were early components, while the most reinforcing activities were located at the ends of the chains and only attainable by performing the earlier activities in a predetermined sequence (Findley et al. 1963). Among the findings were the following: Increased frequency of sleep coupled with decreased duration of sleep casts doubt on the utility of fixed work–rest cycles for long space flights. Creative and intellectual activities fell off over time, probably a result of social isolation. Reading and listening to music retained a similar level of activity throughout. The intensity of complaints increased; during the final stages, the subject showed considerable paranoid-type ideation (from which recovery was rapid following completion of the experiment). Increased frequency and duration in the use of toilet facilities; increased negative complaints, somatic complaints, and requests for health items; increased frequency of sleeping rather than following the full program of

activities; increased duration of dessert eating; and decreased creative manual and verbal activities all indicated progressive behavioral deterioration during the experiment.

Vigilance, monitoring, boredom, and fatigue. Long space missions may alternate between long periods of boredom and long periods of extreme activity, both of which can produce fatigue that may crucially degrade performance on precisely those tasks that make it necessary to have a man on board in the first place. Real and simulated astronaut performance, as affected by these factors, is compatible with previous work; for example, tasks using gross discrete cues are more resistant to fatigue than tasks using minute cues, for which vigilance and alertness are necessary (U.S. School of Aerospace Medicine 1961; Hauty 1958). But findings from simulation studies and from flights already made emphasize our limited understanding of these factors and the need for studies that extend over long time periods (Hartman 1961, pp. 298–299). Vigilance is adversely affected by fatigue, and in some cases during periods of deteriorated vigilance and considerable fatigue subjects have estimated their own competence as much higher than it actually was (Simons et al. 1961). Motivation and previous experience with monotonous environments and especially with the experience of performing throughout a diurnal cycle are important; for example, six experienced pilots maintained performance at consistently high levels over 7-day simulated flights (Simons et al. 1963).

Man is not a good "watch-keeper." However, vigilance is highly susceptible to fatigue, and fatigue may be more easily dispelled in space since considerably less sleep seems required in a weightless environment. Nevertheless, long space trips will have to be organized so that detection of very low signal rates will not be the task of humans. [See ATTENTION; FATIGUE; TIME, *article on* PSYCHOLOGICAL ASPECTS.]

Weightlessness and hypergravity. Some people are emotionally discomforted by the experience of weightlessness, but so far trained astronauts have not been psychologically discommoded either by weightlessness or hypergravity produced by acceleration or deceleration.

Long-term effects of weightlessness are of considerable concern. Loss of that sensory input produced by the force of gravity acting on the body's receptors may combine with other stresses and deprivations to affect deleteriously the astronaut's psychomotor state during gravity-free exposure, particularly when he is suddenly subject to several times the force of earth's gravity during the critical period of re-entry into the atmosphere prior to landing. There are plans to study the effects of weightlessness over long periods of time in manned orbiting laboratories.

Floating the subject in a tank of water can produce partial simulation of weightlessness. A 7-day hydrodynamic environment study indicated gross disruption in psychomotor performance, which might be sufficient to prevent the performance of critical tasks during re-entry. There also was evidence that less sleep may be required and perhaps less fatigue experienced than in an earth environment (U.S. School of Aerospace Medicine 1961).

Compound environmental stress.   Essentially unstudied is the evaluation and measurement of the physiological and psychological effects of simultaneous exposure to multiple stresses. This situation needs detailed understanding so that adverse combinations of stress can be eliminated or minimized through appropriate design of the astronaut's environment. The small amount of data available indicates that psychological effects are not additive even when the physiological variables measured are affected additively (Dean & McGlothlen 1962). Nor is it presently known how to establish tolerance criteria for the various characteristics of a given stress, such as magnitude, duration, and rate of onset, much less for combinations of stresses. Since weightlessness will probably be an important contributor to stress, valid studies will probably require an orbiting laboratory. [See STRESS.]

Further problem areas.   Formidable training and selection problems lie ahead. Environmental and operating-load stress intensities that are sustainable for short periods may be too great for effective performance as flights lengthen. Selecting and training multiple-man teams whose members can tolerate one another over long periods of enforced proximity present a new area for research. Means must be discovered for dealing with the psychological consequences of long periods of isolation and danger. To this end, induced hibernation and the use of drugs will doubtless be explored.

Detecting and developing capacities for adaptation to unusual environments is another area for psychological research. Coping with long periods in space, including coping with physical and symbolic separation from earth, and coping with all the other "artificial" circumstances of life in a space capsule may require "pretailoring" personality types and environments to each other. For many of these studies, the laboratory and the training environment will be the manned orbiting space laboratory, where simulation and reality will converge.

The effects on behavior of intense magnetic fields and prolonged exposure to occasional high-energy cosmic rays need further study. In the United States, no doubt, as equipment improves and the intense controversies concerning priority access to telemetering channel capacity are resolved, the Soviet pattern will be followed and much more information that is useful for understanding the psychology of human behavior in space will be transmitted to earth. Humans under great stress have shown extraordinary physiological and psychological abilities: it may well be that in studying the exertions of astronauts trying to deal with the compound crises that inevitably will face them— perhaps including death—we will come to a better understanding of the psychology of everyday life.

Social implications

Some of the most important present effects of space activities cannot be differentiated from the impact on society of the military missiles from which both United States and Russian space technology has evolved and from the enormous emphasis on science and technology, itself partly sparked by the needs of the space programs. Many of the resources, rationales, and motivations for exploring space on a scale sufficient to produce present social consequences derive from the political–military competition between the Soviet Union and the United States.

We have to speculate almost as much about the current impact of space on society as about potential future consequences. With a few exceptions, neither social scientists nor research fund sources have taken advantage of the opportunities for research that space provides. Before-and-after studies on the social effects of anticipatable space events are few and fragmentary. There have been few longitudinal studies initiated about the influence of space events on the values and behavior of children as well as adults. These facts are revealing in themselves for estimating the significance of space activities, at least for the American social science community—especially since many of its members were made aware of the research possibilities well before Sputnik (Michael 1957; Mead et al. 1958).

Attitudes and values.   A forthright analysis of the present situation is made even more difficult by the frequency of blatant assertions, usually optimistic, often naive, by political, engineering, scientific, and business leaders concerning the social implications of space, about which they have little or no real knowledge. However, the agencies and spokesmen involved have done little to support research that could test the validity of these assertions. The United States National Aeronautics and Space Administration (NASA) has been somewhat of an exception, since the legislation establishing the agency required that it undertake long-term research assessing the potential peaceful and scientific benefits of space activities. While NASA has been less than enthusiastic in fulfilling this obligation, its establishing legislation has encouraged it to be more systematically self-conscious about its social impact than any other government agency ever has been. Of the small amount of research that has been done on the social implications of space activities, a large part has been supported by NASA.

In the United States, the allocation of funds for space activities and the composition of programs have steadily reflected increasing sensitivity to those political values that are paramount when jobs and constituencies can be affected by the geographic placement of major installations. Political infighting has been intensified by increased competition between corporations seeking major contracts and between the civilian NASA and the U.S. Air Force, which seeks a larger role. There is some informal evidence that the Russian program is subject to similar internal competition as to whether the program emphasis should be on manned or unmanned exploration, scientific or military objectives, etc.; but the details are obscure.

The impact of space on public attitudes and values is nominal or minor, at least as far as adults are concerned, although this varies with the interests, education, and values of the responding populations. What few studies there are indicate that Americans were less upset by, but more confused about, the implications of Sputnik than their public spokesmen claimed (Michael 1960). Since then, despite generally favorable American support for space activity, there has been no large percentage of the public that assigns it very high priority compared to other major social issues or that prefers to expend funds on space rather than on more immediate social needs (Rohles et al. 1963; Michael 1963). Even among scientists, there is considerable disagreement over the priorities and aims of the space program ("Space Program" 1964). Business executives seem to be the only partial exception to this pattern. They have been consistently more enthusiastic than other groups about space expenditures, but there are several alternative social needs to which even they give higher priority.

The orbiting of Sputnik 1 caused important changes in views of the world regarding Russian technological capability (U.S. Information Agency 1961). Except for a leveling up of relative positions

in space capabilities, the general pattern has probably not fundamentally changed since then. At that time, the general public in Great Britain and France felt that Russia was clearly superior to the United States in over-all scientific accomplishment and that it still would be in ten years. West Germany and, with less conviction, Italy viewed the balance in favor of the United States. (That the United States led in some specific sciences was not disputed by any country.) All four nations believed the U.S.S.R. to be ahead *in space*, and only West Germany thought that the United States would catch up by 1971. The outcomes of particular space missions do not appear to have resulted in fundamental shifts in estimates of the present and long-range destiny and attributes, scientific or otherwise, of either nation (at least as far as the unclassified data indicate).

Education. Sputnik also stimulated a burst of American interest in education. Spurred by competition with the Soviet Union, the United States has placed increased emphasis on improved quality and quantity in science and engineering. To some extent, curriculum improvement has carried over to other educational subjects, and some school systems have rejected alleged progressive education methods in favor of the "fundamentals."

Because it needs skilled personnel, NASA has initiated an extensive predoctoral training program as well as offering research grants in a variety of scientific areas. Universities most able to further the space agency's mission-oriented investment get most of the funds. The size and pattern of NASA's funding program, plus the growing appreciation by congressmen of the economic and prestige values of a top academic institution in their district, have substantially deepened controversy about the location and the number of "centers of excellence" to be supported by federal funds (Lindveit 1964).

Through its postdoctoral and doctoral grants, its technician training programs, and its use of local talent to help operate overseas stations, NASA is contributing to education abroad and, hopefully, helping to develop a technician and scientist base in the emerging nations.

One education-related factor contributing to social disruption has been the very high rate of professional obsolescence in the space-oriented industries. Older professionals often must return to school, while recent graduates have an unprecedented opportunity to displace their seniors by virtue of their fresh knowledge.

Civilian economy and entrepreneurship. One persistent American justification for its space program has been the belief that the new technology can also be applied to civilian life. To date, the carry-over has been limited. The technology is often too expensive for civilian use, and there seem to be few entrepreneurs willing to risk investing in untried technologies to gain new civilian markets. Also, recent studies (generated by curiosity about the low utilization of space technology) suggest that new information moves slowly and informally even through advanced technological organizations.

The aerospace industry is very important in the American economy (and in the Soviet economy as well). It is, in effect, a major government subsidy, and the vast sums expended contribute importantly to American prosperity as well as to diminishing further the traditional and ideologically important distinction between government and the private economy. For the former reason alone, many believe the space program should be continued at the present scale of several billion dollars a year. However, recent concern about program costs probably presage some eclipsing of the space effort by more immediate national needs and more politically attractive ways for spending government funds.

International cooperation. At least 18 major international scientific organizations, half of them private, have space-oriented research projects under way or are planning such research. Many of these arrangements have been bilateral, but relatively few have been multilateral, so that the full international potential of this research area is yet to be exploited (Schwartz 1962). The outstanding space venture involving international cooperation is the effort to operate the U.S. Communications Satellite Corporation, a consortium of 17 nations that will own and operate an international commercial satellite system. Problems pertaining to multinational management of an American corporation are yet to be worked out. [See INTERNATIONAL ORGANIZATION.]

Management. The exceeding complexity of space equipment and the development programs have led to new, highly sophisticated, integrative techniques being applied to engineering, operations, and management. These techniques regulate and pace human intellectual action much as assembly lines did human physical action. Maintaining creativity and individuality in a technology dependent on these attributes, but that operates in such ways as to submerge them, presents a significant social problem in the space industry.

In the future. Long-run social implications depend on political and technological factors operating essentially independently of space activities. Two decades is a speculative limit, although, given the extensive changes occurring everywhere, even

this may be too long for useful forecasts. But within this period earth societies will be confronted by space activities containing a broad range of potential problems and opportunities, and the social science research required to prepare for them will be wide-ranging too (Bloomfield 1962; Michael 1961). A few challenges are outlined here.

Weather. Weather satellites and deep space probes will contribute to better local weather forecasting and, eventually, to forecasts extending over six months to a year or more. (Large-scale weather modification, if at all possible, is probably more than twenty years off.) If used, accurate local weather forecasts—dependent in part on regular satellite observations—will require radical social reorganization, especially in the newer nations. In particular, farmers will have to change farming styles if they are to take advantage of the forecasts. Distribution, credit, and government administration will all be profoundly modified in consequence. But the inertia of social systems, especially in farm cultures, probably means that for many years the impact of such weather forecasts will be slight in underdeveloped areas. If forecast-oriented behavior is imposed in the interests of productivity, then there will be the usual deep disruptions that go with major cultural changes.

Long-range or short-range predictions of drought, flood, typhoon, etc. will offer new opportunities to protect people and resources. However, predictable disasters will subject governments to intense demands for appropriate action. Political disruption, international humanitarianism, and international blackmail will thereby increase.

Foreknowledge of weather extremes in specific regions and of favorable or adverse growing conditions in different regions producing the same commodity for international sale will mean that private and national profits based on the relative scarcity of fuels or farm products will eventually have to give way to multinational preplanning based on advance information about supply and demand. And new means will have to be invented to compensate for serious national and private economic losses when bad weather is forecast a season in advance for specific resort areas.

Communications. Satellites will increase the number of relatively cheap communications channels; this will provide special opportunities for establishing closer multinational working relationships, with all the socially important advantages and disadvantages of rapid communication. With such inexpensive and convenient facilities, executives will be able to communicate more by telephone and private television rather than struggle with the inconveniences and dangers of physical transportation. Thus the communications satellite may compete with the supersonic jet plane.

Live television in east–west directions is unlikely to develop into a major form of entertainment, since the time differences between major transmitting regions would make viewing inconvenient and tape-recorded programs probably can be more economically transported by aircraft to transmission centers. On the other hand, television transmission in a north–south direction offers a great potential for cultural exchange and education between the Southern Hemisphere and the more developed northern nations. With sufficient research on teaching by television, it might be possible to provide some education for people in preliterate and nonliterate areas now deprived of teachers and of access to visual experience of the larger world. What could be taught this way, and what could be used by the emerging nations to facilitate their cultural development, remains to be discovered. How commercially valuable channels will be provided for such nonprofit use is also an unanswered question.

Satellite video transmission raises disturbing problems about control of what is transmitted and what is received. Opportunities for propaganda, signal jamming, and misinterpretation of the content of another nation's programs are at least as great as the opportunities for enhancing international harmony. The audiovisual imagery of different cultures varies in language, pacing, style, and taste. There is much to be learned if this medium is to be used for mutual benefit.

The implications of space activities for peace and war are mostly unclear. Observation satellites, especially those operating under international auspices, should reduce the chances for undetected clandestine preparation for conventional wars; but within a few years they may be relatively useless for predicting when well-hidden missiles might be launched. The United States and the Soviet Union joined the rest of the United Nations in passing by acclamation UN Resolution 1884, expressing their intention to refrain from orbiting such weapons. As of now, there seems to be no valid argument for lunar bombardment stations. At present, the U.S. Air Force's chief argument for putting a man in space is to discover if there is some unexpected military role for him. As with so many other space activities, it will be what is done on earth to solve the problem of the function of warfare that will determine what happens in space.

Values and viewpoints. It is unlikely that presently anticipated space activities will deeply affect the values and viewpoints of very many people on earth. Most people are selectively attentive and tend to organize new experience so that it fits their conventional viewpoints, and this is the way most adults so far have interpreted space activities. Whether the excitement and deep interest that many young people have shown will influence their adult lives—and if so, in what ways—is not known. Certainly, only an infinitesimal portion of today's youth will play a direct role in space activities.

Attention to space has made it legitimate to speculate seriously about intelligent extraterrestrial life and to make small efforts to search for it via radiotelescope. The chance of discovering intelligent life in other solar systems by this method is exceedingly slight, and the distance between solar systems is so great that an exchange of messages would very probably take many years at least, even at the speed of light. Thus, there would be no sustained basis for social or psychological involvement with extraterrestrial intelligent forms. Growing recognition that the universe is very likely populated with sentient intelligence will affect some philosophies and doctrines, but it is no more likely to affect the values of most people than does relativity theory today.

Space-derived scientific discoveries will contribute to major changes in scientific theory about the nature of the universe and of life. What the practical consequences will be is, of course, unknown —most likely the philosophical consequences will be significant for very few. We could better anticipate the social impact if we learned more about how complex and radical ideas are transformed into popular commonplaces and rationalizations. Space activities are an excellent means for such study—if we would grasp the opportunity.

The long-range impact on the average man's attitudes and values of following the adventures of men in orbit and on the moon will (as with explorers and heroes in the past) depend on how the society exploits these accomplishments at least as much as it depends on the deeds themselves.

Population control. Contrary to popular fantasy, space will not solve our population problem. The rate of increase in population positively precludes rocketing people off the planet frequently enough and in large enough numbers. Indeed, those who moved to space colonies would have to practice birth control in order not to overcrowd the colonies.

The significant influences that space activities may have for man and his societies over the next two decades most likely will derive from (1) weather satellites; (2) communications satellites; (3) the proliferation of multinational space-oriented institutions; (4) the greater knowledge of human behavior gained from studying the effects of technological change on societies involved in selecting, training, predicting the performance, and studying the behavior under extreme stress of astronaut crews; and (5) the increased attention to, and argument over, national and international social priorities as emphasized by the increased competition among space activities and other programs that need, on an enormous scale, skilled personnel and financial and physical resources.

DONALD N. MICHAEL

[*See also* FATIGUE; PERCEPTION, *article on* PERCEPTUAL DEPRIVATION; STRESS.]

BIBLIOGRAPHY

BLOOMFIELD, LINCOLN (editor) 1962 *Outer Space Prospects for Man and Society.* Englewood Cliffs, N.J.: Prentice-Hall.

DEAN, ROBERT D.; and McGLOTHLEN, CARL L. 1962 *The Effect of Environmental Stress Interactions on Performance.* Seattle, Wash.: Boeing Co., Aerospace Division.

FINDLEY, JACK D.; MIGLER, BERNARD M.; and BRADY, JOSEPH V. 1963 *A Long Term Study of Human Performance in a Continuously Programmed Experimental Environment.* Technical Report, Space Research Laboratory, Univ. of Maryland. Univ. of Maryland, Institute for Behavioral Research, and Walter Reed Army Institute of Research.

GORBOV, F. D. 1962 Certain Problems of Space Psychology. *Voprosy psikhologii* (Problems of Psychology) [1962], no. 6:3–13. → First published as "Nekotorye voprosy kosmicheskoi psikhologii." Translated by the U.S. Defense Documentation Center, Alexandria, Va., AD–428547.

HARTMAN, BRYCE O. 1961 Time and Load Factors in Astronaut Proficiency. Pages 278–308 in Symposium on Psychophysiological Aspects of Space Flight, Brooks Air Force Base, Texas, 1960, *Psychophysiological Aspects of Space Flight.* New York: Columbia Univ. Press.

HAUTY, GEORGE T. 1958 Human Performance in the Space Travel Environment. *Air University Quarterly Review* 10, no. 2:89–107.

KORCHIN, SHELDON J.; and RUFF, GEORGE E. 1964 Personality Characteristics of Mercury Astronauts. Pages 197–207 in G. H. Grosser, H. H. Wexler, and M. Greenblat, *The Threat of Impending Disaster: Contributions to the Psychology of Stress.* Cambridge, Mass.: M.I.T. Press.

LINDVEIT, EARL W. 1964 Science, Education, and Politics. *Educational Record* 45:41–48.

MEAD, MARGARET et al. 1958 Man in Space: A Tool and Program for the Study of Social Change. New York Academy of Sciences, *Annals* 72:165–214.

MICHAEL, DONALD N. 1957 Man-Into-Space: A Tool and Program for Research in the Social Sciences. *American Psychologist* 12:324–328.

MICHAEL, DONALD N. 1959 What *Saturday Review* Readers Think About Man in Space. *Saturday Review* April 4:60–63. → Analysis of reader responses to detailed questionnaire on knowledge of and attitudes about space activities.

MICHAEL, DONALD N. 1960 The Beginning of the Space Age and American Public Opinion. *Public Opinion Quarterly* 24:573–582.

MICHAEL, DONALD N. 1961 *Proposed Studies on the Implications of Peaceful Space Activities for Human Affairs.* Washington: Brookings Institution. → Available through University Microfilms, Ann Arbor, Mich.

MICHAEL, DONALD N. 1963 The Problem of Interpreting Attitudes Toward Space Activities. Pages 105–110 in Colloquium on the Law of Outer Space, *Proceedings, Fourth.* Norman: Univ. of Oklahoma, Research Institute.

Pervyi pol'et cheloveka v kosmicheskoe prostranstvo (The First Manned Flight Into Outer Space). 1961 *Pravda* April 25, p. 1, col. 4–6 ff.

ROHLES, FREDERICK H. JR.; GRUNZKE, M. E.; and REYNOLDS, H. H. 1963 Chimpanzee Performance During the Ballistic and Orbital Project Mercury Flights. *Journal of Comparative and Physiological Psychology* 56:2–10.

RUFF, GEORGE E.; and KORCHIN, SHELDON J. 1964 Psychological Responses of Mercury Astronauts to Stress. Pages 208–220 in G. H. Grosser, H. H. Wexler, and M. Greenblat, *The Threat of Impending Disaster: Contributions to the Psychology of Stress.* Cambridge, Mass.: M.I.T. Press.

SCHWARTZ, LEONARD E. 1962 *International Organizations and Space Cooperation.* Durham, N.C.: Duke Univ., World Rule of Law Center.

SELLS, SAUL B.; and BERRY, CHARLES A. (editors) 1961 *Human Factors in Jet and Space Travel: A Medical–Psychological Analysis.* New York: Ronald.

SIMONS, DAVID G.; FLINN, D. E.; and HARTMAN, B. 1963 Psychophysiology of High-altitude Experience. Pages 127–164 in Neal M. Burns, R. M. Chambers, and E. Hendler (editors), *Unusual Environments and Human Behavior: Physiological and Psychological Problems of Man in Space.* New York: Free Press.

SIMONS, DAVID G.; HENDERSON, B. W.; and RIEHL, J. L. 1961 Personal Experiences in Space Equivalent Flight. Pages 39–49 in Symposium on Psychophysiological Aspects of Space Flight, Brooks Air Force Base, Texas, 1960, *Psychophysiological Aspects of Space Flight.* New York: Columbia Univ. Press.

Space Program: Results of Poll of AAAS Members. 1964 *Science* 145:368 only.

U.S. INFORMATION AGENCY 1961 *The Image of the U.S. Versus Soviet Science in West European Public Opinion: A Survey in Four West European Countries.* Survey Research Studies, Attitude and Opinion Series, WE-3. Washington: Government Printing Office.

U.S. MANNED SPACECRAFT CENTER, HOUSTON, TEXAS 1963 *Mercury Project Summary, Including Results of the Fourth Manned Orbital Flight, May 15 and 16, 1963.* Washington: Government Printing Office. → See especially Chapter 10, "Astronaut Training," and Chapter 18, "Aeromedical Observations."

U.S. SCHOOL OF AEROSPACE MEDICINE 1960 *Lectures in Aerospace Medicine, 1960.* Brooks Air Force Base, Tex.: U.S. Air Force, Aerospace Medical Center. → See especially Chapter 18, "Psychophysiological Problems of Manned Space Vehicles." Contains verbatim dialogue of subjects experiencing hallucinations during 7- to 30-day simulated space flights.

U.S. SCHOOL OF AEROSPACE MEDICINE 1961 *Lectures in Aerospace Medicine, 1961.* Brooks Air Force Base, Tex.: U.S. Air Force, Aerospace Medical Center. → See especially Chapter 14, "Experimental Approaches to the Psychophysiological Problems of Manned Space Flight."

VOLYNKIN, IU. M. et al. 1962 The First Manned Space Flights. Akademiia Nauk SSSR, Otdelenie Biologicheskikh Nauk, *Mediko–Biologicheskie issledovaniia* [1962]: 203 only. → First published as "Pervye kosmicheskie pol'ety cheloveka." Translated by the U.S. Defense Documentation Center, Alexandria, Va., AD–294537.

SPATIAL ECONOMICS

I. THE PARTIAL EQUILIBRIUM
    APPROACH   *Edgar M. Hoover*
II. THE GENERAL EQUILIBRIUM
    APPROACH   *Leon N. Moses*

I

THE PARTIAL EQUILIBRIUM APPROACH

Spatial economics deals with *what* is *where,* and *why.* The "what" refers to every type of economic entity, i.e., production establishments, other kinds of businesses, households, and public and private institutions. "Where" refers basically to location in relation to other economic activity, i.e., to questions of proximity, concentration, dispersion, and similarity or disparity of spatial patterns. The "where" can be defined in broad terms such as regions or metropolitan areas, or in microgeographic terms such as zones, neighborhoods, or sites. The "why" refers to explanations within the somewhat elastic limits of the economist's competence.

Location theory describes this kind of analysis when the emphasis is upon alternative locations for specified kinds of activities, such as industry. *Regional analysis* is concerned with groupings of interrelated economic activities in proximity, within specified areas or types of areas; and the *theory of interregional trade* refers to the economic relationships between such areas.

Decision units and their interdependence. The explanations provided by spatial economic theory are ultimately in terms of the economic motivation and behavior of individual decision units and the ways in which their decisions react upon each other. A decision unit in this context can be, say, a business enterprise, a household, a public institution, or a labor union local. Here, as elsewhere in economic theorizing, simplifying assumptions about motivation are used—for example, the assumption that a business firm will prefer locations that provide higher rates of return to the investments of its owners, or the assumption that households will prefer locations with higher and more dependable levels of real income.

Location theory views a decision unit (most often a business establishment or a household) as weighing the desirability of alternative locations. The unit, wherever located, needs to obtain certain "inputs" (e.g., labor services, materials, electric energy, police protection, information) and needs to dispose of certain "outputs" (e.g., goods produced in a factory, labor services of members of a household, services provided by a hospital). The unit functions as a converter of inputs into outputs within technical limits described by its "production function" (for example, a shoe factory as such can convert various alternative combinations of leather, plastics, labor, energy, and so on into various alternative combinations of shoes and by-products). Finally, the unit derives from its activity a residual "return" which is the measure of satisfaction of its objectives.

From the standpoint of a particular decision unit, with a production function that gives it a limited range of alternative ways of combining inputs and producing outputs, some locations are better than others. Thus, the terms on which outputs can be disposed of will depend on access to established markets for such outputs; labor and other service inputs of the types required will be available on more favorable terms in some places than in others; land for cultivation or building will be available in different qualities and at different prices in various locations.

The process by which the decision unit weighs all these location factors and makes a choice of location and production technology is describable, as first clearly pointed out by Predöhl (1928), in terms of marginal substitutions. Such analysis is not peculiar to location economics but is part and parcel of the more general body of economic theory of rational firm and household behavior. The distinctive task of spatial economics is to identify and account for the development of systematic spatial configurations of advantage for economic activities, as they arise out of the interaction of different decision units upon one another in ways strongly conditioned by distance. There is an analogy here to the work of the physicist who identifies systematic spatial patterns of the microstructure of matter (e.g., in molecules, atoms, or crystals) and explains them in terms of the interaction of attractive and repulsive forces between units.

Some of the more important ways in which decision units interact in a systematic spatial way can be cited. For example, sellers of a product compete for markets; users of a material compete for the source of supply; firms in a labor market compete for labor; economic activities in a city compete for space. Such interrelationships appear as forces of mutual repulsion or dispersion between the competing units. At the same time, when one unit supplies a good or service to another, either or both will have an interest in proximity for the sake of reducing transport cost and inconvenience. And many kinds of production and exchange are subject to important economies of scale, calling for some degree of spatial concentration. Suppliers of complementary products and services find themselves attracted to the same markets, and buyers of jointly produced goods or services find themselves attracted to the same sources. Here we have forces of mutual attraction or agglomeration. Both the repulsive and the attractive forces can apply either as between like decision units (e.g., similar households, or firms in the same industry) or as between unlike units that are complementary or competitive (e.g., a seller and a buyer of a product, a household and an employer, or a supermarket chain and a bank both thinking of buying the same parcel of urban land).

A general equilibrium theory of spatial economic relations takes cognizance simultaneously of all the important types of spatial interdependence of firms, households, and other decision units. A partial equilibrium theory focuses on just one or a few selected relationships, which can then be explored with greater attention to realistic detail, while other elements are taken as given. Thus, by making the necessary simplifying assumptions, we can focus on, say, the way in which complexes of metals industries locate in response to given market, raw material, and technological situations; the allocations of land in an urban central business district; the patterns of residence adopted by people employed in an industrial area; the development of reciprocal trade between two regions; or the choice of a good site for a new suburban shopping center.

The remainder of this article describes some of the various lines of partial equilibrium spatial analysis that have been most extensively developed by economic theorists. In each case the point of departure is the simplest case, in which all but a very few variables are ignored. Some indication is given of the ways in which this type of analysis can gradually approach reality by successive relaxations of the initial simplifying assumptions.

Transport orientation. "Transport orientation" refers to one of the classic cases of location determination under highly simplified assumptions. It was first set forth by the engineer Wilhelm Launhardt in 1885, further developed by the economist Alfred Weber (1909), and later elaborated by Tord Palander (1935) and others [see WEBER, ALFRED]. It is assumed the producer's revenues from the sale of output are determined by the cost of transport to one specified market; that the cost of each transported input is similarly determined by cost of transport from one specified source; and that no other considerations of location preference exist. All costs and prices are assumed to be constant, irrespective of the scale of output.

Under these assumptions, the optimum location is simply the location for which the combined costs of procuring and assembling inputs and delivering outputs is least per unit of output. The principal use of the analysis is in evaluating the effects on location of (1) the relative weight and relative transportability of an industry's materials and products and (2) the patterns of variation in transport cost—the existence of route networks and of nodes thereon, the cost or service differentials reflecting length or direction of haul, volume or size of shipments, mode of transport, or other factors. All these considerations can be weighed as determinants of the type of transport orientation of a specified kind of production; that is, whether production is likely to be optimally located at the market, at a source of material, or at some intermediate point, such as a junction of routes, of modes of transport, or of rate zones.

If the various inputs are required in fixed proportions, as assumed by Weber and others, the optimum production location will also be the point of minimum total transport costs of inputs and outputs; but as Leon Moses (1958) has shown, this need not be the case if the mix of inputs can be varied in response to spatial differences in their relative unit costs.

Spatial competition for markets. One of the most drastic simplifications in Weber's basic transport orientation case is that all prices and costs are independent of quantities produced and sold. Relaxing this highly artificial assumption makes it possible to analyze the various ways in which producers compete for markets and the ways in which location patterns are affected by economies of scale and geographic concentration.

If the amount of output that a producer can sell in any one market without lowering his price is limited, he is likely to find it advantageous to sell in more than one market, and perhaps in a whole range of markets constituting his *market area*. Thus, one kind of situation in which producers in different locations interact through competition for markets is that in which each supplies a market area wherein he can deliver the product at a lower price than his competitor can. One branch of spatial economic analysis considers the way in which the size and shape of contiguous market areas are determined for producers whose locations are taken as fixed. The key factors here are (1) the difference between the f.o.b. (before transport cost is added) prices at the producers' locations; (2) the way in which transport costs are related to length of haul; (3) whether or not the same tariff for transportation applies to all producers. If, for example, one producer must ship at a higher tariff because his product is less compactly packed, more perishable, or shipped in smaller lots than that of his competitor, he will be under an added disadvantage at markets at longer distances, and his market area may be entirely surrounded by that of his rival who ships at a lower tariff.

The laws of market areas, first set forth in systematic form by Frank A. Fetter (1924) and subsequently elaborated by others, permit useful insights into some of the ways in which the structure of transport costs influences the location of producers in relation to their markets and the extent to which a reduction of either production costs or transport rates may enlarge the market that can be economically served from a given production location. An enterprise facing a choice among locations can use these principles under some circumstances in estimating the relative advantages, in terms of the market area and net sales revenues, of alternative locations.

In its most simplified form, market-area theory assumes that market areas are discrete because (1) the products from competing centers are highly interchangeable rather than differentiated, (2) transport costs rise continuously with distance, and (3) the output of a producer sells at a uniform f.o.b. price plus freight, rather than under a discriminatory delivered-price system involving freight absorption by the seller. This combination of conditions is rather uncommon in practice and is perhaps most closely approached in the case of the sales territories of the several separated branches of a given firm that seeks to minimize total delivery expense.

But where different firms are competing for markets and are selling somewhat differentiated products, the market areas of different production centers often overlap to a high degree. To some extent this reflects the fact that transport charges do not always rise continuously with added distance but stay constant over substantial ranges of added length of haul. More important is the fact that sellers can and do discriminate among buyers according to the buyer's location, most often by partial or complete absorption of the added transport cost of sales to the more distant markets. Full freight absorption means selling at a uniform delivered price to all markets and tends, of course, to produce a very great degree of market-area overlap and cross-hauling of products. This and a great

variety of other systems of setting prices in space, such as basing-point systems, have been documented and analyzed in great detail by many writers in terms of (1) theoretical rationale from the standpoint of the seller's interest; (2) historical origins and evolution; and (3) conformity with norms of "workable competition" and with the public interest in efficient location and allocation of resources.

Market areas and supply areas. The types of market-area analysis just discussed apply essentially to products that are produced at fewer points than those at which they are consumed or bought. For certain products, however—mainly agricultural ones—the characteristic situation is that of widely dispersed producers selling to a relatively small number of consuming or collecting centers. This is the inverse of the characteristic market-area situation. Accordingly, the various simplified and complex types of market-area analysis have their counterparts in the field of supply-area analysis. The most familiar examples of rather discrete supply areas are urban milksheds. The effects of various transport rate patterns and pricing policies of buyers have been worked out, in fairly close analogy to the effects of transport rate patterns and pricing policies of sellers in the market-area analysis discussed above.

Many situations in the real world are composite, with a single seller or production point serving several markets while at the same time a market is supplied by several sellers at different locations. This is particularly likely to occur where transport costs of the product in question are small relative to either (1) other considerations of production location, such as labor costs, or (2) qualitative differences between the brands of rival producers.

Competition for space. Another classic approach to spatial analysis, pioneered by Thünen, focuses upon the competition between producers for space on which to operate and upon the role of land rent as the price and allocator of space [see the biography of THÜNEN]. This approach is the main root of those branches of spatial analysis which, under the broad rubric of "land utilization theory," address themselves to the question of how to use a specified area rather than where to locate a specified kind of activity.

This line of analysis uniquely points up the dual economic role that space plays—it provides *utility* as a necessary and generally scarce production input, and it causes *disutility* by imposing costs of transport or communication to bridge distances.

In the simplest case, the choice of location for the producer is assumed to rest on just two factors: the net price per unit received for his output and the price he has to pay (per acre) for the use of land, i.e., rent. The net prices realized for outputs are assumed to depend only on transport costs to a single specified market. All other location factors (such as cost of transported inputs or labor) are ignored.

The factor of access to market thus acts centripetally on producers, while the balancing centrifugal force is the higher rent resulting from competitive bidding for the space nearer the market. Each industry or kind of land use, depending on its technical production characteristics and the transportability of its output, strikes its own compromise between nearness to market and cheap land; and the equilibrium pattern of land uses is envisaged, in the simplest such case, as a systematic series of concentric ring-shaped zones, each devoted to a particular use.

Given the net price receivable for outputs at a specified location, the individual producer's profit possibilities will be greater the lower is the rent charged for the land. In general, his production function will allow considerable substitution between land and other production factors (e.g., more or less intensive cultivation of a crop, or high-rise versus lower buildings in a city). The higher the rent, the more "intensive" is the most efficient way of producing the specified product at that location. There is a maximum rent that the producer can afford to pay to occupy that specified location. The pattern of such maximum, or ceiling, rents tolerated by a specified land use at a series of different locations is described by a "rent gradient" (along one line) or a "rent surface" (over a whole area).

A rent gradient or surface rises to a peak at the point of best access to market (e.g., a town where produce from the surrounding countryside is consumed, or the heart of the central business district in the case of many types of urban commercial land uses). The gradients or surfaces corresponding to different land uses have different heights and slopes. Competition in the real estate market, together with the incentive for owners of land to realize maximum returns, implies that each land use will tend to pre-empt those areas for which its rent surface is the highest one.

This theoretical approach is most applicable to situations in which the main factors affecting the choice of location for a variety of competing uses are (1) rents and (2) some other spatial differential that is common to all the principal alternative uses and is related systematically and continuously to distance—e.g., market access, in the illustrations cited. In practice, this applies to extensive extractive land uses like agriculture and forestry and (on a much more local scale) the main classes of urban land use within a city or metropolitan area.

With this general type of analysis it is possible to derive useful insights, for planning or prognosis, into the shifts in land-use patterns likely to result from changes in demand for products, technological and transport changes, and land-use controls. Some of the more obvious variations on the simplest case have been developed by Thünen and succeeding generations of theorists; they include, for example, the existence of cheaper transport along certain routes, variations in the desirability of land other than those due to access to markets, labor cost differentials, economies of scale, multicrop farming systems and other land-use combinations, trade barriers, and imperfections in the real estate market.

Competition for labor. Many important and interesting questions of spatial economics relate to the spatial interaction between people and jobs. Labor is an essential input of all productive activities, and variations in the cost and availability of manpower influence the choice of location for many activities. At the same time, location theory includes the analysis of the locational behavior of the household as a decision unit with labor services for sale and with certain environmental preferences and other "input requirements." Commuting and migration are two ways in which the labor supply adapts itself to job location.

One of the oldest components of the theory of labor cost differentials rests on the proposition that living costs are lower in predominantly agricultural areas, so that a lower money wage in such areas is consistent with the equality of real wages, which is a condition for equilibrium under full labor mobility. "Equalizing differences" in money wages between areas are defined by Ohlin (1933) as those which simply reflect differences in the cost of living. In the more advanced countries, however, locally produced foodstuffs account for a smaller part of the consumer budget, and interregional differences in consumer prices within the country are narrower. Moreover, the cost of living as measured by statistical indexes omits some important considerations, such as amenity and style of life, that enter into choice of residence.

A second well-established component of the theory explicitly involves demographic behavior (fertility, mortality, and migration). Since various economic and social impediments to labor mobility exist, labor tends to be abundant and cheap where natural increase outruns the growth of labor demand. Further insight here calls for evaluation of the complex ways in which fertility and mortality are influenced by income level and the local pattern of economic opportunities, and also for more detailed analysis of the determinants of spatial mobility. The selectivity of migration plays a vital role here: mobility depends to such an extent on the age, family status, financial resources, education, and other characteristics of the individual that the pattern of manpower characteristics in areas of high unemployment and heavy out-migration contrasts sharply with the pattern in flourishing areas with heavy in-migration.

Certain important locational effects arise from the fact that (since most adults are members of households) labor is often a jointly supplied service. Specifically, labor markets highly specialized in activities employing mainly men are likely to have a surplus of female "complementary" labor which may be attractive to a quite different range of industries.

Still another principal component of the theory of labor cost differentials involves the factors of size, diversity, and productivity in a labor market. This is mentioned in the next section, in the discussion of local external economies. [See WAGES, article on STRUCTURE.]

Agglomeration. Among the most important questions to which spatial economic theory is addressed is the degree to which a particular economic activity, or a complex of closely related activities, is concentrated in a small number of locations. The term "agglomeration" refers in a broad sense to such concentration.

Perhaps the simplest basis for spatial concentration is economies of scale for the individual production unit, such as a steel works or oil refinery [see ECONOMIES OF SCALE]. If large units are much more efficient than small ones, one large unit can serve a number of market locations more cheaply than a number of smaller decentralized units can, even though the total delivery cost is greater. (Similarly, the economies of concentration in a single large plant can outweigh extra costs of material assembly involved in drawing materials from a larger range of sources of supply.) In the case where scale economies and access to markets are the principal locational factors, production units will be larger when markets are more concentrated and when transport is cheap. Some degree of spatial concentration through scale economies underlies the class of situations discussed earlier in regard to spatial competition for markets, in which individual producers sell to many markets and can adopt discriminatory systems of delivered prices.

The agglomeration of a single activity by virtue of internal economies of scale, as just described, often has important indirect agglomerative effects by providing external economies to related activities [see EXTERNAL ECONOMIES AND DISECONOMIES]. For example, fully equipped commercial testing laboratories can operate economically only where they can command a sizable volume of business; and firms using such services can save time and money by locating in a center where such service is available. Similarly, the sheer volume of demand for interregional transport (freight and passenger) to and from a large metropolitan area provides the basis for much more efficient, varied, and flexible transport services than a smaller center can support; and this advantage in transport service is an attraction to a wide range of transport-using activities.

Scale economies within individual units, specialization (division of labor among production units), and close contact among units are the elements in an external-economies type of agglomeration. Where there is a large concentration of activities in proximity, more and more particular operations, processes, or services can be undertaken on an efficient scale by separate units that serve other units in the area. In smaller areas, such specialized activities are either absent altogether or have to be provided within the firms that use them—at higher costs, because they are on a relatively smaller-scale basis. To return to the initial example of testing services for industrial products or materials, in a major industrial center various fully equipped and efficient commercial laboratories are available to provide quick service, while in a distant small town the manufacturer needing such testing service has to choose among (1) providing it himself on a small and less efficient scale, (2) having it done at a distance by a commercial facility, with costly delay and inconvenience, or (3) doing without it.

From the standpoint of the user of specialized goods and services, there are three advantages of quick access to a large source of supply—cheapness, variety, and flexibility. First, the specialized producers or providers of services who exist in large agglomerations can provide their goods or services at lower cost because of their own scale economies. Second, more different grades and varieties are available at any one time, which is an important attraction to the buyer who needs to make selective comparisons (the shopper for fashionable clothes, the theatergoer, the employer who needs unusual types of labor, the manufacturer who needs highly specialized technical assistance on production or sales-promotion problems). Third, access to a large source of supply gives greater assurance of ability to meet rapidly changing and unforeseen needs and reduces the penalty arising from instability of requirements. Costly delays and inventory requirements are lessened when a firm's sudden need for additional labor, repair services, or materials is so small relative to local supplies that the firm can count on its need being met.

Agglomeration via external economies is manifest both on a large interregional distance scale (urban versus nonurban regions, large metropolitan areas versus smaller urban areas) and on a microgeographic intraregional scale (downtown versus outlying areas of a city or even smaller specialized areas within a city, such as shopping districts, garment districts, financial districts, or automobile rows). The distance scale depends partly on the urgency of the need for close personal contact and proximity among the units involved, and partly on the extent to which advantages of spatial concentration are offset by various disadvantages of crowding, such as high cost of space, traffic congestion, noise, and pollution.

The role of external economies in agglomeration and urbanization has been particularly well described by Florence (1948) and Lichtenberg (1960). Its importance as a field of analysis is rapidly increasing because of the increasingly urban and interdependent character of economic activities and the emergence of distinctively urban economic and social problems of the first magnitude; the increasing importance of activities that are related to others through transmission of information requiring quick, close, and detailed contact; and the increasing awareness of the important role that the industrial structure of a region plays in determining its opportunities for growth and adjustment to changing conditions.

EDGAR M. HOOVER

[See also CENTRAL PLACE; GEOGRAPHY, *article on* ECONOMIC GEOGRAPHY; REGIONAL SCIENCE; RENT; TRANSPORTATION, *article on* ECONOMIC ASPECTS.]

BIBLIOGRAPHY

ALONSO, WILLIAM 1964 *Location and Land Use: Toward a General Theory of Land Rent.* Cambridge, Mass.: Harvard Univ. Press.

BERRY, BRIAN J. L.; and PRED, ALLAN 1961 *Central Place Studies: A Bibliography of Theory and Applications.* Bibliography Series, No. 1. Philadelphia: Regional Science Research Institute. → Reprinted in 1965, with additions through 1964.

CHISHOLM, MICHAEL 1962 *Rural Settlement and Land Use: An Essay in Location.* London: Hutchinson University Library.

FETTER, FRANK A. 1924 The Economic Law of Market Areas. *Quarterly Journal of Economics* 38:520–529.

FLORENCE, P. SARGANT 1948 *Investment, Location, and Size of Plant: A Realistic Inquiry Into the Structure of British and American Industries.* Cambridge Univ. Press.

GREENHUT, MELVIN L. 1963 *Microeconomics and the Space Economy: The Effectiveness of an Oligopolistic Market Economy.* Chicago: Foresman.

HOOVER, EDGAR M. 1948 *The Location of Economic Activity.* New York: McGraw-Hill.

ISARD, WALTER 1956 *Location and Space-economy: A General Theory Relating to Industrial Location, Market Areas, Trade and Urban Structure.* Cambridge, Mass.: Technology Press of M.I.T.; New York: Wiley.

ISARD, WALTER et al. 1960 *Methods of Regional Analysis: An Introduction to Regional Science.* New York: Wiley; Cambridge, Mass.: M.I.T. Press.

LICHTENBERG, ROBERT M. 1960 *One-tenth of a Nation: National Forces in the Economic Growth of the New York Region.* Cambridge, Mass.: Harvard Univ. Press.

LÖSCH, AUGUST (1940) 1954 *The Economics of Location.* New Haven: Yale Univ. Press. → First published as *Die räumliche Ordnung der Wirtschaft.*

MEYER, J. R. 1963 Regional Economics: A Survey. *American Economic Review* 53:19–54.

MOSES, LEON N. 1958 Location and the Theory of Production. *Quarterly Journal of Economics* 72:259–272.

NORTH, DOUGLASS C. 1955 Location Theory and Regional Economic Growth. *Journal of Political Economy* 63:243–258.

NOURSE, HUGH O. 1967 Regional Economics. Unpublished manuscript.

OHLIN, BERTIL (1933) 1957 *Interregional and International Trade.* Harvard Economic Studies, Vol. 39. Cambridge, Mass.: Harvard Univ. Press.

PALANDER, TORD 1935 *Beiträge zur Standortstheorie.* Uppsala (Sweden): Almqvist & Wiksell.

PONSARD, CLAUDE 1958 *Histoire des théories économiques spatiales.* Rennes (France): Colin.

PREDÖHL, ANDREAS 1928 The Theory of Location in Its Relation to General Economics. *Journal of Political Economy* 36:371–390.

WEBER, ALFRED (1909) 1957 *Theory of the Location of Industries.* Univ. of Chicago Press; Cambridge Univ. Press. → First published as *Über den Standort der Industrien. Teil 1: Reine Theorie des Standorts.*

II

THE GENERAL EQUILIBRIUM APPROACH

Central to most general equilibrium models of location is a system of equations that emphasizes the interdependence of regions due to linkages between economic activities. Thus, in such models an exogenous change in demand for a commodity in one region may affect interregional trade and the spatial distribution of consumption, production, etc., of all commodities in all regions. These models represent a distinct departure from tradition in location theory. Problems in this field were first investigated formally by Weber (1909) and other European scholars who were contemporaries of Walras. Their analyses drew, however, most heavily on the partial equilibrium logic of Marshall. Their theoretical formulations did not lend themselves to consideration of mutual-interdependence issues and tended to obscure the relationship of location theory to branches of economic theory, particularly interregional trade theory, that dealt with general equilibrium problems.

Mutual-interdependence models of location and regional interaction are of two varieties: (1) highly abstract formulations that extend Walras' reasoning to spatial phenomena; (2) models that are more restrictive in their assumptions and less general in their intent but which lend themselves to empirical application. The latter will be dealt with at greater length here. Not all of the more operational techniques, however, will be reviewed. The approach of some of them is so highly aggregative that they cannot deal adequately with factors affecting the geographic distribution of production, trade, and optimum location of investment in new capacity for individual industries. For this reason, multisector multiplier and regional growth models, while important tools of regional and interregional analysis, will not be discussed (but see Chipman 1951; Isard et al. 1960; Borts 1960). Moreover, the results of some of the aggregative formulations—economic base analysis is an example—can be derived from those that are reviewed below (Andrews 1958).

This article will concentrate on two types of models: those that employ input–output techniques and those that employ linear programming [*see* INPUT–OUTPUT ANALYSIS; PROGRAMMING]. The most important difference between the two is that the former rule out optimization by fixing geographic patterns of production and/or trade. Efforts by scholars to develop techniques that determine relative, as well as absolute, patterns of production and trade and that are concerned with the optimum use of resources led to the application of linear programming to spatial analysis.

We shall begin by considering a group of input–output models. First, the derivation of trade balances for regions is dealt with. Second, the linkages between regions or nations involved in the usual input–output system are described. Third, several full-scale regional input–output techniques that are theoretically capable of analyzing the effects of trade linkages between many regions are considered. A group of linear programming models is then reviewed.

Input–output techniques

Derivation of trade balances. Data on trade between regions of a country are not usually available, and estimates of such trade are thought to be less reliable than estimates of regional output

and final demand. Given information on output and final demand and a matrix of technical coefficients, individual industry balances of trade for a region with respect to all other regions can be derived. Let $_gx_j$ be output of industry j in region g and $_gc_j$ be *total* consumption of the output of industry j in region g; then $_ge_j$, the net trade balance of industry j in region g with respect to all other areas, is

$$_ge_j = {}_gx_j - {}_gc_j .$$

A positive e indicates a net export balance, a negative e a net import balance. An over-all trade balance for the region is obtained by summing the e's for all industries in the region.

Total consumption, c above, is the sum of final demands, y, and intermediate or interindustry demands. The latter are derived by multiplying the known regional outputs by technical coefficients of production, that is,

$$_gc_i = \sum_{j=1}^{n} {}_ga_{ij}\, {}_gx_j + {}_gy_i .$$

The technical coefficient $_ga_{ij}$ is the amount of the output of industry i required to produce a unit of the output of industry j in region g.

There are difficulties in deriving commodity trade balances by the above technique. Coefficients of production vary between regions as a result of differences in methods of production, differences in prices, which affect the coefficients because they are in dollar terms, differences in the product mix of industries, etc. Yet, since *regional* input–output coefficients are not usually known, *national* coefficients are often employed, with resulting errors in the estimates of intermediate demands. It is also difficult to obtain information on consumption by the final demand sectors, particularly investment and government.

Import and export balances for individual industries have sometimes been derived as a first step in studies whose object is to determine the industries that might be encouraged to locate or expand in a region. Although the size of the import balance, or regional excess demand for the output of an industry, is only one element in such an analysis—costs of producing and transporting the inputs and outputs of an industry are also considered—it is viewed as particularly important. This outlook reflects a belief that narrowing regional differentials in factor prices and production costs are leading to an increased market orientation of nonprimary industry. Some studies, unfortunately, appear to settle the issue of a region's comparative advantage by a ranking of industries in terms of the size of regional excess demand. Virtue is found in those patterns of investment that contribute most to self-sufficiency, an approach that partakes of regional mercantilism.

Locational analyses based on balances of trade employ general equilibrium techniques to only a very limited degree. After the initial input–output calculations are made, an industry-by-industry approach is adopted. In general such analyses do not take into account in a systematic way the manner in which the introduction of new capacity for any one industry will affect the costs of production of all other industries in a region. Changes in outputs that are induced by cost changes are, therefore, not taken into account. Also neglected are the constraints that may exist on expansion. While factors of production are more mobile for regions of a country than they are internationally, regional supply functions for some factors may be inelastic unless there is substantial unemployment. If factor supplies and other things impose constraints on industry expansion, a pattern of investment should be selected that minimizes or maximizes some meaningful economic variable. Such an objective requires a general equilibrium system of an optimizing character. Several systems of this type are discussed below.

Trade linkages in national models. As was indicated above, balance of trade studies begin with known outputs. The main objective of most inter-industry studies is, however, to determine outputs, and the objective of regional input–output systems is to determine what effects a change, say, in final demand, in one or more regions will have on all others. The simplest approach to the latter issue is that adopted in national input–output analyses. These are in effect two-region systems, one region being the nation under study and the other the rest of the world. In such models we are given the technical coefficients of production of the region or nation, $_{g}a_{ij}$, for $i, j = 1, 2, \cdots, n$ industries; the final demands, $_{g}y_{j}$, of all exogenous sectors other than foreign trade; and a set of imports, $_{g}m_{j}$, and exports, $_{g}e_{j}$. In matrix notation these are represented by $_{g}A$, $_{g}Y$, $_{g}M$, and $_{g}E$. Imports are arranged in two categories, competing and noncompeting goods, the latter being those for which there are no counterparts in the region under study. Imports of these goods are entered in an exogenous import row and have no effect on regional output. Output of each of the industries in the nation or region, g, being studied is found by solving the following set of simultaneous equations:

$$_{g}X = [I - {}_{g}A]^{-1}[{}_{g}Y + ({}_{g}E - {}_{g}M)].$$

Here $_{g}X$ is the $n \times 1$ vector of outputs in region g; $[I - {}_{g}A]^{-1}$ is the inverse of $[I - {}_{g}A]$, the $n \times n$ identity matrix minus the $n \times n$ matrix of technical coefficients; $_{g}Y$ is the $n \times 1$ vector of final demands; $({}_{g}E - {}_{g}M)$ is the $n \times 1$ vector of the differences between imports and exports for each of the competing-goods industries. Negative values for these differences are precluded. Thus, if the imports of any good exceed the sum of exports and all other final demands, a zero value is assigned to the final demand for the good. Effectively, it is treated as a noncompeting good.

In the above approach imports and exports are not explained within the model. There are, for example, no functions relating region g's imports of all goods to its income. Since regional linkages are external to the system, it is not possible to determine the effects on region g of such things as an exogenous increase in demand for a non-traded good in the rest of the world. We shall now consider a variety of regional input–output techniques that can determine the effects of such changes.

The Leontief intranational model. In its most general form Leontief's intranational model (see Research Project . . . 1953) involves a complex hierarchy of goods and regions. The place of any particular good within the hierarchy depends upon the degree of spatial aggregation required to obtain a balance, or equality, between regional production and consumption. An empirical application of the model employs the simpler hierarchy traditional to international trade theory, that of traded and nontraded goods, although they are referred to as national and local goods. National goods are those for which a balance between production and consumption can be struck only at the national level. Local goods are those for which there is a balance between production and consumption for each region into which the nation is divided for purposes of the study. The outline of the model's structure presented below is in terms of this simpler hierarchy.

Assume there are n industries, the first h being national and the remaining $n - h$ local. There are r regions. A national bill of final demand, Y, for all goods, a national matrix of technical coefficients, A, and a set of locational constants, $_{g}\beta_{d}$, for the *national goods* are given. The locational constant $_{g}\beta_{d}$ indicates the proportion of total output of a national good, d, produced by region g. These constants may be determined from past data on the geographic distribution of production. By definition, the locational constants for each national good sum to unity.

Total outputs of both national and local goods are determined by solving

$$X = [I - A]^{-1}Y.$$

A regional allocation of total output of each national good is then obtained by applying the locational constants as follows:

$$_g x_d = {}_g\beta_d\, x_d, \quad \begin{aligned} & d = 1, 2, \cdots, h, \text{ national industries;} \\ & g = 1, 2, \cdots, r, \text{ regions.} \end{aligned}$$

In this expression $_g x_d$ represents the amount of national good d that is produced in region g and x_d represents the total output of national good d. Since the locational constants for each national good sum to unity, we are assured that the above procedure precisely allocates total output of each national good to the regions.

Derivation of regional outputs of nontraded goods is somewhat more involved. For this purpose it is convenient to think of the national matrix of technical coefficients as having been arranged so that all national-goods industries appear first. The coefficients are then in four meaningful blocks:

$$\begin{bmatrix} A_1 & A_2 \\ A_3 & A_4 \end{bmatrix} \equiv \begin{bmatrix} \{a_{df}\} & \{a_{dl}\} \\ \{a_{ld}\} & \{a_{lq}\} \end{bmatrix}, \quad \begin{aligned} & d, f = 1, 2, \cdots, h, \\ & \text{national industries;} \\ & l, q = h + 1, h + 2, \cdots, \\ & n, \text{ local industries.} \end{aligned}$$

Technical coefficients in the $\{a_{df}\}$ or A_1 block pertain to the requirements of national-goods industries for the outputs of other national-goods industries per unit of their output; coefficients in the $\{a_{dl}\}$ or A_2 block describe the requirements of local-goods industries for the outputs of national-goods industries per unit of the former's outputs, etc.

Regional outputs of local goods are determined as follows:

$$_g X = [I - A_4]^{-1}[A_3\, {}_g X_d + {}_g Y_l], \quad \begin{aligned} & g = 1, 2, \cdots, r \\ & d = 1, 2, \cdots, h \\ & l = h + 1, \cdots, n. \end{aligned}$$

Here $[I - A_4]^{-1}$ is the inverse of the block of coefficients that pertain to the requirements of local-goods industries for the outputs of local-goods industries; $A_3\, {}_g X_d$ gives the intermediate requirements of local-goods industries in region g for production of the already determined regional outputs of national goods; $_g Y_l$ is the final demand for local goods in region g.

The intranational model being considered determines all outputs. It also determines individual commodity and, therefore, aggregate trade balances for each region with respect to all others. Balances of trade between individual pairs of regions remain unknown. This is one of the senses in which the model is intranational rather than interregional. It is part of the logic of the system that the effect on a particular region of a change in final demand for national goods is the same regardless of the region in which the change takes place. Similarly, the effect on any given region of a change in final demand for local goods is the same regardless of the region (if other than itself) in which the change takes place.

The hierarchy of goods and regions, whether of a simple or complex variety, assumed by the intranational model is difficult to establish in reality. The empirical application of the system finally settled upon a definition of goods and regions that in some sense minimized departures from strict production–consumption balance for the entire group of industries designated as local (see Isard 1953). The empirical difficulty raises a question as to the kind of theoretical framework that would produce a strict hierarchy of goods and regions. The answer is provided by Lösch's general equilibrium model of location (1940).

Lösch assumed a uniform transport surface, every point being on a straight-line connection with every other; freight rates given and the same in all directions; population evenly distributed and with identical tastes, so that each point in space has an identical demand function for each commodity; factor supplies everywhere the same; identical production functions and U-shaped cost curves for each commodity everywhere; and intermediate inputs, if required, present everywhere, so that only final goods are transported. Economies of scale in production ensure that the economy is not composed of self-sufficient households. Transport costs, on the other hand, impose limits on market areas and the extent of specialization. Lösch concluded that under competitive equilibrium conditions, with all consumers served and profits of all firms zero, the surface is covered by a network of hexagonal market areas of different sizes or orders, one for each good. The hexagons pertaining to any given good are everywhere the same. Each hexagon of a given size contains an equal number of hexagonal market areas of all lower-order goods and is itself completely contained in the next-higher-order market. This is the strict hierarchy involved in the Leontief intranational model.

Interregional models. To describe an interregional input–output system, we assume a closed economy divided into $b, g = 1, 2, \cdots, r$ regions and producing $i, j = 1, 2, \cdots, n$ goods. Technical coefficients, $_g a_{ij}$, are given for each region and may differ between them. For each region there is also given a set of trade or supply coefficients, $_{bg} t_i$, for every good, showing the relative regional composition of that region's purchases of every commodity. Thus, the coefficient $_{34}t_2 = .40$ indicates that for every dollar spent on the output of industry 2 by the sectors of region 4, 40 cents' worth is purchased in region 3. Each region's trade coefficients for each commodity add to unity: $\sum_{b=1}^{r} {}_{bg}t_i = 1$, $i = 1, 2, \cdots, n$. Regional final demands, $_g y_i$, are given.

From the trade and technical coefficients a new set of coefficients is derived, which describes the interregional and interindustry structure of every region:

$$\bar{A} \equiv \{{}_{bg}a_{ij}\} = \{{}_{bg}t_{i\ g}a_{ij}\}, \qquad \begin{aligned} i, j &= 1, 2, \cdots, n; \\ b, g &= 1, 2, \cdots, r. \end{aligned}$$

Hereafter $\bar{A}$ will be described as the interregional input–output matrix. Consider one element of this $nr \times nr$ matrix, say, $_{34}a_{12} = .20$. The coefficient indicates that for each dollar's worth of commodity 2 produced in region 4, 20 cents' worth of commodity 1 is purchased from region 3. Since the trade coefficients for each good in a region add to unity, the sum of all a's in any column of the interregional input–output matrix yields a technical coefficient for the relevant region and industry: $\sum_{b=1}^{r} {}_{bg}a_{ij} = {}_g a_{ij}$.

In interregional systems, outputs of an area are determined by the amounts that the endogenous sectors of an area *ship* on final demand account rather than the amounts that its exogenous sectors consume. Shipments on final demand account, $_b y_j^*$, are determined from the usual final demands and the trade coefficients:

$$_b y_j^* = \sum_{g=1}^{r} {}_{bg}t_{j\ g}y_j, \qquad j = 1, 2, \cdots, n.$$

Regional outputs of all goods are then obtained in the usual way, namely,

$$X = [I - \bar{A}]^{-1} Y^*.$$

Here X and Y^* are the vectors, respectively, of regional outputs and of shipments on final demand account, and $[I - \bar{A}]^{-1}$ is the inverse of the interregional input–output matrix. The system yields balances of trade for individual commodities and for the aggregate of all commodities between pairs of regions or for a single region with respect to all others.

The intranational model described above determines all outputs by fixing the *relative regional outputs* of national goods and the trading patterns of a class of goods, i.e., those designated as local. Interregional input–output systems allow relative, as well as absolute, levels of regional output of all goods to vary but *fix relative trading patterns of*

all goods in one way or another. The model developed by Isard (1951) has a set of trade coefficients for every industry in every region. The models of Chenery and Clark (1959) and of Moses (1955), on the other hand, have a single set of trade coefficients for all sectors within a region— the assumption employed in the above description of an interregional input–output system. There are, however, differences between the latter two models.

Chenery and Clark assume that any region is more efficient than any other region in supplying its requirements of all goods that it actually produces. Each area, then, fully utilizes existing capacity before resorting to imports. Unless a capacity constraint is encountered, trade coefficients must therefore be zero or one. If such a constraint is encountered, trade coefficients will take on intermediate values, but they then cannot be stable. Moreover, this approach can be used only for a two-region system, since it has no mechanism for assigning the imports of a region to a number of different areas.

The theory of spatial competition of traditional location analysis provides the basis for the determination and stability of the coefficients employed by Moses and, with some adaptation, Isard. Thus, assume that each industry produces a single homogeneous product, so that the output of a given industry from one region is a perfect substitute in production or consumption for the output of the same industry from any other region. Each industry in each region is assumed to have *excess* capacity and to produce at constant cost. Regional supply functions of the factors of production are perfectly elastic at given factor prices, up to some limit representing regional endowments. Factors of production are perfectly mobile within each region, industry is perfectly competitive, and transport costs per unit of output increase continuously with distance but do not vary with the quantity shipped. In these circumstances there are perfectly defined market and supply areas for every site where a good is produced and consumed. Trade coefficients then reflect the aggregation of market and supply areas into regions. The world of reality departs from perfect competition, transport rate structures have many peculiarities, etc. There may, as a result, be significant differences in market and supply boundaries of different industries in a region and, therefore, intraregional differences in trade coefficients, as suggested by the Isard model.

The most questionable aspect of interregional input–output systems is their assumption of stable trading patterns. A theoretical framework can be developed, as was done above, under which trade coefficients would be stable, but it is extremely unlikely that the conditions of this framework will be met in reality. The evidence for stability that has been presented is not convincing, because all economic activity was grouped into a few gross industries and regions, with changes over time in individual market and supply areas probably balancing out (Moses 1955).

The main virtue of regional input–output models is their operational character. This is achieved at a heavy cost in terms of theoretical interest. They have no mechanism for explaining trade patterns. Aside from reductions in final demand, they have no way of explaining the disappearance of an industry from a region. Nor are they so constructed that their internal logic points to situations in which new industries will emerge in a region. The above criticism is not removed by the introduction of dynamic elements. In dynamic formulations investment in new capacity is typically related to rates of change in output of industries found in each region in the initial period. In this respect the best that has so far been done with the various input–output models is to incorporate and investigate the conclusions of separate locational and interregional trade analyses. Thus, in one study (Isard & Kuenne 1953) the ideal location of a new integrated steel plant was determined from a separate location study. The impact on the area of the mill's output was then investigated by a regional input–output analysis that involved a limited application of the trade-coefficient approach. In this approach the indirect effects that the region would have on itself because of its effects on other regions were ignored. This limited impact approach has been adopted in a number of studies (see, for example, Hirsch 1964; Moore & Peterson 1955).

Regional input–output studies have sometimes had the objective of projecting all economic activity in an area over a considerable period of time. In only one study, however, that of Berman and her co-workers (1960), has the important topic of factor redistribution, and labor migration in particular, been faced. In this study population projections derived by demographic techniques and employment projections derived by input–output analysis were made to square with one another, and it was concluded that a significant change would take place in historical migration trends.

Interregional linear programming models

The intranational model and all of the fixed-trade interregional models treated above face a serious difficulty if a capacity constraint is encountered

anywhere in the system. If the "predicted" output of even a single industry in a single region exceeds the region's capacity to produce the good, then a strict application of the model's logic requires that the final demand program be declared infeasible. This is surely undesirable if the good is transportable and other regions have sufficient excess capacity to produce the required output. An obvious solution is to alter trading patterns, at least at the margin. In what way, however, should they be altered? If some particular region can deliver the required amounts of the good at a lower price, either because of a production or transport cost advantage, a well-formulated economic model would assign to it the task of supplying the requirements. The issue then is the following: if choice and optimization can be introduced into multiregion systems, why not eliminate the fixed, exogenously given patterns of trade and/or output entirely and formulate models that determine all outputs and trade by means of an optimizing scheme? Several techniques for doing this, all of them of a programming variety, are presented below. Their connections with the theory of interregional trade are very clear. They encompass much of what is valuable in traditional location theory but, because of their general equilibrium character, also go beyond it.

The first model to be considered involves cost minimization and is related to the well-known transportation problem of linear programming. It builds directly on a study by Henderson (1958). The existence of intermediate inputs for current production is ignored at first, and attention is focused on a number of final products. The following notation is employed:

$i = 1, 2, \cdots, n$, final consumption products;

$b, g = 1, 2, \cdots, r$, regions;

$e = 1, 2, \cdots, m$, primary factors of production;

$_b w_e$ = price of a unit of primary factor e in region b;

$_b a_{ei}$ = quantity of primary factor e required to produce a unit of good i in region b;

$_b k_i$ = capacity, or maximum rate of output, of plant and equipment producing good i in region b;

$h = 1, 2, \cdots, z$, routes or modes of transportation connecting each pair of regions, the routes between regions being entirely independent of one another.

$_{bg}^h s_i$ = shipment of commodity i from region b to region g by route or mode h;

${}^{h}_{bg}K$ = capacity or maximum quantity of all goods that can be transported by route h between regions b and g, it being assumed that all goods are identical in their use of transport capacity;

${}^{h}_{bg}t_e$ = quantity of primary factor e required to transport a unit of *any* commodity from region b to region g by route h;

${}_{b}D_e$ = endowment of primary factor e in region b;

${}_{b}y_i$ = final demand for commodity i in region b.

It should be noted that factors of production are perfectly mobile within regions, regional factor supply functions are perfectly elastic up to the limit imposed by endowment, and demand functions are perfectly inelastic with respect to both income and price. The assumption that goods are identical in their use of transport capacity and primary inputs for transport is employed to keep an involved notational scheme from becoming even more complicated.

The problem is to determine a regional allocation of output and trade in all goods that satisfies the fixed demands at minimum total cost, subject to the constraints on capacities and factor endowments. The system is written as follows: minimize

$$(1) \quad C = \sum_{b=1}^{r} \sum_{b=g=1}^{r} \sum_{e=1}^{m} \sum_{i=1}^{n} \sum_{h=1}^{z} [{}_{b}w_e \, ({}_{b}a_{ei} + {}^{h}_{bg}t_e)] \, {}^{h}_{bg}s_i,$$

subject to

$$(2) \quad \sum_{b=1}^{r} \sum_{h=1}^{z} {}^{h}_{bg}s_i \geqslant {}_{g}y_i, \qquad \begin{array}{l} g = 1,2,\cdots,r, \text{ regions,} \\ i = 1,2,\cdots,n, \text{ industries;} \end{array}$$

$$(3) \quad \sum_{g=1}^{r} \sum_{h=1}^{z} {}^{h}_{bg}s_i \leqslant {}_{b}k_i, \qquad \begin{array}{l} b = 1,2,\cdots,r, \\ i = 1,2,\cdots,n; \end{array}$$

$$(4) \quad \sum_{i=1}^{n} {}^{h}_{bg}s_i \leqslant {}^{h}_{bg}K_i, \qquad \begin{array}{l} h = 1,2,\cdots,z, \text{ routes,} \\ b,g = 1,2,\cdots,r; \end{array}$$

$$(5) \quad \sum_{i=1}^{n} \sum_{g=1}^{r} \sum_{h=1}^{z} ({}_{b}a_{ei} + {}^{h}_{bg}t_e) \, {}^{h}_{bg}s_i \leqslant {}_{b}D_e,$$

$$\begin{array}{l} e = 1,2,\cdots,m, \\ b = 1,2,\cdots,r. \end{array}$$

Equation (1) states the objective—to minimize the total cost of producing and transporting all commodities. The constraints have the following meanings: (2) total shipments of each commodity into each region must be at least great enough to satisfy final demand; (3) total shipments, this being the same as output, of each commodity by each region to all regions must be less than or equal to the maximum possible rate of output; (4) total shipments of all commodities by any route must be less than or equal to the capacity of that route; (5) total requirements of each primary factor in

a region for production and transport must be less than or equal to the endowment. All shipments are nonnegative.

The introduction of intermediate inputs changes the model in only one way. The first set of constraints, equations (2) above, must be rewritten to state that the total pool of a good available in a region minus the region's intermediate demand for the good must be at least as great as its final demand for the good. A region's pool of a good is defined as total shipments into it from all other areas plus the amount of the good it produces itself minus its total exports of the good.

The minimum-cost, feasible solution is the same as would be achieved by a perfectly competitive economy. The entire system is a set of linked interregional trade problems, the linkages being due to capacities and factor endowments. If these constraints did not exist or were not encountered in a particular problem, total production and transport of each commodity would be assigned to the least-cost region and route, i.e., would be determined by absolute advantage. The existence of binding constraints on factors and transport provides a solution based on considerations of comparative advantage. Moreover, in a multiregion system with positive transport costs, comparative advantage is defined in terms of markets to be served, as well as commodities produced.

The dual to the above minimizing problem is a maximizing problem that determines the delivered price of every good in every region and the quasi rent of each productive capacity, transport capacity, and factor endowment. Delivered price is determined by the marginal supply source. Thus, if any region's demand for a commodity is satisfied by more than one region, price in the consuming area will be equal to the unit production and transport cost of the least efficient supplying source. Capacity in every other area that supplies this region receives a quasi rent, or return above its cost. Capacities that are not fully utilized earn no such return.

The quasi rents are key variables for analysis of the location of investment in new capacity and the retirement of existing capacity. For this purpose it is convenient to think in terms of a planned economy that has set aside a given sum for investment in additional capacity. It is also convenient to assume that the cost of providing additional capacity to produce each good in each region and of providing additional capacity on each transport route is given. The task of the planning authority is to allocate investment among goods, regions, and routes in an optimal manner. Since final demands are fixed, the obvious criterion of optimality is to allocate investment so as to achieve the greatest reduction in total cost. The significance of the quasi rents can now be seen. Each is in fact the reduction in total system cost that would be realized if the associated capacity were increased sufficiently to permit an additional unit of output or transport. From the initial set of quasi rents, the changes that take place in the quasi rents as additional capacity is added, and the cost of providing each type of capacity, the given total investment can be assigned in an optimal manner. If, instead of taking the total amount of investment as given, we assume that an interest rate is given, the optimum level, as well as allocation, of investment in commodities, regions, and routes can be determined.

Input–output models were criticized above because they had no internal rules governing the emergence of productive capacity for particular goods in regions which have not previously had such capacity. The programming technique does not have this weakness, since in all cases of zero capacity some small fictitious quantity can be assigned. Unit costs of production and transport are determined for these capacities. The model will then determine in what regions, if any, new industry should be introduced.

The quasi rents for factors of production, so far ignored, have interpretations similar to those for capacity. They indicate how much total cost would be reduced if a region had enough of a particular primary factor to produce and transport an additional unit of output. Obviously the quasi rents will be zero in all cases where the optimal solution involves less than full employment for a factor. The optimal solution, therefore, indicates the areas from which mobile factors should migrate—those in which they are less than fully employed and earn zero quasi rents—and those which should attract them. As stated, there is some asymmetry in the system. It determines optimal patterns of interregional trade in goods but not optimal patterns of interregional migration. To include a set of relationships that would change the situation would be misleading, since there is at present no way of quantifying the social, as well as the economic, costs of migration.

The model that has been described determines optimal patterns of output, trade, and employment of primary factors. It determines geographic patterns of price and, when extended to include investment, optimal expansions in capacity for production and transport. It indicates the regions from which mobile factors should migrate and the re-

gions which should attract them, if such decisions are made on the basis of economic considerations alone. With the two extensions suggested above, the results of the model reflect a network of comparative advantages that are defined in terms of production functions for goods and transport, supply prices of primary factors, propensities to consume, and the initial distribution of capacities. An empirical application of this type of model has been attempted by Moses (1960).

A second interregional linear programming model (see Lefeber 1958; Stevens 1958; Kuenne 1963) is almost the converse of the one presented above. It takes as given the prices of final goods in each region, rather than the minimum prices of primary factors of production. Instead of a perfectly inelastic demand for each good in each region, it assumes that demands are perfectly elastic and that a certain minimum quantity of each good is to be delivered to each region. The primal problem of this model maximizes the value of output of final goods, rather than minimizing the cost of satisfying a fixed set of demands. Given a set of final goods prices, it determines an optimal point on the production frontier of the entire economy.

The treatment given demand in both of these programming models is inadequate: one assumes a perfectly elastic demand for each commodity, the other a perfectly inelastic demand. Samuelson (1952), however, has suggested a programming formulation for a single-commodity multiregion spatial competition problem that involved regular supply, as well as demand, functions. In this formulation, total consumer surplus, as defined by Marshall, was maximized, subject to constraints imposed by demand and supply considerations in each region. Smith (1963) has provided an interpretation to the dual of this problem which shows that it involves the minimization of rents. Recently, Takayama and Judge (1964) have demonstrated that the Samuelson spatial competition problem is in reality a quadratic programming problem. They have suggested a method of solution that can be applied either to a single homogeneous good or to a number of goods produced and consumed in many regions. In the latter case, however, all of the goods must be for final consumption only.

LEON N. MOSES

[*See also* REGIONAL SCIENCE.]

BIBLIOGRAPHY

ANDREWS, RICHARD B. 1958 Comment re Criticisms of the Economic Base Theory. *Journal of the American Institute of Planners* 24:37–40.

BERMAN, BARBARA R.; CHINITZ, BENJAMIN; and HOOVER, EDGAR M. 1960 *Projection of a Metropolis: Technical Supplement to the New York Metropolitan Region Study.* Cambridge, Mass.: Harvard Univ. Press.

BORTS, GEORGE H. 1960 The Equalization of Returns and Regional Economic Growth. *American Economic Review* 50:319–347.

CHENERY, HOLLIS B.; and CLARK, PAUL G. 1959 *Interindustry Economics.* New York: Wiley. → See especially pages 308–332.

CHIPMAN, JOHN S. 1951 *The Theory of Inter-sectoral Money Flows and Income Formation.* Baltimore: Johns Hopkins Press.

HENDERSON, JAMES M. 1958 *The Efficiency of the Coal Industry: An Application of Linear Programming.* Cambridge, Mass.: Harvard Univ. Press.

HIRSCH, WERNER Z. 1964 [A General Structure for Regional Economic Analysis.] Introduction to Conference on Regional Accounts, Second, Miami Beach, Fla., 1962, *Elements of Regional Accounts: Papers.* Baltimore: Johns Hopkins Press.

ISARD, WALTER 1951 Interregional and Regional Input–Output Analysis: A Model of a Space-economy. *Review of Economics and Statistics* 33:318–328.

ISARD, WALTER 1953 Some Empirical Results and Problems of Regional Input–Output Analysis. Pages 116–181 in Research Project on the Structure of the American Economy, *Studies in the Structure of the American Economy: Theoretical and Empirical Explorations in Input–Output Analysis.* New York: Oxford Univ. Press.

ISARD, WALTER; and KUENNE, ROBERT E. 1953 The Impact of Steel Upon the Greater New York–Philadelphia Industrial Region. *Review of Economics and Statistics* 35:289–301.

ISARD, WALTER et al. 1960 *Methods of Regional Analysis: An Introduction to Regional Science.* New York: Wiley; Cambridge, Mass.: The Technology Press of M.I.T. → See especially pages 182–231.

KUENNE, ROBERT E. 1963 Spatial Economics. Pages 395–454 in Robert E. Kuenne, *The Theory of General Economic Equilibrium.* Princeton Univ. Press.

LEFEBER, LOUIS 1958 *Allocation in Space: Production, Transport and Industrial Location.* Amsterdam: North-Holland Publishing.

LÖSCH, AUGUST (1940) 1964 *The Economics of Location.* New Haven: Yale Univ. Press. → First published as *Die räumliche Ordnung der Wirtschaft.*

MOORE, FREDERICK T.; and PETERSON, JAMES W. 1955 Regional Analysis: An Interindustry Model of Utah. *Review of Economics and Statistics* 37:368–383.

MOSES, LEON N. 1955 The Stability of Interregional Trading Patterns and Input–Output Analysis. *American Economic Review* 45:803–832.

MOSES, LEON N. 1960 A General Equilibrium Model of Production, Interregional Trade, and Location of Industry. *Review of Economics and Statistics* 42:373–397.

RESEARCH PROJECT ON THE STRUCTURE OF THE AMERICAN ECONOMY 1953 *Studies in the Structure of the American Economy: Theoretical and Empirical Explorations in Input–Output Analysis,* by Wassily Leontief et al. New York: Oxford Univ. Press.

SAMUELSON, PAUL A. 1952 Spatial Price Equilibrium and Linear Programming. *American Economic Review* 42:283–303.

SMITH, VERNON L. 1963 Minimization of Economic Rent in Spatial Price Equilibrium. *Review of Economic Studies* 30:24–31.

STEVENS, BENJAMIN H. 1958 An Interregional Linear Programming Model. *Journal of Regional Science* 1: 60–98.

TAKAYAMA, T.; and JUDGE, G. G. 1964 Equilibrium Among Spatially Separated Markets: A Reformulation. *Econometrica* 32:510–524.

WEBER, ALFRED (1909) 1957 *Theory of the Location of Industries.* Univ. of Chicago Press; Cambridge Univ. Press. → First published as *Über den Standort der Industrien. Teil 1: Reine Theorie des Standorts.*

SPEARMAN, C. E.

Charles Edward Spearman (1863–1945) is known for two major contributions to behavioral science: a methodological one—what we now call factor analysis; and a substantive one—the development of a rational basis for determining the concept of general intelligence and for validating intelligence testing. In addition, his name is associated eponymously with the Spearman rank-order correlation coefficient. But few psychologists today would agree with his judgment that his most important work was the enunciation of noegenetic cognitive laws.

Spearman's work on factor analysis and on intelligence are historically intertwined, and it would be difficult to say whether his philosophical interest in the notion of a single general ability forced him to study statistical correlational methods more creatively or whether his intrinsic love of clear and ingenious methods generated his two-factor theory of intelligence. The former is more likely. In any case, his 1904 article, "'General Intelligence' Objectively Determined and Measured," is a landmark in psychological thought and involves both of his major interests.

Factor analysis

Methodologically, Spearman began by recognizing that E. L. Thorndike, Clark Wissler, and James McKeen Cattell had failed to discover the structure of abilities through correlational methods; more particularly, they had been unable to find a general factor, because they had not allowed for the systematic influence of random error of measurement. Spearman demonstrated the *attenuating* effect of error on the correlation coefficient. Furthermore, he realized that the attenuation correction formula made it possible to discover what any two intercorrelated variables, X and Y, have in common with any other two intercorrelated variables, W and Z. This insight, backed by an evaluation of the standard error of the tetrad difference, led to the invention of factor analysis capable of demonstrating a single common factor plus specific factors. This made it possible to explain the individual differences in test scores as due primarily to differences in a *single general ability* as well as to something quite specific to each test. As Cyril Burt has pointed out, the beginning of the concept of factor analysis may be found in Karl Pearson's work, but Spearman's development of the concept cannot be explicitly traced to Pearson.

In the first quarter of this century the study, by tests, of individual differences grew apace, and Spearman's discovery of factor analysis, as well as his statistical contributions in such formulae as the rank correlation coefficient and the Spearman–Brown prophecy formula, prevented the work in this field from becoming completely chaotic. (Since the more active and less scholarly failed to understand what Spearman was saying, the field became a sorry mess notwithstanding, especially in intelligence testing.) Spearman's two-factor theory of intelligence—or of "g" as he preferred to symbolize the discovered general factor—states that any cognitive performance is a function of two "factors"— the general ability common to most cognitive performances and an ability specific to a given test. Since it is possible to determine this general factor objectively, disputes about the validity of intelligence tests can be settled by assessing the loadings of the tests on the general factor. High loadings have been found particularly for analogies, classifications, and series—either in words or in perception material—and for problem solving.

Two major developments followed in psychology. In the first place, Spearman's important example taught psychologists to look beyond particular concrete criteria and test scores to underlying factors. Not all learned the lesson; some self-styled practical psychologists called factor analysis "mysticism"—a curious name for a basically scientific procedure. Second, it gave to intelligence testing a more positive theoretical basis than had the basically atheoretical empirical approaches of men like Binet and Wechsler, whom Spearman severely criticized, and whose work ultimately led, as Spearman and others clearly foresaw, to the scientifically cynical view that "intelligence is what intelligence tests measure." If the methodological elegance of Spearman's contributions had been more generally appreciated, many pointless experiments based on arbitrary "intelligence tests" would never have been conducted and the generations of psychologists who were working between 1900 and 1925 would have been spared many wrong leads and outright misconceptions.

Even among those who took up factor analysis, Spearman's theories soon ran into difficulties (see, e.g., Thurstone 1947). Godfrey Thompson pointed out that an alternative model could fit the same

statistics (1939). Experiments also appeared showing that the correlational hierarchy requiring the postulation of a single general ability was found only with *certain* choice of variables. Spearman has been reproached by some for arbitrarily removing variables that produced "group factors," and his first major book, *The Nature of "Intelligence" and the Principle of Cognition* (1923), certainly shows how impatient he was to establish a general factor. At that time he was concerned only with purifying the concept of intelligence. By the time his second book, *The Abilities of Man*, appeared in 1927, he had accepted the reality of several group factors— perseveration, oscillation, persistence, and fluency —and had, with his students and associates, done more than anyone else to define them.

It was at this point that Hotelling, Truman Kelley, and Thurstone generalized Spearman's factor analysis into what we now know as multiple factor analysis, and in so doing they incorporated purely mathematical notions that lay ready for such integration with Spearman's methodological ones. As a result, all broad factors found then assumed equal status. Psychologists, unfortunately, have been slower than physicists to perceive the importance of mathematical models to the scientific growth of their ideas, and around 1930, when Thurstone began to publish, only a minority— though an impressive minority—reacted favorably or even intelligently to these radical ideas. Among clinicians, for example, a common reaction was that factors were "unreal abstractions" unrelated to their problems. Or, again, psychologists teaching the history or methodology of their discipline often mistook multiple factor analysis for a revival of faculty psychology, oblivious to the vast difference between creating a faculty by giving it a name and discovering a functional unity by correlation. The manipulative experimenters, in the classical tradition of Wundt, were puzzled by the absence of manipulation in factor analytic investigations, for Spearman, although he was trained by Wundt (he obtained his PH.D. at Leipzig in 1908), rejected the fine atomism of experiments on perception and sensation and sought instead to "connect the psychics of the laboratory with those of real life" (quoted in Burt & Myers 1946, p. 68). Incidentally, gestalt psychology, which was moving in the same direction at the same time, never recognized that what we now call the multivariate experimental method, built on procedures implicit in and developed on the basis of Spearman's work, contains an effective holistic and "real life" treatment of social and general behavior.

Both Spearman's method and his specific views on ability and other structures have necessarily been further developed, as are all fertile contributions to science. Factor analysis is now multiple factor analysis; and multivariate experimental design, assessing the simultaneous effects of many variables, is recognized as a new principle of research. The general factor that Spearman sought is now regarded as being a second order rather than a primary factor, and it is thought to consist perhaps of two factors—fluid and crystallized general intelligence.

Noegenetic laws

Spearman's cognitive laws have not had the important impact on the development of psychology that his contributions to methodology and his work on intelligence have had. His interest in establishing these laws was rooted in his profound sense of the history and philosophy of science, which made him keenly aware of the absence of any adequate general laws in psychology. He believed that English associationism (of Locke, Hume, Bain, et al.) was the only existent systematic attempt to formulate such laws (apart from a few theories limited, for example, to perception, such as the Weber–Fechner law or the merely descriptive reflexological laws of conditioning), but he regarded the laws of association as only anoegenetic explanations of the *reproduction* of mental content, not as explanatory of the genesis of *new* mental content. The noegenetic laws, in contrast, assert that the perception of two fundaments tends to evoke a relation between them, and that the presentation of a fundament and a relation will tend to educe a new fundament. This applies in principle to even the simplest cognitive activity, as well as to the processes determined by the general intelligence factor. Whether the "tendency" to perceive a relation between, say, π and e, eventuates in a perception depends on the intelligence of the perceiver. An analogies test, for example, immediately illustrates in its two parts both of these noegenetic laws. In his penultimate (and slender) book, *Creative Mind* (1930), Spearman developed further the implications of his noegenetic laws, aware that this aspect of his work had received little recognition.

Spearman's last major work, *Psychology Down the Ages* (1937), was an ambitious attempt to describe and interpret the development of psychology over two thousand years. The book has many powerful ideas and insights, even if Spearman's earnest commitment to the validity of his own theories prevented it from being an ideally detached history; Cyril Burt has described it as an attempt to show "how all the acceptable formula-

tions were really dim foreshadowings of the fundamental noegenetic laws" (see Burt & Myers 1946, p. 71). The book permitted Spearman, in his early seventies, a leisurely return to the contemplative philosophical interests of his youth.

In Spearman's case, it seems particularly necessary to relate his scientific creativity to his life and his personality. It would be hard to imagine a life pattern less similar to the academic norm. Coming from an English family of established status and some eminence, Spearman became an officer in the regular army because, he said, this offered him more leisure and freedom to study than did other professions. He served in the Burmese war and held the rank of major. Resigning after the Boer War, at 40, he was recommended by McDougall to a newly created position at University College, London. His first book, *The Nature of "Intelligence,"* appeared in his sixtieth year. Although a person of very definite opinions, whose students worked on thesis topics that fitted into his own monumental work (and enjoyed it), he possessed remarkable charm and a capacity to stimulate and reassure. As Burt, who worked with and succeeded him, remarked, "Few have possessed his gift of coördinating the research interests of pupils . . . on one single dominating and fertile theme" (see Burt & Myers 1946, p. 71). On retiring he went to America and with a former student, Karl Holzinger, worked on a unitary-traits project.

In addition to making a major contribution to the theory of human abilities in the first quarter of the twentieth century, Spearman gave great impetus to those multivariate experimental methods that have since revolutionized other areas, and thus he takes his place with the few great names in psychology during that period.

RAYMOND B. CATTELL

[*For discussion of the subsequent development of Spearman's ideas, see* EXPERIMENTAL DESIGN; FACTOR ANALYSIS; INTELLIGENCE AND INTELLIGENCE TESTING; NONPARAMETRIC STATISTICS, *article on* RANKING METHODS; *and the biographies of* CATTELL; KELLEY; THORNDIKE; THURSTONE.]

WORKS BY SPEARMAN

1904   "General Intelligence" Objectively Determined and Measured. *American Journal of Psychology* 15:201–293.
(1923) 1927   *The Nature of "Intelligence" and the Principle of Cognition.* 2d ed. London: Macmillan.
1927   *The Abilities of Man: Their Nature and Measurement.* London: Macmillan.
(1930) 1931   *Creative Mind.* New York: Appleton.
1937   *Psychology Down the Ages.* 2 vols. London: Macmillan.

1950   SPEARMAN, C. E.; and JONES, LLEWELLYN W. *Human Ability.* London: Macmillan. → A continuation of Spearman's *The Abilities of Man* (1927).

SUPPLEMENTARY BIBLIOGRAPHY

BURT, CYRIL; and MYERS, C. S. 1946 Charles Edward Spearman, 1863–1945. *Psychological Review* 53:67–71.

THOMAS, FRANK C. 1935 *Ability and Knowledge: The Standpoint of the London School.* London: Macmillan.

THOMPSON, GODFREY (1939) 1951 *The Factorial Analysis of Human Ability.* 5th ed. Boston: Houghton Mifflin.

THOMPSON, GODFREY 1947 Charles Spearman: 1863–1945. Royal Society, London, *Obituary Notices of Fellows* 5:373–385.

THURSTONE, LOUIS L. 1947 *Multiple-factor Analysis: A Development and Expansion of* The Vectors of Mind. Univ. of Chicago Press.

SPECIALIZATION AND EXCHANGE

Modern economies, whether capitalistic or socialistic, whether fully developed or not, are characterized by specialization of the means of production and by exchange of goods and services. The earliest and most common form of specialization is that of labor. Interrelated with it, particularly in modern developed economies, is specialization of machines. In manufacturing, the advantages of both are best realized through specialization of plants and, in some cases, of enterprises. Finally, there is regional and local specialization. All of these forms of specialization imply an exchange economy.

Specialization of labor. The advantages of specialization of labor were recognized at least as early as the times of Plato and Xenophon and were pointed out by several of the mercantilist writers before Adam Smith. In the *Republic* (II), Plato indeed regarded the city-state as having come into being because of the mutual needs and the resulting interdependence of individuals. Out of this interdependence arises the division of labor, the specialization of individuals in different occupations in accordance with their natural gifts, and the mutual exchange of their products for those of others out of self-interest. A further consequence of exchange is the development of markets and the use of a currency to facilitate transactions. All goods are produced in greater quantities and are of superior quality than otherwise.

By the time Adam Smith wrote *The Wealth of Nations*, the concept of the division of labor must have been familiar to him from the works of William Petty, Bernard Mandeville, Adam Ferguson, Francis Hutcheson, and others. Smith, however, surpassed their treatment of the subject not only in the thoroughness of his analysis but even more in the importance he attributed to the phenomenon in his theory of economic progress: "The greatest improvement in the productive powers of labour, and the greater part of the skill, dexterity, and judgment with which it is any where directed, or applied, seem to have been the effects of the division of labour" ([1776] 1950, vol. 1, p. 5).

Smith's description of the "trade of the pin-maker" served to illustrate how a single manufacturing process could be subdivided into a number of distinct operations, each performed by a specialized worker. He applied the term "division of labor," second, to the quite different case of the separation into production stages of the whole process of manufacture, from raw material to finished product, of a commodity such as woolen cloth (*ibid.*, p. 7); and, third, to the case in which a handicraft worker specialized exclusively in the production of a single commodity, such as nails (*ibid.*, p. 8).

Bücher (1893, pp. 290–293 in the 1901 edition) supplemented Smith's treatment by adding a fourth and a fifth type of division of labor: the specialization of workers by vocation or occupation, which Smith probably had in mind when he referred to the "separation of different trades and employments from one another" ([1776] 1950, vol. 1, p. 7); and what Bücher called the displacement of labor by machines, the latter taking over and performing production steps previously done by hand. This change in technique is called an increase in the division of labor, on the ground that it involves an increase in the variety of different employments of workers: there are now workers engaged in making the machines as well as in operating them.

Smith found the advantages of the division of labor to be (1) the increase in skill acquired by each workman, (2) the saving in time through concentration on a single task, and (3) the stimulus provided for the invention of labor-saving machines. Cannan has pointed out that Smith ignored (*ibid.*, p. 12n.), and in fact in a degree denied (*ibid.*, pp. 17–18), the advantage (stressed by Plato) to be gained by the assignment of individuals to the tasks for which they are best fitted. However, Babbage ([1832] 1963, chapter 19) convincingly developed the proposition that an important gain from specialization of labor was that it permitted the utilization of precisely the degree of skill or strength requisite for each process, with a consequent saving in costs.

Babbage also recognized that specialization

of labor was as effective in "mental" as in mechanical operations (*ibid.*, chapter 20); and he illustrated the point by reference to the various managerial functions involved in the operation of a mine that could be allocated to different specialists. The extent to which the principle of the division of labor has been applied in managerial organization of the modern corporation is well known (see, e.g., Florence 1953, chapter 4).

Although impressed mainly by the advantages of labor specialization, Smith did briefly recognize one disadvantage: When workers are confined to a few simple operations, they become stupid and ignorant ([1776] 1950, vol. 2, p. 267). Marx quoted Smith with bitter approval and added that the division of labor is a capitalist method of increasing relative surplus value by crippling the individual workers (1867–1879, vol. 1, p. 400 in 1906 edition). The further point that a high degree of specialization of labor increases the unemployed worker's difficulty in finding new employment was stressed by Marshall ([1890] 1961, p. 260).

It has also been claimed (e.g., in Lachmann 1951, p. 426) that specialization of labor produces increased inequality of income, for it promotes a wider spread between the performance and income of individuals of different abilities. Lampman (1957, p. 522) has pointed out, however, that any such tendency appears to be offset by other circumstances tending to reduce the dispersion of worker incomes—such as the elimination of lower-skill jobs by the development of specialized machines.

Specialization of machines. Adam Smith's view that the division of labor is the primary source of economic progress was early disputed by Lauderdale (1804, pp. 285–304), who maintained that it is not so much through the division of labor as it is through the substitution of tools and machines for labor that mankind comes to enjoy "that extended opulence which expands itself throughout civilized society" (1804, p. 297). Babbage ([1832] 1963, pp. 173–175) illustrated the way in which a machine may be expected to replace labor in a given process as soon as an individual worker concentrates on a very limited and simple operation. Machines contribute to economic progress by providing sources of power that greatly supplement human power; they make possible operations too delicate for the human hand and the production of articles (e.g., replaceable parts of a larger implement) with an accuracy not otherwise obtainable; they reduce the burden-

someness of labor; they are economical of materials; they speed up production; and they result in a reduction in costs of production—provided that they are used to capacity (see also Marshall [1890] 1961, vol. 1, pp. 255–266).

While a machine may initially be as specialized as was the worker whom it replaces, it is likely, on further development, to combine a series of operations or even a whole production process. In fact, in recent years, with the development of automatic and semiautomatic mechanisms, machines are often specialized only in the sense that they concentrate on the production of a single commodity or class of commodities. Kimball ([1913] 1947, pp. 461–462) describes, for example, an automatic plant for the production of automobile frames which is essentially one great machine automatically transforming steel plates into the finished product. With the development of modern high-speed electronic computers and data-processing machines, the modern assembly line can turn out a wide variety of different color combinations, body styles, accessory equipment, and types of engines in the automobiles it produces. As a result of automation the machine process has in a sense become less specialized.

While the division of labor, particularly in the earlier phases of the industrial revolution, contributed to mechanization, the latter has in more recent times come to determine in turn the pattern of the division of labor. On the assembly line, the specialization of labor conforms to the pattern of production laid out by the engineers. Many types of machine processes still require manual feeding, control, or regulation; and in these cases the division of labor essentially takes the form of specialization of workers in repetitive operations necessary because automation has not yet reached these processes. The division of labor in these cases is simply the labor counterpart of the specialization of machines. However, in wide ranges of modern industry, automation is releasing labor from the most monotonous tasks, substituting electronic controls for manual controls. The process is accompanied by the development of new varieties of specialization of labor necessary for the development and maintenance of automation systems.

Adam Smith's important observation that the extent of the division of labor is limited by the size of the market ([1776] 1950, book 1, chapter 3) is equally applicable to the specialization of machines. A large enterprise can fully employ more highly specialized machinery and labor and thus can reduce its cost per unit of output below that of its smaller competitors (Marshall [1890] 1961, vol. 1, pp. 285, 315).

Similarly, Chamberlin has ascribed the economies of scale of the individual plant or enterprise to "(1) increased specialization, made possible in general by the fact that the aggregate of resources is larger, and (2) qualitatively different and technologically more efficient units or factors, particularly machinery, made possible by a wise selection from among the greater range of technical possibilities opened up by the greater resources" ([1948] 1957, pp. 175–176). A somewhat different way of viewing economies of scale (e.g., McLeod & Hahn 1949) attributes them to the presence of indivisibilities in the factors of production; as size of plant increases, a more nearly optimum proportion of the factors can be realized, with resulting decline in cost per unit. In a small plant a highly specialized machine cannot be fully utilized, and yet a different production technique that did not employ the specialized machine would be even less economical. Under these circumstances an increase in size of plant, with fuller utilization of specialized units, yields economies of scale even in the absence of either increased specialization or a change in technique.

At any given stage in the development of techniques, the extent to which it is profitable to carry specialization of labor and machines varies with the type of production process. For example, a large spinning firm does not exhibit a higher degree of specialization than one of 20,000 spindles (see Robinson [1931] 1959, pp. 17–19). In many industries large plants differ from small ones only in the number of identical machines employed. Safety-razor blades, for example, are made by a standard set of machines, each set contributing a relatively small proportion of the plant's output; the technical economies of specialization of machines are attained equally by a small plant and by a large plant. On the other hand, in the case of such industries as farm machinery, automobiles, and typewriters, the output of a single plant of most efficient scale will account for 5 per cent or more of the total output of the industry [see Bain 1954; see also ECONOMIES OF SCALE].

Specialization of plants and firms. Full utilization of a plant's most specialized machinery and labor is most likely to be achieved when the plant concentrates on the production of a single type of a commodity so that it may obtain the economies that go with long and uninterrupted runs. The result tends to be the specialization of plants and, to some extent, of firms. For example, a spinning mill may specialize on a narrow range of counts, or a plant producing electric motors may specialize on a single size of motor.

Although individual business enterprises may specialize to the same extent, there are important circumstances in modern developed economies that favor the multiplant, multiproduct firm: the desirability of spreading risks, the advantages of vertical and horizontal integration, and the economies of marketing, finance, and managerial organization (Robinson [1931] 1959, chapters 3–8).

As an industry grows, the increasing specialization of firms, the development of by-product industries, and the expansion of subsidiary industries that supply means of production are all sources of what Marshall called external economies ([1890] 1961, vol. 1, book 4, chapters 9–11). More broadly viewed, the whole industrial structure of the economy changes in response to economic growth and technological change. New industries come into existence and old industries subdivide. The industrial operations of an economy are an interrelated whole whose pattern of specialization is constantly changing, constantly revealing a new industrial fabric as economic progress occurs. [See Young 1928; see also EXTERNAL ECONOMIES AND DISECONOMIES.]

Regional and local specialization. Well before Torrens and Ricardo, the view was developed (e.g., by Gervaise in 1720) that a nation, by specializing in the production of one commodity and exporting it in exchange for commodities in the production of which other countries specialize, could acquire the imported commodities with a smaller amount of labor than it would take to produce them at home (Schumpeter 1954, pp. 373–376). Although this view might be liberally interpreted to imply an understanding of the principle of comparative advantage, Adam Smith's illustrations ([1776] 1950, vol. 1, pp. 422–423) suggest that he at least was thinking in terms of the absolute advantage (and, particularly, natural advantage) of one country in the production of a particular commodity. Somewhat later, in 1808, Torrens made it clear that a country's specialization in the production of one commodity rather than another depends upon the existence of a comparative, not necessarily an absolute, advantage in the production of the first commodity as against the other (Schumpeter 1954, p. 607).

Regions, like nations, are differently endowed with resources (factors of production), and it follows that regional specialization, in accordance with the principle of comparative advantage, leads to increased efficiency in production. Regions differ in climate, qualities of soil, mineral resources, transportation facilities and their cost, quality and wage rates of different types of labor, and interest rates on borrowed capital. Some of these differences would not persist in the presence of perfect mobility of capital and labor; but interregional mobility of these factors, while greater than international mobility, is far from perfect.

Florence (1953, pp. 37–43) has measured the degree of regional localization for different industries and has shown that it varies greatly. Agriculture is moderately localized by climatic, soil, and transportation circumstances. Mining and quarrying necessarily are highly localized. Some industries have become localized by the necessity of having easy access to one or more of the essential raw materials (e.g., steel). Other industries are located close to the markets for their products and consequently are dispersed (e.g., baking). Some industries have become concentrated in particular regions without reference to either sources of raw materials or markets for products (e.g., cotton textiles); their location is to be explained by the availability of sources of labor or power, an advantageous situation with regard to transportation facilities, or even by historical accident. Still other industries are localized by their dependence upon other industries (e.g., textile machinery). [See SPATIAL ECONOMICS.]

Once an industry has become established in a region, there are substantial advantages in what Weber called agglomeration (1909, p. 20 in 1929 edition)—the concentration of related industries at a single point (usually a metropolitan area) within a region. Marshall ([1890] 1961, vol. 1, book 4, chapter 10), who included these advantages among his external economies arising from the general development of an industry, stressed the importance of a locally available supply of trained labor with the special skills particularly required, and the existence of subsidiary and auxiliary industries. Others have pointed to the advantage offered by easily available services for replacement and repair of machinery; to the convenience to customers when the industry is concentrated in a single location (Weber 1909, pp. 129–130 in 1929 edition); to the availability of expert services (Florence 1953, p. 85); and to the possibility of a higher degree of specialization of plants when they are closely associated in a particular locality (*ibid.*; Stigler 1951, p. 192).

Exchange. For Adam Smith the specialization of labor is feasible only in an economy in which exchange of products between workers or firms is possible; it must be a market economy. In fact, Smith believed that the division of labor originated in a propensity in human nature "to truck, barter, and exchange one thing for another" ([1776] 1950, vol. 1, p. 15). The inconvenience of barter results, in turn, in the invention of money, and thus in the emergence of a price system. In this way, "society itself grows to be what is properly a commercial society" (*ibid.*, p. 24). Since the extent of the division of labor is limited by the extent of the market, economic progress requires the development of improved means of transportation and the expansion of trade from a local basis to a world basis (*ibid.*, book 1, chapter 3).

Actually, trade and exchange preceded the appearance of the division of labor (Bücher 1893, p. 296 in 1901 edition). Exchange of surpluses among household producing-units in primitive communities is a common phenomenon, often unaccompanied by specialization of labor by households or even within the household. On the other hand, extensive division of labor within the household can develop without resulting in exchange (*ibid.*, pp. 304–305). However, division of labor within the household is the beginning of the development of separate occupations; and the development of labor specialization in occupations is the essential basis for the development of trade. So Smith's hypothetical anthropology was not too far from the truth.

For Smith, exchange performs the function of enabling the laborer to dispose of his surplus product and to obtain in turn an equivalent value of the surplus product of other laborers ([1776] 1950, vol. 1, p. 17). There is no gain from trade; exchange simply makes possible the specialization of labor, which is the source of increased production. Similarly, foreign trade provides an outlet for a country's surplus produce, which arises from specialization in the production of those commodities which it can produce more cheaply than other countries can and which it exchanges for the surplus products of other countries.

That exchange is not simply a device for disposing of surpluses but is mutually advantageous in a positive way is implicit in the principle of comparative advantage as applied to either international or interregional trade (see Ohlin 1933, chapter 2). If, for example, the endowment of factors in region A gives it a comparative advantage in the production and export of agricultural products, and that in region B gives it a comparative advantage in the production and export of manufactured products, the effect of interregional trade will be to improve the terms of trade of agricultural products for manufactured products in A and those of manufactured products for agricultural products in B. The real income of the factors of production will increase in both regions. [*See* INTERNATIONAL TRADE, *article on* THEORY.]

Similarly, the development of the marginal utility theory of value was accompanied by a recognition of the mutual gains from exchanges between individual buyers and sellers (e.g., Jevons 1871, pp. 153–158 in 1879 edition). Although the price of the commodity is equal to its marginal utility for both buyer and seller, the exchange results in an increase in total utility for each of them. Marshall ([1890] 1961, vol. 1, pp. 124–137) analyzed the gains from trade by means of the concept of consumer's surplus—the excess of the price which a consumer would be willing to pay for a unit of a commodity, rather than go without it, over the price that he actually does pay [*see* CONSUMER'S SURPLUS]. More recent analysis can demonstrate the gains from trade more effectively by means of indifference curve analysis. [*See* UTILITY.]

BERNARD F. HALEY

BIBLIOGRAPHY

BABBAGE, CHARLES (1832) 1963 *On the Economy of Machinery and Manufactures.* 4th ed., enl. New York: Kelley.

BAIN, JOE S. 1954 Economies of Scale, Concentration, and the Condition of Entry in Twenty Manufacturing Industries. *American Economic Review* 44:15–39.

BÜCHER, KARL (1893) 1912 *Industrial Evolution.* New York: Holt. → First published as *Die Entstehung der Volkswirtschaft.*

CHAMBERLIN, EDWARD H. (1948) 1957 Proportionality, Divisibility, and Economies of Scale. Pages 169–204 in Edward H. Chamberlin, *Towards a More General Theory of Value.* New York: Oxford Univ. Press. → First published in the *Quarterly Journal of Economics.*

FLORENCE, P. SARGANT (1953) 1961 *The Logic of British and American Industry: A Realistic Analysis of Economic Structure and Government.* Rev. ed. London: Routledge.

JEVONS, W. STANLEY (1871) 1965 *The Theory of Political Economy.* 5th ed. New York: Kelley.

KIMBALL, DEXTER S. (1913) 1947 *Principles of Industrial Organization.* 6th ed. New York: McGraw-Hill.

LACHMANN, L. M. 1951 The Science of Human Action. *Economica* New Series 18:412–427.

LAMPMAN, ROBERT J. 1957 The Effectiveness of Some Institutions in Changing the Distribution of Income. *American Economic Review* 47, no. 2:519–528.

LAUDERDALE, JAMES MAITLAND (1804) 1819 *An Inquiry Into the Nature and Origin of Public Wealth, and Into the Means and Causes of Its Increase.* 2d ed., enl. Edinburgh: Constable.

MCLEOD, A. N.; and HAHN, F. H. 1949 Proportionality, Divisibility, and Economies of Scale: Two Comments. *Quarterly Journal of Economics* 63:128–137.

MARSHALL, ALFRED (1890) 1961 *Principles of Economics.* 9th ed. 2 vols. New York and London: Macmillan. → A variorum edition.

MARX, KARL (1867–1879) 1925–1926 *Capital: A Critique of Political Economy.* 3 vols. Chicago: Kerr. → Volume 1: *The Process of Capitalist Production.* Volume 2: *The Process of Circulation of Capital.* Volume 3: *The Process of Capitalist Production as a Whole.* Volume 1 was published in 1867. The manuscripts of Volumes 2 and 3 were written between 1867 and 1879. They were first published posthumously in German in 1885 and 1894.

OHLIN, BERTIL (1933) 1957 *Interregional and International Trade.* Harvard Economic Studies, Vol. 39. Cambridge, Mass.: Harvard Univ. Press.

ROBINSON, E. A. G. (1931) 1959 *The Structure of Competitive Industry.* Rev. ed. Univ of Chicago Press.

SCHUMPETER, JOSEPH A. (1954) 1960 *History of Economic Analysis.* Edited by E. B. Schumpeter. New York: Oxford Univ. Press.

SCITOVSKY, TIBOR 1951 *Welfare and Competition: The Economics of a Fully Employed Economy.* Chicago: Irwin.

SMITH, ADAM (1776) 1950 *An Inquiry Into the Nature and Causes of the Wealth of Nations.* 6th ed. 2 vols. London: Methuen. → A paperback edition was published in 1963 by Irwin.

STIGLER, GEORGE J. 1951 The Division of Labor Is Limited by the Extent of the Market. *Journal of Political Economy* 59:185–193.

WEBER, ALFRED (1909) 1957 *Theory of the Location of Industries.* Univ. of Chicago Press; Cambridge Univ. Press. → First published as *Über den Standort der Industrien.* Teil 1: Reine Theorie des Standorts.

YOUNG, ALLYN A. 1928 Increasing Returns and Economic Progress. *Economic Journal* 38:527–542.

SPECK, FRANK G.

Frank Gouldsmith Speck (1881–1950), American anthropologist, was born in Brooklyn, New York. After being trained by Franz Boas at Columbia University, he became a Harrison fellow at the University of Pennsylvania in 1907 and founded the department of anthropology there. Under his leadership a program of undergraduate and graduate instruction was initiated. He remained the senior member of the department for forty years and was chairman for most of this period. He was the author of the first monograph in the "Anthropological Publications" that the museum of the University of Pennsylvania began to publish in 1909, and he was the founder of the Philadelphia Anthropological Society, which celebrated its fiftieth anniversary in 1962.

Speck's boyhood interest in Indians, natural history, and languages reached scholarly fruition in his mature years, when the wide range of his specialized interests and the nature of his field work made him a unique figure in American anthropology. His interest in the field of natural history, combined with his anthropological knowledge, led to pioneer articles in "ethnoscience," such as his "Ethnoherpetology of the Catawba and Cherokee Indians" (1946). While still an undergraduate he became interested in eastern Algonquian languages (Pequot–Mohegan and Delaware Mohican), which were thought by some to have already died out; however, he found and interviewed surviving speakers of these languages. This continuing interest in retrieving Indian languages from oblivion gave Speck a head start in anthropological linguistics and set a pattern for further studies. He expanded his knowledge to include other Algonquian tongues, learning to speak several of them and recording texts. Speck attained competence in the languages of four other linguistic stocks: Uchean, Muskhogean, Siouan, and Iroquoian. In his *Catawba Texts* (1934) he salvaged all that he could from the last speakers of this eastern Siouan language.

Speck did his first ethnological field work in 1904 among the displaced Yuchi of Oklahoma, when the state was still the Indian Territory (1909; 1910). He also published material on southeastern Indians: Creek (1907*a*), Chickasaw (1907*b*), and Osage (1907*c*). The investigation of the remnants of the Algonquian tribes of the eastern United States occupied him for many years thereafter. In his last years he studied Iroquois groups, stimulating a fruitful revival of interest in these Indians. Thus, while other American ethnologists were devoting themselves chiefly to Indians west of the Mississippi, Speck, almost singlehanded, was surveying Indian communities of Algonquian tradition, however much acculturated, from Labrador, through New England, Delaware, and Virginia, to the few surviving Machapunga in North Carolina. Few ethnologists have been known personally in so many communities or over so wide a geographical area or been so warmly welcomed. Speck studied Indians with delight, lived with them, and befriended them.

In addition to his work on languages, Speck collected a formidable body of folklore, some in text; did pioneer work in ethnomusicology, beginning with his publication of *Ceremonial Songs of the Creek and Yuchi Indians* (1911); studied religious beliefs with particular interest; and systematically collected material on decorative art and technology. His monographs cover such subjects as moose-hair embroidery, wampum, Cherokee basketry, the use of birch bark, gourds and masks, the double-curve motif in decorative art, and shamanism. Speck's discovery of the hunting-territory system of the northern Algonquians is well known, as is his defense of its aboriginality as a form of private property. This ran counter to the then current unilinear doctrine of cultural evolution, according to which this form of ownership was impossible at the hunting stage of human development. He began mapping hunting territories before 1915. His empirical approach prepared him for local variations and led him to modify some of his original conceptions. In the 1920s he also made and published detailed and definitive maps of the linguistic and ethnic boundaries of the Indians of southern New England. His monographic studies of the Naskapi (1935) and the Penobscot (1940) are among the few publications available that give a rounded picture of the life of the Indians of the eastern woodlands.

Speck's interest in arts and crafts led to indefatigable collecting, which became an integral part of his field work. Although no precise records are available, thousands of objects must have passed through his hands in the course of his career. In addition to the museum of the University of Pennsylvania, half a dozen other museums in the United States and several in Canada benefited from his collecting activity, as did the Pitt-Rivers Museum in England and the Danish National Museum.

The details that reached the printed page in Speck's work were never assembled in haste. They were always evaluated against a wide-ranging and masterly knowledge of relevant linguistic and ethnographic facts and historical documents. Speck was always an ethnohistorian, although this term appears only in his later writings. In this perspective particularly, the geographical scope, variety, and quality of his observations and interpretations of data can be seen as a unique contribution to North American ethnology.

A. IRVING HALLOWELL

[*See also* INDIANS, NORTH AMERICAN; *and the biographies of* BOAS; KROEBER.]

WORKS BY SPECK

1907*a*   *The Creek Indians of Taskigi Town.* American Anthropological Association, Memoirs, Vol. 2, part 2. Lancaster, Pa.: New Era.
1907*b*   Notes on Chickasaw Ethnology and Folk-lore. *Journal of American Folk-lore* 20:50–58.
1907*c*   Notes on the Ethnology of the Osage Indians. Pennsylvania, University of, Department of Archaeology, *Transactions* 2, part 2:159–171.
1909   *Ethnology of the Yuchi Indians.* University of Pennsylvania, Museum Anthropological Publications, Vol. 1, no. 1. Philadelphia: The Museum.
1910   Yuchi. Pages 1003–1007 in *Handbook of American Indians.* Washington: U.S. Bureau of American Ethnology.

1911   *Ceremonial Songs of the Creek and Yuchi Indians.* University of Pennsylvania, Museum Anthropological Publications, Vol. 1, no. 2. Philadelphia: The Museum.

1934   *Catawba Texts.* New York: Columbia Univ. Press.

1935   *Naskapi: The Savage Hunters of the Labrador Peninsula.* Norman: Univ. of Oklahoma Press.

1940   *Penobscot Man: The Life History of a Forest Tribe in Maine.* Philadelphia: Univ. of Pennsylvania Press.

1946   Ethnoherpetology of the Catawba and Cherokee Indians. *Journal of the Washington Academy of Sciences* 36:355–360.

WORKS ABOUT SPECK

HALLOWELL, A. IRVING   1951   Frank Gouldsmith Speck: 1881–1950. *American Anthropologist* New Series 53: 67–75.

WALLACE, ANTHONY F. C.   1951   The Frank G. Speck Collection. American Philosophical Society, *Proceedings* 95:286–289.

WITTHOFT, JOHN   1951   Anthropological Bibliography: 1903–1950. *American Anthropologist* New Series 53: 75–87.

SPECTRAL ANALYSIS

See TIME SERIES.

SPECULATION, HEDGING, AND ARBITRAGE

Arbitrage is the simultaneous purchase and sale of equivalent assets at prices which guarantee a fixed profit at the time of the transactions, although the life of the assets and, hence, the consummation of the profit may be delayed until some future date. The key element in the definition is that the amount of profit be determined with certainty. It specifically excludes transactions which guarantee a minimum rate of return but which also offer an option for increased profits.

Hedging is the simultaneous purchase and sale of two assets in the expectation of a gain from different subsequent movements in the price of those assets. Usually the two assets are equivalent in all respects except maturity.

Speculation is the purchase or sale of an asset in the expectation of a gain from changes in the price of that asset.

Arbitrage. Arbitrage can occur in a number of ways. For example, a wholesale egg merchant in Chicago may find that eggs are being quoted in New York at a price that exceeds the Chicago price by more than the costs of transportation between New York and Chicago. He can then buy eggs in Chicago, simultaneously sell them for delivery in New York next week, and ship the eggs for an assured profit. The key consideration is that the instant the transactions are completed, the profit is assured, even though delivery may not take place

until later. Similarly, a foreign exchange arbitrageur may be able to buy British pounds sterling in New York for $2.80 and sell them on the Swiss market for $2.8010. Since, in this case, there are no "shipping" costs, the entire difference, except for minor transaction costs, is profit.

In the pursuit of these profits, arbitrageurs tend to force prices in all markets toward equality. The arbitrageur's transactions tend to raise prices in the cheap market and depress prices in the expensive one. Because of transaction costs and transportation costs, literal equality will not be achieved. But neglecting the former costs, completely effective arbitrage would eliminate the incentive to shop among markets. To the extent that arbitrageurs, through specialization, can seek out market imperfections more efficiently than other market participants can, they will increase social welfare.

Because arbitrage profits are riskless, they are hard to get. Since most obvious opportunities are quickly eliminated by the activity itself, most actual arbitrage activity involves more complicated operations than are suggested by the above examples. The foreign exchange arbitrageur is more likely to use his dollars to buy German marks, use those marks to buy pounds, and sell those pounds for dollars (Grubel 1963). Such profits as do exist are a recompense for the detailed attention and time invested in seeking out those opportunities.

Many operations customarily designated as arbitrage are not arbitrage at all. For example, if the egg merchant in the previous example had purchased eggs in Chicago at a price lower than in New York, but lower by less than costs of transport, in the hope that Chicago prices would go to a par with New York, he would not be engaging in bona fide arbitrage because the profit is not assured.

Hedging. An understanding of hedging requires an understanding of the elements of the theory of asset holding. Individuals will hold inventories of assets only in the expectation of increases in the value of those assets by at least enough to cover the costs of carrying the assets. In the case of financial assets, these carrying costs are largely the costs of the money tied up. In the case of physical inventories, there will also be costs of storage and spoilage or deterioration. Set against these costs will be certain benefits from the inventory: for merchants, for example, the inventory may be the means to increased sales or commissions.

The net costs of carrying inventory may be positive or negative, but in economic equilibrium the marginal cost of a unit of inventory must be equal to the expected price appreciation of that unit of inventory (Working 1933; Brennan 1958). This introduces an asymmetry into the behavior of expected changes in prices of storable assets. At no time can the expected price one period from now be greater than the current price by more than the marginal cost of storage for that period. Once the difference becomes equal to the costs of storage, an increase in expected future price will increase today's price as well. On the other hand, there is no similar lower limit on the extent of expected price decreases: if prices are expected to fall, current prices will be depressed by a reduction in the amount of inventories held until the marginal value of those inventories is equal to the expected price decline. But while inventories can be accumulated indefinitely, they can be reduced only to zero.

When inventories are increased, the holder exposes himself to increased capital risk from fluctuations in the price of the goods being held. If the merchant is a risk averter, increasing his inventory increases his subjective costs of storage. To reduce that risk, he may hedge by selling for future delivery at some fixed price some or all of the inventory he owns. By doing so, he passes the risk to the speculator who buys the futures contracts.

Traditionally, this reduction in risk is supposed to be the primary advantage of hedging. To illustrate this argument, assume that a Chicago wheat merchant purchases 1,000,000 bushels of No. 2 soft red winter wheat in July at $1.45 a bushel for his inventory. He is now exposed to the risk of changes in the value of his inventory due to fluctuations in the price of his wheat: he is speculating on the price of wheat. If he prefers, however, he may sell futures contracts on the Chicago Board of Trade, promising delivery of 1,000,000 bushels of No. 2 soft red winter wheat any time in December at the price currently quoted for December futures, say, $1.52. If he does so, he is clearly "hedging," as we have defined it, since his wealth is now affected only by relative movements in the prices of the wheat and of the futures contracts. Conventional usage stresses the fact that by waiting until December and delivering his wheat on the futures contracts, the merchant is assured of a seven-cent gain on each and every bushel of wheat he owns. (Note that since he must pay storage costs on the wheat from July to December, this is not necessarily a profitable transaction.) This traditional view likens hedging to an arbitrage in which the merchant has eliminated his risk by passing it on to the speculator who purchases the futures contract.

This transaction, however, is not genuine arbitrage, nor is it typical of hedging at all. To be sure, the price of actual wheat will gain by seven cents relative to Chicago December futures *if* the wheat is held until December. It is possible, however, that some temporary shortage in supplies (due either to a spurt in demand or to a natural catastrophe) might occur, so that in October the price of wheat might rise to $1.52 or higher without a concomitant rise in the December futures. In such an event, the merchant would make a profit by selling the wheat and buying back the futures contract in October, since he would experience the same or a greater relative movement in prices while paying storage charges for a shorter period of time. In addition, by selling the wheat he would earn a commission which he would not get if he delivered the wheat on the futures contract. In other words, his hedge is really an option to benefit from a certain minimum relative price movement, but with freedom to take a larger gain if the opportunity arises.

In view of this, the premium of the December futures contract price over the actual wheat price in July is rarely enough to cover the actual costs of storing wheat from July to December. If the premium were usually that large, any amateur could earn a riskless profit, since hedging would result in zero profits at worst and positive profits whenever random events made it possible. As a result, hedging rarely takes the form of the textbook example.

In the usual case, hedging is undertaken in the hope or expectation that the gain on the hedge transaction will be greater than the current difference between the price of the futures contract and the price of the corresponding physical commodity. This may arise as in the illustration above or in a number of other ways. For example, the hedger may feel that wheat in Indianapolis is cheap relative to Chicago wheat and will rise by more, relative to the Chicago futures contract, than will Chicago wheat. Note that the Indianapolis wheat is not deliverable on the Chicago futures contract without incurring the cost of shipment to Chicago, and so the prospect of actual delivery is even more remote than in the earlier case. Similarly, the wheat hedged might be No. 1 white wheat at Toledo—different both in grade and in location from the Chicago futures contract.

Notice that, in financial terminology, the merchant has bought a "callable" asset and has sold an asset (bought a liability) with a maturity of five months. This is just the reverse of the bank that accepts ("buys") a demand deposit (a call liability) and invests the funds in (buys) a five-month loan or Treasury security. The merchant buys "short-lived assets" and "long-lived liabilities"; the bank buys "long-lived assets" and "short-lived liabilities."

In both cases hedger and bank alike can (and do) benefit from appropriate changes in the relative prices of the assets they hold. Their position is much safer than outright holding of either the asset or the liability alone, but it retains some risk and some hope of gain in each case (Cootner 1963). This is true even though in practice bank demand deposits are rather long-lived assets (Samuelson 1945).

These examples are known as "short" hedges, because the futures contracts are sold short first and bought back, or delivered against, later. Another form of hedge, the "long" hedge, arises when, for example, a merchant is asked in March, at a time when he has no wheat on hand, to deliver wheat to a flour mill at a fixed price of $2.00 in May. The merchant has the option of buying the wheat in March and holding it until May, or, if he feels that the current price difference between March and May wheat is too small, of *buying* May wheat futures. In the latter case, he would wait until May, take delivery of wheat on the futures contract, and in turn deliver the wheat to the flour mill (an unlikely procedure). Or he could hold the futures contract as protection until a lot of wheat of suitable price and quality becomes available, say in April, and then liquidate the contract. The transactions involving the initial purchase of futures and later selling the futures or taking delivery are called long hedges—protection against price rises.

Although transactions involving futures constitute most of what we call hedges, futures markets are not a prerequisite to hedging. One might buy shares of one textile company while selling those of another if one had feelings about the *relative* prosperity of the former but little assurance about the *over-all* prospects of the industry.

Regardless of whether merchants hedge to eliminate risk or to anticipate movements of relative prices, the hedge generally has less risk associated with it than does holding of either of the two assets constituting the hedge: the variance in value of the hedge is less than that of the assets themselves. When a merchant hedges, however, he need not reduce his risk exposure, since the lower risk per unit of inventory can be offset by holding a larger total volume of inventory. Since a larger level of inventories permits an individual merchant to increase his profitable sales opportunities, he has an incentive to hedge in order to increase inventories. Thus, even if the expected gain from holding a bushel of wheat outright is greater than the expected gain from holding a bushel of wheat hedged, the merchant may prefer to hedge in order to be able to finance a larger inventory holding. A common figure used in trade circles is that banks will permit a merchant to finance three to five times as much hedged inventory as unhedged.

Thus, the merchant may assume the same total risk in hedged contracts as he would have if he had held a smaller volume unhedged. In doing so, he exercises his opinion that he is better able to predict relative price movements than changes in the absolute level of prices and has increased the rate of return associated with the risk by specializing in the area in which he has a comparative advantage.

Hedging provides the economic rationale for the speculator. When the merchant hedges to reduce his personal risk, he does not change the total risk faced in the market. The risk of price fluctuation is merely transferred from the merchant to the futures speculator. The speculator accepts that risk voluntarily, in expectation of making money from the futures price changes.

For speculators as a group actually to earn a profit requires that merchants be willing to sell for future delivery at prices lower than those they expect in the future. One reason why they might do so is that by hedging, they eliminate risk; and the difference between the price at which they sell and the price they expect in the future is the risk premium—somewhat analogous to the premium one pays for insurance (over and above the actuarial value of the risk). Speculators, like insurance companies, would not furnish their services without being paid the premium. In this view, the speculator receives what the merchant is willing to pay for his services. Whether the speculator actually makes money or whether he is willing to accept the risk for the love of the gamble has been a matter of some controversy. The weight of the evidence now is that speculators do make money (Cootner 1960; Houthakker 1957), although some writers disagree (see Telser in Cootner 1960).

If speculators do make money, futures prices must rise over the period that they own futures, and fall during the period that they are "short" futures. Since hedgers are usually short and speculators usually long, Keynes (1930) argued that futures prices will normally rise over the lifetime of each contract. More recently, Cootner (1960) has shown that in agricultural commodities, hedgers are frequently long (and speculators are short) in the period prior to harvest when inventories are low. In cases where that pattern usually obtains, if speculators are to profit, futures prices must fall prior to harvest and rise thereafter. In short, payment of risk premiums would imply a seasonal pattern for futures prices.

In the view of hedging presented here, however,

the individual merchant, by hedging and paying the risk premium, gets the opportunity to increase his merchandising profits by an equal or greater amount. While this is true for every merchant individually, it can be true for the market as a whole only if speculation (1) increases the average price to the consumer or (2) reduces the costs of merchandising. The evidence on this point is that (1) is not true but that (2) is likely to be true, although it has not been proved (Working 1953).

The social value of speculation. In a world characterized by uncertainty, speculation is essential to the allocation of economic resources over time. There is no question of whether or not speculation should be permitted; the only economic issue is who will perform the service most effectively. The sometimes-heard charge of "overspeculation" is incorrectly framed: The issue is not one of amount but, rather, whether it is done well or poorly.

The role of speculation is to allocate resources among periods. If one expects, as did Joseph and the Pharaoh in the Old Testament, seven lean years to follow the seven fat, economic theory tells us that social welfare can be increased by refraining from some present consumption and storing the unconsumed goods until the lean years are upon us, so long as the price expected in the lean years is greater than today's price by at least the costs of storage (including capital costs). If the future is certain (Samuelson 1957), there is no need for speculation, but with uncertainty, whoever carries the inventories is exposed to the risk that the expected lean years will not materialize. Unless that risk is taken, resources will be used wastefully today and unnecessary hardship will be induced tomorrow, relative to intertemporal distribution under certainty.

Although the issue is stated in terms of grain, it is formally identical with the problem of financing fixed capital investment. The terminology of capital markets is less precise, but the suppliers of capital for investment projects play a similar role in determining whether resources should be "nonconsumed" today so as to permit greater production of goods in the future.

In futures markets, the influence of the speculator is easier to see. If the speculator anticipates higher prices in the future, he buys futures contracts, tending to force up their price. As indicated in our hedging example, this gives a larger prospective profit to the hedger for carrying inventory and causes him to increase his holdings. Thus, if speculators as a group make correct judgments, their self-interest results in correct intertemporal decisions.

Several studies of commodity markets before and after futures trading have been undertaken. All suggest that prices are more stable with futures trading than without: that prices do not fall as low or rise as high after the introduction of futures trading (e.g., Working 1960). This implies that futures traders tend to buy at low prices and sell at high ones, i.e., that they profit. Despite this evidence, periods of very low prices or very high prices still are often blamed on speculators, and futures trading has been regulated or prohibited on many occasions. Interestingly enough, however, because it works very well, futures trading has sometimes been banned when, for political or social motives, interference with the economic mechanism is desired. Abolition of foreign exchange futures markets frequently accompanies foreign exchange controls, and some regulation of bond speculation was introduced in the United States in the 1960s because the speculation interfered with the operation of monetary policy intended to destabilize bond prices (Cootner 1964).

Even among those who recognize that futures markets may reduce the range of price variation, there are some who believe that speculative activity may cause prices to move more frequently between the narrower boundaries. According to this view, alternate waves of buying and selling may cause excessive fluctuations: price changes over successive periods would be positively correlated. On the other hand, in a *perfect* market, future price changes would be completely independent of past history. The price at the end of the previous day would discount all factors of importance known at that time—a price change would result only from new information. To a very close approximation, if we correct for the seasonality of risk premiums, speculative markets seem to be perfect (Cootner 1960; 1964; Working 1934).

PAUL H. COOTNER

[See also DECISION MAKING, *article on* ECONOMIC ASPECTS; ECONOMIC EXPECTATIONS; INTERNATIONAL MONETARY ECONOMICS, *article on* EXCHANGE RATES.]

BIBLIOGRAPHY

BRENNAN, MICHAEL J. 1958 The Supply of Storage. *American Economic Review* 48:50–72.

COOTNER, PAUL H. 1960 Returns to Speculators: Telser Versus Keynes. *Journal of Political Economy* 68:396–404. → A reply by Lester G. Telser appears on pages 404–415; a rejoinder by Cootner appears on pages 415–418.

COOTNER, PAUL H. 1963 Speculation in the Government Securities Market. Pages 267–310 in Commission on

Money and Credit, *Fiscal and Debt Management Policies*. Englewood Cliffs, N.J.: Prentice-Hall.

COOTNER, PAUL H. (editor) 1964 *The Random Character of Stock Market Prices*. Cambridge, Mass.: M.I.T. Press.

GRUBEL, HERBERT G. 1963 A Multicountry Model of Forward Exchange: Theory, Policy, and Empirical Evidence 1955–1961. *Yale Economic Essays* 3:105–169.

HOUTHAKKER, HENDRIK S. 1957 Can Speculators Forecast Prices? *Review of Economics and Statistics* 39:143–151.

KEYNES, JOHN MAYNARD (1930) 1960 *A Treatise on Money*. Volume 2: The Applied Theory of Money. London: Macmillan.

LARSON, ARNOLD B. 1960 Measurement of a Random Process in Futures Prices. Stanford University, Food Research Institute, *Food Research Institute Studies* 1:313–324.

SAMUELSON, PAUL A. 1945 The Effect of Interest Rate Increases on the Banking System. *American Economic Review* 34:16–27.

SAMUELSON, PAUL A. 1957 Intertemporal Price Equilibrium: A Prologue to the Theory of Speculation. *Weltwirtschaftliches Archiv* 79:181–221.

TELSER, LESTER G. 1955 Safety First and Hedging. *Review of Economic Studies* 23, no. 1:1–16.

WORKING, HOLBROOK 1933 Price Relations Between July and September Wheat Futures at Chicago Since 1885. Stanford University, Food Research Institute, *Wheat Studies of the Food Research Institute* 9:187–238.

WORKING, HOLBROOK 1934 A Random-difference Series for Use in the Analysis of Time Series. *Journal of the American Statistical Association* 29:11–24.

WORKING, HOLBROOK 1953 Hedging Reconsidered. *Journal of Farm Economics* 35:544–561.

WORKING, HOLBROOK 1960 Price Effects of Futures Trading. Stanford University, Food Research Institute, *Food Research Institute Studies* 1:3–31.

SPEECH

See COMMUNICATION; LANGUAGE; LINGUISTICS; PERCEPTION, *article on* SPEECH PERCEPTION; SEMANTICS AND SEMIOTICS.

SPEECH COMMUNITY

See under LINGUISTICS.

SPEECH PERCEPTION

See under PERCEPTION.

SPENCER, HERBERT

Herbert Spencer (1820–1903), the English philosopher–scientist, was a leading figure in the intellectual revolution of the nineteenth century. Although largely ignored today, Spencer in his own time was enormously influential and played a significant role in the development of biology, psychology, sociology, and anthropology.

He dealt with the evolution of phenomena of all classes, from the inorganic to the superorganic. For the various social sciences, the primary significance of Spencer is that he was among the first to affirm that human society can be studied scientifically and to do so from an evolutionary point of view. With E. B. Tylor and Lewis H. Morgan, Spencer ranks among the three great cultural evolutionists of the nineteenth century.

Spencer was born in Derby in the English Midlands. He came from a family of staunch Dissenters, and the influence of this background is evident in his writings on ethics and political theory. He was educated at home by his father and later by an uncle who wanted him to attend Cambridge. Spencer declined, however, feeling himself unfit for a university career.

From an early age Spencer demonstrated a marked inclination toward science, and especially toward scientific generalization. At 17 he went to work for the London and Birmingham Railway and during his years with the railroads became a civil engineer, in fact if not in name. His engineering background influenced his approach to various fields, especially biology (1864–1867, vol. 1, pp. 122–123).

Evolution

Spencer's interest in evolution began with his examination of fossils taken from railroad cuts. To learn more about geology and paleontology, he purchased a copy of Charles Lyell's *Principles of Geology*. Spencer wrote in his *Autobiography*:

I name this purchase chiefly as serving to introduce a fact of considerable significance. I had during previous years been cognizant of the hypothesis that the human race has been developed from some lower race; though what degree of acceptance it had from me memory does not say. But my reading of Lyell, one of whose chapters was devoted to a refutation of Lamarck's views concerning the origin of species, had the effect of giving me a decided leaning to them. ([1904] 1926, vol. 1, p. 176)

After leaving the railroads, Spencer began his literary career, obtaining a position as subeditor of the *Economist*. In 1850 Spencer's first book, *Social Statics*, appeared. For the most part, this was a work of political philosophy, but here and there it foreshadowed some of his later ideas on evolution ([1904] 1926, vol. 2, pp. 7–8).

In 1851 Spencer was asked to review W. B. Carpenter's *Principles of Physiology*. Spencer later wrote,

In the course of such perusal as was needed to give an account of its contents, I came across von Baer's formula expressing the course of development through which every plant and animal passes—the change from homogeneity to heterogeneity. . . . this phrase of von Baer expressing the law of individual development, awakened my attention to the fact that the law which holds of the ascending stages of each individual organism is also the law which holds of the ascending grades of organisms of all kinds. ([1904] 1926, vol. 1, pp. 384–385)

The following year, 1852, Spencer published in the *Leader* his now-famous article, "The Development Hypothesis," in which he openly rejected special creation and espoused organic evolution.

Spencer's notion of evolution was further elaborated in the writings that followed. He perceived that evolution involves not only an increase in heterogeneity but also an increase in definiteness and in integration ([1904] 1926, vol. 1, p. 501). The term "evolution" itself, which Spencer made current, he used for the first time in "On Manners and Fashion" ([1854] 1891, p. 23).

Years later, in discussing his first use of the term, he wrote, "I did not . . . introduce it in the place of 'epigenesis,' or any word of specially biological application, but as a word fit for expressing the process of evolution throughout its entire range, inorganic and organic" (Duncan 1908, p. 551n). In explaining why he had replaced the term "progress," which he had used as late as April 1857 in his article "Progress: Its Law and Cause," Spencer noted that " 'progress' has an anthropocentric meaning, and that there [is] needed a word free from that" (*ibid.*).

In some of his later writings Spencer defined the general process of evolution in the following terms: *Evolution is a change from a state of relatively indefinite, incoherent, homogeneity to a state of relatively definite, coherent, heterogeneity* (1862, p. 367 in the 1912 edition; 1898a, p. 353).

While he had discussed the evolution of various things in earlier articles, it was in "Progress: Its Law and Cause" (1857b) that Spencer first applied the concept of evolution systematically to the universe at large, and especially to human society:

The advance from the simple to the complex, through a process of successive differentiations, is seen alike in the earliest changes of the Universe to which we can reason our way back, and in the earliest changes which we can inductively establish; it is seen in the geologic and climatic evolution of the Earth; it is seen in the unfolding of every single organism on its surface, and in the multiplication of kinds of organisms; it is seen in the evolution of Humanity, whether contemplated in the civilized individual, or in the aggregate of races; it is seen in the evolution of Society in respect alike of its political, its religious, and its economical organization; and it is seen in the evolution of all those endless concrete and abstract products of human activity. . . . ([1857b] 1915, p. 35)

While becoming increasingly interested in general evolution, Spencer continued to be concerned with organic evolution. In 1855, in the first edition of *Principles of Psychology*, he wrote that "Life under all its forms has arisen by a progressive, unbroken evolution; and through the immediate instrumentality of what we call natural causes" (1855, vol. 1, p. 465 in the 1871 edition).

When Darwin's *Origin of Species* appeared in 1859, Spencer received it warmly and in fact over the years defended it against attack (Duncan 1908, p. 149; Spencer 1895; Wallace 1905, vol. 2, p. 32). What Darwin supplied that Spencer had not was a satisfactory mechanism—natural selection—to account for organic evolution. Spencer had relied on the inheritance of acquired characteristics as the major causal factor in organic evolution and was somewhat chagrined at failing to hit upon the principle of natural selection himself ([1904] 1926, vol. 1, p. 390).

Sociological work

In 1858 Spencer conceived the idea of surveying the fields of biology, psychology, sociology, and ethics from an evolutionary point of view. By 1860 his ideas for this scheme had crystallized, and he issued a prospectus announcing the future publication of his Synthetic Philosophy. The work was to include three volumes entitled *The Principles of Sociology*, in which Spencer proposed to deal with "General facts, structural and functional, as gathered from a survey of Societies and their changes: in other words, the empirical generalizations that are arrived at by comparing the different societies, and successive phases of the same society" ([1904] 1926, vol. 2, p. 481). Thus, before the theoretical works of any other classical evolutionist had appeared, Spencer already had a clear notion of a comparative science of society based on evolutionary principles.

In propounding a science of sociology Spencer was preceded by Auguste Comte, and during Spencer's lifetime, as afterward, his critics asserted that he was indebted to Comte. Spencer denied such allegations and affirmed that he had not read Comte when in 1850, in *Social Statics*, he first began to deal with concepts such as the social organism and to see that in individual and social organisms "progress from low types to high types is progress from uniformity of structure to multiformity of structure" (*ibid.*, vol. 2, p. 488). Thus, Spencer argued, Comte's ideas could not have entered into his thinking on comparative sociology.

The first volume of the Synthetic Philosophy was *First Principles* (1862), in which Spencer dealt with the principle of evolution at great length, exhibiting and discussing many examples of it. When writing the two volumes of *Principles of Biology* (1864–1867) and the 1870–1872 two-volume second edition that recast *Principles of Psychology* (1855), Spencer had drawn largely on his own store of knowledge and ideas. But he realized that when he began to deal with sociology, he would require "an immense accumulation of facts so classified and arranged as to facilitate generalization" ([1904] 1926, vol. 2, p. 171). Accordingly, in 1867, several years before he expected to begin work on *Principles of Sociology* (1876–1896), he hired the first of three researchers who were to read and extract cultural data from ethnographic and historical sources and organize them according to a system of headings and subheadings that Spencer had devised.

The results of this undertaking were published as separate volumes under the general title of *Descriptive Sociology* (see 1873–1934), a work which, according to George P. Murdock, "clearly foreshadowed the development of the present Human Relations Area Files" (1954, p. 16). This series of publications, today very little known, marks Spencer as the founder of systematic, inductive, comparative sociology.

Eight large folio volumes of *Descriptive Sociology* appeared between 1873 and 1881, when the series was discontinued because it was a financial failure which Spencer could no longer afford to carry. However, he never abandoned the idea of this series and in his will provided funds for the compilation and publication of the remainder of the projected volumes of *Descriptive Sociology*. Nine volumes of the series were published after Spencer's death.

In 1872, at the urging of Edward L. Youmans, his most energetic American disciple, Spencer wrote *The Study of Sociology* (1873). In part, the book was written to demonstrate that a science of sociology is possible. "There can be no complete acceptance of Sociology as a science," wrote Spencer, "so long as the belief in a social order not conforming to natural law, survives" (1873, p. 360). Such a belief was prevalent at that time, especially among historians, who tended to base their view on man's supposed possession of free will. A thoroughgoing determinist, Spencer main-

tained that causation operates in human behavior just as it does in other spheres of nature and regarded free will as an illusion (1855, vol. 1, pp. 500–504 in the 1871 edition).

Spencer's disdain for conventional historians extended to their published works. "I take but little interest in what are called histories," he wrote, "but am interested only in Sociology, which stands related to these so-called histories much as a vast building stands related to the heaps of stones and bricks around it" ([1904] 1926, vol. 2, p. 185).

Spencer further charged historians with failing to present the essential facts of human history. He wrote,

That which constitutes History, properly so called, is in great part omitted from works on the subject. Only of late years have historians commenced giving us, in any considerable quantity, the truly valuable information. As in past ages the king was everything and the people nothing; so, in past histories the doings of the king fill the entire picture, to which the national life forms but an obscure background. . . . That which it really concerns us to know, is the natural history of society.   ([1854–1859] 1963, p. 67)

Later he added, "The only history that is of practical value, is what may be called Descriptive Sociology. And the highest office which the historian can discharge, is that of so narrating the lives of nations, as to furnish materials for a Comparative Sociology; and for the subsequent determination of the ultimate laws to which social phenomena conform" (*ibid.*, pp. 69–70). This essay has been taken to be the opening gun in the intellectual movement that gave rise to the New History of James Harvey Robinson and others (Barnes 1925, p. 3).

The Study of Sociology had a very strong impact in the United States, where according to Charles Horton Cooley, it "probably did more to arouse interest in the subject than any other publication before or since" (Cooley 1920, p. 129). William Graham Sumner was very much impressed by the work, finding that "it solved the old difficulty about the relation of social science to history, rescued social science from the dominion of cranks, and offered a definite and magnificent field for work . . ." ("Sketch of William Graham Sumner" 1889, pp. 265–266; a similar statement may be found quoted in Hofstadter 1944, p. 41). *The Study of Sociology* served Sumner as a textbook for a course he established at Yale, which appears to have been the first course in sociology ever taught in an American university (Starr 1925, p. 387).

Well before the publication of the final volume

of *Principles of Sociology* in 1896, Spencer was already a philosopher–scientist of distinction and acclaim. His books were widely read, and his views commanded great attention. *Principles of Biology* had been adopted as a textbook at Oxford, and *First Principles* and *Principles of Psychology* were used by William James as textbooks for two of his courses at Harvard. Spencer had, in short, become a towering figure in the world of learning. Yet he always shunned the academic limelight. When, in 1867, he was asked to become a candidate for the professorship of mental philosophy and logic at University College, London, Spencer declined. Between 1871 and 1903 he was offered no fewer than 32 academic honors, but with one or two exceptions, he refused them all (Spencer [1904] 1926, vol. 2, pp. 146–147; Duncan 1908, pp. 588–589).

Spencer lived seven years beyond the publication of the third volume of *Principles of Sociology*, devoting himself mostly to controversial writing. He died in 1903, at the age of 83.

Conception of society

In *Principles of Sociology* Spencer pointed to a number of parallels between biological organisms and human societies and, in fact, spoke of society as a kind of organism. So often was Spencer attacked for making this analogy, that he took pains to make his position clear:

Analogies between the phenomena presented in a physically coherent aggregate forming an individual, and the phenomena presented in a physically incoherent aggregate of individuals [forming a society] . . . cannot be analogies of a visible or sensible kind; but can only be analogies between the systems, or methods, of organization. Such analogies as exist result from the one unquestionable community between the two organizations: *there is in both a mutual dependence of parts.* This is the origin of all organization; and determines what similarities there are between an individual organism and a social organism. ([1871] 1966, vol. 15, p. 411)

Spencer is widely known as an evolutionist. What is less generally recognized is that he was also a thoroughgoing functionalist. He saw social structures arising out of social functions: "There can be no true conception of a structure without a true conception of its function. To understand how an organization originated and developed, it is requisite to understand the need subserved at the outset and afterwards" ([1876–1896] 1925–1929, vol. 3, p. 3). Spencer also spoke of "the general law of organization that difference of functions entails differentiation and division of the parts performing them . . ." (*ibid.*, vol. 2, p. 441). He illustrated

this principle by showing, for example, how military functions had given rise to elaborate military organization among the Incas and the Spartans (*ibid.*, pp. 580–584). Much of *Principles of Sociology* is devoted to tracing the increased specialization of functions and accompanying differentiation of structures that characterize cultural evolution.

It was Spencer who coined the term "superorganic," which, following its use by Kroeber in 1917 in his article "The Superorganic," has been accepted as designating the unique and distinct elements in human behavior, and therefore as synonymous with "culture." But by "superorganic" Spencer meant no more than what the term means literally: something beyond the purely biological. To him the term was essentially equivalent to "social," and he included within it the behavior of bees, rooks, beaver, and bison, as well as that of man ([1876–1896] 1925–1929, vol. 1, pp. 4–7).

Spencer did not, however, conceive of human society simply as a response to a "social instinct." He held that "social phenomena depend in part on the natures of the individuals and in part on the forces the individuals are subject to, . . ." (*ibid.*, p. 14). In fact, he believed that practical considerations that increased chances of survival lay at the root of human sociality: "Living together arose because, on the average, it proved more advantageous to each than living apart; . . ." Once in existence, social life was perpetuated because "maintenance of combination [of individuals in society] is maintenance of the conditions to more satisfactory living than the combined persons would otherwise have" ([1892–1893] 1914, vol. 1, p. 134).

Yet if Spencer saw societies as something more than mere aggregations of individuals behaving instinctually, he nevertheless did not regard the behavior of social animals and that of man as sufficiently different to warrant distinguishing them terminologically. In *Principles of Sociology* he almost never used the word "culture," although Tylor had already given the term its anthropological definition in his *Primitive Culture* in 1871. However, while he perceived this difference between human and subhuman behavior as one of degree rather than of kind, Spencer was nevertheless impressed by its enormous magnitude. He remarked that the "various orders of super-organic products, [of human societies] . . . constitute an immensely-voluminous, immensely-complicated, and immensely-powerful set of influences" ([1876–1896] 1925–1929, vol. 1, pp. 13–14). He maintained that these orders so transcend all others "in extent, in complication, in importance, as to make them relatively insignificant" (*ibid.*, p. 7).

Spencer never thought of himself as a materialist and, in fact, considered the section of *First Principles* entitled "The Unknowable" to be a "repudiation of materialism" ([1904] 1926, vol. 2, p. 75). Despite his repeated disclaimers, however, materialistic and mechanistic interpretations permeated much of Spencer's writings. For him, the universe consisted basically of matter and energy and was to be explained in these terms. In the concluding paragraph of *First Principles* Spencer wrote that "the deepest truths we can reach, are simply statements of the widest uniformities in our experiences of the relations of Matter, Motion, and Force; . . ." (1862, p. 509 in the 1912 edition).

In view of this mechanistic attitude it is not surprising that Spencer should have perceived and expressed the fundamental importance of energy to the evolution of culture. He was, in fact, perhaps the first to make this relationship explicit:

Based as the life of a society is on animal and vegetal products, and dependent as these are on the light and heat of the Sun, it follows that the changes wrought by men as socially organized, are effects of forces having a common origin with those which produce all the other orders of changes. . . . Not only is the energy expended by the horse harnessed to the plough, and by the labourer guiding it, derived from the same reservoir as is the energy of the cataract and the hurricane; but to this same reservoir are traceable those subtler and more complex manifestations of energy which humanity, as socially embodied, evolves. (*ibid.*, pp. 203–204)

Spencer was among the earliest social scientists to argue that culture change is better explained in terms of sociocultural forces than as the result of actions of important men. He maintained, for example, that it is unrealistic to think of Lycurgus as having originated the Spartan constitution ([1876–1896] 1925–1929, vol. 2, p. 376n). He also maintained that it was not the personal initiative of Cleisthenes that brought about democratic organization in Athens, but rather that his political reorganization was prompted by, and was successful only because of, the large number of non-clan-organized persons living in that city at the time (*ibid.*, pp. 424–425).

Not only did Spencer deny that great men create social and political institutions, he held that their rise was not a matter of deliberate choice at all: "society is a growth and not a manufacture" (*ibid.*, vol. 3, p. 321). He went as far as to deny that recognition of "advantages or disadvantages of this or that arrangement, furnished motives for establishing or maintaining" a form of government, and argued instead that "conditions and not intentions determine [it]" (*ibid.*, vol. 2, p. 395).

Spencer was very much impressed with the importance of war in the development of complex societies, and in fact this is one of the recurring themes of *Principles of Sociology*. He also called attention to the effect of environment on institutions, maintaining, for example, that rugged, mountainous terrain, like that of Greece, fosters the development of confederacies rather than of strongly centralized monarchies (*ibid.*, pp. 373, 395).

Spencer also appreciated the importance of economic factors in the origin and development of customs and institutions. He showed the important role played by commerce and industry in widening the base of Athenian oligarchy and paving the way for Greek democracy (*ibid.*, pp. 391–393, 424–425). He also argued that representative government and the democratic state resulted from an increased concentration of people in towns, from the rise of artisan and merchant classes, and from expanding production and commerce (*ibid.*, pp. 421–423).

Development of social institutions

Like other evolutionists of the period, Spencer dealt at length with the problem of primal human social organization. Many pages of *Principles of Sociology* are devoted to the development of marriage and forms of the family, early concepts of property, and the like. With regard to most of these issues, Spencer's thinking was sound and modern. For example, he did not believe that the incest taboo is innate (*ibid.*, vol. 1, p. 610). Nor did he believe that sexual promiscuity was the earliest stage of human marriage (*ibid.*, p. 662). He did, however, think that promiscuity was at one time common and that the resulting difficulty in establishing paternity led to the early reckoning of kinship in the female line (*ibid.*, p. 647). But he had reservations in this regard and pointed out that even in primitive matrilineal societies a term for "father" always existed, implying a consciousness of male kinship (*ibid.*, p. 648).

Spencer likewise did not believe that polygyny had preceded monogamy but held that monogamy went back as far as any form of marriage (*ibid.*, p. 679). Similarly, he rejected the notion of an early stage of "primitive communism," i.e., common ownership of all forms of property. While recognizing that everywhere "land is jointly held by hunters because it cannot be otherwise held" (*ibid.*, p. 645), he noted that among contemporary primitive peoples, tools, utensils, weapons, and ornaments are habitually owned individually and concluded that a similar situation probably prevailed in very early times.

In *Principles of Sociology* Spencer proposed a theory about the origin of religion that came to be known as the ghost theory. According to this view, the concept of a soul that inhabits the human body was the earliest supernatural belief entertained by man, and this notion was later extended to animals, plants, and inanimate objects. Eventually, through further extensions and differentiations, the concept of the soul was transfigured into that of gods of myriad forms and powers. This hypothesis came very close to Tylor's theory of animism, and the two men entered into a dispute over priority of authorship.

A belief in rectilinear evolution—the view that cultural evolution proceeds in a straight line, without interruptions or regressions—has been attributed to the classical evolutionists, including Spencer. But Spencer held no such view. "Though, taking the entire assemblage of societies, evolution may be held inevitable . . . ," he wrote, "yet it cannot be held inevitable in each particular society, or even probable" (*ibid.*, p. 96). Likewise, Spencer was not a unilinear evolutionist: "Like other kinds of progress, social progress is not linear but divergent and re-divergent. Each differentiated product gives origin to a new set of differentiated products" (*ibid.*, vol. 3, p. 331).

Although Spencer (*ibid.*, vol. 1, pp. 549–556) did propose a sequence of stages of political evolution, he was far more concerned with process than with stages. Moreover, he saw the process by which societies develop as consisting, by and large, in responses to particular problems posed by the cultural and natural environments, rather than in movement through a universal and necessary series of stages.

Spencer's advocacy of individualism and laissez-faire led him to champion the philosophy of social Darwinism. He held that the rapid elimination of unfit individuals from society through natural selection would benefit the race biologically and that the state should therefore do nothing to relieve the condition of the poor, whom he assumed to be the less fit. Spencer also maintained that the economic system works best if each individual is allowed to seek his own private interests and that consequently the state should not intervene in the economy except to enforce contracts and to see to it that no one infringes upon the rights of others. He believed that in the ensuing competition, the fittest business enterprises and economic institutions would survive. These views were set forth at length in *Social Statics* (1850) and *The Man Versus the State* (1884).

Spencer never abandoned his belief in the inheritance of acquired characteristics, a theory which, while essentially biological, also affected his social theory. He argued, for example, that "the constitutional energy needed for continuous labour, without which there cannot be civilized life . . . is an energy . . . to be acquired only by inherited modifications slowly accumulated" ([1876–1896] 1925–1929, vol. 2, p. 270).

Certain cultural peculiarities among peoples of the world Spencer attributed to innate psychological differences. He spoke, for instance, of "the independence of the Greek nature," which was unlike Oriental natures, and held that it was because of this nature that the ancient Greeks "did not readily submit to the extension of sacerdotal control over civil affairs" (*ibid.*, vol. 3, p. 265).

Yet, despite such views, Spencer only rarely resorted to the idea of inherent psychological differences to explain cultural differences. Almost invariably he explained cultural phenomena primarily by the interplay of cultural and environmental factors. He did not believe that "racial" differences involve any truly fundamental differences in psychology and did not impute to preliterate peoples a "prelogical" mentality (*ibid.*, vol. 1, p. 100).

Influence

Although Spencer's direct influence on present-day anthropology and sociology is slight, his indirect influence has been considerably greater. The most important link between Spencer and contemporary social science is Émile Durkheim, who although critical of Spencer on a number of points, was influenced by Spencer's treatment of comparative sociology, typologies of human society, the division of labor, and social structure, function, and integration.

Through Durkheim, Spencer influenced A. R. Radcliffe-Brown, and it is probably fair to say that the core of what Radcliffe-Brown derived from Durkheim—the concept of society as a functioning system, susceptible of scientific study—Durkheim had derived from Spencer. Radcliffe-Brown's students in turn were taught principles and ideas deriving from Spencer, although mostly those dealing with function rather than with evolution. The line of descent of this aspect of Spencer's influence was summed up by Howard Becker as follows: "'From Spencer to Durkheim to British and British-influenced functional anthropology to structural–functional sociology in the United States' . . . may not be a drastic distortion of the actual 'who to whom' sequence" (Becker 1954, p. 132).

Evolutionism, Spencer's other signal contribution to cultural anthropology, has had less continuous acceptance than functionalism. In fact, it virtually disappeared from the scene during the great reaction against it in the first fifty years of the twentieth century. However, the wave of anti-evolutionism appears spent, and the last two decades have seen the resurgence of evolution, led by Leslie A. White and Julian H. Steward in the United States and V. Gordon Childe in England. Anthropologists have come to accept cultural evolution as a fact and to see it as a process of increasing structural differentiation and functional specialization, the very terms in which Spencer first portrayed it more than a century ago.

ROBERT L. CARNEIRO

[*For the historical context of Spencer's work, see* EVOLUTION; *and the biography of* DARWIN; *for discussion of the subsequent development of his ideas, see* SOCIAL DARWINISM; *and the biographies of* CARVER; CHILDE; DURKHEIM; GIDDINGS; HANKINS; RADCLIFFE-BROWN; ROSS; SUMNER; WARD, LESTER F.]

WORKS BY SPENCER

(1850) 1954 *Social Statics: The Conditions Essential to Human Happiness Specified, and the First of Them Developed.* London: Routledge; New York: Humanities.

(1852) 1915 The Development Hypothesis. Volume 1, pages 1–7 in Herbert Spencer, *Essays: Scientific, Political, and Speculative.* New York: Appleton.

(1854) 1891 On Manners and Fashion. Volume 3, pages 1–51 in Herbert Spencer, *Essays: Scientific, Political, and Speculative.* London: Williams & Norgate. → First published in the *Westminster Review.*

(1854–1859) 1963 *Education: Intellectual, Moral, and Physical.* Paterson, N.J.: Littlefield.

(1855) 1920–1926 *Principles of Psychology.* 3d ed. 2 vols. New York: Appleton.

(1857a) 1915 Transcendental Physiology. Volume 1, pages 63–107 in Herbert Spencer, *Essays: Scientific, Political, and Speculative.* New York: Appleton. → First published in the *National Review* as "The Ultimate Laws of Physiology."

(1857b) 1915 Progress: Its Law and Cause. Volume 1, pages 8–62 in Herbert Spencer, *Essays: Scientific, Political, and Speculative.* New York: Appleton. → First published in the *Westminster Review.*

(1858–1874) 1915 *Essays: Scientific, Political, and Speculative.* 3 vols. New York: Appleton.

(1860) 1966 Prospectus of a System of Philosophy. Pages 297–303 in Jay Rumney, *Herbert Spencer's Sociology: A Study in the History of Social Theory.* New York: Atherton. → Written in 1858; first published in 1860.

(1862) 1958 *First Principles.* New York: DeWitt Revolving Fund.

(1864–1867) 1914 *The Principles of Biology.* 2 vols. New York: Appleton.

(1871) 1966 Specialized Administration. Volume 15, pages 401–444 in *The Works of Herbert Spencer.* Osnabrück (Germany): Zeller.

(1873) 1961 *The Study of Sociology.* Ann Arbor: Univ. of Michigan Press.

1873–1934 *Descriptive Sociology: Or, Groups of Sociological Facts, Classified and Arranged by Herbert Spencer.* Compiled and abstracted by David Duncan,

Richard Scheppig, and James Collier. 17 vols. London: Williams & Norgate.

(1876–1896) 1925–1929 *The Principles of Sociology.* 3 vols. New York: Appleton.

(1884) 1950 *The Man Versus the State.* 2d ed. London: Watts.

(1892–1893) 1914 *The Principles of Ethics.* 2 vols. New York: Appleton.

1895 Lord Salisbury on Evolution. *Nineteenth Century* 38:740–757.

1898a What Is Social Evolution? *Nineteenth Century* 44:348–358.

(1898b) 1914 *Various Fragments.* New York: Appleton.

1902 *Facts and Comments.* London: Williams & Norgate; New York: Appleton.

(1904) 1926 *An Autobiography.* 2 vols. London: Watts.

The Evolution of Society: Selections From Herbert Spencer's Principles of Sociology. Edited by Robert L. Carneiro. Univ. of Chicago Press, 1967.

The Works of Herbert Spencer. 21 vols. Osnabrück (Germany): Zeller, 1966–1967.

SUPPLEMENTARY BIBLIOGRAPHY

BARKER, ERNEST (1915) 1959 *Political Thought in England 1848–1914.* 2d ed. Oxford Univ. Press.

BARNES, HARRY E. 1925 *The New History and the Social Studies.* New York: Century.

BARNES, HARRY E.; and BECKER, HOWARD (1938) 1961 *Social Thought From Lore to Science.* 3d ed., rev. & enl. 2 vols. New York: Dover.

BECKER, HOWARD 1954 Anthropology and Sociology. Pages 102–159 in John P. Gillin (editor), *For a Science of Social Man.* New York: Macmillan.

CLODD, EDWARD (1897) 1907 *Pioneers of Evolution From Thales to Huxley.* Rev. ed. London: Cassell.

COOLEY, CHARLES H. 1920 Reflections Upon the Sociology of Herbert Spencer. *American Journal of Sociology* 26:129–145.

DUNCAN, DAVID 1908 *The Life and Letters of Herbert Spencer.* London: Methuen.

DURANT, WILLIAM JAMES (1926) 1933 *The Story of Philosophy.* New rev. ed. New York: Simon & Schuster. → In paperback, 1962, Washington Square.

ELLIOT, HUGH 1917 *Herbert Spencer.* London: Constable.

ENSOR, R. C. K. 1946 *Some Reflections on Herbert Spencer's Doctrine That Progress Is Differentiation.* Oxford Univ. Press.

FISKE, JOHN (1874) 1903 *Outlines of Cosmic Philosophy: Based on the Doctrine of Evolution.* 4 vols. Boston: Houghton Mifflin.

HØFFDING, HARALD (1894–1895) 1955 *A History of Modern Philosophy.* 2 vols. New York: Dover. → First published as *Den nyere filosofis historie.*

HOFSTADTER, RICHARD (1944) 1959 *Social Darwinism in American Thought.* Rev. ed. New York: Braziller.

HOLT, HENRY 1923 *Garrulities of an Octogenarian Editor.* Boston: Houghton Mifflin.

HUDSON, WILLIAM H. (1894) 1904 *An Introduction to the Philosophy of Herbert Spencer.* New York: Appleton.

KROEBER, A. L. (1917) 1952 The Superorganic. Pages 22–51 in A. L. Kroeber, *The Nature of Culture.* Univ. of Chicago Press. → First published in Volume 9 of the *American Anthropologist* New Series.

MACPHERSON, HECTOR 1900 *Spencer and Spencerism.* New York: Doubleday.

MELDOLA, RAPHAEL 1910 *Evolution: Darwinian and Spencerian.* Oxford: Clarendon.

MORGAN, C. LLOYD 1898 Mr. Herbert Spencer's Biology. *Natural Science* 13:377–383.

MUNRO, THOMAS 1963 *Evolution in the Arts and Other Theories of Culture History.* Cleveland (Ohio) Museum of Art.

MURDOCK, GEORGE P. 1954 Sociology and Anthropology. Pages 14–21 in John P. Gillin (editor), *For a Science of Social Man: Convergences in Anthropology, Psychology, and Sociology.* New York: Macmillan.

PARSONS, TALCOTT (1937) 1949 *The Structure of Social Action: A Study in Social Theory With Special Reference to a Group of Recent European Writers.* Glencoe, Ill.: Free Press.

ROYCE, JOSIAH 1904 *Herbert Spencer: An Estimate and Review.* New York: Fox, Duffield.

RUMNEY, JAY 1934 (1966) *Herbert Spencer's Sociology: A Study in the History of Social Theory.* New York: Atherton.

Sketch of William Graham Sumner. 1889 *Popular Science Monthly* 35:261–268.

STARR, HARRIS E. 1925 *William Graham Sumner.* New York: Holt.

THOMSON, J. ARTHUR 1906 *Herbert Spencer.* London: Dent.

TILLETT, A. W. 1914 *Spencer's Synthetic Philosophy: What It Is All About.* London: King.

TYLOR, E. B. 1877 Mr. Spencer's *Principles of Sociology. Mind* 2:141–156.

WALLACE, ALFRED RUSSEL 1905 *My Life: A Record of Events and Opinions.* 2 vols. New York: Dodd.

WEBB, BEATRICE (1926) 1950 *My Apprenticeship.* London and New York: Longmans.

WHITE, LESLIE A. 1947 Evolutionary Stages, Progress, and the Evaluation of Cultures. *Southwestern Journal of Anthropology* 3:165–192.

SPENGLER, OSWALD

Oswald Spengler (1880–1936), German universal historian, was born in Blankenburg, in the Harz mountains. Of Protestant parentage, he was descended on his father's side from a line of mining engineers; his mother's family was artistically inclined. Both inheritances came together in Spengler—in his scientific interests on the one hand and his stylistic ability and talent for bold, intuitive theoretical formulations on the other.

After attending a humanist Gymnasium in Halle, he studied mathematics and the natural sciences at the universities of Munich, Berlin, and Halle. He obtained his doctor's degree at Halle with a dissertation on Heraclitus. Spengler's preoccupation with this pre-Socratic Greek philosopher foreshadowed some of the main ideas of his major work: he was to translate "everything flows" into historical relativism and "war, the father of all things" into a self-consciously tough, "heroic" world view. Spengler was a lone wolf—a bachelor, and also an outsider to the German world of learning. Having taught at a number of schools, the last a Hamburg Realgymnasium, he moved to Munich as a private scholar in 1911, at which time he conceived the idea for the work which was to stir up the entire historical profession.

The Decline of the West (1918–1922) was revolutionary less in its basic ideas than in the impressive breadth of its canvas—a feature for which it was readily attacked by professional scholars—and in its elaborate systematization of cultural and historical pessimism. Spengler's immediate inspiration was his perception that the civilization of the West since the late nineteenth century was exhibiting the same symptoms as ancient civilization in its decline. He acknowledged the influences primarily of Goethe and Nietzsche; to them he owed "practically everything." From Goethe he derived his "method," particularly his way of relating scientific insights to cultural phenomena, and his latent historical relativism. From Nietzsche he acquired the "questioning faculty," his approach to cultural criticism.

In the work of Edward Gibbon, decline had been a historical theme closely circumscribed by time and space; for Spengler it became a metaphysical one. While Gibbon had seen decline in a broader context of the long-range history of human progress, Spengler used it as an argument against the existence of progress. This difference is a measure of Spengler's dramatic break with the premises of the eighteenth-century Enlightenment. His historicism and antirationalism carried the tradition of German romanticism to its ultimate conclusions; he called his work a "German philosophy." His ponderousness and lack of humor in fact took him far afield from both Goethe and Nietzsche. Thus the blue flower of German romanticism blossomed for the last time in an icy, apocalyptic twentieth-century setting.

The Decline of the West is described in the subtitle as a "morphology of history." History is not the study of a coherent evolution (Spengler *contra* Hegel); it is a comparative study of cultures. Spengler dismissed with vehemence the traditional periodization of world history in terms of ancient, medieval, and modern. Instead he concentrated on eight separate cultures: those of Egypt, India, Babylon, China, classical antiquity, Islam, the West (Faustian culture), and Mexico. Each one of these "powerful cultures" imprints upon mankind its own form, has its own idea, passions, life, and death (Spengler's historical relativism). Each one, like a plant, goes through the appointed course of youth, maturity, and decline (Spengler's determinism). Each "culture," in Spengler's terms, produces its "civilization," the latter representing a late, declining phase of that culture: a civilization is "a conclusion, the thing become succeeding to the thing becoming, rigidity following expansion," intellect replacing the soul. For the linear view of history Spengler thus substituted a cyclical theory such as had last been elaborated in the West by Vico in the early eighteenth century (though one had been propounded in the nineteenth century by the Russian writer Nikolai I. Danilevskii).

According to this theory, historical events are symbolic of the "metaphysical structure of historical mankind." There is a "morphological relationship" between diverse expressions of human activity—between differential calculus and the dynastic state of the time of Louis XIV, for instance, or between the ancient polis and Euclidean geometry. Furthermore, Spengler saw "contemporaneity" in phenomena widely separated in time—in the Trojan war and the crusades, in Homer and the song of the Nibelungs, and so forth. Napoleon was not a pupil of Alexander the Great but his alter ego. Altogether, historical data, instead of being subject to the law of cause and effect, follow a compelling "fate." Spengler called his work grandiloquently a "philosophy of fate." In effect, while he could hardly pass for a philosopher, he was one of the twentieth century's outstanding visionaries.

Applied to twentieth-century Western civilization, Spengler's theories opened up impressive social perspectives. His insights into atomized life in the big city (the "megalopolis"), into an age of masses, money, and a new Caesarism are penetrating. For all his mystical vision, Spengler actually raised the very issues that agitate contemporary sociologists. And what is more, many of his predictions have come true.

Spengler's immediate impact on Germany was electrifying. Although accused of charlatanism by most professional scholars, he became one of the most widely read and discussed authors in the 1920s. At the same time, a number of pamphlets that he wrote after the war, while serving as sketches for and elaborations of his general work, drew him deeper and deeper into the bitter political struggles of the Weimar Republic. *Preussentum und Sozialismus* (1920) was particularly influential, orphic but compelling. It exhorted the Germans to live up to a type that Spengler, in *The Decline of the West*, had called the "last race": strong, heroic, Prussian. Spengler's politics added up to a violent rejection of liberalism, democracy, and the West, and they contributed vitally to the undermining of the young German republic, which

was to him nothing but a "business enterprise." While Spengler is considered by some to have paved the way for National Socialism, he disagreed with the Nazis on various basic issues (such as race) and many times repudiated the movement (*Neubau des Deutschen Reiches* 1924; *The Hour of Decision* 1933b). The Nazis, however, used him as one of their ideological fathers, although after Hitler's seizure of power they dismissed him harshly as a magician of decline, a sadist, and so forth. In the end Spengler died a lonely, almost forgotten man.

After World War II *The Decline of the West*, its prophecies seemingly borne out by events, came into its own, especially in the United States. Arnold Toynbee's universal history—which conquered America in the late 1940s—was really something of a Spenglerian heresy, Spengler tempered by British empiricism. Spengler, indeed, left a lasting imprint upon modern "metahistorians" like Toynbee, sociologists like Sorokin, and anthropologists like Kroeber. Finally, a pessimistic mid-twentieth century saw itself reflected in Spengler's grand scheme.

KLEMENS VON KLEMPERER

WORKS BY SPENGLER

(1918–1922) 1926–1928 *The Decline of the West*. 2 vols. Authorized translation with notes by Charles F. Atkinson. New York: Knopf. → Volume 1: *Form and Actuality*. Volume 2: *Perspectives of World History*. First published as *Der Untergang des Abendlandes*.

(1920) 1942 *Preussentum und Sozialismus*. Munich: Beck. → Reprinted in Spengler (1933a).

1924 *Der Neubau des Deutschen Reiches*. Munich: Beck. → Reprinted in Spengler (1933a).

(1931) 1932 *Man and Technics: A Contribution to a Philosophy of Life*. New York: Knopf. → First published as *Der Mensch und die Technik: Beitrag zu einer Philosophie des Lebens*.

1933a *Politische Schriften*. Munich: Beck.

(1933b) 1934 *The Hour of Decision*. New York: Knopf. → First published as *Jahre der Entscheidung*.

Reden und Aufsätze. 3d ed. Munich: Beck, 1951. → Published posthumously. Contains *Heraklit* and other writings first published between 1904 and 1936.

Letters, 1913–1936. Translated and edited by Arthur Helps. New York: Knopf, 1966. → First published in German.

SUPPLEMENTARY BIBLIOGRAPHY

ADORNO, T. W. 1950 Spengler nach dem Untergang. *Der Monat* 2, no. 20:115–128.

HELLER, ERICH (1952) 1959 *The Disinherited Mind*. New York: Meridian.

HUGHES, H. STUART 1952 *Oswald Spengler: A Critical Estimate*. New York: Scribner.

MEINECKE, FRIEDRICH (1923)1959 Über Spenglers Geschichtsbetrachtung. Pages 181–195 in Friedrich Meinecke, *Werke*. Volume 4: Zur Theorie und Philosophie der Geschichte. Munich: Oldenbourg.

SCHROETER, MANFRED 1922 *Der Streit um Spengler: Kritik seiner Kritiker.* Munich: Beck.

SCHROETER, MANFRED 1949 *Metaphysik des Untergangs: Eine kulturkritische Studie über Oswald Spengler.* Munich: Leibniz.

SOROKIN, PITIRIM A. (1950) 1963 *Modern Historical and Social Philosophies.* New York: Dover. → First published as *Social Philosophies of an Age of Crisis.*

SPIER, LESLIE

Leslie Spier (1893–1961), American anthropologist, was born in New York City and educated in the New York public schools. He graduated from the College of the City of New York in 1915 with a degree in engineering. His interest in social science began when he spent a summer doing field work as an archeologist with the Geological Survey of New Jersey. Spier entered Columbia University as a graduate student in anthropology and came under the influence of Boas; as an assistant in anthropology at the American Museum of Natural History he was also influenced by Wissler and Lowie.

Spier's first university appointment was at the University of Washington, where he established a department of anthropology. There he combined teaching with research among the tribes of the Puget Sound area. He taught at Yale from 1933 to 1939, at the University of New Mexico from 1939 until his retirement in 1955, and for shorter periods at Chicago, Harvard, and other universities.

Throughout his academic career, Spier continued to do field work among North American Indians. He resisted the lure of far-off places and "untouched" tribes in order to pursue systematically the problems that had gained his attention early in his career. His field work was largely in two geographic areas—among the tribes around Puget Sound and in the Southwest, where he passed over the picturesque Pueblos in order to concentrate on the peripheral peoples who were less well known but of equal theoretical importance. His major ethnographic contributions were *Havasupai Ethnography* (1928), an ethnographic classic; *Klamath Ethnography* (1930); and *Yuman Tribes of the Gila River* (1933).

Spier made his chief theoretical contributions to anthropology in ethnology, where his major interests were in exploring the relations of peoples over time and analyzing cultural process. His doctoral dissertation, *The Sun Dance of the Plains Indians* (1921), is a model of culture-historical analysis. Mapping the distribution of the different elements in a single widely distributed ceremonial complex, he identified a clustering of traits in a central area, which he suggested was the probable place of origin—a conclusion that was supported by an analysis of the organizational structure of the ceremony. The final section of the study deals with the integration of the ceremonial complex into the different Plains cultures, foreshadowing theoretical concern with cultural themes and configurations in anthropology. However, Spier rejected as too subjective the attempts of Benedict and others to categorize culture wholes in terms of "pattern" or "ethos."

Spier's interest in the relationships of Southwestern cultures began with archeological research in the Little Colorado valley. In *An Outline for a Chronology of Zuñi Ruins* (1917) he developed a statistical method for establishing chronological relationships. This unpretentious paper is important chiefly for the light it throws on the movements of peoples in the area and the linkages it suggests between the Puebloan and Mexican tribes. Similar interests dominated his studies among the Yumans of the Gila and Colorado basins. On the basis of cultural distributions he suggested a new alignment of peoples, refuting the supposed isolation of the Puebloan peoples and placing the Southwest in a wider geographical and historical perspective.

Pursuing the idea that all cultural phenomena, even responses to cultural disorganization, have historical antecedents, Spier traced the aboriginal complex of beliefs and practices that provided the basic pattern of the Ghost Dance, a nativistic movement that swept the northern Plains in 1890, and identified the specific sources of the Christian accretions (1935).

Spier's major contributions deal with the analysis of specific historical conditions rather than with the development of general theories of historical process. He was critical of generalizations for which broad or universal validity was claimed. He emphasized the accidental and unpredictable, as opposed to the directional, in culture growth, but he recognized the existence of a universal pattern of human adaptation as well as regional patterns that allow predictions of limited scope. Although change is accidental, subject to influences lying outside the cultural system, "borrowing" and innovation are not random, but selective. However diverse the sources of cultural elements, they are altered and given new meanings in terms of pre-existing patterns.

Spier served as editor of the *American Anthropologist* and of the *Southwest Journal of Anthropology*, which he founded in 1944 and edited until

1961. He also edited several series of monographs. Although he received many honors from his colleagues, he eschewed publicity. He did not write for mass media, and he made no attempt to popularize his ideas beyond the circle of his students and colleagues. He did not become involved in large government programs or in the direction of huge projects. As an editor and critic Spier was one of the best-informed anthropologists, but he continued to pursue his own interests and problems, uninfluenced by changing fashions in research. He died in New Mexico in 1961.

RUTH BUNZEL

[*See also* DIFFUSION, *article on* CULTURAL DIFFUSION; HISTORY, *article on* CULTURE HISTORY; INDIANS, NORTH AMERICAN; *and the biographies of* BOAS; LOWIE; WISSLER.]

WORKS BY SPIER

1917   *An Outline for a Chronology of Zuñi Ruins.* American Museum of Natural History, Anthropological Papers, Vol. 18, part 3. New York: The Museum.
1918   *The Trenton Argillite Culture.* American Museum of Natural History, Anthropological Papers, Vol. 22, part 4. New York: The Museum.
1921   *The Sun Dance of the Plains Indians: Its Development and Diffusion.* American Museum of Natural History, Anthropological Papers, Vol. 16, part 7. New York: The Museum.
1923   Southern Diegueno Customs. Pages 297–358 in *Phoebe Apperson Hearst Memorial Volume.* University of California Publications in American Archaeology and Ethnology, Vol. 20. Berkeley: Univ. of California Press.
1925a   *An Analysis of Plains Indian Parfleche Decoration.* University of Washington Publications in Anthropology, Vol. 1, No. 3. Seattle: Univ. of Washington Press.
1925b   *The Distribution of Kinship Systems in North America.* University of Washington Publications in Anthropology, Vol. 1, No. 2. Seattle: Univ. of Washington Press.
1927   *The Ghost Dance of 1870 Among the Klamath of Oregon.* University of Washington Publications in Anthropology, Vol. 2, No. 2. Seattle: Univ. of Washington Press.
1928   *Havasupai Ethnography.* American Museum of Natural History, Anthropological Papers, Vol. 29, part 3. New York: The Museum.
1929a   *Growth of Japanese Children Born in America and in Japan.* University of Washington Publications in Anthropology, Vol. 3, No. 1. Seattle: Univ. of Washington Press.
1929b   Problems Arising From the Cultural Position of the Havasupai. *American Anthropologist* New Series 31:213–222.
1930   *Klamath Ethnography.* University of California Publications in American Archaeology and Ethnology, Vol. 30. Berkeley: Univ. of California Press.
1930   SPIER, LESLIE; and SAPIR, EDWARD *Wishram Ethnography.* University of Washington Publications in Anthropology, Vol. 3, No. 3. Seattle: Univ. of Washington Press.
1933   *Yuman Tribes of the Gila River.* University of Chicago Publications in Anthropology, Ethnological Series. Univ. of Chicago Press.
1935   *The Prophet Dance of the Northwest and Its Derivatives: The Source of the Ghost Dance.* General Series in Anthropology, No. 1. Menasha, Wis.: Banta.
1936a   *Cultural Relations of the Gila River and Lower Colorado Tribes.* Yale University Publications in Anthropology, No. 3. New Haven: Yale Univ. Press.
1936b   *Tribal Distribution in Washington.* General Series in Anthropology, No. 3. Menasha, Wis.: Banta.
1946   *Comparative Vocabularies and Parallel Texts in Two Yuman Languages of Arizona.* University of New Mexico Publications in Anthropology, No. 2. Albuquerque: Univ. of New Mexico Press.
1954   Some Aspects of the Nature of Culture. *New Mexico Quarterly* 24:301–321.
1959   Some Central Elements in the Legacy. Pages 146–155 in Walter R. Goldschmidt (editor), *The Anthropology of Franz Boas: Essays on the Centennial of His Birth.* American Anthropological Association, Memoirs, No. 89. Menasha, Wis.: The Association.

SUPPLEMENTARY BIBLIOGRAPHY

BASEHART, HARRY W.; and HILL, W. W. 1965 Leslie Spier: 1893–1961. *American Anthropologist* New Series 67:1258–1277. → Contains an extensive bibliography.

SPIETHOFF, ARTHUR

Arthur Spiethoff (1873–1957), German economist, made his most lasting contribution in business-cycle research. He began to work in this field at an early age, and it is here that he did pioneer work. To work on the problem of the business cycle he had to transcend his intellectual origins in the German historical school and develop a new general theory of economics. His "historical–realistic," or "intuitive," theory, in combination with a theory of economic style and with new methods of generalizing and patterning the results of extremely detailed investigation of essential elements, created the framework for a comprehensive explanation of business cycles—an "analytical description."

Spiethoff saw himself as the heir and executor of Gustav Schmoller. He appreciated Schmoller's grasp of the living, historical reality of economics accessible by observation and intuition. He considered theoretical speculation for its own sake to be fruitless, but approved of, and himself mastered, purely theoretical analysis as a necessary preliminary or an auxiliary to other analysis.

Business cycles

In his research on the business cycle, Spiethoff's point of departure was the work of Clément Juglar, who had been the first to establish the cyclical nature of business booms and depressions, basing his findings on historical and statistical research. Juglar distinguished between boom, crisis, and stagnation and regarded the boom as the "sole cause" of stagnation. A generation later, Spiethoff (together with a group of researchers, including Mikhail I. Tugan-Baranovskii and Albert Aftalion) renewed the systematic empirical and analytical study of specific problems related to business cycles.

Spiethoff delivered his first lecture outlining a theory of the business cycle in Berlin in 1901 (see 1902). The lecture gave evidence of years of historical and statistical research and of a high degree of methodological rigor. Numerous specialized studies on the problem of the business cycle followed. In the celebrated article "Krisen," published in 1923, he gave a comprehensive exposition of what he called economic *Wechsellagen* (states of alternation), but he considered even this exposition to be merely a preliminary survey. It appeared in English as "Business Cycles" in 1953 and was reprinted in 1955 as *Die wirtschaftlichen Wechsellagen: Aufschwung, Krise, Stockung*, supplemented by the statistical material on which the article was based and which was published for the first time in Volume 2 of the 1955 work. This statistical material, going back a century, is essential to Spiethoff's theory of the business cycle. Another article, "Overproduction," in the *Encyclopaedia of the Social Sciences* (1933), is a concise treatment of a related important problem.

Spiethoff's over-all treatment of business cycles conforms to the methods of the historical–realistic theory. An initial conceptual clarification of the basic characteristics of business cycles is followed by a close analysis of the significance for cyclical developments of capital investment, production, consumption, and prices. This analysis yields a "model cycle," which specifies the decisive characteristics of particular stages. The model, derived from the careful study of more than a century of economic evolution, claims to present only typical and essential elements, rather than any regular sequence, such as decline, ascent, boom, and capital scarcity.

As early as 1902, Spiethoff made a major advance in business-cycle theory by attempting to explain systematically the origin, development, and cessation of the business boom. The cessation of the boom is equivalent to the *genesis* of overproduction, as distinct from the *continuation* of overproduction, which is the essential ingredient of business stagnation. The crisis is not part of the regular cycle, inasmuch as it may, but need not, occur. Describing and explaining the crisis raises new problems. Spiethoff always saw business cycles

in terms of increasing or decreasing capital investment: capital goods and means of production are more central to them than are consumers' goods. Spiethoff asserted that this observation made possible a causal explanation of cycles and created the basis of all modern theories.

Although Spiethoff did attribute great importance to capital investment, his theory interrelates so many causes, conditions, and characteristic factors that it cannot really be called an "overinvestment theory," as, for instance, Gottfried Haberler and Alvin Hansen have stated. Spiethoff also took into account psychological circumstances, crop fluctuations, the "accelerator" phenomenon, and monetary and credit factors. His *Schichtenlehre* (doctrine of levels), to use a term coined by Adolf Löwe (*Der Stand . . . 1933*, p. 157), is the first attempt to provide an organic synthesis of empiricism and theory, as well as an effective combination of elements that are essential from the standpoint of realistic (intuitive) theory. Hence, it is not a classical formulation of the descriptive–empirical approach, as W. A. Jöhr (1957) has asserted.

According to Schumpeter (1954, p. 1127), Spiethoff was the first economist after Marx to recognize that business cycles are not simply insignificant attendant phenomena of capitalist development but constitute, instead, the essential form of this development.

Spiethoff was also one of the first to observe that the business cycle is only part of a larger rhythm, each phase of which spans several decades, and that economic developments in the period studied by him—the period from 1822 to 1913—were governed by this rhythm. Spiethoff coined the term *Wechselspannen* to designate the alternation of periods predominantly characterized by prosperity with those predominantly characterized by stagnation. Much research was later done on these *Wechselspannen*, or Kondratieff cycles, as they came to be called. Spiethoff himself was not able to provide a systematic analysis of the "riddle of the long waves," but occasionally he attempted speculative explanations.

The much-discussed question of the necessity, or the inevitability (according to Haberler), of the business cycle was answered positively by Spiethoff, who considered the cycle to be based on fundamental traits of the economic style of fully developed capitalism. The consistent application of the historical theory permits this positive answer to what is often called the problem of the periodicity, or regular recurrence, of business cycles.

A second frequently discussed problem is that

of the compatibility of the theory of the business cycle with the theory of an economic "system," for example, a dynamic system. In terms of pure historical–realistic theory, it is the economic style which represents what the system does. Thus, the central issue is the relation of cycles to a given economic style, rather than the course of these cycles within the framework of a system. Spiethoff rejected the notion advanced by Irving Fisher, Friedrich Lutz, and Walter Eucken that the phenomenon of the business cycle is not a "general problem to be solved by means of pure dynamic theory" (Lutz in *Der Stand* . . . 1933, p. 163). Spiethoff's factual research demonstrated the untenability of that viewpoint. Indeed, hardly any significant theory of the business cycle has adopted the "nihilistic" thesis that "the" cycle does not exist. Schumpeter, Haberler, and Jöhr, for example, assume a general cycle phenomenon.

Thus, with regard to Spiethoff's business-cycle theory, it has been said that the "modern researcher will look in vain for a rigorously 'pure' model of the business cycle or for the effects of 'deficit spending' or for his familiar tools, such as the multiplier, the principle of acceleration, preference for liquidity, and marginal inclination toward consumption and investment. Rudiments of these, however, as well of Keynesian and post-Keynesian thinking are to be found in Spiethoff's writings . . ." (Nicol 1957, p. 21*). Spiethoff would have considered many of the present "oscillation models," which explain, for example, the course of business cycles as a purely mechanical process involving a combination of the multiplier and accelerator principles and which eliminate all psychic components, as interesting intellectual exercises, but remote from reality.

Since Spiethoff's theory of the business cycle is a "historical" one, its validity is limited to the advanced capitalist economic style of the so-called free market. Consequently, the business cycle is related, for example, to particular psychological premises, a given historical environment, and especially to the possibility of technological innovation and the opening up of new markets.

Theory of economic styles

Spiethoff's research on the business cycle was the focal point of his work, but it was also part of his wider effort to evolve a new theory of economics. His contributions to the Sombart *Festgabe* (1932), to the Schmoller *Festgabe* (1938), and to the Alfred Weber *Festgabe* (1948), are milestones along this road. We might add Spiethoff's publications in English: "The 'Historical' Character of Economic Theories" (1952) and "Pure Theory and Economic Gestalt Theory: Ideal and Real Types" (1953).

As in the case of business cycles, Spiethoff approached his general theory with new methods, in the tradition of Schmoller, Max Weber, and Sombart, working toward a historical–realistic theory of economic styles. All of Spiethoff's scientific lifework, built up quite systematically, reflects the fruitful employment of these methods. This is true not only of his business-cycle research but also of his highly important theory of the capital and money market or his extensive investigations of land utilization and housing. His heuristic tools are most fully developed in his advanced conception of a general science of political economy, which he did not live to elaborate in full but for which the theoretical concept of economic style is crucial.

The economic style is an open-ended set of phenomena that is continuously complemented and modified by new experiential research rather than exclusively by "system-compatible" data. Spiethoff believed that this concept would permit the resolution of the perennial dilemma of economics: the quest for general knowledge, in the face of the historical variability of most economic phenomena. In the strictest sense, an absolute theory can be formulated only for fundamental economic phenomena, but a certain "general validity" at least may be claimed within the scope of an economic style, such as the style of the era of the free market.

The concept of economic style is designed to deal with the fact that "economy and society" constitute a complex of economic phenomena that are internally related in many ways with one another as well as with extraeconomic factors, such as political ones. They must be comprehended and explained as a meaningful whole.

Going beyond the theories of economic stages, which stress general patterns of economic evolution, the concept of economic style deals in theoretical terms with the typical variations in economic life. These variations determine the number of economic styles as well as of "historical theories." Together, these constitute the general science of political economy, which is complemented by the absolute theory of basic patterns and is supported by the methods and perceptions of the theory of logic. The validity of historical theories is limited to the particular economic styles on which they are founded, but they may be considered generally valid for those styles.

The definition of economic styles is, therefore, an important problem. They are defined by those characteristics whose regular appearance, interplay, and change from one epoch to another bring about the style changes of the economy. These characteristics include, for example, Sombart's "economic spirit" (*Wirtschaftsgeist*), variable natural and technological foundations, the social structure, the economic structure, and the course of economic events.

Spiethoff's scholarly contributions included considerable editorial activity. For many years he was the editor of *Schmollers Jahrbuch*, of the political science division of the *Enzyklopädie der Rechts- und Staatswissenschaft*, of the *Bonner staatswissenschaftliche Untersuchungen* (together with Herbert von Beckerath and Joseph Schumpeter), and of many volumes of a series on business cycles. He also edited the 1932 Sombart *Festgabe*, a Schmoller *Festgabe* in 1938, and (after World War II) the *Hand- und Lehrbücher aus dem Gebiet der Sozialwissenschaften* (with Edgar Salin), and two volumes of a collection of articles by Joseph Schumpeter (with Erich Schneider).

GUSTAV CLAUSING

[*See also* BUSINESS CYCLES *and the biographies of* KONDRATIEFF; JUGLAR; SCHMOLLER; SCHUMPETER.]

WORKS BY SPIETHOFF

1902   Vorbemerkungen zu einer Theorie der Überproduktion: Vortrag, gehalten am 17. Dezember 1901 in der Staatswissenschaftlichen Vereinigung zu Berlin. *Jahrbuch für Gesetzgebung, Verwaltung und Volkswirtschaft im Deutschen Reich* 26:721–759. → Now called *Schmollers Jahrbuch*.

1909a   Die äussere Ordnung des Kapital- und Geldmarktes. *Jahrbuch für Gesetzgebung, Verwaltung und Volkswirtschaft im Deutschen Reich* 33:445–467.

1909b   Der Kapitalmangel in seinem Verhältnisse zur Güterwelt. *Jahrbuch für Gesetzgebung, Verwaltung und Volkswirtschaft im Deutschen Reich* 33:1417–1437.

1909c   Das Verhältnis von Kapital, Geld und Güterwelt. *Jahrbuch für Gesetzgebung, Verwaltung und Volkswirtschaft im Deutschen Reich* 33:927–951.

1918a   Die Kreditkrise. *Schmollers Jahrbuch für Gesetzgebung, Verwaltung und Volkswirtschaft im Deutschen Reiche* 42:571–614.

1918b   Die Krisenarten. *Schmollers Jahrbuch für Gesetzgebung, Verwaltung und Volkswirtschaft im Deutschen Reiche* 42:223–266.

1920   Der Begriff des Kapital- und Geldmarktes. *Schmollers Jahrbuch für Gesetzgebung, Verwaltung und Volkswirtschaft im Deutschen Reiche* 44:981–1000.

(1923) 1953   Business Cycles. *International Economic Papers* 3:75–171. → First published as "Krisen" in Volume 6 of the *Handwörterbuch der Staatswissenschaften*.

1932   Die allgemeine Volkswirtschaftslehre als geschichtliche Theorie: Die Wirtschaftsstile. Pages 51–84 in *Festgabe für Werner Sombart*. Schmollers Jahrbuch für Gesetzgebung, Verwaltung und Volkswirtschaft im Deutschen Reiche, Vol. 56, No. 6. Munich: Duncker & Humblot.

1933   Overproduction. Volume 11, pages 513–517 in *Encyclopaedia of the Social Sciences*. New York: Macmillan.

1934   *Boden und Wohnung in der Marktwirtschaft, insbesondere im Rheinland*. Bonner staatswissenschaftliche Untersuchungen, Vol. 20. Jena: Fischer.

1938   SPIETHOFF, ARTHUR (editor) *Gustav von Schmoller und die deutsche geschichtliche Volkswirtschaftslehre: Festgabe zur hundertsten Wiederkehr seines Geburtstages 24. Juni 1938*. Schmollers Jahrbuch für Gesetzgebung, Verwaltung und Volkswirtschaft im Deutschen Reiche, Vol. 62, No. 4–6. Berlin: Duncker & Humblot.

1948   Anschauliche und reine volkswirtschaftliche Theorie und ihr Verhältnis zu Einander. Pages 567–664 in *Synopsis: [Festgabe für] Alfred Weber, 30.VII. 1868–30.VII. 1948*. Edited by Edgar Salin. Heidelberg: Schneider.

1952   The "Historical" Character of Economic Theories. *Journal of Economic History* 12:131–139.

1953   Pure Theory and Economic Gestalt Theory: Ideal and Real Types. Pages 444–463 in Frederic C. Lane and Jelle C. Riemersma (editors), *Enterprise and Secular Change: Readings in Economic History*. Homewood, Ill.: Irwin.

1955   *Die wirtschaftlichen Wechsellagen: Aufschwung, Krise, Stockung*. 2 vols. Zürich: Polygraphischer Verlag; Tübingen: Mohr. → Volume 1: *Erklärende Beschreibung*. Volume 2: *Lange statistische Reihen über die Merkmale der wirtschaftlichen Wechsellagen*.

SUPPLEMENTARY BIBLIOGRAPHY

ACKLEY, GARDNER 1954   Spiethoff's Views on the Business Cycle. *Kyklos* 7:283–285. → A review of Spiethoff (1923).

Arthur Spiethoff zum 70. Geburtstag. Schmollers Jahrbuch für Gesetzgebung, Verwaltung und Volkswirtschaft im Deutschen Reiche, Vol. 67, No. 4–5. 1943 Berlin: Duncker & Humblot.

CLAUSING, GUSTAV 1958   Arthur Spiethoffs wissenschaftliches Lebenswerk. *Schmollers Jahrbuch für Gesetzgebung, Verwaltung und Volkswirtschaft im Deutschen Reiche* 78:257–290.

Der Stand und die nächste Zukunft der Konjunkturforschung: Festschrift für Arthur Spiethoff. 1933 Berlin: Duncker & Humblot. → See especially pages 154–160 by Adolf Löwe and pages 161–165 by Friedrich Lutz.

EUCKEN, WALTER (1940) 1951   *The Foundations of Economics: History and Theory in the Analysis of Economic Reality*. Univ. of Chicago Press. → First published as *Die Grundlagen der Nationalökonomie*.

HABERLER, GOTTFRIED (1937) 1958   *Prosperity and Depression: A Theoretical Analysis of Cyclical Movements*. 4th ed., rev. & enl. Harvard Economic Studies, Vol. 105. Cambridge, Mass.: Harvard Univ. Press; London: Allen & Unwin.

JÖHR, WALTER ADOLF 1957   Konjunktur. Volume 6, pages 97–132 in *Handwörterbuch der Sozialwissenschaften*. Stuttgart: Fischer.

KAMP, MATHIAS ERNST 1958   *Gedenkrede auf Arthur Spiethoff*. Bonn: Hanstein. → Includes a bibliography of works by and about Spiethoff.

LANE, FREDERIC C. 1956   Some Heirs of Gustav von Schmoller. Pages 9–39 in *Architects and Craftsmen in*

History: Festschrift für Abbott Payson Usher. Tübingen: Mohr.

LANE, FREDERIC C.; and RIEMERSMA, JELLE C. (editors) 1953 Enterprise and Secular Change: Readings in Economic History. Homewood, Ill.: Irwin. → See pages 431–443, "Introduction to Arthur Spiethoff," and some important remarks in the "Conclusion" by F. C. Lane.

NICOL, HELEN O. 1957 [A Book Review of] Arthur Spiethoff, Die wirtschaftlichen Wechsellagen. Weltwirtschaftliches Archiv, Schrifttum 78:19*–22*.

SCHUMPETER, JOSEPH A. (1954) 1960 History of Economic Analysis. Edited by E. B. Schumpeter. New York: Oxford Univ. Press.

SCHWEITZER, ARTHUR 1941 Spiethoff's Theory of the Business Cycle. University of Wyoming Publications 8:1–30. → Contains a bibliography.

WEIPPERT, GEORG 1941–1942 Walter Euckens Grundlagen der Nationalökonomie. Zeitschrift für die gesamte Staatswissenschaft 102:1–58; 271–337.

WEIPPERT, GEORG 1943 Zum Begriff des Wirtschaftsstils. Schmollers Jahrbuch für Gesetzgebung, Verwaltung und Volkswirtschaft im Deutschen Reiche 67:417–478.

SPINOZA

Benedictus (Baruch) de Spinoza (1632–1677) was born to a family of Portuguese origin settled in the Jewish community at Amsterdam. He received a thorough Hebrew education in preparation, evidently, for a rabbinical career. He himself sought and gained instruction in Latin, which proved to be the key for him to the whole Western philosophical tradition, which naturally lay outside the Jewish curriculum. Further study of non-Judaic traditions led to his dramatic expulsion from the synagogue and the community, with the formula of anathema read out against him. Thenceforth, Spinoza lived outside the community into which he had been born. Generally supporting himself as a lens grinder, a trade in which he achieved some repute, and with the help of a small annuity from an admirer, Spinoza lived first in Rijnsburg, near Leiden, from 1653 to 1663; then in Voorburg, outside The Hague, from 1663 to 1670; and, for the rest of his life, in The Hague itself. During this time, he was in contact with various religious and philosophical "libertine" groups, such as the Collegiants, the Baptists, and the Socinians, as well as with men of predominantly secular interests, such as Johan De Witt and the tolerationist politiques around him; Coenraad van Beuningen, an aristocratic religious freethinker; Henry Oldenburg, the secretary of the Royal Society, who corresponded with Spinoza both on his own behalf and on that of his particular patron, the chemist Robert Boyle; the scientist Christiaan Huygens; the polymath Gottfried Wilhelm von Liebniz; the philosophical mystic Walter von Tschirnhaus; and the "atheist" Adriaan Koerbagh.

By far the most important group to which Spinoza belonged was that formed by those with whom he talked and corresponded about philosophical problems—Lodewijk Meyer, Pieter Balling, Jarig Jelles, Johan Hudde, Albert Burgh—men in varying degrees equipped to understand Spinoza's developing thought. Stimulated by the enormous impact of Cartesianism, particularly by the problems raised by Cartesian dualism, the group dealt with metaphysical, physical, scriptural, political, and ethical matters, of which the chief record is Spinoza's preserved correspondence. In 1670 Spinoza published at Amsterdam—anonymously and under a false imprint—the Tractatus theologico–politicus (see Chief Works, vol. 1; and The Political Works); the book was banned in 1674 for its impiety—that is, for its naturalistic critique of scriptural documents and its consequent denial of revelation through scripture.

Spinoza died, apparently of tuberculosis aggravated by his lens grinding, in 1677; he was buried in the New Church at The Hague, where his grave is still to be seen. In 1677 his friends, under Meyer's direction, edited the Opera postuma, published by Jan Rieuwertz, also a member of the circle; though generally attacked by Leibniz, Bayle, More, Limborch, William King, and a host of others, the Ethics (part of the Opera postuma; see Chief Works, vol. 2) made a considerable impression on philosophers, religious and secular, particularly English and French deists.

Although Spinoza's systematic philosophy had greater solidity than did Descartes's, Spinoza's philosophy may nevertheless be called Cartesian: his "geometrical method" is an extension into formal rhetoric of the Cartesian effort to mathematicize thinking and expression. One of Spinoza's early works (Renati des Cartes principiorum philosophiae pars I et II 1663) is the presentation more geometrico of the Cartesian system, evidently made for the benefit of his study group. His pantheism, however, is his solution to Cartesian radical dualism. He might also be called a Hobbist: different as were their ideas of human nature and its government, Spinoza owed more to Hobbes's formulations on causality and necessity than to Aristotle, Machiavelli, or Bruno, whose works he also knew.

Because of the interlocking nature of Spinoza's system, which unites God and nature, thought and extension, mind and matter, metaphysics and ethics—and, thus, politics—it is difficult to extract his specific contributions to the social sciences. As in the case of Descartes's, Spinoza's method provided an important scientific model for organizing thoughts about man, individual and collective; he adapted the mechanist psychology of Descartes and Hobbes to an ethical view of behavior, in which "ideal" behavior—and, consequently, optimal political and social arrangements—result from the mind's acquiescence in the necessary moral laws of a rational and benevolent deity, united at all points of time and space with his creation. Spinoza's pantheism, with its radical grant of divinity to "nature" (or matter), is rare in Western philosophy and caused an enormous theological polemic to be raised against him.

Spinoza attempted a reformation both of thought and of thinking; using Euclidean and Cartesian geometry as his rhetorical and logical models, he formulated his thought in definitions, postulates, propositions, corollaries, proofs, lemmas, and explanations. Following from his fundamental assumption of pantheism, his psychology postulates a closer connection between man's intellectual and emotional lives than does the Cartesian psychology: Spinoza did not regard the body as properly dominated by the mind, but rather presented mind and body acting as one because they *are* one. Desire (or appetite) is the essence of a man, all of whose emotions may be related to perceptions of pleasure or pain. All emotions, even the approved ones, are *confused ideas* which because of their intellectual inadequacy leave the mind passive; in this way, the passions are related to infirmity of soul and mind, since the result of an adequate idea is activity (i.e., action rather than passion). Part IV of the *Ethics* is entitled "Of Human Bondage, or the Strength of the Emotions," and Part V, "Of the Power of the Understanding, or of Human Freedom." The mind is charged with understanding how it is a part of nature and, therefore, by definition, a part of God. When it has achieved such understanding, it will necessarily be aligned with what exists, or with the good, and will, thus, be good. In such harmony, no emotion or passion can flaw the balance reached; by simple understanding the mind can reach truth and, thus, enjoy the highest pleasure. All lesser pleasures (love, lust, desire for gain, etc.) automatically lose their power to tempt the mind to passion or passivity.

Another way to remove the intellectual infirmity caused by the emotions is to form a clear and distinct idea of the emotions themselves. Each emotion so understood, then, will cease to be a passion, or put another way, the mind becomes less passive with respect to it and more capable of controlling it. Theoretically, all emotions can thus be brought

under the mind's control; by understanding his "nature" a man comes to understand nature at large and, thus, to perfect himself morally. Here, as elsewhere, Spinoza used the language of hedonism: absolute pleasure and pain are understood as absolute good and evil. However, his strong stoical strain led him to redefine pleasure as intellectual understanding and pain as moral, ethical, psychological, and intellectual confusion.

Unlike Descartes's, Spinoza's psychology does not derive from physiology; indeed, he deduced his psychology from his metaphysical postulate, with which the *Ethics* begins and ends, that God is naturally *in* all things, and, therefore, *is* all things, including the human mind and body. Since nature is divine, it is necessarily good. Such errors as a man commits, either intellectual or moral, are the result of his misinterpretation of the natural order —or are intellectual errors which the human mind has the power to correct. Though Spinoza established no direct connection between the psychology of his *Ethics* and his political treatises, it is clear that the truly free Spinozan man lives well in society and that a society made up of men truly free is rational, naturally permitting the greatest possible liberty to each of its members. The exact nature of that "liberty" is much debated: in the public sphere, men were restricted in their freedom to act by their sense of mutual need; in the intellectual sphere, Spinoza argued for liberty of thought as a psychological fact rather than a moral principle. Like Hobbes, Spinoza presupposed a contractual relation between governor and governed, by which a concept of justice is validated. Unlike Hobbes, however, Spinoza was led by his idea of a perfect natural order to have confidence in human intellection and human nature; he emphasized the rights under natural law and favored, not an absolute sovereignty, but a democratic form of government. Spinoza's true freedom, as his psychology made plain, was achieved by intellection and was not a voluntarist matter. True knowledge aligned men "necessarily" with cosmic order, to allay those passions that make them "enemies by nature" so that they may create "a union or agreement of minds."

ROSALIE L. COLIE

[*For the historical context of Spinoza's work, see the biographies of* DESCARTES *and* HOBBES; *for discussion of the subsequent development of his ideas, see* EMOTION; SOCIAL CONTRACT; SYMPATHY AND EMPATHY.]

WORKS BY SPINOZA

1663 *Renati des Cartes principiorum philosophiae pars I et II.* Amsterdam.

Benedicti de Spinoza opera quotquot reperta sunt. 4 vols. Edited by J. van Vloten and J. P. N. Land. The Hague: Nijhoff, 1914.

Chief Works. Translated from the Latin with an introduction by R. H. M. Elwes. 2 vols. New York: Dover, 1955. → Volume 1: *Introduction. Theologico–Political Treatise. A Political Treatise.* Volume 2: *On the Improvement of the Understanding of Ethics.*

Opera. Edited by Carl Gebhardt. 4 vols. Heidelberg: Winter, 1925.

Opera postuma. Amsterdam: Rieuwertz, 1677.

The Political Works: The Tractatus theologico–politicus in part, and *The Tractatus politicus* in full. Edited and translated by A. G. Wernham. Oxford: Clarendon, 1958.

SUPPLEMENTARY BIBLIOGRAPHY

BIDNEY, DAVID (1940) 1962 *The Psychology and Ethics of Spinoza: A Study in the History and Logic of Ideas.* 2d ed. New York: Russell.

DUNIN-BORKOWSKI, STANISLAUS VON 1933–1936 *Spinoza.* 4 vols. Münster (Germany): Aschendorff. → Volume 1: *Der Junge De Spinoza* (First published separately in 1910). Volumes 2–4: *Aus den Tagen Spinozas.* Part 1: Das Entscheidungsjahr 1657. Part 2: Das neue Leben. Part 3: Das Lebenswerk.

HAMPSHIRE, STUART 1951 *Spinoza.* Harmondsworth (England): Penguin.

JOACHIM, HAROLD H. (1901) 1964 *A Study of the Ethics of Spinoza (Ethica ordine geometrico demonstrata).* New York: Russell.

McKEON, RICHARD 1928 *The Philosophy of Spinoza: The Unity of His Thought.* New York: Longmans.

PARKINSON, GEORGE H. R. 1954 *Spinoza's Theory of Knowledge.* Oxford: Clarendon.

VERNIÈRE, PAUL 1954 *Spinoza et la pensée française avant la Révolution.* 2 vols. Paris: Presses Universitaires de France.

WOLFSON, HARRY A. (1934) 1948 *The Philosophy of Spinoza: Unfolding the Latent Processes of His Reasoning.* 2 vols. Cambridge, Mass.: Harvard Univ. Press. → A paperback edition was published in 1961 by World.

SPORT

See LEISURE.

STAGNATION

Central to the definition of "stagnation," in economics, is a situation in which total output (or output per capita) is constant, falling slightly, or rising only sluggishly, or a situation in which unemployment is chronic and growing. Such conditions may exist in particular industries, in wider sectors of an economy, or in the economy as a whole. Only the last of these will be treated here.

Economists have analyzed the occurrence of stagnation in the following widely different circumstances:

(1) Stagnation during certain stages of the business cycle in industrial economies. This type of stagnation is temporary, for it marks a transition in the cyclical process. Its description and explanation are thus part of the general theory of business cycles and will not be discussed here [*see* BUSINESS CYCLES].

(2) Stagnation in the advanced stages of economic growth. This is a more permanent stagnation. It plays an important role in the classical analysis of economic maturity marked by the advent of the "stationary state" and in the Keynesian analysis of the "secular stagnation" of an advanced capitalist economy.

(3) Stagnation in poor, underdeveloped countries. Here stagnation may persist because the economy is dominated by unchanging traditional patterns of economic and social life, which have remained untouched by outside forces and in which there is no incentive to change. Or it may persist if the economy is in the grip of certain types of "vicious circles" that defeat all efforts to advance and that hold the economy in a state of "static equilibrium" at low levels of income. This type of stagnation is analyzed in the theories of the economic development of poor countries.

(4) Stagnation in economies facing difficulties in adapting to changed external circumstances, suffering from the aftermath of severe shocks such as wars and plagues, from gross maladministration of economic affairs, or from political instability. This type of stagnation is discussed more by economic historians than by economists.

(5) Stagnation of economies that seem to be suffering an inexplicable decline in enterprise and "vigor." The last two types of stagnation, unlike the first three, are not due to inherent characteristics of the economic system but are the consequence of external changes or internal decline, which may have occurred for either economic or noneconomic reasons, or both.

A rigorous exposition of persistent and prolonged stagnation as it appears in the classical stationary state, in the Keynesian theory of underemployment equilibrium, or in the theories of economic development cannot be presented in the space available here. Consequently, we shall confine ourselves to a discussion of the general nature of the problem as it appears in these various contexts, together with a brief reference to the treatment of the subject by economic historians.

Stagnation in classical theory. The classical economists were particularly interested in the question of economic progress, but that growth could continue forever seemed inconceivable to them. For one reason or another progress would have to cease at some point, and in a fully mature economy, population and capital accumulation would both become stagnant, with wages at a subsistence level and profits at a minimum. For these economists the "stationary state" was not just an analytical tool, as it was later for Alfred Marshall, but a condition that would eventually be reached in historical time. Thus, to understand fully their conceptions of the causes of stagnation, the reader should examine their theories of economic growth [*see* ECONOMIC GROWTH, *article on* THEORY; *and the biographies of* MALTHUS; RICARDO; SMITH, ADAM].

For Adam Smith, capital accumulation, on which progress depended, both promoted and was promoted by a progressive division of labor; but a country's resources, climate, and location set limits to the amount of capital it could absorb even under the most favorable conditions. Hence, continued accumulation would eventually drive down the rate of profit to a point at which net investment became zero and the economy stagnated because resources permitted no further advance. Yet Smith regarded such a state as far in the future. He was more concerned with the imminent checks to progress arising from political and legal institutions inimical to risk bearing and to individual initiative, from the perverse effects of monopolistic organization, and from the stultifying consequences of government intervention in commerce and international trade, for these could lead to stagnation long before the full potentialities of the economy had been realized. Thus, Smith found eighteenth-century China a country of considerable wealth but stagnating because her laws and institutions did not permit full use of her resources. He considered neglect of foreign commerce and industry a particularly important cause of China's arrested growth, since it limited the extent to which division of labor could be carried out.

The stagnation of the "stationary state" that Ricardo envisaged was *au fond* the result of diminishing returns to labor applied to land. As population increased in response to an increased output made possible by increased investment, the demand for food would rise; but more food could be produced only at increasing cost, because less fertile land would have to be brought under cultivation and existing land used more intensively. This would raise the price of food, and a progressively larger share of the increment in output would have to be paid out in wages, thus driving down the rate of profit and reducing the incentive to accumulate, on which continuing progress depended. Eventually, capital accumulation would cease, and the economy would stagnate: it would have reached the "stationary state."

Nevertheless, according to Ricardo, technological advance could stave off stagnation for a long time,

and an individual country could continue to progress "for ages," since the relevant condition, given free trade, was the ability of the whole world to produce foodstuffs. And even if stagnation did occur, a reasonable standard of living might still be possible, since the subsistence wage that would prevail would be in part culturally determined. If workers insisted on a high standard of living and were willing to restrict their numbers, the subsistence wage might be considerably above the physiological minimum. In spite of these elements of optimism, however, Ricardo was (unjustifiably) labeled a "pessimist"; and economics was called by Carlyle the "dismal science."

Although the Malthusian image of the stationary state was much the same as that of Ricardo, Malthus took issue with Ricardo on a number of significant questions. In particular, he greatly emphasized the importance of the demand for commodities in maintaining the profitable employment of capital and labor, arguing that a deficiency of demand could lead to stagnation in which both capital and labor were redundant relative to the opportunities for employing them profitably. Here he clearly foreshadowed some aspects of modern Keynesian theory, even though he did not quite get to the heart of the matter. Moreover, in the exposition of his argument Malthus came close to some of the fundamental notions in the modern theories of so-called "balanced growth" when he discussed the importance of a supply of commodities consistent with the "structure and habits of society" ([1820] 1964, book 2, chapter 1, section 3).

Malthus analyzed at length the conditions in what today would be called the underdeveloped countries, illustrating his arguments by reference to Ireland and Spanish America. There he found that the grossly unequal distribution of income and wealth, especially of land, and the absence of adequate foreign markets for raw materials disastrously reduced both the peasant's incentive to produce and the landlord's incentive to invest. Consistent with his general sociological views about the nature of man, he stressed the "indolence" of laborers. But he was well aware that much of the apparent indolence might be accounted for by the fact that there was little for laborers to do in the "actual state of things," and by the absence of the stimulus to work and to consumption that a brisk demand for labor might provide. He pointed out that where such demand existed, as in the vicinity of a "new mine," for example, the demand for labor and produce together induced a rapid increase in cultivation. Lack of demand and ignorance and indolence, promoted by inequality of property and deficiency of commerce in landlord and peasant alike, and not capital deficiency, he warned, made it likely that ". . . Spanish America may remain for ages thinly peopled and poor, compared with her natural resources" (*ibid.*, section 4, p. 343). It would follow that to overcome this type of stagnation the appropriate policies would be to promote land reform, to extend the export market for raw materials and improve the terms on which they could be sold, to provide the appropriate incentives (consumer goods?) to overcome the "indolence" of workers, and to overcome "ignorance" through education and "technical assistance." Malthus is famous for his population theory, but it is clear that he anticipated much twentieth-century thought in his analysis of the causes of stagnation and in the means of curing it implicit in that analysis.

Keynesian stagnation. Another version of the stagnation of a mature capitalist economy appeared in the late 1930s, with the Keynesian analysis of the relation, as a country grows in wealth, between the strength of the propensity to save and the inducement to invest. According to this analysis, as capital accumulation proceeds, the return to investors can be expected to fall, leading to a level of investment insufficient to absorb the desired saving of the economy at full employment. As a result, the equilibrium level of national income may be consistent with extensive unemployment. Alvin H. Hansen (1938; 1939), a leading Keynesian "stagnationist," developed this analysis with respect to the historical evolution of capitalism in the United States. He attempted to show how reduced opportunities for investment, coupled with an increased propensity to save, had created a growing gap between actual and potential national output. He thought that as trade cycle succeeded trade cycle, the troughs would become deeper and the booms weaker, with a growing core of unemployment. This process he called "secular stagnation," and he thought it characteristic of "mature economies," especially when there was also a decline in the rate of increase of population. [*See the biographies of* HANSEN *and* KEYNES, JOHN MAYNARD.]

In both Keynesian and classical theory, stagnation resulted from a decline in the inducements to invest. In the former, however, stagnation took the form of unemployment and loss of potential output, while in the latter, it appeared in the form of a cessation of saving as well as of investment, with full employment at "subsistence" wage levels.

The secular stagnation theory, coming as it did during the great depression of the 1930s and casting doubt on the efficiency of unsupervised capitalism—which events had already brought under

suspicion—aroused great controversy, and a number of writers set out to refute in detail Hansen's evidence for the alleged decline of investment opportunities in the United States. The controversy died shortly after the end of World War II, partly because events did not appear to support the thesis that investment opportunities were drying up and partly because the monetary and fiscal policies that the Keynesians advocated, as well as the task of "maintaining full employment," had become widely accepted by governments.

Stagnation in poor countries. Interest in stagnation due to full development or "maturity" was replaced after World War II by interest in the problems of the stagnating economies of poor countries; for all but a tiny minority of the peoples of the world, static or only sluggishly rising incomes have long seemed more "normal" than significant growth. Most of the literature on the development of the poor countries contains explicitly or by implication some theory of stagnation—that is, an explanation of why per capita incomes have for such a long time failed to increase significantly. Two broad types of explanation have been offered. One views stagnation in terms of the circular "static equilibrium" of societies bound by a traditional culture. The other attempts to discover why societies where considerable change has taken place and which have in fact experienced substantial periods of growth often fail to maintain the impetus, tending either to fall back to low levels of per capita income or to advance only apathetically.

Lack of incentive to invest. If one accepts the notion that the growth of an economy in the long run is characterized by an S-shaped curve, the stagnation of the traditional society can be regarded as the counterpart, at the bottom of the curve, of the stagnation of maturity at the top. Both types of stagnation occur because of the lack of incentive to further capital investment.

The absence of significant net investment in traditional societies is attributed by many to the absence of any notion of productive accumulation, or even of progress, and to acceptance of values and institutions which are inimical to innovation. Unchanging technology is held to be, almost by definition, a characteristic of "traditional" stagnation. As a result, economic life continues year after year in a repeating pattern, with no underlying tendency for output to increase appreciably. Some economists, however, have held that the presence of certain economic conditions, such as markets too small to permit the use of more productive technology, incomes too low to permit saving, and inadequate means of transport or sources of power, are sufficient explanations of the failure of an economy to grow.

Failure to maintain growth. Very few countries have such a rigid traditional structure that significant change has never taken place, and in many of them there have been periods in which considerable increases in income have occurred; yet such periods often have not led to sustained economic advance. Explanations of the type of stagnation in which potential economic growth is constantly aborted emphasize certain types of circular causation. Among the chief characteristics of a backward economy, according to many (e.g., Leibenstein 1957), is not only stagnating per capita income but also a tendency, when equilibrium is disturbed, for any forces that increase income to call forth even stronger forces that will again depress it. The relation between increases in income and in population, where technology is relatively primitive and arable land is not easily extended, is held to be one of the more important examples of this type of cause of stagnation. If, with an increase in income, no surplus for investment becomes available because of increased consumption as the population increases, then periods of rising per capita income may well be only temporary. This kind of problem, which was also at the center of classical analysis, is aggravated by advances in medicine and public health which permit the population to grow independently of economic conditions.

A large number of characteristics of poor economies which are inimical to growth have been discussed in the literature, but many of them are merely descriptions of the accompaniments of poverty: ignorance and superstition, low standards of education, disease, inability to save, apathy, etc. There is no doubt that material and technical backwardness of the mass of the people makes the elimination of poverty extremely difficult, particularly when political institutions and the attitudes of the wealthier classes do not favor productive enterprise. But a major objection to all of the theories which insist on the closed and unbreakable nature of "vicious circles" arises from the fact that a number of countries whose conditions would seem to fit the requirements of such theories have in fact been able to break out largely by their own efforts. It should be noted, however, that many of these countries had unusually favorable opportunities for international trade.

Stagnation following external shocks or severe decline. In addition to the stagnation discussed in economic theory and the apparent stagnation of traditional and primitive societies described primarily by anthropologists, there are periods of stagnation in more advanced economies which historians have explained in various ways.

An excellent modern discussion of an economic stagnation which can be traced largely to the difficulties of adjusting to radically changed external conditions can be found in Svennilson's analysis of the European economy between the World Wars (1954). Some of the major heavy industries in the large industrial countries of Europe found themselves ill-equipped to meet postwar circumstances. Stagnation in these industries spread to other sectors of the European economy, giving rise to very slow rates of growth for a number of countries, with severe consequences not only for international trade but for intra-European trade as well. This, in turn, intensified the problems of adjustment. It is clear that stagnation in advanced countries, like poverty in backward countries, often creates economic and, perhaps even more important, political and social conditions which are antagonistic to the very changes required to overcome it. A variety of circular economic, political, and social causal relationships give rise to cumulative movements in which tendencies to stagnation or decline reinforce each other, particularly after an economy has suffered a shock or when adaptation to changed external conditions requires substantial alterations in the existing economic structure.

Many of the notorious examples of stagnation in history have been explained primarily as the consequences of conditions and events which brought about a preceding decline. For our purposes we must distinguish between the causes of decline and the reasons for the subsequent stagnation. Since wars, internal political fissions, and general breakdown of law and order have often been engendered by decline brought on by other causes, the resulting inability of the economy to recover quickly has been explained with reference to the damage caused by such prior events. Many great empires and civilizations of the past seem to have suffered before their final "collapse" long periods in which agriculture, industry, and trade were stagnant. Among the more prominent explanations advanced by historians have been the excessive luxury of courts, the corruption of the ruling classes, and the growth of a despotic, extortionate, and expensive bureaucracy, all of which led to financial disorder and particularly to disastrously heavy taxation of agriculture, which destroyed the foundations of the rural economy. The income taken from agriculture was not used productively, but in ostentatious consumption.

Thus taxation and the unproductive consumption of the ruling classes were apparently important causes of the stagnation of the agriculture and industry of Athens in the fourth century B.C., where decline was hastened also by the loss of export markets. The break-up of the Islamic empire after the eighth century and the stagnation of many of its constituent parts were also associated with oppressive taxation of agriculture, unheeding luxury expenditure, and corruption and mismanagement of rulers. In Iraq, for example, the economy had been stagnating long before the Mongol invaders arrived in the thirteenth century and sacked Baghdad. The neglect and final destruction of the irrigation system on which the area depended resulted in a long period of stagnation. Later, in the eighteenth century, the Ottoman Empire was in a state of economic anarchy also largely because of the decayed and degenerate state of government. Neither the ruling class, nor the military, nor the intellectuals were concerned about economic conditions, especially the state of agriculture; and oppression of the rural population, general misrule, and bureaucratic corruption were prevalent. Similar conditions have a central place in the historians' descriptions of the closing periods of the Roman Empire, the Byzantine Empire, and even of the stagnation in Spain after the sixteenth century.

Some scholars have attempted sweeping theories to explain the decline and stagnation of particular types of societies. The great fourteenth-century Arab historian and philosopher, Ibn Khaldūn (1375–1382), postulated, with many illustrations, an inevitable decline of "group feeling" in empires in full maturity, and also the rise of luxurious habits of rulers and a growing "tameness" among the people as characterizing the "senility" of the society. Schumpeter, considering modern capitalism, also noted a tendency to self-destruction "which, in its earlier stages, may well assert itself in the form of a tendency toward retardation of progress" (1942, p. 162). And Toynbee (1934–1939) explained why some civilizations suffer "arrest" and enter periods of "petrifaction."

As is to be expected, any attempt to isolate specific "causes" for historical events is fraught with serious difficulties. Simple economic "models" do not attempt to deal with those sociological and political aspects of stagnation that are as important as, if not more important than, the economic aspects. Economists may fruitfully try to explain in economic terms why an economy may stagnate in the modern world, and they have come up with some useful relationships which can be used in the formulation of economic policies. But stagna-

tion sets in for different reasons in different circumstances, and all explanations, including the so-called economic ones, rest, in the last analysis, on as yet unexplained characteristics of human psychology and sociology: attitudes toward procreation, "propensities" to save and invest, aptitudes for innovating "enterprise," religious values or superstitions, and apathetic acceptance of the apparently inevitable. To explain the sufficient conditions for stagnation is also to explain the necessary conditions for sustained progress; and this has not yet been achieved.

EDITH PENROSE

[*See also* ECONOMIC GROWTH.]

BIBLIOGRAPHY

CIPOLLA, CARLO M. 1952 The Decline of Italy: The Case of a Fully Matured Economy. *Economic History Review* Second Series 5:178–187.

HAMMOND, MASON 1946 Economic Stagnation in the Early Roman Empire: The Tasks of Economic History. *Journal of Economic History* 6 (Supplement):63–90.

HANSEN, ALVIN H. 1938 *Full Recovery or Stagnation?* New York: Norton.

HANSEN, ALVIN H. (1939) 1944 Economic Progress and Declining Population Growth. Pages 366–384 in American Economic Association, *Readings in Business Cycle Theory.* Philadelphia: Blakiston. → First published in Volume 29 of the *American Economic Review.* Expounds the theory of secular stagnation.

HIGGINS, BENJAMIN 1959 *Economic Development: Problems, Principles and Policies.* New York: Norton. → A useful discussion of the classical and modern theories of stagnation, together with bibliographical references, may be found in chapters 3, 5, and 7 and Part 4.

IBN KHALDŪN (1375–1382) 1958 *The Muqaddimah: An Introduction to History.* 3 vols. Translated from the Arabic by Franz Rosenthal. New York: Pantheon. → See especially Volume 1, Chapter 3, sections 10–13.

LEIBENSTEIN, HARVEY (1957) 1963 *Economic Backwardness and Economic Growth: Studies in the Theory of Economic Development.* New York: Wiley.

MALTHUS, THOMAS ROBERT (1820) 1964 *Principles of Political Economy Considered With a View to Their Practical Application.* 2d ed. New York: Kelley. → A reprint of the 1836 edition. See especially Book 2 on the progress of wealth.

MILL, JOHN STUART (1848) 1965 *Principles of Political Economy, With Some of Their Applications to Social Philosophy.* Edited by J. M. Robson. 2 vols. Collected Works, Vols. 2–3. Univ. of Toronto Press. → See especially Book 4, Chapter 6, "Of the Stationary State."

MOSSÉ, CLAUDE 1962 *La fin de la démocratie athénienne: Aspects sociaux et politiques du déclin de la cité grecque au IVe siècle avant J.-C.* Paris: Presses Universitaires de France.

RICARDO, DAVID (1817) 1951 *Works and Correspondence.* Volume 1: On the Principles of Political Economy and Taxation. Cambridge Univ. Press. → See especially Chapter 2, "On Rent"; Chapter 5, "On Wages"; and Chapter 6, "On Profits." See also Chapter 19, "On Sudden Changes in the Channels of

Trade." A paperback edition of this volume was published in 1963 by Irwin.

SCHUMPETER, JOSEPH A. (1942) 1950 *Capitalism, Socialism, and Democracy.* 3d ed. New York: Harper; London: Allen & Unwin. → A paperback edition was published by Harper in 1962.

SMITH, ADAM (1776) 1950 *An Inquiry Into the Nature and Causes of the Wealth of Nations.* Edited by Edwin Cannan. 6th ed. 2 vols. London: Methuen. → For the effects on employment of a stationary state, see Book 1, Chapter 8, "On the Wages of Labour." See also Book 3, "Of the Different Progress of Opulence in Different Nations," and Book 4, "Of Systems of Political Economy." A paperback edition was published in 1963 by Irwin.

SVENNILSON, INGVAR 1954 *Growth and Stagnation in the European Economy.* Geneva: United Nations, Economic Commission for Europe.

TOYNBEE, ARNOLD J. (1934–1939) 1947 *A Study of History.* Abridgment of Vols. 1–6 by D. C. Somervell. Issued under the auspices of the Royal Institute of International Affairs. Oxford Univ. Press.

STAMP, JOSIAH CHARLES

Josiah Charles Stamp, first baron Stamp of Shortlands, Kent (1880–1941), economist and economic adviser to the British government, was born at Bexley, Kent, and entered the British civil service as a clerk at a salary of about $3 a week. For 21 of his 23 years in the civil service he devoted himself to the analysis and development of taxation. The structure of the British income tax that emerged from World War I and was elaborated in the report of the Royal Commission on the Income Tax (Great Britain . . . 1920) is in large measure his achievement.

Because of his lucidity and ability in explaining this complicated instrument of government to industrialists, he was persuaded to become a director of Nobel Industries. So began in 1919 the second phase of his career, the management of corporations. In 1926, when Nobel was bought by Imperial Chemical Industries, he remained as a director of this large-scale enterprise. In addition, he was chairman of the board of the largest railway amalgamation in Great Britain, the London, Midland and Scottish, an officer of a dozen or more financial and educational institutions, and, from 1928, a director of the Bank of England. From 1924 to 1929 he served on the international commissions which developed the Dawes and Young plans for German reparations and in the process evolved the Bank for International Settlements.

From 1935 on, in a third phase of Stamp's career, the British government increasingly used him as a consultant on economic policy. Typically, he set in motion a rationalization of the statistical services that enabled the various departments, especially the Treasury, to organize the economy speedily for the prosecution of World War II. When war broke out in 1939 he was chief economic adviser to the government. On the night of April 16, 1941, Stamp, his wife, his eldest son, and their domestic staff were in their bomb shelter when the house received a direct hit in an air raid. No one survived.

In his upwardly mobile career, from a minor clerkship to the peerage of England, Stamp personified the Puritan ethic; he was a teetotaler and a nonsmoker, and he was once referred to as the "busiest man in England." He earned a London University B.SC. in 1911 by examination without ever attending a lecture and a D.SC. in 1916 with a brilliant dissertation on taxation. From 1924 on he published several series of lectures, including a presidential address and sectional addresses to the British Association for the Advancement of Science, all of which give evidence of his continued intellectual growth and production. Honorary degrees, medals, and awards, including a peerage, were given him.

Stamp's early papers show his grasp of classical economic theory, his capacity to analyze the usage of current terms, his massive work on the illogical structure of the British tax statistics, and his practical judgment concerning those adjustments that would lead to the attainment of tax policy goals with greater efficiency and no loss of total revenue. A major new concept, excess profits, together with convincing arguments for the ethical correctness of taxing them at a higher rate, entered the British tax structure after 1915. These ideas were foreshadowed in an analytical paper by Stamp on unearned income, where he distinguished between two types of economic surpluses: (*a*) those necessary for the continuation of productive enterprise, and (*b*) those created by unusual scarcities or demands. He returned to this problem, in 1932, when he first advanced the index of profits. He saw clearly even before 1920 the imperfections of the excess profits duty, although it produced 25 per cent of the revenue during World War I. He also saw that a capital levy in a society with high income taxes would merely be an anticipation of future revenue. In all of these writings, while showing a knowledge of the historical development of the income tax structure and of differences between British principles and those of Europe and the United States, Stamp presented what was principally an analytical and statistical argument, highly technical and adapted closely to the exigencies and idiosyncrasies of Britain's particular circumstances. With A. L. Bowley and others at the London School of Economics, he developed acceptable methods for calculating the gross national product of the United Kingdom.

Stamp's contributions to nontechnical economic issues or to general social questions, through his public lectures and addresses to learned societies, aim at clarifying a confused public debate or illustrating the essential complexity of problems that look simple if approached solely from the point of view of economics, statistics, or ethics. In the *Calculus of Plenty* (1935), a close economic analysis of the concept of "plenty" showed it to mean either (*a*) physical or scientific potentiality, (*b*) unused or unmarketed production, or (*c*) idle capacity—or some combination of these. He deplored the quantification of any one of these three as if it were independent of restraints from the others. "Large dynamic ideas are scientifically dangerous if they remain unmeasured" (see *The Calculus of Plenty* 1935). By measurement, Stamp meant precision of classification, exactness of the crude figures, and elegance in the derived statistics.

As an economist, Stamp did much to clarify and expand specialized aspects of economic doctrine related to the national income, the national capital, and problems in the economics and ethics of taxation. As a master statistician he provided the tools for economic analysis and theory testing rather than the analyses or the theories.

JOHN MOGEY

WORKS BY STAMP

(1916) 1920 *British Incomes and Property: The Application of Official Statistics to Economic Problems . . . With Supplementary Tables From 1914 to 1918.* London School of Economics and Political Science, Studies in Economics and Political Science, No. 47. London: King.
(1918–1936) 1937 *The National Capital and Other Statistical Studies.* London: King. → Contains eight previously published essays.
(1921) 1936 *The Fundamental Principles of Taxation in the Light of Modern Developments.* Rev. ed. London: Macmillan.
(1922) 1930 *Wealth and Taxable Capacity, Being the Newmarch Lectures for 1920–1921 on Current Statistical Problems in Wealth and Industry.* 3d ed. London: King.
1924 *Studies in Current Problems in Finance and Government and "The Wealth and Income of the Chief Powers" (1914).* London: King.
1929 *Some Economic Factors in Modern Life.* London: King.
1932 *Industrial Profits in the Last Twenty Years: A New Index Number.* London: Royal Statistical Society. → Presidential address delivered on June 21, 1932. Also published in Volume 95 of the *Journal of the Royal Statistical Society.*
1934 Eugenic Influences in Economics. *Eugenics Review* 26:107–119. → The Galton lecture delivered before the Eugenics Society on February 16, 1934.
(1934–1936) 1937 *The Science of Social Adjustment.* London: Macmillan. → Includes Stamp 1934 and 1935.
1935 *The Calculus of Plenty.* London: British Science Guild.

SUPPLEMENTARY BIBLIOGRAPHY

BEVERIDGE, WILLIAM 1941 The Right Hon. Lord Stamp, G.C.B., G.B.E., F.B.A. *Nature* 147:567–568.
BEVERIDGE, WILLIAM 1959 Josiah Charles Stamp. Supplement 6, pages 817–820 in *Dictionary of National Biography: 1949–1950.* Oxford Univ. Press.
BOWLEY, ARTHUR LYON 1941 Lord Stamp. *Journal of the Royal Statistical Society* 104:193–196.
Economics of Plenty. 1935 *Nature* 136:809–810. → A review of Stamp's *The Calculus of Plenty* 1935.
GREAT BRITAIN, ROYAL COMMISSION ON THE INCOME TAX 1920 *Report.* Papers by Command, Cmd. 615. London: H.M. Stationery Office.
HENDERSON, HUBERT DOUGLAS 1941 Josiah Charles Stamp, Baron Stamp of Shortlands (June 21, 1880 to April 16, 1941). *Economic Journal* 51:338–347.
JONES, JAMES HARRY 1964 *Josiah Stamp, Public Servant: The Life of the First Baron Stamp of Shortlands.* New York and London: Pitman.
WILLCOX, WALTER FRANCIS 1941 Josiah Charles Stamp, 1880–1941. *Journal of the American Statistical Association* 36:546–547.

STANDARD OF LIVING

See CONSUMERS, *article on* CONSUMPTION LEVELS AND STANDARDS.

STATE

I. THE INSTITUTION   *Morton H. Fried*
II. THE CONCEPT   *Frederick M. Watkins*

I
THE INSTITUTION

"L'état," Louis XIV is reported to have said, "c'est moi." The clarity and ease of application of this definition are somewhat exceeded by its lack of utility. As a definition, however, it suffers only slightly more from the outrages of controversy than most other attempts to set out succinctly the essence of the institutional phenomenon known as the state. At one extreme of argument the state is identified with one or more highly specific features, such as organized police powers, defined spatial boundaries, or a formal judiciary. At the other end of the definitional spectrum the state is regarded simply as the institutional aspect of political interaction; no concrete structures are specified, and the state, being coterminous with society, vanishes in universality.

Nineteenth-century theorists, whether in moral philosophy or the emerging disciplines of political science, sociology, and anthropology, accepted a more or less rigid concept of the state as a complex of specific mechanisms of government which could be described in their own contemporary societies and which could be recognized in some form in the classical Mediterranean civilizations. Differences in gross types of polity did not disturb these thinkers. Aristotle, after all, had provided for at least three polarities, monarchy, aristocracy, and polity, each with its nonideal form, tyranny, oligarchy, and democracy; this system of classification has remained without essential change to the present day, although its utility has declined sharply of late.

Though the Aristotelian approach predated the evolutionary orientation, it had several features that enabled it to fit very well into the mainstream of nineteenth-century thought. Foremost among these were its reliance on conventional logic and the fact that it had been developed, albeit long before, in a theoretical matrix of historical change. In political theory the difference between pure and corrupt forms and the possibility of passage from one type to another was evidently compatible with newer emphases on evolution and progress. The revolution in thought, which, at least temporarily, undermined the analysis of the state as a complex of concrete institutions, began toward the end of the nineteenth century with the emergence of functionalism. It was in the twentieth century that new ways of looking at the state, stimulated by the parallel development of behavioral and operational approaches, began to show competitive degrees of refinement.

Definition of the state. According to George Sabine, the word "state" was fixed as a generic term for a body politic by Machiavelli early in the sixteenth century, at which time it seems to have been current in the form *stato*. Somewhat earlier, similar and related forms were used to designate "status" and "estate." Slightly divergent in etymology, both words are traced to the Latin *status*, the participial form of *stare*, "to stand." Considering the continuing problem of the relationship of the state to the existence of socioeconomic classes, the philological interdependence of state, estate, and status is of some interest.

In some definitions, such as those contributing to or inspired by Marxist theory, the state coincides with all societies composed of two or more classes involved in relations of dominance and subordination, primarily in the sphere of economics, but also in other sectors of social life. It is this postulated identity that underlies the concept of the

withering away of the state and is proposed as rationalization and justification for the dictatorship of the proletariat: when only one class is in possession of society, the state, by this definition, must become a null category.

Equipped with a definition that furnishes a logical point of emergence and an equally logical point of expiration for the state, one may reasonably attempt to isolate characteristic features or mechanisms whereby the state may be recognized and its variations plotted. It is not surprising, moreover, that a considerable portion of the literature devoted to this subject is polemical and normative, given to proofs of the historical superiority of one system as opposed to another or to the inevitability of the emergence and the ultimate demise of the state. With regard to the latter points, an important focus of problems is found in the conditions and processes whereby states are precipitated; these subjects have long had particular fascination for anthropologists and more recently have attracted political scientists, who, rather than speculating on these questions from a distance, are going into the field to study the political systems of newly established states.

For various reasons, some political in the most restricted sense and others having to do with the dialectical character of the expansion of knowledge and the growth of theory, functionalism developed within sociology and anthropology partly as a counter to the dominant position of evolutionary orientations in nineteenth-century thought. Functionalism brought some changes in the formulation of problems; the quest for origins was abandoned, if not attacked on theoretical and methodological grounds. Concurrently, the emphasis on process in the analysis of systems and subsystems redirected attention toward types of societies that previously had been omitted from the field of study. This trend was reinforced by implicit or explicit subscription to cultural relativism; if no people lacked technology and religion, so too none lacked the state. In some approaches this led to virtual elimination of the term "state" and its content; the state was equated with political organization. The further development of operationalism and behavioral orientations encouraged these views. The strategy of operationalism concentrated research on the study of clearly separable parts of the political process and their interactions. The analysis of political systems as a whole, the implicit focus of evolutionary studies, was abandoned on the ground that the state, taken as a totality, was a variable congeries of complex institutions and an unwieldy research subject. Concomitantly, the growth of be- haviorism, in a sense the operational phase of psychology, encouraged the study of the micro- processes of politics, decision making in particular. Moreover, a branch of mathematics specially geared to this type of problem analysis was developed. Game theory and complex statistical techniques capable of determining regularities in multivariate situations have greatly enhanced the prestige of the small-scale study. [*See* SYSTEMS ANALYSIS.]

It is not unlikely that the future will see a *rapprochement* between these now divergent ap- proaches. At present, however, conflict and paro- chialism overshadow harmony and the search for common denominators. As a result, it is impossible to offer a unified definition of the state that would be satisfactory even to a majority of those seriously concerned with the problem.

Territoriality. At first, the association of the state with a territory seems unlikely to encounter disagreement from any analyst, whatever his theo- retical commitment. But difficulties do appear. In some simple cultures attachment to place is *ad hoc* and relates not to bounded areas but to scattered features of the environment, such as sources of water or windfall foods. Even with respect to stra- tegic features, the concept of exclusive access is not universal. Unfortunately, it is probable that a completely definitive statement about the relations between truly primitive societies and their habitats, considered as domains, will remain beyond the power of anthropology to offer. There are no longer any such societies available for study. Interesting results are being obtained, however, from compar- ative observations of other primates; these show a range of situations, including the relatively close tie of a group to a locality as well as cases of both peaceful overlapping of territories and relatively easy movement of individuals from one resource area into that occupied by another group [*see* SOCIAL BEHAVIOR, ANIMAL, *article on* PRIMATE BEHAVIOR].

Vagueness in regard to the association between society and territory interfered in the attempt of the U.S. government to repair some of the inequities that attended the westward spread of the dominant culture. Skilled witnesses, attorneys, and federal judges tried to establish cash values for territories from which various Indian tribes, particularly in the area of the Great Basin and adjacent Califor- nia, had been dispossessed, but there was incessant wrangling over which tribe had occupied exactly what stretch of ground.

More crucial to the discussion are those situa- tions in which kinship rather than territoriality furnishes the basis of association. Two facts must be added immediately. First, proximity plays a role in the organization of all kinship groups, and to that extent all such groups are territorial. Second, the development of complex political organization does not extinguish kinship but leads to its reinter- pretation, the loss of some old functions and the emergence of new ones. A kinship society, however, is one in which social relationships are primarily determined by pre-existing sociogenetic ties, with other principles of affiliation playing minor roles. Basically, apart from the network and ideology of sociogenetic and affinal kinship, there are no loci of power from which regular sanctions emanate. As indicated above, some scholars do not regard this as sufficient ground for withholding the desig- nation of state. But it should be asked whether there is any value in a term stretched so broadly that it pertains simultaneously to both an acepha- lous, territorially unfocused aggregate of kin and a formally organized, territorially demarcated, elaborately coordinated society, composed of mem- bers whose only bonds are those of participation in the same social system or even in overlapping but largely discrete segments of a complex system. [*See* STATELESS SOCIETY.]

There are other problems in the association of a state with a defined and bounded territory. The analysis of feudalism, for example, raises questions of this kind. Even in its European setting, where feudalism was tied so clearly to a territorially based manorialism, actual political ties did not always correlate with location; feudal hierarchies rarely can be understood in territorial terms, although they possess territorial elements [*see* FEUDALISM]. Perhaps a more illuminating case is that of the Berber rule in portions of north Africa until the middle of the last century. In that system a rela- tively high degree of governmental complexity existed in the context of general territorial ambi- guity.

Sovereignty. Territoriality in many of its fea- tures raises questions of sovereignty—the identifi- cation and monopoly of paramount control in a society. The concern with the paramountcy of con- trol is important. All complex societies and some of the simpler ones can be described as collections of administrative subsystems. Such a society has a kind of cellular structure which represents the areal spread of the political system. Thus, a federal system comprises provinces or "states," which in turn consist of smaller units down to the lowest level of formal political control, such as wards, or precincts. These low-level units can be adapted to urban or rural settlement, to a nomadic life, to capitalism, socialism, or any other system of property ownership.

While most systems provide for considerable local power in carrying out the frequently vague or ambiguous prescriptions of higher authority, an implementation that often requires extensive *ad hoc* decision making, there are always provisions guaranteeing the final authority of the higher administrative echelons. The maintenance of channels of communication between levels is one of the most important of state tasks.

At best, sovereignty is a relative concept, though some states claim total power and attempt to wield it. Other polities (feudal, for example) exclude certain areas from control and thus circumscribe and reduce the sovereign power, as in the instance of the Magna Charta. Anthropologists and sociologists, particularly those working in premodern African states, have made fairly intensive analyses of the structural limits on the power of the ruler who has been found to be inhibited in the exercise of his office by the necessity of relying on advisers and agents and by the weight of ritual, if not tradition. These limitations can have the effect of an unwritten constitution, but what is not always realized is that they compromise the power of the ruler without compromising the power of the sovereignty concerned. Rulers, including dictators and despots, are only one focal manifestation of the power of the organized political state. It is obvious that this power must be transmitted and thus shared, but this does not eliminate it.

The inefficiency of physical means of communication and the lack of understanding of individual and group psychodynamics have interfered with the exercise of sovereignty. In addition to problems arising out of the necessity to parcel out authority to a bureaucracy, all complexly organized societies have been subject to what Karl Wittfogel has called the rules of diminishing administrative returns. This means that conflicts between higher and lower levels of authority may be decided by default of the superior level, which cannot apply its force to every issue and trouble spot but must husband it, defending strategic regions or institutions. The contest is particularly acute in some societies, although it is endemic in all. If the gap between the claims of sovereignty and the availability of force grows too great, the state may be destroyed. This may be the result of internal pressures, as a new group comes to power, or it may be accomplished externally,

with conquest sweeping aside the outworn pretensions of sovereignty.

The failure to deal with problems of sovereignty has sometimes adversely affected field work in the social sciences. This is a particular matter of concern when a society has been described as if it were politically autonomous when, in fact, it has been under the firm control of a superior political establishment and therefore has suffered significant changes in its system of administration, economic allocation, warfare, and other major aspects of social life. The errors of description become errors of interpretation when observations made on such societies are purported to represent pristine conditions in the development of a political system. One empirical index of the magnitude of such errors is apparent in the failure of such studies to predict or even prepare us for the massive anticolonial revolutions sweeping much of the world. These studies have also been almost useless in furnishing guides to the developments that have taken place since the establishment of new states, especially in Africa.

In the first half of the nineteenth century, the jurist John Austin tied his definition of law, and implicitly the concept of the state, to the concept of sovereignty. He held that positive law, on which formal government rested, could only exist in conjunction with a determinate locus of power and ultimate authority. Though no state has yet seen total power vested in the ruling forces, the wisdom of Austin's suggestion is revealed by its utility. This value, however, diminishes as the frame of the problem moves from the evolution of the state to the functioning of particular political systems. [*See* SOVEREIGNTY.]

Legitimacy.   Sovereignty involves the source of ultimate power in a society. Power is the ability to make and carry out decisions that are binding on the rest of the population. As such, it is essentially divorced from moral or value judgments. It is through the concept of legitimacy that ideology is blended with politics. One of the basic functions of legitimacy, in other words, is to offer an excuse for and justify the existence of the state; beyond this, it also justifies specific social orders and hierarchies and the means of maintaining them.

Related to this meaning of legitimacy, yet distinct, is the technical meaning of the term made familiar by Max Weber, which deals with the basis of acceptance by a population of a specific polity and system of rule. This conception both flows from and reinforces notions of social solidarity and integration. When used by Weber and his followers, the concept of legitimacy was superficially freed from connections with specific ideologies, but a deep current akin to utilitarianism, or to the older and now generally discredited concept of social contract, runs in it and is manifested in implications that all political systems ultimately rest upon the consent of the governed. [*See* LEGITIMACY.]

Without attempting to summarize the Weberian typology of modes of legitimizing authority, it is interesting to note that two of the types form a progression: The charismatic leadership of the magically potent warrior chief, which, with the delegation and routinization of power, becomes patrimonial. If development continues, it tends to be in the direction of increasing bureaucratization, which shows increasing rationalization of the process of government.

Since the time of Weber problems in the structure of bureaucracy have commanded increasing attention among sociologists. Such scholars as Peter Blau and Amitai Etzioni have expanded the theoretical frame of analysis and its appplications. Others, following the lead of political philosophers such as Michels, have stressed elitist elements and have taken more programmatic lines, becoming advocates of a timocracy based on managerial ability. The descriptive analysis of bureaucratic organization has been undertaken in relation to a wide variety of cultures. Some analyses have focused on societies long famed for bureaucratic complexity, such as traditional China, and have involved the overlapping labors of specialists from a number of different disciplines. Others have pioneered in less well known traditions, primarily in work on African kingdoms, such as Fallers' study of Soga organization. Still other inquiries have been made into bureaucratic formations in industry and commerce, where these have not been branches of the state, yet have exerted statelike power not only over their employees but also over sectors of the public that have been affected by their pricing, marketing, or other policies, or their influence on decision making in formal organs of the state. All of these studies, particularly the last mentioned, have shown deep awareness of the interpenetration of political and economic behavior and institutions. [*See* TRADE AND MARKETS.]

State and economy. Politics has been defined by Harold Lasswell as the study of "who gets what, when, and how." The distinction between economics and politics is in large measure a heuristic device of the analyst and a measure of his specialization. A case may be made, however, to show that one index of the complexity of a social system is

the discreteness of its several subsystems of allocation. Another way of putting this is to remark that the development of the state parallels the development of semi-independent sectors of economic and political action. A number of profound questions flow from the foregoing statement. Some have to do with the integration of culture: it may be asked how far changes may develop in one cultural sector without necessitating at least compensatory changes in other sectors. Related to this question is the important problem of core and superstructure, raised not only in Marxist philosophy but in many other materialistic approaches to the nature of culture and society. It is interesting to consider the recent attempt to remold the economy of China by the primary means of applying tremendous political pressure to the population. In this attempt the Chinese Communist party rallied behind a slogan borrowed from Lenin, "the primacy of politics," and vaunted ideological means over economic means of reforming the culture. The differences between economics and politics are made very clear when one compares the political–ideological view of the Chinese economy with what can be gathered of its statistical reality [*see* CHINESE SOCIETY; ECONOMIC DATA, *article on* MAINLAND CHINA].

Conversely, a nineteenth-century myth still circulates in some quarters, spreading the fantasy that a state can exist that plays no role in the economy. No such state has yet existed, and there are ample theoretical grounds for believing it impossible. So-called laissez-faire governments had no hesitation in applying crushing force to the unpropertied in order to keep them in that status. The use of its power to maintain a specific social order is one of the primary aspects of the state, and the analysis of ancient, classical, and exotic legal codes confirms that the points in the social order that are considered strategic have invariably been definable as economic statuses. The codes of ancient Mesopotamian states, whether of Lipit-Ishtar or Hammurabi, of the Mediterranean civilizations, and of ancient China, as well as what is known of the legal structure of the Inca empire, indicate the same proliferating of law in the overlapping areas of property and status. The one area that competes most strongly with these is that of administrative law and rules of procedure. However, the sanctions involved in maintaining procedure are frequently couched in terms of a defense of the paramount status of the ruler, offenses against which may be regarded as the serious crime of lese majesty, or treason.

Among the various theories of the origin of the state are several that stress economic factors; one approach portrays the state as the precipitate of the social organization of the economy at a particular level of productive and distributive efficiency. According to the economic ideas of Karl Polanyi, the pristine state was a solution to the problems of organization of increasingly complex redistributive economies. The theory is broadly synthetic, relying also on Weberian notions about the development and routinization of bureaucracy, on Marxian notions of incipient class struggle, and on the ecological notions of Wittfogel, which relate the growth of complex government to the need for directing a large labor force carrying out socially compulsory tasks of irrigation and flood control.

This particular problem has attracted considerable attention in anthropology. Contributions have been made by archeologists and by some ethnographers. The former have produced evidence on the antiquity and importance of irrigation structures in civilizations in Asia and the New World. Ethnographers have observed societies presently dependent on irrigation works or drainage control and have attempted to evaluate the pressure such social tasks place on the political network. [See Urban Revolution.]

State and religion.   There have been many states that have wedded the mechanisms of government to a particular sacred establishment, not merely in a supportive way but also to create an identity between political and religious hierarchies. The question of whether any state has ever existed completely free of religious ties is somewhat more difficult to answer, since it raises serious problems of definition.

As already indicated, the concept of legitimacy, which explains the basis of state sovereignty, is essentially an ideological rationalization of *de facto* political power. In every state the ideology of legitimacy is associated with extensive ritual, with ceremonies that are anything but hollow, even if they may not conform to a narrow definition of religion. Anthropologists have long been aware of the relations between ritual and social organization and are becoming increasingly concerned with this topic. Whether their attention has focused on the role and significance of the golden stool in Ashanti kingship or on the ceremonial first plowing which is a responsibility of the ruler in almost all of the states whose agrarian economies rested on irrigation, those who have studied political activity in simple states have become familiar with the interdependence of state and ritual, governance and myth.

Because so many early states either were theocracies or conceived of the political ruler as a god, there has been no shortage of theories attributing the origin of the state to the emergence of a powerful priesthood. Such theories tend to neglect or misinterpret the negative cases, such as ancient China, where the priesthood occupied an ancillary position. More importantly, however, such theorizing tends to miss the main question: Regardless of the alternate roles occupied by those who filled leadership positions, what were the conditions that demanded or at least supported the development and concentration of such new and extreme forms of social power? It is particularly the problem of supplying an excuse and rationale for this power that implicates the religious subsystem of the culture. Though there have obviously been a great many ways of linking religion and governance, the reasons for doing so remain few and simple. [See Ritual; Myth and symbol; Religion.]

State and law.   Quite obviously, as E. A. Hoebel has reminded us, the number of legal systems will shrink considerably if among the criteria of such systems is possession of marble edifices: courts of law above whose portals is inscribed, *Fiat justitia, ruat caelum*. Most of those concerned with the problem of defining law will readily grant that elaborate courthouses are dispensable; indeed, they will give up the courthouse *in toto*. However, can they also give up the court?

Ultimately this question comes down to the distinction between law and custom. According to the historical school of jurisprudence, the distinction was inconsequential. The emphasis was on compliance rather than on the means of securing compliance. The problem, of course, is both real and practical: the state, as we have seen, cannot constantly mobilize its force at each point in its structure. On the other hand, it is well established that laws are not broken simply because police power is not being exerted. For the most part, social norms are maintained because of socialization; trouble cases, if they exceed a small minority of all cases, are evidence of a potentially fatal gap between ideology and polity. The majority of laws, then, are followed as if they were customs. Laws that are remote from customary behavior are very difficult to enforce; the weight of police needed to secure compliance may completely outweigh the objectives of the original proscriptions. Although there are many examples of this, the reaction of the population of the United States to the federal prohibition on the sale of alcoholic beverages has become a classic illustration.

The previous discussion of sovereignty and its

natural, i.e., systemic, limitations suggests a possible answer to the question of the distinction between custom and law. It would seem that the essential criterion that differentiates the two is that concentrated force is available to make the breaking of a law both dangerous and expensive, whereas the breach of custom initiates a crisis that requires only a strong ego.

Beyond this point lies a vast field only partially explored by social scientists. Legal systems are by definition normative and thus fit only approximately, at best, with actual behavior. The sociology of law has made only limited excursions into the amount of variation between legal codes and customary patterns in different societies. Many other questions remain to be investigated, such as the reasons for the high incidence of specific types of illegal behavior in particular societies. Other questions are best treated in a broad comparative frame; these have to do with variations in justice and equity by class and social status and the evaluation of the strength of bureaucracy in replacing conventional legality with its own administrative codes. These phenomena are by no means limited to modern Western society and the states it has influenced but seem to be a functional aspect of bureaucratic organization, wherever found. [*See* LEGAL SYSTEMS, *article on* COMPARATIVE LAW AND LEGAL SYSTEMS; *and the articles listed in the guide under* LAW.]

State and nation. One of the intellectual functions of the historical school of jurisprudence was the attempt to counteract the predominance of the Roman concept of *jus gentium* in the legal theory of the time. This was made particularly clear in the romantic and fervidly nationalistic writings of von Savigny and is most conspicuously intertwined with the development of the modern German state. According to the principles of *jus gentium*, the law of the state was to incorporate, wherever possible, those elements that seemed common to all traditions. This was an appropriate attempt for an expansionistic empire with goals of universality, as Rome was at the height of its political maturity. The romantics, particularly the Germans, whose political thought was already showing affinity for the blight of racism, exalted a different goal and were driven to establish the identity of a population sharing the myth of common descent and a common culture with one sharing a common government.

One of Maine's great contributions was to show how the life of the state rests upon legal fictions. The romantic nationalistic theory of the state introduced and emphasized fictions that extended far beyond the area of jural personality. Fictions of commonality, at best, were and remain selectively distilled myths whose main reality lies in their ability to lead a population to internal violence and external aggression. Beyond wedding the state with a xenophobic notion of race, the romantic-historical approach assisted in the creation of a mystique which, in a familiar phrase, places the state above society.

The philosophy of one folk–one state helped cause some relatively minor nuisances before it matured as a major irritant in the attempt to draw a rational map of Europe after World War I. Little thought was given at that time to the effects of the spread of the thesis of self-determination to areas then held as colonies. The rapid emergence of scores of new nations after World War II is only a foretaste of what may be expected as today's minorities demand separate statehood tomorrow.

In conjunction with this problem, it is interesting to note that Marxist theory strongly criticizes all schemes that attempt to link the state and ethnicity. Class solidarity is seen, of course, as the product of the most enlightened form of association. Since class solidarity is thought to be the means of polarizing the struggle against the state, the state acts to counter it and, as one technique to that end, creates dissension by favoring bourgeois nationalism and ethnic chauvinism. Such is the theory, but within the orbit of this theory, the last decade has seen the formal assertion of principles startlingly like those of nationalism. [*See* COMMUNISM, *article on* NATIONAL COMMUNISM; NATION; NATIONALISM.]

State and war. Although several states have passed through long periods of peace, there is a deep and abiding association between the state as a form of social organization and warfare as a political and economic policy. From the viewpoint that the state is an institutional invention of post-neolithic times, it can be convincingly argued that the development of the state has been paralleled by growth in the scale of war. Although much of this growth can be attributed to technological advances, the state clearly provides a means for organizing violence on such a large scale as to lend a new quality to war. In addition, the state has provided an improved economic basis for the constant maintenance of military forces and has marshaled and multiplied the motives and justifications for the use of organized force.

Unfortunately, there is no convincing theory in which confidence can be placed in the attempt to eliminate war as a means of attaining national goals. Indeed, with few exceptions, such as the work of Quincy Wright, the serious literature of the social sciences has conspicuously ignored the subject of war, which is usually left to the province of the historian [*see* WAR]. In recent years, however, there has been a significant growth of interest in such studies within the power-wielding circles of the great states and in the decision-making echelons of the United Nations.

A supranational agency, a state above states, meets many of the logical requirements of a body capable of suppressing wars. Given sufficient force and the authority to use it autonomously, such a body might be capable of rendering the resort to violence socially and economically unwise for any state or its ruling class or party. It is also capable, theoretically, of carrying out functions calculated to reduce or remove the necessity of choosing war as an instrument of policy. It might do this by enhancing its provision of the office of third party in the arbitration of disputes and by enforcing its decisions. Hopefully, it would also expand its work directly within member states to modify conditions that are discovered to breed war. Unfortunately, all of these functions, and several others not here mentioned, require that the United Nations, or another supranational body, be given forces and powers that conflict with the earlier established notion of state sovereignty. [*See* INTERNATIONAL ORGANIZATION.]

The problem will be exacerbated when the possession of nuclear armaments spreads to small states whose ruling cliques or classes cherish grand ambitions which they are willing, or which they are forced, to place ahead of the demands of international responsibility. When that situation is reached, even more than in the anxious present, the structural affinity of the national state for war will constitute a constant threat to the existence of all states, no matter how large or prosperous. The danger is already perceived. It may provide the stimulus that will enable the major powers to cooperate effectively and sacrifice some portion of their individual sovereignties, so that the benefits of complex society can be preserved and expanded and the viability of the human race protected.

MORTON H. FRIED

BIBLIOGRAPHY
A guide to related articles and a combined bibliography appear after the article that follows.

II

THE CONCEPT

The state is a geographically delimited segment of human society united by common obedience to a single sovereign. The term may refer either to the society as a whole or, more specifically, to the sovereign authority that controls it.

As the above definition shows, the concept of the state is closely related to the concept of sovereignty, which was first developed in the field of jurisprudence. It starts from the essentially legalistic assumption that all political societies are, or ought to be, united under a determinate rule of law. Since laws emanating from several authorities are likely to come into conflict, it follows that there can be no determinate law of the land unless there is, within that land, a supreme law-making authority whose decisions are final. If the law of the land is to prevail, moreover, it must be backed by effective sanctions. Thus coercive power, as well as legal authority, are both essential to the juristic concept of sovereignty. The state is a territory in which a single authority exercises sovereign powers both *de jure* and *de facto*. [*See* SOVEREIGNTY.]

In the history of political thought, the term "state" has enjoyed wide currency, both as a normative and as a descriptive concept. Normative theorists, convinced that the concentration of coercive powers in the hands of a single determinate authority is indispensable to the maintenance of public order in any given territory, have frequently tried to show that obedience to the state is the highest form of political obligation. Descriptive theorists, without necessarily committing themselves to the normative proposition that the state is supremely valuable, have likewise been disposed, in many cases, to single it out among all social institutions as the only one that is distinctively "political" and to regard the description and analysis of the state as the central problem of political science. In the remainder of this article I shall consider the role of both these usages, first the normative and then the descriptive, in the development of modern political thought.

The normative concept

The primary value of the concept "state," historically speaking, lies in its normative contribution to the early development of Western political institutions. When the word "state" first appeared in its present sense in the course of the sixteenth century, its significance was clearly revolutionary. The men who used it were consciously opposed to existing political traditions. For them the state was not a present fact but a desirable objective. By giving new meaning to the old concept "sovereignty," which then meant "kingship," they hoped to overcome the traditional pluralism of Western politics and thereby to place the maintenance of public order on new and sounder foundations. Their efforts were largely successful. For several centuries the establishment and maintenance of states was widely accepted as the proper goal of political action. At a formative stage of their development the political thought and institutions of the modern world were shaped by this belief.

The political conditions against which the new concept was directed were an outgrowth of the Middle Ages. During the centuries that followed the fall of Rome, the political organization of the Western world was extremely pluralistic. Theoretically the medieval political system was dualistic, being based on the idea that the pope and emperor, as vicars of Christ, were jointly responsible for the governance of Christendom, the former being the final authority in spiritual questions, the latter in secular ones. In practice, however, the division of authority went even farther. The secular realm in particular was broken down into a complex network of overlapping jurisdictions, each of which was recognized as being vested with prescriptive or contractual rights of its own. Under these conditions no territorial ruler had either the power or the authority to maintain an effective rule of law. Conflict and insecurity were endemic to the system. [*See* CHRISTIANITY.]

The modern state is the product of a long and ultimately successful struggle to overcome these difficulties. It was accomplished by a gradual increase in the power of territorial princes at the expense of all other authorities. By the fourteenth century the kings of France had already gone a long way toward reducing the independent powers of the church and toward controlling the feudal magnates. Other kings, in varying degree, were similarly successful. This involved the violation of many vested rights and encountered much resistance. Because of the sacredness of their office, however, kings had a great advantage over most of their rivals in the general competition. As a result of their efforts the foundation of the modern state was well under way by the end of the Middle Ages.

Machiavelli. It was not until the sixteenth century, however, that the concept "state" gained currency. Niccolò Machiavelli was the man who introduced the word in its modern sense into the vocabulary of politics. His use of the term was a reflection of the special problems then being faced by his native Italy. In many respects Italy had been a leader in the development of modern political institutions. For various reasons feudalism had never flourished there. This meant that there were comparatively few traditional interests to stand in the way of an effective concentration of power. But the form that concentration took in Italy was an uncommon one. A traditional bone of contention between popes and emperors, the country as a whole had no king to serve as a focus for the creation of a single state. Renaissance Italy was a patchwork of republics and principalities, all vying with one another in a ruthless competition for power. This was the world that Machiavelli knew, the world that found expression in his theory of the state.

"Reason of state" was the central principle of Machiavelli's thought. Although the phrase itself does not appear in his own works, the idea is implicit in everything he wrote. According to this principle, politics consists essentially in an all-out struggle for power. The proper objective of political action is to maximize the power of the state. All things are permitted, on the sole condition that they are "rationally" calculated to further the objective. Like so many men of the Renaissance, Machiavelli was magnificently confident in the possibility of achieving results by the use of rational techniques. The state to him was an artifact, a work of art created by the skill and genius of statesmen. To teach the basic rules of that art was the purpose of his political writings.

Machiavelli's theory was too extreme to be widely influential in its original form. The difficulty lay in his disregard for the problem of legality. Accustomed to thinking of political authority in terms of the rule of law, the Western world was reluctant to accept a system that subordinated all other considerations to the pure pursuit of power. It is true that reason of state was a concept that could not be entirely neglected. Beginning with Giovanni Botero, who seems to have invented the term, books devoted to the subject began to appear in most of the principal countries and languages of Europe. They were greeted with some uneasiness, however, and "Machiavellian" gained international currency as a word of popular opprobrium. [*See* MACHIAVELLI.]

Bodin. It was Jean Bodin who first succeeded in formulating the concept "state" in an acceptable way. Bodin was a Frenchman whose view of politics was largely shaped by conditions in sixteenth-century France. Unlike the Italian republics and principalities, the French monarchy was a typical large-scale state, and its problems were typical modern problems.

In that country the pluralistic traditions and institutions of the Middle Ages, though greatly affected by the expansion of royal power, were still much more formidable than they had been in Renaissance Italy. This led, with the advent of the Reformation, to a serious political crisis. In accordance with the traditions of Christian dualism, the church had the right and duty to defend the true faith against heretical kings. In a time of religious disunity, when the claim to orthodoxy was in dispute between two or more rival churches, no ruler could avoid appearing as a heretic to some part of the population. This meant, in France, that a strong Protestant minority felt justified in disputing the authority of their Catholic kings. Some of them, known as monarchomachs, even went so far as to maintain that heretical rulers ought to be forcibly deposed and, if necessary, killed. Although the Protestants were unable to control the country as a whole, they were strong enough to dominate a number of provincial parliaments and other local agencies that had survived from the feudal period and to use the traditional privileges of those agencies as legal justification for their resistance to the king. Thus the unity of the kingdom was effectively broken, and the country was committed to a long and exhausting period of religious warfare.

Bodin's epoch-making theory of sovereignty was an idea developed in response to this situation. He adhered to the position of the *politiques*, a loosely associated group of theorists and statesmen who deplored the trend toward religious extremism and who believed that law and order were political values that ought to be preserved at all costs. This led him to the conclusion that there ought to be, in every state, a single recognized lawmaker, or sovereign, whose decisions were recognized as having final authority. As against the sovereign no vested interests and no sort of jurisdiction, secular or spiritual, could rightfully prevail. For Bodin sovereignty was a matter not so much of power as of legal right. The value of a coherent legal order was the premise from which he deduced the need for a sovereign authority. Unlike Machiavelli's, his view of the state was squarely in line with the Western tradition of respect for the rule of law. Through him the concept was firmly established in the repertory of Western political thought. [See BODIN.]

The cult of the state reached its highest point in the seventeenth and eighteenth centuries. From the end of the Thirty Years' War to the French Revolution absolute monarchy reigned almost without a challenge as the standard form of political organization. After more than a century of religious warfare most people were ready to accept the Bodinian position as the only possible basis for the maintenance of public order. The most serious limitation on the authority of princes had been eliminated by the Treaty of Westphalia in 1648, which expressly confirmed the right of secular sovereigns to determine the religious duties of their subjects. In secular matters, also, their su-

premacy was generally recognized. It is true that in some countries, most notably in England, some vestiges of the older pluralism still managed to survive. But these were rare exceptions, and even in England the theoretical dualism of king-in-parliament soon gave way, in practice, to the sovereignty of parliament. Thus western Europe, for more than a century, was ruled by a number of clearly determinate sovereigns, hereditary monarchs in most cases, who exercised an unlimited right to make and enforce the laws within their respective states. The obligation of the subject to obey the sovereign was the highest form of duty. [See MONARCHY.]

Erosion of the normative concept

Ever since the French Revolution the normative power of the concept "state" has steadily eroded. Indeed the process had already started by the beginning of the eighteenth century. As the fear of religious warfare faded, people came to feel that the maintenance of law and order was not enough, in itself, to justify political action. Individual happiness and social justice came also to be reckoned as values, values in terms of which it was right to make demands. In the eighteenth century the primary inspiration for such demands was the philosophy of the Enlightenment. Legal equality, intellectual freedom, and laissez-faire economics were the liberal ideas that first gave men the vision of a better world to come. Nationalism and socialism, later on, gave rise to similar hopes. To people inspired by such ideas obedience to the state was no longer acceptable as the highest form of political obligation. If sovereigns would consent to become reformers, well and good; if not, reform would have to be achieved in defiance of them. Although the philosophers of the Enlightenment long persisted in the hope of achieving their purposes through the "enlightened despotism" of existing rulers, the final outcome of their efforts was the French Revolution. This was only the first of a long series of revolutionary movements which led, in the course of the nineteenth and twentieth centuries, to a marked and progressive deterioration of the authority of the state.

Anarchism and socialism. One consequence of the modern age of revolution has been to encourage the development of philosophic anarchism. An anarchistic element was implicit from the beginning in the theory of liberalism. Although most liberals recognized the need for a rule of law enforced by coercive sanctions, they emphasized the spontaneous self-regulation of society by noncoercive institutions, such as the free market. To them, the government was best that governed least. This greatly reduced the dignity and importance of the state and led a few individuals—William Godwin, for example—to the extreme conclusion that a government that had wholly ceased to exist would be the best government of all.

It was not until the nineteenth century, however, in connection with the rise of socialism, that anarchism really flourished. Athough some, like Saint-Simon, believed in using the powers of government for the attainment of social justice, the more important socialists thought of the state quite simply as an agency of economic oppression and regarded the elimination of all coercive authority as one of their principal objectives. This was the view of Marx and Engels. It was also that of Proudhon, whose influence in the early socialist movement was second only to their own. Although twentieth-century socialists have generally abandoned this position, it still enjoys wide currency as part of the orthodox doctrine of the modern communist movement, as established by Lenin. [*See* ANARCHISM; MARXISM.]

The theory of popular sovereignty. In most cases, however, the modern reaction against the cult of the state has taken a different form. The usual thing has been to recognize the need for coercive authority but to reduce the prestige of actual rulers by making a sharp distinction between the sovereign and the government. This follows the line which had already been developed in the *Social Contract* of Jean Jacques Rousseau (1762). The outstanding feature of Rousseau's political thought was his insistence that sovereignty was an inalienable right of the people and that no government, even as delegate of the people, could properly claim any share whatever in the exercise of sovereign powers, including legislation. Though few of his successors were willing to follow him all the way in denying the legislative authority of governments, his doctrine of popular sovereignty was widely influential. [*See the biography of* ROUSSEAU.] In their contest with the monarchy the leaders of the French Revolution relied heavily on the proposition that the third estate, as representatives of the people, were the rightful rulers of France. In subsequent revolutions similar claims were made on behalf of the nation or the proletariat. The result, in each case, was to attack the position of established state authorities by appealing to an alternative and presumably more popular source of sovereignty.

Revolutionary in its origins, the theory of popular sovereignty was destined in the course of the nineteenth and twentieth centuries to become the only widely accepted basis of political legitimacy. It is true that after the French Revolution conservative theorists tried for a time to defend and strengthen the old connection between sovereignty and government. Burke, with his emphasis on the importance of maintaining political traditions, and Hegel, with his more elaborate theory of the state as the ultimate achievement of a rational "world spirit," were among the more notable defenders of the older conception. [*See the biographies of* BURKE; HEGEL.] There were also attempts, especially by the papacy, to counteract the more extreme pretensions of popular sovereignty by showing that God is the one true source of political authority and that to rebel against established governments is a sin against God himself. Even among the liberals, moreover, the theory of popular sovereignty met some resistance. For example, most liberal governments felt free to claim imperial rights in colonies without any appeal to popular consent on the ground that non-European peoples were not yet ripe for self-government. In the long run, however, the idea of popular sovereignty could nowhere be successfully withstood. During the nineteenth and twentieth centuries colonial empires and traditional monarchies alike have repeatedly had to make way for movements claiming the indefeasible right of national self-determination. Most governments today, no matter how oppressive they may be in fact, find it necessary to justify themselves as representatives of the people. In that sense democracy is the well-nigh universal norm of contemporary politics.

This development has led to a marked devaluation of the normative concept of the state. In the days when the sovereign was an actively ruling monarch the entire power and prestige of the state was concentrated in his person. The aura of kingship created a vast distance between him and his subjects and lent special dignity to the civil and military servants who executed his will. Under democratic conditions this view of the state as a thing apart is not easy to maintain. Though allegiance to a democracy may be symbolized by flags, anthems, and uniforms, and even by a royal family, the authority to which these symbols point is no longer that of a prince over his subjects but that of a sovereign people, collectively, over its own individual members. Under these circumstances the state is hard to distinguish from the citizens in whose name and over whom its authority is being exercised. Sovereignty thus conceived is little more than a bloodless legal fiction. Attention shifts from the state to the government, which, though it makes no claim to sovereignty, does all the actual ruling. [*See* DEMOCRACY.]

Constitutional democracy. The erosion of the concept is especially clear in the case of constitutional democracy. When the powers of government are limited by the provisions of a constitution, written or unwritten, it is hard to say who, if anyone, is in a position to exercise sovereignty. Although the government is supposed to reflect the will of the "sovereign" people, actual decisions are the outcome of a complex political process in which many different agencies, both private and public, are allowed to play a part. Since the rights and duties of these various agencies are defined by the constitution, it is sometimes said that in constitutional democracies the constitution itself is sovereign. This is true in the sense that obedience to the constitution is apt, in such societies, to acquire much of the normative value once associated with obedience to a king. But a constitution, unlike a king, is not a person with a mind and will of its own; it is a collection of laws and usages that have to be defined and enforced by someone. Like other democratic processes, the process of making constitutional decisions is diffuse. Even in Great Britain, where the rights of Parliament from a legal standpoint are virtually unlimited, there is in practice no single agency with absolute power to change the constitution. Although the powers of a constitutional democracy are in a very real sense derived from the consent of the governed, the process of eliciting that consent is highly complex. To say where sovereignty lies in such a system is almost impossible. [See CONSTITUTIONS AND CONSTITUTIONALISM.]

For normative purposes, therefore, the concepts of state and sovereignty have lost much of their former significance. To jurists, who must stop somewhere in their search for a final legal authority, these concepts will always be meaningful. To dependent peoples throughout the world the idea of independent statehood is still an object of aspiration. It would be an exaggeration to say, therefore, that the concepts of state and sovereignty have lost *all* normative value. The fact remains, however, that the effect of modern democracy in all of its forms has been to devalue them. A large part of the world is at present ruled by communist regimes, which expressly promise an ultimate "withering away of the state" and justify their continuing use of coercive power in terms of social justice and the interests of the proletariat. Where communism does not prevail, the words to conjure with are "people," "country," "nation," and "race." Few people today would regard obedience to the state, as such, as the highest form of duty. Bodin's

theory of the state as the ultimate value of politics is practically extinct.

The descriptive concept

In addition to its normative role the concept "state" has also played an important part in the attempt to create a descriptive science of politics. There was a time, indeed, when most people would have agreed that political power is nothing more or less than sovereign power and that the proper subject of political science is the study of the state. *Staatswissenschaft*, the nearest German equivalent for the English "political science," reflects a point of view which was by no means limited to the German-speaking world. Thus James W. Garner's *Introduction to Political Science*, an influential American textbook which appeared in 1910, starts from the proposition that "political science begins and ends with the state." This view of the discipline was once the standard one, but few would subscribe to it today.

The idea that the state alone can provide the basis for truly political behavior goes back to the beginnings of Western political thought. For Plato and Aristotle the city-state, or polis, was the ultimate expression of man's intrinsic capacity for social action. Although many social needs could be met by lesser associations, such as the family and the village, the city-state alone, in the opinion of these early philosophers, was sufficiently comprehensive to enable man to realize his full potentialities and thus to develop that "good life" which was the proper goal of his social existence. The good man was one who lived in close and harmonious association with all his fellow citizens in a perfectly integrated polis. To the founders of Western political thought, therefore, the city-state was a form of human association generically different from all others. Lesser units, like the family, were too small to be self-sufficient; greater units, like the vast barbarian empires of the East, were too large to meet the human need for social communication. Only the city-state was both large enough and small enough to enable men to achieve a truly lawful and human form of social life. That is why political science, to the ancient Greeks, could begin and end with the polis. [See PLATO; ARISTOTLE.]

The influence of this tradition is clearly reflected in modern political thought. It is true that the modern state is in many ways quite different from the ancient polis. Its territorial extent is normally far greater, and its relationship to the social life of its members is correspondingly less intimate. Instead of being regarded as an aspect of the common life of a close-knit community of citizens, the modern state often appears as an external agency of control, ruling over a more or less random and heterogeneous collection of subjects. The British and Hapsburg empires are typical cases in point. Different as such aggregates may be from the ancient polis, however, the modern state resembles its predecessor in ways that might seem to entitle it, also, to be regarded as the central concern of a specialized science of politics.

The essential point is that the modern state, like the ancient polis, is both large enough and small enough to provide a uniquely effective form of social integration. In all modern societies the rights and duties of men are defined by a wide variety of associations and enforced by various agencies. Some, like the family, are less comprehensive—others, like the Roman Catholic church, more comprehensive—than any single state. Large or small, however, these "private" associations are rarely self-sufficient. In pursuit of their respective goals they make rival claims which often lead to conflict. The distinctive function of the state is to regulate such conflicts. In territories where a sovereign is available to decide between rival claims and to enforce its decisions if need be with adequate coercive sanctions, it is possible to achieve a substantial degree of social coherence. Thus the modern state, like the ancient polis, is a form of association to be distinguished from all others by virtue of its unique capacity for achieving integrative action. The idea that political science begins and ends with the state is a reflection of the idea that this type of action, and this type alone, is essentially political.

This idea no longer corresponds, however, to the theory and practice of contemporary political scientists. Although problems of state and sovereignty are occasionally discussed, they are rarely regarded as central to the discipline. In the United States especially, attention is now focused mainly on problems of political power and on the nature and operation of political systems in general. The tendency is to regard politics not as a function specifically limited to one particular type of social organization, the state, but as a particular functional aspect of social life in general. According to this point of view, the power relationships that exist in trade unions or professional associations are no less "political" than those existing within a national government and no less worthy of attention. Some scholars believe, indeed, that the "micropolitical" rather than the "macropolitical" is the most promising line of approach and that the study of all

larger political structures should be based on a thorough knowledge of small groups and of face-to-face relationships. This is not to say that contemporary political scientists are uninterested in the larger forms of political organization; the modern state is too powerful an institution to be neglected by students of politics. Typically, however, the interest today is not in the *state* as such, but in the *governments* or *political processes* that operate within it. [*See* GOVERNMENT; POLITICAL PROCESS.]

This shift of interest away from the state may be taken, at least in part, as a reflection of the increasingly nonlegalistic character of contemporary political science. The concepts of state and sovereignty have traditionally rested on the assumption that the determination and enforcement of legal rights is the most important technique of social integration. The political tradition of the West, with its long-standing commitment to the maintenance of an effective "rule of law," is based on this assumption. When the problems of politics are thought of in this way, it is natural for political science and jurisprudence to be closely associated and to share many common concepts. To modern social scientists, however, the juristic approach to political problems is comparatively uncongenial. Important as law may be in society, it is only one among many possible agencies for the control of social behavior. Contemporary political scientists generally believe that they ought to study political power in all of its manifestations, not just in its legal aspects.

The state does not, of course, have to be defined in legalistic terms. Because of the coercive aspect of law, power as well as authority have always been associated with the idea of the state. The familiar distinction between sovereignty *de facto* and *de jure* is a reflection of this fact. This being so, there is no reason why political scientists, with their special interest in problems of power, should not confine their attention to the *de facto* aspects of sovereignty and treat the state quite simply in these terms. Considered without reference to the problems of legal authority, the distinctive feature of the state, as compared with other associations, is its attempt to monopolize coercive power within its own territory. Although the limiting case of absolute monopoly is never reached in fact, it has often been approximated. From the standpoint of a purely descriptive political science it is sufficient, therefore, to define the state in terms of the limit and to study the conditions that accompany the greater or lesser degrees of monopoly that have been achieved in particular times and places. Thus defined, the concept "state" has no necessary connection with the making and enforcing of law and is compatible with a wholly nonlegalistic approach to the problems of politics.

Even in this form, however, the concept is little used. The difficulty is that it places excessive emphasis on the coercive aspects of political life. In the days of absolute monarchy it was not unnatural to think of politics as a one-way relationship of command and obedience between a ruler and his subjects. The interaction between a sovereign people and its government cannot be so simply understood. Although modern governments may act coercively, they lack that ultimate identification with the sovereign state which constituted the peculiar strength of the older monarchies. The concept "the sovereignty of the people" still remains as a useful political catch phrase, but it is too abstract to throw much light on the realities of contemporary politics. That is why political scientists generally prefer to use other terms in describing the phenomena that once were subsumed under the concept "state."

FREDERICK M. WATKINS

[*Directly related are the entries* AUTHORITY; GOVERNMENT; INTERNATIONAL POLITICS; NATION; POWER; SOCIAL STRUCTURE; SOVEREIGNTY. *Other relevant material may be found in* POLITICAL ANTHROPOLOGY; POLITICAL SCIENCE; POLITICAL THEORY.]

BIBLIOGRAPHY

ALLEN, JOHN W. (1928) 1957 *A History of Political Thought in the Sixteenth Century.* 3d ed. London: Methuen.

BODIN, JEAN (1576) 1962 *The Six Bookes of a Commonweale.* Edited by Kenneth D. McRae. Cambridge, Mass.: Harvard Univ. Press. → A facsimile reprint of the English translation of 1606, corrected and supplemented in the light of a new comparison with the French and Latin texts.

BOSANQUET, BERNARD (1899) 1951 *The Philosophical Theory of the State.* 4th ed. London: Macmillan. → The 1951 publication is a reprint of the 1923 4th edition.

BOTERO, GIOVANNI (1589) 1956 The Reason of State. Pages 1–224 in Giovanni Botero, *The Reason of State and The Greatness of Cities.* New Haven: Yale Univ. Press; London: Routledge. → First published as *Della ragion di stato.*

CASSIRER, ERNST 1946 *The Myth of the State.* New Haven: Yale Univ. Press. → A paperback edition was published in 1955 by Doubleday.

CHANG, SHERMAN HSIAO-MING (1931) 1965 *The Marxian Theory of State.* New York: Russell.

COKER, FRANCIS W. 1910 *Organismic Theories of the State: Nineteenth Century Interpretations of the State as Organism or as Person.* Columbia University Studies in History, Economics, and Public Law, Vol. 38, No. 2. New York: Columbia Univ. Press.

CONFERENCE ON NEW APPROACHES IN SOCIAL ANTHROPOLOGY, JESUS COLLEGE, CAMBRIDGE, ENGLAND, 1963 1965 *Political Systems and the Distribution of Power.* A.S.A. Monograph No. 2. London: Tavistock; New York: Praeger.

EASTON, DAVID 1965 *A Systems Analysis of Political Life.* New York: Wiley.

EMERSON, RUPERT 1928 *State and Sovereignty in Modern Germany.* New Haven: Yale Univ. Press.

FALLERS, LLOYD A. (1956) 1965 *Bantu Bureaucracy: A Century of Political Evolution.* Univ. of Chicago Press. → First published as *Bantu Bureaucracy: A Study of Integration and Conflict in the Political Institutions of an East African People.*

FORTES, MEYER; and EVANS-PRITCHARD, E. E. (editors) (1940) 1961 *African Political Systems.* Oxford Univ. Press.

FRIED, MORTON H. 1960 On the Evolution of Social Stratification and the State. Pages 713–731 in Stanley Diamond (editor), *Culture in History: Essays in Honor of Paul Radin.* New York: Columbia Univ. Press.

FRIED, MORTON H. 1968 *On the Evolution of Stratification and the State.* New York: Random House.

GARNER, JAMES W. 1910 *Introduction to Political Science: A Treatise on the Origin, Nature, Functions, and Organization of the State.* New York: American Book.

GLUCKMAN, MAX 1965 *Politics, Law and Ritual in Tribal Society.* Oxford: Blackwell; Chicago: Aldine.

HAMMOND, MASON 1951 *City-state and World State in Greek and Roman Political Theory Until Augustus.* Cambridge, Mass.: Harvard Univ. Press.

HEGEL, GEORG W. F. (1821) 1942 *Philosophy of Right.* Translated with notes by T. M. Knox. Oxford: Clarendon.

HOCKING, WILLIAM E. 1926 *Man and the State.* New Haven: Yale Univ. Press.

HOEBEL, E. ADAMSON 1954 *The Law of Primitive Man: A Study in Comparative Legal Dynamics.* Cambridge, Mass.: Harvard Univ. Press.

LASKI, HAROLD J. (1935) 1956 *The State in Theory and Practice.* London: Allen & Unwin.

LEACH, EDMUND R. 1954 *Political Systems of Highland Burma: A Study of Kachin Social Structure.* London School of Economics and Political Science; Cambridge, Mass.: Harvard Univ. Press.

LENIN, VLADIMIR I. (1917) 1964 The State and Revolution: The Marxist Theory of the State and the Tasks of the Proletariat in the Revolution. Volume 25, pages 381–492 in Vladimir I. Lenin, *Collected Works.* 4th ed. Moscow: Progress. → First published in Russian.

LINDSAY, A. D. (1943) 1959 *The Modern Democratic State.* Vol. 1. Oxford Univ. Press.

LOWIE, ROBERT (1922) 1962 *The Origin of the State.* New York: Russell.

MacIVER, ROBERT M. (1926) 1955 *The Modern State.* Oxford Univ. Press.

MAINE, HENRY J. S. (1861) 1960 *Ancient Law: Its Connection With the Early History of Society, and Its Relations to Modern Ideas.* Rev. ed. New York: Dutton; London and Toronto: Dent. → A paperback edition was published in 1963 by Beacon.

MAIR, LUCY P. (1962) 1964 *Primitive Government.* Baltimore: Penguin.

MARITAIN, JACQUES 1951 *Man and the State.* Univ. of Chicago Press.

MEINECKE, FRIEDRICH (1924) 1962 *Machiavellism: The Doctrine of Raison d'État and Its Place in Modern*

History. New York: Praeger. → First published as *Die Idee der Staatsräson in der neueren Geschichte*.

OPPENHEIMER, FRANZ (1907) 1926 *The State: Its History and Development Viewed Sociologically*. New York: Vanguard. → First published in German as *Der Staat*.

POLANYI, KARL; ARENSBERG, CONRAD M.; and PEARSON, HARRY W. (editors) 1957 *Trade and Market in the Early Empires: Economies in History and Theory*. Glencoe, Ill.: Free Press.

ROMMEN, HEINRICH 1945 *The State in Catholic Thought: A Treatise in Political Philosophy*. St. Louis, Mo., and London: Herder. → Based on the author's *Der Staat in der katholischen Gedankenwelt* (1935).

ROUSSEAU, JEAN JACQUES (1762) 1961 *The Social Contract*. London: Dent.

SABINE, GEORGE H. (1937) 1962 *A History of Political Theory*. 3d ed. New York: Holt.

SCHAPERA, ISAAC 1956 *Government and Politics in Tribal Societies*. London: Watts.

SWARTZ, MARC J.; TURNER, VICTOR W.; and TUDEN, ARTHUR (editors) 1966 *Political Anthropology*. Chicago: Aldine.

WATKINS, FREDERICK M. 1934 *The State as a Concept of Political Science*. New York: Harper.

WEBER, MAX (1921–1924) 1949 Power. Part 2, pages 159–264 in Max Weber, *From Max Weber: Essays in Sociology*. Translated and edited by Hans H. Gerth and C. Wright Mills. New York: Oxford Univ. Press.

WITTFOGEL, KARL A. 1957 *Oriental Despotism: A Comparative Study of Total Power*. New Haven: Yale Univ. Press. → A paperback edition was published in 1963.

WRIGHT, QUINCY (1942) 1965 *A Study of War*. 2d ed. Univ. of Chicago Press.

STATE TRADING
See under INTERNATIONAL TRADE CONTROLS.

STATELESS SOCIETY

There is probably considerable common-sense agreement among those interested in what is meant by a stateless society. Brief definition of the concept does little that is positive to increase understanding, but it may focus disagreement and so lead to clarification. To cover data so varied, a definition must be abstract and employ terms which are themselves the subject of controversy.

Positive definition is desirable, yet we will start out with an etymologically negative concept. Most of the current alternatives for defining a stateless society, such as acephalous, uncentralized, or anarchic, are equally negative; for example, Middleton and Tait (1958) called a book on the subject *Tribes Without Rulers*. Furthermore, "decentralized" suggests the distribution of something from the center, which in the present case does not exist.

What a stateless society *is* ultimately depends upon what are held to be the characteristics of the state. Thus, a stateless society is one that has no specialized political roles, let alone institutionalized political structures composed of a plurality of roles. By specialized we mean formal, named, and recognized roles that are played by specialists, not by any or every full member of the society. A specialist is also, properly speaking, full-time. However, this is ambiguous, since the conventional (though highly variable) full-time working day is specific only to industrial societies. Stateless societies do not differentiate between working and leisure hours in this way. Specialization also implies special qualifications—training for achieved roles or inherent qualities for ascribed positions. Specialists are at least mainly and most importantly involved in the concerns associated with their specialization, and they are publicly held to be so.

By political we mean that aspect of social activity which is primarily concerned with power—with getting certain things done, with making decisions and getting them carried out, or preventing things from being done, by and on behalf of some collectivity of persons. In the societies with which we are concerned, the control of violence both in its relatively internal and external aspects looms large, but we would not subscribe to a definition of the political that relates it directly to the use of physical force, for although this possibility is present somewhere in any system of political action, it is essentially an ultimate sanction, usually very indirect and significantly overlaid with other important and conventional mechanisms. In our definition, stateless societies have political action, which is universal, but they do not have either purely or even primarily political institutions or roles.

There is a very fine and at points ambiguous distinction between the ritual and the political. Ritual mechanisms often achieve certain ends, get things done, and even coerce and secure obedience, and it is difficult to see how the essential distinction can be other than that between physical and supernatural forces. Coercion is political when it is backed by a chain of command, when it is part of an ordered series of roles whose players recognize the obligation to support an institution in which the right to secular command is held to inhere. It does not matter whether the reason for this recognition is a perception of rational ends that are properly and regularly to be secured in that way or a perception of an organized following that will support the command and enforce it against opposition, thus involving the ultimate sanction of physical force.

Ritual coercion primarily depends not upon its setting in a chain of command, nor upon followers recognizing a leader's right to give commands for the common good, but upon the recognized right and obligation to invoke or express the operation of supernatural forces. Backing comes not from recognition of the right to command as inherent in a role, but from recognition of the efficacy of the supernatural forces invoked or expressed and the necessity of bowing and conforming to them. On this basis an apparent or rudimentary chain of command may emerge, and certainly economic motivations may reinforce the process, but the roots of ritual coercion are different from those of political coercion.

The negative starting point of the usual definitional approach to stateless societies is no coincidence. It is due to the fact that these societies first attracted the theoretical interest of scholars who were themselves socialized in states, where the concept of the state had been a consuming object of cultural interest for at least four centuries, from the time of Machiavelli, if not for nearly two and a half millenniums, from the time of Aristotle and Plato. The stateless society has understandably never been such an object of intellectual interest for anyone socialized in one. We are therefore justified in endeavoring to ignore the whole body of philosophical speculation on the state while concentrating on theoretical implications of the empirical facts of stateless societies insofar as they are known and to seek a more positive definition from this point of view. We may then briefly note how, in principle, stateless societies may acquire state forms through endogenous or exogenous change.

The passage from stateless to state forms is difficult to document, because stateless societies have no history of their own and dubious efforts at reconstruction are involved. Migration, climatic change, or improvements in technology may lead to increase in food supply, growth of population, congestion, hardening of boundaries, competition for resources, and attempts at permanent domination by one group over others. These developments will be accompanied by the emergence of new roles and greater specialization. The routinization of charismatic leadership is the most plausible general characterization. Prophets may arise in response to external threats and can easily turn eventually into hereditary ruling dynasties. By such changes the quality of society is radically transformed. However, no doubt the spread of state forms has occurred to an important extent through direct conquest and also through emulation.

To see the state as metaphysically ubiquitous in society and even present in the subhuman herd (Meyer [1884–1902] 1953–1958, vol. 1, pp. 10–12) does not assist understanding in this context. Rather, I stand with Vinogradoff (1920–1922, vol. 1, p. 93) in holding that the state, which has assumed a monopoly of political coordination, ruling, and making laws and enforcing them eventually with coercion, did not exist in ancient times. The commonwealth was not centered in one sovereign body, and the necessary political elements that are never absent from any human society were distributed among many other formations. This emphasis confronts us with the wide range of empirical variation and also the variable quality and direction of interest found in field reports and analyses based on them.

Definition of stateless society

There is no a priori reason why societies negatively defined by their lack of state forms should have many significant features in common. Attempts to delineate the empirical variations of the state cross-culturally have not been very satisfactory so far. Yet despite the enormous cultural variety of stateless societies, it is somewhat astonishing how frequently certain formal characteristics echo through the literature about them. These may be grouped under five very general headings.

(1) Stateless societies are *multipolities*. (2) *Ritual superintegration* is achieved in diverse ways beyond the level of the political community. (3) Potentially disruptive action is channeled and constrained in the *complementary opposition* of groups and categories at several levels, and integrative action may also follow the same lines. (4) The several levels of action share a graded and *distributive legitimacy*. (5) *Intersecting kinship* ties provide an essential, pervasive framework. These five characteristics—multipolity, ritual superintegration, complementary opposition, distributive legitimacy, and intersecting kinship—are cumulative and interlocking rather than exclusive. It is their combination that is sufficiently frequent to be significant.

Multipolity.   All serious investigators have described stateless societies as multipolities. However varied their approaches, they found that whatever level of grouping or crystallization of activity had the greatest clustering and concentration of political functions defined an entity which was to them essentially less than a "society" in the complete, though not autarchic, sense. When Evans-Pritchard used the term "tribe" in the clear yet culturally specific sense of the largest group recognizing a moral obligation to settle feuds and other disputes by arbitration, his definition resulted in splitting what had been and still are regarded as tribes into multitribes; in the case of the Nuer and the Kenya Luo, there were then dozens of different tribes in this new sense. When applied by his followers to other peoples, such as the Dinka (Lienhardt 1958) and the Lugbara (Middleton 1965), this anomaly became so excessive and contradictory to common sense—the Dinka consisting of literally hundreds of tribes—that there has been a reversal to the older, common-sense meaning of tribe, while qualifying terms such as subtribe (Middleton 1963, p. 82; 1965, p. 36) are used for its more precisely defined components.

The other part of this dilemma may be seen, perhaps, in Boas' (1897) vacillating use of tribe with reference to the Kwakiutl: as applied to that society it refers variously to the dialect group, the subdialect group, the corporate territorial communities within the latter, and even on occasion the component local "clans." Such ambiguity should be deplored, but it is an apparent consequence of seeking a single level of polity.

Even when major political functions cluster at a particular level of grouping that may reasonably be called the political community, so much of the fabric of social life, such a high proportion and frequency of activity in kinship, marriage, economic exchange, and ritual, and such important meanings and identities lie essentially outside or extend beyond this limit that for the member and for the investigator alike "society," however defined, must be considerably more inclusive than the political community. This applies even more when political functions are distributed at several levels rather than clustering significantly at one, or when they attach to temporary, *ad hoc*, situational, and occasional groupings of persons according to recognized principles rather than to permanent or corporate groupings.

Society is that field within which the requisites of social life are effectively met. A further characteristic of the stateless society is that it need not be an absolutely and uniquely bounded entity in space or time, but that its effective field may differ from one person to another and certainly from one family or primary settlement to another. Categorical limits may obtain where natural factors such as seas, deserts, or mountains provide them, or where the movement of peoples results in clearly juxtaposed boundaries of language and culture, but both social intercourse and most cultural elements show a remarkable capacity for transcending the apparent boundaries of mutually unintelligible languages. As this relativity is essential, it is important that it should be so recognized and not explained away as exceptional. However, there are usually at least relative discontinuities in the distribution of social and cultural features, so that for any local group society has effective working limits, although they may differ somewhat for different purposes and have distinctly different limits for several neighboring groups, which nonetheless regard themselves as essentially belonging together.

Ritual superintegration. Ritual superintegration is the most general basis for this wider-than-political effective social field. Of course, such effective social fields exist for persons and for groups in states also, but it seems logical and useful to distinguish between those situations where the effective social field lies for most, if not the vast majority of purposes, conclusively within the boundaries of the state, and those situations where it extends significantly beyond any zone of common political action. Thus ". . . there was no one who had authority over all the Tallensi; no one who could exact tax, tribute or service from all. They never united for war or self-protection against a common enemy" (Fortes 1940, pp. 240–241). Although fighting and warfare between sections and clans of the Tallensi were comparatively frequent, there were nonpolitical sanctions and ceremonies that brought them all together and expressed their unity. "These festivals are periods of ritually sanctioned truce, when all conflicts and disputes must be abandoned for the sake of ceremonial co-operation. . . . In this festival cycle, therefore, the widest Tale community emerges. . . . It is not a fixed political entity but a functional synthesis" (*ibid.*, p. 263). Tallensi chiefs had no authority beyond the lineage, but they had wider ritual duties. Their office was modeled on the remote chiefship of Mampurugu, but neither that chief nor any of his subchiefs had any economic, juridical, administrative, or military rights over the Tallensi chiefs (*ibid.*, p. 257). There is the same extension of common ritual action beyond the furthest limits of effective and legitimate political authority in all the societies from which examples are drawn here. The mechanisms of ritual superintegration vary, but very frequently they have a heavy kinship component, which is sufficiently important to be singled out under the heading of intersecting kinship.

Complementary opposition. The idea of complementary opposition arose from the work of social anthropologists on segmentary lineage systems, publication of which began in 1940 and continued during the following two decades (Evans-

Pritchard 1940*a*; 1940*b*; Fortes 1944; 1945; 1953; Mayer 1949; Southall 1952; Smith 1956; Middleton & Tait 1958). In this work there is a constant re-iteration of certain closely interlocking concepts, social processes, and structural features, and there is a gradual crystallization of terminology. Evans-Pritchard (1940*a*, p. 147) wrote of "the principle of contradiction in political structure," stating that there is "always contradiction in the definition of a political group, for it is a group only in relation to other groups. . . . A section which from the point of view of its members comprises opposed segments is seen by members of other sections as an unsegmented unit." Elsewhere (1940*b*, pp. 293, 296) Evans-Pritchard wrote of the "balanced opposition of political segments" and of "complementary tendencies towards fission and fusion which . . . enable us to speak of a system and to say that this system is characteristically defined by the relativity and opposition of its segments." The term "complementary opposition" gradually came to be accepted (Middleton & Tait 1958).

We may distinguish three dimensions of meaning in the concept of complementary opposition—the classical, the composite, and the extended. The classical refers to the original context of superordinate and subordinate segments in a lineage system. But even in the prototypical Nuer case, the actual segments through which the principle of complementary opposition operates are usually territorial sections, not lineage segments as such. The composite may be derived from Fortes' study of the Tallensi (1945, p. 7), where the idea of complementarity is used with the dual foci of the external Bogar cult and the Earth cult, which have an asymmetrical relationship to the major cleavage between Talis and Namoos. Complementarity here refers not only to lineage relationships but also to the ways in which lineage segments are tied together in many complementary and cross-cutting interconnections. For example,

. . . in spatial relations every maximal lineage belongs to one set of adjacent lineages in the Bogar cult and to a different set of adjacent lineages in the Earth cult. It has, therefore, two intersecting fields of politico-ritual relations so adjusted that its loyalties to the other component lineages of one field are counterbalanced by its loyalties to the component lineages of the other field. . . . Their organization in two complementary configurations around polar symbols checks the dangers of disruptive conflicts that might spring from them. (Fortes 1945, pp. 107–108)

Analogous interconnections of lineages that are not those of clanship appear in Winter's account of the Amba (1958, p. 154). Thus, the Tallensi Earth cult and external Bogar cult are complementary, as are the Talis and Namoos, and the manner in which both cleavages are transcended in unity during the cycle of the Great Festivals is formally analogous to the transcendence of cleavage between subordinate segments by superordinate segments in lineage structure.

Intersecting kinship. It seems convenient and logical to extend the concept of complementary opposition to embrace analogous cleavages and transcendent interconnections in nonunilineal systems. In the first place, even in unilineal systems much of the countervailing motivation that transcends segmental oppositions is derived not only from superordinate agnatic bonds but also from cross-cutting cognatic ties. It is the latter ties that are paramount in the complementary oppositions of ego-centered categories in nonunilineal systems such as those of the Ifugao and Kalinga. Here personal kinship ties individuals to series of other individuals who are not in corporate groups. However, the Kalinga local community has something of the corporate identity, based on a dense clustering of cognatic ties, which the Nuer territorial section has in conjunction with its dominant lineage. The privileged intervention in a feud by an Ifugao neutral (Barton 1919) and the reconciliation of hostile communities by a Kalinga pact holder (Barton 1949) must be put in the same class of events as the reconciliation of warring Nuer segments by a leopard-skin chief. Furthermore, it is hard to see how any dualistic cleavage, social or ideological, such as that of the Winnebago expounded by Radin (1923) and explored by Lévi-Strauss ([1958] 1963, p. 133ff.), can fail to have the quality of complementary opposition.

The order, balance, and equilibrium that obtain throughout a society as perceived by its members depend largely on the complementary opposition of groups and categories of varying permanence. This mechanism is, of course, not peculiar to stateless societies, but it is of particular importance in them (Smith 1956). It is the self-regulating mechanism whereby, without any titular office or institution that represents or embodies sovereign authority within a bounded society, individuals who interact with one another, directly or indirectly, are ordered and positioned with respect to one another by their own reciprocal activities in dyadic relations and in joint action. This is achieved either through groups or situational categories, which are formed by and give expression to generally accepted principles, whereby the rivalry and hostility between parties in one context are mitigated by the cross-cutting obligations of some of them in another context (cf. Eliot 1948, pp. 59–60). Aggression heightens solidarity, while it is balanced by counteraggression. Despite the ever-present threat and the occasional actuality of violence, suffering, and death for the individual, the social structure is maintained in dynamic equilibrium according to relatively constant principles. The technological means of destruction are also relatively limited, and membership might fluctuate, clan turn into tribe, lineage turn into clan or vice versa, villages split and re-form, kindreds appear and disappear, without appreciable alteration in the over-all structure.

Distributive legitimacy. The characteristic of distributive legitimacy follows from the other four characteristics. As there are many polities within a single society, however differently defined and bounded from within, tensions and conflicts are worked out through the complementary opposition of groups and categories formed on various bases and at several levels. Legitimate political action also belongs to multiple points and levels, without any overriding monopoly or delegation from above, although different types of action are followed and appropriately sanctioned in each context.

States cannot be multipolities, and although they have often been connected by ritual as well as contractual links, the locus and supremacy of the state have usually remained unambiguous. For states, legitimacy is correspondingly indivisible and undistributed. Although complementary opposition is an important and neglected phenomenon, possibly recognized under other names, it does not itself define the state. While intersecting kinship is undoubtedly ubiquitous, it makes a relatively minor contribution to the constitution of the state.

Stateless societies as working systems

In the course of history stateless societies have been unevenly distributed in terms of the types of ecology and world areas in which they are found. Oceania, sub-Saharan Africa, and the Americas all lay largely outside the sphere of the large-scale literate civilizations—with obvious exceptions such as the Maya, Aztec, and Inca in America and the Muslim peoples in Africa—until these vast areas and myriad peoples were overrun by Europeans during the last three centuries. Until then, peoples with state organization were exceptional, although some important cases and many incipient instances existed in Africa (see Lowie 1948, p. 11) and Oceania.

The five cumulative characteristics discussed above will be documented by as representative a selection of stateless societies as space and the uneven quality of ethnographies permit. These societies are the Kung Bushmen of southern Africa, the Siriono and the Nambikuara Indians of South America, the Murngin and the Tiwi of Australia, the Kwakiutl and other North American Indians, the Nuer of Sudan and the Turkana of Kenya, the Kalinga and the Ifugao of the Philippines, the Plateau Tonga of Zambia, and the Siane and the Star Mountain peoples of New Guinea. These include hunters and gatherers, and agricultural and pastoral peoples; they are patrilineal, matrilineal, and bilateral in descent; they are grouped in nomadic bands, settled villages, localized lineages, kindreds, and age organizations.

It may give a misleading impression to describe any one level of grouping in a stateless society as the political community. But among hunters and gatherers the band is usually taken as such, in the sense of the largest continuously coactive group. It consists of only a few dozen or at the very most a few hundred individuals. But even in the band there often seem to be several alternative levels rather than a single unique level of grouping. Bands may combine or split seasonally; some may become extinct while new ones are formed; and it may be relatively easy for members to switch from one band to another. Bands may be exogamous or not, depending upon the relation between kinship structure and residence rules.

There is considerable ambiguity as to the existence of tribal groupings in which bands are found. Rather than accept the idea that there is an unequivocal tribal identity, I would insist that it is of the essence of the stateless society that the widest sense of common identity should positively attach to different levels and differently based clusterings for different purposes and occasions. Tribal names may be the names of languages rather than of social groups, or they may have some general connotation such as "people" without precise limitation of reference. Frequently they are derived from popular misconceptions, geographical directions, or terms of abuse applied by hostile neighbors (Elkin [1938] 1954, pp. 25, 37). In fact, the dominant sense of identity and community properly pertains to different levels for different purposes and occasions because of the different spread and distribution of such relevant features as language, kinship systems, clan or age group names, myths of origin, and similar economies and ways of life. In the case of agricultural and pastoral peoples with large, dense populations, the potential number of relevant levels of identity is greater than for groups with small, sparse populations. There may be seemingly distinctive identities attaching to such names as Kung, Tiv, Gisu, Nath (Nuer), Kwakiutl, and so forth, but very often there are more and less inclusive categories that, on occasion, are more meaningful. Such meanings attach most strongly to nuclear zones, while peripheral to them there may be more significant cross-cutting classifications. A Tiv can prove he is a Tiv by genealogy although his genealogy includes non-Tiv peoples (Bohannan 1958, pp. 35–36). Northern and southern Aranda find one another's systems incomprehensible (Lévi-Strauss [1962] 1963, p. 52).

The Kung bands recently studied by Marshall (1960) averaged twenty-five members, although earlier reports mentioned fifty to one hundred members. They are fluctuating groups of cognatic kin, displaying deep solidarity in joint exploitation of a harsh environment. There are no larger continuing or corporate groupings, but these bands are obviously not complete societies, for on the average each member has almost one-third of his nuclear kin in other bands. Affinal, agnatic, and cognatic links form multiple chains of interconnection from band to band. The number of personal names is limited, and all who possess the same one regard each other as kin and recognize associated obligations. Such categories of fictive kin run from band to band far beyond the range of any one individual's acquaintance and form the bases of interband feasts and rituals when the opportunity arises.

Siriono bands (Holmberg 1950) are more isolated and self-sufficient, rarely meeting one another. However, marriage and the transfer of membership between bands do occur. There is no evident authority over the band beyond diffuse disapproval and spontaneous and collective criticism and upbraiding that may be evoked by particularly callous and disruptive behavior. Men exercise authority over wives and children, but beyond this level political aspects of activity are hardly discernible. However, the band is closely knit by intersecting kinship ties, and a limited number of general kinship categories clearly define the relationship of all band members to one another. The harshness of the environment in relation to the Siriono's simple technology reinforces the solidarity of the band's common residence in a single forest shelter, although individual members can go hunting for days and weeks at a time without others being concerned. Here human society seems reduced to its smallest proportions.

Murngin bands (Warner 1937) have a local patriclan core with other attached relatives, but membership in the band fluctuates with the seasonal requirements of the food quest and the performance of numerous rituals. The band is the war-making group and the largest group with any continuity and solidarity. To this extent it may be seen as a political community. There is no violent conflict within it, or with the patriclans of its members' wives and mothers, so that there are changing networks of interclan obligations. Kinship and ritual are elaborated in and beyond the band through a number of interlocking systems involving clans, phratries, and special associations. The social world of the individual is classified into seven lines of descent extending over five generations, 71 kin categories forming eight intermarrying subsections. It is obvious that for any individual, family, or band, the effective field of society includes a much wider complex of interacting and interlocking groups and categories.

The Kwakiutl (Boas 1897; Codere 1950) depend more on fishing than on hunting and are exceptional in the richness of their natural resources and the relative density of population. There is a system of social stratification into nobles, commoners, and slaves, although they lack cultivation and domestic animals. The details of the Kwakiutl traditional social structure will never be altogether certain, but it is known that they lived in seashore villages composed of large houses, each probably occupied by a different descent group. One or several such villages made up the basic political community, which was also the usual fighting unit. There was intense rivalry for prestige between individuals, between brothers, between descent groups, and between political communities. Food, blankets, canoes, houses, coppers, songs and rituals, marriage, murder, and warfare were all exploited for display, consumption, acquisition, and destruction in the endless battle for prestige and rank. Many political communities were tied together in this circulatory process, their chiefs intermarrying, interfeasting, ambushing, and exterminating one another, although close kin ties between polities imposed certain restrictions on their fighting. The elaborate winter rituals also combined several neighboring polities. Order depended on kinship and ritual ramifications combined with the overriding prestige motivation. There were no specific political authorities or sanctions. Chiefs were ranked descent-group heads. They fought for rank, and their people fought and paid to share in it. When the burden was too great they refused, and the chief was powerless. With imperceptible changes of emphasis the same stateless complex transcended many tribal and language barriers throughout the Northwest Pacific Coast.

There are very few accounts of ethnic groups in aboriginal North America that have not confused linguistic, societal, and political units. Cumulative historical scholarship shows, for example, that neither the League of the Iroquois nor its component parts were states and that relations between the tribes were constantly fluctuating and even hostile; however, like other stateless societies they were characterized by the possibility of extending ritual relationships beyond the limits of political communities.

There is no good reason to suppose that the North American Indians fall outside the range of stateless societies, although individual visionary experiences and ritual associations, whose contribution to political order still cannot be precisely defined, were especially common, and there was considerable coherence and continuity of cultures and societies. It seems likely that the appearance and disappearance, splitting and amalgamation, and conquest and defeat of groups and subgroups took place within a fairly consistent structure of kin groups, settlements, and elaborate symbolic activities, each aspect of which might metamorphose gradually at different points from one type of system to another.

The Siane (Salisbury 1962) have 17 "tribal" groups, each composed of from two to nine patri-clan villages containing several wards focused on large communal men's houses with separate quarters for women and children. The clan village is the feud unit and is described as "sovereign," but the whole tribe (or sometimes phratry) is exogamous and constitutes a quasi kin group, to every member of which a kin term can be applied and chartered by myth. When one clan fights, the others in its tribe or phratry remain neutral. They celebrate ancestor festivals together. Violence within the phratry is limited to club fighting.

In the Star Mountains of New Guinea (Pouwer 1964) linguistically defined "tribes" are composed of parish polities divided into hamlets, which are aggregates of nuclear families. The parish is the war unit, yet certain parishes have sacred meeting houses that are the ritual centers for several other parishes. Hamlets are ephemeral and within them fighting is rare. There are 45 patriclans common to several tribes, and a common culture extends beyond language boundaries.

The Ifugao (Barton 1919) have no continuously cohesive group larger than the extended family, although bilateral kinship is traced in concentric circles, as it were, as far as seventh cousins, exogamy extending to second or third cousins. Larger named districts are recognized, but they never meet or act together. There are no political authorities; killing and the acquisition of heads for supernatural power and prestige are highly valued, violence being restricted only by the inherent conflict of ramifying bilateral kinship obligations. Members of kindreds do assist one another both in offense and defense, but since each person belongs to many different ego-centered kindreds, he is always faced with a complicated balancing of opposing interests and obligations. The nearer his kinship to a plaintiff and the higher his rank, the stronger is his obligation and self-interest to back and defend the plaintiff and the larger his share of compensation received. The nearer his kinship to a defendant, the heavier is his contribution to compensation and the stronger his motive to enforce good behavior. A's share of compensation received by B from C may even be canceled out by what he had to contribute to C to enable him to pay it. Moreover, the closer the kin relationship, the more adequate one is as a substitute victim in a feud. Some Ifugao traders from distant regions made personal pacts of mutual obligation to protect and avenge, which tended to escalate into territorial treaties.

The Kalinga (Barton 1949) live in larger, concentrated settlements that form the nuclei of more cohesive regions, whose most prestigeful leaders may enter into pacts that further enhance their prestige and enable all feuds to be settled between them. All the obligations of reciprocal kinship, including exogamy, obtain between pact holders. Pacts are initiated and reaffirmed by exchange feasting, drinking, dancing, flirting, and gift giving.

This striking type of social system, still not well integrated in the mainstream of anthropological thought, is common in most parts of Indonesia, but more isolated examples are found in all major regions of the world.

The Plateau Tonga (Colson 1951) display a singular lack of distinctively political activities in contrast to other African cultivators. They live in small villages having a vague matrilineal core to which other kin and nonkin are attached. There is no larger continuous group than the village, but the feuding organization is based on matrilineages scattered through several villages. The named matriclans are common not only to the Tonga but also to similar neighboring peoples, each associated with an animal and linked together by joking relationships. Although matrilineages rather than villages organize raids, all fellow villagers can be held responsible for one another's misdemeanors in the context of feuding. Ancestor worship also draws lineage members from beyond the confines of the village. Varying clusters of villages are linked in allegiance to rain shrines of fluctuating repute, whose owners are regarded as representing first settlers and nominal owners of the country. Through them peace is ritually sanctioned when the first fruits are annually presented and the local spirits express their demands. The claims of men on the bridewealth of their classificatory sisters' daughters or great-granddaughters give rise to intricate links between matrilineages that bind neighborhoods together.

Nuer society (Evans-Pritchard 1940*a*; 1940*b*) is arranged in an articulated segmentary series of territorial units, one inside the other, whose common action and coherent interrelation derive from the agnatic core that runs through each, although these agnates may be a minority of the whole. It is the dialectic between the territorially based communities and the agnatic cores on which they are structured and the networks of personal kinship ties that criss-cross between them that provide the operational mode of Nuer society. The political community is the largest segment capable of joint action and of settling internal disputes by standardized processes, and there are some dozens of these among the Nuer. Many of the clans are dispersed all over the country, creating personal and corporate obligations between members and sections of different polities. Initiation into the age organization is coordinated within three or four divisions of the country and held jointly by some smaller polities, while the social age equivalence established by it is recognized by all Nuer. Certain prophets acquired a reputation extending over many polities and could even induce occasional joint political action in warfare. The definition of a Nuer polity is contingent purely upon which level of segmentary grouping empirically acts as such and does so with sufficient consistency to permit its actions to be regarded as morally obligatory. This recognition is strongly influenced by the kinship and ritual relations that extend far beyond the usual field of political action.

Turkana society (Gulliver 1955; 1958) has no permanent residential grouping or authority beyond the extended family, but the orderly activity of much larger temporary collections of individuals is coordinated primarily by the principles that cluster around the age organization. Father and son belong to opposite-named alternations, so that every temporary gathering of men is precipitated into momentary moieties. Youths are initiated into new named age groups about every five years at some 25 centers. Through informal canvassing one name comes to be adopted for the same age set all over the country. Age organization both defines and emphasizes social age. The oldest men available at any time or place are the most potent ritually and are nearest the deity; they pray for rain and stop fights by walking between combatants. Homicide is almost unknown among the Turkana, since it is believed to prevent rain, the greatest disaster to nomadic pastoralists in semi-desert country. The Turkana secure their general social needs and protection further by developing personal kin networks, to which they add stock associates through the exchange of cattle. Large exogamous patriclans are dispersed throughout Turkana society and among neighboring related peoples. Age organization gives a common identity to all Turkana and a spatial framework that can precipitate any chance assembly into agreed relationships and orderly common action. The Turkana never fought their related Jie neighbors, but they fought the equally related Karamojong and Dodoth, as well as the unrelated Samburu Masai and Marile, with whom they also intermarried.

Discussion

Having presented these few highly compressed examples, so diverse geographically and structurally, yet all maintaining social life without state forms through certain basic common principles, we may introduce some further recurrent themes. Few of the names by which these peoples are ethnographically known are their real names, and usually there is a cultural continuum along which social relations and cultural characteristics are clustered and concentrated at different times and places and for different purposes in a variable manner, yet according to coherent principles. Either cultural transformations are essentially gradual and phase into each other without discernible points of confrontation or clear lines of divergence, or even if there are marked boundaries, say, in language, they do not coincide with those of other cultural phenomena, as when zones of warfare, intermarriage, clanship, and ritual observance fall at different points so that again the net outcome is one of relativity. This situation can only obtain where large continuous areas are occupied by equally stateless societies. Clearer distinctions naturally appear where there is confrontation with more politically specialized groups or with recent migrants of a radically different culture that is not yet integrated.

None of the peoples discussed above have an unambiguous, categorical tribal designation, with the possible exception of the Turkana. The case of the Turkana is particularly interesting and in some respects represents the polar opposite to that of the Murngin. The latter have minute and elaborate local differentiations of many kinds, to the point that they insist that even clans have separate named languages although in fact they may not significantly differ. The result is that Murngin society consists of a large though fluctuating number of highly diverse parts. On the other hand, since the Turkana have no permanent groups beyond the family, they require a rather precise framework of principles to order their wider relationships. The spatial recognition of this framework provides an unusually clear group definition, although it is far larger than the effective social field for any Turkana individual or group. Thus, paradoxically, Turkana homogeneity differentiates the people and Murngin diversity does not; both arrangements serve the same general end in the maintenance of stateless society. These societies are not only stateless, but most of them are essentially nameless. They have designations, but these are specific to purpose, time, and place and must not be used to define the unique limits of the society. Distinctions that make unique names acceptable, recognized, meaningful, and necessary are part of the process of imperative over-all political coordination and specialization, out of which state structures arise from stateless situations that are logically incompatible with them.

Leadership.   Certain characteristics of leadership and of behavior in situations of serious conflict are noticeably recurrent in these examples. Leadership depends to a surprising extent on personal qualities of achievement within ascribed limits of eligibility. Thus it seems that any Kung who belongs to a group that has general rights in an area can form a band if he can get people to follow him. Once established, his position becomes hereditary among his cognatic descendents. However, if these descendents fail, the position lapses although the band may continue. Leadership must be valued, although it is not indispensable. The leader has no imperative authority, and apart from his undoubted prestige he seems to have far more obligations than rights. He supplies initiative in leading the band from camp to camp and in planning hunting and other activities. The more successful he is, the greater is the dependence upon him. Lévi-Strauss strengthens the idea of recurrent characteristics of leadership in his account (1944) of the Nambikuara, who are formally rather similar to the Kung but culturally and geographically close to the Siriono. There is free choice of membership between bands, which unite in a temporary village for cultivation during

the rains and then disperse again. Multiple kin ties run through many bands, so that a family may be more closely tied to another in a different band than it is to any in the same one. Chiefs are the relatively stable nuclei round which bands fluctuate and cluster. Chiefs have no political authority or sanctions; their efficacy depends fundamentally on doing better than others in the food quest and all essential social activities and on supplying initiative and leadership by consent of the group, which is their only basis of legitimacy. They have to work harder and be more generous than others in food-giving and entertainment. It would be impossible for them to satisfy these demands were it not for their effective monopoly of polygyny, through the practice of secondary unions, which the band grants as long as they succeed, and which in turn permits them success through the extra womanpower of subsidiary wives who supply labor, hunting assistance, sexual gratification, and general support rather than conventional childbearing and domestic services. Yet the chiefs' motivation is for prestige more than for women or food. Although they nominate their successors formally, this act can only ratify informal support by popular consent. The chiefs' ambivalence, reluctance, and even refusal to assume the heavy burdens of leadership, also found in many far more specialized institutions of chiefship, are highly intelligible in this small-scale example. Leadership at its most elemental naturally depends on being judged better than the led, but even here ascribed aspects of the leader himself or of his family and descent group are frequently taken into account.

The Nuer who is the "bull," or leader of his lineage segment and of the territorial group focused upon it, acquires this position through a similar combination of descent, ability, and good fortune in establishing a successful family. The leopardskin chiefs, through whom armed conflicts may be resolved, must come from particular lineages, but within this wide area of eligibility their position as ritual conciliators depends solely upon the consensual insistence of the people. Among the Siane, the big man's pre-eminence depends upon his age and his success in oratory, in founding a large family, and on his example of industry, wealth, generosity, and bravery. Any man can aspire to this position, and the status of figurehead so achieved depends upon general consent, although it is easier for one who stands in the structural category of "eldest brother."

In principle, any Tonga man (and even woman in some cases) can form a village and become a headman if he has the necessary qualities for attracting and holding such a following. But as soon as such a position is achieved it acquires hereditary qualities, although there is a wide group of possible successors. As with the Nambikuara and Kung leaders, the Tonga headman has additional responsibilities but very few privileges and no political authority or sanctions.

The most general level of Turkana leadership is determined by the age organization, which designates the most senior person present as nearest the divinity. The Kwakiutl chiefs were hereditary heads of kin groups occupying clearly defined relative positions in a hierarchy of rank, but where each one came into this hierarchy at any time depended upon his personal achievements and the backing of his followers in the fluctuating hazards of the potlatch. Shamanistic divination offered those of lower status an arduous path to the personal achievement of another form of pre-eminence and prestige.

Head-hunting was the chief personal path to high status for Kalinga men, but birth into a family whose head already enjoyed wealth and high status was such an advantage that it was usually from this combination that pre-eminent positions of ritual influence and superintegration as *pangats* and pact holders were achieved and frequently passed on within the family. So great were the prestige at stake and the supernatural sanction and loss of face involved that a Kalinga pact holder would even kill a transgressing kinsman himself rather than fail in fulfilling a pact obligation.

Conflict resolution. For the Kung, the Siriono, and many other hunting and gathering peoples, the sheer quest for food and physical and social survival are all-engrossing, and physical violence or armed conflict between groups hardly ever occurs. But in other cases, especially among the larger-scale stateless societies of agricultural and pastoral peoples, ingenious ritual mechanisms of conflict resolution are important. This is true also of many Australian peoples, despite the fact that they do not practice agriculture.

It is certainly a common characteristic of stateless societies, in all major regions where they are found, that the highest levels of leadership and the widest levels of integration are secured and set in a ritual context. Legitimacy is distributive or pluralistic in that it belongs to several groups and categories, which are interlocked and functionally differentiated within the same social system yet not hierarchically ordered, and which are integrated yet not coordinated by any over-all political authority. There are frequently several distinct sources of leadership—typically, some arising from the structure of groups and interlocking categories, based on personal achievement within ascribed limits of eligibility, and some arising from more purely personal factors of a supernatural character, related to divination and personal experiences of revelation often developing outside the highest status levels. Examples are the shaman diviners in Kwakiutl and many stateless societies in Asia, or the prophets and diviners in Nuer, Turkana, Tonga, and many other African societies. There are also many instances from Africa, Asia, Oceania, and the Americas in which different levels of conflict were delimited by methodical restrictions, as in the progressive limitation of open warfare to adult males, to fighting only with clubs or sticks instead of with more harmful weapons, to wrestling matches and other formalized types of conflict that provide cathartic relief with little danger of serious injury.

In many of these cases it is difficult to resist the conclusion that in the very foundations of these simple social systems there are various mechanisms biased in the direction of maintenance, collective survival, and equilibrium. The techniques of conflict resolution would so often remain inoperative were it not for a priori sanctions of supernatural beliefs, reinforced by conveniently built-in motivations of prestige, greed, and even sexual gratification. Not only in the very small-scale societies, but also in the relatively small local groups of even the larger ones, there is constant reference to the fact that violent and continued conflict does not commonly occur in primary local groups because it is mutually recognized by all as too inconvenient and uncomfortable, so that those inclined to cause it are restrained by the spontaneous pressure of opinion against them or are ultimately forced to leave the group. It is important to note that this is characteristic of societies in any part of the world (such as the Nuer and the Siane) in which the expression of violence is approved and common in other contexts.

The stateless society is both an empirical, historical fact and a comment on political theory. From the time of Plato and Aristotle to the twentieth century political theory has been Western-oriented and ethnocentric, normative rather than empirical. Information about the stateless societies, which existed throughout the greater part of the world until recent centuries, was for practical reasons lacking and was in any case used as a negative foil for Western experience rather than valued for its own sake. Since the major interest was in the problems of political philosophy arising out of the cumulative Western experience, the incentive to understand the internal workings of stateless societies as empirical phenomena was doubly lacking. Some exceptions may be found, as in the case of the great historical jurisprudents, such as Maine, Maitland, Pollock, and Seebohm. Despite the excellence of their historical researches, their accounts of earlier phases of Western societies inevitably left crucial gaps, while effective data on contemporary stateless societies were still not available to them. Indeed, no adequate accounts of the political structure and workings of Oriental states have been available to the West until very recently, let alone of stateless societies outside the Western world, which, although smaller and in a sense simpler, are more difficult to penetrate and understand. Most works on political philosophy make brief initial reference to a largely hypothetical situation in which the institution of the state as generally understood is lacking, but this is a negative construct with about as much reality as the noble savage. There are two main attitudes: one in which the emergence of the state, so fundamental to society as we know it, is regarded as a boundary on the other side of which society hardly exists as a recognizable part of our common humanity; and another in which it is maintained that the state, as the fundamental institution of society, is already implicit in a herd of buffalo or a troop of monkeys and to that extent necessarily also attributable to early man.

Positive emphasis on stateless societies as political entities worthy of empirical study in their own right came only with twentieth-century anthropology, and ironically (one wonders whether also necessarily), at a stage of world history when they were hardly any longer to be found as going concerns. It is difficult to get out of the habit of looking at these small stateless societies in negative terms. They do lack the definitive territorial boundaries, exclusive sovereignty, and central monopoly of legitimate force that characterize states. We must regard states as a further evolved form of human polity than stateless society. But the latter have very positive characteristics. The most general and important is the fact that fundamental responsibility for the maintenance of society itself is much more widely dispersed throughout its varied institutions and its whole population, at least, usually, all its adult males. The remarkable spectacle of societies positively maintaining themselves at a high level of integration without any obvious specialized means of enforcement has un-

doubtedly led to new insight and attention to the fundamental responsibilities of all citizens, which for most people are obscured by the ubiquity of specialized political institutions. In stateless societies every man grows up with a practical and intuitive sense of his responsibility to maintain constantly throughout his life that part of the fabric of society in which at any time he is involved. Stateless societies are so constituted that the kaleidoscopic succession of concrete social situations provides the stimulus that motivates each individual to act for his own interest or for that of close kin and neighbors with whom he is so totally involved, in a manner which maintains the fabric of society. It is a little like the classical model of laissez-faire economics translated into the political field. But if every man is thus for himself, he is so only within a very tight framework of reciprocal obligation that he cannot avoid absorbing. The lack of specialized roles and the resulting multiplex quality of social networks mean that neither economic nor political ends can be exclusively pursued by anyone to the detriment of society, because these ends are intertwined with each other and further channeled by ritual and controlled by the beliefs which ritual expresses.

AIDAN SOUTHALL

[*See also* POLITICAL ANTHROPOLOGY; STATE; TRIBAL SOCIETY.]

BIBLIOGRAPHY

BARTON, ROY F. 1919 *Ifugao Law.* University of California Publications in American Archaeology and Ethnology, Vol. 15, No. 1. Berkeley: Univ. of California Press.

BARTON, ROY F. 1949 *The Kalingas: Their Institutions and Custom Law.* Univ. of Chicago Press. → Published posthumously.

BERNDT, RONALD M. 1964 Warfare in the New Guinea Highlands. *American Anthropologist* New Series 66 (Special Publication) no. 4, part 2:183–203.

BOAS, FRANZ 1897 The Social Organization and the Secret Societies of the Kwakiutl Indians. Based on personal observations and on notes made by George Hunt. Pages 311–738 in U.S. National Museum, *Annual Report, 1895.* Washington: The Museum.

BOHANNAN, L. (1958) 1964 Political Aspects of Tiv Social Organization. Pages 33–66 in John Middleton and David Tait (editors), *Tribes Without Rulers: Studies in African Segmentary Systems.* London: Routledge.

CODERE, HELEN F. 1950 *Fighting With Property: A Study of Kwakiutl Potlatching and Warfare, 1792–1930.* American Ethnological Society, Monograph No. 18. New York: Augustin.

COLSON, ELIZABETH 1951 The Plateau Tonga of Northern Rhodesia. Pages 94–168 in Elizabeth Colson and Max Gluckman (editors), *Seven Tribes of British Central Africa.* Oxford Univ. Press.

EASTON, DAVID 1959 Political Anthropology. *Biennial Review of Anthropology* [1959]:210–262.

ELIOT, T. S. (1948) 1949 *Notes Towards the Definition of Culture.* New York: Harcourt.

ELKIN, A. P. (1938) 1954 *The Australian Aborigines.* 3d ed. Melbourne: Angus & Robertson. → A paperback edition was published in 1964 by Doubleday.

EVANS-PRITCHARD, E. E. (1940a) 1963 *The Nuer: A Description of the Modes of Livelihood and Political Institutions of a Nilotic People.* Oxford: Clarendon.

EVANS-PRITCHARD, E. E. (1940b) 1961 The Nuer of the Southern Sudan. Pages 272–296 in Meyer Fortes and E. E. Evans-Pritchard (editors), *African Political Systems.* Oxford Univ. Press.

EVANS-PRITCHARD, E. E. 1949 Luo Tribes and Clans. *Rhodes–Livingstone Journal* 7:24–40.

FORTES, MEYER (1940) 1961 The Political System of the Tallensi of the Northern Territories of the Gold Coast. Pages 239–271 in Meyer Fortes and E. E. Evans-Pritchard (editors), *African Political Systems.* Oxford Univ. Press.

FORTES, MEYER 1944 The Significance of Descent in Tale Social Structure. *Africa* 14:362–384.

FORTES, MEYER 1945 *The Dynamics of Clanship Among the Tallensi: Being the First Part of an Analysis of the Social Structure of a Trans-Volta Tribe.* Published for the International African Institute. Oxford Univ. Press.

FORTES, MEYER 1953 The Structure of Unilineal Descent Groups. *American Anthropologist* New Series 55:17–41.

GULLIVER, PHILLIP H. 1955 *The Family Herds: A Study of Two Pastoral Tribes in East Africa, the Jie and the Turkana.* London: Routledge.

GULLIVER, P. H. 1958 The Turkana Age Organization. *American Anthropologist* New Series 60:900–922.

GULLIVER, PAMELA; and GULLIVER, P. H. 1953 *The Central Nilo-Hamites.* London: International African Institute.

HART, CHARLES W. M.; and PILLING, ARNOLD R. 1960 *The Tiwi of North Australia.* New York: Holt.

HODGE, FREDERICK W. (1907–1910) 1959 *Handbook of American Indians North of Mexico.* 2 vols. U.S. Bureau of American Ethnology, Bulletin No. 30. Parts 1–2. New York: Pageant.

HOLMBERG, ALLAN R. 1950 *Nomads of the Long Bow: The Siriono of Eastern Bolivia.* Smithsonian Institution, Institute of Social Anthropology, Publication No. 10. Washington: Government Printing Office.

LA FONTAINE, J. S. 1959 *The Gisu of Uganda.* London: International African Institute.

LEVINE, ROBERT A. 1960 The Internalization of Political Values in Stateless Societies. *Human Organization* 19:51–58.

LÉVI-STRAUSS, CLAUDE 1944 The Social and Psychological Aspects of Chieftainship in a Primitive Tribe: The Nambikuara of Northwestern Mato Grosso. N.Y. Academy of Sciences, *Transactions* 2d Series 7:16–32.

LÉVI-STRAUSS, CLAUDE (1958) 1963 *Structural Anthropology.* New York: Basic Books. → First published in French.

LÉVI-STRAUSS, CLAUDE (1962) 1963 *Totemism.* Boston: Beacon. → First published as *Le totémisme aujourd'hui.*

LIENHARDT, GODFREY (1958) 1964 The Western Dinka. Pages 97–135 in John Middleton and David Tait (editors), *Tribes Without Rulers: Studies in African Segmentary Systems.* London: Routledge.

LOWIE, ROBERT H. (1922) 1962 *The Origin of the State.* Rev. & enl. New York: Russell. → An enlarged and revised version of articles first published in the *Freeman* in 1922.

LOWIE, ROBERT H. (1935) 1956 *The Crow Indians.* New York: Rinehart.

LOWIE, ROBERT H. (1948) 1960 Some Aspects of Political Organization Among the American Aborigines. Pages 262–290 in Robert H. Lowie, *Selected Papers in Anthropology.* Berkeley: Univ. of California Press. → First published in Volume 78 of the *Journal of the Royal Anthropological Institute of Great Britain and Ireland.*

MAIR, LUCY P. (1962) 1964 *Primitive Government.* Baltimore: Penguin.

MARSHALL, LORNA 1960 !Kung Bushman Bands. *Africa* 30:325–355.

MAYER, PHILIP 1949 *The Lineage Principle in Gusii Society.* International African Institute, Memorandum No. 24. Oxford Univ. Press.

MEYER, EDUARD (1884–1902) 1953–1958 *Geschichte des Altertums.* 5 vols. Basel: Schwabe.

MIDDLETON, JOHN 1963 The Yakan or Allah Water Cult Among the Lugbara. *Journal of the Royal Anthropological Institute of Great Britain and Ireland* 93:80–108.

MIDDLETON, JOHN 1965 *The Lugbara of Uganda.* New York: Holt.

MIDDLETON, JOHN; and TAIT, DAVID (editors) (1958) 1964 *Tribes Without Rulers: Studies in African Segmentary Systems.* London: Routledge.

MOSS, CLAUDE R. 1920 Nabaloi Law and Ritual. University of California Publications in American Archaeology and Ethnology, Vol. 15, No. 3. Berkeley: Univ. of California Press.

POUWER, JAN 1964 A Social System in the Star Mountains: Toward a Reorientation of the Study of Social Systems. *American Anthropologist* New Series 66 (Special Publication) no. 4, part 2:133–161.

RADIN, PAUL 1923 The Winnebago Tribe. U.S. Bureau of American Ethnology, *Annual Report* 37:35–560.

SALISBURY, RICHARD F. 1962 *From Stone to Steel: Economic Consequences of a Technological Change in New Guinea.* London and New York: Melbourne Univ. Press; Cambridge Univ. Press.

SMITH, M. G. 1956 On Segmentary Lineage Systems. *Journal of the Royal Anthropological Institute of Great Britain and Ireland* 86, part 2:39–80.

SOUTHALL, A. W. 1952 *Lineage Formation Among the Luo.* International African Institute, Memorandum No. 26. Oxford Univ. Press.

SWADESH, MORRIS 1948 Motivations in Wootka Warfare. *Southwestern Journal of Anthropology* 4:76–93.

VINOGRADOFF, PAUL 1920–1922 *Outlines of Historical Jurisprudence.* 2 vols. Oxford Univ. Press. → Volume 1: *Introduction. Tribal Law.* Volume 2: *The Jurisprudence of the Greek City.*

WARNER, W. LLOYD (1937) 1958 *A Black Civilization: A Social Study of an Australian Tribe.* Rev. ed. New York: Harper.

WATSON, JAMES B. (editor) 1964 New Guinea: The Central Highlands. *American Anthropologist* New Series 66 (Special Publication) no. 4, part 2.

WINTER, E. H. 1958 The Aboriginal Political Structure of Bwamba. Pages 136–166 in John Middleton and David Tait (editors), *Tribes Without Rulers: Studies in African Segmentary Systems.* London: Routledge.

STATES' RIGHTS
See CONSTITUTIONAL LAW; FEDERALISM.

STATICS AND DYNAMICS
IN ECONOMICS

Since the end of the nineteenth century, economic analysis has been fairly rigidly compartmentalized into statics and dynamics. Various, sometimes conflicting definitions of these terms have appeared in the literature; some have based the distinction on the nature of the subject matter studied, while others have emphasized the difference in analytic approach. Utilizing the first of these viewpoints, we may distinguish between a *stationary* economic phenomenon—that is, one that does not change with the passage of time—and a *developing* or *changing* phenomenon. But no matter which type of phenomenon we study, we may focus upon it an analytic apparatus which we describe as *dynamic*—that is, one that takes explicit account of the role of the passage of time in the structure of the subject—or we can subject it to a *static* analysis, which deals with its mechanism at a given moment and abstracts from the effect of past events on the present and future. For example, an investigation of the determination of the level of employment at a given moment and its dependence on current consumption, investment, and governmental demand may be considered static in character, but a discussion of the same problem that considers how the relationship between today's supply of capital equipment and its growth affects tomorrow's investment demand and how this process can generate a time path of investment demand can be considered a dynamic analysis. (For further discussion of the definitions, see Samuelson 1947, pp. 315–317; Frisch 1935–1936.)

In earlier periods of economic analysis, the distinction between statics and dynamics was not very clear-cut. Characteristically, the object of the economist was to provide useful advice to the rulers of the body politic rather than systematic studies defensible under the canons of scientific analysis. Such a pragmatic concern justified the construction of a pastiche composed of both static and dynamic relationships that switched from one approach to the other whenever it became convenient. For example, monetary theorists, in their discussions of the effects of an increase of the supply of currency, turned rather early to an examination of the sequence of events whereby the initial stimulation of production and prosperity resulting from an injection of funds may gradually be dissipated by translation into a rise in price levels that is ultimately diffused throughout the economy. Cantillon and Hume were among those who described this process perspicaciously and in considerable detail.

The marriage of the two analytic approaches attained its apex in the work of the early classical economists, including Malthus and Ricardo, and culminated in the work of J. S. Mill. In these writings a purely static theory of wages, profits, and rent was wedded to a mechanism that accounted for the rates of growth of capital and population. In rough outline the model may be described as follows: In the short run wages are determined by the demand for labor, which increases with the supply of capital. But if the demand for labor is high, causing high wages, population growth is encouraged; and this gradually increases the supply of labor and reduces wages. Profits are thereby increased, stimulating investment both by enhancing its profitability and by augmenting the supply of funds that are normally used for this purpose. Thus, the levels of capital supply, population, and labor supply will grow with the passage of time, and in this process wages will frequently be kept up by high demand for labor. But, in the classical model, this process cannot continue indefinitely. The supply of natural resources, including land, being fixed, a growing population must result in an ever increasing ratio of labor supply to resources. Here enters the principle of diminishing returns, which states that if the supply of natural resources remains constant, increased labor supply will, at least after some point, yield diminishing marginal returns; that is, further increments in the labor supply will add less to the national product than did previous increments. Ultimately, then, the capital–population growth process will reduce per capita output and hence will decrease either wages or profits or both. Reduced profits will cause decreased investment, decreased demand for labor, and decreased wages. And when wages have been reduced to a minimal level representing either the amount necessary to provide subsistence or some habitual minimum living standard, population growth will cease. In sum, in this analysis the "law" of diminishing returns ultimately brings growth to a halt and then, finally, takes the economy into a stationary state where wages and profits are low and the general welfare is in a sorry condition.

From this model the classical economists derived a number of policy conclusions, among them their approbation of such measures as late marriage, which reduces the rate of growth of population, and their general denigration of activities designed to enforce increases in wage rates, which in their view could only temporarily ameliorate the lot of the laboring classes and would do so at a heavy cost—the increased imminence of the unhappy stationary state.

From our point of view, this construct is significant because it shows how an unsophisticated mélange of statics and dynamics can sometimes serve the needs of policy more effectively than a structure that is analytically pure. By bringing the static relationship between wages and the demand for labor together with the dynamics of population growth and marginal productivity, the classicists were able to derive conclusions which, right or wrong, were at least relevant for public decisions. (For further information on the classical and other earlier dynamic models, see Adelman 1961, chapters 3–5; Baumol [1951] 1959, chapters 2, 3.)

Toward the end of the nineteenth century, when economic analysis began more self-consciously to follow the precepts of scientific method, statics and dynamics were more rigidly compartmentalized. At first this meant in practice that systematic dynamic analysis was largely abandoned and was confined primarily to some casual observations about the time processes that underlay the well-developed static constructs. These observations ranged from the apologetic comments of John Bates Clark, who commended dynamic analysis to the care of the future economists, to Walras' suggestive discussion of *tâtonnements* and Edgeworth's recontracting model. Both of the latter economists were fully cognizant of the difficulties besetting the equilibrium assumptions of static price theory, recognizing that in a world of imperfect knowledge initial pricing and supply bids were unlikely to approximate their equilibrium levels. They therefore described, in rather vague terms, intertemporal processes whereby the market, by trial and error, might gradually approach the price and output levels predicted by static theory.

Only in the last few decades has dynamic analysis developed into the independent and complex body of theoretical matter to be described presently. However, before that development occurred, a related analytic approach, *comparative statics*, provided a substantial contribution to economics.

Comparative statics. Comparative statics is a method of theoretical investigation of the consequences of a change in some datum in an economic model. For example, to determine the effects of a tax rate change on the level of output of a firm, a comparative statics study examines the two relevant equilibrium outputs—the equilibrium output

under the old tax rate and the modified equilibrium output that would result from the imposition of the alternative tax arrangement. In effect, the comparative statics approach starts from an equilibrium position, then imposes an experimental variation on one or more of the parameters of the model and examines what has happened after the smoke has cleared away and the system has had time to settle down to a new equilibrium. But this method abstracts entirely from the time path of the variables of the model during the adjustment process. It considers a dynamic process (the time-consuming adjustment of the system to the change in parameters) but disregards everything but its end points—the initial equilibrium from which the process of change started out and the terminal equilibrium point at which the process comes to rest. This is why contemporary terminology distinguishes sharply between comparative statics analysis and dynamic analysis. However, the two are not unrelated. Implicit in every theorem of comparative statics is an adjustment process for which only dynamics can account. This, in part, constitutes what Samuelson (1947, chapter 9) has called the *correspondence principle*. He has also shown, by investigating the mathematics of the dynamic process, that if this process is unstable (if its time path does not converge toward an equilibrium value), the corresponding comparative statics analysis is likely to yield nonsense results. This principle will be explained and illustrated below, after some of the necessary tools of dynamic process analysis have been introduced.

It is probably no exaggeration to say that comparative statics has yielded some of the most fruitful portions of economic analysis. Both in terms of our insight into the workings of the economy and in its guidance for policy, comparative statics may well have contributed more than either pure statics or pure dynamics. Almost every branch of economic theory has made effective use of the approach. Two typical results of comparative statics are the macroeconomic conclusion, from the Keynesian model, that a fall in the supply of money will reduce the (equilibrium) level of employment, and the microeconomic result that a rise in price must decrease the (equilibrium) quantity of a commodity demanded by a utility-maximizing consumer if the item is not an inferior good (a commodity whose consumption declines when income rises).

Methodology of comparative statics. In recent decades comparative statics has developed an effective and fairly standardized mathematical methodology. (For descriptions of the method, see Samuelson 1947, chapter 9; Henderson & Quandt

1958, chapters 2, 3; Bushaw & Clower 1957.) The analysis involves the following steps:

(1) Formulate an expression describing the determination of the value of the variable that constitutes the objective of the person(s) directly involved and that therefore is maximized in equilibrium; for example, write out the functional relationship between the level of profit of a firm and the length of time for which an investment is retained.

(2) Write out the first-order and second-order maximum conditions of this expression, for example, the condition that the first derivative of the profit function with respect to the length of the investment period be zero and that the second derivative be negative.

(3) Vary a parameter in the problem (for example, allow for a change, di, in the rate of interest, i, that the firm confronts) and use the first-order maximum condition to determine what compensating change in the other variables (for example, in the period of investment, dt) is necessary to bring the situation back to equilibrium.

(4) Use the preceding step to determine the marginal effect of the change in the parameter on the other variables of the system, for example, to determine dt/di.

(5) Use the second-order condition and any other economic information to determine the sign of this marginal yield figure, for example, to determine whether a rise in the rate of interest will cause a profit-maximizing firm to lengthen its investment period, that is, to find whether $dt/di > 0$.

A relatively simple illustration should make these steps clearer. Suppose that the firm in question is growing timber and that the revenue it gets when it sells the product depends upon the length of time, t, a tree has been permitted to grow. Revenue, $R(t)$, will then be a function of time. But this amount will be available only t periods in the future, and its present value will be smaller by a discounting factor that represents the loss of earnings resulting from not having the money during the interim. Suppose an investment. I, could grow continually at a constantly compounded rate of interest, ρ, so that $dI/dt = \rho I$ (where we no longer use the symbol i to represent the interest rate, because i denoted interest compounded only at discrete points in time). Then we must have $I(t) = I(0)e^{\rho t}$. Therefore, the present value, $I(0)$, of $R(t) \equiv I(t)$, obtainable t periods in the future, must be given by $I(0)e^{\rho t} = R(t)$, or

$$(1) \qquad I(0) = e^{-\rho t}R(t).$$

We have now completed step 1 of our comparative statics analysis; that is, we have found the

function expressing the determination of the variable, $I(0)$, whose value is to be maximized.

Step 2, giving first-order and second-order maximum conditions, yields

$$(2) \qquad dI(0)/dt = -\rho e^{-\rho t}R(t) + e^{-\rho t}dR(t)/dt = 0$$

and

$$(3) \qquad d^2I(0)/dt^2 < 0.$$

In step 3 we allow for a change in the interest rate, ρ, and determine the compensating change in the investment period, t, necessary to maintain the maximum condition (2). To do this we calculate the total differential of (2), $d[dI(0)/dt]$, and require that it be equal to zero, that is, that there be no change in the first derivative from its optimal (zero) value. We thus obtain

$$d[dI(0)/dt] = [d^2I(0)/dt^2]dt + [\partial(dI(0)/dt)/\partial\rho]d\rho = 0.$$

By direct differentiation of (2) with respect to ρ, we see that

$$\partial[dI(0)/dt]/\partial\rho = -e^{-\rho t}R(t) - \rho[dI(0)/dt] = -e^{-\rho t}R(t),$$

since, by (2), $dI(0)/dt = 0$. Thus, we have

$$(4) \quad d[dI(0)/dt] = [d^2I(0)/dt^2]dt - [e^{-\rho t}R(t)]d\rho = 0.$$

Step 4 requires us to solve (4) for $dt/d\rho$, the marginal effect of the change in ρ on the equilibrium value of t. We obtain directly

$$\frac{dt}{d\rho} = \frac{e^{-\rho t}R(t)}{d^2I(0)/dt^2}.$$

Our final step consists in evaluation of the sign of the preceding expression. Now we know that $e^{-\rho t}$ is positive for any value of t. Moreover, in any economic context we expect our tree to have a positive value; that is, $R(t) > 0$. Finally, by (3), the denominator of our fraction is negative. Hence, we conclude that $dt/d\rho < 0$; that is, a rise in the interest rate must reduce the optimal life of a tree grown for lumber. In our simple illustration the conclusion is not very startling, but when applied to more complex problems this same comparative statics procedure has provided very helpful and far less obvious results.

It should be noted that much of this analysis might be described as qualitative, in that only the sign of $dt/d\rho$, not its magnitude, is evaluated. But for many policy problems even this limited information can be very helpful. For example, evidence that a tax cut will stimulate employment can be useful even if the extent of the increase in employment is not clear. Thus, it is desirable to develop this sort of qualitative calculus, whereby from qualitative information (such as the signs of the second derivatives) one derives qualitative results. However, it is not always possible to do so. For example, we cannot determine the sign of the difference between two terms simply from the information that each term, by itself, is positive. Only when we know their relative magnitudes can we hope to determine the sign of the term that results when we subtract one from the other. Samuelson (1947) and Lancaster (1965) have explored the theory of qualitative comparative statics analysis and have characterized the sorts of results that can and cannot be derived with the aid of these procedures. Meanwhile, the applications of comparative statics analysis have continued to grow, with some of the most interesting contributions being those of Metzler (1945), Patinkin (1956), and Samuelson.

Stock–flow analysis. A number of writers, notably Bushaw and Clower (1957), have also produced comparative statics analyses of the important relationship between stocks and flows. They have pointed out that in a general equilibrium model the market for a typical commodity is characterized by *two* equilibrium conditions, one of them requiring that the excess demand for stocks be zero and the other specifying the same requisite for flows. Thus, even if the demand for stocks of some item exceeds the supply, flows may be in equilibrium (at a nonzero level) because any further speeding up of production of the good would raise its cost prohibitively. These observations and the more complex model to which they give rise offer illumination on such issues as the relationship between the liquidity preference (money stock equilibrium) and loanable funds (flow equilibrium) models of interest rate determination and Lerner's (1944) distinction between the marginal efficiency of investment (flow) and the marginal efficiency of capital (stock). [*See* STOCK–FLOW ANALYSIS.]

Methods of dynamic analysis. Dynamic analysis proper has developed a totally distinct methodology. By definition, these procedures must take explicit account of the passage of time and its economic influence.

Period analysis. The nonmathematical approach to dynamics took the form of period analysis, which was used frequently in business cycle theory, particularly in the work of Dennis Robertson (1926) and in the Swedish works of the 1930s, for example, Lindahl (1939). In period analysis, time is artificially partitioned into discrete intervals, sometimes referred to as "weeks" or "days" (which, of course, do not correspond to the calendar intervals bearing similar names). The developments in any particular period were taken to depend on the

events that preceded it, and the consequences of these interconnections were then determined. The multiplier process, whereby an injection of funds into the expenditure stream can provide a convergent sequence of additions to national income, is an illustration of period analysis. Suppose 90 per cent of additions to income are spent during the period after they are received and that somehow an autonomous $1,000 increase in income occurs during the first "day" of our study. As a consequence of this increase in income, an additional $900 will be spent during the second day, and that amount will constitute added income for those who receive these payments. During the third day, these persons will, in turn, spend $\frac{9}{10}$ of this amount, that is, $\frac{9}{10}(\$900) = \$810$, and so on, ad infinitum. (Some standard references on period analysis are Robertson 1926, appendix to chapter 5; Lindahl 1939, part 1. For a summary discussion, see also Baumol [1951] 1959, chapter 8.)

Difference equations. Period analysis has also adopted an extremely suitable mathematical technique—the difference equation. This is an equation in which the value of some variable during period t is a function of the values of this and perhaps other variables during earlier periods. For example, if $I(t)$, $P(t)$, and $S(t)$ represent the values of inventory, production, and sales of some commodity during period t, then we have

$$I(t + 1) \equiv I(t) + P(t) - S(t).$$

This identity is a very simple first-order linear difference equation. It is said to be linear because none of the terms contain anything but the first power of a variable; that is, the terms do not contain $[I(t)]^2$ or $\log P(t)$ or any other more complex expression. Moreover, the relationship in the preceding equation is said to be first order because it contains no time difference greater than one period; that is, only variables at periods t and $t + 1$ enter the equation. The following is an illustrative second-order linear difference equation in one variable, $A(t)$, advertising expenditure at time t:

$$A(t + 1) = 0.9A(t) + 0.1[A(t) - A(t - 1)].$$

This equation states that next period's advertising expenditure, $A(t + 1)$, is a weighted average of the current advertising outlay, $A(t)$, and the current rate of growth of advertising outlay, $A(t) - A(t - 1)$. The most remarkable feature of such a relationship is the long-term prediction of the future that it allows. Given a limited amount of information about advertising expenditure in the past, the equation can be used to make a series of predictions of advertising expenditures that *must* hold as long as the equation retains its validity, that is, as long as it is legitimate for *any* year, t. For example, suppose we take $t - 1 = 1960$, $t = 1961$, and $t + 1 = 1962$. If statistics indicate that $A(t - 1) = A(1960) = 150$ and $A(t) = A(1961) = 200$, our equation becomes

$$A(1962) = 0.9A(1961) + 0.1[A(1961) - A(1960)]$$
$$= 0.9(200) + 0.1(50) = 185.$$

Now, utilizing the information $A(1962) = 185$ and $A(1961) = 200$, we can employ the same equation to make a prediction about advertising in 1963 (this time setting $t = 1962$):

$$A(1963) = 0.9A(1962) + 0.1[A(1962) - A(1961)]$$
$$= 0.9(185) + 0.1(-15) = 165.$$

In the same way our difference equation can be used in turn to make forecasts for 1964, 1965, etc., going on into the indefinite future. Of course, if the history of advertising follows no such readily predictable pattern, then the facts can only be represented adequately by a relationship more complicated than the second-order, single-variable difference equation given above.

Where, as in our first illustration, difference equations contain several distinct variables, such as $I(t)$, $S(t)$, and $P(t)$, it will take several simultaneous equations to constitute a determinate system capable of making predictions about the time path in question. Normally, we expect the system to contain as many equations as there are variables. Such a linear difference equation system, whether it contains one or several equations, can usually be solved. The solution of such a system consists of a set of relations expressing each variable as an explicit function of time, for example, $I(t) = f(t)$. These relations give us the value of each variable for any given calendar date, t; that is, the solution gives explicitly the time path of each variable.

The solution also enables us to characterize qualitatively the time path of each variable. In the linear case, these time paths are of four different types: stable, explosive, stable (or damped) oscillatory, and explosive oscillatory. The time path of a variable, $A(t)$, is said to be *stable* (or *damped*) if, with the passage of time, the value of $A(t)$ approaches some equilibrium value, A_c, as a limit, that is, if after some interval of time the value of $A(t)$ becomes and remains as close to A_c as we may prespecify. The time path of a variable is called *explosive* if the value of the variable either increases or decreases indefinitely and without limit, that is, if the value of the variable eventually exceeds any prespecified positive number or eventually falls below any prespecified negative number.

A time path is termed *oscillatory* if it is characterized by periodic increases and decreases in the value of the variable, that is, if the variable falls, then rises, then falls, etc., and does so at regular repetitive intervals of time. It is termed *nonoscillatory* or *monotonic* if the value of the variable continually rises, continually falls, or remains absolutely constant. Thus, for example, a time path is called *stable oscillatory* if the variable alternately takes values above and below its equilibrium level but its range of oscillation about that value grows constantly smaller.

To illustrate the concept of a solution, consider the very simple first-order linear difference equation $A_t = CA_{t-1}$. This gives us successively

$$A_1 = CA_0,$$
$$A_2 = CA_1 = C(CA_0) = C^2A_0,$$
$$A_3 = CA_2 = C(C^2A_0) = C^3A_0,$$

which yields the general solution

$$A_t = C^tA_0.$$

We see that if $0 < C < 1$, this solution will be stable and nonoscillatory because each A_t will be successively smaller than the preceding value of A, and, indeed, A_t will approach zero asymptotically. Similarly, if $C > 1$, the time path will be explosive—A_t will grow without limit.

Moreover, if C is negative, our time path will be oscillatory. If A_0 is positive, then A_1 will be negative, A_2 will be positive, etc. (It will be stable and oscillatory if $0 > C > -1$ and explosive oscillatory if $C < -1$.)

Thus, we conclude that even with a given model different values of the parameters can lead to different types of time paths. A model may be stable for some more or less wide ranges of parameter values and unstable for others, and it is often possible to specify these ranges from the structure of the model, as has just been done in our very simple case. It should be noted that the solution is also influenced by the initial value of our variable, A_0, although in a *linear* difference equation model the long-run characteristics of the time path are unaffected by such initial conditions.

We can use our difference equation analysis to illustrate a subject that was mentioned earlier—Samuelson's correspondence principle. Consider the following simple dynamic model describing a specific economic problem—the economic decline of a city. Let us suppose that the lower the per capita income in the city (and hence, the poorer its amenities), the more middle-class inhabitants will move to the suburbs in a given period, but the more rapid this exodus, the more quickly will per capita income decline. Thus, we have a cumulative process that can be described by the following equations:

$$\Delta Y_t = G - kM_t \quad \text{and} \quad M_t = -w\Delta Y_{t-1},$$

where ΔY_t is the rate of growth of per capita income in the city in period t, G is the exogenous growth rate per period, reflecting perhaps a rising national output per capita, M_t is the number of middle-class migrants in period t, and k and w are positive constants. The first of our equations states that per capita income growth will be reduced below its exogenously determined rate by an amount proportional to migration from the city. The second (behavioral) equation alleges that migration is strictly proportional to the rate of decrease of per capita income in the previous period. Combining these equations, we obtain our basic difference equation,

$$\Delta Y_t = G + kw\Delta Y_{t-1}.$$

This equation can yield a stable time path only if $kw < 1$, for otherwise a change in ΔY_{t-1} will lead to a still larger change in ΔY_t, and so on, ad infinitum. This is analogous to the stability requirement $C < 1$ in our previous model.

Let us now find the equilibrium value of ΔY_t. This is a value, E, such that if $\Delta Y_{t-1} = E$, then we will also have (for the next period) $\Delta Y_t = E$. Hence, substituting E for both ΔY_t and ΔY_{t-1} in our difference equation, we have

$$E = G + kwE, \quad \text{or} \quad E = G/(1 - kw).$$

This shows that if the system is stable ($kw < 1$), it will have reasonable comparative statics properties; a rise in G, the exogenous growth rate, will also increase E, the equilibrium growth rate of per capita income. But if the system is unstable, so that $(1 - kw)$ is negative, it will no longer yield obviously sensible comparative statics results. A rise in the exogenous growth rate will then reduce the equilibrium rate of growth, and, indeed, only a negative exogenous growth rate can yield a positive equilibrium growth rate!

This, then, illustrates graphically the substance of the correspondence principle showing that an unstable system is likely to yield nonsensical comparative statics results. This is so because of the way in which the value of kw enters both the dynamic and comparative statics solutions, a relationship that can be extended to much more complex systems.

In general, after some initial period of time, the path of a variable generated by a linear difference equation system will either be stable or explosive, and it will either be oscillatory or monotonic. Fur-

thermore, it will retain its pattern throughout the remainder of its history, since more complex time paths, even time paths that switch from one of these characteristics to another, are ruled out by linearity. This restricts considerably the uses to which linear difference equation models can be put in economic analysis. For example, because they can generate oscillatory behavior, a number of linear business cycle models have been constructed. But, as Hicks (1950) and Goodwin (1951) have pointed out, these models suffer from a serious defect. For, aside from what may be considered the very exceptional case, on the "razor's edge" borderline between stability and instability (the special case $C = -1$ in our model $A_t = CA_{t-1}$), the cycles generated by linear models must either gradually disappear (if their time path is stable) or the amplitudes of the cycles must increase without limit (the explosive case). Only by the use of nonlinear models can we generate cycles with any degree of constancy in their amplitude.

Differential equations. Another mathematical tool that has proved particularly useful in dynamic analysis is the differential equation. A simple example is the equation describing the behavior of a variable, y, whose rate of change, dy/dt, is proportionate to its own value, so that $dy/dt = ky$. Such a relationship would hold, for example, where interest on a bank deposit was compounded continuously, so that at every moment of time the principal would be increasing at a constant k per cent. We know that a function that satisfies this relationship is $y = ae^{kt}$, where a is a constant. This last function is the solution to the preceding differential equation, and it obviously specifies the time path of the variable y. In particular, we see that if k is positive, ae^{kt} must increase indefinitely as t becomes larger, so that the time path of y will be explosive (without oscillation). On the other hand, if k is negative, so that $-k = c > 0$, then $ae^{kt} = ae^{-ct} = a/e^{ct}$. Hence, $y = a/e^{ct}$ will get closer and closer to zero as t increases. Thus, if k is negative, the time path of y will be stable (and nonoscillatory).

The preceding differential equation is said to be of first order because it contains only a first derivative of y. An example of a third-order linear differential equation with constant coefficients is

$$d^3y/dt^3 = \alpha d^2y/dt^2 + \beta dy/dt + \gamma y + \delta.$$

Such an equation will also yield a determinate time path for y. While the resulting time path may be more complex than those that can arise in the first-order case, it will still fall within one of the four types that characterize linear difference equations. And, once again, one may have recourse to multivariable differential equation systems composed of several simultaneous equations, or it may be appropriate to employ nonlinear differential equations that are more flexible in the time paths they generate. Mixed difference–differential equation models involving both derivatives and lagged variable values have also occurred in the literature. (For further materials on difference and differential equations and their applications in economic dynamics, see Samuelson 1947, chapters 10, 11, appendix B; Goldberg 1958; Allen 1956, chapters 1–4; Baumol [1951] 1959, chapters 9–16.)

Stochastic dynamic models.   A number of dynamic (difference and/or differential equation) models in which stochastic (random) elements play an important role have been used in both theoretical and empirical applications. For example, Frisch (1933) proposed a business cycle model in which the dynamic equation generated a damped oscillatory time path, so that if left to itself, the model produced cycles that would tend to disappear. However, he superimposed on this structure a "shock variable"—a random element that caused unpredictable and sometimes sharp displacements in the time path. These shocks were meant to correspond to exogenous events, such as wars and crop failures, that can affect significantly the workings of the economy. Even with a linear model it was shown that such shocks can prevent the system from settling down to an equilibrium. Thus, the random shocks yield a time path characterized by fluctuations of varying initial amplitude and timing.

Dynamic stochastic models are found extensively in the econometrics literature dealing with specification and estimation of simultaneous equation systems. Here, following the pioneering work of Koopmans (1950) and his colleagues at the Cowles Commission, random shock variables in each of the relevant equations have provided the basis for probabilistic analysis of the statistical properties of the systems.

Evaluation of dynamic models.   Unfortunately, the dynamic mathematical models that have so far been developed have suffered from two serious shortcomings. First, there has been little empirical evidence supporting the choice of the values of the coefficients or even the types of functional relationships utilized (linear or nonlinear, difference or differential, of first or of some higher order). Second, and perhaps even more serious, it is possible to show that the predicted behavior of the variables of such models is often highly sensitive to changes in functional relationships and coefficient values. For example, a small change in the value of a coefficient can lead to drastic qualitative changes in

time paths; it can transmute stability into explosion, or monotonicity into oscillation. Since econometrics has up to this point provided so little empirical basis for the choice of dynamic models and since the implications of these models are so highly dependent on the assumed structure, we can as yet have little confidence in the applicability of the results of most dynamic analyses, either as descriptions of reality or as satisfactory bases for policy.

So far these models have mainly served negative purposes. They have functioned most effectively as counterexamples indicating cases where persuasive arguments were not in fact conclusive and where apparently attractive policy measures might fail to serve the purposes for which they were designed. For example, it has sometimes been alleged that profitable speculation must always mitigate fluctuations (they must always be stabilizing). The argument is that if a speculator is to make a profit, he must purchase when price is low and sell when price is high. Hence, his actions will raise prices in the one case and reduce them in the other, on both counts making for a more stable price level. A somewhat more explicit set of dynamic models was able to show that this argument was oversimplified and that when price trends as well as price levels were taken into account the profit-making speculator might easily aggravate any cyclical behavior that was present in the system.

Similarly, it can be shown that a policy of raising net government expenditure when national income is low and decreasing net government outlays when income is high may well worsen business cycles unless the changes in government expenditure are perfectly timed. Moreover, this defect may plague discretionary and other types of contracyclical policies as well as automatic contracyclical policy measures of the sort just described. Thus, even if dynamic models have been most effective in providing such negative conclusions, they clearly can be extremely important both for understanding the workings of the economy and for the formulation of economic policy. (For discussions of the effectiveness of contracyclical measures, see Friedman 1953; Phillips 1954; Baumol 1961.)

Despite the unsolved problems of dynamic analysis, there is a sense in which it may be considered indispensable for the progress of economics. In reality the economy is never fully in equilibrium. Therefore, the applicability of static and comparative statics analyses is necessarily somewhat limited. When things are in flux, only a dynamic model can account for everything that is going on. However, this argument should not be pushed too far, for in no science do theoretical constructs correspond perfectly to reality. One must always work with models that provide approximative illumination, and there can be little doubt that the economists' static models have often successfully served this purpose.

Recent developments—growth models. In recent years the major focus of dynamic analysis has shifted from business cycles to longer-term economic growth. Recent writings in growth theory have ranged from illuminating observations firmly based on empirical evidence, an approach most effectively developed in the work of W. A. Lewis (1955), to the highly abstract growth model of von Neumann (1938). In between lies a spectrum of work running the full gamut of applicability and technical sophistication. Leibenstein (1954; 1957), Kaldor (1957; 1961), and Robinson (1956) have produced growth analyses whose mathematical complexity is not very great but which are extremely suggestive. For example, one of the Leibenstein models (1954, chapters 4–6) shows that an economy whose population grows at a fixed rate must somehow surpass some minimum increase in per capita income before it will "take off" and embark on a long-term course of growth. Any smaller increase in per capita income must, in his model, prove transitory, with the economy soon reapproaching a subsistence output level.

Kaldor's model seeks to describe the interactions among the distribution of income, the development of technology, and economic growth. His argument, roughly speaking, is that the level of investment is largely determined by technical progress in an economy that tends in the long run to approximate full employment. But in such a system, the distribution of income must adapt itself to permit desired savings to equal investment demand. Thus, for example, if the latter exceeds the former, there will be excess demand, causing prices to rise and the share of profits in national income to increase. Since profit earners' collective propensity to save exceeds that of wage earners, the resulting redistribution of income will increase the level of desired savings until it becomes equal to investment demand.

There has also been considerable interest in the model developed by Harrod (1948) and Domar (1957), in which the acceleration principle of investment demand and the multiplier theorem of saving analysis are employed to investigate the characteristics of a growth path that balances supply and demand. Savings, S (the supply of resources available for investment), is assumed to be proportional to the level of income, Y, so that $S = kY$. The demand for capital, C, is also assumed to be pro-

portional to output (income), Y, so that the demand for net investment, I (which is the rate of growth of capital), becomes proportionate to the *rate of growth* of Y, that is, $I = dC/dt = adY/dt$. The two equations together then tell us that if demand for and supply of investment are to be equal, we must have $kY = adY/dt$. The time path of income that satisfies this first-order differential equation is said to exhibit the "warranted rate of growth." Several paradoxical conclusions follow. The equation shows, for example, that if there is overproduction (if more goods are saved or unconsumed than are wanted for investment), the way to remedy the situation is to increase production even faster (increase dY/dt)! For in this way the demand for new equipment can be stimulated sufficiently to take up the otherwise undemanded output. The time path that satisfies the Harrod–Domar requirements can readily be shown to involve a geometric rate of growth of income.

The highly mathematical growth models of recent years all have their origin in von Neumann's original construct (1938). His magnificent piece of reasoning also foreshadows important portions of game theory and of the duality theory of linear programming. The von Neumann economy is a highly artificial construct in which the production function is characterized by constant returns to scale and perfectly fixed input–output coefficients. It is assumed that there are no scarce resources to limit the expansion of the economy, and the model is perfectly closed, with consumers appearing only as factors of production who use up outputs in the course of their own productive efforts. Finally, it is assumed that some positive amount of each and every input is employed in the production of each output. Using these highly restrictive assumptions, which have been considerably relaxed in later work by Kemeny, Morgenstern, and Thompson (1956), von Neumann was able to show, among other things, that there is a unique (maximal) growth rate for the entire economy and that this growth rate is the appropriate discounting rate of interest for the economy.

Dorfman, Samuelson, and Solow (1958) have developed what they call the turnpike theorem, which asserts that in the long run an optimal growth path for an economy must approximate the time path called for in the von Neumann model. Although short-run output maximization may be achieved through time paths that differ very significantly from the von Neumann path, the longer the period considered, the more closely will the optimal path approximate von Neumann's. The authors suggest that their result is analogous to the routing of a trip, which, if it is very short, should often follow the side roads that lead most directly to one's destination. But on a long journey, time will be saved by going out of one's way to take the turnpike (the von Neumann route). Harold W. Kuhn has shown (in unpublished work) that the analogy is somewhat misleading because the optimal time paths only approach the "turnpike," as it were, asymptotically and may in fact never coincide with the von Neumann path at any point in their history. Moreover, Kuhn has shown that the turnpike theorem does not hold for as general a set of circumstances as the authors originally believed. Nevertheless, the theorem remains an illuminating and substantial contribution to the literature of economic growth theory. Since the appearance of the Dorfman–Samuelson–Solow volume, the number of abstract growth models has grown enormously, broadening the analysis to include a wider range of technological circumstances and production relationships. [*See* ECONOMIC GROWTH, *article on* MATHEMATICAL THEORY; *see also* Solow 1956; Phelps 1961; Uzawa 1964.]

WILLIAM J. BAUMOL

[*Directly related are the entries* BUSINESS CYCLES, *article on* MATHEMATICAL MODELS; ECONOMIC EQUILIBRIUM.]

BIBLIOGRAPHY

ADELMAN, IRMA (1961) 1964 *Theories of Economic Growth and Development.* Stanford Univ. Press.

ALLEN, R. G. D. (1956) 1963 *Mathematical Economics.* 2d ed. New York: St. Martins; London: Macmillan.

BAUMOL, WILLIAM J. (1951) 1959 *Economic Dynamics: An Introduction.* 2d ed. New York: Macmillan.

BAUMOL, WILLIAM J. 1961 Pitfalls in Contracyclical Policies: Some Tools and Results. *Review of Economics and Statistics* 43, Feb.:21–26.

BUSHAW, D. W.; and CLOWER, R. W. 1957 *Introduction to Mathematical Economics.* Homewood, Ill.: Irwin.

DOMAR, EVSEY 1957 *Essays in the Theory of Economic Growth.* Oxford Univ. Press.

DORFMAN, ROBERT; SAMUELSON, PAUL A.; and SOLOW, ROBERT M. 1958 *Linear Programming and Economic Analysis.* New York: McGraw-Hill.

FRIEDMAN, MILTON (1953) 1959 *Essays in Positive Economics.* Univ. of Chicago Press. → See especially "The Effects of a Full-employment Policy on Economic Stability: A Formal Analysis," pages 117–132.

FRISCH, RAGNAR (1933) 1965 Propagation Problems and Impulse Problems in Dynamic Economics. Pages 155–185 in American Economic Association, *Readings in Business Cycles.* Homewood, Ill.: Irwin.

FRISCH, RAGNAR 1936 On the Notion of Equilibrium and Disequilibrium. *Review of Economic Studies* 3, Feb.:100–105.

GOLDBERG, SAMUEL 1958 *Introduction to Difference Equations: With Illustrative Examples From Economics, Psychology, and Sociology.* New York: Wiley.

GOODWIN, R. M. 1951 The Nonlinear Accelerator and the Persistence of Business Cycles. *Econometrica* 19: 1–17.

HARROD, R. F. (1948) 1960 *Towards a Dynamic Economics: Some Recent Developments of Economic Theory and Their Application to Policy.* London: Macmillan; New York: St. Martins.

HENDERSON, JAMES M.; and QUANDT, RICHARD E. 1958 *Microeconomic Theory: A Mathematical Approach.* New York: McGraw-Hill.

HICKS, J. R. 1950 *A Contribution to the Theory of the Trade Cycle.* Oxford: Clarendon.

KALDOR, NICHOLAS 1957 A Model of Economic Growth. *Economic Journal* 67:591–624.

KALDOR, NICHOLAS 1961 Capital Accumulation and Economic Growth. Pages 177–222 in International Economic Association, *The Theory of Capital: Proceedings.* New York: St. Martins.

KEMENY, J. G.; MORGENSTERN, OSKAR; and THOMPSON, G. L. 1956 A Generalization of the von Neumann Model of an Expanding Economy. *Econometrica* 24: 115–135.

KOOPMANS, TJALLING C. (editor) 1950 *Statistical Inference in Dynamic Economic Models.* New York: Wiley.

LANCASTER, K. J. 1965 The Theory of Qualitative Linear Systems. *Econometrica* 33:395–408.

LEIBENSTEIN, HARVEY 1954 *A Theory of Economic–Demographic Development.* Princeton Univ. Press.

LEIBENSTEIN, HARVEY (1957) 1963 *Economic Backwardness and Economic Growth: Studies in the Theory of Economic Development.* New York: Wiley.

LERNER, ABBA P. 1944 *The Economics of Control: Principles of Welfare Economics.* New York: Macmillan. → See especially "Capital, Investment, and Interest," pages 323–345.

LEWIS, W. ARTHUR 1955 *The Theory of Economic Growth.* Homewood, Ill.: Irwin.

LINDAHL, ERIK 1939 *Studies in the Theory of Money and Capital.* London: Allen & Unwin.

METZLER, LLOYD A. 1945 The Stability of Multiple Markets: The Hicks Conditions. *Econometrica* 13: 277–292.

PATINKIN, DON (1956) 1965 *Money, Interest, and Prices: An Integration of Monetary and Value Theory.* 2d ed. New York: Harper.

PHELPS, EDMUND S. 1961 The Golden Rule of Accumulation: A Fable for Growthmen. *American Economic Review* 51:638–643.

PHILLIPS, A. W. 1954 Stabilization Policy in a Closed Economy. *Economic Journal* 64:290–323.

ROBERTSON, DENNIS HOLME (1926) 1949 *Banking Policy and the Price Level.* Rev. ed. New York: Kelley.

ROBINSON, JOAN 1956 *The Accumulation of Capital.* Homewood, Ill.: Irwin; London: Macmillan.

SAMUELSON, PAUL A. (1947) 1958 *Foundations of Economic Analysis.* Harvard Economic Studies, Vol. 80. Cambridge, Mass.: Harvard Univ. Press. → A paperback edition was published in 1965 by Atheneum.

SOLOW, ROBERT M. 1956 A Contribution to the Theory of Economic Growth. *Quarterly Journal of Economics* 70:65–94.

UZAWA, HIROFUMI 1964 Optimal Growth in a Two-sector Model of Capital Accumulation. *Review of Economic Studies* 31, no. 1:1–24.

VON NEUMANN, JOHN (1938) 1945 A Model of General Economic Equilibrium. *Review of Economic Studies* 13, no. 1:1–9. → First published in German.

STATISTICAL ANALYSIS, SPECIAL PROBLEMS OF

I
OUTLIERS

In a series of observations or readings, an *outlier* is a reading that stands unexpectedly far from most of the other readings in the series. More technically, an outlier may be defined to be a reading whose *residual* (explained below) is excessively large. In statistical analysis it is common practice to treat outliers differently from the other readings; for example, outliers are often omitted altogether from the analysis.

The name "outlier" is perhaps the most frequently used in this connection, but there are other common terms with the same meaning, such as "wild shot," "straggler," "sport," "maverick," "aberrant reading," and "discordant value."

Perspective. It is often found that sets of parallel or similar numerical readings exhibit something close to a "normal" pattern of variation [see DISTRIBUTIONS, STATISTICAL, *article on* SPECIAL CONTINUOUS DISTRIBUTIONS]. From this finding of normal variation follows the interest of statisticians in simple means (that is, averages) of homogeneous sets of readings, and in the method of least squares for more complicated bodies of readings, as seen in regression analysis and in the standard methods of analysis for factorial experiments [see LINEAR HYPOTHESES].

Sometimes a set of readings does not conform to the expected pattern but appears anomalous in some way. The most striking kind of anomaly—and the one that has attracted most attention in the literature of the past hundred years—is the phenomenon of outliers. One or more readings are seen to lie so far from the values to be expected from the other readings as to suggest that some special factor has affected them and that therefore they should be treated differently. Outliers have often been thought of simply as "bad" readings, and the problem of treating them as one of separating good from bad readings, so that conclusions can be based only on good readings and the bad observations can be ignored. Numerous rules have been given for making the separation, the earliest being that proposed by B. Peirce (1852). None of these rules has seemed entirely satisfactory, nor has any met with universal acceptance.

Present-day thinking favors a more flexible approach. Outliers are but one of many types of anomaly that can be present in a set of readings; other kinds of anomalies are, for example, heteroscedasticity (nonconstant variability), nonadditivity, and temporal drift. The question of what to do about such anomalies is concerned with finding a satisfactory specification (or model) of the statistical problem at hand. Since no method of statistical analysis of the readings is uniquely best, tolerable compromises must be sought, so that as many as possible of the interesting features of the data can be brought out fairly and clearly. It is important that outliers be noticed, but the problem of dealing with them is not isolated from other problems of statistical analysis.

An illustration. Suppose that a psychologist arranges to have a stimulus administered to a group of 50 subjects and that the time elapsing before each subject gives a certain response is observed. From the resulting set of times he wishes to calculate some sort of mean value or measure of "central tendency," for eventual comparison with similar values obtained under different conditions. [See STATISTICS, DESCRIPTIVE, *article on* LOCATION AND DISPERSION.]

Just as he is about to calculate a simple arithmetic mean of the 50 readings, the psychologist notices that 3 of the readings are considerably larger than all the others. Should he include these outliers in his calculation, discard them, or what? Several different answers seem reasonable, according to the circumstances.

It may occur to the psychologist that the outliers have been produced by some abnormal condition, and he therefore inquires into the conduct of the trial. Perhaps he discovers that, indeed, three of the subjects behaved abnormally by going to sleep during the test, these being the ones yielding the longest response times. Now the psychologist needs to consider carefully what he wants to investigate. If he decides that he is interested only in the response times of subjects who do not go to sleep and explicitly defines his objective accordingly, he may feel justified in discarding the outlying readings and averaging the rest. But, on the other hand, he may decide that the test has been incorrectly administered, because no subject should have been allowed to go to sleep; then he may discard not only the outliers but all the rest of the readings and order a repetition to be carried out correctly.

In experimental work it is often not possible to verify directly whether some abnormal condition was associated with an outlier; nothing special is known about the reading except that it is an outlier. In that case, the whole distributional pattern of the readings should be examined. Response times, in particular, are often found to have a skew distribution, with a long upper tail and short lower tail, and this skewness may be nearly removed by taking logarithms of the readings or by making some other simple rescaling transformation [*see* STATISTICAL ANALYSIS, SPECIAL PROBLEMS OF, *article on* TRANSFORMATIONS OF DATA]. The psychologist may find that the logarithms of his readings have a satisfactorily normal pattern without noticeable outliers. If he then judges that the arithmetic mean of the log-times, equivalent to the geometric mean of the original times, is a satisfactory measure of central tendency, his outlier problem will have been solved without the rejection or special treatment of any reading.

Finally, it may happen that even after an appropriate transformation of the readings or some other modification in the specification, there still remain one or more noticeable outliers. In that case, the psychologist may be well advised to assign reduced weight to the outliers when he calculates the sample mean, according to some procedure designed to mitigate the effect of a long-tailed error distribution or of possible gross mistakes in the readings.

Thus, several actions are open to the investigator, and there is no single, simple rule that will always lead him to a good choice.

Terminology. An outlier is an observation that seems discordant with some type of pattern. Although in principle any sort of pattern might be under consideration, as a matter of fact the notion of outlier seems rarely to be invoked, except when the expected pattern of the readings is of the kind to which the method of least squares is applicable and fully justifiable [*see* LINEAR HYPOTHESES, *article on* REGRESSION]. That is, we have a series of readings $y_1, y_2, \cdots, y_n$, and we postulate, in specifying the statistical problem, that

$$(1) \qquad y_i = \mu_i + e_i, \qquad i = 1, 2, \cdots, n,$$

where the e_i are "errors" drawn independently from a common normal distribution having zero mean and where the expected values, μ_i, are specified in terms of one or several unknowns. For a homogeneous sample of readings (a single, simple sample) it is postulated that all the μ_i are equal to the common mean, μ; for more complicated bodies of readings a "linear hypothesis" is usually postulated, of form

$$(2) \qquad \mu_i = \mu + x_{i1}\beta_1 + x_{i2}\beta_2 + \cdots + x_{ir}\beta_r,$$

where the x_{ij} are given and μ and the β_j are parameters. The object is to estimate (or otherwise discuss the value of) some or all of the parameters,

$\mu, \beta_1, \beta_2, \cdots$, and the variance of the error distribution.

Let Y_i denote the estimate of μ_i obtained by substituting in the right side of (2) the least squares estimates of the parameters—that is, the parameter values that minimize the expression $\sum_i (y_i - \mu_i)^2$, given the assumed relationship among the μ_i. The residuals, z_i, are defined by

$$z_i = y_i - Y_i.$$

Relative to the specification (1) and (2), an outlier is a reading such that the corresponding absolute value of z is judged to be excessively large.

Causes of outliers. It is convenient to distinguish three ways in which an outlier can occur: (*a*) a mistake has been made in the reading, (*b*) no mistake has been made, but the specification is wrong, (*c*) no mistake has been made, the specification is correct, and a rare deviation from expectation has been observed.

In regard to (*a*), a mistake may be made in reading a scale, in copying an entry, or in some arithmetic calculation by which the original measurements are converted to the reported observations. Apparatus used for making measurements may fail to function as intended—for example, by developing a chemical or electrical leak. A more subtle kind of mistake occurs when the intended plan of the investigation is not carried out correctly even though the act of observation itself is performed perfectly. For example, in a study of ten-year-old children it would be a mistake to include, by accident, as though relating to those children, material that was in fact obtained from other persons, such as teachers, parents, or children of a different age.

In regard to (*b*), the specification can be wrong in a variety of ways [*see* ERRORS, *article on* EFFECTS OF ERRORS IN STATISTICAL ASSUMPTIONS]. The errors may have a nonnormal distribution or may not be drawn from a common distribution at all. The expression (2) for the expected values may be incorrect, containing too few terms or terms of the wrong sort.

In regard to (*c*), any value whatsoever is theoretically observable and is consistent with any given normal distribution of errors. But readings differing from the mean of a normal distribution by more than some three or four standard deviations are so exceedingly rare as to be a virtual impossibility. Usually the normal-law linear-hypothesis specification cannot be regarded as more than a rough approximation to the truth. Moreover, one can never entirely rule out the possibility that a mistake of some sort has been made. Thus, when a reading is seen to have a large residual, explanation (*a*) or (*b*) usually seems more plausible than (*c*). However, if one wishes to reach a verdict on the matter, one will do well to examine, not just the outliers, but all the readings for evidence of mistakes and of an incorrect specification.

Preferred treatment. Suppose that it could be known for sure whether the cause of a particular outlier was of type (*a*), (*b*), or (*c*) above. What action would then be preferred?

(*a*) If it were known that the outlying reading had resulted from a mistake, the observer would usually choose, if he could, either to correct the mistake or to discard the reading. One sufficiently gross error in a reading can wreck the whole of a statistical analysis. The danger is particularly great when the data of an investigation are processed by an automatic computer, since it is possible that no one examines the individual readings. It is of great importance that such machine processing yield a display of the residuals in some convenient form, so that gross mistakes will not pass unnoticed and the conformity of the data to the specification can be checked [*see* COMPUTATION].

However, it is not invariably true that if the observer becomes aware that a reading was mistaken, and if he cannot correct the mistake, he will be wise to discard the reading, as though it had never been. For example, suppose that a new educational test is tried on a representative group of students in order to establish norms—that is, to determine the distribution of crude scores to be expected. When the trial is finished and the crude scores have been obtained, some circumstance (perhaps the occurrence of outliers) prompts an investigation of the trial, and then evidence comes to hand that about a quarter of the students cheated, a listing of those involved being available. Should the scores obtained by the cheaters be discarded and norms for the test be based on the scores of the non-cheaters? Surely that would be misleading, for if the possibility of cheating will persist in the future, as in the trial, the scores of the cheaters should obviously not be excluded. If, on the other hand, a change in the administration of the test will prevent such cheating in the future, then for a correct norming the scores that the cheaters would have obtained, had they not been allowed to cheat, must be known. It would be rash to assume that these scores would be similar to the scores of the actual noncheaters. But that is what is implied by merely rejecting the cheaters' scores. Conceivably, a change in the administration of the test might even have affected the scores of those who did not cheat. Thus, the trial would have to be run afresh under the new system of administration in order to yield a fair distribution of scores. (For further discussion of this sort of situation, see Kruskal 1960.)

(*b*) Consider now the next imagined case, where it is known that no mistakes in observation were made but that the specification was wrong. What to do with any particular reading would then be a secondary question; attention should first be directed toward improving the specification. The appropriateness of the expression (2) for the expected values, μ_i, may possibly be improved by transformation of the observations, y_i, or the associated values, x_{ij}, or by a change in the form of the right side so that further terms are introduced or a nonlinear function of the parameters is postulated. Sometimes it is appropriate to postulate unequal variances for the errors, e_i, depending perhaps on the expectations, μ_i, or on some associated *x*-variable. A consequence of making such changes in the specification will usually be that the standard least squares method of analysis will be applied to modified data.

As for the assumption that the distribution of the errors, e_i, is normal, there are many situations where this does seem to agree roughly with the facts. In no field of observation, however, are there any grounds for thinking that the normality assumption is accurately true, and in cases where it is roughly true, extensive investigation has sometimes revealed a frequency pattern having somewhat longer tails than those of a normal distribution. Jeffreys (1939), Tukey (1962), Huber (1964), and others have considered various systems of assigning reduced weight to readings having large residuals, in order to make the least squares method less sensitive to a possibly long-tailed distribution of errors, while preserving as nearly as possible its effectiveness when the error distribution is normal and not greatly changing the computational procedure. One such modified version of the least squares method is described below.

(*c*) Finally, suppose that it were known that an outlier was caused neither by a mistake in observation nor by an incorrect specification, but that it was simply one of the rare deviations that must occasionally occur. Then one would wish to perform the usual statistical analysis appropriate to the specification; the outlier would be included with full weight and treated just like the other observations. This is so because the ordinary least squares estimates of the parameters (together with the usual estimate of common variance) constitute a set of sufficient statistics, and no additional information can be extracted from the configuration of the readings [*see* SUFFICIENCY].

Conclusions. This exposition has considered what action would be preferred if it were known for sure whether an outlier had arisen (*a*) from a mistake, (*b*) from an incorrect specification, or (*c*) by mere chance, the specification and the technique of observation both being correct. It has been shown that a different action would be preferred in each case. Usually, no such knowledge of the cause of an outlier is available in practice. A compromise is therefore necessary.

Obviously, all reasonable efforts should be made to prevent mistakes in observation and to find a specification and a method of statistical analysis consonant with the data. That is so in any case, although outliers may naturally stimulate a closer scrutiny of the specification and a more vigorous search for mistakes. But however careful one is, one can never be certain that undetected mistakes have not occurred and that the specification and plan of statistical analysis are completely appropriate. For the purpose of estimating parameters in a linear hypothesis like (2) above, some modification of the customary least squares procedure giving reduced weight to outliers seems to be advisable. The harmful effects of mistakes in observation and of a long-tailed distribution of errors are thereby mitigated, while negligible damage is done if no mistakes or specification errors have been made. Suitable computational procedures have not yet been fully explored, but it seems likely that considerable attention will be directed to this topic in the near future.

A modified least squares method. One type of modified least squares method for estimating the parameters for the statistical specification indicated at (1) and (2) above is as follows:

Positive numbers, K_1 and K_2, are chosen, with $K_2 > K_1$. Instead of taking as estimates of the parameters the values that minimize the sum of squares $\sum_i (y_i - \mu_i)^2$, one takes the values that minimize the sum of values of a function,

$$\sum_i \psi(y_i - \mu_i),$$

where $\psi(\cdot)$ is the square function for small values of the argument but increases less rapidly for larger values and is constant for very large values. Specifically, one minimizes the following composite sum:

$$(3) \quad \sum_{(1)} (y_i - \mu_i)^2 + \sum_{(2)} (2K_1|y_i - \mu_i| - K_1^2) + \sum_{(3)} (2K_1 K_2 - K_1^2),$$

where $\sum_{(1)}$ denotes the sum over all values of i such that $|y_i - \mu_i| \le K_1$, $\sum_{(2)}$ denotes the sum over all values of i such that $K_1 < |y_i - \mu_i| \le K_2$, and $\sum_{(3)}$ denotes the sum over all remaining values of i. Minimizing (3) is, roughly speaking, equivalent to the ordinary least squares method modified by giving equal weight to all those readings whose residual does not exceed K_1 in magnitude, reduced weight (inversely proportional to the magnitude of the residual) to those readings whose residual exceeds K_1 but not K_2 in magnitude, and zero weight to those readings whose residual exceeds K_2 in magnitude. The minimization is a problem in quadratic programming [*see* PROGRAMMING]. If K_1 is large enough for most readings to come in the sum $\sum_{(1)}$, there are rapidly converging iterative procedures. The necessity of iterating comes from the fact that until the parameters have been estimated and the residuals calculated, it is not possible to say with certainty which readings contribute to the sum $\sum_{(1)}$, which to $\sum_{(2)}$, and which to $\sum_{(3)}$. As soon as all the readings have been correctly assigned, a single set of linear equations determines the values of the parameters, as in the ordinary least squares method. The ordinary method results when K_1 is set so large that all readings come in $\sum_{(1)}$. At another extreme, if K_1 is chosen to be infinitesimally small but K_2 is chosen to be very large, all readings come in $\sum_{(2)}$, and the result is the method of least absolute deviations. For general use, as a slight modification of the ordinary least squares method, K_1 and K_2 should be chosen so that only a small proportion of the readings come in $\sum_{(2)}$ and scarcely any in $\sum_{(3)}$. For example, K_1 might be roughly equal to twice the estimated standard deviation of the error distribution, and K_2 might be three or four times as large as K_1.

Such a procedure leads to the exclusion of any very wild reading from the estimation of the parameters. Less wild readings are retained with less than full weight.

F. J. ANSCOMBE

[*See also* DISTRIBUTIONS, STATISTICAL, *article on* MIXTURES OF DISTRIBUTIONS; NONPARAMETRIC STATISTICS, *article on* ORDER STATISTICS.]

BIBLIOGRAPHY

ANSCOMBE, F. J. 1967 Topics in the Investigation of Linear Relations Fitted by the Method of Least Squares. *Journal of the Royal Statistical Society* Series B 29:1–52. → Includes 23 pages of discussion and recent references.

ANSCOMBE, F. J.; and TUKEY, JOHN W. 1963 The Examination and Analysis of Residuals. *Technometrics* 5:141–160.

CHAUVENET, WILLIAM 1863 *Manual of Spherical and Practical Astronomy.* Philadelphia: Lippincott. → See especially the appendix on the method of least squares, sections 57–60.

DANIEL, CUTHBERT 1960 Locating Outliers in Factorial Experiments. *Technometrics* 2:149–156.

[GOSSET, W. S.] 1927 Errors of Routine Analysis, by Student [pseud.]. *Biometrika* 19:151–164.

HUBER, PETER J. 1964 Robust Estimation of a Location Parameter. *Annals of Mathematical Statistics* 35:73–101.

JEFFREYS, HAROLD (1939) 1961 *Theory of Probability.* 3d ed. Oxford: Clarendon.

KRUSKAL, WILLIAM H. 1960 Some Remarks on Wild Observations. *Technometrics* 2:1–3.

PEIRCE, BENJAMIN 1852 Criterion for the Rejection of Doubtful Observations. *Astronomical Journal* 2:161–163.

TUKEY, JOHN W. 1962 The Future of Data Analysis. *Annals of Mathematical Statistics* 33:1–67.

WRIGHT, THOMAS W. 1884 *A Treatise on the Adjustment of Observations, With Applications to Geodetic Work and Other Measures of Precision.* New York: Van Nostrand. → See especially sections 69–73.

II
TRANSFORMATIONS OF DATA

It is often useful to apply a transformation, such as $y = \log x$ or $y = 1/x$, to data values, x. This change can simplify relationships among the data and improve subsequent analysis.

Many transformations have been used, including $y = \sqrt{x}$, $y = x^c$, where c is a constant, and $y = \frac{1}{2} \log [x/(1 - x)]$. Sometimes a beneficial transformation is constructed empirically from the data themselves, rather than given as a mathematical expression.

The general effect of a transformation depends on the shape of its plotted curve on a graph. It is this curve, rather than the mathematical formula, that has central interest. Transformations with similar curves will have similar effects, even though the formulas look quite different. Graphical similarity, however, must be judged cautiously, as the eye is easily fooled.

The benefits of transforming

The relationship of y to other variables may be simpler than that of x. For example, y may have a straight-line relationship to a variable u although x does not. As another example, y may depend "additively" on u and v even though x does not.

Suppose the variance of x is not constant but changes as other variables change. In many cases it is possible to arrange for the variance of y to be nearly constant.

In some cases the distribution of y may be much more like the normal (Gaussian) distribution or some other desired distribution than is that of x.

Thus, the benefits of transforming are usually said to be (1) simpler relationships, (2) more stable variance, (3) improved normality (or closeness to another standard distribution). Where it is necessary to choose between these, (1) is usually more important than (2), and (2) is usually more important than (3). However, many authors have remarked that frequently (although not invariably) a single transformation achieves two or all three at once.

In some cases analysis of y, however illuminating, is not to the point, because some fact about x itself is needed (usually the expected value) and the corresponding fact about y is not an acceptable substitute. If so, it is often better not to transform, although sometimes it is desirable and feasible to obtain the necessary fact about x from information about y.

The ultimate profit. The benefits listed above are not ultimate profit but merely a means to achieve it. The ultimate profit, however, is difficult to describe, for it occurs during the creative process of interpreting data. A transformation may directly aid interpretation by allowing the central information in the data to be expressed more succinctly. It may permit a subsequent stage of analysis to be simpler, more accurate, or more revealing.

Later in this article an attempt will be made to illustrate these elusive ideas. However, the first examples primarily illustrate the immediate benefits, rather than the ultimate profit.

Some simple examples

Some of the most profitable transformations seem almost as basic as the laws of nature. Three such transformations in psychology are all logarithmic: from sound *pressure* to the decibel scale of sound *volume* in the study of hearing; from light intensity to its logarithm in the study of vision; and from tone *frequency* in cycles per second to tone *pitch* on the musical scale. In each case many benefits are obtained.

To simplify curves. Transformations may be used to display the relationship between two variables in a simple form—for example, as a straight line or as a family of straight lines or of parallel curves. One or both variables may be transformed. Figure 1 is a simple illustration, using hypothetical data.

One easy way to transform while plotting is to use graph paper with a special scale. Two widely used special scales are the logarithmic scale and the normal probability scale, which correspond, respectively, to the logarithmic and "probit" transformations. [*See* GRAPHIC PRESENTATION.]

To stabilize variance. The analysis of many experiments is simpler if the variance of response is approximately constant for different conditions.

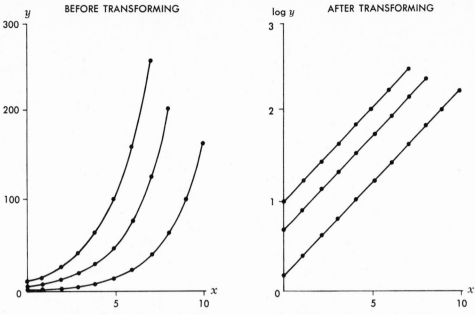

Figure 1 — The effect of the logarithmic transformation

Crespi (1942, pp. 483–485) described very clearly how he first used the *time* required by a rat to run down a 20-foot runway as a measure of its eagerness to obtain food but found that the response variance differed greatly for experimental conditions with different average responses. This hampered the intended analyses of variance, which require approximate constancy of variance. However, the transformation to *speed* = (20 feet)/(time) removed this difficulty entirely. In short, the reciprocal transformation helpfully stabilized the variance.

Furthermore, Crespi indicated reasons why in this context speed should be better than time as a measure of eagerness. It happens quite often that performance times, latency times, reaction times, and so forth can benefit from a reciprocal or a logarithmic transformation.

To improve normality. Many statistical techniques are valid only if applied to data whose distribution is approximately normal. When the data are far from normal, a transformation can often be used to improve normality. For example, the distribution of personal income usually is skewed strongly to the right and is very nonnormal. Applying the logarithmic transformation to income data often yields a distribution which is quite close to normal. Thus, to test for difference of income level between two groups of people on the basis of two samples, it may well be wiser to apply the usual tests to logarithm of income than to income itself.

To aid interpretation. In a letter to *Science*, Wald (1965) made a strong plea for plotting spectra (of electromagnetic radiation) as a function of frequency rather than of wavelength; frequency plots are now much commoner. Frequency and wavelength are connected by a reciprocal transformation, and most of the reasons cited for preferring the frequency transformation, both in Wald's letter and in later, supporting letters, have to do with ease of interpretation. For example, frequency is proportional to the very important variable, energy. On a frequency scale, but not on a wavelength scale, the area under an absorption band is proportional to the "transition probability," the half-width of the band is proportional to the "oscillator strength," the shape of the band is symmetrical, and the relationship between a frequency and its harmonics is easier to see.

To quantify qualitative data. Qualitative but ordered data are often made quantitative in a rather arbitrary way. For example, if a person orders *n* items by preference, each item may be given its numerical rank from 1 to *n* [*see* NONPARAMETRIC STATISTICS, *article on* RANKING METHODS]. In such cases the possibility of transforming the ranks is especially relevant, as the original space between the ranks deserves no special consideration. Quite often the ranks are transformed into "normal scores," so as to be approximately normally distributed [*see* PSYCHOMETRICS].

To deal with counted data. Sometimes the number of people, objects, or events is of interest. For example, if qualified applicants to a medical school are classified by age, ethnic group, and other characteristics, the number in each group might be under study. [*See* COUNTED DATA.]

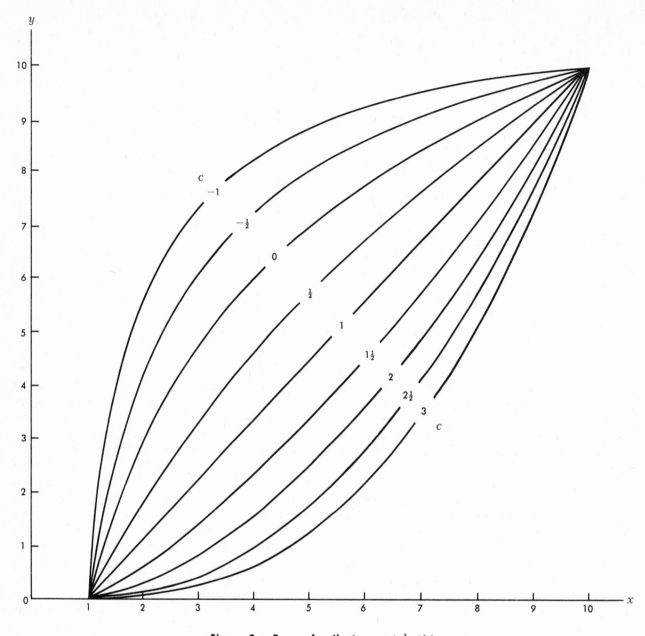

Figure 2 — Power family $(y = a + bx^c)$*

* For $c = 0$, $y = a + b \log x$.

If the observed values have a wide range (say, the ratio of largest to smallest is at least 2 or 3), then a transformation is especially likely to be beneficial. Figure 2 shows a whole family of transformations which are often used with counted data and in many other situations as well. Each of these is essentially the same as $y = x^c$ for some constant c. (For greater ease of comparison, however, the plotted curves show $y = a + bx^c$. By a standard convention, $y = \log x$ substitutes for $y = x^0$, in order to have the curves change smoothly as c passes through the value 0. No other function would serve this purpose.)

For example, suppose the observed values x come from Poisson distributions, which are quite common for counted data. Then the variance of x equals its expected value, so different x's may have very different variances. However, the variance of $y = \sqrt{x} = x^{\frac{1}{2}}$ is almost constant, with value $\frac{1}{4}$ (unless the expected value of x is very close to 0). For various purposes, such as testing for equality, y is better than x. Often, simpler relationships also result from transforming.

Other values of c are also common. In only four pages Taylor (1961) has displayed 24 sets of counted biological data to which values of c over the very wide range from 0.65 to −0.54 are appropriate!

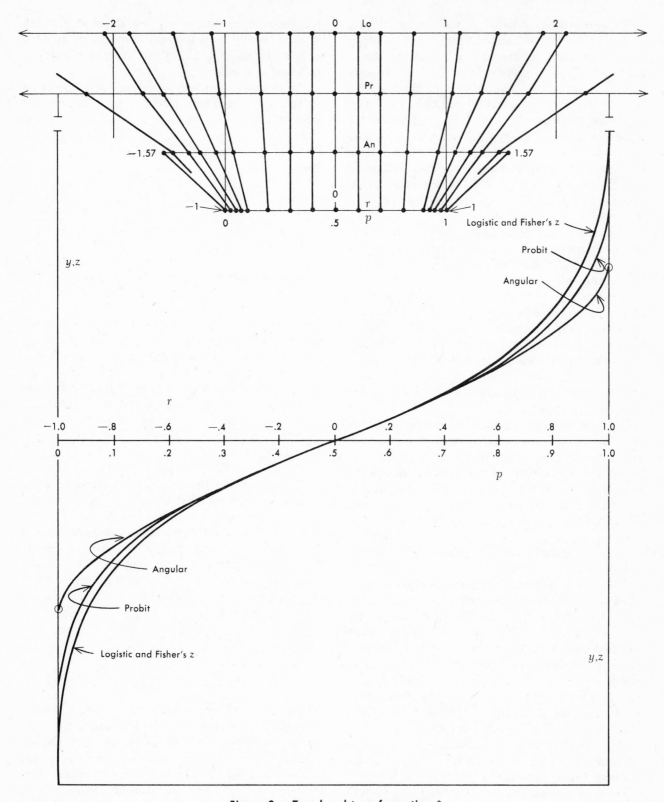

Figure 3 — Two-bend transformations*

* In the top part of the figure, the scale shown on the Lo axis is used for the Pr, An, and r axes as well.

If the observations include 0 or cover a very wide range, it is common to use various modifications, such as $y = (x + k)^c$, with k a small constant, often $\frac{1}{2}$ or 1. There has been considerable investigation of how well various modifications stabilize the variance under certain assumptions, but most of these modifications differ so slightly that interest in them is largely theoretical.

To deal with fractions. A very common form of data is the fraction or percentage, p, of a group who have some characteristic (such as being smokers). If the observed percentages include some extreme values (say, much smaller than 10 per cent or much larger than 90 per cent), a transformation is *usually* beneficial. Figure 3 shows the three transformations most frequently used with fractions: angular, probit, and logistic. Their formulas are given in Table 8, below. Of course, nothing prevents the use of transformations in the absence of extreme values, or the use of other transformations.

The upper part of Figure 3 displays the three transformations in a different way, showing how they "stretch the ends" of the unit interval relative to the middle.

Suppose a study is designed to compare different groups of men for propensity to smoke. The variance of p (the observed proportion of smokers in a sample from one group) depends on the true proportion, p^*, of that group. For extreme values of p^*, the variance of p gets very small. The nonconstant variance of p hinders many comparisons, such as tests for equality.

One possible remedy is to transform. Each of the three transformations mentioned is likely to make the variance more nearly stable. Each can be justified theoretically in certain circumstances. (For example, if p has the binomial distribution, the angular transformation is indicated.) However, transforming fractions often has practical value, even in the absence of such theory, and this value may include benefits other than variance stabilization.

There is an important caution to keep in mind when using the angular transformation for proportions, the square root transformation for Poisson data, or other transformations leading to theoretically known variances under ideal conditions. These transformations may achieve stabilization of variance even where ideal conditions do not hold. The stabilized variance, however, is often much larger than the theoretically indicated one. Thus, when using such transformations it is almost always advisable to use a variance estimated from the transformed values themselves rather than the variance expected under theoretical conditions.

To deal with correlation coefficients. Fisher's z-transformation is most commonly used on correlation coefficients, r, and occasionally on other variables which go from -1 to $+1$ [*see* MULTI-VARIATE ANALYSIS, *articles on* CORRELATION]. In Figure 3 the curve of Fisher's z-transformation coincides with the curve of the logistic trans-

formation, because the two are algebraically identical if $r = 2p - 1$. Generally speaking, remarks similar to those made about fractions apply to correlation coefficients.

To improve additivity. Suppose x is influenced by two other variables, u and v; for example, suppose x has the values shown in Table 1, for two

Table 1 — Values of x

	v_1	v_2	v_3	
u_1	27	28	35	$a_1 = -10$
u_2	47	48	55	$a_2 = +10$

$$b_1 = -3 \quad b_2 = -2 \quad b_3 = +5 \qquad m = 40$$

unspecified values of u and three unspecified values of v. Examine the values of x. You will note that the difference between corresponding entries in the two rows is always 20, *whichever column they are in.* Likewise, the difference between corresponding entries in any two columns is independent of the particular row they are in. (The difference is 1 for the first two columns, 7 for the last two columns, and 8 for the first and third columns.) These relations, which greatly simplify the study of how x depends on u and v, are referred to as *additivity.* (For a discussion of additivity in another sense, see Scheffé 1959, pp. 129–133.)

An alternative definition of additivity, whose equivalence is established by simple algebra, is phrased in terms of addition and accounts for the name. Call x additive in u and v if its values can be reconstructed by adding a row number (shown here as a_i) and a column number (shown here as b_j), perhaps plus an extra constant (shown here as m). For example, considering x_{11} in the first row and column,

$$27 = (-10) + (-3) + 40,$$

while, in general,

$$x_{ij} = a_i + b_j + m.$$

The extra constant (which is not essential, because it could be absorbed into the row numbers or the column numbers) is commonly taken to be the "grand mean" of all the entries, as it is here, and the row and column numbers are commonly taken, as here, to be the row and column means less the grand mean. [*See* LINEAR HYPOTHESES, *article on* ANALYSIS OF VARIANCE.]

To understand how additivity can be improved by a transformation, consider tables 2 and 3. Neither is additive. Suppose Table 2 is transformed by $y = \sqrt{x}$. This yields Table 4, which is

Table 2 — Values of x

	v_1	v_2	v_3
u_1	1	4	9
u_2	4	9	16
u_3	9	16	25

Table 3 — Values of x

	v_1	v_2	v_3
u_1	1.2	4.1	9.2
u_2	4.3	9.4	16.2
u_3	9.1	16.5	25.4

Table 4 — Values of y

	v_1	v_2	v_3	a_i
u_1	1	2	3	−1
u_2	2	3	4	0
u_3	3	4	5	+1
b_j	−1	0	+1	$3 = m$

clearly additive. The same transformation applied to Table 3 would yield values which are additive to a good approximation. Usually, approximate additivity is the best one can hope for.

Whether or not a transformation can improve additivity depends on the data. Thus, for tables 5 and 6, which are clearly nonadditive, no one-to-one transformation can produce even approximate additivity.

Table 5 — Values of x

	v_1	v_2
u_1	1	0
u_2	0	1

Table 6 — Values of x

	v_1	v_2	v_3
u_1	0	1	2
u_2	1	2	0
u_3	2	0	1

The concept of additivity is also meaningful and important when x depends on three variables, u, v, and w, or even more. Transformations are just as relevant to improve additivity in these cases.

Empirical transformations. Sometimes transformations are constructed as tables of numerical values and are not conveniently described by mathematical formulas. In this article such transformations are called empirical.

One use of empirical transformations is to improve additivity in u and v. J. B. Kruskal (1965) has described a method for calculating a monotonic transformation of x, carefully adapted to the given data, that improves additivity as much as possible according to a particular criterion.

Sometimes it is worthwhile to transform quantitative data into numerical ranks $1, 2, \cdots$ in order of size [*for example, this is a preliminary step to many nonparametric, or distribution-free, statistical procedures; for discussion, see* NONPARAMETRIC STATISTICS, *article on* RANKING METHODS]. This assignment of ranks can be thought of as an empirical transformation which leaves the data uniformly distributed. If normal scores are used instead of ranks, the empirical transformation leaves the distribution of the transformed data nearly normal.

Basic concepts

Linear transformations. A linear transformation $y = a + bx$, with b not 0, is often convenient, to shift the decimal point (for example, $y = 1,000x$), or to avoid negative values (for example, $y = 5 + x$) or for other reasons. Such transformations (often called coding) have no effect whatsoever on the properties of interest here, such as additivity, linearity, variance stability, and normality. Thus, linearly related variables are often considered equivalent or even the "same" in the context of transformations. To study the form of a transformation, a linearly related variable may be plotted instead. Thus, the comparison of power transformations $y = x^c$ in Figure 2 has been simplified by plotting $y = a + bx^c$, with a and b chosen for each c to make the curve go through two fixed points.

Monotonic transformations. A transformation is called (monotonic) increasing if, as in $y = \log x$, y gets larger as x gets larger. On a graph its curve always goes up as it goes to the right. A decreasing transformation, like $y = 1/x$ (where x is positive), goes the other way.

Data transformations of practical interest (in the sense of this article) are almost always either increasing or decreasing, but not mixed. The term "monotonic" (or, more precisely, "strictly monotonic") covers both cases. Sometimes the word "monotone" is used for "monotonic."

Region of interest. The region of interest in using a transformation is the region on the x-axis in which observed data values might reasonably be found or in which they actually lie. The characteristics of a transformation are relevant only in its region of interest. In particular, it need be monotonic only there.

Even though $y = x^2$ is not monotonic (it increases for x positive and decreases for x negative), it can be sensible to use $y = x^2$ for observations, x, that are necessarily positive.

Mild and strong transformations. If the graph of a transformation is almost a straight line in the region of interest, it is described as mild, or almost linear. If, on the contrary, it is strongly curved, it is called strong. Note, however, that visual impressions are sensitive to the sizes of the relative scales of the x-axis and y-axis.

A very mild transformation is useful, as a preliminary step, only when the subsequent analysis seeks maximum precision. On the other hand, if a strong transformation is appropriate, it may provide major benefits even for very approximate methods, such as visual inspection of graphical display (and for precise analysis also, of course).

The strength of a transformation depends critically on the region of interest. For x from 1 to 10, $y = \log x$ is fairly strong, as Figure 2 shows. From 5 to 6 it is quite mild, and from 5 to 5.05 it is virtually straight. From 1 to 1,000,000 it is very strong indeed.

Effect of transforming on relations among averages. Transforming can change the relationship among average values quite drastically. For example, consider the hypothetical data given in Table 7 for two rats running through a 20-foot channel. Which rat is faster? According to average time, rat 2 is slightly faster, but according to average speed, it is only half as fast! Thus, even the answer to this simple question may be altered by transformation. More delicate questions are naturally much more sensitive to transformation. This shows that use of the correct transformation may be quite important in revealing structure.

Table 7—Hypothetical times and speeds

	Time (seconds)	Corresponding speed (feet per second)
Rat 1		
Trial 1	50.0	0.4
Trial 2	10.0	2.0
Trial 3	5.6	3.6
Average	21.9	2.0
Rat 2		
Trial 1	20.0	1.0
Trial 2	20.0	1.0
Trial 3	20.0	1.0
Average	20.0	1.0

The effect of transformations on expected values and variances. The transform of the expected value does *not* equal the expected value of the transform, although they are crude approximations of each other. This is clearer in symbols. Because interest usually lies in estimating the expected value, $E(x)$, from information about $y = f(x)$, rather than vice versa, it is convenient to invert the transformation and write $x = g(y)$, where g is f^{-1}. Then, to a crude approximation,

$$E(x) = E[g(y)] \cong g[E(y)].$$

The milder the transformation is, the better this approximation is likely to be, and for linear transformations it is precisely correct.

In practice one usually uses an estimate for $E(y)$, often the average value, $\bar{y}$. Substituting the estimate for the true value is a second step of approximation: $E(x)$ is crudely approximated by $g(\bar{y})$.

One simple improvement, selected from many which have been used, is

$$E(x) \cong g[E(y)] + \tfrac{1}{2}g''[E(y)] \cdot \text{var}(y),$$

where g'' denotes the second derivative of g and $\text{var}(y)$ denotes the variance of y. (This approximation, since it is based on a Taylor expansion through the quadratic term, is exact if $g(y)$ is a quadratic polynomial, a situation that occurs for $y = \sqrt{x+k}$.) Substituting estimates, such as $\bar{y}$ for $E(y)$ and s_y^2, the sample variance, for $\text{var}(y)$ is a second step of approximation:

$$E(x) \cong g(\bar{y}) + \tfrac{1}{2}g''(\bar{y}) \cdot s_y^2.$$

Advanced work along these lines is well represented by Neyman and Scott (1960).

For variances, the simplest approximation is

$$\text{var}(x) \cong \text{var}(y) \cdot \{g'[E(y)]\}^2,$$

where g' is the first derivative of g. This is fairly good for mild transformations and perfect for linear ones. After estimates are substituted, the estimate becomes

$$\text{var}(x) \cong s_y^2 \cdot [g'(\bar{y})]^2.$$

One-bend transformations. Most transformations of practical use have only one bend (as in Figure 2) or two bends (as in Figure 3). A curious fact is that the increasing one-bend transformations most often used bend downward, like $y = \log x$, rather than upward, like $y = x^2$. For decreasing transformations, turn the graph upside down and the same thing holds true.

Some important families of one-bend transformations are

$y = \log(x + k)$,	logarithmic family;
$y = \sqrt{x+k}$,	square-root family;
$y = x^c$,	power family;
$y = e^{cx}$ (or 10^{cx} or k^x),	exponential family;
$y = (x + k)^c$,	"simple" family.

Here k and c are constants, and $e \cong 2.718$ is a familiar constant. The region of interest is generally

Table 8 — Two-bend transformations

Forward forms	Backward forms	Names
$y = \arcsin \sqrt{p}$ $= \sin^{-1} \sqrt{p}$	$p = \sin^2 y$	angular arcsine inverse sine
$y = \text{Erf}^{-1}(p)$ $= \Phi^{-1}(p)$ $y = \Phi^{-1}(p) + 5$ (often)	$p = \text{Erf}(y) = \Phi(y)$ $=$ normal probability up to y	probit[a] normit phi-gamma
$y = \frac{1}{2} \log \frac{p}{1-p}$	$p = \frac{e^{2y}}{e^{2y}+1}$	logistic[b] logit
$z = \frac{1}{2} \log \frac{1+r}{1-r}$ $= \text{arctanh } r$	$r = \frac{e^{2z}-1}{e^{2z}+1}$	Fisher's z[b] z hyperbolic arctangent

a. Under the name "probit" the addition of 5 is usual, to avoid negative values.
b. Natural logarithms are generally used here.

restricted either to $x \geqslant 0$ or to $x \geqslant -k$. Of course, each family also includes linearly related transformations (for example, $y = a + bx^c$ is in the power family).

The "simple" family (named and discussed in Tukey 1957) obviously includes two of the other families and, by a natural extension to mathematical limits, includes the remaining two as well.

Two-bend transformations. Only those two-bend transformations mentioned above (angular, probit, logistic, and z) are in general use, although the log–log transformation, given by $y = \log(-\log x)$, is sometimes applied. A whole family of varying strengths would be desirable (such as $p^c - (1 - p)^c$), but no such family appears to have received more than passing mention in the literature.

Several formulas and names for two-bend transformations are presented in Table 8. Tables of these transformations are generally available. (For references, consult Fletcher et al. 1946 and the index of Greenwood & Hartley 1962.)

When to use and how to choose a transformation

Many clues suggest the possible value of transforming. Sometimes the same clue not only gives this general indication but also points to the necessary transformation or to its general shape.

When using a transformation, it is *essential* to visualize its plotted curve over the region of interest. If necessary, actually plot a few points on graph paper. (In several published examples the authors appear to be unaware that the transformations are so mild as to be useless in their context.)

If a quantity, such as the expected value, is needed for x itself, consider whether this quantity is best found by working directly with x or indirectly through the use of some transform. However, need should be judged cautiously; although it is often real, in many cases it may vanish on closer examination.

A word of caution: "outliers" can simulate some of the clues below and falsely suggest the need for transforming when, in fact, techniques for dealing with outliers should be used [*see* STATISTICAL ANALYSIS, SPECIAL PROBLEMS OF, *article on* OUTLIERS].

Some simple clues. Very simple and yet very strong clues include counted data covering a wide range, fraction data with some observations near 0 or 1, and correlation coefficient data with some values near -1 or $+1$. Generally, observations which closely approach an *intrinsic boundary* may benefit by a transformation which expands the end region, perhaps to infinity.

If several related curves present a complex but systematic appearance, it is often possible to simplify them, as in Figure 1. For example, they might all become straight lines, or the vertical or horizontal spacing between curves might become constant along the curves.

A very nonnormal distribution of data is a clue, although, by itself, a weak one. For this purpose, nonnormality is best judged by plotting the data on "probability paper" [*see* GRAPHIC PRESENTATION]. The general shape of a normalizing transformation can be read directly from the plot.

Nonconstant variance. Suppose there are many categories (such as the cells in a two-way table) and each contains several observations. Calculate the sample variance, s_{ij}^2, and the average value, a_{ij}, in each category. If the s_{ij}^2 vary substantially, make a scatter plot of the s_{ij}^2 against the a_{ij}. If the s_{ij}^2 tend to change systematically along the a-axis, then a variance-stabilizing transformation is possible and often worthwhile. Usually the scatter plot is more revealing if plotted on paper with both scales logarithmic, so that $\log s_{ij}^2$ is plotted against $\log a_{ij}$.

To choose the transformation, the relationship between the s_{ij}^2 and the a_{ij} must be estimated. Using even a crude estimate may be better than not transforming at all. Suppose the estimated relationship is $s_{ij}^2 = g(a_{ij})$. (Commonly, this is $s_{ij}^2 = ka_{ij}^c$. This is a straight line on log–log paper. Taylor [1961] contains many such examples.) It can be shown that $y = \int [\sqrt{g(x)}]^{-1} dx$ stabilizes the variance (approximately). If $s_{ij}^2 = ka_{ij}$ (for Poisson distributions, $k = 1$), this leads essentially to $y = \sqrt{x}$. For $s_{ij}^2 = ka_{ij}^c$, it leads essentially to $y = x^d$, with $d = 1 - c/2$ (or $y = \log x$ if $d = 0$).

Removable nonadditivity. When nonadditivity can be removed by a transformation, it is almost always worthwhile to do so. To recognize nonadditivity is often easy, either by direct examination or by the size of the interaction terms in an analysis of variance [see LINEAR HYPOTHESES, *article on* ANALYSIS OF VARIANCE]. To decide how much of it is removable may be harder.

With experience, in simple cases one can often recognize removable nonadditivity by direct examination and discover roughly the shape of the required transformation. If Tukey's "one degree of freedom for non-additivity" (see Moore & Tukey 1954; or Scheffé 1959, pp. 129–133) yields a large value of F, some nonadditivity is removable. Closely related is the scatter-plot analysis of residuals given by Anscombe and Tukey (1963, sec. 10). Kruskal's method (1965) directly seeks the monotone transformation leaving the data most additive.

How to choose the transformation. In addition to the methods mentioned above, one or more transformations may be tried quite arbitrarily. If significant benefits result, then the possibility of greater benefits from a stronger, weaker, or modified transformation may be investigated.

A whole family of transformations can, in effect, be tried all at once, with the parameter values chosen to optimize some criterion. The important paper by Box and Cox (1964) gives a good discussion of this method. Another useful approach is provided in Kruskal (1965).

An illustration—galvanic skin response

It has long been known that electrical resistance through the skin changes rapidly in response to psychological stimuli—a phenomenon known as galvanic skin response (GSR) or electrodermal response. Originally, the only scale used for analyzing GSR was that of electrical resistance, R, measured in ohms (or in kilohms). As early as 1934, Darrow (see 1934; 1937) suggested the use of electrical conductance, $C = 1/R$, measured in mhos (or in micromhos), and later $\log C$, as well as various modifications. More recently, other scales, such as $\sqrt{C}$, have also been used, and the topic has continued to receive attention up to the present.

Although agreement on "the best scale" has not been reached, many authors who treat this question agree that R is a very poor scale and that both C and $\log C$ provide substantial improvement. Most experimenters now use either C or $\log C$, but a few still use R (and some fail to specify which scale they are using), more than thirty years after Darrow's original paper!

Lacey and Siegel (1949) have discussed various transformations, using their own experimental results. Their final recommendation is C. Using 92 subjects, they measured the resistance of each one twice, first while the subject was sitting quietly, then just after the subject had received an unexpected electric shock. Call the two values R_0 (before shock) and R_1 (after shock). Each subject received only one shock, and presumably all the shocks were of the same strength.

For any scale y (whether R, $\log C$, C, or another), let y_0 and y_1 be the two values (before and after) and let $GSR = y_1 - y_0$. (A separate question, omitted here, is whether $y_1 - y_0$ itself should be transformed before use as the GSR.)

The major use of GSR is to measure the strength of a subject's response to a stimulus. For this use it is desirable that the size of the GSR not depend on extraneous variables, such as the subject's basal resistance. Thus, in the equation $y_1 = y_0 + GSR$ the value of GSR should be independent of y_0. This is a form of additivity.

Figure 4 shows GSR plotted against y_0 for the two scales R and C. On the R scale it is obvious that the GSR has a strong systematic dependence on R_0 (in addition to its random fluctuation). The C scale is in strong contrast, for there the GSR displays relatively little systematic dependence on C_0. The corresponding plot for the intermediate $\log C$ scale (not shown here) displays a distinct but intermediate degree of dependence.

Another desirable property, often specified in papers on this topic, is that y_0 should be approximately normal. Plots on "probability paper" (not shown here) display $\log C_0$ as quite nicely straight but $\sqrt{C_0}$ and $\sqrt{R_0}$ as definitely curved (skew), and C_0 and R_0 as even more curved. Thus, a conflict appears: the requirement of normality points to the $\log C$ scale, while additivity points to the C scale. For the major use of GSR, additivity is more important and must dominate unless some resolution can be found.

An intermediate scale might provide a resolution. Schlosberg and Stanley (1953) chose $\sqrt{C}$. A significantly different intermediate scale, with a plausible rationale, is $\log (R - R^*)$, where R^* depends only on the electrodes, electrode paste, and so forth. For the data of the Lacey and Siegel study, the

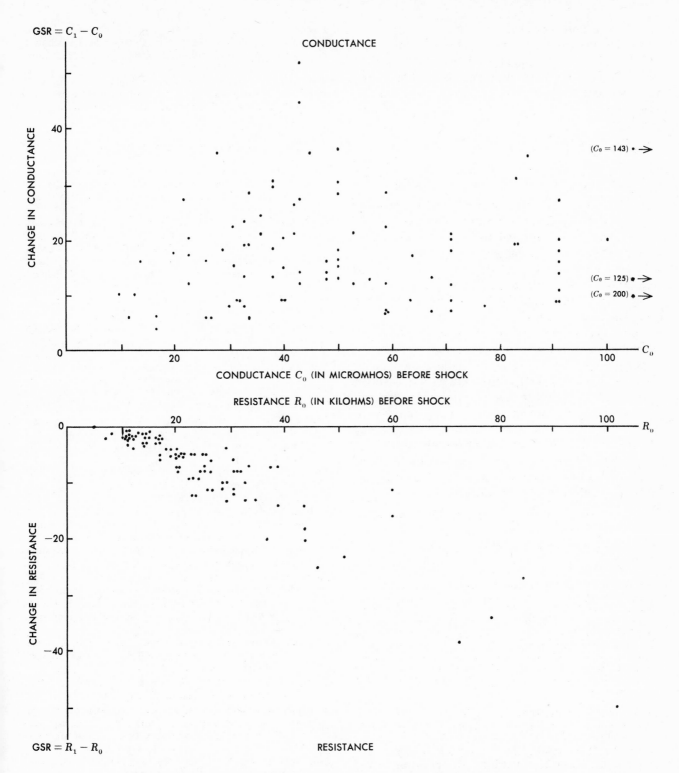

Figure 4 — Galvanic skin response (GSR) plotted against initial level on two scales*

* GSR represents postshock level of resistance or conductance minus preshock level. The same 92 observations are plotted in both parts of the figure.

Source: Data from Lacey & Siegel 1949.

value of R^* should be a little more than 4 kilohms.

Some other topics

Multivariate observations can be transformed. Even linear transformations are significant in this case, and these have been the main focus of interest so far. [*See* FACTOR ANALYSIS; MULTIVARIATE ANALYSIS.]

Where detailed mathematical assumptions can safely be made, transformations can sometimes be used in a more complex way (based on the maximum likelihood principle) to obtain greater precision. This is often called the Bliss–Fisher method. How widely this method should be used has been the subject of much controversy. An article by Fisher (1954, with discussion) gives a good statement of that author's views, together with concise statements by five other eminent statisticians.

Similarity and dissimilarity measures of many kinds are sometimes transformed into spatial distances, by the technique of multidimensional scaling. Briefly, if δ_{ij} is a measure of dissimilarity between objects i and j, multidimensional scaling seeks points (in r-dimensional space) whose interpoint distances, d_{ij}, are systematically related to the dissimilarities. The relationship between δ_{ij} and d_{ij} may usefully be considered a transformation (for further information on multidimensional scaling, see Kruskal 1964).

An ingenious and appealing application of transformations (to three sets of data) appears in Shepard (1965). In each case the data can be represented by several plotted curves on a single graph. Each curve is essentially unimodal, but the peaks occur at different places along the x-axis. The x-variable is monotonically transformed so as to give the different curves the same shape, that is, to make the curves the same except for location along the x-axis. The transformed variables appear to have subject-matter significance.

JOSEPH B. KRUSKAL

[See also ERRORS; GRAPHIC PRESENTATION.]

BIBLIOGRAPHY

General discussion of transformations accompanied by worthwhile applications to data of intrinsic interest may be found in Bartlett 1947, Box & Cox 1964, Kruskal 1965, Moore & Tukey 1954, and Snedecor 1937. Actual or potential applications of great interest may be found in Lacey & Siegel 1949, Shepard 1965, Taylor 1961, and Wald 1965. For tables, consult Fletcher, Miller & Rosenhead 1946, and Greenwood & Hartley 1962. Large and useful bibliographies may be found in Grimm 1960 and Lienert 1962.

ANSCOMBE, F. J.; and TUKEY, JOHN W. 1963 The Examination and Analysis of Residuals. *Technometrics* 5: 141–160.

BARTLETT, M. S. 1947 The Use of Transformations. *Biometrics* 3:39–52. → Down-to-earth, practical advice. Widely read and still very useful.

BOX, G. E. P.; and COX, D. R. 1964 An Analysis of Transformations. *Journal of the Royal Statistical Society* Series B 26:211–252. → Starts with a very useful general review. The body of the paper, although important and equally useful, requires some mathematical sophistication.

CRESPI, LEO P. 1942 Quantitative Variation of Incentive and Performance in the White Rat. *American Journal of Psychology* 55:467–517.

DARROW, CHESTER W. 1934 The Significance of Skin Resistance in the Light of Its Relation to the Amount of Perspiration (Preliminary Note). *Journal of General Psychology* 11:451–452.

DARROW, CHESTER W. 1937 The Equation of the Galvanic Skin Reflex Curve: I. The Dynamics of Reaction in Relation to Excitation-background. *Journal of General Psychology* 16:285–309.

FISHER, R. A. 1954 The Analysis of Variance With Various Binomial Transformations. *Biometrics* 10: 130–151. → Contains a statement of the Bliss–Fisher method and a controversy over its scope. Do not overlook the important 11-page discussion, especially the remarks by Cochran and Anscombe, whose views are recommended.

FLETCHER, ALAN; MILLER, JEFFERY C. P.; and ROSENHEAD, LOUIS (1946) 1962 *An Index of Mathematical Tables.* 2d ed. 2 vols. Reading, Mass.: Addison-Wesley.

GREENWOOD, J. ARTHUR; and HARTLEY, H. O. 1962 *Guide to Tables in Mathematical Statistics.* Princeton Univ. Press.

GRIMM, H. 1960 Transformation von Zufallsvariablen. *Biometrische Zeitschrift* 2:164–182.

KRUSKAL, JOSEPH B. 1964 Multidimensional Scaling by Optimizing Goodness of Fit to a Nonmetric Hypothesis. *Psychometrika* 29:1–27.

KRUSKAL, JOSEPH B. 1965 Analysis of Factorial Experiments by Estimating Monotone Transformations of the Data. *Journal of the Royal Statistical Society* Series B 27:251–263.

LACEY, OLIVER L.; and SIEGEL, PAUL S. 1949 An Analysis of the Unit of Measurement of the Galvanic Skin Response. *Journal of Experimental Psychology* 39: 122–127.

LIENERT, G. A. 1962 Über die Anwendung von Variablen-Transformationen in der Psychologie. *Biometrische Zeitschrift* 4:145–181.

MOORE, PETER G.; and TUKEY, JOHN W. 1954 Answer to Query 112. *Biometrics* 10:562–568. → Includes Tukey's "One Degree of Freedom for Non-additivity" and an interesting example of how to choose a transformation, explained clearly and with brevity.

MOSTELLER, FREDERICK; and BUSH, ROBERT R. (1954) 1959 Selected Quantitative Techniques. Volume 1, pages 289–334 in Gardner Lindzey (editor), *Handbook of Social Psychology.* Cambridge, Mass.: Addison-Wesley.

NEYMAN, J.; and SCOTT, E. L. 1960 Correction for Bias Introduced by a Transformation of Variables. *Annals of Mathematical Statistics* 31:643–655.

SCHEFFÉ, HENRY 1959 *The Analysis of Variance.* New York: Wiley. → See especially pages 129–133.

SCHLOSBERG, HAROLD S.; and STANLEY, WALTER C. S. 1953 A Simple Test of the Normality of Twenty-four Distributions of Electrical Skin Conductance. *Science* 117:35–37.

SHEPARD, ROGER N. 1965 Approximation to Uniform Gradients of Generalization by Monotone Transformations of Scale. Pages 94–110 in David I. Mostofsky (editor), *Stimulus Generalization.* Stanford Univ. Press.

SNEDECOR, GEORGE W. S. (1937) 1957 *Statistical Methods: Applied to Experiments in Agriculture and Biology.* 5th ed. Ames: Iowa State Univ. Press. → See especially pages 314–327.

TAYLOR, L. R. 1961 Aggregation, Variance and the Mean. *Nature* 189:732–735.

TUKEY, JOHN W.   1957   On the Comparative Anatomy of Transformations. *Annals of Mathematical Statistics* 28:602–632.

WALD, GEORGE   1965   Frequency or Wave Length? *Science* 150:1239–1240. → See also several follow-up letters, under the heading "Frequency Scale for Spectra," *Science* 151:400–404 (1966).

III
GROUPED OBSERVATIONS

When repeated empirical measurements are made of the same quantity, the results typically vary; on the other hand, ties, or repetitions of measurement values, often occur, because measurements are never made with perfect fineness. Length, for example, although theoretically a continuous quantity, must be measured to the closest inch, centimeter, or some such; psychological aptitudes that are conceptually continuous are measured to a degree of fineness consonant with the test or instrument used. In many cases it is desirable and efficient to measure less finely than current techniques permit, because the expense of refined measurement may outweigh the value of the added information. Also, grouping of measurements is often carried out after they are made, in order to enhance convenience of computation or presentation.

No matter how the data are obtained, unless there are only a few it is usually convenient to present them in groups or intervals; that is, the data are organized in a table that shows how many observations are in each of a relatively small number of intervals. The motivations are clarity of description and simplification of subsequent manipulation. Table 1 presents an example of such grouped data. (The data are taken from Wallis & Roberts 1956; this work should be consulted for

Table 1 — Thirty-two persons grouped according to their body weight (in pounds)

Weight	Number of persons	Mid-value of class
137.5–147.5	2	142.5
147.5–157.5	5	152.5
157.5–167.5	4	162.5
167.5–177.5	5	172.5
177.5–187.5	7	182.5
187.5–197.5	5	192.5
197.5–207.5	3	202.5
207.5–217.5	0	212.5
217.5–227.5	0	222.5
227.5–237.5	0	232.5
237.5–247.5	1	242.5

details of computation and for the useful discussion in secs. 6.2.1, 7.4.5, and 8.5.2.) If it is assumed that the weights were originally measured only to the nearest pound, then there is no ambiguity at the class boundaries about which group is appropriate for each measurement. Some information is, of course, lost when the data are recorded in these coarser groups. Such loss of information can, however, be compensated for by making some more observations, and so a purely economic problem results: which is cheaper—to make fewer but finer measurements or to make more but coarser measurements?

A second problem is that most mathematical and statistical tools developed for the treatment of data of this kind presuppose exact measurements, theoretically on an infinitely fine scale. To what extent can use be made of these tools when the data are grouped? How must the theory be modified so that it may legitimately be applied to grouped observations?

Another problem is that bias may arise in cases where an observation is more likely to fall in some part of a relatively wide group than in other parts of that group. Theoretically this holds, of course, for any size of group interval, but when group intervals are less than one-quarter of the standard deviation of the distribution, there will, in practice, be little trouble.

Usually one refers all the observations falling in a group to the midpoint of that group and then works with these new "observations" as if they were exact. What does such a procedure imply? Is it justified? And what should be done if the grouping is very coarse or if there are open intervals to the right and/or left? What should be done in the case where the groups can only be ranked, because their limits have no numerical values?

Estimation of μ and σ in the normal case.   Most work on problems of grouped observations has centered about simple normal samples, where one is interested in inferences about mean and variance. Suppose N observations are regarded as a random sample from a normal population with mean μ and standard deviation σ. The observations have fallen in, say, k groups. The maximum likelihood (ML) estimators of μ and σ can be found whether or not the grouping is into equal intervals and whether or not the end intervals are open. The method is a bit troublesome because of its iterative character, but tables have been constructed for facilitation of the work (see Gjeddebæk 1949; advice on finer details is given in Kulldorff 1958*a*; 1958*b*). The ML method can be used with assurance in cases where there is some doubt about the admissibility of using the so-called simple estimators of μ and σ.

The simple estimators are obtained if all observations are referred to the midpoints of their respective groups and standard estimators m and s are calculated for the mean and standard deviation, as outlined in Wallis and Roberts (1956, secs. 7.4.5, 8.5.2). These estimators of μ and σ have almost the same variances and expected mean squares as the ML estimators when the grouping intervals are not wider than 2σ, and N, the sample size, is no more than 100. The simple estimators have biases that do not go to zero as N increases. If, however, interval width is no more than 2σ and $N \leqslant 100$, the bias is negligible.

If the grouping is equidistant with groups of size $h\sigma$, and $N < 100$, the efficiencies, E, of the ML mean (or of the simple mean, m) relative to the ungrouped mean are as presented in Table 2.

Table 2 — *Efficiency of the ML and simple estimators of the mean from grouped data, relative to the ungrouped mean*

h	E (in per cent)
0.2	99.7
0.4	98.7
0.6	97.1
0.8	94.9
1.0	92.3
1.2	89.3
1.4	86.0
1.6	82.4
1.8	78.7
2.0	75.0

Here E indicates how many ungrouped observations are equivalent to 100 grouped observations made with the group size in question. The above figures can be obtained from a formula given by R. A. Fisher (1922), $E = (1 + h^2/12)^{-1}$. If the phase relationship between true mean and group limits is taken into account, there are only very small changes (see Gjeddebæk 1956).

ML grouped and simple estimators of σ have an efficiency of about 58 per cent for $h = 2$. For estimating σ, groups should not be wider than 1.6σ, so that "phase relationship" will not play a role. For equidistant grouping with intervals of length 1.6σ, all efficiencies for estimating σ will be about 70 per cent.

Practical conclusions. Because σ depends on both natural variation and measurement variation, it may be seen, for example, that measurements of height in man lose little efficiency when recorded in centimeters rather than in millimeters. It will also be seen that if a considerable reduction of cost per observation can be obtained by measuring with a coarse scale, the information obtained per unit of cost may be increased by such coarse measuring. Even with such large group intervals as 2σ, it is necessary to make only four grouped observations for each three ungrouped observations to obtain the same amount of information about μ.

An instance can be quoted of the advantage of refraining from using a scale to its utmost capacity. Consider the routine weighing of such things as tablets or other doses of substances weighing between 200 and 600 milligrams. Sometimes, in practice, even tenths of milligrams are taken into account here. The last significant figure obtained by such a weighing will, as a rule, require preposterous labor and will divert attention from the foregoing, more important figures. Thus, carrying out the weighing to this point will do more harm than good in the long run. Also, the accuracy of reading ought to be kept in reasonable proportion to the accuracy inherent in the measured pieces; in other words, observations ought to be grouped with due regard to the size of their natural variation. Here the table of efficiencies will be useful, as it immediately reveals at what point the coarseness of a scale essentially influences the accuracy. In this connection it is worthwhile to stress that an impression of great accuracy from a result with many decimal places is misleading if the natural variation of the results makes illusory most of the decimal places. For example, it was an exaggeration of scientific accuracy when it was said that every cigarette smoked by a person cuts off 14 minutes and 24 seconds from his lifetime. Of course, there was some publicity value in the statement. If, however, you are told that whenever you have smoked 100 cigarettes you have lost a day and a night of your lifetime, you will conclude that some scientist has given this opinion with due regard to the obvious uncertainty of such an estimate. From the viewpoint of a statistician, this statement seems a bit more honest, despite the fact that exactly the same thing is expressed as before. (Example 82C of section 3.10 of Wallis & Roberts 1956 gives a similar provocative use of figures.)

Sheppard correction. When the variance, σ^2, is estimated from data grouped into intervals of width $h\sigma$, it has been proposed that the best estimator of σ^2 is $s^2 - (h^2/12)\sigma^2$, where $-(h^2/12)\sigma^2$ is the so-called Sheppard correction. There has been persistent confusion about a statement by R. A. Fisher that the Sheppard correction should be avoided in hypothesis testing. Given N grouped observations, calculate the simple estimators m of the mean and s^2 of the variance, with the size of group intervals,

$h\sigma$, the same for the two calculations. From the efficiency, E (see discussion above), it follows that the variance of m is $(\sigma^2/N)(1 + h^2/12)$. According to Sheppard, $s^2 - (h^2/12)\sigma^2$ is the best estimator of σ^2; thus, it must follow that the best estimator of the quantity $\sigma^2(1 + h^2/12)$ is simply s^2, and hence the best estimator of the variance of m is s^2/N. That is the same expression used for ungrouped observations, and so s^2 should be used without Sheppard's correction when m and s^2 are brought together in a testing procedure or in a statement of confidence limits for μ. Obvious modifications may be made when h is different for the grouping used to calculate m and s^2. Sheppard's correction should also be avoided in analysis of variance, as the same group intervals are used for "within" and "between" estimators of the variance. In practice, Sheppard's correction is not very useful, because an isolated estimate of variance is seldom required. For that case, however, the correction is well justified. A serious drawback is that it cannot be used when grouping is not equidistant. Here the maximum likelihood method seems to be the only reasonable precise one.

When the Sheppard-corrected estimator of σ^2 is available, it has the same efficiency as the ML estimator, at least for N less than 100 (see Gjeddebæk 1959a and the above discussion of the inconsistency of the simple estimators for large N).

Very coarse groups. When a grouping must be very coarse, the problem arises of where to place the group limits most efficiently. The problem is compounded because the efficiency depends on the site of the unknown true mean. Sometimes—for example, for quality-control purposes—it is known where the true mean ought to be, so the theory is often useful in these instances (see Ogawa 1962).

To investigate the consequences of very wide grouping, consider the weights example once again. Let the groups be very wide—40 pounds. Depending on which group limits are deleted, one of the four situations illustrated in Table 3 results. The ML method presupposes an underlying normal distribution, and therefore it gives rather small s-values in the last two extreme situations, but all in all, Table 3 demonstrates an astonishingly small effect of such coarse grouping. [*For a discussion of optimum grouping, see* NONPARAMETRIC STATISTICS, *article on* ORDER STATISTICS.]

Grouping ordinal data. If the group limits have no numerical values by nature but are ranked, a different set of problems arises. By use of probits the group limits may be given numerical values, and then the situation may be treated according to the principle of maximum likelihood. In reality a two-step use of that principle is involved, and this gives rise to distribution problems. (The method is discussed in Gjeddebæk 1961; 1963.) From a hypothesis-testing point of view, the grouping of ordinal data may be regarded as the introduction of ties [*see* NONPARAMETRIC STATISTICS, *article on* RANKING METHODS, *for a discussion of such ties*].

Other aspects. Extensions of techniques using grouped data to distributions other than the normal, to multivariate data, and to procedures other than estimation of parameters are possible and have been investigated. For example, Tallis and Young (1962) have discussed the multivariate case and have given hints on hypothesis testing. Kulldorff (1961) has investigated the case of the exponential distribution, and Gjeddebæk (1949; 1956; 1957; 1959a; 1959b; 1961; 1963) has worked on methods parallel to t-testing and F-testing. In addition, P. S. Swamy (1960) has done considerable work on these extensions. A comprehensive treatment of rounding errors is given by Eisenhart (1947).

N. F. GJEDDEBÆK

[*See also* STATISTICS, DESCRIPTIVE.]

Table 3 — Alternate groupings of 32 persons according to their body weight (in pounds)

WEIGHT	NUMBER OF PERSONS	MEAN Simple	MEAN ML	STANDARD DEVIATION Simple	STANDARD DEVIATION ML
Situation 1					
107.5–147.5	2				
147.5–187.5	21	177.5	177.7	22.0	21.9
187.5–227.5	8				
227.5–267.5	1				
Situation 2					
117.5–157.5	7				
157.5–197.5	21	175.0	175.1	24.2	24.1
197.5–237.5	3				
237.5–277.5	1				
Situation 3					
127.5–167.5	11				
167.5–207.5	20	175.0	174.7	18.0	17.1
207.5–247.5	1				
Situation 4					
137.5–177.5	16				
177.5–217.5	15	178.8	178.9	19.6	18.5
217.5–257.5	1				
Results of 10-pound grouping for comparison		176.6	176.6	21.0	21.0

BIBLIOGRAPHY

EISENHART, CHURCHILL 1947 Effects of Rounding or Grouping Data. Pages 185–233 in Columbia University, Statistical Research Group, *Selected Techniques of Statistical Analysis for Scientific and Industrial Research, and Production and Management Engineering*, by Churchill Eisenhart, Millard W. Hastay, and W. Allen Wallis. New York: McGraw-Hill.

FISHER, R. A. (1922) 1950 On the Mathematical Foundations of Theoretical Statistics. Pages 10.308a–10.368 in R. A. Fisher, *Contributions to Mathematical Statistics.* New York: Wiley. → First published in the *Philosophical Transactions,* Series A, Volume 222, of the Royal Society of London.

FISHER, R. A. (1925) 1958 *Statistical Methods for Research Workers.* 13th ed. New York: Hafner. → Previous editions were also published by Oliver & Boyd. See especially section 19, Appendix D, "Adjustment for Grouping."

GJEDDEBÆK, N. F. 1949 Contribution to the Study of Grouped Observations: I. Application of the Method of Maximum Likelihood in Case of Normally Distributed Observations. *Skandinavisk aktuarietidskrift* 32: 135–159.

GJEDDEBÆK, N. F. 1956 Contribution to the Study of Grouped Observations: II. Loss of Information Caused by Groupings of Normally Distributed Observations. *Skandinavisk aktuarietidskrift* 39:154–159.

GJEDDEBÆK, N. F. 1957 Contribution to the Study of Grouped Observations: III. The Distribution of Estimates of the Mean. *Skandinavisk aktuarietidskrift* 40:20–25.

GJEDDEBÆK, N. F. 1959a Contribution to the Study of Grouped Observations: IV. Some Comments on Simple Estimates. *Biometrics* 15:433–439.

GJEDDEBÆK, N. F. 1959b Contribution to the Study of Grouped Observations: V. Three-class Grouping of Normal Observations. *Skandinavisk aktuarietidskrift* 42:194–207.

GJEDDEBÆK, N. F. 1961 Contribution to the Study of Grouped Observations: VI. *Skandinavisk aktuarietidskrift* 44:55–73.

GJEDDEBÆK, N. F. 1963 On Grouped Observations and Adjacent Aspects of Statistical Theory. *Methods of Information in Medicine* 2:116–121.

KULLDORFF, GUNNAR 1958a Maximum Likelihood Estimation of the Mean of a Normal Random Variable When the Sample Is Grouped. *Skandinavisk aktuarietidskrift* 41:1–17.

KULLDORFF, GUNNAR 1958b Maximum Likelihood Estimation of the Standard Deviation of a Normal Random Variable When the Sample Is Grouped. *Skandinavisk aktuarietidskrift* 41:18–36.

KULLDORFF, GUNNAR 1961 *Contributions to the Theory of Estimation From Grouped and Partially Grouped Samples.* Uppsala (Sweden): Almqvist & Wiksell.

OGAWA, JUNJIRO 1962 Determinations of Optimum Spacings in the Case of Normal Distribution. Pages 272–283 in Ahmed E. Sarhan and Bernard G. Greenberg (editors), *Contributions to Order Statistics.* New York: Wiley.

STEVENS, W. L. 1948 Control by Gauging. *Journal of the Royal Statistical Society* Series B 10:54–98. → A discussion of Stevens' paper is presented on pages 98–108.

SWAMY, P. S. 1960 Estimating the Mean and Variance of a Normal Distribution From Singly and Doubly Truncated Samples of Grouped Observations. Calcutta Statistical Association *Bulletin* 9, no. 36.

TALLIS, G. M.; and YOUNG, S. S. Y. 1962 Maximum Likelihood Estimation of Parameters of the Normal, Log-normal, Truncated Normal and Bivariate Normal Distributions From Grouped Data. *Australian Journal of Statistics* 4, no. 2:49–54.

WALLIS, W. ALLEN; and ROBERTS, HARRY V. 1956 *Statistics: A New Approach.* Glencoe, Ill.: Free Press.

IV

TRUNCATION AND CENSORSHIP

Statistical problems of truncation and censorship arise when a standard statistical model is appropriate for analysis except that values of the random variable falling below—or above—some value are not measured at all (truncation) or are only counted (censorship). For example, in a study of particle size, particles below the resolving power of observational equipment will not be seen at all (truncation), or perhaps small particles will be seen and counted, but will not be measurable because of equipment limitations (censorship). Most of the existing theory for problems of this sort takes the limits at which truncation or censorship occurs to be known constants. There are practical situations in which these limits are not exactly known (indeed, the particle-size censorship example above might involve an inexactly ascertainable limit), but little theory exists for them. Truncation is sometimes usefully regarded as a special case of selection: if the probability that a possible observation having value x will actually be observed depends upon x, and is, say, $p(x)$ (between 0 and 1), selection is occurring. If $p(x) = 1$ between certain limits and 0 outside them, the selection is of the type called (two-sided) truncation.

More particularly, if values below a certain lower limit, a, are not observed at all, the distribution is said to be truncated on the left. If values larger than an upper limit, b, are not observed, the distribution is said to be truncated on the right. If only values lying between a and b are observed, the distribution is said to be doubly truncated. One also uses the terms "truncated sampling" and "truncated samples" to refer to sampling from a truncated distribution. (This terminology should not be confused with the wholly different concept of truncation in sequential analysis.)

In *censored sampling,* observations are measured only above a, only below b, or only between a and b; but in addition it is known how many unmeasured observations occur below a and above b. Censorship on the left corresponds to measuring observations only above a; censorship on the right corresponds to measuring only below b; and double censorship corresponds to measuring only between a and b. In the case of double censorship, the total sample consists of l, the number of observations to the left of the lower limit a; r, the number of observations to the right of the upper limit b; and $X_1, \cdots, X_n$, the values of the observations occurring between the limits. In one-sided censorship, either l or r is 0. A second kind of censorship arises when, without regard to given limits a or b, the l

smallest and/or r largest observations are identified but not measured. This is type II censorship. In consequence, "type I censoring" is a name applied to the case described earlier. (In older literature the word "truncation" may be used for any of the foregoing.)

Some of the definitions mentioned above may be illustrated by the following examples:

Suppose X is the most advanced year of school attained for people born in 1930 where the information is obtained by following up records of those who entered high school; then the distribution is truncated on the left, because every possible observation is forced to be larger than 8. In particular, every observation of a sample from this distribution must be larger than 8. Censorship on the left, in this case, would occur if the sample were drawn from the population of people born in 1930 and if, in addition to noting the most advanced year of school attained by those who entered high school, the number of sample members who did not enter high school were ascertained. Similarly, if two hours is allowed for an examination and the time of submission is recorded only for late papers, the distribution of time taken to write the examination is censored on the left at two hours.

Truncation on the right would apply to a 1967 study of longevity of people born in 1910, as inferred from a comprehensive survey of death certificates. Censorship on the right would occur in this case if the sample were based on birth certificates, rather than death certificates, since then the number of individuals with longevity exceeding the upper observable limit would be known.

The distribution of height of U.S. Navy enlistees in records of naval personnel is a doubly truncated distribution because of minimum and maximum height requirements for enlistment. An example of type II censorship on the right would be given by the dates of receipt of the first 70 responses to a questionnaire that had been sent out to 100 people.

Goals. In dealing with truncated distributions, a key issue is whether the conclusions that are sought should be applicable to the entire population or only to the truncated population itself. For instance, since the navy, in purchasing uniforms, need consider only those it enlists, the truncated, not the untruncated, population is the one of interest. On the other hand, if an anthropologist wished to use extensive navy records for estimating the height distribution of the entire population or its mean height, his inferences would be directed, not to the truncated population itself, but to the untruncated population. (Perhaps this anthropologist should not use naval enlistees at all, since the sample may not be representative for other reasons,

such as educational requirements and socioeconomic factors.) In a study in which treated cancer patients are followed up for five years (or until death, if that comes sooner), the observed survival times would be from a distribution truncated on the right. This is also a natural example of censored sampling. The censored sample would provide the information relevant to setting actuarial rates for five-year (or shorter) term insurance policies. For assessing the value of treatment the censored sample is less adequate, since the remainder of the survival-time distribution is also important.

In cases in which the truncated population itself is of interest, few essentially new problems are posed by the truncation; for example, the sample mean and variance remain unbiased estimators of these parameters of the truncated population, and (at least with large samples) statistical methods that are generally robust may ordinarily be confidently applied to a truncated distribution. On the other hand, if data from the truncated sample are to be used for reaching conclusions about the untruncated distribution, special problems do arise. For instance, the sample mean and variance are not reasonable estimators of those parameters in the untruncated distribution, nor are medians or other percentiles directly interpreted in terms of the untruncated distribution. The situation for means and variances in censored samples, although not identical, is similar.

Estimation and testing under censorship. Suppose, now, that a sample of observations is censored and that the purpose is to make estimates of parameters in the population. In this case the data consist of $l, X_1, \cdots, X_n$, and r. Let $N = l + n + r$. Usually N is regarded as fixed. For type II censorship, if both l and r are less than $N/2$, then the sample median has the same distributional properties as it would if no censorship had been imposed. Similarly, such statistics as the interquartile range, certain linear combinations of order statistics, and estimates of particular percentiles may be more or less usable, just as if censoring had not occurred (depending upon the values of l, n, and r). This fact allows censoring to be deliberately imposed with advantage where the investigator knows enough to be sure that the sample median or other interesting quantiles will be among $X_1, \cdots, X_n$ and where the cost of taking the sample is greatly reduced by avoiding exact measurement of a substantial part of the sample. Generally, the precision obtainable from a sample of size N where censorship has been imposed can never be greater than the precision obtainable from a sample of size N from the same distribution without censoring (Raja Rao 1958), but the censored sample may be cheaper to observe. Sometimes censorship is deliberately imposed for another reason. If the investigator fears that some of the observations in samples are actually errors (coming from a "contaminating" distribution), he may deliberately choose to censor the smallest one or two (or more) and the largest one or two (or more) and use only the intermediate values in the statistical analysis. Censorship of this form is called "trimming"; it is akin to a related technique called Winsorizing. [See STATISTICAL ANALYSIS, SPECIAL PROBLEMS OF, *article on* OUTLIERS; NONPARAMETRIC STATISTICS, *article on* ORDER STATISTICS.]

Since censorship will generally cause some off-center part of the distribution to be the one furnishing $X_1, \cdots, X_n$, it is clear that the sample mean, $\bar{X}$, based only on those observations will generally be a seriously biased estimator of the population mean, μ; similarly, s^2, the sample variance of $X_1, \cdots, X_n$, will tend to be too small to be a good estimator of the population variance, σ^2. Thus, in using a censored sample to reach conclusions about the parameters (other than quantiles), such as the mean and standard deviation of the population, it is necessary to make some assumptions about the underlying distribution in order to arrive at estimators with known properties.

Even with strong assumptions, it is difficult to obtain procedures such as confidence intervals of exact confidence coefficient. (Halperin 1960 gives a method for interval estimation of location and scale parameters with bounded confidence coefficient.) If samples are large, then more satisfactory results are available through asymptotic theory.

With respect to testing hypotheses where two samples singly censored at the same point are available, it has been shown by Halperin (1960) that Wilcoxon's two-sample test can be applied in an adapted form and that for samples of more than eight observations with less than 75 per cent censoring, the normal approximation to the distribution of the (suitably modified) Wilcoxon statistic holds well.

Normal distributions and censorship. The case which has been most studied is, naturally, that of the normal distribution. For type I censorship, by use of a and b, together with l, r, and $X_1, \cdots, X_n$, it is possible to calculate the maximum likelihood estimators in the normal case. The calculation is difficult and requires special tables. Among other methods for the normal distribution are those based on linear combinations of order statistics. [See NONPARAMETRIC STATISTICS, *article on* ORDER STATISTICS.]

Cohen (1959) gives a useful treatment of these problems, and a rather uncomplicated method with good properties is offered by Saw (1961), who also presents a survey of the more standard estimation methods. It is interesting to observe that a sample of size N which is censored on one side and contains n measured values is more informative about μ, the population mean, than would be an uncensored sample of n observations (Doss 1962). The additional information is obviously furnished by l (or r). The same thing is true in the estimation of σ, providing that censored observations lie in a part of the distribution with probability less than one-half (Doss 1962). Although in uncensored samples from the normal distribution the sample mean, $\bar{X}$, and standard deviation, s, are statistically independent, they are not so with one-sided censoring; indeed, the correlation between $\bar{X}$ and s grows as the fraction censored increases (Sampford 1954).

Estimation and testing under truncation. Samples from distributions truncated at points a and b generally give less information relating to that part of the distribution which has been sampled than do samples from the same distribution with censoring at those points. (In the case of type I censorship, l and r do afford some idea of whether the center or the left-hand side or the right-hand side is furnishing the observations $X_1, \cdots, X_n$.) It follows that no distribution-free relationships between percentiles, location parameters, or dispersion parameters of the untruncated distribution and the truncated one can hold. To reach any conclusions about the untruncated population, it is essential to have some assumptions about the underlying probability law.

If certain statistics are jointly sufficient for a random sample from the untruncated distribution, then those same statistics remain sufficient for a sample from the truncated distribution (Tukey 1949; Smith 1957).

The amount of information in the truncated sample may be greater than, less than, or equal to that afforded by an untruncated sample of the same size from the same distribution. Which of these alternatives applies depends upon what the underlying distribution is and how the truncation is done (Raja Rao 1958).

For the normal distribution, a truncated sample is always less informative about both μ and σ than an untruncated sample having the same number of observations (Swamy 1962). (However, an inner truncated sample from a normal distribution, that is, one in which only observations *outside* an interval are observed, may be more informative about σ^2 than an untruncated sample with the same number of observations.)

Testing two-sample hypotheses from truncated samples can be done on the basis of distributional assumptions. In addition, a little can be said about distribution-free procedures. Lehmann showed that if two continuous distributions, F and G, are being compared by Wilcoxon's test (or any rank test), where $G = F^k$, then whatever F is, the distribution of the test statistic depends only on k and the two sample sizes. Truncation on the right at point b gives the truncated cumulative distribution functions $F_b(x) = F(x)/F(b)$ and $G_b(x) = F^k(x)/F^k(b)$, so it is still true that $G_b(x) = [F_b(x)]^k$. Thus, truncation on the right does not affect the properties of Wilcoxon's test against Lehmann (1953) alternatives. On the other hand, truncation on the left at point a leads to the relations $G_a(x) = F^k(x)/[1 - F^k(a)]$ and $F_a(x) = F(x)/[1 - F(a)]$, and it is not true that $G_a(x) = [F_a(x)]^k$. Further, it can be shown that the noncentrality parameter of the test, $P(X < Y)$, declines as a grows (that is, as more and more of the distribution is truncated). Thus, truncation on the left does affect the test against Lehmann alternatives. By a similar argument, if F and G are related by $1 - G = (1 - F)^k$, then truncation on the left leaves the relationship unaltered, while truncation on the right does not.

In comparing two treatments of some disease where time to recurrence of the disease is of interest, *random* censorship is sometimes encountered. For example, death by accidental injury may intervene before the disease has recurred. Such an observation has been subjected to censorship by a random event. Problems of this sort are treated by Gehan (1965).

Bivariate cases.   The bivariate case occurs when truncation or censorship is imposed on each member of a sample, or possible sample, in terms of one variable, say, X, while another variable, Y, is the one of principal interest. For example, in studying income data, an investigator might take as his sample all tax returns submitted before the delinquency date. He would then have censored the sample on the date of submission of the tax return, but his interest would apply to some other properties of these data, such as the taxable income reported. This kind of bivariate truncation or censoring is common in social science. Estimation of the parameters of the multivariate normal distribution when there is truncation or censorship has been treated by Singh (1960) in the case of mutually independent variables. The estimation equations in the case of truncation are the usual univariate equations, which may be separately solved. But in the presence of censorship, when only the number of unobservable vectors is known and there is no information as to which components led to unobservability, the estimating equations require simultaneous solution.

If X and Y are independent, the truncation on X does not affect the distribution of Y. Otherwise, in general, it will; and it may do so very strongly. When dependence of X and Y exists, then censorship or truncation affords opportunities for large and subtle bias, on the one hand, and for experimental strategies, on the other. For example, the selection of pilots, students, domestic breeding stock, all represent choosing a sample truncated in terms of one variable (an admission score or preliminary record of performance), with a view to ensuring large values of a different variable in the truncated (retained) portion of the population. Generally, the larger the correlation between X and Y, the greater the improvement obtainable in Y by truncation on X. [*See* SCREENING AND SELECTION.]

A second example of truncation of one variable with the eye of purpose fixed on a second is afforded by "increased severity testing." This engineering method may be illustrated by taking a lot of resistors designed to tolerate a low voltage over a long service life and exposing them to a short pulse of very high voltage. Those not failing are assumed satisfactory for their intended use, provided that service life is not shortened as a result of the test. This is seen as an example of bivariate truncation if one attributes to each resistor two values: X, its service life at the high voltage, and Y, its service life at the low voltage. Truncation on X presumably increases the mean value of Y in the retained, or truncated, population. Analogues of this may have relevance for psychology in such areas as stress interviews or endurance under especially difficult experimental tasks.

In the bivariate case, truncation of one variable can greatly affect the correlation between the two variables. For example, although height and weight exhibit a fairly strong correlation in adult males, this correlation virtually disappears if we consider only males with height between 5 feet 6 inches and 5 feet 9 inches. Although there is considerable variation in weight among men of nearly the same height, little of this variation is associated with variation in height. On the other hand, *inner* truncation—omitting cases with intermediate values of one variable—will produce spuriously high correlation coefficients. Thus, in a sample of males of heights less than 5 feet 4 inches or greater than 6 feet 6 inches, virtually all the variation in weight will be associated with variation in height. In a linear regression situation, where there is inner or outer truncation, the slope of the regression line continues to be unbiasedly estimated. But the correlation coefficient has a value that may depend so strongly on the truncation (or, more generally, selection) that there may be little if any relationship between the correlations in the truncated and untruncated populations. [*See* ERRORS, *article on* NONSAMPLING ERRORS.]

To show how truncation can enormously affect the correlation coefficient, consider X and Y, two random variables with a joint distribution such that

$$Y = \alpha + \beta X + e,$$

where α and β are constants and where e is a random variable uncorrelated with X. This kind of simple linear structure frequently arises as a reasonable assumption. Assume that β is not 0.

Let σ_e^2 and σ_X^2 be the variances of e and X respectively; immediate computation then shows that the covariance between X and Y is $\beta \sigma_X^2$, while the variance of Y is $\beta^2 \sigma_X^2 + \sigma_e^2$. It follows that ρ^2, the square of the correlation coefficient between X and Y, is

$$\rho^2 = \frac{\beta^2}{\beta^2 + (\sigma_e^2 / \sigma_X^2)}.$$

Hence, if the structure stays otherwise the same but the marginal distribution of X is changed so that σ_X^2 becomes very large, ρ^2 becomes nearly unity. In particular, if the marginal distribution of X is changed by truncating *inside* the interval $(-d, d)$, it is readily shown that as d becomes indefinitely large, so will σ_X^2.

Similarly, if σ_X^2 becomes nearly 0, so will ρ^2. In particular, if X is truncated outside a small enough interval, σ_X^2 will indeed become nearly 0.

Still more difficulties arise if truncation in a bivariate (or multivariate) population is accomplished not by truncation on X or Y alone but on a function of them. If X and Y were utterly independent and a sample were drawn subject to the restraint $|X - Y| \leqslant a$, then all the points (X, Y) in the sample would be required to lie in a diagonal strip of slope 1 and vertical (or horizontal) width $2a$ units. Obviously, very high "correlation" might be observed! Some follow-up studies embody a bias of just this form. Suppose that survival of husband and wife is to be studied by following up all couples married during a period of 40 years. Suppose further that A_H, the age of the husband at marriage, and A_W, the age of the wife at marriage, are highly correlated (as they are) and that L_H and L_W, their lifetimes, are completely independent of each other statistically. Then the correlation between L_H and L_W observed in a follow-up study may be very high

or very low, depending upon how the sample is truncated. Consider several methods:

(1) All couples married in the 40-year period are followed up until all have died—making a study of about a hundred years' duration; then there is no truncation of L_H or L_W, and since (by assumption) they are statistically independent, the observed correlation will, except for sampling error, be zero.

(2) All couples whose members have both died during the 41st year of the study furnish the sample values of L_H and L_W; now there will be a very high correlation. Write $L_H = A_H + T_H$ and $L_W = A_W + T_W$, where T represents life length after marriage. The curious sampling scheme just proposed ensures that $|T_H - T_W| \leqslant 1$, so T_H and T_W are highly correlated and A_H and A_W are also correlated; hence L_H and L_W in such a truncated sample will be highly correlated.

(3) All couples whose members have both died by the end of the 40th year (the cases "complete" by then) furnish the data. In this not infrequently used design, a fictitious correlation will be found. Those couples married during the last year and with both members dead will have values of T_H and T_W which are nearly equal, and they will have correlated values of A_H and A_W; such couples will contribute strongly to a positive correlation. Those couples married two years before the end of the study and with both members dead will have values of T_H and T_W differing at most by 2, and correlated values of A_H and A_W; they will also contribute—not quite so strongly—to a positive correlation. By continuation of this reasoning, it is seen that the same kind of bias (diminishing with progress toward the earliest marriage) affects the entire sample. A detailed numerical example of this problem is given by Myers (1963).

It is probably wise to view with great caution studies that are multivariate in character (involve several observable random aspects) and at the same time use samples heavily truncated or censored on one or more of the variables or—especially—on combinations of them.

LINCOLN E. MOSES

BIBLIOGRAPHY

COHEN, A. CLIFFORD JR. 1959 Simplified Estimators for the Normal Distribution When Samples Are Singly Censored or Truncated. *Technometrics* 2:217–237.

DOSS, S. A. D. C. 1962 On the Efficiency of BAN Estimates of the Parameters of Normal Populations Based on Singly Censored Samples. *Biometrika* 49:570–573.

GEHAN, EDMUND A. 1965 A Generalized Wilcoxon Test for Comparing Arbitrarily Singly-censored Samples. *Biometrika* 52:203–223.

HALPERIN, MAX 1960 Extension of the Wilcoxon–Mann–Whitney Test to Samples Censored at the Same Fixed Point. *Journal of the American Statistical Association* 55:125–138.

LEHMANN, E. L. 1953 The Power of Rank Tests. *Annals of Mathematical Statistics* 24:23–43.

MYERS, ROBERT J. 1963 An Instance of the Pitfalls Prevalent in Graveyard Research. *Biometrics* 19:638–650.

RAJA RAO, B. 1958 On the Relative Efficiencies of BAN Estimates Based on Doubly Truncated and Censored Samples. National Institute of Science, India, *Proceedings* 24:366–376.

SAMPFORD, M. R. 1954 The Estimation of Response-time Distributions: III. Truncation and Survival. *Biometrics* 10:531–561.

SAW, J. G. 1961 Estimation of the Normal Population Parameters Given a Type I Censored Sample. *Biometrika* 48:367–377.

SINGH, NAUNIHAL 1960 Estimation of Parameters of a Multivariate Normal Population From Truncated and Censored Samples. *Journal of the Royal Statistical Society* Series B 22:307–311.

SMITH, WALTER L. 1957 A Note on Truncation and Sufficient Statistics. *Annals of Mathematical Statistics* 28:247–252.

SWAMY, P. S. 1962 On the Joint Efficiency of the Estimates of the Parameters of Normal Populations Based on Singly and Doubly Truncated Samples. *Journal of the American Statistical Association* 57:46–53.

TUKEY, JOHN W. 1949 Sufficiency, Truncation, and Selection. *Annals of Mathematical Statistics* 20:309–311.

STATISTICAL IDENTIFIABILITY

Identifiability is a statistical concept referring to the difficulty of distinguishing among two or more explanations of the same empirical phenomena. Unlike traditional statistical problems (for example, estimation and hypothesis testing), identifiability does not refer to sampling fluctuations stemming from limited data; rather, nonidentifiability, or the inability to distinguish among explanations, would exist even if the statistical distribution of the observables were fully known.

A model represents an attempt to describe, explain, or predict the values of certain variables as the outputs of a formally described mechanism. Yet it is evident that given any specified set of facts or observations to be explained, an infinite number of models are capable of doing so. One way of describing all scientific work is as the task of distinguishing among such eligible models by the introduction of further information.

The problem of identification, as usually encountered, is essentially the same phenomenon in a more restricted context. Suppose that the *form* of the explanatory model is regarded as specified, but

that it involves unknown parameters. Suppose further that the observational material to be explained is so abundant that the basic statistical distributions may be regarded as known. (In practice this will rarely be the case, but identifiability considerations require thinking in these terms.) An important task then is to select from all possible *structures* (sets of values for the unknown parameters) contained in the model the particular one that, according to some criterion, best fits the observations. It may happen, however, that there are two, several, or even an infinite number of structures generating precisely the same distribution for the observations. In this case no amount of observation consistent with the model can distinguish among such structures. The structures in question are thus *observationally equivalent*.

It may, however, be the case that some specific parameter or set of parameters is the same in all observationally equivalent structures. In such a case, that set is said to be *identifiable*. Parameters whose values are not the same for all observationally equivalent structures are not identifiable; their values can never be recovered solely by use of observations generated by the model.

In its simplest form lack of identifiability is easy to recognize. Suppose, for example, that a random variable, X, is specified by the model to be distributed normally, with expectation or mean the difference between two unknown parameters, $EX = \theta_1 - \theta_2$. It is evident that observations on X can be used to estimate $\theta_1 - \theta_2$, which is identifiable, but that the individual parameters, θ_1 and θ_2, are not identifiable. The θ_i can be recovered only by combining outside information with observations on X or by changing the whole observational scheme. In cases such as this, the θ_i are sometimes said not to be *estimable*. Observations on X do restrict the θ_i, since their difference can be consistently estimated, but can never distinguish the true θ_i generating the observations from among all θ_i with the same difference. Although one way of describing the situation is to note that the likelihood function for a random sample has no unique maximum but has a ridge along the line $\theta_1 - \theta_2 = \bar{x}$, the sample average, it is instructive to note further that the problem persists even if the model is non-stochastic and X is a constant.

(In the context of the general linear hypothesis model, the concept of *estimability* has been developed by R. C. Bose, C. R. Rao, and others, apparently independently of the more general identifiability concept. [*See* LINEAR HYPOTHESES, *article on* REGRESSION; *for history, references, and dis-*

cussion, see Reiersøl 1964.] Estimability of a linear parameter, in the linear hypothesis context, means that an unbiased estimator of the parameter exists; within its domain of discussion, estimability is equivalent to identifiability.)

In more complicated cases, lack of identifiability may be less easy to recognize. Because of rounding errors or sample properties, numerical "estimates" of unidentifiable parameters may be obtained, although such estimates are meaningless. As a fanciful, although pertinent, example, suppose that in the situation of the previous paragraph there were two independent observations on X, say, X_1 and X_2, and that, by rounding or other error, these observations were regarded as having expectations not quite equal to $\theta_1 - \theta_2$, say,

$$EX_1 = .99\theta_1 - 1.01\theta_2,$$
$$EX_2 = 1.01\theta_1 - .99\theta_2.$$

It is then easy to see that the least squares (and maximum likelihood) estimators would appear to exist and would be

$$\hat{\theta}_1 = -\frac{99}{4}X_1 + \frac{101}{4}X_2,$$

$$\hat{\theta}_2 = -\frac{101}{4}X_1 + \frac{99}{4}X_2,$$

so that $\hat{\theta}_1 - \hat{\theta}_2 = \frac{1}{2}(X_1 + X_2)$, which last does make good sense. The effect of underlying nonidentifiability, with the coefficients slightly altered from unity, is that the variance of $\hat{\theta}_1$ (or $\hat{\theta}_2$) is very large, about 2,500 times the variance of $\frac{1}{2}(X_1 + X_2)$.

In other cases numerical estimates may be obtained in finite samples when in fact no consistent estimator exists and, for example, the matrix inverted in obtaining the numbers is guaranteed to be singular in the probability limit. In such cases it is of considerable interest to know what restrictions on the form or parameters of the model are necessary or sufficient for the identification of subsets of parameters. Analyses of identifiability are typically devoted to this question.

The identification problem can arise in many contexts. Wherever a reasonably complicated underlying mechanism generates the observations, and the parameters of that mechanism are to be estimated, the identification problem may be encountered. Examples are factor analysis and the analysis of latent structures. [See FACTOR ANALYSIS and LATENT STRUCTURE; for the analysis of identifiability in factor analysis, see Reiersøl 1950a.] A further example occurs in the analysis of accident statistics, where the occurrence of approximately negative binomial counts led to the concept of accident proneness on the false assumption that

a negative binomial can *only* be generated as a mixture of Poisson distributions. [*See* DISTRIBUTIONS, STATISTICAL, *articles on* SPECIAL DISCRETE DISTRIBUTIONS *and* MIXTURES OF DISTRIBUTIONS; FALLACIES, STATISTICAL.]

An important case, and one in which the analysis is rich, is that of a system of simultaneous equations such as those frequently encountered in econometrics. The remainder of this article is accordingly devoted to a discussion of identifiability in that context.

Identifiability of a structural equation

Suppose the model to be investigated is given by

$$(1) \qquad \boldsymbol{u}_t = \boldsymbol{A}\boldsymbol{x}_t = [\mathbf{B} \quad \boldsymbol{\Gamma}] \begin{bmatrix} \boldsymbol{y}_t \\ \boldsymbol{z}_t \end{bmatrix},$$

where $\boldsymbol{u}_t$ is an M-component column vector of random disturbances (with properties to be specified below) and $\boldsymbol{x}_t$ is an N-component column vector of variables, partitioned into $\boldsymbol{y}_t$, the M-component vector of *endogenous* variables to be explained by the model, and $\boldsymbol{z}_t$, the $\Lambda = (N - M)$-component vector of *predetermined* variables determined outside the current working of the model (one element of $\boldsymbol{z}_t$ can be taken to be identically unity).

The elements of $\boldsymbol{z}_t$ can thus either be determined entirely outside the model (for example, they can be treated as fixed) or represent lagged values of the elements of $\boldsymbol{y}_t$. The assumption that $\boldsymbol{z}_t$ is determined outside the current working of the model requires, in any case, that movements in the elements of $\boldsymbol{u}_t$ not produce movements in those of $\boldsymbol{z}_t$. In its weakest form this becomes the assumption that the elements of $\boldsymbol{z}_t$ are asymptotically uncorrelated with those of $\boldsymbol{u}_t$, in the sense that

$$\operatorname*{plim}_{T \to \infty} \left\{ \frac{1}{T} \sum_{t=1}^{T} \boldsymbol{z}_t' \boldsymbol{u}_t \right\} = 0,$$

where the prime denotes transposition and plim denotes stochastic convergence (convergence in probability). As with all prior assumptions required for identification, this assumption is quite untestable within the framework of the model.

The t subscript denotes the number of the observation and will be omitted henceforth. In (1), $\boldsymbol{A}$ is an $M \times N$ matrix of parameters to be estimated and is partitioned into $\mathbf{B}$ and $\boldsymbol{\Gamma}$, corresponding to the partitioning of $\boldsymbol{x}$. As the endogenous variables are to be explained by the model, $\mathbf{B}$ (an $M \times M$ square matrix) is assumed nonsingular. Finally, the $\boldsymbol{u}$ vectors for different values of t are usually assumed (serially) uncorrelated, with common mean $\mathbf{0}$ and with common covariance matrix $\boldsymbol{\Sigma}$. Thus, $\boldsymbol{\Sigma}$ is $M \times M$ and is in general unknown and not diagonal, as its typical element is the covariance between contemporaneous disturbances from different equations of the model. (Normality of u is also generally assumed for estimation purposes but has so far been of little relevance for identifiability discussions in the present context; for its importance in another context, see Reiersøl 1950b.)

Such models occur frequently in econometrics, in contexts ranging from the analysis of particular markets to studies of entire economies. The study of identification and, especially, estimation in such models has occupied much of the econometric literature since Haavelmo's pathbreaking article (1943).

For definiteness, this article will concentrate on the identifiability of the first equation of (1), that is, on the identifiability of the elements of the first row of A, denoted by A_1. In general, one is content if A_1 is identifiable after the imposition of a normalization rule, since the units in which the variables are measured are arbitrary. This will be understood when A_1 is spoken of as identifiable.

It is not hard to show that the joint distribution of the elements of y, given z, depends only on the parameters Π and Ω of the *reduced form* of the model,

$$(2) \quad \begin{aligned} y &= \Pi z + v, \\ \Pi &= -B^{-1}\Gamma, \\ v &= B^{-1}u, \\ \Omega &= B^{-1}\Sigma B^{-1\prime}, \end{aligned}$$

so that observations generated by the model can at most be used to estimate Π and Ω (the variance–covariance matrix of the elements of v). Since the elements of z are assumed asymptotically uncorrelated with those of u, such estimation can be consistently done by ordinary least squares regression, provided that the asymptotic variance–covariance matrix of the elements of z exists. On the other hand, if (1) is premultiplied by any nonsingular $M \times M$ matrix, the resulting structure has the same reduced form as the original one, so that all such structures are observationally equivalent. Unless outside information is available restricting the class of such transformations to those preserving A_1 (up to a scalar multiple), A_1 is not identifiable.

Examination of the nonstochastic case, in which $u = 0$, provides another way to describe the phenomenon. Here the investigator can, at most, obtain values of the Λ predetermined variables and observe the consequences for the endogenous variables. This can be done in, at most, Λ independent ways. Let the N-rowed matrix whose tth column consists of the tth observation on x so generated be denoted by X. Then X has rank Λ in the most favorable circumstances (which are assumed to hold here), and $AX = 0$. It is easy to see that Π can be recovered from this.

On the other hand, $A_1X = 0$ expresses all that observational evidence can tell about A_1. Since X has rank Λ and has $M = N - \Lambda$ rows and since A has rank M, the rows of A are a basis for the row null space of X, whence the true A_1 can be distinguished by observational information from all vectors which are not linear combinations of the rows of A but not from vectors which are. The second part of this corresponds to the obvious fact that, without further information, there is nothing to distinguish the first equation of (1) from any linear combination of those equations. If, returning to the stochastic case, one replaces X by $\begin{bmatrix} \Pi \\ I \end{bmatrix}$, the same analysis remains valid. The condition that $A_1 \begin{bmatrix} \Pi \\ I \end{bmatrix} = 0$ embodies all the information about A_1 which can be gleaned from the reduced form, and the reduced form, as has been noted, is all that can be recovered from observational evidence, even in indefinitely large samples.

This is the general form of the classic example (Working 1927) of a supply and a demand curve, both of which are straight lines [*see* DEMAND AND SUPPLY]. Only the intersection of the two curves is observable, and the demand curve cannot be distinguished from the supply curve or any other straight line through that intersection. Even if the example is made stochastic, the problem clearly remains unless the stochastic or other specification provides further (nonobservational) information enabling the demand curve to be identified.

Thus, the identification problem in this context is as follows: what necessary or sufficient conditions on prior information can be stated so that A_1 can be distinguished (up to scalar multiplication) from all other vectors in the row space of A? Equivalently, what are necessary or sufficient conditions on prior information that permit the recovery of A_1, given Π and Ω?

If A_1 cannot be so recovered, the first equation of (1) is called *underidentified*; if, given any Π and Ω, there is a unique way of recovering A_1, that equation is called *just identified*; if the prior information is so rich as to enable the recovery of A_1 in two or more different and nonequivalent ways, that equation is called *overidentified*. In the last case, while the true reduced form yields the same A_1 whichever way of recovery is followed, this is in general not true of sample estimates obtained without imposing restrictions on the reduced form. The problem of using overidentifying information to avoid this difficulty and to secure greater efficiency is the central problem of simultaneous equation estimation but is different in kind from the identification problem discussed here (although the two overlap, as seen below).

Homogeneous linear restrictions on a single equation

The most common type of prior identifying information is the specification that certain variables in the system do not in fact appear in the first equation of (1), that is, that certain elements of A_1 are zero. Such exclusion restrictions form the leading special case of homogeneous linear restrictions on the elements of A_1.

Thus, suppose φ to be an $N \times K$ matrix of known elements, such that $A_1\varphi = 0$. Since A_1 can be distinguished by observational information from any vector not in the row space of A, it is obviously sufficient, for the identification of A_1, that the equation $(\eta'A)\varphi = 0$ be satisfied only for η' a scalar multiple of $(1 \quad 0 \quad \cdots \quad 0)$. If there is no further information on A_1, this is also necessary. This condition is clearly equivalent to the requirement that the rank of $A\varphi$ be $M - 1$, a condition known as the *rank condition*, which is due to Koopmans, Rubin, and Leipnik (1950, pp. 81–82), as is much of the basic work in this area.

Since the rank of $A\varphi$ cannot exceed that of φ, a necessary condition for the identifiability of A_1 under the stated restrictions is that the number of those restrictions which are independent be at least $M - 1$, a requirement known as the *order condition*. In the case of exclusion restrictions, this becomes the condition that the number of predetermined variables excluded from the first equation of (1) must be at least as great as the number of included endogenous variables.

While the order condition does not depend on unknown parameters, the rank condition does. However, if the order condition holds and the rank condition does not fail identically (because of restrictions on the other rows of A), then the rank condition holds almost everywhere in the space of the elements of A. This has led to a neglect of the rank condition in particular problems, a neglect that can be dangerous, since the rank condition may fail identically even if the order condition holds. Asymptotic tests of identifiability (and of *over*identifying restrictions) are known for the linear restriction case and should be used in doubtful cases.

The difference between the rank of $A\varphi$ (appearing in the rank condition) and the rank of φ (appearing in the order condition) is the number of restrictions on the reduced form involving φ (see Fisher 1966, pp. 45–51).

Other restrictions

The case of restrictions other than those just discussed was chiefly investigated by Fisher, in a series of articles leading to a book (Fisher 1966), which in part examined questions opened by Koopmans, Rubin, and Leipnik (1950, pp. 93–110; Wald 1950, on identification of individual parameters, should also be mentioned). While generalizations of the rank and order conditions tend to have a prominent place in the discussion, other results are also available. The restrictions considered fall into two categories: first, restrictions on the elements of Σ; second, more general restrictions on the elements of A_1.

Working (1927) had observed, for example, that if the supply curve is known to shift greatly relative to the demand curve, the latter is traced out by the intersection points. When such shifting is due to a variable present in one equation but not in the other, the identifiability of the latter is due to an exclusion restriction. On the other hand, such shifting may be due to a greater disturbance variance, which suggests that restrictions on the relative magnitude of the diagonal elements of Σ can be used for identification. This is indeed the case, provided those restrictions are carefully stated. The results are related to the conditions for the *proximity theorem* of Wold (1953, p. 189) as to the negligible bias (or inconsistency) of least squares when the disturbance variance or the correlations between disturbance and regressors are small.

Wold's work (1953, pp. 14, 49–53, and elsewhere) on recursive systems, which showed least squares to be an appropriate estimator if B is triangular and Σ diagonal, and Fisher's matrix generalization (1961) to block-recursive systems, suggested the study of identifiability in such cases and the extension to other cases in which particular off-diagonal elements of Σ are known to be zero (disturbances from particular pairs of equations uncorrelated). Special cases had been considered by Koopmans, Rubin, and Leipnik (1950, pp. 103–105) and by Koopmans in his classic expository article (1953, p. 34). Aside from the generalization of the rank and order conditions, the results show clearly the way in which such restrictions interact with those on A to make the identifiability of one equation depend on that of others.

Finally, certain special cases and the fact that equations nonlinear in the parameters can frequently (by Taylor series expansion) be made linear in the parameters but nonlinear in the variables, with nonlinear constraints on the parameters, led to the study of identification with nonlinear (or nonhomogeneous) constraints on A_1. This is a much more difficult problem than those already discussed, as it may easily happen that the true A_1 can be distinguished from any other vector in some neighborhood of A_1 without over-all identifiability holding. As might be expected, local results (based on the rank and order conditions) are fairly easy to obtain, but useful global results are rather meager.

Other specifications of the model

The Taylor series argument just mentioned, as well as the frequent occurrence of models differing from (1) in that they are linear in the parameters and disturbances but not in the variables, also led Fisher to consider identifiability for such models. In these models, it may turn out that nonlinear transformations of the structure lead to equations in the same form as the first one, so that the result that A_1 can be observationally distinguished from vectors not in the row space of A can fail to hold (although such cases seem fairly special). Provided a systematic procedure is followed for expanding the model to include all linearly independent equations resulting from such transformations, the rank and order conditions can be applied directly to the expanded model. In such application, linearly independent functions of the same variable are counted as separate variables. It is clear also that such nonlinear transformations are restricted if there is information on the distribution of the disturbances, but the implications of this remain to be worked out.

A somewhat similar situation arises when the assumption that the elements of u are not serially correlated is dropped and the elements of z include lagged values of the endogenous variables. In this case it is possible that the lagging of an equation can be used together with linear transformation of the model to destroy identification. In such cases there may be underidentified equations of the reduced form as well as of the structure. This possibility was pointed out in an example by Koopmans, Rubin, and Leipnik (1950, pp. 109–110) but was shown to be of somewhat limited significance by Fisher (1966, pp. 168–175). He showed that the problem cannot arise if there is sufficient independent movement among the present and lagged values of the truly exogenous variables, a result connected to one of those for models nonlinear in the variables. In such cases the rank condition remains

necessary and sufficient. The problem in nearly or completely self-contained models awaits further analysis.

Is identifiability discrete or continuous?

Identifiability is apparently a discrete phenomenon. A set of parameters apparently either is or is not identifiable. This was emphasized by Liu (1960, for example), who pointed out that the prior restrictions used to achieve identification, like the very specification of the model itself, are invariably only approximations. Liu argued strongly that if the true, exact specification and prior restrictions were written down, the interrelatedness of economic phenomena would generally make structural equations underidentified.

Liu's argument that badly misspecified structures and restrictions that are used to lead to identification in fact only lead to trouble is clearly true; true, also, is his contention that econometric models and restrictions are only approximations and that those approximations may not be good ones. More troublesome than this, however, are the apparent implications of his argument as to the possibility of having a "good" approximation. If identifiability disappears as soon as any approximation enters in certain ways, no matter how close that approximation might be to the truth, then structural estimation ceases altogether to be possible.

This issue of principle was settled by Fisher (1961), who showed that identifiability can be considered continuous, in the sense that the probability limits of estimators known to be consistent under correct specification approach the true parameters as the specification errors approach zero, a generalization of Wold's proximity theorem. If the equation to be estimated is identifiable under correct specification, the commission of minor specification errors leads to only minor inconsistency.

A number of other questions are then raised, however. Among them are the following: How good does an approximation have to be to lead to only minor inconsistency? To what extent should only approximate restrictions be imposed to achieve identification? What about overidentification, where the trade-off may be between consistency and minor gains in variance reduction? What can be said about the relative robustness of the different simultaneous equation estimators to the sorts of minor specification error discussed by Liu?

Clearly, once identifiability is considered continuous, the identification problem tends to merge with the estimation problem, rather than be logically prior to it. It seems likely that both can best be approached through an explicit recognition of the approximate nature of specification, for example, by a Bayesian analysis with exact prior restrictions replaced by prior distributions on the functions of the parameters to be restricted [*see* BAYESIAN INFERENCE]. Work on this formidable problem is just beginning (see, for example, Drèze 1962; Reiersøl 1964).

FRANKLIN M. FISHER

[*See also* DISTRIBUTIONS, STATISTICAL, *article on* MIXTURES OF DISTRIBUTIONS; LATENT STRUCTURE; SIMULTANEOUS EQUATION ESTIMATION.]

BIBLIOGRAPHY

DRÈZE, JACQUES 1962 The Bayesian Approach to Simultaneous Equations Estimation. O.N.R. Research Memorandum No. 67. Unpublished manuscript, Northwestern University.

FISHER, FRANKLIN M. 1961 On the Cost of Approximate Specification in Simultaneous Equation Estimation. *Econometrica* 29:139–170.

FISHER, FRANKLIN M. 1966 *The Identification Problem in Econometrics.* New York: McGraw-Hill.

HAAVELMO, TRYGVE 1943 The Statistical Implications of a System of Simultaneous Equations. *Econometrica* 11:1–12.

KOOPMANS, TJALLING C. 1953 Identification Problems in Economic Model Construction. Pages 27–48 in William C. Hood and Tjalling C. Koopmans (editors), *Studies in Econometric Method.* Cowles Commission for Research in Economics, Monograph No. 14. New York: Wiley.

KOOPMANS, TJALLING C.; RUBIN, H.; and LEIPNIK, R. B. (1950) 1958 Measuring the Equation Systems of Dynamic Economics. Pages 53–237 in Tjalling C. Koopmans (editor), *Statistical Inference in Dynamic Economic Models.* Cowles Commission for Research in Economics, Monograph No. 10. New York: Wiley.

LIU, TA-CHUNG 1960 Underidentification, Structural Estimation, and Forecasting. *Econometrica* 28:855–865.

REIERSØL, OLAV 1950a On the Identifiability of Parameters in Thurstone's Multiple Factor Analysis. *Psychometrika* 15:121–149.

REIERSØL, OLAV 1950b Identifiability of a Linear Relation Between Variables Which Are Subject to Error. *Econometrica* 18:375–389.

REIERSØL, OLAV 1964 Identifiability, Estimability, Phenorestricting Specifications, and Zero Lagrange Multipliers in the Analysis of Variance. *Skandinavisk aktuarietidskrift* 46:131–142.

WALD, A. (1950) 1958 Note on the Identification of Economic Relations. Pages 238–244 in Tjalling C. Koopmans (editor), *Statistical Inference in Dynamic Economic Models.* Cowles Commission for Research in Economics, Monograph No. 10. New York: Wiley.

WOLD, HERMAN 1953 *Demand Analysis: A Study in Econometrics.* New York: Wiley.

WORKING, E. J. (1927) 1952 What Do Statistical "Demand Curves" Show? Pages 97–115 in American Economic Association, *Readings in Price Theory.* Edited by G. J. Stigler and K. E. Boulding. Homewood, Ill.: Irwin. → First published in Volume 41 of the *Quarterly Journal of Economics.*

STATISTICAL INFERENCE
See STATISTICS, *article on* THE FIELD.

STATISTICS

The articles under this heading provide an introduction to the field of statistics and to its history. The first article also includes a survey of the statistical articles in the encyclopedia. At the end of the second article there is a list of the biographical articles that are of relevance to statistics.

I. THE FIELD — *William H. Kruskal*
II. THE HISTORY OF STATISTICAL METHOD — *M. G. Kendall*

I
THE FIELD

A scientist confronted with empirical observations goes from them to some sort of inference, decision, action, or conclusion. The end point of this process may be the confirmation or denial of some complicated theory; it may be a decision about the next experiment to carry out; or it may simply be a narrowing of the presumed range for some constant of nature. (The end point may even be the conclusion that the observations are worthless.) An end point is typically accompanied by a statement, or at least by a feeling, of how sure the scientist is of his new ground.

These inferential leaps are, of course, never made only in the light of the immediate observations. There is always a body of background knowledge and intuition, in part explicit and in part tacit. It is the essence of science that a leap to a false position—whether because of poor observational data, misleading background, or bad leaping form—is sooner or later corrected by future research.

Often the leaps are made without introspection or analysis of the inferential process itself, as a skilled climber might step from one boulder to another on easy ground. On the other hand, the slope may be steep and with few handholds; before moving, one wants to reflect on direction, where one's feet will be, and the consequences of a slip.

Statistics is concerned with the inferential process, in particular with the planning and analysis of experiments or surveys, with the nature of observational errors and sources of variability that obscure underlying patterns, and with the efficient summarizing of sets of data. There is a fuzzy boundary, to be discussed below, between statistics and other parts of the philosophy of science.

Problems of inference from empirical data arise,

not only in scientific activity, but also in everyday life and in areas of public policy. For example, the design and analysis of the 1954 Salk vaccine tests in the United States were based on statistical concepts of randomization and control. Both private and public economic decisions sometimes turn on the meaning and accuracy of summary figures from complex measurement programs: the unemployment rate, the rate of economic growth, a consumer price index. Sometimes a lack of statistical background leads to misinterpretations of accident and crime statistics. Misinterpretations arising from insufficient statistical knowledge may also occur in the fields of military and diplomatic intelligence.

There is busy two-way intellectual traffic between statisticians and other scientists. Psychologists and physical anthropologists have instigated and deeply influenced developments in that branch of statistics called multivariate analysis; sociologists sometimes scold statisticians for not paying more attention to the inferential problems arising in surveys of human populations; some economists are at once consumers and producers of statistical methods.

Theoretical and applied statistics.   Theoretical statistics is the formal study of the process leading from observations to inference, decision, or whatever be the end point, insofar as the process can be abstracted from special empirical contexts. This study is not the psychological one of how scientists actually make inferences or decisions; rather, it deals with the consequences of particular modes of inference or decision, and seeks normatively to find good modes in the light of explicit criteria.

Theoretical statistics must proceed in terms of a more or less formal language, usually mathematical, and in any specific area must make assumptions—weak or strong—on which to base the formal analysis. Far and away the most important mathematical language in statistics is that of probability, because most statistical thinking is in terms of randomness, populations, masses, the single event embedded in a large class of events. Even approaches like that of personal probability, in which single events are basic, use a highly probabilistic language. [*See* PROBABILITY.]

But theoretical statistics is not, strictly speaking, a branch of mathematics, although mathematical concepts and tools are of central importance in much of statistics. Some important areas of theoretical statistics may be discussed and advanced without recondite mathematics, and much notable work in statistics has been done by men with modest mathematical training. [*For discussion of nonstatistical applications of mathematics in the social sciences, see, for example,* MATHEMATICS; MODELS, MATHEMATICAL; *and the material on mathematical economics in* ECONOMETRICS.]

Applied statistics, at least in principle, is the informed application of methods that have been theoretically investigated, the actual leap after the study of leaping theory. In fact, matters are not so simple. First, theoretical study of a statistical procedure often comes after its intuitive proposal and use. Second, there is almost no end to the possible theoretical study of even the simplest procedure. Practice and theory interact and weave together, so that many statisticians are practitioners one day (or hour) and theoreticians the next.

The art of applied statistics requires sensitivity to the ways in which theoretical assumptions may fail to hold, and to the effects that such failure may have, as well as agility in modifying and extending already studied methods. Thus, applied statistics in the study of public opinion is concerned with the design and analysis of opinion surveys. The main branch of theoretical statistics used here is that of sample surveys, although other kinds of theory may also be relevant—for example, the theory of Markov chains may be useful for panel studies, where the *same* respondents are asked their opinions at successive times. Again, applied statistics in the study of learning includes careful design and analysis of controlled laboratory experiments, whether with worms, rats, or humans. The statistical theories that enter might be those of experimental design, of analysis of variance, or of quantal response. Of course, nonstatistical, substantive knowledge about the empirical field—public opinion, learning, or whatever—is essential for good applied statistics.

Statistics is a young discipline, and the number of carefully studied methods, although steadily growing, is still relatively small. In the applications of statistics, therefore, one usually reaches a point of balance between thinking of a specific problem in formal terms, which are rarely fully adequate (few problems are standard), and using methods that are not as well understood as one might hope. (For a stimulating, detailed discussion of this theme, see Tukey 1962, where the term "data analysis" is used to mean something like applied statistics.)

The word "statistics" is sometimes used to mean, not a general approach like the one I have outlined, but—more narrowly—the body of specific statistical methods, with associated formulas, tables, and traditions, that are currently understood and used. Other uses of the word are common, but they are not likely to cause confusion. In particular, "statistics" often refers to a set of numbers describing some empirical field, as when one speaks of the mortality statistics of France in 1966. Again, "a statistic" often means some numerical quantity computed from basic observations.

Variability and error; patterns. If life were stable, simple, and routinely repetitious, there would be little need for statistical thinking. But there would probably be no human beings to do statistical thinking, because sufficient stability and simplicity would not allow the genetic randomness that is a central mechanism of evolution. Life is not, in fact, stable or simple, but there are stable and simple aspects to it. From one point of view, the goal of science is the discovery and elucidation of these aspects, and statistics deals with some general methods of finding patterns that are hidden in a cloud of irrelevancies, of natural variability, and of error-prone observations or measurements.

Most statistical thinking is in terms of variability and errors in observed data, with the aim of reaching conclusions about obscured underlying patterns. What is meant by natural variability and by errors of measurement? First, distinct experimental and observational units generally have different characteristics and behave in different ways: people vary in their aptitudes and skills; some mice learn more quickly than others. Second, when a quantity or quality is measured, there is usually an error of measurement, and this introduces a second kind of dispersion with which statistics deals: not only will students taught by a new teaching method react in different ways, but also the test that determines how much they learn cannot be a perfect measuring instrument; medical blood-cell counts made independently by two observers from the same slide will not generally be the same.

In any particular experiment or survey, some sources of variability may usefully be treated as constants; for example, the students in the teaching experiment might all be chosen from one geographical area. Other sources of variability might be regarded as random—for example, fluctuations of test scores among students in an apparently homogeneous group. More complex intermediate forms of variability are often present. The students might be subdivided into classes taught by different teachers. Insofar as common membership in a class with the same teacher has an effect, a simple but important pattern of dependence is present.

The variability concept is mirrored in the basic notion of a *population* from which one samples. The population may correspond to an actual population of men, mice, or machines; or it may be con-

ceptual, as is a population of measurement errors. A population of numerical values defines a distribution, roughly speaking, and the notion of a *random variable*, fluctuating in its value according to this distribution, is basic. For example, if a student is chosen at random from a school and given a reading-comprehension test, the score on the test—considered in advance of student choice and test administration—is a random variable. Its distribution is an idealization of the totality of such scores if student choice and testing could be carried out a very large number of times without any changes because of the passage of time or because of interactions among students. [*For a more precise formulation, see* PROBABILITY.]

Although much statistical methodology may be regarded as an attempt to understand regularity through a cloud of obscuring variability, there are many situations in which the variability itself is the object of major interest. Some of these will be discussed below.

Planning. An important topic in statistics is that of sensible planning, or design, of empirical studies. In the above teaching example, some of the more formal aspects of design are the following: How many classes to each teaching method? How many students per class to be tested? Should variables other than test scores be used as well—for example, intelligence scores or personality ratings?

The spectrum of design considerations ranges from these to such subject-matter questions as the following: How should the teachers be trained in a new teaching method? Should teachers be chosen so that there are some who are enthusiastic and some who are skeptical of the new method? What test should be used to measure results?

No general theory of design exists to cover all, or even most, such questions. But there do exist many pieces of theory, and—more important—a valuable statistical point of view toward the planning of experiments.

History. The history of the development of statistics is described in the next article [*see* STATISTICS, *article on* THE HISTORY OF STATISTICAL METHOD]. It stresses the growth of method and theory; the history of statistics in the senses of vital statistics, government statistics, censuses, economic statistics, and the like, is described in relevant separate articles [*see* CENSUS; COHORT ANALYSIS; ECONOMIC DATA; GOVERNMENT STATISTICS; LIFE TABLES; MORTALITY; POPULATION; SOCIOLOGY, *article on* THE EARLY HISTORY OF SOCIAL RESEARCH; VITAL STATISTICS]. Two treatments of the history of statistics with special reference to the social sciences are by Lundberg (1940) and Lazarsfeld (1961).

It is important to distinguish between the history of the word "statistics" and the history of statistics in the sense of this article. The word "statistics" is related to the word "state," and originally the activity called statistics was a systematic kind of comparative political science. This activity gradually centered on numerical tables of economic, demographic, and political facts, and thus "statistics" came to mean the assembly and analysis of numerical tables. It is easy to see how the more philosophical meaning of the word, used in this article, gradually arose. Of course, the abstract study of inference from observations has a long history under various names—such as the theory of errors and probability calculus—and only comparatively recently has the word "statistics" come to have its present meaning. Even now, grotesque misunderstandings abound—for example, thinking of statistics as the routine compilation of uninteresting sets of numbers, or thinking of statistics as mainly a collection of mathematical expressions.

Functions. My description of statistics is, of course, a personal one, but one that many statisticians would generally agree with. Almost any characterization of statistics would include the following general functions:

(1) to help in summarizing and extracting relevant information from data, that is, from observed measurements, whether numerical, classificatory, ordinal, or whatever;

(2) to help in finding and evaluating patterns shown by the data, but obscured by inherent random variability;

(3) to help in the efficient design of experiments and surveys;

(4) to help communication between scientists (if a standard procedure is cited, many readers will understand without need of detail).

There are some other roles that activities called "statistical" may, unfortunately, play. Two such misguided roles are

(1) to sanctify or provide seals of approval (one hears, for example, of thesis advisers or journal editors who insist on certain formal statistical procedures, whether or not they are appropriate);

(2) to impress, obfuscate, or mystify (for example, some social science research papers contain masses of undigested formulas that serve no purpose except that of indicating what a bright fellow the author is).

Some consulting statisticians use more or less explicit declarations of responsibility, or codes, in their relationships with "clients," to protect themselves from being placed in the role of sanctifier. It is a good general rule that the empirical scientist use only statistical methods whose rationale is clear to him, even though he may not wish or be able to follow all details of mathematical derivation.

A general discussion, with an extensive bibliography, of the relationship between statistician and client is given by Deming (1965). In most applied statistics, of course, the statistician and the client are the same person.

An example. To illustrate these introductory comments, consider the following hypothetical experiment to study the effects of propaganda. Suppose that during a national political campaign in the United States, 100 college students are exposed to a motion picture film extolling the Democratic candidate, and 100 other students (the so-called control group) are not exposed to the film. Then all the students are asked to name their preferred candidate. Suppose that 95 of the first group prefer the Democratic candidate, while only 80 of the second group have that preference. What kinds of conclusions might one want about the effectiveness of the propaganda?

(There are, of course, serious questions about how the students are chosen, about the details of film and questionnaire administration, about possible interaction between students, about the artificiality of the experimental arrangement, and so on. For the moment, these questions are not discussed, although some will be touched on below.)

If the numbers preferring the Democratic candidate had been 95 and 5, a conclusion that a real effect was present would probably be reached without much concern about inferential methodology (although methodological questions would enter any attempt to estimate the magnitude of the effect). If, in contrast, the numbers had both been 95, the conclusion "no effect observed" would be immediate, although one might wonder about the possibility of observing the tie by chance even if an underlying effect were present. But by and large it is the middle ground that is of greatest statistical interest: for example, do 95 and 80 differ enough in the above context to suggest a real effect?

The simplest probability model for discussing the experiment is that of analogy with two weighted coins, each tossed 100 times. A toss of the coin corresponding to the propaganda is analogous to selecting a student at random, showing him the motion picture, and then asking him which candidate he prefers. A toss of the other coin corresponds to observing the preference of a student in the control group. "Heads" for a coin is analogous, say, to preference for the Democratic candidate. The hypothetical coins are weighted so that their probabilities of showing heads are unknown (and in general not one-half), and interest lies in the difference between these two unknown heads probabilities.

Suppose that the students are regarded as chosen randomly from some large population of students, and that for a random propagandized student there is a probability p_A of Democratic preference, whereas a random nonpropagandized student has probability p_B of Democratic preference. Suppose further that the individual observed expressions of political preference are statistically independent; roughly speaking, this means that, even if p_A and p_B were known, and it were also known which groups the students are in, prediction of one student's response from another's would be no better than prediction without knowing the other's response. (*Lack* of independence might arise in various ways, for example, if the students were able to discuss politics among themselves during the interval between the motion picture and the questionnaire.) Under the above conditions, the probabilities of various outcomes of the experiment, for any hypothetical values of p_A and p_B, may be computed in standard ways.

In fact, the underlying quantities of interest, the so-called parameters, p_A and p_B, are not known; if they were, there would be little or no reason to do the experiment. Nonetheless, it is of fundamental importance to think about possible values of the parameters and to decide what aspects are of primary importance. For example, is $p_A - p_B$ basic? or perhaps p_A/p_B? or, again, perhaps $(1 - p_B)/(1 - p_A)$, the ratio of probabilities of an expressed Republican preference (assuming that preference is between Democratic and Republican candidates only)? The choice makes a difference: if $p_A = .99$ and $p_B = .95$, use of a statistical procedure sensitive to $p_A - p_B$ (= .04 in this example) might suggest that there is little difference between the parameters, whereas a procedure sensitive to $(1 - p_B)/(1 - p_A)$ (in the example, .05/.01 = 5) might show a very large effect. These considerations are, unhappily, often neglected, and such neglect may result in a misdirected or distorted analysis. In recent discussions of possible relationships between cigarette smoking and lung cancer, controversy arose over whether ratios or differences of mortality rates were of central importance. The choice may lead to quite different conclusions.

Even apparently minor changes in graphical presentation may be highly important in the course of research. B. F. Skinner wrote of the importance to his own work of shifting from a graphical record that simply shows the times at which events occur (motion of a rat in a runway) to the logically equivalent *cumulative* record that shows the number of events up to each point of time. In the latter form, the *rate* at which events take place often becomes visually clear (see Skinner 1956, p. 225). This general area is called descriptive statistics, perhaps with the prefix "neo." [*See* STATISTICS, DESCRIPTIVE; GRAPHIC PRESENTATION; TABULAR PRESENTATION.]

As suggested above, the assumption of statistical independence might well be wrong for various reasons. One is that the 100 students in each group might be made up of five classroom groups that hold political discussions. Other errors in the assumptions are quite possible. For example, the sampling of students might not be at random from the same population: there might be self-selection, perhaps with the more enterprising students attending the motion picture. Another kind of deviation from the original simple assumptions (in this case planned) might come from balancing such factors as sex and age by stratifying according to these factors and then selecting at random within strata.

When assumptions are in doubt, one has a choice of easing them (sometimes bringing about a more complex, but a more refined, analysis) or of studying the effects of errors in the assumptions on the analysis based on them. When these effects are small, the errors may be neglected. This topic, sometimes called *robustness* against erroneous assumptions of independence, distributional form, and so on, is difficult and important. [*See* ERRORS, *article on* EFFECTS OF ERRORS IN STATISTICAL ASSUMPTIONS.]

Another general kind of question relates to the design of the experiment. Here, for example, it may be asked in advance of the experiment whether groups of 100 students are large enough (or perhaps unnecessarily large); whether there is merit in equal group sizes; whether more elaborate structures—perhaps allowing explicitly for sex and age—are desirable; and so on. Questions of this kind may call for formal statistical reasoning, but answers must depend in large part on substantive knowledge. [*See* EXPERIMENTAL DESIGN.]

It is important to recognize that using better measurement methods or recasting the framework of the experiment may be far more important aspects of design than just increasing sample size. As B. F. Skinner said,

. . . we may reduce the troublesome variability by changing the condition of the experiment. By discovering, elaborating, and fully exploiting every relevant variable, we may eliminate *in advance of measurement* the individual differences which obscure the difference under analysis.   (1956, p. 229)

In the propaganda experiment at hand, several such approaches come to mind. Restricting cneself to subjects of a given sex, age, kind of background, and so on, might bring out the effects of propaganda more clearly, perhaps at the cost of reduced generality for the results. Rather than by asking directly for political preference, the effects might be better measured by observing physiological reactions to the names or pictures of the candidates, or by asking questions about major political issues. It would probably be useful to try to follow the general principle of having each subject serve as his own control: to observe preference both before and after the propaganda and compare the numbers of switches in the two possible directions. (Even then, it would be desirable to keep the control group—possibly showing it a presumably neutral film—in order to find, and try to correct for, artificial effects of the experimental situation.)

Such questions are often investigated in side studies, ancillary or prior to the central one, and these pilot or instrumental studies are very important.

For the specific simple design with two groups, and making the simple assumptions, consider (conceptually in advance of the experiment) the two observed proportions of students expressing preference for the Democratic candidate, P_A and P_B, corresponding respectively to the propagandized and the control groups. These two *random variables*, together with the known group sizes, contain all relevant information from the experiment itself, in the sense that only the proportions, not the particular students who express one preference or another, are relevant. The argument here is one of sufficiency [*see* SUFFICIENCY, *where the argument and its limitations are discussed*]. In practice the analysis might well be refined by looking at sex of student and other characteristics, but for the moment only the simple structure is considered.

In the notational convention to be followed here, random variables (here P_A and P_B) are denoted by capital letters, and the corresponding parameters (here p_A and p_B) by parallel lower-case letters.

Estimation.   The random variables $100P_A$ and $100P_B$ have binomial probability distributions depending on p_A, p_B, and sample sizes, in this case 100 for each sample [*see* DISTRIBUTIONS, STATISTICAL, *article on* SPECIAL DISCRETE DISTRIBUTIONS]. The fundamental premise of most statistical methods is that p_A and p_B should be assessed on the basis of P_A and P_B in the light of their possible probability distributions. One of the simplest modes of

assessment is that of point estimation, in which the result of the analysis for the example consists of two numbers (depending on the observations) that are regarded as reasonable estimates of p_A and p_B [*see* ESTIMATION, *article on* POINT ESTIMATION]. In the case at hand, the usual (not the only) estimators are just P_A and P_B themselves, but even slight changes in viewpoint can make matters less clear. For example, suppose that a point estimator were wanted for p_A/p_B, the ratio of the two underlying probability parameters. It is by no means clear that P_A/P_B would be a good point estimator for this ratio.

Point estimators by themselves are usually inadequate in scientific practice, for some indication of *precision* is nearly always wanted. (There are, however, problems in which point estimators are, in effect, of primary interest: for example, in a handbook table of natural constants, or in some aspects of buying and selling.) An old tradition is to follow a point estimate by a "±" (plus-or-minus sign) and a number derived from background experience or from the data. The intent is thus to give an idea of how precise the point estimate is, of the spread or dispersion in its distribution. For the case at hand, one convention would lead to stating, as a modified estimator for p_A,

$$P_A \pm \sqrt{\frac{P_A(1-P_A)}{100}},$$

that is, the point estimator plus or minus an estimator of its standard deviation, a useful measure of dispersion. (The divisor, 100, is the sample size.) Such a device has the danger that there may be misunderstanding about the convention for the number following "±"; in addition, interpretation of the measure of dispersion may not be direct unless the distribution of the point estimator is fairly simple; the usual presumption is that the distribution is approximately of a form called normal [*see* DISTRIBUTIONS, STATISTICAL, *article on* SPECIAL CONTINUOUS DISTRIBUTIONS].

To circumvent these problems, a confidence interval is often used, rather than a point estimator [*see* ESTIMATION, *article on* CONFIDENCE INTERVALS AND REGIONS]. The interval is random (before the experiment), and it is so constructed that it covers the unknown true value of the parameter to be estimated with a preassigned probability, usually near 1. The confidence interval idea is very useful, although its subtlety has often led to misunderstandings in which the interpretation is wrongly given in terms of a probability distribution for the parameter.

There are, however, viewpoints in which this last sort of interpretation is valid, that is, in which the parameters of interest are themselves taken as random. The two most important of these viewpoints are Bayesian inference and fiducial inference [*see* BAYESIAN INFERENCE; FIDUCIAL INFERENCE; PROBABILITY, *article on* INTERPRETATIONS]. Many variants exist, and controversy continues as the philosophical and practical aspects of these approaches are debated [*see* LIKELIHOOD *for a discussion of related issues*].

Hypothesis testing. In the more usual viewpoint another general approach is that of hypothesis (or significance) testing [*see* HYPOTHESIS TESTING; SIGNIFICANCE, TESTS OF]. This kind of procedure might be used if it is important to ascertain whether p_A and p_B are the same or not. Hypothesis testing has two aspects: one is that of a two-decision procedure leading to one of two actions with known controlled chances of error. This first approach generalizes to that of decision theory and has generated a great deal of literature in theoretical statistics [*see* DECISION THEORY]. In this theory of decision functions, costs of wrong decisions, as well as costs of observation, are explicitly considered. Decision theory is related closely to game theory, and less closely to empirical studies of decision making [*see* GAME THEORY; DECISION MAKING].

The second aspect of hypothesis testing—and the commoner—is more descriptive. From its viewpoint a hypothesis test tells how surprising a set of observations is under some *null hypothesis* at test. In the example, one would compute how probable it is under the null hypothesis $p_A = p_B$ that the actual results should differ by as much as or more than the observed 95 per cent and 80 per cent. (Only recently has it been stressed that one would also do well to examine such probabilities under a variety of hypotheses other than a traditional null one.) Sometimes, as in the propaganda example, it is rather clear at the start that some effect must exist. In other cases, for example, in the study of parapsychology, there may be serious question of any effect whatever.

There are other modes of statistical analysis, for example, classification, selection, and screening [*see* MULTIVARIATE ANALYSIS, *article on* CLASSIFICATION AND DISCRIMINATION; SCREENING AND SELECTION]. In the future there is likely to be investigation of a much wider variety of modes of analysis than now exists. Such investigation will mitigate the difficulty that standard modes of analysis, like hypothesis testing, often do not exactly fit the inferential needs of specific real problems. The standard modes must usually be regarded as approximate, and used with caution.

One pervasive difficulty of this kind surrounds what might be called exploration of data, or data-dredging. It arises when a (usually sizable) body of data from a survey or experiment is at hand but either the analyst has no specific hypotheses about kinds of orderliness in the data or he has a great many. He will naturally wish to explore the body of data in a variety of ways with the hope of finding orderliness: he will try various graphical presentations, functional transformations, perhaps factor analysis, regression analysis, and other devices; in the course of this, he will doubtless carry out a number of estimations, hypothesis tests, confidence interval computations, and so on. A basic difficulty is that any finite body of data, even if wholly generated at random, will show orderliness of some kind if studied long and hard enough. Parallel to this, one must remember that most theoretical work on hypothesis tests, confidence intervals, and other inferential procedures looks at their behavior in isolation, and supposes that the procedures are selected in advance of data inspection. For example, if a hypothesis test is to be made of the null hypothesis that mean scores of men and women on an intelligence test are equal, and if a one-sided alternative is chosen after the fact in the same direction as that shown by the data, it is easy to see that the test will falsely show statistical significance, when the null hypothesis is true, twice as often as the analyst might expect.

On the other hand, it would be ridiculously rigid to refuse to use inferential tools in the exploration of data. Two general mitigating approaches are (1) the use of techniques (for example, multiple comparisons) that include explicit elements of exploration in their formulation [*see* LINEAR HYPOTHESES, *article on* MULTIPLE COMPARISONS], and (2) the splitting of the data into two parts at random, using one part for exploration with no holds barred and then carrying out formal tests or other inferential procedures on the second part.

This area deserves much more research. Selvin and Stuart have given a statement of present opinions, and of practical advice [*see* Selvin & Stuart 1966; *see also* SURVEY ANALYSIS; SCALING *and* STATISTICAL ANALYSIS, SPECIAL PROBLEMS OF, *article on* TRANSFORMATIONS OF DATA, *are also relevant*].

Breadth of inference. Whatever the mode of analysis, it is important to remember that the inference to which a statistical method directly relates is limited to the population actually experimented upon or surveyed. In the propaganda example, if the students are sampled from a single university, then the immediate inference is to that university only. Wider inferences—and these are usually wanted—presumably depend on subject-matter background and on intuition. Of course, the breadth of direct inference may be widened, for example, by repeating the study at different times, in different universities, in different areas, and so on. But, except in unusual cases, a limit is reached, if only the temporal one that experiments cannot be done now on future students.

Thus, in most cases, a scientific inference has two stages: the direct inference from the sample to the sampled population, and the indirect inference from the sampled population to a much wider, and usually rather vague, realm. That is why it is so important to try to check findings in a variety of contexts, for example, to test psychological generalizations obtained from experiments within one culture in some very different culture.

Formalization and precise theoretical treatment of the second stage represent a gap in present-day statistics (except perhaps for adherents of Bayesian methodology), although many say that the second step is intrinsically outside statistics. The general question of indirect inference is often mentioned and often forgotten; an early explicit treatment is by von Bortkiewicz (1909); a modern discussion in the context of research in sexual behavior is given by Cochran, Mosteller, and Tukey (1954, pp. 18–19, 21–22, 30–31).

An extreme case of the breadth-of-inference problem is represented by the case study, for example, an intensive study of the history of a single psychologically disturbed person. Indeed, some authors try to set up a sharp distinction between the method of case studies and what they call statistical methods. I do not feel that the distinction is very sharp. For one thing, statistical questions of measurement reliability arise even in the study of a single person. Further, some case studies, for example, in anthropology, are of a tribe or some other group of individuals, so that traditional sampling questions might well arise in drawing inferences about the single (collective) case.

Proponents of the case study approach emphasize its flexibility, its importance in attaining subjective insight, and its utility as a means of conjecturing interesting theoretical structures. If there is good reason to believe in small relevant intercase variability, then, of course, a single case does tell much about a larger population. The investigator, however, has responsibility for defending an assumption about small intercase variability. [*Further discussion will be found in* INTERVIEWING; OBSERVATION, *article on* SOCIAL OBSERVATION AND SOCIAL CASE STUDIES.]

Other topics

Linear hypotheses.   One way of classifying statistical topics is in terms of the kind of assumptions made, that is—looking toward applications—in terms of the structure of anticipated experiments or surveys for which the statistical methods will be used. The propaganda example, in which the central quantities are two proportions with integral numerators and denominators, falls under the general topic of the analysis of counted or qualitative data; this topic includes the treatment of so-called chi-square tests. Such an analysis would also be applicable if there were more than two groups, and it can be extended in other directions. [*See* COUNTED DATA.]

If, in the propaganda experiment, instead of proportions expressing one preference or the other, numerical scores on a multiquestion test were used to indicate quantitatively the leaning toward a candidate or political party, then the situation might come under the general rubric of linear hypotheses. To illustrate the ideas, suppose that there were more than two groups, say, four, of which the first was exposed to no propaganda, the second saw a motion picture, the third was given material to read, and the fourth heard a speaker, and that the scores of students under the four conditions are to be compared. Analysis-of-variance methods (many of which may be regarded as special cases of regression methods) are of central importance for such a study [*see* LINEAR HYPOTHESES, *articles on* ANALYSIS OF VARIANCE *and* REGRESSION]. Multiple comparison methods are often used here, although —strictly speaking—they are not restricted to the analysis-of-variance context [*see* LINEAR HYPOTHESES, *article on* MULTIPLE COMPARISONS].

If the four groups differed primarily in some quantitative way, for example, in the number of sessions spent watching propaganda motion pictures, then regression methods in a narrower sense might come into play. One might, for example, suppose that average test score is roughly a linear function of number of motion picture sessions, and then center statistical attention on the constants (slope and intercept) of the linear function.

Multivariate statistics.   "Regression" is a word with at least two meanings. A meaning somewhat different from, and historically earlier than, that described just above appears in statistical theory for multivariate analysis, that is, for situations in which more than one kind of observation is made on each individual or unit that is measured [*see* MULTIVARIATE ANALYSIS]. For example, in an educational experiment on teaching methods, one might look at scores not only on a spelling examination, but on a grammar examination and on a reading-comprehension examination as well. Or in a physical anthropology study, one might measure several dimensions of each individual.

The simplest part of multivariate analysis is concerned with association between just two random variables and, in particular, with the important concept of correlation [*see* STATISTICS, DESCRIPTIVE, *article on* ASSOCIATION; MULTIVARIATE ANALYSIS, *articles on* CORRELATION]. These ideas extend to more than two random variables, and then new possibilities enter. An important one is that of partial association: how are spelling and grammar scores associated if reading comprehension is held fixed? The partial association notion is important in survey analysis, where a controlled experiment is often impossible [*see* SURVEY ANALYSIS; EXPERIMENTAL DESIGN, *article on* QUASI-EXPERIMENTAL DESIGN].

Multivariate analysis also considers statistical methods bearing on the joint structure of the means that correspond to the several kinds of observations, and on the whole correlation structure.

Factor analysis falls in the multivariate area, but it has a special history and a special relationship with psychology [*see* FACTOR ANALYSIS]. Factor-analytic methods try to replace a number of measurements by a few basic ones, together with residuals having a simple probability structure. For example, one might hope that spelling, grammar, and reading-comprehension abilities are all proportional to some quantity not directly observable, perhaps dubbed "linguistic skill," that varies from person to person, plus residuals or deviations that are statistically independent.

The standard factor analysis model is one of a class of models generated by a process called mixing of probability distributions [*see* DISTRIBUTIONS, STATISTICAL, *article on* MIXTURES OF DISTRIBUTIONS]. An interesting model of this general sort, but for discrete, rather than continuous, observations, is that of latent structure [*see* LATENT STRUCTURE].

Another important multivariate topic is classification and discrimination, which is the study of how to assign individuals to two or more groups on the basis of several measurements per individual [*see* MULTIVARIATE ANALYSIS, *article on* CLASSIFICATION AND DISCRIMINATION]. Less well understood, but related, is the problem of clustering, or numerical taxonomy: what are useful ways for forming groups of individuals on the basis of several measurements on each? [*See* CLUSTERING.]

Time series. Related to multivariate analysis, because of its stress on modes of statistical dependence, is the large field of time series analysis, sometimes given a title that includes the catchy phrase "stochastic processes." An observed time series may be regarded as a realization of an underlying stochastic process [*see* TIME SERIES]. The simplest sort of time series problem might arise

when for each child in an educational experiment there is available a set of scores on spelling tests given each month during the school year. More difficult problems arise when there is no hope of observing more than a single series, for example, when the observations are on the monthly or yearly prices of wheat. In such cases—so common in economics—stringent structural assumptions are required, and even then analysis is not easy.

This encyclopedia's treatment of time series begins with a general overview, oriented primarily toward economic series. The overview is followed by a discussion of advanced methodology, mainly that of spectral analysis, which treats a time series as something like a radio signal that can be decomposed into subsignals at different frequencies, each with its own amount of energy. Next comes a treatment of cycles, with special discussion of how easy it is to be trapped into concluding that cycles exist when in fact only random variation is present. Finally, there is a discussion of the important technical problem raised by seasonal variation, and of adjustment to remove or mitigate its effect. The articles on business cycles should also be consulted [*see* BUSINESS CYCLES].

The topic of Markov chains might have been included under the time series category, but it is separate [*see* MARKOV CHAINS]. The concept of a Markov chain is one of the simplest and most useful ways of relaxing the common assumption of independence. Methods based on the Markov chain idea have found application in the study of panels (for public opinion, budget analysis, etc.), of labor mobility, of changes in social class between generations, and so on [*see, for example,* PANEL STUDIES; SOCIAL MOBILITY].

Sample surveys and related topics. The subject of sample surveys is important, both in theory and practice [*see* SAMPLE SURVEYS]. It originated in connection with surveys of economic and social characteristics of human populations, when samples were used rather than attempts at full coverage. But the techniques of sample surveys have been of great use in many other areas, for example in the evaluation of physical inventories of industrial equipment. The study of sample surveys is closely related to most of the other major fields of statistics, in particular to the design of experiments, but it is characterized by its emphasis on finite populations and on complex sampling plans.

Most academically oriented statisticians who think about sample surveys stress the importance of probability sampling—that is, of choosing the units to be observed by a plan that explicitly uses random numbers, so that the probabilities of possible samples are known. On the other hand, many actual sample surveys are not based upon probability sampling [for *a discussion of the central issues of this somewhat ironical discrepancy, see* SAMPLE SURVEYS, *article on* NONPROBABILITY SAMPLING].

Random numbers are important, not only for sample surveys, but for experimental design generally, and for simulation studies of many kinds [*see* RANDOM NUMBERS; SIMULATION].

An important topic in sample surveys (and, for that matter, throughout applied statistics) is that of nonsampling errors [*see* ERRORS, *article on* NONSAMPLING ERRORS]. Such errors stem, for example, from nonresponse in public opinion surveys, from observer and other biases in measurement, and from errors of computation. Interesting discussions of these problems, and of many others related to sampling, are given by Cochran, Mosteller, and Tukey (1954).

Sociologists have long been interested in survey research, but with historically different emphases from those of statisticians [*see* SURVEY ANALYSIS; INTERVIEWING]. The sociological stress has been much less on efficient design and sampling variation and much more on complex analyses of highly multivariate data. There is reason to hope that workers in these two streams of research are coming to understand each other's viewpoint.

Nonparametric analysis and related topics. I remarked earlier that an important area of study is robustness, the degree of sensitivity of statistical methods to errors in assumptions. A particular kind of assumption error is that incurred when a special distributional form, for example, normality, is assumed when it does not in fact obtain. To meet this problem, one may seek alternate methods that are insensitive to form of distribution, and the study of such methods is called nonparametric analysis or distribution-free statistics [*see* NONPARAMETRIC STATISTICS]. Such procedures as the sign test and many ranking methods fall into the nonparametric category.

For example, suppose that pairs of students—matched for age, sex, intelligence, and so on—form the experimental material, and that for each pair it is determined entirely at random, as by the throw of a fair coin, which member of the pair is exposed to one teaching method (A) and which to another (B). After exposure to the assigned methods, the students are given an examination; a pair is scored positive if the method A student has the higher score, negative if the method B student has. If the two methods are equally effective, the number of positive scores has a binomial distribution with basic probability $\frac{1}{2}$. If, however, method A is superior, the basic probability is greater than $\frac{1}{2}$; if

method B is superior, less than $\frac{1}{2}$. The number of observed positives provides a simple test of the hypothesis of equivalence and a basis for estimating the amount of superiority that one of the teaching methods may have. (The above design is, of course, only sensible if matching is possible for most of the students.)

The topic of order statistics is also discussed in one of the articles on nonparametric analysis, although order statistics are at least as important for procedures that do make sharp distributional assumptions [*see* NONPARAMETRIC STATISTICS, *article on* ORDER STATISTICS]. There is, of course, no sharp boundary line for distribution-free procedures. First, many procedures based on narrow distributional assumptions turn out in fact to be robust, that is, to maintain some or all of their characteristics even when the assumptions are relaxed. Second, most distribution-free procedures are only partly so; for example, a distribution-free test will typically be independent of distributional form as regards its level of significance but not so as regards power (the probability of rejecting the null hypothesis when it is false). Again, most nonparametric procedures are nonrobust against dependence among the observations.

Nonparametric methods often arise naturally when observational materials are inherently nonmetric, for example, when the results of an experiment or survey provide only rankings of test units by judges.

Sometimes the form of a distribution is worthy of special examination, and goodness-of-fit procedures are used [*see* GOODNESS OF FIT]. For example, a psychological test may be standardized to a particular population so that test scores over the population have very nearly a unit-normal distribution. If the test is then administered to the individuals of a sample from a different population, the question may arise of whether the score distribution for the different population is still unit normal, and a goodness-of-fit test of unit-normality may be performed. More broadly, an analogous test might be framed to test only normality, without specification of a particular normal distribution.

Some goodness-of-fit procedures, the so-called chi-square ones, may be regarded as falling under the counted-data rubric [*see* COUNTED DATA]. Others, especially when modified to provide confidence bands for an entire distribution, are usually studied under the banner of nonparametric analysis.

Dispersion. The study of dispersion, or variability, is a topic that deserves more attention than it often receives [*see* VARIANCES, STATISTICAL STUDY OF]. For example, it might be of interest to compare several teaching methods as to the resulting heterogeneity of student scores. A particular method might give rise to a desirable average score by increasing greatly the scores of some students while leaving other students' scores unchanged, thereby giving rise to great heterogeneity. Clearly, such a method has different consequences and applications than one that raises each student's score by about the same amount.

(Terminology may be confusing here. The traditional topic of analysis of variance deals in substantial part with means, not variances, although it does so by looking at dispersions among the means.)

Design. Experimental design has already been mentioned. It deals with such problems as how many observations to take for a given level of accuracy, and how to assign the treatments or factors to experimental units. For example, in the study of teaching methods, the experimental units may be school classes, cross-classified by grade, kind of school, type of community, and the like. Experimental design deals with formal aspects of the structure of an experimental layout; a basic principle is that explicit randomization should be used in assigning "treatments" (here methods of teaching) to experimental units (here classes). Sometimes it may be reasonable to suppose that randomization is inherent, supplied, as it were, by nature; but more often it is important to use so-called random numbers. Controversy centers on situations in which randomization is deemed impractical, unethical, or even impossible, although one may sometimes find clever ways to introduce randomization in cases where it seems hopeless at first glance. When randomization is absent, a term like "quasi experiment" may be used to emphasize its absence, and a major problem is that of obtaining as much protection as possible against the sources of bias that would have been largely eliminated by the unused randomization [see EXPERIMENTAL DESIGN, *article on* QUASI-EXPERIMENTAL DESIGN].

An important aspect of the design of experiments is the use of devices to ensure both that a (human) subject does not know which experimental treatment he is subjected to, and that the investigator who is measuring or observing effects of treatments does not know which treatments particular observed individuals have had. When proper precautions are taken along these two lines, the experiment is called *double blind*. Many experimental programs have been vitiated by neglect of these precautions. First, a subject who knows that he is taking a drug that it is hoped will improve his memory, or reduce his sensitivity to pain, may well change his behavior in response to the knowledge of what is

expected as much as in physiological response to the drug itself. Hence, whenever possible, so-called placebo treatments (neutral but, on the surface, indistinguishable from the real treatment) are administered to members of the control group. Second, an investigator who knows which subjects are having which treatments may easily, and quite unconsciously, have his observations biased by preconceived opinions. Problems may arise even if the investigator knows only which subjects are in the same group. Assignment to treatment by the use of random numbers, and random ordering of individuals for observation, are important devices to ensure impartiality.

The number of observations is traditionally regarded as fixed before sampling. In recent years, however, there have been many investigations of sequential designs in which observations are taken in a series (or in a series of groups of observations), with decisions made at each step whether to take further observations or to stop observing and turn to analysis [see SEQUENTIAL ANALYSIS].

In many contexts a response (or its average value) is a function of several controlled variables. For example, average length of time to relearn the spellings of a list of words may depend on the number of prior learning sessions and the elapsed period since the last learning session. In the study of response surfaces, the structure of the dependence (thought of as the shape of a surface) is investigated by a series of experiments, typically with special interest in the neighborhood of a maximum or minimum [see EXPERIMENTAL DESIGN, *article on* RESPONSE SURFACES].

Philosophy. Statistics has long had a neighborly relation with philosophy of science in the epistemological city, although statistics has usually been more modest in scope and more pragmatic in outlook. In a strict sense, statistics is part of philosophy of science, but in fact the two areas are usually studied separately.

What are some problems that form part of the philosophy of science but are not generally regarded as part of statistics? A central one is that of the formation of scientific theories, their careful statement, and their confirmation or degree of confirmation. This last is to be distinguished from the narrower, but better understood, statistical concept of testing hypotheses. Another problem that many statisticians feel lies outside statistics is that of the gap between sampled and target population.

There are other areas of scientific philosophy that are not ordinarily regarded as part of statistics. Concepts like explanation, causation, operationalism, and free will come to mind.

A classic publication dealing with both statistics and scientific philosophy is Karl Pearson's *Grammar of Science* (1892). Two more recent such publications are Popper's *Logic of Scientific Discovery* (1935) and Braithwaite's *Scientific Explanation* (1953). By and large, nowadays, writers calling themselves statisticians and those calling themselves philosophers of science often refer to each other, but communication is restricted and piecemeal. [*See* SCIENCE, *article on* THE PHILOSOPHY OF SCIENCE; *see also* CAUSATION; POWER; PREDICTION; SCIENTIFIC EXPLANATION.]

Measurement is an important topic for statistics, and it might well be mentioned here because some aspects of measurement are clearly philosophical. Roughly speaking, measurement is the process of assigning numbers (or categories) to objects on the basis of some operation. A measurement or datum is the resulting number (or category). But what is the epistemological underpinning for this concept? Should it be broadened to include more general kinds of data than numbers and categories? What kind of operations should be considered?

In particular, measurement *scales* are important, both in theory and practice. It is natural to say of one object that it is twice as heavy as another (in pounds, grams, or whatever—the unit is immaterial). But it seems silly to say that one object has twice the temperature of another in any of the everyday scales of temperature (as opposed to the absolute scale), if only because the ratio changes when one shifts, say, from Fahrenheit to Centigrade degrees. On the other hand, it makes sense to say that one object is 100 degrees Fahrenheit hotter than another. Some measurements seem to make sense only insofar as they order units, for example, many subjective rankings; and some measurements are purely nominal or categorical, for example, country of birth. Some measurements are inherently circular, for example, wind direction or time of day. There has been heated discussion of the question of the meaningfulness or legitimacy of arithmetic manipulations of various kinds of measurements; does it make sense, for example, to average measurements of subjective loudness if the individual measurements give information only about ordinal relationships?

The following are some important publications that deal with measurement and that lead to the relevant literature at this date: Churchman and Ratoosh (1959); Coombs (1964); Pfanzagl (1959); Adams, Fagot, and Robinson (1965); Torgerson (1958); Stevens (1946); Suppes and Zinnes (1963). [*See* STATISTICS, DESCRIPTIVE; *also relevant are* PSYCHOMETRICS; SCALING; UTILITY.]

Communication and fallacies. There is an art of communication between statistician and nonstatistician scientist: the statistician must be always aware that the nonstatistician is in general not directly interested in technical minutiae or in the parochial jargon of statistics. In the other direction, consultation with a statistician often loses effectiveness because the nonstatistician fails to mention aspects of his work that are of statistical relevance. Of course, in most cases scientists serve as their own statisticians, in the same sense that people, except for hypochondriacs, serve as their own physicians most of the time.

Statistical fallacies are often subtle and may be committed by the most careful workers. A study of such fallacies has intrinsic interest and also aids in mitigating the communication problem just mentioned [*see* FALLACIES, STATISTICAL; *see also* ERRORS, *article on* NONSAMPLING ERRORS].

Criticisms

If statistics is defined broadly, in terms of the general study of the leap from observations to inference, decision, or whatever, then one can hardly quarrel with the desirability of a study so embracingly characterized. Criticisms of statistics, therefore, are generally in terms of a narrower characterization, often the kind of activity named "statistics" that the critic sees about him. If, for example, a professor in some scientific field sees colleagues publishing clumsy analyses that they call statistical, then the professor may understandably develop a negative attitude toward statistics. He may not have an opportunity to learn that the subject is broader and that it may be used wisely, elegantly, and effectively.

Criticisms of probability in statistics. Some criticisms, in a philosophical vein, relate to the very use of probability models in statistics. For example, some writers have objected to probability because of a strict determinism in their *Weltanschauung*. This view is rare nowadays, with the success of highly probabilistic quantum methods in physics, and with the utility of probability models for clearly deterministic phenomena, for example, the effect of rounding errors in complex digital calculations. The deterministic critic, however, would probably say that quantum mechanics and probabilistic analysis of rounding errors are just temporary expedients, to be replaced later by nonprobabilistic approaches. For example, Einstein wrote in 1947 that

. . . the statistical interpretation [as in quantum mechanics] . . . has a considerable content of truth.

Yet I cannot seriously believe it because the theory is inconsistent with the principle that physics has to represent a reality. . . . I am absolutely convinced that one will eventually arrive at a theory in which the objects connected by laws are not probabilities, but conceived facts. . . . However, I cannot provide logical arguments for my conviction, but can only call on my little finger as a witness, which cannot claim any authority to be respected outside my own skin.   (Quoted in Born 1949, p. 123)

Other critics find vitiating contradictions and paradoxes in the ideas of probability and randomness. For example, G. Spencer Brown sweepingly wrote that

. . . the concept of probability used in statistical science is meaningless in its own terms [and] . . . , however meaningful it might have been, its meaningfulness would nevertheless have remained fruitless because of the impossibility of gaining information from experimental results.   (1957, p. 66)

This rather nihilistic position is unusual and hard to reconcile with the many successful applications of probabilistic ideas. (Indeed, Spencer Brown went on to make constructive qualifications.) A less extreme but related view was expressed by Percy W. Bridgman (1959, pp. 110–111). Both these writers were influenced by statistical uses of tables of random numbers, especially in the context of parapsychology, where explanations of puzzling results were sought in the possible misbehavior of random numbers. [See RANDOM NUMBERS; *see also* PARAPSYCHOLOGY.]

Criticisms about limited utility.   A more common criticism, notably among some physical scientists, is that they have little need for statistics because random variability in the problems they study is negligible, at least in comparison with systematic errors or biases. This position has also been taken by some economists, especially in connection with index numbers [*see* INDEX NUMBERS, *article on* SAMPLING]. B. F. Skinner, a psychologist, has forcefully expressed a variant of this position: that there are so many important problems in which random variability is negligible that he will restrict his own research to them (see Skinner 1956 for a presentation of this rather extreme position). In fact, he further argues that the important problems in psychology as a field are the identification of variables that can be observed directly with negligible variability.

It often happens, nonetheless, that, upon detailed examination, random variability is more important than had been thought, especially for the design of future experiments. Further, careful experimental design can often reduce, or bring under-

standing of, systematic errors. I think that the above kind of criticism is sometimes valid—after all, a single satellite successfully orbiting the earth is enough to show that it can be done—but that usually the criticism represents unwillingness to consider statistical methods explicitly, or a semantic confusion about what statistics is.

Related to the above criticism is the view that statistics is fine for applied technology, but not for fundamental science. In his inaugural lecture at Birkbeck College at the University of London, David Cox countered this criticism. He said in his introduction,

. . . there is current a feeling that in some fields of fundamental research, statistical ideas are sometimes not just irrelevant, but may actually be harmful as a symptom of an over-empirical approach. This view, while understandable, seems to me to come from too narrow a concept of what statistical methods are about.   (1961)

Cox went on to give examples of the use of statistics in fundamental research in physics, psychology, botany, and other fields.

Another variant of this criticism sometimes seen (Selvin 1957; Walberg 1966) is that such statistical procedures as hypothesis testing are of doubtful validity unless a classically arranged experiment is possible, complete with randomization, control groups, pre-establishment of hypotheses, and other safeguards. Without such an arrangement—which is sometimes not possible or practical—all kinds of bias may enter, mixing any actual effect with bias effects.

This criticism reflects a real problem of reasonable inference when a true experiment is not available [*see* EXPERIMENTAL DESIGN, *article on* QUASI-EXPERIMENTAL DESIGN], but it is not a criticism unique to special kinds of inference. The problem applies equally to any mode of analysis—formal, informal, or intuitive. A spirited discussion of this topic is given by Kish (1959).

Humanistic criticisms.   Some criticisms of statistics represent serious misunderstandings or are really criticisms of *poor* statistical method, not of statistics per se. For example, one sometimes hears the argument that statistics is inhuman, that "you can't reduce people to numbers," that statistics (and perhaps science more generally) must be battled by humanists. This is a statistical version of an old complaint, voiced in one form by Horace Walpole, in a letter to H. S. Conway (1778): "This sublime age reduces everything to its quintessence; all periphrases and expletives are so much in disuse, that I suppose soon the only way to [go about] ·making love will be to say 'Lie down.' "

A modern variation of this was expressed by W. H. Auden in the following lines:

> Thou shalt not answer questionnaires
> Or quizzes upon World-Affairs,
>   Nor with compliance
> Take any test. Thou shalt not sit
> With statisticians nor commit
>   A social science.

> From "Under Which Lyre: A Reactionary Tract for the Times." Reprinted from *Nones*, by W. H. Auden, by permission of Random House, Inc. Copyright 1946 by W. H. Auden.

Joseph Wood Krutch (1963) said, "I still think that a familiarity with the best that has been thought and said by men of letters is more helpful than all the sociologists' statistics" ("Through Happiness With Slide Rule and Calipers," p. 14).

There are, of course, quite valid points buried in such captious and charming criticisms. It is easy to forget that things may be more complicated than they seem, that many important characteristics are extraordinarily difficult to measure or count, that scientists (and humanists alike) may lack professional humility, and that any set of measurements excludes others that might in principle have been made. But the humanistic attack is overdefensive and is a particular instance of what might be called the two-culture fallacy: the belief that science and the humanities are inherently different and necessarily in opposition.

Criticisms of overconcern with averages. Statisticians are sometimes teased about being interested only in averages, some of which are ludicrous: 2.35 children in an average family; or the rare disease that attacks people aged 40 on the average —two cases, one a child of 2 and the other a man of 78. (Chuckles from the gallery.)

Skinner made the point by observing that "no one goes to the circus to see the average dog jump through a hoop significantly oftener than untrained dogs raised under the same circumstances . . ." (1956, p. 228). Krutch said that "Statistics take no account of those who prefer to hear a different drummer" (1963, p. 15).

In fact, although averages are important, statisticians have long been deeply concerned about dispersions around averages and about other aspects of distributions, for example, in extreme values [*see* NONPARAMETRIC STATISTICS, *article on* ORDER STATISTICS; *and* STATISTICAL ANALYSIS, SPECIAL PROBLEMS OF, *article on* OUTLIERS].

In 1889 the criticism of averages was poetically made by Galton:

> It is difficult to understand why statisticians commonly limit their inquiries to Averages, and do not revel in more comprehensive views. Their souls seem as dull to the charm of variety as that of the native of one of our flat English counties, whose retrospect of Switzerland was that, if its mountains could be thrown into its lakes, two nuisances would be got rid of at once. (p. 62)

Galton's critique was overstated even at its date, but it would be wholly inappropriate today.

Another passage from the same work by Galton refers to the kind of emotional resistance to statistics that was mentioned earlier:

> Some people hate the very name of statistics, but I find them full of beauty and interest. Whenever they are not brutalized, but delicately handled by the higher methods, and are warily interpreted, their power of dealing with complicated phenomena is extraordinary. They are the only tools by which an opening can be cut through the formidable thicket of difficulties that bars the path of those who pursue the Science of man. (1889, pp. 62–63)

One basic source of misunderstanding about averages is that an individual may be average in many ways, yet appreciably nonaverage in others. This was the central difficulty with Quetelet's historically important concept of the average man [*see the biography of* QUETELET]; a satirical novel about the point, by Robert A. Aurthur (1953), has appeared. The average number of children per family in a given population is meaningful and sometimes useful to know, for example, in estimating future population. There is, however, no such thing as the average family, if only because a family with an average number of children (assuming this number to be integral) would not be average in terms of the reciprocal of number of children. To put it another way, there is no reason to think that a family with the average number of children also has average income, or average education, or lives at the center of population of the country.

Criticisms of too much mathematics. The criticism is sometimes made—often by statisticians themselves—that statistics is too mathematical. The objection takes various forms, for example:

(1) Statisticians choose research problems because of their mathematical interest or elegance and thus do not work on problems of real statistical concern. (Sometimes the last phrase simply refers to problems of concern to the critic.)

(2) The use of mathematical concepts and language obscures statistical thinking.

(3) Emphasis on mathematical aspects of sta-

tistics tends to make statisticians neglect problems of proper goals, meaningfulness of numerical statistics, and accuracy of data.

Critiques along these lines are given by, for example, W. S. Woytinsky (1954) and Corrado Gini (1951; 1959). A similar attack appears in Lancelot Hogben's *Statistical Theory* (1957). What can one say of this kind of criticism, whether it comes from within or without the profession? It has a venerable history that goes back to the early development of statistics. Perhaps the first quarrel of this kind was in the days when the word "statistics" was used, in a different sense than at present, to mean the systematic study of states, a kind of political science. The dispute was between those "statisticians" who provided discursive descriptions of states and those who cultivated the so-called *Tabellenstatistik*, which ranged from typographically convenient arrangements of verbal summaries to actual tables of vital statistics. Descriptions of this quarrel are given by Westergaard (1932, pp. 12–15), Lundberg (1940), and Lazarsfeld (1961, especially p. 293).

The *ad hominem* argument—that someone is primarily a mathematician, and hence incapable of understanding truly statistical problems—has been and continues to be an unfortunately popular rhetorical device. In part it is probably a defensive reaction to the great status and prestige of mathematics.

In my view, a great deal of this kind of discussion has been beside the point, although some charges on all sides have doubtless been correct. If a part of mathematics proves helpful in statistics, then it will be used. As statisticians run onto mathematical problems, they will work on them, borrowing what they can from the store of current mathematical knowledge, and perhaps encouraging or carrying out appropriate mathematical research. To be sure, some statisticians adopt an unnecessarily mathematical manner of exposition. This may seem an irritating affectation to less mathematical colleagues, but who can really tell apart an affectation and a natural mode of communication?

An illuminating discussion about the relationship between mathematics and statistics, as well as about many other matters, is given by Tukey (1961).

Criticisms of obfuscation. Next, there is the charge that statistics is a meretricious mechanism to obfuscate or confuse: "Lies, damned lies, and statistics" (the origin of this canard is not entirely clear: see White 1964). A variant is the criticism that statistical analyses are impossible to follow, filled with unreadable charts, formulas, and jargon.

These points are often well taken of specific statistical or pseudostatistical writings, but they do not relate to statistics as a discipline. A popular book, *How to Lie With Statistics* (Huff 1954), is in fact a presentation of horrid errors in statistical description and analysis, although it could, of course, be used as a source for pernicious sophistry. It is somewhat as if there were a book called "How to Counterfeit Money," intended as a guide to bank tellers—or the general public—in protecting themselves against false money.

George A. Lundberg made a cogent defense against one form of this criticism, in the following words:

. . . when we have to reckon with stupidity, incompetence, and illogic, the more specific the terminology and methods employed the more glaring will be the errors in the result. As a result, the errors of quantitative workers lend themselves more easily to detection and derision. An equivalent blunder by a manipulator of rhetoric may not only appear less flagrant, but may actually go unobserved or become a venerated platitude. (1940, p. 138)

Criticisms of sampling per se. One sometimes sees the allegation that it is impossible to make reasonable inferences from a sample to a population, especially if the sample is a small fraction of the population. A variant of this was stated by Joseph Papp: "The methodology . . . was not scientific: they used sampling and you can't draw a complete picture from samplings" (quoted in Kadushin 1966, p. 30).

This criticism has no justification except insofar as it impugns *poor* sampling methods. Samples have always been used, because it is often impractical or impossible to observe a whole population (one cannot test a new drug on every human being, or destructively test all electric fuses) or because it is more informative to make careful measurements on a sample than crude measurements on a whole population. Proper sampling—for which the absolute size of the sample is far more important than the fraction of the population it represents—is informative, and in constant successful use.

Criticisms of intellectual imperialism. The criticism is sometimes made that statistics is not the whole of scientific method and practice. Skinner said:

. . . it is a mistake to identify scientific practice with the *formalized constructions* [italics added] of statistics and scientific method. These disciplines have their place, but it does not coincide with the place of scientific research. They offer *a* method of science but not, as is so often implied, *the* method. As formal disciplines they arose very late in the history of science, and most of the facts of science have been discovered without their aid.   (1956, p. 221)

I know of few statisticians so arrogant as to equate their field with scientific method generally. It is, of course, true that most scientific work has been done without the aid of statistics, narrowly construed as certain formal modes of analysis that are currently promulgated. On the other hand, a good deal of scientific writing is concerned, one way or another, with statistics, in the more general sense of asking how to make sensible inferences.

Skinner made another, somewhat related point: that, because of the prestige of statistics, statistical methods have (in psychology) acquired the honorific status of a shibboleth (1956, pp. 221, 231). Statisticians are sorrowfully aware of the shibboleth use of statistics in some areas of scientific research, but the profession can be blamed for this only because of some imperialistic textbooks— many of them not by proper statisticians.

Other areas of statistics

The remainder of this article is devoted to brief discussions of those statistical articles in the encyclopedia that have not been described earlier.

Grouped observations.   The question of grouped observations is sometimes of concern: in much theoretical statistics measurements are assumed to be continuous, while in fact measurements are always discrete, so that there is inevitable grouping. In addition, one often wishes to group measurements further, for simplicity of description and analysis. To what extent are discreteness and grouping an advantage, and to what extent a danger? [See STATISTICAL ANALYSIS, SPECIAL PROBLEMS OF, *article on* GROUPED OBSERVATIONS.]

Truncation and censorship.   Often observations may reasonably follow some standard model except that observations above (or below) certain values are proscribed (truncated or censored). A slightly more complex example occurs in comparing entrance test scores with post-training scores for students in a course; those students with low entrance test scores may not be admitted and hence will not have post-training scores at all. Methods exist for handling such problems. [See STATISTICAL ANALYSIS, SPECIAL PROBLEMS OF, *article on* TRUNCATION AND CENSORSHIP.]

Outliers.   Very often a few observations in a sample will have unusually large or small values and may be regarded as outliers (or mavericks or wild values). How should one handle them? If they are carried along in an analysis, they may distort it. If they are arbitrarily suppressed, important information may be lost. Even if they are to be suppressed, what rule should be used? [See STATISTICAL ANALYSIS, SPECIAL PROBLEMS OF, *article on* OUTLIERS.]

Transformations of data.   Transformations of data are often very useful. For example, one may take the logarithm of reaction time, the square root of a test score, and so on. The purposes of such a transformation are (1) to simplify the structure of the data, for example by achieving additivity of two kinds of effects, and (2) to make the data more nearly conform with a well-understood statistical model, for example by achieving near-normality or constancy of variance. A danger of transformations is that one's inferences may be shifted to some other scale than the one of basic interest. [See STATISTICAL ANALYSIS, SPECIAL PROBLEMS OF, *article on* TRANSFORMATIONS OF DATA.]

Approximations to distributions.   Approximations to distributions are important in probability and statistics. First, one may want to approximate some theoretical distribution in order to have a simple analytic form or to get numerical values. Second, one may want to approximate empirical distributions for both descriptive and inferential purposes. [See DISTRIBUTIONS, STATISTICAL, *article on* APPROXIMATIONS TO DISTRIBUTIONS.]

Identifiability—mixtures of distributions.   The problem of identification appears whenever a precise model for some phenomenon is specified and parameters of the model are to be estimated from empirical observations [see STATISTICAL IDENTIFIABILITY]. What may happen—and may even fail to be recognized—is that the parameters are fundamentally incapable of estimation from the kind of data in question. Consider, for example, a learning theory model in which the proportion of learned material retained after a lapse of time is the ratio of two parameters of the model. Then, even if the proportion could be observed without any sampling fluctuation or measurement error, one would not separately know the two parameters. Of course, the identification problem arises primarily in contexts that are complex enough so that immediate recognition of nonidentifiability is not likely. Sometimes there arises an analogous problem, which might be called identifiability of the model. A classic example appears in the study of accident statistics: some kinds of these statistics are satisfactorily fitted by the negative binomial distribution, but that distribution itself may be obtained as the outcome of several quite different, more fundamental models. Some of these models illustrate the important concept of mixtures. A mixture is an important and useful way of forming a new distribution from two or more statistical distributions. [*See* DISTRIBUTIONS, STATISTICAL, *article on* MIXTURES OF DISTRIBUTIONS.]

Applications. Next described is a set of articles on special topics linked with specific areas of application, although most of these areas have served as motivating sources for general theory.

Quality control. Statistical quality control had its genesis in manufacturing industry, but its applications have since broadened [*see* QUALITY CONTROL, STATISTICAL]. There are three articles under this heading. The first is on acceptance sampling, where the usual context is that of "lots" of manufactured articles. Here there are close relations to hypothesis testing and to sequential analysis. The second is on process control (and so-called control charts), a topic that is sometimes itself called quality control, in a narrower sense than the usage here. The development of control chart concepts and methods relates to basic notions of randomness and stability, for an important normative concept is that of a *process in control*, that is, a process turning out a sequence of numbers that behave like independent, identically distributed random variables. The third topic is reliability and life testing, which also relates to matters more general than immediate engineering contexts. [*The term "reliability" here has quite a different meaning than it has in the area of psychological testing; see* PSYCHOMETRICS.]

Government statistics. Government statistics are of great importance for economic, social, and political decisions [*see* GOVERNMENT STATISTICS]. The article on that subject treats such basic issues as the use of government statistics for political propaganda, the problem of confidentiality, and the meaning and accuracy of official statistics. [*Some related articles are* CENSUS; ECONOMIC DATA; MORTALITY; POPULATION; VITAL STATISTICS.]

Index numbers. Economic index numbers form an important part of government statistical programs [*see* INDEX NUMBERS]. The three articles on this topic discuss, respectively, theory, practical aspects of index numbers, and sampling problems.

Statistics as legal evidence. The use of statistical methods, and their results, in judicial proceedings has been growing in recent years. Trademark disputes have been illuminated by sample surveys; questions of paternity have been investigated probabilistically; depreciation and other accounting quantities that arise in quasi-judicial hearings have been estimated statistically. There are conflicts or apparent conflicts between statistical methods and legal concepts like those relating to hearsay evidence. [*See* STATISTICS AS LEGAL EVIDENCE.]

Statistical geography. Statistical geography, the use of statistical and other quantitative methods in geography, is a rapidly growing area [*see* GEOGRAPHY, *article on* STATISTICAL GEOGRAPHY]. Somewhat related is the topic of rank–size, in which are studied—empirically and theoretically—patterns of relationship between, for example, the populations of cities and their rankings from most populous down. Another example is the relationship between the frequencies of words and their rankings from most frequent down. [*See* RANK–SIZE RELATIONS.]

Quantal response. Quantal response refers to a body of theory and method that might have been classed with counted data or under linear hypotheses with regression [*see* QUANTAL RESPONSE]. An example of a quantal response problem would be one in which students are given one week, two weeks, and so on, of training (say 100 different students for each training period), and then proportions of students passing a test are observed. Of interest might be that length of training leading to exactly 50 per cent passing. Many traditional psychophysical problems may be regarded from this viewpoint [*see* PSYCHOPHYSICS].

Queues. The study of queues has been of importance in recent years; it is sometimes considered part of operations research, but it may also be considered a branch of the study of stochastic processes [*see* QUEUES; OPERATIONS RESEARCH]. An example of queuing analysis is that of traffic flow at a street-crossing with a traffic light. The study has empirical, theoretical, and normative aspects.

Computation. Always intertwined with applied statistics, although distinct from it, has been computation [*see* COMPUTATION]. The recent advent of high-speed computers has produced a sequence of qualitative changes in the kind of computation that is practicable. This has had, and will continue to have, profound effects on statistics, not only as regards data handling and analysis, but also in theory, since many analytically intractable problems can now be attacked numerically by simulation on a high-speed computer [*see* SIMULATION].

Cybernetics. The currently fashionable term "cybernetics" is applied to a somewhat amorphous body of knowledge and research dealing with information processing and mechanisms, both living and nonliving [*see* CYBERNETICS *and* HOMEOSTASIS]. The notions of control and feedback are central, and the influence of the modern high-speed computer has been strong. Sometimes this area is taken to include communication theory and information theory [see INFORMATION THEORY, *which stresses applications to psychology*].

WILLIAM H. KRUSKAL

BIBLIOGRAPHY

GENERAL ARTICLES

BOEHM, GEORGE A. W. 1964 The Science of Being Almost Certain. *Fortune* 69, no. 2:104–107, 142, 144, 146, 148.

KAC, MARK 1964 Probability. *Scientific American* 211, no. 3:92–108.

KENDALL, M. G. 1950 The Statistical Approach. *Economica* New Series 17:127–145.

KRUSKAL, WILLIAM H. (1965) 1967 Statistics, Molière, and Henry Adams. *American Scientist* 55:416–428. → Previously published in Volume 9 of *Centennial Review*.

WEAVER, WARREN 1952 Statistics. *Scientific American* 186, no. 1:60–63.

INTRODUCTIONS TO PROBABILITY AND STATISTICS

BOREL, ÉMILE F. E. J. (1943) 1962 *Probabilities and Life.* Translated by M. Baudin. New York: Dover. → First published in French.

GNEDENKO, BORIS V.; and KHINCHIN, ALEKSANDR IA. (1945) 1962 *An Elementary Introduction to the Theory of Probability.* Authorized edition. Translated from the 5th Russian edition, by Leo F. Boron, with the editorial collaboration of Sidney F. Mack. New York: Dover. → First published as *Elementarnoe vvedenie v teoriiu veroiatnostei.*

MORONEY, M. J. (1951) 1958 *Facts From Figures.* 3d ed., rev. Harmondsworth (England): Penguin.

MOSTELLER, FREDERICK; ROURKE, ROBERT E. K.; and THOMAS, GEORGE B. JR. 1961 *Probability With Statistical Applications.* Reading, Mass.: Addison-Wesley.

TIPPETT, L. H. C. (1943) 1956 *Statistics.* 2d ed. New York: Oxford Univ. Press.

WALLIS, W. ALLEN; and ROBERTS, HARRY V. 1962 *The Nature of Statistics.* New York: Collier. → Based on material presented in the authors' *Statistics: A New Approach* (1956).

WEAVER, WARREN 1963 *Lady Luck: The Theory of Probability.* Garden City, N.Y.: Doubleday.

YOUDEN, W. J. 1962 *Experimentation and Measurement.* New York: Scholastic Book Services.

ABSTRACTING JOURNALS

Mathematical Reviews. → Published since 1940.

Psychological Abstracts. → Published since 1927. Covers parts of the statistical literature.

Quality Control and Applied Statistics Abstracts. → Published since 1956.

Referativnyi zhurnal: Matematika. → Published since 1953.

Statistical Theory and Method Abstracts. → Published since 1959.

Zentralblatt für Mathematik und ihre Grenzgebiete. → Published since 1931.

WORKS CITED IN THE TEXT

ADAMS, ERNEST W.; FAGOT, ROBERT F.; and ROBINSON, RICHARD E. 1965 A Theory of Appropriate Statistics. *Psychometrika* 30:99–127.

AURTHUR, ROBERT A. 1953 *The Glorification of Al Toolum.* New York: Rinehart.

BORN, MAX (1949) 1951 *Natural Philosophy of Cause and Chance.* Oxford: Clarendon.

BORTKIEWICZ, LADISLAUS VON 1909 Die statistischen Generalisationen. *Scientia* 5:102–121. → A French translation appears in a supplement to Volume 5, pages 58–75.

BRAITHWAITE, R. B. 1953 *Scientific Explanation: A Study of the Function of Theory, Probability and Law in Science.* Cambridge Univ. Press. → A paperback edition was published in 1960 by Harper.

BRIDGMAN, PERCY W. 1959 *The Way Things Are.* Cambridge, Mass.: Harvard Univ. Press.

BROWN, G. SPENCER, *see under* SPENCER BROWN, G.

CHURCHMAN, CHARLES W.; and RATOOSH, PHILBURN (editors) 1959 *Measurement: Definitions and Theories.* New York: Wiley.

COCHRAN, WILLIAM G.; MOSTELLER, FREDERICK; and TUKEY, JOHN W. 1954 *Statistical Problems of the Kinsey Report on Sexual Behavior in the Human Male.* Washington: American Statistical Association.

COOMBS, CLYDE H. 1964 *A Theory of Data.* New York: Wiley.

COX, D. R. 1961 *The Role of Statistical Methods in Science and Technology.* London: Birkbeck College.

DEMING, W. EDWARDS 1965 Principles of Professional Statistical Practice. *Annals of Mathematical Statistics* 36:1883–1900.

GALTON, FRANCIS 1889 *Natural Inheritance.* London and New York: Macmillan.

GINI, CORRADO 1951 Caractère des plus récents développements de la méthodologie statistique. *Statistica* 11:3–11.

GINI, CORRADO 1959 Mathematics in Statistics. *Metron* 19, no. 3/4:1–9.

HOGBEN, LANCELOT T. 1957 *Statistical Theory; the Relationship of Probability, Credibility and Error: An Examination of the Contemporary Crisis in Statistical Theory From a Behaviourist Viewpoint.* London: Allen & Unwin.

HUFF, DARRELL 1954 *How to Lie With Statistics.* New York: Norton.

KADUSHIN, CHARLES 1966 Shakespeare & Sociology. *Columbia University Forum* 9, no. 2:25–31.

KISH, LESLIE 1959 Some Statistical Problems in Research Design. *American Sociological Review* 24:328–338.

KRUTCH, JOSEPH WOOD 1963 Through Happiness With Slide Rule and Calipers. *Saturday Review* 46, no. 44:12–15.

LAZARSFELD, PAUL F. 1961 Notes on the History of Quantification in Sociology: Trends, Sources and Problems. *Isis* 52, part 2:277–333. → Also included in Harry Woolf (editor), *Quantification*, published by Bobbs-Merrill in 1961.

LUNDBERG, GEORGE A. 1940 Statistics in Modern Social Thought. Pages 110–140 in Harry E. Barnes, Howard Becker, and Frances B. Becker (editors), *Contemporary Social Theory.* New York: Appleton.

PEARSON, KARL (1892) 1957 *The Grammar of Science.* 3d ed., rev. & enl. New York: Meridian. → The first and second editions (1892 and 1900) contain material not in the third edition.

PFANZAGL, J. 1959 *Die axiomatischen Grundlagen einer allgemeinen Theorie des Messens.* A publication of the Statistical Institute of the University of Vienna, New Series, No. 1. Würzburg (Germany): Physica-Verlag.

→ Scheduled for publication in English under the title *The Theory of Measurement* in 1968 by Wiley.

POPPER, KARL R. (1935) 1959 *The Logic of Scientific Discovery*. Rev. ed. New York: Basic Books; London: Hutchinson. → First published as *Logik der Forschung*. A paperback edition was published in 1961 by Harper.

SELVIN, HANAN C. 1957 A Critique of Tests of Significance in Survey Research. *American Sociological Review* 22:519–527. → See Volume 23, pages 85–86 and 199–200, for responses by David Gold and James M. Beshers.

SELVIN, HANAN C.; and STUART, ALAN 1966 Data-dredging Procedures in Survey Analysis. *American Statistician* 20, no. 3:20–23.

SKINNER, B. F. 1956 A Case History in Scientific Method. *American Psychologist* 11:221–233.

SPENCER BROWN, G. 1957 *Probability and Scientific Inference*. London: Longmans. → The author's surname is Spencer Brown, but common library practice is to alphabetize his works under Brown.

STEVENS, S. S. 1946 On the Theory of Scales of Measurement. *Science* 103:677–680.

SUPPES, PATRICK; and ZINNES, JOSEPH L. 1963 Basic Measurement Theory. Volume 1, pages 1–76 in R. Duncan Luce, Robert R. Bush, and Eugene Galanter (editors), *Handbook of Mathematical Psychology*. New York: Wiley.

TORGERSON, WARREN S. 1958 *Theory and Methods of Scaling*. New York: Wiley.

TUKEY, JOHN W. 1961 Statistical and Quantitative Methodology. Pages 84–136 in Donald P. Ray (editor), *Trends in Social Science*. New York: Philosophical Library.

TUKEY, JOHN W. 1962 The Future of Data Analysis. *Annals of Mathematical Statistics* 33:1–67, 812.

WALBERG, HERBERT J. 1966 When Are Statistics Appropriate? *Science* 154:330–332. → Follow-up letters by Julian C. Stanley, "Studies of Nonrandom Groups," and by Herbert J. Walberg, "Statistical Randomization in the Behavioral Sciences," were published in Volume 155, on page 953, and Volume 156, on page 314, respectively.

WALPOLE, HORACE (1778) 1904 [Letter] To the Hon. Henry Seymour Conway. Vol. 10, pages 337–338 in Horace Walpole, *The Letters of Horace Walpole, Fourth Earl of Orford*. Edited by Paget Toynbee. Oxford: Clarendon Press.

WESTERGAARD, HARALD L. 1932 *Contributions to the History of Statistics*. London: King.

WHITE, COLIN 1964 Unkind Cuts at Statisticians. *American Statistician* 18, no. 5:15–17.

WOYTINSKY, W. S. 1954 Limits of Mathematics in Statistics. *American Statistician* 8, no. 1:6–10, 18.

II

THE HISTORY OF STATISTICAL METHOD

The broad river of thought that today is known as theoretical statistics cannot be traced back to a single source springing identifiably from the rock. Rather is it the confluence, over two centuries, of a number of tributary streams from many different regions. Probability theory originated at the gaming table; the collection of statistical facts began with state requirements of soldiers and money; marine insurance began with the wrecks and piracy of the ancient Mediterranean; modern studies of mortality have their roots in the plague pits of the seventeenth century; the theory of errors was created in astronomy, the theory of correlation in biology, the theory of experimental design in agriculture, the theory of time series in economics and meteorology, the theories of component analysis and ranking in psychology, and the theory of chi-square methods in sociology. In retrospect it almost seems as if every phase of human life and every science has contributed something of importance to the subject. Its history is accordingly the more interesting, but the more difficult, to write.

Early history

Up to about 1850 the word "statistics" was used in quite a different sense from the present one. It meant information about political states, the kind of material that is nowadays to be found assembled in the *Statesman's Year-book*. Such information was usually, although not necessarily, numerical, and, as it increased in quantity and scope, developed into tabular form. By a natural transfer of meaning, "statistics" came to mean any numerical material that arose in observation of the external world. At the end of the nineteenth century this usage was accepted. Before that time, there were, of course, many problems in statistical methodology considered under other names; but the recognition of their common elements as part of a science of statistics was of relatively late occurrence. The modern theory of statistics (an expression much to be preferred to "mathematical statistics") is the theory of numerical information of almost every kind.

The characteristic feature of such numerical material is that it derives from a set of objects, technically known as a "population," and that any particular variable under measurement has a distribution of frequencies over the members of the set. The height of man, for example, is not identical for every individual but varies from man to man. Nevertheless, we find that the frequency distribution of heights of men in a given population has a definite pattern that can be expressed by a relatively simple mathematical formula. Often the "population" may be conceptual but nonexistent, as for instance when we consider the possible tosses of a penny or the possible measurements that may be made of the transit times of a star. This concept of a distribution of measurements, rather than a single measurement, is fundamental to the whole subject. In consequence, points of statistical interest concern the properties of aggregates, rather than of individuals; and the elementary parts of theoretical statistics are much concerned with summarizing these properties in such measures as averages, index numbers, dispersion measures, and so forth.

The simpler facts concerning aggregates of measurements must, of course, have been known almost from the moment when measurements began to be made. The idea of regularity in the patterning of discrete repeatable chance events, such as dice throwing, emerged relatively early and is found explicitly in Galileo's work. The notion that measurements on natural phenomena should exhibit similar regularities, which are mathematically expressible, seems to have originated in astronomy, in connection with measurements on star transits. After some early false starts it became known that observations of a magnitude were subject to error even when the observer was trained and unbiased. Various hypotheses about the pattern of such errors were propounded. Simpson (1757) was the first to consider a *continuous* distribution, that is to say, a distribution of a variable that could take any values in a continuous range. By the end of the eighteenth century Laplace and Gauss had considered several such mathematically specified distributions and, in particular, had discovered the most famous of them all, the so-called normal distribution [*see* DISTRIBUTIONS, STATISTICAL, *article on* SPECIAL CONTINUOUS DISTRIBUTIONS].

In these studies there was assumed to be a "true" value underlying the distribution. Departures from this true value were "errors." They were, so to speak, extraneous to the object of the study, which was to estimate this true value. Early in the nineteenth century a major step forward was taken with the recognition (especially by Quetelet) that living material also exhibited frequency distributions of definite pattern. Furthermore, Galton and Karl Pearson, from about 1880, showed that these distributions were often skew or asymmetrical, in the sense that the shape of the frequency curve for values above the mean was not the mirror image of the curve for values below the mean. In particular it became impossible to maintain that the deviations from the mean were "errors" or that there existed a "true" value; the frequency distribution itself was to be recognized as a fundamental property of the aggregate. Immediately, similar patterns of regularity were brought to light in nearly every branch of science—genetics, biol-ogy, meteorology, economics, sociology—and even in some of the arts: distributions of weak verse endings were used to date Shakespeare's plays, and the distribution of words has been used to discuss cases of disputed authorship.

Nowadays the concept of frequency distribution is closely bound up with the notion of probability distribution. Some writers of the twentieth century treat the two things as practically synonymous. Historically, however, the two were not always identified and to some extent pursued independent courses for centuries before coming together. We must go back several millenniums if we wish to trace the concept of probability to its source.

From very ancient times man gambled with primitive instruments, such as astragali and dice, and also used chance mechanisms for divinatory purposes. Rather surprisingly, it does not seem that the Greeks, Romans, or the nations of medieval Europe arrived at any clear notion of the laws of chance. Elementary combinatorics appears to have been known to the Arabs and to Renaissance mathematicians, but as a branch of algebra rather than in a probabilistic context. Nevertheless, chance itself was familiar enough, especially in gambling, which was widespread in spite of constant discouragement from church and state. Some primitive ideas of relative frequency of occurrence can hardly have failed to emerge, but a doctrine of chances was extraordinarily late in coming. The first record we have of anything remotely resembling the modern idea of calculating chances occurs in a fifteenth-century poem called *De vetula*. The famous mathematician and physicist Geronimo Cardano was the first to leave a manuscript in which the concept of laws of chance was explicitly set out (Ore 1953). Galileo left a fragment that shows that he clearly understood the method of calculating chances at dice. Not until the work of Huygens (1657), the correspondence between Pascal and Fermat, and the work of Jacques Bernoulli (1713) do we find the beginnings of a calculus of probability.

This remarkable delay in the mathematical formulation of regularity in events that had been observed by gamblers over thousands of years is probably to be explained by the philosophical and religious ideas of the times, at least in the Western world. To the ancients, events were mysterious; they could be influenced by superhuman beings but no being was in control of the universe. On the other hand, to the Christians everything occurred under the will of God, and in a sense there was no chance; it was almost impious to suppose that events happened under the blind laws of probability. Whatever the explanation may be, it was not until Europe had freed itself from the dogma of the medieval theologian that a calculus of probability became possible.

Once the theory of probability had been founded, it developed with great rapidity. Only a hundred years separates the two greatest works in this branch of the subject, Bernoulli's *Ars conjectandi* (1713) and Laplace's *Théorie analytique des probabilités* (1812). Bernoulli exemplified his work mainly in terms of games of chance, and subsequent mathematical work followed the same line. Montmort's work was concerned entirely with gaming, and de Moivre stated most of his results in similar terms, although actuarial applications were always present in his mind (see Todhunter [1865] 1949, pp. 78–134 for Montmort and pp. 135–193 for de Moivre). With Laplace, Condorcet, and rather later, Poisson, we begin to find probabilistic ideas applied to practical problems; for example, Laplace discussed the plausibility of the nebular hypothesis of the solar system in terms of the probability of the planetary orbits lying as nearly in a plane as they do. Condorcet (1785) was concerned with the probability of reaching decisions under various systems of voting, and Poisson (1837) was specifically concerned with the probability of reaching correct conclusions from imperfect evidence. A famous essay of Thomas Bayes (1764) broke new ground by its consideration of probability in inductive reasoning, that is to say, the use of the probabilities of observed events to compare the plausibility of hypotheses that could explain them [see BAYESIAN INFERENCE].

The linkage between classical probability theory and statistics (in the sense of the science of regularity in aggregates of natural phenomena) did not take place at any identifiable point of time. It occurred somewhere along a road with clearly traceable lines of progress but no monumental milestones. The critical point, however, must have been the realization that probabilities were not always to be calculated a priori, as in games of chance, but were measurable constants of the external world. In classical probability theory the probabilities of primitive events were always specified on prior grounds: dice were "fair" in the sense that each side had an equal chance of falling uppermost, cards were shuffled and dealt "at random," and so on. A good deal of probability theory was concerned with the pure mathematics of deriving the probabilities of complicated contingent events from these more primitive events whose probabilities were known. However, when

sampling from an observed frequency distribution, the basic probabilities are not known but are parameters to be estimated. It took some time, perhaps fifty years, for the implications of this notion to be fully realized. Once it was, statistics embraced probability and the subject was poised for the immense development that has occurred over the past century.

Once more, however, we must go back to another contributory subject—insurance, and particularly life insurance. Although some mathematicians, notably Edmund Halley, Abraham de Moivre, and Daniel Bernoulli, made important contributions to demography and insurance studies, for the most part actuarial science pursued a course of its own. The founders of the subject were John Graunt and William Petty. Graunt, spurred on by the information contained in the bills of mortality prepared in connection with the great plague (which hit England in 1665), was the first to reason about demographic material in a modern statistical way. Considering the limitations of his data, his work was a beautiful piece of reasoning. Before long, life tables were under construction and formed the basis of the somewhat intricate calculations of the modern actuary [see LIFE TABLES]. In the middle of the eighteenth century, some nations of the Western world began to take systematic censuses of population and to record causes of mortality, an example that was soon followed by all [see CENSUS; VITAL STATISTICS]. Life insurance became an exact science. It not only contributed an observable frequency distribution with a clearly defined associated calculus; it also contributed an idea that was to grow into a dynamic theory of probability—the concept of a population moving through time in an evolutionary way. Here and there, too, we find demographic material stimulating statistical studies, for example, in the study of the mysteries of the sex ratio of human births.

Modern history

1890–1940. If we have to choose a date at which the modern theory of statistics began, we may put it, somewhat arbitrarily, at 1890. Francis Galton was then 68 but still had twenty years of productive life before him. A professor of economics named Francis Ysidro Edgeworth (then age 45) was calling attention to statistical regularities in election results, Greek verse, and the mating of bees and was about to propound a remarkable generalization of the law of error. A young man named Karl Pearson (age 35) had just been joined by the biologist Walter Weldon at University College, London, and was meditating the lectures that ultimately became *The Grammar of Science*. A student named George Udny Yule, at the age of 20, had caught Pearson's eye. And in that year was born the greatest of them all, Ronald Aylmer Fisher. For the next forty years, notwithstanding Russian work in probability theory—notably the work of Andrei Markov and Aleksandr Chuprov—developments in theoretical statistics were predominantly English. At that point, there was something akin to an intellectual explosion in the United States and India. France was already pursuing an individual line in probability theory under the inspiration of Émile Borel and Paul Lévy, and Italy, under the influence of Corrado Gini, was also developing independently. But at the close of World War II the subject transcended all national boundaries and had become one of the accepted disciplines of the scientific, technological, and industrial worlds.

The world of 1890, with its futile power politics, its class struggles, its imperialism, and its primitive educational system, is far away. But it is still possible to recapture the intellectual excitement with which science began to extend its domain into humanitarian subjects. Life was as mysterious as ever, but it was found to obey laws. Human society was seen as subject to statistical inquiry, as an evolutionary entity under human control. It was no accident that Galton founded the science of eugenics and Karl Pearson took a militant part in some of the social conflicts of his time. Statistical science to them was a new instrument for the exploration of the living world, and the behavioral sciences at last showed signs of structure that would admit of mathematical analysis.

In London, Pearson and Weldon soon began to exhibit frequency distributions in all kinds of fields. Carl Charlier in Sweden, Jacobus Kapteyn and Johan van Uven in Holland, and Vilfredo Pareto in Italy, to mention only a few, contributed results from many different sciences. Pearson developed his system of mathematical curves to fit these observations, and Edgeworth and Charlier began to consider systems based on the sum of terms in a series analogous to a Taylor expansion. It was found that the normal curve did not fit most observed distributions but that it was a fair approximation to many of them.

Relationships between variables.   About 1890, Pearson, stimulated by some work of Galton, began to investigate bivariate distributions, that is to say, the distribution in a two-way table of frequencies of members, each of which bore a value of two variables. The patterns, especially in the biological field where data were most plentiful, were equally typical. In much observed material there were relationships between variables, but they were not of a mathematically functional form. The length and breadth of oak leaves, for example, were dependent in the sense that a high value of one tended to occur with a high value of the other. But there was no formula expressing this relationship in the familiar deterministic language of physics. There had to be developed a new kind of relationship to describe this type of connection. In the theory of attributes this led to measures of *association* and *contingency* [see STATISTICS, DESCRIPTIVE]; in the theory of variables it led to *correlation* and *regression* [see LINEAR HYPOTHESES; MULTIVARIATE ANALYSIS, *articles on* CORRELATION].

The theory of statistical relationship, and especially of regression, has been studied continuously and intensively ever since. Most writers on statistics have made contributions at one time or another. The work was still going strong in the middle of the twentieth century. Earlier writers, such as Pearson and Yule, were largely concerned with linear regression, in which the value of one variable is expressed as a linear function of the others plus a random term. Later authors extended the theory to cover several dependent variables and curvilinear cases; and Fisher in particular was instrumental in emphasizing the importance of rendering the explanatory variables independent, so far as possible.

Sampling.   It was not long before statisticians were brought up against a problem that is still, in one form or another, basic to most of their work. In the majority of cases the data with which they were presented were only samples from a larger population. The problems then arose as to how reliable the samples were, how to estimate from them values of parameters describing the parent population, and, in general, what kinds of inference could be based on them.

Some intuitive ideas on the subject occur as far back as the eighteenth century; but the sampling problem, and the possibility of treating it with mathematical precision, was not fully appreciated until the twentieth century.

Classical error theory, especially the work of Carl Friedrich Gauss in the first half of the nineteenth century, had considered sampling distributions of a simple kind. For example, the chi-square distribution arose in 1875 when the German geodesist Friedrich Helmert worked out the distribution of sample variance for sampling from a normal population. The same chi-square distribution was independently rediscovered in 1900 by

Karl Pearson in a quite different context, that of testing distributional goodness of fit [see COUNTED DATA; GOODNESS OF FIT]. In another direction, Pearson developed a wide range of asymptotic formulas for standard errors of sample quantities. The mathematics of many so-called small-sample distribution problems presented difficulties with which Pearson was unable to cope, despite valiant attempts. William Gosset, a student of Pearson's, produced in 1908 one of the most important statistical distributions under the pseudonym of "Student"; and this distribution, arising from a basic small sample problem, is known as that of Student's *t* [see DISTRIBUTIONS, STATISTICAL].

It was Student and R. A. Fisher (beginning in 1913) who inaugurated a new era in the study of sampling distributions. Fisher himself made major contributions to the subject over the ensuing thirty years. In rapid succession he found the distribution, in samples from a normal population, of the correlation coefficient, regression coefficients, multiple correlation coefficients, and the ratio of variances known as *F*. Other writers, notably John Wishart in England, Harold Hotelling and Samuel Wilks in the United States, and S. N. Roy and R. C. Bose in India, added a large number of new results, especially in the field of multivariate analysis. More recently, T. W. Anderson has advanced somewhat farther the frontiers of knowledge in this rather difficult mathematical field.

Concurrently with these spectacular mathematical successes in the derivation of sampling distributions, methods were also devised for obtaining approximations. Again R. A. Fisher was in the lead with a paper (1928) introducing the so-called *k*-statistics, functions of sample values that have simplifying mathematical properties.

The question whether a sampling method is random is a subtle one. It does not always trouble an experimental scientist, when he can select his material by a chance mechanism. However, sometimes the data are provided by nature, and whether they are a random selection from the available population is difficult to determine. In the sampling of human beings difficulties are accentuated by the fact that people may react to the sampling process. As sampling methods spread to the social sciences, the problems of obtaining valid samples at low cost from a wide geographical scatter of human beings became increasingly important, and some new problems of respondent bias arose. In consequence, the sampling of humans for social inquiry has almost developed into a separate subject, dependent partly on psychological matters, such as how questions should be framed to avoid

bias, and partly on expense. By 1960 sampling errors in social surveys were well under control; but many problems remained for exploration, notably those of drawing samples of individuals with relatively rare and specialized characteristics, such as retail pharmacists or sufferers from lung cancer. Designing a sample was accepted as just as much a matter of expertise as designing a house [see INTERVIEWING; SAMPLE SURVEYS; SURVEY ANALYSIS].

The control of the sample and the derivation of sampling distributions were, of course, only means to an end, which was the drawing of accurate inferences from the sample that ultimately resulted. We shall say more about the general question of inference below, but it is convenient to notice here the emergence, between 1925 and 1935, of two branches of the subject: the theory of estimation, under the inspiration of Fisher, and the theory of hypothesis testing, under the inspiration of Karl Pearson's son Egon and Jerzy Neyman [see ESTIMATION; HYPOTHESIS TESTING].

Estimation. Up to 1914 (which, owing to World War I, actually means up to 1920), the then current ideas on estimation from a sample were intuitive and far from clear. For the most part, an estimate was constructed from a sample as though it were being constructed for a population (for example, the sample mean was an "obvious" estimate of the parent population mean). A few writers—Daniel Bernoulli, Laplace, Gauss, Markov, and Edgeworth—had considered the problem, asked the right questions, and sometimes found partial answers. Ideas on the subject were clarified and extended in a notable paper by Fisher (1925). He introduced the concepts of optimal estimators and of efficiency in estimation, and emphasized the importance of the so-called method of maximum likelihood as providing a very general technique for obtaining "best" estimators. These ideas were propounded to a world that was just about ripe for them, and the theory of estimation developed at a remarkable rate in the ensuing decades.

The related problem of gauging the reliability of an estimate, that is, of surrounding it with a band of error (which has associated with it a designated probability) led to two very different lines of development, the confidence intervals of Egon Pearson and Neyman and the "fiducial intervals" of Fisher, both originating between 1925 and 1930 [see ESTIMATION, *article on* CONFIDENCE INTERVALS AND REGIONS; FIDUCIAL INFERENCE]. The two proceeded fairly amiably side by side for a few years, and at the time it seemed that they were equivalent; they certainly led to the same results in simpler cases. However, it became clear about 1935 that they were conceptually very different, and a great deal of argument developed which had not been resolved even at the time of Fisher's death in 1962. Fortunately the controversy, although embittered, did not impede progress. (Omitted at this point is any discussion of Bayesian methods, which may lead to intervals resembling superficially those of confidence and fiducial approaches; Bayesian methods are mentioned briefly below.) [See BAYESIAN INFERENCE for a detailed discussion.]

Hypothesis testing. In a like manner, the work of Neyman and Pearson (beginning in 1928) on the theory of statistical tests gave a very necessary clarity to procedures that had hitherto been vague and unsatisfactory. In probabilistic terms the older type of inference had been of this type: If a certain hypothesis were true, the probability that I should observe the actual sample that I have drawn, or one more extreme, is very small; therefore the hypothesis is probably untrue. Neyman and Pearson pointed out that a hypothesis could not be tested *in vacuo* but only in comparison with other hypotheses. They set up a theory of tests and—as in the case of estimation, with which this subject is intimately linked—discussed power, relative efficiency, and optimality of tests. Here also there was some controversy, but for the most part the Neyman–Pearson theory was generally accepted and had become standard practice by 1950.

Experimental design and analysis. Concurrently with developments in sampling theory, estimation, and hypothesis testing, there was growing rapidly, between 1920 and 1940, a theory of experimental design based again on the work of Fisher. Very early in his career, it had become clear to him that in multivariate situations the "explanation" of one variable in terms of a set of dependent or explanatory variables was rendered difficult, if not impossible, where correlations existed among the explanatory variables themselves; for it then became impossible to say how much of an effect was attributable to a particular cause. This difficulty, which still bedevils the general theory of regression, could be overcome if the explanatory variables could be rendered statistically independent. (This, incidentally, was the genesis of the use of orthogonal polynomials in curvilinear regression analysis.) Fisher recognized that in experimental situations where the design of the experiment was, within limits, at choice, it could be arranged that the effects of different factors were "orthogonal," that is, independent, so

that they could be disentangled. From this notion, coupled with probabilistic interpretations of significance and the necessary mathematical tests, he built up a most remarkable system of experimental design. The new methods were tested at the Rothamsted Experimental Station in England but were rapidly spread by an active and able group of disciples into all scientific fields.

Some earlier work, particularly by Wilhelm Lexis in Germany at the close of the nineteenth century, had called attention to the fact that in sampling from nonhomogeneous populations the formulas of classical probability were a poor representation of the observed effects. This led to attempts to split the sampling variation into components; one, for example, representing the inevitable fluctuation of sampling, another representing the differences between the sections or subpopulations from which members were drawn. In Fisher's hands these ideas were extended and given precision in what is known as the analysis of variance, one of the most powerful tools of modern statistics. The methods were later extended to cover the simultaneous variation of several variables in the analysis of covariance. [See LINEAR HYPOTHESES, article on ANALYSIS OF VARIANCE.]

It may be remarked, incidentally, that the problems brought up by these various developments in theoretical statistics have proved an immense challenge to mathematicians. Many branches of abstract mathematics—invariants, symmetric functions, groups, finite geometries, n-dimensional geometry, as well as the whole field of analysis—have been brought effectively into play in solving practical problems. After World War II the advent of the electronic computer was a vital adjunct to the solution of problems where even the resources of modern mathematics failed. Sampling experiments became possible on a scale never dreamed of before.

Recent developments. So much occurred in the statistical domain between 1920 and 1940 that it is not easy to give a clear account of the various currents of development. We may, however, pause at 1940 to look backward. In Europe, and to a smaller extent in the United States, World War II provided an interregnum, during which much was absorbed and a good deal of practical work was done, but, of necessity, theoretical developments had to wait, at least as far as publication was concerned. The theory of statistical distributions and of statistical relationship had been firmly established by 1940. In sampling theory many mathematical problems had been solved, and methods of approach to outstanding problems had been devised. The groundwork of experimental design had been firmly laid. The basic problems of inference had been explicitly set out and solutions reached over a fairly wide area. What is equally important for the development of the subject, there was about to occur a phenomenal increase in the number of statisticians in academic life, in government work, and in business. By 1945 the subject was ready for decades of vigorous and productive exploration.

Much of this work followed in the direct line of earlier work. The pioneers had left sizable areas undeveloped; and in consequence, work on distribution theory, sampling, and regression analysis continued in fair volume without any fundamental change in concept. Among the newer fields of attention we may notice in particular sequential analysis, decision function theory, multivariate analysis, time series and stochastic processes, statistical inference, and distribution-free, or nonparametric, methods [*see* DECISION THEORY; MARKOV CHAINS; MULTIVARIATE ANALYSIS; NONPARAMETRIC STATISTICS; QUEUES; SEQUENTIAL ANALYSIS; TIME SERIES].

Sequential analysis. During World War II it was realized by George Barnard in England and Abraham Wald in the United States that some types of sampling were wasteful in that they involved scrutinizing a sample of fixed size even if the examination of the first few members already indicated the decision to be made. This led to a theory of sequential sampling, in which the sample number is not fixed in advance but at each stage in the sampling a decision is made whether to continue or not. This work was applied with success to the control of the quality of manufactured products, and it was soon also realized that a great deal of scientific inquiry was, in fact, sequential in character. [*See* QUALITY CONTROL, STATISTICAL.]

Decision functions. Wald was led to consider a more general approach, which linked up with Neyman's ideas on hypothesis testing and developed into a theory of decision functions. The basic idea was that at certain stages decisions have to be made, for example, to accept or reject a hypothesis. The object of the theory is to lay down a set of rules under which these decisions can be intelligently made; and, if it is possible to specify penalties for taking wrong decisions, to optimize the method of choice according to some criterion, such as minimizing the risk of loss. The theory had great intellectual attraction and even led some statisticians to claim that the whole of statistics was a branch of decision-function theory, a claim

that was hotly resisted in some quarters and may or may not stand up to deeper examination.

Multivariate problems. By 1950 the mathematical development of some branches of statistical theory had, in certain directions, outrun their practical usefulness. This was true of multivariate analysis based on normal distributions. In the more general theory of multivariate problems, several lines of development were pursued. One part of the theory attempts to reduce the number of effective dimensions, especially by component analysis and, as developed by psychologists, factor analysis [*see* FACTOR ANALYSIS]. Another, known as canonical correlation analysis, attempts to generalize correlation to the relationship between two vector quantities. A third generalizes distribution theory and sampling to multidimensional cases. The difficulties are formidable, but a good deal of progress has been made. One problem has been to find practical data that would bear the weight of the complex analysis that resulted. The high-speed computer may be a valuable tool in further work in this field. [*See* COMPUTATION.]

Time series and stochastic processes. Perhaps the most extensive developments after World War II were in the field of time series and stochastic processes generally. The problem of analyzing a time series has particular difficulties of its own. The system under examination may have a trend present and may have seasonal fluctuations. The classical method of approach was to dissect the series into trend, seasonal movement, oscillatory effects, and residual; but there is always danger that an analysis of this kind is an artifact that does not correspond to the causal factors at work, so that projection into the future is unreliable. Even where trend is absent, or has been abstracted, the analysis of oscillatory movements is a treacherous process. Attempts to apply harmonic analysis to economic data, and hence to elicit "cycles," were usually failures, owing to the fact that observed fluctuations were not regular in period, phase, or amplitude [*see* TIME SERIES, *article on* CYCLES].

The basic work on time series was done by Yule between 1925 and 1930. He introduced what is now known as an autoregressive process, in which the value of the series at any point is a linear function of certain previous values plus a random residual. The behavior of the series is then determined, so to speak, partly by the momentum of past history and partly by unpredictable disturbance. In the course of this work Yule introduced serial correlations, which measure the relationship between terms of the series separated by specified time intervals. It was later realized that these functions are closely allied to the coefficients that arise in the Fourier analysis of the series.

World War II acted as a kind of incubatory period. Immediately afterward it was appreciated that Yule's method of analyzing oscillatory movements in time series was only part of a much larger field, which was not confined to movements through time. Earlier pioneer work by several writers, notably Louis Bachelier, Eugen Slutsky, and Andrei Markov, was brought together and formed the starting point of a new branch of probability theory. Any system that passes through a succession of states falls within its scope, provided that the transition from one state to the next is decided by a schedule of probabilities and is not purely deterministic. Such systems are known as stochastic processes. A very wide variety of situations falls within their scope, among them epidemics, stock control, traffic movements, and queues. They may be regarded as constituting a probability theory of movement, as distinct from the classical systems in which the generating mechanism behind the observations was constant and the successive observations were independent. From 1945 onward there was a continual stream of papers on the subject, many of which were contributed by Russian and French authors [*see* MARKOV CHAINS; QUEUES].

Some philosophical questions. Common to all this work was a constant re-examination of the logic of the inferential processes involved. The problem of making meaningful statements about the world on the basis of examination of only a small part of it had exercised a series of thinkers from Bacon onward, notably George Boole, John Stuart Mill, and John Venn, but it remained essentially unsolved and was regarded by some as constituting more of a philosophical puzzle than a barrier to scientific advance. The specific procedures proposed by statisticians brought the issue to a head by defining the problem of induction much more exactly, and even by exposing situations where logical minds might well reach different conclusions from the same data. This was intellectually intolerable and necessitated some very searching probing into the rather intuitive arguments by which statisticians drew their conclusions in the earlier stages of development of the subject.

Discussion has been centered on the theory of probability, in which two attitudes may be distinguished: subjective and objective [*see* PROBABILITY, *article on* INTERPRETATIONS]. Neither approach is free from difficulty. Both lead to the same calculus of probabilities in the deductive

sense. The primary problem, first stated explicitly by Thomas Bayes, however, is one of induction, to which the calculus of probabilities makes no contribution except as a tool of analysis. Some authorities reject the Bayesian approach and seek for principles of inferences elsewhere. Others, recognizing that the required prior probabilities necessitate certain assumptions, nevertheless can see no better way of tackling the problem if the relative acceptability of hypotheses is to be quantified at all [*see* BAYESIAN INFERENCE]. Fortunately for the development of theoretical statistics, the philosophical problems have remained in the background, stimulating argument and a penetrating examination of the inferential process but not holding up development. In practice it is possible for two competent statisticians to differ in the interpretation of data, although if they do, the reliability of the inference is often low enough to justify further experimentation. Such cases are not very frequent, but important instances do occur; a notable one is the interpretation of the undeniable observed relationship between intensity of smoking and cancer of the lung. Differences in interpretation are particularly liable to occur in economic and social investigations because of the difficulty of performing experiments or of isolating causal influences for separate study.

Robustness and nonparametric methods. The precision of inferences in probability is sometimes bought at the expense of rather restrictive assumptions about the population of origin. For example, Student's *t*-test depends on the supposition that the parent population is normal. Various attempts have been made to give the inferential procedures greater generality by freeing them from these restrictions. For example, certain tests can be shown to be "robust" in the sense that they are not very sensitive to deviations from the basic assumptions [*see* ERRORS]. Another interesting field is concerned with tests that depend on ranks, order statistics, or even signs, and are very largely independent of the form of the parent population. These so-called distribution-free methods, which are usually easy to apply, are often surprisingly efficient [*see* NONPARAMETRIC STATISTICS].

The frontiers of the subject continue to extend. Problems of statistical relationship, of estimation in complicated models, of quantification and scaling in qualitative material, and of economizing in exploratory effort are as urgent and lively as ever. The theoretical statistician ranges from questions of galactic distribution to the properties of subatomic particles, suspended, like Pascal's man, between the infinitely large and the infinitely small. The greater part of the history of his subject lies in the future.

M. G. KENDALL

[*The following biographies present further details on specific periods in the history of statistical method. Early Period:* BABBAGE; BAYES; BERNOULLI FAMILY; BIENAYMÉ; GALTON; GAUSS; GRAUNT; LAPLACE; MOIVRE; PETTY; POISSON; QUETELET; SÜSSMILCH. *Modern Period:* BENINI; BORTKIEWICZ; FISHER, R. A.; GINI; GIRSHICK; GOSSET; KEYNES, JOHN MAYNARD; KŐRÖSY; LEXIS; LOTKA; PEARSON; SPEARMAN; STOUFFER; VON MISES, RICHARD; VON NEUMANN; WALD; WIENER; WILKS; WILLCOX; YULE.]

BIBLIOGRAPHY

There is no history of theoretical statistics or of statistical methodology. Westergaard 1932 is interesting as an introduction but is largely concerned with descriptive statistics. Walker 1929 has some valuable sketches of the formative period under Karl Pearson. Todhunter 1865 is a comprehensive guide to mathematical work up to Laplace and contains bibliographical information on many of the early works cited in the text of this article. David 1962 is a modern and lively account up to the time of de Moivre. The main sources for further reading are in obituaries and series of articles that appear from time to time in statistical journals, especially the "Studies in the History of Probability and Statistics" in Biometrika *and occasional papers in the* Journal of the American Statistical Association.

BAYES, THOMAS (1764) 1958 An Essay Towards Solving A Problem in the Doctrine of Chances. *Biometrika* 45:296–315. → First published in Volume 53 of the Royal Society of London's *Philosophical Transactions.* A facsimile edition was published in 1963 by Hafner.

BERNOULLI, JACQUES (1713) 1899 *Wahrscheinlichkeitsrechnung (Ars conjectandi).* 2 vols. Leipzig: Engelmann. → First published posthumously in Latin.

CONDORCET, MARIE JEAN ANTOINE NICOLAS CARITAT, DE 1785 *Essai sur l'application de l'analyse à la probabilité des décisions rendues à la pluralité des voix.* Paris: Imprimerie Royale.

CZUBER, EMANUEL 1898 *Die Entwicklung der Wahrscheinlichkeitstheorie und ihrer Anwendungen.* Jahresbericht der Deutschen Mathematikervereinigung, Vol. 7, No. 2. Leipzig: Teubner.

DAVID, F. N. 1962 *Games, Gods and Gambling: The Origins and History of Probability and Statistical Ideas From the Earliest Times to the Newtonian Era.* London: Griffin; New York: Hafner.

FISHER, R. A. 1925 Theory of Statistical Estimation. *Cambridge Philosophical Society, Proceedings* 22:700–725. → Reprinted in Fisher 1950.

FISHER, R. A. 1928 Moments and Product Moments of Sampling Distributions. *London Mathematical Society, Proceedings* 30:199–238. → Reprinted in Fisher 1950.

FISHER, R. A. (1920–1945) 1950 *Contributions to Mathematical Statistics.* New York: Wiley.

HUYGENS, CHRISTIAAN 1657 De rationciniis in ludo aleae. Pages 521–534 in Frans van Schooten, *Exercitationum mathematicarum.* Leiden (Netherlands): Elsevir.

KOTZ, SAMUEL 1965 Statistical Terminology—Russian vs. English—In the Light of the Development of Statistics in the USSR. *American Statistician* 19, no. 3:14–22.

LAPLACE, PIERRE SIMON (1812) 1820 *Théorie analytique des probabilités.* 3d ed., revised. Paris: Courcier.

ORE, ØYSTEIN 1953 *Cardano: The Gambling Scholar.* Princeton Univ. Press; Oxford Univ. Press. → Includes a translation from the Latin of Cardano's *Book on Games of Chance* by Sydney Henry Gould.

PEARSON, KARL (1892) 1911 *The Grammar of Science.* 3d ed., rev. & enl. London: Black. → A paperback edition was published in 1957 by Meridian.

POISSON, SIMÉON DENIS 1837 *Recherches sur la probabilité des jugements en matière criminelle et en matière civile, précédées des règles générales du calcul des probabilités.* Paris: Bachelier.

SIMPSON, THOMAS 1757 *Miscellaneous Tracts on Some Curious and Very Interesting Subjects in Mechanics, Physical-astronomy, and Speculative Mathematics.* London: Nourse.

TODHUNTER, ISAAC (1865) 1949 *A History of the Mathematical Theory of Probability From the Time of Pascal to That of Laplace.* New York: Chelsea.

WALKER, HELEN M. 1929 *Studies in the History of Statistical Method, With Special Reference to Certain Educational Problems.* Baltimore: Williams & Wilkins.

WESTERGAARD, HARALD 1932 *Contributions to the History of Statistics.* London: King.

STATISTICS, DESCRIPTIVE

I. LOCATION AND DISPERSION   *Hans Kellerer*
II. ASSOCIATION   *Robert H. Somers*

I
LOCATION AND DISPERSION

A basic statistical need is that of describing a set of observations in terms of a few calculated quantities—descriptive statistics—that express compactly the most salient features of the observational material. Some common descriptive statistics are the sample average, the median, the standard deviation, and the correlation coefficient.

Of course, one is also interested in corresponding descriptive quantities for the underlying population from which the sample of observations was drawn; these population descriptive statistics may usually be thought of as sample descriptive statistics for very large hypothetical samples, so large that sampling variability becomes negligible.

The present article deals with descriptive statistics relating to *location* or position (for instance, the sample average or the median) and to *dispersion* or variability (for instance, the standard deviation). The accompanying article deals with descriptive statistics for aspects of association between two or more statistical variates (for instance, the correlation coefficient).

Most, although not all, descriptive statistics for location deal with a generalized mean—that is, some function of the observations satisfying intuitive restrictions of the following kind: (*a*) a generalized mean must take values between the lowest and highest observations; (b) it must be unchanged under reorderings of the observations; and (c) if all the observations are equal, the generalized mean must have their common value. There are many possible generalized means; those selected for discussion here have useful interpretations, are computationally reasonable, and have a tradition of use.

Descriptive statistics of dispersion supply information about the scatter of individual observations. Such statistics are usually constructed so that they become larger as the sample becomes less homogeneous.

Descriptive statistics of location

Generalized means. An important family of location measures represents the so-called central tendency of a set of observations in one of various senses. Suppose the observations are denoted by $x_1, x_2, \cdots, x_n$. Then the ordinary average or arithmetic mean is

$$(1) \qquad \frac{1}{n}\sum_{i=1}^{n} x_i.$$

If, however, a function, f, is defined and the average of the $f(x_i)$'s is considered, then an associated generalized mean, M, is defined by

$$f(M) = \frac{1}{n}\sum f(x_i).$$

The summation is from 1 to n, and f has the same meaning on both sides of the defining equation. For the arithmetic mean, f is the identity function. For the geometric mean (when all x_i's are positive), f is the logarithmic function—that is, $\log M = (1/n) \sum \log x_i$, so that

$$M = \sqrt[n]{x_1 x_2 \cdots x_n}.$$

For this procedure to make sense, f must provide a one-to-one relationship between possible values of the x_i's and possible values of the $f(x_i)$'s. Sometimes special conventions are necessary.

For any such generalized mean, the three intuitive restrictions listed earlier are clearly satisfied when f is monotone increasing. In addition, a change in any single x_i, with the others fixed, changes the value of M. Four of the many generalized means having these properties are listed in Table 1. Since the quadratic mean is important primarily in measuring dispersion, only the first three means listed in Table 1 will be discussed in detail.

The arithmetic mean. The arithmetic mean is perhaps the most common of all location statistics because of its clear meaning and ease of computation. It is usually denoted by placing a bar above the generic symbol describing the observations, thus $\bar{x} = (1/n) \sum x_i$, $\bar{a} = (1/n) \sum a_i$, etc. The population analogue of the arithmetic mean is simply the expectation of a random variable describing the population—that is, $E(X)$, if X is the random variable. [See PROBABILITY, *article on* FORMAL PROBABILITY.]

If the x_i's represent, for example, the wages received by the ith individual in a group, then $\sum x_i$ represents the total wages received, and $\bar{x}$, the arithmetic mean or ordinary average, represents the wages that would have been received by each person if everyone in the group had received the same amount.

The major formal properties of the arithmetic mean are:

(a) The sum of the deviations of the x_i's from $\bar{x}$ is zero: $\sum(x_i - \bar{x}) = 0$.

(b) The sum of squared deviations of the x_i's from x, considered as a function of x, is minimized by $\bar{x}$: $\sum(x_i - \bar{x})^2 \leqslant \sum(x_i - x)^2$ for all x.

(c) If a and b are any two numbers, and if one sets $y_i = ax_i + b$, then $\bar{y} = a\bar{x} + b$, and $\bar{x} = (\bar{y} - b)/a$ when $a \neq 0$. This linear invariance of the arithmetic mean is the basis for so-called coding, changing the origin and scale of the observations for computational convenience. For example,

Table 1 — Four important generalized means

	$f(x)$	Equation for the mean value, M
Arithmetic mean	x	$M = \dfrac{\sum x_i}{n}$
Geometric mean	$\log x$	$\log M = \dfrac{\sum \log x_i}{n}$ so that $M = \sqrt[n]{x_1 x_2 \cdots x_n}$, where $x_i > 0$
Harmonic mean	$\dfrac{1}{x}$	$\dfrac{1}{M} = \dfrac{\sum(1/x_i)}{n}$ so that $M = \dfrac{n}{\sum(1/x_i)}$, where $x_i \neq 0$
Quadratic mean	x^2	$M^2 = \dfrac{\sum x_i^2}{n}$ so that $M = \sqrt{\dfrac{\sum x_i^2}{n}}$, where $x_i \geqslant 0$

instead of finding the average of the x_i's 110, 125, 145, 190, 210, and 300, it is simpler to subtract 100 from each number and multiply by $\frac{1}{5}$: $y_i = \frac{1}{5}(x_i - 100)$. After finding $\bar{y}$ (16 for the x_i's listed here), it is necessary only to reverse the coding process to obtain $\bar{x} = 5\bar{y} + 100$ (180 in this case).

(d) Suppose the x_i's are divided into m subgroups, where the jth subgroup includes n_j of the x_i's ($\sum n_j = n$) and has arithmetic mean $\bar{x}_j$. Then $\bar{x}$, the arithmetic mean for all the x_i's, is

$$(2) \quad \bar{x} = \frac{n_1 \bar{x}_1 + n_2 \bar{x}_2 + \cdots + n_m \bar{x}_m}{n_1 + n_2 + \cdots + n_m} = \frac{\sum n_j \bar{x}_j}{n}.$$

When n is large, it is often advisable to summarize the original observations in a frequency table. Table 2 shows how $\bar{x}$ is calculated in this case.

Table 2 — Observations summarized in a frequency table

CLASS (j)	CLASS INTERVAL	CLASS MARK w_j	FREQUENCY f_j	$w_j f_j$
1	$10 \leqslant x < 15$	12.5	3	37.5
2	$15 \leqslant x < 20$	17.5	22	385.0
3	$20 \leqslant x < 25$	22.5	38	855.0
4	$25 \leqslant x < 30$	27.5	29	797.5
5	$30 \leqslant x < 35$	32.5	8	260.0
Totals			100	2,335.0

The table shows, for example, that 22 of the 100 x_i lie in the interval from 15 to 20. By eq. (2)

$$\bar{x} = \frac{\text{Sum of the statistical values in the 5 classes}}{\sum f_j}.$$

The numerator may be determined approximately by resorting to the "hypothesis of the class mark": the average value of the observations in a class is the class mark—that is, $w_j = \bar{x}_j$ for all j. Up to the accuracy of the approximation this yields

$$(3) \quad \bar{x} \cong \frac{\sum w_j f_j}{\sum f_j} = \frac{\sum w_j f_j}{n}.$$

The numerator summation is now from 1 to m (m = the number of classes). For the data in Table 2, $\bar{x} \cong 2{,}335/100 = 23.35$.

A coding transformation may be employed for easier computation:

$$(4) \quad \bar{x} \cong c \cdot \frac{\sum \left(\dfrac{w_j - x_0}{c} \right) f_j}{n} + x_0.$$

The numbers x_0 and c should be chosen for convenience in computation. In the example, one might take $x_0 = 22.5$ = the class mark of the central class and $c = 5$ = the class width. This transformation

Table 3 — Frequency table with coded observations

Class	$y_j = (w_j - 22.5)/5$	f_j	$y_j f_j$
1	-2	3	-6
2	-1	22	-22
3	0	38	0
4	1	29	29
5	2	8	16
Totals		100	17

yields Table 3, from which $\bar{x} \cong 5(17/100) + 22.5 = 23.35$, as before.

It often happens that the first or last class is "open"—that is, the lowermost or uppermost class boundary is unknown. If there are only a few elements in the open classes, a reasonable choice of class marks may often be made without fear that the arithmetic mean will be much affected. [*Considerations about choice of class width and position, and about the errors incurred in adopting the hypothesis of the class mark, are given in* STATISTICAL ANALYSIS, SPECIAL PROBLEMS OF, *article on* GROUPED OBSERVATIONS.]

Weighted averages, of the form $\sum a_i x_i / \sum a_i$, are often employed, especially in the formation of index numbers. These bear a clear formal relationship to the arithmetic means computed by formula (3) [*see* INDEX NUMBERS].

The geometric mean. One of the subtle problems that concerned thinkers in the Middle Ages was the following: The true, unknown value of a horse is, say, 100 units of money. Two persons, A and B, estimate this unknown value. A's estimate is 10 units, and B's is 1,000. Which is the worse estimate? There are two objections to the answer "B's estimate is worse, because he is off by 900 units, whereas A is only 90 units off": first, the available room for estimating downward is only 100 units, because negative units do not apply, whereas the room for estimating upward (above 100 units) is unlimited; second, since A's estimate is $\frac{1}{10}$ of the true value and B's is 10 times the true value, both estimates are equally poor, relatively speaking. The two errors balance out on the multiplicative average, for $0.1 \cdot 10 = 1$.

An example will illustrate the use of the geometric mean: The number of television viewers in a certain area was 50 on January 1, 1960, and 4,050 on January 1, 1964. It might be in order to assume the same *relative* increase (by a factor of r) for each of the four years involved. Table 4 can then be drawn up. Under the assumption of constant relative increase per year, $50r^4 = 4{,}050$, so that $r = \sqrt[4]{4{,}050/50} = 3$. The corresponding imputed values are given in parentheses in the last

Table 4 — Television viewers in a certain area[a]

Date (Jan. 1)	Observed number	Assumed formula	Observed and imputed[b]
1960	50	50	50
1961		$50r$	(150)
1962		$50r^2$	(450)
1963		$50r^3$	(1,350)
1964	4,050	$50r^4$	4,050

a. Hypothetical data.
b. Imputed values are shown in parentheses.

column of Table 4. Note that the square root of the product of the initial and final numbers, $\sqrt{50 \times 4{,}050}$, is 450, the imputed value at the middle year.

The example indicates that the geometric mean may be appropriate in instances of relative change. This is the situation, for example, in several index problems [see INDEX NUMBERS]. Here multiplication takes the place of the addition employed in the arithmetic mean; hence, the procedure is to extract roots instead of to divide. One justification for the term "geometric mean" comes from considering the geometric sequence 1, 2, 4, 8, 16, 32, 64; the central element, 8, is the same as the geometric mean. Calculating the geometric mean makes sense only when each original value is greater than zero. If the data is grouped as in Table 2, the corresponding geometric mean is

$$(5) \qquad M = \sqrt[n]{w_1^{f_1} w_2^{f_2} \cdots w_m^{f_m}}.$$

The geometric mean of n fractions, x_i/y_i, $i = 1, \cdots, n$, is equal to the quotient of the geometric mean of the x_i's divided by the geometric mean of the y_i's. If X is a positive random variable that describes the underlying population, then the population geometric mean is $10^{E(\log X)}$, where logarithms are taken to base 10.

The harmonic mean. The feature common to the following examples is the employment of reciprocals of the original values.

Example 1: A man travels 2 kilometers, traveling the first at the speed $x_1 = 10$ km/hr and the second at the speed $x_2 = 20$ km/hr. What is the "average" speed? The answer $(10 + 20)/2 = 15$ would usually be misleading, for the man travels a longer time at the lower speed, 10 km/hr, than at the higher speed, 20 km/hr—that is, 1/10 as against 1/20 of an hour. Since speed is defined as distance/time, a better average might be the harmonic mean

$$H = \frac{2}{\dfrac{1}{10} + \dfrac{1}{20}} = 13\tfrac{1}{3} \text{ km/hr.}$$

The point is that speed averaged over time must satisfy the relationship

average speed × total time = total distance,

and only the harmonic average does this (when the individual distances are equal).

The example may be generalized as follows: At first a man travels 60 km at a speed of 15 km/hr and then 90 km at a speed of 45 km/hr. The corresponding weighted harmonic mean is

$$\frac{60 + 90}{60 \cdot \dfrac{1}{15} + 90 \cdot \dfrac{1}{45}} = 25 \text{ km/hr.}$$

Example 2: A market research institute wants to determine the average daily consumption of razor blades by polling 500 persons. Experience has shown that it is better to ask, "How many days does a razor blade last you?" because that is how people usually think. The results of the poll are shown in Table 5, where x_i denotes the number of

Table 5 — Useful life of razor blades*

Number of days $= x_i$	Number of persons $= f_i$	Total consumption per day $= (1/x_i)f_i$
2	100	50
3	150	50
4	200	50
5	50	10
Totals	500	160

* Hypothetical data.

days a razor blade lasts. Column 3 indicates that the 100 persons in the first group use $\tfrac{1}{2} \cdot 100 = 50$ blades a day. The average consumption per person per day is

$$\frac{1}{H} = \frac{\sum (1/x_i)f_i}{\sum f_i} = \frac{160}{500} = .32.$$

Other descriptive statistics of location. There are several location measures that are not conveniently described in the form $f(M) = (1/n)\sum f(x_i)$. Most of these other location measures are based on the order statistics of the sample [see NONPARAMETRIC STATISTICS, *article on* ORDER STATISTICS].

The median. If a set of n observations (n odd) with no ties is arranged in algebraic order, the median of the observations is defined as the middle member of the ordering. For example, the median, $\text{Me}(x)$, of the (ordered) x_i's

2, 17, 19, 23, 38, 47, 98

is 23. If n is even, it is conventional, although arbitrary, to take as median the average of the two middle observations; for example, the conventional median of

$$2, 17, 19, 23, 38, 47$$

is $(19 + 23)/2 = 21$. The same definitions apply even when ties are present. Thus, the median cuts the set of observations in half according to order.

Unlike the descriptive statistics discussed earlier, the median is unaffected by changes in most individual observations, provided that the changes are not too large. For example, in the first set of numbers above, 2 could be changed to any other number not greater than 23 without affecting the median. Thus, the median is less sensitive to outliers than is the arithmetic mean [*see* STATISTICAL ANALYSIS, SPECIAL PROBLEMS OF, *article on* OUTLIERS]. On the other hand, the median is still a symmetric function of all the observations, and not, as is sometimes said, a function of only one observation.

The median minimizes the sum of absolute residuals—that is, $\sum |x_i - x|$ is minimum for $x = \text{Me}(x)$.

A disadvantage of the median is that if the x_i's are divided into subgroups, one cannot in general compute $\text{Me}(x)$ from the medians and sizes of the subgroups.

For a population described by a random variable X the median is any number, Med, such that

$$Pr\{X < \text{Med}\} \leqslant \tfrac{1}{2} \leqslant Pr\{X \leqslant \text{Med}\}.$$

In general, Med is not uniquely defined, although it is when X has a probability density function that is positive near its middle [*see* PROBABILITY]; then Med has a clear interpretation via

$$\begin{aligned} Pr\{X < \text{Med}\} &= Pr\{X \leqslant \text{Med}\} \\ &= Pr\{X > \text{Med}\} = Pr\{X \geqslant \text{Med}\} \\ &= \tfrac{1}{2}. \end{aligned}$$

(See Figure 1.)

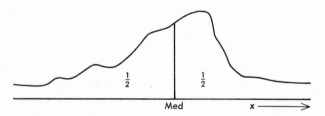

Figure 1 — Probability density function with median, Med, indicated

Table 6 shows how the value of Me is determined *approximately* for grouped observations. The first two columns might represent the frequency distribution of the test scores achieved by 141 subjects. With this as a basis column 3 is derived. The figures in column 3 are found by continued addition (accumulation) of the frequencies given in

Table 6 — Frequencies and cumulative frequencies for approximate determination of median

Class interval	Frequency	Cumulative frequency
$x < 20$	4	4
$20 \leqslant x < 30$	17	21
$30 \leqslant x < 40$	38	59
$40 \leqslant x < 60$	49	108
$60 \leqslant x < 80$	29	137
$80 \leqslant x$	4	141

column 2. The number 59, for example, means that 59 subjects achieved scores of less than 40. In accordance with the definition, the median, Me, is the score achieved by the 71st subject. Since the 59 smallest scores are all less than 40 and since each of the other scores is greater than that, $\text{Me} = 40 + a$, where $0 \leqslant a < 20$, because the fourth class, within which the median lies, has an interval of 20.

The hypothesis that the 49 elements of the fourth class are uniformly distributed [*see* DISTRIBUTIONS, STATISTICAL] over the interval yields the following relationship for a (linear interpolation): $20 : a = 49 : (71 - 59)$, whence $a = 4.9$ and $\text{Me} = 44.9$. The value $71 - 59 = 12$ enters into the equation because the median is the twelfth score in the median class.

The frequency distribution is a good starting point for computing Me because it already involves an arrangement in successive size classes. The assumption of uniform distribution within the median class provides the necessary supplement; whether this hypothesis is valid must be decided in each individual case. Only a small portion of the cumulative sum table is required for the actual calculation.

In the calculation it was presupposed that the variate was continuous—for instance, that a score of 39.9 could be achieved. If only integral values are involved, on the other hand, the upper boundaries of the third and fourth classes are 39 and 59 respectively. In that case we obtain $\text{Me} = 39 + 5 = 44$.

Quartiles, deciles, percentiles, midrange. The concept that led to the median may be generalized. If there are, say, $n = 801$ observations, which are again arranged in algebraic order, starting with the smallest, it may be of interest to specify the variate values of the 201st, 401st, and 601st observations —that is, the first, second, and third *quartiles*, Q_1, Q_2, and Q_3. Obviously, Q_2 is the same as Me. From the associated cumulative distribution, Q_1 and Q_3 may be obtained as follows (see Figure 2, where, for convenience, a smoothed curve has been used to represent a step function): Draw parallels to the x-axis at the heights 201 and 601; let their intersections with the cumulative distribution be P_1 and P_3. The x-coordinates of P_1 and P_3 then yield Q_1 and Q_3 respectively.

If $Q_1 = \$800$, $Q_2 = \$1,400$, and $Q_3 = \$3,000$ in an income distribution, the maximum income of the families in the lower fourth of income recipients is $800 and that of the bottom half is $1,400, while 25 per cent of the population has an income in excess of $3,000.

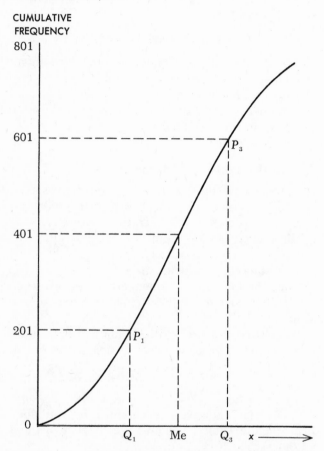

CUMULATIVE
FREQUENCY

Figure 2 — Hypothetical cumulative distribution (smoothed from a step function) showing the graphic method of obtaining quartiles

The variate values of the 81st, 161st, 241st, $\cdots$, 721st observations in the examples where $n = 801$ determine the 1st, 2d, 3d, $\cdots$, 9th *deciles*. Similarly, the *percentiles* in the example are given by the 9th, 17th, 24th, $\cdots$, 793d ordered observations. In general, if the sample size is n, the ith percentile is given by the sample element with ordinal number $[ni/100] + 1$ when $ni/100$ is not an integer and by the simple average of the two elements with ordinal numbers $ni/100$ and $(ni/100) + 1$ when $ni/100$ is an integer. Here "$[x]$" stands for the largest integer in x. [*For further discussion, see* NONPARAMETRIC STATISTICS, *article on* ORDER STATISTICS.]

If the smallest observation is denoted by $x_{(1)}$ and

the largest by $x_{(n)}$, the midrange is $\frac{1}{2}(x_{(1)} + x_{(n)})$ and the quartile average is $\frac{1}{2}(Q_1 + Q_3)$.

Mode. If a variate can take on only discrete values, another useful measure of location is the variate value that occurs most frequently, the so-called mode (abbreviated as Mo). If, for instance, the number of children born of 1,000 marriages, each of which has lasted 20 years, is counted, Mo is the most frequent number of children.

The mode is often encountered in daily life: the most frequent mark in a test, the shoe size called for most often, the range of prices most frequently requested. Generally speaking, the concept of the typical is associated with the mode; consider, for instance, wage distribution in a large factory. The mode is very vivid. However, it possesses concrete significance only when there is a tendency toward concentration about it and when enough observations are available.

In considering a frequency distribution with class intervals that are all of equal width, one convention is to take as the mode the midpoint of the class containing the largest number of elements. This procedure is open to the objection that it does not take into consideration which of the adjoining classes contains a larger number of elements; the mode would be better calculated in such a way that it is closer to the adjacent class that contains the larger number of elements. Several more or less arbitrary ways of doing this have been suggested— for example, by Croxton and Cowden (1939, p. 213) and by Hagood and Price ([1941] 1952, p. 113). On the other hand, for a continuous distribution it makes sense to take the value of x that yields a (relative) maximum as the mode. There may be two or more relative maxima, as may be readily seen from a graph of the distribution.

Further comments on mean values. There exist some quantitative relationships between the mean values.

(*a*) Harmonic mean $\leqslant$ geometric mean $\leqslant$ arithmetic mean. The equal signs apply only to the trivial case where all the observations have the same variate value. This is a purely mathematical result.

(*b*) For a symmetrical distribution (one whose density or frequency function is unchanged by reflection through a vertical line) with exactly one mode, $\bar{x}$, Me, and Mo coincide. For a distribution that is slightly positively skew (that is, one that slopes more gently to the right than to the left— this is not a precise concept), an approximate relationship is Me − Mo $\cong 3(\bar{x} -$ Me). In a positively skew distribution the sequence of the three parameters is Mo, Me, and $\bar{x}$; in negatively skew ones, on the other hand, it is $\bar{x}$, Me, and Mo. Kendall and

Stuart write as follows about this: "It is a useful mnemonic to observe that the mean, median, and mode occur in the same order (or reverse order) as in the dictionary; and that the median is nearer to the mean than to the mode, just as the corresponding words are nearer together in the dictionary" ([1943] 1958, p. 40).

Scales of measurement. There is usually a distinction made between four types of scales on which observations may be made; the distinction is briefly characterized by Senders as follows:

If all you can say is that one object is different from another, you have a *nominal scale.*

If you can say that one object is bigger or better or more of anything than another, you have an *ordinal scale.*

If you can say that one object is so many units (inches, degrees, etc.) more than another, you have an *interval scale.*

If you can say that one object is so many times as big or bright or tall or heavy as another, you have a *ratio scale.*   (1958, p. 51)

Scales of measurement are also discussed by Gini (1958), Pfanzagl (1959), Siegel (1956), and Stevens (1959).

For an interval scale there is a meaningful *unit* (foot, second, etc.) but not necessarily an intrinsically meaningful origin. A ratio scale has both a meaningful unit and a meaningful origin.

Some examples of these four types of scales are:

(*a*) *Nominal scale:* classifying marital status into four categories—single, married, widowed, and divorced; a listing of diseases.

(*b*) *Ordinal scale:* answers to the question "How do you like the new method of teaching?" with the alternative replies "Very good," "Good," "Fair," "Poor," "Very poor."

(*c*) *Interval scale:* measuring temperature on the centigrade, Réaumur, or Fahrenheit scales; measuring calendar time (7:09 A.M., January 3, 1968).

(*d*) *Ratio scale:* measuring a person's height in centimeters; measuring temperature on the absolute (Kelvin) scale; measuring age or duration of time.

It is apparent that the four scales are arranged in our listing according to an increasing degree of stringency. The nominal scale, in particular, is the weakest method of measurement.

The applicability of a given location measure depends upon the scale utilized, as is shown in Table 7. Only the most frequent value can be calculated for every scale, although Gini (1958) and his school have endeavored to introduce other averages appropriate for a nominal scale.

Table 7 indicates that the median, the quartiles,

Table 7 — Scales of measurement required for use of location measures

Location measure	Scale required
Mode	at least a nominal scale
Median, quartile, and percentile	at least an ordinal scale
Arithmetic mean	at least an interval scale
Geometric and harmonic means	ratio scale

and the percentiles are relatively invariant for any strictly monotonic transformation in the sense that, for example,

$$\phi(\text{median } X) = \text{median}(\phi(X)),$$

where ϕ is a strictly monotone transformation. Similarly, the arithmetic mean is relatively invariant for any linear transformation $y = ax + b$, and the geometric and harmonic means are relatively invariant in the transformation $y = ax$ (with $a > 0$ for the geometric mean).

Descriptive statistics of dispersion

If there were no dispersion among the observations of a sample, much of statistical methodology would be unnecessary. In fact, there almost always is dispersion, arising from two general kinds of sources: (*a*) inherent variability among individuals (for instance, households have different annual savings) and (*b*) measurement error (for instance, reported savings may differ erratically from actual savings).

Absolutive measures of dispersion. A first intuitive method of measuring dispersion might be in terms of $\sum(x_i - \bar{x})$, the sum of residuals about the arithmetic mean. This attempt immediately fails since the sum is always zero. A useful measure of dispersion, however, is obtained by introducing absolute values, yielding the *mean deviation* $(1/n)\sum|x_i - \bar{x}|$.

Variance and standard deviation. An even more useful measure of dispersion is the *variance,*

$$(6) \qquad s^2 = \frac{1}{n}\sum(x_i - \bar{x})^2,$$

the average squared deviation between an observation and the arithmetic mean. The positive square root of s^2 is called the *standard deviation.* (Often n, in the above definition, is replaced by $n - 1$, primarily as a convention to simplify formulas that arise in the theory of sampling, although in some contexts more fundamental arguments for the use of $n - 1$ may be given.) [*See* SAMPLE SURVEYS.]

It is of interpretative interest to rewrite s^2 as

$$(7) \qquad s^2 = \frac{1}{2n^2}\sum_i\sum_j(x_i - x_j)^2$$

without mention of $\bar{x}$.

The population variance is $E(X - \mu)^2$, where

$\mu = E(X)$ [see Probability, *article on* formal probability].

The variance and standard deviation may be computed from a table of grouped observations in a manner analogous to that for the arithmetic mean; coding is particularly useful. Suggestions have been made toward compensating for the class width in a grouping [see Statistical analysis, special problems of, *article on* grouped observations].

Variance has an additivity property that is akin to additivity for the arithmetic mean over subgroups. Suppose that the x_i's are divided into two subgroups of sizes n_1, n_2, with arithmetic means $\bar{x}_1$, $\bar{x}_2$, and with variances s_1^2, s_2^2. For convenience, let $p_1 = n_1/n$, $p_2 = n_2/n$. Then, not only does

$$(8) \qquad \bar{x} = p_1\bar{x}_1 + p_2\bar{x}_2,$$

but also

$$(9) \qquad s^2 = p_1 s_1^2 + p_2 s_2^2 + p_1 p_2 (\bar{x}_1 - \bar{x}_2)^2.$$

This relationship may be extended to more than two subgroups, and, in fact, it corresponds to a classic decomposition of s^2 into within and between subgroup terms. [See Linear hypotheses, *article on* analysis of variance.]

Perhaps a more important additivity property of variance refers to sums of observations. [*This is discussed in* Probability, *article on* formal probability, *after consideration of correlation and independence.*]

Other deviation measures of dispersion. The *probable error* is a measure of dispersion that has lost its former popularity. It is most simply defined as $.6745 \times s$, although there has been controversy about the most useful mode of definition. If the x_i's appear roughly normal and n is large, then about half the x_i's will lie in the interval $\bar{x} \pm$ probable error.

Gini has proposed a dispersion measure based on absolute deviations,

$$\Delta = \frac{1}{n(n-1)} \sum_i \sum_{\substack{j \\ i \neq j}} |x_i - x_j|,$$

that has attracted some attention, although it is not widely used.

When the observations are ordered in time or in some other exogenous variate, the mean square successive difference,

$$\delta^2 = \frac{1}{n-1} \sum_1^{n-1} (x_{i+1} - x_i)^2,$$

has been useful. [See Variances, statistical study of.]

Dispersion measures using order statistics. The simplest measure of dispersion based on the order statistics of a sample is the difference between the largest and smallest x_i: the range [see Nonparametric statistics, *article on* order statistics]. As against its advantage of vividness and ease of calculation there is the disadvantage that the range is fixed by the two extreme values alone. Outliers often occur, especially for large n, so that the range is of limited usefulness precisely in such cases. This is not so serious in small samples, where the range is readily employed. There is a simple relationship connecting the sample size, n, the expected range, and the standard deviation under certain conditions.

The basic shortcoming of the range is avoided by using, say, the 10–90 interpercentile range. This is determined by eliminating the top and bottom 10 per cent of the elements that are ordered according to size and determining the range of the remaining 80 per cent. The 5–95 percentile range can be determined similarly. The semi-interquartile range is $\frac{1}{2}(Q_3 - Q_1)$, in which the bottom and top 25 per cent of all the elements are ignored and half the range of the remaining 50 per cent is calculated.

Relative measures of dispersion. The expressions set forth above are absolute measures of dispersion. They measure the dispersion in the same unit chosen for the several variate values or in the square of that unit. The following example shows that there is also need for relative measures of dispersion, however: A study is to be made of the annual savings (a) of 1,000 pensioners and (b) of 1,000 corporation executives. The average income in (a) might be \$1,800, as against \$18,000 in (b). The absolute dispersion in (b) will presumably be considerably greater than that in (a), and a measure of dispersion that allows for the gross differences in magnitude may be desired. Two of the numerous possibilities available are (1) the coefficient of variation, $s/\bar{x}$ or $(s/\bar{x}) \cdot 100$, which measures s as a fraction or a percentage of $\bar{x}$ (this parameter loses its significance when $\bar{x}$ equals 0 or is close to 0), and (2) the quartile dispersion coefficient $(Q_3 - Q_1)/\text{Me}$, which indicates the interquartile range as a fraction of the median. Such measures are dimensionless numbers.

Concentration curves. Another way of describing dispersion is the construction of a concentration (or Lorenz) curve. [*These techniques are discussed in* Graphic presentation.]

Populations and samples. In the above discussion a number of descriptive statistics have been defined, both for sets of observations and for populations. A fundamental statistical question is the inductive query "What can be said about the population mean, variances, etc., on the basis of a sample's mean, variance, etc.?" [*Many of the statistical articles in this encyclopedia deal with aspects of this question, particularly* SAMPLE SURVEYS; ESTIMATION; *and* HYPOTHESIS TESTING.]

HANS KELLERER

BIBLIOGRAPHY

Discussions of the statistics of location and dispersion are found in every statistics text. The following are only a few selected references.

CROXTON, FREDERICK E.; and COWDEN, DUDLEY J. (1939) 1955 *Applied General Statistics.* 2d ed. Englewood Cliffs, N.J.: Prentice-Hall. → Sidney Klein became a joint author with the third edition, published in 1967.
DALENIUS, T. 1965 The Mode: A Neglected Statistical Parameter. *Journal of the Royal Statistical Society* Series A 128:110–117.
FECHNER, GUSTAV T. 1897 *Kollektivmasslehre.* Leipzig: Engelmann.
GINI, CORRADO 1958 *Le medie.* Turin (Italy): Unione Tipografico.
HAGOOD, MARGARET J.; and PRICE, DAVID O. (1941) 1952 *Statistics for Sociologists.* Rev. ed. New York: Holt.
KENDALL, MAURICE G.; and BUCKLAND, WILLIAM R. (1957) 1960 *A Dictionary of Statistical Terms.* 2d ed. Published for the International Statistical Institute with the assistance of UNESCO. Edinburgh and London: Oliver & Boyd.
KENDALL, MAURICE G.; and STUART, ALAN (1943) 1958 *The Advanced Theory of Statistics.* Volume 1: Distribution Theory. New York: Hafner; London: Griffin.
PFANZAGL, J. 1959 *Die axiomatischen Grundlagen einer allgemeinen Theorie des Messens.* Schriftenreihe des Statistischen Instituts der Universität Wien, New Series, No. 1. Würzburg (Germany): Physica-Verlag.
SENDERS, VIRGINIA L. 1958 *Measurement and Statistics: A Basic Text Emphasizing Behavioral Science Application.* New York: Oxford Univ. Press.
SIEGEL, SIDNEY 1956 *Nonparametric Statistics for the Behavioral Sciences.* New York: McGraw-Hill.
STEVENS, S. S. 1959 Measurement, Psychophysics, and Utility. Pages 18–63 in Charles W. Churchman and Philburn Ratoosh (editors), *Measurement: Definitions and Theories.* New York: Wiley.
VERGOTTINI, MARIO DE 1957 *Medie, variabilità, rapporti.* Turin (Italy): Einaudi.
YULE, G. UDNY; and KENDALL, MAURICE G. (1911) 1958 *An Introduction to the Theory of Statistics.* 14th ed., rev. & enl. London: Griffin. → Kendall has been a joint author since the eleventh edition (1937); the 1958 edition was revised by him.
ŽIŽEC, FRANZ (1921) 1923 *Grundriss der Statistik.* 2d ed., rev. Munich: Duncker & Humblot.

II

ASSOCIATION

When two or more variables or attributes are observed for each individual of a group, statistical description is often based on cross-tabulations showing the number of individuals having each combination of score values on the variables. Further summarization is often desired, and, in particular, a need is commonly felt for measures (or indices, or coefficients) that show how strongly one variable is associated with another. In the bivariate case, the primary topic of this article, well-known indices of this kind include the correlation coefficient, the Spearman rank correlation measure, and the mean square contingency coefficient. In this article, the motivations for such measures are discussed, criteria are explained, and some important specific measures are treated, with emphasis throughout on the cross-tabulations of nominal and ordinal measurements. [*For further material on the metric case, see* MULTIVARIATE ANALYSIS, *articles on* CORRELATION.]

Current work in this area is generally careful to make an explicit distinction between a *parameter*—that is, a summary of a population of values (often taken as infinitely large)—and a *statistic*, which is a function of sample observations and most sensibly regarded as a means of making an estimate of some clearly defined population parameter. It is of doubtful value to have a quantity defined in terms of an observed sample unless one is clear about the meaning of the population quantity that it serves to estimate. Recent work on sampling theory presenting, among other things, methods for computing a confidence interval for their γ (illustrated below) is contained in Goodman and Kruskal (1954–1963, part 3).

The correlation coefficient and related measures. In a bivariate normal distribution that has been standardized so that both marginal standard deviations are equal, the correlation coefficient nicely describes the extent to which the elliptical pattern associated with the distribution is elongated. At one extreme, when the distribution is nearly concentrated along a straight line, the correlation coefficient is nearly 1 in absolute value, and each variate is nearly a linear function of the other. At the other extreme, the elliptical pattern is a circle if and only if the correlation coefficient, whose population value is often designated by ρ, is 0. In this case, knowledge of one variate provides no information about the other.

In this bivariate normal case, with equal marginal standard deviations, the regression (conditional expectation) of either variate on the other is a straight line with slope ρ. For the above reasons, it is not unreasonable to adopt ρ as a measure of degree of association in a bivariate normal distribution. The essential idea behind the correlation coefficient was Francis Galton's, but Karl Pearson defined it carefully and was the first to study it in detail. [*See the biographies of* GALTON *and* PEARSON.]

It was pointed out by G. Udny Yule, a student of Pearson's, that ρ also has a useful interpretation even if the bivariate distribution is *not* normal. This interpretation is actually of ρ^2, since $1 - \rho^2$ measures how closely one variate clusters about the least squares linear prediction of it from the other. More generally, it remains true that the two variates have a linear functional relation if and only if $\rho = \pm 1$, but ρ may be 0 without the existence of stochastic independence; in fact, the variates may be functionally related by a properly shaped function at the same time that $\rho = 0$.

More recently, Kruskal (1958, pp. 816–818) has reviewed attempts to provide an interpretation of both Pearson's ρ and the correlation ratios whether or not normality obtains. Both of these measures may be interpreted in terms of expected or average squared deviations, but Kruskal feels that interpretations in these terms are not always appropriate.

In Pearson's early work the assumption of normality was basic, but he soon recognized that one often deals with observations in the form of discrete categories, such as "pass" or "fail" on a test of mental ability. Consequently, he introduced additional coefficients to deal with a bivariate distribution in which one or both of the variables are normal and continuous in principle but become grouped into two or more classes in the process of making the observations. Thus, his biserial correlation coefficient is designed to estimate the value of ρ when one of the normal variables is grouped into two classes, and his tetrachoric coefficient is designed for the same purpose when *both* variables are grouped into two classes, yielding in this latter case a bivariate distribution in the form of a fourfold table (see Kendall & Stuart [1946] 1961, pp. 304–312). More recently, Tate (1955) has pointed out the value of having a measure of association between a discrete random variable that takes the values 0 and 1, and a continuous random variable, especially in the sort of problems that often arise in psychology, where one wishes to correlate a dichotomous trait and a numerically measurable characteristic, such as an ability. He has reviewed two alternative models and both asymptotic and exact distribution theory, all based on normality, and has applied these models to illustrative data.

Yule's "attribute statistics" and recent continuations. Yule's reluctance to accept the assumption of normality in order to measure relationships soon led him to an interest in the relationship between discrete variables, which he referred to as attributes. Most of this work concentrated on dichotomous attributes and, thus, the measurement of relationships in fourfold tables. For this purpose his first proposal was a measure designated Q (for Quetelet, the Belgian astronomer–statesman–statistician); the aspect of the relationship that this represented in quantitative form he designated the "association" of the two attributes (see Yule 1912). The attempt to coin a special term for the aspect of a relationship measured by a particular coefficient has since been largely discarded, and the term "association" is now used more broadly. [*See the biographies of* QUETELET; YULE.]

The computation of Yule's Q is illustrated in Table 1, where it is adapted to a sociological study of the relationship between race and an attitude of alienation from one's social environment. Alienation was measured by a version of Srole's Anomia Scale (1956); the sample is of adults in Berkeley, California, in 1960. The quantification of this relationship in this way, which in the present case gives $Q = (ad - bc)/(ad + bc) = .66$, might be especially useful if the purpose of the study were to compare different years or communities with regard to the extent to which race may condition an attitude of alienation. Of course,

Table 1 — Illustrative fourfold table, relating race to an attitude of alienation from one's social environment*

		RACE (X)				ASSOCIATION MEASURE	
		Negro	White	Total			
ALIENATION (Y)	High	$a = 19$	$b = 55$	74		$Q = \dfrac{ad - bc}{ad + bc} = .66$	
	Low	$c = 6$	$d = 85$	91		$d_{yx} = \dfrac{ad - bc}{(a + c)(b + d)} = .37$	
	Total	25	140	165			
Per cent highly alienated		76%	39%				

* Cell entries are frequencies.

Source: Templeton 1966.

neither an association nor a correlation is in itself evidence of causation. Although the relationship shown here is an objective fact, and therefore a descriptive reflection of social reality with possible consequences for social relations in the United States, it is possible that some other variable, such as socioeconomic status, accounts for at least part of the relationship, and to that extent the relation observed in Table 1 would be considered "spurious" in the Lazarsfeld ([1955] 1962, p. 123) sense.

It might seem more natural to measure the relation between race and alienation by a comparison of rates of alienation in the two racial groups. Thus, there was a difference of $76 - 39 = 37$ percentage points (see bottom row Table 1) in the measured alienation for these two groups at that time and place. This difference might be considered a measure of association, since it, too, would be 0 if the tabulated frequencies showed statistical independence. Theoretically, such a coefficient (sometimes called the "percentage difference") could achieve a maximum of 100 if the distribution were as in Table 2. For comparability, it is customary to divide by 100, producing a coefficient sometimes referred to as d_{yx} (for X an independent variable and Y a dependent one), which has a maximum of 1.0, as do most other measures of association.

A problem in the use of d_{yx}, the difference between rates of alienation, arises when it is noted that the maximum absolute value of d_{yx} (that is, unity) is achieved only in the special situation illustrated in Table 2, where the row and column marginal distributions must necessarily be equal. This dependence of maximum value on equality of the marginal distributions can be misleading—for example, in comparisons of different communities where the number of Negroes remains about the same but the average level of alienation varies. In Table 3, Q is 1.0, while d_{yx} is less than 1.0. Table 3 represents the maximum discrepancy that could be observed in the rates of alienation, given the mar-

ginal distributions of the obtained sample of Table 1, and for this situation the maximum value of d_{yx} is only .65.

In addition to this independence of its maximum as marginals vary, Q has another desirable property, which is shared by d_{yx}: it has an operational interpretation. Both of these coefficients may be interpreted in a way that involves paired comparisons. Thus, $Q = ad/(ad + bc) - bc/(ad + bc)$ represents the probability of a pair having a "concordant ordering of the variables" less the probability of a pair having a "discordant ordering" when the pair is chosen at random from the set of pairs of individuals constructed by pairing each Negro member of the population with, in turn, each white member of the population and disregarding all pairs except those for which the alienation levels of the two individuals differ. By a "concordant ordering" is meant, in this illustration, a situation in which the Negro member of the pair has high alienation and the white has low alienation.

Closely related to this is the interpretation of $d_{yx} = ad/[(a + c)(b + d)] - bc/[(a + c)(b + d)]$, which is also the difference between the probability of a concordant pair and the probability of a discordant pair. In this case, however, the pair is chosen at random from a somewhat extended set of pairs: those in which the two individuals are of different races (here race is taken as X, the independent variable), whether or not they have different levels of alienation. Thus, d_{yx} asks directly: To what extent can one predict, in this population, the ordering of alienation levels of two persons, one of whom is Negro, the other white? On the other hand, Q asks: To what extent can one predict the ordering of alienation levels of persons of different races among those whose alienation levels are not equal? Thus, Q does not distinguish beween the situation of Table 2, in which no white persons are highly alienated, and that of Table 3, in which about 35 per cent of the whites are alienated.

Table 2 — Hypothetical fourfold table showing $d_{yx} = 1$

| | | RACE (X) | | | ASSOCIATION MEASURE |
		Negro	White	Total	
ALIENATION (Y)	High	25	0	25	
	Low	0	140	140	$Q = 1$
					$d_{yx} = 1$
	Total	25	140	165	
Per cent highly alienated		100%	0%		

Table 3 — Hypothetical fourfold table showing the maximum possible value of d_{yx} given the observed marginal distribution

		RACE (X)			ASSOCIATION MEASURE
		Negro	White	Total	
ALIENATION (Y)	High	25	49	74	
	Low	0	91	91	$Q = 1$
					$d_{yx} = .65$
	Total	25	140	165	
Per cent highly alienated		100%	35%		

There is, of course, no reason why one should expect to be able to summarize more than one aspect of a bivariate distribution in a single coefficient. Indeed, some investigators assume that several quantities will be necessary to describe a cross-tabulation adequately, and some go so far as to question the value of summary statistics at all, preferring to analyze and present the whole tabulation with r rows and c columns. This latter approach, however, leads to difficulties when two or more cross-classifications are being compared. The measures of association Q and d_{yx} may be extended to cross-tabulations with more than two categories per variable, as described below. The problems mentioned above extend to such cross-tabulations.

Although correlation theory developed historically from the theory of probability of continuous variables, one may consider the antecedents of "association theory" as lying more in the realm of the logic of classes. Yule's early paper on association traces the origin of his ideas to De Morgan, Boole, and Jevons (in addition to Quetelet); more recently it has been recalled that the American logician Peirce also worked on this problem toward the close of the nineteenth century [*see the biography of* PEIRCE].

The fact that most of the detailed remarks in this article refer to the work of British and American statisticians does not imply that developments have been confined to these countries. In Germany important early work was done by Lipps and Deuchler, and Gini in Italy has developed a series of statistical measures for various types of situations. [*See* GINI.] A comprehensive review of the scattered history of this work is contained in Goodman and Kruskal (1954–1963, parts 1 and 2) and Kruskal (1958). Characteristically, investigators in one country have developed *ad hoc* measures without a knowledge of earlier work, and some coeffi-

cients have been "rediscovered" several times in recent decades.

Measurement characteristics and association

In recent years the distinction between the continuous and the discrete—between quantity and quality—often running through the work of logicians has become less sharp because of the addition of the idea of ordinal scales (rankings), which may be either discrete or continuous. Indeed, a whole series of "levels of measurement" has been introduced in the past twenty-five years (see Torgerson 1958, chapters 1–3), and because of their relevance to the measurement of relationships the matter warrants a brief statement here. [*Other discussions of scales of measurement can be found in* SCALING; *and in* STATISTICS, DESCRIPTIVE, *article on* LOCATION AND DISPERSION.]

As described above, in the past the term "correlation" has referred to a relation between quantities, while the term "association" has been reserved for the relation between qualities. For present purposes it is sufficient to elaborate this distinction only slightly by defining the three categories "metrics," "ordinals," and "nominals." Metrics (for example, height and weight), roughly corresponding to the earlier quantitative variables, are characterized by having an unambiguous and relevant unit of measurement. (Metrics are often further classified according to whether a meaningful zero point exists.) Ordinals (for example, amount of subjective agreement or appreciation) lack a unit of measurement but permit comparisons so that of two objects one can always say that one is less than the other, or that the two are tied, on the relevant dimension. Ordinal scales are for this reason designated "comparative concepts" by Hempel (1952, pp. 58–62). Nominals (for example, types of ideology, geographical regions) are simply classificatory categories lacking any relevant ordering but tied together by some more generic conception. Each of these scales may be either continuous or discrete, except nominals, which are inherently discrete.

Present usage generally retains the term "correlation" for the relationship between metrics (sometimes "correlation" is restricted to ρ and the correlation ratio), and "rank correlation" for the relationship between continuous ordinals, although the term "association" has also been used here. The terms "order association" and "monotonic correlation" have been used for the relationship between discrete ordinals, and the terms "association" and "contingency" are used to refer to the relationship between nominals. (Some statisticians prefer to reserve the term "contingency" for data arising from a particular sampling scheme.)

With ordinal data of a social or psychological origin the number of ordered categories is often small relative to the number of objects classified, in which case the bivariate distribution is most conveniently represented in the form of a cross-classification that is identical in format to the joint distribution over two nominals. Because of the identity of format, however, the different cases are sometimes confused, and as a result a measure of association is used that ignores the ordering of the categories, an aspect of the data that may be crucial to the purposes of the analysis. For this reason it is helpful to conceive of a cross-classification of two ordinals as rankings of a set of objects on two ordinals simultaneously, with ties among the rankings leading to a number of objects falling in each cell of the cross-classification.

Illustrative data, of a type very common in contemporary survey research, are presented in Table 4. In this instance the investigator utilized an additive index of income, education, and occupational prestige to obtain a socioeconomic ranking, which was then grouped into three ordered classes, with observations distributed uniformly over these classes insofar as possible. The alienation scale used in this study is derived from questionnaire responses indicating agreement with 24 such statements as "We are just so many cogs in the machinery of life"; "With so many religions around, one doesn't really know which to believe"; and "Sometimes I feel all alone in the world." Again the results are grouped into three nearly equal classes.

An appropriate coefficient for the measurement of the relation between socioeconomic status and alienation in Table 4 would be gamma (γ), a generalization of Yule's Q, introduced by Goodman and Kruskal (1954–1963, part 1, p. 747). Omitting details of computation, this measure provides in-

Table 4 — Cross-classification of socioeconomic status and alienation*

| | | SOCIOECONOMIC STATUS | | | |
		High	Medium	Low	Total
	High	23	62	107	192
ALIENATION	Medium	61	65	61	187
	Low	112	60	23	195
	Total	196	187	191	574

* Cell entries are frequencies.

Source: Reconstructed from Erbe 1964, table 4(B), p. 207.

formation of the following sort: Suppose one is presented with a randomly chosen pair of individuals from a population distributed in the form of Table 4, the pair being chosen with the restriction that the members be located in different status categories as well as different alienation categories. What are the chances that the individual in the higher status category, say, will also be more alienated? The probability of this event for the population of Table 4 is .215. Similarly, one may ask for the chance that in such a pair of individuals the person with higher status has *less* alienation—this complementary event has probability $1 - .215 = .785$. The difference between these probabilities, $-.570$, is the value of γ, a measure of association with many convenient properties, most of which have been noted in the comments on Q, which is a special case of γ. A slight modification of γ, retaining many of the same properties but yielding an asymmetric coefficient, d_{yx}, has recently been presented by Somers (1962) and was also illustrated above in the special case of a fourfold table. It is asymmetric in that, unlike γ, it will in general have a different value depending on which variable is taken as independent.

This example shows clearly that a distinction must be made between ordinal and nominal measurement; this distinction becomes especially important when, as in Table 4, the number of categories exceeds two. Table 4 cross-tabulates two ordinal variables, while Table 5 presents a representative cross-tabulation of two variables treated by the analysts as nominal variables, that is, categorical groupings with no inherent ordering.

The investigators in the latter case were interested in quantifying, for purposes of comparison, the extent of occupational segregation within the school districts shown in Table 5 and accomplished this by means of a measure of association introduced by Goodman and Kruskal (1954–1963, part 1, p. 759), designated τ_b (not to be confused with the very different τ_b of Kendall [1948] 1963, chapter 3). As a measure of association, τ_b is 0 when

Table 5 — Distribution of occupations of fathers of children in three school districts*

| | | FATHER'S OCCUPATION | | | | |
		Profes-sional	White-collar	Self-employed	Manual	Total
	A	92	174	68	39	373
SCHOOL DISTRICT	B	39	138	90	140	407
	C	11	111	37	221	380
	Total	142	423	195	400	1,160

* Cell entries are frequencies.

Source: Data from Wilson 1959, p. 839, as presented and analyzed in Rhodes et al. 1965, pp. 687–688.

the frequencies are statistically independent and is +1 when the frequencies are so distributed that a knowledge of location of an individual on one variable—here, school district—enables perfect prediction of his location on the other variable. In Table 5 the value of τ_b is .075, indicating that, in the language of Goodman and Kruskal's interpretation, the error of prediction (employing a "proportional" prediction) would be reduced only 7.5 per cent in making predictions of occupational status of father given a knowledge of school district (and the joint frequency distribution), as opposed to making that prediction with a knowledge only of the occupational distribution in the margin. Changing the order of rows or columns does not affect τ_b.

If the frequencies had been distributed as in Table 6, then τ_b would have been 1.0, since knowledge of school district would permit perfect prediction of occupational category.

Because τ_b is intended for nominal variables, the idea of a "negative" association has no meaning, and the measure therefore varies only between 0 and +1.

Whereas Goodman and Kruskal interpreted τ_b in prediction terms as described above, Rhodes and others (1965) in their application have presented an interpretation that motivates this measure as an index of spatial segregation, based on a model of chance interaction. Their work thus provides a

good example of the derivation of a summary statistic that is appropriate to, and interpretable in the light of, the specific research hypothesis that is the investigator's concern. It is, for their research purposes, a largely irrelevant coincidence that their coefficient happens to be Goodman and Kruskal's τ_b, interpretable in another way.

Another special kind of problem may arise in certain analyses where association is of interest. In many types of sociological analysis data are not available for cross-tabulating the *individual* observations but rather are available only on the "ecological" level, in the form of rates. Thus, for example, one might have available only the proportion of persons of high income and the proportion of persons voting for each political party for collectivities such as election districts. The investigator, however, may still be interested in the relation at the individual level. Duncan and others (1961) have discussed this problem in detail and have presented methods for establishing upper and lower bounds for the value of the individual association, given ecological data. Goodman (1959) has discussed and elaborated upon these procedures, and he has shown how it is possible, with minimal assumptions, to make estimates of the value of the individual association from the ecological data.

Multiple and partial association

There is an area in which much work remains to be done: the problem of analysis of simultaneous relations among more than two variables of an ordinal or nominal sort. An article by Lewis (1962) summarizes much of the literature on particular aspects of the problem for nominals, more from the point of view of testing hypotheses of no relation, but dealing indirectly with the choice of descriptive statistics; Goodman (1963) has corrected and modified certain remarks of Lewis'. From a different point of view, several new methods are introduced in Coleman (1964, chapter 6). Goodman and Kruskal (1954–1963, part 1, secs. 11–12) have also discussed ways of extending their conceptions to the partial-association and multiple-association situations, and somewhat different ideas are contained in a brief discussion of the triple dichotomy by Somers (1964).

ROBERT H. SOMERS

[See also MULTIVARIATE ANALYSIS, *articles on* CORRELATION; SURVEY ANALYSIS, *article on* THE ANALYSIS OF ATTRIBUTE DATA; TABULAR PRESENTATION.]

Table 6 — Hypothetical distribution of frequencies enabling perfect prediction of occupation of father, given knowledge of school district

| | | FATHER'S OCCUPATION | | | | |
		Profes-sional	White-collar	Self-employed	Manual	Total
	A	0	373	0	0	373
SCHOOL DISTRICT	B	407	0	0	0	407
	C	0	0	0	380	380
	Total	407	373	0	380	1,160

BIBLIOGRAPHY

COLEMAN, JAMES S. 1964 *Introduction to Mathematical Sociology.* New York: Free Press.

DUNCAN, OTIS DUDLEY; CUZZORT, RAY P.; and DUNCAN, BEVERLY 1961 *Statistical Geography: Problems in Analyzing Areal Data.* New York: Free Press.

ERBE, WILLIAM 1964 Social Involvement and Political Activity: A Replication and Elaboration. *American Sociological Review* 29:198–215.

GOODMAN, LEO A. 1959 Some Alternatives to Ecological Correlation. *American Journal of Sociology* 64:610–625.

GOODMAN, LEO A. 1963 On Methods for Comparing Contingency Tables. *Journal of the Royal Statistical Society* Series A 126:94–108.

GOODMAN, LEO A.; and KRUSKAL, WILLIAM H. 1954–1963 Measures of Association for Cross-classifications. Parts 1–3. *Journal of the American Statistical Association* 49:732–764; 54:123–163; 58:310–364.

GUTTMAN, LOUIS 1941 An Outline of the Statistical Theory of Prediction: Supplementary Study B-1. Pages 253–318 in Social Science Research Council, Committee on Social Adjustment, *The Prediction of Personal Adjustment,* by Paul Horst et al. New York: The Council.

HEMPEL, CARL G. 1952 Fundamentals of Concept Formation in Empirical Science. Volume 2, number 7, in *International Encyclopedia of Unified Science.* Univ. of Chicago Press.

KENDALL, M. G. (1948) 1963 *Rank Correlation Methods.* 3d ed., rev. & enl. New York: Hafner. → The first edition was published by Griffin.

KENDALL, M. G.; and STUART, ALAN (1946) 1961 *The Advanced Theory of Statistics.* Volume 2: Inference and Relationship. New York: Hafner; London: Griffin.

KRUSKAL, WILLIAM H. 1958 Ordinal Measures of Association. *Journal of the American Statistical Association* 53:814–861.

LAZARSFELD, PAUL F. (1955) 1962 Interpretation of Statistical Relations as a Research Operation. Pages 115–125 in Paul F. Lazarsfeld and Morris Rosenberg (editors), *The Language of Social Research: A Reader in the Methodology of Social Research.* New York: Free Press.

LEWIS, B. N. 1962 On the Analysis of Interaction in Multi-dimensional Contingency Tables. *Journal of the Royal Statistical Society* Series A 125:88–117.

RHODES, ALBERT L.; REISS, ALBERT J. JR.; and DUNCAN, OTIS DUDLEY 1965 Occupational Segregation in a Metropolitan School System. *American Journal of Sociology* 70:682–694.

SOMERS, ROBERT H. 1962 A New Asymmetric Measure of Association for Ordinal Variables. *American Sociological Review* 27:799–811.

SOMERS, ROBERT H. 1964 Simple Measures of Association for the Triple Dichotomy. *Journal of the Royal Statistical Society* Series A 127:409–415.

SROLE, LEO 1956 Social Integration and Certain Corollaries: An Exploratory Study. *American Sociological Review* 21:709–716.

TATE, ROBERT F. 1955 Applications of Correlation Models for Biserial Data. *Journal of the American Statistical Association* 50:1078–1095.

TEMPLETON, FREDRIC 1966 Alienation and Political Participation: Some Research Findings. *Public Opinion Quarterly* 30:249–261.

TORGERSON, WARREN S. 1958 *Theory and Methods of Scaling.* New York: Wiley.

WILSON, ALAN B. 1959 Residential Segregation of Social Classes and Aspirations of High School Boys. *American Sociological Review* 24:836–845.

YULE, G. UDNY 1912 On the Methods of Measuring Association Between Two Attributes. *Journal of the Royal Statistical Society* 75:579–652. → Contains ten pages of discussion on Yule's paper.

STATISTICS AS LEGAL EVIDENCE

One of the normal functions of a legal trial is to resolve an uncertain factual situation according to some canon of probability: in criminal cases by evidence that establishes guilt "beyond reasonable doubt," in civil cases by a "preponderance of the evidence." In spite of these probabilistic terms, the law "refuses to honor its own formula when the evidence is coldly 'statistical.'" As a rule, "probabilities are determined in a most subjective and unscientific way" (Hart & McNaughton 1958, p. 54). A plaintiff who established that he was negligently run over by "a bus" and tried to identify the liable defendant by proof that Company X had the only regular bus franchise on the street where he was hit, was denied recovery on the ground that occasionally other buses traveled that street and that probability, however great, was not sufficient identification. In a trial for income tax evasion involving an illegal lottery wheel, expert testimony to the effect that mathematical probabilities suggest that the take from the wheel was twice as large as reported by the defendant was excluded as irrelevant. On the other hand, in an internal investigation of alleged rigging of a civil service examination, a chi-square test for goodness of fit showed that the distribution of the obtained grades, or a more extreme one, was highly improbable under the hypothesis of no cheating. This led to further investigation and eventual proof of chicanery, albeit not proof in court (McCann Associates 1966, p. 16).

However, in a recent Swedish trial for overtime parking, a figure was put to what constitutes insufficient probability for a finding of "guilty." The police constable had marked the position of the valves on two tires on a standard sketch, accurate to the nearest "hour," one valve at the "1 o'clock" position and the other at the "12 o'clock" position. Returning after a time lapse greater than the permitted length of parking, the constable found both valves in the same positions they had been in earlier. The defendant claimed he had left the place and returned. The Court of Appeals considered odds of $(12 \times 12 =)$ 144:1 insufficient and declared registering the position of all four tire valves would have been sufficient—odds of $(12^4 =)$ 20,736:1 ("Parkeringsfrägor . . ." 1962, pp. 24, 25). The court may be pardoned for having overstated the odds by calculating them under the assumption that the positions of the valve markings are statistically independent of each other, which is almost certainly not true.

But this distrust of statistical evidence is directed primarily against statistical proof of individual, specific events. Whenever some measurement of a large universe is at issue, such as the share of a market or the proportion of people holding a certain view, statistical evidence is clearly the best, if not the only, evidence obtainable. It is in such contexts that statistical evidence is playing a growing role in litigation.

Objections to statistical evidence.   Objections to statistical evidence come from two sources: the hesitation to accept sample results in place of complete census counts and—at least in the Anglo-Saxon legal sphere—the evidentiary rule prohibiting hearsay evidence, if the statistic is based on surveys that involve interviews. Of the two, the objection to sampling is less stubborn. The example set by the U.S. Bureau of the Census helped to break the way. Statutes in many states make census and other published governmental statistics prima facie legal evidence, although many "census" data are based on samples and all of them are hearsay evidence many times removed.

The hearsay rule is the more serious obstacle. The law holds that testimony must be open to cross-examination in order to test accuracy of perception, reliability of memory, and sincerity. The law allows exceptions to this rule, thereby inviting certain kinds of surveys (see below), but has been slow to admit statistical evidence in general. Old-fashioned doctrine will often allow testimony of selected witnesses who are far from constituting a representative sample but will refuse admittance of a survey based on a representative sample because, technically, it is hearsay evidence. That a carefully conducted survey is a source of truth superior to the testimony of such selected witnesses has been convincingly argued, and on the whole the courts are learning to appreciate this position.

Areas of acceptance.   Statistical evidence has found more general acceptance in three areas: in proceedings before administrative agencies which are not bound by evidentiary rules; in antitrust cases, where measurements of market shares have become almost indispensable; and in surveys of what the law calls the witness' "state of mind"— a broad area that is specifically exempt from the hearsay rule and that has spawned much statistical evidence. If a respondent is asked, for instance, whether he believes two different trademarks represent the same or different manufacturers, the sur-

vey maker knows what the true facts are; all he wants to find out is whether the interviewee knows them too. Following are the major types of disputes in which survey evidence often forms what is usually the core of proof.

Consumer awareness.   Sometimes the law provides that a trademark or advertising slogan can be protected only as long as it is in sufficient use, that is, sufficiently established in the consumer's mind (*Verkehrsgeltung* in German trademark law).

Confusion of trademarks.   A trademark that is so similar to an already existing one that the two are likely to be confused may not be registered. The similarity might be created by similar words, by similar design, by a similar color, or by any combination of these factors.

Meaning of trademarks.   The requirement of truth in trademark labeling occasionally imposes the burden of finding out what certain words mean; the issue may be, for instance, whether a term such as "English lavender" or "farmer bread" denotes true origin or merely a type of product.

Proprietary or generic name.   Names, originally protected as brand designations, lose their proprietary character if they have in fact become generic terms, designating the type of product rather than one of its brands. In the United States, "Thermos" has become a generic term in this fashion. "Vaseline" has lost its proprietary character in some European countries but not in the United States, where it is a specific brand of petroleum jelly.

Misleading advertising.   The Federal Trade Commission and the Food and Drug Administration in the United States have the duty to prohibit false advertising claims. In such procedures two questions arise, one factual—what the product actually does—and one psychological—what the public, judging from the advertising claims, thinks it does. Thus, it was litigated whether coal made from corncobs can claim to be charcoal. The issue involved both a chemical question—whether wood charcoal is different from corncob charcoal—and a psychological one—what the public understood charcoal to be and whether the difference, if perceived, mattered.

Preparation of legal surveys

There is no need here to discuss the general rules of procedure that must be observed in the preparation of surveys for purposes of legal evidence. But there are several problems peculiar to legal surveys that deserve mention. They derive from a variety of sources: from issues of law that cannot be anticipated with precision because they may be decided only during the very trial for which the evidence is prepared; from the peculiarly strict requirements of legal proof; and, unless it is a "state of mind" survey, from the hearsay rule.

Problems generated by the hearsay rule. At times, choosing a different survey design may circumvent the hearsay rule. When the geographic range of patrons of a drive-in movie theater was at issue, the data were obtained not through interviews with the patrons but through recordings and subsequent tracing of the license numbers of the parked automobiles. In this way the field workers who jotted down the numbers remained competent witnesses even under the hearsay rule.

Occasionally a court may offer to remedy the hearsay defect by allowing the survey evidence to be verified through the testimony of some of the original interviewees. This is a futile and, one may hope, passing remedy. But the dilemma it presents is real. In order to verify the fact of interviewing, the names of the interviewees may have to be presented in court, and there is then no way of protecting these interviewees from being subpoenaed as witnesses. This raises a serious problem of interviewing ethics, since survey interviewees are implicitly reassured of the privileged nature of their answers. If it became widely known that such protection cannot be guaranteed, people might decide to refuse cooperation in surveys. A similar problem, ironically, has arisen for the census itself, which, by law, is a privileged communication. One possible way, incidentally, of insuring privacy to survey respondents is to detach the interviewees' names from their questionnaires, thus making it possible to present their identity to the court but making it impossible to connect any individual with his specific questionnaire answers. This procedure, however, renders cross-examination of survey respondents almost useless, since there is no way of confronting their court testimony with their survey response.

Problems generated by proof requirements. The peculiar requirements of legal evidence affect the preparation of sampling surveys in several ways. There is, first, the prospect of a double scrutiny by opposing counsel. The first scrutiny occurs when the admissibility of the particular piece of evidence is debated; at this stage, the opposing side will try to prove that it is on its face irrelevant to the litigated issue, or that it has such obvious technical flaws that the court would be well advised to refuse its admittance. If the offered evidence overcomes this hurdle, its probative value is then explored in even greater detail through cross-examination like that of any witness.

This double scrutiny is often more exacting than it deserves to be. The discovery of but one serious flaw may endanger the entire piece of evidence. The doctrine of *falsus in uno, falsus in omnibus* is sometimes used to excuse dismissal of a witness' entire testimony if it is found to be untrue in a single instance; and by way of analogy, it may be applied to the witness who presents survey evidence.

This witness, therefore, should always be an expert witness, able to defend the evidence and able to explain the meaning of technical terms, such as "chi-square test," and answer such ever-recurring questions as why the sampling error hardly ever depends on the proportion the sample constitutes of its universe, but only on the absolute size of the sample.

Occasionally, the dangerous pretense is made that survey findings are the results of simple, common-sense procedures whose validity can be appraised without special expertise by any judge or jury. It is essential that both sides have experts; if one side refuses to have one, it does so at its peril. This holds even for the rare, if desirable, situation in which the statistical evidence is prepared by an expert whom the litigants and the court jointly appoint.

The strict requirements of legal proof make it essential that the chain of statistical inferences be meticulously documented. The definition of the universe, the details of the sample design, the details of the sample selection procedure, the communications to the interviewers, their control in the field, and, finally, the analysis of their reports—all should be documented by the respective research instruments and, if necessary, by *ad hoc* working memoranda.

Since the interviewees themselves might have some interest in the litigated issue, its nature—if possible, its very existence—should not be divulged. The safest way of doing this is to keep even the interviewers from learning the purpose of the survey. If this should prove unavoidable, they should certainly not learn which side in the litigation is sponsoring the survey.

Problems generated by legal uncertainties. One of the major difficulties in preparing survey evidence results from legal uncertainties that are likely to be decided only in the very trial for which the evidence is prepared. Foremost among these uncertainties is the definition of the relevant universe to be sampled. In a trademark confusion case, for instance, is it those who were purchasers of the particular brands—or of *any* brand of this type of product—or simply all potential customers? The proper way of solving such a problem is to sample all three universes and to tabulate the results for each separately as well as for all possible combinations.

Another uncertainty concerns the level of precision at which the survey answers will be relevant. It is sometimes impossible to focus the interviewee's attention on a particular issue without giving him some information about the issues in litigation. Thus, one often buys a more precise answer at the price of some contamination and even possible bias.

Consider the following sequence from a questionnaire designed to explore the respondent's knowledge of a certain merger:

Question: Do you recall any mergers of cement companies in this area during the last two or three years?
[If no reference is made to the litigated merger, ask:]
Question: Did you know that the XX-Corporation merged with another company?
[If the answer is yes, ask:]
Question: Do you happen to know the name of that other company?

Since it is difficult to predict which level of precision the court will accept as relevant, the rule must be to begin with the uncontaminated, unaided questions and to make sure that the contamination —if it is necessary—is introduced as late as possible, so that whatever answers were obtained before remain clean. At the very end of the interview even leading questions may be proper, provided their character is openly admitted, just as such questions in cross-examination in court sometimes have their justification.

Then there is the issue of realism, of the significance of merely verbal response. To avoid objections, the real problem situation should be simulated as closely as possible. For instance, instead of taking a housewife's word that if the price differential between two brands reached a certain level, she would switch, the following design was employed in a survey: One sample of housewives was given a choice of buying either brand A or brand B at the same price; a comparable sample was given the choice of A, or B at 1 cent less; a third sample the choice of A, or B at 2 cents less, and so forth. To ensure an actual purchase, the housewife was promised a gift, slightly but clearly more valuable than the price of the purchased merchandise, if she completed the experiment. Actually, the purchase price was also returned to the housewife after she had made the test purchase. In another litigation, where the types of channels used for transmitting telegrams to various places overseas were at issue, the survey maker simply sent a number of real telegrams and produced their overseas receipts in court.

Finally, there is the very special problem that arises in surveys that are to measure confusion. Confusion usually has several dimensions, and the research designed to measure it must consider all of them. In a study designed to measure confusion about trademarks, for example, there is, first, the confusion that will arise in the minds of people who simply do not know what the essential—that is, the protected—features of a trademark are. These people may confuse the two even if they note their difference. Second, there is the optical confusion that results from failure to notice a difference that is obviously too small. And, third, there is the "normal" confusion that must be discounted in the research design: the confusion that will prevail among the fringe of particularly inattentive people, who will register confusion even if there is not the slightest ground for it.

Statistics on validity of proof

This article has been limited to statistical evidence in a narrow sense of the term, that is, mostly sample surveys. But statistical questions may arise with respect to other forms of legal proof, such as blood tests for the establishment of paternity (Ross 1958, p. 466; Steinhaus 1954; Łukaszewicz 1955), lie detector tests (Levitt 1955, p. 440), identification of handwriting (Levin 1956, pp. 632, 637), or with respect to psychiatric diagnosis introduced as evidence (Schmidt & Fonda 1956, p. 262; Ash 1949, p. 272). All of these procedures are far from infallible, and efforts have been made to measure their fallibility in statistical terms. Psychologists, moreover, beginning with Münsterberg (1908), have been occupied with the problem of reliability of observation and testimony. They have accumulated a great amount of statistics on the difficulties of correctly observing moving objects or quickly developing scenes, of correctly identifying voices, on the reliability of children's testimony, or even on the reliability of psychiatric diagnosis (Marston 1924; Hutchins & Slesinger 1928; Gardner 1933, pp. 391, 407; Messerschmidt 1933, p. 422; McGehee 1937, p. 249). What these studies have in common is that they are statistical evidence once removed from the courts: they contain statistics *on* legal evidence, hardly ever evidence itself.

HANS ZEISEL

[*See also* LEGAL REASONING; PSYCHIATRY, *article on* FORENSIC PSYCHIATRY; SAMPLE SURVEYS.]

BIBLIOGRAPHY

ASH, PHILIP 1949 The Reliability of Psychiatric Diagnoses. *Journal of Abnormal and Social Psychology* 44: 272–276.

BAADE, HANS W. 1961 Social Science Evidence and the Federal Constitutional Court of West Germany. *Journal of Politics* 23:421–461.

BARKSDALE, HIRAM 1957 *The Use of Survey Research Findings as Legal Evidence.* Pleasantville, N.Y.: Printers' Ink Books.

BLUM, WALTER J.; and KALVEN, HARRY JR. 1956 The Art of Opinion Research: A Lawyer's Appraisal of an Emerging Science. *University of Chicago Law Review* 24:1–69.

GARDNER, DILLARD S. 1933 The Perception and Memory of Witnesses. *Cornell Law Quarterly* 18:391–409.

HART, HARRY M. JR.; and McNAUGHTON, JOHN T. (1958) 1960 Some Aspects of Evidence and Inference in the Law. Pages 48–72 in Daniel Lerner (editor), *Evidence and Inference: The Hayden Colloquium on Scientific Concept and Method.* Glencoe, Ill.: Free Press. → First published in *Dædalus.*

HUTCHINS, ROBERT M.; and SLESINGER, DONALD 1928 Some Observations on the Law of Evidence-memory. *Harvard Law Review* 41:860–873.

LEVIN, A. LEO 1956 Authentication and Content of Writings. *Rutgers Law Review* 10:632–646.

LEVITT, EUGENE E. 1955 Scientific Evaluation of the "Lie Detector." *Iowa Law Review* 40:440–458.

ŁUKASZEWICZ, J. 1955 O dochodzeniu ojcostwa (On Establishing Paternity). *Zastosowania matematyki* 2:349–379. → Contains a summary in English.

McCANN ASSOCIATES 1966 Chicago Metropol. Sanitary Distr., First Report. Unpublished manuscript.

McGEHEE, EUGENE E. 1937 The Reliability of the Identification of the Human Voice. *Journal of General Psychology* 17:249–271.

MARSTON, WILLIAM M. 1924 Studies in Testimony. *Journal of Criminal Law and Criminology* 15:5–31.

MESSERSCHMIDT, RAMONA 1933 The Suggestibility of Boys and Girls Between the Ages of Six and Sixteen Years. *Journal of Genetic Psychology* 43:422–437.

MÜNSTERBERG, HUGO (1908) 1933 *On the Witness Stand: Essays on Psychology and Crime.* New York: Broadman. → For a slashing retort, see Wigmore 1909.

NOELLE-NEUMANN, ELISABETH; and SCHRAMM, CARL 1961 *Umfrageforschung in der Rechtspraxis.* Weinheim (Germany): Verlag Chemie.

Parkeringsfrågor. II. Tillförlitligheten av det S. K. klocksystemet för parkeringskontroll. 1962 *Svensk juristidining* 47:17–32. → See especially pages 24–25, "Rättsfall från hovrätterna."

PENNSYLVANIA, UNIVERSITY OF, LAW SCHOOL, INSTITUTE OF LEGAL RESEARCH 1956 *Evidence and the Behavioral Sciences.* Edited by A. Leo Levin. Philadelphia: Univ. of Pennsylvania Law School.

RICHARDSON, JAMES R. 1961 *Modern Scientific Evidence: Civil and Criminal.* Cincinnati, Ohio: Anderson.

ROSS, ALF 1958 The Value of Blood Tests as Evidence in Paternity Cases. *Harvard Law Review* 71:466–484.

SCHMIDT, HERMANN O.; and FONDA, CHARLES P. 1956 The Reliability of Psychiatric Diagnosis: A New Look. *Journal of Abnormal and Social Psychology* 52:262–267.

STEINHAUS, HUGO 1954 The Establishment of Paternity. Wrocławskie Towarzystwa Naukowe, *Prace wrocławskiego towarzystwa naukowego* Series A No. 32.

WIGMORE, JOHN H. 1909 Professor Muensterberg and the Psychology of Testimony: Being a Report of the Case of Cokestone v. Muensterberg. *Illinois Law Review* 3:399–434.

ZEISEL, HANS 1960 The Uniqueness of Survey Evidence. *Cornell Law Quarterly* 45:322–346.

STATUS, SOCIAL

Until about 1920 the term *status* was most commonly used to refer to either the legally enforceable capacities and limitations of people or their relative superiority and inferiority. More recently, the rights and duties fixed by law have seemed less significant than those fixed by custom; and thus the nonscalar usage, now often called "status in the Linton sense," after the social anthropologist Ralph Linton (1936), has come to be a synonym for any "position in a social system." While the nonscalar usage of the term has broadened, however, the scalar usage has narrowed. Whereas formerly superiority of status could mean any sort of hierarchical ordering—of power, wealth, or honor—to many it now refers only to esteem, prestige, honor, respect, that is, to various forms of evaluation.

Status in the Linton sense

According to Linton, a status is marked off by the fact that distinctive beliefs about, and expectations for, social actors are organized around it. "Child" is a status because we believe children are less mature than adults and because in American society children are expected to be more submissive to the authority of their parents than are adults. The status "31 years old," on the other hand, although there are beliefs and expectations held of 31-year-olds, is typically not called a status, because the same beliefs and expectations are held of 30-year-olds.

Age, sex, birth, genealogy, and other biological and constitutional characteristics are very common bases of status. Nevertheless, status is a phenomenon, not of the intrinsic characteristics of men, but of social organization. While it is natural in one society to use biology to define a status, in another it is completely irrelevant. Americans mean by the expression "father" the genitor of a child; in many parts of Australia and Africa, people sharply distinguish genitor from father. Americans mean by the expression "brother" the son of one's father; many patrilineal societies mean by it both the son of one's father and the son of one's father's brother. Even where the same characteristic is used, it may be used differently by two different societies. An American of any traceable degree of dark color is a "Negro"; but Brazilians see eight distinct degrees of color, with each corresponding to a distinct status. Nor is it necessary to actually possess an attribute to have the status based on it. What matters is not what you really are but what people believe you to be.

The very substantial number of Negroes who each decade pass into the "white" population have not changed their color, but people believe they are white and organize behavior toward them around this conception.

The term *status* is often not clearly distinguished from the term *role*, and some use the two terms almost interchangeably. But one can make the distinction easily enough if one keeps in mind that status defines *who* a person is (e.g., he is a child, or a Negro, or a doctor), while role defines *what* such a person is expected to do (e.g., he is too young to work; he should not want to push himself ahead; he should care about patients).

A common method of identifying the statuses of a social system is to discover its "list" of status designators. For example, kinship studies typically begin with a list of kin terms and their usage. If father's son and father's brother's son are both brothers, they have a common status; if one is brother and the other is cousin, they have different statuses. Although statuses are often reflected in language in this way, the rule does not seem to be perfectly general. Some distinctions are made by language (e.g., blonde, brunette) that do not seem significant of status, while some distinctions are not made by language (e.g., leader and follower in small, informal groups) that are very indicative of status.

Status as the unit of social systems.   Everyone has more than one status. No status, in any social situation, encompasses the person. Therefore, it is natural to distinguish the status and the person. What appears to many as less natural is that sociologists typically take the status rather than the person as their basic unit in analyzing social systems. The argument that leads to this conclusion has two premises: first, it is argued that persons and statuses are not only distinct concepts; they also identify distinct levels of analysis; second, it is argued that given the typical concerns of sociologists, it is status rather than person that is the more useful level of analysis.

That person and status are independent levels of analysis is claimed for three reasons. First, even though two persons have quite different psychological motives or characters, very often their observable conduct is similar if they have the same status. For example, because of the way medical institutions function, very acquisitive and very altruistic doctors may behave in much the same way if both want to succeed. Second, even though two persons have the same psychological motives or character, very often their observable conduct is different if they have different statuses. Because of differences in the way medicine and business are institutionally structured, very acquisitive doctors behave differently than very acquisitive businessmen. Third, even if two persons with similar character structures are seen in two different statuses, very often their observable conduct is different: for example, the authoritarian son is not the authoritarian father.

If the two levels of analysis are distinct, which is the concern of the sociologist? A social system is a process of interaction between actors, and its structure is made up of the relationships between the actors. If we entertain the idea that the unit of such a system is the person, then either we must discover a basic personality structure from which its behavior derives or we must regard the behavior of the system as being a result of individual differences in the character of its members. For example, we could argue that Russians and Americans are aggressive people, and therefore Russia and the United States are aggressive; or that the influence structure of a small social group is due to the dominance of some personalities and the submissiveness of others. But the first argument does not come to terms with highly differentiated modern society, and the second does not come to terms with processes inherent in the social system itself that most sociologists believe bring about such differentiation in influence.

Status is, therefore, the unit of social systems for most practicing sociologists. However, frequently they do not face the fact that status is an abstract concept; that is, they often want to use status to explain "behavior," meaning by behavior every concrete event that takes place in the "real" world. But status and role will not explain behavior in this sense, any more than will person and character. Status is the unit of sociological analysis because it is the most elementary component of that kind of abstract system, the social system, studied by sociologists, not because it has some priority over other concepts in explaining concrete behavior.

Sets and sequences of statuses and roles.   Social position is always defined relative to a counterposition. A doctor behaves to a patient one way, to a nurse a second way, and to a hospital administrator a third way. The elementary unit of analysis for social systems, therefore, is not the status itself, but the relation of two statuses. Looked at from the point of view of some participant in the system, one of these statuses is his own, or the "subject status," while the second is a definition of the "other," or the "object status." More complicated structures of these elementary relations are still in the process of being defined, and terminology is not yet well established. Following Merton (1957), however, one may say that a set of object statuses of a single subject status is a *role set*; a set of subject statuses of a single person is a *status set*; and a set of subject statuses through time, such that it is necessary and sufficient that the subject occupy an earlier status for him to occupy a later status, is a *status sequence*. Thus, Smith's being a doctor means that he must involve himself in social relations with nurses, patients, other doctors, hospital administrators, and so on (role set); perhaps Smith is also a husband, a father, a deacon of the church, a member of the grand jury (status set); the process by which he became a doctor required that he first be a medical student, then an intern, then a resident (status sequence).

Status as a property of actors.   Status sets, role sets, and status sequences may all be distinguished from *status characteristics*. All three are units, in the same sense that a particle is a unit in physical theories; that is, they are basically elements of which properties are asserted, not themselves properties. That is why status is often thought of as static rather than dynamic and why so little can be done with the concept in the eyes of many sociologists. Status can, however, be treated as a property of actors—that is, as a status characteristic—as well as a unit of a social system, and in this sense it is a dynamic concept. Vice-president of company Q is a status in organization Q and might have various properties, such as centrality in the communication network of the organization. Smith, who is vice-president of Q, may also be a juror in a court trial, and his evidently middle-class status, or even the information that he is a company vice-president, will play a substantial part in organizing the attitudes of other jurors toward him, although vice-president of Q is not a status in the jury itself (Strodtbeck et al. 1957). Thus, status may function in systems other than the system of which it is the elementary unit, because it is a property of actors as well as a unit.

Functions of status in interaction.   Stable interactive systems depend on the emergence of normative expectations. Once emerged, such expectations are not created *de novo* every time two new actors encounter each other. Instead, the two classify themselves in terms already established in society; they identify both themselves and the other; and knowing who they are, relative to each other, they understand what attitude to take toward each other.

Underlying this view of organized social interaction—which stems in a direct line from Cooley (1902), Park (1928), and the Hugheses (1952) to almost every modern sociologist—is the assumption that every actor is sensitive to the attitudes others will take toward him. Every actor, therefore, tends to feel tense and upset if unable to define the social situation in such a way that the behavior of the other is predictable. For if it is not possible to behave in appropriate ways to the other, one may be very embarrassed or even shattered if a serious breach of moral order results.

How one classifies both oneself and others, given an established set of statuses in society, is a matter of the cues in both the situation of the encounter and in the action of the other. One of the more dynamic features of this theory of social interaction, in fact, is the idea that each action implies a status, and each status an action; therefore, each actor reveals how he defines the situation in the way he behaves, and thus provides other actors with cues to their own statuses in the situation. If actors start fairly far apart in their definitions of the situation and if, as a result, their behavior is different from what others expect, the situation is self-corrective in the sense that each readjusts his behavior to the definitions of the others. The path of such readjustments is in the direction of reciprocity, that is, of defining each other in terms of the appropriate reciprocal statuses.

The idea that one's self-conception is mirrored in the behavior of others is of course Cooley's, although the "looking-glass self" is both a more and a less complicated notion. It is less complicated in that it does not concern itself with how adult actors in an encounter use each other's behavior to define the situation; it is more complicated in that it is concerned both with self-image (definitions of the self) and self-esteem (evaluations of the self). What is relevant at this point is the self-image hypothesis, which Huntington (1957) has given some degree of confirmation by showing how medical students come to see themselves as doctors. Where students are involved in an interactive situation with a nurse or patient who expects them to behave like, or even defines them as, doctors, they are more likely to think of themselves as doctors.

Status ambiguity.   The tradition of Park and Hughes leads one inevitably to the study of status ambiguity as a central theoretical problem. If every actor has more than one status, the attitudes of any two statuses may be either compatible or incompatible in their demands on the self and the other. If two statuses that are activated in the same situation are incompatible, it will be difficult for each status occupant to know how to interact with the other, because it will be difficult for him to know which status is the basis of their interaction. For example, a female doctor and a male patient may have a problem in maintaining the doctor–patient interaction in the face of the male–female definition it might also be given. Such ambiguity is a source of strain and discomfort, and thus people tend to do something about either getting out of such situations or changing them. Lenski's analysis of "status crystallization" (1954; 1956) and Homans' analysis of "social certitude" (1961, chapter 12) are essentially concerned with this same process. Lenski, for example, finds that status ambiguity creates so much stress that many want to withdraw from sociable interaction, while many others want to change the social structure so that such situations are redefined.

Status evaluation

The more colloquial use of *status*—and the use still favored by many sociologists—connotes evaluation; hence *honor, esteem, respect,* and *prestige* are its synonyms. Status in this sense is a gratification, and its loss a deprivation. Opportunities to improve status are seized by almost everyone, even in societies that are not achievement-oriented (Lipset & Zetterberg 1956). When status is threatened, its loss is resisted. For example, Short and Strodtbeck (1965) have found that established leaders of adolescent conflict gangs ordinarily restrain their followers; but when threatened with displacement as leaders, they provoke gang aggression, which is status-enhancing in such gangs. In general, when status is lost, people are angry and disturbed. For example, downward social mobility is correlated with prejudice against minority groups; those who have lost status are more aggressive toward such groups than even the lower stationary classes (Greenblum & Pearlin 1953).

How is status evaluation determined? Cooley saw the situation in terms of a respected or accepted *source* and the *self* as a social object. According to this view, self-evaluation is a reflected evaluation: given a significant source, self-evaluation is determined by the source's evaluation. Such a result, for example, is found by Miyamoto and Dornbusch (1956), who asked respondents to rate both themselves and others in their social group on intelligence, likableness, attractiveness, and confidence. The same respondents estimated how well they would be rated by others. Self-evaluations were highly correlated with evaluations made by others and were correlated to an even greater degree with perceptions of these evaluations.

A third element of the evaluation situation has been given an important part in the process by Speier and Garfinkel. Speier (1935), concerned with conferring honor, and Garfinkel (1956), concerned with status degradation, have emphasized the part played by the *public audience*. An audience is a part of the community that also reflects the source's evaluation, rather than evaluating the actor directly and independently. According to Speier and Garfinkel, the source determines self-evaluation, but the stability and force of that evaluation depend on its acceptance by a public. Cooley, of course, was in the first instance concerned with how children derived self-esteem from parents; there the audience seems least important. Speier and Garfinkel are concerned with how society confers honor or dishonor on adult members of the moral community. If it were not for the reflection by the public of the source's evaluation, self-evaluation would be subject to continual counterpressure; those people with whom one daily interacts would not support or grant the honor (or dishonor) derived from the source. In what sense, then, would it be honor or dishonor at all? And how could it remain stable?

The stability of self-evaluation is particularly important because uncertain evaluation apparently makes people very anxious. Status anxiety can lend importance to even the most trivial behavior of the source and the public. For example, how the boss greets an employee may have an exaggerated significance to the employee who does not know where he stands, although the employer does not intend to convey any evaluation at all by what he says or the way he says it. Status anxiety also increases the assertiveness of status claims. The upwardly mobile, for example, can be as prejudiced as the downwardly mobile if their mobility leaves them uncertain as to exactly how they stand in their community. The argument is that they are concerned about validating their not yet accepted status, so that they emphasize their distance from the lower-status classes more than stationary upper classes do (Greenblum & Pearlin 1953). As it happens, mobility is apparently neither necessary nor sufficient to create status anxiety, but Silberstein and Seeman (1959) have confirmed the hypothesis that status anxiety, when it does exist, increases the emphasis on social distance from lower-status classes.

There is a fourth vital element in evaluation situations: since Durkheim it has been understood that status deprivation or gratification is relative to a *referent*. In the *Division of Labor* (1893) Durkheim showed that happiness was relative and depended on comparisons with others; in *Suicide* (1897) he applied his idea to status-related phenomena. The original meaning of *anomie* was not the absence of expectations for behavior but rather the absence of a referent or standard of comparison. Very rapid upward or downward social mobility, Durkheim argued, made the actor uncertain about which others in his society were appropriate standards of comparison—how, then, could he tell if he had enough wealth, privilege, or esteem? The importance of the referent was later demonstrated experimentally by Hyman (1942), and the most important application of the concept was in *The American Soldier* (Stouffer et al. 1949). This study showed that in comparing oneself to others in the same status class, if one has less in the way of privilege, esteem, or reward, one feels *relatively deprived*, whatever the absolute level of advantage. [*See* REFERENCE GROUPS.]

Status differences in small groups. Once status differences have emerged within a group, they are found to correlate highly with participation rates, evaluations of performances by members of the group, and influence over group decision making. A member who has been defined as very good is given more opportunities to participate, seizes such opportunities with greater assurance, is more favorably evaluated (even if the same performance, objectively evaluated, would prove to be a poor one), and is more likely to influence others than a member defined as not very good. Furthermore, because interaction is correlated with the status order in this way, the status order tends to persist. For how can the least-regarded member of the group, once so defined, upset the status order? He is seldom given a chance to participate; if he accepts the evaluations others make of him, he does not make much use of the chances he has; and even if he does, his contribution is evaluated through the distorted image the group has of him. Objective disproof might upset the status order, but such disproof is seldom available; and even when it is available, the group apparently resists its implications. Whyte (1943) found, for example, that a street-corner gang in danger of complete reversal of status abandoned certain activities—in this case the dating of a girls' club—that too visibly demonstrated the superior capacities of lower-status members.

Most of the research results on status differences in groups have been obtained for task-oriented groups, and nontask groups are apparently much less stratified. A task imposes two kinds of constraints on members: They are forced to say what they think should be done about something; and if they disagree, they are forced to resolve their disagreements. If they disagree, resolving dis-

agreements must enhance the status of some members and depress the status of others. But in nontask groups one is less often forced to this extremity, so that quite possibly such groups are less differentiated than task groups. Moreover, it is likely that task groups vary in the degree of stratification as they move from nontask, to task, and back to nontask phases of activity.

A task group may be composed either of status equals (say, all Harvard sophomores) or of status unequals (say pilot, navigator, and gunner in a small bomber crew). If it is composed of status equals, differentiation of status is a gradual process and one that involves struggle and tension. If the group is composed of status unequals, on the other hand, the underlying status order is already determined and there is not nearly the same tension about it. In a study of mock juries, for example, initial differences in education and occupation determined the participation rates and influence of jurors (Strodtbeck et al. 1957). And a study of mental health specialists showed that the lower-status specialists not only deferred to the higher-status ones but also liked them (Hurwitz et al. 1953). The underlying status order in the task group of status unequals is apparently based on stereotyped conceptions of people's worth, brought into the group from the external community. Even those with lower statuses come to believe in these stereotypes, as research on Negroes in biracial work groups shows (Katz et al. 1958).

Stability of status structures. Characteristics such as skin color, technical competence, sex, and ethnicity may come to be differentially evaluated by a society. We can think of these characteristics independently of the particular actors who possess them and analyze the properties of this abstracted status structure. As part of this same status structure one may include all those privileges, advantages, possessions, and symbols that have evaluative significance for the actors of a given society. There is a long history of investigations that have sought to define the conditions under which such status structures are stable.

Weber (1921) argued that those who had high status would tend in time to acquire wealth and those who had wealth would tend in time to acquire status. Benoît-Smullyan (1944) built on this idea the theory that if this natural tendency to conversion is blocked, it will turn itself into a revolutionary impetus to change the status structure. For example, for a half century before the French Revolution the bourgeoisie had been advancing in wealth and thus were able to buy noble status by purchasing army commissions or magistrates' offices. Then the encroached-on nobility, fearing the depreciation of their status, stopped the sale of nobility-bearing offices to the bourgeoisie; the bourgeoisie thus turned to revolution (Barber 1955). Moreover, it has been argued that this theory also holds true for the French peasants' impetus to revolution; although some have believed that the position of the peasants was declining in the half century before the revolution, a case has been made for the view that, in fact, the peasants were rising both in wealth and status before the revolution and that their desire to improve their over-all standing, rather than their reaction against growing degradation, explains their part in the revolution.

Similar interpretations have been offered of populism and progressivism in American politics, of the Ku Klux Klan and more recent radical right movements in the United States, and of the English revolution of 1640. The last of these has provoked a continuing controversy over the question of the rise or decline of the British gentry class before the Puritan revolution. Tawney (1941) has interpreted the revolution of 1640 as a struggle for political power between a rising gentry class and a declining court nobility. On the other hand, Trevor-Roper (1953) has tried to show that the country gentry in fact declined in wealth between 1540 and 1640 and was moved to revolt in order to overthrow the court nobility, which they saw as responsible for their decline. But both arguments involve the same sorts of assumptions: if a status structure is consistent (the terms *crystallized, balanced*, or *congruent* are typical synonyms), it will be stable; if it is not consistent, people experience great tension and strain; and because of this strain, pressures tend to build up in the system that make the status structure unstable.

Status politics of this kind form a regular part of the process of industrialization (Marshall 1949; Lipset 1964). Of great interest in the thesis of Marshall and Lipset is the distinction between short-run and long-run effects of economic change. In the short run one will find, Marshall claimed, a polarization of extremist ideologies: the newly created strata will develop extremist left ideologies as they seek greater equality of political participation in society, while the older strata will become defensive and develop extremist right ideologies that preserve their established monopoly of status. However, in time, as the newer strata come to have a legitimate place in society, with status and power equal to their wealth, the newer strata develop much less extreme ideologies and the older strata become less defensive. Thus, extreme class conflict is a passing phenomenon. This hypothesis has had some success in interpreting changes in both communist and fascist parties in contemporary Europe. First, it appears true that Communist party strength is correlated with early industrial expansion rather than mature capitalism. Second, even where communist parties have not lost strength, they appear to have softened their line in the more mature industrial societies. Third, in the more mature capitalist systems the fascist parties have been peripheral in significance; like the communists, the fascists are most active in the early periods of industrial expansion (Lipset 1964).

Status symbolism. Status is apparently a very contagious phenomenon. Because the value of a status is so communicable, in time almost every aspect of a social system can become part of its status structure. For example, within an organization the status value of an occupation is communicated to the rug, desk, way of being paid, physical location within the office, washroom used, and so on. The only limit yet known to this process is the "equilibrium limit": that is, if the transfer of status value is likely to bring about the kind of situation that would make the status structure unstable, it will probably not occur. Thus, if both white-collar and blue-collar workers in an organization were to use the same parking lot, probably the parking lot would not come to symbolize status.

Most of the elements to which status value becomes communicated are symbolic of the status structure, rather than significant in their own right. The processes associated with such symbols are therefore largely derivative. Nevertheless, they are very interesting in their own right. The study of such processes still rests largely on the work of Veblen (1899). In Veblen's study of status symbolism there are three basic assumptions: first, that possessions and objects of consumption become significant, not so much as economic objects (although to begin with they are economic), but as symbols of prowess and worth; second, that satisfaction with such objects is a matter of comparison with others like oneself (pecuniary emulation); and third, that it is a matter of self-respect to display one's status to others (conspicuous consumption) and, indeed, even to outdo others wherever possible.

Since Veblen only two ideas have been added to our knowledge of such processes. First, the importance of status symbolism depends on the urbanization process, for in smaller communities, in which the past history and present position of everyone is fairly well known, one does not depend on clothing, housing, style of life, and manner to reveal one's status to others. Visible display of status is more common where one fairly often encounters others who have relatively little personal knowledge of one's position (Form & Stone 1957). Second, in an open-class society there is a continual inflationary and deflationary cycle in status symbols. In fashions, for example, the lower-status groups may aspire to the symbols of higher status, so that elite fashions are mass-produced for the nonelites. But the status value of such fashions depreciates, and the elites therefore find it necessary to invent new symbols of their status, thus deflating the status currency. The nonelites, in turn, aspire to the newer status symbols, restarting the process. Possibly, however, the nonelites are left with some sense of having improved their status.

MORRIS ZELDITCH, JR.

[Directly related are the entries GROUPS, article on ROLE STRUCTURE; ROLE. Other relevant material may be found in INTERACTION; SOCIAL STRUCTURE; and in the biographies of BARNARD; COOLEY; LINTON; SIMMEL; WEBER, MAX.]

BIBLIOGRAPHY

ADAMS, J. STACY 1963 Toward an Understanding of Inequity. Journal of Abnormal and Social Psychology 67:422–436.

BALES, ROBERT F. 1950 Interaction Process Analysis: A Method for the Study of Small Groups. Reading, Mass.: Addison-Wesley.

BARBER, ELINOR G. 1955 The Bourgeoisie in Eighteenth Century France. Princeton Univ. Press. → A paperback edition was published in 1967.

BARNARD, C. 1946 Functions and Pathology of Status Systems in Formal Organizations. Pages 46–83 in William F. Whyte (editor), Industry and Society. New York: McGraw-Hill.

BENDIX, REINHARD; and LIPSET, SEYMOUR M. (editors) (1953) 1966 Class, Status, and Power: Social Stratification in Comparative Perspective. 2d ed. New York: Free Press.

BENOÎT-SMULLYAN, ÉMILE 1944 Status, Status Types, and Status Interrelations. American Sociological Review 9:151–161.

BERGER, JOSEPH; COHEN, BERNARD P.; and ZELDITCH, MORRIS JR. 1966 Status Characteristics and Expectation States. Volume 1, pages 29–46 in Joseph Berger, Morris Zelditch, Jr., and Bo Anderson (editors), Sociological Theories in Progress. Boston: Houghton Mifflin.

BIDDLE, BRUCE J.; and THOMAS, EDWIN J. (editors) 1966 Role Theory: Concepts and Research. New York: Wiley.

COHEN, ALBERT K. (1955) 1963 Delinquent Boys: The Culture of the Gang. New York: Free Press.

CONFERENCE ON NEW APPROACHES IN SOCIAL ANTHROPOLOGY, JESUS COLLEGE, CAMBRIDGE, ENG., 1963 1965 The Relevance of Models for Social Anthropology. Edited by Michael Banton. London: Tavistock; New York: Praeger. → See especially the article by Ward H. Goodenough, "Rethinking 'Status' and 'Role': Toward a General Model of the Cultural Organization of Social Relationships."

COOLEY, CHARLES H. (1902) 1956 Human Nature and the Social Order. Rev. ed. In Charles H. Cooley, Two Major Works: Social Organization and Human Nature and the Social Order. Glencoe, Ill.: Free Press. → Each title reprinted with individual title page and pagination. Separate paperback editions were published in 1964 by Schocken.

DURKHEIM, ÉMILE (1893) 1960 The Division of Labor in Society. Glencoe, Ill.: Free Press. → First published as De la division du travail social.

DURKHEIM, ÉMILE (1897) 1951 Suicide: A Study in Sociology. Glencoe, Ill.: Free Press. → First published in French.

FORM, M. H.; and STONE, G. P. 1957 Urbanism, Anonymity, and Status Symbolism. American Journal of Sociology 62:504–514.

GARFINKEL, HAROLD 1956 Conditions of Successful Degradation Ceremonies. American Journal of Sociology 61:420–424.

GREENBLUM, JOSEPH, and PEARLIN, LEONARD I. 1953 Vertical Mobility and Prejudice: A Socio-psychological Analysis. Pages 480–491 in Reinhard Bendix and Seymour M. Lipset (editors), Class, Status, and Power: A Reader in Social Stratification. Glencoe, Ill.: Free Press.

HOMANS, GEORGE C. 1953 Status Among Clerical Workers. Human Organization 12:5–10.

HOMANS, GEORGE C. 1961 Social Behavior: Its Elementary Forms. New York: Harcourt.

HUGHES, EVERETT C. 1945 Dilemmas and Contradictions of Status. American Journal of Sociology 50:353–359.

HUGHES, EVERETT C.; and HUGHES, HELEN M. 1952 Where Peoples Meet: Racial and Ethnic Frontiers. Glencoe, Ill.: Free Press.

HUNTINGTON, MARY JEAN 1957 The Development of a Professional Self-image. Pages 179–187 in The Student–Physician: Introductory Studies in the Sociology of Medical Education. Edited by Robert K. Merton, George G. Reader, and Patricia L. Kendall. Cambridge, Mass.: Harvard Univ. Press.

HURWITZ, JACOB; ZANDER, ALVIN F.; and HYMOVITCH, BERNARD (1953) 1960 Some Effects of Power on the Relations Among Group Members. Pages 800–809 in Dorwin Cartwright (editor), Group Dynamics: Research and Theory. 2d ed. Evanston, Ill.: Row, Peterson.

HYMAN, HERBERT H. 1942 The Psychology of Status. Archives of Psychology 38: Whole no. 269.

JACKSON, ELTON F. 1962 Status Consistency and Symptoms of Stress. American Sociological Review 27:469–480.

KATZ, IRWIN; GOLDSTON, JUDITH; and BENJAMIN, LAWRENCE 1958 Behavior and Productivity in Bi-racial Work Groups. Human Relations 11:123–141.

LENSKI, G. E. 1954 Status Crystallization: A Non-vertical Dimension of Social Status. American Sociological Review 19:405–413.

LENSKI, G. E. 1956 Social Participation and Status Crystallization. American Sociological Review 21:458–464.

LINTON, RALPH 1936 The Study of Man: An Introduction. New York: Appleton.

LIPSET, SEYMOUR M. 1964 The Changing Class Structure and Contemporary European Politics. Dædalus 93:271–303.

LIPSET, SEYMOUR M.; and ZETTERBERG, HANS L. 1956 A Theory of Social Mobility. Volume 3, pages 155–177 in World Congress of Sociology, 3rd, Amsterdam, 1956, *Transactions*. London: International Sociological Association. → Reprinted in the 2d edition of Bendix and Lipset (1953).

MCDILL, EDWARD L.; and COLEMAN, JAMES S. 1963 High School Social Status, College Plans, and Academic Achievement: A Panel Analysis. *American Sociological Review* 28:905–918.

MARSHALL, T. H. (1949) 1964 Citizenship and Social Class. Pages 65–122 in T. H. Marshall, *Class, Citizenship, and Social Development: Essays*. New York: Doubleday. → This essay is based on a lecture delivered at Cambridge in 1949. The collection of essays was first published in England in 1963 as *Sociology at the Crossroads*.

MERTON, ROBERT K. (1957) 1959 Continuities in the Theory of Reference Groups and Social Structure. Pages 281–286 in Robert K. Merton, *Social Theory and Social Structure*. 2d ed., rev. & enl. Glencoe, Ill.: Free Press.

MIYAMOTO, S. FRANK; and DORNBUSCH, SANFORD M. 1956 A Test of the Interactionist Hypotheses of Self-conception. *American Journal of Sociology* 61:399–403.

PARK, ROBERT E. (1928) 1950 The Bases of Race Prejudice. Pages 230–243 in Robert E. Park, *Race and Culture*. Collected Papers, Vol. 1. Glencoe, Ill.: Free Press.

SHORT, JAMES F.; and STRODTBECK, FRED L. 1965 *Group Process and Gang Delinquency*. Univ. of Chicago Press.

SILBERSTEIN, FRED; and SEEMAN, MELVIN 1959 Social Mobility and Prejudice. *American Journal of Sociology* 65:258–264.

SPEIER, HANS (1935) 1952 Honor and the Social Structure. Pages 36–52 in Hans Speier, *Social Order and the Risks of War: Papers in Political Sociology*. New York: Stewart.

STOUFFER, SAMUEL A. et al. 1949 *The American Soldier*. Studies in Social Psychology in World War II, Vols. 1 and 2. Princeton Univ. Press. → Volume 1: *Adjustment During Army Life*. Volume 2: *Combat and Its Aftermath*.

STRODTBECK, FRED L.; JAMES, RITA M.; and HAWKINS, CHARLES (1957) 1958 Social Status in Jury Deliberations. Pages 379–388 in Society for the Psychological Study of Social Issues, *Readings in Social Psychology*. 3d ed. New York: Holt. → First published in Volume 22 of the *American Sociological Review*.

TAWNEY, R. H. 1941 The Rise of the Gentry: 1558–1640. *Economic History Review* First Series 11:1–38.

TREVOR-ROPER, H. R. 1953 *The Gentry: 1540–1640*. Economic History Review, Supplement 1. Cambridge Univ. Press.

VEBLEN, THORSTEIN (1899) 1953 *The Theory of the Leisure Class: An Economic Study of Institutions*. Rev. ed. New York: New American Library. → A paperback edition was published in 1959.

WEBER, MAX (1921) 1946 Class, Status, Party. Pages 180–195 in Max Weber, *From Max Weber: Essays in Sociology*. Translated and edited by Hans H. Gerth and C. Wright Mills. New York: Oxford Univ. Press. → First published as Part 3, Chapter 4 of *Wirtschaft und Gesellschaft*. A paperback edition was published in 1958.

WHYTE, WILLIAM F. (1943) 1961 *Street Corner Society: The Social Structure of an Italian Slum*. 2d ed., enl. Univ. of Chicago Press.

ZELDITCH, MORRIS JR.; BERGER, JOSEPH; and COHEN, BERNARD P. 1966 Stability of Organizational Status Structures. Volume 1, pages 269–294 in Joseph Berger, Morris Zelditch, Jr., and Bo Anderson (editors), *Sociological Theories in Progress*. Boston: Houghton Mifflin.

STEIN, LORENZ VON

Lorenz von Stein (1815–1890) is remembered for his attempt to establish a science of society based on Hegelian idealism and his interpretation of the ideas and events of the French Revolution. He played a major role in introducing class conflict and socialism as public topics in Germany and influenced the academic development of public administration and finance.

Stein was born in Schleswig, then under Danish suzerainty; he died near Vienna. His father was Baron von Wasner, his mother a commoner. Stein spent much of his youth in an orphanage, but in 1832 he succeeded in going to the university. He studied philosophy and law at Jena and Kiel, where he received his doctor of law degree in 1840. Subsequently he went to Paris on a travel grant to undertake research in legal history. There he met Victor Considérant, Étienne Cabet, Louis Blanc, and others, and under their influence his interests shifted to the study of socialist ideas and social movements. With his talent for speedy literary production—which also proved useful for his many newspaper articles—Stein was able to publish his *Sozialismus und Kommunismus des heutigen Frankreich* by 1842; eight years later he produced the three-volume *Geschichte der sozialen Bewegung in Frankreich* (1850a; 1850b). This work established Stein's fame with the politically agitated public of the time.

In 1846 Stein became a professor at Kiel, but in the early 1850s he was dismissed by the Danish authorities for having advocated the independence of Schleswig-Holstein during the revolution of 1848. Since he had also opposed Prussian intervention in his homeland, Prussian authorities forced the Bavarian authorities to withdraw an offer of a professorship at Würzburg. However, with the backing of the Austrian minister of finance, Stein became professor of government (*Staatswissenschaften*) at Vienna in 1854, a position which he held until his retirement in 1885. In 1868 he was ennobled in recognition of his academic achievements and his public service; he had wanted to merit a patent of nobility on his own rather than take on his father's name and title.

Stein's eminent academic career was not matched by success in politics and business. The Prussian victory of 1866 brought to nought his advocacy of Austrian predominance in Germany; before that, the various proposals for reform that he had made as an adviser to the ministry of finance were ignored, and he lost an election for a seat on the Austrian Reichsrat, for which he had tried to qualify as a "Saint-Simonian industrialist." He also ruined himself in a series of industrial speculations.

Stein's exposition of his science of society is contained in the long introduction to his *History*, "The Concept of Society and Its Dynamic Laws." His approach combined the social and socialist theories of Saint-Simon and his followers and of Blanc, on the one hand, with Hegelian views of the individual and the state, on the other. Thus, Stein posited a basic difference between society and the state: society is governed by social laws, the crucial factors determining its functioning being economic interest and class struggle; the state is man's instrument for bringing about personal autonomy and self-realization. Economically dominant groups in pursuit of their material interests always attempt to capture the state, thus provoking class conflicts. It is a "social law" that such groups first strive for economic privileges, then tend to develop into classes, and, finally, become estates and castes. Historically, these phenomena have occurred sequentially, but they may also exist concurrently. Stein believed that the history of France, and of Europe following French precedent, would be a history of class struggles as long as the ruling class—whether aristocratic or bourgeois—refused to accord political rights to that stratum of the subject class that had acquired the education and wealth necessary for social and political independence. He argued that a monarchy, because of its relative independence from the class structure, would be more likely to succeed in social reforms than a bourgeois republic.

Stein and Marx developed their ideas contemporaneously, but Stein wrote and published his work on the class struggle in France before Marx did. Marx read Stein's work and reacted in his customary negative manner; there is no evidence that he was influenced by it. To Marxists (e.g., Marcuse 1954), Stein's juxtaposition of determinist and voluntarist viewpoints and of dialectic and positivist elements has appeared typical of "idealist aberration" and to pragmatists (e.g., Weiss 1963),

typical of "dialectic obscurantism," but this theoretical dualism permitted Stein to be sociologically more perceptive and historically more nearly correct than Marx.

Stein not only believed that social reforms could control the dynamics of class conflict, but he also recognized that unless the workers acquired more education and wealth, a proletarian revolution would necessarily result in a dictatorship over the proletariat. To forestall such an empty victory, it was necessary for the proletariat to be socially mobile, and Stein saw education and a rising standard of living as the main avenues of social mobility. It was the responsibility of the state to safeguard these avenues. However, Stein did not actually advocate major welfare legislation, and for this reason he later opposed the German academic social reformers.

As early as 1852, Stein repudiated the economic determinism of his own *History*. Henceforth he devoted himself to the systematic study of public administration and finance in France, England, and Germany, and in the academic circles of his time this part of his work became more influential than his *History*. Today, however, his earlier insights into the sources of class conflict and the preconditions of political stability appear as an impressive contribution to the study of industrialization and democratization.

GUENTHER ROTH

[*See also* MARXISM *and the biography of* SAINT-SIMON.]

WORKS BY STEIN

(1842) 1848 *Der Sozialismus und Kommunismus des heutigen Frankreich: Ein Beitrag zur Zeitgeschichte.* 2d ed., 2 vols. Leipzig: Wigand.

(1850a) 1959 *Geschichte der sozialen Bewegung in Frankreich von 1789 bis auf unsere Tage.* 3 vols. Edited by Gottfried Salomon. Hildesheim: Olms. → Volume 1: *Der Begriff der Gesellschaft und die soziale Geschichte der Französischen Revolution bis zum Jahre 1830.* Volume 2: *Die industrielle Gesellschaft, der Sozialismus und Kommunismus Frankreichs von 1830 bis 1848.* Volume 3: *Das Königtum, die Republik, und die Souveränität der französischen Gesellschaft seit der Februarrevolution 1848.*

(1850b) 1964 *The History of the Social Movement in France: 1789–1850.* Introduced, edited, and translated by Kaethe Mengelberg. Totowa, N.J.: Bedminster Press. → An abridged version of Stein 1850a.

1852–1856 *System der Staatswissenschaft.* 2 vols. Leipzig: Brockhaus. → Volume 1: *System der Statistik, der Populationistik und der Volkswirtschaftslehre,* 1852. Volume 2: *Der Begriff der Gesellschaft,* 1856.

(1860) 1885–1886 *Lehrbuch der Finanzwissenschaft.* 5th ed., 4 vols. Leipzig: Brockhaus.

(1865–1868) 1869–1884 *Die Verwaltungslehre.* 2d ed., 3 vols. Stuttgart: Cotta.

(1870) 1888 *Handbuch der Verwaltungslehre und des Verwaltungsrechtes mit Vergleichung der Literatur und Gesetzgebung von Frankreich, England und Deutschland.* Stuttgart: Cotta.

SUPPLEMENTARY BIBLIOGRAPHY

ANGERMANN, ERICH 1962 Zwei Typen des Ausgleichs gesellschaftlicher Interessen durch die Staatsgewalt: Ein Vergleich der Lehren Lorenz von Steins und Robert Mohls. Pages 173–205 in Werner Conze (editor), *Staat und Gesellschaft im deutschen Vormärz.* Stuttgart: Klett.

GRÜNFELD, ERNST 1908 *Die Gesellschaftslehre von Lorenz von Stein.* Halle: Kaemmerer.

MARCUSE, HERBERT 1954 The Transformation of the Dialectic Into Sociology: Lorenz von Stein. Pages 374–388 in Herbert Marcuse, *Reason and Revolution: Hegel and the Rise of Social Theory.* 2d ed. New York: Humanities Press.

WEISS, JOHN 1963 Dialectical Idealism and the Work of Lorenz von Stein. *International Review of Social History* 8, no. 1:1–19.

STEREOTYPES

The term "stereotype" originated in the technology of printing, where it has a clearly defined meaning. A body of type is set up; then a mold is made from this type, and a solid metal plate is cast in the mold. This metal plate is the stereotype. Its printing surface is precisely equivalent to that of the original type. The major purpose of stereotyping is to produce a printing surface that can be used for thousands and thousands of impressions without needing to be replaced. Thus, the adjective "stereotyped" has come to mean "mechanically repeated" or—in a broader usage—"hackneyed" or "trite."

During the past forty years the noun "stereotype" has been widely used as a social science concept without ever being precisely defined. Its usage was introduced by the American journalist Walter Lippmann in a book called *Public Opinion* (1922). The major thesis of this book is that in a modern democracy political leaders and ordinary citizens are required to make decisions about a variety of complicated matters that they do not understand. People believe that their conceptions of German soldiers, Belgian priests, or American Ku Klux Klansmen, for example, are accurate representations of the real members of these classes. Not so! said Lippmann. The conception in most cases is actually a stereotype acquired by the individual from some source other than his direct experience. The situation is not usually improved even by direct experience with the social object corresponding to the stereotype because (according to Lippmann) people see mainly what they expect to see rather than what is really there.

Lippmann's book was much admired by social scientists, and in many of their writings (especially textbooks) the term "stereotype" has continued to have essentially the meaning Lippmann gave it. When a concept is referred to as a stereotype, the implication is that (1) it is simple rather than complex or differentiated; (2) it is erroneous rather than accurate; (3) it has been acquired secondhand rather than through direct experience with the reality it is supposed to represent; and (4) it is resistant to modification by new experience. [*See the biography of* LIPPMANN.]

It is unfortunate for the development of social science that attention has been focused on the noun "stereotype" rather than the adjective "stereotyped." When one considers the adjective it becomes obvious that in the realm of concepts (though not in printing technology) stereotypy is a matter of degree. It is also fairly clear that the extent to which an individual's conception of, say, "the German soldier" is stereotyped is not a unidimensional variable. The four characteristics of a stereotype described above can vary independently; as a matter of fact, there is no solid evidence that they are even positively correlated. In these circumstances there would be little scientific value in setting up arbitrary criteria for the extent to which a concept had to have these characteristics in order to be termed a stereotype. It would be more profitable instead to treat the dimensions of stereotypy as quantitative variables and to investigate their variation from individual to individual, from concept to concept, and from situation to situation.

Empirical research. There has actually been very little of such systematic investigation. The only dimension that has been seriously studied is the one of resistance to modification by new experience [*for a discussion of this research, see* ATTITUDES, *article on* ATTITUDE CHANGE; PERSUASION]. On the other hand, there have been very few attempts to set up criteria for classifying an individual's concepts in a particular area into "stereotypes" and "nonstereotypes." In empirical research the term "stereotype" has usually been employed simply as a pejorative designation for "group concept."

This "group concept" usage became established in a classic study by Katz and Braly (1933). A group of 100 white American college students were asked to select from a list of 84 traits those they considered characteristic of each one of ten ethnic groups; then they were asked to choose the five "most typical" traits for each group. An index of *definiteness of stereotype* was constructed by counting the least number of traits required to include 50 per cent of the 500 choices by all subjects. This index ranged from a minimum of 4.6 for Negroes to a maximum of 15.9 for Turks. The six most frequent characterizations of each group were as follows (figures in parentheses indicate the number of students choosing a trait as one of the five "most typical")—*Negroes:* superstitious (84), lazy (75), happy-go-lucky (38), ignorant (38), musical (26), and ostentatious (26); *Turks:* cruel (47), very religious (26), treacherous (21), sensual (20), ignorant (15), and physically dirty (15). Both Negroes and Turks were viewed very unfavorably by these students, but there was considerably more agreement on the characteristics attributed to Negroes.

The Katz and Braly procedure has been repeated many times, for many different ethnic groups, and in many different countries. In one of the more recent studies, a list of 99 adjectives was submitted to a group of 100 Arab students in Beirut, Lebanon (Prothro & Melikian 1954). These adjectives, in Arabic, had been selected from a longer list developed by other students at the same university to characterize members of various ethnic groups. The Arab students characterized Negroes in a manner similar to American students twenty years earlier, but their ratings of Turks were entirely different. The six traits most frequently chosen as "most typical" of Turks were strong (36), militaristic (33), nationalistic (33), courageous (31), progressive (18), and arrogant (17).

Since 1933 the paper-and-pencil questionnaire has been the typical method for investigating stereotypes. Most studies have dealt with beliefs about ethnic groups, but a substantial number have investigated beliefs about occupational groups, social class groups, the two sexes, etc. What conclusions can be drawn from all this research?

One conclusion is that most individuals feel able to make at least a guess about the characteristics of almost any defined social group on the basis of information that a social scientist would consider quite inadequate. Opinions are picked up from other individuals, from the mass media, and—to some extent—from direct personal contact. There are some highly conspicuous national groups—Americans, Russians, French, British, Chinese—about whom the majority of the world's citizens seem now to hold definite opinions.

To what extent are these opinions correct? A great many social scientists accept the "kernel of truth" hypothesis (Klineberg 1950), which asserts that if we could determine objectively and accurately the characteristics of a defined social group and that if we ascertained the beliefs of some other social group about the first, we would find a more than random correspondence between the two sets of characteristics. There will always be some individuals whose beliefs about members of the defined social group are almost completely accurate and others whose beliefs are more wrong than right. However, according to the "kernel of truth" hypothesis, the over-all amount of truth in stereotypes is greater than the amount of error.

This hypothesis is clearly impossible to test in its general form. What can be tested are hypotheses about the accuracy with which specific sets of characteristics are attributed to the members of group X by the members of group Y—*provided we can determine the true distribution of these characteristics in group X.* For obvious reasons, little research of this sort has been done, and the findings have been highly divergent. In at least one study of attitudes toward an ethnic group (Armenians in California) there was a negative relationship between the actual characteristics of the group and the stereotype of it held by nonmembers (LaPiere 1936).

There are many hypotheses about the circumstances under which stereotypes (in the sense of group concepts) are likely to be accurate or inaccurate. One of the most plausible is that of Roger Brown (1965), who argues that beliefs about members of a particular social group are most likely to be accurate if the group consists of people playing a defined social role—for example, the members of a particular occupation, caste, or sex. In this case, "what is prescribed for the category is ordinarily performed by the category and expected from the category" (*ibid.,* p. 172). Social life would be almost impossible if this were not so.

A very widely held belief is that the stereotypes held by educated people are in general more accurate than those of the uneducated and that the concepts of social scientists are most accurate of all. This is certainly Lippmann's view, and it seems very reasonable; however, it has not been demonstrated.

When members of two different ethnic groups are asked to rate both themselves and each other in the Katz and Braly manner, two things usually occur. One is that the array of characteristics selected by group X as most typical of itself is similar to the array of characteristics selected by group Y as most typical of group X. The other is that socially desirable characteristics are more likely to be emphasized in a group's description of itself, while undesirable characteristics are more likely to be emphasized in the description of a group by members of another group—especially if there has been a recent history of conflict between the two groups. A representative study is that of Reigrotski and Anderson (1959), in which large numbers of Belgians, Dutch, French, and Germans were asked to characterize both themselves and the other three nationality groups. From a list of 12 adjectives the ones most frequently selected by the Germans to describe themselves were (in order): hardworking, brave, intelligent, practical, progressive, and peace-loving. On the other hand, the French thought the Germans were most characteristically: domineering, hardworking, cruel, progressive, brave, and intelligent.

When there is agreement between a group's image of itself and the image that members of a second group have of the first, this is usually taken as evidence for a substantial "kernel of truth" in both sets of stereotypes (e.g., Vinacke 1949). The tendency of members of a group to see themselves more favorably than members of other groups see them is generally considered to be a reflection of ethnocentrism; this tendency has been widely demonstrated. In the case of low-status groups, however, such as the American Negroes, lower-caste Hindus, and people in depressed areas, even their own stereotypes of themselves may be unfavorable (Bayton 1941; Bayton & Byoune 1947; Rath & Sircar 1960; Hughes et al. 1960, pp. 244–311).

Although in the great majority of studies the term "stereotype" has been used to mean "group concept," with no attempt to determine either the adequacy of the concept in representing its object or the quality of thinking of the person using the concept, there has been some research in which the investigator tried to study stereotypes in Lippmann's sense of the term. Most of these studies have dealt with ethnic stereotypes, and the major conclusion has been that the more unfavorable an individual's attitude is toward members of a particular group, the more likely are his concepts of such group members to be stereotypes in Lippmann's sense (Bettelheim & Janowitz 1950; Adorno et al. 1950; Secord 1959).

The confusion in the meaning assigned to the term "stereotype" by different authors, especially the contrast in usage by the majority of empirical workers and the majority of textbook writers, has led to a good deal of discussion of the basic concept or concepts involved in the term. Two of the best articles on this subject are those of Fishman (1956) and Vinacke (1957). In the opinion of the present writer, the broad and undiscriminating

usage of the noun "stereotype" is now too well established to be dislodged.

The extreme diversity of research on stereotypes has inhibited authors from attempting to review the entire field. (A review and bibliography of research on ethnic stereotypes can be found in Klineberg 1950 and in Harding et al. 1954.)

JOHN HARDING

[*Directly related are the entries* IDEOLOGY; PREJUDICE. *Other relevant material may be found in* ATTITUDES; CONCEPT FORMATION; ETHNIC GROUPS; RACE; RACE RELATIONS.]

BIBLIOGRAPHY

ADORNO, T. W. et al. 1950 *The Authoritarian Personality.* American Jewish Committee, Social Studies Series, No. 3. New York: Harper.

BAYTON, JAMES A. 1941 The Racial Stereotypes of Negro College Students. *Journal of Abnormal and Social Psychology* 36:97–102.

BAYTON, JAMES A.; and BYOUNE, ETHEL 1947 Racio-National Stereotypes Held by Negroes. *Journal of Negro Education* 16:49–56.

BETTELHEIM, BRUNO; and JANOWITZ, MORRIS (1950) 1964 *Social Change and Prejudice, Including Dynamics of Prejudice.* New York: Free Press. → A reprinting of the authors' *Dynamics of Prejudice*, with a reassessment of its findings.

BROWN, ROGER W. 1965 *Social Psychology.* New York: Free Press.

FISHMAN, JOSHUA A. 1956 An Examination of the Process and Function of Social Stereotyping. *Journal of Social Psychology* 43:27–64.

HARDING, JOHN S. et al. 1954 Prejudice and Ethnic Relations. Volume 2, pages 1021–1061 in Gardner Lindzey (editor), *Handbook of Social Psychology.* Cambridge, Mass.: Addison-Wesley.

HUGHES, CHARLES C. et al. 1960 *People of Cove and Woodlot: Communities From the Viewpoint of Social Psychiatry.* The Stirling County Study of Psychiatric Disorder and Socio-cultural Environment, Vol. 2. New York: Basic Books.

KATZ, DANIEL; and BRALY, KENNETH 1933 Racial Stereotypes of One Hundred College Students. *Journal of Abnormal and Social Psychology* 28:280–290.

KLINEBERG, OTTO 1950 *Tensions Affecting International Understanding: A Survey of Research.* Social Science Research Council, Bulletin No. 62. New York: The Council.

LAPIERE, RICHARD T. 1936 Type-rationalizations of Group Antipathy. *Social Forces* 15:232–237.

LIPPMANN, WALTER (1922) 1944 *Public Opinion.* New York: Macmillan. → A paperback edition was published in 1965 by the Free Press.

PROTHRO, EDWIN T.; and MELIKIAN, LEVON H. 1954 Studies in Stereotypes: III. Arab Students in the Near East. *Journal of Social Psychology* 40:237–243.

RATH, R.; and SIRCAR, N. C. 1960 The Mental Pictures of Six Hindu Caste Groups About Each Other as Reflected in Verbal Stereotypes. *Journal of Social Psychology* 51:277–293.

REIGROTSKI, ERICH; and ANDERSON, NELS 1959 National Stereotypes and Foreign Contacts. *Public Opinion Quarterly* 23:515–528.

SECORD, PAUL F. 1959 Stereotyping and Favorableness in the Perception of Negro Faces. *Journal of Abnormal and Social Psychology* 59:309–314.

VINACKE, W. EDGAR 1949 Stereotyping Among National–Racial Groups in Hawaii: A Study in Ethnocentrism. *Journal of Social Psychology* 30:265–291.

VINACKE, W. EDGAR 1957 Stereotypes as Social Concepts. *Journal of Social Psychology* 46:229–243.

STERILIZATION

See FERTILITY CONTROL; POPULATION, *article on* POPULATION POLICIES.

STERN, WILLIAM

William Stern (1871–1938), German psychologist and philosopher, was born in Berlin and spent the first 25 years of his life there. He received his doctorate in 1892, soon after the establishment of the first psychological laboratories in Germany and in America, and wrote his dissertation under the then young Ebbinghaus, who had fired his enthusiasm for exact empirical studies. At that time an empirical approach to the new discipline of psychology usually meant an exhaustive study of single functions and elements of experience with the assumption that, when enough of them were understood as distinct entities, the resulting knowledge would constitute a working system. In spite of his allegiance to Ebbinghaus, Stern did not entirely accept the limitations of this approach. He had entered the University of Berlin with the intention of studying philosophy and philology and had acquired a broad base in those fields before he started to study psychology. At 19 he realized that he would have to find a way to reconcile his love for empirical investigation with his love for philosophical speculation, and this was to remain his goal for the rest of his life (1930*b*, p. 340).

Between 1892 and 1897 Stern worked on his monograph *Psychologie der Veränderungsauffassung* (1898), which dealt with a series of investigations on the apperception of change. The experimental work that formed the basis for this study included observations that made him aware of the richness and diversity of types of change and led him to the conviction that the prevalent view, which equated all change with change of location, was artificial and unreal.

In 1897 Ebbinghaus left Berlin for a chair in Breslau, and Stern also went to Breslau as a *Privatdozent*. The succeeding years there were marked by intense activity and untiring production. At this time Stern felt that the deeper implications of his work on the experience of change were be-

ing largely ignored by his colleagues, so he set himself, for a time, a variety of more narrowly psychological tasks; they served, he said, as a stockade behind which his metaphysical system could develop. It was only later, he noted, that he fully realized how much this work contributed to the conceptual foundations of his final theory. At the same time, it did much to establish his reputation at home and abroad. Especially in the areas of child psychology and in the applied fields of mental and vocational testing and legal psychology, his observational methods and the ways in which he organized his material helped open up and structure new fields of study. With the more recent development of experimental techniques and rigorous statistical treatment of data, his publications are less frequently quoted, but there is no doubt of the part that they have played.

In the United States Stern is probably best known for his contributions to child psychology, especially for his studies of the development of language in children. He published two important monographs in collaboration with his wife, Clara Stern, based on diaries that she kept during the early development of their own children: *Erinnerung, Aussage, Lüge in der ersten Kindheit* in 1905 and *Die Kindersprache* in 1907. An account of the childhood of Helen Keller (1910), tracing the construction of her world from tactual sensations and the unusual but well-ordered processes by which she acquired language, also appeared at this time. [*See* DEVELOPMENTAL PSYCHOLOGY; *and* LANGUAGE, *article on* LANGUAGE DEVELOPMENT.]

Stern early became interested in the psychology of individual differences, publishing in 1900 a monograph entitled *Über Psychologie der individuellen Differenzen*, which appeared, completely rewritten, in 1911 as *Differentielle Psychologie*. During this period he became involved in the testing of intelligence and of vocational aptitude and was the first to suggest the use of the intelligence quotient to indicate ability. In later years he warned against the overemphasis of such measures, stressing the importance of looking at the role of intelligence in the functioning of the person as a whole, rather than evaluating it as an independent factor. [*See* APTITUDE TESTING; INTELLIGENCE AND INTELLIGENCE TESTING; VOCATIONAL INTEREST TESTING.]

Another field in which Stern worked was that of legal psychology. His interest in this topic resulted in the publication of "Zur Psychologie der Aussage" in 1902 and two volumes of *Beiträge zur Psychologie der Aussage* (1903–1906) soon thereafter. His continuing interest in this field is evidenced by the fact that his last public lecture in 1937 dealt with questions of courtroom procedure. [*See* PSYCHIA-TRY, *article on* FORENSIC PSYCHIATRY.]

In 1906, while he was still a member of the Breslau faculty, Stern cooperated with his former student Otto Lipmann in founding the Institut für Angewandte Psychologie in Berlin, and in 1907 he established the journal *Zeitschrift für angewandte Psychologie*, of which he remained coeditor until he left Germany in 1933. In spite of his manifold activity during the period in Breslau, he found time to reflect on his philosophical system and wrote the first volume of *Person und Sache: System des kritischen Personalismus* (1918–1923).

In 1916 he was appointed director of the psychological laboratory in Hamburg and professor of philosophy, psychology, and pedagogy at what was then the Kolonial Institut there. As the demand for university training increased at the end of World War I, Stern played an important part in the transformation of several loosely organized facilities in Hamburg into a major university. He remained at his post there until the beginning of the Hitler regime. During those years he published a large number of articles and books in different fields of theoretical and applied psychology. He was especially active in introducing tests for vocational guidance and for the selection of gifted children into the Hamburg schools. He also completed the presentation of his philosophical–psychological system (see 1918–1923, vols. 2–3; 1924).

With the advent of Hitler, Stern first sought refuge in Holland, and in 1934 joined the department of psychology headed by William McDougall at Duke University. During his year in Holland, he used his enforced leisure to give a detailed and comprehensive account of his ideas on psychology (1935). At Duke, Stern continued teaching, writing, and giving occasional public lectures until his sudden death in 1938.

Philosophical–psychological system

In describing his philosophical system, Stern said that his basic motive was a striving for concrete unity. He wanted to synthesize the antithetical concepts of mind and body, causality and teleology, associationism and holism. His central idea is the category of "person," to which he assigned the defining property of concrete, purposeful activity, emphasizing that this activity is inner-determined rather than imposed from without and that the person is a genuine whole rather than an aggregate of parts.

With this definition, the category of person is applied to "the human, the sub-human, the super-human, to the organic and inorganic, to individual and societal forms" ([1930*b*] 1961, p. 371). Complementary to the concept of "person" is the concept of "thing." "Thing" refers to everything that is not whole, that is merely aggregated, that is not endowed with purposive, self-originating activity but is instead a sphere of influence for foreign determinants.

Stern called the science that studies the human person in his totality "personalistics." It deals with the topics that the specialized sciences of the person—biology, physiology, pathology, psychology—have in common. Psychology is a branch of personalistics, and in defining it Stern began with the individual person (using the word "person" in its more usual sense). He said the person, in this sense, is "a living whole, unique, striving toward goals, self-contained and yet open to the world around him; he is capable of having experience"; and psychology is, then, "the science of the person as having experience or as capable of having experience. It studies this personal attribute, experience, in regard to the conditions of its appearance, its nature, mode of functioning and regularity, and its significance for personal existence and life considered as a whole" ([1935] 1938, p. 70).

Although the person exists as a biological organism and is connected with objective values, psychology, according to Stern, does not deal with the biosphere or with values as such. The biosphere and values belong to the broader science of personalistics and become part of the subject matter of psychology only as they enter into the experience of the person. Experience, in turn, is to be identified and interpreted in terms of its matrix, the unitary, goal-directed person (*ibid.*, p. viii).

In his book on general psychology (1935), Stern treated those fields that are usually found in such a text—perception, memory and learning, thought and imagination, motivation and affect. The content is unusually rich; a great variety of phenomena are described and classified. Often they are sorted out according to polar dimensions—depth–surface, reactivity–spontaneity, nearness–remoteness, etc. Throughout the book every experience and every process is related to the total person. Stern frequently asked, What is it for? (i.e., What instrumental value does it have for the adaptation of the person to the environment?) and provided answers to that question. In short, with Stern an emphasis on the concrete unity of the person was paramount: he was always a holistic psychologist. His concern was mainly with phenomenological description and teleological explanation and less with causal conditions or effects. Thus his thought is related, on the one hand, to recent existentialism and phenomenology and, on the other, to the functionalism of James, Dewey, or Angell.

In discussing the relation between the person and the world, Stern talked about "the personal world," which is different from other worlds, e.g., the mathematical, physical, or sociological world. Each individual has his own world centered in his person, and this world has its own spatial–temporal structure. Thus, the usual dimensions of above–below, before–behind, right–left are found in the personal world, but they carry meanings beyond those of ordinary mathematical, Euclidean space. One term of a dimension is often given greater value than its opposite. For example, the terms "above," "before," and "right" are often given greater value than their opposites, "below," "after," and "left." In this sort of treatment of the phenomenology of space and time, Stern came close to the existentialists with their "lived space" and "lived time."

He distinguished between degrees of consciousness along a dimension that he called "salience–embeddedness." The greater the salience of a specific experience the greater its relative independence and inner structure. Thus, a thought on which attention is focused, a clearly perceived figure, or a structured act of will is salient. On the other hand, the more embedded an experience, the less clear, structured, and independent it is. Examples are moods or general, unformulated attitudes. The polarity of salience versus embeddedness is similar to, but not the same as, the polarity of figure versus ground in gestalt psychology. Stern accused gestalt theory of dealing only with the salient parts of experience, since it stressed the clearly articulated gestalt; however, the embedded parts, such as feelings, smells, tastes, or empathic experience, should not be forgotten. Gestalt theory committed the error, he felt, of reifying figural units as if they were elements of a higher order. There can be no gestalt without a person who forms gestalten. Figural units are not independent; one always has to consider their relevance to the person and especially their significance for the person's adaptation to the environment.

Stern did not conceive of memory as related to traces having fixed content; rather, the traces become immersed in the total person and alter his disposition to react to immediate stimuli. In discussing thought and intellect, he conceded that they have survival value; but here again he stressed man's capacity to be more than a passive adapter: spontaneous striving toward enhanced status and power activates the intellect more than does mere self-preservation.

In treating the psychology of motivation, Stern dealt not only with reflexes, drives, needs, and instincts but also with "will," which implies conscious anticipation of end and means. He discussed the course of voluntary behavior and distinguished pro-phase, onset of will, execution, and after-phase. Stern's treatment of the psychology of personality consists mainly of a classification of traits and types. For instance, he suggested that one can distinguish between people who are mainly concerned with their own preservation and development and those whose aims are related to the environment, i.e., to other persons, to groups, and to values.

Among Stern's younger contemporaries who were influenced by his thinking and who helped bring some of the broader aspects of his work, especially his stress on the whole person, into the stream of present-day psychology are Heinz Werner and Gordon Allport. On the whole, it may be said that in his most active years his greatest influence was on the new fields in which he was a trail blazer. Beyond this, it is hard to know how far contemporary trends that are in line with his thinking stem from his work and how far he should be thought of as merely anticipating independent developments. For psychologists who feel the need to go beyond a fragmented view of human nature, Stern's personalism, centered as it is in the concrete unity of the person, will always have a special attraction. It may be that, as he himself felt, this will be the most lasting part of his work.

FRITZ HEIDER

[Other relevant material may be found in FIELD THEORY; GESTALT THEORY; PERSONALITY; SELF CONCEPT; and in the biographies of ANGYAL and BÜHLER.]

WORKS BY STERN

(1898) 1906 *Psychologie der Veränderungsauffassung.* 2d ed. Breslau (then Germany): Preuss & Junger.

1900 *Über Psychologie der individuellen Differenzen.* Leipzig: Barth.

1902 *Zur Psychologie der Aussage. Zeitschrift für die gesamte Strafrechtswissenschaft* 22:56 only.

1903–1906 *Beiträge zur Psychologie der Aussage.* 2 vols. Leipzig: Barth.

(1905) 1922 STERN, WILLIAM; and STERN, CLARA *Erinnerung, Aussage, Lüge in der ersten Kindheit.* 3d ed. Leipzig: Barth.

(1907) 1927 STERN, WILLIAM; and STERN, CLARA *Die Kindersprache.* 4th ed. Leipzig: Barth.

1910 *Helen Keller: Persönliche Eindrücke. Zeitschrift für angewandte Psychologie* 3:321–333.

1911 *Differentielle Psychologie in ihren methodischen Grundlagen.* Leipzig: Barth.

(1914) 1930 *Psychology of Early Childhood up to the Sixth Year of Age.* 2d ed. New York: Holt. → First published in German.

1918–1923 *Person und Sache: System des kritischen Personalismus.* 3 vols. Leipzig: Barth. → Subtitle of Volume 1: *Ableitung und Grundlage des kritischen Personalismus;* Volumes 2 and 3: *Die menschliche Persönlichkeit.*

1924 *Wertphilosophie.* Leipzig: Barth.

1930a *Studien zur Personwissenschaft.* Part 1: *Personalistik als Wissenschaft.* Leipzig: Barth.

(1930b) 1961 *William Stern.* Volume 1, pages 335–388 in *A History of Psychology in Autobiography.* Edited by Carl Murchison. New York: Russell.

(1935) 1938 *General Psychology From the Personalistic Standpoint.* New York: Macmillan. → First published in German.

SUPPLEMENTARY BIBLIOGRAPHY

ALLPORT, GORDON W. 1937 The Personalistic Psychology of William Stern. *Character and Personality* 5: 231–246.

ALLPORT, GORDON W. 1938 William Stern: 1871–1938. *American Journal of Psychology* 51:770–773.

WERNER, HEINZ 1938 William Stern's Personalistics and Psychology of Personality. *Character and Personality* 7:109–125.

STERNBERG, LEV Y.

See BOGORAZ, VLADIMIR G., STERNBERG, LEV Y., AND JOCHELSON, VLADIMIR.

STEUART, JAMES DENHAM

Sir James Denham Steuart, British mercantilist, was born in Edinburgh in 1712, the son of Sir James Steuart, solicitor-general for Scotland under Queen Anne and George I. After legal studies at the University of Edinburgh and admission to the Faculty of Advocates there in 1735, he traveled extensively on the Continent. While in Rome, he became a supporter of the Jacobite cause; in 1745 he was involved in the second Jacobite rebellion, and, after the battle of Culloden, was forced to live abroad until 1763. In 1773 he changed his name (in connection with the inheritance of an estate) to Steuart Denham. He died in 1780.

A disciple of Montesquieu and Hume, Steuart embedded his economics in a wider sociological matrix. His main work, *An Inquiry Into the Principles of Political Economy* (1767), attempts a synthesis of contemporary knowledge from the point of view of late mercantilism.

Basing his analysis on the near-Malthusian conviction that "the generative faculty resembles a spring loaded with a weight, which always exerts itself in proportion to the diminution of resistance," Steuart saw economic life in dynamic terms. According to him, two types of society succeed each other: slave societies and free nations. In the former, men work because they are subject to others; in the latter, because they are subject to their own wants. When an agricultural surplus is achieved, free societies split into rural and urban sectors. An exchange economy then develops, desires are released, production is stimulated, well-being is induced, provided only that there is "mutual serviceableness," i.e., adjustment of the various branches of the economy to each other.

As a mercantilist, Steuart did not believe that this adjustment would come about spontaneously. The competitive merchant, as the mediator between the farmers and the urban "free hands," was its prime agent; but it had to be ultimately guaranteed and, if necessary, engineered by the statesman. Population growth, for instance, might bring either "procreation" (mere increase in numbers) or "multiplication" (an increase in numbers that ensures continued serviceableness of all, i.e., social and economic harmony). The government must see to it that there is multiplication rather than procreation, that some trades are encouraged and others discouraged, and that new employment is created for workmen displaced by labor-saving machines, etc.

The government must also manage the market, Steuart maintained: "A statesman must be constantly attentive, and so soon as he perceives a too frequent tendency in any one of the scales to preponderate, he ought gently to load the opposite scale . . . Thus when the scale of demand is found to preponderate, he ought to give encouragement to the establishment of new undertakings, for augmenting the supply, and for preserving prices at their former standard: when the scale of work is on the preponderating hand, then every expedient for increasing exportation must be employed, in order to prevent profits from falling below the price of subsistence" (*The Works . . . ,* vol. 1, pp. 490–491).

Steuart's over-all view of development is pessimistic. A first phase brings a growing population associated with what he calls "infant trade"; a second phase, a static population and "foreign trade"; and a third, a declining population and "inland trade." When industrialization begins, in the first stage, the workers, being as yet semirural, do not wholly depend on wages; costs are low, the country competitive. Later, the workers increasingly depend on wages alone, and these must rise because agriculture finds it difficult to feed rising numbers at stable cost. (Steuart came close to a theory of diminishing returns.) As export prices rise, competitiveness declines. As the home population increases further, and as population shifts away from the land, foodstuffs will be imported. But soon the foreign buyers of industrial goods and providers of agricultural commodities will in their turn become industrialized, and this will create crisis conditions for the more advanced economy, which cannot lower its costs, high wages and profits having been consolidated. To prevent unemployment, home consumption must then be encouraged, wider "inland trade" making up for the deficiency of "foreign trade." This, however, is at best a partial remedy, and emigration from the now relatively overpopulated country will be necessary. Policy will therefore all along have to aim at permanently low cost, especially at the retention of wages at subsistence level. Free trade would help only if all countries had the same costs of production—which is not, in fact, the case.

Steuart's greatest weakness lies in his failure to offer an adequate theory of value and price. His attempt to invalidate Hume's analysis of inflation is hardly convincing either. Steuart argued that from an influx of specie nothing can be concluded as to prices, because it is not certain that people will increase their expenses in proportion to their wealth. It is characteristic of his interventionist outlook that he did not appreciate the near-automatic process involved.

In Britain, Steuart met with scant response. Smith never mentioned him, though some of Smith's arguments may have been aimed at Steuart. He was more appreciated in Germany, especially in the late nineteenth century, by the historical school, because of his historical bent and wide use of the inductive method. Some of his minor writings (for example, his "Considerations on the Interest of the County of Lanark" of 1769, a kind of social survey) deserve to be remembered in this context. Steuart's abiding importance, however, is as a leading representative of the remarkable efflorescence of the social sciences in the Scotland of his day.

WERNER STARK

[See also ECONOMIC THOUGHT, *article on* MERCANTILIST THOUGHT.]

WORKS BY STEUART

Steuart's name is also catalogued as Steuart Denham, Sir James; or Denham, Sir James Steuart.

(1767) 1967 *An Inquiry Into the Principles of Political Economy.* Edited by Andrew S. Skinner. 2 vols. Edinburgh: Oliver & Boyd. → Contains a biographical sketch and an analytical introduction.
The Works, Political, Metaphisical, and Chronological, of the Late Sir James Steuart of Coltness, Bart. 6 vols. London: Cadell & Davies, 1805. → Volumes 1–4 are a reprint of *An Inquiry Into the Principles of Political Economy,* first published in 1767. Volumes 5 and 6 contain various essays, among them Steuart's "Considerations on the Interest of the County of Lanark," first published in 1769.

SUPPLEMENTARY BIBLIOGRAPHY

FEILBOGEN, SIGMUND 1889 James Steuart und Adam Smith. *Zeitschrift für die gesamte Staatswissenschaft* 45:218–260.
JOHNSON, EDGAR A. J. 1937 Steuart: The Political Oeconomist. Pages 209-234 in Edgar A. J. Johnson, *Predecessors of Adam Smith: The Growth of British Economic Thought.* Englewood Cliffs, N.J.: Prentice-Hall.
SEN, S. R. 1957 *The Economics of Sir James Steuart.* Cambridge, Mass.: Harvard Univ. Press.
STANGELAND, CHARLES E. 1904 *Pre-Malthusian Doctrines of Population: A Study in the History of Economic Theory.* Columbia University Studies in History, Economics, and Public Law, Vol. 21, No. 3. New York: Columbia Univ. Press.

STIMULATION DRIVES

Man and lower animals repeatedly do things to provide themselves with a change in stimuli. These activities can range anywhere from a shift in gaze about the room to a complicated sequence of responses that produces a new or different auditory, visual, or tactile experience. Moreover, animals will selectively attend to stimuli which are novel or particularly striking. Much of the time these behaviors do not subserve any of the primary biological drives such as hunger, thirst, sex, or escape from pain. Nor can they be satisfactorily explained in terms of an acquired drive. In keeping with the traditional position that an organism's actions are impelled by drives, stimulation drives have been postulated to account for these otherwise inexplicable behaviors. A curiosity or exploratory drive is one popular interpretation of an animal's apparent desire for commerce with new or different stimuli. Another explanation is that there is a general drive for sensory stimuli that increases in strength with an increase in the duration of stimulus deprivation. A drive for stimulus changes is thought to be operating concomitantly. Its fluctuations in strength are governed by the organism's second-to-second transactions with the environment. This is a relatively new formulation that may or may not prove satisfactory as research progresses.

The adequacy of the curiosity drive as an explanatory concept will be considered first.

The curiosity drive

Several investigators with quite divergent interests have contended that animals possess a fundamental tendency to explore and learn about the world. For example, W. S. Small (1901, p. 214), remembered for the original work on maze learning in rats, was most impressed by the thorough manner in which his animals explored the mazes. He believed that rats have a basic desire to know about their new environment and that this desire for knowledge, which appears so fundamental to the rat's behavior, finds its most highly differentiated expression in man's search for scientific truth. A similar point of view was expressed by the French psychologist Ribot ([1896] 1911, p. 368). He contended that a basic craving for knowledge as manifested by the "all-examining, all-embracing scrutiny of a Goethe" was not different in kind from the activity of an animal "that touches and smells an unknown object." I. P. Pavlov, the Russian physiologist, spoke of an investigatory or "What-is-it?" reflex. Pavlov claimed that this reflex, in animals, results in immediate responsiveness to the slightest changes in the environment and enables animals to engage their receptor organs appropriately ([1927] 1960, p. 12). Pavlov, too, traced the scientific endeavors of man back to this basic propensity of animals to learn about their surroundings.

Research on curiosity behavior.   The notion that there exists a basic tendency to explore has been responsible for a large number of animal studies. These can be divided into two groups: (1) experiments designed to provide information on the motivational aspects of curiosity behavior; (2) experiments concerned with the responsiveness of animals to objects or places differing from one another in degree of novelty. Several reviews of these studies have been written, the most complete being Welker's (1961).

Motivational aspects of curiosity behavior.   Several types of investigations have been used to study the motivational aspects of curiosity behavior. The animals employed most frequently in this kind of research are the white rat and the rhesus monkey. The rewards provided have been exploratory, visual, manipulative, and auditory experiences.

Exploratory rewards.   The white rat is an avid explorer of unfamiliar settings. It seems to rely largely on olfaction, but visual and tactile stimuli are also known to influence curiosity behavior. Permitting the rat to investigate a new region as a reward for executing a specific response provides very satisfactory results. Rats will, for instance, cross an electrically charged grid in order to gain access to an area divided into many compartments. Rats will learn to turn a wheel that removes a barrier separating two compartments and thereby permits entrance into the adjacent one. No food or sexual partner awaits them in this compartment; it is simply a place to be explored, a place somewhat different from the one they had previously occupied. When rewarded, for each correct response, by a 60-second sojourn in a multiunit maze, rats will even learn a brightness-discrimination problem and perform proficiently throughout repeated test sessions.

Visual rewards.   The rhesus monkey proves an excellent subject for the motivational aspects of curiosity behavior since it is a highly visual animal as well as an unflagging manipulator of almost any movable object within reach. In view of these basic propensities, the opportunity to watch environmental events and to manipulate small devices has been employed as reward for responding correctly in various discrimination learning problems.

In one study, results showed unquestionably that monkeys will learn to discriminate yellow from blue if rewarded by the opportunity to view the activities taking place in their environment.

Manipulative rewards.   A color discrimination problem was also used to determine the value of manipulative rewards. Monkeys were presented with a board containing several pairs of screw eyes arranged vertically. One member of each pair was painted red, the other green. Although all of the screw eyes were fitted firmly to the board, the red ones could be removed easily. If the subject grasped one of these, he was permitted to take it from the board and handle it for several seconds. This was, in fact, defined as the correct response to the problem. An error consisted of either touching a red screw eye but not removing it, or touching a green one. Within a few test sessions the monkeys responded differentially to the screw eyes, reaching for and manipulating the red ones, but infrequently touching those painted green. Obviously, discrimination learning occurred, and the only apparent reward for the performance was the opportunity to manipulate the devices.

This work has been extended to the study of manipulative tendencies in mice, kittens, and raccoons. Mice were confined in cages equipped with two levers. One lever was movable, the other was not. The recording apparatus registered automatically the number of times each lever was touched; the results showed an overwhelming preference for the one that could be moved. In other experiments, kittens and raccoons have been found to learn simple maze problems in return for the opportunity to manipulate such items as rubber balls, crumpled paper, or small devices mounted on springs.

Auditory rewards.   The opportunity to hear what is happening in the environment can also serve effectively as a reward for discrimination learning. Rhesus monkeys were tested on a spatial discrimination problem. During testing, a subject was isolated from the rest of the colony and placed in a box located in a sound-treated room. A loudspeaker was fixed to the top of the box, and a microphone with its associated amplifier was placed in the room housing the colony. The box contained two levers. Pressing one of them resulted in 12 seconds of sounds emanating from the colony room. The other lever was "silent." Each monkey showed a distinct preference for pressing the lever that provided the auditory stimuli. When sound reward was made contingent on pressing the previously silent lever, the monkeys changed their response pattern accordingly.

Persistence of curiosity behavior. Behavior maintained by exploratory rewards is found to be extremely persistent. This fact is of especial theoretical significance. For if one postulates that curiosity behavior is an expression of a fundamental drive, then it is imperative that the behavior be strong and persistent. With regard to visual exploration, it has been shown that monkeys will hold open a spring-loaded door several hours a day, day after day, if their efforts are rewarded by a view of a dynamic scene. One situation that invariably elicits considerable interest on the part of the test animal is a view of other monkeys. The persistence of manipulative behavior is also great. Monkeys will, for example, repeatedly manipulate devices throughout a 10-hour test session. The amount of manipulative behavior that takes place over a period of days is highly dependent on the animal's previous experience with the manipulanda. Those data available on responsiveness to auditory rewards are not adequate for evaluating the strength of any underlying motivational mechanism. All that can be said is that no decline in response frequency for sound reward was evident during a long series of weekly test sessions.

Factors that influence drive strength. It is clear that for monkeys the strength of an inferred curiosity drive can be increased by confining the animal to a monotonous environment. In the first experiment to demonstrate this, monkeys were kept in an empty illuminated box for two-hour, four-hour, or eight-hour periods without an opportunity to look outside. On completion of the visual restriction period, a small door for viewing purposes was unlocked and the animal was allowed to push it open. A colony of monkeys was outside. The records showed that the frequency of door openings was positively correlated with the duration of visual restriction.

Fear, on the other hand, serves to suppress curiosity behavior. The explanation is somewhat circular but appears, nonetheless, to be relatively reasonable. The experiments have been designed as follows: Animals are subjected to situations presumed, on the basis of other criteria, to be fear provoking. Any marked reduction in curiosity behavior is attributed to the suppressive effect of fear. For example, rats are shocked in a maze; monkeys are presented a close-up view of a large dog or the sound of its bark; or infant chimpanzees are exposed to a strange object. In each case the animal fails to investigate. The rat freezes; the monkey refuses to open the door to look or press a lever to hear; and the infant chimpanzee retreats to the rear of its cage. In most situations not involving painful stimuli, exploration gradually gains ascendancy over fear. This has been elegantly shown for the infant chimpanzee's behavior toward strange objects. A most orderly increase in curiosity behavior occurs with repetitive exposure to new and different objects.

The influence of hunger and thirst on curiosity behavior has elicited a great deal of interest. The general question posed in this line of experimentation is whether curiosity or exploration functions in the service of the nutritional needs. Clearly, if the amount of curiosity behavior is greater when an animal is hungry or thirsty the probability of finding food or water is increased and curiosity has definite survival value. The results of approximately a score of studies on the rat are markedly inconsistent. Much of the confusion can be traced to a confounding of exploration with the amount of locomotor behavior. In some situations animals locomote more when deprived; in others they locomote less. It is probably correct to say, however, that curiosity behavior increases under conditions of food or water deprivation. The most compelling data that support this statement are those from experiments in which (1) a variety of indices for curiosity, including such behaviors as manipulation, sniffing, and window peeking are used; and (2) the locomotive behavior is controlled by the apparatus design, leaving responsiveness to novelty as the critical variable. The thesis that exploratory tendencies in animals are fundamental is not necessarily contradicted by the findings that exploration increases with food and water deprivation. These experiments do imply, however, that a curiosity drive can interact with hunger and thirst drives.

Research carried out with infant rhesus monkeys has direct relevance to the question of the primacy of the curiosity drive. The infants begin manipulating objects within the first few days of life and learn simple problems for manipulative rewards by the time they are two to three months of age. At an equally early age they operate a lever in order to view objects outside their quarters.

Novelty and stimulus change.   At this point the argument for the existence of a curiosity drive is half complete. The opportunity to look, listen, and manipulate appears to be rewarding for a variety of animals; and performances can be maintained by these rewards throughout prolonged and repeated test sessions. Curiosity, however, implies selective attention to the new and the different. Animals do, in fact, display such selective attention, but the motivational basis for such behavior may be other than curiosity. This particular problem has generated a long series of experiments; a few representative ones will be discussed briefly.

Spontaneous alternation.   In the early studies, white rats were placed in a complex maze containing neither food nor water and the sequence of their movements was carefully noted. It soon became apparent that the rats were not moving about the areas in a haphazard fashion. Rather, when confronted with a choice, they usually entered the maze unit that they had least recently occupied. Later, rats were observed in a simpler situation— a maze constructed in the form of a T. In this apparatus, the animals are started at the stem of the T. On reaching the intersection of the T they enter one of the arms. When, after a few seconds, they are placed again in the maze, they are more likely to enter the opposite arm. This behavior, called spontaneous alternation, was first explained in terms of a response inhibition. It was suggested that the act of turning left or right at the choice-point initiated an inhibitory process, which decreased the probability that the same turn would be repeated on the next trial. Some investigators suggested that an exploratory tendency was responsible for spontaneous alternation, but under ordinary circumstances there was no way to decide whether animals were alternating turns or alternating places, that is, maze arms. Alternating turns by necessity brought the animal to a different place, and alternating places required the animal to make a different turn. By a rather ingenious arrangement of T mazes, it has been shown that rats will repeat the same turn if by doing so they will end up at a different place. Furthermore, they fail to alternate turns if the consequences lead them to the same place. These data were interpreted to mean that spontaneous alternation is an expression of the rat's tendency to respond positively to the more novel aspects of the environment.

Rejection of the familiar.   The above opinion was not without its dissenters. Why, it was asked, could one not say that spontaneous alternation in the T maze reflects an active avoidance of the familiar arm rather than a positive approach to the more novel arm? This is no trivial question. Phrased in more general terms, it relates to the basic orientation of animals toward their environment. Are they attracted to the new or repulsed by the old? The data available support the idea that animals are attracted to new or relatively novel places and things. The experiment offering the most convincing evidence for this idea is one in which rats were forced to remain in the stem of a T maze for several seconds. A glass door permitted them to view either arm but prevented their entry. At the time of their confinement, one arm was painted white, the other black. Then the rats were removed and one of the maze arms was replaced so that both were either black or white. The animals were immediately placed back into the maze and this time they were free to enter either arm. Since the subjects had just been exposed to both black and white, presumably they were equally familiar with each color. And with both arms now being the same color the subjects should show no preference if avoidance of the familiar is the basis for exploratory behavior. Yet, almost every animal entered the newly inserted arm.

Reactions to novelty.   Other experimenters have studied the rat's responsiveness to environmental change simply by introducing a novel object into the subject's cage and recording the amount of time the animal spends touching and sniffing the object. All experiments consistently demonstrate that rats are quick to notice the presence of anything new. The frequency of investigative responses, however, declines sharply within the first few minutes of stimulus exposure. Investigative behavior can be revived immediately by placing something else in the cage. Novelty effects even extend to eating behavior; novel foods are preferred initially to familiar foods.

The influence of novelty on investigative behavior has also been studied in primates, most of the work being carried out on chimpanzees. When presented with a new object, chimpanzees usually start handling it immediately. Like the rat—and, for that matter, like the monkey and the young child—chimpanzees soon become satiated. Introducing another object serves to reinstate manipulative activity. Generally speaking, more heterogeneous objects elicit more manipulative behavior. It has been argued that heterogeneity makes for greater novelty, which in turn increases the subject's responsiveness. This hypothesis is at least partially supported by other data. For instance, the amount of manipulation in young chimpanzees increases with increase in the number of novel stimuli provided by the object.

The curiosity drive as an explanatory concept. Much of these data can be accounted for by postulating the existence of a curiosity drive. The strong tendency to manipulate, look, and listen certainly appears to be basic to the motivational system of the higher organisms. It is extremely difficult to explain these response tendencies in terms of other drives. The evidence on the importance of novelty in maintaining investigative activity lends further support to the curiosity drive concept. Selective attention to the new is precisely what one would expect if behavior is motivated by curiosity.

Curiosity implies, however, that an animal is motivated to learn about its world. It has been formally demonstrated that some animals can learn spatial relationships as well as relationships between events merely through the process of exploring the situation. There is little question that this is so for the young child. Nonetheless, differential attentiveness to environmental stimuli is not necessarily an information-seeking process. There are drives for sensory stimulation and stimulus change, as proposed at the beginning of this paper. It is suggested that animals' responses to certain stimuli do not reflect a desire to learn about them; learning may occur as a consequence of stimulus-seeking behavior.

Sensory drives

Drive for stimulus change. There are data collected whose explanation does not require a concept as elaborate as curiosity; simply, a change in stimulation can function as a reward. It has been shown, for example, that mice, rats, and monkeys confined in a darkened cage will repeatedly press a lever that momentarily turns on a light. Some data suggest that the onset of a neutral auditory stimulus in response to the lever can also reinforce lever-pressing behavior.

The recording of eye movements is another technique that may be employed to study what appears to be a fundamental requirement for stimulus change. Chimpanzees will immediately fixate on a panel when it is first illuminated; but the duration of this fixation drops rapidly, and the animal attends to other things. As discussed earlier, the relative novelty of a stimulus influences attentiveness. It could be argued then that this is the basis for the rewarding effect of stimulus change. But other stimulus characteristics, which before now have commanded little research interest, also affect an animal's responsiveness. Stimulus complexity is one. Lever-pressing frequency for light reward is increased over its normal level when the pattern of light describes a complex geometrical figure. Chimpanzees and man have been shown to fixate longer on complex, than on simple, stimuli.

Stimulus characteristics other than novelty influence the duration of visual attention in the monkey. When provided with a chance to view either of two motion pictures of identical content, they will look at each about the same number of times. But they will watch for longer periods that film which is (1) better focused, (2) more brightly illuminated, (3) oriented right side up, (4) in color, and (5) presented at normal speed. In this connection, chimpanzees looking out of a box will select that one of two windows which provides an undistorted view.

In summary, animals will act to effect a simple stimulus change. The level of responsiveness can be influenced by various stimulus characteristics, stimulus novelty being only one of many. This concept of stimulus change can account for much of the data previously described quite as adequately as can a curiosity drive. Moreover, the notion of stimulus change is trimmed of surplus meaning.

The drive for stimulation. The primary biological drives, such as hunger and thirst, increase in strength with deprivation and are reduced by intake of food and drink. The postulated drive for stimulation appears to behave comparably to these in that drive strength is influenced by the degree of deprivation—in this case, stimulus deprivation. Already mentioned is the fact that the monkey's responsiveness to those visual incentives provided by a view of a monkey colony increases with longer intervals of visual restriction. But there are more compelling data that argue for the existence of a stimulus drive. Monkeys confined in the dark for periods up to eight hours will press a lever for a flash of light more frequently as duration of deprivation increases. Comparable data have been reported for man.

Orderly and predictable satiation effects can be demonstrated also when light is used as a reward. Response frequency for light reinforcement declines during a test session; it varies inversely with the level of ambient illumination in the test box and is reduced by pre-exposure to an irregularly flashing light. There are additional data that indicate that rats, when given control over cage illumination, provide themselves with a nearly constant duration of light daily. This observation suggests the operation of a homeostatic mechanism and places the need for illumination in the same category as the basic physiological needs.

Complete visual deprivation or severe visual restriction continuing for the first several months of life have a profound effect on lever pressing for light reinforcement. Response frequency is inordinately high. It should be noted that in these studies the reinforcement (light) is not confounded with any event associated with seeing, for the subjects had never experienced the world visually.

Animals will learn new problems and maintain performances on previously learned tasks when their efforts are rewarded by visual, auditory, or tactile stimuli. Closely related to this phenomenon are the findings indicating a fundamental tendency to seek stimulus change in the second-to-second transactions with the environment. These data cannot be explained adequately in terms of either primary biological drives or acquired drives. The operation of a curiosity drive has been suggested; and, indeed, most of the findings can be accounted for by this type of motivational agent. The writer, however, prefers to interpret these results in terms of a drive for stimulation and stimulus change. Additional data have been presented to support such a notion.

Irrespective of their eventual interpretation, the experiments discussed here have influenced significantly the theoretical treatment of motivation in man and animals. In fact, it is being argued now that the drive for stimulation is a general and omnipresent motivational mechanism and that hunger, thirst, and sex are more specialized drives peculiar to the particular state of the organism. This represents an extreme position, but it serves to emphasize the increasing role that is being attributed to the stimulation drives as determinants of behavior.

ROBERT A. BUTLER

[Directly related are the entries CREATIVITY; NERVOUS SYSTEM, article on BRAIN STIMULATION; PROBLEM SOLVING. Other relevant material may be found in DRIVES; LEARNING, article on REINFORCEMENT; MOTIVATION.]

BIBLIOGRAPHY

FOWLER, HARRY 1965 Curiosity and Exploratory Behavior. New York: Macmillan.

PAVLOV, IVAN P. (1927) 1960 Conditioned Reflexes: An Investigation of the Physiological Activity of the Cerebral Cortex. New York: Dover. → First published as Lektsii o rabote bol'shikh polusharii golovnogo mozga.

RIBOT, THÉODULE A. (1896) 1911 The Psychology of the Emotions. 2d ed. New York: Scribner. → First published in French.

SMALL, WILLARD S. 1901 Experimental Study of the Mental Processes of the Rat. Part 2. American Journal of Psychology 12:206–239.

WELKER, W. I. 1961 An Analysis of Exploratory and Play Behavior in Animals. Pages 175–226 in Donald W. Fiske and Salvatore R. Maddi (editors), Functions of Varied Experience. Homewood, Ill.: Dorsey Press.

STIRNER, MAX

Max Stirner (the pseudonym of Johann Caspar Schmidt), German philosopher and writer, was born in 1806 in Bayreuth and died in 1856 in Berlin. He studied theology and philology at the universities of Berlin, Erlangen, and Königsberg. After a period spent teaching in secondary schools in Berlin, he became a free-lance writer. His principal source of income was translating, and he was imprisoned several times for debt.

One of the more prominent left-wing Young Hegelians in Berlin, Stirner contributed, with Marx and other young bourgeois radicals, to the Rheinische Zeitung, the journal of the advanced wing of the industrial and banking circles in the Rhineland. Like most Young Hegelians, he wrote there and elsewhere on all kinds of subjects: lengthy reviews of Eugène Sue's Mystères de Paris and Bruno Bauer's Posaune des jüngsten Gerichts; articles entitled "Das unwahre Princip unserer Erziehung oder der Humanismus und Realismus" (1842a), "Kunst und Religion" (1842b), and "Einiges Vorläufige vom Liebesstaat" (1843).

Stirner's major work, Der Einzige und sein Eigenthum, was published in 1844. The book made a strong impression on the German intelligentsia and was widely read and reviewed. Moses Hess, an early German socialist, and Ludwig Feuerbach, the philosopher, wrote critical reviews of the book. Marx and Engels devoted many pages of Die deutsche Ideologie to a refutation of Stirner's ideas. In 1852 his two-volume Geschichte der Reaction appeared but made little impression. His translations of Adam Smith's The Wealth of Nations and J. B. Say's Cours complet d'économie politique pratique, however, were used for many years.

Stirner's political and philosophical viewpoint was opposed to feudalism, bourgeois liberalism, German idealism as represented by Kant, Fichte, and Hegel, and communism. He hated the state and abhorred all social conventions. Holding the individual to be the focal point and center of the world, he asserted that the feelings and thinking of the individual determine the whole scale of social values and that there is nothing objective outside the individual, or the ego. "Humanity" is nothing but an unreal, metaphysical abstraction. Since the individual who creates the world through his imagination and will is the only reality, the world belongs to the individual; the world becomes his possession. Just as Marx said that he had stood Hegel on his head, Stirner might well have said that he had done the same to Fichte, by turning Fichte's idealistic allgemeines Ich into a materialistic, concrete ego.

Although Proudhon was attracted to Stirner's petty bourgeois radicalism, and Friedrich Nietzsche to Stirner's upper bourgeois attitude of individualizing all moral values, the greatest influence exerted by Stirner was upon anarchism, many years after his death. The actual extent of this influence is a matter of dispute. While the claim of his follower, John Henry Mackay, that he was the father of anarchism, is not quite justified—since by 1845 Bakunin had to a large extent developed his anarchistic ideas, if not his system of theories—Max Nettlau, in his *Der Vorfrühling der Anarchie* (1925), calls *Der Einzige und sein Eigenthum* "the best known and easiest to come by book of older anarchism." Georgii Valentinovich Plekhanov also included Stirner among the early anarchists. Max Adler, however, disagreed, arguing that "if . . . [anarchism] . . . is considered only as a definite political trend within the socialist labor movement as it has existed since Bakunin and Kropotkin, then Stirner was as far from anarchism as was Saint-Simon, Fourier, or Marx" (1934, p. 393). Since twentieth-century anarchists, rightly or wrongly, do look upon Stirner as one of their ideological forebears and often quote him, he must be regarded as at least one of the progenitors of modern anarchism.

There is, of course, no doubt that Stirner developed many ideas which cannot in any sense be considered anarchistic. His political individualism, for example, was so extreme that it excluded the possibility that either the will and feelings of masses and classes or collective action by the masses toward a common aim might constitute an original and primary factor of social development. On the other hand, his extreme antistatism, coupled with an attitude which the young Engels once ridiculed with the slogan "À bas aussi les lois," has always been one of the fundamental tenets of anarchism.

Little attention has been paid to Stirner's literary and political journalistic work, despite all the efforts of Mackay and others to publicize it. His translations have been replaced by better ones, or are forgotten, and his history of political reaction is not mentioned any more. *Der Einzige und sein Eigenthum* remains a book which philosophers read, even though few incorporate any of its ideas into their philosophical systems; but the political theoreticians of anarchism often claim that their systems are at least partly derived from Stirner.

JÜRGEN KUCZYNSKI

[For the historical context of Stirner's work, see the biography of HEGEL; for discussion of the subsequent development of Stirner's ideas, see ANARCHISM.]

WORKS BY STIRNER

(1842*a*) 1914 Das unwahre Princip unserer Erziehung oder der Humanismus und Realismus. Pages 237–257 in *Max Stirner's kleinere Schriften und seine Entgegnungen auf die Kritik seines Werkes:* Der Einzige und sein Eigenthum, *aus den Jahren 1842–1848.* 2d ed. Edited by John H. Mackay. Treptow bei Berlin: Zack. → First published in Nos. 100, 102, 104, and 109 of the *Rheinische Zeitung*.

(1842*b*) 1914 Kunst und Religion. Pages 258–268 in *Max Stirner's kleinere Schriften und seine Entgegnungen auf die Kritik seines Werkes:* Der Einzige und sein Eigentum, *aus den Jahren 1842–1848.* 2d ed. Edited by John H. Mackay. Treptow bei Berlin: Zack. → First published in No. 165 of the *Rheinische Zeitung*.

(1843) 1914 Einiges Vorlaeufige vom Liebesstaat. Pages 269–277 in *Max Stirner's kleinere Schriften und seine Entgegnungen auf die Kritik seines Werkes:* Der Einzige und sein Eigentum, *aus den Jahren 1842–1848.* 2d ed. Edited by John H. Mackay. Treptow bei Berlin: Zack. → First published in the *Berliner Monatsschrift* under the pseudonym Ludwig Buhl.

(1844) 1963 *The Ego and His Own: The Case of the Individual Against Authority.* With an introduction by J. L. Walker. New York: Libertarian Book Club. → First published as *Der Einzige und sein Eigenthum.*

1852 *Die Geschichte der Reaction.* 2 vols. Berlin: Allgemeine Deutsche Verlags-Anstalt.

Max Stirner's kleinere Schriften und seine Entgegnungen auf die Kritik seines Werkes: Der Einzige und sein Eigenthum, *aus den Jahren 1842–1848.* 2d ed. Edited by John H. Mackay. Treptow bei Berlin: Zack, 1914.

SUPPLEMENTARY BIBLIOGRAPHY

ADLER, MAX 1934 Max Stirner. Volume 14, pages 393–394 in *Encyclopaedia of the Social Sciences.* New York: Macmillan.

ARVON, HENRI 1954 *Aux sources de l'existentialisme: Max Stirner.* Paris: Presses Universitaires de France.

BASCH, VICTOR (1904) 1928 *L'individualisme anarchiste: Max Stirner.* 2d ed. Paris: Alcan.

BOROWOGO, A. 1925 *Stirner i Dostojewskii.* Moscow: No publisher given.

ELTZBACHER, PAUL (1900) 1960 *Anarchism: Exponents of the Anarchist Philosophy.* London: Freedom Press; New York: Libertarian Book Club. → First published as *Der Anarchismus.*

ENGERT, HORST 1911 *Das historische Denken Max Stirners.* Leipzig: Wigand.

HELMS, HANS G. 1966 *Die Ideologie der anonymen Gesellschaft: Max Stirners "Einziger" und der Fortschritt des demokratischen Selbstbewusstseins vom Vormärz bis zur Bundesrepublik.* Cologne: Du Mont Schauberg.

JENSEN, ALBERT 1916 *Max Stirner: Den anarkistiska individualismens djärvaste apostel, hans liv och åskådning.* Revolutionens Förkämpar, Vol. 6. Stockholm: Holmström.

KURCHINSKII, MIKHAIL A. (1920) 1923 *Der Apostel des Egoismus: Max Stirner und seine Philosophie der Anarchie.* Berlin: Prager. → First published in Russian.

MACKAY, JOHN HENRY (1898) 1910 *Max Stirner: Sein Leben und sein Werk.* Treptow bei Berlin: Zack.

MAUTZ, KURT A. 1936 *Die Philosophie Max Stirners im Gegensatz zum Hegelschen Idealismus.* Berlin: Junker & Dünnhaupt.

NETTLAU, MAX 1925 *Der Vorfrühling der Anarchie: Ihre historische Entwicklung von den Anfängen bis zum Jahre 1864.* Berlin: Kater.

SCHELLWIEN, ROBERT 1892 *Max Stirner und Friedrich Nietzsche: Erscheinungen des modernen Geistes und das Wesen des Menschen.* Leipzig: Pfeffer.

STOCHASTIC PROCESSES

See MARKOV CHAINS; QUEUES; TIME SERIES.

STOCK–FLOW ANALYSIS

The purpose of stock–flow analysis is to describe the formation of economic plans and the determination of market prices in an economy where one or more commodities (e.g., wheat, bonds, money) are traded simultaneously on both capital and current account. Traditional demand and supply analysis is not entirely silent on this subject, but it is uncomfortably vague. Walras and later general equilibrium theorists focused attention on the existence and stability of a set of market-clearing prices in pure stock and pure flow models, i.e., models in which no means exist whereby individuals can convert current income into present wealth, or present wealth into future expenditure. In a pure stock economy, assets can be exchanged only for other assets; in a pure flow economy, income can only be consumed. Explicit analysis of saving, investment, and growth processes is conceptually possible only in the context of a stock–flow model.

Marshall and later partial equilibrium theorists did more justice to the special characteristics of a stock–flow economy. The familiar trichotomy of market equilibria into temporary, short-run, and long-run periods was conceived specifically to deal with transitory saving and investment processes. But this analytical schema was applied systematically only to business transactors. Thus, changes in long-run supply induced by business decisions to vary physical plant were investigated in detail, while changes in long-run demand induced by analogous saving decisions of households were largely ignored. In the end, therefore, Marshall and his followers contributed little more than did Walras and the neo-Walrasians toward the development of a coherent theory of price–quantity behavior in a stock–flow economy.

The existence of this gap in traditional value theory was gradually forced upon the attention of economists by the prolonged debate about the foundations of economic analysis which followed the publication of Keynes's *General Theory* in 1936. Even so, more than 15 years elapsed before the appearance, in 1954, of an explicit model of price determination in a stock–flow economy (see Clower 1954; Clower & Bushaw 1954). Subsequent contributions to stock–flow analysis (particularly Archibald & Lipsey 1958; Chase 1963; Hadar 1965; Smith 1961) have extended its boundaries to include, as special cases, both the general equilibrium theory of money and established microeconomic analysis. Most of this material lies outside the scope of the present discussion. The exposition that follows is intended to provide not a survey of, but an introduction to, the literature of stock–flow analysis.

Basic concepts. The rudiments of stock–flow analysis may be set forth most conveniently by considering an economy in which all commodities are traded in central auction markets at prices established by an independent market authority. In keeping with familiar procedure, we may suppose that individual transactors formulate tentative trading plans at the outset of any given market period, on the basis of given initial asset holdings and given rates of exchange (as reflected in provisional price announcements by the market authority). In general these plans will involve decisions about the quantity of each commodity to be purchased for current consumption, to be purchased to hold for future disposal, to be sold from current production, and to be sold from previously accumulated stocks.

Thus, for any commodity traded in the economy, e.g., the nth, and for any given market period, we may suppose that there are defined the following:

(1) An aggregate *stock demand function*, D_n, which indicates for any given vector of market prices, $\mathbf{P}$, and any given matrix of individual asset holdings, $\mathbf{S}$ (indicating the holdings of each commodity by each individual), the gross quantity of a particular commodity that individuals plan to hold for future disposal at the end of the current market period: $D_n = D_n(\mathbf{P}, \mathbf{S})$.

(2) An aggregate *flow demand function*, d_n, which indicates for any given $\mathbf{P}$ and $\mathbf{S}$ the gross quantity of a particular commodity that individuals plan to consume during the current market period: $d_n = d_n(\mathbf{P}, \mathbf{S})$.

(3) An aggregate *flow supply function*, s_n, which indicates for any given $\mathbf{P}$ and $\mathbf{S}$ the gross quantity of a particular commodity that individuals plan to produce during the current market period: $s_n = s_n(\mathbf{P}, \mathbf{S})$.

(4) An aggregate *stock supply quantity*, S_n, defined as the sum of individual holdings of a particular commodity at the outset of the current market period.

Given the "primitive" demand and supply relations (1) to (4), we may proceed immediately to define various "derived" relations that are relevant for describing market trading plans for each commodity. Specifically, we define *planned net purchases on capital account*—henceforth referred to as *holder excess demand*—as the difference between aggregate stock demand and aggregate stock supply: $Z_n \equiv D_n - S_n$. Similarly, we define *planned net purchases on current account*—henceforth referred to as *user excess demand*—as the difference between aggregate flow demand and aggregate flow supply: $z_n \equiv d_n - s_n$. Finally, we define *market excess demand* by the identity $x_n \equiv z_n + Z_n$. Thus, if N different commodities are traded in the economy, there will in general be $3N$ market trading relations. Depending on the precise character of the commodities traded, however, certain user and holder excess demands may be ignored. Just as in established price theory, moreover, one of the market excess demand relations may be assumed to be defined in terms of the others, by virtue of Walras' law.

Trading equilibrium.   The demand and supply relations of stock–flow analysis, like those of established price theory, are defined by underlying conceptual experiments in which all factors, other than prices, that might influence current economic plans are assumed to be fixed. Thus, the only requirement for individual trading plans to be mutually consistent is that the market authority establish a set of provisional prices such that market excess demand is zero for each and every commodity traded in the economy.

Accordingly, let us suppose that the finalization of individual trading plans in any given market period is preceded by a bargaining process in the course of which provisional market prices are varied in accordance with prevailing conditions of market excess demand. We shall not deal with the details of this process (on this, see Bushaw & Clower 1957; Hadar 1965; Negishi 1962); we shall simply assume that the bargaining process is globally stable and very heavily damped. We may then argue that the process leads rapidly to the announcement by the market authority of a set of market-clearing trading prices, at which binding exchange transactions may be concluded between individual market participants. Since individuals will then be able (at least in principle) to carry out their respective production, consumption, and asset-holding plans precisely as scheduled, it is natural to associate the establishment of such a set of trading prices with the attainment of a state of trading equilibrium.

In a pure stock economy, where individuals trade only on capital account, trading equilibrium will occur if and only if prices are such that *holder* excess demand is zero for every commodity; for in this case, user excess demand is identically zero in every market and $x_n^t \equiv Z_n^t$, where the superscript t denotes the market period. Similarly, in a pure flow economy, where individuals trade only on current account, trading equilibrium will occur if and only if prices are such that *user* excess demand is zero for every commodity; for in this case, holder excess demand is identically zero in every market and $x_n^t \equiv z_n^t$. In a stock–flow economy, however, trading equilibrium requires only that market excess demand be zero for every commodity, and this condition may be satisfied even if user and holder excess demands are not zero, i.e., even if individuals in the aggregate are planning to save or dissave. To be sure, the market clearance condition $x_n^t \equiv z_n^t + Z_n^t = 0$ will automatically be satisfied if user and holder excess demands are both zero. In general, however, this requirement is merely a sufficient, not a necessary, condition for trading equilibrium in a stock–flow economy; for trading equilibrium will also occur if $z_n^t = -Z_n^t$.

The exception to the last rule concerns what might be called a mixed stock–flow economy, in which some commodities are held for future disposal and some commodities are produced and consumed but no asset can be produced or consumed and no commodity other than an asset can be held for future disposal. An example of such a system is provided by the familiar production and exchange economy of contemporary monetary theory in which the only assets are fiat money and bonds. In such models, market excess demand for each commodity is identically equal either to user excess demand or to holder excess demand for the same commodity; hence, trading equilibrium cannot occur if the aggregate stock demand for any commodity differs from aggregate stock supply. However, trading equilibrium may occur even though some individuals plan to save, provided such plans are offset in each market by dissaving plans of other individuals.

Intertemporal equilibrium.   The significance of stock–flow analysis does not lie in what it adds to existing accounts of market bargaining and the determination of equilibrium trading prices. The interest of the subject lies, rather, in the fact that it provides for the first time an explicit conceptual framework to analyze intertemporal saving and investment processes as market phenomena.

In order to indicate the force of these observations, we begin by distinguishing between the formation and the execution of individual economic plans. The bargaining process may be presumed to lead to the establishment of a specific vector of trading prices at the end of any given market period and so to the determination of a set of vectors of mutually consistent production, consumption, and asset-holding plans. However, the theory of bargaining does not itself say anything about *actual trading*; that is an entirely different subject, which requires separate analysis.

The easiest way to characterize the trading process is to suppose that quantities actually produced, consumed, and traded at the conclusion of the bargaining process are precisely as planned. This assumption is logically permissible, of course, only in special circumstances, namely, when no actual transactions take place except in trading equilibrium. Since this restriction is not peculiar to stock–flow analysis, however, we shall accept it without question here and proceed on the assumption that equilibrium trading plans are in fact carried out by individual transactors at the end of each market period. The question then arises: will completion of the trading process in one period and reopening of the bargaining process at the beginning of the next period lead to the establishment of a set of trading prices identical with or different from those established during the first market period?

If we grant the validity of accepted statical theories of household and business behavior, the answer to this question is fairly straightforward. In pure stock economies, the execution of plans at the end of one market period will not alter the real wealth or income of any transactor, nor will any change in the distribution of assets within individual portfolios alter existing asset-holding plans. Thus, the only effect of the trading process will be to eliminate any initial gaps between desired and actual holdings of various commodities; i.e., *individual*, as well as aggregate, holder excess demands will be zero for every commodity at the end of the trading process. Therefore, other things being equal, in a pure stock economy a once-over execution of economic plans will eliminate for all time the need for further trade.

A similar result is obtained for pure flow models. As before, the execution of plans does not alter the real wealth or income of any household or the physical assets of any business. The only effect of the trading process is to permit individuals to produce and consume as desired. Therefore, other things being equal, in a pure flow economy a single

bargaining process will lead to the establishment of a set of trading prices and transactions quantities that will be maintained throughout all subsequent time.

Our conclusions regarding pure stock and pure flow models may be summarized by saying that, in such systems, trading equilibrium implies intertemporal equilibrium. Such models are not without interest as devices for analyzing elementary bargaining processes. Moreover, they may be made to generate nonstationary price and quantity time series by introducing price and income expectations, wage and interest-rate rigidities, trading at disequilibrium prices, etc. Under no circumstances, however, may such models be considered appropriate vehicles for any but preliminary analysis of price–quantity behavior in an asset-holding economy. For this purpose we must have recourse to stock–flow models.

In general, the execution of economic plans in a stock–flow economy will alter both the real income and real wealth of some households and also will lead to changes in the asset holdings of some businesses. Such effects are inevitable, indeed, if *any* transactor in the economy plans to save or dissave at the outset of the trading process. As a rule, therefore, the trading process will in itself lead some individuals to revise their production, consumption, and asset-holding plans. Hence *trading equilibrium does not imply intertemporal equilibrium in a stock–flow economy.*

The truth of the last remark is obvious in cases where the excess user demand for some asset is nonzero in trading equilibrium; for this means that planned production of the asset differs from planned consumption, and hence, that aggregate stocks of the asset will change from one market period to another if plans are executed as scheduled during the trading process. The truth of the remark is less obvious in the case of mixed stock–flow models, where excess user demand is identically zero for every asset and aggregate stocks are necessarily constant over time. Trading equilibrium then requires that holder excess demand be zero for every asset. However, this does not imply constancy over time in the asset holdings of individual transactors following a once-over redistribution of existing asset stocks. For in a stock–flow economy, unlike a pure stock economy, individuals may continue to save and dissave indefinitely, even though aggregate asset stocks never change.

Stability of intertemporal equilibrium. The distinction between trading equilibrium and intertemporal equilibrium is an inherent and distinctive characteristic of stock–flow analysis. To describe individual economic plans in pure stock and pure flow models requires, as it were, just one analytical dimension—prices. All other determinants of individual conduct are specified in advance, and none can be altered by market trading. In such models logic does not compel us to develop separate theories of trading and intertemporal equilibrium, even though we may find it convenient to do so in certain instances. To describe economic plans in a stock–flow model, however, requires two analytical dimensions—prices and individual asset holdings—because individual asset holdings may be altered by market trading. In the case of stock–flow models, therefore, logic does indeed compel us to develop separate theories of trading and intertemporal equilibrium.

The problems posed by this characteristic of stock–flow analysis have to do mainly with the stability of intertemporal equilibrium. As remarked earlier, the stability of intertemporal equilibrium in pure stock and pure flow models is an immediate consequence of the stability of trading equilibrium. Intertemporal disequilibrium may occur in stock–flow systems, however, either because markets fail to clear or because individual transactors choose to save or dissave. Therefore, even if bargaining processes are inherently stable, a stock–flow economy may fail to converge to a state of intertemporal (stationary) equilibrium if individual asset-adjustment processes are unstable. This possibility will most certainly be realized if one or more individuals in the economy invariably save, and add to previously accumulated resources, some fraction of current income (as is presumed to be true, for example, in von Neumann and other linear models of economic growth and also in most theories of the consumption function). In general, however, the saving behavior of individuals will depend on market prices and asset holdings, as well as income. Therefore, even if individual asset-adjustment processes tend to be unstable at some initial set of market prices, intertemporal instability of the economic system may be avoided by appropriate intertemporal adjustments in market prices. Whether intertemporal instability deserves to be regarded as anything more than a theoretical curiosity is an open question at the present time. The answer is of obvious relevance for such practical problems as the lag effects of monetary policy, econometric forecasting of consumption and investment expenditures, and the existence and persistence of structural unemployment. To date, however, the derivation of intertemporal stability conditions for various possible stock–flow systems

has received little explicit attention (Hadar 1965; Negishi 1962).

The preceding discussion does little more than scratch the surface of stock–flow analysis. Because stock–flow analysis involves an integration of balance-sheet with income–expenditure aspects of economic behavior, the subject directly embraces or indirectly bears upon virtually every other branch of contemporary economic analysis: value and monetary theory, the theory of income and employment, the theory of growth and economic development. What needs to be emphasized, however, is not so much the virtual scope of stock–flow analysis as the severely limited extent of actual knowledge about the properties of stock–flow systems.

First, we must recognize that most of the familiar weaknesses of established price theory, e.g., inadequate treatment of expectations phenomena and related problems of market organization, are shared by stock–flow analysis.

Second, we must note that the explicit inclusion of asset variables in the theory of business behavior forces us to think in terms of preference-maximization, rather than profit-maximization, models, which leads to numerous analytical complications and uncertainties not found in established theories. Hardly any work has been done so far in this area of stock--flow analysis.

Third, we should remark that the present literature on the dynamics of multiple markets—which, incidentally, includes nearly all modern treatments of the theory of income and employment—is concerned with the dynamics of *bargaining*, rather than the dynamics of *bargaining and trade*; i.e., it does not deal at all with problems of intertemporal equilibrium. The relevance of this literature for interpreting actual market behavior is dubious, to say the least. However, since a satisfactory account of the intertemporal dynamics of stock–flow systems has yet to be developed, these shortcomings of established theory provide no present grounds for congratulatory remarks about stock–flow analysis.

Finally, a comment is in order concerning a problem of fundamental importance that is only dimly foreshadowed in earlier discussion. The whole of stock–flow analysis and most of contemporary value and monetary theory rest on the assumption that market exchange is a complicated form of barter, involving multiple, rather than double, coincidence of wants. This is reflected in the proposition known as Walras' law, which asserts that units of any given commodity (goods or money) constitute effective means of payment for units of any other commodity. This can only be true in an economy where trading processes in all markets are rigidly synchronized, so that purchases and sales of different commodities can be set off against each other without having recourse to intermediate market transactions. If trading processes are not synchronized, we move from the barter economy of "classical" economics to the money economy of John Maynard Keynes; from a world where supply creates its own demand to a world where demands are directly constrained by current accruals of cash and cash substitutes and where supplies are directly constrained by current levels of factor employment. To investigate the dynamic properties of such systems clearly requires the use of stock–flow models. As of this time, however, stock–flow analysis provides nothing more than a foundation for future research in this area.

ROBERT W. CLOWER

BIBLIOGRAPHY

ARCHIBALD, G. C.; and LIPSEY, R. G. 1958 Monetary and Value Theory: A Critique of Lange and Patinkin. *Review of Economic Studies* 26, Oct.:1–22.

BAUMOL, WILLIAM J. 1962 Stocks, Flows and Monetary Theory. *Quarterly Journal of Economics* 76:46–56.

BAUMOL, WILLIAM J. et al. 1960 A Symposium on Monetary Theory. *Review of Economic Studies* 28, Oct.:29–56.

BURSTEIN, MEYER L. 1963 *Money*. Cambridge, Mass.: Schenkman.

BUSHAW, D. W.; and CLOWER, ROBERT W. 1957 *Introduction to Mathematical Economics*. Homewood, Ill.: Irwin.

CHASE, SAM B. JR. 1963 *Asset Prices in Economic Analysis*. Berkeley: Univ. of California Press.

CLOWER, ROBERT W. 1954 An Investigation Into the Dynamics of Investment. *American Economic Review* 44, no. 1:64–81.

CLOWER, ROBERT W. 1963 Permanent Income and Transitory Balances: Hahn's Paradox. *Oxford Economic Papers* 15:177–190.

CLOWER, ROBERT W.; and BUSHAW, D. W. 1954 Price Determination in a Stock–Flow Economy. *Econometrica* 22:328–343.

HADAR, JOSEF 1965 A Note on Stock–Flow Models of Consumer Behavior. *Quarterly Journal of Economics* 74:304–309.

HICKS, JOHN R. 1956 Methods of Dynamic Analysis. Pages 139–151 in *25 Economic Essays in Honour of Erik Lindahl*. Stockholm: Ekonomisk Tidskrift.

HORWICH, GEORGE 1964 *Money, Capital, and Prices*. Homewood, Ill.: Irwin.

LLOYD, CLIFF L. 1960 The Equivalence of the Liquidity Preference and Loanable Funds Theories and the New Stock–Flow Analysis. *Review of Economic Studies* 27:206–209.

NEGISHI, TAKASHI 1962 The Stability of a Competitive Economy: A Survey Article. *Econometrica* 30:635–669.

SMITH, VERNON L. 1961 *Investment and Production*. Harvard Economic Studies, Vol. 117. Cambridge, Mass.: Harvard Univ. Press; Oxford Univ. Press.

STOCK MARKETS
See SECURITIES MARKETS.

STOUFFER, SAMUEL A.

Samuel A. Stouffer (1900–1960), American sociologist, was a founder of large-scale quantitative social research. His contribution to the analysis of survey data represents a distinctively American approach to sociology. The four volumes of the collaborative magnum opus, Studies in Social Psychology in World War II, of which the two volumes of *The American Soldier* (1949) are best known, remain a landmark and a model in the new tradition of mass production in research, emphasis upon quantitative evidence, avoidance of theoretical speculation except in close contact with the data, and close connection with applied problems. The work has also been a prime target of criticism for those who deplore this trend (e.g., the book reviews quoted in Lerner 1950). Stouffer's career, as his collaborator Paul F. Lazarsfeld has noted (*Social Research* . . . , p. xv), coincides with the development of empirical social research in the United States, and his writings reflect its strengths and limitations.

Stouffer was born and brought up in the little town of Sac City in western Iowa, where his father was publisher of the local newspaper. He attended the small local Methodist college, Morningside, and after a year's graduate work in English at Harvard, he returned to work for a time on the family newspaper. His career as a sociologist began with graduate work at the University of Chicago, where he received his PH.D. in 1930. There he came under the formative influence of L. L. Thurstone and William F. Ogburn, both pioneers in the development and application of quantitative methods in the study of human behavior. Stouffer's quantitative bent was strengthened by his work with Karl Pearson and R. A. Fisher during a postdoctoral year at the University of London. On his return from England he proceeded to take up successive academic positions at the universities of Wisconsin and Chicago. During World War II he served as director of the professional staff in the Research Branch, Information and Education Division, of the War Department, where he mobilized a large staff of research personnel and planned and supervised the extensive studies that culminated in the four volumes including *The American Soldier*. After the war he established the Laboratory of Social Relations at Harvard University, where he remained until his death.

At the outset of Stouffer's career, demography and social statistics were the only aspects of sociology in which a quantitative approach was well developed. These were the areas on which Stouffer's early contributions were focused, and his interest in them continued. He was, for example, consultant to the U.S. Bureau of the Census; furthermore, during the year immediately preceding his death he was embarking upon a study for the Population Council in New York. His early studies—for example, his analysis of differential trends in fertility in Catholics and non-Catholics (*Social Research . . .*, pp. 165–184) and his study, with Lazarsfeld, of the effects of the depression on the family (*ibid.*, pp. 134–153)—are, like his later ones, marked by his strong talent for getting social data to speak with minimal ambiguity. The data for these early studies were obtained from public records, and much ingenuity was required to develop relevant indices and to control for obscuring factors. In his analysis, he always considered plausible alternative interpretations and tried to find ways to reduce interpretive ambiguity.

Whether he worked with available social statistics or, later, with survey data created by the investigator, Stouffer's forte lay in this ingenious interplay, close to the data, of interpretive hypothesis and empirical check. Theoretical questions tended to arise directly from the data before him and to return him quickly to the data for further analysis. His personal style of research fitted the stage of precomputer technology, when the investigator, running his sets of data cards through the counter–sorter himself, could quickly adapt his tactics of analysis to the emerging results. Stouffer's career ended just as the requirements of modern electronic computers were tending to impose a greater separation between the investigator and his data.

Research in Stouffer's style is not mere fact-grubbing, but neither does it often result directly in broader integrations of theory. One of his early contributions to demographic research, however, provided a precedent-setting example of the kind of mathematically formalized small-scale theory that was later to attract much attention in American social research: his theory of internal migration in terms of *intervening opportunities* (*ibid.*, pp. 68–91), which he subsequently elaborated and tested against additional data (*ibid.*, pp. 91–112). Stouffer's model seeks to account for the movement of population between cities, and it asserts, in effect, that the number of people moving between two places will be larger the more opportunities there are in the target area and the fewer the opportunities that are interposed between the target area and the place of origin. According to his initial formulation, all locations within the circular area centering on the city of origin (with the target city falling on the circumference) potentially present intervening opportunities; direction is ignored. His later elaboration takes direction into account in the estimation of intervening opportunities and introduces such further refinements as adjustment for the general accessibility of the target city to migration from sources other than the origin under consideration. The ingenuity of Stouffer's treatment of migration lies less in the mathematical formulation than in the ways in which he was able to coordinate the formal model with data available in census statistics.

During the 1930s the methods of survey research had been developed in the United States under auspices that were largely journalistic or commercial. Stouffer's use of survey methods in the wartime studies under his direction and the later secondary analysis of the data reported in *The American Soldier* had a substantial impact on the improvement of survey design and analysis as a research approach that generates data convenient for quantitative treatment. His approach to survey research had several distinguishing features. One was largely a matter of historical accident: reliance upon self-administered questionnaires rather than on field interviews. More important were his consistent practice of controlling statistically for the effects of many variables on the relationships under examination and his analytic preference for basing interpretative conclusions upon replicated analyses rather than on strong statistical tests of single sets of observations. Also characteristic was his attention to the need for mathematically sophisticated indices of attitudes, as reflected in his sponsorship of work by Guttman and by Lazarsfeld in developing "scalogram" and "latent structure" analysis (Stouffer et al. 1950), and in his own later contribution of the H-technique of scale analysis as a practical improvement upon Guttman's method (*Social Research . . .*, pp. 274–289).

The theoretical concept given the most emphasis in *The American Soldier* is characteristic not only of Stouffer's analytic ingenuity but also of his somewhat data-bound empiricism: the concept of *relative deprivation*. This notion, not formally developed, was invoked to account for such otherwise puzzling findings as that when rank, educational level, and length of Army service are held constant, the *less* the opportunity for promotion afforded by a branch of the Army, the *more* favorably will members of that branch assess their chances of promotion. The explanation is offered that each individual evaluates his chances of promotion in comparison with others who share his situation. The Air Force private, in a service (objectively) characterized by rapid promotion, feels more deprived than the private in Military Police, where promotions are much less frequent. Similar interpretative principles appear to account for a variety of seemingly paradoxical observations. It remained for Robert K. Merton and Alice S. Kitt (1950) to explicate and generalize the theoretical notions that are involved and to relate them to the concept of *reference groups*; in this way they developed a conceptually powerful approach to the analysis of social influences on individual persons. Stouffer asserted, as does Merton, that modest small-scale theories are more useful than theoretical systems in the older, grand style that rarely generated predictions accessible to empirical test. Stouffer's theorizing was more modest, more closely tied to the data than is Merton's, but at a cost.

If Stouffer's practically-oriented yet intellectually curious empiricism at once reflected and tended to reinforce a characteristically American orientation in the social sciences, so also did his emphasis on prediction as a touchstone of scientific merit. The wartime studies provide several examples of moderately effective prediction of behavior from attitudinal data (Stouffer et al. 1950). What is missing, however, is concern with the theoretical articulation of the steps that intervene between antecedent and consequent. Prediction thus comes to be valued in its own right, as a matter of practical achievement, rather than as a criterion of the correctness or utility of theoretical formulations.

For Stouffer, the ideal research method was the controlled experiment, in which outcomes are predicted by prior hypothesis and in which variations in the independent variables are manipulated by the experimenter. Ironically, Stouffer never conducted experimental studies himself, although in his wartime role he sponsored the important experimental work on mass communications by Hovland, Lumsdaine, and Sheffield (1949), and later actively encouraged experimental research in the Harvard Laboratory of Social Relations. Always sophisticated and critical in his appraisal of the essentially descriptive and correlational methods of analysis of which he was master, Stouffer's admiration for the magic of experimentation was somewhat naïve. In his methodological writings (e.g., *Social Research* . . . , pp. 290–299), he came close to viewing the experimental method as a royal road to truth, neglecting the ambiguities that be-

devil the experimenter in his attempts to translate theoretical variables into empirical operations. Yet progress in the sophisticated application of the experimental method in social research has surely resulted from Stouffer's enthusiastic sponsorship.

As the merger of research and theory that both he and Merton had called for became increasingly the order of the day, Stouffer proceeded, in two of his later studies, published in 1949 and 1951, to test a small-scale theory concerning social roles and role conflict (*ibid.*, pp. 39–67). Characteristically, the distinctive contribution of these two studies is in the development of empirical indices of such theoretical concepts as universalism and particularism and in revising the view of role expectations as well-defined social norms, thus yielding more complicated conceptions in closer accord with the facts.

Stouffer's work reflected a meliorist concern with the social problems of the day. He hoped that social research would be socially useful; he held that in the long run the social justification of investment in basic research is in its applications (*ibid.*, p. 4). Yet he was deeply concerned lest the exaggerated claims of enthusiasts should jeopardize the long-run prospects for the development and application of the social sciences. About these long-run prospects, he was firmly optimistic. In the shorter run, he saw the danger of dissipated effort and conspicuous failure if social scientists were too eager to solve those social problems for which their tools were still inadequate. Stouffer was ever confident about the prospects of social science, but modest about its present resources.

Nevertheless, on three occasions, Stouffer did direct his skills in social research to matters of urgent social import. He played a major role in carrying out the studies undertaken as part of Myrdal's monumental analysis of the American Negro problem (1944) and continued to take an interest in problems of race relations throughout his career. His deployment of social research to meet wartime needs has already been noted. During the postwar episode in which civil liberties in the United States suffered serious erosion under the attack of Senator Joseph R. McCarthy, he planned and analyzed an important survey of American attitudes toward communism and civil liberties (1955).

Stouffer's influence, in sum, accentuated certain distinctively American trends in social research: toward quantification and small-scale theoretical formalization, toward large-scale collaborative research organization, toward fusion of pure and applied research interests, away from speculative theoretical synthesis. His writings provided models upon which contemporary practice in survey analysis is built. While he valued empirically based theory, his own preference was for a style of inquiry rather closer to the data than is optimal for the development of theoretical conceptions with powerful generality. Stouffer was a master of such empirical analysis, making social data answer to his questioning as they would never "speak for themselves."

M. BREWSTER SMITH

[*For the historical context of Stouffer's work, see the biographies of* FISHER, R. A.; OGBURN; PEARSON; THURSTONE; *for discussion of the subsequent development of his ideas, see* ATTITUDES; PUBLIC OPINION; REFERENCE GROUPS; SCALING; SURVEY ANALYSIS; *and the biography of* HOVLAND.]

WORKS BY STOUFFER

1949   STOUFFER, SAMUEL A. et al. *The American Soldier.* 2 vols. Studies in Social Psychology in World War II, Vols. 1–2. Princeton Univ. Press. → Volume 1: *Adjustment During Army Life.* Volume 2: *Combat and Its Aftermath.*

1950   Some Afterthoughts of a Contributor to *The American Soldier.* Pages 197–211 in Robert K. Merton and Paul F. Lazarsfeld (editors), *Continuities in Social Research: Studies in the Scope and Method of* The American Soldier. Glencoe, Ill.: Free Press.

1950   STOUFFER, SAMUEL A. et al. *Measurement and Prediction.* Studies in Social Psychology in World War II, Vol. 4. Princeton Univ. Press.

(1955) 1963 *Communism, Conformity, and Civil Liberties.* Gloucester, Mass.: Smith.

Social Research to Test Ideas: Selected Writings. New York: Free Press, 1962. → Contains papers published between 1935 and 1960. A bibliography of Stouffer's writings appears on pages 301–306.

SUPPLEMENTARY BIBLIOGRAPHY

HOVLAND, CARL I.; LUMSDAINE, ARTHUR A.; and SHEFFIELD, FREDERICK D. 1949 *Experiments on Mass Communication.* Studies in Social Psychology in World War II, Vol. 3. Princeton Univ. Press.

HYMAN, HERBERT H. 1942 The Psychology of Status. *Archives of Psychology* No. 269.

LAZARSFELD, PAUL F. 1962 Introduction. In Samuel A. Stouffer, *Social Research to Test Ideas: Selected Writings.* New York: Free Press.

LERNER, DANIEL 1950 *The American Soldier* and the Public. Pages 212–251 in Robert K. Merton and Paul F. Lazarsfeld (editors), *Continuities in Social Research: Studies in the Scope and Method of* The American Soldier. Glencoe, Ill.: Free Press.

MERTON, ROBERT K.; and KITT, ALICE S. 1950 Contributions to the Theory of Reference Group Behavior. Pages 40–105 in Robert K. Merton and Paul F. Lazarsfeld (editors), *Continuities in Social Research: Studies in the Scope and Method of* The American Soldier. Glencoe, Ill.: Free Press.

MYRDAL, GUNNAR (1944) 1962 *An American Dilemma: The Negro Problem and Modern Democracy.* New York: Harper. → A paperback edition was published in 1964 by McGraw-Hill.

YOUNG, DONALD 1961 In Memoriam: Samuel Andrew Stouffer, 1900–1960. *American Sociological Review* 26:106–107.

STOUT, G. F.

George Frederick Stout (1860–1944), English psychologist, was born on Tyneside. He went to Cambridge as a classical scholar of St. John's College and had a brilliant career there, gaining firsts in both parts of the classical tripos in 1881 and 1882 and in Part 2 of the moral science tripos in 1883. He was made a fellow of his college in 1884.

In 1886 Stout went to the University of Aberdeen as lecturer in comparative psychology. (At that time, comparative psychology did not designate the study of animal behavior; it meant treating psychology in a Darwinian rather than a philosophical context. The term thus corresponds rather closely to "functional psychology," which was prevalent in the United States at about the same time [see Angell 1907; Herrnstein & Boring 1965, pp. 499–507].) In 1898 he became Wilde reader in mental philosophy at Oxford, and finally he moved north again to become professor of philosophy at St. Andrews University, where he remained from 1903 until his retirement in 1936.

Stout was essentially what is now disparagingly called an armchair psychologist, but this did not detract from his influence on British psychology, which continued into the years following World War I; the fifth edition of his *Manual of Psychology* (1899) appeared as late as 1938.

His first and most original book was *Analytic Psychology*, which appeared in 1896, to be followed by the *Manual* in 1899 and the *Groundwork of Psychology* in 1903. Thereafter his interests became more philosophical; he was, after all, a professor of philosophy by this time.

During the latter half of the nineteenth century the distinctively British account of mental processes, with its empiricism and associationism, as represented by James Mill and Alexander Bain, was influenced and greatly enriched by contemporary developments in Germany and in particular by the sophisticated epistemology of Kant. The transition from this older position was marked by the publication of James Ward's article "Psychology" in the *Encyclopaedia Britannica* of 1886. This raised arguments against associationism that so far have not been satisfactorily answered.

Stout was a pupil of Ward, with whom he differed on many points of detail but on few of substance. He advanced some distance beyond his teacher, however, and in the fields of perception and cognition he put forward views that are often credited to later writers. For example, the *Manual* contains an early formulation of the gestalt position that, to be sure, lacks experimental evidence but does not differ in any essential from the theories elaborated in Germany during the decade after 1912. Also, in a chapter entitled "Conation and Cognitive Synthesis" in the second volume of *Analytic Psychology*, he developed the theme, later proved and illustrated experimentally by Piaget, that action is a basic component of cognitive structure.

Stout was in no sense a behaviorist, but he held that mind and body are always implicated with one another in two basic ways. First of all, minds are embodied; they are never to be found on their own. Second, the concept of awareness, or consciousness, implies the concepts of objectivity and externality. Yet, only introspective analysis is the proper task of the psychologist, and any discussion of the brain or sense organs involves a departure from the strictly psychological point of view. Thus, a great deal of what we now think of as experimental psychology would have been regarded by Stout as irrelevant to his field. Much of his work, therefore, is of merely historical interest, but even today his type of acute theoretical analysis might usefully precede experimental work on many of the more complex cognitive and perceptual processes.

JAMES DREVER

[*For the historical context of Stout's work, see the biography of* WARD, JAMES; *for discussion of the subsequent development of his ideas, see* DEVELOPMENTAL PSYCHOLOGY, *article on* A THEORY OF DEVELOPMENT.]

WORKS BY STOUT

(1896) 1918 *Analytic Psychology.* 2 vols. London: Allen & Unwin.

(1899) 1938 *Manual of Psychology.* 5th ed. London: University Tutorial Press.

1903 *Groundwork of Psychology.* New York: Hinds & Noble.

1930 *Studies in Philosophy and Psychology.* New York: Macmillan.

1931 *Mind and Matter.* Cambridge Univ. Press. → Based on the Gifford lectures delivered between 1919 and 1921.

1952 *God and Nature.* Cambridge Univ. Press. → Published posthumously. Based on the Gifford lectures delivered between 1919 and 1921.

WORKS ABOUT STOUT

ANGELL, JAMES R. 1907 The Province of Functional Psychology. *Psychological Review* 14:61–91.

HERRNSTEIN, RICHARD J.; and BORING, E. G. (editors) 1965 *A Sourcebook in the History of Psychology.* Cambridge, Mass.: Harvard Univ. Press.

PASSMORE, J. A. 1944 G. F. Stout: 1860–1944. *Australasian Journal of Psychology and Philosophy* 22:1–14. → Now called *Australasian Journal of Philosophy.* Contains a bibliography of Stout's works on pages 11–14.

STRATEGY

The word "strategy," derived from Greek, originally meant the "art of the general," or "generalship." It has long since been broadened to include also the art of the admiral and of the air commander. So dynamic and pregnant a word is bound to be applied also to numerous other kinds of competitive situations, including commerce and games, and today one speaks of testing various "strategies of play" over a broad range of game situations. Such usage is, however, comparatively recent, occurring mostly since World War II. In this article we shall be concerned only with the classic application of the term strategy to war, including relevant aspects of the planning processes prior to, and in preparation for, war.

Strategy is distinguished from the related term "tactics" in ways which are well understood, though variously stated. Thus, the Oxford English *Dictionary* asserts that tactics refers "only to the mechanical movement of bodies set in motion by" strategy. Mahan proposed as a distinction between tactics and strategy the fact of *contact.* Tactics thus refers to the localized hostilities that occur where adversaries are in contact; strategy, to the basic dispositions of strength that constitute the entire conduct of a campaign or of a war. Or one can say that tactics is fighting and strategy is planning where and how to fight, with the "how" construed so as to exclude the details.

Another meaningful and even necessary distinction stresses the different *levels* at which the pertinent operations or decisions take place. Although one might speak appropriately of the "strategy" of a battle, referring thereby to the commander's purpose and essential dispositions of force, one would generally apply the term only to a large and critical battle and to the decisions of the commander in chief. Lesser commanders would be concerned with tactics. The normal connotations of the word "strategy" suggest, however, even higher levels of direction. Some have attempted, though abortively, to introduce terms like "grand strategy" to refer to the very highest levels of decision making affecting the most basic and essential dispositions for the conduct of a war, such as the major decisions made jointly by Churchill and Roosevelt during World War II, the most basic and dominant of these being the decision to defeat Germany first and Japan second.

Although it is pointless to resist established usage, one might note in passing that the use of the term "strategic" to describe a certain kind of aerial bombing has been misleading and therefore unfortunate. "Strategic bombing" applies to a type of operation characterized by deep penetration into the heartland of the enemy country, against targets selected for military or economic (i.e., supportive of the military) reasons or simply for purposes of terrorizing civilians. It is distinguished from "tactical bombing," which includes short-range operations, often in close support of friendly ground forces, and intermediate-range, or "interdiction," bombing, usually against the logistics or supply system of the enemy ground forces. The distinction is essentially one of zones of penetration and attack, with the concurrent implication, at least on the part of its advocates, that the targets for strategic bombing are radically different in kind from those sought in tactical bombing and somehow more fundamental in importance.

Professional neglect of strategic thought

The student in quest of the written strategic thought of the past will be startled to discover how lean it is, especially in a world that has known so much war. Actually, the frequency and persistence of war from remote antiquity to the present—for long periods one might almost speak of its continuity—provide one clue to the scarcity of written works. Men who spent much of their adult lives fighting were apparently content to learn their art in the field and by communication of relevant wisdom through word of mouth.

Moreover, until the early part of the nineteenth century, weapons and methods of fighting changed slowly, as did the conventions which guided those methods. The challenge of sharply changed conditions was generally absent. Even the introduction of gunpowder offered no such change. At the time it was so unimportant that chroniclers neglected to note the precise date of its first use on a European battlefield, sometime in the early fourteenth century. It took two centuries for the crossbow to be displaced by the musket, which developed when the touchhole gave way to the matchlock (late in the fifteenth century), thus permitting use of a trigger.

Another part of the explanation concerns the character and number of the potential users of strategic lore, who would also normally be the contributors to its literature. For most of the span of our civilization the leaders of armies have been aristocrats, often princes and kings, and those surrounding them have been of the same caste, which has never been known as a society of scholars. It is significant that the great Marshal de Saxe, first soldier of France during part of the reign of Louis xv, wrote his brief "Reveries Upon the Art of War" (1757) relatively early in his career, during a period of illness when he could do nothing else, and wrote nothing subsequently. The more modern practitioners of the military arts too have been committed to the idea, no doubt correctly on balance, that the first function of the commander is not strategic decision making but the leadership of military forces, whether large or small. Among the great military powers of modern times, it has always been axiomatic that the avenue to promotion in peacetime and, especially, in war is success in command, not good staff work.

A related conviction long cherished by professional military officers is, in the words of Field Marshal Lord Wavell, "that tactics, the art of handling troops on the battlefield, is and always will be a more difficult and more important part of the general's task than strategy, the art of bringing forces to the battlefield in a favorable position." Of strategy, Wavell added, "the main principles . . . are simple and easy to grasp" (1953, p. 97). It is remarkable that the reflective Wavell should have considered tactics more important as well as more difficult than strategy. The fatal error in his own military career was one of strategic judgment—his approving early in 1941 the commitment of a major portion of his North African forces to the British expedition to Greece without having first disposed of Rommel in the desert. What has been certainly true, however, is that tactics has been much more than strategy the province of the professional soldier, since the former is in many ways more esoteric and makes far heavier demands on military virtues like resolution and courage.

Finally, one should remember that the market for strategic insight has always been a limited one. Actual and potential commanders in chief were never numerous. Until very recently, the great majority of professional military officers could live out their careers without ever being called upon to make or to offer advice upon a strategic decision. Their training took full cognizance of this fact.

Background of strategy

The "roots of strategy" have been traced as far back as the writings, or collected maxims, of Sun Tzu (c. 500 B.C.). His "Art of War," however, is today merely quaint. The Greeks, especially Xenophon and Thucydides, are more important, although they did not write discourses on strategy. But included in their chronicles or histories are long statements, supposedly quoting Greek generals, which often reveal fascinating strategic insight. Another early author, Vegetius ("The Military Institutions of the Romans," c. A.D. 390), deals more with tactics than strategy, though his book is said to have been used by commanders in the Middle Ages and later. Niccolò Machiavelli should also be mentioned, although interestingly enough, his *Art of War* (1521), engrossed with problems of tactics and organizational reform, probably contains less about strategy than some of his other works. Again, the writings of Marshal Maurice de Saxe (1757) and Friedrich II (1747) are absorbed largely in detailed tactical concerns and are interesting today mostly for what they reveal of war in their own times. Only the collection of what are purported to be Napoleon's "maxims" begin to show some live connection with our own times. In short, the roots of *modern* strategy really begin at the end of the eighteenth century.

However, rather than catalogue the contributions of past writers whose works have dissolved into the stream of modern military thinking, it is preferable to look back to see which thinkers stand out as major contributors to the ideas and doctrines that in one form or another represent our living strategic inheritance.

Mahan. Before World War II, theoretical strategy was divided into three parts: naval, air, and land strategy. In the field of naval strategy the figure of the American naval officer Alfred Thayer Mahan was still supreme. His strategic ideas represented mostly the rediscovery of principles that had held sway in sailing days. More clearly than any predecessor, Mahan illuminated the concept of "command of the sea." He distinguished sharply between attaining command, which is the function of the battle fleet, and exercising it, which is done by cruisers and convoy-escort vessels. He felt that mere commerce raiding had always failed to be "decisive of great issues," and being innately conservative, he missed seeing the special strategic potential of the submarine in that role. He died too early (December 1914) to witness its astonishing success against Allied commerce in World War I. Mahan's views and great prestige contributed to the general prewar underestimation of the submarine, even within the German navy. [*See the biography of* MAHAN.]

Corbett and Castex. Another distinguished though less well-known figure in naval strategy was Mahan's civilian British contemporary Julian Corbett, also a naval historian. In France an outstand-

ing figure was Admiral Raoul Castex, who between the wars wrote with insight of the submarine experience of World War I. The very few books on naval strategy published after these writers (e.g., Brodie 1941) were usually attempts to bring the work of these thinkers, especially of Mahan, up to date.

Douhet. In the new field of air strategy there was only one noteworthy writer, the Italian General Giulio Douhet, whose slender body of writings appeared in the decade following World War I. U.S. Brigadier General "Billy" Mitchell was an air propagandist, but except for some commonplace ideas, like applying the notion of concentration of force to the air, he was not truly a thinker on air strategy. The British attach much importance to the views of Lord Trenchard, World War I commander of the Royal Flying Corps and founder of the Royal Air Force, and some of his assistants (e.g., General P. R. C. Groves), whose convictions were more or less parallel to those of Douhet. The leaders of the German Luftwaffe of World War II, as well as of the American air forces, subsequently acknowledged their indebtedness to Douhet.

Douhet (1921) attempted to apply Mahan's concept of command of the sea to air fighting. Actually Douhet exaggerated the similarity of air and naval strategies, and he is more easily and accurately remembered as the prophet of the concept that attributes dominance to strategic bombing. In Douhet's opinion nothing could withstand the power of a large bomber force, which could and should ignore the static battle lines on the ground and proceed to destroy first the enemy's offensive air force, then the factories from which his air power issued, and finally the will to resist of the people at large. Douhet assumed too readily that ground fighting would always be stalled as it was in 1914–1918, and he grossly underestimated the tonnage of bombs required to accomplish the above-described goals against any significant power. In World War II the RAF and the USAAF attempted to carry out his design, with results that were limited but certainly positive, especially against Japan. [*For an evaluation, see* Brodie 1959, *chapters 3 and 4; see also the biography of* DOUHET.]

Clausewitz. In land strategy, certainly the oldest area in which any kind of strategic thinking can be discovered, the towering stature of Karl von Clausewitz, who died in 1831, has not been surpassed or even equaled. Clausewitz is almost alone in the philosophic breadth and grasp he had of this subject. Among the publicists in all strategic fields since his time, only Mahan comes close to his sense of the political constraints on strategy. Clausewitz' book *On War* (1832–1834) is ponderous and difficult to read, and it has suffered from bad translations of corrupted texts. It has had few readers, and the frequent references to, or "quotations" from, his work often distort his essential message.

Far from being the advocate of total or absolute war, as is often charged, Clausewitz might in fact be considered the originator of the modern doctrine of limited war. His often-quoted phrase "War is a mere continuation of politics by other means" was intended simply to stress the necessary dominance of the political aim and thus the necessary subjection of the general to the political leader. This has been generally overlooked or forgotten, but another basic Clausewitz thesis which did not suffer this fate was the importance of destroying the enemy's armed forces, a process distinct from capturing portions of his territory or cities or fortresses. [*See the biography of* CLAUSEWITZ.]

Jomini. An important contemporary of Clausewitz' was the Swiss mercenary Antoine Henri Jomini, a senior officer on Napoleon's staff and later on the staff of Napoleon's enemy, the tsar of Russia. Jomini's continual publications during a very long life, his lucidity, and the fact that he wrote in relatively accessible French rather than forbidding German, resulted in his having, outside of Germany, a far greater influence than Clausewitz. The generals on both sides of the American Civil War are supposed to have been much influenced by him.

He is best summarized as the chief interpreter of Napoleon's strategy and of the elements which brought about its success. We may perceive his continuing influence especially in his exaltation of the doctrine of the offensive. Clausewitz had also appreciated the importance of the offensive, but his views were characteristically more moderate and qualified. Jomini is also famous for coining the phrase (though not originating the thought) "methods change but principles are unchanging." However, he did not deign to present an accompanying list of principles. Such a list was to be the corruption of a later age.

Du Picq and Foch. In France an original mind appeared in the slender but scholarly work of Colonel Ardant du Picq, killed in one of the first battles of the Franco–Prussian War. Du Picq was entirely absorbed with the psychology of the soldier in combat. His realistic insights, because they were not carefully studied, had an unfortunate influence in the pre-World War I school of French military romantics under the intellectual leadership of Ferdinand Foch. Foch and his followers made slogans of quotations from du Picq and Clausewitz

without troubling to understand the subleties of their thought. For example, du Picq's remark "He will win who has the resolution to advance" referred to the omnipresent element of fear in battle. Foch quoted it as a clarion call to the attack. However outstanding his later abilities as a commander, Foch in his pre-1914 role as professor at the École Supérieure de la Guerre and as a writer on strategy was mostly a propagandist and a vulgarizer of his greater predecessors.

The method of all these men consisted in the scrutiny of military history to see what abiding lessons could be derived from the experience of the past. Some, like Clausewitz, du Picq, and Mahan, had been careful and fairly objective historians; others, like Foch, were not averse to distorting history, with which they had little enough familiarity, to serve their pre-existing convictions. We should also notice that none of these figures, including the most recent, were at all interested in applying quantitative measures to their data or conceptions. Douhet's failure to apply even elementary arithmetical calculations to his concepts resulted in the gross exaggerations that oblige us to account him, however insightful, more wrong than right in his prediction of the character of World War II. Perhaps the contemporary strategists contrast most sharply with the old precisely in their different attitude toward quantification.

"Principles of war." Beginning shortly before World War I and continuing into the present, there have been various presentations of the so-called principles of war (the first listing of principles in United States Army training manuals was in *Training Regulations 10-5* of 1921, which simply named the "principles" without explaining them). These "principles," usually presented in lists of six to a dozen numbered maxims, are supposed to be unchanging despite the fantastic changes that have occurred and continue to occur in almost all the factors with which they deal. The propositions usually stress the importance of such commonsense precepts as: avoid undue dispersion of strength in order to maximize the chances for superiority at the decisive point (principle of mass, or concentration); choose firmly your course of action and adhere to it despite distracting pressures (principle of the objective); press vigorously any advantage gained, especially after victory in battle (principle of pursuit); etc. There are occasional additions to, or subtractions from, this list, depending on the whim or bias of the individual compiler.

The utility of these generalizations or "principles" is in encapsulating what otherwise has to be derived from much study, as well as in placing foremost in the commander's mind important ideas that might otherwise be forgotten in the heat of battle. Nevertheless, undue emphasis upon them argues a negation of strategic thinking. When Admiral Halsey declined on the basis of the "principle of concentration" to divide his tremendous force at Leyte Gulf, electing instead to throw the whole of the great Third Fleet against the puny decoy force under Admiral Ozawa, he threw away his chance for destroying the main Japanese fleet. As Winston Churchill put it, "The truths of war are absolute, but the principles governing their application have to be deduced on each occasion from the circumstances, which are always different; and in consequence no rules are any guide to action" (1923–1929, p. 576 in the 1931 edition).

Contemporary strategic thought

Changes wrought by World War II. World War II had an altogether different character from World War I, but among the more conspicuous changes two deserve special mention. The first was the heavy reliance upon scientists to assist not only top military commanders but even heads of government to reach critical tactical and strategic decisions. The role of scientists was particularly prominent in the new field of strategic bombing, where previous war experience was completely lacking and where a flow of new inventions was radically affecting the capabilities of the bombing forces. The outstanding application of analytical skills was in target selection, where economists proved especially invaluable.

The second was the introduction at the very end of the conflict of the atomic bomb, which was in itself a basic strategic change of totally unprecedented importance. It also signaled the beginning of an era of extremely rapid and also extremely costly technological development, which would in turn account for the unparalleled ascendancy of the "superpowers," the Soviet Union and especially the United States. The atomic bomb differed from all previous military inventions in that it was immediately clear that its effects went far beyond the tactical. The bomber airplane had already taken war beyond the battlefield, but nuclear weapons guaranteed that those operations which in World War II we called strategic bombing would be all-important in any war in which they should again occur. However, shortly one began to hear expressions of the fear that even in their initial form those weapons were far too effective for the user's good, as long as reciprocal use also had to be considered.

Furthermore, the rapidity of change that resulted from the development of a wide range of nuclear weapons, combined with the development of fabulous new rockets or "self-propelled missiles" for carrying them, diminished greatly the utility of traditional "military judgment" in selecting the appropriate systems. The professional military man had enough to do to keep abreast of current technological developments pertinent to his work. But decisions about weapons systems had to be made even though these systems might not be ready for six years or more, when the whole technological environment could be significantly different. (A "weapons system" refers to the entire system of utilization, including manning, bases, etc., of any major weapon.)

It was not a wholly new requirement of the military that they think ahead technologically, but certainly the dimensions and complexity of the problem were totally new. Also, apart from technological issues, the fears justly inspired by nuclear weapons, as well as the menacing unknowns posed by the political realignment of world power—accented by the ascendancy of the Soviet Union in Europe, the victory of communism in China, and the decolonization of large parts of Africa, Asia, and the western Pacific—required continuing intensive scrutiny by suitably trained scholars of the changing political constraints on national strategy.

Institutional and intellectual developments. Deriving partly from these realizations on the part of the military, a development took place in the United States that was to have far-reaching consequences for the study of strategy. This was the founding of a number of nonprofit research institutions closely associated with, but autonomous from, the military services, where people with various kinds of scientific training, including the social sciences, and with access to "classified" (i.e., secret) information could devote themselves on a full-time basis to the consideration of national security problems. The prototype of these organizations, and still the best known among them, is The RAND Corporation, originally set up by a contract between the United States Air Force and the Douglas Aircraft Corporation but shortly thereafter made independent from Douglas.

Although it was perhaps not intended by their military sponsors that these research institutions should concern themselves with strategy, it was inevitable that at least some of their personnel would ultimately do so. Able, highly trained men are unlikely to let go unchallenged assumptions which they consider invalid or faulty but which have been fed to them as "givens" or "inputs" for what are supposed to be limited technical inquiries. Furthermore, while in the nuclear age the old division between land, sea, and air strategy makes, from the national point of view, less sense than ever, professional military officers are likely to be affected by loyalty to service interests. At any rate, the new nonprofit research institutions, together with some universities, began to produce from their civilian staffs the new leaders of strategic thought.

Although the larger research efforts conducted by these institutions were likely to be carried on by teams of technical experts, the novel and important ideas that floated into public consciousness were, as always in the past, the product mostly of individuals who seemed to have special gifts for strategic insight. The latter, though certainly more numerous than ever before, are still not a numerous group, yet they have produced most of the ideas on which debate has focused since the end of World War II, some of which have already won overwhelming national and even international acceptance. The more important of these ideas can be divided into two groups, comprising (a) a drastic modification of the previously prevailing notions concerning the conduct of total, or "general," nuclear war, and (b) development of a new body of views concerning "limited war."

With respect to the former, the theory of strategic bombing derived from Douhet and the experience of World War II, and initially carried over almost unchanged into the nuclear era, called for the most rapid possible destruction of the enemy's retaliatory air power, his war-production industries, and the morale of his people, mostly through the slaughter of a large proportion of them. Security of the offensive force was to be gained not through defensive means but by attacking in good time, and nuclear weapons only made it more urgent to strike first. However, civilian theorists began to point out that because general nuclear wars would have to be fought with "forces-in-being," which is to say, forces existing at the outset, the so-called war-production industries counted for little or nothing as targets. Furthermore, the slaughter of populations was contraindicated for strategic as well as humanitarian reasons. There was, therefore, a strong trend toward "city-avoidance" strategies, which is to say that in any sensible target system cities were to be hostages rather than ruins, the main emphasis being on "counterforce" or "damage-limiting" targets, that is, the destruction of enemy retaliatory forces in order to limit damage to oneself.

Security of one's own offensive or retaliatory forces was to be sought not through rapidity of reaction—obviously dangerous to the maintenance of peace—but, especially with missiles, through underground protection ("hardening"), concealment, or mobility. As both major nuclear powers proceeded to make their retaliatory forces markedly less vulnerable, a real targeting dilemma set in, inasmuch as the resulting deterioration of the utility of counterforce strategies did not in itself warrant a return to the concept of city targeting. At any rate, the changes which produced this dilemma were considered highly stabilizing, because far from being anxious to strike while striking was possible, neither side now had much inducement to initiate the mutually destructive exchange.

The prevailing realization was indeed that there could be no conceivable political objectives worth the fighting of a general nuclear war. As a result ideas of limited war were developed, characterized in the main by the concept of having localized aggressions resisted locally rather than by general war or "massive retaliation" (to use a phrase derived from a much-publicized speech on January 12, 1954, by U.S. Secretary of State John Foster Dulles, who was thereby attempting to reject the recently concluded Korean War as a pattern for the future). The modern concept of limited war, it should be noted, is totally different from that of the eighteenth century, inasmuch as it means not a limited mobilization of the total potential force of the state but rather the *withholding* of a tremendously powerful, already mobilized and in fact highly alerted force.

The earlier theorists of limited war saw no essential reason for avoiding tactical use of nuclear weapons, but later a school of thought developed which placed heavy emphasis on the avoidance of nuclear weapons at almost all costs, primarily because of the allegedly "escalatory" effects of any resort to nuclear weapons. "Escalation" (i.e., a heightening of intensity of hostilities) was something which might be deliberately sought as a warning to the enemy of one's resolve, but its obvious dangers made it imperative to keep it tightly controlled. The idea of a deliberate and always measured progression, where necessary, from very limited to very large applications of force fell under the general concept of "controlled response." This concept, with special emphasis on "conventional," or nonnuclear, fighting capabilities, characterized the administration of President John F. Kennedy and Secretary of Defense Robert S. McNamara. [*See* LIMITED WAR; *and* NUCLEAR WAR.]

The intellectual and institutional movement just

described has thus far been almost exclusively American, with some imitation, on an extremely modest scale, in the United Kingdom and in France. There seems to be no comparable emphasis on analytical techniques in the communist countries, where the study of strategy still seems to be the exclusive preserve of the military leaders, except insofar as they are guided on particular issues by the intuitively derived dicta of their political leaders.

Recent research directions. The body of the new strategic inquiry may be divided, somewhat arbitrarily, into three major categories: (1) the formulation and intellectual testing of new strategic concepts by a variety of analytical devices (including war gaming); (2) the formulation of national-defense-policy recommendations concerning particular regions; and (3) recommendations on the selection of "weapons systems," determined largely by what has come to be called "cost–effectiveness" analysis, that is, a rigorous method for finding how to get the most military value for any given sum of money or, conversely, for getting a certain high level of defense potential at minimum cost (see Quade 1964).

These varying efforts, most of them concerned with vast expenditures, have stimulated an appreciation of quantification, which as we have seen, was previously absent from strategic discourse except in mobilization planning. On the other hand, where strategic study used to be based primarily on historical research, most of its new devotees have largely neglected or abandoned military history. Although this neglect or separation has sometimes been defended by appeals to the novelty of the post-World War II strategic universe, there is no doubt that it represents one of the weaknesses or limitations in the new approach. Perhaps the new emphasis on limited war will stimulate a return to relevant historical research, which after all provides our only secure information on how men behave in political crisis and in battle. Besides, the era since World War II has by now developed an important history of its own, which includes a succession of crises and of various kinds of military conflict, including a considerable conventional war in Korea and a new kind of conflict in Vietnam.

The pace of technological development in military armaments is hardly likely to slacken appreciably in the future. For that reason, the special kinds of cost–effectiveness analysis of military systems developed since World War II will no doubt continue to play a prominent part in strategic decision-making processes. On the other hand, there are at least two reasons for expecting that strategic thought will be much less concerned with technological developments than in the score of years following World War II. First, though new weapons systems will appear, and various existing kinds will become more "sophisticated," there do seem to be ceilings on meaningful effectiveness. Already nuclear weapons can be made that are much more powerful than seems to be warranted by most conceivable uses; and the possibility, for example, of using orbiting space vehicles for potentially aggressive military purposes (they are already available for reconnaissance) is not likely to make a major change in the military aspect that the great nuclear powers already present to each other. Second, while the primary problem for strategists in the past was to assemble and effectively utilize superior strength, in the contemporary period the more frequent problem is how to make the available power relevant to objectives likely to be in dispute. Certainly it is no longer necessary at this writing to emphasize, to any government that may have the power to conduct it, the fantastic destructiveness of total nuclear war and the unsuitability of that degree of military conflict for *any* conceivable political objectives.

We may therefore expect, in any strategic analysis, a heightening of the importance of the political environment with respect to the total governance of any military operations. And for that reason we may expect not only the continued dominance of civilian influence in both the analysis and determination of strategic issues but possibly also some lessening of the relative importance of the special nonprofit defense-oriented research organizations described above, for they will not necessarily have a comparative advantage over other intellectual institutions in appraising the political realities of the times.

BERNARD BRODIE

[*See also* DETERRENCE; LIMITED WAR; MILITARY POLICY; MILITARY POWER POTENTIAL; NATIONAL SECURITY; NUCLEAR WAR. *Other relevant material may be found under* INTERNATIONAL RELATIONS; *and* WAR.]

BIBLIOGRAPHY

ARDANT DU PICQ, CHARLES (1880) 1947 *Battle Studies: Ancient and Modern Battles.* Edited by John N. Greely and Robert C. Cotton. Harrisburg, Pa.: Military Service Publishing. → First published in French.

ARON, RAYMOND (1963) 1965 *The Great Debate: Theories of Nuclear Strategy.* Garden City, N.Y.: Doubleday. → First published as *Le grand débat: Initiation à la stratégie atomique.*

BRODIE, BERNARD (1941) 1965 *A Guide to Naval Strategy.* 5th ed. Princeton Univ. Press.

BRODIE, BERNARD (1959) 1965 *Strategy in the Missile Age*. 2d ed. Princeton Univ. Press. → An introduction to modern strategic concepts.

BRODIE, BERNARD 1966 *Escalation and the Nuclear Option*. Princeton Univ. Press. → On the debate concerning nuclear versus conventional strategies.

BULL, HEDLEY (1961) 1965 *The Control of the Arms Race: Disarmament and Arms Control in the Missile Age*. 2d ed. New York: Praeger.

CHURCHILL, WINSTON (1923–1929) 1963–1964 *The World Crisis*. 6 vols. New York: Scribners. → The 1931 edition is a condensation of the 1923–1929 edition.

CLAUSEWITZ, KARL VON (1832–1834) 1943 *On War*. New York: Modern Library. → First published in German as *Vom Kriege*, in three volumes. To date this is the best translation of this great classic, but a new and superior version is at this writing under preparation by an international team of scholars.

CORBETT, JULIAN S. (1911) 1918 *Some Principles of Maritime Strategy*. London: Longmans.

DOUHET, GIULIO (1921) 1942 *The Command of the Air*. New York: Coward-McCann. → First published as *Il domino dell 'aria*.

EARLE, EDWARD M. (editor) 1943 *Makers of Modern Strategy: Military Thought From Machiavelli to Hitler*. Princeton Univ. Press.

FOCH, FERDINAND (1903) 1920 *Principles of War*. New York: Holt. → First published as *Des principes de la guerre*.

FRIEDRICH II, DER GROSSE, KING OF PRUSSIA (1747) 1950 The Instruction of Frederick the Great for His Generals, 1747. Pages 301–400 in Thomas R. Phillips (editor), *The Roots of Strategy*. Harrisburg, Pa.: Military Service Publishing. → For other writings of Frederick the Great, see Earle (1943).

HITCH, CHARLES J.; and McKEAN, R. N. 1960 *The Economics of Defense in the Nuclear Age*. Cambridge, Mass.: Harvard Univ. Press.

JOMINI, HENRI (1836) 1952 *Summary of the Art of War*. Edited by J. D. Hittle. Harrisburg, Pa.: Military Service Publishing. → First published as *Précis de l'art de la guerre*. The 1952 edition is a condensed version.

KAHN, HERMAN (1960) 1961 *On Thermonuclear War*. 2d ed. Princeton Univ. Press.

KAUFMANN, WILLIAM W. 1964 *The McNamara Strategy*. New York: Harper. → An interpretation of the strategic philosophy absorbed by U.S. Secretary of Defense McNamara from certain of his contemporaries.

KISSINGER, HENRY A. (editor) 1965a *Problems of National Strategy: A Book of Readings*. New York: Praeger.

KISSINGER, HENRY A. 1965b *The Troubled Partnership: A Re-appraisal of the Atlantic Alliance*. New York: McGraw-Hill.

KNORR, KLAUS E.; and READ, THORNTON (editors) 1962 *Limited Strategic War*. New York: Praeger.

LUVAAS, JAY 1964 *The Education of an Army: British Military Thought, 1815–1940*. Univ. of Chicago Press.

MACHIAVELLI, NICCOLÒ (1521) 1965 *The Art of War*. Edited with an introduction by Neal Wood. New York: Bobbs-Merrill. → First published as *Arte della guerra*.

MAHAN, ALFRED THAYER (1890) 1963 *The Influence of Sea Power Upon History: 1660–1783*. New York: Hill & Wang.

MAHAN, ALFRED THAYER 1911 *Naval Strategy Compared and Contrasted With the Principles and Practice of Military Operations on Land: Lectures.* . . . Boston: Little.

NAPOLÉON I, EMPEROR OF THE FRENCH (1827) 1950 Military Maxims of Napoleon. Pages 401–441 in Thomas R. Phillips (editor), *The Roots of Strategy*. Harrisburg, Pa.: Military Service Publishing. → First published posthumously in French.

OSGOOD, ROBERT E. (1957) 1960 *Limited War: The Challenge to American Strategy*. Univ. of Chicago Press.

PHILLIPS, THOMAS R. (editor) (1940) 1950 *The Roots of Strategy*. Harrisburg, Pa.: Military Service Publishing.

QUADE, EDWARD S. (editor) 1964 *Analysis for Military Decisions*. Chicago: Rand McNally.

SAXE, MAURICE DE (1757) 1950 My Reveries Upon the Art of War. Pages 177–300 in Thomas R. Phillips (editor), *The Roots of Strategy*. Harrisburg, Pa.: Military Service Publishing. → First published posthumously as *Les rêveries; Ou mémoires sur l'art de la guerre*.

SCHELLING, THOMAS C. 1960 *The Strategy of Conflict*. Cambridge, Mass.: Harvard Univ. Press. → A paperback edition was published in 1963 by Oxford University Press.

SCHELLING, THOMAS C. 1966 *Arms and Influence*. New Haven: Yale Univ. Press.

SNYDER, GLENN H. 1961 *Deterrence and Defense: Toward a Theory of National Security*. Princeton Univ. Press.

SOKOLOVSKII, VASILII D. (editor) (1962) 1963 *Soviet Military Strategy*. Translated, analyzed, and annotated by H. S. Dinerstein, L. Gouré, and T. W. Wolfe. Englewood Cliffs, N.J.: Prentice-Hall. → First published in Russian as *Voennaiia strategiia*.

SUN TZU On the Art of War. Pages 13–63 in Thomas R. Phillips (editor), *The Roots of Strategy*. Harrisburg, Pa.: Military Service Publishing, 1950. → First written as *Ping Fa* c. 500 B.C.

VEGETIUS The Military Institutions of the Romans. Pages 65–175 in Thomas R. Phillips (editor), *The Roots of Strategy*. Harrisburg, Pa.: Military Service Publishing, 1950. → First written as *De re militari* c. A.D. 390. First printed in 1473.

WAVELL, ARCHIBALD 1953 *Soldiers and Soldiering: Or Epithets of War*. London: Cape.

WOLFE, THOMAS W. 1964 *Soviet Strategy at the Crossroads*. Cambridge, Mass.: Harvard Univ. Press.

STRATIFICATION, SOCIAL

I
INTRODUCTION

Social stratification, in its most general sense, is a sociological concept that refers to the fact that both individuals and groups of individuals are conceived of as constituting higher and lower differentiated strata, or classes, in terms of some specific or generalized characteristic or set of characteristics. Borrowed by analogy from the earth sciences, the term "social stratification" has come into general sociological use only since about 1940, although the matters to which it refers have been discussed under the heading "social class" for a very long time. However, in contrast to its earth-science usage the sociological usage of the concept of stratification often includes, implicitly or explicitly, some evaluation of the higher and lower layers, which are judged to be better or worse according to a scale of values. Such matters as relative moral worth, relative equality and inequality, and degrees of justice and injustice are often involved in the concept of social stratification. The concept is therefore widely used in political, ideological, and moral debate and controversy, as well as in social science analysis. But despite the difficulty of separating the context of moral and ideological controversy, on the one hand, from that of social science analysis, on the other, considerable progress, both theoretical and empirical, has been made in the study of social stratification during the last one hundred years. A brief history of this progress provides some necessary background for assessing where social stratification theory stands today and for laying out a conceptual model of what that theory might be in the future.

Origins of social stratification theory

As a relatively undifferentiated notion, the idea of social stratification is found in the Judaeo–Christian Bible, the social thought of the Greeks, and the basic social and religious texts of the Indians and the Chinese. The idea has persisted, in relatively crude form, right up to the present day.

Marxian theory. In the history of the evolution of social stratification theory, Marx is the Copernican hero because his concept of social stratification, in contrast with all previous, common-sense notions in this area, emphasizes the basic importance, as a criterion of stratification, of the individual's or group's location in the economic structure. This emphasis contributed one of the essential foundations for all subsequent stratification theory and, indeed, for all other kinds of sociological analysis. In terms of their structural location in the social system, which is centered on the means of production, men in society are divided by Marx into two strata, or "classes," as he called them (following the generally preferred practice of his time). These two classes are the owners of the means of production and the workers whom they employ.

In the light of present sociological analysis and knowledge, this is too crude a concept of social stratification to cope with empirical social reality. First, it does not provide an adequate account of actual structural differentiation in what has been variously labeled the economic, the productive, and the occupational aspect of society. Modern students of the sociology of work and of social stratification have demonstrated not only that this aspect of society is structurally much more differentiated than Marx said but that actual behavior cannot be understood without taking this greater differentiation into account. For example, the analysis of social stratification needs to take into account such differences as those between owning and managing business roles, between business and professional occupational roles, and between skilled and unskilled labor roles. A second way in which the Marxian concept of social stratification is relatively crude is that it tends to minimize, and therefore has no systematic theoretical place for, a variety of other social-structural factors that are of the greatest importance in society, such as lineage and kinship affiliations in all societies or ethnic affiliations in societies that are ethnically differentiated. Modern theorists and researchers treat ethnic-group stratification, for example, as an important type of stratification in its own right—as indeed it is and has been throughout much of history in many parts of the world (see, for instance, Shibutani & Kwan 1965). Third, Marxian theory tends to minimize, and therefore has no satisfactory theoretical place for, a variety of cultural factors that are as important in the determination of behavior as is the single factor of social stratification. These cultural factors include values, religious ideas, scientific ideas, and legal norms. It is not correct, as Marxian theory holds in the explanation of social stability and change, that social stratification is always the independent variable and cultural factors always dependent variables. Both stability and change are as much determined by cultural factors as by the factor of social stratification. For example, science is probably as much a maker of the modern world as is social stratification.

Marxist analysis has also, of course, been vehemently ideological, in addition to claiming to be scientific. It has always sought to make moral judgments of the world and to change it. Some of the resulting ideological distortion has hindered the progress of social stratification theory. For example, social science has taken a long time to shake off the conceptual confusion resulting from the Marxian moral disapproval of the entrepreneurial and managing roles in society. (For an analysis of the positive functions of entrepreneurs and managers and also for much good appreciation and criticism of Marx, see Schumpeter 1942.) Similarly, the excessively simplified dichotomization of the social stratification structure in the Marxian picture of modern society has exaggerated the amount of class conflict that has occurred and that is inevitable in such a society. To be sure, some conflict is endemic in the structure of every society; and the productive, or occupational, aspect of modern society is certainly one structural source of conflict. But there are other sources, such as religious and ethnic differences, and it may be that these differences have actually engendered more conflict in the modern world than has the occupational difference. In any case, this is a matter for empirical analysis, not for ideological preconception, while Marxian theory has tended to take its stand on the latter.

Max Weber. After Marx, the next great figure in the history of social stratification theory is Max Weber. He made progress in several ways, probably in part because of his desire to correct Marx, who was one of the dominant intellectual figures when Weber's thought was taking shape. Weber's trinitarian model of social stratification—based on the concepts of class, status, and party—introduced a systematic, explicit, and necessary differentiation into stratification theory. Although Marx knew about such "status groups" as the aristocracy and the peasantry, he chose to neglect status as an explicit and independent dimension of stratification. Weber improved stratification theory by making both status and party (or power, as he also called this factor) as independent in principle as class, which for Marx was the sole independent factor. With this trinitarian view, Weber was able to show that any one of these three factors could independently affect the other two and that any one of them could often be translated into, or exchanged for, either of the other two. Even Weber, however, as we now see, did not go far enough in differentiating his conceptual model of social stratification. There are more than three important and independent dimensions of social stratification. We have already referred to two of these other dimensions: kinship and ethnic stratification. Educational stratification is still another dimension that independently affects behavior in society.

Weber's view inevitably had ideological implications; many took this view as a counterideology to the Marxian view of society. At least implicitly, Weber was justifying the functions of the high-ranking status groups, especially those that performed political, military, and civil-service functions. According to Marxian ideology, these groups are viewed as useless, at least for positive tasks; it is their negative function—that is, their "exploitation" of the lower classes—that is of importance. The classic Marxist proposition that in a socialist society the state will wither away is a result of the view that the high-ranking military, political, and civil service roles (and, in some societies, their associated status groups) are essentially useless.

As a product of his times, Weber was not very much concerned with how to make a more precise ordering of social behavior along the three dimensions of social stratification that he analyzed. For example, he defined "class" as "chances on the market," but he said little about the measurable indicators of this concept or about problems of measurement in general. We now feel it necessary to ask Weber a series of questions: how does one measure "chances on the market"? just by current income? by earned or inherited capital as well? by some application of social power, as through influence of the government or of trade unions? Similarly, Weber defined "status" in terms of "honor" and "style of life," but he did not tell us how either is to be reliably and precisely measured. Indeed, it is obvious that he was thinking only of the *higher* ranges of the "honor," or "status," dimension of stratification, not of the middle and lower ones. Present analysis is interested in the whole continuum of "honor," or "prestige," as it is now usually called. And prestige measurement scales range from the least to the most highly ranked points on this continuum. Finally, Weber said little about how to measure "power," and we have had to wait until the recent studies of local-community influence structure to see some improvement in this area [*see* COMMUNITY, *article on* THE STUDY OF COMMUNITY POWER].

The multidimensional approach

In the contemporary period, conceptual developments in stratification theory have come most notably from Parsons (1949*a*; 1949*b*; 1953) and from Davis and Moore (1945). Influenced in part by the general interest in the study of values in modern social science, these theorists have stressed the prestige dimension of social stratification and have treated what Weber called status as a generalized social phenomenon applying to all positions in the occupational structure of society. Prestige is the resultant of two factors: a system of values, and the functional significance of roles as embodied in the occupational structure. Functional significance is determined by the relative capacity of a role for "producing" some service or good in society—services and goods being construed in the most comprehensive way possible, not in the limited economic way intended by Marx when he spoke of production. For example, governmental, religious, artistic, and ideological roles are as functionally significant, as subject to evaluation, and as "productive" in some measure as are the roles of owning capital, managing a business, or tending a machine in a factory.

Parsons, in addition to his interest in the dimension of prestige, has also been interested in the power aspect of social stratification (see especially 1957; 1963). In this area he has stressed two general propositions, neither of which has been universally accepted in social science theory. One is that power is a positive social phenomenon—the capacity for achieving goals in social systems—and not just a negative phenomenon—the capacity to prevent others from acting as they wish. The second proposition is that power is not a zero-sum phenomenon, in which if A has more, then B necessarily has less. Rather, power is a phenomenon that allows increments and their social consequences to be shared by both A and B, although not always in complete equality, of course.

Parsons, Davis, and Moore have sought to be scientific about social stratification theory or at least to reduce its ideological bias when presenting it as scientific theory. But they have had many critics who have charged them with a number of ideological commitments nonetheless—for example, with favoring inequality in social systems, underemphasizing the conflict and power aspects of social stratification, and favoring social stability rather than social change (see the series of critiques of Davis and Moore collected in Bendix & Lipset 1966).

Measurement

Parsons, Davis, and Moore have not been concerned with the problem of improving measurement techniques in social stratification analysis. Fortunately, considerable progress in this respect has come from other contemporary sources. First, there has been a great development of occupational-prestige scales as instruments for measuring this dimension of social stratification. After the pioneering but simple work of George S. Counts in the 1920s, the occupational scale was very much improved by North and Hatt (1949) in the United States and by similar studies in England, France, West Germany, Poland, the Philippines, Northern Rhodesia, Indonesia, and elsewhere. (For an analysis of the comparative study of occupational prestige, with data from studies in 24 different countries, see Hodge et al. 1966.) The results of these

studies show a very large degree of consensus across societies in the relative evaluation of a great many of the different occupational positions included in these scales. This suggests that it is indeed the actual functional significance of an occupational role that determines its relative evaluation, regardless of the society in which it occurs. However, there is enough variability of evaluation to suggest that values differ somewhat across societies and that these value differences result in somewhat different evaluations of the same job in different societies. A business executive, for example, may be somewhat less highly evaluated in socialist Poland than in a society like the United States, which is more favorable to business activities in general. In 1966 a new set of studies on a national sample of the population was being carried out under the auspices of the National Opinion Research Center of the University of Chicago. One of the results obtained was that during the preceding forty years there was considerable stability in the pattern of differential evaluation of occupations in American society (Hodge et al. 1964). The new scale and findings resulting from this project may be as great a benefit to social stratification studies in the next twenty years as the study by North and Hatt has been in the past twenty. Cumulative progress in measurement techniques for the occupational-prestige dimension of social stratification is clearly present and seems likely to continue, perhaps at an even faster pace now that the base of achievement has been made so solid. [*For a description of these techniques, see* STRATIFICATION, SOCIAL, *article on* THE MEASUREMENT OF SOCIAL CLASS.]

Moreover, there has been considerable progress during the last 15 years in evolving techniques for the measurement of the power dimension of social stratification, at least at the local-community level. Studies of this kind have been undertaken chiefly in the United States but also in England, Mexico, and Canada. Sociometric, reputational, and decision-making techniques have all been used, sometimes in combination, and are slowly resulting in improved theory and knowledge. Both sociologists and political scientists have participated in this development. Eventually it will be possible to apply these techniques at the national and societal levels.

A conceptual model

A conceptual model for contemporary social stratification theory should be highly differentiated —that is, it should be multidimensional. It should also have good measurement techniques for each of its differentiated dimensions and be as free as possible of ideological bias. There seem to be at least two sources of resistance to the adoption of such a model. One source is ideological. There are still sociologists who resist a highly differentiated social stratification model because, for ideological reasons, they want the term "class" to refer to some single, simple, and all-explanatory notion. Such a simplistic approach would be more difficult to sustain in the face of a social stratification model that captured the full complexity of social-stratificational reality. Another source of resistance is connected with methodology and with resources for research. The more differentiated the conceptual model for stratification analysis, the greater the resources needed for research studies and the more difficult such studies are likely to be. Up to now, studies using oversimple stratification models and poor measurement techniques have been made by a number of poorly trained sociologists. Such researchers are now conceptually and technologically obsolete, and, like all workers who see their skills being reduced in value or discarded, they resist new ideas and methods.

It is fundamental that social stratification is multidimensional. Contrary to a view held by some, this is the case not only for contemporary industrial societies but for other types of societies and in other historical periods as well. For example, studies of stratification in Hindu caste society (B. Barber 1968) and in seventeenth-century England (Stone 1965.) demonstrate the necessity of a multidimensional model. But it is not only on empirical grounds that the several dimensions of a multidimensional stratification model are justified. On theoretical grounds, each of the dimensions has to be, and can be, justified in terms of the special and independent functions that the specified dimension plays in society. It is desirable, of course, that the analysis of these special and independent functions be derived from, and integrated in, some systematic general theory about behavior and social systems, rather than constructed *ad hoc*. But this is not always possible. Where it is possible, general theory and social stratification theory are the more fruitful for one another.

To say that the several dimensions of stratification are independent of one another, both theoretically and empirically, does not mean that they are not also interdependent—that is, that they affect one another to some extent and yet retain a measure of autonomy. For example, the dimensions of occupational prestige, power, income, and education are to some extent independent. That is to say, in some measure occupational prestige is respected regardless of the amount of power or income. Contrariwise, power or income may achieve goals despite low occupational prestige. But the different dimensions also affect or limit one another because of their interdependence. A certain level of educational attainment may not be able to express itself without a certain level of income. And a certain level of occupational prestige may find itself ineffective because it does not have a certain amount of power. One of the important tasks for a multidimensional theory is to conduct research that leads to more and more precise statements, probably in quantified form, of the various measures of independence and interdependence that the several dimensions of stratification have in regard to one another.

Both theoretical analysis and empirical research have already made quite clear what some of these multiple dimensions, or independently functional variables, of social stratification are. Though the list below includes the most important of these dimensions, it is not necessarily complete. Nor is the order in which they are listed meant to imply any order of relative importance. In principle, each dimension is as important as every other. In any concrete social situation, of course, one may be more important in the determination of behavior than another, but this greater importance holds only for those specific circumstances.

Some dimensions of social stratification

Power.   One way of defining "power" is as the capacity for achieving goals in social systems. Power in this sense is obviously functional for all social systems, large and small, and for all types of societies. In all social systems, some roles have more power, others less, and the result of this differential distribution is a stratified structure of power. Sometimes an individual's or group's differential capacity for power extends over a broad range of social situations, sometimes over quite a narrow one. The degree of specialization, or division of labor, in a society will affect the typical distribution of these ranges that exists in that society. When power is exercised against the moral feelings of the relevant other actors in a social system, it is perceived by these others as illegitimate; when exercised in accord with such feelings, it is perceived as legitimate, or, as it is usually called, authoritative. Power, legitimate and illegitimate, has a number of different social sources in all societies. Therefore it does not stand in any simple one-to-one relation with any of the other dimensions of social stratification (B. Barber 1957, chapter 4).

Occupational prestige.   The different more or less full-time "productive" roles in a society are of differential functional significance for the society and therefore obtain a higher or a lower evaluation, or amount of prestige. In different societies and in different historical periods, the relative amount of prestige obtained by a specific "productive" role may vary somewhat, though not nearly so much as some ideological views of society have held. This variability is a result of the fact that the same necessary function in a social system—for example, the military function and roles—may be somewhat differently valued according to the different sets of values that prevail in different social systems and at different times. However, since the differences among these sets of values are often much exaggerated for ideological purposes and since even such relatively small differences as do exist have to accommodate themselves in some measure to the necessary functional significance of particular roles, it follows that the same specific "productive" role in different societies usually has much the same prestige everywhere. We have already seen that the results of occupational-prestige studies in 24 societies (all contemporary but representing quite different types) show considerable consensus in the relative evaluation of the same role in societies of different types. We have also seen that research shows the stability over time, at least for the United States, of occupational-prestige ratings for specific occupational roles. Prestige, too, of course, to some extent varies independently of the other dimensions of stratification.

Income or wealth. Different roles in society offer different possibilities for earning income and accumulating capital wealth; so too, different roles have different chances of inheriting wealth. Sometimes, highly prestigious and also powerful roles—for example, religious leaders such as "medicine men" in primitive societies or the Catholic pope in modern society—can earn or accumulate little money in their own right or for their own use. Conversely, sometimes roles of low prestige—for example, bandits or thieves—can accumulate large amounts of capital wealth. In the modern type of society, an example of differential chances for earned income can be seen in a comparison of business with professional "productive" roles. On the whole, and partly because of the differential symbolic significance of money as an indicator of achievement in the two areas, professional roles earn less than business roles of equal relative prestige.

The stratification of income and wealth, whether earned or inherited, has considerable social and economic consequences in partial independence of the other dimensions of social stratification. For example, chances for education may be much influenced by relative income and wealth, so that individuals who occupy roles of the same relative prestige but of differential income may find themselves at an advantage or disadvantage vis-à-vis one another in affording educational opportunities to their children. Differential amounts of disposable income are also important in determining differential access to those "style of life" items that are taken as symbolic, sometimes accurately, sometimes inaccurately, of a given amount of occupational prestige or power or education. This is what Veblen (1899) was concerned with in his discussion of patterns of "conspicuous consumption." Both economists and sociologists have studied the independent significance of disposable income as a dimension of social stratification, but much more study, preferably by the two disciplines jointly, would be valuable.

Education and knowledge. The amount of knowledge that individuals have acquired, either formally, through education, or informally, affects the way in which they behave. As a result of differential amounts and types of education and of other learning experiences, the amount of knowledge is differentially distributed and may be conceived of as forming a stratified structure among the individuals in a society. [*See* KNOWLEDGE, SOCIOLOGY OF.] This dimension of stratification produces effects independently of the other dimensions. For example, in studies of the use of psychotherapeutic facilities and of behavior toward relatives who have been released from mental hospitals, it has been shown that amount and type of education and knowledge is the significant determinant of behavior among people of the same level of occupational prestige or income (Freeman & Simmons 1963).

Religious and ritual purity. In terms of the functionally significant religious ideas that prevail in every society, individuals and groups can be regarded as possessing either more or less religious or ritual purity. In a religiously homogeneous society, of course, there is greater consensus about where individuals and groups should be placed with regard to this dimension of stratification; in religiously heterogeneous societies, there is usually more dissensus. Hindu caste society has probably been the society in which religious and ritual purity have been most important in comparison with the other dimensions and structures of stratification. But even in Hindu society the religious dimension has not been all-important (although some religious and literary ideology has held that it has been), nor is it in any one-to-one relationship with other dimensions (B. Barber 1968). Clearly, this has been even truer of other types of society.

Family and ethnic-group position. In all societies, kinship groups and their extensions in the form of ethnic groups perform important functions: procreation, socialization of children, and provision of moral and psychological support between parents and children and between husbands and wives. Families, because of their varying success in performing these functions and because the other services that they perform for the national and local communities also vary, are differentially evaluated. This evaluation results in a stratification of higher-ranked and lower-ranked families, which in turn has an important and independent influence on the way in which members of particular families treat one another and are treated by others. (For a critical summary of some studies providing evidence on this point, see B. Barber 1961.) Moreover, family and ethnic-group position (where there is ethnic heterogeneity in a society) does not stand in a one-to-one relationship with other dimensions of social stratification.

Local-community status. All but the very simplest societies are subdivided into communities that have special problems for which the contributions of local individuals and families are needed. These individuals and families are given a higher or a lower evaluation in the local community in proportion to their contributions to that community's welfare and quite independently of their evaluation on the other dimensions of social stratification (B. Barber 1961). Differential evaluation of position in the local community is an important determinant of the behavior of self and others in the local community and sometimes of behavior outside it as well, when local-community position becomes known in other local communities or in the society as a whole.

Correlations among rankings

According to the multidimensional approach to social stratification, each individual or group in society is conceived of as ranked along each of the several dimensions of social stratification discussed above, as well as along others. The study of social stratification should therefore involve investigation of the ways in which these different relative rankings are correlated with one another, whether positively or negatively. The rankings may all be highly correlated with one another (all high, all medium, or all low in rank) or much less highly correlated (some high, some medium, and some low in rank). A series of analyses and researches have been undertaken to investigate social stratification in these terms. The task of explaining why the various rankings of groups and individuals are often *not* highly correlated has been called the problem of "status inconsistency." (For useful critical summaries of

past discussion and research and for valuable positive statements of their own, see Anderson & Zelditch 1964; Jackson & Burke 1965.) Two general hypotheses, or propositions, underlie the investigation of this phenomenon. The first is that status inconsistency results in types of behavior different from those caused by status consistency, with each specific pattern of inconsistency having its own specific consequences. Thus, it has been said that in the United States the combination of high occupational prestige and low ethnic position results in political liberalism. Unfortunately, this and other empirical generalizations in the study of status inconsistency have not yet been solidly established. For example, it has also been asserted that Catholics, many of whom experience the status inconsistency of having higher occupational prestige than ethnic position, tend to be politically illiberal. Further empirical work is necessary to arrive at more reliable empirical generalizations about the consequences of specific patterns of status inconsistency.

A second general proposition underlying work on status inconsistency is that there is a tendency toward status equilibration, that is, toward highly positive correlation among the individual's several rankings. This proposition should, however, still be taken as a working hypothesis and not as an established empirical generalization. In our own and other societies, various kinds of status inconsistency have lasted long enough—not only throughout an individual's lifetime but over several generations—to raise a strong doubt: are the social processes that maintain status inconsistency not at least as powerful in principle as, and sometimes more powerful in practice than, the processes that lead to status equilibration? The position of the Jews in most societies, the position of the many high-caste Brahman priests in India with low occupational prestige—these are the kinds of empirical phenomena that raise such a doubt.

In the light of this discussion of the problem of status inconsistency, a number of general points should be made as a basis for further work in this field. First, there is no question that for some individuals in all societies, even relatively simple societies, and for many individuals in some societies, there is considerably less than perfect correlation among their rankings on the several different dimensions of social stratification. Second, apparently there are social processes that are conducive to maintaining this lack of perfect correlation over a long period of time, as well as processes for increasing the degree of status consistency. If hypergamous marriage in caste societies or the marriage of the daughters of the *nouveaux riches* to men of distinguished lineage in modern societies are examples of the latter, then ethnic and so-called racial prejudice is an equally compelling example of the former. Still very much an open and important question for social stratification research is what the various empirical tendencies toward status consistency or inconsistency are in different societies and at different historical times. Third and last, it should be assumed in this research that there is nothing inherently or completely functional about status consistency. It may have its dysfunctions as well as its functions. For example, status consistency may lead to social stagnation as well as to social harmony. Contrariwise, status inconsistency may have its functions as well as its better-known dysfunctions. Those who experience status inconsistency may be the more socially creative and liberal, although they may also have the unhappiness and sense of social injustice that sometimes, although not always, comes from status inconsistency.

The structure of stratification systems

When all the individuals in a society or all their associated solidary kinship groups are ranked along any one of the several dimensions of social stratification, there results a distribution of differential rankings that can be conceived of as having a certain structured shape. Because of the differential distribution of capacities among the members of any society and because of society's need for some measure of hierarchy in the patterning of its authority systems, the rankings tend to show some, and often a considerable, degree of hierarchy, which manifests itself in a tapering toward the top of the various stratification structures. If some tapering is universal, the shape of the rest of the structure is more variable. There seem to be two basic shapes, the pyramid and the diamond. The latter is the typical pattern for modernized societies, where there are strong pressures toward social equality as well as a need for increasing numbers of middle-ranking functionaries. In other types of societies, where the opposite forces prevail, the standard shape of the stratification structures has been more pyramidal, the majority of roles (and therefore the individuals who occupy them) ranking very low. In the modern world, a number of fundamental social and cultural changes are resulting in what seems to be a general trend in all societies toward an increasingly diamond-shaped distribution of roles along many of the dimensions of their social stratification systems. In some cases, aspirations toward this type of stratification structure outrun actual achievement. This leads to much

social unrest as well as to great efforts to make social fact conform to social aspiration.

Stratification and social mobility

Social mobility consists in the movements of individuals up and down along any one or several of the dimensions of social stratification [*see* SOCIAL MOBILITY; *see also* Lipset & Bendix 1959]. Because there are several different dimensions of social stratification in any society, the relative importance of different processes of mobility and also the relative amounts and degrees of mobility will vary in different types of social stratification systems (see B. Barber 1957, chapters 14–16). Any discussion of the processes and amounts of social mobility should always make very clear whether they are occurring within an over-all stratification system that is relatively stable in type or in one that is changing (whether slowly or rapidly) from one basic type to another. Otherwise, the phenomena of individual mobility may be confused with those of basic social structure. For example, in both seventeenth-century England and eighteenth-century France only certain individuals were rising from lower strata into the bourgeoisie and the aristocracy. Contrary to what has sometimes been said, the aristocratic stratum itself was not disappearing, nor was the bourgeois stratum becoming more highly evaluated or more politically powerful than the aristocratic stratum. It was a case of individual mobility in both places, not of basic change in the system of social stratification (on England, see Hexter 1950; on France, see E. G. Barber 1955). With regard to social mobility—as is also true of other dynamic social processes—it is necessary to see that individual processes and basic structural processes are different matters, though not, of course, unrelated.

BERNARD BARBER

[*Directly related are the entries* CASTE; ETHNIC GROUPS; KINSHIP; SOCIAL MOBILITY; STATUS, SOCIAL. *Other relevant material may be found in* MINORITIES; POWER; PREJUDICE; PROFESSIONS; SYSTEMS ANALYSIS, *article on* SOCIAL SYSTEMS; *and in the biographies of* HALBWACHS; MARX; VEBLEN; WEBER, MAX.]

BIBLIOGRAPHY

ANDERSON, Bö; and ZELDITCH, MORRIS 1964 Rank Equilibration and Political Behavior. *Archives européennes de sociologie* 5:112–125.

BARBER, BERNARD 1957 *Social Stratification: A Comparative Analysis of Structure and Process.* New York: Harcourt.

BARBER, BERNARD 1961 Family Status, Local-community Status, and Social Stratification: Three Types of Social Ranking. *Pacific Sociological Review* 4:3–10.

BARBER, BERNARD 1968 Social Mobility in Hindu India. Unpublished manuscript. → To be published by Mouton in James Silverberg (editor), *Social Mobility in the Caste System in India.*

BARBER, BERNARD; and BARBER, ELINOR G. (editors) 1965 *European Social Class: Stability and Change.* New York: Macmillan.

BARBER, ELINOR G. 1955 *The Bourgeoisie in Eighteenth Century France.* Princeton Univ. Press. → A paperback edition was published in 1967.

BENDIX, REINHARD; and LIPSET, SEYMOUR M. (editors) 1966 *Class, Status, and Power: Social Stratification in Comparative Perspective.* 2d ed. New York: Free Press. → The first edition was published in 1953.

DAVIS, KINGSLEY; and MOORE, WILBERT E. (1945) 1966 Some Principles of Stratification. Pages 47–53 in Reinhard Bendix and Seymour M. Lipset (editors), *Class, Status, and Power: Social Stratification in Comparative Perspective.* 2d ed. New York: Free Press. → First published in Volume 10 of the *American Sociological Review.*

FREEMAN, HOWARD E.; and SIMMONS, OZZIE G. 1963 *The Mental Patient Comes Home.* New York and London: Wiley.

HEXTER, J. H. (1950) 1961 The Myth of the Middle Class in Tudor England. Pages 71–116 in J. H. Hexter, *Reappraisals in History: New Views on History and Society in Early Modern Europe.* London: Longmans. → First published in Volume 2 of *Explorations in Entrepreneurial History.*

HODGE, ROBERT W.; SIEGEL, PAUL M.; and ROSSI, PETER H. 1964 Occupational Prestige in the United States, 1925–1963. *American Journal of Sociology* 70:286–302.

HODGE, ROBERT W.; TREIMAN, DONALD J.; and ROSSI, PETER H. 1966 A Comparative Study of Occupational Prestige. Pages 309–334 in Reinhard Bendix and Seymour M. Lipset (editors), *Class, Status, and Power: Social Stratification in Comparative Perspective.* 2d ed. New York: Free Press.

JACKSON, ELTON F.; and BURKE, PETER J. 1965 Status and Symptoms of Stress: Additive and Interaction Effects. *American Sociological Review* 30:556–564.

LIPSET, SEYMOUR M.; and BENDIX, REINHARD 1959 *Social Mobility in Industrial Society.* Berkeley: Univ. of California Press.

NORTH, C. C.; and HATT, P. K. 1949 Jobs and Occupations: A Popular Evaluation. Pages 464–473 in Logan Wilson and W. L. Kolb (editors), *Sociological Analysis: An Introductory Text and Case Book.* New York: Harcourt.

PARSONS, TALCOTT (1949a) 1954 An Analytical Approach to the Theory of Social Stratification. Pages 69–88 in Talcott Parsons, *Essays in Sociological Theory.* Rev. ed. Glencoe, Ill.: Free Press.

PARSONS, TALCOTT (1949b) 1954 Social Classes and Class Conflict in the Light of Recent Sociological Theory. Pages 323–335 in Talcott Parsons, *Essays in Sociological Theory.* Rev. ed. Glencoe, Ill.: Free Press.

PARSONS, TALCOTT 1953 A Revised Analytical Approach to the Theory of Social Stratification. Pages 92–128 in Reinhard Bendix and Seymour M. Lipset (editors), *Class, Status, and Power: A Reader in Social Stratification.* Glencoe, Ill.: Free Press.

PARSONS, TALCOTT 1957 The Distribution of Power in American Society. *World Politics* 10:123–143.

PARSONS, TALCOTT 1963 On the Concept of Political Power. American Philosophical Society, *Proceedings* 107:232–262.

SCHUMPETER, JOSEPH A. (1942) 1950 *Capitalism, Socialism and Democracy.* 3d ed. London: Allen & Unwin; New York: Harper. → A paperback edition was published in 1962 by Harper.

SHIBUTANI, TAMOTSU; and KWAN, K. M. 1965 *Ethnic Stratification: A Comparative Approach.* New York: Macmillan.

STONE, LAWRENCE 1965 *The Crisis of the Aristocracy: 1558–1641.* Oxford: Clarendon.

VEBLEN, THORSTEIN (1899) 1953 *The Theory of the Leisure Class: An Economic Study of Institutions.* Rev. ed. New York: New American Library. → A paperback edition was published in 1959.

II

SOCIAL CLASS

Concern with social class and social stratification is as old as social thought. The ancient Greek philosophers were extremely conscious of the effects of stratification, and propositions about stratification may be found throughout many of the writings of Aristotle and Plato. Thus Aristotle, in discussing the conditions for different types of political organization, suggested in essence that constitutional government—limitation on the powers of the political elite—is most likely to be found in societies with large middle classes, while city-states characterized by large lower classes and small middle and upper classes would be more likely to be governed as dictatorships based on mass support, or as oligarchies. This general approach has been elaborated in contemporary studies of the social requisites of democracy. Plato, in the *Republic*, discussed the conditions for a genuine equalitarian communist society and suggested that the family is the key support of inequality—that is, of social stratification. His argument, which is still followed by many contemporary sociologists, was that individuals are motivated to secure for other family members, for whom they feel affection, any privileges that they themselves enjoy. Hence, in every society there is a built-in pressure to institutionalize inequality by making it hereditary. Plato argued that the only way to create a communist society would be to take children away from their parents and to have the state raise them, so as to eliminate the tendency toward inherited social privilege.

Most of contemporary sociological theory and research on social class, however, does not stem from the Greeks. The emphasis of the Enlightenment on the possibility of social laws and of their discovery through observation and comparative study must be taken as one of the principal methodological breakthroughs. Institutional regularities, such as those governing class, status, and political relationships, became objects of disinterested inquiry as things in themselves, thus reversing the notion, dominant in the Middle Ages, that the temporal sphere was nothing more than an auxiliary part of a supernatural plan, subject to the principles of natural law.

The Enlightenment served to erase the assumptions about hierarchy, class, and intergroup relationships that stemmed from the medieval model of an organic Christian civilization. Thus, the basis was being laid for a science of society.

But it was Karl Marx, more than anyone else, who carried this scientific perspective into the study of social class, even going so far as to derive his idea of class from what he called the scientific laws of history. He then not only accepted the premise that social phenomena possess their own laws, but also set out to discover the underlying variables and how they are expressed under differing historical conditions. Thus, if one were to award the title of father of the study of social class to any individual, it would have to be to Marx. He made class the central aspect of his analysis of society and of his theory of social change. Though most latter-day sociologists have disagreed with many, if not most, of Marx's assumptions about stratification, many of the non-Marxist or anti-Marxist ideas on the subject have come about in reaction to Marx's original formulations.

This does not mean, of course, that there were not other important eighteenth-century and nineteenth-century figures who used stratification concepts in a sophisticated manner. Marx obviously was a child of his times; many of his ideas, sometimes in almost identical form, can be found in the writings of others. The Marxist formulation, laid down in the chapter "Social Classes" in *Capital*, that there are three major economic classes in modern society—landlords receiving rent, capitalists profit, and workers wages—is derived directly from Ricardo's *Principles*, published in 1817, a work that also presented the labor theory of value. Adam Smith's great book, *The Wealth of Nations*, is an important work for the study of stratification, as are other writings of the school of Scottish philosophers of his day. The American founding fathers admitted that all complex societies are stratified and that there is an inherent basis of conflict among groups with diverse economic and class interests. Various American Marxist groups have, in fact, sought to legitimate Marxist doctrine as compatible with classic American thought by pointing to the similarities between the ideas pre-

sented in No. 10 of *The Federalist* and various writings of Marx (see especially De Leon 1889–1913). However, these precursors of Marxism influenced sociology primarily through their influence on Marx himself. It was he who formulated the theory of class so powerfully that he defined the terms of the argument for later sociological thinkers.

Types of theoretical approach

Approaches to the fact of social inequality have differed in the extent to which they emphasize change or stability in social systems. These differences in theoretical orientation have to a considerable extent reflected political differences. Reformists or radicals have seen social inequality and social class differences as sources of social change, which they are inclined to favor. Theorists with more conservative political tastes have justified aspects of the existing order by trying to show the functions performed by hierarchy in all social systems. Concern with social change has generally been associated with interest in social classes, that is, groups within stratified collectivities that are said to act politically as agents of change. Those stressing the functional basis of inequality have been interested in social stratification and in the purposes served by differential rewards, particularly in prestige, to various positions in social systems.

Those using the concept of social class to interpret the dynamics of social change have assumed that the creation of new occupational or economic roles has often resulted in the emergence of groups that initially were outside the traditional hierarchical system. As these new groups attempt to stabilize their position within society, they come into conflict with older, privileged strata whose status, economic resources, or power they challenge. The new groups also often develop sets of values, both secular and religious, that enhance their position by undermining the stability of the prior value system and the structure of privilege it justified. Thus historical change is viewed basically as a consequence of the rise of new classes and the downfall of old ones; it is assumed that complex social systems are inherently unstable and that conflicts stemming from inequality cause pressure for changes in the system.

In contrast, functional theorists have assumed that social systems must be treated as if they were in equilibrium. From this point of view, it is necessary to relate the various attributes of the social hierarchy to the conditions for social stability.

Class, therefore, has been seen by these theorists not as an intervening variable in the process of social change but, rather, as a set of institutions that provide some of the conditions necessary for the operation of a complex society. These conditions, basically, amount to the need for a system of differentiated rewards as a means of institutionalizing the division of labor: differentiation by status and income is posited as a necessary part of the system of motivation required to place individuals in the various positions that must be filled if society is to operate.

The interest of students of social change in why men rebel, why they want change, has led to an emphasis within the tradition of class analysis on the way in which inequality frustrates men and leads them to reject the *status quo*. Functional analysts, on the other hand, are much more concerned with how the social system gets men to conform, to seek and remain in various positions in society, including ones that are poorly rewarded or require onerous work. The former, in other words, often ask how systems of stratification are undermined; the latter seek to know how and why they hold together.

It is important to note that while any analysis of social class must necessarily deal with social stratification as well, these two terms are not synonymous. Theories of social class refer to the conditions affecting the existence of strata that have developed or should develop some "consciousness of kind," that is, some sense of existence as a group attribute of society. Stratification refers to the entire complex of hierarchical differentiation, whether group-related or not. Although this article is about social class, much of the discussion in it will involve stratification, since it is impossible to account for the way in which social classes are formed, change, and affect other aspects of society without referring to stratification systems as such.

I have distinguished two polar traditions of social thought that do not, of course, occur in pure form in real life. Marx, the foremost student of class and social change and the advocate, par excellence, of instability and revolution, was also aware of the functional aspects of social stratification. Many of his writings attempt to show how ideologies, values, and patterns of behavior—all at different class levels—serve to maintain the stability of the social order. In fact, Marxian analysis is replete with functional propositions.

The functionalists, on the other hand, are of course aware that change and conflict occur and that men not only accept but also reject the given stratification system. Thus (as is noted in more detail below) the most influential stimulator of functional thought in sociology, Émile Durkheim, sought to show the way in which strains in value emphases within the same system lead individuals and groups to reject the dominant value system and to deviate from expected forms of behavior. Where Marx saw alienation as inherent in social inequality, Durkheim suggested that anomie, or rulelessness, is endemic in all complex social systems. [*See* INTEGRATION, *article on* SOCIAL INTEGRATION.]

To see the way these concerns with stability and change, with alienation, and with the formation of class sentiments have evolved in modern social thought, it is necessary to turn to an examination of the work of some of the key theorists, particularly Marx, Weber, and Durkheim.

The Marxist theory of class

Marxist sociology starts from the premise that the primary function of social organization is the satisfaction of basic human needs—food, clothing, and shelter. Hence, the productive system is the nucleus around which other elements of society are organized. Contemporary sociology has reversed this emphasis by stressing the distribution system, the stratification components of which are status and prestige. To Marx, however, distribution is a dependent function of production.

Stemming from the assumption of the primacy of production is the Marxist definition of class: any aggregate of persons who play the same part in the production mechanism. Marx, in *Capital*, outlined three main classes, differentiated according to relations to the means of production: (1) *capitalists*, or owners of the means of production; (2) *workers*, or all those who are employed by others; (3) *landowners*, who in Marx's theory seemingly differ from capitalists and are regarded as survivors of feudalism ([1867–1879] 1925–1926, vol. 3, pp. 862–863). From Marx's various historical writings, it is clear that he had a more complex view than this of the hierarchical reality and that he realized, for instance, that there is differentiation within each of these basic categories. Thus, the small businessmen, or petty bourgeoisie, were perceived as a transitional class, a group that will be pressed by economic tendencies inherent in capitalism to bifurcate into those who descend to the working class and those who so improve their circumstances that they become significant capitalists.

Although Marx differentiated classes in objective terms, his primary interest was in understanding and facilitating the emergence of class consciousness among the depressed strata. He wished to see created among them a sense of identical class interests, as a basis for conflict with the dominant class. The fact that a group held a number of objective characteristics in common but did not have the means of reaching organized class consciousness meant for Marx that it could not play the role of a historically significant class. Thus, he noted in "The Eighteenth Brumaire of Louis Bonaparte" that the French peasants of that period possessed many attributes that implied a common class situation:

The small-holding peasants form a vast mass, the members of which live in similar conditions, but without entering into manifold relations with one another. Their mode of production isolates them from one another, instead of bringing them into mutual intercourse. The isolation is increased by France's bad means of communication and by the poverty of the peasants. . . . In so far as millions of families live under economic conditions of existence that separate their mode of life, their interests and their culture from those of other classes, and put them in hostile opposition to the latter, they form a class. In so far as there is merely a local interconnection among these small-holding peasants, and the identity of their interests begets no community, no national bond and no political organization among them, they do not form a class. (Marx [1852] 1962, p. 334)

Nikolai Bukharin, one of the leading theoreticians of the Russian Communist party, who was more concerned with sociological theory and research than any other major Marxist figure, attempted to formalize the differences among the workers, the peasants, and the lumpenproletariat (unattached laborers), making the workers a class and the other two not classes. His analysis, based on the events of the early decades of the twentieth century, was elaborated beyond that of Marx (see Table 1).

Table 1 — Bukharin's analysis of class conditions

Class properties	Peasantry	Lumpen-proletariat	Proletariat
1. Economic exploitation	+	−	+
2. Political oppression	+	+	+
3. Poverty	+	+	+
4. Productivity	+	−	+
5. Freedom from private property	−	+	+
6. Condition of union in production, and common labor	−	−	+

Source: Bukharin (1921) 1965, p. 289.

The working class is exploited by a visible common oppressor, is brought together by conditions of work that encourage the spread of ideas and organization among them, and remains in a structured conflict situation with its employers over wages and working conditions. Consequently, over time it can become a conscious class.

Marx, however, did not really anticipate a high correlation between objective class position and subjective revolutionary class consciousness until the point at which the social system in question broke down: if there was to be total class consciousness in any given society, then by definition it would be in the midst of revolution. In normal times, structural factors press deprived strata to become conscious, but the inherent strength of the ruling class prevents class consciousness. The dominant class possesses social legitimacy, controls the media of communication, is supported by the various mechanisms of socialization and social control, such as the school and the church, and, during its period of stability is able to "buy off" those inclined to lead or participate in opposition movements. The Marxist term that characterizes the attitudes of the lower class in the period of the predominance of the other classes is "false consciousness."

Marx was not very concerned with analyzing the behavior of the capitalist upper class. Basically, he assumed that the powerful parts of such a class must be self-conscious and that the state as a vehicle of power necessarily serves the interests of the dominant class in the long run. But more important to Marx than the sociology of the privileged class was that of the workers; the important question for research and action concerned the factors that would bring about working-class consciousness.

The dilemma of the Marxist theory of class is also the dilemma of every other single-variable theory. We can locate a class member objectively, but this may tell us little about the subjective correlates (social outlook, attitudes, etc.) of class position. Marx never actually said that at any given point in history or for any individual there would necessarily have to be a relationship between class position and the attitudes of class members. He did believe, however, that common conditions of existence create the necessary base for the development of common class attitudes, but that at any point in time, sharp discrepancies may exist between class position and class attitudes or behavior. Marx attempted to deal with this problem by his theory of transitional stages in the development of class. The first stage, in which a class is a class "in itself" (the German *an sich*), occurs when the class members do not understand their class position, the controls over them, or their "true class interests." The proletariat, insofar as it is simply fighting for higher wages without recognizing that this is part of a necessary class struggle between themselves and the bourgeoisie that will end in the victory of one or the other, is a class *an sich*. In ideal-type terms the opposite of the class in itself is the class "for itself" (*für sich*). The class *für sich* is a self-conscious class, a large proportion of whose members consciously identify with it and think in terms of the class's struggle with another class. As long as most persons in a lower class think in *an sich* terms, the behavior of class members will be characterized by intraclass competition in which individual members of the class strive to get ahead of other members. In such a period, class conflict will be weak. Only when *für sich* attitudes develop does the class struggle really emerge. Members of a lower class who do not yet identify with their class are, according to Marx, thinking in terms of values or concepts that are functional for the stability of the position of the dominant class. Any individual, therefore, though objectively a member of the lower class, may subjectively be identified with or may be acting in ways which correspond to the position of another class. At different periods varying portions of an underprivileged population may be either *an sich* or *für sich*. One of the purposes of Marxist analysis is the investigation of this discrepancy. In discussing the rise of the bourgeoisie, Marx suggested that the period during which the bourgeoisie was a class *an sich* was longer and required greater effort than the period during which it became self-conscious and took political class action to overthrow feudalism and monarchy ([1847] 1963, pp. 146–147). Implicit in this discussion of the development of the bourgeois class is the idea that the emergence of self-consciousness among the workers will also take a long time. Marx in fact suggested "making a precise study of strikes, combinations and other forms of class activity" in order to find out how the proletariat organizes itself as a class (*ibid.*, p. 147).

Alienation. A key element in the Marxist sociology of the exploited is the concept of alienation. Men are distinguished from animals—are, in fact, less animal and more human—insofar as they become increasingly self-conscious about and freely selective of their work and conditions of life. Insofar as men do not freely choose their work but, rather, do whatever tasks are set before them, simply in order to exist, they remain in a less than human state. If work (or leisure) is imposed on man, so far from being free, he is objectively exploited and alienated from the truly human, that is, autonomous, condition (Marx 1844, pp. 120–134 in the 1964 edition).

Alienation, for Marx, is an objective, not a sub-jective, condition. It signifies lack of autonomy, of self-control. The fact that workers may say that they like their work or social conditions does not mean that they are free actors, even if they think they are. Thus, in a slave society the fact that some slaves may have believed that they preferred to be slaves, and even that they were better off as slaves than as freed men, did not change the fact that objectively they were slaves. Similarly, the fact that a wage worker likes his conditions of work does not affect his position of being alienated and economically exploited or his potential as a free human being. In this sense, class society is akin to slavery. Class society must produce alienated individuals who are distorted, partial people. Marx therefore sought to document the facts about alienation and to understand the conditions under which estrangement, resentment, and, ultimately, political class consciousness would arise. Both class and alienation, he thought, would be eliminated by ending the private ownership of the means of production, for as long as people are working for others, they do not have conscious control over their life space and therefore are not truly human. Fully human society would come about when the production system could produce abundance in an absolute sense, when the machines produced enough food, clothing, and shelter for all men and to have as much as they needed, so that they could then devote themselves not to fighting over the scarce fruits of production but to fostering the activities of the mind. In essence, he was arguing that all class societies were prehuman and that class must disappear. [*See* ALIENATION.]

The Weberian approach to stratification

While Marx placed almost exclusive emphasis on economic factors as determinants of social class, Weber suggested that economic interests should be seen as a special case of the larger category of "values," which included many things that are neither economic nor interests in the ordinary sense of the term. For Weber, the Marxist model, although a source of fruitful hypotheses, was too simple to handle the complexity of stratification. He therefore sought to differentiate among the various sources of hierarchical differentiation and potential cleavage. The two most important sets of hierarchies for Weber were class and status ([1906–1924] 1946, pp. 180–195).

Class. Weber reserved the concept of class for economically determined stratification. He defined a class as being composed of people who have life chances in common, as determined by their power to dispose of goods and skills for the sake of income. Property is a class asset, but it is not the only criterion of class. For Weber, the crucial aspect of a class situation is, ultimately, the market situation.

The existence of large groups of people who can be located in a common class situation need not produce communal or societal action—that is, conscious, interest-determined activity—although it should produce *similar* reactions in the sense that those in the same class situation should exhibit similar behavior and attitudes without having a sense of class consciousness. These similarities, such as patterns of voting behavior or of drinking habits, reflect the effect of variations in life chances among the classes.

Weber, like Marx, was concerned with the conditions under which class consciousness arises. For him, however, there was no single form of class consciousness. Rather, which groups develop a consciousness of common interests opposed to those of another group is a specific empirical question; different groups acquire historical significance at different times and in different places. The extent of consciousness of kind depends to a considerable degree on the general culture of a society, particularly the sets of intellectual ideas current within it. Concepts or values that might foster or inhibit the emergence of class-conscious groups cannot be derived solely from knowledge about the objective economic structure of a society. The existence of different strata subjected to variations in life chances does not necessarily lead to class action. The causal relationship posited by Marx between the fact of group inferiority and other aspects of the structure that might be changed by action had to be demonstrated to people; consciousness of it need not develop spontaneously. The presence or absence of such consciousness is not, of course, a fortuitous matter. The extent to which ideas emerge pointing to a causal relationship between class position and other social conditions is linked to the transparency of the relationship—that is, to how obvious it is that one class will benefit by action directed against another.

An examination of the history of class struggles suggested to Weber that conflicts between creditors and debtors are perhaps the most visible form of conflict flowing from economic differentiation. The conflict between employers and workers is also highly visible under capitalism, but it is essentially a special case of the economic struggle between buyers and sellers, a form of interest tension normal within a capitalist market economy. It involves an act of creative imagination and perception to develop the idea that the tension between employer and worker requires an attack on the entire system of private ownership through the common action of all workers against the capitalist class. Such an act is much more likely to come from the intellectuals, who thereby present the workers with an ideological formula, than from the workers themselves. In this respect, Weber came to conclusions similar to those drawn by Lenin, who also argued that workers by themselves could only reach the stage of economism, of trade union consciousness—that is, of conflict with their employers over wages and working conditions. For Lenin, as for Weber, the emergence of revolutionary class consciousness requires leadership, much of which would be drawn from other strata—in Lenin's case, the elite or vanguard party (Lenin 1902). Weber explicitly formalized the conditions that facilitate the emergence of class consciousness in terms that incorporated the principal elements of the Marxist scheme almost intact, although he made the significant and important addition of common status:

Organized activity of class groups is favoured by the following circumstances: (a) the possibility of concentrating on opponents where the immediate conflict of interests is vital. Thus workers organize against management and not against security holders who are the ones who really draw income without working. . . . (b) The existence of a class status which is typically similar for large masses of people. (c) The technical possibility of being easily brought together. This is particularly true where large numbers work together in a small area, as in the modern factory. (d) Leadership directed to readily understandable goals. Such goals are very generally imposed or at least are interpreted by persons, such as intelligentsia, who do not belong to the class in question. (1922, pp. 427–428 in the 1947 edition)

Weber's condition (a) is essentially a rephrasing of Marx's antagonism factor, though Weber made a distinction, not made by Marx, concerning the direction of the antagonism—in this case, toward the visible overseer. Condition (b) was never explicitly discussed by Marx. Condition (c) is borrowed directly from Marx. As for condition (d), in Marx's works it appears as the role of the party, although Marx never faced up to the problems that arise when a workers' party has a middle-class leadership.

Status. The second major dimension of stratification, status, refers to the quality of perceived interaction. Status was defined by Weber as the positive or negative estimation of honor, or prestige, received by individuals or positions. Thus it involves the felt perceptions of people. Those in a similar status position tend to see themselves as located in a comparable position on the social hierarchy. Since status involves perception of how much one is valued by others, men value it more than economic gain.

Weber argued that since status is manifest, consciousness of kind is more likely to be linked to status differentiation than to class. In other words, those who are in a higher or lower status group are prone to support status-enhancing activities, whether or not these activities can be classed as political. Those groups with high status will be motivated to support values and institutions that seemingly serve to perpetuate their status. Weber regarded economic class as important primarily because it is perceived as a cause of status. Since it is usually easier to make or lose money than it is to gain or lose status, those in privileged status positions seek to dissociate status from class, that is, to urge that status reflects factors such as family origin, manners, education, and the like—attributes that are more difficult to attain or lose than economic wealth.

There is, of course, as Weber pointed out, a strong correlation between status and class positions. However, once a group has attained high status through given achievements, its members try to limit the chances that others will replace them. And this is often done by seeking to deny the original source of individual or family status. The economic and class orders are essentially universalistic and achievement-oriented. Those who get, are. He who secures more money is more important than he who has less. The status order, on the other hand, tends to be particularistic and ascriptive. It involves the assumption that high status reflects aspects of the system that are unachievable. Thus it operates to inhibit social mobility, up or down. Weber, in his writings on status, echoed the functional analysis of the role of style presented by Veblen (1899). For Weber, as for Veblen, the function of conspicuous consumption—that is, of emphasis on pragmatically useless styles of consumption that take many years to learn—was to prevent mobility and to institutionalize the privileges of those who had risen to the top in previous years or epochs. Status groups are therefore identifiable by specific styles of life. Even though the original source of status was economic achievement, a status system, once in existence, operates independently of the class system and even seeks to negate its values. This, as Weber and Veblen both suggested, explains the seemingly surprising phenomenon that even in an industrial capitalist society, money-making is considered vulgar by many in privileged positions, and the children of those who have made money are frequently to be found in noncommercial activities.

Class relations and status relations. The distinction between class and status is also reflected in the different nature of the key set of interactions that characterizes each. Class relations are defined by interaction among unequals in a market situation; status is determined primarily by relations with equals, even though there are many status contacts among unequals. The sanctions, in the case of status, are greater when violating the norms for relations with equals than those for relations with unequals.

One value of differentiating between class and status is that while these two dimensions of stratification are correlated, there are many cases in which they are discrepant. Thus individuals or groups may be higher in status than in class, or vice versa. Weber argued that such discrepancies are important aids to understanding the dynamics of social change and of conflict; he detected an inherent strain between the norms of the market and those of status systems. Markets are the dynamic source of tension for modern industrial society. Success or failure in the market constantly upsets the relative position of groups and individuals: groups high in status and wealth often lose their relative economic position because of market innovations, failure to adjust to change, and the like, while others rise suddenly on the scale of wealth. Those who had status and its frequent concomitant, legitimate access to political authority, exert their influence and power against the *nouveaux riches*. For example, a common interpretation of the behavior of the French bourgeoisie during the Revolution of 1789 is that they had not pressed for economic rights and power because they already possessed all they needed. Rather, they had wanted to force the monarchy and aristocracy to accord them high status. Similarly, Weber's disciple Robert Michels suggested that the political radicalism of many quite wealthy European Jews before World War I was a consequence of their having been denied a status position commensurate with their class level in society (1911, pp. 260–261 in the 1915 edition).

Social structure and political conflict. An industrial society characterized by an elaborate, highly institutionalized status structure *combined* with the class tensions usually found in industrial societies is more likely to exhibit class-conscious politics than is one in which status lines are imprecise and not formally recognized. It has therefore been argued that Marxist, class-conscious parties have been stronger in societies, like the Wilhelmine Germany in which Weber lived most of his life, that maintain a very visible and fairly rigid status system derived from preindustrial society than in class societies, such as the United States, that lack a feudal tradition of estates. Moreover, insofar as the dynamics of a successful industrial society undermine the ascriptive status mechanisms inherited from the feudal precapitalist order, the amount of political conflict arising from class consciousness is reduced. Hence it would seem to follow from Weber's analysis that the growth of industrial capitalism, and the consequent imposition on the stratification system of capitalism's emphases on achievement and universalism, weaken rather than increase class-linked consciousness of kind.

This thesis of Weber's that stresses the consequences of structural changes on class relationships has been paralleled by T. H. Marshall's analysis of the relationship between citizenship and social class (1934–1962, pp. 71–134 in the 1965 edition). Citizenship, for Marshall, is a status that involves access to various rights and powers. In premodern times citizenship was limited to a small elite; social development in European states has consisted to a considerable extent in admitting new social strata—first the bourgeoisie and later the workers—to the status of citizen. The concept of the citizen that arose with the emergence of the bourgeoisie in the eighteenth century involved a claim to universalistic rights in the status order, as well as the political one. Marshall has suggested that class-conscious ideologies of the extreme sort are characteristic of new strata, such as the bourgeoisie or the working class, as they fight for the right to full social and political participation—that is, for citizenship. As long as they are denied citizenship, sizable segments of these classes endorse revolutionary ideologies. In turn, older strata and institutions seeking to preserve their ancient monopolies of power and status foster extreme, conservative doctrines.

From this point of view, the history of political ideologies in democratic countries can be written in terms of the emergence of new social strata and their eventual integration into society and the polity. In Europe, the struggle for such integration took the form of defining a place in the polity for the business strata and the working class alongside the preindustrial upper classes and the church. Unless class conflicts overlapped with continuing controversies concerning the place of religion, as they did in Latin Europe, or concerning the status

of the traditional upper strata, as they did in Germany, intense ideological controversy declined soon after the new strata gained full citizenship rights.

Power, status, and bureaucracy. Power, which in the Marxist analysis derives from class position, is a much more complex phenomenon in the Weberian model. Weber defined power as the chance of a man or group to realize their will even against the opposition of others. Power may be a function of resources possessed in the economic, status, and political systems; both status and class are power resources. Since men want higher status, they tend to try to orient their behavior to that approved by those with the higher status which they value. Power resources can also be found in institutions that command the allegiance of people—religions, parties, trade unions, and the like. Anyone with followers or, like the military, with control of force, may have access to power. In large measure, the relative weight of different power resources is determined by the rules of the political game, whatever these may be in different societies. The structure of legal authority and its degree of legitimacy influence the way in which power is secured.

For Weber, the key source of power in modern society is *not* to be found in the ownership of the means of production. Rather, the increased complexity of modern industrial society leads to the development of vast bureaucracies that become increasingly interconnected and interdependent. The modern state, with its monopoly of arms and administration, becomes the dominant institution in bureaucratized society. Because of the increasing complexity of operating modern social institutions, even economic institutions are brought into a close, dependent relationship with the administrative and military bureaucracies of the state. Increasingly, therefore, as all social institutions become more bureaucratized and the centralized state gains control of other social institutions, the key power resources become rigidly hierarchical large-scale bureaucracies.

Bureaucratization and alienation. This concern with bureaucracy as the key hierarchical power-related structure of the stratification system of industrial society (whether the society is formally capitalist or socialist is irrelevant) led Weber to formulate a source of alienation very different from that of Marx. For Weber, it was not only the wage worker who becomes alienated through his lack of control over his human needs; the bureaucrat is even more subject to obsessive demands. Bureaucracy, in fact, has an inherent tendency to destroy men's autonomy. It is characterized by formalism and it involves, in Weber's terms: (1) subordination; (2) expertise (and hence a rigid division of labor); (3) obeying fixed rules ([1906–1924] 1946, pp. 196–198). Even members of small, nonbureaucratic structures have their freedom reduced if these structures are involved with bureaucracies. In this conclusion, Weber agreed with Marx. However, for Weber the key depersonalizing element is the expectation that the bureaucrat will give absolute loyalty to the organization. Loyalty within a bureaucracy is impersonal; no personal attachments are supposed to interfere with the functioning of the system. Thus the depersonalization of loyalty became the equivalent of what Marx called the alienation of man from his labor. Weber argued that, as a social mechanism, bureaucracy assumes absolute discipline and a high level of predictability. People in bureaucracies fulfill role requirements rather than their personal desires. Rational action in bureaucracies is not an end in itself but, rather, an aspect of the structure of social interaction. Individuals both judge others and interact on the basis of universalistic norms; personal motives are not considered. The bureaucratic structure functions for its own ends, not those of the people within it. In theory, all individuals in bureaucracies are expendable and only positions are important.

Preparation for a bureaucratic career involves increasing conformity. Bureaucracy requires that individuals become highly specialized. Success depends on the individual's ability to conform. As one enters a bureaucracy, he loses much of his freedom to change his life alternatives. He becomes highly specialized and therefore cannot move from one firm or type of job to another. Such specialization, such conformity to narrow role requirements—to the needs of the "machine"—means dehumanization, or alienation from true human choice.

The alienation inherent in bureaucracy is, for Weber, independent of the system of property relations. Socialism means more rather than less alienation, because it involves greater bureaucratization. There is little difference between capitalist and socialist societies in their class relations and their propensity to alienation. The source of alienation lies in bureaucracy, which is inherent in industrial society.

The growth of bureaucratization also has the effect of separating work roles from other activities, with socially destructive consequences. An individual within a bureaucracy has to conform to efficiency rules, production standards, and other impersonal goals that have no meaning in his life outside work, since they are the bureaucracy's goals, not his; he conforms to them while at work, but gets no guidance as to how to behave in other activities. Weber can be interpreted as having believed that the nonbureaucratic part of life was becoming increasingly normless while bureaucratic structures were becoming increasingly normative. As social institutions become more bureaucratized, individuals learn how to behave within bureaucracies but not outside of them.

In a sense, Weber raised Marx's ideas about the nature and consequences of stratification to a higher order of generalization. Marx's conclusions were based mainly on his analysis of social relations under capitalism; this analysis presupposed a social system in which the fruits of production were scarce and control over the means of production was inequitably distributed. Weber, by using more general analytical categories, sought to deal with issues that cut through all complex social systems. Thus he characterized every complex system according to the distribution of economic and honorific life chances in it. While Marx stressed that social stratification is a result of economic scarcity, Weber emphasized that honor and prestige are themselves scarce: economic goods could increase, and everyone could gain in an absolute sense, but, since prestige is determined by relative ranking, if one went up, another went down. The latter form of stratification involves a zero-sum game, and consequently occasions continual tensions in any society with unrestricted social mobility.

Alienation also is presented as a broader category in Weber's work than in that of Marx. Basically, alienation from self involves compulsive conformity to norms: the alienated individual is role-bound. Since such compulsive conformity is inherent in bureaucracy, which Weber saw as the dynamic element in modern society, he was much more pessimistic about the future of society than was Marx.

Much of contemporary writing by intellectuals and social scientists about alienation is derived more from Weber than from Marx. For instance, the ideas advanced by Erich Fromm, David Riesman, William H. Whyte, Robert K. Merton, Arnold Green, and C. Wright Mills concerning the "bureaucratic," "marketeer," or "other-directed" personality, the "organization man," and, in general, the individual who seeks to get ahead by selling his personality, are all related to the effects of bureaucracy on individuals. Weber is the intellectual father of these and all similar discussions. His ideas, therefore, constitute not only a contribution to sociological analysis but also a basic source for the moral criticism of society. They usually have not been perceived as such because Weber's empirical conclusion, that all complex societies will be both stratified and alienative, leads to no positive moral solution. This is because for Weber (as for C. Wright Mills), the only society that really makes individual autonomy possible is the nonbureaucratized society of small producers, and societies of this type are rapidly vanishing.

Functionalist approaches

Although the ideas generated by Marx and Weber remain the most fruitful sources of theory on social stratification, much of contemporary sociology accepts the so-called functionalist approach to the subject. This approach is associated with the names of Émile Durkheim, Kingsley Davis, Talcott Parsons, and Robert K. Merton.

Durkheim and subsequent functionalists have assumed that since modern society has a complex and highly differentiated system of roles, which must be performed, different men must be motivated to perform different roles (Durkheim 1893). They see man as a social animal whose needs are not primarily physical and satiable but, rather, culturally determined and potentially unlimited. However, if all individuals had the same set of unlimited desires, no complex social structure would be possible. Consequently, some social or moral force must shape and limit these potentially unlimited desires. Society prescribes varying goals for different individuals and groups, sets limits on these goals, and prescribes the means that may legitimately be used to attain them.

In analyzing the function of stratification, functionalists see it as the mechanism through which society encourages men to seek to achieve the diverse positions necessary in a complex social system. The vast variety of positions that must be filled differ in their requirements for skill, education, intelligence, commitment to work, willingness to exercise power resources against others, and the like. Functionalist theory posits that in an unstratified society—that is, one in which rewards are relatively equal for all tasks—those positions which require more work, postponement of gratification, greater anxiety, and the like will not be filled by the most able people. The stratification system is perceived, therefore, as a motivation system; it is society's mechanism for encouraging the most able people to perform the most demanding roles in order to have the society operate efficiently.

The theory also suggests that status—honorific prestige—is the most general and persistent form of stratification because what human beings as social animals most require to satisfy their ego needs is recognition from others. Beyond a certain point, economic rewards and power are valued, not for themselves but because economic or power positions are symbolic indicators of high status. Hence, the functionalist school of stratification agrees with Weber that stratification, or differential hierarchical reward, is an inherent aspect of complex society and that status as a source of motivation is inherently a scarce resource.

The emphasis in functional analysis on the need for hierarchical differentiation does not, of course, explain how men evaluate different individuals in the stratification system. Parsons has pointed to three sets of characteristics which are used as a basis of ranking. These are *possessions*, or those attributes which people own; *qualities*, belonging to individuals and including traits that are ascribed, such as race, lineage, or sex, or that are attributed as permanent characteristics, such as a specific ability; and *performances*, or evaluations of the ways in which individuals have fulfilled their roles—in short, judgments about achievements. Societies, according to Parsons, vary considerably in the degree to which their central value systems emphasize possessions, qualities, or performances in locating people on the social hierarchy. Thus, ideally, a feudal social system stresses ascribed qualities, a capitalist society emphasizes possessions, and a pure communist system would assign prestige according to performance. Parsons has stated that no actual society has ever come close to any of these three "ideal-type" models; each society has included elements of all three. However, the variation in the core ideal value does inform the nature of the stratification system, patterns of mobility, and the like (1953).

If we assume, as most functionalists do, that the function of stratification is to act as a system of role allocation, then it follows that a key requisite for an operating social system is a relatively stable system of social rankings. That is, there must be consensus in a society about what sorts of activities and symbols are valued; without such consensus, the society could not operate. Given this assumption, an ongoing system of stratification requires a general set of ideological justifications. There must be various mechanisms which explain, justify, and propagate the system of inequality, and which cause men to accept as legitimate the fact of their own inequality. From an ideal-typical point of view, a system of stratification that is stable would set for various groups within societies goals that could be achieved by all within each group. Feudal societies, which theoretically separate the population from birth into distinct hierarchical strata which cannot be crossed, but within which men may succeed and gain social recognition for doing a good job, represent perhaps the extreme form of stratification as something that adjusts men to the needs of society. Theoretically, in a society in which individuals were socialized to accept attainable positions as the proper and necessary fulfillment of their role in life, men would feel "free" and satisfied. The sense of freedom, of being one's own master and of achieving what one thinks one wants to achieve, exists only where the means–ends relationship defined by society is stable—that is, where men do in fact get what they have been taught to want.

But it is extremely doubtful whether any such system of balanced means–ends relationships within a stratification system ever existed or could exist. The assumption that individuals seek to maximize the esteem in which they are held implies that those who are in low-valued positions are subject to punishment. To be valued negatively means to be told that one is no good, that one is bad. Consequently, it may be argued that there is an inherent tension between the need to maximize esteem and the requirements of a stratification system.

In actual stratification systems, this tension appears to be alleviated by various transvaluational mechanisms. That is, there seems in all societies to be a reverse stratification system, the most enduring form of which is usually found in religion. Inherent in many religions is the belief that wealth and power are associated with sin and evil, while virtue is associated with poverty. Christianity and Hinduism, for example, both posit that righteousness will somehow be rewarded in the hereafter, so that the virtuous poor will ultimately be able to look down upon the wicked rich. This mechanism, which holds out the hope of subsequent reward for adhering to the morality of the present, does not, of course, challenge the existing secular distribution of privilege. It does, however, reflect the inherent tension within stratified society: that there is both acceptance and rejection of the value system by the underprivileged. [See MILLENARISM.]

Durkheim and functionalist theory. Durkheim assumed that preindustrial society had been reasonably stable in that it had prescribed different sets of goals for different strata. He assumed that the lowly in feudal society had not resented not being high and that feudalism had been so organized that a man could and did obtain a sense of self-respect within his own group. Industrial society, he thought, is quite different. Society no longer provides the individual with definitions of means and ends that allow him to attain the goals his society defines as worthwhile. A highly integrated normative order such as feudalism had provided everyone with the possibility of feeling that his life was meaningful and successful within a given castelike stratum. In modern society, however, wealth and power become ends in themselves, and most people, unable to attain high prestige, find their own lives in conflict with social norms. Such conflict of norms leads to anomie, the breakdown of normative order, which becomes a chronic condition in industrial society ([1897] 1951, pp. 246–257).

Industrial society prescribes universalistic goals in monetary or bureaucratic terms. Since the norms of the market place and the bureaucracy prescribe common orientations and similar goals for all, it is inevitable that many men will experience life as failure. For Durkheim, the weakness of the stratification system of industrial society is that, basically, it encourages only one set of values, those involving individual success. This pressure on the individual to achieve results produces anomie— Durkheim's equivalent of alienation. The higher rate of suicide in industrial as compared with traditional society was, in part, explained by Durkheim in these terms. The individual no longer has the sense of being socially integrated that was possible in a *Gemeinschaft* society, that is, one with a strong set of closely related means and ends linked to the religious system. The individual does not have the means to achieve the universalistic goals set by modern society, and the society's normative order does not support him in his daily life, guide his activities, or give him a sense that his life is worthwhile. When the normative structure collapses, when individuals lose their sense of being involved in meaningful means–ends relationships, many break down, engage in obsessive behavior, and lose their ability to relate to achievable goals, and some commit suicide [see SUICIDE, *article on* SOCIAL ASPECTS].

The key to understanding Durkheim's contribution to the discussion of alienation and stratification is his emphasis on a stable society as a prerequisite for an integrated personality. The absence of an established harmony of means and ends, far from producing freedom, produces, according to Durkheim, resentment and apathy—the war of each against all. Durkheim's theory therefore leads to the ironic conclusion that people should feel freest in a closed, integrated system in which they have little choice of occupation or opportunity for social mobility, while in an open, universalistic system they should feel coerced, de-humanized, estranged. In the latter case it follows that they will also experience a need to, in Erich Fromm's words, "escape from freedom." Society's emphasis on success thus becomes the principal source of alienation.

Durkheim's analysis of anomie ties into Weber's discussion of the alienative properties of bureaucracy, for, as Fromm, Merton, Riesman, and others have pointed out, to succeed in a bureaucratic society, one must not simply conform to a work role—one must sell one's personality to one's superiors. This implies that the rules for success are often very imprecise and hence create confusion about means and ends.

Anomie, social change, and rebellion. Durkheim's account of what Merton has called the "seeming contradictions between cultural goals and socially restricted access to these goals" ([1949] 1957, p. 123) is a key aspect of the theory of social change that is inherent in Durkheimian functionalism. Since no complex society can achieve a complete balance between its emphases on ends and means, stratification systems always generate pressure on individuals and strata to deviate systematically from the cultural prescriptions of the society, and hence they foster social change. As Merton put it:

The distribution of statuses through competition must be so organized that positive incentives for adherence to status obligations are provided for *every position* within the distributive order. Otherwise, as will soon become plain, aberrant behavior ensues. It is, indeed, my central hypothesis that aberrant behavior may be regarded sociologically as a symptom of dissociation between culturally prescribed aspirations and socially structured avenues for realizing these aspirations. (*ibid.*, p. 134)

The outcome of the possible relations between approved goals and prescribed means has been analyzed in detail by Merton (*ibid.*, chapter 4) and by numerous other writers [see ALIENATION; INTEGRATION; SOCIAL MOBILITY; VALUES]. These relations create a variety of strains fostering change. Thus innovation in the means of getting ahead occurs among those who feel strongly the culturally prescribed mandate to succeed but lack such culturally approved means to do so as access to capital, skills, education, and proper ascribed background characteristics. Innovation may have positive and negative consequences from the point of view of society. On the positive side is the effort to get ahead by "building a better mousetrap," that is, by providing services that did not exist before, such as credit buying, which was first diffused by Jewish

businessmen. On the negative side are the forms of innovation that are regarded as illegitimate. As Bell has pointed out, organized crime has constituted a major avenue of mobility in American life (1960, pp. 115–136). Minority ethnic groups and those of recent immigrant stock have contributed disproportionately to the ranks of professional criminals.

While Merton has elaborated on the sources of social and individual tensions in this area, more pertinent here is his emphasis that such tensions may also produce rebellion. Rebellion by the lower strata, he has argued, may be viewed as an adaptive response called for when the existing social system is seen as an obstacle to the satisfaction of legitimate needs and wants. In means–ends terms, rebellion involves the establishment of a new set of goals which are attractive to those who feel themselves "outcasts" in the existing system. When rebellion is not a generalized response but is limited to relatively powerless groups, it can lead to the formation of subgroups alienated from the rest of the community but united among themselves. Of course, rebellion may also take a political form in an effort to overthrow the existing society and replace it with one that stresses other values.

Emphasis on these and allied sources of rebellion advances the study of alienation and prospective lower-class rebellion beyond the concern with objective social inferiority and economic exploitation. The study of values in this context helps to explain the phenomenon that many quite poverty-stricken strata in different countries do not rebel and are often even conservative conformists, while other, relatively affluent strata, whose position is improving objectively, may provide the mass base for widespread rebellion (compare Durkheim [1897] 1951, p. 254). It is clearly possible, under the means–ends formula, for a very lowly group to accept its place and income because it has achieved as much as it has been socialized to aspire to. Conversely, a much more well-to-do group whose aspiration levels have been raised sharply as a result of rapid urbanization, greater education, access to international media, recent involvement in industry, and exposure to the blandishments of unions and leftist political parties may experience the phenomenon of unlimited "rising expectations" and hence feel dissatisfied and prove receptive to a new myth which locates "the source of large-scale frustrations in the social structure and . . . portray[s] an alternative structure" that would be more satisfying (Merton [1949] 1957, p. 156).

Functionalist sociology stresses the way in which stratification fulfills certain basic needs of complex social systems and so becomes one of the principal stabilizing mechanisms of complex societies. Like the Marxist and Weberian forms of analysis, it points to ways in which the demands of a stratification system press men to act against their own interests, and alienate them from autonomous choice. However, the focus in functionalism on means–ends relationships reveals the conflict-generating potential of stratification systems, in which goals are inherently scarce resources. Hence, functional analysis, like the other two, locates sources of consensus and cleavage in the hierarchical structures of society.

Empirical studies. A considerable amount of the research on stratification by American sociologists has stemmed directly from functional analysis. Perhaps the most extensive single set of studies is contained in the many volumes by W. Lloyd Warner and his associates reporting on the "social class" (i.e., status) system of a number of American communities (see, for example, Warner 1941–1959). Warner, an anthropologist by training and originally a follower of Durkheim, has argued that any effort to deal in functional terms with the social system of a modern community must relate many of the institutional and behavioral patterns of the community to the needs of the classes within them rather than to the larger system as such. Using the method of reputational analysis (asking people in the community to rank others and seeing who associated with whom as status equals), Warner located five or six social classes ranging from "upper-upper" to "lower-lower." Each of them was found to possess a number of distinct class characteristics, such as intrafamily behavior, associational memberships, and attitudes on a variety of issues. On the whole, Warner sees class divisions as contributing to social stability rather than to conflict, because the strata are separated into relatively distinct elements that have a more or less balanced and integrated culture. He has interpreted his data as indicating that those in lower positions tend to respect those above them in the status hierarchy and to follow their lead on many issues. While most sociologists would agree with Warner concerning the existence of the sort of status groupings that he has described (Weber presented a picture of American status relations in much the same terms), many would disagree with him concerning the degree of consensus within the system as to where individuals are located and would tend to agree more with Merton that tensions and conflicts are inherent in any hierarchical order. It is interesting to note, however, that while the various community studies of the accorded status sys-

tem do suggest considerable ambivalence about where various individuals or families rank, particularly if they are not close to the very top or bottom of the system, investigations concerning the prestige rankings of occupations indicate considerable consensus both within and among a variety of nations [see STRATIFICATION, SOCIAL, *article on* THE MEASUREMENT OF SOCIAL CLASS; *see also* Hodge et al. 1966]. The prestige studies would seem to be in line with the assumption of functionalist theory that consensus in the desirability of different occupational roles is necessary in order to motivate the most competent individuals to seek those positions which are valued most.

Criticism of the functionalist approach. Functionalist theory has been sharply criticized by a number of sociologists who argue that while systems of widespread inequality characterize all existing complex societies, this fact does not demonstrate that inequality is a social requisite for a stable society, as many functionalists argue. Rather, these critics urge that systems of stratification persist and take the varying forms they do because the privileged strata have more power and are able to impose their group interests on the society. The greater rewards in income and status received by various positions reflect greater power than the need to motivate individuals to secure them. The value systems related to stratification therefore reflect the functional needs of the dominant strata, not those of the social system as such (Tumin 1953; Buckley 1958). A Polish sociologist, Wlodzimierz Wesolowski (1962), has suggested that functionalist sociologists, particularly Davis and Moore (1945), who have written the most comprehensive contemporary statement of the functionalist position, are wrong when they emphasize the need for stratification as a system of motivation in the form of material advantage or prestige. He has contended that there are alternative systems of social organization that can sharply reduce inequality in prestige and income while motivating people to seek higher education and fill responsible positions. Hence, class differences that derive from such forms of inequality may decline greatly. Wesolowski, however, agrees with the functionalists that complex social systems will continue to be organized on hierarchical lines, because systems of authority and command are necessary. Men will continue to be divided between those who occupy "positions of authority . . . who have the right (and duty) to give orders, while the others have the duty to obey them" ([1962] 1966, p. 68). And he has noted that Friedrich Engels, Marx's closest intellectual collaborator, "said that in a communist system the State as a weapon of class domination would wither away . . . [and yet] declared that it would be impossible to think of any great modern industrial enterprise or of the organization of the future communist society without authority—or superiority–subordination relationships" (*ibid.*).

Wesolowski agrees with the functionalists that stratification is inevitable because differentials in authority relationships, not variations in income or prestige, are necessary. As he put it, "if there is any functional necessity for stratification, it is the necessity of stratification according to the criterium of authority and not according to the criterium of material advantage or prestige. Nor does the necessity of stratification derive from the need to induce people for the acquirement of qualifications, but from the very fact that humans live collectively" (p. 69).

Wesolowski has presented in general terms a formulation very similar to that of the German sociologist Ralf Dahrendorf, who has tried to reformulate Marx's theoretical assumptions so as to deal more adequately with certain structural changes in Western society—especially those which have resulted in the divorce of ownership from management that is characteristic of the modern corporation (Dahrendorf 1957). Many have argued that this separation negates Marx, since it means the disappearance of the class of private capitalists as a powerful stratum. Dahrendorf, however, has suggested that the only significant difference this change makes is that it is now more meaningful to speak of the differential distribution of *authority* as the basis of class formation than it is to speak of the ownership of the means of production. It is differential access to authority positions and, therefore, to power and prestige that gives rise to contemporary class conflict, for those who are excluded from authority in "imperatively co-ordinated associations" (a term Dahrendorf borrowed from Weber) will be in conflict with those who have command over them. Articulation of manifest interest and organization of interest groups then become the dynamite for social-structural change.

Functionalism and Marxism. In urging that the universality of stratification, or hierarchical differentiation—though not, it should be noted, of social class—is linked to the functional requirements for a power hierarchy, Wesolowski has built an interesting theoretical bridge between Marxist and functionalist sociology. For his and Dahrendorf's lines of reasoning ultimately are not greatly different from the functionalist approach to power presented by Parsons. The latter, of course, does not emphasize the theme of power as self-interested, which is found

in the Marxian tradition, or that of coercion, which was stressed by Weber. Rather, Parsons has suggested that power—in his terms, the ability to mobilize resources necessary for the operation of the system—should be viewed in value-neutral terms, as follows. Inherent in the structure of complex society, especially in the division of labor, is the existence of authority roles, holders of which are obligated to initiate acts that are socially necessary. Most of the things done by those at the summits of organizations or societies are necessary. If individuals and groups are to achieve their goals within the division of labor, it must include a complex system of interactions. The more complex the system, Parsons has argued, the more dependent individuals are on others for the attainment of their goals, that is, the less free or powerful they are. And power is basically control over the allocation of resources and roles so as to make a given system operative. Power, under any system of values, resides in having what people desire, because they will obey for the sake of getting what they desire. Finally, unless the capacity to organize the behavior of those in a system existed, sharply differentiated societies could not operate (1963).

It should be noted that there is a coincidence of the Marxist and functionalist approaches to political power. Both approaches view it as a social utility—as the means, par excellence, through which societies attain their objectives, including the expansion of available resources. Elite theories of power, on the other hand, see it in "zero-sum" terms, that is, they assume a fixed amount of power, so that the gain of one group or individual necessarily involves the loss of others. Two reviews of C. Wright Mills's analysis of the American power elite (Mills 1956)—one by a functionalist, Parsons (1957), and the other by the student of stratification who, among leading American sociologists, stands closest to Marxism, Robert S. Lynd (1956; 1957)—criticized Mills for having a zero-sum game approach to power and for identifying it with domination. That is, both Lynd and Parsons agreed that power should be viewed, both sociologically and politically, in the light of its positive functions as an agency of the general community and that it is erroneous to view power, as Mills did, solely or even primarily in terms of powerholders seeking to enhance their own interests.

There is, of course, a link with stratification theory in Parsons' analysis of power, since he has assumed that what people value most are economic advantage and esteem. It follows from this that those who possess the qualities which place them at the upper levels of the economic and status hierarchies also have the most power. Money and influence, Parsons has noted, are exchangeable for power, since power is the ability to mobilize resources through controlling the action of others [*see* SYSTEMS ANALYSIS, *article on* SOCIAL SYSTEMS].

The dimensions of stratification

The foregoing discussion of the Marxist, Weberian, and functionalist approaches to social class analysis has distinguished a number of issues that continue to concern sociologists. Instead of moving toward one concept of social class, students of stratification have generally reacted to an awareness of the complexity of the subject by differentiating a large number of apparently relevant concepts, most of which are directly derivable from the three traditions discussed above. The differences in approach have, in large measure, reflected variations in the intellectual concerns of the scholars involved.

Contemporary students of stratification continue to be divided into two groups: those who urge that there is a single dimension underlying all stratification and those who believe that stratification may best be conceptualized as multidimensional. That is, they disagree as to whether economic class position, social status, power, income, and the like are related to one underlying factor in most societies, or whether they should be considered as distinct although related dimensions of the stratification system. To some degree this controversy may be perceived as a continuation on a more formal level of the differences between the approaches of Marx and Weber. However, some of those who uphold the single attribute position are far from being Marxists. They do not believe that position in the economic structure determines all other aspects of status; rather, they would argue that statistical analysis suggests the presence of a basic common factor. For analytic purposes, however, the controversy cannot be resolved by statistical manipulation, since some of those who favor a multidimensional approach would argue that even if it turns out that these various aspects of stratification do form part of a single latent attribute, there is enough variation among them to justify the need to analyze the cases in which individuals or groups are ranked higher on certain dimensions than on others.

If we assume, as most contemporary sociologists do, that stratification may most usefully be conceptualized in multidimensional terms, we are confronted with the issues of which dimensions the various theorists emphasize. The dimensions they have suggested may be grouped into three categories: (1) *objective* status, or aspects of stratification that structure environments differently enough to evoke differences in behavior; (2) *accorded* status, or the prestige accorded to individuals and groups by others; (3) *subjective* status, or the personal sense of location within the social hierarchy felt by various individuals. These approaches in turn may be further broken down in terms of important variables, as follows.

Objective class concepts. Perhaps the most familiar component of objective status is power position within the economic structure. This is essentially Marx's criterion for class: persons are located according to their degree of control over the means of production. In the first analysis this serves to distinguish owners from employees. Owners, however, may vary in their degree of economic security and power, as large businessmen differ from small ones, and workers also may vary according to the bargaining power inherent in the relative scarcity of the skills they possess.

Another important concept in this area is extent of economic life chances. Weber perceived economic status not only in terms of ownership but also in terms of the probability of receiving a given economic return, or income. Thus an employee role, such as engineer or lawyer, which gave someone a higher probability of earning high income than a small businessman, would place him in a higher class position. Essentially, this dimension refers to power in the market. Indeed, the simple difference in income received has been suggested as the best way to measure economic class.

Variation in the relative status of different occupations has also been seen as an important criterion for differentiating positions in the economic hierarchy. This approach has increasingly come to be used in studies of social mobility. Occupational prestige is, of course, a form of accorded status, except that what is being ranked are occupations, not individuals or groups.

Another aspect of stratification that is sometimes perceived as an objective one is power, which may be defined as the ability to affect the life chances of others, or conversely as the amount of freedom from control by others. Power may also be conceptualized as the set of probabilities that given role relationships will allow individuals to define their own will—that is, to impose their version of order even against the resistance of others. This dimension is extremely difficult to describe in operational terms: how, for instance, does one compare the different amounts and types of power possessed by labor leaders, Supreme Court justices, factory owners, and professors? It is also argued that power should not be regarded as an aspect of stratification in itself, as if it were comparable with economic class, but, rather, as the dynamic resultant of the forces brought into play in different types of social situations. Authority—legitimate power within a formal structure—is clearly hierarchical, but the rank order of authority usually applies only to a given authority structure within a society, not to the society itself.

Finally, a number of sociological studies have treated education as a major determinant of objective status and as a dimension of stratification. The differences in behavior and attitudes of those who are higher or lower in educational attainments have been demonstrated by empirical research. On the theoretical level, it is argued that education, like the various economic dimensions, affects the life chances of individuals—their degree of security, their status, and their ability to interact with others. People are given differential degrees of respect and influence according to their level of education.

Accorded status. The dimension of accorded status is the one most sociologists tacitly or overtly refer to when they use the term "social class." This dimension involves the amount of status, honor, or deference that a given position commands in a society. Various methods are used to study accorded status, but in any case the location of individuals or groups in the status system depends on the opinion of the individuals who go to make up the system rather than the opinion of the sociologist who observes it. Accorded status, then, is a result of the felt perceptions of others, and a social class based on accorded status is composed of individuals who accept each other as equals and therefore as qualified for intimate association in friendship, marriage, and the like.

Since this concept depends on rankings by others, it is difficult to apply it to large-scale social systems, particularly nations, except at the level of the small uppermost social class. Individuals from different communities cannot rank each other unless they rely on criteria more objective than social acceptability. The social class consisting of individuals who have, roughly speaking, the same attributes will vary with size of community; for instance, the type of individual who may be in the highest social class of a small town will probably be in the middle class of a large city. It has, in fact, been argued that the larger the community, the more likely it is that accorded status will correspond to objective status. In other words, individuals who live in large communities are more prone to make status judgments about others on the basis of knowledge about their jobs, how much their homes are worth, how many years of education they have had, and the like.

Accorded status tends to become an ascribed characteristic, that is, one that can be inherited. "Background," which usually means family identification, is the way in which people define the source of accorded status. This implies that in addition to specific lineage, other visible ascribed characteristics, such as race, ethnicity, and religion, often constitute elements in status placement. In all societies that contain a variety of racial, ethnic, or religious groups, each such group is differentially ranked in honorific or status terms. Those groups which were present first and retain the highest economic and political positions tend to have the highest status. Thus in the United States, such traits as being white, Anglo-Saxon, and Protestant (preferably of the historically earliest American denominations, such as Episcopal, Congregational, or Quaker) convey high status on those possessing them. The status attributes of various socially visible groups are also determined by various typical characteristics of their members. Thus religious or ethnic groups which are poor on the average are of low status, and wealthy members of such groups tend to be discriminated against socially by comparably well-to-do members of more privileged groups (for instance, a well-to-do Baptist will have lower status in most American communities than a comparably affluent Episcopalian).

Status, it should be noted, is a power resource in much the same way as economic position or political authority. Since status involves being accepted by those in high positions, and since the desire for status is universal, men seek to accommodate their actions to those who can confer status on them.

Subjective status. Unlike objective and accorded class concepts, which locate individuals in the stratification hierarchy according to the judgments of analysts or of the community, subjective status categories involve efforts to discover the way in which the individual himself perceives the stratification hierarchy. In sociology there are essentially two main traditions of dealing with subjective positions, one based on the methodological device of self-identification and the other on reference group theory.

Self-identification. The technique of self-identification is used to determine the extent to which given individuals or portions of specific groups see themselves as members of a given class or other group that may be located in terms of stratification. Efforts to locate individuals have involved asking them to place themselves in one of a number of class categories furnished by the investigator in such questions as "Do you think of yourself as a member of the upper, middle, working, or lower class?" (Centers 1949). The number of alternatives furnished respondents may, of course, be larger or smaller than this. Other investigators, instead of following this procedure, have sought to find out what categories people use to describe the social hierarchy (Manis & Meltzer 1963).

Reference group theory. The groups that individuals use as reference points by which to evaluate themselves or their activities are known in sociology as reference groups. They can be, but need not be, groups to which an individual belongs. Thus a person may judge his degree of occupational achievement by comparing his attainments with those which preponderate among his fellow ethnic, racial, or religious group members, people he went to school with, neighbors, or those who are more privileged than he is and whose position he would like to attain. [See REFERENCE GROUPS.]

Reference group theory assumes that individuals rarely use the total social structure as a reference group but, rather, that they judge their own status by comparison with smaller, more closely visible groups. The extent of satisfaction or dissatisfaction with status is held to depend on one's reference groups.

Reference groups are often derivable from structural factors; thus neighborhoods, factories, employers, schoolmates, and the like often constitute relevant reference groups. On the other hand, relevant reference groups may be manipulated, as when organized groups that are competing for support seek to affect the reference groups of those whose support they want so as to increase their sense of satisfaction or dissatisfaction (Lipset & Trow 1957). The formation of class consciousness may be seen as a process in which members of the lower social strata change their reference groups: while class consciousness is dormant or incipient, the lower-class individual relates himself to various small groups; with the full emergence of class consciousness, he relates himself to aspects of the larger social structure.

Objective and subjective orientations

The fact that social class may be conceptualized both objectively and subjectively does not mean that these are in any sense mutually exclusive ways of looking at the social hierarchy. Almost all analysts, regardless of which approach they choose to stress, are interested in examining the interrelations between their conception of class and other factors, which they view either as determinants or as consequences of class variations. Thus, as has been noted, Marx was intensely interested in the subjective reactions of people to their location in the class structure.

It is significant that Richard Centers, who is most identified with the social-psychological approach to class as involving self-definition, initiated his study of the subject as a way of finding out to what extent American workers were class-conscious in the Marxist sense. In fact, Centers' work is more directly inspired by Marx than is that of many sociologists, who are more wont to approach the subject in objective terms.

It should also be noted that there are close links between elements in Marx's thought and contemporary reference group theory. In seeking to suggest hypotheses that would explain the relationship between objective position and anticipated subjective reactions, Marx advanced a theory of relative deprivation. He suggested that although objective improvement in the economic position of the workers could take place under capitalism, this would not prevent the emergence of "true" class consciousness, since the position of the capitalists would improve more rapidly than that of the workers. As he put it, the "material position of the worker has improved, . . . but at the cost of his social position. The social gulf that divides him from the capitalist has widened" ([1849] 1962, p. 98). In another work Marx illustrated this generalization with the story of a man who was very happy with a small house in which he lived until a wealthy man came along and built a mansion next door: then, wrote Marx, the house of the worker suddenly became a hut in his eyes (1898, pp. 268–269 in the 1936 edition).

Similarly, although Marx never dealt with the distinction between class and status on a conceptual level, there are frequent references in his historical writings to distinctions among social strata in various countries. These distinctions actually reflect what would now be called variations among status groups. Perhaps the most interesting formulation related to this question may be found in a major Marxist classic by Engels. In discussing political life in nineteenth-century England, Engels pointed out in very clear terms that status may be an independent source of power, more important in a given situation than economic power:

In England, the bourgeoisie never held undivided sway. Even the victory of 1832 left the landed aristocracy in almost exclusive possession of all the leading government offices. The meekness with which the wealthy middle class submitted to this remained inconceivable to me until the great Liberal manufacturer, Mr. W. A. Forster, in a public speech implored the young men of

Bradford to learn French, as a means to get on in the world, and quoted from his own experience how sheepish he looked when, as a Cabinet Minister, he had to move in society where French was, at least, as necessary as English! The fact was, the English middle class of that time were, as a rule, quite uneducated upstarts, and could not help leaving to the aristocracy those superior government places where other qualifications were required than mere insular narrowness and insular conceit, seasoned by business sharpness. . . .

The English bourgeoisie are, up to the present day, so deeply penetrated by a sense of their social inferiority that they keep up, at their own expense and that of the nation, an ornamental caste of drones to represent the nation worthily at all state functions; and they consider themselves highly honoured whenever one of themselves is found worthy of admission into this select and privileged body, manufactured, after all, by themselves.   ([1880] 1935, pp. 25–26)

Clearly, what Engels was describing is a situation in which an old upper class, which had declined in economic power, continued to maintain its control over the governmental machinery because it remained the highest status group in the society. Those with less status but more economic resources conformed to the standards set up by the higher status group.

Stable and unstable status systems. The relationships among the different dimensions of stratification vary in different types of societies and different periods; they are probably at their weakest during periods of rapid social change involving the rise of new occupational strata, shifts from rural to urban predominance, and changes in the status and authority of key institutions, such as religion and education. Of all the relatively stable types of society, the ones in which the various dimensions of stratification are most closely correlated are rural, caste, and feudal societies. The growth of industrial and urban society in Europe and America has resulted in a system of stratification characterized by wide discrepancies between class and objective status, and between both of these and the subjective attributes of status. Currently, as Western society moves into a "postindustrial" phase characterized by a considerable growth in the white-collar, technological, and service sectors of the economy and a relative decline in employment in manufacturing, the relationships between the dimensions have become more tenuous. Status, economic reward, and power are tied to educational achievement, position in some large-scale bureaucracy, access to political authority, and the like. In a predominantly bureaucratic society, property as such has become a less important source of status and social mobility. Complaints about alienation

and dehumanization are found more commonly among students, intellectuals, and other sectors of the educated middle classes than among the working class. Most recently, sections of the communist movement have openly discussed the revolutionary role of university students and the petty bourgeoisie, and have seen the organized proletariat in Western society as a relatively conservative group, unavailable for radical politics.

These developments may reflect the fact that some of the most politically relevant discontent in the bureaucratic "affluent society" of the 1960s seems to be inherent in social tensions induced by *status inconsistencies*. However, the bulk of resentment against the stratification system is still rooted in objective deprivation and exploitation. The concept of status inconsistency introduced by Lenski (1954), who derived it from Weber, refers to the situation of individuals or groups that are differentially located on various dimensions of stratification. Persons in such a situation are exposed to conflicting sets of expectations: for instance, those who are high in educational attainments but are employed in relatively low-paid occupations tend to be more dissatisfied than those whose stratification attributes are totally consistent. As evidence in support of this assumption it is possible to cite research findings that among the relatively well-to-do, those with discrepant status attributes are more likely to favor change in the power structure and to have more liberal or leftist attitudes than those with status attributes that are mutually consistent (Goffman 1957). Consequently, the increase in status discrepancy inherent in situations of rapid social change should result in an increase in overall discontent and, among those in the more ambiguous status positions (which in the 1960s occurred largely in the well-educated middle strata) in greater receptivity to the myths justifying rebellion. In industrialized societies those who form the underprivileged strata but who have consistent status attributes remain politically on the left but show little interest in radical change. Because all social change generates status discrepancies, rebellious and extremist mass movements are more likely to be found during periods of rapid industrialization and economic growth, and in areas where immigration has caused sudden population growth, than in industrially mature urbanized areas.

Analysis of the consequences of status discrepancies has yielded seemingly contradictory results, largely because some researchers treat all discrepancies as necessarily equal in their effects. For example, institutionalized discrepancies, such as those which result when a member of a minority group becomes rich but is still discriminated against, are equated with inconsistencies between education and occupation, or between occupation and income. Highly visible institutionalized discrepancies should result in more active expression of resentment and more efforts to bring about *social* change than do loosely structured personal inconsistencies. The latter are more likely to be reflected in efforts by the individual to change his personal situation through various forms of mobility, including change in occupation, residence, or organization. The consequences of status discrepancies should therefore be investigated within broad status categories rather than for total societies. For instance, discrepancies among the poor may have effects very different from those they have among the well-to-do. A manual worker with a claim, based on good education or family background, to higher status than his occupational position allows him is more likely to be politically conservative than workers whose status attributes are consistent. Among the well-to-do, however, status inconsistency will impair claims to high positions and will induce favorable attitudes toward liberal or egalitarian ideologies. The effects of status inconsistencies in societies with relatively rigid status lines are quite different from their effects in societies that have relatively fluid stratification systems. Clearly, the concept of status inconsistency, though potentially a useful tool in class analysis, presupposes some systematic treatment of how the relationship between the various dimensions of status varies from one type of stratification to another.

The future of social class. To conclude on a note of irony, it may be observed that in a certain sense history has underwritten one of Marx's basic assumptions, which is that the cultural superstructure, including political behavior and status relationships, is a function of the underlying economic and technological structure. As Marx put it in the Preface to *Capital*: "The country that is more developed industrially only shows, to the less developed, the image of its own future" ([1867–1879] 1925–1926, vol. 1, pp. 8–9). Hence, the most economically developed society should also have the most advanced set of class and political relationships. Since the United States is the most advanced society economically, its class system, regarded as part of its cultural superstructure, should be more appropriate to a technologically advanced society than the class systems of the less developed economies of Europe. In addition, one might argue that

the United States, since it lacks a feudal past, should evolve the institutions of a highly developed society in their purest form. Hence, an unpolitical Marxist sociology would expect the social class relationships of the United States to present an image of the future of other societies that are moving in the same general economic direction. Characteristic of such a social system is a decline in emphasis on social class, that is, a decline of distinct visible strata with a "felt consciousness of kind" (Lipset 1964a; 1964b); the various dimensions of stratification are more likely to operate in a crisscrossing fashion, increasing the numbers who are relatively high on some components of status and low on others. Highly developed societies of this kind, whether variants of the communist or the capitalist model, are more likely to possess systems of social stratification—varied rankings—than social classes.

These comments suggest the need to view stratification in international as well as national terms. (Horowitz 1966). The differences between the average per capita income of the poorest and wealthiest nations are on the order of 40 or 50 to 1, that is, much greater than the differences among social strata within the industrially advanced nations. These variations in national wealth constitute structural parameters that greatly affect the "class" relationships between nations. A Chinese communist has already advanced the thesis that the significant class struggle is between the predominantly rural nations, which are underdeveloped and very poor, and the urbanized, wealthy ones (Piao 1965). He has also argued that the wealth of the latter has to a considerable degree reduced the political expression of class tensions within them, but that this should be seen as a result of exploitation by the economically advanced countries of the underdeveloped ones. Whether this thesis is warranted by the facts of international trade relationships or not, it does seem true that any analysis of class structures and their political consequences must in the future consider the impact of variation in national incomes. Many in the elite of the poorer part of the world see themselves as the leaders of oppressed peoples; the radicalism of the intellectuals, university students, military officers, and the like in the less developed nations can be related to the social and economic inferiority of their countries, rather than to their position in the class structure. Such considerations take us far afield from the conventional Western sociological concerns with class relationships, but they clearly are relevant to any effort at specifying the sources of class behavior and ideologies. As sociology becomes more comparative in outlook and research, we may expect efforts to link class analysis of individual nations to the facts of international stratification.

SEYMOUR M. LIPSET

[*Directly related are the entries* BUREAUCRACY; MARXIST SOCIOLOGY; MASS SOCIETY; MENTAL HEALTH, *article on* SOCIAL CLASS AND PERSONAL ADJUSTMENT; PROFESSIONS; SOCIAL DIFFERENTIATION; SOCIAL MOBILITY; STATUS, SOCIAL. *Other relevant material may be found in* CONFLICT, *article on* SOCIAL ASPECTS; COOPERATION; INDUSTRIALIZATION, *article on* SOCIAL ASPECTS; LEISURE; POWER; SOCIAL STRUCTURE, *article on* SOCIAL STRUCTURAL ANALYSIS; SOCIETY; *and in the biographies of* DURKHEIM; ENGELS; GEIGER; HALBWACHS; LENIN; MADISON; MARX; MICHELS; SOROKIN; VEBLEN; WEBER, MAX.]

BIBLIOGRAPHY

BELL, DANIEL (1960) 1962 *The End of Ideology: On the Exhaustion of Political Ideas in the Fifties.* 2d ed., rev. New York: Collier.

BUCKLEY, WALTER (1958) 1961 Social Stratification and the Functional Theory of Social Differentiation. Pages 478–484 in Seymour M. Lipset and Neil Smelser (editors), *Sociology: The Progress of a Decade.* Englewood Cliffs, N.J.: Prentice-Hall. → First published in Volume 23 of the *American Sociological Review.*

BUKHARIN, NIKOLAI I. (1921) 1965 *Historical Materialism: A System of Sociology.* Translated from the 3d Russian edition. New York: Russell. → First published as *Teoriia istoricheskogo materializma.*

CENTERS, RICHARD (1949) 1961 *The Psychology of Social Classes: A Study of Class Consciousness.* New York: Russell.

DAHRENDORF, RALF (1957) 1959 *Class and Class Conflict in Industrial Society.* Rev. & enl. ed. Stanford Univ. Press. → First published in German.

DAVIS, KINGSLEY; and MOORE, WILBERT E. (1945) 1966 Some Principles of Stratification. Pages 47–53 in Reinhard Bendix and Seymour M. Lipset (editors), *Class, Status, and Power: Social Stratification in Comparative Perspective.* 2d ed., rev. New York: Free Press. → First published in Volume 10 of the *American Sociological Review.*

DE LEON, DANIEL (1889–1913) 1932 *James Madison and Karl Marx: A Contrast and a Similarity.* 3d ed. New York Labor News Co.

DURKHEIM, ÉMILE (1893) 1960 *The Division of Labor in Society.* Glencoe, Ill.: Free Press. → First published as *De la division du travail social.*

DURKHEIM, ÉMILE (1897) 1951 *Suicide: A Study in Sociology.* Glencoe, Ill.: Free Press. → First published in French.

ENGELS, FRIEDRICH (1880) 1935 *Socialism: Utopian and Scientific.* New York: International Publishers. → First published in French.

GOFFMAN, IRWIN W. 1957 Status Consistency and Preference for Change in Power Distribution. *American Sociological Review* 22:275–281.

HODGE, ROBERT W.; TREIMAN, DONALD J.; and ROSSI, PETER H. 1966 A Comparative Study of Occupational Prestige. Pages 309–321 in Reinhard Bendix

and Seymour M. Lipset (editors), *Class, Status, and Power: Social Stratification in Comparative Perspective.* 2d ed., rev. New York: Free Press.

HOROWITZ, IRVING LOUIS 1966 *Three Worlds of Development: The Theory and Practice of International Stratification.* New York: Oxford Univ. Press.

LENIN, VLADIMIR I. (1902) 1961 What Is to Be Done? Volume 5, pages 347–529 in Vladimir I. Lenin, *Collected Works.* 4th ed. Moscow: Foreign Languages Publishing House. → First published as "Chto delat'?"

LENSKI, GERHARD E. (1954) 1961 Status Crystallization: A Non-vertical Dimension of Social Status. Pages 485–494 in Seymour M. Lipset and Neil Smelser (editors), *Sociology: The Progress of a Decade.* Englewood Cliffs, N.J.: Prentice-Hall. → First published in Volume 19 of the *American Sociological Review.*

LIPSET, SEYMOUR M. 1964a The Changing Class Structure and Contemporary European Politics. *Dædalus* 93:271–303.

LIPSET, SEYMOUR M. 1964b Political Cleavages in "Developed" and "Emerging" Polities. Pages 21–55 in Erik Allardt and Yrjö Littunen (editors), *Cleavages, Ideologies and Party Systems: Contributions to Comparative Political Sociology.* Transactions of the Westermarck Society, Vol. 10. Helsinki: The Society.

LIPSET, SEYMOUR M.; and TROW, MARTIN 1957 Reference Group Theory and Trade-union Wage Policy. Pages 391–411 in Mirra Komarovsky (editor), *Common Frontiers of the Social Sciences.* Glencoe, Ill.: Free Press.

LYND, ROBERT S. 1956 Power in the United States. *Nation* 182:408–411. → A review of C. Wright Mills's *The Power Elite.*

LYND, ROBERT S. 1957 Power in American Society as Resource and Problem. Pages 1–45 in Arthur Kornhauser (editor), *Problems of Power in American Democracy.* Detroit, Mich.: Wayne State Univ. Press.

MANIS, JEROME G.; and MELTZER, BERNARD N. 1963 Some Correlates of Class Consciousness Among Textile Workers. *American Journal of Sociology* 69:177–184.

MARSHALL, T. H. (1934–1962) 1964 *Class, Citizenship, and Social Development: Essays.* Garden City, N.Y.: Doubleday. → A collection of articles and lectures first published in England in 1963 under the title *Sociology at the Crossroads, and Other Essays.* A paperback edition was published in 1965.

MARX, KARL (1844) 1963 *Early Writings.* Translated and edited by T. B. Bottomore. London: Watts. → First published in German. Contains "On the Jewish Question," "Contribution to the Critique of Hegel's Philosophy of Right," and "Economic and Philosophic Manuscripts." A paperback edition was published in 1964 by McGraw-Hill.

MARX, KARL (1847) 1963 *The Poverty of Philosophy.* With an introduction by Friedrich Engels. New York: International Publishers. → First published in French. A paperback edition was published in 1964.

MARX, KARL (1849) 1962 Wage Labour and Capital. Volume 1, pages 70–105 in Karl Marx and Friedrich Engels, *Selected Works.* Moscow: Foreign Languages Publishing House. → First published in German in the *Neue Rheinische Zeitung.*

MARX, KARL (1852) 1962 The Eighteenth Brumaire of Louis Bonaparte. Volume 1, pages 243–344 in Karl Marx and Friedrich Engels, *Selected Works.* Moscow: Foreign Languages Publishing House. → First published in German in the journal *Die Revolution.* A paperback edition was published in 1964 by International Publishers.

MARX, KARL (1867–1879) 1925–1926 *Capital: A Critique of Political Economy.* 3 vols. Chicago: Kerr. → Volume 1: *The Process of Capitalist Production.* Volume 2: *The Process of Circulation of Capital.* Volume 3: *The Process of Capitalist Production as a Whole.* Volume 1 was published in 1867. The manuscripts of volumes 2 and 3 were written between 1867 and 1879 and first published posthumously in German in 1885 and 1894.

MARX, KARL (1898) 1962 Wages, Price, and Profit. Volume 1, pages 398–447 in Karl Marx and Friedrich Engels, *Selected Works.* Moscow: Foreign Languages Publishing House. → First published in German.

MERTON, ROBERT K. (1949) 1957 *Social Theory and Social Structure.* Rev. & enl. ed. Glencoe, Ill.: Free Press.

MICHELS, ROBERT (1911) 1959 *Political Parties: A Sociological Study of the Oligarchical Tendencies of Modern Democracy.* New York: Dover. → First published as *Zur Soziologie des Parteiwesens in der modernen Demokratie.* A paperback edition was published in 1966 by Collier.

MILLS, C. WRIGHT 1956 *The Power Elite.* New York: Oxford Univ. Press.

PARSONS, TALCOTT 1953 A Revised Analytical Approach to the Theory of Social Stratification. Pages 92–128 in Reinhard Bendix and Seymour M. Lipset (editors), *Class, Status, and Power: A Reader in Social Stratification.* Glencoe, Ill.: Free Press.

PARSONS, TALCOTT 1957 The Distribution of Power in American Society. *World Politics* 10:123–143.

PARSONS, TALCOTT (1963) 1966 On the Concept of Political Power. Pages 240–265 in Reinhard Bendix and Seymour M. Lipset (editors), *Class, Status, and Power: Social Stratification in Comparative Perspective.* 2d ed., rev. New York: Free Press. → First published in Volume 107 of the American Philosophical Society *Proceedings.*

PIAO, LIN 1965 Long Live the Victory of the People's War. *Peking Review* 8, no. 36:9–39.

TUMIN, MELVIN M. (1953) 1966 Some Principles of Stratification: A Critical Analysis. Pages 53–58 in Reinhard Bendix and Seymour M. Lipset (editors), *Class, Status, and Power: Social Stratification in Comparative Perspective.* 2d ed., rev. New York: Free Press. → First published in Volume 18 of the *American Sociological Review.*

VEBLEN, THORSTEIN (1899) 1953 *The Theory of the Leisure Class: An Economic Study of Institutions.* Rev. ed. New York: New American Library. → A paperback edition was published in 1959.

WARNER, W. LLOYD (editor) 1941–1959 *Yankee City Series.* 5 vols. New Haven: Yale Univ. Press. → An abridged edition was published in 1963 as *Yankee City.*

WEBER, MAX (1906–1924) 1946 *From Max Weber: Essays in Sociology.* Translated and edited by Hans H. Gerth and C. Wright Mills. New York: Oxford Univ. Press.

WEBER, MAX (1922) 1957 *The Theory of Social and Economic Organization.* Edited by Talcott Parsons. Glencoe, Ill.: Free Press. → First published as Part 1 of *Wirtschaft und Gesellschaft.*

WESOLOWSKI, WLODZIMIERZ (1962) 1966 Some Notes on the Functional Theory of Stratification. Pages 64–69 in Reinhard Bendix and Seymour M. Lipset (editors), *Class, Status, and Power: Social Stratification in Comparative Perspective.* 2d ed., rev. New York: Free Press. → First published in the *Polish Sociological Review.*

III

THE MEASUREMENT OF SOCIAL CLASS

Establishing a valid and reliable measure of social class from presumed correlates of class that can be applied in a variety of research situations has proved an elusive task. Since indices are validated by showing that they measure what they profess to measure, the unresolved differences in prevailing conceptions of social class lead to different indices of it, all nominally professing to measure the same thing. In fact, these indices tap only those features of social class emphasized or employed in different conceptual formulations. This article will explore the different techniques of measurement of social class derived from diverse conceptions of it.

Components of social class. As a point of departure we need to develop some ideas about the components of a social class arrangement. The presence or absence of these components will enable us to distinguish the conceptualizations to which different techniques of measurement of social class are appropriate. Most writers would agree that, whatever else may be attributed to them, social classes, if they exist at all, are bounded, ordered, and mutually exclusive. To say that classes are *bounded* merely means that we can write a rule for each class that tells us whether a particular individual is to be included or excluded from membership in it. To talk about the property of *order* is to express in abbreviated form the assumption that there is a criterion according to which the bounded classes can all be arranged into a single hierarchy. *Mutual exclusiveness* means that social class membership is unambiguous, that is, we assume that membership in any one class precludes simultaneous membership in any other class (though movement from class to class may be permitted).

To these components common to most conceptions of social class arrangements may be added two others requiring further discussion: *exhaustiveness* and *awareness*. A social class arrangement is exhaustive if each person in the social system can be assigned membership in a social class. Whether or not any class arrangement is exhaustive is an empirical problem. However, most research operations assume exhaustiveness by adopting a rule, often implicit, assigning all members of a household to the same social class, or a rule relating the social class of a married woman, a child, a single individual, or an institutional inmate to the social class of his spouse, family of origin, or other relative. The exhaustiveness component serves to focus our attention on the problem of establishing a *unit* of social stratification, that is, on the question of the nature of the *elements* that the classes comprise. Typically, it is assumed that the unit of social stratification is the household or the family, and that the position of the unit in the social class arrangement rests largely upon the characteristics of its head.

Individuals in a social system may or may not be *aware* of the existence and form of the class system, their own class membership, the class membership of other individuals, and the rules by which the class membership of individuals is determined. The form and extent of awareness have direct implications for the methods by which social class may be measured. Where all participants in a social class system know the class membership of all other participants, any informant can reveal the class structure of an entire community. If knowledge is less than complete or is not universally shared, informants must be purposively selected. If knowledge extends little beyond awareness of one's own position, each participant can act as little more than an informant about himself. While these are the forms of awareness relevant here, we may note that by themselves they are insufficient to insure the development of class consciousness, which requires manifest consensus. The forms and extent of awareness discussed above insure only latent consensus: they require that the knowledge of various individuals coincide, but they do not require that individuals be aware of this coincidence.

Measurement strategies.   The components of a social class arrangement, particularly the form and extent of awareness, will aid in differentiating alternative strategies for measuring social class. In the small community, where the range of acquaintance extends to most residents and where knowledge of everyone's standing is likely to be universal, one may be able to glean the social class position of all families from invidious comparisons of them solicited from a few informants, as Kaufman (1944) did in rural New York. Clearly, the *size* of a social system is an important parameter that restricts the application of this technique to smaller communities. But the evidence of its applicability, even in smaller places, is less than completely convincing.

In the Kaufman study of a New York rural community, the 14 raters who evaluated the social standing of the other residents formed an average of 6.2 prestige classes (Kaufman 1946). However, the standard deviation of the number of classes formed was 1.6, indicating appreciable disagreement among raters over the broad outlines of the class structure. In a similar study of a Northeastern textile mill community, Lenski found that his 24 raters identified an average of 5.4 strata. Once again, the standard deviation of 1.1 in the number of strata identified pointed "to the conclusion that no system of discrete, perceived social classes existed in the community" (1952, p. 142).

Although raters may disagree over the number of classes in a community and thereby call into question the existence of *bounded* classes, they may still achieve a degree of consensus over the relative standing of families in the community. Kaufman (1944, p. 9) found correlations above .74 between the ratings obtained from his individual raters and the composite scores from all raters combined. While this correlation indicates far less than perfect agreement, it does suggest that in small communities where most families are known to each other—on the average, Kaufman's raters were able to evaluate three-fourths of the nearly five hundred families in the community—there is at least a gross consensus about the hierarchy of the social placement of households.

In large urban centers—or medium-sized places, for that matter—awareness of the social position of others is at best indirect, and the methods discussed above are no longer applicable. But if knowledge of the social position of particular others is greatly reduced in the urban milieu, consensus may still exist about the shape of the social class structure, and individuals may be able to place *themselves* in it accurately. For "the status and role of the individual in relation to the means of production and exchange of goods and services give rise in him to a consciousness of membership in some social class which shares those attitudes, values, and interests" (Centers [1949] 1961, pp. 28–29). If the economic system and the latent social classes it creates are mirrored in the mind of all participants, one may obtain the social class position of persons simply by asking, as Centers did, their class identification.

This type of inquiry appears, however, to be subject to variable responses, depending upon the class categories identified in the question. When asked simply "What social class are you a member of?" or when forced to choose between membership in the "upper," "middle," or "lower" class, 80 to 90 per cent of a national sample—at least in the United States—will place themselves squarely in the middle, with negligible proportions electing the extremes or disavowing the existence of social classes. Adding a "working class" category to the tripartite division "upper," "middle," and "lower" yields a quite different picture: in this forced-choice situation about half the respondents will align themselves with the "working class" (which apparently falls between the "middle" and "lower" classes), while one-third retain their "middle class" identification (Centers [1949] 1961, p. 77). In view of the variation in responses to this question, depending on whether class categories are presented as forced alternatives, and which alternatives are specified, one can hardly use inquiries of this type to reveal the class structure. The inquiry presupposes that the structure exists; and if alternative class affiliations are specified, the researcher presumes to know the classes, their boundaries, and the ways of referring to them.

Just as variation in the number of classes identified by Kaufman's and Lenski's raters challenges the existence of bounded classes, so the exitsence of a social class system with a common representation in the minds of society's members is challenged by direct inquiry about the number of classes. Herman (1962), for example, found from a sample inquiry in a middle-sized satellite city near Philadelphia that, on the average, respondents identified 3.0 classes. This is only about half the number of classes formed by the "expert judges" of Kaufman and Lenski, but the standard deviation of 0.8 is not much smaller than that observed for raters in much smaller communities. Thus this study suggests the absence of a shared image of the class structure among urban dwellers.

Evaluation of social roles and symbols

The absence of common awareness of the class structure, and substantially incomplete awareness of the social placement of particular individuals, shift the focus of attempts to measure social class from a concern with the rating of individuals to the evaluation of more abstract cues that may serve as criteria for estimating the social standing of individuals. Thus Davis (1956) asked respondents to evaluate photographs of living rooms according to the social standing of the people who lived in the homes, and demonstrated that the judgments of the pictures formed a Guttman scale [see Scaling]. Clearly, one can transform the evaluation of such cues into a measure of social status by either (*a*) requesting interviewers to identify respondents' living rooms as most nearly similar to one of the ordered pictures or (*b*) soliciting the same kind of judgment from respondents themselves.

Davis' work is particularly noteworthy because of its concern with relatively intimate cues, accessible in everyday life only to bill collectors, traveling salesmen, and one's friends. Better known, of course, are the studies of more public cues, such as occupational prestige (Counts 1925; National Opinion Research Center [NORC] 1947), in which respondents are required to evaluate the social standings of selected occupations and jobs. The resulting prestige hierarchy of *occupations* is easily transformed into prestige classes of *individuals* by identifying respondents' occupations with the prestige scores derived for similar occupations from such an evaluative study. However, as Duncan points out (1961*a*, pp. 110–114), this procedure requires appreciable guesswork, since prestige ratings for all the possible occupations of a random sample of the population do not exist.

Just as judges of individual families in small communities achieve gross consensus about the ordering of families, so respondents exhibit gross consensus in their evaluation of abstract cues to social class. Davis (1956) found a median correlation of .75 between the scale order of the ratings of living room photographs and each individual's rating of them. Reiss, using data from the NORC study of 1947, reports correlations on the order of .98 between occupational prestige measures derived from ratings by such diverse social groups as college and grade school graduates or respondents judged to be economically "prosperous" and "poor" (Reiss et al. 1962, p. 189). Of course, these correlations between aggregated scores derived by different groups of raters are higher than the average correlation between the ratings given by pairs of *individuals* randomly drawn from the population.

Evidence of the consensus between groups, and to a lesser extent between individuals, on the evaluation of occupations and other abstract social positions certainly does not mean that individuals would group occupations into identical occupational classes if left to their own devices. They *would* group them into prestige classes in such a way that few major discrepancies would be found in the relative position of particular occupations from rater to rater. But if they are instructed merely to form classes of *similar* occupations, respondents need not employ the criterion of prestige at all: kind of work, skills required for performance of the job, and other criteria might come into play. Campbell (1952) asked respondents simply to arrange a list of occupations into groups of similar ones. He found that respondents formed different numbers of groups, invoked different criteria for forming them, and achieved no obvious consensus on the composition of any particular occupational class. Nevertheless, after the respondents had formed groups of similar occupations, they were required to order the groups into social levels. Occupational prestige scores derived from this ordering proved to have a rank correlation of .97 with the scores derived from the NORC study of 1947, which were based solely upon judgments of the social standing of selected occupations as "excellent," "good," "average," "somewhat below average," or "poor." This result and similar ones obtained from comparisons with other occupational prestige studies employing still different procedures indicate that the evaluation of occupations—and possibly other cues to the social status of individuals—is invariant under substantial shifts in method of measurement and despite the fact that respondents do not necessarily divide the occupational world into even roughly identical classes of jobs.

Sociometric techniques

Abandoning the dependence of techniques of measuring social class upon awareness of the class system on the part of members of the society requires identification of social classes without reference to judgments by participants in the system. A procedure that very closely approximates this approach makes use of objective sociometric relations to identify social classes. Many observers have noted that especially "the upper classes are organized into social cliques and exclusive clubs" (Warner [1949] 1960, p. 12). The fact that these cliques and organizations represent networks of sociometric ties suggests that attempts to delimit the boundaries of social classes with reference to interpersonal ties will produce cliques of individuals whose social standing—whether based on the prestige assigned their occupational roles or upon their individual esteem—is fairly homogeneous. Since sociometric techniques need not disclose the *order* of the classes they identify, this approach is not entirely free of reliance upon judgments by participants in the social system.

As a demonstration of the validity of this approach, Duncan and Artis (1951*a*) report an intraclass correlation of .52 between the Sewell Socio-economic Status Scale scores of households involved in mutual visiting relationships in a rural Pennsylvania community. Similar associations are revealed through secondary analysis by the present authors of data on a *hacienda* and a peasant farming community in Costa Rica originally studied by Loomis and his associates (1953). Let Y equal the social status of each family (ascertained from judges' ratings), X_1 equal the average social status

of all families with which visiting relationships are maintained (excluding families related through kinship or common church membership), and X_2 equal the total number of families with which visiting relationships are maintained. For the *hacienda,* where the social status of the 55 resident families was heterogeneous, we find that the standardized partial regression coefficients (the b^* of Walker & Lev 1953, pp. 318–320) associated with the two independent variables are .61 for the social *status* of families connected by sociometric ties (X_1) and −.24 for the *number* of families with which such ties are maintained (X_2); the multiple correlation of Y with the two independent variables is .70. In the small farming village, where the social status of the 47 resident families was more homogeneous, a similar *pattern* of results is found, but the *degree* of association is diminished: the partial regression coefficients in standard form of Y with X_1 and X_2 are .14 and −.10, respectively, while the multiple correlation is .18. In sum, these results indicate both the tendency for families to establish sociometric relations with their status equals and the tendency of higher status families to isolate themselves by forming fewer contacts. However, the magnitude of the observed associations varies, depending in part upon the status homogeneity of communities. In no case are the associations large enough to establish class boundaries unequivocally. As Duncan and Artis conclude in their Pennsylvania study: "If the socioeconomic status score distribution were divided into class intervals, no doubt [sociometric] 'cleavages' could be shown to exist between 'classes' so defined. However, inspection of sociometric charts gives no indication of the most appropriate breaking points for such divisions, and there is, accordingly, no unique solution to the problem of the number of classes and their boundaries" (1951*a*, pp. 24–25).

Objective indicators of social class

The vast majority of social class or social status metrics make little or no reference to awareness of one's own social position, perception of the class position of others, evaluation of social roles and symbols, or sociometric relations. Instead, researchers pursuing substantive interests other than a concern with stratification systems per se have found it expedient to form indices of social status and social class from such objective information as occupational role, ethnic background, income and earnings, individual attainments (especially education), and even material possessions. In our opinion, the formation of indices from these objective items is at best hazardous; it is preferable to treat such objective items as separate dimensions of social stratification rather than combine them into a single index. The reasons for this are several, but the most commanding is that many dependent variables are not identically related to education, occupation, and income. To cite one example, in the indigenous, nonfarm population of the United States, fertility (number of children ever born) appears, when duration of marriage has been controlled, to have an inverse relation to educational attainment and a modest positive relation to income (see, for example, Freedman & Slesinger 1961).

Occupation, education, and income. Among the several objective indicators of social class, occupation is one of the most important. However, distilling a few relatively homogeneous occupational groups from the many thousands of distinct jobs held in the labor force is a difficult task that probably has no fully satisfactory solution. The socioeconomic groupings of detailed occupations worked out by Alba M. Edwards (1933) are still widely used by researchers to ascertain membership in broadly defined social classes. Indeed, the major occupation groups currently employed by the U.S. Bureau of the Census represent only a slight modification of the socioeconomic classification of occupations proposed by Edwards after the 1930 census of population. In devising this classification, Edwards merely arranged the detailed occupational categories of the census into what appeared to be meaningful socioeconomic groups. While the detailed categories purport to be fairly homogeneous with respect to the kinds of work performed, it is difficult to aggregate them into broader groups according to a single, over-all criterion. Edwards was able to effect a skill classification only for most manual occupations, while white-collar employees were differentiated primarily according to type of work. Once Edwards had formed the major occupational groups, he ordered them largely on socioeconomic grounds (for a detailed discussion of these and other problems connected with the Edwards classification, see Hodge & Siegel 1966).

Instead of using the kind of procedure followed by Edwards, one can measure occupational status by directly assigning socioeconomic scores to more detailed occupational groups. Thus Charles (1948), using the educational and income distributions of incumbents, derived a quantitative score for the 177 occupations identified in the 1941 census of Canada in which more than 50 per cent of the gainfully employed males were salaried or self-employed. For each occupation, the average earnings and the percentage of gainfully employed with

nine or more years of schooling were transformed into standard scores, on the basis of the distributions for all 177 occupations, and these two scores were averaged to produce a socioeconomic score for each occupation. The occupations were ordered in terms of these scores, and arbitrary boundaries were chosen to form eight socioeconomic classes. Blishen (1958) devised a quite similar index on the basis of the 1951 census returns for Canada. Bogue (1963, chapter 14) derived a score for each of the occupations identified in the detailed classification of the U.S. Bureau of the Census. This index required use of a factor analytic technique for assigning weights to summary measures of the income and educational distributions of the incumbents of each occupation.

Duncan (1961a) has derived a quite similar index, although his method of summarizing the income and education distribution of detailed occupational groups and of deriving weights for these summary measures differs from Bogue's. On the basis of the classic study of occupational prestige by North and Hatt (National Opinion Research Center 1947), one can assign prestige scores to 45 detailed occupational categories identified in tabulations of the 1950 U.S. census of population. For these 45 titles, Duncan observed that the prestige scores had a multiple correlation of .91 with his summary measures of the education and income levels enjoyed by the occupations' incumbents. In constructing his index of occupational socioeconomic status, Duncan used the multiple regression equation associated with the multiple correlation reported above to establish weights for the two components of his index. These weights, established over the 45 detailed occupational groups of known prestige, could then be applied to the measures of education and income that were known for all occupations, yielding an index of occupational socioeconomic status. The results of Duncan's and Bogue's efforts produced nearly identical measures (for all detailed occupational categories, Bogue reported a correlation of .95 between his scores and Duncan's index).

There apparently is little basis for choosing between these indices, and one might well decide to employ neither. For, as Whelpton and Hollander have pointed out (1940, p. 489), associations between social and economic characteristics and occupational affiliation are redundant insofar as most occupational classifications employ socioeconomic criteria in their construction.

Reliability. Such measures of socioeconomic status as education, occupation, and income recommend themselves not only by their ease of collection but also by their reliability. Adopting objective measures does not, however, relieve one of the responsibility of taking into account the probable effect of measurement errors. Table 1 shows reliability coefficients for years of school completed, occupational socioeconomic status, and income. The values exhibited in Table 1 were calculated from cross-tabulations of 1950 census returns with reports solicited by highly skilled interviewers in the 1950 *Post-Enumeration Survey*. Although the reliability coefficients appear quite large, they are small enough to produce appreciable attenuation in correlations involving objective status indicators. For example, in the 1950 census reports, the correlation (for males 14 and over) between years of school completed and income in 1949 was .325; assuming uncorrelated errors, one would estimate the *true* correlation by $(.325)/(.858)^{\frac{1}{2}}(.822)^{\frac{1}{2}} = .387$, taking the reliability coefficients from Table 1. The squares of the observed and corrected values are .106 and .150, respectively, indicating that errors produce an understatement of the true common variance between education and income by about one-fourth $[= 1 - (.106)/(.150)]$. This correction is intended for illustrative purposes only, since it is not quite legitimate in the present case. If one takes the *Post-Enumeration Survey* results as true values, one can see in the second column of Table 1 that errors in reporting are in fact correlated with the true levels of education, occupational socioeconomic status, and income. The ceiling and floor imposed on most socioeconomic variables tend to produce positive correlations between errors and true scores. A man whose true level of education, occupation, or income is high can *only* under-report his actual level, while a man whose true level is low can *only* overreport his actual level. The precise effects of correlated errors and of possible correlations between errors on different status variables have yet to be evaluated (compare Bogue & Murphy 1964).

Table 1 — Reliability coefficients and correlations of errors for three variables as reported in the 1950 U.S. Census of Population and the 1950 Post-Enumeration Survey (PES)

Variable	Correlation between PES (Y) and Census (X)	Correlation of (Y—X) with Y
Years of school completed[a]	.858	.280
Occupation[b]	.879	.237
Income in 1949[a]	.822	.273

a. Scored according to midpoint of intervals used for tabulation in source.

b. Major occupation groups were scored according to Duncan's Socioeconomic Index, for which see Duncan 1961b, table VII-4, p. 155.

Source: Calculated from U.S. Bureau of the Census 1960.

Style of life

Many common objective measures of social status tend to obscure socioeconomic variation in special populations. For example, American students of social stratification have, with a few notable exceptions, ignored differentiation within the farm population, which is typically treated as a single group. Here, as elsewhere, style of life, as reflected in social participation, residential area, house type, living room equipment, and other visible aspects of status, may serve to array the population hierarchically, if not to segregate it into distinct classes.

Probably the best-known attempts to assess life style through the recording of personal possessions are the several versions of Chapin's Living Room Scale. Actually, Chapin posed his problem as the generic one of measuring socioeconomic status, which he saw as "the position that an individual or a family occupies with reference to the prevailing average standards of cultural possessions, effective income, material possessions, and participation in the group activities of the community" (1935, p. 374). Consequently, the original version of Chapin's scale was based on measures of cultural and material possessions derived from enumeration of household equipment and housing characteristics, lists of membership and degree of involvement in voluntary organizations, and a measure of income. However, "the total of the weights given to living room equipment were found to correlate so highly with the combined weights of the four indices that the equipment of the living room could be taken as a fair index of socio-economic status" (*ibid.*, p. 375).

After almost a decade of experimentation, Chapin finally arrived at a short Social Status Scale, which is derived from an enumeration of 17 items of living room equipment, ranging from radios and newspapers to fireplaces and hardwood floors, plus an evaluation by interviewers of the condition, repair, and orderliness of the respondent's living room and the articles in it. Evidence about the validity of this shortened version comes from its correlation with income and occupation. In a nonrandom sample of residents of several metropolitan areas, 14 per cent of the variance in the short social status scores could be accounted for by income, and 27 per cent by occupation. Associations of the same order of magnitude were observed in an analysis of a more detailed living room scale based on nearly fifty items of household equipment (*ibid.*, pp. 389, 397). Since Chapin's various versions of the Living Room Scale are not very highly intercorrelated with other criteria of socioeconomic position, we are unable to recommend them (or modifications of them) as *single* general measures of socioeconomic status. Rather, we prefer to regard their content as a reflection of one aspect of social status—life style—which is functionally intertwined with other elements into a socioeconomic configuration whose parts are but loosely connected (as revealed by measures of association).

Socioeconomic status of farm families. One interesting application of Chapin's formulation has been in measuring the socioeconomic status of farm families, which cannot be differentiated very well (especially within states or regions) by means of the usual objective indicators, such as education and occupation. Pursuing the facets of socioeconomic status identified by Chapin, Sewell (1940) constructed indices of *material possessions* (house construction, floor and wall finishings, etc.), *cultural possessions* (living room rugs, magazine and newspaper subscriptions, education of husband and wife, etc.), and *social participation* (family attendance at church, farm cooperative, and PTA activities) of Oklahoma farm families. Sewell's Farm Family Socio-economic Status Scale is derived by combining all three of these indices, and, when a measure of effective farm income is added to them, can be shown by the method of tetrad differences to measure a single common factor. The elements of the total index are not, however, dramatically intercorrelated. As one can see in Table 2, the index of social participation bears only

Table 2 — Intercorrelations between components of Sewell's Farm Family Socio-economic Status Scale (data from Oklahoma, circa 1938)[a]

Components	Index of cultural possessions	Effective income index	Index of social participation
Index of material possessions	.790	.555	.318
Index of cultural possessions		.597	.366
Effective income index[b]			.245

a. Correlations based on a sample of approximately 800 families.
b. This measure is excluded from Sewell's final scale.

Source: Adapted from Sewell 1940, p. 80.

modest positive associations with indicators of material and cultural possessions. Thus, the degree of their involvement in the community cannot be predicted from the life style revealed in the objects with which families surround themselves.

Interrelations of status indicators

While the raison d'être of objective indicators of social status often seems to be nothing more than convenience, such indicators are nevertheless functionally intertwined both among themselves and with class identification and life style. Thus *education* is a kind of investment whereby one acquires an *occupation* from which *income* is the return limiting the *life style* one may set and, hence, the *class identification* one may consistently maintain. The ordering imposed upon these variables by their functional interrelation is not meant, of course, to imply that they form a simple causal chain. Quite the contrary. Class identification probably rests as much upon educational attainment as upon life style. Indeed, many ingenious economic devices—such as credit—have become important cogs in the machinery of business precisely because they enable an individual to maintain a class identification he would have to forgo were his life style determined solely by his current money income.

The fact that status variables are functionally interrelated does not imply that they are strongly intercorrelated statistically. On the contrary, they are a loosely associated configuration. Materials from the 1950 U.S. *Census of Population* reveal that for males 30 per cent of the variation in years of school completed and 18 per cent of the variation in income can be accounted for by major occupation group, while 11 per cent of the variation in income can be accounted for by educational attainment. One aspect of these loose connections between objective indicators of social status is that individuals with disparate configurations of occupation, education, and income are free to adopt similar class identifications. Indeed, under the conditions imposed by these loose associations, relatively few individuals will have consistently high or consistently low education, occupational status, and income. The absence in the United States of objective configurations of education, occupation, and income around which classes may crystallize tends, of course, to leave individuals with ambiguous notions about their appropriate class identification. Consensus about one's social class position and that of others becomes nearly impossible to attain. This is perhaps the fundamental reason why class identification and class awareness have not played a central role in the indices of social class typically employed in the United States.

Size of status systems. Clearly, size of place is an important parameter that limits the use of judges' ratings in devising measures of social status. There is also some feeling that size of place is intertwined with the *degree* of association between status variables: while objective status positions are not highly intercorrelated at the societal level of integration, they may be highly intercorrelated in smaller communities, where the status attributes of all families and individuals are more visible and widely known. In large measure, this suggestion is built upon qualitative reports from community studies, the most notable empirical evidence being that amassed under the guidance of W. Lloyd Warner. Using data collected in the Jonesville investigations, Warner ([1949] 1960, p. 172) reported that the common variance (the proportion of the variation in one variable accounted for by another) between pairs of such objective characteristics as occupation, education, income, and house type (measures of the last characteristic having been formed largely from inspection of the size and condition of dwelling units) ranged between 36 and 64 per cent. But there is no reason whatsoever to believe that these associations are either typical of other communities or, for that matter, accurate for Jonesville. First, they are based on a biased sample of individuals whose characteristics are not fully known (Pfautz & Duncan 1950, pp. 208–209). The admission (see McGuire 1950) that the sample is in fact a "blue ribbon" one suggests that the correlations are as high as they are because of the introduction of a correlation between extremes achieved by under-representing the middle sectors of the class structure. Second, Hochbaum and his associates (1955) have demonstrated that in an urban setting (St. Paul, Minnesota) associations between education, occupation, and income fall in a range lower than, and only partially overlapping with, that observed in Warner's reports. Third, associations between these variables reported in other small communities are not appreciably higher than those calculated above for the United States as a whole. Thus Duncan and Artis (1951b) show, for a rural community of 533 households, that 21 per cent of the variation in judges' prestige ratings, 29 per cent of the variation in education (of male household heads), and 20 per cent of the variation in Sewell's Socio-economic Status Score can be accounted for by major occupation group. Income accounts for similar fractions of the variance in judges' prestige ratings, education, and Sewell's Socio-economic Status Score. So far, then, there is no really substantial empirical evidence for assuming greater crystallization of status variables in small communities than in the nation as a whole.

It is reasonable to assume that patterns of organizational membership and interpersonal contacts are more salient features of small-scale status systems than of large urban ones, since in the latter individuals are not known, and membership groups do not extend, throughout the entire community. For example, Kaufman (1944) reports that for a rural New York community, prestige class accounts for 41 per cent of variation in the number of memberships in voluntary associations,

and one can estimate from his report that membership in the local Presbyterian church accounts for 30 per cent of the variation in judges' prestige ratings. No direct comparisons with the correlations to be found in urban settings can be made, but from the files of the National Opinion Research Center we were able to estimate for residents of a suburb of the District of Columbia that 10 per cent of the variance of the number of memberships in voluntary associations could be attributed to either years of school completed or family income. Both associations were much lower than one would expect from Kaufman's study and somewhat lower than the values obtained by Duncan and Artis (1951b), who used a more elaborate measure of participation in formal organizations. These findings suggest that voluntary organizations are an important focus of stratification in small communities but become less important in this respect as scale becomes an obstacle to community-wide organization.

Status consistency. In the United States, the lack of crystallization in the national status structure—as revealed by the modest associations between different status attributes—has encouraged divergent approaches to the measurement of social class. Some researchers, most notably Lenski (1954; 1956), have abandoned the task altogether. Instead, a modified view of the class structure is proposed, in which not only the condition of universal class awareness, but also the condition of mutual exclusiveness of classes, is relaxed. Different variables, such as occupation, educational attainment, ethnic background, class identification, and judgments by others, may be understood as defining different status hierarchies. Since the stratification system is not very crystallized—that is, since these different aspects of status are not highly intercorrelated—individuals will vary in their degree of consistency: some will be quite consistent, experiencing high or low standing on each of the several status indicators, while many will be inconsistent in varying degrees, combining some elements of high status, such as a college education, with elements of low status, such as a modest income. In such a scheme a person does not occupy a single position in a unique hierarchy of mutually exclusive classes; rather, his social status is defined by his positions on several dimensions of stratification, and one aspect of his total position in such a stratification system is held to be the consistency between the levels he occupies on various dimensions of status.

Adopting the formulations implicit in the theory of status consistency may not, of course, be a feasible research strategy to choose in countries with less fluid status systems. However, even the rigidity of the Indian caste system is apparently insufficient to produce extremely high associations between status variables in urban areas. For example, for Poona, India, we can calculate from published tabulations (Sovani et al. 1956, tables 6.1 and 6.3) that an arrangement of castes and an occupational classification similar to the major occupation groups of the U.S. Bureau of the Census account for 10 and 46 per cent, respectively, of the variation in total family income. These values, like similar associations observed for the United States, do not show enough common variance between status variables to rule out a status consistency approach.

The multidimensionality of social stratification systems is implicitly assumed in the status consistency approach. Actually, this multidimensionality is only manifest and is open to empirical evaluation. Indeed, the plethora of social class indicators reviewed above might be defining a single latent continuum. The conclusions about measuring social class that one might derive from the application of latent structure or factor analyses of status variables are hard to specify because in relatively complex situations these techniques often yield several equally plausible representations of the underlying structures [see LATENT STRUCTURE]. For example, in an application of latent structure analysis to the problems of measuring social class, Rossi found that dichotomously represented items covering such features of social status as possession of certain household objects, class identification, education, and interviewer's rating could be treated either "as correlated latent continua with linear tracelines or as essentially unidimensional with parabolic tracelines" (1951, p. 250). Ambiguities such as these leave open the fundamental question of whether the multidimensionality in status variables at the manifest level can be reduced to a single latent continuum. It seems unlikely that more elaborate methodologies will provide any easy answers, especially insofar as they tend to ignore the functional interdependence between status variables.

Selecting measures of social class

How is the individual researcher to choose among the wealth of existing measures of social class without first conducting his own independent investigation of stratification? Our view is quite simple, but provides no explicit rules: selection of an appropriate measure of social class, like the choice between alternative modes of data analysis, depends on the problem to be investigated, and should reflect the interpretation the researcher is likely to make of correlations between social status and the variables regarded as dependent. Thus, in studies of morbidity, differential rates according to social status are apt to be interpreted as a reflection of either differential nutrition and health care or differential exposure to hazardous work environments. Accordingly, in such studies one should employ measures of socioeconomic status, like income or occupation, that have a clear connection with the intervening variables, such as health care, nutrition, and risk, that are thought to specify the relation between mortality and status. Alternative measures, such as class identification, which seem less relevant in studies of morbidity, of course assume greater salience in investigations of other matters (child-rearing practices, for instance). Thus, in selecting a measure of social class the researcher should think his problem through clearly and then make his choice. So selected, different measures of social class can achieve appreciable face validity within the particular context in which they are employed. Reliability is, of course, a more complex matter, but it is no less true in other areas than in stratification research that, to quote Rossi again: "Fruitful empirical work in an area where errors of measurement tend to obscure the fundamental structure can only be possible by the employment of descriptive models in a methodology where such errors are explicitly provided for" (1951, p. 225).

ROBERT W. HODGE AND PAUL M. SIEGEL

[*Directly related are the entries* CASTE; CENSUS; COMMUNITY, *article on* THE STUDY OF COMMUNITY POWER; SOCIAL STRUCTURE, *article on* SOCIAL STRUCTURAL ANALYSIS; STATUS, SOCIAL. *Other relevant material may be found in* HOMELESSNESS; LABOR FORCE, *article on* DEFINITIONS AND MEASUREMENT; LATENT STRUCTURE; SCALING.]

BIBLIOGRAPHY

BLISHEN, BERNARD R. 1958 The Construction and Use of an Occupational Class Scale. *Canadian Journal of Economic and Political Science* 24:519–531.

BOGUE, DONALD J. 1963 *Skid Row in American Cities.* Univ. of Chicago, Community and Family Study Center.

BOGUE, DONALD J.; and MURPHY, EDMUND M. 1964 The Effect of Classification Errors Upon Statistical Inference: A Case Analysis With Census Data. *Demography* 1:42–55.

CAMPBELL, J. D. 1952 Subjective Aspects of Occupational Status. Ph.D. dissertation, Harvard Univ.

CENTERS, RICHARD (1949) 1961 *The Psychology of Social Classes: A Study of Class Consciousness.* New York: Russell.

CHAPIN, FRANCIS S. 1935 *Contemporary American Institutions: A Sociological Analysis.* New York: Harper.

CHARLES, ENID 1948 *The Changing Size of the Family in Canada.* Canada, Bureau of Statistics, Census Monograph No. 1. Ottawa: Cloutier.

COUNTS, GEORGE S. 1925 The Social Status of Occupations: A Problem in Vocational Guidance. *School Review* 33:16–27.

DAVIS, JAMES A. 1956 Status Symbols and the Measurement of Status Perception. *Sociometry* 19:154–165.

DUNCAN, OTIS DUDLEY 1961a A Socioeconomic Index for All Occupations. Pages 109–138 in Albert J. Reiss, Jr. et al., *Occupations and Social Status.* New York: Free Press.

DUNCAN, OTIS DUDLEY 1961b Properties and Characteristics of the Socioeconomic Index. Pages 139–161 in Albert J. Reiss, Jr. et al., *Occupations and Social Status.* New York: Free Press.

DUNCAN, OTIS DUDLEY; and ARTIS, JAY W. 1951a Some Problems of Stratification Research. *Rural Sociology* 16:17–29.

DUNCAN, OTIS DUDLEY; and ARTIS, JAY W. 1951b *Social Stratification in a Pennsylvania Rural Community.* Pennsylvania State College, School of Agriculture, Agricultural Experiment Station, Bulletin 543. University Park, Pa.: The College.

EDWARDS, ALBA M. 1933 A Social-economic Grouping of the Gainful Workers of the United States. *Journal of the American Statistical Association* 28:377–387.

FREEDMAN, RONALD; and SLESINGER, DORIS P. 1961 Fertility Differentials for the Indigenous Non-farm Population of the United States. *Population Studies* 15:161–173.

HERMAN, MARY W. 1962 Class Concepts, Aspirations and Vertical Mobility. Pages 115–152 in G. L. Palmer et al., *The Reluctant Job Changer: Studies in Work Attachments and Aspirations.* Philadelphia: Univ. of Pennsylvania Press.

HOCHBAUM, GODFREY et al. 1955 Socioeconomic Variables in a Large City. *American Journal of Sociology* 61:31–38.

HODGE, ROBERT W.; and SIEGEL, PAUL M. 1966 The Classification of Occupations: Some Problems of Sociological Interpretation. American Statistical Association, Social Statistics Section, *Proceedings* [1965]: 176–192.

KAUFMAN, HAROLD F. 1944 *Prestige Classes in a New York Rural Community.* Cornell University, Agricultural Experiment Station, Memoir No. 260. Ithaca, N.Y.: The University.

KAUFMAN, HAROLD F. 1946 *Defining Prestige in a Rural Community.* Sociometry Monographs, No. 10. New York: Beacon.

LENSKI, GERHARD E. 1952 American Social Classes: Statistical Strata or Social Groups? *American Journal of Sociology* 58:139–144.

LENSKI, GERHARD E. 1954 Status Crystallization: A Nonvertical Dimension of Social Status. *American Sociological Review* 19:405–413.

LENSKI, GERHARD E. 1956 Social Participation and Status Crystallization. *American Sociological Review* 21:458–464.

LOOMIS, CHARLES P. et al. (editors) 1953 *Turrialba: Social Systems and the Introduction of Change.* Glencoe, Ill.: Free Press.

McGUIRE, CARSON 1950 Social Stratification and Mobility Patterns. *American Sociological Review* 15:195–204.

NATIONAL OPINION RESEARCH CENTER 1947 Jobs and Occupations: A Popular Evaluation. *Opinion News* 9, no. 4:3–13.

PFAUTZ, HAROLD W.; and DUNCAN, OTIS DUDLEY 1950 A Critical Evaluation of Warner's Work in Community Stratification. *American Sociological Review* 15: 205–215.

REISS, ALBERT J. JR. et al. 1962 *Occupations and Social Status.* New York: Free Press.

ROSSI, PETER H. 1951 Latent Structure Analysis and Research on Social Stratification. Ph.D. dissertation, Columbia Univ.

SEWELL, WILLIAM H. 1940 *The Construction and Standardization of a Scale for the Measurement of Oklahoma Farm Families: Socio-economic Status.* Agricultural Experiment Station, Technical Bulletin No. 9. Stillwater: Oklahoma Agricultural and Mechanical College. → Permission for the use of Table 2 was granted by the Board of Regents for the Oklahoma Agricultural and Mechanical College, acting for and on behalf of the Oklahoma State University of Agriculture and Applied Sciences and its Agricultural Experiment Station.

SOVANI, N. V.; APTE, D. P.; and PENDSE, R. G. 1956 *Poona: A Re-survey; The Changing Pattern of Employment and Earnings.* Gokhale Institute of Politics and Economics, Publication No. 34. Poona (India): Gadgil.

U.S. BUREAU OF THE CENSUS 1960 *The Post-Enumeration Survey, 1950: An Evaluation Study of the 1950 Census of Population and Housing.* Census Technical Paper No. 4. Washington: Government Printing Office.

WALKER, HELEN; and LEV, JOSEPH 1953 *Statistical Inference.* New York: Holt.

WARNER, W. LLOYD (1949) 1960 *Social Class in America: A Manual of Procedure for the Measurement of Social Status.* New York: Harper.

WHELPTON, P. K.; and HOLLANDER, EDWARD 1940 A Standard Occupational and Industrial Classification of Workers. *Social Forces* 18:488–494.

IV

THE STRUCTURE OF STRATIFICATION SYSTEMS

The study of stratification systems involves three main topics: the degree of inequality of rewards and privileges (in wealth, power, and fame) in different societies and the causes and effects of different amounts and kinds of inequality; the relation between the distribution of the good things of life and the solidarity of categories of people with different levels of reward (such as social classes, ethnic groups, and regions within societies) and the causes and effects of different patternings of solidary groupings in relation to the distribution of privileges; and the patterning of social relations between people of different levels of reward (conflict, domination, ritual equality, and so forth) and its causes and effects. The pattern of a stratification system can be fairly well outlined if we know the amount of inequality in the distribution of rewards, the amount and patterning of solidarity among people at approximately the same level in the distribution, and the relations between "the rich, the wise, and the well-born" and the poor, the ignorant, and the lowly.

Inequality of rewards and privileges

In order to measure the degree of inequality, it is necessary to have quite precise measures of the rewards obtained by the individuals or groups of a society. For this reason, much of what we know about the causes and effects of different degrees of inequality is based on studies of the distribution of income and property. The measurement of the political power of various individuals and groups within a society is very poorly developed, and therefore it is difficult to obtain measurements of the degree of inequality of power in different societies. Likewise, it is very difficult to determine whether fame and social honor are more unequally distributed in some societies than in others, although such men as Alexis de Tocqueville have given strong reasons for believing that societies do differ in this respect.

A final difficulty in the measurement of inequality is that the social groups which are the units of stratification systems vary among societies. Let us suppose, for instance, that in one society all commercial, industrial, and agricultural firms are families, while in another many of the firms are corporations. It may well be that in the corporately organized society there is a concentration of wealth and power in a few firms, while in the society where firms are families the distribution of power and money among firms is more even. At the same time, it may be that in the corporately organized society no families have very great wealth and power, whereas in the society where families are firms the distribution of wealth and power among families is very unequal. When the very structure of the social groups that appropriate money, power, and fame differs, statistical measurements of the distribution of wealth (or power and fame, if they can be measured) ought to be constructed on correspondingly different bases. But if they are so constructed, the measures are not comparable.

With these precautions in mind, I will outline some of the main causes of different degrees of inequality of condition in various societies, especially the distribution of culturally valued competences; the distribution of "tenures," particularly property rights, which allow some part of the people in a society to obtain benefits which are not dependent on their current performances; taxation and social security systems; and the technological organization of societies.

Culturally valued competences. The distribution of culturally valued competences affects the amount and patterning of inequality, because those activities in a society that give high returns have to be carried on in a distinctive language, pattern of etiquette, or technical culture. Part of this is due to the inherent character of highly productive activities. For instance, many of the activities in the urban economy cannot be carried on without writing and, consequently, literacy. Also, most foreign trade must be carried on in foreign languages, so the profits go to multilingual people. Another reason why highly productive activities have to be performed within a distinctive culture is that they are highly interdependent and require communication among the participants. Thus, historical accident may determine that the government and commerce and literature of England will be carried on largely in the dialect of the Midlands. But once this language is chosen for such highly valued activities, competence in that language is closely related to capacity to enter those fields where wealth, power, and fame are to be had.

The capacity to read and write the language of the elite is much more widely distributed in some societies than in others. First, societies differ greatly in their degree of linguistic homogeneity. In Japan, England, France, Germany, Spain, Australia, and some of the Latin American countries that do not have large native Indian populations (Chile, Argentina, and Uruguay, for instance), the traditional spoken languages are dialects of a common root language. Other societies have very substantial linguistic diversity: nearly half the population of the Soviet Union speaks one of the minority languages as a mother tongue; in Peru, Bolivia, the Central American highland republics, and southern Mexico a large proportion of the population speaks an Indian language; and many of the new nations in Africa and Asia have no majority language at all. Under these conditions, whatever language is chosen to be used in carrying on the activities that produce wealth, power, and fame, a substantial proportion of the population will be seriously disadvantaged. Thus, a high degree of inequality of language groups is characteristic of these societies, even where (as in the Soviet Union) substantial efforts are made to create highly valued activities in the various minority cultures. When the powerful language groups exploit their advantage to the fullest, as was typically the case in colonial areas before independence, the resulting degree of inequality is very high.

Whatever the degree of inequality deriving from linguistic heterogeneity, in order to participate in the high-return activities of urban and cosmopolitan society people must learn to read and write. Societies differ a great deal in the degree of inequality of educational opportunity, especially in the degree of advantage derived by urban people from living in cities. In advanced societies elementary schooling exists in both urban and rural areas. In poorer societies generally, the only people who live near enough to schools to send their children are urban people. This means that in poorer societies a large proportion of the population cannot compete for those high-paying, powerful, or prestigious positions that require literacy. In such societies there are thus two radically separate labor markets, marked off by the fundamental cultural variable of literacy, which have different wage rates, different levels of political power, and different chances for fame and social honor. This in turn shows up in a larger degree of income inequality between urban and rural people in underdeveloped societies.

The available information on the literacy rates in urban and rural areas in different societies supports this analysis. For those societies for which we have data on urban and rural literacy rates over a long period of time, it is uniformly the case that rural literacy rates approach the urban rates, although both are, of course, increasing at the same time (UNESCO 1953). It is also true that the difference between the rural and urban rates is quite small in richer societies and quite large in poorer societies, and thus the degree of inequality in cultural preparation for the urban labor market is generally much higher in underdeveloped countries. In the United States an urban employer has little reason for preferring an urban-born worker over a rural-born worker, while in Honduras the urban-born man can probably read, while the rural-born worker is probably illiterate.

Although literacy in the elite language is probably the most important cultural characteristic determining the shape of stratification systems, other cultural competences, such as an educated dialect, technical skills, knowledge of the laws and procedures of urban society and appropriate modes of dress, also affect stratification position. The more culturally homogeneous a society, the less inequality will be caused on such grounds. Although traditional societies vary a great deal in degree of cultural heterogeneity, the general tendency of modernization is to equalize cultural competence, either by cultural homogenization or by increasing, through specification of additional legal, commercial, and literary languages, the diversity of the culture in which the business of the society is carried on.

Distribution of tenures. By "tenure" we refer to a socially defensible right to a flow of rewards —money, power, or fame—which is not dependent on people's current performances (as when people hold property or sinecures). If tenures are unequally distributed, the structure of competences or activities in a population is not sufficient to explain the degree of inequality. For instance, according to the *Return of Owners of Land* of 1873 in England, four-fifths of the land was held by less than 7,000 persons. If land rents form a major part of the income of a society and if power derived from landownership is institutionalized in a House of Lords and in landowners' control of local rural society and if the peaks of the distribution of fame and social honor are reserved for large landlords, then this great inequality of property creates a great inequality of reward and privilege.

In general, property income as a percentage of the total of all personal income declines with modernization (partly because of changes in taxation systems but mostly because urban production is less capital-intensive than agriculture). At the same time, the proportion of jobs that are held on some sort of tenure (mainly based on seniority) tends to increase. Roughly speaking, this results in a redistribution of tenure rights, which tends to increase the rewards of the poor and decrease the rewards of the rich, relatively. Still, there is a persistence of societal differences, at any level of economic development, in the proportion of the good things of life that are rewards for current efforts and skills and the proportion that are held on some type of socially defensible tenure; and there are great variations in the degree of inequality in the distribution of such tenure rights. A comparison of English land tenure with that of either France or the United States, of Japanese land tenure before the postwar land reform with the Malayan distribution, or of Peruvian land tenure with that of Mexico will show that incomes from "rent," as a form of economic return, can be either very unequally or very equally distributed. What effect this has on the total stratification structure will depend on the proportion of total income that is imputable to rent. Likewise, sinecures, or jobs that make no substantial demands on the man who holds them, are much more common, and the benefits from these jobs are more unequally distributed, in some societies than in others.

It is generally true that entrance into tenures is more ascriptively allocated than is entrance to jobs at which one has to work. In other words, land, stocks and bonds, and sinecures are more likely to be distributed by inheritance than are jobs that require skill or exceptional talent. The proportion of a society's income, power, and social honor which is held on some kind of tenure is thus related to the degree of openness of opportunity.

The causes of differences between societies in the degree of inequality in the distribution of tenures are not well known. The main determinants seem to be aspects of the political history of the societies, such as conquest or social revolution, and certain kinds of economic developments, such as plantation or ranch agriculture, which tend to concentrate tenures in a few hands.

Taxation and social security systems. Another major influence on the degree of inequality and its pattern is the system of taxation and social security. The system of taxation is intimately tied to the system of tenures in three ways. First, the social defensibility of a right to a flow of benefits is usually guaranteed, and often obtained, by political means. Thus, the existence of a government with resources of its own derived from taxation or expropriation is a conditioning variable for tenure systems. Second, government and ownership are not usually distinguished sharply and unequivocally in primitive and feudal societies. The medieval manor is both a local government and the lord's property. The modern distinction between taxes and rents or between the national budget and the lord's or king's budget is not clearly drawn in such societies. Third, without very complex accounting and enforcement structures, apportionment of the tax burden in relation to ability to pay is made easier by taxing (or expropriating) tenures than by taxing income. In addition, the distribution of the tax burden has direct influence on the distribution of income.

Governments influence income distributions by redistributive social security, as well as by taxation. Social security arrangements are those techniques by which the lame, the halt, the blind, and the incompetent are allocated their social rights and income. Age, sickness, genetic accident, and social imperfection create people who are "useless" from the point of view of the productive activities of a society. The economic support of these people may be arranged within the family, as the "uselessness" of children is almost always handled. But if the heads of families are biologically or socially imperfect or are in jail, the position of their families is determined by different techniques in different societies. The presence or absence of politically arranged systems of social security, as well as their character and policy if they exist, are fundamental in determining the social status of "useless" people. There is less inequality in societies that care for and support the imperfect than in societies where those with poor biological, social, or moral equipment must fend for themselves.

The following very rough outline will distinguish several types of relationships between taxation and social security systems, on the one hand, and stratification, on the other.

First, there are stateless peoples—that is, peoples who are not subject to coercion by a tax-supported state. For these peoples, the elementary social units that carry on productive, household, and kinship functions also carry on the social insurance functions of society and define the status of children, the aged, the infirm, and the insane. The social unit itself carries the brunt of the malfunctioning of key people.

Second, in intermediate-level societies (feudal systems, traditional empires, medieval mercantile states) a separate governmental structure provides a contingency reserve of power, to guarantee the tenures of the rich against both external enemies and internal revolt and theft. As tax farmers, landholders, and patricians, the rich either perform government functions themselves or collect rents, tributes, taxes, or services from their underlings in order to maintain the governmental structure. Citizenship, in the sense of rights guaranteed by the central government and influence on the central government, is confined to the rich. Social security, beyond that provided for the rich by tenures, remains a local affair within the kin group or manor or merchant company, is provided as charity by the church, or takes the form of a general tolerance of begging. In such societies the government reinforces the inequality of condition, rather than mitigating it. Generally a feudal state's government has a rapidly declining capacity to enforce its will, that is, to collect taxes or guarantee tenures, as one travels out from its center; near the borders of feudal states the lords must maintain their own armies and are not tightly controlled from the center. Thus, even for tenure holders "citizenship" depends on geographical variables. Government guarantees the right of the rich to oppress the poor; and the closer they are to the center, the freer they are to do so.

Finally, as a government grows in power and the size of its budget increases compared with the largest private interests, it becomes capable of resisting these interests and of enforcing its will up to the border. This ability, along with the bureaucratization of government, fulfills the elementary prerequisites of the extension of "citizenship" to the general population. In other words, the government can now guarantee a certain minimum of political rights and social security to all people living within the borders of the nation. Government services, guarantees, and social security payments become the right of every man; taxation of the rich to provide services and income to the poor becomes general instead of taxation to support a government to defend the tenures of the rich. Rent becomes a form of income radically distinct from taxation. Gradually, it becomes an established political principle that citizens have a right to a certain level of living and should not be allowed to fall below that level. Social insurance functions tend to move more and more under the sway of the government, and charity comes to be enforced by law, rather than pleaded for by begging.

Broadly speaking, then, increases in the level of taxation for central government functions first increase the amount of inequality, by protecting the rich, and then decrease it, by taxing the rich for the benefit of all citizens. There are, of course, numerous variations in taxation systems and social security systems that cause variations and deviations from the pattern outlined here. [See TAXATION and WELFARE ECONOMICS.]

The economic and technological base.   Technology affects the degree of inequality of reward in two different ways. First, various types of technical and economic activity either require or cause different degrees of inequality within the productive organization itself. Different technological systems require different distributions of skills. A research organization, for instance, requires a relatively high degree of skill by all, whereas a mine generally requires many unskilled workers and a few highly skilled ones. In addition, large cooperative undertakings tend to give rise to a complex hierarchy of authority, and rewards tend to be associated with authority both because people in authority have the power to take more rewards and because it seems fair to most people that different degrees of responsibility should meet with different levels of reward.

The combination of skill requirements and authority systems of the technical organization of productive groups in a society thus to a large extent determines the shape of the distribution of rewards. Early modern armies, for example, required many men to do the handwork of fighting and few to plan, train, and lead. Modern armies require a good many skills of very different types, and they use relatively less hand labor as it becomes more efficient to kill men by machines. Therefore, the distribution of ranks (and consequently of pay and deference) in armies is much less unequal than it used to be. Armies today have a much larger group in the middle ranks and a smaller group at the very bottom. Likewise, it has been argued that the complex authority system required to construct, maintain, and distribute the

benefits from a complex irrigation system has tended to create a very high degree of inequality in societies where the economic base is irrigated agriculture (Wittfogel 1957; cf. Eberhard 1952).

A second effect of technology on the degree of inequality of reward is that technological systems have different degrees of productivity. This has two implications. First, societies with different technological bases will have different amounts of resources to distribute unequally, after some base line of sufficiency is reached. Thus, an increase in wealth seems to increase the level of inequality. In addition, in complex societies different people will be involved in different technological systems. If some of these are "high-wage" industries while others are "low-wage," if some give special access to political power (people involved in military technology, for instance), or if different technical systems offer differential chances of becoming famous (acting in movies, as opposed to running motels, for instance), then the mix of industries in a society helps determine its stratification system. As a general rule the technological systems introduced late in a country's development give a greater return to the individuals involved in them than do the older industries. Those who, because of tenures that compel them to remain in the older technological systems, skills that tie them to the older industries, or inertia and family tradition, are bound up with declining industries tend to be disadvantaged compared with those in new industries and occupations.

Societies also vary in their flexibility, or labor mobility. Low labor mobility tends to give rise to an oversupply of labor (with consequent lowering of wages and returns) in the older sections of the economy. Low incomes in older sectors, along with the compensating excessive wages in the new industries, which have to attract labor over the barriers of low labor mobility, tend to increase the degree of inequality in societies. [See LABOR FORCE, article on MARKETS AND MOBILITY.]

It seems that a considerable part of rural poverty in otherwise rich societies can be explained on such grounds: regional inequalities between areas that have an industrial structure based on older industries and areas in which innovation is concentrated seem to derive from low labor mobility. But whether societies with highly flexible labor markets in fact tend to have less regional inequality of income, to a degree over and above that which can be explained by the concentration of illiteracy or minority language in certain regions, has not been investigated sufficiently.

In sum, then, the amount of inequality of reward

in different societies is determined to a large extent by the amount of inequality in the distribution of cultural competences, especially the ability to read and write the elite language; by the importance of property and sinecure income in the total income of society and by the degree of inequality of property; by the degree of development of taxation and social security and by variations in tax and social security systems; and by the mix of industries of a society, their total productivity, the requirements of their technical systems for inequality within the enterprise, and the conditions under which new industries compete with old industries for the labor force of the society.

Patterns of group solidarity

Societies vary not only in the ways in which the total distribution of their valuables is structured but also in the type of relation that obtains between the degree of inequality they exhibit and the structure of their solidary groups. This has two major aspects. First, how does the distribution of good things in the society relate to the other bases men have for feeling themselves to have a common destiny with other men? Second, how does the distribution of rewards itself cause men to associate to improve their positions? Since men's sense of justice interacts with their sense of self-interest when they judge the fairness of the distribution of rewards in society, and since a large share of public policy (especially taxation, social security, tariff policy, and policy toward monopolies) is directly relevant to the degree of inequality, solidary groupings of men who share a common position in the stratification system have great political importance.

Economic interest and pre-existing groups. As implied in the previous discussion of the causes of different degrees of inequality, depressed ethnic groups, rural regions, and regions whose industrial structures emphasize older industries will tend to have distinctive positions in the distribution of rewards, although more so under some conditions than others. Most societies have at least one ethnic group that occupies a distinctive position in the economic system, for example, the Europeans in Algeria or South Africa, the Negroes in the United States, the Chinese in southeast Asia, the Tamils in Ceylon and east Africa. The mutual reinforcing of common interest and common cultural tradition tends to make such groups solidary internally, while the surrounding society often combines communal hostility with opposing economic interests when dealing with such groups.

Likewise, most societies have at least one and often several regions that have a certain amount of regional solidarity and political organization and distinctive positions in the regional distribution of income. For example, the following areas represent more or less well organized and politically powerful concentrations of poverty on a regional basis: the south in the United States and in Italy; central Asia in the Soviet Union; the northeast in Brazil; the southern tier of states in Mexico and also the central area (except for the capital city itself); Java, as compared with Sumatra, in Indonesia; and the central region of the Congo (Kinshasa), as opposed to Katanga. When such regional groups with divergent positions in the distribution of the good things of a society exist, they can form a basis for common action of the relatively poor communities of a society against the relatively rich. Conversely, if a group of the rich can gain control of regional organizations (even though the region as a whole is poor) and appear to act in the name of the region, they can extend their power a great deal. Examples would be the plantation owners in the American south, the great landowners of Prussia, and the oil sheiks in the Arabian areas.

The same thing that can be said of stratification within a society in this respect can also be said of the world as a whole. Undoubtedly the main determinant of a man's income level is what country he happens to be born in, and the defense of the interests of the world's poor in international politics rests heavily on the diplomatic apparatus of the world's poor nations. [See PEACE.]

Just as the coincidence of a common economic fate with solidary ties on other grounds, such as ethnicity or region, strengthens the political capacity of a group, so the division of the poor or the rich into diverse communal or regional groups can limit the scope of pure class organization. Ethnicity, region, and community are bases of solidarity and organized action in politics and in the economic structure. These may or may not be important in a society. If they are important, it may be true that such natural "acting groups" occupy different stratification positions as a whole and act to affect the stratification system. Thus, although the politics of some major industrial cities in the United States have been run by the poor of those cities for some time, the poor are organized to affect politics as ethnic groups, rather than as the poor. This means that the strength of the lower class as a whole on economic questions is probably less than it would otherwise be.

Mutual association. The distribution of privileges is also related to the kind of solidarity that, arising from common conditions of life, provides one of the possible bases for group formation. Both informal social life and formal organization to defend collective interests tend to follow the lines of the distribution of privileges. However, the form taken by this relationship between group life and the class system varies among different societies, depending on the way in which the determinants of solidarity are related to the distribution of privileges. Probably the most important of these determinants are the size of work places, the degree of residential segregation of the social classes, and the degree to which the rewards of social classes are formally allocated to large categories of people defined by an abstract criterion, as when voters are selected by a property qualification.

The larger the size of work places or the more social life tends to be restricted to class equals, the more militant the unions and political parties of the social classes tend to be and the more closely the structure of solidarity in the society is likely to be intertwined with the distribution of rewards (Lipset et al. 1954). The more ecologically differentiated the cities in which people live (so that poor homes are geographically concentrated in slums and rich homes in good neighborhoods), the fewer members of other classes any given man will be likely to meet and the more social relations will be correlated with the structure of social classes. And finally, the more formal privileges are distributed according to abstract criteria that are applied to a large number of people uniformly, the more relevant collective action is likely to be to changing a man's conditions of life and the more closely group life will correspond to the class structure. For instance, a universal property qualification for voting is more likely to unite the poor to obtain equal representation than is a process of individual qualification of voters that is so administered as to be generally discriminatory against the poor, even if the two systems have exactly the same effect. Likewise, if all the workers in a factory have their wages determined by the setting of one basic wage rate, they are more likely to act in common than if wage rates are negotiated individually, even if the same amount of money is spent for wages in the two situations.

Conversely, when the rich and poor meet at work (although, of course, not as equals), especially in small enterprises; when the rich live next to the poor (although, of course, in richer houses); and when the rich treat the poor as individuals (although, of course, not as if they were rich individuals), the degree of class solidarity on both sides is likely to be lower, for the rich sympathize with the lot of the poor and the poor develop attachments to the rich.

Relations between the classes

On the fundamental question of how the social classes treat each other, there is much less theory and research. It is quite clear that societies vary in this respect. For instance, in the United States, outside the South, and in the Soviet Union it is considered very ill-mannered for a man to emphasize his superior social position or to insist on deferential treatment from those whose social standing is not as high. In contrast, many racially stratified societies and countries that have not destroyed their feudal aristocracies during the course of modernization have maintained organized patterns of deference. Likewise, in those societies that are generally called liberal, greatly unequal power is supposed to be limited to specific purposes rather than used to the full in all situations; while, in many feudal and semifeudal areas, it is considered perfectly legitimate for men to use all the power at their disposal to govern in detail all aspects of the lives of their inferiors. In some societies the lower classes treat the upper classes as open enemies or objects of hostility, while in other societies they are polite and suppress (or do not have) such hostility.

Within any society there are clear variations in the way superiors in different walks of life treat inferiors: usually a general in an army or the captain of a merchant ship or a plantation boss acts in a more authoritarian way than an equally rich and powerful superior in retail trade or manufacturing. Part of the variation between societies can again be explained by their mix of industries: a society whose economic base is plantation agriculture is likely to have basically authoritarian relations between the social classes in daily life, while a society with an economic base in wholesale commerce and international banking (e.g., Switzerland, the Netherlands) will have less open authoritarianism, even if the degree of inequality is the same.

Another major variable explaining differences among societies in this regard seems to be the ideological residue of social revolutions. Equalitarianism of manners was apparently not as prevalent in the United States before the War of Independence, and certainly it was not as prevalent in the Russian empire before the 1917 revolution and in Mexico before the revolution of 1910–1920. It is likewise certain that the manners of colonial populations toward Europeans changed after the anticolonial revolutions of recent years; and Europeans are not nearly as arrogant in their behavior as they were when these peoples were their subjects. Whether this ideological equalitarianism will spread to the symbolic behavior of classes toward each other within former colonial societies is not yet clear, but the tendency to generalize the revolutionary ideology is obviously present, for example, in Indian attempts to reduce discrimination against Untouchables.

Although the whole area of the comparative study of stratification systems is very underdeveloped, the theory of the causes of the way the rich treat the poor and of the way the poor react is probably the least developed part.

ARTHUR L. STINCHCOMBE

[*See also* BUREAUCRACY; EQUALITY; LITERACY; POVERTY; SOCIAL MOBILITY; STATELESS SOCIETY; WELFARE STATE; *and the biographies of* MARX; OSSOWSKI; TOCQUEVILLE; TROTSKY.]

BIBLIOGRAPHY

BENDIX, REINHARD 1956 *Work and Authority in Industry: Ideologies of Management in the Course of Industrialization.* New York: Wiley. → One of the few systematic studies of the way social classes treat each other in different societies.

BUKHARIN, NIKOLAI I. (1921) 1926 *Historical Materialism: A System of Sociology.* London: Allen & Unwin. → First published as *Teoriia istoricheskogo materializma.* Probably still the best introduction to the Marxist theory of the causes of differences in stratification systems.

CLARK, COLIN (1940) 1957 *The Conditions of Economic Progress.* 3d ed. New York: St. Martins. → An analysis of the effect of modernization on occupational and income distributions.

DEUTSCH, KARL W. 1953 *Nationalism and Social Communication: An Inquiry Into the Foundations of Nationality.* Cambridge, Mass.: M.I.T. Press; New York: Wiley. → Perhaps the best account to date of the development of stratification positions of ethnic groups in several European societies and in India.

EBERHARD, WOLFRAM 1952 *Conquerors and Rulers: Social Forces in Medieval China.* Leiden (Netherlands): Brill. → Maintains that riches created by irrigation invite conquest, thus causing high degrees of inequality; for an argument in opposition to this one, see Wittfogel 1957.

INKELES, ALEX; and ROSSI, PETER H. 1956 National Comparisons of Occupational Prestige. *American Journal of Sociology* 61:329–339. → Shows that most occupations in the modern sectors of different economies have the same relative standing in different countries.

KUZNETS, SIMON 1956— Quantitative Aspects of the Economic Growth of Nations. Part 1—. *Economic Development and Cultural Change* 5—. → A continuing study by Simon Kuznets, usually included as a supplement to No. 4 of each volume. A rich source of information on the dynamics of the creation and distribution of money, the fundamental reward in stratification systems.

LAMARTINE YATES, PAUL 1961 *El desarrollo regional de México.* Mexico City: Banco de Mexico, Investigaciones Industriales. → A very good monograph on the causes of regional inequality in a developing country, with suggestions for policies of equalization.

LIPSET, SEYMOUR M. et al. (1954) 1959 The Psychology of Voting: An Analysis of Political Behavior. Volume 2, pages 1124–1175 in Gardner Lindzey (editor), *Handbook of Social Psychology.* Cambridge, Mass.: Addison-Wesley. → An empirical analysis of the determinants of class solidarity in political behavior.

LOCKWOOD, DAVID 1958 *The Black-coated Worker. A Study in Class Consciousness.* London: Allen & Unwin. → An analysis of white-collar unionism which shows that class solidarity is dependent on the allocation of rewards according to abstract classifications of people.

MARSHALL, T. H. (1934–1949) 1950 *Citizenship and Social Class, and Other Essays.* Cambridge Univ. Press. → The title essay provides a historical analysis of the distribution of legal, political, and social security rights among social classes in Great Britain.

SAHLINS, MARSHALL D. 1958 *Social Stratification in Polynesia.* Seattle: Univ. of Washington Press. → Provides empirical support for the proposition that richer societies have more inequality.

STINCHCOMBE, ARTHUR L. 1961 Agricultural Enterprise and Rural Class Relations. *American Journal of Sociology* 67:165–176. → An analysis of the internal structure of enterprises in different types of agriculture and its effect on the class structure.

STINCHCOMBE, ARTHUR L. 1965 Social Structure and Organizations. Pages 142–193 in James G. March (editor), *Handbook of Organizations.* Chicago: Rand McNally. → Contains analyses of stratification within organizations, of the distribution of power and wealth among organizations and its relation to revolutionary movements, and of the properties and development of such communal groups as ethnic groups and regions.

TROTSKY, LEON (1931–1933) 1957 *The History of the Russian Revolution.* Translated by Max Eastman. 3 vols. Ann Arbor: Univ. of Michigan Press. → Volume 1: *The Overthrow of Tsarism.* Volume 2: *The Attempted Counter-revolution.* Volume 3: *The Triumph of the Soviets.* First published in Russian. One of the best accounts of the development of class organizations in Russia.

UNESCO 1953 *Progress of Literacy in Various Countries: A Preliminary Statistical Study of Available Census Data Since 1900.* Paris: UNESCO.

WITTFOGEL, KARL A. 1957 *Oriental Despotism: A Comparative Study of Total Power.* New Haven: Yale Univ. Press. → A paperback edition was published in 1963.

V

CLASS CULTURE

Controversies similar to those that have marked attempts to define *class* and to determine whether classes "really exist" are now beginning to arise over the concept of *class culture.* The implications raised by Marx about class formation and class action are being echoed by questions about the formation and consequences of a lower-class culture (or culture of poverty). On a practical level, the existence of a separate lower-class culture may be taken as a reason for attempting to alter that culture rather than altering the conditions that may have fostered its development. The strong reactions to the U.S. Department of Labor's recent (1965) report on the Negro family stem from precisely this question: Can we eliminate poverty and approach equality through changing lower-class conditions such as inferior educational and occupational opportunities, or must we attempt to change certain lower-class cultural forms directly?

The question of whether we can speak of a class culture is similar to the question of whether we can speak of a class. The ambiguities about the concept of class culture stem from the ambiguities about the concept of class. We shall therefore briefly review some of the discussion about the concept of class, which will help to throw light upon similar discussions about class culture.

Definitions of social class

There is a vast literature on the definition of *class*, or *social class*. A distinction is sometimes made between the two terms: the former is defined in terms of objective criteria such as economic power, while the latter is defined in terms of subjective criteria such as class consciousness. Various writers make use of terms such as *stratum*, *socioeconomic status*, and *occupational class* as alternatives to *class*, but the general tendency, which will be followed here, is to use only the single term *class*, or *social class* (Pfautz 1953).

"Realist" definitions.   For the sake of sanity, and of perspective, three major questions are here singled out of the vast literature on class: (1) Is a social class a social group—rather than an aggregate or category of individuals—marked off by patterns of interaction and by barriers to interaction with members of other classes? (2) Are members of a social class conscious of the existence of class division, of economic or political class interests, and of their own membership in a class? (3) Is there a distinctive culture or way of life for each social class? These three criteria—class interaction (the social class as a group), class consciousness, and class culture—form the core of most "realist" attempts to define social class. Since they are three closely related ideas, they are often discussed together. Schumpeter (1919–1927), MacIver and Page (1949), and Ossowski (1957), among many others, have all made explicit reference to the factors of class interaction, class consciousness, and class culture as criteria for distinguishing a separate class.

The idea that a separate class of people in a society would develop a distinctive class culture or way of life is an old one. Particularly in cases where the barriers to interaction between members of different classes are circumscribed by law or custom, as in a caste society or estate society, we would expect the separate development of class

cultures within a wider cultural framework that holds the separate castes or estates together as part of a total society. However, once we are dealing with "classes" where there are no legal or customary boundaries that must be adhered to, we can no longer be so definitive in our conclusions about the existence of separate class cultures.

"Nominal" definitions.   Most recent research on social class uses a "nominal" definition. Studies that report findings on the lower class, working class, middle class, or upper class usually define class in terms of an index such as occupation, education, or income, or some combination of these indices. The use of a combined index raises the question whether each component of the index is measuring the same thing. It has long been recognized that there may be different status hierarchies and that one should distinguish, for example, between such factors as economic status, social status, and political status (Weber 1921). The general idea that an individual may be ranked differently according to different criteria leads to the question of the degree of correspondence between the different rankings, and a field of empirical investigation has emerged that seeks to identify the consequences of ranking consistency or inconsistency. Marshall (1956) has suggested that inconsistency on different rankings has been increasing in complex societies and that this is the reason for the present interest in the multidimensional aspects of class status.

In using a nominal definition, whether unidimensional or multidimensional, the researcher sidesteps the question of whether classes really exist, and thus he can carry out his research. Although, at one level, this literature avoids tangling with the "real" issues of social class, at another level it is of great importance because it provides us with information about the relationship between social classes, nominally defined, and other variables. Thus, social class has been either positively or negatively correlated with family stability, juvenile delinquency, mental disorders, aspirations, membership in voluntary organizations, and so forth. One strength of some of these empirical studies is that, properly used and interpreted, they can provide us with data on the relationship between nominally defined social classes and variables that can be seen as indices of the factors of basic "realist" concern—class interaction, class consciousness, and class culture.

Feudal European societies are frequently contrasted with contemporary Western societies in order to illustrate a declining sharpness of class boundaries. As a result, the advisability of research on social classes in contemporary societies has been carefully questioned (Rose 1958; Wrong 1964). Gradations of rank are said to be more characteristic of modern society than are discrete social classes; moreover, social mobility is common. We therefore may not find sharp class barriers to communication or strongly developed class consciousness or completely distinctive class cultures. But while we would not expect to find them in fully developed form, we may find them to a degree. To what extent are there class barriers to communication (the literature on interclass marriages would be relevant), to what extent do we find class consciousness, and to what extent are there separate class cultures?

Class culture as a concept

To what degree is it possible to speak of distinctive class cultures or subcultures, and to what degree does the existence of a common culture cut across all social classes? To what degree can we speak of separate class values, attitudes, behavior, and beliefs—of a separate class way of life? At one extreme, each class would have separate and unique cultural forms. At the other extreme, a common culture would cut across the whole society without any differences, modifications, or variations by social class. Rodman (1963) has reviewed the literature pertaining to the question of whether society is based upon a common value system or a class-differentiated value system. He points out that those who hold either extreme position are partly right and partly wrong and that we must consider the range of values to be found in the different classes; the overlapping ranges result in a common core of values, while the extremes of the ranges suggest that some classes (particularly the lower class) have developed unique values.

Insofar as it may be possible to generalize about the relationship between class status and cultural forms, we are dealing with at least the following issue: To what extent do the conditions of class life influence cultural patterns? Since conditions are most pressing within the lower class, in a way that is difficult for members of the lower class to avoid or control, we would expect to find the most fully developed variations from the dominant culture within the lower class. Indeed, this appears to be so; at least, most of the discussion of class culture deals with lower-class culture, or the culture of poverty. Some authors have sought to describe a culture of poverty. Others have objected to these attempts, on the grounds that there is a vast amount of heterogeneity to be found among lower-class members (Bernard 1966). As a result, it has been suggested that we should talk about the lower classes rather than *the* lower class; and that we should talk about subcultures of poverty rather than *the* culture of poverty.

Since much of the research on social class is based upon a nominal definition of class, the controversy about the utility of the concept of lower-class culture should not be surprising. Lower-class conditions that are implied by an occupational category, such as unskilled labor, or by an income category, are obviously not all-powerful in determining cultural forms. We must therefore expect a good deal of cultural heterogeneity within a nominally defined social class. As a result, the discussion that follows contains many references to the objections that have been raised to the notion of a class culture; and even where such objections are not specifically raised, the attempt to describe separate lower-class, working-class, middle-class, and upper-class cultures must be seen in a context of homogeneity stemming from class conditions, tempered by heterogeneity stemming from other considerations.

Lower-class culture

A good deal has been written about lower-class culture, the culture of poverty, or the culture of the underprivileged. In general, most authors take the position that there are certain features of lower-class status that tend to lead to the development of certain cultural forms. Allison Davis (1946) has referred to the culture of underprivileged workers in an analysis based upon evidence from a city in the United States. Raymond T. Smith (1956) has identified a lower-class cultural tradition in British Guiana, and he has made tentative comparisons of his data with published data on lower-class communities in Peru and Scotland. Walter B. Miller (1958) has referred to the focal concerns of lower-class American culture in an essay based upon his studies of gang delinquency. Oscar Lewis (1961) has briefly spelled out an introductory statement on the culture of poverty based upon his extensive materials on families in Mexico, and he has specifically suggested the existence of some universal features of the culture of poverty that transcend national boundaries. Many others have addressed themselves to a description and understanding of lower-class culture, including Cohen and Hodges (1963), Hylan Lewis (1967), and Rainwater (1966).

What are the features attributed to the so-called lower-class culture? Walter B. Miller (1958) singles out six major focal concerns of lower-class culture—concerns that revolve about "trouble," "toughness," "smartness," "excitement," "fate," and "autonomy." Smith (1956) refers to the peripheral position of men within the lower-class family. Oscar Lewis (1961) mentions the following, among many other traits of the culture of poverty: gregariousness, violence, consensual marriages, authoritarianism, present-time orientation, tolerance, and fatalism. Cohen and Hodges (1963) report the following features, among others: most interaction with kin and neighbors, maintenance of separate kin networks by husband and wife, less participation in voluntary organizations, a preference for the familiar, authoritarianism, intolerance, anomie, distrust, toughness, extrapunitiveness. More comprehensive details from studies on social class differences, focusing particularly upon the lower class, can be found in the reviews by Herzog (1963) and Chilman (1965) and in the continuing coverage of the subject provided by *Poverty and Human Resources Abstracts*.

A mere listing of lower-class cultural traits, however, is not especially helpful. In the first place, the meaning of a trait, such as a concern about toughness or authoritarianism, is not self-evident. For example, the tolerance reported by Oscar Lewis (1961, p. xxvii) is "a high tolerance for psychological pathology of all sorts," while the intolerance reported by Cohen and Hodges (1963, p. 321) is "above all toward the ethnic minority group." The original reports must therefore be read for a clear account of the meaning of the traits. A second reason for the inadequacy of a listing is that many of the authors are concerned with the cultural patterning of the traits, that is, the sense in which they form an integrated cultural system (W. B. Miller 1958, pp. 6–7). For example, Oscar Lewis acknowledges that some of the traits he lists are "also found in the middle and upper classes. However, it is the peculiar patterning of these traits which defines the culture of poverty" (1961, p. xxvii).

One example from the literature may help to epitomize some of the basic features of lower-class culture. Rainwater (1966, pp. 206–207) has condensed a good deal of detail in his elaboration of three different kinds of survival strategies in the lower class: an expressive life style, which may lead to immediate gratification; a violent strategy; and a depressive strategy. He suggests that "when the expressive strategy fails or when it is unavailable there is . . . the great temptation to adopt a *violent strategy* in which you force others to give you what you need. . . . Finally . . . there is the *depressive strategy* in which goals are increasingly constricted to the bare necessities for survival. . . ."

One important point that underlies all discussions of class culture revolves about the distinction that must be made between statistically significant class differences and characteristics of a class. There is a danger that the statistically significant difference—which may be represented by a finding that 25 per cent of lower-class adults are "authoritarian" in comparison to 15 per cent of middle-class adults—will be converted into an unqualified statement that authoritarianism is a lower-class characteristic.

Researchers are ordinarily very careful in pointing out the qualifications to their findings, but the reader who is looking for the characteristics of the culture of poverty all too frequently singles out the tentatively stated findings and ignores the carefully stated qualifications. For example, in an article entitled "Characteristics of the Lower Blue-collar Class," Cohen and Hodges carefully point out that they are reporting statistically significant differences between the lower class and other classes and that to take their descriptions literally, "even though these descriptions point to real and important differences, is to subscribe to a caricature" (1963, p. 332).

Hylan Lewis (1967) has written a careful evaluation of the concept of the culture of poverty stemming from an account of his own research among low-income groups. First, he documents a variety of life styles that are to be found among low-income people. Second, he points to a variety of practical and theoretical dangers arising from the unqualified use of the class-culture concept. Finally, he introduces the idea that much of the behavior of low-income people can be seen as a pragmatic response to the stresses and deprivations of life. Insofar as lower-class behavior is pragmatically based, it is responsive to the overpowering conditions of life rather than to cultural guidelines; from this perspective lower-class culture, whatever its characteristics may be, takes on lesser importance.

A related view has been elaborated by Rodman (1963; 1966) with his concept of the lower-class "value stretch." From this perspective, a major lower-class problem is the inability to behave in accordance with the dominant values because of deprived conditions. A major response is to "stretch" the dominant values (or to develop alternative values without abandoning the dominant values) so that some degree of desirability becomes attached to behavior that is more in accord with lower-class conditions. The result is the existence of a wider range of values within the lower class, with less commitment to each level of that range.

The working, middle, and upper classes

Since there are no universally accepted definitions of *working class*, *middle class*, or *upper class*, any attempt to delineate the culture of these "classes" is an approximation at best. Since contemporary societies are better characterized in terms of "nonegalitarian classlessness" (Ossowski 1957) than in terms of discrete classes, any division into classes for purposes of analysis is arbitrary. Agreement does not exist on the number of classes to be found in a community or in a society. The arbitrary criteria used to assign individuals and families to specific classes and the arbitrary terms assigned to different classes often make comparability between different studies difficult. For example, *working class* and *lower class* are sometimes used interchangeably. And even when they are not, the criteria used to separate *working class* from *lower class* (or *upper-lower class* from *lower-lower class*) may differ, and the exact cutting points on these criteria may differ. With these qualifications firmly in mind, we can proceed to a brief account of some of the cultural characteristics of the working, middle, and upper classes.

Working-class culture. Kahl (1957), in summarizing the literature, has characterized the working class by the basic value orientation of "getting by." The working-class man usually cannot look forward to much promotion or pay increase; he has little commitment to his job and more commitment to outside interests. Thus, his interests turn to his family and to the pleasures of consumption. S. M. Miller and Frank Riessman (1961) refer to the following characteristics of a working-class subculture: stability and security; traditionalism; intensity; person-centeredness; pragmatism and anti-intellectualism; and excitement. Gans (1962) characterizes the working-class subculture as one that stresses the importance of family life and peer group life above the importance of work commitment and work advancement; he refers to this as "person-oriented" behavior. Perhaps two characteristics stand out most clearly: the concern for stability and security; and the person orientation of the working class.

Middle-class culture. Many of the cultural characteristics attributed to the middle class—concerns for individual development, deferred gratification, occupational success and advancement—are frequently part of the dominant value system in society. However, other classes, because of their conditions of life, do not stress these characteristics as much, if at all. In a summary statement Kahl (1957) distinguishes between a lower-middle-class concern about respectability, which is manifested by a desire for children to attend college as well as by a strong interest in religion and home ownership, and an upper-middle-class stress upon success in a career, upon which the family's style of living is based. Kahl (*ibid.*, p. 201) also mentions an emphasis on "individual initiative combined with smooth group functioning," on "planning for the future," and on "activity, accomplishment, practical results." Gans (1962) characterizes a middle-class subculture as emphasizing the importance of the nuclear family, child rearing, the husband's career, and education in terms of its contribution to career advancement. He also refers to a "professional upper-middle-class culture," which is similar to the middle-class culture but in which more stress is placed upon individual self-expression and development within the nuclear family and within the work world. Finally, Seeley and his associates (1956, p. 357) refer to a "premium on foresight and control," "prudent calculation," faith in education and technique, an "orientation towards the future," and a child-centered home as characteristics of the middle class.

For all the reasons mentioned above, and in addition because of the frequently heterogeneous population composition of the middle classes and because of the dominant nature of the middle-class values, we must not expect to find a neatly delimited group that shares these values. In particular, because of the dominance of these values, we must expect a good deal of agreement with them in other classes.

Upper-class culture. If one uses group interaction in defining a social class, the upper class frequently qualifies best. The upper class is also conscious of its position in society and stresses marriage within the class in order to preserve the favored position of its members. Moreover, certain subcultural customs tend to set the upper class off from the rest of society. Kahl refers to "the skills of graceful living" and the emphasis upon tradition, familism, and lineage as characteristics of the upper class. Baltzell (1958) refers to different speech patterns, a past-time orientation, a "being" rather than a "doing" orientation, and an emphasis upon lineage as characteristics of the upper class. In short, the upper class typically consists of a relatively small group of families with inherited wealth and position who are in intimate contact with each other, who stress endogamy, and who value and practice a graceful style of living that sets them somewhat apart from other classes.

If the defining criteria of a social class are the variables of group interaction, class consciousness, and class culture, then social classes exist only in small measure in most contemporary societies. If we assume gradations of rank according to a variety of criteria and if we use arbitrary indices and cutting points in order to delimit a social class, then we have nominally defined social classes. Most research has been done on nominally defined social classes, and despite the variability of the definitions, there has been enough consistency to provide us with information about social class differences. One feature of this empirical research is that it has provided us with information on certain cultural attributes on which there are social class differences. As a result, it has been possible to describe briefly, if approximately, some features of lower-class, working-class, middle-class, and upper-class culture. But it has not been possible to present, without qualification, the unique and distinctive features of any class culture because of the vast amount of overlapping that is found.

HYMAN RODMAN

[See also ELITES; STATUS, SOCIAL.]

BIBLIOGRAPHY

BALTZELL, E. DIGBY 1958 Philadelphia Gentlemen: The Making of a National Upper Class. Glencoe, Ill.: Free Press.

BERNARD, JESSIE 1966 Marriage and Family Among Negroes. Englewood Cliffs, N.J.: Prentice-Hall.

CHILMAN, CATHERINE S. 1965 Child-rearing and Family Relationship Patterns of the Very Poor. Welfare in Review 3:9–19.

COHEN, ALBERT K.; and HODGES, HAROLD M. JR. 1963 Characteristics of the Lower Blue-collar Class. Social Problems 10:303–334.

DAVIS, ALLISON 1946 The Motivation of the Underprivileged Worker. Pages 84–106 in William Foote Whyte (editor), Industry and Society. New York: McGraw-Hill.

GANS, HERBERT (1962) 1964 The Urban Villagers: Group and Class in the Life of Italian–Americans. New York: Free Press.

HERZOG, ELIZABETH 1963 Some Assumptions About the Poor. Social Service Review 37:389–402.

KAHL, JOSEPH A. 1957 The American Class Structure. New York: Rinehart.

LEWIS, HYLAN 1967 Culture, Class and Poverty. Washington: Health and Welfare Council of the National Capital Area. → Contains three essays by Lewis. See especially "Culture, Class and the Behavior of Low Income Families."

LEWIS, OSCAR 1961 The Children of Sánchez: Autobiography of a Mexican Family. New York: Random House.

MACIVER, ROBERT M.; and PAGE, CHARLES H. (1949) 1961 Society: An Introductory Analysis. New York: Holt.

MARSHALL, T. H. 1956 General Survey of Changes in Social Stratification in the Twentieth Century. Volume 3, pages 1–17 in World Congress of Sociology, Third, Amsterdam, Transactions. London: International Sociological Association.

MILLER, S. M.; and RIESSMAN, FRANK 1961 The Working Class Subculture: A New View. Social Problems 9:86–97.

MILLER, WALTER B. 1958 Lower Class Culture as a Generating Milieu of Gang Delinquency. Journal of Social Issues 14, no. 3:5–19.

OSSOWSKI, STANISŁAW (1957) 1963 Class Structure in the Social Consciousness. New York: Free Press. → First published as Struktura klasowa w społecznej świadomości.

PFAUTZ, HAROLD W. 1953 The Current Literature on Social Stratification: Critique and Bibliography. American Journal of Sociology 58:391–418.

Poverty and Human Resources Abstracts. → Published since 1966 by the Institute of Labor and Industrial Relations, University of Michigan and Wayne State University.

RAINWATER, LEE 1966 Crucible of Identity: The Negro Lower-class Family. Dædalus 95:172–216.

RODMAN, HYMAN 1963 The Lower-class Value Stretch. Social Forces 42:205–215.

RODMAN, HYMAN 1966 Illegitimacy in the Caribbean Social Structure: A Reconsideration. American Sociological Review 31:673–683.

ROSE, ARNOLD M. 1958 The Concept of Class and American Sociology. Social Research 25:53–69.

SCHUMPETER, JOSEPH A. (1919–1927) 1951 Imperialism and Social Classes. New York: Kelley. → Contains two works, first published as "Zur Soziologie der Imperialismen," 1919, and "Die sozialen Klassen im ethnisch homogenen Milieu," 1927. A paperback edition was published in 1955 by Meridian.

SEELEY, JOHN R. et al. 1956 Crestwood Heights: A Study of the Culture of Suburban Life. New York: Basic Books.

SMITH, RAYMOND T. 1956 The Negro Family in British Guiana: Family Structure and Social Status in the Villages. London: Routledge.

U.S. DEPARTMENT OF LABOR 1965 The Negro Family: The Case for National Action. Washington: Government Printing Office.

WEBER, MAX (1921) 1946 Class, Status, Party. Pages 180–195 in Max Weber, From Max Weber: Essays in Sociology. Translated and edited by Hans H. Gerth and C. Wright Mills. New York: Oxford Univ. Press. → First published as Part 3, Chapter 4 of Wirtschaft und Gesellschaft. A paperback edition was published in 1958.

WRONG, DENNIS H. 1964 Social Inequality Without Social Stratification. Canadian Review of Sociology and Anthropology 1:5–16.

STRESS

The concept of stress has come into increasing prominence in the biological and social sciences since World War II. As in the use of the term in engineering, where it is applied to forces exerted on inorganic objects, "stress" suggests excessive demands made on men and animals, demands that produce disturbances of physiological, social, and psychological systems. The important biological, social, and psychological consequences of stress galvanize scientific interest and mobilize efforts to understand and control them. The entire subject has been reviewed and analyzed recently by Lazarus (1966).

"Stress," as the term is used in the social sciences, has been applied to phenomena as diverse as metabolic imbalance following surgery, failure to succeed in an experimental task, personal bereavement, psychopathological reactions connected with military combat or life in a concentration camp, and the societal disruptions produced by naturally occurring disasters. The term "stress" is thus loose, in that it is applied to a host of phenomena related only by their common analogy with the engineering concept, and, at the same time, exceedingly broad, in that it covers phenomena at the physiological (Selye 1956), social (Smelser 1962), and psychological (Lazarus 1966) levels of analysis that may be described in a common theoretical language of causes, intervening processes, and effects. Whether phenomena as different as metabolic imbalance, symptoms of psychopathology, and social disturbance have anything in common beyond this loose analogy is an open issue, but the idea of stress as applied to a host of biological and social phenomena has intuitive appeal to laymen and scientists alike and gives the appearance to many of permitting the synthesis of these phenomena within some common system of thought. The term "stress" has, at the very least, the value of being a generic one, unifying a wide variety of phenomena, concepts, and empirical research.

This article deals with psychological stress. Within the field of psychological stress there are several distinct problem areas. One concerns the processes and conditions that produce stress reactions. A second has to do with the ways in which the conditions resulting in psychological stress are coped with. A third deals with the measurement of the reactions and with the links between these reactions and the intervening stress processes postulated by theory.

Psychological stress phenomena

Before we deal with key theoretical and methodological issues, let us consider the phenomena that define the subject matter of psychological stress so that we have some common empirical bases for a discussion of concepts and findings. What kinds of stimulus conditions have been studied as deter-minants of psychological stress reactions, and what reactions in response to these stimuli define the field?

Stimuli eliciting psychological stress. The following stimulus conditions are typical of research into stress under natural circumstances: military combat, imprisonment in concentration camps, isolation as produced, for example, by shipwreck, the imminence of death from such diseases as cancer and heart attack, the prospect of major surgery, the anticipation of a crucial scholastic examination, the death of close family members, the onslaught of and adaptation to such crippling diseases as paralytic polio, and warnings or actual impacts of various disasters, such as floods, tornadoes, and explosions. [See DISASTERS.]

Many types of experimentally produced, laboratory stimulus situations have also been employed in the study of psychological stress. Some typical ones are making the subject believe he has neurotically misperceived reality, producing failure on the part of the subject in the performance of some skilled or intellectual task, ridiculing or verbally assaulting the subject, creating the belief in the subject that he is in danger of electrocution or likely to sustain severe bodily injury, creating in the subject the anticipation of painful electric shock, and having the subject watch a disturbing motion picture.

These stimulus conditions have been chosen by research workers mainly because of the psychological and physiological disturbances they are known to create and not because the researchers want to test a controversial theoretical analysis of psychological stress processes. They are worthy of study for their own sake as well as aiding in the general understanding of how people react to various forms of stress. Experimental work on stress is designed to create laboratory analogues of processes or effects that are observed in natural situations, in order to study those processes and effects under better controlled conditions (see Lazarus & Opton in Spielberger 1966).

Characteristics of the person that interact with the stimulus conditions have been heavily emphasized in both the naturalistic and the experimental approaches. A frequent observation under all these conditions is that individual differences in reaction loom very large, and personality variables that account for this have been sought with rather limited success (Opton et al. 1967).

Response variables indicating stress. With regard to response, four classes of measures have been employed as indicators of stress reaction. Three of these are the classical, defining attributes of (negatively toned) emotional states: disturbed affect as reported by the individual (for example, fear, anxiety, anger, and depression); motor-behavioral patterns that permit the observer to make inferences about such emotions (for example, postures, facial patterns, flight and attack), and physiological correlates of emotion (for example, secretions of adrenal hormones, such as epinephrine, norepinephrine, and hydrocortisone, and autonomic nervous system reactions, including increased skin conductance, heart rate, blood pressure, and skin temperature, to name a few of the most common).

Cognitive functioning. The fourth category of stress-reaction measure, disturbance in cognitive functioning, has been employed to indicate stress reactions because impairment of skilled performance and of perception, learning, and judgment is often observed under stress-producing conditions. However, impairment is by no means inevitable; many studies have revealed significant improvement in functioning under stress. Thus, paradoxically, conditions of stress can be viewed as being damaging to performance but as also being capable of improving performance. The conceptual and methodological aspects of this problem have been discussed at considerable length by Lazarus, Deese, and Osler (1952) and more recently by Sarason (1960).

One of the generalizations usually accepted is that the disruption or facilitation of performance appears to depend on such factors as the nature of the task, the characteristics of the individual who is exposed to the stress conditions, and the intensity of stress. Specifically, difficult or complex tasks requiring great concentration or abstraction are more vulnerable to the effects of stress than simple, repetitive tasks; some individuals appear more vulnerable to impairment than others, although it is not at all clear which personality variables are involved; and only under mild or moderate degrees of stress does facilitation of performance appear to take place.

Attempts at understanding impaired functioning. The problem of accounting for impairment of functioning under stress conditions poses controversial questions that have prompted much theorizing and empirical research. Two contrasting points of view are examples of attempts to understand the principles underlying performance changes with stress.

One of these positions is represented by Farber (1955), who emphasizes the drive properties of the anxiety that is produced by stress conditions. Following Hullian reasoning, he argues that high drive, or high anxiety, will increase the strength of all responses, correct as well as incorrect ones, in task performances connected with learning. If

the task is difficult or complex—that is, if it contains many competing responses—high drive will impair performance, because a larger number of incorrect, competing responses will be facilitated. If the task is simple and contains small numbers of competing responses, performance will be facilitated by high drive, since comparatively fewer incorrect responses will be strengthened. An active controversy over this view exists. Sarason (1960) has reviewed the literature and the arguments, citing studies with findings not consistent with this formulation and noting critiques of the drive viewpoint. [*See* DRIVES.]

An alternative class of viewpoints about the effects of stress on performance is represented by Korchin (1964) and Easterbrook (1959), who have argued that impairment of performance results from the narrowing or restricting of perception that occurs under stress. Just why this restriction of the perceptual field occurs is not entirely clear. An interpretation can be made in terms of interference or in motivational terms. In terms of motivation, the individual is motivated under stress to select from the environment only that which is relevant to the danger. Thus, he may ignore features of the situation that seem momentarily irrelevant, ultimately narrowing his perceptions to a damaging extent. The experimental task may also decrease in importance in the face of other problems that are posed by the stress conditions. Although to the experimenter the performance of the task may be the central criterion of adaptation, to the subject it may be comparatively unimportant.

In any event, a central concern is the mechanism or mechanisms underlying impairment and improvement in functioning under stress. And since it is difficult, without further knowledge of the determining conditions, to predict which way, if at all, performance will be affected, inferences about psychological stress from changes in performance contain unresolved difficulties.

Some key theoretical issues in the field of psychological stress may be expressed by the questions: What are the antecedents of stress reactions? What processes of coping are generated and by what conditions are they produced? What observable consequences do each of the coping processes have? These issues are complex. Let us consider some of the main ones.

Threat, frustration, and conflict

The terminological confusion that exists in the area of threat, frustration, and conflict has already been touched upon. Theoretical solutions, of course, carry with them terminological conventions upon which there is not necessarily wide agreement (see Lazarus 1966). Still, we must seek some sort of clarity. The word that most clearly connotes the psychological aspects of stress is "threat." The characteristics of threat must be defined and differentiated from other similar or overlapping concepts, such as frustration and conflict.

Threat refers to the anticipation of harm of some kind, an anticipation that is created by the presence of certain stimulus cues signifying to the individual that there is to be an experience of harm. This experience of harm may be called the "confrontation" (researchers into the psychological aspects of disaster call it the "impact"). Threat refers not to this confrontation but rather to the anticipation of it. The immediate stimulus configuration resulting in threat merely heralds the coming of harm. Threat is thus a purely psychological concept, an interpretation of a situation by the individual. Although the anticipated harm could be some physical injury, the meaning of the term "harm" is usually broadened to include damage to important goals and values.

Both frustration and conflict are concepts often confused with threat, even though they have specific meanings of their own. All three have been considered as antecedents of aggression, regression, anxiety, and defense. When these terms are used loosely, their distinctive features and their possibly different roles in behavior tend to be obscured.

Frustration is the actual blockage of some goal-oriented behavior. We speak of a motive's being frustrated or thwarted when a goal cannot be attained or when gratification is delayed. In such cases, frustration refers to a present or continuing confrontation with harm in the form of a goal that has already been blocked. The reasons for frustration are multiple; one of them is the presence of motivational conflict.

Conflict occurs when two goals are incompatible —that is, require contradictory behavior—or when the gratification of one goal frustrates the other. By definition, when conflict exists, then frustration is inevitable. Conflict is therefore one antecedent of frustration. If "conflict" is defined more broadly, to include the opposition between an external force or obstacle and the motive, then "conflict" and "frustration" tend to be interchangeable terms, although their emphases are slightly different. Conflict focuses on the motives involved, frustration on the blockage of motive gratification. From the point of view of psychological stress theory, it is the threatening and frustrating aspects of conflict that are important. [*See* CONFLICT, *article on* PSYCHOLOGICAL ASPECTS.]

Threat in its anticipatory sense is not routinely distinguished from frustration. Most experiments or naturalistic observations in the field of psychological stress have not clearly isolated these elements. For example, the classic observations of Grinker and Spiegel (1945) on war neuroses and Bettelheim (1960) on the concentration camp found that there is great frustration or confrontation with harm in the form of social degradation, hunger, physical injury, isolation from loved ones, and so forth. But there is also threat, in the sense that the present conditions signify continuing or future harm, perhaps even death. Grinker and Spiegel appear to emphasize the threat aspect of military combat. The emphasis on anticipation of harm is nowhere more clearly emphasized than in the literature on disaster (for example, Janis 1962). Psychologists and sociologists in their work on disaster distinguish a warning period in which the individual anticipates the impact of a disastrous storm or flood. Reactions that are observed include anxiety, defense mechanisms, disorganized thinking, and so on—in other words, the same consequences that are commonly attributed to frustration.

Failure to consider the separate aspects of threat and frustration is widespread in the experimental literature on aggression, where the emphasis is placed on frustration as the antecedent of aggression. The same trend has been followed by recent analytic writers on aggression, such as Berkowitz (1962). The threat and frustration components are never isolated in such research. Therefore, it is not clear to what extent anticipation or confrontation accounts for the observed stress reactions.

There are some observations in which threat alone has been isolated and in which the very reactions usually attributed to frustration have been observed. Some of the work on disaster mentioned above constitutes one example, especially where a warning period is distinguished before the calamity has actually happened. An experiment by Shannon and Isbell (1963) is another example. These authors exposed several groups of dental patients to varying procedures connected with the injection of an anesthetic, sometimes employing no anesthetic and sometimes merely going through all the motions of an injection short of actual needle insertion. Following their carefully designed procedures, they found that stress response consisting of an elevated level of hydrocortisone (an adrenal cortical hormone associated with stress) in the blood followed the anticipation of the injection and was as great as that found when the needle was actually inserted and the drug actually injected. In effect, it was not the actual physical pain, tissue damage, or drug effects that produced the stress reaction but merely the realization that an injection would be experienced. There appears to be a sound basis for viewing the various stress reactions as based on threat. There is no clear agreement among researchers about what aspects of the stimulus condition produce the stress reaction. Sometimes threat is emphasized and sometimes frustration. Often the distinction is simply overlooked. It is clearly an unresolved issue in stress research.

Threat and anxiety

The tendency to treat anxiety as the only intervening variable in psychological stress analysis poses some theoretical difficulty in which controversial issues reside. Conflict, or the frustration produced by conflict, is commonly said to result in anxiety, which in turn triggers some form of defense. This analysis is confusing for two reasons. First, it is often implied that the defense is activated by the pain or discomfort of anxiety. But if this is the case, why is the responsibility for defense placed exclusively on anxiety and not, for example, on anger or depression, which are also distressing affects? Actually, in the clinical literature the assumption that anger and depression may lead to defense is common, as when manic states are considered to be defenses against "underlying" depression or when positive feelings are treated as reaction formations against anger. But this view provides a plurality of intervening variables. Anxiety cannot then be considered to be *the* intervening variable promoting defenses.

The second problem with treating anxiety as the only intervening variable is that when such affective disturbances as anxiety are taken as the "cause" of defense, the actual cognitive processes producing it are underemphasized. If anxiety is the reaction to anticipated harm as heralded by stimulus cues, then it is not the pain or discomfort of the anxiety that generates the defense but rather the recognition by the individual that there is danger. Indeed, Freud, whose analyses of these problems have most influenced later researchers, shifted his views about anxiety during the course of his prolific career and finally regarded anxiety as the signal of danger. But to what psychological structure or agency is the signal useful? In Freud's analysis, anxiety signals the ego about the danger. But the main function of the ego is to distinguish safe from unsafe conditions. Why then should the structure which already has the function of interpreting reality need to be informed about what it already "knows" to be harmful? The role of

anxiety, both as the intervening variable in psychological stress analysis and as an affective response, remains the subject of intense disagreement. The role of anxiety touches on the problem of consciousness or awareness, about which there is also continuous debate. [*See* ANXIETY.]

Cognitive processes and threat

There is an increasing realization that cognitive processes are involved in threat and in the production of anxiety and other affects. Some of the difficulties inherent in the treatment of anxiety as the intervening variable in psychological stress can be resolved by regarding it entirely as a response to threat and by making threat itself the intervening variable. This has the virtue of emphasizing the cognitive activity preceding anxiety. Anxiety then becomes an affective response to the anticipation of harm (which is the definition of threat). Whether the response is anxiety, fear, anger, depression, guilt, or shame depends on the way the individual evaluates the situation and on the consequences of any form of adaptive response he might make.

Cognitive processes and emotion.   The role of cognitive processes in emotion in general is becoming increasingly emphasized in present day psychological thought and research. An example is the major work of Arnold (1960), in which emotion is understood in terms of the individual's evaluation or appraisal of the personal significance of the stimulus. If the stimulus is appraised as beneficial, a positive emotion, such as joy or contentment, will ensue. If it is appraised as harmful, a negatively toned emotional state, such as fear or anger, will result. Emotion itself consists of an action tendency with respect to the stimulus, an action tendency that has motor and physiological correlates. In this way, Arnold links emotion to the cognitive process of appraisal. Appraisal means the evaluation of the significance of the cues at hand. If they are taken to signify the imminence of harm, threat and stress reactions are produced. [*See* EMOTION.]

Experimental study.   One important and widely cited piece of recent research (Schachter & Singer 1962) highlights the importance of cognitive processes in the production of different kinds of emotion. Some subjects were given epinephrine injections and others given a placebo under various experimental conditions. The epinephrine produced the expected sympathetic nervous system activation. By means of trained "stooges," two different social atmospheres were created. In one, a euphoric condition was created by having the stooge act in an appropriate fashion. In the other, an anger condition was produced by having the stooge react with anger about the injection procedure, so that he gradually went into a rage. Based on behavioral ratings and self-report data, the findings clearly indicate that the quality of the emotion experienced by the experimental subject as a result of the physiological arousal was dependent on the nature of the social atmosphere and the cognitions created by this atmosphere. Anger occurred when the social situation stimulated anger, and euphoria occurred in the euphoric social situation. The social atmosphere thus yielded a conception that shaped the actual emotional effects of the epinephrine injection.

The experiment conducted by Schachter and Singer is important because it turns attention to the neglected cognitive determinants of emotion and provides a clear refutation of the widespread assumption that emotion can be conceptualized purely in terms of physiological arousal. This assumption has now been effectively challenged, emphasizing a theoretical issue of great importance. As Arnold (1960) has insisted, the quality of emotional states depends on appraisal of the personal significance of the situation. The argument can easily be extended to stress reactions that include negatively toned emotional states like fear and anger.

Relevant dimensions of cognitive appraisal. If the concept of appraisal in the production of threat is to have more than merely subjective referents, then we must be able to specify the necessary and sufficient conditions of threat and nonthreat appraisals. There is little systematic work along these lines. The factors determining appraisal are classifiable into those that reside in the external stimulus configuration and those that are within the psychological structure of the individual, as traits or dispositions. A few examples will be suggested.

Ratio of harm-producing to harm-combating aspects. Relevant to the stimulus configuration is something that might be referred to as the balance of power between the harm-producing stimulus and the counterharm resources of the individual. Threat is aroused when the former heavily outweighs the latter. If the individual believes that he can readily overcome or reverse the danger, threat is minimal or absent. Empirical examples can be found in which, for example, the casualty rates in military combat are positively correlated with incidence of psychological breakdown or where the experience and skill of the individual minimizes or reduces the threat that originally existed in his early states of contact

with the dangerous conditions (Epstein 1962). Janis (1958) and Mechanic (1962) have each emphasized this line of reasoning.

Imminence of harm. Another, less emphasized factor in the stimulus configuration is the imminence of the confrontation with harm. Threat is more intense when the harm is more imminent. For example, Epstein (1962) has evaluated approach and avoidance tendencies of parachute jumpers during the twenty-four-hour period preceding the jump, leading up to it, and culminating in the landing. As the time of final commitment to the jump approached, avoidance tendencies (evidence of threat) increased to a maximum, until they actually exceeded the approach (positive) tendencies.

Another example of the role of imminence of confrontation comes from Mechanic's study (1962) of the reactions of a group of graduate students facing a crucial examination. More students reported anxiety and more symptoms of anxiety were observed as the date of the examination grew nearer. Changes were also noted in the type of adaptive solutions displayed by the students as the deadline neared.

Another, more anecdotal example of the role of the imminence of confrontation with harm in determining the degree of threat may be found in people's reactions to the prospect of their own deaths. Even though the prospect itself may be exceedingly threatening, the fact that it may be regarded as long distant (not imminent) greatly reduces the intensity of the threat. Under conditions that make it appear imminent, threat is greatly intensified.

Ambiguity of cues. The role of ambiguity of the stimulus cues has been dealt with at some length by Janis (1962). As in projective stimuli, ambiguity encourages the operation of factors within the psychological structure of the individual. In Janis' terms, the new and ambiguous information will be assimilated to the previously existing psychological set or expectation of the person. If he has previously interpreted the situation as benign, an ambiguous cue will be interpreted in a way that is consistent with this idea; similarly, if he has previously interpreted the situation as dangerous, ambiguous information will become part of his fearful outlook and be assimilated to it.

Motives and beliefs. Concerning factors within the psychological structure, patterns of motivation and belief systems are fundamental to threat appraisal. Studies may be found (for example, Vogel et al. 1959) which demonstrate that threat is minimal when the stimulus conditions occur in the presence of a weak motive and greater when a powerful motive is engaged. In effect, what is threatening depends on the motive characteristics of the individual. In the absence of individually oriented assessments of motivation, researchers in the field of psychological stress have tended to emphasize shared or widespread sources of threat, sometimes recognizing that the conditions employed were not of equal threat value to all individuals studied. Sources of threat are universal or widespread because of shared cultural or experiential factors. Even such widespread threats as death are subject to motivational and cognitive factors as sources of individual differences. For example, recent researchers have noted wide variations in what it is about death that is actually feared, and there are great individual variations in conceptions of what will happen to the person after death.

Belief systems about the nature of one's transactions with the environment appear to play an interesting part in the appraisal of threat. We can regard the individual who is, for example, chronically anxious as believing that the environment is hostile or dangerous or that his own resources are too limited to cope with danger. Questionnaires about anxiety often contain items reflecting such beliefs. Observations by Persky and his associates (Persky et al. 1959) show that subjects with such beliefs (identified by measures of chronic anxiety) are more readily threatened by a strange experimental situation (as measured by the amount of increase of hydrocortisone in the blood) than nonanxious subjects. Yet the latter react more to specific threats within the total experimental situation. The former subjects are threatened by any new situation, whereas the latter are comfortable in novel situations but are threatened by specifically harmful features of the situation. [See ATTITUDES; THINKING, *article on* COGNITIVE ORGANIZATION AND PROCESSES.]

Not everyone would agree with this particular interpretation of the effects of measured anxiety on threat appraisal in novel situations. For example, there are questions about the actual meaning of scales presumably measuring anxiety and about the conceptualization of the processes that underlie the reaction patterns just described. But regardless of theory and current difficulties concerning the assessment and labeling of personality variables, the facts appear to be that certain people are likely to appraise new situations as threatening and in fact give stress reactions almost chronically to many types of situations that do not especially disturb others. On the basis of personality measures

like anxiety scales, it is possible to predict with some success the level of stress reaction the individual will show in social contexts to which he has not yet become accustomed.

Coping processes and reactions to threat

The patterns of reaction that define the presence of threat are variable and complex. They are often not in agreement with each other, as, for example, when the individual denies any affective distress but gives evidence of it in behavioral or physiological changes. The same condition that produces stress reaction in one individual results in no evidence of threat in another. Furthermore, one individual will react with anger and attack, while another will show fear and flee. Some of these variations represent individual differences in the psychodynamics of threat production. Other disagreements arise from difficulties of measurement.

The concept of reaction.   A major source of variation in reaction has to do with the kinds of coping processes that are generated by threat. In introducing the concept of coping process, the term "reaction" to threat requires some additional comment. Unfortunately, "reaction" usually connotes a passive and automatic state not necessarily involving active efforts to master or cope with a danger. This passive implication is not at all intended here, nor is it implied in any of the theory and research on coping processes. It is precisely because threat must be coped with and the individual must employ his experience and resources to meet it that the prediction of stress reactions is so complex. Different individuals bring different resources to the situation, and processes of coping are required that sensitively reflect the options available to the individual and the consequences of any action taken. In a valuable study of psychological stress in graduate students brought about by doctoral examinations, Mechanic (1962) examines in some detail the strategies of adaptation that are selected. The focus in this work is on how the student deals or copes with threat. But an additional principle that makes the study of coping processes valuable is that the stress reaction as observed in behavior depends on the kind of coping process the individual adopts. For example, attack as a means of coping with threat will appear behaviorally, and perhaps even physiologically, to be different from flight or avoidance. Thus, to understand the observed reaction we must correctly identify the active choices that the individual makes in coping with threat.

Evaluation of coping processes.   There is a strong tendency in the literature to distinguish between various types of coping processes—for example, those in which the individual attempts directly to alter the threatening conditions themselves and those in which he attempts to change only his appraisal of them so that he need not feel threatened. The former are often referred to as adaptive behavior or as coping devices, whereas the latter are usually called defenses. It is generally assumed that coping devices are healthier, since they offer some means of actually mastering or changing the situation. By using defenses, the individual may become more comfortable but remain vulnerable to external danger. A persistent issue in the discussion of this problem relates to what is healthy and what is not. Some theorists point out that defensive processes may be adaptive, at least in preventing psychological disorganization where no adaptive solution is really possible. Others regard coping processes as healthy and defenses as pathological. The problem of criteria for healthy or effective processes of coping as opposed to pathological ones remains an important and controversial issue within psychological stress theory and research. There is little agreement among the experts about this issue.

Aggression—cognitive aspects of coping. If we are to understand the observable reaction pattern to stress it is important to consider the coping processes that produce it. Perhaps more research has been performed on aggression than on any other threat reaction, making it a fine illustration of the type of issue that arises in this work.

The trend toward postulating and investigating cognitive processes as antecedents of threat may be found in the research on aggression. The earlier conception of aggression as an instinctual drive has fallen out of favor even among orthodox psychoanalysts because of the circularity of this approach. In its place is the view that aggression is a response to frustration. Aggression or attack may be regarded as a form of coping with the conceived source of the harm. But attack is one of many coping reactions, and it is necessary to specify the conditions that determine attack as the coping process rather than avoidance or defense mechanism.

The role of cognitive processes in the production of aggression as a means of coping with threat is illustrated in some of the findings of research reviewed by Berkowitz (1962). For example, when the antecedent frustrating condition created by the experimenter is not arbitrary or capricious and appears to the subject to occur through no fault of the frustrating agent, aggression will not occur as readily as when the frustration appears arbi-

trary. Either it is inhibited or it is weaker, an issue on which much research centers (see Berkowitz 1962). Furthermore, if the social sanctions against attack are weakened, aggression will be more apt to occur. And if there are strong internal moral sanctions against aggression, direct, behaviorally expressed aggression is also less likely, presumably because it is inhibited from expression. Finally, if the frustrating agent is powerful or prestigious and capable of harmful retaliation against any attack, direct aggression is also less likely on the part of the threatened or frustrated individual. These findings support the concept of an evaluating individual who perceives the social forces of a situation and his own place within it and whose behavior is shaped by this appraisal. [See AGGRESSION.]

Defense mechanisms as a form of coping

The concept of defense mechanism has been widely accepted and applied in psychological stress theory and in clinical practice. Fundamentally, defense is regarded as consisting of a variety of psychological processes that have in common the distortion of reality as a means of reducing threat (or anxiety, in the typical formulation). Defense is contrasted with more active forms of coping in which the actual conditions of threat are altered. For example, when the individual who is threatened with failure attempts to learn what he must know to pass an examination, he is attempting to influence the actual forces involved in the threat. But when he distorts the actual realities, by convincing himself that he cannot fail, he is engaging in defense. [See DEFENSE MECHANISMS.]

There has been comparatively little progress in the theory of defense since its basic outlines were expounded in Freudian theory. Theories of defense are largely descriptive; that is, they specify the types of strategies but do not specify the processes and conditions that determine them. Or if they do, they are not stated in ways that lend themselves to clear empirical testing. Thus, much controversy centers on the details of the concept of defense. For example, there is little agreement about patterns of defenses within the same individual or about which ones underlie each type of psychopathology. Unresolved is the question of whether a given defense is a general trait of the personality that can be activated by any threat or whether it is linked to a specific kind of threat. Psychologists who attempt to measure "defense preferences" assume the former position, whereas Freudian theory appears to take the latter position. In the latter viewpoint each defense is related to a particular stage of psychosexual development (and its particular instinctual drive—for example, oral, anal aggressive, or Oedipal) and to a particular set of symptoms of psychopathology. But this conceptual neatness is not readily supported by the observable patterns with which the clinician deals. It remains an assumption that is often challenged. Also unresolved is the matter of distinguishing such defense behaviors as those associated with denial from instances where threat is absent. In both cases the individual says, "I am not angry or distressed," but in one case this report reflects a defense against threat, while in the other the statement correctly describes an internal state. The observable signs that permit the identification of these inferred processes are not well established.

Contributing stimulus conditions. Some interesting efforts have been made to pin down the stimulus conditions under which one or another defense will occur.

Projection. A study by Bramel (1962) is illustrative. He found that projection as a defense does not occur as readily when the person who might be the object of the projection is negatively evaluated by the threatened individual. Ratings of desirable and undesirable characteristics of experimental partners were made before the experiment proper began by a group of male subjects. Then while a fake physiological indicator, supposedly indicating their sexual arousal, was attached to them, the subjects observed photographs of men. By manipulating the indicator, the experimenter in effect was able to convincingly suggest that the subject had homosexual impulses. The indicator was made to rise sharply when the subject looked at pictures of the most provocative males. Following this threatening information, the subject was asked to evaluate homosexual tendencies in the original partner, a task which permitted the projection or attribution of the undesirable impulse to another individual like himself. Control subjects not having the threatening experience showed no tendency to project the homosexuality on the other person. Where the partner had been evaluated in positive terms, threatened subjects attributed homosexuality to him with significantly larger frequency. Bramel concludes that projection, as a defense against threat, requires a positively regarded object and will not be useful in reducing threat if the object is seen as an undesirable character. Moreover, Bramel argues, projection occurs in his study because the threatening information was so convincing that it could not readily be denied.

Denial. Clinical research also points to situational determinants of denial defenses. Research with the patient who is dying of cancer shows him to be under great social pressure to accept the myth that he will recover. Relatives and friends and other visitors to the patient are extremely uneasy about facing openly with the patient the dreadful outlook. In their hospital visits they encourage the denial of the truth. The patient, fearful of losing contact with his loved ones, who appear to withdraw uneasily when the terminal nature of the disease is faced, is pressured into a denial process both by his own wish and by the social pressure, although often he gives evidence that the defense is not fully successful and that below the surface of awareness he recognizes the truth. The work cited above points up more recent efforts to pin down some of the external situational factors that determine which defense is selected as a means of coping with threat. There is as yet only a trickle of data on this very important problem.

Personality factors. Personality factors also determine the choice of defenses. Defenses may be treated as personality dispositions, traits which operate to some extent in spite of situational variations. Studies have demonstrated that such dispositions operate to determine the success of a defense-oriented communication in reducing threat. For example, Lazarus and Alfert (1964) utilized a disturbing motion picture depicting a primitive ritual of adolescence called "subincision," in which a series of genital operations with a flint knife is shown. If nothing is said about the film events, autonomic and subjective evidence of disturbance rises dramatically during the operation scenes and falls during benign scenes. If the threatening events of the film are pointed up in an orientation passage or sound track, the level of stress reaction is even greater. If the pain or other dangers of the operation are denied convincingly in an orientation passage prior to the film presentation, or if an attitude of intellectualized detachment is presented, the over-all level of stress reaction is markedly lowered. But the effectiveness of these defensive orientation passages in reducing the stress reaction depends on measured defensive dispositions. Subjects typically disposed to denial as a preferred defense get more relief from the denial orientation than from the intellectualized detachment. They seem better able to adopt the attitude presented. Similarly, subjects inclined to deal with threat by intellectualization gain most from the intellectualization passage and little from the denial statements. The utilization of defensive orientations to reduce threat appears to depend, in part, on defensive dispositions within the personality.

Comparatively little research has been done on

the conditions that determine particular strategies of coping with threat. Naturalistic observation in the field provides abundant hypotheses about these conditions. If we are to extend our knowledge beyond the point of mere ability to describe the psychological strategies of defense, it will be necessary to employ effective laboratory analogues of these processes to test the often contradictory assumptions about these forms of coping with threat.

Methodological issues

One difficult methodological problem concerns the setting in which stress reactions and their causes occur.

Naturalistic observations. A considerable literature exists in which naturalistic observations have been made of people in real life stress situations. While there are many examples, the work of Grinker and Spiegel (1945) on battle, that of Janis (1958) on the threat of surgery, and that of Bettelheim (1960) on the concentration camp are classic ones. Although these studies offer rich hypotheses about the sources of stress and the mechanisms of stress production and reduction, it is difficult to isolate systematically the variables that are operating, since the situations studied are enormously complex, the measurement of reactions comparatively informal, and the assessment of causes often retrospective.

Laboratory studies. In contrast are the laboratory studies of stress in which control and measurement of the variables are comparatively precise. However, levels of stress are usually mild or moderate, since ethical and practical considerations limit the extent and the range of situations that are possible with human subjects. Moreover, the very fact that a subject conceives of the situation as experimental raises the question whether laboratory analogues are good models of real life situations. What is gained in control may be lost in artificiality of the setting. The issue is basic to all experimentation and generates protagonists for either the naturalistic or the laboratory orientation. The difficulties of each cannot be wholly eliminated. Therefore, the fullest theoretical analysis of psychological stress will ultimately derive from the wise integration of both kinds of data.

Measurement. It is difficult to discuss the field of psychological stress without touching on the measurement of such key variables as threat. The experimenter must be able to infer degree of threat and the nature of the coping process on the basis of the pattern of reaction that he observes. As previously noted, the response variables in psychological stress analysis include different levels—for example, subjectively reported affect, observed motor-behavioral adjustments, and physiological reactions that may include a dozen or so different autonomic nervous system response variables and a number of adrenal hormones found in the blood or urine. Investigators have differed widely over the kinds of response variables they have emphasized and over the number they have observed.

Problem of agreement among measurements. One fundamental problem in measurement has been the low order of correlation that is found between different measures presumably indicating stress reaction. Even within a response class (for example, among different autonomic nervous system measures, such as heart rate, electrical conductivity of the skin, respiration, blood pressure, and so forth), the correlation is low to moderate at best. Sometimes this poor correlation may be attributed to methodological errors or technological limitations. For example, it has been shown that particular procedures for measuring heart-rate variations will increase the agreement between heart rate and the level of skin conductance above what is usually obtained, and Lazarus and his associates (Lazarus et al. 1963) have demonstrated that intraindividual approaches yield higher agreement between measures than interindividual approaches do. Intraindividual analysis has made it possible to show considerable agreement between autonomic measurement and self-report ratings of disturbance. But even if all the methodological and technical difficulties of measurement were overcome, it is doubtful that very high correlations would ever be found between the different stress-response indicators. And if the measures employed to index stress reaction do not agree substantially, theoretical as well as methodological questions may be raised about the justification of treating any one of them as a stress-response measure.

There are excellent theoretical reasons why disagreement exists between stress indicators. These reasons can be summarized by the general statement that each indicator, while indeed dependent on threat appraisal, is also dependent on different specific psychological and physiological intervening processes. In any study, some of these processes are not relevant to the investigator's concern and constitute a kind of nuisance variance in the system, while other processes convey important information about psychological stress mechanisms.

Response specificity. An example of variance that can be a nuisance in some cases is based on response specificity in psychophysiology and psychosomatic medicine (Engel 1960). This concept was introduced partly to explain the absence of correlation between autonomic nervous system indicators. Each indicator involves some particular tissue system—for example, the sweat glands, the heart muscle, the blood vessels, and so on. It has been shown that certain individuals may be consistently more reactive in one measure—say, blood pressure—than in another. In effect, subjects are constitutionally different, and if the investigator is measuring only one indicator he may overestimate reactivity in one subject and underestimate it in another, depending on whether he has chosen the sensitive or insensitive measure. Naturally, then, two different indicators may not agree very well with each other. From the point of view of measuring stress reaction, this constitutional variation is a nuisance that interferes with accurate inferences. From the point of view of psychosomatic disease, however, it is of the utmost importance, since one individual may develop the disorder of hypertension rather than some other disease just because of this constitutional quirk that makes him respond to threat with heightened blood pressure. [See PSYCHOSOMATIC ILLNESS.]

Stimulus specificity. The concept of stimulus specificity, in contrast to response specificity, suggests that the pattern of autonomic reaction will be different for different sources of threat or in different kinds of emotional reactions (Lacey et al. 1963). Recent evidence, for example, suggests that the physiological patterns of fear and anger may be different. Thus, from the point of view of measurement of stress reaction, stimulus specificity requires that we employ the appropriate indicators in order to identify the particular pattern that is generated by the specific threat; otherwise, it might be missed or the degree of threat incorrectly estimated. Moreover, if our interest lies in identifying the process of coping with threat, the precise nature of the response is important since it will tell us something about the coping process. Yet both stimulus specificity and response specificity, however they are ultimately defined and understood, occur at the expense of agreement among autonomic indicators of threat. The more response variation depends on the stimulus or the physical constitution of the individual, the less agreement can we expect to find among indicators.

Individual differences and environment. On the psychological side, the pattern of reaction of the individual across different types and levels of response reveals something about the nature of his transactions with the environment, his particular psychodynamics. And different kinds of measures reveal different features of these transactions. For example, if the individual wishes to create the impression that he is brave, he may refuse to admit to fear in military combat even though he is very frightened. Or, in other contexts, he may deny anger. In such a situation, autonomic and adrenal evidence of stress reaction will probably be found. The pattern of evidence may appear different if the reaction is fear than if the reaction is anger. Here we have lawful disagreement between two legitimate response indicators of stress reaction, reported disturbances of affect and physiological arousal.

Sometimes psychologists have relied on expressive indicators of emotion to correct for the lack of candidness of the individual. But even expressive indicators such as gestures, facial expressions, and body postures may be employed by the individual to conceal how he feels or to create a social impression he thinks is desirable, since the individual also knows that his styles and expressive movements contain socially relevant information.

The point is that no single class of indicators, behavioral or physiological, is free from the influence of other variables that have nothing to do with threat. For example, adrenal cortical hormonal substances are increased in the blood as a result of psychologically based threats as well as physical assaults. Thus, walking up a hill on the golf course in exuberance will result in some of the same kinds of physiological arousal as sitting quietly and experiencing anxiety. Similarly, autonomic nervous system measures are also subject to such irrelevant influence. Temperature and humidity changes, and indeed even air pollution, will have substantial effects. In other words, the indicators we use physiologically to measure stress reaction also tend to vary with anything that makes the individual more aroused or activated.

The dilemma posed here is that the measurement of stress relevant processes is exceedingly complex, and no simple, single class of measurement device can solve the problem adequately. The clinician knows this when he carefully observes many features of a reaction: subjective report, gestures, the goal directedness of acts, the consistency over time of what the individual reports, and evident signs of physiological reactions, such as flushing or pallor. The pattern of these reactions provides the basis of inferences about internal psychological activity.

It has been suggested that the shortcomings of one measuring device should be compensated for by the simultaneous use of others. Then, only where there is agreement between a number of indicators can we afford to make an inference about anxiety (or threat or defense). But we cannot expect the various indicators to be always in high agreement, especially if we recognize that each approach reveals something different about the individual's psychodynamics. It is only through these very disagreements that we recognize efforts on the part of individuals to present themselves socially in a certain way or to utilize defenses or other forms of coping. When irrelevant artifacts in our measurement techniques have been ruled out, then the apparent contradictions between stress-response indicators are no longer necessarily contradictory but serve as crucial sources of inference about the underlying processes relevant to psychological stress.

RICHARD S. LAZARUS

[*See also* ANXIETY; FATIGUE. *Other relevant material may be found in* AGGRESSION; DEFENSE MECHANISMS; MOTIVATION; PSYCHOLOGY, *article on* CONSTITUTIONAL PSYCHOLOGY; SPACE, OUTER, *article on* SOCIAL AND PSYCHOLOGICAL ASPECTS.]

BIBLIOGRAPHY

ARNOLD, MAGDA B. 1960 *Emotion and Personality.* 2 vols. New York: Columbia Univ. Press. → Volume 1: *Psychological Aspects.* Volume 2: *Neurological and Physiological Aspects.*

BERKOWITZ, LEONARD 1962 *Aggression: A Social Psychological Analysis.* New York: McGraw-Hill.

BETTELHEIM, BRUNO 1960 *The Informed Heart: Autonomy in a Mass Age.* Glencoe, Ill.: Free Press.

BRAMEL, DANA 1962 A Dissonance Theory Approach to Defensive Projection. *Journal of Abnormal and Social Psychology* 64:121–129.

EASTERBROOK, J. A. 1959 The Effect of Emotion on Cue Utilization and the Organization of Behavior. *Psychological Review* 66:183–201.

ENGEL, BERNARD T. 1960 Stimulus–Response and Individual-response Specificity. *AMA Archives of General Psychiatry* 2:305–313.

EPSTEIN, SEYMOUR 1962 The Measurement of Drive and Conflict in Humans: Theory and Experiment. Volume 10, pages 127–209 in *Nebraska Symposium on Motivation.* Edited by Marshall R. Jones. Lincoln: Univ. of Nebraska Press.

FARBER, I. E. 1955 The Role of Motivation in Verbal Learning and Performance. *Psychological Bulletin* 52:311–327.

GRINKER, ROY R.; and SPIEGEL, JOHN P. 1945 *Men Under Stress.* Philadelphia: Blakiston. → A paperback edition was published in 1963 by McGraw-Hill.

JANIS, IRVING L. 1958 *Psychological Stress: Psychoanalytic and Behavioral Studies of Surgical Patients.* New York: Wiley.

JANIS, IRVING L. 1962 Psychological Effects of Warnings. Pages 55–92 in George W. Baker and Dwight W. Chapman (editors), *Man and Society in Disaster.* New York: Basic Books.

KORCHIN, SHELDON J. 1964 Anxiety and Cognition. Pages 58–78 in Martin Scheerer Memorial Meetings on Cognitive Psychology, University of Kansas, 1962, *Cognition: Theory, Research, Promise.* New York: Harper.

LACEY, JOHN I. et al. 1963 The Visceral Level: Situational Determinants and Behavioral Correlates of Autonomic Response Patterns. Pages 161–196 in Symposium on Expression of the Emotions in Man, New York, 1960, *Expression of the Emotions in Man.* Edited by Peter H. Knapp. New York: International Universities Press.

LAZARUS, RICHARD S. 1966 *Psychological Stress and the Coping Process.* New York: McGraw-Hill.

LAZARUS, RICHARD S.; and ALFERT, ELIZABETH 1964 The Short Circuiting of Threat by Experimentally Altering Cognitive Appraisal. *Journal of Abnormal and Social Psychology* 69:195–205.

LAZARUS, RICHARD S.; DEESE, J.; and OSLER, S. F. 1952 The Effects of Psychological Stress Upon Performance. *Psychological Bulletin* 49:293–317.

LAZARUS, RICHARD S.; SPEISMAN, J. C.; and NORDKOFF, A. M. 1963 The Relationship Between Autonomic Indicators of Psychological Stress: Heart Rate and Skin Conductance. *Psychosomatic Medicine* 25:19–30.

MECHANIC, DAVID 1962 *Students Under Stress: A Study in the Social Psychology of Adaptation.* New York: Free Press.

OPTON, E. M. JR.; ALFERT, ELIZABETH; and LAZARUS, RICHARD S. 1967 Personality Determinants of Psychophysiological Response to Stress: A Theoretical Analysis and an Experiment. Unpublished manuscript.

PERSKY, HAROLD et al. 1959 Effect of Two Psychological Stresses on Adrenocortical Function. *Archives of Neurology and Psychiatry* 81:219–226.

SARASON, IRWIN G. 1960 Empirical Findings and Theoretical Problems in the Use of Anxiety Scales. *Psychological Bulletin* 57:403–415.

SCHACHTER, STANLEY; and SINGER, JEROME E. 1962 Cognitive, Social, and Physiological Determinants of Emotional State. *Psychological Review* 69:379–399.

SELYE, HANS 1956 *The Stress of Life.* New York: McGraw-Hill.

SHANNON, IRA L.; and ISBELL, G. M. 1963 *Stress in Dental Patients: Effect of Local Anesthetic Procedures.* Technical Report No. SAM-TDR-63-29. Brooks Air Force Base, Texas: USAF School of Aerospace Medicine.

SMELSER, NEIL J. (1962) 1963 *Theory of Collective Behavior.* London: Routledge; New York: Free Press.

SPIELBERGER, CHARLES D. (editor) 1966 *Anxiety and Behavior.* New York: Academic Press. → See especially "The Study of Psychological Stress: A Summary of Theoretical Formulations and Experimental Findings," by R. S. Lazarus and E. M. Opton, Jr.

VOGEL, WILLIAM; RAYMOND, SUSAN; and LAZARUS, RICHARD S. 1959 Intrinsic Motivation and Psychological Stress. *Journal of Abnormal and Social Psychology* 58:225–233.

WITHEY, STEPHEN B. 1962 Reaction to Uncertain Threat. Pages 93–123 in George W. Baker and Dwight W. Chapman (editors), *Man and Society in Disaster.* New York: Basic Books.

STRIKES

See under LABOR RELATIONS.

STRONG, WILLIAM DUNCAN

William Duncan Strong (1899–1962), American anthropologist, was born in Portland, Oregon. The Strong family played an active role in the development of the Oregon and Washington territories. Strong's grandfather was one of the first federal judges of the Oregon and Washington territories; his father, Thomas Nelson Strong, was a surveyor for the Northern Pacific Railroad and subsequently became an attorney for the Tshimsian and other Alaskan and Pacific Coast tribes. The early and deep personal involvement of young Strong with American Indian culture was further reinforced by his godfather, William Duncan, who was a well-known missionary to the Tshimsian.

Considering the "long and warm association" of his family with the American Indian (see "Knickerbocker Views . . ." 1961, p. 61), it was hardly surprising that Strong decided to major in anthropology at the University of California at Berkeley, where he received his PH.D. in 1926. It was at Berkeley that he came under the influence of Alfred Louis Kroeber. Kroeber's teaching was, without doubt, the major influence on Strong's career. The young graduate student had a deep interest in zoology and a keen sense of history, and hence he was particularly receptive to Kroeber's conception of anthropology as a strongly empirical discipline in which ethnology, linguistics, physical anthropology, and archeology all contribute to an understanding of the historical patterns of cultural phenomena.

Both Strong's early association with living Indian cultures and his graduate training formed the basis of his conviction that ethnological and archeological research should be closely associated. In his first major publications, which were based on his ethnological field work in southern California (1927; 1929), as well as in subsequent publications, Strong demonstrated that the ethnological present could never be satisfactorily explained without a knowledge of the past and that an understanding of prehistoric cultures of the American Indian should be based, when possible, on ethnological knowledge of the living cultures (1936; 1940).

The value of this approach was particularly well illustrated in "The Plains Culture Area in the Light of Archaeology" (1933) and in *An Introduction to Nebraska Archeology* (1935a). In these studies Strong combined ethnological, historical, and archeological data which led to a better understanding of the recent nomadic Plains Indian culture by showing that it had been largely agricultural and sedentary before the introduction of the horse.

Strong joined the Smithsonian Institution in 1931 and remained there until 1937. Under its auspices he carried out field work in Honduras (1935b; Smithsonian Institution . . . 1938) and continued his work in the Great Plains as well (1940).

Strong's next appointment was at Columbia University, where he taught until he died. He began to excavate in coastal Peru (Strong et al. 1943) and became particularly interested in the problems of the cultural relationships among pre-Columbian cultures. Strong first defined the scope of this problem in *Cross Sections of New World Prehistory* (1943), in which he evaluated the significance of the archeological work done in Latin America in 1941 and 1942 by the members of the first project of the Institute of Andean Research. In this publication Strong briefly outlined what were to become some of the major problems of archeological research after World War II: the definition of an early, basic New World culture analogous to Spinden's hypothetical Archaic culture (Willey 1953, p. 375) and the delineation of the prehistoric patterns of cultural development as a basis for the comparative study of culture process and culture history (1943, p. 41).

This interest in the comparative study of developmental culture patterns became more sharply focused after further field work in the Virú Valley in northern coastal Peru, carried out in 1946 in collaboration with other participants in a new project of the Institute of Andean Research (Strong & Evans 1952). The project led to the development by several persons, more or less independently, of a sequential ordering of Peruvian prehistory. At the Chiclín conference (Willey 1946), Strong joined R. Larco Hoyle in proposing a developmental sequence for the economic, social, political, and artistic aspects of the successive prehistoric cultures of coastal Peru (1948, p. 100).

It is of interest to note that Strong insisted that these cultural epoch sequences, his own as well as those presented by Wendell C. Bennett, Julian Steward, and others, must be constantly re-evaluated on the basis of archeological field research (1948, p. 100; 1951, p. 273). He felt that these developmental classifications were temporarily useful to express the results of prehistoric field research in culturally significant and comparable terms.

As a teacher and a humanist, Strong's concern was for man as a living being, and he constantly stressed the significance of archeological data for anthropology as a whole. Because of his insistence on the need to combine ethnological and archeological data and on the complementarity of the functional and the historical approaches, he was in the mainstream of significant archeological research throughout his career (Willey 1953, pp. 372, 375, 378, 381, 383).

The increase in specialization which tends to separate archeology and ethnology is a serious problem. Strong's work stands as an eloquent reminder of the fruitfulness of an integrated anthropological approach.

JACQUES BORDAZ

[*Directly related are the entries* ARCHEOLOGY, *article on* THE FIELD; HISTORY, *article on* CULTURE HISTORY; HUNTING AND GATHERING, *article on* NEW WORLD PREHISTORIC SOCIETIES. *Other relevant material may be found in the biography of* KROEBER.]

WORKS BY STRONG

1927   An Analysis of Southwestern Society. *American Anthropologist* New Series 29:1–61.
1929   *Aboriginal Society in Southern California.* University of California, Publications in American Archaeology and Ethnology, Vol. 26. Berkeley: Univ. of California Press.
1933   The Plains Culture Area in the Light of Archaeology. *American Anthropologist* New Series 35:271–287.
1935a   *An Introduction to Nebraska Archaeology.* Smithsonian Miscellaneous Collections, Vol. 93, No. 10. Washington: Smithsonian Institution.
1935b   *Archeological Investigations in the Bay Islands, Spanish Honduras.* Smithsonian Miscellaneous Collections, Vol. 92, No. 14. Washington: Smithsonian Institution.
1936   Anthropological Theory and Archaeological Fact. Pages 359–370 in *Essays in Anthropology in Honor of Alfred Louis Kroeber.* Berkeley: Univ. of California Press.
1938   SMITHSONIAN INSTITUTION–HARVARD UNIVERSITY ARCHEOLOGICAL EXPEDITION TO NORTHWESTERN HONDURAS, 1936 *Preliminary Report on the Smithsonian Institution–Harvard University Archeological Expedition to Northwestern Honduras, 1936,* by William D. Strong, Alfred Kidder, and A. J. Drexel Paul, Jr. Washington: The Institution.
1940   From History to Prehistory in the Northern Great Plains. Pages 353–394 in Smithsonian Institution, *Essays in Historical Anthropology of North America in Honor of John R. Swanton.* Smithsonian Miscellaneous Collections, Vol. 100. Washington: Smithsonian Institution.
1943   *Cross Sections of New World Prehistory: A Brief Report on the Work of the Institute of Andean Research, 1941–1942.* Smithsonian Miscellaneous Collections, Vol. 104, No. 2. Washington: Smithsonian Institution.
1943   STRONG, WILLIAM DUNCAN; WILLEY, GORDON R.; and CORBETT, JOHN M. *Archaeological Studies in Peru: 1941–1942.* Columbia Studies in Archaeology and Ethnology, Vol. 1. New York: Columbia Univ. Press.
1948   Cultural Epochs and Refuse Stratigraphy in Peruvian Archaeology. Pages 93–102 in Wendell C. Bennett (editor), *A Reappraisal of Peruvian Archaeology.* Society for American Archaeology, Memoirs, No. 4. Menasha, Wis.: The Society.
1951   Cultural Resemblances in Nuclear America: Parallelism or Diffusion? Volume 1, pages 271–279 in International Congress of Americanists, 29th, New York, 1949, *Selected Papers.* Univ. of Chicago Press.
1952   STRONG, WILLIAM DUNCAN; and EVANS, CLIFFORD JR. *Cultural Stratigraphy in the Virú Valley, Northern Peru: The Formative and Florescent Epochs.* Columbia Studies in Archaeology and Ethnology, Vol. 4. New York: Columbia Univ. Press.
1957   *Paracas, Nazca, and Tiahuanacoid Cultural Relationships in South Coastal Peru.* Society for American Archaeology, Memoirs, No. 13. Salt Lake City, Utah: The Society.
1961   Knickerbocker Views of the Oregon Country: Judge William Strong's Narrative, with a Foreword by William Duncan Strong. *Oregon Historical Quarterly* 62:57–87. → See pages 57–62 for Strong's Foreword.

SUPPLEMENTARY BIBLIOGRAPHY

SOLECKI, RALPH; and WAGLEY, CHARLES 1963 William Duncan Strong: 1899–1962. *American Anthropologist* New Series 65:1102–1111. → An obituary written by two of Strong's Columbia University colleagues; includes a detailed list of his positions and honors and a complete bibliography.
WILLEY, GORDON R. 1946 The Chiclín Conference for Peruvian Archaeology. *American Antiquity* 12:132–134.
WILLEY, GORDON R. 1953 Archeological Theories and Interpretations: New World. Pages 361–385 in International Symposium on Anthropology, New York, 1952, *Anthropology Today: An Encyclopedic Inventory.* Univ. of Chicago Press.

STRUCTURAL–FUNCTIONAL ANALYSIS

See FUNCTIONAL ANALYSIS.

STRUCTURALISM

See the introductory article under PERCEPTION *and the biographies of* TITCHENER *and* WUNDT.

"STUDENT"

See GOSSET, WILLIAM SEALY.

STUMPF, CARL

Friedrich Carl Stumpf, German psychologist, philosopher, and music theorist, was born in 1848 in Wiesentheid, Lower Franconia, and died in 1936 in Berlin. His father was the medico-legal officer of a county court. Both of his parents were very musical. While attending secondary schools in Kitzingen, Bamberg, and Aschaffenburg, Stumpf was taught to play several musical instruments; ultimately, he learned to play six instruments and taught himself the theory of harmony and counterpoint.

In 1865 Stumpf matriculated at the University of Würzburg, where he initially studied Catholic theology and then philosophy with Franz Brentano. Next he went to study with Hermann Lotze at Göttingen, where he also took courses in the natural sciences. After receiving his doctorate, he was habilitated at Göttingen as *Privatdozent* in philosophy. Between 1873 and 1893 he held chairs successively at Würzburg, Prague, Halle, Munich, and finally at Berlin, where he founded the psychological institute of the university. Stumpf became dean and then rector of the university, a privy councilor, and a member of the Academy of Sciences.

Work in music. Stumpf began his work on *Tonpsychologie* (the psychology of musical sounds) while still at Würzburg. His monograph on the Bellacoola Indians (1886) pioneered research on non-European music and stimulated the use of recording devices in such research. In Berlin, together with his students Otto Abraham and Erich von Hornbostel, he set up a collection of Edison wax cylinders and established a record archive, affiliated with the psychological institute.

Stumpf's work on *Tonpsychologie* is his most permanent scientific achievement. He coined the term and was the first to deal with the subject systematically. In his major work, with the same title (1883–1890), he used Helmholtz' researches, which were primarily physical and physiological, as a point of departure and then shifted to a psychological focus—a focus on the sensation of tone and the function of that sensation, rather than on the organ of hearing. He regarded the experience of the blending of tones as the basic factor in consonance, which he traced back hypothetically to "specific synergies" in the brain processes. In a later work, *Die Anfänge der Musik* (1911), he modified his position, having been impressed by the arguments of Hugo Riemann, who found the concept of blending inadequate for triads and for chords of more than three notes. Stumpf therefore introduced the term "concordance" (or "concord") for all major and minor triads, together with their inversions. He regarded all other chords as "discordances" (or "discords"). This aspect of his theory did not stand up against the theory of Felix Krueger or against that of Stumpf's own students, especially von Hornbostel.

Stumpf's ethnological studies, including studies of music, particularly his *Anfänge der Musik*, qualify him as the founder of comparative musicology, or ethnomusicology. He also continued the kind of research Helmholtz had done, using the physical method of interference to break down vocal and instrumental chords and build them up again. He presented his findings in *Die Sprachlaute* (1926), a book written late in life as a substitute for the planned third volume of his *Tonpsychologie*. Thus, Stumpf harnessed physics, physiology, psychology, ethnology, philosophy, and above all, aesthetics to the service of the systematic study of music, and eventually he won acceptance of this subject as an independent discipline by the faculty of philosophy of the University of Berlin.

Psychology. As a psychologist, Stumpf formulated a theory of space perception and a theory of emotions. His first (psychological) book dealt with space perception (1873). Boring has described it as a nativistic theory which argues that both color and extension are equally "part-contents" of visual sensation ([1929] 1950, p. 363). Stumpf's theory of emotions is akin to those of Wundt, James, and C. Lange, who derived emotions from organic sensations. Stumpf introduced the concept of "emotional sensations" as a special class of sensations, related to tickling, itching, and cutaneous pain, and he believed that these emotional sensations constitute the basis of all emotionality. Pleasure and pain (or displeasure) were for him merely another special class of sensations rather than a separate class of psychic phenomena. This view has not, however, prevailed.

At the turn of the century Stumpf created something of a stir with his attempt to re-establish with regard to the body–soul problem the theory of mutual causation (or causal interdependence), which was by then considered obsolete. This effort was aimed at Wundt in particular (it was only one of the many areas in which Stumpf was at odds with Wundt and his school). But again, Stumpf's view was not accepted, not even by the gestalt theorists among his own students.

Philosophy. Stumpf's third area of interest, besides music and psychology, was that of logic and epistemology. Stumpf's work here is sometimes considered similar to that of von Meinong and Husserl, since all three were students and intellectual descendants of Lotze and Brentano, but Stumpf and the two slightly younger philosophers really have nothing fundamentally in common. Indeed, Stumpf criticized von Meinong and Husserl, incisively although respectfully. He rejected von Meinong's theory of "impossible" objects and Husserl's "pure" phenomenology as impracticable. Although he approved of Husserl's rejection of "psychologism," in the *Logische Untersuchungen*, he could not go along with the fundamental cleavage Husserl proposed between psychology and philosophy, and he took issue sharply with the Marburg school of Neo-Kantianism (1891). He considered Kant's misconception and neglect of psychology to be the basic failing of his philosophical system.

According to Stumpf, the fundamental task of epistemology is to establish those immediately evident "rational insights" that become organized into axioms of different degrees of abstraction and generality. In these fundamental insights, logic must cooperate with psychology; their content is not the subject of logic alone. Stumpf believed that the theory of probability is important for developing knowledge from its a priori fundaments; however, he saw probability as concerned not with judgments or facts but rather with judgments on man's subjective knowledge about facts. As in the *Tonpsychologie*, Stumpf made a rigorous distinction between phenomena and functions, that is, between objects of experience (sensory and memory contents), on the one hand, and actions and experiences or states, on the other. Thus, he called the doctrine of phenomena so defined "phenomenology" and separated it strictly from "psychology," the doctrine of functions.

More particularly, psychology is, according to Stumpf, the doctrine of elementary functions, the complex ones being the subject of the other *Geisteswissenschaften*. Psychology thus becomes a low-level, elementary *Geisteswissenschaft;* this definition is similar to the one offered by Dilthey in his 1894 article, "Ideen über eine beschreibende und zergliedernde Psychologie." Thus, Stumpf defined phenomenology in a somewhat different way than did Husserl, namely, in a more narrow sense and less specifically in terms of methodology. In addition to phenomena and functions, Stumpf distinguished "correlates," or "structures," of functions, these being the concepts, facts, and values that he made the substance of a special science called "eidology," which might also be called *Ideenwissenschaft*, and is best translated as "theory of ideas," in the Platonic sense. Finally, there remain relationships as distinct objects of inquiry; these are treated in the "sciences of relations."

In ethics Stumpf followed Brentano in combating relativism and so for once found himself in agreement with Wundt. Stumpf doubted the assumption that the amount of "happiness" in the world is increasing, although he was convinced that there is a progressive refinement of ethical sensibility.

Stumpf also made excursions into metaphysics, but these were no more successful than his complicated classification of the sciences. His accomplishments as a psychologist were significant for his time, especially his work as an experimenter, although here, too, his views have hardly endured in any essential respect. Some of the leading gestalt theorists, including Max Wertheimer and Wolfgang Köhler, were among his students—Köhler succeeded him at Berlin—but they largely rejected his basic position. It is in the area of musical theory that Stumpf's influence has been most lasting.

ALBERT WELLEK

[*For the historical context of Stumpf's work, see the biographies of* HELMHOLTZ; HUSSERL; JAMES; LOTZE; WUNDT; *for discussion of the subsequent development of his ideas, see* AESTHETICS; HEARING; PERCEPTION, *article on* DEPTH PERCEPTION; PHENOMENOLOGY; PSYCHOPHYSICS; SENSES.]

WORKS BY STUMPF

1873   *Ueber den psychologischen Ursprung der Raumvorstellung.* Leipzig: Hirzel.

1883–1890   *Tonpsychologie.* 2 vols. Leipzig: Hirzel.

(1886) 1922   Lieder der Bellakula-Indianer. Pages 87–103 in A. J. Ellis et al., *Abhandlungen zur vergleichenden Musikwissenschaft.* Munich: Drei Masken. → First published in Volume 2 of the *Vierteljahrsschrift für Musikwissenschaft.*

1891   *Psychologie und Erkenntnistheorie.* Munich: Franz.

1898–1924   STUMPF, CARL (editor) *Beiträge zur Akustik und Musikwissenschaft.* 9 vols. Leipzig: Barth.

(1900–1903) 1909   *Leib und Seele* und *Der Entwicklungsgedanke in der gegenwärtigen Philosophie.* 3d ed. Leipzig: Barth. → These two works were originally published separately.

1907   *Erscheinungen und psychische Funktionen.* Berlin: Reimer.

1908a   *Die Wiedergeburt der Philosophie.* Leipzig: Barth.

1908b   *Vom ethischen Skeptizismus.* Berlin: Universitäts-Buchdruckerei von Gustav Schade.

1910   *Philosophische Reden und Vorträge.* Leipzig: Barth.

1911   *Die Anfänge der Musik.* Leipzig: Barth.

1924   [Autobiography of] Carl Stumpf. Volume 5, pages 205–265 in *Die deutsche Philosophie der Gegenwart in Selbstdarstellungen.* Edited by Raymund Schmidt. Leipzig: Meiner.

1926   *Die Sprachlaute: Experimentell-phonetische Untersuchungen nebst einem Anhang über Instrumental-Klänge.* Berlin: Springer.

1927   *William James nach seinen Briefen.* Berlin: Pan-Verlag Rolf Heise.

1928   *Gefühl und Gefühlsempfindung.* Leipzig: Barth.

1939–1940   *Erkenntnislehre.* 2 vols. Edited by Felix Stumpf. Leipzig: Barth.

SUPPLEMENTARY BIBLIOGRAPHY

BORING, EDWIN G. (1929) 1950   *A History of Experimental Psychology.* 2d ed. New York: Appleton. → See especially pages 362–371, "Carl Stumpf."

DILTHEY, WILHELM 1894   Ideen über eine beschreibende und zergliedernde Psychologie. Akademie der Wissenschaften, Berlin, *Sitzungsberichte* 2:1309–1407. → Reprinted in 1964 in Volume 5 of Dilthey's *Gesammelte Schriften.*

STYLE

Style is any distinctive, and therefore recognizable, way in which an act is performed or an artifact made or ought to be performed and made. The wide range of applications implied in this definition is reflected in the variety of usages of the word in current English. (Definitions and illustrations in the *Shorter Oxford English Dictionary* take up almost three columns.) They may be conveniently grouped into descriptive and normative usages. Descriptions may classify the various ways of doing or making, according to the groups or countries or periods where these were or are habitual—for example, the gypsy style of music, the French style of cookery, or the eighteenth-century style of dress; it may take its name from a particular person, as in "Ciceronian style," or even denote one individual's manner of doing something ("This is not my style."). In a similar way institutions or firms may have a distinctive way of procedure or production, publishers have a "house style" and provide authors with a "style sheet" indicating how to quote titles of books, etc.

Often styles are described by some characteristic quality that is experienced as expressive of psychological states—"a passionate style," "a humorous style"; frequently, also, these characterizations shade over into intrasensory (synesthetic) descriptions, as in a "sparkling," a "drab," or a "smooth" style of writing or playing. Equally often, the distinctive quality to be described is derived from a particular mode of performance or production and transferred to others of similar character, as in a "theatrical" style of behavior, a "jazzy" style of ornament, a "hieratic" style of painting. Finally, there are the terms now reserved for categories of style, such as the "Romanesque" or the "Baroque" style, which have sometimes been extended in their application from the descriptions of architectural procedures to the manner of performance in other arts and beyond to all utterances of the societies concerned during the periods covered (Baroque music, Baroque philosophy, Baroque diplomacy, etc.; see Wellek & Warren 1949, chapter 11).

As in most terms describing distinctions—including the very words "distinction" and "distinguished"—the term "style" stripped of any qualifying adjective can also be used in a normative sense, as a laudatory term denoting a desirable consistency and conspicuousness that makes a performance or artifact stand out from a mass of "undistinguished" events or objects: "He received him in style"; "This acrobat has style"; "This building lacks style." Huckleberry Finn, describing a "monstrous raft that was as long going by as a procession" remarked, "There was a power of style about her. It *amounts* to something being a raftsman on such a raft as that" (Mark Twain, *Huckleberry Finn*, chapter 16). To the anthropologist, perhaps, every raft has a "style" if he chooses to use this term for the way of producing any such craft habitual in any society. But to Mark Twain's hero the term connotes a raft with a difference, one sufficiently elaborate to impress. This connotation is illustrated in Winston Churchill's reply to a barber who had asked him what "style of haircut he desired": "A man of my limited resources cannot presume to have a hair *style*—get on and cut it" (*News Chronicle*, London, December 19, 1958).

Intention and description. It might have saved critics and social scientists a good deal of trouble and confusion if Churchill's distinction had been applied in the usage of the term—that is, if the word "style" had been confined to cases where there is a choice between ways of performance or procedure. Historically, this is clear. Thus, the word "style" was adopted for the alternative forms of dating in use during the period between the introduction and acceptance of the Gregorian calendar in England. When the "old style" gradually fell out of use, nobody continued to speak of the "style" of dating a letter.

But usage apart, the indiscriminate application of the word "style" to any type of performance or production which the user, rather than the performer or producer, is able to distinguish has had grave methodological consequences. It may be argued (and will be argued in this article) that only against the background of alternative choices can the distinctive way also be seen as expressive. The girl who chooses a certain style of dress will in this very act express her intention of appearing in a certain character or social role at a given occasion. The board of directors that chooses a contemporary style for a new office building may equally be concerned with the firm's image. The laborer who puts on his overalls or the builder who erects a bicycle shed is not aware of any act of choice, and although the outside observer may realize that there are alternative forms of working outfits or sheds, their characterization as "styles" may invite psychological interpretations that can lead him astray. To quote the formulation of a linguist, "The pivot of the whole theory of expressiveness is the concept of *choice*. There can be no question of style unless the speaker or writer has the possibility of choosing between alternative forms of expression. Synonymy, in the widest sense of the term, lies at the root of the whole problem of style" (Ullmann 1957, p. 6).

If the term "style" is thus used descriptively for alternative ways of doing things, the term "fashion" can be reserved for the fluctuating preferences which carry social prestige. A hostess may set the fashion in a smaller or wider section of the community for a given style of decoration or entertainment. Yet the two terms may overlap in their application. A fashionable preference can become so general and so lasting that it affects the style of a whole society. Moreover, since considerations of prestige sometimes carry with them the suspicion of insincerity and snobbery, the same movement may be described as a fashion by its critics and as a style by its well-wishers.

Etymology. The word "style" derives from Latin *stilus*, the writing instrument of the Romans. It could be used to characterize an author's manner of writing (Cicero, *Brutus*, 100), although the more frequent term for literary style was *genus dicendi*, "mode of speech" (Leeman 1963). The writings of Greek and Roman teachers of rhetoric still provide the most subtle analyses ever attempted of the various potentialities and categories of style. The effect of words depends on the right choice of the noble or humble term, with all the social and psychological connotations that go with these stratifications. Equal attention should be paid to the flavor of archaic or current usages (Gombrich 1966*a*). Either usage can be correct if the topic so demands it. This is the doctrine of *decorum*, of the appropriateness of style to the occasion. To use the grand manner for trivial subjects is as ridiculous as to use colloquialisms for solemn occasions (Cicero, *Orator*, 26). Oratory, in this view, is a skill that slowly developed until it could be used with assurance to sway the jury. But corruption lurks close to perfection. An overdose of effects produces a hollow and affected style that lacks virility. Only a constant study of the greatest models of style (the "classical" authors) will preserve the style pure (Curtius 1948, p. 249).

These doctrines, which also have an application to music, architecture, and the visual arts, form the foundation of critical theory up to the eighteenth century. In the Renaissance, Giorgio Vasari discussed the various manners of art and their progress toward perfection in normative terms. The word "style" came only slowly into usage as applied to the visual arts, although instances multiply in the late sixteenth century and in the seventeenth century (Białostocki 1961). It became established as a term of art history in the eighteenth century, largely through J. J. Winckelmann's *History of Ancient Art* (1764). His treatment of Greek style as an expression of the Greek way of life encouraged Herder and others to do the same for the medieval Gothic and, thus, paved the way for a history of art in terms of succeeding period styles. It is worth noting that the names for styles used in art history derive from normative contexts. They denote either the (desirable) dependence on a classical norm or the (condemned) deviations from it (Gombrich 1966*b*, pp. 83–86). Thus, "Gothic" originated from the idea that it was the "barbaric" style of the destroyers of the Roman Empire (Frankl 1960). "Baroque" is a conflation of various words meaning "bizarre" and "absurd" (Kurz

1960). "Rococo" was coined as a term of derision about 1797 by J. L. David's pupils for the meretricious taste of the age of Pompadour (Kimball 1943). Even "Romanesque" started its career about 1819 as a term denoting "the corruption of the Roman style," and "mannerism," equally, signified the affectation that corrupted the purity of the Renaissance (Gombrich 1966*b*, pp. 99–106). Thus, the sequence of classical, postclassical, Romanesque, Gothic, Renaissance, mannerist, baroque, rococo, and neoclassical originally recorded the successive triumphs and defeats of the classical ideal of perfection (Panofsky 1960). While the eighteenth-century Gothic revival brought the first challenge to this view, it was only in the nineteenth century that the whole repertory of "historical styles" was available for the architect, a state of affairs which made the century increasingly style-conscious and led to the insistent question, "What is the style of *our* age?" (George Boas 1941). Thus, the concepts of style developed by critics and historians reacted back on the artists themselves. In the course of these debates the relation between style and the progress of technology came increasingly to the fore.

Technology and fashion

The distinctive way an act is performed or an artifact made is likely to remain constant as long as it meets the needs of the social group. In static groups the forces of conservatism are, therefore, likely to be strong and the style of pottery, basketry, or warfare may not change over long periods (Franz Boas 1927). Two main forces will make for change: technological improvements and social rivalry. Technological progress is a subject extending far beyond the scope of this article, but it must be mentioned because of its effect on choice situations. Knowledge of better methods might be expected to change the style of artifacts irresistibly, and indeed, where the technical aim is paramount —as in warfare, athletics, or transport—the demonstrably better method is likely to change the style of procedure as soon as it is known and mastered.

What is relevant here for the student of style is that the older method may yet be retained within certain limited contexts of ritual and ceremony. The queen still drives to Parliament in a coach, not in an automobile, and is guarded by men with swords and lances, not with Tommy guns. The Torah is still in scroll form, while the world has adopted the more convenient codex. It is clear that the expressive value of the archaic style will tend to increase with the distance between the normal technological usages and the methods reserved for these distinctive occasions. The more rapid technical progress becomes, the wider will be the gap between adoption and rejection. In our technological society, even the retention of the "vintage car" is symptomatic of a "style of life."

We are here touching on the second factor making for change—the element of social rivalry and prestige. In the slogan "Bigger and better," "better" stands for technological improvement with reference to a statable purpose, "bigger" for the element of display that is such a driving force in competitive groups. In medieval Italian cities rival families vied with each other in building those high towers that still mark the city of San Gimignano. Sometimes civic authority asserted its symbolic rights by forbidding any of these towers to rise higher than the tower of the town hall. Cities, in their turn, might vie with each other to have the biggest cathedral, just as princes would outdo each other in the size of their parks, the splendor of their operas, or the equipment of their stables. It is not always easy to see why competition suddenly fastens on one element rather than another, but once the possession of a high tower, a large orchestra, or a fast motorcycle has become a status symbol within a given society, competition is likely to lead to excesses far beyond the need of the technological purpose.

It might be argued that these developments belong to the realm of fashion rather than of style, just as the improvement of method belongs to technology. But an analysis of stability and change in style will always have to take into account these two influences. The pressures of fashion, like those of technology, provide an additional dimension of choice for those who refuse to go with the fashion and, thus, desire to assert their independence. Clearly, this independence is only relative. Even a refusal to join in the latest social game is a way of taking up a position toward it. Indeed, it might make those who adopt this course willy-nilly more conspicuous than the followers of fashion. If they have sufficient social prestige, they might even find themselves to be creators of a nonconformist fashion which will ultimately lead to a new style of behavior.

The above distinction between technical and social superiority is of necessity artificial, for technological progress tends to create prestige for the society in which it originated, which will carry over into other fields. Admiration for Roman power and for the ruins of Rome led to the fashion for all things Roman in the Renaissance, and the admiration of Peter the Great and Kemal Pasha for

Western superiority even led to a forced change to Western dress and hairstyles in their countries. The fashions for American jazz or American slang so much deplored by conservative Europeans on both sides of the Iron Curtain are reminders of the legendary prestige of American technology and power, just as the rush to learn the Russian language can be traced back to the success of the first Sputnik. Here, as always, however, the reaction of the nonconformist provides the best gauge for the potential attractions of the style. Leaders of underdeveloped nations, such as Gandhi, have defiantly resisted Westernization in their style of dress and behavior and exalted the virtues of uncorrupted technological primitivity.

Style in art has rarely been analyzed in terms of these pressures, but such an analysis might yield worthwhile results, for the various activities which, since the eighteenth century, have gradually become grouped together under the name of art (Kristeller 1951–1952) once served a variety of practical purposes in addition to increasing prestige. In architecture both aspects interacted from the very beginning, the erection of the Egyptian pyramids, for example, displaying both technological and organizational skills and competitive pride. Opinions tend to differ about the relative proportions of technological and prestige elements in the succession of medieval architectural styles; the technology of stone vaulting offered a clear advantage in view of fire risks, but it is still an open question whether the introduction of the Gothic rib and the subsequent competition in light and high structures was motivated principally by technical considerations. Clearly, considerations of prestige, of outdoing a rival city or a rival prince, have always played a part in architectural display. At the same time, architectural history exhibits many reactions away from these dual pressures, toward simpler styles or more intimate effects. The rejection of ornament in neoclassical architecture, the conspicuous simplicity of Le Petit Trianon—not to speak of Marie Antoinette's *hameau* at Versailles —are cases in point. The Gothic revival drew its strength from the associations of that style with a preindustrial age. Indeed, the history of architecture provides perhaps the most interesting conflict of motives. When, in the nineteenth century, technology and engineering improved the use of iron constructions, architects adopted, for a time, the ritualistic attitude that this new material was essentially inartistic: the Eiffel Tower was a display of engineering, not of art. But ultimately, it was the prestige of technology within our industrial society that assured the embodment of the new methods in a new technological "functional" style (Pevsner 1936). Now even functionalism, the conspicuous look of technological efficiency, has become a formal element of expression in architecture and, as such, sometimes influences design at least as much as genuine adaptation to a purpose. The best example for this interaction of technology and fashion in the visual arts is the adoption of "streamline" patterns to designs not intended to function in rapid currents.

Even the development of painting and sculpture could be seen in the light of these dual influences if it is accepted that image making usually serves a definite function within society. In tribal societies the production of ritual masks, totem poles, or ancestral figures is usually governed by the same conservative traditions of skill as is the production of other artifacts. When the existing forms serve their purpose, there is no need for change and the craftsman's apprentice can learn the procedures from his master. However, foreign contacts or playful inventions may lead to the discovery of "better" methods of creating images—better, at least, from the point of view of naturalistic plausibility. Whether these methods are accepted, ignored, or deliberately rejected will depend largely on the function assigned to images within a given society. Where the image functions mainly in a ritualistic context, changes will be discouraged even though they cannot be entirely prevented. The conservative styles of Egypt and Byzantium are cases in point. On the other hand, when the principal function of painting and sculpture lies in their capacity to evoke a story or event before the eyes of the spectator (Gombrich 1960), demonstrable improvements in this capacity will tend to gain ready acceptance and displace earlier methods, which may then only linger on in confined, sacred contexts. This prestige of improved methods can be observed at least twice in the history of art: in the development of Greek art from the sixth to the fourth century B.C. and in the succession of styles in Europe from the twelfth to the nineteenth century.

The invention of such illusionistic devices as foreshortening, in the fifth century B.C., or of perspective, in the fifteenth century A.D., gave to the arts of Greece and Florence a lead which is expressed in the prestige and the diffusion of these styles over the whole of the civilized world. It took centuries until the momentum of such spectacular superiority was spent and a reaction set in.

Even in this realm of artistic styles, however, the introduction of better illusionistic devices could and did lead to tensions where rejection was as powerful a means of expression as was acceptance.

This reaction became particularly important after the method of achieving the then main purpose of art—convincing illustration—had been mastered in fourth-century Greece and sixteenth-century Italy. It was felt that technical progress was no longer needed once the means had been perfected to suit the ends, as in the (lost) paintings by Apelles or in the masterpieces by Leonardo, Raphael, and Michelangelo. Subsequent innovations in the dramatic use of light and shade (Caravaggio and Rembrandt) or in the rendering of movement (Bernini) were rejected by critics as obscuring rather than helping the essential purpose of art and were considered an illicit display of technical virtuosity at the expense of clarity. Here lie the roots of that philosophy of style that is essential to the whole development of criticism in the Western tradition. The perfect harmony between means and ends marks the classical style (Gombrich 1966b); periods in which the means are not yet quite sufficient to realize the ends are experienced as primitive or archaic, and those in which the means are said to obtrude themselves in an empty display are considered corrupt. To evaluate this criticism, we would have to ask whether display could not and did not develop into an alternative function of art with its own conventions and code.

Evolution and disintegration of styles

It is clear that from the normative point of view there is an intrinsic destiny which artistic styles are likely to follow and that this will overtake different activities at different points in time. The classic moment in epic poetry may have been achieved in Homer; that of tragedy, in Sophocles; that of oratory, in Demosthenes; that of sculpture, in Praxiteles; and that of painting in Apelles or Raphael. Symphonic music may have reached its perfect balance between ends and means, its classic moment, in Mozart, three hundred years after Raphael's paintings.

It has indeed been argued that such phenomena as mannerism or the baroque, however they may be valued, occur in the development of any art which has reached maturity and, perhaps, overripeness. In that "late" phase, the increasingly hectic search for fresh complexities may lead to an "exhaustion" of the style when all permutations have been tried (Munro 1963). Although there is a certain superficial plausibility in this interpretation, which accounts for some stretches of historical development, it must never be forgotten that terms such as "complexity" and "elements" do not here refer to measurable entities and that even the relationship of means to ends is open to contrasting interpretations. What may appear to one critic as the classic moment of an art may carry, for another, the seeds of corruption, and what looks like the final stage of exhaustion of a style to one interpreter may be seen from another point of view as the groping beginnings of a new style. Cézanne, the complexity of whose art is beyond doubt, saw himself as the primitive of a new age of art, and this ambiguity adheres to any great artist, who can always be described as representing the culmination of a preceding evolution, a new beginning, or (by his adversaries) an archcorruptor. Thus, the naturalism of Jan van Eyck can be seen as the climax of late Gothic tendencies in the descriptive accumulation of minute details (Huizinga 1919, chapter 21) or as the primitive start of a new era. The style of J. S. Bach can be experienced as late complexity or as archaic grandeur. For the same reasons almost any style can be convincingly described as transitional.

It is evident, moreover, that the units, or styles, by which the evolution is traced will always be rather arbitrarily chosen. Aristotle gave the lead in his famous sketch of the evolution of tragedy (*Poetics* 1448b3–1449a) but to do so, he had first to set off tragedy from comedy or mime. In a similar way, we may either describe the evolution of painting or of one of its branches, and we may find, for instance, that what was a late phase for portrait painting (e.g., mannerism) was an early one for landscape painting.

If the analysis of styles in terms of the inner logic of their evolution has, nevertheless, yielded illuminating results, this must be attributed less to the validity of alleged historical laws than to the sensitivity of critics. Heinrich Wölfflin (1888), for example, used this framework in order to draw attention to the artistic means available to a given master and developed a vocabulary for a debate, which, however inconclusive it is bound to be, will increase our awareness of the traditions within which the masters concerned operated. By placing an *oeuvre* into a continuous chain of developments, we become alerted to what its creator had learned from predecessors, what he transformed, and how he was used, in his turn, by later generations. We must only guard against the temptation of hindsight to regard this outcome as inevitable. For every one of the masters concerned, the future was open, and although each may have been restricted in his choice by certain characteristics of the situation, the directions the development might have taken are still beyond computation. Ackerman has provided a fuller criticism of this type of stylistic determinism (Ackerman & Carpenter 1963). But

these strictures do not invalidate the search for a morphology of style that should underpin the intuitions of the connoisseur.

Style and period. The analysis of stylistic traditions in terms of the means peculiar to individual arts cuts across another approach, which is less interested in the "longitudinal" study of evolution than in the synchronic characterization of all activities of a particular group, nation, or period. This approach to style as an expression of a collective spirit can be traced back to romantic philosophy, notably to Hegel's *Philosophy of History* (1837). Seeing history as the manifestation of the Absolute in its growing self-awareness, Hegel conceived of each stage of this process as a step in the dialectical process embodied in one particular nation. A nation's art, no less than its philosophy, religion, law, mores, science, and technology, will always reflect the stage in the evolution of the Spirit, and each of these facets will thus point to the one common center, the essence of the age. Thus, the historian's task is not to find out what connections there may be between aspects of a society's life, for this connection is assumed on metaphysical grounds (Hegel 1837, pp. 53, 63–64 in the 1944 edition). There is no question, for instance, whether the Gothic style of architecture expresses the same essential attitude as scholastic philosophy or medieval feudalism. What is expected of the historian is only to demonstrate this unitary principle.

It matters little in this context whether the historian concerned thinks of this unitary principle as the "Hegelian spirit" or whether he looks for some other central cause from which all the characteristics of a period can be deduced. In fact, the history of nineteenth-century historiography of art (and its twentieth-century aftermath) can largely be described as a series of attempts to get rid of the more embarrassing features of Hegel's metaphysics without sacrificing his unitary vision. It is well known that Marx and his disciples claimed to do precisely this when they turned Hegel's principle upside down and claimed that material conditions are not the manifestation of the spirit, but rather the spirit is an outflow or superstructure of the material conditions of production. It was these conditions (to remain with our previous example) which led to medieval feudalism and which are reflected in scholastic philosophy no less than in Gothic architecture.

What distinguishes all these theories from a genuinely scientific search for causal connections is their a priori character. The question is not whether, and in what form, feudalism may have influenced the conditions under which cathedrals were constructed, but how to find a verbal formula that makes the assumed interdependence of style and society immediately apparent. In this conviction the various holistic schools of historiography agreed, regardless of whether they belonged to the materialist Hegelian left-wing or to the right-wing of *Geistesgeschichte*. As Wölfflin, one of the most subtle and sophisticated analysts of style, formulated his program in his youth, in 1888: "To *explain* a style then can mean nothing other than to place it in its general historical context and to verify that it speaks in harmony with the other organs of its age" ([1888] 1964, p. 79; for a detailed discussion of these ideas as related to style in art, see Schapiro 1953). What matters in the present context is that this holistic conviction became widely accepted by historians and artists alike. As Adolf Loos, the pioneer of modern architecture in Austria, put it: "If nothing were left of an extinct race but a single button, I would be able to infer, from the shape of that button, how these people dressed, built their houses, how they lived, what was their religion, their art, and their mentality" (Kulka 1931, p. 25).

It is the old classical tag *Ex ungue leonem* ("The claw shows the lion") applied to the study of culture. By and large, historians and anthropologists have preferred to display their skill for interpretation where the results were foreknown rather than risk being proved wrong by fresh evidence.

Stylistic physiognomics

Seductive as the holistic theory of style has proved to be, it is still open to criticism on methodological grounds. It is true that both individuals and groups exhibit to our mind some elusive unitary physiognomy. The way a person speaks, writes, dresses, and looks merges for us into the image of his personality. We therefore say that all these are expressions of his personality, and we can sometimes rationalize our conviction by pointing out supposed connections (Pear 1957). But the psychologist knows that it is extremely hazardous to make inferences from one such manifestation to all the others even when we know the context and conventions extremely well. Where this knowledge is lacking, nobody would venture such a diagnosis. Yet, it is this paradoxically which the diagnosticians of group styles claim to be able to do (Gombrich 1963). More often than not, they are simply arguing in a circle and inferring from the static or rigid style of a tribe that its mentality must also be static or rigid. The less collateral evidence there is, the more easily will this kind of diagnosis be accepted—particularly if it is part of a system of polarities in which, for instance, dynamic cultures are opposed to static ones or intuitive mentalities to rational ones.

The weaknesses of this kind of procedure in both history and anthropology are obvious. The logical claims of cultural holism have been subjected to dissection and refutation in K. R. Popper's *The Poverty of Historicism* (1957). There is no necessary connection between any one aspect of a group's activities and any other.

This does not mean, however, that style cannot sometimes provide a fruitful starting point for a hypothesis about certain habits and traditions of a group. One of these possibilities has been mentioned already. There certainly are conservative groups or societies which will tend to resist change in all fields, and other societies (like ours) in which prestige attaches to experimentation as such (Peckham 1965). It might be argued that contrasting characteristics of style may flow from these contrasting attitudes. The static societies may tend to value solid craftsmanship and the refinements of skill, while the dynamic groups may favor the untried even where it is the unskilled. But such generalizations are subject to the same qualifications as the ones criticized in the preceding section. There is no real common gauge by which to compare the skill of Picasso with that of a conservative Chinese master. Once more, therefore, the evaluation of expressiveness will largely depend on a knowledge of choice situations. In such a situation the twentieth-century art lover may indeed prefer originality to skill, while the Chinese would select the skillful, rather than the novel, painting. The same applies to such dominant values of a society as love of luxury or its rejection. What constitutes luxury may change, but it may still be true to say that at the fashionable courts of Europe, around 1400, the more precious and shiny artifact or painting would have been preferred, while a Calvinist paterfamilias would have thrown the same gaudy bauble out of the window. Such basic attitudes may, indeed, color the style of several arts at the same time.

It might even be argued that social values such as the traditional English love of understatement will influence the choice of means and styles in various fields and favor the rejection of display in architecture, of "loud" colors in painting, and of emotionalism in music. But, although there is an intuitive truth in such connections, it is only too easy to point to opposite features in the grandiloquent vulgarity of English Victorian town halls, the shrill colors of pre-Raphaelite paintings, or the emotionalism of Carlyle's tirades.

What is true of national character as allegedly

"expressed" in art is even more conspicuously true of the spirit of the age. The baroque pomp and display of the *Roi soleil* at Versailles is contemporaneous with the classical restraint of Racine. The functionalist rationalism of twentieth-century architecture goes hand in hand with the irrationalism of Bergson's philosophy, Rilke's poetry, and Picasso's painting. Needless to say, it is always possible to reinterpret the evidence in such a way that one characteristic points to the alleged "essence" of a period, while other manifestations are "inessential" survivals or anticipations, but such *ad hoc* explanations invalidate rather than strengthen the unitary hypothesis.

The diagnostics of artistic choice

To escape from the physiognomic fallacy, the student of style might do worse than return to the lessons of ancient rhetoric. There, the alternative vocabularies provided by social and chronological stratifications provided the instrument of style. We are familiar with similar stratifications in the styles of speech, dress, furnishings, and taste which allow us to size up a person's status and allegiance with reasonable confidence. Taste in art is now similarly structured between the cheap and the highbrow, the conservative and the advanced. No wonder that artistic choices offer themselves as another badge of allegiance. But what is true today need not always have been true (Haskell 1963, introduction). The temptation to overrate the diagnostic value of artistic style stems partly from an illicit extension of our experience in modern society.

It is possible that this situation in art did not fully arise before the French Revolution, which polarized European political life into right-wing reactionaries and left-wing progressives. While the champions of reason clung to the neoclassical style, its opponents became medievalizers in architecture, painting, and even dress to proclaim their allegiance to the age of faith. From then on, it was not exceptional for an artistic movement to be identified with a political creed. Courbet's choice of working-class models and subjects was felt to be an act of defiance that stamped him as a socialist. In vain did some artists protest that their radicalism in painting or music did not imply radical political views (Pelles 1963). The fusion and confusion of the two was strengthened by the critics' jargon, which spoke of the avant-garde (Poggioli 1962) and revolutionaries in art, and by the artists who copied the politicians in issuing manifestoes.

But, although the divisions of our societies are possibly reflected in the range of our art, it would be rash to conclude that the allegiance can be read off the badge, as it were. There was a time, in the early 1920s, when abstract painting was practiced in revolutionary Russia and when opposition to these experiments could rally the opponents of "cultural Bolshevism." Now abstract art is denounced in Russia, where "social realism" is extolled as the healthy art of the new age. This change of front, in its turn, has made it possible for abstract art to be used as a subsidiary weapon in the cold war, in which it now has come to stand for freedom of expression. The toleration of this style of painting in Poland, for instance, is indeed a social symptom of no minor importance.

There are perhaps two lessons which the student of style can learn from this example. The first concerns the "feedback" character of social theories. Soviet Russia, having adopted the Marxist version of Hegelianism as its official creed, could not look at any artistic utterance but as a necessary expression of a social situation. Deviation and nonconformity in art were therefore bound to be interpreted as symptoms of potential disloyalty, and a monolithic style appealing to the majority became a theoretical necessity. We in the West, happily, do not suffer from the same state religion, but the Hegelian conviction is still sufficiently widespread among critics and politicians to encourage a political interpretation of stylistic changes—our newspapers prefer to ask of every new movement in art or architecture what it stands for, rather than what its artistic potentialities may be. The second lesson suggested by this contemporary experience in East and West is that one cannot opt out of this game. Once an issue has been raised in this form, once a badge has been adopted and a flag hoisted, it becomes hard, if not impossible, to ignore this social aspect. One might pity the anticommunist Pole who would like to paint a brawny, happy tractor driver, but one would have to tell him that this subject and style has been pre-empted by his political opponents. The harmless subject has become charged with political significance, and one person alone cannot break this spell.

These two observations underline the responsibility of the social scientist in his discussion of style. Here, as always, the observer is likely to interfere with what he observes.

Morphology and connoisseurship

The distinctive character of styles clearly rests on the adoption of certain conventions which are learned and absorbed by those who carry on the tradition. These may be codified in the movements learned by the craftsman taught to carve a ritual mask, in the way a painter learns to prime his canvas and arrange his palette, or in the rules of harmony, which the composer is asked to observe.

While certain of these features are easily recognizable (e.g., the Gothic pointed arch, the cubist facet, Wagnerian chromaticism), others are more elusive, since they are found to consist not in the presence of individual, specifiable elements but in the regular occurrence of certain clusters of features and in the exclusion of certain elements.

We become aware of these hidden taboos when we encounter an instance of their infringement in a bad imitation. We then say with conviction that Cicero would never have ended a sentence in that fashion, that Beethoven would never have made this modulation, or that Monet would never have used that color combination. Such apodictic statements seem to restrict severely the artist's freedom of choice. Indeed, one approach to the problem of style is to observe the limitations within which the artist or craftsman works. The style forbids certain moves and recommends others as effective, but the degree of latitude left to the individual within this system varies at least as much as it does in games. Attempts have been made to study and formulate these implicit rules of style in terms of probabilities. The listener who is familiar with the style of a piece of music will be aware at any moment of certain possible or probable moves, and the interaction between these expectations and their fulfillment or evasion is a necessary part of the musical experience. Not surprisingly, this intuition is confirmed by mathematical analysis, which shows the relative frequency of certain sequences within a given style of composition (Cohen 1962). Music, with its limited number of permutations of discrete elements, is, however, a rather isolated case, which cannot be readily generalized. Even so, the analysis of literary style in terms of word order, sentence length, and other identifiable features has also yielded promising results for statistical morphology (Ellegård 1962; Kreuzer & Gunzenhäuser 1965). No systematic attempt to extend this method to the analysis of style in the visual arts is known to the present writer. Certainly, methods of prediction and completion could even be applied in these cases. We would not expect the hidden corner of a brownish Rembrandt painting to be light blue, but it may well be asked if observations of this kind stand in need of statistical confirmation.

The limitations of scientific morphology are perhaps all the more galling when we realize that a style, like a language, can be learned to perfection by those who could never point to its rules (Hayek 1963; Gombrich 1966b, p. 127). This is true not only of contemporaries who grow into the use of their styles and procedures in learning the craft of building or gardening but also of the most skillful forger, mimic, or parodist, who may learn to understand a style from within, as it were, and reproduce it to perfection without bothering about its syntax. Optimists like to state that no forgery can be successful for a long time, because the style of the forger's own period is bound to tell and tell increasingly with distance, but it must be recognized that this argument is circular and that any forgeries of the past which were sufficiently successful simply have not been detected. The possibility exists, for instance, that certain busts of Roman emperors which are universally held to date from antiquity were in fact made in the Renaissance, and it is equally likely that many Tanagra figures and Tang horses in our collections are modern. Some forgeries, moreover, were unmasked only on external evidence such as the use of materials or of tools unknown in the alleged period of their origin (Kurz 1948). It is true that this achievement of the successful forger also suggests that the understanding of style is not beyond the reach of the intuitively minded and that the great connoisseur who is pitted against the forger has at least as much chance as has his opponent.

Confronted with a painting, a piece of music, or a page of prose attributed to a particular author or age, the connoisseur can also say with conviction that this does not look or sound right. There is no reason to doubt the authority of such statements, though it would be incautious to consider them infallible. It has happened that an essay published under Diderot's name was deleted from the author's canon on stylistic grounds but had to be restored to it when the original draft in his hand was found. If such independent evidence came more frequently to light, the fame of the connoisseur would probably suffer, but he would still be sure to score quite an impressive number of hits. For the time being, at any rate, the intuitive grasp of underlying *Gestalten* that makes the connoisseur is still far ahead of the morphological analysis of styles in terms of enumerable features.

E. H. GOMBRICH

[See also ARCHITECTURE; FASHION; FINE ARTS; LITERATURE; MUSIC. *A detailed guide to related articles can be found under* ART.]

BIBLIOGRAPHY

ACKERMAN, JAMES S.; and CARPENTER, RHYS 1963 *Art and Archaeology.* Englewood Cliffs, N.J.: Prentice-Hall. → Contains a chapter on "Style" with a bibliography by J. S. Ackerman.

BIAŁOSTOCKI, JAN 1961 Das Modusproblem in den bildenden Künsten. *Zeitschrift für Kunstgeschichte* 24: 128–141. → The best survey to date of the adaptation of ancient rhetorical categories, including the concept of style, to the criticism of the visual arts before the nineteenth century.

BOAS, FRANZ (1927) 1955 *Primitive Art.* New ed. New York: Dover.

BOAS, GEORGE (1941) 1950 Il faut être de son temps. Pages 194–210 in George Boas, *Wingless Pegasus: A Handbook of Art Criticism.* Baltimore: Johns Hopkins Press. → An essay on the nineteenth-century notion of art having to express its age.

COHEN, JOEL E. 1962 Information Theory and Music. *Behavioral Science* 7:137–163.

CONFERENCE ON STYLE, INDIANA UNIVERSITY, *1958* 1960 *Style in Language.* Edited by Thomas A. Sebeok. Cambridge, Mass.: M.I.T. Press.

COOPER, LANE (1907) 1923 *Theories of Style, With Especial Reference to Prose Composition: Essays, Excerpts, and Translations.* New York: Macmillan.

CURTIUS, ERNST ROBERT (1948) 1963 *European Literature and the Latin Middle Ages.* New York: Harper. → First published in German. The classic book on the influence of ancient rhetoric on medieval literary style.

ELLEGÅRD, ALVAR 1962 *A Statistical Method for Determining Authorship:* The Junius Letters, 1769–1772. Gothenburg Studies in English, No. 13. Goteborg (Sweden): The University.

FRANKL, PAUL 1960 *The Gothic: Literary Sources and Interpretations Through Eight Centuries.* Princeton Univ. Press.

GOMBRICH, E. H. (1960) 1961 *Art and Illusion: A Study in the Psychology of Pictorial Representation.* 2d ed., rev. London: Phaidon; New York: Pantheon.

GOMBRICH, E. H. 1963 *Meditations on a Hobby Horse, and Other Essays on the Theory of Art.* London: Phaidon.

GOMBRICH, E. H. 1966a The Debate on Primitivism in Ancient Rhetoric. *Journal of the Warburg and Courtauld Institutes* 29:24–38.

GOMBRICH, E. H. 1966b *Norm and Form: Studies in the Art of the Renaissance.* London: Phaidon.

HASKELL, FRANCIS 1963 *Patrons and Painters: A Study in the Relations Between Italian Art and Society in the Age of the Baroque.* London: Chatto; New York: Knopf.

HATZFELD, HELMUT A. 1953 *A Critical Bibliography of the New Stylistics Applied to the Romance Literatures, 1900–1952.* University of North Carolina Studies in Comparative Literature, No. 5. Chapel Hill: Univ. of North Carolina Press.

HAUSER, ARNOLD (1958) 1963 *The Philosophy of Art History.* Cleveland and New York: World. → First published as *Philosophie der Kunstgeschichte.*

HAYEK, FRIEDRICH A. VON 1963 Rules, Perception, and Intelligibility. British Academy, *Proceedings* 48:321–344.

HEGEL, GEORG WILHELM FRIEDRICH (1837) 1956 *The Philosophy of History.* New York: Dover. → First published as *Vorlesungen über die Philosophie der Weltgeschichte.* The basic text for understanding Hegel's notions of *Volksgeist* and *Zeitgeist.*

HUIZINGA, JOHAN (1919) 1924 *The Waning of the Middle Ages: A Study in the Forms of Life, Thought and Art in France and the Netherlands in the 14th and 15th Centuries.* London: Arnold. → First published in Dutch. A paperback edition was published in 1954 by Doubleday.

KIMBALL, S. FISKE (1943) 1964 *The Creation of the Rococo.* New York: Norton.

KREUZER, HELMUTH; and GUNZENHÄUSER, R. 1965 *Mathematik und Dichtung: Versuche zur Frage einer exakten Literaturwissenschaft.* Munich: Nymphenburger Verlagshandlung.

KRISTELLER, PAUL O. 1951–1952 The Modern System of the Arts: A Study in the History of Aesthetics. *Journal of the History of Ideas* 12:496–527; 13:17–46.

KUBLER, GEORGE 1962 *The Shape of Time: Remarks on the History of Things.* New Haven: Yale Univ. Press.

KULKA, HEINRICH (editor) 1931 *Adolf Loos: Das Werk des Architekten.* Vienna: Schroll.

KURZ, O. 1948 *Fakes: A Handbook for Collectors and Students.* London: Faber.

KURZ, O. 1960 Barocco: Storia di una parola. *Lettere italiane* 12, no. 4.

LAUSBERG, HEINRICH 1960 *Handbuch der literarischen Rhetorik: Eine Grundlegung der Literaturwissenschaft.* Munich: Hueber.

LEEMAN, ANTON DANIEL 1963 *Orationis ratio: The Stylistic Theories and Practice of the Roman Orators, Historians, and Philosophers.* 2 vols. Amsterdam: Hakkert.

MILES, JOSEPHINE (1957) 1964 *Eras and Modes in English Poetry.* 2d ed., rev. & enl. Berkeley: Univ. of California Press. → Combines statistical studies of words and notions with a general discussion (in Chapter 13) of style and change.

MUNRO, THOMAS 1963 *Evolution in the Arts and Other Theories of Culture History.* Cleveland Museum of Art.

PANOFSKY, ERWIN 1960 *Renaissance and Renascences in Western Art.* Stockholm: Almqvist & Wiksell.

PEAR, T. H. 1957 *Personality, Appearance, and Speech.* London: Allen & Unwin. → A discussion of the social implications of accent and dress.

PECKHAM, MORSE 1965 *Man's Rage for Chaos: Biology, Behavior and the Arts.* Philadelphia: Chilton.

PELLES, GERALDINE 1963 *Art, Artists and Society: Origins of a Modern Dilemma; Painting in England and France, 1750–1850.* Englewood Cliffs, N.J.: Prentice-Hall.

PEVSNER, NIKOLAUS (1936) 1958 *Pioneers of Modern Design From William Morris to Walter Gropius.* Rev. ed. New York: Doubleday. → A paperback edition was published in 1964 by Penguin.

POGGIOLI, RENATO 1962 *Teoria dell'arte d'avanguardia.* Bologna (Italy): "Il Mulino."

POPPER, KARL R. 1957 *The Poverty of Historicism.* Boston: Beacon.

QUENEAU, RAYMOND (1947) 1964 *Exercices de style.* Paris: Gallimard.

SCHAPIRO, MEYER (1953) 1961 Style. Pages 81–113 in Morris Philipson (editor), *Aesthetics Today.* Cleveland, Ohio: World.

Special Issue on Baroque Style in Various Arts. 1946 *Journal of Aesthetics and Art Criticism* 5, no. 2.

Second Special Issue on Baroque Style in Various Arts. 1955 *Journal of Aesthetics and Art Criticism* 14, no. 2.

ULLMANN, STEPHEN 1957 *Style in the French Novel.* Cambridge Univ. Press.

WELLEK, RENÉ; and WARREN, AUSTIN (1949) 1965 *Theory of Literature.* 3d ed. New York: Harcourt.

WINCKELMANN, JOHANN J. (1764) 1880 *The History of Ancient Art.* 4 vols. Boston: Osgood. → First published in German.

WÖLFFLIN, HEINRICH (1888) 1964 *Renaissance and Baroque.* London: Collins. → First published in German.

STYLE OF LIFE

See STRATIFICATION, SOCIAL, *article on* THE MEASUREMENT OF SOCIAL CLASS.

SUÁREZ, FRANCISCO

Born in Granada in 1548, Francisco Suárez followed the tradition of the Jesuits whose theological writings constitute an important contribution to the Iberian "golden age." After completing his secondary studies with distinction, he attended the University of Salamanca, then at the peak of its development with an enrollment of six thousand students. There he seems to have studied canon law from about 1561 to 1564. He then entered the Society of Jesus and pursued his philosophical and theological studies for another six years. Having been "proctor of repetitions" and professor of philosophy in various colleges and novitiates, he became a theologian and remained such for more than forty years. He taught brilliantly in the houses of the order at Valladolid, Segovia, and Ávila, at the Jesuit college of Rome, 1580–1585, and finally at the universities of Alcalá, 1585–1597, and Coimbra, 1597–1617. He died at Coimbra in 1617.

Suárez' voluminous works constitute an entire "summa" of theoretical and practical theology. The most important of his writings is probably the *De legibus* (see Suárez 1612–1621). In this work he related the metaphysical order to the political or juridical order. In Part III, he set forth the basis of his doctrine in the form of a dialectic of liberty. Since man is naturally free and obligated only to his Creator, it might appear that any authority of man over man is mere usurpation and tyranny. However, it must not be forgotten that the nature of man transcends the individual: "Firstly, man is a social animal whose true nature tends toward life in common" ([1612–1621] 1944, *De legibus*, Part III, chapters 1, 3). All social arrangements required for that development, such as the family and the state, are therefore not only legitimate but necessary.

The creation of the state, then, proceeds from natural law. But inasmuch as it is a moral organism, it requires for its actual realization the active intervention of united human wills. Political society needs an efficient cause based on the free decision of its citizens: it demands, as the foundation of community life, a moral act which expresses the will to live together and the readiness to accept a constitutional *modus vivendi*. Thus, the organization of political union calls for an explicit dec-laration of the desire to live in common and a mutual recognition of an authority which thereafter acts in the name of all. In 1620 he wrote in *De opere sex dierum*: "such a political union [*communitas*] does not occur without a certain agreement, whether explicit or assumed, on mutual aid, nor without a certain subordination of individual families and persons to a superior or ruler of that union. Without such subordination, no political union can endure" (1856–1878, vol. 3, book V, chapter 7, section 3).

Hence, there lies at the base of political society a consensus of citizens, a union ("some special moral agreement among themselves") that is made manifest in a desire to render service to itself and to recognize the brotherhood of its members. These psychological conditions constitute, so to speak, the materials necessary for the creation of any given state, but the preordained structure of political society requires further the presence of a very strong "power of jurisdiction" for the realization and preservation of that unity.

With respect to this question of political authority, Suárez was heir to the rather pessimistic Biblical and Augustinian tradition which considered the authority of kings to be the consequence of original sin. He restated this position with the qualification that authority derives from natural law. It is only the constraining aspect of authority which has been magnified by sin. Suárez was influenced in this matter by Luther and received, in addition, a well-developed theory of sovereignty from Bodin. He asserted that the surrender of authority to the prince meant that the populace lost all rights to participate in government—this despite his doctrine that the sovereign's power derives from the consensus of the citizens. He should therefore be classed among the defenders of a certain type of absolutism—that of the Roman Catholic monarchies of his time.

Nonetheless, both Suárez and Bodin believed that sovereignty is subject to limitations, whether internal or external. Created for the general wellbeing of the citizenry, it cannot derogate justice without creating a detestable tyranny. Moreover, the ruler must respect the conditions under which he was invested with sovereignty (such as constitutional rights and customs). Finally, the sovereign ruler must respect those other values necessary for the development of human kind: the rights of individual conscience, the rights of peoples. The subtlety of Suárez' views in this regard allowed him to define the indirect authority of the church over the citizens of diverse countries—as, for example, the authority granted the Church of England by the Thirty-nine Articles—with such acumen that his analysis remains even today the authoritative statement on the subject.

Suárez, by his lofty conception of the human will and of its natural and supernatural authority, found the means of rescuing political philosophy from sordid realism by defining the conditions under which a state might prosper without sacrificing either the aspirations of its subjects or the primacy of the international order.

PIERRE MESNARD

[*For the historical context of Suárez' work, see* INTERNATIONAL LAW; NATURAL LAW; SOVEREIGNTY; *and the biographies of* AUGUSTINE; BODIN; LUTHER.]

BIBLIOGRAPHY

BATTAGLIA, FELICE   1946   [A Book Review of] *Le dottrine politiche da Lutero a Suarez,* by Giuseppe Santonastaso. *Giornale di metafisica* 2:553–555.

BROUILLARD, R.   1941   La théologie pratique. Volume 14, part 2, cols. 2691–2728 in *Dictionnaire de théologie catholique contenant l'exposé des doctrines de la théologie catholique, leurs preuves et leur histoire.* Paris: Letouzey & Ané.

DUMONT, P.   1941   Théologie dogmatique. Volume 14, part 2, cols. 2649–2691 in *Dictionnaire de théologie catholique contenant l'exposé des doctrines de la théologie catholique, leurs preuves et leur histoire.* Paris: Letouzey & Ané.

GIACON, CARLO   1945   *Suarez.* Brescia (Italy): "La Scuola."

HAMILTON, BERNICE   1963   *Political Thought in Sixteenth-century Spain: A Study of the Political Ideas of Vitoria, De Soto, Suárez and Molina.* Oxford: Clarendon.

MESNARD, PIERRE   (1936) 1951   *L'essor de la philosophie politique au XVIe siècle.* 2d ed. Paris: Vrin.

MONNOT, P.   1941   Suarez: I. Vie et oeuvres. Volume 14, part 2, cols. 2638–2649 in *Dictionnaire de théologie catholique contenant l'exposé des doctrines de la théologie catholique, leurs preuves et leur histoire.* Paris: Letouzey & Ané.

MÚGICA, PLÁCIDO   1948   *Bibliografía suareciana.* Universidad de Granada, Cátedra Suárez.

RAZÓN Y FE   1948   *Centenario de Suarez: 1548–1948.* Madrid: Razón y Fe.

SCOTT, JAMES BROWN   1933   Suárez and the International Community. Pages 44–50 in Catholic University of America, *Francisco Suárez: Addresses in Commemoration of His Contribution to International Law and Politics.* Washington: Catholic Univ. of America.

SOLÁ, FRANCISCO DE P.   1948   *Suárez y las ediciones de sus obras: Monografía bibliográfica con ocasión del IV centenario de nacimento, 1548–1948.* Barcelona: Editorial Atlántida.

SUÁREZ, FRANCISCO   (1612–1621) 1944   *Selections From Three Works of Francisco Suárez. De legibus, ac Deo legislatore, 1612. Defensio fidei catholicae, et apostolicae adversus anglicanae sectae errores, 1613. De triplici virtute theologica, fide, spe, et charitate, 1621.* 2 vols. Oxford: Clarendon. → Volume 1 contains selections from the Latin editions; Volume 2 contains the translations.

SUÁREZ, FRANCISCO   *R.p. Francisci Suárez ... Opera omnia.* 28 vols. Paris: Vivès, 1856–1878. Translations in the text were provided by the editors.

Suárez: Modernité traditionelle de sa philosophie. 1949   *Archives de philosophie* 18, no. 1:3–128.

WILENIUS, REIJO   1963   *The Social and Political Theory of Francisco Suárez.* Acta philosophica Fennica, No. 15. Helsinki: No publisher given.

ZARAGÜETA BENGOECHEA, JUAN   1941   El problema del ser en la metafísica de Suárez. Granada, Universidad de, *Boletín de la Universidad de Granada* 13, no. 62:59–81.

ZARAGÜETA BENGOECHEA, JUAN   1941   La teoría suareciana de la causalidad: Los valores ético-jurídicos en el pensamiento de Suárez. Granada, Universidad de, *Boletín de la Universidad de Granada* 13, no. 63:173–219.

SUBLIMATION
See DEFENSE MECHANISMS.

SUB-SAHARAN AFRICAN SOCIETY
See under AFRICAN SOCIETY.

SUBSIDIES

Subsidies exist in the shadowland of economics where transactions are decided by government decree rather than by the free choices of buyers and sellers in the market place. Their forms and objectives vary greatly. Some attempt to provide defense or other facilities for emergency use; others to stimulate the domestic economy; others to improve the balance of international payments; and still others to improve the welfare of specific groups.

There is no developed economic theory for subsidies. The values or benefits conferred by subsidies pass in one direction only, since a compensating flow of goods or services is not required. With few exceptions, the subsidies involve transfers of real income from one group to another, most commonly from taxpayers generally or from the consuming public in the form of higher prices to the producers of designated commodities. The transfers are effected through the coercive power of the state. Enactments of subsidy laws often closely resemble, in reverse, the imposition of taxes, so that many subsidies may be described as negative taxes, and the techniques of tax analysis may be used to examine the effects of a subsidy. [*See* PUBLIC EXPENDITURES *and the general article under* TAXATION.] However, subsidies typically arise in emergent situations, to which normative concepts do not necessarily apply.

In terms of a narrow definition, like that used

in compiling the national economic accounts, subsidies constitute a limited class of money payments, by government to business enterprises, for which there is no corresponding value of current production. In this context, they are distinguished both from other classes of government payments without recompense, namely transfers and grants-in-aid, and from the basic stream of government expenditures designated "purchases of goods and services." The distinction between the former and subsidies is in terms of recipient: transfer payments are made to individuals, mostly for social security purposes, and grants-in-aid are paid to other government units for the support of specified programs. However, these definitions are not uniformly applied in all countries. [See NATIONAL INCOME AND PRODUCT ACCOUNTS.]

Subsidies reported in this way are a minor item in the national income and product accounts of major industrial countries, usually less than 2 per cent of gross national product. When put in terms of government budget totals, however, they may reach as much as 10 per cent of total government expenditures, as in Italy and the United Kingdom. Budgeted outlays of this magnitude are conspicuous in published government statements and have to be specifically justified, a necessity which many governments prefer to avoid.

The United States accounts show only the item "subsidies less current surplus of government enterprises." This tends to minimize the total reported by netting out gross subsidies against profit-making operations. For example, the Post Office makes excessive payments to airlines and shipping companies for carrying mail and renders some services below cost, particularly to publishers of magazines and books, but the true amount of subsidies to these groups is minimized in the over-all postal deficit, since some other classes of mail more than pay their way.

In a broader definition, subsidies include all kinds of measures whose effects on production and income distribution are similar to those resulting from direct subsidy payments. This brings into consideration a host of benefits in such forms as tax concessions, price supports, protection against competition, and provision of goods and services below cost. Since exemption from taxes results in a situation where no funds change hands, there is nothing to report in a compilation of actual transactions; but tax remissions are a much more important source of subsidy in some countries than direct payments. Similarly, tariffs, import quotas, and special preferences for domestic producers have important price-increasing impacts which are only partly measurable. In contrast to direct payments, some of these other benefits may come to public attention only rarely, and the issues may not be readily understood when they do. They tend to be hidden in legislation whose ostensible goal is some kind of social good and, being thus cloaked in patriotism or high ideals, may encounter ready public acceptance.

The significance of any such measure, as well as the occasion to use it, inevitably depends upon the circumstances and structure of the community in which it is applied. From this institutional viewpoint, subsidies appear to be phenomena belonging to the mixed economies of the industrial West; for they typically attempt to modify the results experienced in markets whose behavior in other respects remains unrestricted. In the planned economies of the communist countries, an industry may be protected and encouraged, or the reverse, as part of the everyday procedures through which the controlled market operates; so any change in its situation might be a subsidy, or none might be a subsidy, depending on how one appraised its prior position and the planners' intent. The underdeveloped countries, too, attempt a high degree of centralized planning and control, partly because they lack a labor force with the training and initiative necessary for independent action. Programs to assist or preserve developing industries are commonly employed, but a different frame of reference must be used in interpreting them.

In the developed countries, the justification for subsidy programs derives mainly from three sources: first, national security considerations, including preparedness for possible future wars; second, government commitments to aid industry or local area groups that cannot cope with difficulties they have encountered; and finally, responses to pressures created by lobbying and other political activities of self-seeking groups. Often, these various bases for support operate in combination. For example, agricultural subsidies may result partly from the desire to be self-sufficient in the production of basic food supplies, partly from the relative decline in farm income, and partly from the influence farm spokesmen wield in government circles. At the outset the emphasis is likely to be placed on temporary aspects, on the need for dealing with an emergency, but in the course of time, as a subsidy becomes semipermanent, the emphasis shifts toward preserving the position of those who would be harmed by its elimination.

Most of the industrial countries now have subsidy programs relating to several important fields, most notably agriculture, housing, transportation, business expansion, regional development, and foreign trade. Within these fields the specific subsidies provided and the methods of application vary widely from country to country.

Sometimes two or more subsidies are applied in a given field, but their effects are not always mutually reinforcing, so that the problem may be perpetuated rather than solved. Here again, agricultural subsidies serve to illustrate the point. Recent programs in some countries have been designed to limit production, keep surpluses off the market, and raise the prices received by farmers. At the same time, subsidies may be provided in the form of research to increase efficiency and teach farmers to use the most advanced methods of production. Frequently the efforts to limit and those to expand output are carried on simultaneously. Growing farm surpluses, based on increasing yields per acre, are then the result of improved technology as well as of high support prices.

Agriculture is almost universally subsidized today by guaranteed prices for domestic production, and the guarantees are supported by tariffs or other import controls, organization of marketing, and in a few countries, state trading (Food and Agriculture Organization 1960). Worthy of special mention is the British system of deficiency payments, which requires that products be sold at world market prices but then pays farmers the difference between market prices and specified higher prices calculated in the process of budget making. The payments are a direct charge on the budget but consumers receive the benefit of low food prices, and this more than compensates for the tax burden because the half of the food supply that must be imported is subject neither to tax nor to the higher prices imposed by tariff–import control systems. In most other countries the public pays the subsidy in higher prices; but in many countries various devices are used to minimize the impact on living costs. Although charges on the government budget are thus avoided, this approach may lead in the end to direct expenditures. In the United States the public not only pays higher prices but also, via the tax route, covers the losses the government incurs by buying high and selling low and the carrying-charges on government-held surpluses. [See AGRICULTURE, article on PRICE AND INCOME POLICIES.]

Housing subsidies go back in a number of European countries to World War I, when war damage and bans on new construction created severe shortages, and in the United States to the collapse of construction in the great depression. The decades since have been devoted to experimentation in improving housing conditions, with subsidies or grants-in-aid being made available in some country, at some time, for every phase of housing activity. The subsidies provided included provision of sites, capital grants to cover part of building costs, annual contributions to rents or debt service, low-cost credit or credit guarantees, and tax incentives. After World War II, clear-cut budget allocations and subsidies were the rule in Great Britain, Sweden, and the Netherlands. In West Germany, building was ostensibly private for the most part, but income tax concessions were so favorable to saving for this purpose that lenders were encouraged to make some loans at no interest cost (Wendt 1962, p. 142). In the United States, the main reliance was placed on mortgage insurance, which through the early 1960s involved no net losses to the federal government, so that the subsidy was only contingent. [See HOUSING, article on ECONOMIC ASPECTS.]

Transportation has also been widely subsidized. In nationalized European systems outright subsidies may be provided in some cases to cover operating deficits, and rate differentials often result in subsidies to some commodities, or to passenger travel, at the expense of other traffic. Some governments also make capital grants to railways, shipping lines, and airlines for new equipment or other special purposes. The United States, France, and Italy provide direct subsidies to shipbuilders to cover the difference between domestic and foreign costs of construction. Operating subsidies, tax benefits, and special credit arrangements are also available for shipping lines of some countries. Most of these subsidies represent nationalistic efforts to protect domestic interests against foreign competition, often with the stated objective of having available a national merchant marine for wartime use. Another form of subsidy, hidden but controversial, is the flag preference, which requires that all or part of a country's trade be carried by ships of its own registry. [See TRANSPORTATION, article on ECONOMIC ASPECTS.]

Direct subsidies for business expansion are now largely of two kinds—research and development expenditures and investment allowances. The former are sometimes open and explicit, at other times packaged into military, other national, or local government programs. The competitive building of supersonic air transports by France and England and by the United States provides one of the better publicized illustrations. The investment stimulants, mainly tax concessions, are much more important in cost and in value to recipients.

Most countries have provided some kind of allowances or accelerated depreciation in order to spur business investment and over-all economic growth. Sweden alone exercises a degree of control to ensure the use of investment funds for stabilization purposes.

Mineral industries in particular have been frequent beneficiaries of subsidies. In the United States, percentage depletion and permission to charge off the bulk of new exploration costs as current expense enable oil producers to avoid income taxes and accumulate great fortunes. The original subsidies increased greatly in value as tax rates were raised, and later, when prices were threatened by foreign competition in the late 1950s, producer pressures induced the government to establish import quotas—a secondary subsidy to protect the values already established.

The use of tariffs to protect against foreign competition in effect combines an all-inclusive excise tax and a subsidy that returns the tax to domestic producers. The effects of import quotas are more difficult to assess, but they may have an even more severe price-increasing effect because they exclude competition that tariffs might still leave open.

Reaction to the fallacies of protectionism, clearly revealed in the depression of the 1930s, has led to a world-wide drive to reduce trade barriers. GATT (the General Agreement on Tariffs and Trade) stands as a watchdog against restrictive policies, and it has had to be alert to a never-ending series of forays. Despite progress toward economic integration, competition for world markets is keen, and efforts to promote exports prevail all around the globe. Bounties, drawback, special credits, preferential freight rates, information services, and credit or exchange guarantees are among the devices being used for this purpose. [*See* INTERNATIONAL TRADE CONTROLS.]

Experience teaches that subsidy programs, once established, long outlast the emergency or other need that was the occasion for their adoption. Vested interests quickly develop and strenuously fight proposals that would adversely affect them. Such interests tend to develop inside the government as well as out, so that a mutually supporting bureaucracy and industrial establishment may command a great deal of political power. Furthermore, the benefits conferred tend to be capitalized. Thus, price supports are readily capitalized into the sales value of farmland, and the allotments for growing tobacco in the United States have been bid up to values per acre that far exceed the price of land suitable for growing tobacco. Finally, the persistent use of protective devices and technological ad-

vances in various parts of the world result in excess capacity, making it difficult for an industry group to face unrestricted competition.

It should be noted that not all subsidies are undesirable. Some merely involve a choice between direct government action and providing incentives by which others will be induced to get things done. Constructively applied, they can be helpful in promoting economic development or realizing social improvements. Many subsidies, however, involve heavy costs, not only in use of government resources but in various kinds of economic inefficiencies and inequities, misallocation of resources, lower real incomes, and international friction, heightened by retaliatory policies abroad. There is a definite presumption, therefore, in favor of avoiding subsidies except where their justification is clear.

One approach to preventing abuses is to set up rules for government policy makers. Among proposed rules are the following: subsidies should always be regarded as exceptions to the normal conduct of government or commercial business; they should be open and publicized rather than concealed; they should be temporary and if possible self-eliminating; their costs should be justified in terms of the benefits obtained; they should be discontinued or reduced when the need justifying their adoption disappears or dwindles.

In practice, however, such rules tend to be disregarded, so the actual pattern of subsidies is part of a patchwork of government intervention that gives effect to nationalistic tendencies and political pressures of a provincial character. Perhaps the problem can be partly solved only by international agreement. Relevant articles of the Common Market's Rome Treaty permit subsidies with valid internal objectives but rule out those of a self-seeking character and provide for international review of doubtful cases. The application of these principles on a still wider basis would undoubtedly be helpful.

V LEWIS BASSIE

[*See also* INTERNATIONAL TRADE CONTROLS, *article on* TARIFFS AND PROTECTIONISM.]

BIBLIOGRAPHY

FOOD AND AGRICULTURE ORGANIZATION OF THE UNITED NATIONS 1960 *An Enquiry Into the Problems of Agricultural Price Stabilization and Support Policies.* Rome: The Organization.

MYRDAL, GUNNAR (1960) 1963 *Beyond the Welfare State: Economic Planning and Its Implications.* Yale University, School of Law, Storrs Lectures on Jurisprudence, 1958. New Haven: Yale Univ. Press.

U.S. LIBRARY OF CONGRESS, LEGISLATIVE REFERENCE SERVICE 1960 *Subsidy and Subsidylike Programs of the*

U.S. *Government.* Washington: Government Printing Office. → Materials prepared for the Joint Economic Committee of the U.S. Congress.

WENDT, PAUL F. 1962 *Housing Policy: The Search for Solutions.* Berkeley: Univ. of California Press.

SUBSISTENCE ECONOMY

See HUNTING AND GATHERING; PASTORALISM; PEASANTRY; *and the articles listed in the guide under* AGRICULTURE.

SUFFICIENCY

Sufficiency is a term that was introduced by R. A. Fisher in 1922 to denote a concept in his theory of point estimation [*see* FISHER, R. A.]. As subsequently extended and sharpened, the concept is used to simplify theoretical statistical problems of all kinds. It is also used, sometimes questionably, in applied statistics to justify certain summarizations of the data, for example, reporting only sample means and standard deviations for metric data or reporting only proportions for counted data.

The sufficiency concept may be explained as follows. Suppose that the probabilities of two given samples have a ratio that does not depend on the unknown parameters of the underlying statistical model. Then it will be seen that nothing is gained by distinguishing between the two samples; that is, nothing is lost by agreeing to make the same inference for both of the samples. To put it another way, the two samples may be consolidated for inference purposes without losing information about the unknown parameters. When such consolidation can be carried out for many possible samples, the statistical problem becomes greatly simplified.

The argument can best be given in the context of a simple example. Consider tossing a coin four times, with "heads" or "tails" observed on each toss. There are $2^4 = 16$ possible results of this experiment, so the sample space has 16 points, which are represented in Table 1 [*see* PROBABILITY, *article on* FORMAL PROBABILITY]. For example, the point *THHT* represents the experimental result: tosses 1 and 4 gave tails, while tosses 2 and 3 gave heads. For later convenience, the 16 points are arranged

Table 1 — Sample points in coin-tossing experiment

NUMBER OF HEADS

0	1	2	3	4
TTTT	HTTT	HHTT	THHH	HHHH
	THTT	HTHT	HTHH	
	TTHT	HTTH	HHTH	
	TTTH	THHT	HHHT	
		THTH		
		TTHH		

in columns according to the number of occurrences of *H*.

If one makes the usual assumptions that the four tosses are independent and that the probability of heads is the same (say, p) on each toss, then it is easy to work out the probability of each point as a function of the unknown parameter, p: for example, $Pr(THHT) = p^2(1 - p)^2$ [*see* DISTRIBUTIONS, STATISTICAL, *article on* SPECIAL DISCRETE DISTRIBUTIONS]. In fact, each of the 6 points in column 3 has this same probability. Therefore, the ratio of the probabilities of any 2 points in column 3 has a fixed value, in fact the value 1, whatever the value of p may be, and, as stated earlier, it is not necessary to distinguish between the points in column 3. A similar argument shows that the 4 points in column 2 need not be distinguished from each other; the same is true for the 4 points in column 4. Thus, the sample space may be reduced from the original 16 points to merely the 5 columns, corresponding to the number of *H*'s. No further reductions are justified, since any 2 points in different columns have a probability ratio that depends on p.

To see intuitively why the consolidations do not cost any useful information, consider a statistician who knows that the experiment resulted in one of the 6 points in column 3 but who does not know just which of the 6 points occurred. Is it worth his while to inquire? Since the 6 points all have the same probability, $p^2(1 - p)^2$, the *conditional* probability of each of the 6 points, given that the point is one of those in column 3, is the known number $\frac{1}{6}$ [*see* PROBABILITY, *article on* FORMAL PROBABILITY]. Once the statistician knows that the sample point is in column 3, for him to ask "which point?" would be like asking for the performance of a random experiment with known probabilities of outcome. Such an experiment can scarcely produce useful information about the value of p, or indeed about anything else.

Another argument has been advanced by Halmos and Savage (1949). Our statistician, who knows that the observed sample point is in column 3 but who does not know which one of the 6 points was observed, may try to reconstruct the original data by selecting one of the 6 points at random (for example, by throwing a fair die or by consulting a table of random numbers [*see* RANDOM NUMBERS]). The point he gets in this way is not likely to be the point actually observed, but it is easy to verify that the "reconstructed" point has exactly the same distribution as the original point. If the statistician now uses the reconstructed point for inference about p in the same way he would have used the original point, the inference will perform exactly as if the original point had been used. If it is agreed that an inference procedure should be judged by its performance, the statistician who knows only the column, and who has access to a table of random numbers, can do as well as if he knew the actual point. In this sense, the consolidation of the points in each column has cost him nothing.

When a (sample) space is simplified by consolidations restricted to points with fixed probability ratio, the simplified space is called *sufficient:* the term is a natural one, in that the simplified space is "sufficient" for any inference for which the original space could have been used. The original space is itself always sufficient, but one wants to simplify it as much as possible. When all permitted consolidations have been made, the resulting space is called *minimally* sufficient (Lehmann & Scheffé 1950–1955). In the example the 5-point space consisting of the five columns is minimally sufficient; if only the points of column 3 had been consolidated, the resulting 11-point space would be sufficient, but not minimally so.

It is often convenient to define or describe a consolidation by means of a statistic, that is, a function defined on the sample space. For example, let B denote the number of heads obtained in the four tosses. Then B has the value 0, 1, 2, 3, 4 for the points in columns 1, 2, 3, 4, 5, respectively. Knowledge of the value of B is equivalent to knowledge of the column. It is then reasonable to call B a (*minimal*) sufficient statistic. ($B + 2$, B^3, and $\sqrt{B}$, for example, would also be minimal sufficient statistics.) More generally, a statistic is sufficient if it assigns the same value to 2 points only if they have a fixed probability ratio. In Fisher's expressive phrase, a sufficient statistic "contains all the information" that is in the original data.

The discussion above is, strictly speaking, correct only for discrete sample spaces. The concepts extend to the continuous case, but there are technical difficulties in a rigorous treatment because of the nonuniqueness of conditional distributions in that case. These technical problems will not be discussed here. (For a general treatment, see Volume 2, chapter 17 of Kendall & Stuart [1943–1946] 1958–1966, and chapters 1 and 2 of Lehmann 1959, where further references to the literature may be found.)

The discovery of sufficient statistics is often facilitated by the Fisher–Neyman factorization theorem. If the probability of the sample point (or the probability density) may be written as the product of two factors, one of which does not involve the parameters and the other of which depends on

the sample point only through certain statistics, then those statistics are sufficient. This theorem may be used to verify these examples: (*i*) If B is the number of "successes" in n Bernoulli trials (n independent trials on each of which the unknown probability, p, of success is the same), then B is sufficient. (*ii*) If $X_1, X_2, \cdots, X_n$ is a random sample from a normal population of known variance but unknown expectation μ, then the sample mean, $\bar{X}$, is sufficient. (*iii*) If, instead, the expectation is known but the variance is unknown, then the sample variance (computed around the known mean) is sufficient. (*iv*) If both parameters are unknown, then the sample mean and variance together are sufficient. (In all four cases, the sufficient statistics are minimal.) In all these examples, the families of distributions are of a kind called *exponential*. [*For an outline of the relationship between families of exponential distributions and sufficient statistics, see* Distributions, statistical, *article on* special continuous distributions.]

In the theory of statistics, sufficiency is useful in reducing the complexity of inference problems and thereby facilitating their solution. Consider, for example, the approach to point estimation in which estimators are judged in terms of bias and variance [*see* Estimation]. For any estimator, T, and any sufficient statistic, S, the estimator $E(T|S)$—formed by calculating the conditional expectation of T, given S—is a function of S alone, has the same bias as T, and has a variance no larger than that of T (Rao 1945; Blackwell 1947). Hence, nothing is lost if attention is restricted to estimators that are functions of a sufficient statistic. Thus, in example (*ii*) it is not necessary to consider all functions of all n observations but only functions of the sample mean. It can be shown that $\bar{X}$ itself is the only function of $\bar{X}$ which is an unbiased estimator of μ (Lehmann & Scheffé 1950–1955) and that $\bar{X}$ has a smaller variance than any other unbiased estimator for μ.

Sufficiency in applied statistics. In applied statistical work, the concept of sufficiency is often used to justify the reduction, especially for publication, of large bodies of experimental or observational data to a few numbers, the values of the sufficient statistics of a model devised for the data [*see* Statistics, descriptive]. For example, the full data may be 500 observations of a population. If the population is normal and the observations are independent, example (*iv*) justifies reducing the record to two numbers, the sample mean and variance; no information is lost thereby.

Although such reductions are very attractive, particularly to editors, the practice is a dangerous one. The sufficiency simplification is only as valid as the model on which it is based, and sufficiency may be quite "nonrobust": reduction to statistics sufficient according to a certain model may entail drastic loss of information if the model is false, even if the model is in some sense "nearly" correct. A striking instance is provided by the frequently occurring example (*iv*). Suppose that the population from which the observations are drawn is indeed symmetrically distributed about its expected value μ, and that the distribution is quite like the normal except that there is a little more probability in the tails of the distribution than normal theory would allow. (This extra weight in the tails is usually a realistic modification of the normal, allowing for the occurrence of an occasional "wild value," or "outlier.") [*See* STATISTICAL ANALYSIS, SPECIAL PROBLEMS OF, *article on* OUTLIERS.] In this case the reduction to sample mean and variance may involve the loss of much or even most of the information about the value of μ: there are estimators for μ, computable from the original data but not from the reduced data, considerably more precise than $\bar{X}$ when the altered model holds.

Another reason for publication of the original data is that the information suppressed when reducing the data to sufficient statistics is precisely what is required to test the model itself. Thus, the reader of a report whose analysis is based on example (*i*) may wonder if there were dependences among the n trials or if perhaps there was a secular trend in the success probability during the course of the observations. It is possible to investigate such questions if the original record is available, but the statistic B throws no light on them.

J. L. HODGES, JR.

BIBLIOGRAPHY

BLACKWELL, DAVID 1947 Conditional Expectation and Unbiased Sequential Estimation. *Annals of Mathematical Statistics* 18:105–110.

FISHER, R. A. (1922) 1950 On the Mathematical Foundations of Theoretical Statistics. Pages 10.308a–10.368 in R. A. Fisher, *Contributions to Mathematical Statistics.* New York: Wiley. → First published in Volume 222 of the *Philosophical Transactions*, Series A, of the Royal Society of London.

HALMOS, PAUL R.; and SAVAGE, L. J. 1949 Application of the Radon–Nikodym Theorem to the Theory of Sufficient Statistics. *Annals of Mathematical Statistics* 20:225–241.

KENDALL, MAURICE G.; and STUART, ALAN (1943–1946) 1958–1966 *The Advanced Theory of Statistics.* 3 vols. 2d ed. New York: Hafner; London: Griffin. → Volume 1: *Distribution Theory*, 1958. Volume 2: *Inference and Relationship*, 1961. Volume 3: *Design and Analysis, and Time-series*, 1966 (1st ed.). The first editions of volumes 1 and 2 were by Kendall alone.

LEHMANN, E. L. 1959 *Testing Statistical Hypotheses.* New York: Wiley.

LEHMANN, E. L.; and SCHEFFÉ, HENRY 1950–1955 Completeness, Similar Regions, and Unbiased Estimation. *Sankhyā: The Indian Journal of Statistics* 10:305–340; 15:219–236.

RAO, C. RADHAKRISHNA 1945 Information and the Accuracy Attainable in the Estimations of Statistical Parameters. Calcutta Mathematical Society, *Bulletin* 27:81–91.

SUGGESTION

The concept of "suggestion" originally was intimately associated with *hypnos* and was introduced in the mid-nineteenth century by Alexandre Bertrand in France and James Braid in England as an explanation of hypnotic phenomena. It thus replaced the theory of animal magnetism and other fluidistic theories. Suggestion became a universally recognized psychological concept during the famous controversy between the schools of Salpêtrière and Nancy in the 1880s and 1890s.

Hypnotic suggestion. Early usage of the word "suggestion" referred to very specific phenomena. By monotonous verbal phrases, sometimes accompanied by eye fixation, hand movements before the eyes or handstrokes on the forehead ("passes"), or regular soft sounds, a sleeplike, hypnotic state was induced in the subject, and in this state different phenomena were produced: catalepsis, contractures, automatic movements, anesthesia, analgesia, hallucinations, illusions, posthypnotic amnesia, posthypnotic actions, etc. The automatic and uninterested way in which these suggested acts are performed has generally been emphasized as a characteristic of hypnotic suggestion.

As long as the term "suggestion" was used exclusively in connection with hypnosis, we can assume it related to functionally rather homogeneous phenomena. However, this narrow concept of suggestion did not prevail with time. Gradually, miscellaneous phenomena with some similarity to hypnotic suggestion were included in the concept of suggestion.

Expansion of the suggestion concept. Social scientists soon found it useful to incorporate the hitherto exclusively medical concept of suggestion into their theories of social interaction. Such well-known sociologists as Gabriel Tarde, Scipio Sighele, and Gustave Le Bon regarded suggestion as the basic mechanism in social process. These authors considered suggestion in its different forms as a unitary phenomenon. Manifestations of suggestion in different contexts were believed to differ in degree, not in kind. Such pioneers of social psychology as Edward A. Ross and William McDougall also viewed different suggestion phenomena as parts of a continuum. In addition to hypnosis, induced illusions, impressionability through leading questions, uncritical beliefs, conformity to fashion, and mass suggestion were mentioned as examples of suggestion. Everyday suggestion acts were considered less-pronounced forms of the same kind of behavior that could be observed in hypnotized individuals. [*See* LE BON; MCDOUGALL; ROSS; *and* TARDE.]

Testing and experimental psychology. During the 1890s the awakening interest in individual differences and efforts to measure these differences also included considerable concern for the individual's suggestibility. Probably as many suggestibility tests as intelligence tests were constructed in the decades around the turn of the century. This is a noteworthy fact, which bears witness to the importance attached to suggestion at that time.

The expansion of the suggestion concept that can be traced in medicine and in the work of the early sociologists and social psychologists is somewhat paralleled in differential and experimental psychology. It is possible to follow the way in which the term "suggestion," operationally defined in tests or experimental procedures, successively covered wider and wider functional areas. After having first been limited to the production of simple motor and sensory reactions, the suggestion experiments and tests gradually included more complex phenomena, such as change of judgment, opinion, and attitude.

Analysis of the suggestion concept

The question naturally has arisen whether all the phenomena called suggestion and suggestibility really belong together functionally or have been arbitrarily brought together by some superficial similarities.

Qualitative analysis. On the basis of qualitative analysis, Asch (1952) has sought to refute the interpretation of suggestibility in terms of automatisms and baseless beliefs, analogous to the mechanisms in hypnosis, that has often been applied to behaviors shown by the subjects in prestige-suggestion experiments. By means of introspective analysis Asch has attempted to demonstrate that the subject's reactions in such experiments are sensible and reasonable, quite different from the uncritical and automatic actions of a hypnotized individual.

Correlation and factor analysis. A quantitative way of determining the extent of the relations between the functions tapped by different suggesti-

bility tests has been the analysis of correlations between the tests. Some early groping efforts were made (e.g., Brown 1916; Aveling & Hargreaves 1921). No clear pattern appeared, however, in these studies, which embraced rather small numbers of variables. More extensive factor analyses have been made by Eysenck (1943; 1947) and Stukát (1958). In the Eysenck studies two factors were identified: "primary" and "secondary" suggestibility. Primary suggestibility has been characterized by Eysenck (1947, p. 165) as execution of a motor movement after the experimenter has repeatedly suggested to the subject that such a movement will occur, without the subject's conscious participation in the movement. Typical of the tests that define this factor is Hull's body-sway test, where the subject stands straight with his eyes closed and listens to repeated verbal suggestions to the effect that he will fall forward. Other primary-suggestibility tests involve hand or arm movements, such as "hand rigidity" and "arm levitation." The tests that belonged to this factor were rather highly intercorrelated, and they also correlated clearly with hypnotizability.

Eysenck's notion of secondary suggestibility is characterized by the subject's perceptions being influenced by indirect suggestions. This factor had very high loadings in "heat illusion" and "progressive weights" tests, for example. In the former test an electric current is sent through a metal wire, heating it by degrees. The subject holds the wire and is told to report as soon as he feels it getting warmer. The test is repeated, but this time no current is sent through the wire, although the subject believes that it is. In Binet's progressive-weights test, the subject lifts a series of weights, of which only those in the first sequence are successively heavier, while the rest are of the same weight. The subject's tendency to judge the equal weights as successively heavier constitutes the measure of his suggestibility.

On the whole, the secondary-suggestibility tests showed less functional unity than the tests of primary suggestibility. While the latter had an average correlation of .50, the corresponding figure for the former was only .15.

The possibility of a "tertiary," or "prestige," type of suggestibility has also been discussed; this refers to procedures in which the individual's attitude changes when he is told the attitude of experts or a majority. In Stukát's factor analyses the existence of a primary-suggestibility factor was convincingly verified. The primary-suggestibility tests had a clear personality-trait character: they had high reliability coefficients and there were consistently high intercorrelations between different tests in spite of considerable situational variations. The primary-suggestibility factor was largely unconnected with other types of suggestibility. [See FACTOR ANALYSIS.]

Other results of factor analysis were less clear-cut. Some group factors seemed to be related to Eysenck's secondary suggestibility, being characterized by the influence of an experimentally and impersonally induced set upon cognitive functions, but they were functionally too narrow to warrant an identification with it. Other factors were interpreted as personal or prestige suggestibility. The fact that these group factors, impersonal as well as personal, were intercorrelated, was a basis for an interpretation on the second-order level. The feature common to these related factors is that they all represent tests in which different subjective influences, such as set, expectation, and need for conformity, direct the individual's perceptions, memory, and judgments. This second-order factor can be regarded as a secondary-suggestibility factor, but it apparently covers a broader functional area than the secondary-suggestibility factor in Eysenck's analyses.

It thus seems reasonable to distinguish between two kinds of suggestibility: a "primary" form, found in hypnosis and in ideomotor acts of an automatic character which are produced by monotonous verbal stimuli; and secondary suggestibility, characterized by the influence of different experimentally induced subjective factors upon cognitive functions. These influences can be personal or social as well as impersonal (e.g., expectation). In this broad sense, the secondary form includes prestige suggestibility, which thus does not constitute an independent, "tertiary" category.

Concomitants of suggestibility

Suggestibility and age. Suggestibility has usually been assumed to decrease with age, at least during the individual's developing years. This belief has been experimentally corroborated for secondary suggestibility but not for primary suggestibility. Cohn and Dieffenbacher (1911) and Messerschmidt (1933a) found that suggestibility decreased with age among children who were tested with different "illusion" tests. No such age trend appeared, however, between the ages of 5 and 16 in another of Messerschmidt's studies (1933b). In Stukát's investigation (1958), different age gradients appeared for primary- and secondary-suggestibility tests. The slope was steeper for secondary tests of a personal kind (e.g., leading questions, majority suggestions) than for tests with an impersonal influence (e.g., a weight-comparison test similar to Binet's). The age curves for prestige-suggestibility tests likewise have shown considerable decrease between the ages of 6 and 18.

In Barber and Calverley's study (1963), children had higher composite scores on a number of tests of primary suggestion. The "adult" level was reached at 14 to 15 years of age. Instructions designed to produce positive motivation resulted in adults' manifesting a suggestibility level similar to that of children.

Suggestibility and sex. Comparisons between males and females have been made in a great number of investigations. Girls and women have most often been found to be more suggestible than boys and men, both in primary and secondary suggestibility. As to primary suggestibility, women exceeded men in hypnotic susceptibility, although the differences were not significant (e.g., Barry et al. 1931). Aveling and Hargreaves (1921) reported that girls were more suggestible than boys on tests of hand rigidity and arm levitation. Eysenck (1947) reports that neurotic women were significantly more suggestible than neurotic men on the body-sway test but that there was no difference between sexes in normal subjects. In a number of primary-suggestibility tests, Stukát (1958) found more, but not a significantly higher degree of, suggestibility among females than among males; this was the case for children as well as adults.

A very extensive study of sex differences in secondary-suggestibility tests was performed by Brown (1916), who administered 26 different tests to college students, assessing such things as liminal sensations. Most of the differences were indicative of greater female suggestibility, and some of the differences were significant. Other studies have revealed similar results (e.g., Stukát 1958). A few authors report no differences (e.g., Cohn & Dieffenbacher 1911). Thus, in general, females are somewhat more suggestible than males, and mostly so perhaps in personal and prestige secondary suggestibility. The intraindividual differences of each sex are, however, considerably greater than the intersex differences. [See INDIVIDUAL DIFFERENCES, article on SEX DIFFERENCES.]

Suggestibility and neuroticism. The controversy between the Salpêtrière and Nancy schools fundamentally concerned the question of whether suggestibility was a pathological "stigma" present only in hysterical neurotics (Salpêtrière) or a normal trait characterizing all individuals (Nancy). A large body of clinical and experimental data showing that everybody is suggestible to some degree has settled this controversy in favor of the Nancy school. There is, however, a related question, namely, whether neurotics are more suggestible than normal subjects. Here the results have been inconsistent.

Using the body-sway test, Eysenck (1947) found neurotic patients more suggestible than normal ones, while other studies (e.g., Baumgartner 1931) showed no differences with the same test. Nor did Stukát (1958) find any consistent differences between normal persons and neurotics on a number of primary-suggestibility tests. The results of the relatively few studies that have included tests of the secondary type reflect somewhat higher suggestibility among neurotics (e.g., Stukát 1958). There is some evidence that neurotics are more easily influenced by prestige suggestions. Although neurotics constitute a rather heterogeneous group of individuals, such traits and symptoms as anxiety, inferiority feelings, lack of confidence, etc., are predominant in most groups of neurotics. These characteristics probably account for greater need to conform and greater willingness to submit to the expressed opinions of other people. In addition to such relatively constant traits, the greater suggestibility of neurotics may be partly caused by the specific situation in which they happen to be. The fact that a person suffers from acute disturbances and that he is hospitalized may increase his suggestibility, especially in situations that are connected with his illness.

Suggestibility and personality. Parallel to, and sometimes intermingled with, the discussion and study of suggestibility and neuroticism is the question of the relation between suggestibility and personality type. Most often suggestibility has been associated with hysteria and hysterical personalities. The assumed greater suggestibility among hysterics has been ascribed to different mental mechanisms by different authors. Janet (1919) explained it in terms of the hysteric's disposition to shrink his sphere of consciousness, to dissociate, and to be unable to synthesize mentally. According to Janet, this makes the hysterical mind fragmentary and an easy prey to suggestion. Bleuler (1916) has emphasized the vivid and labile affectivity of hysterics, whose emotions are far more important than their intellectual processes. However, Bleuler also points out that hysterics are characterized not only by positive but also by negative suggestibility and autosuggestibility. [See HYSTERIA.]

The experimental studies that have examined the belief generally held by clinicians that there is a close association between suggestibility and hysteria have provided somewhat inconsistent results. On the whole, however, they have not given much support to traditional belief with respect to either primary or secondary suggestibility.

Lindberg (1940) found higher secondary suggestibility (olfactory and visual) in hysterics than in asthenics and syntonics but a lower degree than was found in a group of oligophrenics. Kehlet and Paerregaard (1956) found more secondary suggestibility in female hysterics than in female non-hysterics. Eysenck (1943) and Stukát (1958) report no differences in a number of different suggestibility tests, both primary and secondary. In Stukát's investigation the most suggestible groups were oligophrenics and asthenics. A few studies refer to the relation between different Rorschach indices and suggestibility. In his *Psychodiagnostics* (1921) Rorschach maintained that there is a connection between emotional lability, primarily represented by color–form (CF) responses, and "affective" suggestibility. This belief has been only partially substantiated by experimental research. Linton (1954) correlated cojudge suggestibility in the autokinetic situation with several Rorschach measures. The suggestibility variable had its highest correlation with the ratio of color-to-movement responses (C:M), and the result thus to some extent supported Rorschach's hypothesis. On the other hand, Stukát (1958) found no consistent relations between different Rorschach indices or patterns and a number of suggestibility tests. [See PROJECTIVE METHODS, *article on* THE RORSCHACH TEST; *and the biography of* RORSCHACH.]

Theories

Primary suggestibility. Weitzenhoffer (1953) has classified existing theories of primary suggestibility, including hypnosis, according to what is assumed to be the basic process; there are thus neurophysiological, dissociation, conditioned-response, and transference theories. Of these, the existing neurophysiological theories must be considered quite unsatisfactory. The basic mechanism behind suggestibility has been said to be inhibition of the ganglion cells in the brain (Heidenhain 1880), a functional dissociation between nerve cells (Sidis 1898), or a shift of nervous energies from the central nervous system to the vasomotor system (McDougall 1926), but the empirical support for these hypotheses is weak. The transference theories are likewise based on meager empirical evidence. They can be said mainly to express the often reported experience that in hypnosis an emotional relation between the hypnotist and his subject is often developed. Most of these theories are formulated in psychoanalytic terminology, which makes it difficult to link them to general psychological concepts. The theories that lay emphasis on dissociation (e.g., Janet 1919; Sidis 1898) no doubt touch upon a central factor in primary suggestibility. The observations of hypnotic behavior, as well as of waking suggestion situations, bear witness to the automatic and disintegrated character of the individual's actions, which are strikingly different from normal conscious and "willed" behavior. However, as has been pointed out by Hull (1933), the dissociation is more apparent than real, and the autonomy of the dissociated elements is often far from complete. Another criticism that can be directed against the dissociation theories is that they have been mainly superficially descriptive, that is, not integrated with larger and well-established systems, and are therefore of a limited explanatory value.

The theories that seem to be most satisfactory are those which interpret primary suggestibility in terms of conditioned response. Pavlov (1927) regarded suggestibility as the most simple form of the typical conditioned reflex in man. Among others, Welch (1947) has elaborated this idea. He calls attention to the striking similarity between the initial stages of hypnosis induction (and waking suggestions of the body-sway type) and an ordinary conditioning experiment, as illustrated in the paradigm (Figure 1). [See LEARNING, *article on* CLASSICAL CONDITIONING.]

While Welch believes that such a simple conditioning model may satisfactorily explain the early phases of primary suggestibility, a more complicated process involving abstract conditioning seems to be necessary to explain other hypnotic phenomena. Although the conditioning theories leave a great deal of the primary-suggestibility phenomena

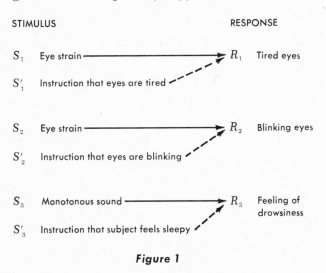

STIMULUS   RESPONSE

S_1 Eye strain ————————————→ R_1 Tired eyes

S'_1 Instruction that eyes are tired

S_2 Eye strain ————————————→ R_2 Blinking eyes

S'_2 Instruction that eyes are blinking

S_3 Monotonous sound ——————→ R_3 Feeling of
                                                                    drowsiness
S'_3 Instruction that subject feels sleepy

Figure 1

Source: Adapted from Welch 1947, p. 361, diagram 1.

unexplained, there is some empirical support for them in the significant correlations that have been found between suggestibility and conditionability (Stukát 1958).

Secondary suggestibility. McDougall defined suggestion (in situations where it was clear that he meant secondary suggestibility) as a "process of communication resulting in the acceptance with conviction of the communicated proposition in the absence of logically adequate grounds for its acceptance" (1908, p. 97). This conception of suggestibility as nonlogical behavior is representative of most older theories. In opposition to this "suggestion doctrine," Asch (1952) has maintained that suggestion is most often a rational process. According to Asch's qualitative analysis of the subject's responses to prestige suggestions, the individual does not change his judgments or evaluations arbitrarily but because there is a change in the object of judgment. The source of prestige provides a context in which a statement can be interpreted. The subject's reaction toward prestige suggestions is ordinarily not a passive, automatic, and uncritical acceptance, analogous with the behavior of a hypnotized individual; rather the subject acts sensibly and does as well as is possible in a vague and difficult situation.

Leaving aside the question of the rational or irrational character of suggestible behavior, Sherif (1936) and Coffin (1941) have also emphasized that a suggestion primarily functions as a frame of reference. If the external stimulus situation is well structured, the frame of reference is almost completely made up of the properties of the objective situation. If, on the other hand, the situation is vague and unstructured, organization still takes place, but now internal factors, such as set, attitude, etc., are important determinants. This makes it reasonable to include secondary suggestibility among the large group of phenomena that have been intensively studied under the headings "central dynamics of cognition," "central directive state," "functional determinants," etc. A large number of studies have adequately established that cognitive functions are determined not only by the objective stimulus situation but also by various internal factors, such as needs, past learning, and mental set.

Postulating that secondary suggestibility is a special case of the central dynamics of cognition, Stukát has derived a number of hypotheses which have been experimentally tested. The results clearly support the hypotheses that, in secondary-suggestibility situations of a personal type, the suggestion effects are greater when (1) there are a greater number (up to a certain limit) of unanimously influencing individuals; (2) the social status of the influencing individual is higher; (3) the influencing individual is older in relation to the subject (among children and adolescents). Further, he verified the hypotheses that (4) reproof tends to increase and praise to decrease an individual's suggestibility toward propositions from other persons; (5) an individual is more suggestible if the atmosphere of the situation is anxiety-arousing than if the situation is calm. As to impersonal secondary suggestibility, it was found that (6) an individual's suggestibility is greater when his expectation is greater. For secondary suggestibility in general, (7) a high negative correlation exists between the degree of stimulus structure and the subject's tendency to yield to suggestions.

These results are in rather close agreement with the findings from several other investigations. Asch (1956) and Rosenberg (1961) have reported an increase in conformity when the number of cojudges increased up to four. Higher-partner prestige has been found to increase conformity tendencies (Rosenberg 1961). Interestingly, it has been found (e.g., Harvey & Consalvi 1960) that the second-status member, the one only one step from the top, was significantly more conforming than either the leader or the lowest-status man. Investigations (e.g., Di Vesta 1959) have shown the effects of prior reinforcement: previous success engenders greater resistance to social influence, while failure has an opposite effect. Stimulus structure as a factor in suggestibility has been demonstrated in studies where conformity was greater for the more difficult than for the easier items in tests when the subjects were given incorrect hints (e.g., Coffin 1941). Other experimental studies (e.g., Di Vesta 1959) have further confirmed the "functional determinants" character of secondary suggestibility (or "conformity" or "persuasibility"), since they have demonstrated that the individual's tendency to yield to social influences is related to such variables as subjective certainty, confidence, dependency, and self-esteem. [See GROUPS, especially the article on GROUP FORMATION.]

Thus, the secondary-suggestibility phenomena, which have often been regarded as specific and isolated from other psychological functions, can be included naturally in the more general field of functional determinants in cognition. As a consequence of such an integration, the same explanatory concepts can be used for secondary suggestibility as for this wider area. Stukát (1958) has applied the "hypothesis theory" of Postman and Bruner to secondary suggestibility. The central concept in the theory is "hypothesis," that is, "expectancies or predispositions of the organism which serve to select, organize, and transform the stimulus information that comes from the environment" (Postman 1951, p. 249). The stronger the hypothesis, the less is the amount of appropriate stimulus information required to confirm it. The hypothesis strength is postulated to be determined by a number of factors, namely, the frequency of past confirmation of the hypothesis, the number of alternative hypotheses available, motivational and cognitive support, and consensual validation. There is good general agreement between this model and the data from the experimental studies of secondary suggestibility mentioned above. A limitation of the theory as an explanatory device for suggestibility is its failure to take account of the fact that social influence ("consensual validation") can act both as a motivational factor and as a source of cognitive information. A good deal of recent experimentation and discussion has aimed at determining the relative effect of "normative" and "informational" influence (e.g., Di Vesta 1959). Although the results so far have given more evidence about the importance of motivational than of rational cognitive factors in conformity behavior, this question still constitutes an interesting problem.

KARL-GUSTAF STUKÁT

[Directly related are the entries ATTITUDES, article on ATTITUDE CHANGE; BRAINWASHING; CONFORMITY; HYPNOSIS; PERSUASION. Other relevant material may be found in MORAL DEVELOPMENT; and in the biographies of CHARCOT; JANET; MESMER.]

BIBLIOGRAPHY

ASCH, SOLOMON E. (1952) 1959 Social Psychology. Englewood Cliffs, N.J.: Prentice-Hall.

ASCH, SOLOMON E. 1956 Studies of Independence and Conformity: I. A Minority of One Against a Unanimous Majority. Psychological Monographs 70, no. 9.

AVELING, F.; and HARGREAVES, H. L. 1921 Suggestibility With and Without Prestige in Children. British Journal of Psychology 12:53–75.

BARBER, THEODORE X.; and CALVERLEY, DAVID S. 1963 "Hypnotic-like" Suggestibility in Children and Adults. Journal of Abnormal and Social Psychology 66:589–597.

BARRY, HERBERT JR.; MACKINNON, D. W.; and MURRAY, H. A. JR. 1931 Studies in Personality: A. Hypnotizability as a Personality Trait and Its Typological Relations. Human Biology 3:1–36.

BAUMGARTNER, MAXINE 1931 The Correlation of Direct Suggestibility With Certain Character Traits. Journal of Applied Psychology 15:1–15.

BLEULER, EUGEN (1916) 1951 Textbook of Psychiatry. New York: Dover. → First published in German.

BROWN, WARNER 1916 *Individual and Sex Differences in Suggestibility.* Berkeley: Univ. of California Press.

COFFIN, THOMAS E. 1941 Some Conditions of Suggestion and Suggestibility: A Study of Certain Attitudinal and Situational Factors Influencing the Process of Suggestion. *Psychological Monographs* 53, no. 4.

COHN, JONAS; and DIEFFENBACHER, JULIUS 1911 *Untersuchungen über Geschlechts-, Alters-, und Begabungsunterschiede bei Schülern.* Beihefte zur Zeitschrift für angewandte Psychologie und psychologische Sammelforschung, no. 2. Leipzig: Barth.

DI VESTA, FRANCIS J. 1959 Effects of Confidence and Motivation on Susceptibility to Informational Social Influence. *Journal of Abnormal and Social Psychology* 59:204–209.

EYSENCK, HANS J. 1943 Suggestibility and Hypnosis: Experimental Analysis. Royal Society of Medicine, London, *Proceedings* 36:349–354.

EYSENCK, HANS J. 1947 *Dimensions of Personality.* London: Routledge.

HARVEY, O. J.; and CONSALVI, CONRAD 1960 Status and Conformity to Pressures in Informal Groups. *Journal of Abnormal and Social Psychology* 60:182–187.

HEIDENHAIN, RUDOLF (1880) 1906 *Hypnotism: Or, Animal Magnetism.* 5th ed. London: Routledge. → First published as *Der sogenannte thierische Magnetismus: Physiologische Beobachtungen.*

HULL, CLARK L. 1933 *Hypnosis and Suggestibility: An Experimental Approach.* New York: Appleton.

JANET, PIERRE (1919) 1925–1928 *Les médications psychologiques: Études historiques, psychologiques et cliniques sur les méthodes de la psychothérapie.* 2d ed. 3 vols. Paris: Alcan. → Volume 1: *L'action morale, l'utilisation de l'automatisme.* Volume 2: *Les économies psychologiques.* Volume 3: *Les acquisitions psychologiques.*

KEHLET, H.; and PAERREGAARD, G. 1956 Experimentelle undersøgelser over suggestibilitet hos neurotikere med og uden hysteriske traek. *Nordisk psykiatrisk medlemsblad* 10:148–158.

LINDBERG, BENGT J. 1940 Suggestibility in Different Personality Types. *American Journal of Psychology* 53:99–108.

LINTON, HARRIET B. 1954 Rorschach Correlates of Response to Suggestion. *Journal of Abnormal and Social Psychology* 49:75–83.

McDOUGALL, WILLIAM (1908) 1950 *An Introduction to Social Psychology.* 30th ed. London: Methuen. → A paperback edition was published in 1960 by Barnes and Noble.

McDOUGALL, WILLIAM 1926 *Outline of Abnormal Psychology.* New York: Scribner.

MESSERSCHMIDT, RAMONA 1933a Responses of Boys Between the Ages of Five and Sixteen Years to Hull's Postural Suggestion Test. *Journal of Genetic Psychology* 43:405–421.

MESSERSCHMIDT, RAMONA 1933b The Suggestibility of Boys and Girls Between the Ages of Six and Sixteen Years. *Journal of Genetic Psychology* 43:422–437.

PAVLOV, IVAN P. (1927) 1960 *Conditioned Reflexes: An Investigation of the Physiological Activity of the Cerebral Cortex.* New York: Dover. → First published as *Lektsii o rabote bol'shikh polusharii golovnogo mozda.*

POSTMAN, LEO J. 1951 Toward a General Theory of Cognition. Pages 242–272 in Conference on Social Psychology at Crossroads, University of Oklahoma, 1950, *Social Psychology at the Crossroads.* New York: Harper.

RORSCHACH, HERMANN (1921) 1942 *Psychodiagnostics.* 3d ed. Bern: Huber; New York: Grune. → First published in German.

ROSENBERG, LEON A. 1961 Group Size, Prior Experience, and Conformity. *Journal of Abnormal and Social Psychology* 63:436–437.

SHERIF, MUZAFER (1936) 1965 *The Psychology of Social Norms.* New York: Octagon.

SIDIS, BORIS (1898) 1927 *The Psychology of Suggestion: A Research Into the Subconscious Nature of Man and Society.* New York: Appleton.

STUKÁT, KARL-GUSTAF 1958 *Suggestibility: A Factorial and Experimental Analysis.* Stockholm: Almqvist & Wiksell.

WEITZENHOFFER, ANDRÉ M. (1953) 1963 *Hypnotism: An Objective Study in Suggestibility.* New York: Wiley.

WELCH, LIVINGSTON 1947 A Behavioristic Explanation of the Mechanism of Suggestion and Hypnosis. *Journal of Abnormal and Social Psychology* 42:359–364.

SUICIDE

I
SOCIAL ASPECTS

Suicide has been an object of fundamental concern to Western men of all cultural periods, though the importance given to suicide itself, as well as the degree to which it has entered into other concerns, has varied greatly from one period to another. "Suicide," said Goethe, "is an incident in human life which, however much disputed and discussed, demands the sympathy of every man, and in every age must be dealt with anew" ([1811–1833] 1908, vol. 2, p. 125).

This is not to say that suicide has failed to interest people in other cultures but, rather, that the reasons have usually been different. In feudal Japan, for instance, suicide was an ultimate act of honor, redemption, or union. In the Western world, however, suicide has always been regarded as fundamentally problematic. Possibly because suicide in the West has nearly always been interpreted as voluntary self-destruction, with no element of social constraint or obligation, philosophers from Plato to Camus have used it as a starting point for reflection on the eternal problems of human existence. Indeed, ambivalence toward the fact of his own existence is one of Western man's most persistent characteristics; life and death, the relation of man to man, and the relation of man to himself have been subject to continual questioning, and suicide has been seen as relevant to all of these. In such a climate of thought, it is not surprising that neither settled opinion nor emotional consensus has ever been reached concerning the nature of suicide.

Early writings. Early Western writers on suicide were primarily concerned either with its desirability (including its honorability) or with its morality. But all of them, whether Greek, Roman, Jew, or Christian, were concerned to some degree with the particular facts of actual cases of suicide. Most importantly, from our point of view, they implicitly assumed that before one could properly judge the actor in the case, one had also to know his *intentions*, the *situation* in which he found himself, and the nature and outcome of his *actions*.

After the normative arguments against suicide by Augustine, the Council of Arles, and the Council of Bourges, there is little evidence that the normative evaluation of suicide was considered to be very problematic until the seventeenth century. But there remained the cognitive problem of deciding which set of facts concerning intentions, situations, and actions should be imputed to the category of suicide. Most important to Christian thinkers was the problem of categorizing "martyrs": were they suicides or not? This cognitive problem was to be just as difficult for sociologists in the twentieth century as for theologians in the fifth century (see Halbwachs 1930).

The nineteenth century. The fundamental forms of thought about suicide, including the implicit assumptions that suicide must be studied as a form of normative action and that suicide is connected with the problem of man's relation to God and man's relation to man, were all part of the literary and common-sense background of sociological thought about suicide in the nineteenth century. But there were many other, more specific influences on these nineteenth-century works.

Almost all of the many works on suicide in the eighteenth and nineteenth centuries included extensive and detailed considerations of the historical cases, the literary examples, and the philosophical treatments of suicide. The works of Appiano Buonafède, Louis F. Bourquelot, Carl F. Stäudlin, Albert des Étangs, Pierre J. C. Debreyne, Alexandre Brière de Boismont, and Alfred Legoyt, to mention but a few, were greatly concerned with such sources. Among the literary, philosophical, and historical influences on the developing sociology of suicide, three can be singled out as most important.

(1) Knowledge of the high frequency of suicide among the upper classes in ancient Rome, and of the honorableness of suicide among the Romans, led to the idea that suicide is fundamentally a matter of social custom. According to Voltaire and other thinkers of the Enlightenment, suicide in a society where suicide is neither the custom nor positively valued or expected was due to a failing, weakness, or disease. This background assumption helped to produce both the psychological theory that suicide is caused by insanity (or character weakness, or disequilibrium), a theory of great influence even today (Dahlgren 1945; Achille-Delmas 1932; Deshaies 1947), and the sociological theory that suicide is caused by a failure of the normative control of individuals by society (Brière de Boismont 1856; Morselli 1879; Durkheim 1897; Cavan 1928).

(2) In the eighteenth century, suicide became a focal point in the ethical argument between the *philosophes* and the church supporters. Largely as an outgrowth of this struggle, the relation of religion to suicide became a leading concern of the nineteenth-century sociologists. Specifically, this tradition of thought was largely responsible for the explanations of the great statistical increase in suicide in nineteenth-century Europe in terms of meaninglessness of life, lack of discipline, self-centeredness, moral disorganization, and materialism. These developments are dealt with more fully below.

(3) Death, especially death by suicide, was a favorite theme in the literature of the romantic movement. Indeed, the most important contribution of this literary tradition to the developing sociology of nineteenth-century Europe was probably that it helped to focus attention on suicide. Largely because of its treatment in literature, suicide was seen by the educated public as a fundamental social problem. Nineteenth-century Europeans, especially the French, were as frightened of *la manie du suicide* (as Tissot [1840] called it) as twentieth-century Americans are of juvenile delinquency and the Mafia. But the literary concern with suicide also provided the core of certain very important, specific "theoretical" explanations. Of fundamental importance was the prime romantic symbol of an isolated, lonely hero of a poetic (or intellectual) bent who wanders far from human society in search of the impossible and, failing of the impossible, becomes increasingly melancholy and enamored of eternity. The idea that self-imposed isolation produces "melancholy," and thence suicide, was hardly novel; indeed, Robert Burton's seventeenth-century treatise, *The Anatomy of Melancholy*, had carefully documented its classical sources. But this prime symbol of romanticism contained the most unclassical ideas of both egoism and anomie. In-

deed, the romantic image of suicide seems to have been so much the mythical model which the sociologists of suicide had in mind that both Morselli ([1879] 1882, p. 297) and Durkheim (1897) had a strong tendency to treat egoism and anomie as almost identical. It is even possible to specify the work of Chateaubriand, especially as treated by Brière de Boismont (1856, pp. 39–40), as the major source of Durkheim's idea of anomic suicide (Douglas 1965, pp. 20–26).

Some of the fundamental ideas about suicide which the sociologists inherited from history, philosophy, literature, and common sense became the cores of the various sociological theories of suicide. There were other influences on these theories which will be described later. But the sociologists of the period were dependent upon these nonscientific and, most importantly, nonempirical sources for their ideas about suicide as a specific phenomenon. Though this is somewhat less true today, the sociological study of suicide is in substantially the same condition.

The definition of suicide

A great number of different definitions of suicide have been proposed by the students of suicide during the first two hundred years of the term's general use. Almost all of these definitions have included, to varying degrees and in various combinations, one or more of the following conceptual dimensions: (a) the initiation of an act that leads to the death of the initiator; (b) the willing of an act that leads to the death of the willer; (c) the willing of self-destruction; (d) the loss of will; (e) the motivation to be dead (or to die, or to be killed) which leads to the initiation of an act that leads in turn to the death of the initiator; (f) the knowledge of an actor concerning the relations between his acts and the objective state of death; (g) the degree of *central integration of the decisions* of an actor who decides to initiate an action that leads to the death of the actor; (h) the degree of *firmness* or *persistence* of the decision to initiate an act that leads to the death of the initiator; (i) the *degree of effectiveness* of the act in producing death. (For a detailed presentation of the various definitions, see Schneider 1954, pp. 9–59; for an analysis of the definitions of suicide, see Douglas 1965.)

The great profusion and confusion of definitions of suicide have been very largely the result of combining an abstract, a priori approach to defining the concept with an assumption of "verbal realism" —i.e., the assumption that if the same name is in fact used to refer to a set of phenomena, then that set of phenomena must in fact have some shared property that is designated by the shared word. Durkheim and almost all other sociologists and psychologists who have attempted to carefully define suicide, have assumed that one should arbitrarily define the concept to fit his scientific methods and his theoretical purposes but that the definition should not differ too much from common usage (Durkheim [1897] 1951, pp. 41–42). Durkheim further assumed that the most common definition of suicide was that of death caused by an action initiated by the actor with the *intention* of causing his own death. Since, however, teleology is anathema to positivists, Durkheim decided that intentions are too "intimate" to yield valid information and that, consequently, "knowledge" by the actor of the deadly consequences of his actions should be the fundamental factor in deciding that a death is a suicide, even if the consequences are relatively uncertain (*ibid.*, pp. 43–46).

Unfortunately, Durkheim's *definition* of suicide was quite irrelevant to his *work* on suicide. As Maurice Halbwachs most astutely argued, Durkheim was almost totally dependent on the official suicide statistics for his data, so the only definition that really mattered was that (rather, *those*) which the officials had in mind when they categorized the causes of deaths. Since Halbwachs believed that one could not know what definitions these officials used, he concluded that sociologists must be satisfied with no definition at all (Halbwachs 1930). Actually, the coroners and doctors who do the categorizing seem generally to be firm believers in the common-sense theory of teleology. Moreover, the laws governing the certification of cause of death very generally specify "intention" as necessary for a classification of suicide. Benoît-Smullyan (1948) has also pointed out that since Europeans do not generally consider self-sacrifices to be suicides, Durkheim's "altruistic suicides" would not be included in the official statistics on suicide. Consequently, it seems clear that Durkheim's definition of suicide was not so much irrelevant to his data as it was a complete distortion of the meaning of the data.

With the exception of Halbwachs' work, the published sociological works on suicide since Durkheim's *Suicide* have generally assumed that Durkheim's definition is best; they have even failed to note Halbwachs' valid criticism of it. They have, however, also either implicitly assumed "intention" to be a necessary factor, or else they have totally avoided the problem. The result has been both confusion and a failure to recognize the problems involved in defining suicide. The sociology of suicide is in obvious need of a system of categories which will describe the observed phenomena that are significant in terms of a theory of suicide. Such descriptive categories must be worked out in partial independence of the theories in order to aid their development, but they must also be worked out in partial dependence on developing theories. However, the first critically important thing for sociologists to do is to make direct observations of the empirical phenomena which are called suicide in any society, so that definitions will be relevant and so that the meanings of the data will be known to the theorists.

Official statistics on suicide

Largely because of the rapid acceleration in statistics-keeping in eighteenth-century Europe, the systematic recording and tabulating of suicides had become standard practice in many of the governmental regions of Europe by the first quarter of the nineteenth century. The basic ideas of "moral statistics," especially the fundamental idea that a given incidence of a phenomenon such as suicide is regularly associated with a given population, had been clearly formulated in the eighteenth century, certainly by 1741, when Johann Peter Süssmilch published his famous treatise on the "divine order" underlying demographic phenomena. The traditions of "political arithmetic," of studying racial and national character, and of comparative studies of suicide rates were synthesized by Adolphe Quetelet (1835) in order to produce his "average man" theory of suicide rates. Quetelet's fundamental idea was that each stable "social system" produces a stable, average personality type about which the individual personalities tend to cluster. The average man, therefore, has a given, stable probability of committing suicide in a given period of time.

Quetelet's probabilistic theory was specifically intended to explain the observed regularity (or order) in the official suicide statistics. This regularity, which was first observed for the different nations of Europe, seemed to the moral statisticians to be a remarkable demonstration of the deterministic, lawlike nature of the actions of individuals. Since the seventeenth century, Europeans had believed suicide to be more frequent in some nations than in others. The French considered suicide to be as English as gambling (they seem to have believed that more Englishmen preferred death to life because the fog made living so unworthwhile), though Voltaire thought this impression was due to more newspaper coverage of suicide in England. But before the nineteenth century, the explanations of these (assumed) regular differences in

suicide frequencies always involved the assumption that the individual will was the ultimate cause of the action. In the early nineteenth century both the psychiatric theory that all suicides are insane (and, therefore, do not cause their own actions) and the direct comparison of national suicide rates (without any real consideration of the individuals who committed the actions) combined to eliminate the individuals (or wills, or personalities) from consideration as possible causes of suicide. Quetelet's early work on the comparisons of social rates of suicide (work that gained much support from the researches of Gustave F. Étoc-Demazy and André M. Guerry) was quickly given a metaphysical basis by the English positivists, especially by Henry Thomas Buckle. This largely eliminated Quetelet's variable of average personality; the direct comparison of other external, objective data (such as geographical–ecological distributions and marriage rates) with suicide rates was now an established method with a metaphysical justification, that of positivistic determinism.

Largely because of the vast influence of Brière de Boismont's great work on suicide (1856), based primarily on case studies of 4,595 suicides, including 1,328 suicide notes (a source of data first used by Guerry as early as 1833), and 265 attempted or planned suicides, the more important works on suicide by Wagner (1864) and Morselli (1879) did not deny causal significance to various individual factors, such as motives. They did, however, consider the comparative analysis of officially computed suicide rates to be necessary for establishing causes of suicide ". . . such as the most positive mode of psychological study would fail to discover in the individual" (Morselli [1879] 1882, p. 10). Durkheim's sociologistic theory of suicide proposed that suicide rates are a *sine qua non* of the sociological study of suicide, and the great influence of his *Suicide* (the first edition of which appeared in 1897, although it was not translated into English until 1951) quickly made the statistical approach almost identical with the sociological approach, especially in the United States. Indeed, Kruijt (1960) and others have recently assumed the two to be totally identical.

Validity of official data. Since sociologists have relied almost exclusively on the official statistics and coroners' reports on suicide for the data from which to develop and test theories of suicide, the question of the validity of the official data is absolutely critical in any evaluation of these sociological works. Throughout the nineteenth century most students of suicide were highly critical of the official statistics on suicide. Esquirol (1838), Brière de Boismont (1856), Legoyt (1881), Strahan (1893), and many others believed the official statistics grossly underestimated the actual number of suicides. Even Morselli (1879) most emphatically warned against the dangerous misuse of suicide statistics. But the sociologists, especially Durkheim (who included very little consideration of the value of his data in *Suicide*), consistently assumed that the evidence was good enough for the kinds of positivistic (i.e., objective, by definition) analyses they wanted to make. In general, they argued that (*a*) the stability of the statistics shows that there are no significant errors in them and (*b*) there are no good reasons to conclude that there are consistent biases in the data, i.e., the errors cancel each other out.

The first argument is based on the mistaken assumption that errors cannot be patterned or stable. Buckle (1857–1861, p. 18) even noted that the frequency of incorrectly addressed letters is extremely stable from year to year without noting the obvious implication for stable suicide statistics. Though contemporary sociologists (especially Americans) who have used the official records on suicide rarely have explicitly considered their value as evidence, they seem generally to have assumed that the second argument given above is correct. The most fundamental reasons for denying the validity of the argument, and therefore the adequate validity of the statistics, are as follows.

(1) It seems quite likely that the official categorizers of suicide in different nations, states, and cities have used different abstract and operational definitions of suicide. We have noted above that the formal definitions of suicide by the students of suicide have varied greatly and in a most complex fashion. But there have been some consistent differences in definitions between groups, such as those between the psychiatrists, the psychologists, and the sociologists. Why would one not expect to find similar consistent differences in the abstract and operational definitions of suicide used by different groups of official categorizers of causes of death? A coroner of a large city who will categorize a cause of death as suicide only if a suicide note is found clearly will produce results consistently different from those of a coroner in another city who uses a different rule-of-thumb definition, such as that there must be an eyewitness report, a clearly perceptible motive, etc. Only "verbal realism" can lead one to assure a priori that the coroner in Lapahaw, Georgia, applies the word "suicide" in a fashion substantially similar to the way the word is applied by the coroner in Los Angeles, California.

(2) It also seems most plausible to assume that there are consistent differences in the abstract and operational definitions of the *terms* of the different definitions, such as "cause," "responsible," "sane," "death," and "intention." For example, some official agencies will not categorize the cause of death as suicide if death occurs three days after the injurious act; and it is worth observing here that all bureaucracies create *ad hoc* rules of thumb in order to effectively apply general policy to their own particular problems.

(3) A great deal of evidence has been presented by Herman Krose, Georg von Mayr, Halbwachs (1930, pp. 19–39), and Achille-Delmas (1932) which has shown both that (*a*) there are consistent differences in the administrative practices of dealing with suicide (and related categories) and that (*b*) changes (hence, differences) in administrative practices regarding suicide produce immediate and highly significant changes in suicide rates. Two brief examples are instructive. Halbwachs (1930, pp. 33–34) found that, though a ruling in 1866 made certification of cause of death by a doctor or public health official obligatory throughout France, in fact almost all rural deaths escaped certification; certification of cause of deaths in public places was made by police officials, and certification by family doctor was universally acceptable. He also found that a reform in the Prussian Bureau of Statistics in 1883 produced a 20 per cent stable increase in the suicide rate, beginning in 1884 (Douglas 1965, pp. 259–377).

These and other facts strongly suggest that the relationship between statistical organizations and the suicide rates they produce is subject to the following principle: other things being equal, suicide rates vary directly with the degree of professional medical training of the categorizers, the average rate of man-hours devoted to "cause of death" categorization, and the independence of the categorizers from "interested parties" (for which see below). This general principle leads us to expect, among other things, that (*a*) urbanization and suicide rates will vary directly; (*b*) both industrialization and the wealth of populations will vary directly with suicide rates (a possible explanation of the great increase in suicide rates of Europe in the nineteenth century and of developing nations today); and (*c*) periods of general disorganization or reorganization, such as wars, will produce decreases in suicide rates (because the officials are fewer and have more important things to do). And, in general, these predictions are strongly supported.

(4) The most important set of "other things" that are not equal, and which we must expect to cause great biases in official statistics on suicide,

are the various *social meanings* of suicide, especially as they relate to approval or disapproval. Because of his positivist philosophy, his peculiar theory of "social pathology," and his theory of "juridical norms," Durkheim assumed that all groups in Europe were equally against suicide. With the partial exception of the works of Halbwachs (1930) and Cavan (1928), almost all sociological theories of suicide since Durkheim have implicitly assumed the normative definitions of suicide to be both invariant and highly negative. This is a totally fallacious and most unfortunate assumption. In his brilliant study of French attitudes toward suicide, Albert Bayet (1922) conclusively demonstrated that over a long period of time there was a consistently far more negative (even horrified) attitude toward suicide on the part of the "simple," uneducated population (largely rural) than on the part of the more educated, upper-class population. Such patterned differences in the normative meanings of suicidal actions might produce different frequencies in actual (or real) suicidal actions, but they would seem far more likely to produce differences in the frequency and strength of attempts to conceal suicide both by the suicidal individual and by his significant others. Moreover, one would expect that the more a primary group has to lose from having one of its members socially categorized as a suicide, the greater will be the frequency and strength of attempts to conceal suicide. These two factors make up what can be called a group coefficient of attempted concealment of suicidal actions. We must also expect, however, that different groups will have different coefficients of success in such attempts, the major determinants of which would seem to be degree of social influence and degree of *social integration* of the group (or individual) making the attempt at concealment. Obviously, these two coefficients could produce many biasing effects on official statistics, the most likely of which seems to be that, given a certain degree of negative normative definition of suicidal action, *the degree of social integration of the suicide's primary group into the general community will vary directly with the coefficient of attempted concealment and with the coefficient of success in attempted concealment.* This means, of course, that official statistics on suicide will tend to be biased in such a direction that they will support an *integration* theory of suicide, such as Durkheim's.

(5) Over half a century before the publication of Durkheim's *Suicide*, Jean-Étienne Esquirol (1838) had established that some methods of committing suicide make valid categorization of the cause of death more difficult. Since, moreover, there seem

to be patterned variations between social categories in suicide methods, we must expect biases in official statistics from this source. For example, women use barbiturates and gas far more frequently than do men. Suicides by barbiturates and gas are very difficult to distinguish from accidents. Since such doubtful cases are almost always categorized as "accidental" or "accidental suicide," we must expect bias in the direction of lower official suicide rates for women.

Two conclusions regarding the official statistics on suicide seem justified: (*a*) we have little specific, systematic knowledge about the means employed by different statistical bureaus to arrive at these figures; (*b*) what knowledge we do have about these figures and the means of arriving at them strongly supports our arguments that they are highly biased in certain directions. In general, at the present time there seems to be no adequate justification for using official statistics on suicide to build or test a *scientific* theory of suicide. There seems to be every reason for not using them (Douglas 1965, pp. 259–377).

Sociology and the official data. Almost every published theory of suicide that has been called sociological has depended on the official statistics on suicide for its testing. This means, of course, that the *testing* of these theories is subject to all of the biases of the official statistics and therefore cannot generally be accepted.

But this does not necessarily mean that the theories of suicide are themselves wrong. All the so-called sociological theories have been general abstract theories which the authors believed to be applicable to a great variety of social behavior—for instance, to all deviant behavior. These theorists have never derived their general theories from the official statistics, still less from any actual observations of cases of suicide. On the other hand, they have always known from the beginning most of the patterns of suicide shown by the official statistics, so that they have been able to select (no doubt unconsciously) just those patterns for consideration in the testing stage which their theories can "predict." In spite of rhetorical disclaimers that any such bias exists, the fact remains that all published sociological theories of suicide have been supported at a high level of statistical significance by "tests" using the official statistics on suicide. Moreover, since all of these works after Durkheim's *Suicide* have included only the most perfunctory consideration of alternative theories for explaining the same data, there is at present no justification for considering any one theory better than any other, unless one were to consider sophistication of argument an acceptable criterion, in which case Durkheim would hold the field unopposed (Douglas 1965, pp. 112–259).

Major theories of suicide

Durkheim's sociologistic theory. In *Suicide* Durkheim was, of course, primarily concerned with proving by demonstration that sociology is a scientific discipline *sui generis*. The work was a polemic in a great ideological war; and as Halbwachs has said (1930, p. 3), its argumentative power has made it convincing (though, I would add, only to those already convinced of its general position). To achieve his goal of demonstration, Durkheim made use of the mass of published material on suicide statistics, the many statistical relations already established between suicide rates and social relations by the flourishing school of "moral statisticians," and the methods of analysis developed by Bertillon and many others. Earlier sociologists, especially Morselli (1879), had considered "society," and in particular the morals of a society, to be the most important cause of a given suicide rate. It was from these previous works that Durkheim took his specific ideas, such as "egoism" and "lack of moral restraint," about what caused suicide rates to vary. But previous theorists, with the major exception of Quetelet, had proposed multifactored explanations; Durkheim proposed a general synthesis. In general, he took his notion of statistical relations and methods from the moral statisticians and, like many of the moral statisticians before him, turned to the romantics, and the psychologists whom they had influenced, for his fundamental causal variables. Durkheim's own contribution was to translate "egoism," "need for an external, moral authority," and similar psychological variables into "social" (or cultural) variables which he finally reduced to the two opposing moral dimensions of egoism–altruism and anomie–fatalism.

Unfortunately for Durkheim's ambitious program, *Suicide* (1897) is an extremely uneven work. The theory presented in Books 1 and 2 is for the most part extremely positivistic, relating external (or "objective") variables to other external variables. In Book 3, however, the theory is radically different: internal variables are related both to each other and to external variables. The positivistic version is the one usually given primacy by American sociologists (see, for example, Gibbs & Martin 1964); but the later version is the more considered, developed, and tenable theory. The core of the latter is very simple, though its presentation is confused by Durkheim's penchant for multiple terms (e.g., "disintegration," "disorder," "disequilibrium," "lack of unity or cohesion"), *petitio principii*, and lack of conceptual clarity. He assumes that for all societies there is some optimal equilibrium or integration of egoism–altruism, on the one hand, and anomie–fatalism, on the other. Any change in the relative strengths of these ideas (or forces) will produce an increase in "social disintegration," which will lead in turn to an increase in the suicide rate and in the particular type of social relation associated with the "force" that is on the increase. Hence, there is a statistical relation between suicide rates and the incidence of different types of social relations.

The critical flaw in the work is the lack of any means of measuring these forces of egoism, anomie, etc., either independently of each other or independently of a change in suicide rates. Yet Durkheim assumed that these were the fundamentally important variables: any change in suicide rates or social relations meant to him that one or more of the forces was increasing relative to the others. But how did he determine which force was increasing? We must conclude that he inferred it from the associated changes in social relations, and that, for the most part, he assumed he knew from common sense what these changes meant. Unfortunately, the concrete examples Durkheim gives us will not support the notion that his common sense was superior, as a scientific instrument, to anyone else's (Douglas 1965, pp. 7–112).

The major contribution of Durkheim's *Suicide* was its grand conception of the general nature of sociological theory. Durkheim's intentions in this work went much too far beyond the possibilities of the theory and data of his day—and of ours.

Halbwachs' theory of suicide. The work of Maurice Halbwachs (1930) began as a supplement to Durkheim's *Suicide* but became a radical reorientation of sociological theory. Halbwachs concluded that Durkheim, in spite of his extensive use of replicative analyses, had overlooked the high degree of overlap of the variables he found to be related to suicide rates. The only fundamentally significant independent relation, Halbwachs argued, is between suicide rates and the degree of complexity of a society: thus, the rural style of life (or sociocultural system) is simpler than the urban and therefore has a lower suicide rate. But Halbwachs also rejected Durkheim's sociologism. He maintained that there is a complementary relation between the motives imputed to suicides and social situations of isolation. To support his theory, Halbwachs presented the most extensive and thorough analysis of official statistics in all of the sociological literature. As we have already said, however, it seems clear that there is a fundamental bias in the official statistics in the direction of underestimating rural rates (Douglas 1965, pp. 195–209).

Social disorganization theories. Unlike almost all other recent sociological works on suicide, the various "ecological" works on suicide have been done quite outside the tradition initiated by Durkheim. Ruth Cavan's *Suicide* (1928), the first of these works, was predominantly influenced by Morselli. Most ecological studies of suicide have relied heavily on some form of social disorganization theory. Various population variables, such as high mobility and complexity, are hypothesized as the causes of a relative lack of effect of social values on behavior (this being the meaning that "social disorganization" usually has for these writers), which in turn is hypothesized as the cause of suicide and similar deviant acts.

The social disorganization approach to suicide involved certain extreme assumptions which have more recently been shown to be clearly unacceptable. For one thing, it assumed cultural homogeneity of values and behavior patterns, that is, it was taken for granted that all of the many ethnic groups of cities like Chicago shared the same values and behavior practices with regard to any form of "deviance," such as suicide was thought to be. An extensive literature has attacked this assumption when applied to delinquency, and Bayet (1922) has amassed enough evidence to prove that attitudes toward suicide may vary considerably even in a nation with a supposedly homogeneous culture. The social disorganization approach also assumed that cultural values are the only social meanings that determine rates of suicidal actions. But there is no evidence whatsoever in favor of this assumption—and, indeed, it was contradicted by Cavan's own arguments concerning the importance of spite and other purely personal motives in causing suicide (Cavan 1928).

Cavan's work, the earliest of the significant ecological works on suicide in America, did not involve the so-called ecological fallacy (for which see Robinson 1950). In fact, Cavan clearly recognized the fundamental principle involved in this fallacy, even to the extent of criticizing the statistical arguments of Morselli and Durkheim in terms of it (1928, p. 289). Realizing what was needed in order to avoid this fallacy, she did attempt to provide evidence regarding individual cases of suicide. In general, she argued that social disorganization causes individual disorganization, and that the latter manifests itself in patterns of increasing inability to cope with crisis situations. In an attempt to demonstrate the validity of this theory, she presented lengthy selections from the personal documents of two individuals who committed suicide. Though it seems clear now that the attempted demonstration involves an imposition of the general category of "individual disorganization" upon the statements of the individuals, it is also clear that Cavan's work, which was followed in most important details by that of Schmid (1928), involved more consideration of real cases of suicide than any other sociological work to appear before the later 1960s. Moreover, her material on the case of Marion is still among the best available on real cases of suicide (see the discussion in Douglas 1965, pp. 140–167, 471–483).

Recent sociological theories. Most of the recent sociological theories of suicide have been formulated ostensibly within a Durkheimian content, yet most of them are psychosocial theories that are actually quite different from Durkheim's.

The one theory that actually seems to be sociologistic in the Durkheimian manner is that proposed by Gibbs and Martin (1964). This theory, although derived from far too simple an interpretation of Durkheim's *Suicide*, is true to its positivistic aspect in rejecting any consideration of real cases of suicide and in attempting to relate official statistics on official categories (such as marriage) to official statistics on suicide. The basic idea of the theory is that the more socially integrated (or less "conflictful") a set of statuses (such as age, race, marital status), the more frequently that set of statuses will be occupied by members of the society and the less frequently it will be associated with suicide. This whole approach suffers from all of the weaknesses already detected in Durkheim's and from some important additional ones. Thus there is almost no consideration of the real-world (as opposed to official) social meanings of statuses, whereas Durkheim did at least make use of well-informed common sense to provide him with social meanings for the status categories he was interested in analyzing. In addition, the "testing" of the theory involved the analysis of only four of the truly immense number of statuses in our society, and all four of these are the standard categories used in analyses of official data on suicide, so that any sociologist making an analysis of the relations between these categories and suicide rates knows what the relations are before he begins (Douglas 1965, pp. 121–135).

Most of the other recent theories of suicide that purport to be sociological—the most significant is that of Henry and Short (1954)—include psychological variables. They almost all agree that socioeconomic status change (or "reverse of fortune," as Brière de Boismont called it) is the basic sociological cause of suicide, but each proposes a different personality theory (frustration–aggression theory, self theory, loss-of-meaning theory, etc.) to explain why some few individuals commit suicide when confronted with a given status change and almost all others do not. The basic problem is that status change is "significantly" related to an immense number of things. These statistical works never involve any demonstration that other factors are not causing both the supposed cause and the suicide. They rarely include consideration of the many alternative, conflicting theories that purport to explain the same official statistics. They generally involve careful arrangement and choice of data so that statistically "significant" results can be obtained. For example, in the work by Henry and Short (1954), social classes in America are dichotomized into high and low, an arrangement which completely obscures the U-functional relationship almost always found to exist between socioeconomic status and official suicide rates in the Western world. Moreover, theoretical argument in these works is frequently quite divorced from statistical analysis; in some cases, the two can be related only through the addition of many *ad hoc* assumptions (see, for instance, the analysis of Henry & Short 1954 in Douglas 1965, pp. 209–229). In some of these works, changes in the population bases for the official suicide statistics were actually not taken into consideration. For example, some of the most important analyses made by Henry and Short were for periods during which new states were being added almost each year to the U.S. Death Registration Area. This fact had led Dublin and Bunzel (1933) to use only the original Death Registration Area, but Henry and Short completely overlooked the whole problem.

However, a few of these psychosocial works, as this mingling of psychological and sociological approaches can be called, have introduced valuable new orientations into the study of suicide. Thus Breed's interviews of the surviving families of individuals who committed suicide (1963) have finally introduced into sociology a research method long established in psychiatry. This method has moved sociologists one step further toward direct observation of real-world cases of suicidal events. Indeed, it has shown them that henceforth they must consider the effects of a suicide on others as part of the suicide phenomenon. The case studies reported by psychologists (Deshaies 1947; Schneider 1954) and the sociocultural studies of suicide made by a few anthropologists and psychiatrists (Devereux 1931; Hendin 1964) make clear what should have been obvious to sociologists long ago: suicidal ac-

tions are socially meaningful actions, and individuals commit them in order to communicate something to themselves and others about themselves and about others. Even an individual whose primary goal is a state of nonbeing will not commit suicide unless he can do so in such a way as to communicate, to himself and possibly to others as well, just the right meanings. The empirical study of suicidal actions as socially meaningful—cognitively, affectively, and normatively—opens new directions of highly fruitful research and theory (Douglas 1965, especially pp. 377–543).

Only the most comprehensive observation and description of the everyday actions and statements relevant to suicide are likely to result in scientifically useful empirical and theoretical generalizations concerning suicidal actions as socially meaningful actions. Systematic analyses of existing case studies have, however, already resulted in some very important generalizations concerning the social meanings of suicidal actions in the Western world. The best attempt to generalize about suicide in this way for a non-Western society is by Devereux (1931); there are some important contributions to such an approach in other works (see, for instance, Bohannan 1960).

Perhaps the most important high-level generalization about suicide that can be made at this time is that the situated meanings of suicidal acts are often very different from their *abstract* meanings. In other words, the meaning of a suicidal act for those who are directly involved with it will very rarely be the same as the meaning it has for those who are not so involved, and will certainly not be the same as for the individual who, by committing suicide, is trying to communicate something (Douglas 1965, pp. 406–440). This finding has two fundamental implications for all investigation of the social meanings of suicide and, perhaps, for all of sociology. First, it is not possible to predict or explain specific types of social events, such as suicide, in terms of abstract social meanings, such as values favoring suicide. Second, it is not possible to study the situated social meanings of suicide, which are most important in its causation, without reference to actual instances of suicidal acts with which the individuals to be questioned have been directly involved. This generalization leads one to question the value of any method for investigating any realm of social action if it attempts to abstract members of society from the involvements of their everyday lives.

This does not imply that there are no patterns of meanings common to all the events that members of a society call "suicide" or "suicidal." When one looks at the meanings imputed to particular suicidal actions, one does find that certain general features tend to recur. Most importantly, any suicidal action is usually believed to mean something fundamental about the self of the individual committing it, or about the situation (especially the persons involved) in which he committed it, or about both of these. Whether the specific meanings realized will be directed to the actor's self or to his situation will depend on the imputations of causality made by the various persons in the situation: will they see the individual as the cause of his own actions—that is, as "responsible" for them —or will they see him as having been caused ("driven") to do them by circumstances (loss of job, family trouble, etc.)? The individual committing the suicidal action often attempts to place one of these two general constructions upon the action by pointing out in some way the external cause that is to be "blamed" for his suicide.

There is no one meaning or set of meanings that can be imputed to all (or even most) suicidal actions. Just what meanings are imputed in each case will depend on (1) the intentions of the various actors; (2) the socially perceived ways in which the actions are committed; (3) the specific patterns of suicidal meanings that are realized; (4) the argument processes before, during, and after the suicidal actions. It should be clearly noted that whether or not actions are *socially* categorized as "suicidal" depends on precisely the same sort of process. The obvious example is that of individuals who with various ends in mind (avoiding embarrassment to their families, loss of insurance money, or disgrace to themselves), arrange suicides that are designed to be taken for accidents.

It is probably not possible for individuals to construct any meanings they please for their actions, though individual creativity does extend the limits immensely, and all cases include imponderable idiosyncrasies. However, the limits remain. There are, first of all, various criteria of plausibility of motives, or rationality, though it is very likely that in some instances individuals intend their actions to be considered implausible or irrational. Second, a relatively few patterns of situated meaning play important parts in most interpretations of particular suicidal actions, and it therefore seems likely that individuals take these patterns into consideration when attempting to construct the meanings of their actions for others. The most common patterns of this sort in the Western world are those involving such motives as the search for help (Sacks 1966), sympathy, escape, repentance, expiation of guilt, self-punishment, and "seriousness" (Douglas 1965, pp. 440–511).

Much careful description and analysis in this area remain to be done (*ibid*, pp. 511–540). However, the basic problems and the most appropriate methods for solving them now seem clear, and there is great promise of rapid development in both the empirical and the theoretical study of suicide.

JACK D. DOUGLAS

[*See also* DEVIANT BEHAVIOR; INTEGRATION, *article on* SOCIAL INTEGRATION; SOCIOLOGY, *article on* THE EARLY HISTORY OF SOCIAL RESEARCH; *and the biographies of* DURKHEIM; HALBWACHS; QUETELET.]

BIBLIOGRAPHY

ACHILLE-DELMAS, FRANÇOIS 1932 *Psychologie pathologique du suicide.* Paris: Alcan.

BAYET, ALBERT 1922 *Le suicide et la morale.* Paris: Alcan.

BENOÎT-SMULLYAN, ÉMILE 1948 The Sociologism of Émile Durkheim and His School. Pages 499–537 in Harry Elmer Barnes (editor), *Introduction to the History of Sociology.* Univ. of Chicago Press.

BOHANNAN, PAUL (editor) 1960 *African Homicide and Suicide.* Princeton Univ. Press.

BREED, WARREN 1963 Occupational Mobility and Suicide Among White Males. *American Sociological Review* 28:179–188.

BRIÈRE DE BOISMONT, ALEXANDRE 1856 *Du suicide et de la folie suicide.* Paris: Baillière.

BUCKLE, HENRY THOMAS (1857–1861) 1913 *The History of Civilization in England.* 2d ed. 2 vols. New York: Hearst.

CAVAN, RUTH S. 1928 *Suicide.* Univ. of Chicago Press.

DAHLGREN, KARL G. 1945 *On Suicide and Attempted Suicide.* Lund (Sweden): Universitets Bokhandel.

DESHAIES, GABRIEL 1947 *La psychologie du suicide.* Paris: Presses Universitaires de France.

DEVEREUX, GEORGE 1931 *Mohave Ethnopsychiatry and Suicide.* Washington: Government Printing Office.

DOUGLAS, JACK D. 1965 The Sociological Study of Suicide: Suicidal Actions as Socially Meaningful Actions. Ph.D dissertation, Princeton Univ.

DOUGLAS, JACK D. 1966 The Sociological Analysis of Social Meanings of Suicide. *Archives européennes de sociologie* 7:249–275.

DOUGLAS, JACK D. 1967 *The Social Meanings of Suicide.* Princeton Univ. Press.

DUBLIN, LEONARD I.; and BUNZEL, BESSIE 1933 *To Be or Not to Be: A Study of Suicide.* New York: Smith & Haas.

DURKHEIM ÉMILE (1897) 1951 *Suicide: A Study in Sociology.* Glencoe, Ill.: Free Press. → First published in French.

ESQUIROL, JEAN-ÉTIENNE D. (1838) 1845 *Mental Maladies.* Philadelphia: Lea & Blanchard. → First published as *Des maladies mentales considérées sous les rapports médical-hygiéniques et médico-légal.*

GIBBS, JACK P.; and MARTIN, WALTER T. 1964 *Status Integration and Suicide.* Eugene: Univ. of Oregon.

GOETHE, JOHANN WOLFGANG VON (1811–1833) 1908 *Poetry and Truth From My Life.* 2 vols. London: Bell. → First published in German.

GUERRY, ANDRÉ M. 1833 *Essai sur la statistique morale de la France.* Paris: Crochard.

HALBWACHS, MAURICE 1930 *Les causes du suicide.* Paris: Alcan.

HENDIN, HERBERT M. 1964 *Suicide and Scandinavia: A Psychoanalytic Study of Culture and Character.* New York: Grune.

HENRY, ANDREW F.; and SHORT, JAMES F. JR. 1954 *Suicide and Homicide: Some Economic, Sociological and Psychological Aspects of Aggression.* Glencoe, Ill.: Free Press.

KRUIJT, CORNELIUS S. 1960 *Zelfmoord: Statistich-sociologische verkenningen. Suicide: Sociological and Statistical Investigations.* Assen (Netherlands): Van Gorcum. → Contains a summary in English.

LEGOYT, ALFRED 1881 *Le suicide ancien et moderne.* Paris: Droiun.

MORSELLI, ENRICO (1879) 1882 *Suicide.* New York: Appleton. → First published in Italian.

QUETELET, ADOLPHE (1835) 1842 *A Treatise on Man and the Development of His Faculties.* 2 vols. Edinburgh: Chambers. → First published in French.

ROBINSON, W. S. 1950 Ecological Correlations and the Behavior of Individuals. *American Sociological Review* 15: 351–357.

SACKS, HARVEY 1966 The Search for Help: No One to Turn to. Unpublished manuscript.

SCHMID, CALVIN F. 1928 *Suicides in Seattle, 1914 to 1925: An Ecological and Behavioristic Study.* University of Washington, Publications in the Social Sciences, Vol. 5, no. 1. Seattle: Univ. of Washington Press.

SCHNEIDER, PIERRE-B. 1954 *La tentative de suicide.* Neuchâtel (Switzerland): Delachaux & Niestlé.

STRAHAN, SAMUEL 1893 *Suicide and Insanity.* London: Sonnenschein.

SÜSSMILCH, JOHANN P. (1741) 1788 *Die göttliche Ordnung in den Veränderungen des menschlichen Geschlechts, aus der Geburt, dem Tode und der Fortpflanzung.* 3 vols. Berlin: Verlag der Buchhandlung der Realschule.

TISSOT, JOSEPH 1840 *De la manie du suicide et de l'esprit de révolte: De leur causes et de leur remèdes.* Paris: Lagrange.

WAGNER, ADOLF H. G. 1864 *Die Gesetzmässigkeit in den scheinbar willkührlichen menschlichen Handlungen vom Standpunkte der Statistik.* Part 2. Statistik willkührlichen Handlungen. Hamburg (Germany): Boyes & Geisler.

II

PSYCHOLOGICAL ASPECTS (1)

The clear definition and meaningful classification of various suicidal phenomena are fundamental to advancements in the treatment, prevention, and investigation of self-destruction in man. The purpose of this article is to present some new conceptions of suicidal phenomena, first by identifying current confusions and then by proposing a taxonomic scheme that attempts to embrace many of the diverse aspects of self-destructive behavior.

Definition

As a beginning, a straightforward definition of suicide might read: "Suicide is the human act of self-inflicted, self-intentioned cessation." At least five points are to be noted in this brief definition: (1) it states that suicide is a human act; (2) it combines both the decedent's conscious wish to be dead and his actions to carry out that wish; (3) it implies that the motivations of the deceased may have to be inferred and his behaviors interpreted by others, using such evidence as a suicide note, spoken testimony, or retrospective reconstruction of the victim's intention; (4) it states that the goal of the action relates to death, rather than to self-injury, self-mutilation, or inimical or self-reducing behaviors; and (5) it focuses on the concept of the cessation of the individual's conscious introspective life. (An explication of the concept of "cessation" may be found in Shneidman 1964.)

Difficulties of definition. Assuming the validity of the definition of suicide cited above—that a human being, with the intention of stopping his life, inflicts upon himself the equivalent of a mortal wound—the meaning would seem clear enough if it were stated that a certain individual had "committed suicide." On the other hand, confusions of meaning arise immediately if a specific individual is labeled as "suicidal." Although suicide seems to be not too difficult to define, suicidal phenomena are, in fact, very complicated. Some of the current confusions relating to the term "suicidal" may be listed as follows.

(1) The word "suicidal" is used indiscriminately to cover different categories of behavior. For example, one cannot be sure whether it is being used to convey the idea that an individual has (*a*) committed suicide, (*b*) attempted suicide, (*c*) threatened suicide, (*d*) exhibited depressive behavior with or without suicidal ideation, or (*e*) manifested generally self-destructive or inimical patterns. Of recent writers, Stengel and Cook (1958) especially have emphasized the importance of differentiating specifically between data on attempted suicide and data regarding individuals who have committed suicide. But the fact remains that the classification of suicidal behavior currently most common in everyday clinical and research use is a rather homely, supposedly commonsense division: in its barest form it implies that all humanity can be divided into two groupings, suicidal and nonsuicidal; and then, with seeming meaningfulness, it divides the suicidal category into subgroups of committed, attempted, and threatened. Although this elaboration is more sophisticated than the suicidal-versus-nonsuicidal view of life, it remains neither theoretically nor practically adequate for understanding or treatment.

(2) There is constant confusion in respect to the temporal dimension of suicidal acts. One sees the word "suicidal" used to convey the information that an individual *was* self-destructive (or mani-

fested behavior in any of the other categories listed immediately above), *is* currently self-destructive, or *will be* so. This obviously contains confusions among statements that are postdictive (relating to the past), "paridictive" (relating to the more-or-less present), and predictive (relating to the future). Most diagnoses of individual "suicidality" are *post hoc* definitions in that they refer to those cases in which an individual is labeled as "suicidal" only after he has committed suicide. Statistics on suicide are, of course, based primarily on *post hoc* definitions of suicide. The primary difficulty in all such cases lies in determining whether or not the individual actually intended to kill himself. The case of the individual who writes a suicide note and then shoots himself is fairly clear, but many cases of death are unclear or equivocal as to mode of death. For example, in the case of an individual who "jumps or falls" from a high place or who is found dead of barbiturate poisoning, the question is often raised whether the case was suicidal or accidental. The coroner's traditional concern has been with assessing whether God (natural and accidental deaths) or man (suicidal or homicidal deaths) is responsible. The term "suicide" as used by coroners in the certification of death is a medicolegal term and includes, as a *sine qua non*, the concept that the person played a major role in bringing about his own demise, that is, that it was his intention to die. It should be obvious that statistics on suicide can be greatly influenced (in any city or country) by the manner in which these equivocal deaths are labeled.

(3) There are confusions relating to the characteristics of suicidal behaviors. In many past and current investigations of self-destructive behaviors, several different dimensions of behavior have unfortunately been thrown together. (If one were, for example, studying homicidal phenomena, it is unlikely that he would fail to differentiate among homicides committed on the highway, in the bedroom, during armed robberies, on the field of battle, etc.—and yet a comparable lack of discrimination has been characteristic of many studies of suicidal phenomena.) These issues also relate to the phenomenologic and semantic confusions in the use of the word "suicidal." Some individuals who "die by their own hand" do not necessarily "commit suicide." That is to say, they do not, in their own minds, kill themselves or seek death. Instead of fleeing into a vaguely conceptualized "death," they behave so as to escape from aspects of life. For some the concept of death, or final cessation of being, does not enter into their thinking. They rather indulge in either a planned or a momentary impulsive act—and termination of life is the result. Then we say that they have "committed suicide," whereas such an individual might conceivably have left a note which states that ". . . all I did was to swallow those pills . . . I just wanted some relief at that moment. . . . The tension was so great I had to do something. . . . I did not know what I was doing or what would happen. . . . It was a gamble. . . . I was desperate. . . ." Operationally, it would seem that the key characteristics of suicidal behaviors do not lie in the differences in method (shooting, sedation, cutting, hanging) but rather in the differences in the individual's life phase, in the lethality of his acts, and in his intention vis-à-vis death, as indicated below in (4), (5), and (6), respectively. That is, it may very well be that the confusions listed above in (1), (2), and (3) might, in large measure, be avoided by making the very distinctions suggested in the subsequent paragraphs.

(4) Many confusions arise because each individual's attitudes toward his own death are biphasic: that is, any adolescent or adult, at any given moment, has (*a*) more or less long-range, pervasive, relatively habitual orientations toward his own death. These characterological orientations are an integral part of his total psychological make-up and reflect his philosophy of life, need systems, aspirations, identifications, conscious beliefs, etc. And he is also capable of having (*b*) relatively short-lived, acute, fairly sudden shifts of his orientations toward his own death. Indeed, this is what is usually meant when one says that an individual has "become suicidal." It is therefore crucial in any complete assessment of an individual's orientations toward his own death to know both his habitual and his current (today's) orientations. Failure to make this distinction is one reason why many current efforts to relate "suicidal state" to psychological test data or to case-history data have been barren and confusing. For individuals in their "normal" (usual for them) state, their habitual and their current orientations toward their own demise will be the same; for individuals who are acutely disturbed, their current orientations toward their demise will often reflect this perturbation. "Being suicidal" involves being disturbed, although not necessarily psychotic.

(5) Popular accounts of "suicidal" behaviors often focus on the method used (for example, wrist cutting) or on the precipitating cause (ill health, losing money) without regard for one of the key dimensions in the assessment of suicidal behavior, namely lethality. The primary clinical goal of any suicide prevention agency is to keep

people out of the coroner's department. Thus, an individual's unhappiness, perturbation, loneliness, alcoholism, schizophrenia, homosexuality, depression, etc., are relevant in suicide prevention primarily as they bear on the assessment of his lethality potential. To say that an individual has "threatened" suicide or has "attempted" suicide is relatively uninformative without some indications of the potentialities of a lethal outcome with which the threat or attempt was made. Recently, at the Suicide Prevention Center in Los Angeles specific procedures have been evolved for the rapid assessment of the lethality of an individual's suicidal potential (see Litman & Farberow 1961; Tabachnick & Farberow 1961).

(6) The most obfuscating confusions relating to suicidal phenomena may occur if the individual's intentions in relation to his own cessation are not considered. "Suicide" also has an administrative definition. In the United States (and most of the countries reporting to the World Health Organization), "suicide" defined from the point of view of the coroner or vital statistician is simply one of the four modes of death, the others being natural, accidental, and homicide (N–A–S–H). This traditional fourfold classification of all deaths leaves much to be desired. Its major deficiency is that it emphasizes relatively adventitious details in the death (that is, whether the individual was invaded by a lethal virus or a lethal bullet, which may make little difference to the deceased) and, more important, it erroneously treats the human being as a Cartesian biological machine rather than appropriately treating him as a psychosocial organism, thus obscuring the individual's intentions in relation to his own cessation. Further, the traditional N–A–S–H classification of deaths completely neglects the concepts of contemporary psychology regarding intention and purpose, the multiple determination of behavior, unconscious motivation, etc.

Much of the problem arises because of a confusion between methods and purpose. Although it is true that the act of putting a shotgun in one's mouth and pulling the trigger with one's toe is almost always related to lethal self-intention, this particular isomorphic relationship between method and intent does not hold for most other means, such as ingesting barbiturates or cutting oneself with a razor. Individuals can attempt to attempt suicide, attempt to commit suicide, or attempt to be nonsuicidal. Cessation intentions may range all the way from deadly ones, through the wide variety of ambivalences, rescue fantasies, cries for help, and psychic indecisions, all the way to clearly

formulated nonlethal intention in which a semantic usurpation of a "suicidal" mode has been consciously employed.

Deaths classified by intention. As a way out of this impasse it is suggested that all deaths—in addition to their being labeled as natural, accidental, suicide, or homicide—also be designated as *intentioned*, *subintentioned*, or *unintentioned* (Shneidman 1963).

Intentioned deaths. An intentioned cessation is one in which the deceased played a direct, conscious role in his own demise. The death was due primarily to the decedent's conscious wish to stop his conscious life and to his actions in carrying out that wish. In this category would be individuals who seek their own demise, initiate or participate in their own demise, or take calculated risks where the odds are critically unfavorable to their survival, as in Russian roulette, where the individual bets his life on the objective probability of as few as five out of six chances that he will survive.

Subintentioned deaths. Subintentioned deaths are those in which the deceased played an important indirect, covert, partial, or unconscious role in his own demise. The death is suspected to be due in some part to the actions of the decedent which seemed to reflect his unconscious wishes to hasten his death, as evidenced by his own carelessness, foolhardiness, neglect of self, imprudence, resignation to death, mismanagement of alcohol or drugs, disregard of life-saving medical regimen, brink-of-death patterns, etc. This concept of subintentioned death is similar in some ways to Karl Menninger's concepts (1938) of chronic suicide, focal suicide, and organic suicide, except that these relate to self-defeating ways of continuing to live, whereas the notion of subintentioned death relates to ways of stopping the process of living.

In terms of the traditional N–A–S–H classification of modes of death, it is important to note that some instances of all four types can be found in the category of subintentioned deaths, depending upon the particular details of each case. There is a growing literature on the role of the individual in his own natural, accidental, suicidal, or homicidal death. Subintentioned deaths involve what might be called the psychosomatics of death, that is, cases in which essentially psychological processes—like fear (including fear of voodoo), anxiety, derring-do, hostility, withdrawal, etc.—seem to play some role in exacerbating the catabolic or physiological processes which bring on termination, as well as those cases in which the individual seems to play an indirect, largely unconscious role in inviting or hastening his own demise [see PSY-CHOSOMATIC ILLNESS; see also Gengerelli & Kirkner 1954; Macdonald 1961; Weisman & Hackett 1961; Weiss 1957; Wolfgang 1959].

It can be noted that the subintentioned death implies more than ambivalence toward wanting to be dead and wishing to be rescued (the to-be-or-not-to-be inner dialogue) found in practically every suicide. It rather reflects the active indirect (largely unconscious) participation of the individual in hastening his own demise.

Unintentioned deaths. Unintentioned deaths are those in which the deceased played no significant psychological role in his own cessation. The death was due entirely to failures within the body or to assault from without (by a bullet, a blow, a steering wheel, etc.) in a decedent who, rather unambivalently, wished to continue to live. Such a person at the time of his death is, as it were, going about his business (even though he may be lying in the hospital) with no conscious intention or strong drive in the direction of effecting or hastening his demise. What happens is that something from the outside—outside of his mind—happens to him. This lethal "something" may be a cerebral vascular accident, a myocardial infarction, some malfunction, some catastrophic catabolism, some invasion—whether by bullet or by virus—which he did not, in any part, himself generate. "It" happens to "him."

Practical applications. A practical application of the above schematization of death in terms of the individual's intention has been made since 1960 in Los Angeles. This procedure, labeled the "psychological autopsy" (Curphey 1961; Litman et al. 1963), has been used in those cases that are equivocal as to *mode* of death. The procedure consists of the use of especially adapted interview techniques to generate psychological information about the deceased. Survivors, friends, and professional acquaintances of the deceased are interviewed. Clues are sought, especially in relation to the prodromal aspects of suicide. A judgment is made along traditional lines (for example, probable suicide, probable accident, probable natural cause, suicide-accident undetermined, suicide-natural undetermined, etc.). An additional judgment is also made in terms of the intentioned, subintentioned, and unintentioned categories. Although one would, a priori, expect all suicidal deaths to be intentioned and all natural, accidental, and homicidal deaths to be unintentioned, the findings in the Los Angeles procedures indicate that the relationship between traditional modes of death and types of intention is a complicated one, with the crucial role occupied by subintentioned deaths.

It might be protested, inasmuch as the assessments of these intentioned states involve the appraisal of unconscious factors, that some workers (especially lay coroners) cannot legitimately be expected to make the psychological judgments required for this type of classification. To this, one answer would be that medical examiners and lay coroners make judgments of this nature every day of the week. The fact is that in the situation of evaluating a possible suicide, the coroner often acts (sometimes without realizing it) as psychiatrist and psychologist and as both judge and jury in a quasi-judicial way. This is because certification of death as suicide does, in itself, imply some judgments of reconstruction of the victim's motivation or intention. Making these judgments is an inexorable part of a coroner's function. It might be much better for these psychological dimensions to be made explicit and for an attempt, albeit crude, to be made to use them, rather than for these psychological dimensions to operate on an unverbalized level.

Theoretical and taxonomic positions

We now turn from our consideration of the definitional problems of suicide to a brief historical résumé of the major theoretical and taxonomic positions in relation to suicidal phenomena.

Durkheim and other sociological positions. In this century (or at least since 1897, the date of the publication of Durkheim's *Le suicide*) there have been two major approaches to the definition and understanding of suicide: the sociological and the psychological. The former historically is identified primarily with Émile Durkheim, French sociologist (1897). Durkheim was interested not so much in suicidal phenomena *per se* as he was in the explication of his own sociological method. He used the analysis of suicidal phenomena as the occasion to work out four types of factors in suicide—altruistic, egoistic, anomic, and fatalistic—but discussed only the first three.

There are studies generally classified as "sociological" (in the sense that they present statistical or ecological data, but not in the sense that they follow Durkheim's interest in explaining the variety of man's moral commitments to his society) which are worthy of note, among them Sainsbury (1955) and Stengel and Cook (1958) in England, and Dublin (1963) in the United States. Dublin's book, especially, furnishes the student with an encyclopedia of statistical information about suicide phenomena.

Freudian and other psychological positions. The psychological approach is identified primarily with Freud, who is generally acknowledged to have first stated comprehensive psychological insights into suicide. Freud's conceptualization of suicide (1917a; 1917b) was that of a primarily intrapsychic phenomenon, stemming from within the mind, primarily the unconscious mind, of the individual. In one of his formulations Freud envisaged suicide as being the result of a process wherein feelings of love and affection which had originally been directed toward an internalized love object had become, as a result of rejection and frustration, angry, hostile feelings; however, because the object had become internalized and part of the self, the hostile feelings were then directed toward the self. Thus suicide, from a psychoanalytic point of view, might be described as murder in the 180th degree.

The classical Freudian approach not only tended rather systematically to ignore social factors but also tended to focus on a single complex or psychodynamic constellation. But we now know that individuals kill themselves for a number and variety of psychologically felt motives: not only hate and revenge, but also dependency, shame, guilt, fear, hopelessness, loyalty, fealty to self-image, pain, and even ennui. Just as no single formula or pattern can be found to explain all human homosexuality or prostitution, so no single psychological pattern is sufficient to contain all human self-destruction. (For a comprehensive review of this topic, see Litman 1967.)

Synthesis—the concept of self. The synthesis of the psychological position, with its clinical emphasis on the individual internal drama within the single mind, and the sociological position, discussed in the previous article, remains to be accomplished. A recent study bearing on this point (Shneidman & Farberow 1960) emphasized the interplay between both the social and psychological factors as mutually enhancing roles in each individual's suicide. This finding is consistent with that of Halbwachs (1930), whose position—unlike that of his mentor, Durkheim—was that the "social" and "psychopathological" explanations of suicide are complementary rather than antithetical. A synthesis of these two lies in the area of the "self," especially in the ways in which social forces are incorporated within the totality of the individual. In understanding suicide, one needs to know the thoughts and feelings and ego functionings and unconscious conflicts of an individual, as well as how he integrates with his fellow man and participates morally as a member of the groups within which he lives.

Taxonomic positions. Not many classifications of suicidal phenomena have been proposed. Durkheim's classification distinguished between anomic, egoistic, and altruistic suicide (1897). To this can be added Menninger's classification of the sources of suicidal impulses, namely the wish to kill, the wish to be killed, and the wish to die (1938). Menninger also classified subsuicidal phenomena into chronic suicide (asceticism, martyrdom, addiction, invalidism, psychosis); focal suicide (self-mutilation, malingering, multiple accidents, impotence and frigidity); and organic suicide (involving the psychological factors in organic disease). A composite listing of other rubrics would include the following: suicide as communication; suicide as revenge; suicide as fantasy crime; suicide as unconscious flight; suicide as magical revival or reunion; suicide as rebirth and restitution. A classification of suicidal types in terms of cognitive or logical styles has been proposed (Shneidman 1961). This classification, which stemmed from the logical analysis of suicide notes, divides the thinking styles of suicides into three types: logical, catalogical, and paleological.

Thus, in general, we see that the term "suicidal" is a broad one, starting from a base line of the individual who consciously and advertently takes his own life, through those individuals who by virtue of their unconscious mechanisms hasten their demise, through those individuals who indulge in partial or focal or chronic suicide, and perhaps even to those many individuals who by their own daily inimical acts truncate and diminish the full scope of their potential self-actualizations.

A concluding note concerning the current professional status of suicide prevention: Since 1955 there has been a marked spurt in interest in suicide prevention activities. In the United States, in 1958, there were 3 suicide prevention centers; in 1960, there were 5; in 1964, 9; in 1965, 15; and in 1967, 40. A Center for Studies of Suicide Prevention was established within the National Institute of Mental Health (NIMH) in 1966. A new multidisciplinary profession, *suicidology*—the scientific and humane study of human self-destruction—has come into being; special training courses in suicidology are offered at Johns Hopkins University.

EDWIN S. SHNEIDMAN

[*See also* DEATH. *Other relevant material may be found in* PSYCHOANALYSIS; SELF CONCEPT; MEDICAL CARE; *and in the biography of* DURKHEIM.]

BIBLIOGRAPHY
The bibliography for this article is combined with the bibliography of the article that follows.

III
PSYCHOLOGICAL ASPECTS (2)

The continuum of suicidal activity comprises total self-destruction (death); self-injury (but nonlethal), including crippling, maiming, painful and nonpainful activities; threats and other verbalized indications of intention toward self-destruction or self-injury; feelings of despair, depression, and unhappiness (which may not include thoughts of self-injury, but frequently do); and thoughts of separation, departure, absence, and relief and release. Somewhere within this continuum the thought or impulse becomes translated into action. The clinical impression is that once the psychological defenses against suicidal activity have been breached and the action has occurred, the possibility for further future acting out when emotional tension and strain recur is facilitated. It seems likely also that increasingly serious behavior results, possibly because of feelings of guilt or of feelings that such behavior is necessary in order to communicate with equivalent impact. The factor that determines the behavior remains puzzling. Perhaps the controls developed through coping mechanisms and defense patterns, brought to bear at different levels of dysfunctioning (Menninger 1963), play a crucial role, and the intensive study of these might provide the understanding necessary for suicide prevention for different individuals in various suicidal situations.

Characteristics of the suicidal person. The identification of the suicidal person is not especially difficult once the process has begun. Most persons considering self-destruction will identify themselves by communicating this tendency either behaviorally or verbally long before any specific act occurs. The typical suicidal person will generally reveal all or most of the following characteristics: (1) ambivalence—the desire, either conscious or unconscious or both, to live and to die, present at the same time; (2) feelings of hopelessness and helplessness, futility, and inadequacy to handle problems; (3) feelings of either physical or psychological exhaustion, or both; (4) marked feelings of unrelieved anxiety or tension, depression, anger, and/or guilt; (5) feelings of chaos and disorganization with inability to restore order; (6) mood swings, for example, from agitation to apathy or withdrawal; (7) cognitive constriction, inability to see alternatives, limitation of potentialities; (8) loss of interest in usual activities, such as sex, hobbies, and work; (9) physical distress, such as insomnia, anorexia, psychasthenia, and psychosomatic symptoms.

Prediction of lethal behavior. The more difficult problem is the evaluation of the suicidal person in terms of the relatively immediate potentiality of lethal acting out. The suicidal crisis presents the professional person with the need for quick appraisal. A schedule, evolved from experiences in the Suicide Prevention Center in Los Angeles, lists the following criteria used in evaluation of the emergency situation (see Litman & Farberow 1961). (1) Age and sex: older white males generally have the highest suicidal potentiality; a young female, on the other hand, is usually less lethally suicidal. (2) Suicidal plans: specificity about time, place, and method, plus the means for carrying out a plan, indicate high suicidal danger; vague, diffuse talk by a nonpsychotic about dying indicates that the situation is less serious. (3) Resources: external sources of support and interest, such as family, relatives, friends, physician, or hospital, are helpful; when the patient's resources are exhausted the suicidal potentiality rises. (4) Prior suicidal behavior: a past history of suicidal behavior indicates greater present danger, and the seriousness of the prior suicide attempt adds an additional important consideration. (5) Onset of suicidal behavior: the acute suicidal crisis may be more immediately serious but also more amenable to intervention. The chronically suicidal person, especially the alcoholic or borderline schizophrenic, who presents repeated feelings of depression, is the more serious long-term therapeutic problem. (6) The medical situation: many patients visit physicians with minor physical complaints which are in reality indications of severe depression. Studies (Motto & Greene 1958; Robins et al. 1959; Dorpat & Ripley 1960; and Shneidman & Farberow 1961) have indicated that more than 50 per cent of the patients who had committed suicide had seen their physicians within three months prior to their deaths. (7) Loss of a loved one: where death, separation, quarrel, or divorce from someone close has recently occurred, the suicidal potentiality is increased. (8) Communication: if communication still exists between the patient and others the suicidal risk is lowered; when the communication breaks and the person withdraws the danger increases. (9) Reaction of the referring person: if interest and concern about the patient continue, this is helpful. If, however, the referring person is angry, rejecting, and attempting to rid himself of responsibility, the potentiality is increased.

Psychological theories

The psychological theories have been summarized by Jackson (1957), who divided them roughly into nonpsychoanalytic and psychoanalytic.

Nonpsychoanalytic formulations. The nonpsychoanalytic formulations refer to "exhaustion" causing restriction of the field of consciousness so that an "organic depression" occurs; failure of adaptation; a disturbance of balance of will to live from a dynamic fixation of infantile attachment; infantile protest and hostility against harsh, restraining figures; narcissism in a rigid personality; compensations for homicidal impulses against members of the immediate family; and spite in children.

Psychoanalytic formulations. Most of the psychoanalytic theories stem from two of Freud's theoretical contributions: his elaboration of the dynamics of depression in *Mourning and Melancholia* (1917*b*) and his postulations of the death instinct in *Beyond the Pleasure Principle* (1920). Depression, and consequently suicide, occurs as a result of strong, aggressive urges directed against an introjected object formerly loved but now hated. Menninger (1938) adopts the concept of a death instinct and elaborates it by postulating three elements in suicide: a wish to kill, a wish to be killed, and a wish to die. Zilboorg (1936; 1937) considers suicide a way of thwarting outside forces and one method of gaining immortality. O'Connor (1948) adds the feeling that the person achieves omnipotence by a return to early power narcissism. Palmer (1941) suggests that arrested psychosexual development as a result of the unavailability of important figures at crucial stages is the basic mechanism. Garma (1943) stresses the loss of an important love object, suicide being used to recover it. Bergler (1946) describes the introjection suicide, aggression against guilt feelings; hysteric suicide, unconscious dramatization of how one does not want to be treated; and the miscellaneous type, such as paranoid schizophrenics reacting to voices. Farberow (1961), in the collection *The Cry for Help*, summarizes his contributors' several theoretical approaches to suicide. To the formulations already presented above, some of his contributors add frustrated dependency; longing for spiritual rebirth and seeking to re-establish contact with the self by destruction of the ego; strong inferiority feelings and veiled aggression in dependent individuals with "pampered life style"; a depressive, hateful type of personality structure developed from interpersonal experiences; alienation and feelings of disparity between idealized self and real self; and the person's attempts to validate his self according to his own "constructions."

Contributing factors

From the variety of theories and multitude of factors in suicide, it is apparent that suicidal phenomena are both widespread and complex. They reflect common sociological roots and influences and, at the same time, express singular personal experiences and impulses. A psychology of suicide must take as many such factors as possible into account if understanding is to be attained. A single schema encompassing the major factors which enter into the understanding of any suicidal event can, as yet, be only a desirable goal. The following factors are necessary considerations in any comprehensive overview of suicidal behavior.

Sociological background. It is obvious that any event needs to be viewed in the setting within which it occurs, but suicide especially has varying significance when it takes place in such widely different countries as, for example, Denmark, Italy, Japan, or the southern part of the United States. National differences are further compounded by racial, religious, and economic factors. Similarities and specific differences will be found. Studies of suicide in some of the tribes of east Africa (Bohannan 1960) and in aboriginal tribes of central India (Elwin 1943) have shown motives remarkably similar to those of Western cultures, for example, domestic strife or loss of social status, as well as features specific to these tribes, such as intervention by the gods or bewitchment by ghosts.

Fluctuations of economic status or the changing political scene influence suicide. For example, suicide has varied with economic depressions, as when the rate soared in the United States during the depression of the mid-1930s and dropped markedly during the war years of the 1940s. An investigation by Arkun (1963) of the suicide rates in Turkey during the periods from 1927 to 1946 (after sweeping social reforms) and 1950 to 1960 (after World War II) showed startling changes in rates which, during the earlier period, could be attributed to the upheavals in the culture of Turkey and especially to the change in the role of women because of the reforms of Ataturk. Japan's suicide rate has always been high; but whereas in ancient times the traditions of hara-kiri and sep-puku were prominent, today much of the suicide rate is contributed to by a younger age group, such as students in universities who are faced with failure or fear of it (Iga 1961).

Cultural background.   Cultures often surround death with taboos and rituals which illustrate feelings about death and dying and which include attitudes toward suicide. Myths and folklore illustrate some of the attitudes, as in the history of the Vikings and the tales of Valhalla, and contribute to the condemnation or condoning of suicide.

The culture may also determine interpersonal relationships that influence the occurrence of suicide. Hendin (1964) examines the "Scandinavian suicide phenomenon" and arrives at an explanation for the high suicide rates in Denmark and Sweden in contrast to those in Norway by a determination of the "psychosocial characteristics." Using psychoanalytic methods, he finds differences in the psychodynamic constellations of the three countries, such as in dependency aspects, attitudes toward performance and accomplishment, handling of aggression and guilt feelings, relationships between the sexes, methods of discipline, and other dynamic features.

Individual demographic characteristics.   Epidemiological aspects of suicide, such as age, sex, nationality, race, religion, marital status, education, financial status, have all been studied exhaustively for various countries (Dublin 1963). Where the individual falls in respect to each of these provides immediately invaluable information about the suicidal person. Important to include here also is the physical and mental status of the individual. A chronic, debilitating, or possibly fatal illness such as emphysema, cardiac disease, or cancer, or a recurrent mental illness which hospitalizes the individual for several months every two or three years will obviously influence the individual suicide (Farberow et al. 1963; Shneidman et al. 1962).

Psychological factors.   It is within the psychological factors that the core of the problem of understanding suicide is met. These factors include not only the current personality status and psychodynamic constellations of the individual in question but also the motivations for his suicidal behavior, the reasons why his actions, thoughts, or feelings lead him to suicide. The categorization of motivations into interpersonal and intrapersonal factors seems to offer a meaningful classification of many of the various phenomena. The distinction is arbitrary, of course, for it is practically impossible for a suicide to occur without both types of

relationships being involved. Nevertheless, one or the other aspect will often predominate.

Interpersonal motivations in suicide occur when the suicidal person attempts by his behavior either to bring about an action on the part of another person or persons or to effect a change in attitude or feeling within another person or persons, or both. The suicidal behavior can thus be seen as a means to influence, persuade, force, manipulate, stimulate, change, dominate, reinstate, etc., feelings or behavior in someone else. The other person is most often someone who has been in a close relationship, such as spouse, fiancée, or member of the family. Infrequently, the object of the behavior is more generalized, and it may be society itself.

Interpersonal motivations can be found, of course, in all ages but are usually predominant in the younger and middle-aged groups. A typical example is that of the girl between the ages of 20 and 25 who is reacting with strong feelings of rejection to a quarrel with a loved one or to divorce or separation. Her emotional state is one of agitation, dependency, immaturity, poor judgment, and impulsivity. Her suicidal behavior is used to express anger or feelings of rejection and to force a change in the rebuffing person or to arouse guilt feelings in him. Much of the behavior is still verbal, some is impulsive acting out, and most of it contains an "appeal" element (Stengel & Cook 1958).

Less often the aim is the expiation of or the need to express the guilt the person feels for having done something either imaginary or real in the relationship with another person. Ambivalence about dying is relatively low, inasmuch as the person, despite the fact that he is engaging in suicidal behavior, does not usually wish to die.

Intrapersonal motivations appear most often in older persons and thus in situations in which ties with others have dissipated. The individual's action seems aimed primarily at expressing the pressures and stresses from within and at fulfilling important needs in himself. The typical person is a male aged 60 or over who has recently suffered the death of a loved one, whose physical condition has deteriorated so that there is illness or pain, or whose children are married and so live their own separate lives. There are intense feelings of loneliness, feelings of not being needed any longer, of no longer being able to work effectively, perhaps because of physical condition, or of feeling that life has been lived and holds no more. The mood is often depressed, withdrawn, and physically and emotionally exhausted. There may be strong need for expiation and for atonement stemming from excessive feelings of guilt. An important dynamic is the need to maintain "psychological integrity" (Appelbaum 1963) or self-esteem or self-concept, even by the paradoxical act of self-destruction. Ambivalence is again low inasmuch as the person, if he embarks on a suicidal course, usually does so with full intent to die. [*See* AGING, *article on* PSYCHOLOGICAL ASPECTS.]

Some cases of suicide occur in which it is difficult to distinguish whether interpersonal or intrapersonal motivations are predominant. Rather it seems that each is equally present, although perhaps not always in the same strength at the same time. A typical example is a middle-aged person, the precipitating suicidal stimulus is the death of a loved one, separation, divorce, loss of job, loss of status, or sometimes a crippling, debilitating illness. Such a person is generally depressed, anxious, frustrated, and sometimes agitated, showing poor judgment and disorganization which will sometimes extend to psychotic or near-psychotic proportions. Marked symptoms of frustrated dependency, hostility, and aggression, perhaps because of rejection or masochism, and the two elements "appeal" and "ordeal" are readily seen (Stengel 1956). The ordeal element is especially apparent in the greater ambivalence about dying and the marked tendency to leave survival up to fate, destiny, or chance. Suicidal attempts are usually more lethal, but there are also more provisions for rescue, both conscious and unconscious.

Importance of work. Work takes on special significance for this group. Often with premature dissolution of relationships in the middle-aged group, work becomes the principal source of self-significance and self-esteem. The nonpersonal aspects of the work itself, rather than the people involved with whom interaction on the job occurs, become important. So long as the person is able to function in his job and to lose himself in its details, there is sufficient defense against suicidal impulses. For the very severely and chronically depressed person, work may provide a cover for the feeling of emptiness and void from which he is continually trying to escape. The routine of work keeps him busy and prevents him from thinking about himself. Not to work provides him with time during which he is free to think about himself and to feel useless and empty. Once the work is lost, perhaps through some personal difficulty, physical crisis, or enforced retirement, a crucial defense seems to be breached and suicidal impulses will burst through.

Can any suicide be entirely intrapersonal? One suggestion has been that this may occur only in the psychotic. However, the problem may well be only one of understanding on the part of the observer. The psychotic may be reacting entirely on an interpersonal basis but in a bizarre or devious process which simply is not comprehended by others.

Feelings about death and the afterlife. Most often the individual simply reflects the prevailing attitudes of his culture about suicide, death, or life after death. However, the individual may arrive at his own conceptualizations, which may vary markedly. Convictions of eternal peace after death, of the possibility of reunion with a deceased loved one, visions of hell-fire and brimstone, or of pain and unmitigated suffering, belief in the supernatural, or faith in magic may be key factors in an individual's suicidal behavior.

Communication. Seen as a communication process, suicidal behavior often achieves clearer perspective. In most instances, the suicidal activity occurs at the end of a long train of events that have finally led the person to the decision that life is no longer worth living. Accompanied by many communications along this course, the suicidal act itself then becomes a communication which may have many meanings and much significance. The communication in suicidal behavior can be grouped under five headings. (1) Form: the communication may be verbal, including written, or nonverbal and behavioral. (2) Directness or indirectness: the communication may be straightforward and clear, or disguised and indirect. Withdrawal, giving away prized possessions, remarks about not needing articles, fantasies of death, burial, or rescue from dangerous situations may occur. (3) Substance or content: the communication may contain expressions of affect, either fixing or expiating guilt or blame, explanations of the suicidal act, or instructions and directions to survivors, as in wills and suicide notes (Shneidman & Farberow 1957a; Tuckman et al. 1959). (4) Object of the communication: in most interpersonal situations, the communication is directed to a specific person or persons; in intrapersonal motivations it is more often directed to society in general. (5) Purpose: the communication may be overt or indirect in aim. Sometimes it is a cry for help, a plea to be stopped or to be rescued, a means for expression of hostility and hate, a final fixing of blame, a way to cause shame or arouse guilt, or a way to assume blame, absolve others, and expiate one's own guilt.

Countersuicidal controls

The factors that mitigate against suicide are as important as those that influence toward it. In many instances, the fact that self-destruction is not chosen as the way out of seemingly unbearable situations—as in the concentration camps of Germany, or when the individual is subject to continuous pain and discomfort in the terminal stages of cancer—impresses the observer. The controls may be external or internal.

External controls. External controls refer to all the controls that society may bring to bear on an individual to keep him conforming and alive, such as taboos, religion, myths, mores, group and subgroup identifications, marriage, family, children. Also significant are the actions of others toward the individual. Indications of support, understanding, interest, and concern, especially on the part of the "significant other" but also by hospital and professional personnel, may be the essential preventive factor.

Internal controls. Internal controls may stem from the ideals, standards, morality, conscience, or feelings of responsibility of the individual. In addition, the ego structure of the individual may provide him with flexibility, adaptability, independence, and feelings of self-esteem which will permit him to endure severe emotional stress. Or he may be more vulnerable because of rigidity, overdependence, and poor self-concept.

Psychology of the survivors

The suicide has great impact on the survivors, regardless of whether it had predominantly interpersonal or intrapersonal motives. These reactions generally vary directly in intensity with distance of relationship with the suicidal person. Among the group in a close relationship, the spouse, children, family, relatives, close friends, or therapist, a variety of feelings and reactions may be aroused. These may include (1) strong feelings of loss, accompanied by sorrow and mourning; (2) strong feelings of anger for (a) being made to feel responsible, or (b) being rejected in that what was offered was refused; (3) guilt, shame, or embarrassment with feelings of responsibility for the death; (4) feelings of failure or inadequacy that what was needed could not be supplied; (5) feelings of relief that the nagging, insistent demands have ceased; (6) feelings of having been deserted, especially true for children; (7) ambivalence, with a mixture of all the above; (8) reactions of doubt and self-questioning whether enough was attempted; (9) denial that a suicide has occurred, with a possible conspiracy of silence among all concerned; and (10) arousal of one's own impulses toward suicide.

Among those in a more distant relationship,

such as neighbors, employer or fellow employees, the hospital, or society, the reactions may also be those of (1) anger because of (a) a feeling that the suicidal person has rejected his social and moral responsibilities, or (b) being made to feel responsible, or (c) an implied accusation of not enough concern, interest, or caring about its members and fellow man; (2) guilt that not enough was offered to make the person want to live; (3) rejection, resulting from the suicidal person's obvious choice to do without them; and (4) uneasiness, manifested by a vague need for self-examination to determine what was wrong or to rationalize the discomfort away.

NORMAN L. FARBEROW

[See also DEATH. *Other relevant material may be found in* DEPRESSIVE DISORDERS; MEDICAL CARE; *and in the biography of* DURKHEIM.]

BIBLIOGRAPHY

APPELBAUM, STEPHEN A. 1963 The Problem-solving Aspect of Suicide. *Journal of Projective Techniques and Personality Assessment* 27:259–268.

ARKUN, NEZAHAT 1963 *Intiharin psikodinamikleri.* Istanbul (Turkey): Baha Matbaasi.

BERGLER, EDMUND 1946 Problems of Suicide. *Psychiatric Quarterly (Supplement)* 20:261–275.

BOHANNAN, PAUL (editor) 1960 *African Homicide and Suicide.* Princeton Univ. Press.

CURPHEY, THEODORE J. 1961 The Role of the Social Scientist in the Medicolegal Certification of Death from Suicide. Pages 110–117 in Norman L. Farberow and Edwin S. Shneidman (editors), *The Cry for Help.* New York: McGraw-Hill.

DORPAT, THEODORE L.; and RIPLEY, HERBERT S. 1960 A Study of Suicide in the Seattle Area. *Comprehensive Psychiatry* 1:349–359.

DUBLIN, LOUIS I. 1963 *Suicide: A Sociological and Statistical Study.* New York: Ronald.

DURKHEIM, ÉMILE (1897) 1951 *Suicide: A Study in Sociology.* Glencoe, Ill.: Free Press. → First published in French.

ELWIN, VERRIER 1943 *Maria Murder and Suicide.* Oxford Univ. Press.

FARBEROW, NORMAN L. 1961 Summary. Pages 290–321 in Norman L. Farberow and Edwin S. Shneidman (editors), *The Cry for Help.* New York: McGraw-Hill.

FARBEROW, NORMAN L.; and SHNEIDMAN, EDWIN S. (editors) 1961 *The Cry for Help.* New York: McGraw-Hill. → Contains a bibliography on suicide, 1897–1957, on pages 325–388.

FARBEROW, NORMAN L.; SHNEIDMAN, E. S.; and LEONARD, C. V. 1963 *Suicide Among General Medical and Surgical Hospital Patients with Malignant Neoplasms.* U.S. Veterans Administration, Medical Bulletin No. 9. Washington: Veterans Administration.

FARBEROW, NORMAN L. et al. 1966 Suicide Among Patients With Cardiorespiratory Illnesses. *Journal of the American Medical Association* 195:422–428.

FREUD, SIGMUND (1917a) 1959 The Psychogenesis of a Case of Homosexuality in a Woman. Volume 2, pages

202–231 in Sigmund Freud, *Collected Papers.* International Psycho-analytic Library, No. 10. London: Hogarth; New York: Basic Books.

FREUD, SIGMUND (1917*b*) 1959 Mourning and Melancholia. Volume 4, pages 152–170 in Sigmund Freud, *Collected Papers.* International Psycho-analytic Library, No. 10. London: Hogarth; New York: Basic Books. → Authorized translation from the German under the supervision of Joan Riviere. The first English edition was published in 1925.

FREUD, SIGMUND (1920) 1950 *Beyond the Pleasure Principle.* Authorized translation from the 2d ed., by C. J. M. Hubback. International Psycho-analytic Library, No. 4. New York: Liveright. → First published as *Jenseits des Lustprinzips.* A paperback edition, translated by James Strachey, was published in 1959 by Bantam Books.

GARMA, ANGEL (1943) 1944 Sadism and Masochism in Human Conduct: Part 2. *Journal of Clinical Psychopathology and Psychotherapy* 6:355–390. → First published in Spanish.

GENGERELLI, JOSEPH A.; and KIRKNER, FRANK J. (editors) 1954 *The Psychological Variables in Human Cancer.* A symposium presented at the Veterans Administration Hospital, Long Beach, California, October 23, 1953. Berkeley: Univ. of California Press.

HALBWACHS, MAURICE 1930 *Les causes du suicide.* Paris: Alcan.

HENDIN, HERBERT M. 1964 *Suicide and Scandinavia: A Psychoanalytic Study of Culture and Character.* New York: Grune.

IGA, MAMORU 1961 Cultural Factors in Suicide of Japanese Youth With Focus on Personality. *Sociology and Social Research* 46:75–90.

JACKSON, DON D. 1957 Theories of Suicide. Pages 17–21 in Edwin S. Shneidman and Norman L. Farberow (editors), *Clues to Suicide.* New York: McGraw-Hill.

KUBIE, LAWRENCE S. 1964 Multiple Determinants of Suicidal Efforts. *Journal of Nervous and Mental Disease* 138:3–8.

LITMAN, ROBERT E. 1967 Sigmund Freud on Suicide. Unpublished manuscript.

LITMAN, ROBERT E.; and FARBEROW, NORMAN L. 1961 Emergency Evaluation of Self-destructive Potentiality. Pages 48–59 in Norman L. Farberow and Edwin S. Shneidman (editors), *The Cry for Help.* New York: McGraw-Hill.

LITMAN, ROBERT E. et al. 1963 Investigations of Equivocal Suicides. *Journal of the American Medical Association* 184:924–929.

MACDONALD, JOHN M. 1961 *The Murderer and His Victim.* Springfield, Ill.: Thomas.

MENNINGER, KARL A. 1938 *Man Against Himself.* New York: Harcourt.

MENNINGER, KARL A. 1963 *The Vital Balance: The Life Process in Mental Health and Illness.* New York: Viking.

MOTTO, JEROME A.; and GREENE, CLARA 1958 Suicide and the Medical Community. *Archives of Neurology and Psychiatry* 80:776–781.

NATIONAL INSTITUTE OF MENTAL HEALTH *Bulletin of Suicidology.* → Published since 1967.

O'CONNOR, WILLIAM A. 1948 Some Notes on Suicide. *British Journal of Medical Psychology* 21:222–228.

PALMER, D. M. 1941 Factors in Suicide Attempts: Review of 25 Consecutive Cases. *Journal of Nervous and Mental Disease* 93:421–442.

RIDOUT, AILEEN B. 1962 Suicide as a Factor in Public Health. *Journal of the Royal Institute of Public Health and Hygiene* 25:115–128.

ROBINS, ELI et al. 1959 The Communication of Suicidal Intent: A Study of 134 Consecutive Cases of Successful (Completed) Suicide. *American Journal of Psychiatry* 115:724–773.

SAINSBURY, PETER 1955 *Suicide in London: An Ecological Study.* London: Chapman. → A paperback edition was published in 1956 by Basic Books.

SHNEIDMAN, EDWIN S. 1961 Psycho-logic: A Personality Approach to Patterns of Thinking. Pages 153–190 in Conference on Contemporary Issues in Thematic Apperceptive Methods, Fels Research Institute, 1959, *Contemporary Issues in Thematic Apperceptive Methods.* Edited by Jerome Kagan and Gerald S. Lesser. Springfield, Ill.: Thomas.

SHNEIDMAN, EDWIN S. 1963 Orientations Toward Death: A Vital Aspect of the Study of Lives. Pages 200–227 in Robert W. White (editor), *The Study of Lives: Essays on Personality in Honor of Henry A. Murray.* New York: Atherton.

SHNEIDMAN, EDWIN S. 1964 Suicide, Sleep, and Death: Some Possible Interrelations Among Cessation, Interruption, and Continuation Phenomena. *Journal of Consulting Psychology* 28:95–106.

SHNEIDMAN, EDWIN S. (editor) 1967 *Essays in Self Destruction.* New York: International Science Press.

SHNEIDMAN, EDWIN S.; and FARBEROW, NORMAN L. (editors) 1957*a* *Clues to Suicide.* New York: McGraw-Hill.

SHNEIDMAN, EDWIN S.; and FARBEROW, NORMAN L. 1957*b* Some Comparisons Between Genuine and Simulated Suicide Notes in Terms of Mowrer's Concepts of Discomfort and Relief. *Journal of General Psychology* 56:251–256.

SHNEIDMAN, EDWIN S.; and FARBEROW, NORMAN L. 1960 A Socio-psychological Investigation of Suicide. Pages 270–293 in Henry P. David and J. C. Brengelmann (editors), *Perspectives in Personality Research.* New York: Springer.

SHNEIDMAN, EDWIN S.; and FARBEROW, NORMAN L. 1961 Statistical Comparisons Between Attempted and Committed Suicides. Pages 19–47 in Norman L. Farberow and Edwin S. Shneidman (editors), *The Cry for Help.* New York: McGraw-Hill.

SHNEIDMAN, EDWIN S.; FARBEROW, NORMAN L.; and LEONARD, C. V. 1962 *Suicide: Evaluation and Treatment of Suicidal Risk Among Schizophrenic Patients in Psychiatric Hospitals.* U.S. Veterans Administration, Medical Bulletin No. 8. Washington: Veterans Administration.

STENGEL, ERWIN 1956 The Social Effects of Attempted Suicide. *Journal of the Canadian Medical Association* 74:116–120.

STENGEL, ERWIN; and COOK, NANCY G. 1958 *Attempted Suicide: Its Social Significance and Effects.* London: Chapman.

TABACHNICK, NORMAN D.; and FARBEROW, NORMAN L. 1961 The Assessment of Self-destructive Potentiality. Pages 60–77 in Norman L. Farberow and Edwin S. Shneidman (editors), *The Cry for Help.* New York: McGraw-Hill.

TUCKMAN, JACOB; KLEINER, R. J.; and LAVELL, M. 1959 Emotional Content of Suicide Notes. *American Journal of Psychiatry* 116:59–63.

WEISMAN, AVERY D.; and HACKETT, THOMAS P. 1961

Predilection to Death: Death and Dying as a Psychiatric Problem. *Psychosomatic Medicine* 23:232–256.

WEISS, JAMES M. A. 1957 The Gamble With Death in Attempted Suicide. *Psychiatry* 20:17–25.

WESTERMARCK, EDWARD A. (1906–1908) 1924–1926 *The Origin and Development of the Moral Ideas.* 2d ed. 2 vols. London: Macmillan.

WOLFGANG, MARVIN E. 1959 Suicide by Means of Victim-precipitated Homicide. *Journal of Clinical and Experimental Psychopathology and Quarterly Review of Psychiatry and Neurology* 20:335–349.

ZILBOORG, GREGORY 1936 Suicide Among Civilized and Primitive Races. *American Journal of Psychiatry* 92:1347–1369.

ZILBOORG, GREGORY 1937 Considerations in Suicide, With Particular Reference to That of the Young. *American Journal of Orthopsychiatry* 7:15–31.

SULLIVAN, HARRY STACK

I. LIFE AND WORK   *Alfred H. Stanton*
II. INTERPERSONAL THEORY   *Patrick Mullahy*

I
LIFE AND WORK

Harry Stack Sullivan (1892–1949), American psychiatrist, who conceived of psychiatry as the study of interpersonal relations, was born in Norwich, New York, into an Irish Catholic home. Little information is available about his early life. He was the only surviving child of a shy and retiring farmer and his partially invalid wife. A lonely child, he had serious difficulties learning how to get along with other children at school, and for many years his only friends were the animals on the farm. He often spoke of the drastic reorganization of his personality during adolescence, but nothing more specific is known. He attended the Chicago College of Medicine and Surgery and, after receiving his M.D. in 1917, worked as a civilian with the U.S. Army during World War I. In 1922 he became a liaison officer for the Veterans Administration at Saint Elizabeths Hospital in Washington. He had learned something about psychoanalysis as a medical student, but it was at Saint Elizabeths that he first encountered psychiatry as a specialty and developed his long-standing interest in schizophrenic patients.

Saint Elizabeths Hospital was a major center of psychiatric activity. William Alanson White had introduced many new treatments there—in particular, the application of Freud's psychoanalytic principles to the diagnosis and treatment of hospital patients. White's influence on Sullivan was profound and freely recognized by Sullivan throughout his life, but Smith Ely Jelliffe, Edward J. Kempff,

Ernest Hadley, and others also helped to make the hospital a center for the attempt to reorganize psychiatric thought and practice on psychoanalytic and psychological principles. While Sullivan's duties were only those of a consultant, he had diagnostic interviews with a large number of schizophrenic patients, and his ability to reach patients who had been thought beyond contact was soon recognized. He became progressively convinced that the interviews he had as a consultant had important effects upon the patient and could not, therefore, be sharply distinguished from treatment.

Sullivan's approach to psychiatry led to his moving to Sheppard and Enoch Pratt Hospital near Baltimore. He also attended staff conferences at the neighboring Johns Hopkins University's Phipps Clinic and, thus, came to know Adolf Meyer and his group, notably Clara Thompson. He was assistant physician at Sheppard Pratt from 1923 to 1925 and then became director of clinical research, a position he held until 1930. This position gave him the opportunity for the detailed study of schizophrenic patients that was needed if the patients were to be understood regularly in "human" terms. With detailed records on several hundred patients, he demonstrated that even the most disturbed patients do not develop any type of symbol activity that is entirely outside the realm of the human, no matter how bizarre it may appear to be; it is, therefore, never impossible to understand the patient in some sense if sufficient contact with him is possible. This is important because many people respond intuitively to much of schizophrenic behavior as if it were *not* human.

Sullivan was strongly influenced by psychoanalytic studies of schizophrenic patients but always related psychoanalytic interpretations to the broader concepts developed by nonpsychoanalytic psychiatrists. A most important influence was the work of Adolf Meyer—above all, his early work. Sullivan noted with approval Meyer's insistence that "mental illnesses" could be profitably considered "reaction types" to situations confronting the patient. If the biography of the patient were fully known, it would explain much of his pathological reaction. In a paper from this period, Sullivan identified the so-called conservative aspects of early schizophrenia as "*attempts by regression* to genetically older thought processes . . . *successfully to reintegrate masses of life experience* which had failed of structuralization into a functional unity, and finally lead by that very lack of structuralization to multiple dissociations in the field of relationship of the individual not only to external reality, including the social milieu, but to his personal reality" (1924, p. 24).

The concept of "illness" as a problem-solving effort became intrinsic to his whole work; he considered the more static descriptions of Eugen Bleuler, Emil Kraepelin, and John T. MacCurdey to be clinically sterile in comparison with dynamic formulations that recognize a teleological aspect to the disturbance. His clinical observations led him to emphasize the existence not only of the conserving aim but of the frequent conserving effect of a schizophrenic episode. In contrast to the usual view at that time—that nearly all such patients were damaged, if they recovered at all—he mentioned patients who were more competent after the episode than before and undertook a number of studies to try to identify the factors responsible. One of Sullivan's characteristic conclusions was that the patient's own appraisal of his circumstances—his foreseeable future, as it were—was a major contributing factor to the outcome of a psychotic episode.

During much of the period of his study of patients at Sheppard Pratt, Sullivan lived on the grounds, and he made his home available to all his co-workers for discussions of clinical problems. These discussions made him progressively more aware that the interactions of the patient with other persons is a primary determinant of the outcome of his "effort to reintegrate masses of life experience." This led in 1929 to his organizing a special admission ward for young male schizophrenic patients that would function almost independently of the rest of the hospital and depart from its customary practices. He selected his staff with great care, with a preference for candidates who had experienced psychological disturbances similar to those of the patients. All staff members were men—no women were allowed on the ward. Sullivan not only had frequently lengthy informal interviews with the patients but also talked freely and informally with the staff, often in the evenings at his home. This type of indirect intervention was based upon a number of newly developed views—a recognition of the potential benefits to be gained when persons with similar backgrounds share their experience and of the therapeutic import of human interactions other than the patient's interview with the psychiatrist. Although the experience of the ward was never analyzed systematically, the outcomes for the patients were extraordinarily favorable. They continued to be favorable under William Silverberg, Sullivan's successor (Sullivan 1931a, p. 290).

Sullivan did not by any means work in intellec-tual isolation. As these experiences with therapy led him to recognize the importance of interpersonal relations, he turned freely to social scientists for help. In particular, he came to know, and often to work with, Lawrence K. Frank, W. I. Thomas, Ruth Benedict, Harold D. Lasswell, and Edward Sapir. He was instrumental in organizing two influential national colloquia on personality investigation, which explicitly recognized the need for collaboration between the social sciences and psychiatry in developing the study of personality. He asserted the view that psychiatry *is* the study of interpersonal relations, a discipline *sui generis,* synonymous in a sense with social psychology, and that the concepts of personality and of its structure are, in effect, working hypotheses that account for the interpersonal relations that constitute the core material of the psychiatrist's useful observations. Personality and its disorders manifest themselves only in interpersonal relations, and it is by the psychiatrist's participant observation of his patient in such relationships that he does his clinical and scientific work (Sullivan 1938, pp. 32–33). Psychiatry then is a *social* science (regardless of what its practitioners may think), and recognition of this prevents many common misconceptions.

Sullivan moved to New York in 1930; there he turned his attention to the obsessive disorders and collaborated with Sapir, the linguist and cultural anthropologist. Sapir organized a highly significant seminar in culture and personality at Yale in 1932 and 1933, to which Sullivan made important contributions. Many prominent social scientists who later studied culture and personality trace their interest, in large part, to this seminar. The depression and financial pressures forced Sullivan to move back to Washington around 1933.

The years which immediately followed were less productive ones for Sullivan. He finished and rewrote a book-length manuscript, but it did not satisfy him; it did not proceed from the clearly interpersonal approach he had adopted by this time and which he was to elaborate in his later writings. (The manuscript was never published.) He devoted much of his time to teaching, largely by the individual supervision of practitioners, an art in which he excelled.

In 1933 he took part in founding the William Alanson White Foundation, with branches in Washington and New York. The establishment of the Washington School of Psychiatry and of the journal *Psychiatry* followed later, in 1936 and 1938, respectively. The journal, of which he was the editor, quickly became a leading organ for reporting on the growing body of work on interpersonal relations. The school, then temporarily in a short-lived, unhappy partnership with the Washington–Baltimore Psychoanalytic Institute, soon took the leadership in developing both teaching and research in the field. Lasswell was very active in the school for a short time, before the demands of the impending war forced his withdrawal. Several highly experienced psychiatrists and psychoanalysts gave great strength to the school and the journal. During these years, Sullivan also worked on a joint research project with Charles Johnson at Fiske University and collaborated with Dexter Bullard and his staff at Chestnut Lodge Sanitarium.

Sullivan had taught almost continuously after going to Sheppard Pratt in 1923—at the University of Maryland School of Medicine, at Yale, and for a short time at the Georgetown School of Medicine—as well as doing a great deal of graduate psychiatric teaching and supervision, but it was at the Washington School that his educational abilities were to flower. A relatively full presentation of his psychiatric formulations was delivered as the first William Alanson White Lectures of the school, which were later published (William Alanson White Association 1952). Only the students in the lecture courses he gave at the school had the opportunity to hear him develop these formulations further. The generalizations he made on the basis of his clinical observation were made explicit in a series of brilliant clinical discussions held (and recorded) for some years at Chestnut Lodge. In spite of his untimely death, these materials were sufficiently developed to provide a reasonably reliable statement of his views (1953; 1954; 1956).

Sullivan was very active as a consultant to the chief of the Selective Service before, and at the time of, the entry of the United States into World War II. Only after the war, however, did he become fully involved in broader fields of public affairs. He characteristically called for a "remobilization for enduring peace and social progress." Since the newly organized World Health Organization did not represent psychiatrists, Sullivan was active in helping to create the World Federation for Mental Health; he served on the preparatory commission which led to its foundation and which ensured the inclusion in it of other social and behavioral scientists. The newly organized United Nations Educational, Scientific, and Cultural Organization asked him to take part in what was to be an influential discussion of tensions which cause wars; he later continued as a consultant to UNESCO. But these activities did not prevent him from producing a stream of theoretical, analytical, and expository papers on the subject of his interpersonal theories. When he died suddenly in Paris, on a consultation, he left a mass of unpublished but relatively finished work which contains some of his most developed thought.

Sullivan never married; however, while in Baltimore he took James Sullivan into his home to live with him as an adopted son. His friendships were many, deep, and lasting and were usually intellectually productive. Yet, gifted with a trenchant, often ironic wit and not disposed to compromise, he also earned his full share of professional enemies. His love of music provided him with such relaxation as came his way; combined with an ability in physics, this love of music led to an early and lasting interest in electronics and recordings. He put this interest to use in his professional work, being among the first to try to record psychiatric interviews. He was also interested in experimental plant breeding and in horses and dogs. In his personal affairs, he was likely to be thoroughly impractical and at times became dependent on his friends. But personal difficulties would deter him only momentarily from developing a program or organizing a meeting whose necessity he had noted.

He was plagued almost throughout his adult life by poor health, suffering from heart disease, which twice was nearly fatal; the discovery of penicillin enabled him to live his last six, most productive years. His death was the result of a massive apoplexy. Although his thought led him far from his childhood beliefs, it was at his own request that he was buried with a Roman Catholic military service.

ALFRED H. STANTON

[*For the historical context of Sullivan's work, see* PSYCHIATRY; PSYCHOANALYSIS, *article on* CLASSICAL THEORY; *and the biographies of* BENEDICT; KRAEPELIN; MEYER; SAPIR; THOMAS. *For discussions relevant to Sullivan's ideas, see* PSYCHOANALYSIS, *article on* EGO PSYCHOLOGY; SCHIZOPHRENIA; *and the biography of* HORNEY.]

BIBLIOGRAPHY

The bibliography for this article is combined with the bibliography of the article that follows.

II

INTERPERSONAL THEORY

Harry Stack Sullivan is known primarily for his theory of interpersonal relations, though he is also well known for his system of psychotherapy, to which it is closely related. Essentially, Sullivan's theory holds that human experience primarily consists of interactions or transactions between people, whether the people are real, imaginary (as in many dreams and psychotic experiences), or a blend of both the real and imaginary. Thus, Sullivan's theory tends to merge with social psychology except that it emphasizes problems which are connected with psychotherapy. He rejected individual psychology (the psychology of individual differences) partly because he thought that individuality cannot be scientifically understood, since no individual can be understood apart from his relationships with others. However, in a given sociocultural context, what a person has "in common" with others, as it is manifested or made manifest in behavior, can be the object of scientific investigation. Sullivan did not profess to know the extent to which human behavior embodies principles or laws which transcend any given sociocultural setting. If there are such principles of human behavior, they appear to be as yet little understood, if at all.

Sullivan's intellectual heritage included Freudian psychoanalysis, the psychiatry of Adolf Meyer, and American social psychology going back to Charles Horton Cooley. Such anthropologists as Edward Sapir and Ruth Benedict also exerted some influence on his thinking, though it seems to have been exaggerated. [*See the biographies of* COOLEY *and* MEYER.]

While Sullivan did not emphasize biological determinants—perhaps in reaction to Freud—his theory leaves room for them logically. He asserted that there are four generic factors which enter into, and have a causative influence on, any act: biological potentiality, maturation, the "results" of previous experience, and foresight. However, it should be added that no one yet knows how much weight should be given to biological determinants.

Continuous effects of experience. It is hardly an exaggeration to say that an individual's history influences every moment of his life, for it provides a dynamic structure and definition for his experiences. Since interpersonal relations begin at birth and are normally significantly correlated with the orderly sequence of biological maturation, Sullivan held that a thorough understanding of people's interpersonal relations requires an understanding of the development of their personalities, as well as a study of their present relationships. It must be stressed that for Sullivan, personality development is primarily the ever-increasing elaboration and modification of the individual's social relations in connection with the demands, limitations, and opportunities of his society. However, he did not agree with Freud that the basic structure of personality is laid down during the first five years of a person's life. Personality structure takes fifteen or twenty, or even more than twenty, years for its essential development, depending partly on sociocultural conditions and partly on the idiosyncrasies of each individual's career. Favorable or unfavorable influences may significantly modify development at any of the "eras," or stages of development, which Sullivan distinguished. The quality and kind of interpersonal relations that one experiences in the home, school, playground, summer camp, and neighborhood are crucially important. But in human life there is nothing static. Everything changes. Some things change quickly; others, slowly and imperceptibly, although the latter too can have a cumulative effect. Hence, significant personality change, for better or for worse, can occur at any time in life, depending to a great extent on the nature and course of one's social life —on one's interpersonal relations. Therefore, from a Sullivanian point of view, social structure and social change, as they are encountered directly as well as indirectly, are very significant in an individual's life experience. [*See* PERSONALITY, *article on* PERSONALITY DEVELOPMENT.]

The development of the self

It is largely by means of the self that the limitations, facilitations, and opportunities of a society are mediated in personality. The self begins to develop in late infancy and grows through several stages—namely, infancy, childhood, the juvenile era, preadolescence, early adolescence, and late adolescence, normally culminating in maturity. But, these stages of development are not instinctually determined. Sullivan's formulations held that before one can enter into any stage (except the first) in the normal course of development, one must have successfully "negotiated" the previous stage, for an arresting of development, due to environmental circumstances, can occur at any era and gravely handicap further growth. For such reasons, there are many "chronically juvenile" people who are chronologically adult.

Infancy. The first two stages are normally lived through in the home under the supervision of authoritative adults, on whom the powerless offspring depends not only for his physical survival but also for the necessities of psychological development. As Sullivan said, the mother or mothering one ("mother surrogate") provides the basic patterns of being human. For example, an infant's activities arising from the tension of needs are said to induce a certain tension in the mothering one, experienced by her (or him) as tenderness and as an impulsion to activities more or less suited to the relief of the infant's needs. In the course of time, the manifest activities of the mothering one toward the relief of the infant's needs come to be experienced by him as tender behavior. Thus, the needs of the infant, whose satisfaction requires the cooperation of the mothering one, take on the character of a general need for tenderness. Sullivan claimed that the need for tender behavior is an interpersonal need because its fulfillment requires the cooperation of another person who has a complementary need to manifest appropriate activity, a need to behave tenderly. [See AFFECTION; INFANCY.]

Empathy. It is not clear in Sullivan's later work just how the tender attitude of the mothering one is communicated to the infant long before he can grasp the meaning of her behavior. In earlier lectures (1940–1945), he maintained that empathy, an as yet not understood mode of emotional contagion or communion between infant and mothering one, is the vehicle by which approving and disapproving attitudes are somehow conveyed, from ages 6 to 27 months. In later lectures (*The Interpersonal Theory of Psychiatry* 1953) Sullivan maintained that it is by means of empathy that anxiety is induced in the infant when the mothering one is anxious or otherwise upset or disapproving. The infant's experiences of anxiety and his gradually developing power to distinguish between increasing and diminishing anxiety serve to canalize his behavior in various ways because he strives to avoid anxiety. Thus, as Leon Salzman (1962) has pointed out, Sullivan thought that anxiety is the "mainspring" of all human development. The self or self-dynamism develops in order to avoid or minimize anxiety and gain approval from the significant adults, who embody various cultural attitudes and values. [See SYMPATHY AND EMPATHY.]

Childhood. Childhood begins with the development of language—that is, the capacity for articulate speech, a development of several years' duration. Since language is a very powerful tool for communication, it contributes greatly to the development of the self. From early childhood, the social responsibility experienced by the mothering one brings about an alteration of tender behavior because of the necessity of "training" and educating the child along socially approved or permissible lines. Thus, certain behaviors of the child that were previously tolerated are now so strongly disapproved of that they become inhibited, sublimated, or, in some instances, dissociated (i.e., functionally split off from the developing self-dynamism).

The juvenile era. The juvenile era appears upon the maturation of the need for compeers. According to Sullivan, it is the time for becoming "social." For the first time, limitations and peculiarities of the home are open to remedy by the school and by the society of one's peers. Schooling is a wholly necessary experience for anyone growing up in a complex industrial society. The school not only imparts skills and subject matters but also, as a rule, provides the youngster with a broader outlook on life.

During the juvenile era, one begins to acquire supervisory patterns of the self, which pertain not only to moral conduct but to behavior generally. These supervisory patterns, developed in connection with authoritative figures in the home, school, and church, tend to make the juvenile more self-critical. Normally, there is a considerable elaboration of the self. The youngster learns patterns of cooperation, competition, and compromise.

Preadolescence. Preadolescence extends roughly from $8\frac{1}{2}$ to 12 years of age. During this era, the capacity to love matures: a relationship in which the satisfactions and security of another person, a "chum," a member of one's own sex, are as important to one as one's own satisfactions and security. The intimacy which flowers between the two chums has essentially nothing to do with sex. Preadolescence is *not* a homosexual stage. The preadolescent relationship encourages the "consensual validation" of personal experiences. For the first time, one can communicate freely with another human being. In the process of communication, personal inadequacies carried over from previous stages may be alleviated or overcome. [See IDENTITY, PSYCHOSOCIAL.]

Adolescence and late adolescence. In Western society, adolescence is a notoriously difficult period for many people. New adjustments have to be accomplished; new relationships, for which there is no precedent in personal experience, have to be established; and one is expected to put away childish things once and for all. So, adolescence is a time of trial and of opportunity. Many people who have developed various inadequacies during the previous eras founder in adolescence because they cannot handle the new demands and opportunities that life presents at this time. Early adolescence is the period from the "eruption" of true genital interest, experienced as lust, to the patterning of sexual behavior. Normally, there is a change in the type of object needed for the intimacy, previously experienced, during preadolescence, with a chum or close friend. The change is influenced by the concomitant maturation of the genital lust dynamism. There is a movement of interest toward members of the opposite sex.

In Sullivan's formulation, late adolescence extends from the patterning of preferred genital activity to the establishment of a fully human repertory of interpersonal relations—both personal and social—insofar as opportunity permits. For a great many warped, immature people, the failure to achieve late adolescence is the "last blow," the culminating defeat. [*See* ADOLESCENCE.]

The functions of the self system

It is self-system functions which prevent many people from getting very far in late adolescence. The self, which comes into being largely in order to protect or enhance one's security, normally operates according to the structure and direction it has acquired progressively during the eras of development. It provides a framework for one's experiences. The problems of adolescents are manifested as inadequate and inappropriate personifications of the self—that is, as warped "self concepts"; adolescents are unable to grasp the fact that their personifications of themselves are distorted, because any tendency to gain insight stirs up anxiety when, otherwise, the incongruity and inappropriateness of situations might be evident. Since no one can transcend his own experiences, no one with an inadequate personification of himself can perceive others with any particular refinement except in terms of his own personification and imagined criticisms of himself. These limitations ensure an inadequate grasp of what others are like. A person's conceptions of others tend to be stereotypes, embodying prejudices, intolerances, fears, hatreds, aversions, and revulsions, which are sometimes compensated for by spurious idealizations of others. Security operations ("defense mechanisms") are employed extensively. [*See* DEFENSE MECHANISMS; SELF CONCEPT.]

Maturity. Sullivan held that the difference between the normal and the mentally ill is one of degree only. But, in a mature person, the outstanding achievements of each of the developmental eras will be manifested. He will, for example, have the ability to relate intimately with another person or persons. He will have insight into the needs which customarily characterize one's interpersonal relations, the circumstances appropriate to their satisfaction, and the more or less remote goals for whose attainments one will forgo current opportunities for satisfaction or for the enhancement of one's prestige.

In Sullivan's lectures, there seems to be too much emphasis on the restrictive functions of the self. His work with patients appears to have led him to a too limited and rigidly deterministic view of the entire personality. His theory does not leave enough room for growth and independence, although it can be rectified without being abandoned.

Anxiety. Anxiety is a central explanatory concept in interpersonal theory. Operationally, any felt threat to self-esteem constitutes anxiety or, more generally, any felt threat to one's emotional well-being or interpersonal security. Anxiety arises and operates only in interpersonal relations. It is the motivating force of selective inattention, a process whereby one inadequately perceives or grasps relevant factors in many situations and, thereby, often fails to profit from experience. Selective inattention is a function of the self. [*See* ANXIETY.]

Modes of experience. A knowledge of Sullivan's ideas on the three "modes of experience" provides a better grasp of his theory. As the self begins to develop, it tends to restrict and channel awareness, which is manifested soon after birth. This awareness is apparently of a very diffuse, unstructured kind, presumably quite different in many ways from the consciousness of adults, lacking the attributes of self-consciousness and the controls over awareness exercised by the supervisory patterns of the self.

Prototaxic mode. Some psychologists regard the period from birth to about 1½ years of age as the "sensorimotor stage," wherein the infant receives impressions and reacts without the intervention of a mediating self. Hence, there is no distinction between the self and the external world. Piaget called this state of affairs an undifferentiated absolute of self and environment (Allport 1961, p. 112). [*See* DEVELOPMENTAL PSYCHOLOGY, *article on* A THEORY OF DEVELOPMENT; SENSORY AND MOTOR DEVELOPMENT.]

Sullivan's notion of the prototaxic, or "primitive," mode of experience is similar but more elaborate. It forms the basis of memory (retention), although it ordinarily defies formulation and hence, discussion. The infant has not yet learned how to differentiate and categorize experience. Thus, distinctions in terms of "now," "before," "after," "here," "there," "I," "you," etc., are lacking. Of course, he undergoes and registers experience, perhaps from moment to moment, but he is apparently unable to discriminate the order of events impinging on his senses. Sullivan thought that all the infant "knows" are momentary states, merging and vanishing like raindrops into the vast reservoir of memory. He may register earlier and later states but without discerning any serial connection between them. The alternation of need and satisfaction is first experienced in the prototaxic mode. But, within the flux of experience, the infant gradually "prehends" or registers a recurrent pattern of events—such as the nipple–lips sequence—which serves as a sign that the state called satisfaction is about to supervene. Sullivan inferred that anxiety tension also is first experienced in the prototaxic mode.

The prototaxic mode is not confined to infancy. Sullivan "presumed" that from the beginning to the end of life individuals continue to undergo these momentary prototaxic experiences (1953). If Sullivan's assumption is valid, it may be that all differentiated experiences occur in connection with, and rest on, the prototaxic mode. He thought that some dream processes, certain schizophrenic episodes in which he held that the person's experiences are "cosmic," and perhaps some experiences that are classed as mystical occur in the prototaxic mode (personal communication to the writer in 1945).

Parataxic mode. With increasing maturation and learning, the infant gradually begins to make some discrimination between himself and the world. He learns to make elementary discriminations in his experience. Thus, the original global experience is sundered into parts or various, diverse aspects, which, however, are not logically connected. They may, or may not, occur together, depending on circumstances. In the language of traditional psychology, the sundered or disconnected aspects of experience may become associated when circumstances (categorized in terms of laws of association) permit. These "elements" of experience are lived or perceived as concomitant but not yet (if ever) recognized as being connected or related in any sort of orderly fashion; this is experience in the parataxic mode. The youngster, because of his limited store of experience and knowledge, takes this mode for granted and, in a manner of speaking, as the natural way of things.

Suppose a youngster is beaten or otherwise mistreated by his mother for no evident cause—a not too rare occurrence. And suppose further that shortly after, the youngster is subjected to "sweetness and light" and "love," also without evident cause. Let us assume that the mother is a bit immature and "neurotic" and that this sequence of behavior is a common occurrence. To an intelligent adult observer her behavior is inconsistent—is, in fact, senseless in relation to the proper upbringing of a child. To the youngster, there is no inconsistency. That is the way things happen; that is the way life is, although the child may wish things

were different or try to circumvent them. While this illustration may seem oversimplified, it is essentially the sort of thing that happens in countless homes where one or both parents are immature and, perhaps, anxiety-ridden or otherwise disturbed. A recurrent pattern of this sort will often be assimilated by the child into his developing self system. Thus, the child may for years experience the incongruous and irrational behavior of his parents without ever questioning it. Furthermore, even in more normal homes, children are subjected to various kinds of irrational behavior, chiefly because the parents reflect the inadequacies, prejudices, and superstitions, as well as the virtues, of their sociocultural background. The life of almost any person is inextricably bound up with the social order of which he is a member.

Selective inattention, which, as suggested above, often makes it difficult to profit from experience, including formal education, occurs in the parataxic mode. Illusory me–you patterns, or "parataxic distortions," occur in the parataxic mode; they often manifest themselves in our dealings with strangers, with acquaintances, perhaps with friends, and certainly in "romantic" attachments, in which the partners often sustain a great many illusions about each other, as well as in disturbed marital relationships. Often, it is anxiety which stimulates these distorted perceptions. But, experience in the parataxic mode also is often a normal occurrence. Much of our living and talking is carried on in this mode.

Syntaxic mode. In the main, any experience that one can discuss occurs in either the parataxic or syntaxic mode. The syntaxic mode begins to appear at the end of infancy or the beginning of childhood and involves an appeal to principles that are accepted as true by the hearer—what Sullivan calls consensual validation. "A consensus has been reached," he says, "when the infant or child has learned the precisely right word for a situation, a word which means not only what it is thought to mean by the mothering one, but also means that to the infant" (1953, pp. 183–184). Summarily, what distinguishes syntaxic operations from everything else that occurs between people is that under appropriate circumstances, they can work quite precisely.

Assumptions underlying Sullivan's theory

In order to round out this outline of Sullivan's theory, I wish to point out certain assumptions underlying his theory. First, any living organism may be "considered" in relation to three ultimate factors: its "communal" existence with a necessary environing medium, its organization, and its functional activity. By and large, while Sullivan recognized the communal existence of man at all levels (physical, biological, psychological, sociocultural), he stressed the psychological and sociocultural levels. In regard to organization, the smallest useful abstraction in the study of the human being is the "dynamism," defined as "the relatively enduring pattern of energy transformations which recurrently characterize the organism in its duration as a living organism" (1953, p. 103). Personality may be conceived as a network of dynamisms hierarchically arranged. Sullivan held that the dynamisms of interest to the psychiatrist are the relatively enduring patterns of energy transformations which recurrently characterize interpersonal relations. They constitute personality, of which the self is a substructure or subdynamism. Since structure and function are two aspects of the same thing in nature, functional activity also is conceived in terms of dynamisms. Thus, love and hate are dynamisms, involving characteristic patterns of activity in interpersonal relations. [*See* PERSONALITY, *article on* THE FIELD.]

A second assumption is that, given a biological substrate, man is a sociocultural being. As sociologists have pointed out, man, and man alone, has a culture. One becomes a *human* being through the processes of acculturation. Complementary to this is the fact that man has a superior neuropsychic structure. Thus, man can employ signs and symbols as no animal can, making possible the marvelous development of mind.

A third assumption is that human beings are all much more human than unique, whether they are mentally healthy, mentally disordered, or whatever. Partly for this reason, Sullivan ignored the psychology of individual differences. Neither would he countenance the notion that people who suffer mental illness, such as schizophrenics, are subhuman.

A fourth assumption is that human behavior on both the biological and cultural levels is directed toward the maintenance of euphoria, a state of well-being. Experiencing needs and anxiety lowers one's euphoria and motivates behavior for a restoration of well-being or, insofar as circumstances permit, for the maintenance of a level of well-being at which one can function adequately. To be sure, euphoria is never absolute. On the physiological level, there is a more or less rhythmic cycle of euphoria and the tension of needs. But, anxiety is a much more complex affair, having to do basically with cultural demands, expectations, restrictions, and opportunities. Among other things, anxiety interferes with the satisfaction of needs. For example, it may make one nauseous or sexually frigid or impotent. If severe and prolonged, it tends to undermine whatever self-confidence and self-assurance one possesses. It very frequently hinders the development of various capacities.

A fifth assumption is that in the processes of acculturation, physiological needs become "conditioned" in various complex ways. A basic drive such as hunger becomes, in the course of personality development, thoroughly "invaded" and structured. A much more spectacular example is the sexual drive, which can be profoundly distorted, inhibited, and, in many cases, denied satisfaction. The meaning of sexual behavior is learned. Interpersonal relations provide definition and direction to sexual behavior.

Finally, one of the most significant of all of Sullivan's "theorems" is the theorem of reciprocal motivational patterns: "Integration in an interpersonal situation is a reciprocal process in which (1) complementary needs are resolved or aggravated; (2) reciprocal patterns of activity are developed or disintegrated; and (3) foresight of satisfaction, or rebuff, of similar needs is facilitated" (1953, p. 198).

A few illustrations will make this theorem clearer. For example, a baby has a need for tenderness, and the normal mother has a need to give tenderness. The baby gradually learns more and more effective nursing behavior, while the mother learns —if she has not already learned—the reciprocal patterns of tender behavior. Later on, in childhood, the youngster may discover that when he manifests a particular need, he is rebuffed, and then all evidence (manifest activity) of the need disappears. Instead, he may manifest mischievous or malevolent behavior if some vital need such as the need for tenderness has been painfully thwarted by the mothering one. Finally, he will anticipate the fulfillment or thwarting of his needs, in accordance with previous experience.

This theorem is applicable to every stage of development and, to a degree, throughout life. Furthermore, it provides a handle for exploring interpersonal relations and their distortions as no other known theory does. [*See* INTERACTION, *article on* INTERACTION AND PERSONALITY.]

Mental illness and psychotherapy

Sullivan's interpretation of functional mental illness is logically based on his theory of interpersonal relations. He did not think there is any absolute difference between the experience and behavior of normal people and the mentally ill.

Even the experiences of schizophrenics are essentially no different from what perhaps everyone experiences during sleep at some time in his life —namely, nightmares. Functional mental illness, like mental health, is an outcome of interpersonal relations. Essentially, mental illness is an expression or manifestation of interpersonal relations complicated by parataxic distortions (illusory me-you patterns), dissociated emotional and motivational patterns, and an enormously time-consuming and energy-consuming set of security operations. It is these things which result in the "difficulties in living" from which patients suffer. Mental illness ultimately stems from, first and foremost, inadequacies and irrational restrictions in the upbringing of the patient and, second, inadequacies and irrational restrictions in the society of which the patient is a member—shortcomings which are sometimes enhanced by rapid and confusing social changes. [See MENTAL DISORDERS; NEUROSIS.]

Sullivan regarded as damnable and destructive the point of view that the person who comes to the psychiatrist for help is a "case." The patient is, rather, a suffering human being, a victim of circumstances over which he had little or no control. On the other hand, sentimentality has no place in therapy. Patients are not cured or helped by "love."

The nature of the person's problems or difficulties dictates the procedures and techniques employed by the psychiatrist in treatment. These difficulties do *not* have to do with sexual problems, except incidentally, although the patient may *present* sexual problems as his actual difficulties. Sexual problems are symptoms of disordered interpersonal relations. However, when they are properly understood, they may provide clues to what is impairing the patient's ability to live with people and, in the process of treatment, may disappear.

The psychiatric interview. Psychotherapy is an interview: an interpersonal situation of a special kind. In the interview, the psychiatrist or interviewer is always a "participant observer"—never simply a "mirror," as Freud thought. The interviewer must *at all times* be alert to the fact that he is interacting with his patient and that the situation in which he is involved often gives rise to many parataxic distortions in his patient. To the extent that the psychiatrist is unconscious of his participation in the interview, he does not know or understand what is happening. Even silence is a form of interaction, but the silence of the interviewer on certain occasions during the interview can be fatal to further therapy, since, for example,

it may signify to the patient that his therapist does not understand. On the other hand, Sullivan taught that silence at times is preferable to statements that reflect lack of understanding. Therapy is not effected by word magic. There must be no hocus-pocus in word or deed and no "social hokum" of any kind.

The psychiatric interview is, then, a situation of a primarily vocal, though not merely verbal, communication, in a more or less voluntarily integrated relationship between two people, on a progressively unfolding expert–client basis. Its purpose is the progressive elucidation of the patient's characteristic patterns of living, patterns that are experienced as very troublesome or especially valuable. Perhaps needless to say, it is a process from which the patient expects to derive benefit. In other words, therapy aims at significant improvement of the patient's interpersonal relations so that he will be appreciably more able to achieve the satisfactions and security he needs. At the same time, it aims at the removal of handicaps which stand in the way of the client's effective use of his abilities. Sullivan's guiding principles in psychiatric diagnosis and prognosis were to determine what the outstanding difficulties in living and the (potential or actual) abilities or liabilities and assets of the patient are, and to determine what can or might be done by primarily vocal, psychological therapeutic procedures. These have to be learned in a series of consultations. [See INTERVIEWING, *article on* THERAPEUTIC INTERVIEWING.]

In seeking the information the psychiatrist needs from the patient, he must realize the necessity of contending with the client's self-system functions, evolved, however inadequately, to protect self-esteem and to ward off anxiety. Sullivan said:

Unless the interviewee is revealing data bearing on his aptitudes for living, on his successes, or on his unusual abilities as a human being, the operations of the self-system are always in opposition to achieving the purpose of the interview. That is, it always opposes the clear revelation of what the interviewee regards as handicaps, deficiencies, defects, and what not, and it does not facilitate communication except in the realms where that which is communicated clearly enhances his sense of well-being, his feeling of making a favorable impression.   (1954, p. 104)

However, it should never be forgotten that the self also stands in the way of unfavorable change. Hence, clumsy, inept handling of the patient's self-system functions may precipitate graver problems. When this happens, the patient may have greater and greater difficulty in having a restful sleep, may become more and more discouraged and "sicker," or may resort to dissociation. Consequently, the therapist must employ his skill to avoid arousing unnecessary anxiety, while obtaining dependable indices of what the interviewee considers to be his misfortunes, unfortunate incidents in the past, handicaps, etc.

It is the pattern of the course of events in the interview which provides the data that the psychiatrist must obtain if he is to help the patient. In other words, he observes the ways in which the interpersonal occurrences (statements, questions, emotional expressions, silences, pauses) follow one another, what striking inconsistencies occur, the timing and stress of what the patient says, the slight misunderstandings that may happen on occasion, the times when the patient gets off the subject, perhaps the volunteering of information not asked for, etc. From such events the psychiatrist learns to infer the information he requires. Perhaps needless to say, he is skilled in the eliciting of information as well as in the evaluation of the client's statements.

Free association. With any patient, the technique of free association has to be used with discrimination and discretion, if only because many people can ramble on and on indefinitely—"free associating" until they grow old or bankrupt. This technique is generally not suited to certain kinds of patients, such as schizophrenics and obsessional neurotics. Where free association was useful, Sullivan employed it when he wanted to know something that the patient was unable to recall because it was "repressed." In this way, the patient's blind spots were attacked, and he often learned that his personality had the faculty to present unknown data by more or less free flow of thought.

Sullivan mapped out the areas of the patient's experience which, normally, the psychiatrist must deal with in therapy. These are (*a*) current events (including his current job) in the patient's life, outside the treatment situation; (*b*) his current relations with the psychiatrist in the treatment situation; and (*c*) the events of the patient's past. It is perhaps not difficult to understand why current relationships provide information regarding the patient's difficulties, but one may wonder about the reasons for delving into the past. One reason is that the patient's difficulties may be masked by a variety of sophisticated operations or stratagems. A knowledge of the past provides information about the handicaps he has, since it reveals when arrests of development occurred and their probable consequences. For example, if a client has gotten bogged down in the juvenile era, he may be very facile at

competition, cooperation, and compromise but have little or no ability to achieve intimacy with people. That tells one a great deal, partly because intimacy is probably the greatest source of happiness in life and a bulwark against misfortune, suffering, and sorrow.

The length of time required for therapy varies, of course, with the individual and his psychiatrist's skill. If the therapy proceeds successfully, there is normally a growing insight into one's interpersonal relations—although sometimes patients are benefited without much insight—and a gradual modification or reorganization of one's way of life.

The Psychiatric Interview (1954) gives an excellent formal outline of Sullivan's therapeutic procedures and techniques and is brilliantly supplemented by a lecture given by Mary Julian White, entitled "Sullivan and Treatment," which vividly portrays Sullivan in action with patients (1952).

Because of its power, one may surmise that interpersonal theory will be considerably elaborated and refined in the coming years.

PATRICK MULLAHY

[*Other relevant material may be found in* INTERACTION, *article on* INTERACTION AND PERSONALITY; INTERVIEWING, *article on* THERAPEUTIC INTERVIEWING; MOTIVATION, *article on* HUMAN MOTIVATION; PERSONALITY, *article on* PERSONALITY DEVELOPMENT; PSYCHIATRY; PSYCHOANALYSIS; SELF CONCEPT.]

BIBLIOGRAPHY

ALLPORT, GORDON W. 1961 *Pattern and Growth in Personality.* New York: Holt.

KLINEBERG, OTTO 1952 Discussion. Pages 215–221 in William Alanson White Association, *The Contributions of Harry Stack Sullivan: A Symposium on Interpersonal Theory in Psychiatry and Social Science.* New York: Hermitage.

SALZMAN, LEON 1962 *Developments in Psychoanalysis.* New York: Grune & Stratton.

SULLIVAN, HARRY STACK (1924) 1962 Schizophrenia; Its Conservative and Malignant Features: A Preliminary Communication. Pages 7–22 in Harry Stack Sullivan, *Schizophrenia as a Human Process.* New York: Norton.

SULLIVAN, HARRY STACK (1924–1933) 1962 *Schizophrenia as a Human Process.* New York: Norton. → Contains Sullivan's major articles from 1924 to 1933, with an introduction by Helen Swick Perry.

SULLIVAN, HARRY STACK (1931*a*) 1962 Socio–Psychiatric Research: Its Implications for the Schizophrenia Problem and for Mental Hygiene. Pages 256–270 in Harry Stack Sullivan, *Schizophrenia as a Human Process.* New York: Norton.

SULLIVAN, HARRY STACK (1931*b*) 1962 The Modified Psychoanalytic Treatment of Schizophrenia. Pages 272–294 in Harry Stack Sullivan, *Schizophrenia as a Human Process.* New York: Norton.

SULLIVAN, HARRY STACK (1938) 1964 The Data of Psychiatry. Pages 32–55 in Harry Stack Sullivan, *The*

Fusion of Psychiatry and Social Science. New York: Norton.

SULLIVAN, HARRY STACK (1940–1945) 1953 *Conceptions of Modern Psychiatry.* With a critical appraisal of the theory by Patrick Mullahy. 2d ed. New York: Norton. → First published in the February 1940 and May 1945 issues of *Psychiatry.*

SULLIVAN, HARRY STACK 1949 Psychiatry: Introduction to the Study of Interpersonal Relations. Pages 98–121 in Patrick Mullahy (editor), *A Study of Interpersonal Relations.* New York: Hermitage.

SULLIVAN, HARRY STACK 1953 *The Interpersonal Theory of Psychiatry.* Edited by Helen Swick Perry and Mary Ladd Gawel. New York: Norton.

SULLIVAN, HARRY STACK 1954 *The Psychiatric Interview.* Edited by Helen Swick Perry and Mary Ladd Gawel. New York: Norton.

SULLIVAN, HARRY STACK 1956 *Clinical Studies in Psychiatry.* Edited by Helen Swick Perry, Mary Ladd Gawel, and Martha Gibbon. New York: Norton.

SULLIVAN, HARRY STACK 1964 *The Fusion of Psychiatry and Social Science.* With an introduction by Helen Swick Perry. New York: Norton.

THOMPSON, CLARA (1949) 1962 Harry Stack Sullivan, the Man. Pages xxxii–xxxv in Harry Stack Sullivan, *Schizophrenia as a Human Process.* New York: Norton. → Contains biographical material by the best informed of his early associates.

WHITE, MARY JULIAN 1952 Sullivan and Treatment. Pages 117–150 in William Alanson White Association, *The Contributions of Harry Stack Sullivan.* New York: Hermitage.

WILLIAM ALANSON WHITE ASSOCIATION 1952 *The Contributions of Harry Stack Sullivan: A Symposium on Interpersonal Theory in Psychiatry and Social Science.* Edited by Patrick Mullahy. New York: Hermitage.

SUMNER, WILLIAM GRAHAM

William Graham Sumner (1840–1910) was one of the founders of the science of sociology in the United States. He studied political economy at Yale, graduating in 1863, and then studied French and Hebrew at Geneva, ancient languages and history at Göttingen, and Anglican theology at Oxford. In 1866 he returned to a tutorship at Yale. Ordained as an Episcopal clergyman, he served parishes in New York City and Morristown, New Jersey, but gave up the ministry when, in 1872, he was appointed to a professorship of political and social science at Yale. During the next 38 years at Yale he achieved a reputation as teacher, polemicist, and scholar.

An abrupt change seems to have occurred in Sumner's career in the early 1890s. Before that time, he had been nationally known as an economist and essayist, fighting brilliantly against tariffs, socialism, sentimental social movements, and big government; thus, his undergraduate courses were enormously popular. After 1890 he increasingly deserted economics for sociology; polemics gave way to research, and the rostrum to the study. Consequently, his public reputation waned. Yet, the early and popular Sumner now merits only a few paragraphs in American social histories as a representative social Darwinian, whereas the later Sumner is given whole chapters in histories of sociological thought. Sumner the economist represented a current of opinion, but Sumner the sociologist was a brilliant innovator.

Economic views. As a professor of economics Sumner steadily championed individualism and laissez-faire and, just as insistently, condemned governmental regulation ("interference") and social reform movements. He believed the economic, political, and social worlds to be governed by natural laws. According to these laws, perfect competition results in a struggle for existence, and the fittest survive in the social, as in the natural, order. To the extent that the social order is rational, interference with it is irrational; to the extent that it is beneficent, interference is pernicious. In any case, interference will eventually prove futile, for the laws, such as those of supply and demand, are relatively fixed.

Sumner fought ardently for free trade and sound money. He spoke of the sacredness of private property. In a famous essay entitled "The Forgotten Man" (1883a), he praised the sober citizen who always has to bear the costs of protective tariffs, governmental social services, and high wages secured through union activity. One of his essays was entitled "What Social Classes Owe to Each Other" (see 1883b), and his blunt answer to the question implied by the title was: nothing. The title of another notable essay, "The Absurd Effort to Make the World Over" (1894), is indicative of Sumner's stark social philosophy. He was constantly engaged in controversy, and his drastic, uncompromising language not only revealed his impatience with any suggestion of sentimentality, but even implied that he regarded tact as hypocrisy.

Shift to sociology. In 1875 Sumner adopted Spencer's newly published *The Study of Sociology* for use in one of his classes [*see the biography of* SPENCER]. This is the basis for the claim that Sumner gave the first university course in sociology. The use of the Spencer volume was significant, for it marked the beginning of Sumner's shift from political economy to sociology. Initially, Spencer's work may have appealed to Sumner simply because of its individualistic, laissez-faire philosophy. On careful reading, however, Spencer's

Study of Sociology revived an excitement Sumner had known ten years before at Oxford, when he and his friends were reading Henry Thomas Buckle's *History of Civilization in England*. It had seemed to them then that it was necessary to develop a true social science and that it must be based upon history in the broadest sense. Now Spencer's volume was pointing the way—a way made increasingly plain when the first of the three volumes of his *Principles of Sociology* appeared in 1876. Spencer's work convinced Sumner that such a social science was indeed feasible, that it must be achieved by induction from ethnographic and historical materials, and that Spencer had found the correct guiding principle—evolution. Sumner had to agree, however, with those of Spencer's critics who asserted that bias and prepossession kept Spencer from being genuinely scientific.

The seed sown in Sumner's mind by Spencer began to germinate when Sumner read the work of an obscure Czech scholar, Julius Lippert, whose *Evolution of Culture* first appeared in 1886 (Murdock 1933). Drawing, like Spencer, on ethnographical material, Lippert traced the evolution of specific cultural traits (such as the use of tools or fire), of institutions, and of ideas. To Sumner it seemed that Lippert, like Spencer, Gumplowicz, and Tylor, hovered on the brink of a social science of sufficient scope to include the whole social life of man.

From 1890 on, Sumner felt it his duty to develop an inductive science of society. (He called it sociology reluctantly, since he disliked the word partly because of its impure etymology, partly because it had been invented and used by philosophers, and partly because it had been seized upon by sentimentalists. "Societology" might be better; "the science of society" would be best of all, but it yields neither a convenient adjective nor an adverb.) Whereas Spencer had employed half a dozen young scholars to collect ethnographical material, Sumner thriftily collected all his own; to that end he learned eight languages in addition to the six already at his command. His absorption in his herculean task precluded further polemics; he now saw economics as merely one important aspect of the science of society.

Folkways and mores.   Sumner himself succinctly described how he came to make his greatest contribution to sociology:

In 1899 I began to write out a text-book of sociology from material which I had used in lectures during the previous ten or fifteen years. At a certain point in that undertaking I found that I wanted to introduce my own treatment of the "mores." I could not refer to it anywhere in print, and I could not do justice to it in a chapter of another book. I therefore turned aside to write a treatise on the "Folkways."   (1906, preface)

The treatise *Folkways* made sociological history. Its subtitle is "A Study of the Sociological Importance of Usages, Manners, Customs, Mores, and Morals."

To Sumner, a study of folkways is to a science of society what the study of the cell is to biology. Or, in terms of a further analogy, he asserted that as habits are to the individual, so folkways are to the group: they are men's customary acts. They have their origin in the repetition of the small acts that satisfy the fundamental needs all men feel; hence, they tend toward uniformity within a group. The same psychological processes are involved in the making of folkways as in the formation of habits. Folkways group themselves around men's major interests in life: the maintenance, protection, perpetuation, and security of the individual in his society. This is to say, then, that they cluster to form social institutions.

Folkways thus become the human means of adjustment to the conditions of life. Certain ways of adjustment survive because they are "expedient," but with time they tend to become more and more arbitrary, positive, and imperative in the compulsion they exert on people, and it is as if they exert social pressure to conformity in and of themselves. A notable characteristic of the folkways is that they exhibit a "strain toward consistency": those in one area of life will come to make sense in terms of those in other areas, until there emerges a noticeable pattern of consistency. There may also be a strain toward "improvement."

Certain folkways become mores. (Sumner coined the term "folkways," but he borrowed "mores" from the Latin word for "customs.") The mores are "the popular habits and traditions, when they include a judgment that they are conducive to societal welfare, and when they exert a coercion on the individual to conform to them, although they are not coördinated by any authority" (Sumner & Keller 1927, vol. 1, p. 34). Mores are both fewer and more coercive than folkways; when they are laid down by society as ethical principles, they constitute morals. Folkways are conventions whose observance makes social intercourse easy, agreeable, satisfying; mores are actions people should perform because they are socially important. A person merely earns disapproval for breaking folkways; he is usually punished, often severely, for breaking mores.

Mores constitute an ideal of "the man as he should be"; a child acquires an awareness of this ideal before he is capable of reasoning about the rationality or desirability of the particular mores, and he takes their rightness for granted. Negative mores are taboos; these are generally supported by a greater element of "philosophy" or of religious sanction than positive injunctions. To say "thou shalt not" often implies that the tabooed action would displease the ghosts or spirits. Laws are those folkways and mores which are given the added "specific sanction of the group as it is organized politically" (1906, p. 56). Like the folkways, mores form accretions around nuclei of social interests, about such "institutions" as those connected with sex and the family, with worship and the church. (Sumner defined an institution as "a concept, idea, notion, doctrine, interest, and a structure"; 1906, p. 53.) The mores have their strongest hold upon the "ever conservative" masses of society. However, both folkways and mores, conservative as they are, change and evolve, since individuals constantly—often unconsciously—make minute variations in their observance of them and these variations are then imitated. This evolution helps to keep even the most traditional society adaptable.

Sumner presented practically all of his analysis of folkways and mores in the first two chapters of *Folkways*. The remaining four-fifths of the book is primarily a demonstration of the power of mores "to make anything right and to prevent the condemnation of anything" (1906, p. 52)—slavery, cannibalism, asceticism, unusual sexual practices, and so on.

Other sociological concepts. *Folkways* ranks, by common agreement, as one of the most influential works in American sociology, despite the fact that it is not a systematic treatise. In addition to inventing and developing the concepts of folkways and mores, Sumner coined the now indispensable word "ethnocentrism," made the contrast between "in-group" and "out-group," and distinguished between institutions that are "crescive" and those that are "enacted." Many of his ideas stimulated work in other areas: studies of social control, for example, stress the power of the mores. Analyses of socialization, of the relativism of culture, of social and cultural change, of the lack of rationality in human sanctions and social control, and of the nature of institutions are all enriched by perceptions in *Folkways*.

The "text-book of sociology" Sumner began to write in 1899 was eventually published in 1927—seventeen years after Sumner himself had died

—as the first three volumes of *The Science of Society*, with Sumner's disciple, Albert G. Keller, as coauthor. (The fourth volume, the "Case-book," presented a compendium of ethnographic material used by Sumner and Keller as evidence upon which their principles were based; Maurice R. Davie collaborated on this volume.) This large work describes the body of social institutions of which the folkways and mores are the cells.

The theory underlying *The Science of Society* may be briefly summarized. All men are driven by four powerful forces: hunger, love, vanity, and fear. Folkways and mores, clustering around these drives and their satisfaction, produce universal institutions. Out of the need to satisfy hunger, in all its ramifications, grow the institutions of "self-maintenance," of economics. These lead immediately to governmental institutions, since men must live together peaceably and defend themselves and each other if they would survive. Out of the drive of sex–love grow the institutions of marriage and the family; from fear (Sumner usually spoke of it as "ghost-fear") grow the elemental forms of religion. Vanity alone produces no universal institutions, since it is protean in form and yields no benefits for societal survival.

The main body of the three volumes traces in detail the evolution of all mankind's major social institutions. It is precisely here that Sumner's vast work fails, for he accepted assumptions commonly held by anthropologists at the turn of the century, when he began his work, but long since renounced by 1927, when the work was published. Sumner assumed that evolution is unilinear, that all institutions begin in simplicity and develop toward complexity through definite "stages," and that the institutions of primitive people now alive represent arrested development at the various stages through which civilized man has evolved. The comparative method that Sumner employed is quite outmoded, and the value of his posthumous work, for all its scholarship, is far less than the insights of *Folkways*.

Sumner's style. In all stages of his career Sumner used language vividly. He perceived the strength of simple Anglo-Saxon words and the subtle complexities of Latin ones—and when each could be most tellingly employed. On the first page of *Folkways*, for example, he made his point in terse language: "The first task of life is to live" and "Men begin with acts, not with thoughts." His coined word "folkways" has all the plainness of the people who make folkways, whereas the Latin "mores" suggests the involved rationalizations of the people's significant customs. Sumner could use impressive Latinisms: "The aleatory element [was an aspect of man's] most elementary experience which was irrational and defied all expedient methods" (1906, p. 6).

He used paradox effectively. An example is his phrase "antagonistic cooperation"—by which he meant that people usually cooperate when it is necessary or advantageous but without yielding their self-interest. (Sumner renounced the idea of a social instinct; he considered it evident that antagonistic cooperation would, of itself, produce society.) He could impress his ideas upon both readers and hearers by his choice of words. Thus: "If we do not like the survival of the fittest, we have only one possible alternative, and that is the survival of the unfittest. The former is the law of civilization; the latter is the law of uncivilization."

Sumner was clearly anthropological in his approach to his materials. His research for *Folkways* and *The Science of Society* was principally ethnographical. Keller quotes Sumner as once saying, as he pointed to a vast wall in the university library, "What I'd like to do would be to cover that wall-space, or a bigger one, with drawers and then set a lot of men to work filling them with notes. Up and down would be tribes and peoples. Crosswise would run topics, like property, marriage. There'd be a third dimension, too: the length of the drawers. Then we'd get somewhere, after a while!" (Keller 1933, p. 30). This vision of his bore fruit in G. P. Murdock's establishment of the Cross-cultural Survey or Human Relations Area Files.

To Sumner, sociology and anthropology were one; but even by the time of the publication of *Folkways* American sociology, with Ward, Giddings, Small, Cooley, and Thomas, was taking the psychological turn it followed for decades and American anthropology was beginning to follow the path Boas had begun to hew for it—and this was neither the path of social anthropology nor of Sumner's "science of society."

JAMES G. LEYBURN

[*For the historical context of Sumner's work, see* SOCIAL CONTROL, *article on* THE CONCEPT; SOCIAL DARWINISM; *for discussion of the subsequent development of his ideas, see* INTEGRATION, *article on* SOCIAL INTEGRATION; MARRIAGE, *article on* FAMILY FORMATION; REFERENCE GROUPS; SOCIAL CHANGE; SOCIETY; *and the biographies of* HANKINS; ODUM; ROSS; THOMAS.]

WORKS BY SUMNER

(1883a) 1918 The Forgotten Man. Pages 465–495 in William Graham Sumner, *The Forgotten Man, and Other Essays.* New Haven: Yale Univ. Press.

(1883b) 1952 *What Social Classes Owe to Each Other.* Caldwell, Ohio: Caxton.

(1894) 1911 The Absurd Effort to Make the World Over. Pages 195–210 in William Graham Sumner, *War, and Other Essays.* New Haven: Yale Univ. Press.

(1906) 1959 *Folkways: A Study of the Sociological Importance of Usages, Manners, Customs, Mores, and Morals.* New York: Dover. → A paperback edition was published in 1960 by New American Library.

1927 SUMNER, WILLIAM GRAHAM; and KELLER, ALBERT G. *The Science of Society.* 4 vols. New Haven: Yale Univ. Press. → All four volumes were begun by Sumner; he asked Keller to continue the work on them, and Keller, in turn, invited Maurice R. Davie to help complete Volume 4.

The Challenge of Facts, and Other Essays. New Haven: Yale Univ. Press, 1914. → A collection of essays, most of them previously published.

Earth-hunger, and Other Essays. New Haven: Yale Univ. Press, 1913. → A collection of essays, most of them previously published.

Essays of William Graham Sumner. 2 vols. Edited by Albert G. Keller and Maurice R. Davie. New Haven: Yale Univ. Press, 1940. → Contains essays written or published between 1881–1910. A complete bibliography appears in Volume 2, pages 479–507.

The Forgotten Man, and Other Essays. New Haven: Yale Univ. Press, 1918. → Contains essays published between 1876 and 1906.

War, and Other Essays. New Haven: Yale Univ. Press, 1911. → Includes essays written or published between 1881 and 1909.

SUPPLEMENTARY BIBLIOGRAPHY

DAVIE, MAURICE R. 1963 *William Graham Sumner: An Essay of Commentary and Selections.* New York: Crowell.

KELLER, ALBERT G. 1933 *Reminiscences (Mainly Personal) of William Graham Sumner.* New Haven: Yale Univ. Press.

LIPPERT, JULIUS (1886–1887) 1931 *The Evolution of Culture.* Translated and edited by George P. Murdock. New York: Macmillan. → First published as *Kulturgeschichte der Menschheit in ihrem organischen Aufbau.*

MURDOCK, GEORGE P. 1933 Lippert, Julius. Volume 9, pages 490–491 in *Encyclopaedia of the Social Sciences.* New York: Macmillan.

SPENCER, HERBERT (1873) 1961 *The Study of Sociology.* Ann Arbor: Univ. of Michigan Press.

STARR, HARRIS E. 1925 *William Graham Sumner.* New York: Holt.

SUNDT, EILERT LUND

Eilert Lund Sundt (1817–1875), a pioneer in Norwegian social science and demography, was the author of a large number of works in social statistics and social anthropology that deal with the population of Norway. Sundt came from a middle-class family in the southern part of Norway. His father was captain of a coastal trader and later became a post-office clerk. Sundt was the youngest of 13 children. Encouraged by his mother, he went to the University of Christiania (now Oslo), where he studied theology, graduating in 1846. His outstanding academic work won him a fellowship to study church history.

While employed as a Sunday-school teacher at the Christiania prison, Sundt had an experience of great importance for his later life: he came into contact with several gypsies among the inmates. He began to study these people and to travel extensively in Norway to collect material on their way of life; he also learned their language. After several years of study he published *Beretning om fante- eller landstrygerfolket i Norge* (1850; "Account of the Gypsy People in Norway"). In this book he established the Hindu extraction of the Norwegian gypsies. He gave an account of their history, their ways and their thinking, and their relationship with the rest of the Norwegian population, and he made suggestions for the future treatment of gypsies in Norway. The book also contained a glossary of Romany, the gypsy language.

Sundt's study of this lowest stratum of Norwegian society led him to undertake more general field studies of the poor. He covered large parts of the country on foot, doing statistical research. He was also familiar with the existing literature of the social sciences; chiefly, perhaps, he was influenced by the works of Quetelet and by the British *Reports of the Poor Law Commission* and the *Reports of the Register-General*. Beginning in 1850 an annual grant from the Norwegian parliament permitted him to continue his research, but in 1869 these grants were discontinued by members of parliament who failed to understand the importance of his work.

In 1855, after five years of further study, he published two demographic essays: *Om dødeligheden i Norge* (1855a; "On Mortality in Norway") and *Om giftermaal i Norge* (1855b; "On Marriage in Norway"). In the study of mortality he presented life tables he had computed for Norway for the period 1821–1850, as well as the results of his investigations into the variable conditions of mortality in different parts of the country. The work on marriage remains one of the classics of demography, because Sundt was the first demographer to observe fluctuations in the growth of populations (for which he coined the term "wave movements"). He showed that the heavy mortality of the years of crop failure in 1742 and 1743 had produced such a fluctuation. This fluctuation was accentuated by further crop failures and famine in the year 1773 and between 1808 and 1812. The consequent variation in the size of cohorts, with

peaks recurring at intervals of about thirty years, led in the late 1830s to an absolute decline in the actual number of births and beginning with the end of the 1840s to a very substantial increase in that number.

Sundt's theory involved him in polemics with those who held that changes in the number of marriages and births are determined only by economic growth or decline. The number of births at a given time is not, he argued, directly determined by whether times are good or bad, although such factors may cause slight postponements or accelerations, but by the number of marriages, and this in turn is a function primarily of the size of the marriageable population.

An analogous issue became important a century later, when P. K. Whelpton and others drew attention to cohort fertility—the number of children couples have in the course of their reproductive life—as against period rates, for example, the number of children born in a year, which are based on cross-sectional data. The Swedish demographer Gustav Sundbärg, who wrote a paper on Sundt in 1894, introduced the term "Eilert Sundt's law" to designate the pattern Sundt discovered in population fluctuations.

In the following years, Sundt published a series of works in two extensive and separate fields: one dealing with the everyday life, customs, and habits of the Norwegian people, the other dealing with work among the Norwegians. In 1857 there appeared *Om sædeligheds-tilstanden i Norge* ("On the State of Morality in Norway"), in which, among other things, he entered into an exhaustive discussion of courting customs, particularly the widespread peasant habit of "night wooing," or bundling, which morally outraged Norway's urban citizens. In 1858 he published the first community study ever undertaken in northern Europe: *Om Piperviken og Ruseløkbakken: Undersøgelser om arbeidsklassens kaar og saedervi Christiania* (1858a; "On Piperviken and Ruselökbakken: Investigations Into the Living Conditions and Mores of the Working Class in Christiania"). The book was based on statistical observation of nearly three hundred families, comprising almost fifteen hundred persons, in two poor districts of Christiania and discussed their economic conditions, family income, housing conditions, reading habits, and so on. This was followed by a monograph, *Om ædruelighed-tilstanden i Norge* (1859a; "On Temperance Conditions in Norway"), and by *Om renligheds-stellet i Norge* (1869; "On Cleanliness in Norway").

Sundt planned to write what he called "the natural history of Norwegian labor." As part of this project he published three works: *Om bygnings-skikken paa landet i Norge* (1862a; "On House Construction in the Norwegian Countryside"), *Fiskeriets bedrift* (1862b; "On the Fishing Trade"), and *Om husfliden i Norge* (1867; "On Domestic Industry in Norway"); however, he never completed this work.

From 1857 to 1866 Sundt was editor-in-chief of a periodical called *Folkevennen* ("The People's Friend"), which was of great importance in furthering popular education. In 1864 he founded the Workers' Association of Christiania—at that time a nonpolitical organization but today the most important affiliated society of the Norwegian Labor party.

JOHAN VOGT

[*See also* DEMOGRAPHY; FERTILITY; NUPTIALITY; POPULATION.]

WORKS BY SUNDT

1850   *Beretning om fante- eller landstrygerfolket i Norge* (An Account of the Gypsy People in Norway). Christiania: Abelsted.
1855a   *Om dødeligheden i Norge* (On Mortality in Norway). Christiania: Mallings.
1855b   *Om giftermaal i Norge* (On Marriage in Norway). Christiania: Mallings.
1857   *Om sædeligheds-tilstanden i Norge* (On the State of Morality in Norway). Christiania: Abelsted.
1858a   *Om Piperviken og Ruseløkbakken: Undersøgelser om arbeidsklassens kaar og saederi Christiania* (On Piperviken and Ruselökbakken: Investigations Into the Living Conditions and Mores of the Working Class in Christiania). Christiania: Mallings.
1858b   *Om Røros og Omegn* (On Röros and the Surrounding Districts). Christiania: No publisher given.
1859a   *Om ædrueligheds-tilstanden i Norge* (On Temperance Conditions in Norway). Christiania: Abelsted.
1859b   *Fortsat beretning om fantefolket* (A Continued Account of the Gypsy People). Christiania: Abelsted.
1862a   *Om bygnings-skikken paa landet i Norge* (On House Construction in the Norwegian Countryside). Christiania: Mallings.
1862b   *Fiskeriets bedrift* (On the Fishing Trade). Christiania: No publisher given.
1862c   *Anden aars-beretning om fantefolket* (Second Annual Account of the Gypsy People). Christiania: Abelsted.
1863   *Tredje aars-beretning om fantefolket* (Third Annual Account of the Gypsy People). Christiania: Abelsted.
1865   *Fjerde aars-beretning om fantefolket* (Fourth Annual Account of the Gypsy People). Christiania: Abelsted.
1867   *Om husfliden i Norge* (On Domestic Industry in Norway). Christiania: Abelsted.
1869   *Om renligheds-stellet i Norge* (On Cleanliness in Norway). Christiania: Abelsted.

SUPPLEMENTARY BIBLIOGRAPHY

ALLWOOD, MARTIN S. 1957 *Eilert Sundt: A Pioneer in Sociology and Social Anthropology.* Oslo: Norli. → Contains a bibliography.
CHRISTIE, NILS 1958 *Eilert Sundt som fanteforsker og sosialstatistiker* (Eilert Sundt as Investigator and Social Statistician). Universitetet i Oslo, Institutet for Sosiologi, Stensilserie. Oslo: The Institute.
CHRISTOPHERSEN, HALFDAN C. 1962 *Eilert Sundt: En dikter i kjensgjerninger.* Oslo: Gyldendal Norsk Forlag.

SUPEREGO
See PSYCHOANALYSIS.

SUPPLY AND DEMAND
See DEMAND AND SUPPLY.

SUPRANATIONALISM
See INTERNATIONAL INTEGRATION.

SURVEY ANALYSIS

I
METHODS OF SURVEY ANALYSIS

The ways in which causal inferences are drawn from quantitative data depend on the design of the study that produced the data. In experimental studies the investigator, by using one or another kind of experimental control, can remove the effects of the major extraneous causal factors on the dependent variable. The remaining extraneous causal factors can be turned into a chance variable if subjects are assigned randomly to the experimental "treatments." In principle, then, there should be only two sources of variation in the dependent variable: (1) the effects of the independent variables being studied; (2) the effects of the random assignment and of other random phenomena, especially measurement error. By using the procedures of statistical inference, it is possible to arrive at relatively clear statements about the effects of the independent variables. But in survey research (or "observational research," as it is usually called by statisticians) neither experimental control nor random assignment is available to any significant degree. The task of survey analysis is therefore to manipulate such observational data after they have been gathered, in order to separate the effects of the independent variables from the effects of the extraneous causal factors associated with them.

In the survey the association of the independent and extraneous variables occurs naturally; in the field experiment, or quasi-experimental design, the extraneous variables usually result from the experimenter's deliberate introduction of a stimulus or his modification of some condition, both of which result in a set of problems different from those considered here [see EXPERIMENTAL DESIGN, *article on* QUASI-EXPERIMENTAL DESIGN].

Among the classics of survey analysis are Émile Durkheim's attempt to explain variations in suicide rates by differences in social structure (1897); the studies of soldiers' attitudes conducted by the Research Branch of the U.S. Army during World War II and reanalyzed afterward in *The American Soldier* (Stouffer et al. 1949); and the series of voting studies that began with *The People's Choice* (Lazarsfeld et al. 1944).

As these examples suggest, survey analysis differs from other nonexperimental procedures for analyzing and presenting quantitative data, notably from probability sampling procedures and demographic analysis. In contrast with the statistical analysis of sample surveys, survey analysis often deals with total populations; even when the data of survey analysis come from a probability sample, the conventional statistical problems of estimating parameters and testing hypotheses are secondary concerns (Tukey 1962). And although survey analysis has historical roots that go back to the earliest work in demography, it differs from demography in the source of its data and, therefore, in the operations it performs on these data. Until recently, demographic analysis had largely relied on reworking the published tables of censuses and registers of vital statistics, while survey analysts usually constructed their own tables from individual questionnaires or interviews. Although these differences are still important, survey analysts have begun to use some demographic techniques, and demographers have resorted to survey analysis of specially gathered interview data in such areas as labor mobility and family planning. Perhaps the most striking evidence of the convergence of these two lines of inquiry is in the widespread use of the one-in-a-thousand and one-in-ten-thousand samples of the 1960 *U.S. Census of Population*. These samples allow the analyst of census data to prepare whatever tables he may wish. As other national censuses make their data available in this form, demographic analysis will more closely resemble survey analysis.

The causal emphasis of survey analysis also serves to distinguish it from more narrowly descriptive procedures. It differs from the "social survey," which, at least in Great Britain, has usually been a statistical account of urban life, especially among the poor. And although it shares with census reports, market research, and opinion polling a re-

liance on tabular presentation, survey analysis is unlike these fields in seeking to link its data to some body of theory. The theory may be as simple as the proposition that a set of communications has changed certain attitudes [see COMMUNICATION, MASS, *article on* EFFECTS]. Or it may involve an explicit structure of variables, as in analyses of the reasons that people give for having done one thing rather than another [see REASON ANALYSIS].

Survey analysis has a role to play in the construction of formal theories, whether they use explicit mathematical relations or are only implicitly mathematical, as in computer simulation. Some mathematical models are indeed useful in the analysis of survey data (Coleman 1964). But survey analysis as it is defined here usually limits itself to identifying variables important enough to be included in the formal theories.

The background of survey analysis

Two basic elements in survey analysis are the use of rates as dependent variables and the explanation of differences in rates by means of their statistical associations with other social phenomena. Both of these features first appeared in Graunt's *Natural and Political Observations Made Upon the Bills of Mortality* (1662), which included the first data on urban and rural death rates. This one small book thus makes Graunt a major figure in the history not only of survey analysis but also of statistics and demography. With the exception of the life table, which Graunt invented but which was improved significantly a generation later by the astronomer Edmund Halley, Graunt's methods set the pattern for statistical analysis until the middle of the nineteenth century [see VITAL STATISTICS].

Although Graunt had already noted the approximate constancy of certain rates over time (e.g., the excess of male births over female), the German pastor Johann Peter Süssmilch was the first to notice that suicide, a voluntary act, also showed the same constancy. He thus initiated the field of "moral statistics," which was to make much of nineteenth-century statistics, especially in France, resemble modern sociology. But the major figure in the development of moral statistics was the Belgian astronomer Adolphe Quetelet, who made three important contributions to survey analysis: (1) he used multivariate tables to explore the relations between the rates of crime or marriage and such demographic factors as age and sex; (2) he applied the calculus of probability to explaining the constancy of social rates over time; and (3) he helped to establish organized bodies of statisticians, including the Statistical Society of London (later the Royal Statistical Society), and he organized several international statistical congresses.

Whether or not Quetelet was right in trying to explain the stability of rates by drawing on the theory of errors of observation is still a subject of controversy (Hogben 1957; Lazarsfeld 1961). There can be no question, however, that the organization of the statistical societies in England during the 1830s and 1840s was followed by increased application of statistical data to social problems, notably in the statistical demonstrations by John Snow and Thomas Farr of the relation between polluted water and cholera, and in several studies on the differences in the rates of mortality in large and small hospitals.

By the last decade of the nineteenth century the use of tables for causal analysis had reached a high stage of development, both in England and on the continent of Europe. This was also the period when Charles Booth, disturbed by a socialist claim that a third of the people of London were living in poverty, was conducting his monumental study of the London poor, a study initially intended to uncover the cause of poverty. In France, at about the same time, Émile Durkheim drew on the accumulated work in moral statistics to produce the first truly sociological explanation of differences in suicide rates. The two men and their studies could hardly have been more different. Booth, the successful businessman and dedicated conservative, primarily sought accurate data on the poor of London; his original hope for causal analysis was never realized. Durkheim, the brilliant and ascetic university professor, saw in his analysis of official statistics the opportunity to make sociology a truly autonomous discipline. And yet the two men were alike in one important error of omission: both failed to recognize their need for the statistical tools being developed at the same time in the work of Francis Galton, Karl Pearson, and G. Udny Yule.

By 1888 Galton's research on heredity and his acquaintance with Quetelet's use of the normal distribution had led him to the basic ideas of correlation and regression, which were taken up and developed further by Pearson, beginning in 1892 (the year in which Booth was president of the Royal Statistical Society). Three years later, in his first paper on statistics, Yule (1895) called attention to Booth's misinterpretation of some tabular data. Where Booth had claimed to find no association between two sets of variables, Yule computed correlation coefficients that ranged from 0.28 to 0.40; a similar table in which Durkheim ([1897] 1951, p. 87) saw "not the least trace of a relation" yields an even higher correlation. According to the then-current theory, the coefficient of correlation had meaning only as a parameter of a bivariate normal distribution; Yule had no "right" to make such a computation, but he made it anyway, apparently believing that an illegitimate computation was better than no computation at all.

Two further papers of Yule's showed the wisdom of this judgment and laid the foundations for much of modern survey analysis. He proved that the use of the correlation coefficient to measure association does not depend on the form of the underlying distribution; in particular, it need not be normal. In the same paper he also gave the formulas of multiple and partial regression and correlation (1897). Two years later he applied these ideas to a survey analysis of "panel" data on poverty—a multiple regression of changes in poverty rates on three independent variables (1899). In these four years Yule showed how the statistical part of survey analysis could be made truly quantitative. But although some economists and psychologists were early users of multiple regression, it was not until the 1960s that other survey analysts, notably sociologists and students of public opinion, came to see its importance [see LINEAR HYPOTHESES, *article on* REGRESSION].

Not content to deal only with continuous variables, Yule also took in hand the analysis of tabular data and set forth its algebraic basis (1900). Although this material appeared in every edition of his *Introduction to the Theory of Statistics* (Yule & Kendall [1911] 1958, chapters 1–3), it had even less effect on survey analysis than did his work on continuous variables. It was finally brought to the attention of social scientists by Lazarsfeld in 1948 (see Lazarsfeld & Rosenberg 1955, pp. 115–125), as the basis for his codification of survey analysis.

A new area of application for survey analysis began to appear in the 1920s, first in the form of market research and later in opinion polling, communications research, and election research. Among the factors that promoted these new developments were the change in American social psychology and sociology from speculation to empirical research, the wide availability of punched-card machines, and a new interest in the use of formal statistical procedures, notably at Chicago, where William F. Ogburn and Samuel A. Stouffer taught both correlational and tabular techniques in the 1930s. By the time of World War II, survey analysis had advanced to the point where Stouffer was able, as already mentioned, to organize a group of experienced survey analysts to conduct hundreds of attitude surveys among American soldiers.

Three major developments have shaped survey analysis since the 1940s. The emphasis on closer relations between theory and research has led to greater concern with conceptualization and index formation, as well as with the causal interpretation of statistical relations. The rise of university research bureaus has increased both the quantity and the quality of survey analysis. And the advent of the large computer has brought survey analysts to contemplate once again the vision that Yule had placed before them in 1899—the possibility of replacing the crude assessment of percentaged tables with the more powerful methods of multiple regression and other multivariate procedures.

The structure of survey analysis

Analysis is the study of variation. Beginning with the variation in a dependent variable, the analyst seeks to account for this variation by examining the covariation of the dependent variable with one or more independent variables. For instance, in a sample where 57 per cent prefer the conservative party and 43 per cent the liberal party, the analytic question is why people divide between the two parties. If everyone preferred the same party, there would be no variation and, *within this sample,* no problem for analysis. The answer to this question comes from examining how the distribution of preferences is affected by a set of independent variables, such as the sex of the individual, the social class of his family, and the size of his community. This combination of a single dependent variable and a set of independent variables is the most common structure examined in survey analysis; it also serves as the building block for other, more complex structures—for example, a study with several dependent variables.

The sequence of steps in the analysis of an ideal experiment is determined largely by the design of the study. In real life, of course, an experimenter almost always confronts new problems in his analysis. The survey analyst, however, has so many more options open to him at each step that he cannot specify in advance all of the steps through which an analysis should go. Nevertheless, it is useful to conceive of analysis as a series of cycles, in which the analyst goes through the same formal sequence of steps in each cycle, each time changing some essential aspect of his problem. A typical cycle can be described as follows.

(1) *Measuring the parameters of some distribu-* *tion.* The concrete form of this step may be as simple as computing percentages in a two-variable table or as complicated as fitting a regression plane to a large set of points. Indeed, the parameters may not even be expressed numerically; in conventional survey analysis (i.e., analysis using percentaged contingency tables) two-variable relations may be classified simply as "large" or "small."

(2) *Assessing the criteria for an adequate analysis.* The reasons survey analysts give for stopping one line of investigation and starting another often appear superficial: they have run out of time, cases, or interest. On further investigation, however, it usually appears that they have stopped for one or more of the following reasons: (*a*) statistical completeness—that is, a sufficiently high proportion of the variation in the dependent variable has been accounted for by the variation in the independent variables; (*b*) theoretical clarity—that is, the meanings of the relations already found and the nature of the causal structure are sufficiently clear not to need further analysis; (*c*) unimportance of error—that is, there is good reason to believe that the apparent findings are genuine, that they are not the result of one or another kind of error. These three reasons, then, can be regarded as criteria for an adequate analysis.

(3) *Changing the analytic model.* With these criteria in mind, the analyst decides whether to stop the analysis or to continue it, either by adding more variables or by changing the basic form of the analysis (for example, from linear to curvilinear regression).

In practice, there are two major sets of procedures by means of which the steps involved in each cycle are taken. One rests on the construction of percentaged contingency tables, the other on the different kinds of multivariate statistical analysis. Despite the extensive use of correlational techniques by psychologists, survey analysis has on the whole been dominated by percentaged contingency tables. One reason for this dominance is economic: with punched-card machines, running several tables takes less time than computing a single correlation coefficient on a desk calculator. The advent of the large electronic computer has brought a revolutionary change in this situation, and statistical computations that might have taken months, if they were done at all, can now be done in minutes. This change has led to new interest in multivariate statistical techniques and to some questioning of the place of tabular methods in survey analysis. Since many textbooks explain the basic ideas of multivariate statistical procedures, it will be necessary to consider in detail only the logic of tabular analysis.

Percentaged contingency tables

Let us recall the illustration of a sample in which 57 per cent prefer the conservative party and 43 per cent the liberal party. Further, let us call the dependent variable (party preference) A and the three independent variables (sex, social class, and size of community) B, C, and D. For simplicity, let each variable take only two values: A_1 (conservative) and A_2 (liberal), B_1 and B_2, and so on. Tabular analysis then begins by considering the distribution of the dependent variable, as in Table 1.

Table 1 — Percentage distribution of A*

A_1	57%
A_2	43
Total	100%
	($n = 1,000$)

* Hypothetical data.

In this simple distribution, 57 per cent of the sample 1,000 cases have the value A_1 and 43 per cent have the value A_2. Analysis proper begins when a second variable is introduced and the association between them is examined by means of a two-variable table. However, instead of looking at a two-variable table, it is intuitively more appealing to consider once again the distribution of A— or, rather, *two* distributions of A, one for those people classified as B_1 and the other for those who are B_2, as in Table 2.

Table 2 — Percentage distribution of A for those who are B_1 and B_2*

	B_1	B_2
A_1	45%	66%
A_2	55	34
Total	100%	100%
	($n = 420$)	($n = 580$)

* Hypothetical data.

Perhaps the simplest measurement of association is to compare these two univariate distributions—that is, to note the 18 percentage-point difference in the proportion of B_1's and B_2's who respond A_1. These two distributions are, of course, the two columns of a 2×2 table. The point of separating them is to stress the concept of two-variable association as the comparison of univariate distributions.

The same sort of link between different levels appears when a third variable is introduced. This three-variable "elaboration," or multivariate analysis, as Lazarsfeld has called it (not to be confused with the statistical concept of the same name, which is here called multivariate statistical analysis), involves the re-examination of a two-variable association for the two separate subgroups of people classified according to the values of the third variable, C, as in Table 3.

Table 3 — Associations of A and B for those who are C_1 and C_2*

	C_1		C_2	
	B_1	B_2	B_1	B_2
A_1	25%	38%	72%	76%
A_2	75	62	28	24
Total	100%	100%	100%	100%
	($n = 240$)	($n = 160$)	($n = 180$)	($n = 420$)

* Hypothetical data.

It is necessary to give a numerical measure of the association in each "partial" table, but the above reasoning applies no matter what measure is chosen. Elaboration, then, is simply the comparison of these two measures of association. That is, when the third variable, C, is introduced, the association between A and B becomes a composite dependent variable; elaboration is the relation between C and some measure of the association between A and B.

This approach to elaboration is another way of describing *statistical interaction*, or the extent to which the association between A and B depends on the value of C. In the usual discussion of interaction, however, it also appears as something new in the treatment of association. The simple formalization presented here emphasizes the common thread that runs through the treatment of one, two, three, or more variables: the measure of the degree of relation for a given number of variables becomes the dependent variable when a new independent variable is introduced.

Lazarsfeld has distinguished three ideal types of configurations that result when the relation between A and B is examined separately for C_1 and C_2. The disappearance of the original relation is called "explanation" when C is causally prior to both A and B, and "interpretation" when C intervenes between A and B. The third type of elaboration, "specification," is essentially an extreme form of interaction, in which at least one partial relation is larger than the original relation or is of opposite sign. A full discussion of elaboration and many examples are given in Hyman (1955, chapters 6, 7).

Lazarsfeld's several discussions of elaboration have clarified much of what a survey analyst does in practice; they have also led Simon, Blalock, Boudon, and Duncan (whose work is discussed below, in the section on causal structures) to mathematize the idea of a causal structure and to extend it beyond the three-variable level. The fundamental ideas of elaboration have thus stood the test of time. However, the percentaged contingency table—the tool that most survey analysts have used to carry out the ideas of elaboration—now appears less satisfactory than it formerly did.

Alternatives to tabular analysis

The value of a technique should be judged against the available alternatives to it. The best alternatives to tabular analysis now seem to be multiple regression (for quantitative dependent variables) and multiple discriminant analysis (for qualitative dependent variables). Two procedures are necessary because tabular analysis, of course, treats quantitative and qualitative variables in essentially the same way. Compared with these techniques, tabular analysis appears to have three principal shortcomings, as follows.

(1) *Lack of a measure of statistical completeness.* The square of the multiple correlation coefficient is the proportion of the variation in the dependent variable that is accounted for by the regression on the independent variables. In regression the analyst always knows how far he has gone toward the goal of complete explanation (usually linear). By the late 1960s no comparable statistic adequate for a large number of independent variables had yet become available in tabular analysis; the analyst therefore does not know whether he has gone far enough or, indeed, whether the introduction of additional variables makes an appreciable addition to the explanatory power of those already included.

(2) *Ambiguity of causal inferences.* Even with very large samples, the number of independent variables that can be considered jointly is usually no more than four or five; percentage comparisons involving many variables are usually based on too few cases to be statistically stable. It is often possible, however, to find many more variables that have appreciable effects on the dependent variable. This inability to examine the joint effects of *all* of the apparently important independent variables makes the interpretation of *any* relation between the independent and dependent variables inherently ambiguous. Suppose, for example, that one

can examine the effects of only three variables at once; that variables B, C, D, E, and F all have appreciable associations with the dependent variable, A; and that, as is usually the case, all of these independent variables are intercorrelated. Then it is impossible to draw clear conclusions from any three-variable table, since what appears to be the effect of, say, B, C, and D is also the effect of E and F, but in some unknown and inherently unknowable degree. Maurice Halbwachs had this kind of argument in mind when he said that Durkheim's attempt to discern the effects of religion by areal comparisons was fundamentally impossible; any comparison between Catholic areas and Protestant areas involves differences in income, social norms, industrialization, and many other factors [see SUICIDE, *article on* SOCIAL ASPECTS]. In contrast, the procedures of multivariate statistics can handle dozens or even hundreds of variables at the same time, so that it is relatively easy to ascertain the meaning of an observed relation between independent and dependent variables.

There is another reason why the percentaged table is an unsatisfactory tool of causal analysis. As Campbell and Clayton (1961) have shown, unwanted regression effects produced by the less than perfect association between the independent variables may be confounded with the causal effects that the analyst wants to examine. These regression effects are particularly dangerous in panel studies.

(3) *Lack of a systematic search procedure.* At the beginning of an analysis the main task is to find the independent variables that are the best predictors of the dependent variables, and the dependent variables that are most predictable from the independent variables. The complex intercorrelations among the independent variables make this a slow task in tabular analysis. In contrast, "stepwise" regression and discriminant programs rapidly arrange the independent variables in the order of their predictive power, and modern programs allow such analyses to be repeated for other dependent variables in a few seconds. Sonquist and Morgan (1964) have devised a computer program that simulates some aspects of the search behavior of a tabular analyst (see also Sterling et al. 1966).

Problems of multivariate statistics. In emphasizing the defects of tabular analysis and the virtues of multivariate statistics, the above section presented a somewhat one-sided picture. Such procedures as regression and discriminant analysis have serious problems of their own. For example, to treat a nominally scaled variable such as race or geographical region as an independent variable, one must first transform it into a set of "dummy variables" (for instances of this procedure, see Draper & Smith 1966, section 5.3).

Another problem arises in detecting and representing statistical interaction. In their standard forms, multivariate statistical procedures assume that there is no interaction. However, several ancillary procedures for detecting interaction are available—for example, analysis of variance, the examination of residuals from the regression, the Sonquist–Morgan "Automatic Interaction Detector" (1964), and the stratification of the sample by one or more of the interacting variables, with separate regressions in each part. Similarly, it is possible to represent interaction by appropriate modifications of the standard equations (see Draper & Smith 1966, chapter 5).

On balance, the method of choice appears to be multivariate statistical procedures for the early and middle phases of a survey analysis, and tables for presenting the final results. An examination of current journals suggests that this judgment is increasingly shared by social scientists who engage in survey analysis.

The meanings of statistical results

In every cycle of analysis there are problems of imputing or verifying the meanings of variables and relations—that is, there are problems of conceptualization and validation. Much of the meaning that one imputes to variables and relations comes from sources other than the statistical data —from the precipitate of past research and theory, from the history of the phenomena studied, and from a wide range of qualitative procedures. Indeed, it is the skillful interweaving of survey and ancillary data that often distinguishes insightful survey analysis from routine manipulation.

Although conceptualization and validation are partly matters of judgment, the wide range of questions in the typical survey provides an objective basis for imputing meanings to observed variables. At one extreme there are such simple procedures as examining the association between a variable of uncertain meaning and one or more additional variables whose meaning is less in question. For example, a self-estimate of "interest in politics" may be validated by seeing how strongly this interest is associated with reading political news, discussing politics with friends, and voting in elections. At the other extreme, the common meanings of large numbers of variables may be extracted by some "rational" scaling procedure, such as Guttman scaling, latent structure analysis,

or factor analysis. Again, computer programs have made such procedures much less expensive than they once were, and therefore more desirable than arbitrarily constructed scales.

Causal structures

Although survey analysts have always aimed at uncovering causes, the idea that the independent and dependent variables should all be located in a determinate structure of relations—usually represented by a set of boxes and arrows—has not yet been generally accepted. Few survey analyses have gone beyond Lazarsfeld's three types of elaboration. The first significant methodological advance on Lazarsfeld's formalization was made by Simon (1954); drawing on a large body of work in econometrics, Simon showed how Lazarsfeld's idea of time order, which had been treated separately from the statistical configurations of his three variables, could be combined with them in a system of simultaneous equations. Blalock (1964) took up Simon's suggestions and showed how they can be applied to empirical data. Boudon (1965) has developed a theory of "dependence analysis," which, along with extending the models of Simon and Blalock, shows the relations between these models, ordinary least-squares regression, and the work of Sewall Wright on "path coefficients" (a line of inquiry independently pursued in biology since 1918). Finally, Duncan (1966) has applied the ideas of path analysis to a set of sociological examples and has shown how path analysis can make loose verbal formulations of the causal structure explicit and consistent.

Statistical inference in survey analysis

The statistical theory of sample surveys has dealt almost entirely with descriptive studies, in which the usual problem is to estimate a few predesignated parameters. Where survey analysts have tried to apply this theory, they have often ignored or argued away two important assumptions: (1) that nonrandom errors, such as those produced in sampling, interviewing, and coding, are negligible, and (2) that all of the hypotheses tested were stated before examining the data.

Few survey investigators know the direction and magnitude of the nonrandom errors in their work with any accuracy, for measurement of these errors requires a specially designed study. Stephan and McCarthy (1958) reported the results of several empirical studies of sampling procedures. Such studies provide a rough guide to the survey investigator; precise data on the actual operation of survey procedures are probably available only in large research organizations that frequently repeat the same kind of survey. Without such knowledge, the interpretation of statistical tests and estimates in precise probabilistic terms may be misleading. An apparently "significant" relation may result from nonrandom error rather than from the independent variable, and a relation that apparently is not significant may stem from a nonrandom error opposite in sign and approximately equal in magnitude to the effect of the independent variable.

Lack of information about the nonrandom errors casts doubt on *any* inference from data, not simply on the inferences of formal statistics. However, the practices of many survey analysts justify emphasizing the effects of this lack of knowledge on the procedures of statistical inference, especially on tests of significance. All too often the words "significant at the .05 level" are thought to provide information on the random variables without there being any knowledge of the nonrandom variables —as if this phrase were a certificate of over-all methodological quality.

Even when there is no problem of nonrandom error, the history of the hypothesis being tested affects the validity of probability computations. The survey analyst seldom begins a study with a single specific hypothesis in mind. What hypotheses he has are usually diffuse and ill-formulated, and the data of the typical survey are so rich and suggestive that he almost always formulates many more hypotheses after looking at the results. Indeed, the original analyst usually examines such a small proportion of the hypotheses that can be studied with his data that libraries of survey data have been established to facilitate "secondary analysis," or the restudy of survey data for purposes that may not have been intended by the original investigator.

In the typical survey conducted for scientific purposes the analyst alternates between examining the data and formulating hypotheses that he explores further in the same body of data. This kind of "data dredging" is a necessary and desirable part of survey analysis; to limit survey analysis to hypotheses precisely stated in advance of seeing the data would be to make uneconomical use of a powerful tool. However, the analyst pays a price for this flexibility: although it is legitimate to explore the implications of hypotheses on the same body of data that suggested them, it is *not* legitimate to attach probability statements to these hypotheses (Selvin & Stuart 1966). The situation is analogous to testing a table of random numbers for randomness: the a priori probability of finding six consecutive fives in the first six digits exam-

ined is $(0.1)^6$, a quantity small enough to cast doubt on the randomness of the process by which the table was generated. If, however, one hunts through thousands of digits to find such a sequence (and the longer one looks, the greater the likelihood of finding it), this probability computation becomes meaningless. Similarly, the survey analyst who leafs through a pile of tables until he finds an "interesting" result that he then "tests for significance" is deceiving himself; the procedure designed to guard against the acceptance of chance results actually promotes their acceptance. The use of computers has exacerbated this problem. Many programs routinely test every relation for significance, usually with procedures that were intended for a single relation tested alone, and many analysts seem unable to resist dressing their dredged-up hypotheses in ill-fitting probabilistic clothes.

The analyst who wants to perform a statistical test of a dredged-up hypothesis does not have to wait for a new study. If he has foreseen this problem, he can reserve a random subsample of his data at the outset of the analysis, dredge the remainder of his data for hypotheses, and then test a small number of these hypotheses on the reserved subsample. The analyst who was not so foresighted or who has dredged up too many hypotheses to test on one subsample may be able to use a large data library to provide an approximate test. For example, an analyst who wants to test a dredged-up relation involving variables A, B, and C would look through such a library until he found another, comparable study with these same variables. He would then divide the sample of this study into a number of random subsamples and see how his dredged-up relation fares in these independent replications. If all or most of the subsamples yield relations in the same direction as his dredged-up relation, he can be reasonably confident that it was not the result of chance.

This procedure is simple, and it will become even simpler when the questions in the data libraries are put on magnetic tape, as the responses are now. However, this "backward replication" does raise some methodological problems, especially concerning the comparability of studies and questions. Neither this procedure nor the use of reserved subsamples has yet been studied in any detail by survey methodologists or statisticians.

HANAN C. SELVIN

[*See also* EVALUATION RESEARCH; EXPERIMENTAL DESIGN; LINEAR HYPOTHESES; MULTIVARIATE ANALYSIS; PANEL STUDIES; SAMPLE SURVEYS; SCIENCE, *article on* THE PHILOSOPHY OF SCIENCE; SOCIOLOGY; STA-

TISTICS, DESCRIPTIVE; TABULAR PRESENTATION; *and the biographies of* BOOTH; DURKHEIM; GALTON; GRAUNT; OGBURN; PEARSON; QUETELET; STOUFFER; SÜSSMILCH; YULE.]

BIBLIOGRAPHY

BLALOCK, HUBERT M. JR. 1964 *Causal Inferences in Nonexperimental Research.* Chapel Hill: Univ. of North Carolina Press.

BOUDON, RAYMOND 1965 A Method of Linear Causal Analysis: Dependence Analysis. *American Sociological Review* 30:365–374.

BOUDON, RAYMOND 1967 *L'analyse mathématique des faits sociaux.* Paris: Plon.

BOUDON, RAYMOND; and LAZARSFELD, PAUL F. (editors) 1966 *L'analyse empirique de la causalité.* Paris and The Hague: Mouton.

CAMPBELL, DONALD T.; and CLAYTON, K. N. 1961 Avoiding Regression Effects in Panel Studies of Communication Impact. *Studies in Public Communication* 3: 99–118.

COLEMAN, JAMES S. 1964 *Introduction to Mathematical Sociology.* New York: Free Press.

DRAPER, N. R.; and SMITH, H. 1966 *Applied Regression Analysis.* New York: Wiley.

DUNCAN, OTIS DUDLEY 1966 Path Analysis: Sociological Examples. *American Journal of Sociology* 72:1–16.

DURKHEIM, ÉMILE (1897) 1951 *Suicide: A Study in Sociology.* Glencoe, Ill.: Free Press. → First published in French.

GRAUNT, JOHN (1662) 1939 *Natural and Political Observations Made Upon the Bills of Mortality.* Edited and with an introduction by Walter F. Willcox. Baltimore: Johns Hopkins Press.

HOGBEN, LANCELOT T. 1957 *Statistical Theory: The Relationship of Probability, Credibility and Error; an Examination of the Contemporary Crisis in Statistical Theory From a Behaviourist Viewpoint.* London: Allen & Unwin.

HYMAN, HERBERT H. 1955 *Survey Design and Analysis: Principles, Cases, and Procedures.* Glencoe, Ill.: Free Press.

LAZARSFELD, PAUL F. 1961 Notes on the History of Quantification in Sociology—Trends, Sources and Problems. Pages 147–203 in Harry Woolf (editor), *Quantification: A History of the Meaning of Measurement in the Natural and Social Sciences.* Indianapolis, Ind.: Bobbs-Merrill.

LAZARSFELD, PAUL F.; BERELSON, BERNARD; and GAUDET, HAZEL (1944) 1960 *The People's Choice: How the Voter Makes Up His Mind in a Presidential Campaign.* 2d ed. New York: Columbia Univ. Press.

LAZARSFELD, PAUL F.; and ROSENBERG, MORRIS (editors) 1955 *The Language of Social Research: A Reader in the Methodology of Social Research.* New York: Free Press. → A revised edition is scheduled for publication in 1968.

MOSER, CLAUS A. 1958 *Survey Methods in Social Investigation.* New York: Macmillan.

SELVIN, HANAN C. 1965 Durkheim's *Suicide:* Further Thoughts on a Methodological Classic. Pages 113–136 in Robert A. Nisbet (editor), *Émile Durkheim.* Englewood Cliffs, N.J.: Prentice-Hall.

SELVIN, HANAN C.; and STUART, ALAN 1966 Data-dredging Procedures in Survey Analysis. *American Statistician* 20, no. 3:20–23.

SIMON, HERBERT A. 1954 Spurious Correlation: A Causal Interpretation. *Journal of the American Statistical Association* 49:467–479.

SONQUIST, JOHN A.; and MORGAN, JAMES N. 1964 *The Detection of Interaction Effects: A Report on a Computer Program for the Selection of Optimal Combinations of Explanatory Variables.* University of Michigan, Institute for Social Research, Survey Research Center, Monograph No. 35. Ann Arbor: The Center.

STEPHAN, FREDERICK F.; and McCARTHY, PHILIP J. 1958 *Sampling Opinions: An Analysis of Survey Procedure.* New York: Wiley.

STERLING, T. et al. 1966 Robot Data Screening: A Solution to Multivariate Type Problems in the Biological and Social Sciences. *Communications of the Association for Computing Machinery* 9:529–532.

STOUFFER, SAMUEL A. et al. 1949 *The American Soldier.* 2 vols. Studies in Social Psychology in World War II, Vols. 1–2. Princeton Univ. Press. → Volume 1: *Adjustment During Army Life.* Volume 2: *Combat and Its Aftermath.*

TUKEY, JOHN W. 1962 The Future of Data Analysis. *Annals of Mathematical Statistics* 33:1–67.

WOOLF, HARRY (editor) 1961 *Quantification: A History of the Meaning of Measurement in the Natural and Social Sciences.* Indianapolis, Ind.: Bobbs-Merrill.

YULE, G. UDNY 1895 On the Correlation of Total Pauperism With Proportion of Out-relief. *Economic Journal* 5:603–611.

YULE, G. UDNY 1897 On the Significance of Bravais' Formulae for Regression, &c., in the Case of Skew Correlation. Royal Society of London, *Proceedings* 60:477–489.

YULE, G. UDNY 1899 An Investigation Into the Causes of Changes in Pauperism in England, Chiefly During the Last Two Intercensal Decades. Part I. *Journal of the Royal Statistical Society* 62:249–286.

YULE, G. UDNY 1900 On the Association of Attributes in Statistics: With Illustrations From the Material of the Childhood Society, etc. Royal Society of London, *Philosophical Transactions* Series A 194:257–319.

YULE, G. UDNY; and KENDALL, M. G. (1911) 1958 *An Introduction to the Theory of Statistics.* 14th ed., rev. & enl. London: Griffin. → M. G. Kendall has been a joint author since the eleventh edition (1937). The 1958 edition was revised by Kendall.

II

THE ANALYSIS OF ATTRIBUTE DATA

Modern social research requires the study of the interrelations between characteristics that are themselves not quantified. Has someone completed high school? Is he native born? Male or female? Is there a relation between all such characteristics? Do they in turn affect people's attitudes and behavior? How complex are these connections: do men carry out their intentions more persistently than women? If so, is this sex difference related to level of education?

Some answers to some of these questions have been made possible by two developments in modern social research: improved techniques of collecting data through questionnaires and observations, and sampling techniques that make such collecting less costly. Empirical generalizations in answer to questions like those above proceed essentially in two steps. First, people or collectives have to be measured on the characteristics of interest. Such characteristics are now often called *variates*, to include simple dichotomies as well as "natural" quantitative variables, like age, or "artificial" indices, like a measure of anxiety. The second step consists in establishing *connections* between such variates. The connections may be purely descriptive, or they may be causal chains based on established theories or intuitive guesswork.

In order to take the second step and study the connection between variates, certain procedures have been developed in *survey analysis*, although the procedures apply, of course, to any kind of data, for instance, census data. Attitude surveys have greatly increased the number of variates that may be connected, and thus the problems of studying connections have become especially visible. The term "survey" ordinarily excludes studies in which there are observations repeated over time on the same individuals or collectives; such studies, usually called panel studies, are not discussed in this article [see PANEL STUDIES].

It makes a difference whether one deals with quantitative variables or with classifications allowing only a few categories, which often may not even be ordered. Connections between quantitative variables have long been studied in the form of correlation analysis and its many derivatives [see MULTIVARIATE ANALYSIS, *articles on* CORRELATION]. Correlation techniques can sometimes also be applied to qualitative characteristics, by assigning arbitrary numbers to their subdivisions. But some of the most interesting ideas in survey analysis emerge if one concentrates on data where the characterization of objects cannot be quantified and where only the frequencies with which the objects fall into different categories are known. As a matter of fact, the main ideas can be developed by considering only dichotomies, and that will be done here. The two terms "dichotomy" and "attribute" will be used interchangeably.

Dichotomous algebra

Early statisticians (see Yule & Kendall 1911) showed some interest in attribute statistics, but such interest was long submerged by the study of quantitative variables with which the economists and psychologists were concerned. Attribute statistics is best introduced by an example which a few decades ago one might have found as easily in a textbook of logic as in a text on descriptive statis-

tics. The example will also permit introduction of the symbolism needed for this exposition.

Suppose there is a set of 1,000 people who are characterized according to sex (attribute 1), according to whether they did or did not vote in the last election (attribute 2), and according to whether they are of high or low socioeconomic status (SES, attribute 3). There are 200 high-status men who voted and 150 low-status women who did not vote. The set consists of an equal number of men and women. One hundred high-status people did not vote, and 250 low-status people did vote. There are a total of 650 voters in the whole set; 100 low-status women did vote. How many low-status men voted? How is the whole set divided according to socioeconomic status?

There are obviously three attributes involved in this problem. It is convenient to give them arbitrary numbers and, for each attribute, to assign arbitrarily a positive sign to one possibility and a negative sign to the other. The classification of Table 1 is then obtained.

Table 1

Number	Attribute	Sign Assignment	
		+	−
1	Sex	Men	Women
2	Vote	Yes	No
3	SES	High	Low

The problem assigns to some of the combinations of attribute possibilities a numerical value, the proportion of people who belong to the "cell." The information supplied in the statement of the problem can then be summarized in the following way:

$$p_{123} = .20,$$
$$p_{1\overline{23}} = .15,$$
$$p_1 = p_{\overline{1}},$$
$$p_{\overline{2}3} = .10,$$
$$p_{2\overline{3}} = .25,$$
$$p_2 = .65,$$
$$p_{\overline{123}} = .10.$$

Here the original raw figures are presented as proportions of the whole set; a bar over an index indicates that in this special subset the category of that attribute to which a negative sign has been assigned applies. For example, $p_{\overline{2}3}$ is the number of people who did not vote and are of high status; this proportion has the numerical value $100/1,000 = .10$. The number of indices that are attached to a proportion is called its *stratification level*. The problem under discussion ends with two questions. Their answers require the computation of two proportions, $p_{12\overline{3}}$ and p_3.

The derivation of the missing frequencies can

be done rather simply in algebraic form. For the present purpose it is more useful to derive them by introduction of so-called fourfold tables. The point of departure is, arbitrarily, the fourfold table between attributes 1 and 2. This table is then stratified by introducing attribute 3, giving the scheme of Table 2, in which the information presented in the original problem is underscored. The principal findings are starred.

The tabular form makes it quite easy to fill in the missing cells by addition and subtraction, and this also permits answers to the two questions of the original problem in symbolic, as well as in numerical, form:

The proportion of low-status men voting is given by

$$p_{12\bar{3}} = p_{2\bar{3}} - p_{\bar{1}2\bar{3}} = .15,$$

and the proportion of high-status people is

$$p_3 = p_{\bar{2}3} + (p_2 - p_{23}) = .5.$$

If it were only a task of dividing and recombining sets, the problem would now be solved. But in survey analysis a new element enters which goes beyond the tradition of a calculus of classes. One is interested in the *relation* between attributes, and to express that relation an additional notion and an additional symbol are required. Taking the left side of Table 2, it is reasonable to ask how many men would have voted if sex had no influence on political behavior. The proportion of joint occurrence of two independent events is the product of the two separate proportions ($p_1 \times p_2$), and therefore, under independence, $.65 \times .5 \times 1,000 = 325$ male voters would have been expected. Actually there are 350, indicating that men have a slightly higher tendency to vote than women. If the difference between the empirical and the "independent" figures for all four cells of the fourfold table had been computed, the same result—25 cases, or a difference of 2.5 per cent of the total set—would have been obtained. (Problems of statistical significance are not relevant for the present discussion.)

Here it is useful to introduce the symbolic abbreviation $|12|$,

$$
\begin{aligned}
.025 = |12| &= p_{12} - p_1 p_2 \\
&= -(p_{\bar{1}2} - p_{\bar{1}} p_2) \\
&= -(p_{1\bar{2}} - p_1 p_{\bar{2}}) \\
&= p_{\bar{1}\bar{2}} - p_{\bar{1}} p_{\bar{2}},
\end{aligned}
\tag{1}
$$

which may be called the *cross product* or the *symmetric parameter of second level*. The quantity $|12|$ is the basis of many measures of association in 2×2 tables [see STATISTICS, DESCRIPTIVE, *article on* ASSOCIATION]. Note that $|12| = -|1\bar{2}|$ and, in general, $|ij| = -|i\bar{j}| = |\bar{i}\bar{j}|$.

Cross products can also be computed for the stratified fourfold tables on the right side of Table 2, and by mere inspection new factual information emerges. In the high-status stratum, men and women have the same tendency to vote, and the stratified cross product vanishes. In the low-status stratum, the relation between sex and voting is very marked. The basic question of survey analysis is whether the relation between such cross products of different stratification levels can be put into a general algorithm that can be used to draw substantive inferences. The rest of this presentation is given to the development of the relevant procedures.

In the context of this presentation, with the exception of one case to be mentioned presently, interest is confined to whether the cross product is positive, is negative, or vanishes. This last case occurs when the two attributes are independent. If men and women furnish the same proportion of voters, the cross product will be zero. The same fact can, of course, also be expressed in a different way: the proportion of men is the same among voters and among nonvoters. In empirical studies the cross product will rarely vanish perfectly; it will just be very small. It is a problem in the theory of statistical hypothesis testing to decide when an empirical cross product differs enough from a hypothesized value (often zero) so that the difference is statistically significant. Concern here, however, is

Table 2[a]

			Vote 2 +	Vote 2 −	Total				Vote 2 +	Vote 2 −	Total				Vote 2 +	Vote 2 −	Total
	TOTAL SAMPLE												SES 3 +				
Sex 1	+		350	150	500	Sex 1	+		200	50	250	Sex 1	+		150*	100	250
	−		300	200	500		−		200	50	250		−		100	150	250
Total			650	350	1,000	Total			400	100	500*	Total			250	250	500*

a. Asterisk represents principal finding. Underscoring indicates the original information.

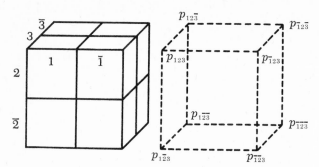

Figure 1 — The dichotomous cube and the relative position of third-level proportions

only with general logical relations between cross products, and discussion of sampling and measurement error is excluded.

The eight third-level class proportions of a three-attribute dichotomous system can be arranged in the form of a cube. Such a dichotomous cube consists of eight smaller cubes, each corresponding to one of the third-level proportions. The dichotomous cube and the relative position of the third-level proportions are shown in Figure 1.

A second-level proportion can be *expanded* in terms of its third-level components. Thus, for example, $p_{1\bar{2}} = p_{12\bar{3}} + p_{1\bar{2}\bar{3}}$. No proportion can be negative. Therefore, *if a second-level proportion vanishes, so do its components;* for example, if $p_{\bar{1}2} = 0$, then it follows that $p_{\bar{1}23} = p_{\bar{1}2\bar{3}} = 0$.

Consider now the proportions that lie in the front sheet of the dichotomous cube. Keeping them in their same relative position, they are as shown in Table 3, where the entries are the proportions corresponding to the frequencies in the middle part of Table 2. Table 3 is a fourfold table that summarizes the relation between attributes 1 and 2 within only a part of the complete set of individuals—those who possess attribute 3. Such a table is called a *stratified fourfold table*. The stratified table is bordered by marginal entries of the second level which are the sums of the respective rows and columns, as indicated in the margins of Table 3, as well as by the first-level proportion p_3, the sum of all the entries. The question of dependence or independence of two attributes can also be raised for a stratified table. A conditional cross product could be constructed from the stratified table by first dividing each entry by p_3. But because it makes the whole discussion

Table 3 — Front sheet of dichotomous cube

	1	$\bar{1}$	Total
2	p_{123}	$p_{\bar{1}23}$	p_{23}
$\bar{2}$	$p_{1\bar{2}3}$	$p_{\bar{1}\bar{2}3}$	$p_{\bar{2}3}$
Total	p_{13}	$p_{\bar{1}3}$	p_3

more consistent and avoids repeated computation of proportions, it is preferable to remain with the original proportions, computed on the base of the total set.

An obvious question, then, would concern the proportion of the high-status men who would have voted if sex had no influence on political behavior. Under this hypothesized independence the proportion would be given by $p_{13}p_{23}/p_3^2$. The actual proportion of the high-status men who voted is given by p_{123}/p_3. An obvious measure of the relationship between sex and voting within the high-status group is supplied by the difference between this actual proportion and the theoretical one. As an alternative development, if within the subset of individuals who possess attribute 3 there is no relation between attributes 1 and 2, then one would expect to find that there is the same proportion of individuals with attribute 1 in the entire subset as there is in that part of the subset which also possess attribute 2. That is,

$$\frac{p_{13}}{p_3} = \frac{p_{123}}{p_{23}}$$

or

$$\begin{vmatrix} p_{123} & p_{23} \\ p_{13} & p_3 \end{vmatrix} = 0.$$

This determinant will be taken as the definition of the *stratified cross product* between attributes 1 and 2 among the subset possessing attribute 3. The symbol $|12; 3|$ is used for this cross product. In general, then, $|ij; k|$ is defined by

$$(2) \qquad |ij; k| = \begin{vmatrix} p_{ijk} & p_{jk} \\ p_{ik} & p_k \end{vmatrix}.$$

Note that $|ij|$ can be represented as

$$\begin{vmatrix} p_{ij} & p_j \\ p_i & 1 \end{vmatrix}.$$

The elements in the back sheet of the dichotomous cube make up the stratified fourfold table shown in Table 4, which summarizes the relation between attributes 1 and 2 within that subset of individuals who *lack* attribute 3. The cross product of such a stratified fourfold table is defined by

$$\left| ij; \bar{k} \right| = \begin{vmatrix} p_{ij\bar{k}} & p_{j\bar{k}} \\ p_{i\bar{k}} & p_{\bar{k}} \end{vmatrix}.$$

It should be noted that eq. (2) suffices to define both $|ij; k|$ and $|ij; \bar{k}|$ if the index k is permitted to range through both barred and unbarred integers designating particular attributes.

Six fourfold tables can be formed from the ele-

Table 4 — Back sheet of dichotomous cube

	1	$\bar{1}$	Total
2	$p_{12\bar{3}}$	$p_{\bar{1}2\bar{3}}$	$p_{2\bar{3}}$
$\bar{2}$	$p_{1\bar{2}\bar{3}}$	$p_{\bar{1}\bar{2}\bar{3}}$	$p_{\bar{2}\bar{3}}$
Total	$p_{1\bar{3}}$	$p_{\bar{1}\bar{3}}$	$p_{\bar{3}}$

ments of the dichotomous cube, one for each of the six sheets. Each of these stratified tables can be characterized by its cross product. Thus, six conditional cross products, $|12; 3|$, $|12; \bar{3}|$, $|23; 1|$, $|23; \bar{1}|$, $|13; 2|$, and $|13; \bar{2}|$, can be formed from the elements of a dichotomous cube.

As can be seen from Figure 1, a dichotomous cube is completely known if the absolute frequency for each of its eight "cells" is known. These eight ultimate frequencies form what is called a *fundamental set;* if they are known, one can compute any of the many other combinations which may be of interest, some of which were used in the introductory example. The number of these possible combinations is large if one thinks of all stratification levels and of all combinations of absence and presence of the three attributes. The search for other fundamental sets, therefore, has always been of interest. Yule (see Yule & Kendall 1911) investigated one which consists of the so-called positive joint frequencies—the frequencies on all stratification levels which have no barred indices, together with the size of the sample (obviously, if the sample size is known, the remaining seven terms in a fundamental set can also be given in the form of proportions).

If one is looking for something like a calculus of associations, the question arises whether a fundamental set whose terms include cross products could be developed. One might then start with the following elements: N, the total number of individuals; p_1, p_2, p_3, the first-level proportions; and $|12|$, $|23|$, $|13|$, the three possible second-level cross products. But these are only seven elements, and so far no third-level data have been utilized. The eighth element must be of the third level, somehow characterizing the dichotomous cube as a whole (that is, depending explicitly on the third-level proportions).

One might choose as the eighth element one of the six stratified cross products, but there is no good reason for choosing one in preference to another. Also, any one of these would lack the symmetry which one can reasonably require of a parameter representing the whole cube.

The choice of the eighth parameter can be determined by three criteria: (a) The parameter should be *symmetric;* that is, its value should not be affected if the numbering of the attributes is changed around. For example, $|ij|$ is symmetric, since $|ij| = |ji|$. (b) The parameter should be *homogeneous,* in the sense that each of its terms should involve the same number of subscripts. (c) The parameter should be such that it can be used, together with lower-level class proportions, to *evaluate any third-level proportion.*

The second-level cross products $|ij| = p_{ij} - p_i p_j$ obviously satisfy the first two conditions. That condition (a), symmetry ($|12| = |21|$), and condition (b), homogeneity, are satisfied can be seen by inspection. That a condition analogous (for second-level proportions) to the third one is satisfied can be demonstrated by equations like

$$p_{i\bar{j}} = p_i p_j - |ij|,$$

which can be verified for any combination of bars and indices.

A homogeneous, symmetric parameter of third level can be built up from lower-level proportions and parameters as follows:

$$(3) \quad p_{ijk} = p_i p_j p_k + p_i |jk| + p_j |ik| + p_k |ij| + |ijk|.$$

The introduction of a new mathematical quantity often, at first sight, seems arbitrary, and indeed it is, in the sense that any combination of old symbols can be used to define a new one. The utility of an innovation and its special meaning can only evolve slowly, in the course of its use in the derivation of theorems and their applications. It will be seen that most of the subsequent material in this presentation centers on symmetric parameters of level higher than that of the cross product.

The quantity $|ijk|$, implicitly defined by eq. (3), quite evidently satisfies the criteria of homogeneity and symmetry; that it can be used together with lower-level class proportions to compute any third-level class proportion will now be shown.

If the indices i, j, and k are allowed to range through any three different numbers, barred or unbarred, it is easily shown that the quantities $|ij\bar{k}|$, $|i\bar{j}k|$, and so forth thus defined are not independent but are related to one another and to $|ijk|$ as follows:

$$|ijk| = -|ij\bar{k}| = -|i\bar{j}k| = -|\bar{i}jk| = |i\bar{j}\bar{k}|$$
$$= |\bar{i}j\bar{k}| = |\bar{i}\bar{j}k| = -|\bar{i}\bar{j}\bar{k}|.$$

As a mnemonic, note that if in $|ijk|$ an odd number of indices is barred, the symmetric parameter changes its sign; if an even number is barred, the value of $|ijk|$ remains unchanged. This is easily proved by showing that

$$|ijk| + |ij\bar{k}| = 0.$$

Once the third-level symmetric parameter is defined and computed by eq. (3), the computation of any desired third-level class proportion is possible. For example,

$$p_{\bar{1}\bar{2}\bar{3}} = p_{\bar{1}}p_{\bar{2}}p_{\bar{3}} + p_{\bar{1}}|2\bar{3}| + p_{\bar{2}}|\bar{1}\bar{3}| + p_{\bar{3}}|\bar{1}\bar{2}| + |\bar{1}\bar{2}\bar{3}|$$

$$= p_{\bar{1}}p_{\bar{2}}p_{\bar{3}} - p_{\bar{1}}|23| + p_{\bar{2}}|13| - p_{\bar{3}}|12| + |123|.$$

With the introduction of the third-level symmetric parameter, a three-attribute dichotomous system can now be completely summarized by *a new fundamental set* of eight data: N, p_1, p_2, p_3, $|12|, |13|, |23|, |123|$.

Through the symmetric parameter, cross products of all levels can be connected. To keep a concrete example in mind, refer to Table 2, where the relation between sex and voting is reported for the whole sample and for two SES strata. It will be seen presently that the following formulas form the core of survey analysis.

Symmetric parameters are substituted into the form

$$|ij; k| = \begin{vmatrix} p_{ijk} & p_{ik} \\ p_{jk} & p_k \end{vmatrix},$$

yielding

$$|ij; k| =$$

(4)

$$\begin{vmatrix} p_i p_j p_k + p_i|jk| + p_j|ik| + p_k|ij| + |ijk| & p_i p_k + |ik| \\ p_j p_k + |jk| & p_k \end{vmatrix}.$$

In the last determinant the second row multiplied by p_i is subtracted from the first row, and then the second column multiplied by p_j is subtracted from the first column. This leaves the right side of (4) as

$$\begin{vmatrix} |ijk| + p_k|ij| & |ik| \\ |jk| & p_k \end{vmatrix}.$$

Thus,

(5) $\qquad |ij; k| = p_k|ijk| + p_k^2|ij| - |ik|\,|jk|.$

By a similar computation,

(6) $\qquad |ij; \bar{k}| = -p_{\bar{k}}|ijk| + p_{\bar{k}}^2|ij| - |ik|\,|jk|.$

Eqs. (5) and (6) are, of course, related to each other by the general rule of barred indices expressed above.

It is worthwhile to give intuitive meaning to eqs. (5) and (6). Suppose the relation between sex (i) and voting (j) is studied separately among people of high and low SES (k). Then $|ij; k|$ is the cross product for sex and voting as it prevails in the high SES group. Eq. (5) says that this stratified interrelation is essentially the cross product $|ij|$ as it prevails in the total population corrected for the

relation that SES has with both voting and sex, given by the product $|ik|\,|jk|$. But an additional correction has to be considered: the "triple interaction" between all three attributes, $|ijk|$.

Subtracting eq. (6) from eq. (5), using the fact that $p_k + p_{\bar{k}} = 1$, and rearranging terms, one obtains

$$|ijk| = |ij; k| - |ij; \bar{k}| + |ij|\,(p_k - p_{\bar{k}}).$$

The symmetric parameter thus, in a sense, "measures" the *difference in the association* between i and j under the condition of k as compared with the condition of $\bar{k}$. This is especially true if $p_k = p_{\bar{k}}$, that is, if the two conditions are represented equally often—and often it is possible to manipulate marginals to produce such an equal cut (either by choosing appropriate sample sizes or by dichotomizing at the median).

By dividing eq. (5) and eq. (6) by p_k and $p_{\bar{k}}$, respectively, and adding the two, one obtains

(7) $\qquad \dfrac{|ij; k|}{p_k} + \dfrac{|ij; \bar{k}|}{p_{\bar{k}}} = |ij| - \dfrac{|ik|\,|jk|}{p_k p_{\bar{k}}}.$

The formula on the left side is analogous to the traditional notion of partial correlation: a weighted average of the two stratified cross products. It may be called the partial association between i and j with k partialed out.

Relation to measures of association. It is very important to keep in mind the difference between a partial and a stratified association. It can happen, for instance, that a partial association is zero, while the two stratified ones have nonzero values, one positive and one negative.

It was mentioned before that the cross products are not "measures of association." They form, however, the core of most of the measures which have been proposed for fourfold tables (Goodman & Kruskal 1954). A typical case is the "per cent difference," which may be exemplified by a well-known paradox [see STATISTICS, DESCRIPTIVE, *article on* ASSOCIATION]. Suppose that the three attributes are i, physical prowess; j, intelligence; and k, SES. Designate f_{ij} as the difference between the percentage of intelligent people in the physically strong group and in the physically weak group. It can easily be verified that $f_{ij} = |ij|/p_i p_{\bar{i}}$. The corresponding relation for the subset of high SES people would be

$$f_{ij;k} = \dfrac{|ij; k|}{p_{ik} p_{\bar{i}k}}.$$

Substituting this expression into eq. (7), one obtains

(8) $f_{ij}p_i p_{\bar{i}} = f_{ij;k}\dfrac{p_{ik}p_{\bar{i}k}}{p_k} + f_{ij;\bar{k}}\dfrac{p_{i\bar{k}}p_{\bar{i}\bar{k}}}{p_{\bar{k}}} + f_{ki}f_{kj}p_k p_{\bar{k}}.$

The f-coefficients are asymmetric. The first subscript corresponds to the item which forms the basis for the percenting; thus, f_{kj} is the difference between the per cents of intelligent people in the high SES subset and in the low SES subset. Now eq. (8) permits the following interpretation: Suppose that the high SES subset has a higher percentage of intelligent people but a lower percentage of physically strong people than the low SES subset ($f_{ki} < 0$ and $f_{kj} > 0$). Then it can happen that *in each SES subset* the physically stronger people *are more often relatively intelligent, while in the total group*—high and low SES combined—*the opposite is true*:

$$f_{ij;k} > 0, \qquad f_{ij;\bar{k}} > 0, \qquad \text{but } f_{ij} < 0.$$

Consider one more example of introducing a traditional measure into eq. (7). Suppose someone wants to use the well-known phi-coefficient, which is defined by

$$\phi_{ij} = \frac{|ij|}{\sqrt{p_i p_{\bar{i}} p_j p_{\bar{j}}}}.$$

With the use of the obvious symbol, the phi-coefficient applied to a stratified fourfold table would be

$$\phi_{ij;k} = \frac{|ij; k|}{\sqrt{p_{ik} p_{\bar{i}k} p_{jk} p_{\bar{j}k}}}.$$

By introducing the last two expressions into eq. (7), one would obtain a relation between stratified and unstratified phi-coefficients.

This is a good place to say a word about the relation between the Yule tradition and the tenor of this presentation. In a rather late edition Yule included one page on "relations between partial associations." He attached little importance to that approach: "In practice the existence of these relations is of little or no value. They are so complex that lengthy algebraic manipulation is necessary to express those which are not known in terms of those which are. It is usually better to evaluate the class frequencies and calculate the desired results directly from them" (Yule & Kendall 1911, p. 59 in the 1940 edition). The few computations Yule presented were indeed rather clumsy. It is easy to see what brought about improvement: the use of determinants, an index notation, and, most of all, the symmetric parameters. Still, it has to be acknowledged that Yule drew attention to the approach which was later developed. Incidentally, Yule reported the theorem on the weighted sum of stratified cross products (eq. 7). It appeared in earlier editions only as an exercise, but in later editions it was called "the one result which has important theoretical consequences." The consequences he

had in mind were studies of spurious factors in causal analysis, which he discussed under the title "illusory associations." It will presently be seen what he had in mind.

Modes of explanation in survey analysis

Eq. (7) is undoubtedly the most important for survey analysis. To bring out its implication, it is preferable to change the notation. Assume two original attributes, x and y. Their content makes it obvious that x precedes y in time sequence. If $|xy| > 0$, then this relation requires explanation. The explanation is sought by the introduction of a test factor, t, as a stratification variable. The possible combinations form a dichotomous cube, and eq. (7) now takes the form

$$(9) \qquad |xy| = \frac{|xy; t|}{p_t} + \frac{|xy; \bar{t}|}{p_{\bar{t}}} + \frac{|xt| \, |ty|}{p_t p_{\bar{t}}}.$$

This *elaboration* leads to two extreme forms, which are, as will be seen, of major interest. In the first case, the two stratified relations vanish; then eq. (9) reduces to

$$(10) \qquad |xy| = \frac{|xt| \, |ty|}{p_t p_{\bar{t}}}.$$

In the second, the test factor, t, is unrelated to x (so that $|xt| = 0$), and then

$$(11) \qquad |xy| = \frac{|xy; t|}{p_t} + \frac{|xy; \bar{t}|}{p_{\bar{t}}},$$

which also results if $|ty| = 0$. This form will turn out to be of interest only if one of the two stratified relations is markedly stronger than the other. Call eq. (11) the S form (emphasis on the stratified cross products) and eq. (10) the M form (emphasis on the "marginals").

To this formal distinction a substantive one, the time order of the three attributes, must be added. If x is prior to y in time, then t either can be located *between* x and y in time or can *precede* both. In the former case one speaks of an *intervening* test variable, in the latter of an *antecedent* one. Thus, there are four major possibilities. It is, of course, possible that t is subsequent in time to both x and y. But this is a case which very rarely occurs in survey analysis and is therefore omitted in this presentation.

Given the two forms of eq. (9) and the two relevant time positions of t, essentially four modes arise with two original variables and one test variable, as shown in Table 5. If a relation between two variables is analyzed in the light of a third, either with real data or theoretically, only these four modes or combinations thereof are sought, irrespec-

Table 5

		STATISTICAL FORM	
		S	M
POSITION OF t	Antecedent	SA	MA
	Intervening	SI	MI

tive of whether they are called interpretation, understanding, theory, or anything else.

Before this whole scheme is applied to concrete examples, the restriction put on the paradigm of Table 5 should be re-emphasized. Only one test variable is assumed. In actual survey practice it is highly unlikely that in eq. (9) the stratified cross products would disappear after one step. Instead of reaching eq. (10), one is likely to notice just a lowering of the first two terms on the right side of eq. (9). As a result, additional test variables must be introduced. But these further steps do not introduce new ideas. One stops the analysis at the point where one is satisfied with a combination of the four modes summarized in Table 5.

The notion of sequence in time also can be more complicated than appears in this schematic presentation. Sometimes there is not enough information available to establish a time sequence. Thus, when a positive association between owning a product and viewing a television program that advertises it is found, it is not necessarily known whether ownership preceded listening or whether the time sequence is the other way around. Additional information is then needed, if one is to proceed with the present kind of analysis. In other cases a time sequence might be of no interest, because the problem is of a type for which latent structure analysis or, in the case of quantitative variables, factor analysis is more appropriate [see LATENT STRUCTURE; FACTOR ANALYSIS]. The problem at hand is to "explain" an empirically found association between x and y. But "explain" is a vague term. The procedures which lead to the main paradigm show that there exist four basic modes of explanation, the combination of which forms the basis for survey analysis. It is also reasonable to relate each type to a terminology which might most frequently be found in pertinent literature. But although the basic types or modes of analysis are precisely defined, the allocation of a name to each of them is somewhat arbitrary and could be changed without affecting the main distinctions. Now each of the four types in the paradigm will be taken up and exemplified.

Specification.   In cases of the type SA, the test variable, t, is usually called a condition. General examples easily come to mind, although in practice

they are fairly rare and are a great joy to the investigator when they are found. For example: the propaganda effect of a film is greater among less-educated than among highly educated people; the depression of the 1930s had worse effects on authoritarian families than on other types.

Three general remarks can be made about this type of finding or reasoning: First, it corresponds to the usual stimulus–disposition–response sequence, with x as the stimulus and the antecedent t as the disposition. Second, the whole type might best be called one of *specification*. One of the two stratified associations will necessarily be larger than the original relationship. The investigator specifies, so to speak, the circumstances under which the original relationship holds true more strongly. Third, usually one will go on from the specification and ask why the relationship is stronger on one side of the test dichotomy than it is in the total group. This might then lead to one of the other types of analysis. Durkheim (1897) used type SA in discussing why relatively fewer married people commit suicide than unmarried people. He introduced as a test variable "a nervous tendency to suicide, which the family, by its influence, neutralizes or keeps from development." This is type SA exactly. It does not appear to be a convincing explanation, because the introduction of the hypothetical test variable (tendency to suicide) sounds rather tautological. A more important question is why the family keeps this tendency from development, which leads to type MI, as will be seen later.

Contingency.   The type SI is also easily exemplified. In a study of the relationship between job success (y) and whether children did or did not go to progressive schools (x), it is found that if the progressively educated children come into an authoritarian situation (t), they do less well in their work than others; on the other hand, if they come into a democratic atmosphere, their job success is greater.

The relation between type of education and job success is elaborated by an intervening test factor, the work atmosphere. This is a "contingency." In many prediction studies the predicted value depends upon subsequent circumstances that are not related to the predictor. An example is the relation between occupational status and participation in community activities. White-collar people participate more if they are dissatisfied with their jobs, whereas manual workers participate more if they are satisfied.

Correcting spurious relationships.   Type MA is used mainly in rectifying what is usually called a *spurious relationship*. It has been found that the more fire engines that come to a fire (x), the larger the damage (y). Because fire engines are used to reduce damage, the relationship is startling and requires elaboration. As a test factor, the size of the fire (t) is introduced. It might then be found that fire engines are not very successful; in large, as well as small, fires the stratified relation between x and y vanishes. But at least the original positive relation now appears as the product of two marginal relations: the larger the fire, the more engines called out, on the one hand, and the greater the damage, on the other hand.

Interpretation.   Type MI corresponds to what is usually called *interpretation*. The difference between the discovery of a spurious relationship and interpretation in this context is related to the time sequence between x and t. In an interpretation, t is an intervening variable situated between x and y in the time sequence.

Examples of type MI are numerous. Living in a rural community rather than a city (x) is related to a lower suicide rate (y). The greater intimacy of rural life (t) is introduced as an intervening variable. If there were a good test of cohesion, it would undoubtedly be found that a community's being a rural rather than an urban one (x) is positively correlated with its degree of cohesion (t) and that greater cohesion (t) is correlated with lower suicide rates (y). But obviously some rural communities will have less cohesion than some urban communities. If cohesion is kept constant as a statistical device, then the partial relationship between the rural–urban variable and the suicide rate would have to disappear.

Differences between the modes.   It might be useful to illustrate the difference between type MA and type MI in one more example. During the war married women working in factories had a higher rate of absence from work than single women. There are a number of possible elaborations, including the following:

The married women have more responsibilities at home. This is an intervening variable. If it is introduced and the two stratified relations—between marital status and absenteeism—disappear, the elaboration is of type MI. The relation is interpreted by showing what intervening variable connects the original two variables.

The married women are prone to physical infirmity, as crudely measured by age. The older women are more likely to be married and to have less physical strength, both of these as a result of their age. Age is an antecedent variable. If it turns

out that when age is kept constant the relation between marital status and absenteeism disappears, a spurious effect of type MA is the explanation. Older people are more likely to be married and more likely to need rest at home.

The latter case suggests, again, an important point. After the original relationship is explained, attention might shift to $|ty|$, the fact that older people show a higher absentee rate. This, in turn, might lead to new elaborations: Is it really the case that older women have less physical resistance, be they married or single? Or is it that older women were born in a time when work was not as yet important for women and therefore have a lower work morale? In other words, after one elaboration is completed, the conscientious investigator will immediately turn to a new one; the basic analytical processes, however, will always be the same.

Causal relations.   One final point can be cleared up, at least to a degree, by this analysis. It suggests a clear-cut definition of the *causal* relation between two attributes. If there is a relation between x and y, and if for every conceivable *antecedent* test factor the partial relations between x and y do *not* disappear, then the original relation should be called a causal one. It makes no difference here whether the necessary operations are actually carried through or made plausible by general reasoning. In a controlled experiment there may be two matched groups: the experimental exposure corresponds to the variable x, the observed effect to y. Randomization of treatments between groups makes sure that $|xt| = 0$ for any antecedent t. Then if $|xy| \neq 0$ and there have been no slip-ups in the experimental procedure, the preceding analysis always guarantees that there is a causal relation between exposure, x, and effect, y. There are other concepts of causal relations, differing from the one suggested here [*see* CAUSATION].

This has special bearing on the following kinds of discussion. It is found that the crime rate is higher in densely populated areas than in sparsely populated areas. Some authors state that this could not be considered a true causal relation, but such a remark is often intended in two very different ways. Assume an intervening variable—for instance, the increased irritation which is the result of crowded conditions. Such an interpretation does not detract from the causal character of the original relationship. On the other hand, the argument might go this way: crowded areas have cheaper rents and therefore attract poorer, partly demoralized people, who are also more likely to *be* criminals to begin with. Here the character of the inhabitants is antecedent to the characteristics of the area. In this case the original relationship is indeed explained as a spurious one and should not be called causal.

Variables not ordered in time. Explanation consists of the formal aspect of elaboration and some substantive ordering of variables. Ordering by time sequence has been the focus here, but not all variables can be ordered this way. One can distinguish orders of complexity, for example, variables characterizing persons, collectives, and sets of collectives. Other ordering principles could be introduced, for instance, degree of generality, exemplified by the instance of a specific opinion, a broader attitude, and a basic value system. What is needed is to combine the formalism of elaboration with a classification of variables according to different ordering principles. This covers a great part of what needs to be known about the logic of explanation and inference in contemporary survey analysis.

Higher-level parameters

This presentation has been restricted to the case of three attributes, but symmetric parameters can be developed for any level of stratification. Their structure becomes obvious if the parameter of fourth level is spelled out as an example:

$$
\begin{aligned}
p_{1234} = p_1 p_2 p_3 p_4 \\
+ p_1|234| + p_2|134| + p_3|124| + p_4|123| \\
(12) \qquad + p_{12}|34| + p_{13}|24| + p_{14}|23| \\
+ p_{23}|14| + p_{24}|13| + p_{34}|12| \\
+ |1234|.
\end{aligned}
$$

It is possible for lower-level symmetric parameters to vanish while some higher-level ones do not, and the other way around. The addition of $|1234|$ to the fundamental set would permit the analysis of questions like these: We already know that economic status affects the relation between sex and voting; is this contextual effect greater for whites or for Negroes? If an antecedent attribute (3) only lowers $|12; 3|$, would a fourth intervening attribute explain the residual relation by making $|12; 34| = 0$? The theorems needed to cope with a larger number of attributes in a survey analysis are often interesting by themselves but are too complex for this summary.

A substantive procedure can always be put into a variety of mathematical forms. Thus, for example, attributes can be treated as random variables, x_i, that can assume the values zero and one. Then the symmetric parameters play the role of covariances, and the difference between two stratified cross products corresponds to what is called interaction. Such translations, however, obscure rather than clarify the points essential for survey analysis. Starting from the notion of spurious correlation, Simon (1954) has translated the dichotomous cube into a system of linear equations that also permits the formalization of the distinction between the *MA* and the *MI* types. In such terminology, however, specifications (*SA* and *SI*) cannot be handled. In spite of this restriction, Blalock (1964) has productively applied this variation of survey analysis to problems for which the symmetric parameters of higher than second level may be negligible.

Polytomous systems have also been analyzed from a purely statistical point of view. A fourfold table is the simplest case of a contingency table that cross-tabulates two polytomous variates against each other. Thus, some of its statistical properties fall under the general heading of nonparametric statistics (Lindley 1964). An additional possibility is to start out with another way to characterize a fourfold table. Instead of a difference, $p_{12}p_{\overline{12}} - p_{1\overline{2}}p_{\overline{1}2}$, that is identical with the cross product, one can build formulas on the so-called odds ratio (Goodman 1965) $p_{12}p_{\overline{12}}/p_{1\overline{2}}p_{\overline{1}2}$. This leads to interesting comparisons between two stratified tables but has not been generalized to the more complex systems that come up in actual survey analysis. Eq. (12) forms the basis of this extension (Lazarsfeld 1961).

PAUL F. LAZARSFELD

[*See also* COUNTED DATA.]

BIBLIOGRAPHY

BLALOCK, HUBERT M. JR. 1964 *Causal Inferences in Nonexperimental Research.* Chapel Hill: Univ. of North Carolina Press.

BOUDON, RAYMOND 1965 Méthodes d'analyse causale. *Revue française de sociologie* 6:24–43.

CAPECCHI, VITTORIO 1967 Linear Causal Models and Typologies. *Quality and Quantity—European Journal of Methodology* 1:116–152.

DURKHEIM, ÉMILE (1897) 1951 *Suicide: A Study in Sociology.* Glencoe, Ill.: Free Press. → First published in French.

GOODMAN, LEO A. 1965 On the Multivariate Analysis of Three Dichotomous Variables. *American Journal of Sociology* 71:290–301.

GOODMAN, LEO A.; and KRUSKAL, WILLIAM H. 1954 Measures of Association for Cross Classifications. Part 1. *Journal of the American Statistical Association* 49:732–764. → Parts 2 and 3 appear in volumes 54 and 58 of the *Journal of the American Statistical Association.*

HYMAN, HERBERT H. 1955 *Survey Design and Analysis: Principles, Cases and Procedures.* Glencoe, Ill.: Free Press. → See especially Chapter 7.

LAZARSFELD, PAUL F. 1961 The Algebra of Dichotomous Systems. Pages 111–157 in Herbert Solomon (editor), *Item Analysis and Prediction.* Stanford Univ. Press.

LINDLEY, DENNIS V. 1964 The Bayesian Analysis of Contingency Tables. *Annals of Mathematical Statistics* 35:1622–1643.

NOWAK, STEFAN 1967 Causal Interpretation of Statistical Relationships in Social Research. *Quality and Quantity—European Journal of Methodology* 1:53–89.

SELVIN, HANAN C. 1958 Durkheim's *Suicide* and Problems of Empirical Research. *American Journal of Sociology* 63:607–619.

SIMON, HERBERT A. (1954) 1957 Spurious Correlation: A Causal Interpretation. Pages 37–49 in Herbert A. Simon, *Models of Man: Social and Rational.* New York: Wiley. → First published in Volume 49 of the *Journal of the American Statistical Association.*

YULE, G. UDNY; and KENDALL, MAURICE G. (1911) 1950 *An Introduction to the Theory of Statistics.* 14th ed., rev. & enl. London: Griffin. → See especially chapters 1–4, dealing with attribute data. M. G. Kendall has been a joint author since the eleventh edition (1937).

III
APPLICATIONS IN ECONOMICS

The development of economic theory and analysis requires an understanding of the forces that shape the decisions of firms, households, and governments. These forces can sometimes be deduced from general principles, such as profit maximization, or inferred from observations of economic behavior under different or changing prices, income, interest rates, etc. But the range of analysis, interpretation, and understanding is vastly enlarged by surveys, which elicit information directly from decision makers. Personal interviews can ascertain far more than simply the facts of the decision maker's situation and behavior; they can also uncover the amount of information available to him, his insight and understanding of the situation, his purposes and expectations, and the various constraints on his behavior. It is important to know, for example, not only what interest rates people are paying but also whether they know what the rate is, whether they see any alternative to borrowing, and what purposes their borrowing serves (in addition to the obvious one).

Interviews frequently throw light in a negative way on forces affecting decisions, by showing that substantial numbers of people do not have sufficient information or insight (understanding of the meaning of the information possessed) to be affected by particular factors. For example, interviews commonly show that many people believe—mistakenly—that during an inflationary period one should buy *more* bonds (not shift to stock) or take out *more* life insurance. In some cases individuals may, however, have adequate substitutes for detailed information and understanding, as when they know, without being able to compute an interest rate, that banks provide cheaper credit.

More important, detailed interviews frequently reveal that decision makers have purposes other than profit maximization and expense minimization, which are practically the sole objectives assumed in many theories of economic behavior. A man whose main desire is to be an excellent doctor or to run a successful business may be less concerned with avoiding income taxes than with getting his job done. Indeed, surveys offer the most direct and promising approach to interdisciplinary research, in which the variables to be explained or predicted pertain to behavior of various sorts and the explanatory variables incorporate theoretical constructs from economics, sociology, psychology, anthropology, etc.

Surveys vary from simple collections of limited facts—the call reports of member banks to the Federal Reserve System, the survey of manufacturers, the decennial census, etc.—to detailed personal interviews of heads of families or business firms. Survey data are used to estimate simple over-all statistics—such as the proportion of households with two cars, inside plumbing, their own home, or debt payments of more than 20 per cent of their income—and to study complex relations based on differences between subgroups or between representative individuals in society. It is the search for functional relations that brings such an endeavor within the sphere of science. The goal is not to explain differences in individual behavior, many of which cancel out even in small-group averages, but to find the forces that affect large parts of the population in the same way. Data that were originally collected for other purposes can often be used to analyze subgroup differences, but survey data have the advantage of being tailor-made for the analytical purposes at hand. Repeated surveys can provide data on changes over time in the characteristics and behavior of a population or of subgroups within a population. Panel studies are particularly useful in the study of subgroups over time, since they place little reliance on the memories of individuals.

History and development. The few surveys of economic behavior or conditions of families conducted before World War II used nonprobability samples and were largely descriptive, rather than analytical. They were concerned mostly with the plight of the workingman or the composition of the budget of a typical workingman's family (see Williams & Zimmerman 1935).

Since World War II there has been rapid improvement in techniques for the sampling of human populations and for eliciting information from them. At the same time, economists have focused increasingly on policy issues and on explanation and prediction of behavior, and this has led to an accelerated demand for information. Surveys have been expanded and improved to estimate the growth of population, the extent of unemployment, patterns of migration, the quality of housing, the extent of poverty, and the plight of special groups, such as the aged. Furthermore, the emphasis in survey analysis has shifted from measurement to explanation of behavior. Survey data can be and are used to test hypotheses regarding behavior, although this has commonly meant using data from a survey designed with other purposes in mind. When important problems are involved— such as the effects of medical insurance on the utilization of medical services, of taxes on incentives, or of local taxes on business location—special studies have been designed.

Major sources of survey data. Since surveys employing probability samples are relatively new and expensive, they have been conducted on a large scale in only a few countries, primarily the economically advanced ones. In the United States the major surveys have been carried on by the Bureau of Labor Statistics, the Bureau of the Census, and the Survey Research Center of the University of Michigan.

The surveys by the Bureau of Labor Statistics include the 1935–1936 expenditure survey (conducted jointly with the United States Department of Agriculture), the 1941–1942 survey of family spending and saving in wartime, the 1950 expenditure survey, and the 1960–1961 expenditure survey. The primary purpose of these surveys was to devise weights for a cost-of-living index, but other uses have been found for the data. The surveys increased over the years in quality, coverage, and availability for secondary analyses. The 1950 study appeared in 18 volumes and also led to a two-volume conference work (Conference on Consumption and Savings 1960).

The Bureau of the Census, which pioneered in probability sampling, has been responsible not only for the samples connected with the decennial censuses of population and housing but also for current population surveys (quarterly, with rotating panel samples for measuring population, labor force, and unemployment), housing surveys, special surveys of the aged, special studies embedded within the current population surveys (including such things as buying plans, home additions and repairs, ownership of major durables, migration, and income), and surveys of manufacturers (replacing the census of manufacturers).

The Survey Research Center of the University

of Michigan has conducted annual surveys of consumer finances since 1947, initially with the support and cooperation of the Federal Reserve Board and since 1960 with a variety of sponsors. The results appeared in the *Federal Reserve Bulletin* through 1959; since then they have appeared in annual volumes issued by the Survey Research Center. These volumes also provide summaries of surveys of consumer attitudes, expectations, and major past purchases, plus such special topics as attitudes toward a tax cut or toward federal expenditure programs. In addition, the Survey Research Center has conducted studies on a variety of special economic topics: the utilization of medical services in Michigan, attitudes toward innovations in household goods, the determinants of family income, the effects of private pension plans on saving, the economic impact of auto accidents in Michigan, and attitudes toward public expenditure programs—to cite just a few. (A complete bibliography can be obtained from the Survey Research Center.)

National studies on economic topics have also been conducted in the United States by the Market Surveys Section of the Department of Agriculture's Agricultural Marketing Service, by the National Opinion Research Center of the University of Chicago, and by National Analysts and other private survey organizations. Survey centers with a state or local focus have been established at Columbia University (Bureau of Applied Social Research), the University of Wisconsin, the University of California (Berkeley), and the University of Illinois.

Major expenditure or saving surveys have been conducted, although not regularly, in Great Britain, Puerto Rico, Ceylon, India, Japan, Sweden, Israel, and Mexico. In addition, there have been numerous small-scale studies of restricted areas.

Surveys on economic topics are carried on continually by the Government Social Survey in Great Britain and the Danish National Institute of Social Research and, less regularly, by the Institut National de la Statistique et des Études Économiques (INSEE) and the newly formed Centre de Recherche Économique sur l'Épargne in France, the Swedish Central Bureau of Statistics, the Polish Radio and Television Service's Public Opinion Research Center, the Forschungsstelle für Empirische Sozialökonomie in Germany (Cologne), the National Council of Applied Economic Research in India (New Delhi), and the Indian government's National Sample Survey. New survey centers are being established in Peru and at the Royal College in Kenya (Nairobi). Centers exist in Chile and Argentina as well, but these focus mainly on sociological or political questions. Of course, single surveys are sometimes done without the establishment of a permanent organization.

Sampling methods. Scientific surveys require probability samples of the population being studied. Since complete lists of people or families are rare, some other sampling frame is required. The one generally adopted is geographic. Everyone is assumed to have some place of residence. A probability sample of people can be developed by sampling the map and taking those who live in the sampled areas. Lists of people, from various sources, have also been used, of course—even rice-ration coupon book lists (in Ceylon); and many special studies use samples of special lists. [*See* SAMPLE SURVEYS.]

A simple probability sample would, however, be expensive and relatively inefficient. Hence, most samples are multistage clustered stratified samples, frequently with interlaced controls. The primary sampling units, roughly counties, are ordered on the basis of a number of criteria—such as region, rate of population growth, and per cent of labor force employed in manufacturing—and are sampled with a population interval that assures proper stratification. Interviews are clustered—in selected counties, in selected areas within counties, and in selected clusters of addresses within those areas—to minimize travel costs or, rather, to maximize the information per dollar spent on traveling and interviewing. Suburbs of the largest metropolitan areas are pooled, stratified by type, and sampled, so that the particular suburban localities of one area in a given sample may represent not all the suburbs of that area, but rather suburbs of that type in several areas.

In general, however, a subsection of a probability sample, selected without using the sampling units (geographic location) as a criterion, is a probability sample of the subgroup it deals with, for instance, a given age or occupation group. In most recent samples, even the regional subsamples are probability samples.

Sometimes, however, a probability sample would have to be unduly large to provide sufficient precision in the information about some subgroup, such as the aged, or those with hospital experience, or women of childbearing age. In this case, unless complete lists are available, some sort of screening is generally required. Either the group is selected from previous interview studies and revisited or a large number of addresses are visited, with interviews being taken only if the right kind of person lives at the address.

A probability sample can be inefficient or even misleading if clustering is overdone, and can be biased if serious attempts are not made to secure information from a large proportion of the sample selected. Those difficult to interview often vary widely—the very young, the very old, the very rich, families in which all members work, individuals suffering financial reverses, etc.

The precision of a sample is almost independent of the size of the population it represents and from which it is selected. Hence, it does not take a substantially larger sample to represent the whole United States than to represent California or Chicago. Once a national sample is developed and interviewers are hired and trained, there are substantial economies in doing a continuing series of national sample surveys; only the last stage of sampling needs to be repeated (selection of addresses). Furthermore, there are no problems in generalizing the results to a broad population and in relating survey data to national aggregates from other sources.

On the other hand, special samples sometimes become themselves an analytical device, since they isolate those at extremes of a behavioral continuum or uncover what is behind the decisions that have had the greatest economic effect.

Methods of eliciting information. The reliability of information is a far more important problem, and more in need of further work, than sampling techniques. It is not always true that facts are more reliably reported than attitudes. Memories are fallible, and people misunderstand questions. A growing body of literature and unpublished studies indicates that it is difficult to make general statements regarding reliability, which seems to depend very much on the content of the questions, as well as on the interviewer's training and procedures. The most dramatic illustration of the nature of the problem arose when the U.S. Census Bureau changed the sample it used for the current population surveys. The first time the new sample was used, estimates of unemployment jumped markedly. It turned out that the cause of the jump was not the sample change but the better training of the new interviewers, who followed their instructions more carefully, asked all the questions, and found more people in the labor force, hence more unemployed (Hansen 1954; U.S. Department of Commerce 1954).

It has proved difficult to get people to look up records, and their memories for financial data are often poor. Hence, when *changes* in financial magnitudes are required, the common practice is to rely on reinterviews. The difficulties with reinterviews are that people move and that the probability of securing two interviews even for those who do not move is somewhat lower than the chance of a single interview. Three different panels have been embedded into the surveys of consumer finances of the Survey Research Center, which also carried on a special panel study interviewing people five times over a three-year period. The Center is currently reinterviewing a panel several times in a study of the effects of the tax cut of 1964–1965 in the United States. The Bureau of the Census' current population surveys use a rotating panel to increase precision in estimating changes in the labor force, and the bureau conducted a reinterview study for the Federal Reserve Board in 1963–1964 to secure data on assets and savings.

For collecting information on attitudes, expectations, buying plans, and motives, a technique known as fixed-question–open-answer has been used, in which the verbatim replies to a uniform question are analyzed and converted into categories at a central office. This is done under close supervision and with intensive reworking, to assure uniformity, which is crucial when comparisons between surveys are needed. On the other hand, elaborate scaling techniques have not commonly been used in economic surveys, partly because these surveys usually have not contained numerous questions that attempt to measure the same attitude or purpose.

While prime reliance has been placed on personal interviews, some use has been made of telephone and mail questionnaires. Telephone inquiries are particularly useful for brief follow-up questions or for locating scattered people sampled from lists. Answers to open-ended questions tend to be briefer and more noncommittal, and there are more serious limits to what can be asked. Response rates to mail questionnaires have varied from very low to very high, depending on the content, the sample, the amount of work required, and (to a small extent) the procedures. Answers again tend to be more noncommittal, and there is the added difficulty of knowing who actually replied.

Treatment of missing information. However representative the original sample is, the survey results can be biased because of nonresponse, that is, cases where there is no interview at all. There will also be missing items of information in otherwise satisfactory interviews. Some of the resulting bias can be reduced by weighting subgroups for nonresponse and by assigning values to some of the more crucial bits of missing information on the basis of other information known about the respondent from previous surveys. But the problem

cannot be avoided, and any estimates from a sample imply some assumption about the missing pieces. If it is known that most of the nonresponse came, say, from families with two wage earners and no children, then similar families who were interviewed can be "weighted up" to represent the missing ones. The more information available about the nonresponse cases, the more likely it is that such weighting can be designed to reduce bias. Sometimes interviews are simply duplicated to make up for missing interviews, but this is a relatively crude procedure. It is better to weight up fifty similar cases by 2 per cent than to duplicate one case. [See ERRORS, article on NONSAMPLING ERRORS.]

When the sampling is not done everywhere at uniform rates—for example, when the rate in lower-income areas is half that in higher-income areas—weights are used to make the final results representative, the weights being the inverse of the sampling ratios. This was commonly done with the early surveys of consumer finances, in which higher-rent dwellings were oversampled and upper-income people were oversampled for reinterviewing.

Analysis of survey data. Rapid development has taken place in the techniques of analysis of survey data, which present a challenge because of their very richness. In economic studies some measure of economic capacity—such as income, total consumption, or wealth—is usually an important classifying characteristic, but the effects of economic capacity on any particular thing—such as home ownership or expenditure on durables—may well vary between rural areas and cities or between old and young. While much survey data is produced only in the form of tables, usually by age or income or family size, increasingly the analysis moves to more complex procedures. Many problems arise, and some theoretical or statistical assumptions must be imposed to make the analysis manageable.

A much used procedure is multiple regression, which assumes that each explanatory factor can be converted into some numerical scale and that these variables have a linear additive relationship with the variable to be explained. Since many of the explanatory factors—occupation, region, etc.—are not themselves scaled, it has become common to introduce "dummy variables" to represent each subclass (except one) of each such factor (Hill 1959; Suits 1957). A dummy variable takes on the value 1 if the individual belongs to the subclass, 0 if he does not.

The assumption of additive effects has remained troublesome. By comparison, the cross-product of two dummy variables introduces only a limited form of interaction effect. It isolates only one of four possible corners of a two-way table; the corner isolated depends on the definitions of the dummy variables. Most recently the search for interaction effects has been formalized and programmed for machine computation (Sonquist & Morgan 1964). This flexible approach produces findings that would otherwise be uncovered only by accident or by many repeated regressions for various subgroups. For example, it has been found that the effects of insurance on the utilization of medical care are important only for adult females; that nonwhite wives are more likely to work than white wives, but the difference is great only at the stage in the family life cycle when there are children in school; that a measure of achievement motivation is related to hourly earnings, but only for middle-aged male college graduates; and that having a private pension is associated with higher (not lower) savings for those persons who have at least $500 in assets—an asset level that seems to indicate that the individual has learned how he can save.

Limitations.   Sample surveys are not appropriate vehicles for securing all kinds of information. It would be useful to know the extent of illegal gambling, or the number of abortions in the United States, or how many people cheat on their income taxes, but it is doubtful that such information would be freely given. It is possible to study popular attitudes about such things, how attitudes of different groups in the population differ, and how attitudes change over time.

In the financial area, individuals easily remember large, irregular, salient matters, such as the price or payment arrangements for a new car or the size of a hospital bill, and regular payments, such as the rent or the mortgage. Other details of family expenditure, however, are generally difficult to recall, and it has never proved easy to get people to keep records. Indeed, only a few keep any records of their expenditures on any regular basis—and these individuals may be atypical in other ways as well.

Some matters are likely to be regarded as private information. In the United States, where most people are employed by others on a regular basis, income is not a particularly sensitive item, nor is installment credit; but assets (particularly with older people) and small loan debts do seem to be sensitive.

It should be kept in mind, however, that where memories are poor or people are sensitive, it may well be possible to secure approximate information, sufficient for many purposes. It is not necessary to know a man's income to the dollar to classify him for analytical purposes.

The paucity of published studies of response errors belies both the amount of research that has been done and the growing interest in methodology. It is, however, quite impossible to determine the accuracy of each of the hundred bits of information secured in a survey, and it will remain necessary to rely on general impressions as to what respondents can be expected to be able and willing to recall in an interview. As long as errors are distributed randomly, or at least independently of the explanatory factors being investigated, they do not lead to spurious positive findings, although they reduce the possibility of finding real relationships.

Forecasting short-run changes.   Surveys are used both to forecast short-run changes in the behavior of consumers or businessmen and to develop a behavioral theory of what it is that brings about these changes. A continuing series of surveys asking about expectations, attitudes, buying plans, and recent major purchases provides evidence on short-run changes in the propensity to consume (or invest). Analyses of such data provide evidence as to the causes of changes in attitudes and how such changes are related to subsequent economic behavior. Once consumers become affluent enough to have some real freedom of action—particularly when the use of cars and appliances and other forms of consumer investment allow postponement or speeding up of investments—changes in "consumption" can become more volatile than changes in business investment.

Since many of the consumer's decisions involve commitment to a pattern of payments (and depreciation) into the future, his views of the future can be expected to affect his decisions. Thus, it is argued, the consumer's confidence and optimism about his own and his country's economic future can and will affect his propensity to make expenditures. The original and continuing work in this area is that of George Katona (1960; 1964) and Eva Mueller (1963). Also, data on buying plans and on a few consumer attitudes are collected by the U.S. Bureau of the Census in its current population surveys.

In the United States, surveys of business investment intentions and other expectations, based on mail questionnaires, have been carried on both by the government (the Securities and Exchange Commission and the Department of Commerce) and by private groups (market research firms and magazines like *Business Week*). In Europe expectational data are collected much more frequently and from larger samples, but the questions relate only to the direction of change. Such questions are easier to answer. The pooled results, industry by industry, are sent to the firms, to induce them to continue cooperating.

Further uses of survey data. Survey analysis provides information on such points as the shape of the consumption function, the role of interest rates, asset preferences and the demand for money, and factors affecting investment decisions. The relationships discovered can be incorporated into systems of equations describing large sectors of an economy, or the economy as a whole. At a simpler level, information relating initial conditions to subsequent actions can be used to construct a Markov process describing the behavior of variables over time. For example, the relation of a respondent's father's education to his own provides evidence on intergenerational change in education levels and can be used to estimate the distribution of education in the population several generations hence (Morgan et al. 1962). It is, of course, necessary to use a sample of sons, not fathers, since not only may a father have more than one son, but an individual son's education may be affected by the number of brothers and sisters he has. Survey data pertaining to brand loyalty have also been treated and analyzed in terms of Markov processes. [See Markov chains.]

Surveys repeated over time can also be used to study processes of social change, not only by indicating over-all changes but also by identifying the subgroups of society in which changes are occurring most rapidly. There are interpretive problems, of course, when age groups are involved, since the age of an individual, the year he was born (his generation, or "cohort"), and the year of the survey are related perfectly to one another. Hence, it is never possible to hold two of them constant and vary the third. However, if it can be assumed that chronological age does not matter, it is possible to separate time trends from differences between generations. Or if the year of a man's birth does not matter, it is possible to separate age effects from time trends, or to find separate time trends for each age group. Or if it can be assumed that there are no major trends, repeated surveys can separate the effects of age from those of cohort (year of birth).

Repeated surveys also allow one to investigate whether the changes in the over-all aggregate of a dependent variable are due to changes in the population structure, changes in the way certain factors affect behavior, or changes in trends unrelated to the variables that have been measured.

JAMES N. MORGAN

[*Directly related are the entries* CONSUMERS, *articles on* CONSUMER ASSETS *and* CONSUMER BEHAVIOR; CONSUMPTION FUNCTION; CROSS-SECTION ANALYSIS; INDEX NUMBERS, *articles on* PRACTICAL APPLICATIONS *and* SAMPLING; PANEL STUDIES; PREDICTION AND FORECASTING, ECONOMIC; SAMPLE SURVEYS.]

BIBLIOGRAPHY

ANDERSON, ODIN; and FELDMAN, JACOB (1954) 1956 *Family Medical Costs and Voluntary Health Insurance: A Nationwide Survey.* New York: McGraw-Hill. → First published as *National Family Survey of Medical Costs and Voluntary Health Insurance.*

BARLOW, ROBIN; MORGAN, JAMES N.; and WIRICK, GROVER 1960 A Study of Validity in Reporting Medical Care in Michigan. American Statistical Association, Social Statistics Section, *Proceedings* [1960]: 54–65.

BREAK, GEORGE F. 1957 Income Taxes and Incentives to Work: An Empirical Study. *American Economic Review* 47:529–549.

CAPLOVITZ, DAVID 1963 *The Poor Pay More: Consumer Practices in Low-income Families.* New York: Free Press.

CONARD, ALFRED et al. 1964 *Automobile Accident Costs and Payments: Studies in the Economics of Injury Reparation.* Ann Arbor: Univ. of Michigan Press.

CONFERENCE ON CONSUMPTION AND SAVINGS, UNIVERSITY OF PENNSYLVANIA, *1959* 1960 *Proceedings.* 2 vols. Edited by Irwin Friend and Robert Jones. Philadelphia: Univ. of Pennsylvania Press.

EISNER, ROBERT 1957 Interview and Other Survey Techniques and the Study of Investment. Pages 513–601 in Conference on Research in Income and Wealth, *Problems of Capital Formation: Concepts, Measurement, and Controlling Factors.* Princeton Univ. Press.

FERBER, ROBERT 1959 *Collecting Financial Data by Consumer Panel Techniques.* Urbana: Univ. of Illinois, Bureau of Economic and Business Research.

FERBER, ROBERT 1962 Research on Household Behavior. *American Economic Review* 52:19–63.

FRIEND, IRWIN; and BRONFENBRENNER, JEAN 1955 Plant and Equipment Programs and Their Realization. Pages 53–111 in Conference on Research in Income and Wealth, *Short Term Economic Forecasting.* Princeton Univ. Press.

HANSEN, MORRIS 1954 Questions and Answers. *American Statistician* 8, no. 4:33–34.

HELLER, WALTER W. 1951 The Anatomy of Investment Decisions. *Harvard Business Review* 29, no. 2:95–103.

HILL, T. P. 1959 An Analysis of the Distribution of Wages and Salaries in Great Britain. *Econometrica* 27:355–381.

INTERNATIONAL LABOR OFFICE 1961 *Family Living Studies: A Symposium.* Studies and Reports, New Series, No. 63. Geneva: The Office.

JUSTER, FRANCIS T. 1964 *Anticipations and Purchases: An Analysis of Consumer Behavior.* Princeton Univ. Press.

KATONA, GEORGE 1960 *The Powerful Consumer: Psychological Studies of the American Economy.* New York: McGraw-Hill.

KATONA, GEORGE 1964 *The Mass Consumption Society.* New York: McGraw-Hill.

KATONA, GEORGE; and MORGAN, JAMES N. 1952 The Quantitative Study of Factors Determining Business Decisions. *Quarterly Journal of Economics* 66:67–90.

KISH, LESLIE; and LANSING, JOHN B. 1954 Response Errors in Estimating the Value of Homes. *Journal of the American Statistical Association* 49:520–538.

KLEIN, LAWRENCE R.; and LANSING, JOHN B. 1955 Decisions to Purchase Consumer Durable Goods. *Journal of Marketing* 20, October: 109–132.

LAMALE, HELEN 1959 *Methodology of the Survey of Consumer Expenditures in 1950.* Philadelphia: Univ. of Pennsylvania Press.

LANSING, JOHN; GINSBURG, GERALD; and BRAATEN, KAISA 1961 *An Investigation of Response Error.* Urbana: Univ. of Illinois, Bureau of Economic and Business Research.

LANSING, JOHN B.; and WITHEY, STEPHEN B. 1955 Consumer Anticipations: Their Use in Forecasting Consumer Behavior. Pages 381–453 in Conference on Research in Income and Wealth, *Short Term Economic Forecasting.* Princeton Univ. Press.

LIVIATAN, NISSAN 1963 Tests of the Permanent-income Hypothesis Based on a Reinterview Savings Survey. Pages 29–59 in *Measurement in Economics: Studies in Mathematical Economics and Econometrics in Memory of Yehuda Grunfeld.* Stanford Univ. Press. → A "Note" by Milton Friedman and a reply by Liviatan appear on pages 59–66.

LYDALL, HAROLD F. 1957 The Impact of the Credit Squeeze on Small and Medium Sized Manufacturing Firms. *Economic Journal* 67:415–431.

MCNERNEY, WALTER J. et al. 1962 *Hospital and Medical Economics.* 2 vols. Chicago: Hospital Research and Educational Trust. → See especially Volume 1, pages 61–357.

MARQUARDT, WILHELM; and STRIGEL, WERNER 1959 *Der Konjunkturtest: Eine neue Methode der Wirtschaftsbeobachtung.* Berlin: Duncker & Humblot.

MORGAN, JAMES N. 1958 A Review of Recent Research on Consumer Behavior. Volume 3, pages 93–219 in Lincoln Clark (editor), *Consumer Behavior: Research on Consumer Reactions.* New York: Harper.

MORGAN, JAMES N.; BARLOW, ROBIN; and BRAZER, HARVEY 1965 A Survey of Investment Management and Working Behavior Among High-income Individuals. *American Economic Review* 55, no. 2: 252–264.

MORGAN, JAMES N.; and SONQUIST, JOHN A. 1963 Problems in the Analysis of Survey Data, and a Proposal. *Journal of the American Statistical Association* 58: 415–434.

MORGAN, JAMES N. et al. 1962 *Income and Welfare in the United States.* New York: McGraw-Hill.

MORRISSETT, IRVING 1957 Psychological Surveys in Business Forecasting. Pages 258–315 in Rensis Likert and Samuel P. Hayes (editors), *Some Applications of Behavioral Research.* Paris: UNESCO.

MUELLER, EVA 1957 Effects of Consumer Attitudes and Purchases. *American Economic Review* 47:946–965.

MUELLER, EVA 1960 Consumer Attitudes: Their Influence and Forecasting Value. Pages 149–179 in Universities–National Bureau Committee for Economic Research, *The Quality and Economic Significance of Anticipations Data.* Princeton Univ. Press.

MUELLER, EVA 1963 Ten Years of Consumer Attitude Surveys: Their Forecasting Record. *Journal of the American Statistical Association* 58:899–917.

MUELLER, EVA; and MORGAN, JAMES N. 1962 Location Decisions of Manufacturers. *American Economic Review* 52, no. 2: 204–217.

MUELLER, EVA; WILKEN, ARNOLD; and WOOD, MARGARET 1961 *Location Decisions and Industrial Mobility in Michigan.* Ann Arbor: Univ. of Michigan, Institute for Social Research.

NETER, JOHN; and WAKSBERG, JOSEPH 1964a Conditioning Effects From Repeated Household Interviews. *Journal of Marketing* 28, April: 51–56.

NETER, JOHN; and WAKSBERG, JOSEPH 1964b A Study of Response Errors in Expenditures Data From Household Interviews. *Journal of the American Statistical Association* 59:18–55.

ORCUTT, GUY H. et al. 1961 *Microanalysis of Socioeconomic Systems: A Simulation Study.* New York: Harper.

SIRKIN, MONROE G.; MAYNES, E. SCOTT; and FRECHTLING, JOHN A. 1958 The Survey of Consumer Finances and the Census Quality Check. Pages 127–168 in Conference on Research in Income and Wealth, *An Appraisal of the 1950 Census Income Data.* Princeton Univ. Press.

SONQUIST, JOHN A.; and MORGAN, JAMES N. 1964 *The Detection of Interaction Effects: A Report on a Computer Program for the Selection of Optimal Combinations of Explanatory Variables.* Monograph No. 35. Ann Arbor: Univ. of Michigan, Institute for Social Research, Survey Research Center.

STONE, RICHARD 1963 Consumers' Wants and Expenditures: A Survey of British Studies Since 1945. In Colloque International sur les Besoins de Biens de Consommation, Grenoble, 11–15 September, 1961, *Actes.* Paris: Éditions du Centre National de la Recherche Scientifique. → Reprinted in mimeographed form by the Department of Applied Economics, Cambridge University.

SUITS, DANIEL B. 1957 Use of Dummy Variables in Regression Equations. *Journal of the American Statistical Association* 52:548–551.

THEIL, H. 1955 Recent Experiences With the Munich Business Test. *Econometrica* 23:184–192.

TOBIN, JAMES 1959 On the Predictive Value of Consumer Intentions and Attitudes. *Review of Economics and Statistics* 41:1–11. → See the comments by George Katona on page 317.

U.S. DEPARTMENT OF COMMERCE, SPECIAL ADVISORY COMMITTEE ON EMPLOYMENT STATISTICS 1954 *Measurement of Employment and Unemployment by the Bureau of the Census in Its Current Population Survey.* Washington: Government Printing Office.

WILLIAMS, FAITH M.; and ZIMMERMAN, CARLE C. 1935 *Studies of Family Living in the United States and Other Countries: An Analysis of Material and Method.*

U.S. Department of Agriculture, Miscellaneous Publication No. 223. Washington: Government Printing Office.

WIRICK, GROVER; and BARLOW, ROBIN 1964 The Economic and Social Determinants of the Demand for Health Services. Pages 95–125 in Conference on the Economics of Health and Medical Care, University of Michigan, 1962, *The Economics of Health and Medical Care*. Ann Arbor: Univ. of Michigan.

SÜSSMILCH, JOHANN PETER

Johann Peter Süssmilch (1707–1767), German demographer, was born in Berlin, the son of a corn merchant. He was interested in medicine at an early age, but his parents did not want him to become a physician and sent him to the university at Halle to study Latin and jurisprudence. After he had been there for a while, he decided instead that he would study Protestant theology and enter the ministry. In 1728 he went to the University of Jena to study philosophy, mathematics, and physics.

In 1736 Süssmilch was appointed chaplain to Marshal von Kalckstein's regiment, and he accompanied the regiment during the First Silesian War. The foreword to his famous book *Die göttliche Ordnung in den Veränderungen des menschlichen Geschlechts, aus der Geburt, dem Tode und der Fortpflanzung desselben erwiesen* ("The Divine Order in the Changes in the Human Race . . .") was signed in 1741, "advancing on Schweidnitz." After the war was over he performed pastoral duties, primarily in Berlin, while he carried on his demographic studies. In 1745 he was elected a member of the Akademie der Wissenschaften.

Although Süssmilch wrote on a wide variety of subjects—philosophy, religion, politics, science, and even linguistics—all of his work is profoundly connected with his analytical theory of population. His book on population, *Die göttliche Ordnung*, is the first complete and systematic treatise on the subject. The work was first published in 1741 and was revised in 1761, but it is best known in the fourth, posthumous edition of 1775.

Süssmilch's theory of population was influenced by William Derham and by John Graunt and William Petty. From Derham's *Physico-theology*, published in London in 1713, Süssmilch took the idea that divine providence has established a balance between the size of the population and the supply of food required for subsistence; from Graunt and Petty he learned that it may be possible to discern an underlying order in vital statistics. Süssmilch's assertion of a divine order in population trends reflects the desire, shared by most eighteenth-century scientists, to detect the pattern of the "natural order." He was convinced that if he succeeded in measuring fecundity and mortality, the vital statistics he discovered would agree with the eternal laws of God, whom he compared to an "infinite and exact Arithmeticus . . . who has determined for all things in their temporal state their score, weight, and proportion."

Although works in political arithmetic exerted a certain influence on Süssmilch, he did not use their rather speculative methods of estimating from faulty or inadequate data. He was one of the first to perceive that the consistency and stability of estimates depends on the number of observations. "One must collect a mass of particular cases over many years and sum up the data for whole provinces before it is possible to detect the concealed rules. Only then does the conformity of these rules to the natural order become apparent" (1741, vol. 1, p. 64).

To obtain reliable estimates, Süssmilch extracted demographic data from many Protestant parish registers. As population mobility was limited and the number of non-Protestants in Prussia was small, the data were fairly representative of the total population. He established the absolute frequencies of births and of deaths and measured the relative growth of population by comparing these quantities, deriving what he called a "rate of special mortality." Arranging the deaths by age groups and comparing the rates for these groups with the rate for a stationary population, he developed a life table. He measured fertility by comparing the number of christened children to the number of married people; as this proportion proved to be relatively constant, he estimated the "general fecundity" of a state by counting the number of married couples.

Süssmilch's rate of special mortality averaged 125/100, that is, he found about 125 births per 100 deaths. He used this rate to predict population growth, estimating that the population tended to double every century. This "divine order" of growth might, however, be disturbed by plagues and wars. Climatic or social obstacles might prevent or defer marriage, thus lengthening the period required for doubling the population. Having established the stability of over-all birth rates and mortality ratios, Süssmilch observed that the rate of growth in urban districts was significantly lower than in rural districts. He therefore concluded that urbanization was a social factor restraining growth. He did not see any definite limits to the tendency of population to increase. Estimating the population capacity of the world at 14,000 million and the population of the world of his time at 1,000 million, he judged that population could grow without any difficulties for the next several centuries.

In order to follow the natural order and to obey divine providence, political measures should support the tendency of population to increase. This interpretation of natural and divine order by Süssmilch conformed well with the mercantilist theories of his time, which emphasized the advantages of a large population for the wealth and military power of the state.

Süssmilch was highly respected as a learned man at the court of Frederick II of Prussia. Christian Wolf, in his Preface to the first edition, called *Die göttliche Ordnung* "a proof that the theories of probability may be utilized for the comprehension of human life." Süssmilch's work, nevertheless, did not have much influence. An abbreviated Dutch translation is the only foreign edition, and the last German reprint dates from 1798. There are at least two reasons for this neglect of Süssmilch's ideas and methods. First, the Achenwall school of statistics rejected Süssmilch's concern with the philosophical implications of population growth, centering its attention more exclusively on the numerical frequency and stability of vital processes. Second, the pessimistic Malthusian theory of population ran counter to Süssmilch's optimistic views. It was not until modern statistics had to deal with actual demographic problems that the abundance of ideas and the methodological achievements of *Die göttliche Ordnung* were finally acknowledged.

I. ESENWEIN-ROTHE

[*For the historical context of Süssmilch's work, see* POPULATION *and the biographies of* GRAUNT *and* PETTY.]

WORKS BY SÜSSMILCH

(1741) 1788 *Die göttliche Ordnung in den Veränderungen des menschlichen Geschlechts, aus der Geburt, dem Tode und der Fortpflanzung desselben erwiesen.* 3 vols. Berlin: Verlag der Buchhandlung der Realschule. → Translations of extracts in the text were provided by I. Esenwein-Rothe.

1752 *Der königlichen Residenz Berlin schneller Wachsthum und Erbauung.* Berlin: Haude.

1758 *Gedanken von den epidemischen Krankheiten und dem grösseren Sterben des 1757ten Jahres.* Berlin: Haude.

1766 *Versuch eines Beweises, dass die erste Sprache ihren Ursprung nicht von Menschen, sondern allein vom Schöpfer erhalten habe.* Berlin: Haude.

SUPPLEMENTARY BIBLIOGRAPHY

BONAR, JAMES (1931) 1966 *Theories of Population From Raleigh to Arthur Young.* New York: Kelley.

CRUM, FREDERICK S. 1901 The Statistical Works of Süssmilch. *Journal of the American Statistical Association* 7:335–380.

DERHAM, WILLIAM (1713) 1742 *Physico-theology: Or, a Demonstration of the Being and Attributes of God, From His Works of Creation.* 10th ed. London: Innys.

ELSTER, LUDWIG 1924 Bevölkerungswesen: III. Bevölkerungslehre und Bevölkerungspolitik. Volume 2, pages 735–812 in *Handwörterbuch der Staatswissenschaften.* 4th ed. Jena (Germany): Fischer.

HORVATH, ROBERT 1962 *L'ordre divin* de Süssmilch: Bicentenaire du premier traité spécifique de démographie (1741–1761). *Population: Revue trimestrielle* 17:267–288.

JOHN, VINCENZ 1884 *Geschichte der Statistik: Ein quellenmässiges Handbuch für den akademischen Gebrauch wie für den Selbstunterricht.* Volume 1: Von dem Ursprung der Statistik bis auf Quetelet (1835). Stuttgart (Germany): Enke.

JOHN, VINCENZ 1894 J. P. Süssmilch. Volume 37, pages 188–195 in *Allgemeine deutsche Biographie.* Leipzig: Duncker & Humblot.

KARLSSON, OSKAR 1925 Die Bedeutung Johann Peter Süssmilchs für die Entwicklung der modernen Bevölkerungs-statistik. Dissertation, University of Frankfurt.

KNAPP, GEORG F. 1874 *Theorie des Bevölkerungs-wechsels: Abhandlungen zur angewandten Mathematik.* Brunswick (Germany): Vieweg.

KNORS, HERMANN 1925 Johann Peter Süssmilch: Sein Werk und seine Bedeutung. Dissertation, University of Erlangen.

LANDRY, ADOLPHE (1945) 1949 *Traité de démographie.* 2d ed., rev. Paris: Payot.

LAZARSFELD, PAUL F. 1961 Notes on the History of Quantification in Sociology—Trends, Sources and Problems. *Isis* 52:277–333. → Also published in 1961 on pages 147–203 in Henry Woolf (editor), *Quantification: A History of the Meaning of Measurement in the Natural and Social Sciences.* Indianapolis, Ind.: Bobbs-Merrill.

MEITZEL, S. 1926 Johann Peter Süssmilch. Volume 7, pages 1172–1173 in *Handwörterbuch der Staatswissenschaften.* 4th ed. Jena (Germany): Fischer.

MOHL, ROBERT VON (1855–1858) 1960 *Die Geschichte und Literatur der Staatswissenschaften in Monographien dargestellt.* 3 vols. Graz (Austria): Akademische Druck- und Verlagsanstalt.

REICHARDT, HELMUT 1959 Süssmilch, Johann Peter. Volume 10, pages 267–268 in *Handwörterbuch der Sozialwissenschaften.* Stuttgart (Germany): Fischer.

REIMER, KARL F. 1932 Johann Peter Süssmilch: Seine Abstammung und Biographie. *Archiv für soziale Hygiene und Demographie* New Series 7:820–827.

ROSCHER, WILHELM G. F. (1874) 1924 *Geschichte der National-oekonomik in Deutschland.* 2d ed. Munich and Berlin: Oldenbourg.

SCHULZE, KARL 1922 Süssmilch's Anschauungen über die Bevölkerung. Dissertation, University of Halle.

Die Statistik in der Wirtschaftsforschung: Festgabe für Rolf Wagenführ zum 60. Geburtstag. Edited by Heinrich Strecker and Willi R. Bihn. 1967 Berlin: Duncker & Humblot. → See especially "Johann Peter Süssmilch als Statistiker," by I. Esenwein-Rothe.

TRIPPENSEE, GOTTFRIED G. 1925 Staat und Gesellschaft bei Bielfeld, Süssmilch und Darjes: Ein Beitrag zur Ideengeschichte des preussischen Staates. Dissertation, University of Giessen.

WAPPÄUS, JOHANN E. 1859–1861 *Allgemeine Bevölker-
ungsstatistik: Vorlesungen.* 2 vols. Leipzig: Hinrichs.
WESTERGAARD, HARALD L. 1932 *Contributions to the
History of Statistics.* London: King.
WILLCOX, W. F.; and CRUM, F. S. 1897 A Trial Bibliography of the Writings of Johann Peter Süssmilch,
1707–1767. *Journal of the American Statistical Association* 5:310–314.

SUTHERLAND, EDWIN H.

Edwin H. Sutherland (1883–1950), American
sociologist, did more than any other individual to
shape the substantive theory and methodological
orientation of contemporary criminology. He started out as an adherent of the popular "multiple-
factor theory," which holds that the causes of
crime lie in a set of concrete circumstances; when
enough of these circumstances are added together,
they produce criminal behavior. In the 1930s,
however, Sutherland became committed to systematic theory, in the sense of a parsimonious set of
general propositions, applicable to all instances of
a class of phenomena and admitting of no exceptions. This commitment can be seen in the development of the theory of differential association
(*Sutherland Papers*, pp. 13–29), in his explanation
of rates of crime during wartime (*ibid.*, pp. 120–
127), and in the later work of his students—for
example, Donald R. Cressey (1953), Albert K.
Cohen (1955), and Lloyd E. Ohlin (Cloward &
Ohlin 1960).

Sutherland was unreservedly a *sociological* criminologist. He took his doctorate at the University
of Chicago in 1913 and taught at the University
of Illinois, the University of Minnesota, and the
University of Chicago before becoming head of
the department of sociology at Indiana University.
Consequently his work reflects the influences of
the giants of American sociology: Cooley, Thomas,
Park, Burgess, and Mead. A dominant theme of
this sociology was that personality and conduct
develop through the progressive incorporation, in
the course of communicative interaction, of the
definitions and perspectives current in the cultural
milieu. Sutherland applied this point of view to
problems of criminology with passionate consistency. As he understood it, this approach meant the
repudiation of biologism, whether in the bald form
of Lombrosian and neo-Lombrosian anatomical
theories (*Sutherland Papers*, pp. 273–290) or in
the attenuated form of theories emphasizing intelligence or other presumably hereditary qualities
(*ibid.*, pp. 308–326). He also repudiated all theories that explain crime as a function of distinct
character types or psychodynamic mechanisms.
Hence he was severely critical of the role of psy-

chiatry in criminological theory and in correction
—an attitude that came to characterize sociological
criminology as a whole in the United States.

Sutherland's own theory of differential association is a radical statement of the position that criminal behavior is learned in essentially the same way
as any other part of the surrounding culture. According to this theory, a person becomes criminal
or delinquent because, through association with
others, primarily in intimate personal groups, he
encounters "an excess of definitions favorable to
violation of law over definitions unfavorable to
violation of law" (*ibid.*, p. 9). The theory, first
published in the 1939 edition of his *Principles of
Criminology* (see 1924), was repeatedly revised
in its details, but not in its main features. Although
Sutherland was never satisfied with the way in
which the theory handled certain problems, such
as that of differential susceptibility to the effects
of criminal and anticriminal associations, he continued to be guided by the methodological conviction that the only successful solution would be to
reformulate the theory so that it would continue
to meet the tests of generality and internal consistency, rather than to tack on, in multiple-factor
fashion, additional variables as discrete and unin-
tegrated appendages. Subsequent to Sutherland,
the outstanding work on differential association
has been done by Cressey (1964). (For assessment and criticism of the theory of differential
association, see Cressey 1964; Glaser 1960; Short
1960; McKay 1960; and Glueck 1956.)

The theory of differential association describes,
on the social psychological level, what happens
when a person is exposed to conflicting criminal
and anticriminal cultures. For Sutherland it implied that, on a societal level, the cause of crime
is culture conflict (*Sutherland Papers*, pp. 20–
21). Moreover, he related crime rates to the actual
structure of social relationships in a society. At
first he formulated this theory in terms of social
disorganization but later recast it as "differential
group organization"—that is, the interaction between organization for and organization against
criminal behavior (*ibid.*, pp. 11, 21, 125–127).

Sutherland's annotated study *The Professional
Thief* (1937) was an early classic in the sociology
of occupations. It was not couched explicitly in
terms of differential association, but his analysis
of the process of becoming a professional criminal
was entirely consistent with that theory. His monograph *White Collar Crime*, published in 1949,
again illustrated his methodological orientation,
but in a somewhat different way. Sutherland perceived the crimes of businessmen, performed in
the course of their occupational activity, as prob-

lematic for criminological theory, in the sense that such theory had generally been based upon data derived from lower-class or blue-collar criminals; he saw the crimes of businessmen and corporations as a body of data against which any comprehensive theory of criminal behavior would have to be tested and which, he was persuaded, no extant theory could accommodate. Sutherland felt that the theory of differential association explained these data better than any other theory. Certainly this monograph and related papers have opened up for research a new field rich with implications for general criminological theory.

ALBERT K. COHEN

[*See also* CRIME; CRIMINOLOGY.]

WORKS BY SUTHERLAND

(1924) 1960 SUTHERLAND, EDWIN H.; and CRESSEY, DONALD R. *Principles of Criminology.* 6th ed. Philadelphia: Lippincott. → First published as *Criminology,* under the sole authorship of Sutherland.
1936 SUTHERLAND, EDWIN H.; and LOCKE, HARVEY J. *Twenty Thousand Homeless Men: A Study of Unemployed Men in the Chicago Shelters.* Philadelphia: Lippincott.
(1937) 1960 CONWELL, CHIC *The Professional Thief: By a Professional Thief.* Annotated and interpreted by Edwin H. Sutherland. Univ. of Chicago Press.
(1949) 1961 *White Collar Crime.* New York: Holt.
The Sutherland Papers. Edited by Albert K. Cohen et al. Indiana University Publications, Social Science Series, No. 15. Bloomington: Indiana Univ. Press, 1956. → Articles first published between 1925 and 1951.

SUPPLEMENTARY BIBLIOGRAPHY

CLOWARD, RICHARD A.; and OHLIN, LLOYD E. 1960 *Delinquency and Opportunity: A Theory of Delinquent Gangs.* Glencoe, Ill.: Free Press.
COHEN, ALBERT K. (1955) 1963 *Delinquent Boys: The Culture of the Gang.* New York: Free Press.
CRESSEY, DONALD R. 1953 *Other People's Money: A Study in the Social Psychology of Embezzlement.* Glencoe, Ill.: Free Press.
CRESSEY, DONALD R. 1964 *Delinquency, Crime and Differential Association.* The Hague: Nijhoff.
GLASER, DANIEL 1960 Differential Association and Criminological Prediction. *Social Problems* 8:6–14.
GLUECK, SHELDON 1956 Theory and Fact in Criminology. *British Journal of Delinquency* 7:92–109.
McKAY, HENRY D. 1960 Differential Association and Crime Prevention: Problems of Utilization. *Social Problems* 8:25–37.
SHORT, JAMES F. JR. 1960 Differential Association as a Hypothesis: Problems of Empirical Testing. *Social Problems* 8:14–25.

SWANTON, JOHN REED

John R. Swanton (1873–1958) spent his entire scientific career at one institution, the Bureau of American Ethnology of the Smithsonian Institution. No other staff member has exemplified more faithfully the bureau's tradition of historical anthropology, and none has left a larger monument of accomplishment. Born in Gardiner, Maine, Swanton was trained at Harvard, receiving his bachelor's degree in 1896 and his master's in 1897. After two years of graduate study in ethnology and linguistics under Franz Boas at Columbia, he was awarded the PH.D. at Harvard in 1900 and immediately joined the staff of the Bureau of American Ethnology, where he remained until his retirement in 1944.

Swanton's first field work was in British Columbia in 1900–1901 and southeast Alaska in 1903–1904 as a member of the Jesup North Pacific Expedition organized by Boas. He contributed two volumes on the Haida Indians to the Jesup expedition monograph series: *Contributions to the Ethnography of the Haida* (1905a) and *Haida Texts —Masset Dialect* (1908a). The former is still regarded as the definitive work on this tribe. In all, Swanton wrote some twenty monographs and papers on the languages, ethnology, and folklore of the Northwest Coast Indians, including one of the basic works on the Tlingit: "Social Conditions, Beliefs, and Linguistic Relationship of the Tlingit Indians" (1908b).

Swanton's Northwest Coast work led to further and highly significant contributions to ethnological theory. He was the first to oppose the nineteenth-century dogma of linear evolutionism, which postulated a universal progression from original promiscuity, through group marriage to matrilineal clans, then to patrilineal clans, and finally to the bilateral family and patrilineal descent. In three papers (see 1904; 1905b; 1906) Swanton showed that the clan structure was absent among many of the most primitive American groups, while the individual family was universally present; that tribes having matrilineal clans were for the most part more culturally advanced than those which were clanless or traced descent in the paternal line; that there was no evidence that maternal descent had preceded paternal descent or that any system of kinship was correlated with any stage of cultural development.

Around 1905 Swanton's interests shifted to the southeastern United States, which became his permanent area of specialization. It was an area peculiarly suited to his talents and interests. The smaller tribes had disappeared completely; and the larger ones, such as the Creek, Choctaw, Chickasaw, and Caddo, had long since been removed to reservations in Indian Territory. Field work among these highly acculturated groups could in itself yield only meager results to an ethnologist bent on reconstructing their early history and culture, although Swanton did make an assiduous effort, on numerous field trips, to extract as much information as possible. Fortunately, however, there was an abundance of documentary material—Spanish, French, English, and American—on the southeastern Indians, beginning with the chronicles of the De Soto expedition of 1540; and Swanton utilized this mine of information most effectively. With an unsurpassed knowledge of the historical literature, supplemented by gleanings from his own field work, he produced 16 large monographs and over one hundred shorter papers, in which he recorded everything that was known on the early history, tribal movements, languages, social organization, material culture, and religion of the Natchez, Chitimacha, Atakapa, Caddo, Timucua, Tunica, Creek, Choctaw, Chickasaw, and other Muskhogean and Siouan tribes of the area. These massive contributions to the aboriginal history of the southeast, with their skillful meshing of ethnology and history, laid the groundwork for the discipline now known as ethnohistory.

Swanton was one of the founders of the American Anthropological Association and later its president and the editor of its journal, the *American Anthropologist*. He was a member of the National Academy of Sciences and served as president of the American Folklore Society, president of the Anthropological Society of Washington, and chairman of the U.S. De Soto Expedition Commission. He was awarded the Loubat Prize and the Viking Fund Medal in recognition of his monumental contributions to anthropology. In 1940, on the occasion of his fortieth year with the Smithsonian Institution, his colleagues honored him with a volume, *Essays in Historical Anthropology of North America in Honor of John R. Swanton.*

Swanton was a lifelong adherent of the Swedenborgian faith. He was a kind and gentle man, a man of high ideals with a deep sense of social justice and fairness. He was modest to the point of shyness, yet courageous and determined in opposing any form of intolerance, aggression, or injustice.

HENRY B. COLLINS

[*Directly related are* HISTORY, *article on* ETHNOHISTORY; INDIANS, NORTH AMERICAN; *and the biography of* BOAS.]

WORKS BY SWANTON

1904 The Development of the Clan System and of Secret Societies Among the Northwestern Tribes. *American Anthropologist* New Series 6:477–485.
1905a *Contributions to the Ethnology of the Haida.* American Museum of Natural History, Memoirs, Vol. 8, Pt. 1. Leiden (Netherlands): Brill; New York: Stechert.
1905b The Social Organization of American Tribes. *American Anthropologist* New Series 7:663–673.
1905c *Haida Texts and Myths.* U.S. Bureau of American Ethnology, Bulletin No. 29. Washington: Government Printing Office.
1906 A Reconstruction of the Theory of Social Organization. Pages 166–178 in *Boas Anniversary Volume: Anthropological Papers Written in Honor of Franz Boas.* New York: Stechert.
1908a *Haida Texts—Masset Dialect.* American Museum of Natural History, Memoirs, Vol. 14, Part 2. New York: Stechert.
1908b Social Conditions, Beliefs, and Linguistic Relationship of the Tlingit Indians. Pages 391–486 in U.S. Bureau of American Ethnology, *Twenty-sixth Annual Report.* Washington: Government Printing Office.
1909 *Tlingit Myths and Texts.* U.S. Bureau of American Ethnology, Bulletin No. 39. Washington: Government Printing Office.
1911 *Indian Tribes of the Lower Mississippi Valley and Adjacent Coast of Mexico.* U.S. Bureau of American Ethnology, Bulletin No. 43. Washington: Government Printing Office.
1911 THOMAS, CYRUS; and SWANTON, JOHN REED *Indian Languages of Mexico and Central America and Their Geographical Distribution.* U.S. Bureau of American Ethnology, Bulletin No. 44. Washington: Government Printing Office.
1912 DORSEY, JAMES O.; and SWANTON, JOHN REED *A Dictionary of the Biloxi and Ofo Languages.* U.S. Bureau of American Ethnology, Bulletin No. 47. Washington: Government Printing Office.
1919 *A Structural and Lexical Comparison of the Tunica, Chitimacha, and Atakapa Languages.* U.S. Bureau of American Ethnology, Bulletin No. 68. Washington: Government Printing Office.
1922 *Early History of the Creek Indians and Their Neighbors.* U.S. Bureau of American Ethnology, Bulletin No. 73. Washington: Government Printing Office.
1928 Social Organization and Social Usages of the Indians of the Creek Confederacy. Pages 23–472 in U.S. Bureau of American Ethnology, *Forty-second Annual Report.* Washington: Government Printing Office.
1931 *Source Material for the Social and Ceremonial Life of the Choctaw Indians.* U.S. Bureau of American Ethnology, Bulletin No. 103. Washington: Government Printing Office.
1942 *Source Material on the History and Ethnology of the Caddo Indians.* U.S. Bureau of American Ethnology, Bulletin No. 132. Washington: Government Printing Office.
1946 *The Indians of the Southeastern United States.* U.S. Bureau of American Ethnology, Bulletin No. 137. Washington: Government Printing Office.
1952 *The Indian Tribes of North America.* U.S. Bureau of American Ethnology, Bulletin No. 145. Washington: Government Printing Office.

SUPPLEMENTARY BIBLIOGRAPHY

FENTON, WILLIAM N. 1959 John Reed Swanton: 1873–1958. *American Anthropologist* New Series 61:663–668.
KROEBER, A. L. 1940 The Work of John R. Swanton. Pages 1–9 in Smithsonian Institution, *Essays in Historical Anthropology of North America in Honor of John R. Swanton.* Smithsonian Miscellaneous Collections, Vol. 100. Washington: The Institution.

SMITHSONIAN INSTITUTION 1940 *Essays in Historical Anthropology of North America in Honor of John R. Swanton.* Washington: The Institution.

STEWARD, JULIAN H. 1960 John Reed Swanton. Volume 34, pages 329–349 in National Academy of Sciences, *Biographical Memoirs.* Washington: The Academy.

SYMBIOSIS
See ECOLOGY.

SYMBOLS
See MYTH AND SYMBOL; SEMANTICS AND SEMIOTICS. *Related material may be found in* CONSENSUS; CULTURE, *article on* CULTUROLOGY.

SYMPATHY AND EMPATHY

The terms "sympathy" and "empathy" have presented a semantic confusion for the behavioral scientist wholly out of proportion to the frequency with which they have been used. The principal contentions revolve around whether sympathy and empathy (1) are voluntary or involuntary capacities, (2) are emotionally neutral or negative, and (3) involve only affective or affective–cognitive elements. Sympathy means "with suffering or passion," and, as the concept has been used both in theory and in empirical research, the connotations of negative affect predominate. Marked deviations from the etymological structure of the word and from general usage seem contraindicated. The following definition of sympathy, therefore, is offered. Sympathy is the capacity to apprehend the pain, suffering, or signs of negative emotions in man or animals and to respond to these with appropriate negative feelings. Sympathy is often an immediate, predominantly emotional awareness, but it is no less sympathetic when it is delayed and involves cognitive or reflective elements. The communication of sympathy is not required by the definition. Sympathy may involve "shared" feelings, but not all shared feelings can be communicated. Finally, the concept of sympathy, as used, has implied a fundamental capacity in man to respond to suffering, albeit by no specific neuropsychic structures. The definition, however, is not much altered by using the active form: that sympathy is the apprehending of suffering.

The concept of *Einfühlung* (Lipps 1903a) was translated by Titchener (1909, p. 21) as "empathy." Empathy literally means "in suffering or passion," but in this instance the etymology of the word and its use in aesthetics and in psychology differ. The connotations of empathy are emotionally neutral, lying between sympathy and antipathy but including the joyous emotions. Empathy may be defined as the self-conscious effort to share and accurately comprehend the presumed consciousness of another person, including his thoughts, feelings, perceptions, and muscular tensions, as well as their causes. Empathy may more briefly be defined as the self-conscious awareness of the consciousness of others. Empathy as used in psychology requires the empathizer to maintain an awareness of the imaginative nature of the transportation of oneself into another. In aesthetics, by contrast, the empathizer is supposed to "lose himself in contemplation." Empathy, unlike sympathy, denotes an active referent. In empathy one attends to the feelings of another; in sympathy one attends to the suffering of another, but the feelings are one's own. In empathy I try to feel your pain. In sympathy I know you are in pain, and I sympathize with you, but I feel my sympathy and my pain, not your anguish and your pain. Empathy as an act and "empathetic understanding" as a therapeutic process are not necessarily coterminous.

It is almost impossible to consider the concepts of sympathy and empathy apart from the systems of thought in which they were embedded and the times in which they flourished. It was against the impending doom predicted by Malthus, Hobbes's perpetual war, and, more immediately, Hume's subordination of reason to passion that Adam Smith took up arms in his *Theory of Moral Sentiments* (1759) and again in the *Wealth of Nations* (1776; see Allport 1954). Later, to challenge Darwin's and T. H. Huxley's preoccupation with the role of competition in the theory of natural selection, Kropotkin (1890–1896) collected a remarkable natural history of "mutual aid" in man and animals. Cooley (1902) reacted to Spencer's (1855) and Ward's (1883) biological and psychological reduction of sociology. And McDougall, who was thoroughly versed in the Scottish transcendentalism and the evolutionary theory out of which the concept of sympathy grew, wrote militantly to preserve "purpose" in a psychology rapidly becoming mechanistic (1908). Therefore, it has been the conceptual ill-fate of sympathy and empathy that they have endured more by contrast with opposing ideas than by the clarity of their own exposition [*see* Allport 1954, pp. 18–21; *see also the biographies of* DARWIN; HOBBES; HUME; MALTHUS].

Sympathy

Adam Smith. In the sense that there were "poets before Homer and kings before Agamemnon," there were social philosophers before Adam Smith who had used the concept of sympathy, but within modern times Smith was the first person to define sympathy with some degree of precision and to use it in a systematic manner. In his two major works, *The Theory of Moral Sentiments* (1759) and *Wealth of Nations* (1776), Smith developed a distinction between the inner, psychological states of man and the institutional, or legal, aspects of his relationships. In *The Theory of Moral Sentiments* Smith was concerned with the nature of morality and the theory of moral motivation; in the *Wealth of Nations* he was concerned with an objective analysis of the institutional aspects of virtue, especially prudence. The *Wealth of Nations* was not, as some have maintained, based upon a psychology of individualism; therefore it is ironic that, notwithstanding his moral concerns, Smith's major works should have contributed in such a singular manner to nineteenth-century, laissez-faire individualism.

Adam Smith began his discussion "On the Propriety of Action" with the observation that "How selfish soever man may be supposed, there are evidently some principles in his nature which interest him in the fortune of others and render their happiness necessary to him, though he derives nothing from it . . ." ([1759] 1948, p. 73). Upon the basis of this "unselfish interest in the fortune of others," Smith provided the classic description of sympathy. It is, he wrote, "by changing places in fancy with the sufferer, that we come either to conceive or to be affected by what he feels . . ." ([1759] 1948, p. 74). There are certain emotions, like grief and joy, which arouse sympathy merely when they are perceived in others. But, in general, we are more easily moved to sympathy when the occasion that arouses the emotion is known. On the other hand, there are passions whose expression excites us with no sympathy until we are first acquainted with the condition that provokes them. Furious retaliation, even in righteous anger, may make us exasperated with the victim rather than with the wrongdoer until we know its provocation. This complication, in the otherwise simple tendency to "change places in fancy with the sufferer," seems to depend, according to Smith, upon the degree of social involvement and the intrusion of cognitive elements into an otherwise affective tendency. Grief and joy are terminable in the person himself; resentment, by contrast, raises concerns about the rights of others and thus dampens feelings of sympathy.

Theory of social control. This consideration led Adam Smith quite naturally into an incipient the-

ory of social control, which is worth stating briefly because it illustrates his systematic extension of the concept of sympathy. When the expressions of emotion in a person are in reasonable concord with the sympathetic emotions of an "impartial spectator," they appear to the latter as just and proper; but, if the impartial spectator, "upon bringing the case home to himself," finds the expressions of passion inordinate and inappropriate, he cannot sympathize with them. In any case there is a disparity between the passions of the persons and the sympathetic emotions of the impartial spectator, for they are affected unequally. In order to understand the person, the impartial spectator

put[s] himself in the situation of the other and . . . bring[s] home to himself every little circumstance of distress which can possibly occur to the sufferer. He must adopt the whole case of his companion, with all its minutest incidents, and strive to render as perfect as possible that imaginary change of situation upon which his sympathy is founded. (Smith [1759] 1948, pp. 84–85)

The person principally involved, on the other hand, longing "for that relief which nothing can afford him but the entire concord of the affections of the spectators with his own" ([1759] 1948, p. 85), tries to flatten the pitch of his emotions to harmonize as much as possible with those of the impartial spectator. Upon these reciprocal human endeavors, the attempt of the impartial spectator to sympathize with the emotions of the sufferer and the attempt of the latter to subdue the expression of his emotions, are founded the two sets of virtues which are fundamental to Smith's conception of society. Upon the former is founded the virtue of "benevolence" and upon the latter the virtue of "self-command." Thus, for Smith, as for some of the Stoics by whom he was considerably influenced, individual happiness and social well-being follow from the control of one's emotions by the principle of self-restraint. It is, as he wrote, "to feel much for others and little for ourselves, . . . to restrain our selfish and to indulge our benevolent affections, . . ." that grace and propriety are produced among mankind ([1759] 1948, p. 88). In the service of this principle is pressed not only the Stoical rationalization that between one situation and another there is no essential difference but also the Christian ideal that improper action will be followed by punishment.

In the final analysis, Smith was too much the man of his age to disavow himself completely of its prevailing psychological hedonism. Man's basically egoistic nature must be contained. The principle of self-command was an element in his socialization. It became clear in the *Wealth of Nations*, where Smith developed the idea of institutionalization of self-command, that the crucial idea was social approbation rather than sympathy; that the latter subserves the former. Men could exist in a society without sympathy and benevolence but not without justice. Justice was the pillar upon which society was founded, and justice depended upon social awareness and, in the final analysis, upon a pre-established natural harmony and the fear of death. [*See* SMITH, ADAM.]

Herbert Spencer and Lester F. Ward. Herbert Spencer (1855) and Lester F. Ward (1883) both used the concept of sympathy in a manner not dissimilar from Smith's. Ward defined sympathy as "the painful sensation which results to high nervous organizations at the sight of suffering in others" ([1883] 1926, vol. 1, p. 395). Sympathy, Ward wrote, arises only when the direct feelings of others are affected. The pain felt by the sympathizer and the direct pain of the sufferer are different, but the feeling of sympathetic pain is real, albeit produced not by stimulation of the external pain receptors but rather by a cognition or an idea ([1883] 1926, vol. 2, p. 369). Sympathy, as Ward used it in his sociology, became the basis of man's moral nature —of honesty, benevolence, justice, and all those virtues that confirm man's essential humanity. Man's moral nature springs from his rational faculties and must be traced back to its origin in sympathy. Through what Karl Pearson came later to call "the law of sympathy," sympathy, according to Ward, diffuses first to one's immediate companions and children, then to the clan, the tribe, the race, and ultimately even to lower animals [(1883) 1926, vol. 1, p. 461; *see also the biographies of* PEARSON; SPENCER].

Since, for Ward, society was an association of individuals who were not by nature social ([1883] 1926, vol. 1, p. 460), the "egoistic basis of altruism" (vol. 2, p. 368) became the great moral paradox. To describe the extension of sympathy to larger and less personal social aggregates was not at all to explain why one person was moved to sympathize with another. This Ward deduced in a manner consistent with his hedonistic position. To feel sympathy is to experience real pain. In order for the sympathizer to terminate his pain, he must help the sufferer to escape. Although Ward regarded this as a "negative social force," it was admittedly a real one. But the "great moral paradox" remained unanswered, for "why" sympathy should be a feature of egoistic man in the first place is

never revealed. The concept of sympathy, once admitted, may be explained within a hedonistic psychology, but its presence there is always anomalous. [*See the biography of* WARD, LESTER F.]

Charles Horton Cooley. Cooley also recognized the great moral paradox and attempted to resolve it (1902). The individual and society are two names for the same set of phenomena viewed from different perspectives. Man and society are not mutually antagonistic. The basis for Adam Smith's preoccupation with the control of man's passions disappeared by definition. Man is not born antisocial. He enters the world innocent, unself-conscious, unmoral, and with an inborn capacity for sociability. It is from society that man acquires his higher mental and moral life. With this conceptualization of society the concept of sympathy assumes another meaning. Sympathy for Cooley denotes "the sharing of any mental state that can be communicated"; it refers to a kind of communion, "an entering into and sharing the mind of someone else" (1902, p. 102). Sympathy as pity or compassion and sympathy as communion have nothing to do with one another. Since, for Cooley, society exists in the minds of men, sympathy provides the conceptual means whereby men can reach one another. Love, which is the normal, healthy expansion of human nature, provides the motive to do so. The concept of sympathy, as Cooley used it, had clearly transcendental and even pan-psychic implications, which were to be more fully explored by Max Scheler. [*See the biography of* COOLEY.]

P'etr Kropotkin. During this same period, for reasons already referred to, P'etr Kropotkin published an important series of articles, later reprinted as *Mutual Aid: A Factor of Evolution*. Kropotkin, while admitting that "life is a struggle," contended that the struggle is more against adverse, mostly natural circumstances than against adversaries, and that "fitness" is no more important than "mutual aid." In support of this position, Kropotkin presented a wide variety of examples showing the development of social institutions for mutual aid, the alleviation of suffering, and the elimination of open conflict. Because biologists, poets, and historians have emphasized the dramatic, warlike elements, scientists conclude that aggression is an inherent characteristic of life. But the study of the natural history of mutual aid among man and animals, Kropotkin insisted, shows that this is wrong. Men everywhere are found in groups, and groups at all times have been characterized as much by cooperation as by conflict. Despite their obviously evolutionary bias, Kropotkin's efforts are lately being more fully appreciated. [See KROPOTKIN.]

William McDougall. One of the more sophisticated attempts to integrate the concept of sympathy in a systematic manner was made by William McDougall (1908; 1923). In order to understand where in McDougall's system the concept of sympathy fits, it is necessary first to discuss briefly his theory of motivation and sentiments. An instinct, according to McDougall, is a mental structure, inferred from behavior, having three component parts. The cognitive, or afferent, portion of the instinct makes possible the perceptual preparation of the response. The conative, or efferent, portion of the instinct determines the behavioral expression. Both of these parts of the instinct are modifiable by learning, and here instinct and intelligence combine. The third component of the instinct contains an unalterable central core of emotional excitement. For each of McDougall's 13 main instincts there are corresponding primary emotions. The primary emotions are the indicators of instinctive energies at work. Since two instincts can be excited at once, the primary emotions can be blended into secondary emotions, but secondary emotions are usually experienced in relation to objects for which sentiments have already been acquired. A sentiment, as McDougall defined it, is an organized and enduring system of emotional dispositions focused on the idea of an object deriving from the individual's experience with that object. Sentiments are the units of character; instincts are the units of motivation. The organizing principle for both comes from the "self-regarding sentiment," which is fed primarily by the instincts of submission and assertion. It develops from the "me" and the objects and ideas associated with "me." Like Adam Smith's principle of self-command, it is the master sentiment.

Clearly, a system of impulsive tendencies, confederated around the notion of the self, would be insufficient for explaining the structure of society, especially in its more highly organized forms, which, according to McDougall, were always characterized by a common purpose, cohesion, and altruism. For this purpose, McDougall invoked two explanatory notions—the "tender emotions" and the "nonspecific innate tendencies." The former are associated originally with the parental instinct but are capable of including any person toward whom no hostility is felt. The nonspecific innate tendencies include the so-called "social instincts"—suggestion, imitation, and sympathy. In placing sympathy in this category, McDougall made it clear that no particular emotion is unavoidably associated with sympathy, but that the capacity for sym-pathy itself was an innate tendency in man. Of sympathy there are two kinds. The more basic of the two is called "primitive passive sympathy," and it depends upon a special perceptual adaptation of each of the principal instincts for the reception of the emotional expression of that same instinct in others. In this way the instinct of fear can be excited by the sight of a threatening object or by the bodily and facial expression of fear in another person.

Sympathy, in this sense, has nothing to do with altruism. Only the confluence of the tender emotions with primitive sympathy moves one to alleviate the suffering of another. By itself, the easiest way to terminate sympathetic suffering would be to avert one's gaze. Sympathy may be an innate human characteristic, but sympathy alone cannot account for altruism. For altruism there must be an amalgamation of sympathy and the tender emotions. This was McDougall's solution to Ward's "great moral paradox." In this manner altruism could be explained in animals possessing egoistic tendencies.

Active sympathy is less important in McDougall's thinking. Active, or voluntary, sympathy is a social process whereby the individual seeks the sympathy of others because he wants them to share his feelings. It is not hard to explain sharing pleasurable emotions, since sharing pleasurable emotions intensifies the feelings of both parties. It is more difficult to explain the sharing of unpleasant emotions. This, for McDougall, depends upon the gregarious instinct, which when activated with sympathy, tends to decrease the emotional expression of all sufferers and thereby to reduce the suffering. [See McDOUGALL.]

Max Scheler. Max Scheler (1913) made a serious attempt to construct a theory of sympathy, per se, from a phenomenological viewpoint. His position, which is complicated, extremely difficult to render into English, and not always consistent, cannot be presented in detail, nor can we engage the doubtlessly justifiable contention that his thinking itself represented an unconscious transmutation of certain antiempirical prejudices into a pretended science. But in order to grasp Scheler's idea of sympathy, it is necessary to understand his theory of values and his treatment of the alter ego problem, the latter being the crux of any phenomenological social psychology.

As a result of his critical analysis of the various conceptions of sympathy, especially the "analogical inference" approach of Smith, Spencer, and Ward, and Lipps's "projective empathy" theory, Scheler comes to the conclusion that both theories overestimate the difficulties involved in knowing others and underestimate the difficulties in knowing ourselves. If there is anything immediately obvious to one human being, it is the suffering of another human being. The problem for Scheler, and indeed for Cooley too, is that if one is concerned only with the pure emotional experience, as that which distinguishes man from animals, all one has immediately given is his own self and the bodily appearances and movements of the other person. The existence of the other self whose emotions are supposed to be expressed by bodily movements is never proved. Scheler's particular solution to this problem is that a stream of experience exists in which there is no distinction between the self and the other. Whatever may be the metaphysical deficiencies in Scheler's solution, they need not detain us here. The solution itself provides the basis for his theory of sympathy.

One person, says Scheler, can never experience the bodily feelings of another person. The physical separation of man is complete. But one person can perceive, directly and veridically, another person's feelings—his terror in his cry, his shame in his blush, his joy in his smile. But genuine sympathy is not merely a matter of shared-feeling states. Genuine sympathy is an intentional act, a movement, like love, which intends to generate, from the lowest to the highest, the values potential in mankind. The lowest of these values is the vegetative level, with the vital, mental, and spiritual values ascending in that order. Therefore, the moral values of sympathy, for Scheler, depend not upon the fact of sympathy, but upon the level of emotional value potential in it. When the person concentrates upon his own emotional state, there is no sympathy and nothing of moral value is generated—the only effect is to increase the total amount of suffering present. In genuine sympathy, the sorrow of the other person is grasped as *his* sorrow, and the sympathizer's sorrow is directed toward this fact. The person's sorrow and the other's sympathy are phenomenologically two different facts. The sympathy comes immediately from the other person's sorrow; it is not the result of a contrived "changing places in fancy," nor does it take place only in the presence of the other's sorrow. Genuine sympathy intends (*meint*) not one's own feelings, but the center of awareness of the other person. It involves emotional "participation." [See PERCEPTION, *article on* PERSON PERCEPTION.]

There have been criticisms of Scheler's philosophical and ethical positions, especially of his assertion that the act of sympathy is more important than the social consequences of it, which suggests a view of human welfare inconsistent with a philosophy of sympathy. Moreover, Scheler took a particularly negative view of empirical psychology and research. [*See the biography of* SCHELER.]

Empathy

The concept of empathy has a shorter history than the concept of sympathy and fewer conceptual proliferations. Theodor Lipps (1903*a*) used the concept *Einfühlung* in the psychological description of the aesthetic experience. The appearance to the senses of a beautiful object, said Lipps, may or may not be the stimulus for the aesthetic experience, but one's pleasure derives from one's active encounters with it in imagination. According to Lipps, the distinction between the self and the object dissolves. One finds one's self absorbed in contemplation of the object, and whatever movements, rhythm, or forces flow phenomenally in the object flow in the self. This is not like a psychotic experience: the observer knows who he is, for the experience happens to the "contemplative self," not the real self (1905). In true aesthetic contemplation, involuntary imitative empathy may move the self or it may satisfy itself by mere perception that relaxes the imitative tendency, but, in either case, Lipps was primarily concerned with describing the motor and sensory characteristics of the creative imagination. [*See* AESTHETICS.]

In Lipps's thinking, as in Scheler's, the epistemological and the psychological theories are inseparable. For Lipps, psychology is concerned with immediate experience, but the object of that experience is an indispensable datum rather than a phenomenal characteristic (1903*a*). The most important term in Lipps's psychology is apperception, which is an inner organizing force concerned with knowledge of the self. Knowledge of things comes from sensations, while *Einfühlung* gives knowledge of other selves. *Einfühlung* becomes more complicated in Lipps's theory, however, because every object of thought can have this transfusion of the self into it. This is more than the subject's view of the object. As Titchener wrote, "Not only do I see gravity and modesty and pride . . . , but I feel or act them in the mind's muscles" (1909, p. 21). This kinesthetic mimicry is the heart of empathetic knowledge.

The concept of empathy has been utilized by personality theorists, perhaps because, as Allport suggests (1937, p. 531), the understanding of personality is similar to aesthetic understanding. The apprehension of the consciousness of another self, however, which is the distinctive function of empathetic knowledge in Lipps's psychology, remains unclear. It is equally unsatisfactory in G. H. Mead's theory of knowledge of the other selves, where it is also solved by the assumption that in empathy the consciousness of the other self is sensed immediately. [*See* Allport 1937, pp. 532–533; *see also the biography of* MEAD.]

Empathy, or empathetic understanding, is the term currently preferred by psychotherapists to designate the process and technique whereby the therapist consciously adopts the "internal frame of reference" of the patient without losing his own identity [Rogers 1959; *see also* MENTAL DISORDERS, TREATMENT OF, *article on* CLIENT-CENTERED COUNSELING].

Empirical investigations

Sympathy. Turning now to empirical investigations, one finds a conspicuous absence of research on sympathy; and what has been done is almost unrelated to any of the theories of sympathy. Glancing briefly at the results of these studies, the classic finding from Murphy's research (1937) remains the relationship between sympathy and aggression in children—both are dependent upon general activity level. The relationship between activity and sympathy was also reported by Hofstätter (1956, pp. 155–161). The amount of sympathy in children, at least, bears no simple relationship to chronological age or to situational factors. It is worth noting, however, that the lack of enthusiasm for sympathy as a research concept cannot derive from ambiguities of behavioral manifestations, for sympathy, as a general trait in children, has been clear enough to permit high interobserver agreement. These basically genetic studies of sympathy have usually been interpreted within a conditioning framework (G. Murphy 1947). More recent work suggests that sympathy in adolescents emanates from a background of relative deprivation where the person projects his own history of deprivation onto others and then tries to meet their needs. Some similar investigations of sympathy as a function of personality variables like acceptance of dependency and affiliative needs and guilt have recently been made, but it would be premature to generalize from these preliminary investigations. There is a strong suggestion, however, that the past treatment of one's affective needs influences one's capacity for sympathetic relationships.

Empathy. On the other hand, what has passed for empathy in empirical research may be only one dimension of it. Empathy and empathetic understanding have been operationalized in two ways: (1) in terms of the summed discrepancies between the subject's and a close associate's, or group's, trait ratings of a person, and (2) in terms of the summed discrepancies of a person's actual ratings of himself and the subject's presumption of how the person would rate himself. A wide variety of psychological variables have been studied and manipulated—self-confidence and humor, values, anxiety, and group atmosphere. Some objections to these procedures are inherent in the conception of empathy itself, especially the confounding of projection and empathy and of empathy and identification. Freud's statement that "a path leads from identification by way of imitation to empathy" (1921) is well known. Clearly, where identification occurs, empathy is lost. The confounding of empathy and projection, however, has been amenable to some empirical investigation. If the amount of projection involved in empathy is inversely related to accurate perception of individual differences, then a number of critical reviews suggest that studies of empathy have been methodologically inadequate (for example, Cronbach 1955). Some studies have tried experimentally to separate projection from empathy, while some have tried to demonstrate the influence of personal preferences and frustration on ratings of others. Less frequently investigated but possibly important in empathetic ability may be general intelligence and stereotypy. Nevertheless, significant, if low-order, correlations are usually found across instruments (Cline & Richards 1961) and across individuals (Cline & Richards 1960), suggesting that a factor like empathy may exist.

LAUREN G. WISPÉ

[*Directly related are the entries* EMOTION *and* AFFECTION. *Other relevant material may be found in* PERSONALITY, *article on* PERSONALITY DEVELOPMENT; MORAL DEVELOPMENT; PHENOMENOLOGY; *and* SOCIAL PSYCHOLOGY.]

BIBLIOGRAPHY

ALLPORT, GORDON W. 1937 *Personality: A Psychological Interpretation.* New York: Holt.

ALLPORT, GORDON W. 1954 The Historical Background of Modern Social Psychology. Volume 1, pages 3–56 in Gardner Lindzey (editor), *Handbook of Social Psychology.* Cambridge, Mass.: Addison-Wesley.

CLINE, VICTOR B.; and RICHARDS, JAMES M. JR. 1960 Accuracy of Interpersonal Perception: A General Trait? *Journal of Abnormal and Social Psychology* 60:1–7.

CLINE, VICTOR B.; and RICHARDS, JAMES M. JR. 1961 The Generality of Accuracy of Interpersonal Perception. *Journal of Abnormal and Social Psychology* 62: 446–449.

COOLEY, CHARLES H. (1902) 1956 *Human Nature and the Social Order.* Rev. ed. In Charles H. Cooley, *Two Major Works: Social Organization and Human Nature* and the Social Order. Glencoe, Ill.: Free Press. → Each title reprinted with its own title page and pagination. Separate paperback editions were published in 1964 by Schocken.

CRONBACH, LEE J. 1955 Processes Affecting Scores on "Understanding of Others" and "Assumed Similarity." *Psychological Bulletin* 52:177–193.

FREUD, SIGMUND (1921) 1955 Group Psychology and the Analysis of the Ego. Volume 18, pages 67–143 in *The Standard Edition of the Complete Psychological Works of Sigmund Freud.* London: Hogarth; New York: Macmillan. → First published in German.

HOFSTÄTTER, PETER R. (1956) 1964 *Sozialpsychologie.* 2d ed. Berlin: Gruyter.

KROPOTKIN, P'ETR (1890–1896) 1955 *Mutual Aid: A Factor of Evolution.* Boston: Extending Horizons. → Thomas Huxley's "The Struggle for Existence" is included in this book.

LIPPS, THEODOR 1903a Einfühlung, innere Nachahmung und Organempfindungen. *Archiv für die gesamte Psychologie* 20:185–204.

LIPPS, THEODOR (1903b) 1909 *Leitfaden der Psychologie.* 3d ed. Leipzig: Engelmann.

LIPPS, THEODOR 1905 "Einfühlung" Geometrie. *Archiv für die gesamte Psychologie* 4:465–519.

McDOUGALL, WILLIAM (1908) 1950 *An Introduction to Social Psychology.* 30th ed. London: Methuen. → A paperback edition was published in 1960 by Barnes and Noble.

McDOUGALL, WILLIAM 1923 *Outline of Psychology.* New York: Scribner.

MURPHY, GARDNER 1947 *Personality: A Biosocial Approach to Origins and Structure.* New York: Harper.

MURPHY, LOIS (BARCLAY) 1937 *Social Behavior and Child Personality: An Exploratory Study of Some Roots of Sympathy.* New York: Columbia Univ. Press.

ROGERS, CARL R. 1959 A Theory of Therapy, Personality, and Interpersonal Relationships, as Developed in the Client-centered Framework. Volume 3, pages 184–256 in Sigmund Koch (editor), *Psychology: A Study of a Science.* New York: McGraw-Hill.

SCHELER, MAX (1913) 1954 *The Nature of Sympathy.* London: Routledge. → First published as *Zur Phänomenologie und Theorie der Sympathiegefühle.* The 2d revised and enlarged edition—which was later translated into English—was published in 1923 as *Wesen und Formen der Sympathie.*

SMITH, ADAM (1759) 1948 The Theory of Moral Sentiments. Pages 3–277 in *Adam Smith's Moral and Political Philosophy.* Edited by Herbert Schneider. New York: Hafner.

SMITH, ADAM (1776) 1950 *An Inquiry Into the Nature and Causes of the Wealth of Nations.* 2 vols., 6th ed. Edited, with an introduction, notes, marginal summary, and an enlarged index by Edwin Cannan. London: Methuen. → A paperback edition was published in 1963 by Irwin.

SPENCER, HERBERT (1855) 1920–1926 *Principles of Psychology.* 2 vols., 3d ed. New York: Appleton.

TITCHENER, EDWARD B. 1909 *Lectures on the Experimental Psychology of the Thought-processes.* New York: Macmillan.

WARD, LESTER F. (1883) 1926 *Dynamic Sociology: Or Applied Social Science, as Based Upon Statical Sociology and the Less Complex Sciences.* 2 vols. 2d ed. New York: Appleton.

SYNDICALISM

Syndicalism is a philosophy and a style of revolutionary or quasi-revolutionary labor-union action that first took shape in the French unions of the last decade of the nineteenth century. The philosophy was further elaborated in the writings of Georges Sorel and other intellectuals. For about a generation it played a significant role in France, Italy, Spain, and other countries as the most spectacular labor protest against the industrial order, against the central state, and against the increasing tendency of socialism to make its peace with the existing political order.

The term comes from the French *syndicat*, a group for the defense of common interests. A labor union is a *syndicat ouvrier*, or simply a *syndicat*. In French, *syndicalisme* is labor unionism in general. But the term was taken over in English to mean specifically the revolutionary unionism which the French call *syndicalisme révolutionnaire*, or *anarcho-syndicalisme*. Similarly the French took from English the term *trade-unionisme* to designate English-style reformist unionism.

The word *syndicalism*, with or without accompanying adjectives, has been harnessed to a wide variety of uses, some metaphorical and some polemic. Some writers have used it to identify systems of occupational or other group organization, voluntary or state-directed; others, to label general theories of political and juridical pluralism. For still others, it has served to stigmatize an abuse of bargaining power by labor or other sectional interests at the expense of the general interest. These connotations are not those of the historical core of syndicalism.

Antecedents. As the syndicalist outlook developed first in the French unions, it combined many of the ideas current among radical groups of the nineteenth century. Proudhon was the strongest intellectual influence among the elite of French workingmen. From him and the Proudhonists of the First International, the syndicalists took their belief in the self-governing workshop as the unit of a free and decentralized society, their stress on the workers' own efforts as the means of the workers' emancipation, and their distrust of coercive state authority. From the Marxists, they took their emphasis on the class struggle as a principle of explanation and as a guide to action. From the French revolutionary tradition, as well as from the Blanquists and from the Bakuninists of the First International, they acquired their acceptance of violence and their stress on the role of a militant elite in the process of social emancipation. From the Paris Commune came further justification for revolt against the centralizing state. The method of the general strike, peaceful or revolutionary, had been in the air since Owenites and Chartists had preached it in Britain in the 1830s, and the First International had revived it. The anarchists who joined the French unions in large numbers in the 1890s brought a new infusion of Proudhonian and Bakuninist ideas and contributed the ideas of opposition to political action in general and to the socialist parties in particular.

Basic concepts. The concepts which were crucial to the syndicalist outlook were these: The class war is the dominant characteristic of modern society and the method of social change; the working class must achieve its own liberation from employer authority, the wage system, and the oppressive state; the workers must not rely on political action. The antithesis of party compromise and parliamentary betrayal was the workers' direct action. This might take many forms of pressure on employers or government: boycott, sabotage (much discussed but little used), mass demonstration, or strikes. All strikes, won or lost, help deepen workers' class consciousness. Any one of them may lead to the supreme form of direct action, the revolutionary general strike.

In the unions, central authority and the power of elected and appointed officials must be kept to a minimum, for they dull the revolutionary spirit. The general strike will come not from the action of powerful, rich unions but from the will of a conscious militant minority galvanizing the torpid mass of workers into a "sudden leap of awareness." That elite is the driving force in history. The workers, isolated in the nation by social injustice, have no fatherland but that of class, that of the international proletariat. The unions must oppose nationalism and militarism. The labor union, organ of struggle against capitalism, will in the future be "an organization for production and distribution" and "the basis of social reorganization." Functional organization and economic representation, in a pluralistic society based on free consensus, will replace the oppressive political state.

Unlike Marxian socialism, syndicalism was not interested in the conquest of the state by political party activity. It attempted no serious analysis of the historical process. Nor did it count on historical determinism to realize its ends.

Unlike anarchism, syndicalism relied on the occupational group and the class rather than the individual. It accepted a degree of organization which alarmed "pure" anarchists. The organization, the union, had tasks of immediate amelioration as well as of final social emancipation. The union, rather than the libertarian commune, was to be the nucleus of the freely federated society of the future.

French syndicalism. Syndicalism in France reflected the failure to develop satisfactory organic or working relationships between socialist parties and the labor unions. In the 1880s and 1890s the still-weak unions were being torn apart by rival socialist parties—five "national parties" by the late 1890s—fighting for union support. Political neutrality was a doctrine of self-protection for the unions. Syndicalist ideas also reflected the state of the unions. Emphasis on the role of active minorities and the unpredictable general strike idealized the conditions of unions without mass membership, financial resources, or central authority, and without collective bargaining rights against hostile employers.

The French unions before 1914 were divided more or less evenly between reformists and revolutionists. But the revolutionary views prevailed as the official doctrine of the General Confederation of Labor (CGT) well before they were proclaimed by Sorel. They were implicit in union structure, practices, and pronouncements and explicit in the writings of a remarkable elite of union activists, mostly self-taught intellectuals: Émile Pouget, Victor Griffuelhes, Georges Yvetot, Paul Delesalle, Pierre Monatte, Alphonse Merrheim, Léon Jouhaux, and earliest and foremost, Fernand Pelloutier.

Pelloutier was a personal link with the theorists outside the unions, for he was a friend of Sorel's. As it is easier for outsiders to read books than to study union documents and practices, it is through Sorel and his followers that most people know syndicalism. Werner Sombart's convenient explanation that Sorel had produced the theory of syndicalism has survived all the disclaimers of Sorel and his followers.

These disclaimers did not arise from false modesty. The syndicalist ideas had already made their way in the unions at a time when Sorel was still a revisionist socialist. In 1898 he first published the articles collected as "L'avenir socialiste des syndicats." Here he found his model not in the syndicalist French unions, about which he was silent, but in the strong, disciplined, reformist English trade unions. Here he praised cooperatives but not the general strike.

Even after Sorel embraced syndicalism, he had little influence on the course of labor thinking or behavior in France. He had two important followers in his syndicalist phase. Edouard Berth elaborated on his anti-intellectual themes and followed his master's course from syndicalism to royalist, anti-Semitic nationalism. Hubert Lagardelle was a more coherent expositor of syndicalism than Sorel, more realistic and constructive, less bitterly and unjustly polemic. Unlike Sorel, he had close contacts with the union movement, and he was active in the Socialist party. He gave to the labor movement that devoted service which Sorel and Berth preached as the intellectual's function. As editor of the *Mouvement socialiste* from 1899 to 1914, he made it a distinguished international review that published many of the most interesting discussions of practice and theory by syndicalist activists and theoreticians. Lagardelle refused to follow the more original Sorel into the royalist camp and regarded as "monstrous" his mentor's attempt to couple syndicalism with reactionary monarchism.

The unionists did not share Sorel's pessimistic view of the world; they were optimistic in that expectation of an imminent social revolution which was part of the radical mood of the generation before 1914. The unionists denounced socialist intellectuals for their party politics, but they did not make a cult of anti-intellectualism and antirationalism, as did Sorel and Berth.

The unionists often seemed to urge direct action for its own sake, but they did not urge violence for its own sake, as did the intellectuals. The general strike was for the intellectuals a great social myth. But the union people saw it as a real tactic for pragmatic purposes.

Even their modest gains in organizational strength were enough to close the "heroic period" of the syndicalist unions, and on the eve of World War I they were moving toward reformism. When in 1914 their members marched off to war without a protest from the Confederation, the foundations of syndicalist dogma and practice collapsed. Syndicalist union leaders cooperated with the French government and the Socialist party. Their share in wartime economic direction and in factory representation gave them a new appreciation of the role of the state, of the problems of political power, and of the complexities of the economy. But for another generation after the war most of them continued to pay verbal tribute to old syndicalist slogans, to the confusion of their followers. The communists entered into this heritage of extremist temperament. A handful of faithful "pure syndicalists" guarded a small, independent source of revolutionary ardor, if no longer of expectation.

Italian syndicalism.   The ideas and organizational forms of the French greatly influenced the Italians. Sorel was far more popular and influential in Italy than in his own land. But the syndicalists never gained a preponderant position in the General Confederation of Labor (CGL), and they withdrew from it to found their own, much smaller union central.

Italian syndicalists took a more flexible view of political action than the French, working for a time in the Socialist party and even sitting in the parliament. Arturo (not to be confused with Antonio) Labriola, the most interesting of the theorists, argued that it would be idiotic to ignore the fact of parliamentary politics. Even a revolutionary party had to make use of existing institutions as a condition of its existence.

Labriola analyzed some of the phenomena which in Italy held back class consciousness and created networks of common interests between proletarians and bourgeois—notably the great number of social groups between the extremes of class identification and the traditional, exclusivist regional feelings. Sorel never attempted this sort of realistic analysis.

The syndicalist vision of workers' control seemed for a moment almost a reality in the wave of Italian factory occupations in 1920. But these futile occupations were not the work of the syndicalists, whose unions had by then declined to impotence.

Spanish syndicalism.   In Spain the syndicalist current merged with the much older anarchist stream to create the strongest and the most militant syndicalist union center to function anywhere, one which endured after syndicalism everywhere else had spent its force. The National Confederation of Labor (CNT) had its chief center in Barcelona, where it drew strength from Catalan resistance to Castilian centralization in the state and in the Socialist party and from resentment with management intransigence and weak governmental protection of workers.

The CNT stressed spontaneity, local autonomy, "libertarian communism," freedom from bureaucracy in structure, and hostility to state, employers, and church in action, far more than even the French or Italian unions. It carried class warfare and local and regional general strikes to a heroic pitch but almost always to defeat, in intermittent, bloody uprisings. In its third and last decade of effective existence, after 1927, the CNT was controlled by the secret organization of the Iberian Anarchist Federation (FAI), which reaffirmed a violent intransigence against those CNT leaders who advanced more realistic, moderate methods than their own.

In 1936 the CNT militia helped save the republican regime from the first shocks of the Franco revolt. To save the republic, CNT leaders joined first the Catalan government and then the national government of Largo Caballero, showing the world the novelty of anarchosyndicalist cabinet ministers. In Catalonia, when the Civil War began, the CNT took over and ran many factories in the most significant attempt ever made to put syndicalist ideas into practice. These activities were stifled when, in May 1937, government and communist armed forces reduced the CNT center of power in Barcelona. Franco's victory confirmed the tragic fate of a movement which had discovered the reality of politics too late for its own or the republic's survival.

Syndicalism in other countries. From Spain and Portugal, Italy and France, syndicalism had spread to Argentina, Uruguay, Chile, Mexico, and other Latin American countries. For the first two decades of this century it constituted the major current in the new labor movements of a number of these nations. In almost all of them the syndicalists were reduced to impotence by the early 1920s, and the downfall of Spanish anarchosyndicalism ended what influence they had retained.

Syndicalist ideas played a role in the labor movements of a number of other countries. They were a major current in the Dutch unions just before and after the turn of the century, represented by the interesting, theoretically oriented leader, Christian Cornelissen. In the disciplined German union movement, syndicalism was a significant though minor current that drew the support of Robert Michels.

In the United States an indigenous syndicalism appeared in the Industrial Workers of the World (IWW). This most colorful and radical of American labor organizations began in 1905 with a recognition of the possibility of independent working-class politics but by 1908 came under the control of the opponents of political action. The "Wobblies," as IWW members were called, were activists to the core, rough in language, and little interested in theory. Proposing the revolutionary expropriation of the propertied classes and the abolition of the wage system, they advanced a crude theory of the social organization of the future by industrial unions.

The IWW fought for better working conditions for some of the most exploited workers in America —the unskilled, migratory, and often homeless workers of the Pacific slope and the foreign factory workers in Eastern cities—but it generally refused the discipline of collective bargaining. It defied all authority—of employers and government, of public opinion (often molded by employer propaganda), and of the mainstream of organized labor. Taking seriously its rejection of all wars but the class war, the IWW paid dearly for its opposition

to American involvement in World War I. The leadership was decimated, and the organization was shattered by government prosecutions and harassment and by government-abetted vigilante actions. A hopelessly impractical organizational structure, internal dissensions, and the competing, new appeal of communism to revolutionaries completed the downfall in the 1920s of an organization which had carried antiauthoritarianism and worker exclusivism to fatal extremes.

Norway was the one northern European country in which a group strongly influenced by syndicalism was for a time dominant in a mass labor movement. That group was the "Trade Union Opposition of 1911," led by the talented Martin Tranmael, who had worked in the United States and had been impressed by the IWW. Although it favored sabotage and other forms of "direct action," the "Opposition of 1911" worked effectively with the left wing of the Labor party. When it won out in the Norwegian labor movement, it did not attempt revolutionary political or industrial action. Tranmael himself, elected general secretary of the Labor party in 1918, was the most influential leader in the Norwegian labor movement between the wars.

In Sweden a small syndicalist labor federation, which split from the main trade-union movement in 1910, remained active into the 1960s. Although its behavior differed little from the practice of other unions then, its publication was an outlet for interesting dissident comments on Swedish society. The federation loyally maintained the vestiges of the once significant anarchosyndicalist International Workingmen's Association, founded in 1922.

Russia seemed to be in the process of a partially syndicalist upheaval after the February Revolution. Workers seized factories and operated them through factory committees, soviets, and trade unions; Lenin for a time found it politic to endorse "workers' control." Abroad these developments helped to foster the idea of a "workers' revolution" in Russia and to win for communism the support of old-time syndicalists. After several years of feverish debate on workers' control, the Bolsheviks managed to put a stop to what Lenin called "syndicalist twaddle." With the defeat of the Workers' Opposition group, branded as "anarchosyndicalist" by its opponents, the state asserted its full control over the economy, and the party its control over the unions. Defeated in Russia, the idea of workers' control was to reappear in the Yugoslav works councils and the revived works council movement in many countries after World War II.

In the labor unrest which shook Britain in the years just before 1914, the word *syndicalism* was much bruited about. There was something of the syndicalist spirit in the heightened class consciousness and militant strike action of certain groups of industrial workers, notably the miners. The militancy reappeared after the first few years of war in the protest movements led by local shop stewards and in demands for workers' control. Syndicalist concepts influenced the British guild socialists, many of them middle class, who stressed the role of unions or "national guilds" of producers as administrative agencies of the cooperative commonwealth. But the guild socialists' temper was rational and moderate, and they left to a democratized, pluralistic government an essential role in their complex utopia.

Evaluation. Syndicalism claims our attention less as a constructive political and economic doctrine than as a trenchant ethical criticism of institutions and as a libertarian way of facing authority. It related widespread labor exploitation and unrest to a romantic notion of the autonomy and the primacy of the working class. But its demands for workers' control were based on excessively optimistic concepts of workers' psychology, and its vision of economic organization was rudimentary and quixotic.

Its critique of the modern state and of liberal democracy and its stress upon functional association helped to stimulate pluralist speculation. But, although the syndicalists were not altogether economic determinists, they carried the overemphasis on economic factors, which prevailed in the late nineteenth century, in many ways even further than did the Marxists. Their stress upon the "apolitical" character of their own action arose from an oversimplified view of societal processes which obscured the political nature both of their goal—total revolutionary change—and of their method—the general strike.

The syndicalist assertion of the need for spontaneity within the workers' organization threw new light on the comparative moderation, smugness, and bureaucratization already setting in among the socialist parties and reformist trade unions. The syndicalist language of extremism flashed warnings of the strange interplay of the rational and the irrational and of the latent sources of violence in social behavior—among intellectuals as well as among manual workers.

The refusal of most syndicalists to recognize the reality and legitimacy of political action left many of them in France and Italy unable to distinguish between democratic politics and the claims of a totalitarian party and the authoritarian state. Other, far more brutal movements put into practice the much bruited about. There was something of the violence that the syndicalists had advocated or con-

doned and their rather mystical view of elite leadership but sacrificed all of the syndicalists' ethical concerns and their generous solidarity.

VAL R. LORWIN

[*See also* ANARCHISM; LABOR UNIONS. *Other relevant material will be found in* MARXISM; SOCIALISM; *and in the biography of* SOREL.]

WORKS BY SYNDICALISTS

GRIFFUELHES, VICTOR 1908 *L'action syndicaliste.* Paris: Rivière.

JOUHAUX, LÉON 1920 *Le syndicalisme et la C.G.T.* Paris: La Sirène.

LABRIOLA, ARTURO; MICHELS, ROBERT et al. 1908 *Syndicalisme & socialisme.* Paris: Rivière.

LAGARDELLE, HUBERT 1911 *Le socialisme ouvrier.* Paris: Giard et Brière.

PEIRATS, JOSÉ 1952–1955 *La C.N.T. en la revolución española.* 3 vols. Buenos Aires: Ediciones C.N.T.

PELLOUTIER, FERNAND (1902) 1946 *Histoire des bourses du travail.* Paris: Costes. → Published posthumously with a preface by Georges Sorel.

SOREL, GEORGES (1898) 1921 *L'avenir socialiste des syndicats.* Pages 77–133 in Georges Sorel, *Matériaux d'une théorie du prolétariat.* 2d ed. Paris: Rivière.

SOREL, GEORGES (1908) 1950 *Reflections on Violence.* Translated by T. E. Hulme and J. Roth, with an introduction by Edward Shils. Glencoe, Ill.: Free Press. → First published in French. A paperback edition was published in 1961 by Collier.

WORKS ABOUT SYNDICALISM

BRENAN, GERALD (1943) 1950 *The Spanish Labyrinth: An Account of the Social and Political Background of the Civil War.* 2d ed. Cambridge Univ. Press.

BRISSENDEN, PAUL F. (1917) 1957 *The I.W.W.: A Study of American Syndicalism.* 2d ed. New York: Russell.

COLE, G. D. H. (1913) 1919 *The World of Labour: A Discussion of the Present and Future of Trade Unionism.* 4th ed. London: Bell.

COLE, G. D. H. 1953–1960 *A History of Socialist Thought.* 5 vols. New York: St. Martins; London: Macmillan. → Volume 1: *Socialist Thought: The Forerunners 1789–1850,* 1953. Volume 2: *Marxism and Anarchism 1850–1890,* 1954. Volume 3: *The Second International 1889–1914,* 2 parts, 1956. Volume 4: *Communism and Social Democracy 1914–1931,* 2 parts, 1958. Volume 5: *Socialism and Fascism 1931–1939,* 1960.

DOLLÉANS, ÉDOUARD (1939) 1946 *Histoire du mouvement ouvrier.* Volume 2: 1871–1936. Paris: Colin.

GEORGES, BERNARD; and TINTANT, DENISE 1962 *Léon Jouhaux: Cinquante ans de syndicalisme.* Volume 1: Des origines à 1921. Paris: Presses Universitaires de France.

GOETZ-GIREY, ROBERT 1948 *La pensée syndicale française: Militants et théoriciens.* Paris: Colin.

LEROY, MAXIME 1913 *La coutume ouvrière.* 2 vols. Paris: Giard et Brière.

LORWIN, LEWIS L. (1912) 1914 *Syndicalism in France.* 2d rev. ed. New York: Longmans; London: King. → First published as *The Labor Movement in France.*

LORWIN, VAL R. 1954 *The French Labor Movement.* Cambridge, Mass.: Harvard Univ. Press.

MAITRON, JEAN 1951 *Histoire du mouvement anarchiste en France (1880–1914).* Paris: Société Universitaire d'Éditions et de Librairie.

MICHELS, ROBERT 1926 *Storia critica del movimento socialista italiano dagli inizi fino al 1911.* Florence: La Voce.

WIARDI BECKMAN, HERMAN B. 1931 *Het syndicalisme in Frankrijk.* Amsterdam: Querido.

SYSTEMS ANALYSIS

I
GENERAL SYSTEMS THEORY

General systems theory is best described not as a theory in the sense that this word is used in science but, rather, as a program or a direction in the contemporary philosophy of science. The outlook represented by this direction stems from various sources, and its adherents emphasize different aspects of the program. However, all the variants and interpretations have a common aim: the integration of diverse content areas by means of a unified methodology of conceptualization or of research.

The scientific background. The traditional outlooks of the physical and biological sciences may be taken as examples of divergent methodologies or conceptualizations. In the eighteenth century, theoretical physics, at least the branch known as mechanics, already appeared in full mathematical garb. So firmly established were the mathematical principles of mechanics that this discipline seemed to be a realization of the rationalists' program—the derivation of knowledge from first principles by deduction alone. Indeed, the theorems of mechanics were in no way less rigorously derived nor less certain of experimental corroboration than were the theorems of geometry. Because mechanics was the branch of physics which matured first, the notion was not uncommon in the beginning of the nineteenth century that all the laws of being and becoming were manifestations of mechanical laws—in other words, that the universe was a strictly determined clockwork, whose operation would be completely understandable to an intelligence sufficiently vast to grasp the totality of its components and the relations among them.

Biology, in contrast, was at that time an almost wholly descriptive—at most an inductive, hardly ever a deductive—science. Life was tacitly assumed to be a phenomenon *sui generis*, apart from events governed by mechanical laws. At least, no serious attempts were made to derive the former from the latter. Therefore, a gap existed between the physical and the biological sciences. The basic terms of the latter—for example, organism, survival, reproduction, development, behavior, senescence, death—had no counterpart in the physical sciences.

Reductionism and vitalism. With the fundamental discoveries in the middle of the nineteenth century—the laws of thermodynamics—and with the maturation of chemistry, the relationship between the physical and the biological sciences began to change. Physiologists began to look upon basic life processes as they looked on physicochemical events, and, as such, these processes seemed in no way to differ from similar events occurring in nonliving environments. In particular, the laws of conservation of matter and energy were shown to be valid in living organisms, and the living organism began to appear to the physiologists as a machine. Thus the point of view known as *reductionism* emerged. Reductionism is essentially a program which seeks to derive events occurring at one level of organization from those occurring at another, presumably both a simpler and a more fundamental level. The reduction of chemistry to physics has been largely successful. The reduction of physiology to chemistry and physics was viewed by the reductionists as their most significant task.

Opposed to the reductionists' program were the *vitalists*, who maintained that life is a phenomenon *sui generis* and that therefore the reductionists' program was futile.

It should be clear that such a controversy can never be settled to the satisfaction of either party. As long as the reduction of *all* life phenomena to physics and chemistry has not been carried out, the vitalists can keep insisting that it never can be carried out. On the other hand, there is no ground for supposing that something cannot be done just because it has not been done.

Bertalanffy's theory of systems. On occasions, the vitalists have attempted to support their position by specific evidence: for example, the apparent teleological nature of some life processes (the so-called principle of entelechy or "equifinality" emphasized by Hans Driesch 1908) and the apparent violations by living organisms of the second law of thermodynamics. Although these arguments have since been shown to be irrelevant to the issue, they stimulated lively discussions which led to one of the early formulations of general systems theory by Ludwig von Bertalanffy (1956; 1962).

Bertalanffy pointed out that apparent goal seeking was not an exclusive characteristic of living systems. He called attention to an essential difference between an *isolated* system of chemical reactions and an *open* one, in which sources and sinks were present. In an isolated system, after equilibrium has been attained, the relative concentration of substances depends, of course, on the initial concentrations of the reactants (because of the conservation of mass); thus, the final state of the system depends on the initial conditions. In an open system, however, a steady state may be attained in which the final concentrations are virtually independent of the initial conditions. Moreover, if the steady state is disturbed, as by adding or removing quantities of reacting substances, it will re-establish itself, being determined by the characteristics of the entire system rather than by any specific state of the system. Thus, an open system will appear to exhibit "equifinality" to a naive observer. It will appear to have a "will of its own" or a "purpose": to maintain the steady state—which, incidentally, is just what living systems are to a large extent engaged in doing by means of their well-known homeostatic (steady-state restoring) mechanisms.

It is noteworthy that the systems cited by Bertalanffy as examples of entities exhibiting characteristics of equifinality were open systems, i.e., those to which the operation of the classical version of the second law of thermodynamics does not apply. Thus, by calling attention to the fundamental feature of living organisms as open systems, Bertalanffy refuted both of the specific arguments put forward by the vitalists.

What is a system?

The classification of systems by the nature of their relation to their environments and the search for laws governing the behavior of each class can be said to be problems posed by a general systems theory. Once one has raised the general questions about possible laws governing the behavior of systems, the problem of rigorous definition of a "system" comes to the fore. In common usage, the word refers to widely separated concepts. Engineers are concerned with systems as functionally related aggregates of technological devices. Physiologists single out functionally related portions of living organisms (circulatory, digestive, nervous systems). Social scientists speak of economic and political systems; philosophers, about systems of thought.

It is, of course, by no means necessary to derive from what may be an accident of usage the idea that all the "systems" which have been so named have something important in common. On the other hand, one need not dismiss such an idea out of hand. Thus the question looms as to what to include in and what to exclude from the definition of "systems," in order to stretch the concept to the limit of generality without at the same time destroying its usefulness.

I subscribe to the view that a definition of "system" must be such that other than physical entities (perhaps language) are included. At the same time, the definition must exclude entities whose principles of organization cannot be at least partially specified. Therefore, I accept the definition of a system as (1) something consisting of a set (finite or infinite) of entities (2) among which a set of relations is specified, so that (3) deductions are possible from some relations to others or from the relations among the entities to the behavior or the history of the system.

According to this definition, both the solar system and a language qualify as systems. In the former, the entities are the sun and the planets; the relations among them are specifiable as position and velocity vectors and forces of gravitational attraction. Other relations (e.g., Kepler's laws of planetary motion) and the history of the system, past and future, are derivable from the given relations. In a language, there are also identifiable entities—phonemes, morphemes, sentences, and the like—and relations between these are given in terms of syntactic rules. In a larger sense, a language system may also include the referential world and even the speakers. In this sense, semantic and pragmatic relations are added to the syntactic ones. "Social system" is a term so widely used that its meaning is assumed to be obvious. However, in the context of a systems theory, "social system" would have to be defined *de novo* every time some class of entities (individuals, families, institutions) and relations among them (communication channels, influence, obligations) are singled out for attention.

The organismic approach

As has been said, early explicit programmatic formulations of general systems theory were outlined by Bertalanffy. Another biologist, Ralph W. Gerard (1958), has offered a formulation which carries an even stronger biological flavor. According to Gerard, a "system" is primarily a living system, and the process which defines it is the maintenance of an organization which we know as life. There is a hierarchy of systems, in which the larger ones frequently include the smaller ones as components or subsystems. Thus, cells form organized aggregates known as tissues or organs; these, in turn, are components of a biological individual. Individuals stand in relation to each other as families or tribes (social arrangements) or as species (interbreeding aggregates). Along the scale of social organization, we have the aggregates characteristic of human beings—institutions, political units, and societies. Along the scale of biological organization, organisms and populations stand in symbiotic, predatory, or parasitic relation to each other, forming ecological systems (ecosystems). To view an ecosystem as an "epiorganism" is not merely to indulge in metaphorical analogies. Metabolic chains and cycles are traceable through a biological community quite as precisely as through the various specialized cells of a single organism. Herbivores eat plants; carnivores eat herbivores and smaller carnivores. Under proper conditions, the ecosystem may reach an equilibrium quite analogous to the homeostatically maintained metabolic equilibrium of the individual organism.

Thus, in Gerard's scheme, the hierarchy of living systems from cell to society, or the entire biota, constitutes one dimension. The levels of organization are the horizontal rows of a matrix, of which the vertical columns are three aspects of living systems: (1) structural, (2) behavioral, and (3) evolving. Structure, in Gerard's view, is a description of the interrelations among the components of a system: the arrangement of its parts and the potential influence which they may have upon each other. For example, the topology of neural tracts, together with the catalogue of their potential action (excitatory or inhibitory), reveals the structure of a nervous system; an organizational chart reveals the structure of an institution.

According to Gerard, *behavior* refers to the short-term reversible changes of state of a living system, its immediate responses to environmental stimuli, the functions performed by its homeostatic devices in maintaining certain steady states, etc. Nervous activity and metabolic processes belong under this rubric, as well as the behavior patterns of higher animals and the short-term actions of organized social bodies. Finally, the third rubric deals with the long-term, typically irreversible changes—the development of the embryo, the growth of an individual, the history of a society, the evolution of a species.

The three aspects just described could be called "being" (structure), "acting" (behavior), and "becoming" (history). The intersections of their respective columns with the rows of the matrix (the levels of organization) determine particular fields of inquiry. For example, anatomy is the study of structure at the level of the individual; history is the study of development at the level of a society;

embryology is the discipline in the same column as history but at the level of the individual (early stage); and histology deals with structure at the level of the cell.

It has already been said that general systems theory is not, strictly speaking, a scientific theory but, rather, an outlook. Gerard's scheme represents this outlook in its most purely programmatic garb, inasmuch as the matrix of levels and of their three aspects does not imply any theoretical assertion. However, the scheme does represent a possibly fruitful way of *viewing* the world of living systems, in the sense that it is suggestive of dependencies and analogies.

James G. Miller (1955) has proposed a program for listing hypotheses (which, when verified, could become general propositions) concerning similarities or differences between analogous events taking place on different levels of system organization. These "levels" in Miller's conceptual scheme are identical with those in Gerard's. For example, living systems grow; is there one law of growth on the cell level, and another law—perhaps similar, perhaps very different—which applies to the growth of the individual, the group, the society, etc.? Living systems process information and utilize it to maintain their viability. Are there propositions concerning information processing which can be maintained (with possible modifications) about all levels of organizations?

The mathematical approach

In my view, the most fundamental feature which distinguishes a system from other aggregates or from an arbitrarily circumscribed portion of the world is the possibility of describing it in purely structural terms. Here the word "structural" refers not necessarily to specific components or physical features but, rather, to relations (which may be relations among parameters as well as relations among parts). A system, roughly speaking, is a bundle of relations. For this reason a general systems theory, in my opinion, ought to single out purely relational isomorphisms that are abstracted from content.

As an example, consider a mathematical formulation of the growth of some system. Specifically, let a physical system be a solid body with a boundary, and let growth be the result of ingestion of substances from the outside through the boundary at a constant rate per unit of surface. Moreover, let the substance which makes up the system break down inside the system at a constant rate per unit mass and be excreted. Then, since the surface is proportional to the two-thirds power of the volume, while mass is proportional to the volume, we have the equation

$$dm/dt = am^{\frac{2}{3}} - bm,$$

where m is the mass and a and b are constants (Bertalanffy 1957). Such will be the "law of growth" of all physical systems of this sort, regardless of size or internal organization. On the other hand, if the system is essentially one-dimensional (i.e., grows only at the ends at a constant rate, while breaking down at a constant rate per unit mass), its law of growth will be

$$dm/dt = a - bm.$$

Evidently not the "level" of the system but, rather, its geometry is likely to be the determinant of its law of growth. If so, then attempts to specify particular laws of growth for "cells," "populations," "corporations," etc., will prove futile.

Isomorphisms. The objections to the so-called organismic general systems theory, centered on levels of organization, have stimulated an altogether different approach to the subject: one founded on *mathematical homologies* rather than organismic homologies. The strictest mathematical homology is called an *isomorphism.* Two mathematical objects are isomorphic if there exists a one-to-one correspondence between the elements of one and those of the other and if the relations among the elements are preserved by the same correspondence. If two physical systems obey the same mathematical law, they are also isomorphic to each other. A famous example of such isomorphism is that between a mechanical harmonic oscillator and an electrical circuit with an inductance, a resistance, and a capacitance. As is well known, the differential equation of the former is

$$m \frac{d^2x}{dt^2} + r \frac{dx}{dt} + kx = f(t),$$

where x is the displacement of the mass m; r is a coefficient of friction; k is the elasticity modulus, associated with the restoring force; and $f(t)$ is an impressed force, which may be a function of time. The differential equation of the electrical system is given by

$$L \frac{d^2q}{dt^2} + R \frac{dq}{dt} + Cq = E(t),$$

where q is charge, L the inductance, R the resistance, C the capacitance, and $E(t)$ an impressed electromotive force.

The isomorphism is apparent from the identical forms of the equations. Any law of behavior derived from the equation with respect to one system has an exact analogue with respect to the other.

Moreover, a fundamental set of "homologies" is established between mass and inductance, between electrical resistance and friction, between capacitance and elasticity—homologies which possibly would not have occurred to one preoccupied with the specific *content* of the events rather than with their mathematical structure. Yet the homologies are quite "real." For example, the heat produced by "overcoming" electrical resistance is the same sort of heat as that produced by overcoming friction.

Classification of systems. Here, then, is a unifying principle, which truly abstracts from the content of phenomena and concentrates on the structural and dynamic relations, in terms of which the phenomena are described. If we follow the definition of "system" given above to its logical conclusion—namely, as a specified set of entities and a set of relations among them—then it would seem that the method of mathematical homology is the most natural foundation of a general systems theory. For an exact specification of relations is practically synonymous with a mathematical specification. The system is specified as a particular mathematical model and is seen at once to be isomorphic to all systems specified in terms of models of the same type.

In this light, the classification of systems derives from a classification of mathematical models. For example, all systems involving monomolecular chemical reactions are representable by systems of the first-order, first-degree linear differential equations. Moreover, closed systems are isomorphic to homogeneous systems of equations (without constant terms), while open systems are isomorphic to nonhomogeneous systems of equations (which include constant terms). The absence or the presence of the "equifinality" that was attributed by the vitalists to specific life forces is directly derivable from the nature of such equations, depending on whether they are or are not homogeneous. Bimolecular reactions are represented by systems of the second degree. These systems are much more complex than linear ones and may have special features like thresholds, which divide the phase space into "watersheds," so that the steady state which finally obtains may be determined by the direction of a chance fluctuation about an unstable equilibrium.

Integration of knowledge

Realizations of such systems are not confined to chemistry. Ecological systems can also, in principle, be represented by systems of differential equations, from which their characteristic features, such as presence or absence of stable equilibria, oscillations, etc., can be derived. To the extent that systems of equations of this sort can be supposed to underlie any phenomenon whatsoever—chemical, biological, or social (e.g., mass behavior)—these phenomena must exhibit homological laws, so that concepts from one field of investigation are compellingly translated into those of another, in the same way that capacitance is translated into elasticity, whatever our preconceived notions may be about the nature of either.

This interchangeability of concepts can already be seen in the fusion of biological and social theories: for example, in the way Malthus influenced Darwin, who, in turn influenced Herbert Spencer and Karl Marx. The essential orientation of all these writers is characterized by an emphasis on the "massive," deterministic aspects of both biological and social phenomena. The general systems orientation led to a much more precise, mathematical statement of similar ideas. Some examples of mathematico–sociological and mathematico–historical theories were elaborated by Lewis F. Richardson (1960) and Nicolas Rashevsky (1953). Likewise, John W. Thompson (1961) has outlined a physicalist approach which links the concepts of meteorology and sociology.

The mathematical homology method solves the problem of "integrating" knowledge stemming from disparate disciplines via the translation rules that are rigorously derived from mathematical models. The method provides a basis for resolving the interminable controversies regarding terminology in the behavioral sciences—whether, for example, "power," as it is understood in political science has any relation to "power" as it is understood in sociology, or whether either has any relation to "influence" or "status" as these are understood in social psychology, or whether "energy" as this term is used in psychodynamics has any bearing on physical energy. If a term enters as a homologous variable or parameter in two or more isomorphic models, then the term plays the same part in the respective theories; if it does not, then the opposite is true.

Precision and specification. The mathematical model approach to general systems theory has one serious, at times crippling, drawback. To define a system, a much more precise specification of entities and relations is required than our knowledge usually warrants. Here a word must be said to forestall a possible misunderstanding of what is meant by "precise" in a rigorous theory. Precision is often understood in terms of accuracy of measurement or in terms of the degree of determinism of deduced conclusions. Thus, celestial mechanics is precise (it is sometimes referred to as an exact

science) in the sense that positions of heavenly bodies are calculated with great accuracy and the predictions of the theory are extremely reliable. In this sense, meteorology is not "precise," because the determination of variables relevant to the prediction of weather is much more difficult than the determination of variables relevant to celestial mechanics.

Nevertheless, the systems studied in meteorology are as precisely *defined* as those studied in celestial mechanics. One knows what one means by the state of a meteorological system—namely, the distribution of temperatures, pressures, wind velocities, etc.—and one is sure that the state of the system determines a certain succession of states in time. Only the difficulty of determining the precise state at a given time and the enormity of the calculations make it impossible for us to predict the weather as precisely as we predict eclipses. In short, we must distinguish between precise results and precise specifications.

To be precisely *specified*, a system need not even be deterministic. The variables of interest may be the probabilities of states; by means of stochastic models, we can calculate the distributions of these probabilities at future times, given some initial distribution. This sort of theory is no less precise than a deterministic one. In short, a system is precisely defined if the states in which it can be are precisely specified (not necessarily actually determined) and the laws of progression of these states (which may be probabilities) are precisely postulated (not necessarily actually verified).

The organismic approach reconsidered. When we say that many events do not lend themselves to the above sort of description, we mean that it is difficult to *specify* the states and to *postulate* the dynamic laws which determine their progression. At times we can say a great deal more about systems if we forgo attempts at such precise specifications. For example, a great deal can be said about living systems without any rigorous specification of "states" and of dynamic laws. We know that all living systems come into being; maintain themselves in more or less steady states in the midst of a changing environment; enter into symbiotic or predatory relations to each other; mature; reproduce themselves, if they are individual organisms—and also, frequently, if they are aggregates (e.g., bee hives); grow old; and cease to exist as organized systems. Furthermore, detailed analysis establishes more specific laws of existence for living systems: for example, the need for outside sources of energy. Similar analysis establishes general conditions of existence of organized social aggregates: for example, the existence of channels of at least internal communication of internalized codes of behavior.

There is no doubt that analysis of this sort yields knowledge and that much of this knowledge can be organized into systematic descriptions and predictions even without the aid of rigorous systems analysis in the mathematical sense of the word "rigorous." To the extent that the organismic approach to a general systems theory can bypass the obstacles to mathematical analysis mentioned above, the organismic approach has its special heuristic advantages. It can therefore be viewed as complementary to the mathematical approach to a general systems theory.

Technological systems

We have traced the current interest in general systems theory to two classes of investigators, the biologists and the mathematicians. The former have had a long-felt need to spell out some features of the organismic view (always predominant in biology) which can contribute to the pressing problem of integrating knowledge. The latter have contributed the rigor of formal analysis to the formulation of a systems theory whose integrative power derives from the process of abstraction characteristic of mathematical thought. There is still a third source of ideas which feeds general systems theory: the modern conception of a technological system.

The structure of a technological system (i.e., an aggregate of interrelated technological devices) is completely known, since such systems are designed by men. Consequently, the problem is not to discover what the important elements are and how they are related but, rather, to determine the overall behavior of a system whose structure is specified. Once methods of solving these problems are developed, the systems engineer can pose the problem of optimal system synthesis: what elements to use and how to relate them to each other in order to achieve a performance that is optimal in some given respect.

General systems theory contributes to the solution of such problems by placing them in a general structural context abstracted from specific content. For example, the emergence of cybernetics can be viewed as a development in the spirit of general systems theory. Cybernetics is a science which deals with the information-processing aspects (as distinguished, say, from the energy-transforming aspects) of all systems, regardless of their physical nature. This point of view has greatly facilitated the development of automatic control, telecom-munications, and computing technologies. The influence of cybernetics, however, has not been confined to technology. The ideas of information theory (which underlie cybernetics) have helped to unify thinking in such apparently very disparate fields as systems engineering, economics, and neurophysiology by singling out the concepts underlying all of them, such as homeostasis (maintenance of dynamic equilibria) and transmission of information.

The future of general systems theory

In short, the task of general systems theory is to find the most general conceptual framework in which a scientific theory or a technological problem can be placed without losing the essential features of the theory or the problem. The proponents of general systems theory see in it the focal point of resynthesis of knowledge. There was a time when the man of knowledge was a generalist rather than a specialist, that is, he embodied the knowledge of principles rather than skills. He was the philosopher and the sage, and his epistemological creed was most clearly stated by Plato, who believed that all real knowledge comes from within rather than from without, that is, from the contemplation of what *must* be rather than what seems to be.

The rise of science and of experimental method puts this extreme rationalist view under a shadow. The legitimate sources of scientific knowledge came to be restricted to data derived from direct contact with the observable world. However, there was a price to be paid for this: the fragmentation of knowledge into specialties. Hand in hand with the fragmentation, however, new syntheses have appeared. Mathematical physics is the best-known example, and the evolutionary principle as the key theme of biology is another. "Systematization" of the social sciences has also been attempted, the works of Marx and Toynbee being among the most ambitious of such attempts.

The main theme of general systems theory is, I believe, the explicit fusion of the mathematical approach with the organismic. The key task of general systems theory is to show how the organismic aspect of a system emerges from the mathematical structure. At times, classical mathematical methods suffice to bring this out; for example, organismic aspects emerge from the properties of systems of differential equations, including trends toward equilibrium states that are independent of initial conditions, stability properties, etc.

However, classical mathematics is not able to handle complex structural features. Organization is best depicted as a network, and the mathematical theory of networks derives largely from certain branches of topology and abstract algebra rather than from analysis, which underlies classical mathematics. Thus the salient feature of a nervous system, of an institution, or of international systems may well reside in the vastly complex network of relations which constitute them: for example, functional neural pathways, lines of communication and authority, links of alliances or rivalries in international trade. If the "nature" of the system is indeed embodied in the quality and interrelations of these connections, then there is hope that knowledge of wholes will emerge from knowledge of the parts.

Moreover, in the system theoretic view, the whole can be viewed as a unit no less than a part can. Hence, the fate of the components of a system may be viewed as determined by the fate of the whole system as legitimately as the other way around. For example, the organism goes through certain stages of maturation because its cells differentiate, but the process of differentiation is also the result of the maturation. The organism dies because the cells die, but the converse is also true. National policies are set by leaders, but the selection of leaders depends at least in part on the inertia of ongoing policies.

These observations are rather commonplace and do not in themselves constitute theories. However, a rigorous *deduction* of these principles as system properties may well involve profound theoretical discoveries. Therein lies the promise of general systems theory.

ANATOL RAPOPORT

[*Directly related are the entries* CYBERNETICS *and* INFORMATION THEORY.]

BIBLIOGRAPHY

ASHBY, W. ROSS 1958 General Systems Theory as a New Discipline. *General Systems* 3:1–6.

BERTALANFFY, LUDWIG VON 1956 General System Theory. *General Systems* 1:1–10.

BERTALANFFY, LUDWIG VON 1957 Quantitative Laws in Metabolism and Growth. *Quarterly Review of Biology* 32:217–231.

BERTALANFFY, LUDWIG VON 1962 General System Theory: A Critical Review. *General Systems* 7:1–20.

BOULDING, KENNETH E. 1956 General System Theory: The Skeleton of Science. *General Systems* 1:11–17.

DRIESCH, HANS (1908) 1929 *The Science and Philosophy of the Organism.* 2d ed. Vol. 2. London: Macmillan. → See especially Part 3.

FOSTER, CAXTON C.; RAPOPORT, ANATOL; and TRUCCO, ERNESTO 1957 Some Unsolved Problems in the Theory of Non-isolated Systems. *General Systems* 2: 9–29.

GERARD, RALPH W. 1958 Units and Concepts of Biology. *Behavioral Science* 3:197–206.

MILLER, JAMES G. 1955 Toward a General Theory for the Behavioral Sciences. *American Psychologist* 10: 513–531.

MILLER, JAMES G. 1965a Living Systems: Basic Concepts. *Behavioral Science* 10:193–237.

MILLER, JAMES G. 1965b Living Systems: Structure and Process; Cross-level Hypotheses. *Behavioral Science* 10:337–411.

RAPOPORT, ANATOL 1967 Mathematical Aspects of General Systems Analysis. Unpublished manuscript.

RASHEVSKY, NICOLAS 1953 Outline of a Mathematical Approach to History. *Bulletin of Mathematical Biophysics* 15:197–234.

RICHARDSON, LEWIS F. 1960 *Arms and Insecurity.* Edited by Nicolas Rashevsky and Ernesto Trucco. Pittsburgh: Boxwood; Chicago: Quadrangle Books.

THOMPSON, JOHN W. 1961 Meteorological Models in Social Dynamics. *Human Relations* 14:43–62.

II
SOCIAL SYSTEMS

"System" is the concept that refers both to a complex of interdependencies between parts, components, and processes that involves discernible regularities of relationship, and to a similar type of interdependency between such a complex and its surrounding environment. System, in this sense, is therefore the concept around which all sophisticated theory in the conceptually generalizing disciplines is and must be organized. This is because any regularity of relationship can be more adequately understood if the whole complex of multiple interdependencies of which it forms part is taken into account.

Social systems and the action system

Methodologically, one must distinguish a theoretical system, which is a complex of assumptions, concepts, and propositions having both logical integration and empirical reference, from an empirical system, which is a set of phenomena in the observable world that can be described and analyzed by means of a theoretical system. An empirical system (e.g., the solar system as relevant to analytical mechanics) is never a totally concrete entity but, rather, a selective organization of those properties of the concrete entity defined as relevant to the theoretical system in question. Thus, for Newtonian solar system mechanics, the earth is "only" a particle with a given mass, location in space, velocity, and direction of motion; the Newtonian scheme is not concerned with the earth's geological or human social and cultural characteristics. In this sense, any theoretical system is abstract.

As a theoretical system, the social system is specifically adapted to describing and analyzing social interaction considered as a class of empirical systems. These systems are concerned with the behavior, as distinguished from the metabolic physiology, of living organisms. Among the categories of organisms, our interest in this article centers on human social interaction, which is organized on the symbolic levels we call "cultural." However, one should remember that such interaction is a late evolutionary product and is continuous with a very broad range of interaction phenomena among other organisms. All bisexual reproduction, for example, requires highly structured interactive relations between the organisms of the two sexes. Various kinds of interspecies ecological relations constitute another example, one to which human relations with domesticated animals are relevant.

The aspects of behavior which directly concern "cultural-level" systems I call *action*. Action in this technical sense includes four generic types of subsystems, the differentiation among which has gained fairly clear definition during modern intellectual history.

The first is simply the organism, which, though quite properly treated as a concrete entity in one set of terms, becomes, on a more generalized level, a set of abstract components (i.e., a subsystem) in the culturally organized system of action.

A second subsystem is the social system, which is generated by the process of interaction among individual units. Its distinctive properties are consequences and conditions of the specific modes of interrelationship obtaining among the living organisms which constitute its units.

Third is the cultural system, which is the aspect of action organized about the specific characteristics of symbols and the exigencies of forming stable systems of them. It is structured in terms of patternings of meaning which, when stable, imply in turn generalized complexes of constitutive symbolisms that give the action system its primary "sense of direction," and which must be treated as independent of any particular system of social interaction. Thus, although there are many ramifications into such areas as language and communication, the prototypical cultural systems are those of beliefs and ideas. The possibilities of their preservation over time, and of their diffusion from one personality and/or social system into another, are perhaps the most important hallmarks of the independent structure of cultural systems.

Fourth, the analytical distinction between social and cultural systems has a correlative relation to the distinction between the organism and those other aspects of the individual actor which we gen-

erally call the personality. With the achievement of cultural levels of the control of behavior, the primary subsystems of action can no longer be organized—or structured primarily—about the organic base, which, in the first instance, is anatomical or "physical." Personality, then, is the aspect of the living individual, as "actor," which *must* be understood in terms of the cultural and social content of the learned patternings that make up his behavioral system. Here, "learned" refers not only to the problem of the origin of the patterns in the heredity–environment sense, but also to the problem of the kind and level of their content. The connection between these two problems partly reflects the fact that we have no evidence that cultural content is, at what we call here the level of pattern, determined through the genes. Thus, there is no evidence of a hereditary "propensity" to speak one language rather than another, although the genetically determined capacities to learn and use language are generally fundamental.

Thus, we treat the social system, when evolved to the action level, as one of four primary subsystems of action, all of which articulate with the organic bases of life and with organic adaptation to the environment in the broadest biological sense.

There is a sense in which the social system is the core of human action systems, being the primary link between the culture and the individual both as personality and as organism—a fact for which "culture and personality" theorists have often not adequately accounted. As the principal source of the independence of cultural systems from restrictive organic and environmental conditions, it has been the primary locus of the "operation bootstrap" of human evolution. The secret of this evolutionary capacity evidently lies in the possibility for "reverberation" among the intercommunicating members of a social system, each of whom is both an actor orienting himself to his situation in terms of complex, cultural-level, intended meanings and an object of orientation meaningful to orienting actors. Furthermore, each person is both actor and object to himself as well as to others. Interaction at the symbolic level thus becomes a system analytically and, very appreciably, empirically independent of its presymbolic bases (though still grounded in them), and is capable of development on its own.

Insight into this basic complex of facts constitutes a principal foundation of modern social science theory. It has been attained by convergence from at least four sources: Freud's psychology, starting from a medical–biological base; Weber's sociology, which worked to transcend the problems of the German intellectual tradition concerning idealism–materialism; Durkheim's analysis of the individual actor's relations to the "social facts" of his situation; and the social psychology of the American "symbolic interactionists" Cooley and Mead, who built upon the philosophy of pragmatism. [*See* INTERACTION, *article on* SOCIAL INTERACTION.]

In dealing with social systems, one must distinguish terminologically between an actor as a unit in a social system and the system as such. The actor may be either an individual or some kind of collective unit. In both cases, the actor within a system of reference will be spoken of as acting in a *situation* consisting of other actor-units within the same system of reference who are considered as objects. The system as a whole, however, functions (but does not "act" in a technical sense) in relation to its environment. Of course, the system references are inherently relative to particular scientific problems. When a collective (i.e., social) system is said to act, as in the case of a government conducting foreign relations, this will mean that it and the objects of its action constitute the social system of reference and that these objects are situation, not environment, to the acting collectivity.

The social system and its environments

A social system, like all living systems, is inherently an open system engaged in processes of interchange (or "input–output relations") with its environment, as well as consisting of interchanges among its internal units. Regarding it as an open system is, from some viewpoints, regarding it as a part of—i.e., a subsystem of—one or more superordinate systems. In this sense, it is interdependent with the other parts of the more comprehensive system or systems and, hence, partly dependent on them for essential inputs. Here the dependence of the organism on its physical environment for nutrition and respiration is prototypical. This is the essential basis of the famous concept of *function* as it applies to social systems, as to all other living systems.

For any system of reference, functional problems are those concerning the conditions of the maintenance and/or development of the interchanges with environing systems, both inputs from them and outputs to them. Functional significance may be determined by the simple criterion of the dysfunctional consequences of failure, deficit, or excess of an input to a receiving system, as asphyxiation is the consequence of failure in oxygen input, and so oxygen input is judged to be functionally

significant for the organism. Function is the only basis on which a theoretically systematic ordering of the structure of living systems is possible. In this context functional references certainly need beg no question about how structural arrangements have come about, since the biological concepts of variation, selection, and adaptation have long since provided a framework for analyzing the widest variety of change processes.

Goal-attaining processes explicitly intended to fulfill functional requirements constitute a limiting, but very important, case. Outputs in this sense have primary functional significance only for the system which receives them and which is situational or environmental to the system of reference, although they have secondary functional significance to the latter. For example, although economic output ("produced" goods) goes to "consumers," the maintenance of certain levels of salable output clearly has great significance to producing organizations. It is its inputs that have primary functional significance for any given system of reference. The "factors of production" of economic theory are classic examples, being the critical inputs of the economy.

In a crucial sense, the relation between any action system—including the social—and any of its environments is dual. On the one hand, the particular environment constitutes a set of objects which are "exterior" to the system in the Cartesian–Durkheimian sense. On the other hand, through interpenetration, the environmental system is partially and selectively included in the action system of reference. Internalization of cultural and social objects in the personality of the individual is certainly the prototypical case of interpenetration, but the principle it involves should be generalized to all the relations between action systems and their environments.

Thus, neither the individual personality nor the social system has any *direct* relation to the physical environment; their relations with the latter are mediated entirely through the organism, which is action's primary link with the physical world. This, after all, is now a commonplace of modern perceptual and epistemological theory (Ayer 1956, pp. 130–133). In essentially the same sense, neither personalities nor social systems have direct contact with the ultimate objects of reference, with the "ultimate reality" which poses "problems of meaning" in the sense sociologists associate above all with the work of Max Weber. The objects that personalities and social systems know and otherwise directly experience are in our terminology cultural objects, which are human artifacts in much the same sense as are the objects of empirical cognition. Hence, the relations of personalities and social systems with ultimate "nonempirical reality" are in a basic sense *mediated* through the cultural system.

Emphasis on their lack of direct contact with what is "out there" concerns in both cases certain qualities of the environing systems as objects. There is, however, important contact with the physical and supernatural environments through the interpenetration of the latter into action systems. Hence, such concepts as knowledge are not naive illusions but modes of the organization of the relations between the various action systems and their environments (Whitehead [1929] and Mead [1938] based their analysis of action on philosophical positions similar to that assumed here). We must regard the relations between the subsystems of action, and between the action system and the systems of nonaction, as *pluralistic*. That is, there will be no one-to-one correspondence between any two interdependent and interpenetrating systems, but there will be a complex relation which can perhaps be understood by theoretical analysis. This is true of "heredity and environment," "culture and personality," and the "ideal" and "real" factors in social systems.

It is necessary to consider the various environments of a living system, because each such environment is engaged in one of the interchange relations with the system, and the specialized natures of these relations serve as the primary bases of the internal differentiation of the system. For instance, the nutrition and elimination systems, the respiratory system, and the locomotor system of an organism are differentiated from each other on this basis. This, as noted, is the essential meaning of the controversial (in social, not biological, science) concept of function. The basis of differentiation *is* functional, since it consists in the differing input–output relations of the system with its various environments and, following from that, the internal relations between the differing parts of the system itself.

Society and societal community

On the understanding that all social systems are systems of interaction, the best reference point among their many types, for general theoretical purposes, is the society. The definition of this concept presents considerable difficulties, the history of which cannot occupy us here. For present purposes, I shall define society as the category of social system embodying, at the requisite levels of evolutionary development and of control over the con-

ditions of environmental relations, the greatest self-sufficiency of any type of social system. [*See* SOCIETY.]

By self-sufficiency (a criterion which has figured prominently in Western thought on the subject since Aristotle at least), I mean the capacity of the system, gained through both its internal organization and resources and its access to inputs from its *environments*, to function autonomously in implementing its normative culture, particularly its values but also its norms and collective goals. Self-sufficiency is clearly a degree of generalized adaptive capacity in the sense of biological theory.

The term "environment" is pluralized here to emphasize the fact that the relevant environment is not just physical, as in most formulations of general biological theory, but also includes the three basic subsystems of action other than the social, which have been outlined above.

The core structure of a society I will call the societal community. More specifically, at different levels of evolution, it is called tribe, or "the people," or, for classical Greece, *polis*, or, for the modern world, *nation*. It is the collective structure in which members are united or, in some sense, associated. Its most important property is the kind and level of solidarity—in Durkheim's sense—which characterizes the relations between its members.

The solidarity of a community is essentially the degree to which (and the ways in which) its collective interest can be expected to prevail over the unit interests of its members wherever the two conflict. It may involve mutual respect among the units for the rights of membership status, conformity with the value and norms institutionalized in the collectivity, or positive contribution to the attainment of collective goals. The character of solidarity varies with the level of differentiation in the society, differentiation which is evident in the structures of the roles in which a given individual is involved, of the system's subcollectivities, and of its norms and specified value orientations. The best-known basis for classifying the types of solidarity is Durkheim's two categories, mechanical and organic (see Parsons 1960*a*).

Both types of solidarity are characterized by common values and institutionalized norms. In the case of mechanical solidarity, however, the patterns of action expected from units are also uniform for all units in the system: relative to one another, the units are *segments*, since they are not functionally differentiated. Durkheim analyzed crime as the prototypical violation of the obligations of mechanical solidarity. For full members of the community, no matter how highly differentiated the society, the treatment of the criminal should ideally be always the same, regardless of *who* commits the crime, even though this ideal is frequently and seriously deviated from. At the societal community level in differentiated societies, the core of the system of mechanical solidarity lies in the patterns of citizenship, in T. H. Marshall's sense (1949). These patterns can be conveniently subdivided into the components of civil–legal citizenship, political citizenship, and social citizenship. In modern American society, the bill of rights and associated constitutional structures, such as the fourteenth amendment, comprise the most directly relevant institutions in this field.

Organic solidarity concerns those aspects of the societal system in which roles, subcollectivities, and norms are differentiated on a functional basis. Here, though common value patterns remain of the first importance to the various subsystems at the relevant levels of specification, expectations of behavior differ according to role and subcollectivity. Solidarity, then, involves the integration of these differing expectations with respect to the various bases of compatible functioning, from mutual noninterference to positive mutual reinforcement. [*See* INTEGRATION.]

Organic solidarity seems to be particularly important in three primary structural contexts. Most familiar is the one Durkheim himself particularly stressed, the economic division of labor, where the most important institutional patterns are contract and property. Second is what we ordinarily call the area of political differentiation, that of both the organization of authority and leadership and the various modes of participation in collective decision making, which involve the interplay of information and influence bearing on collective action. The third is the area of the society's relations with its cultural involvements. This particularly concerns the society's articulation with the religious system, but also (and the more so, the more differentiated both the society and the culture) with the arts, the system of intellectual disciplines, and the relationship between the patterns of moral obligation and those of law.

Organic solidarity and pluralism. In all three contexts, organic solidarity is associated with the phenomenon generally called pluralism. In none of these cases is the structure of a subsystem articulating with the societal community ascribed to the structure of the latter. On the contrary, as a function of the level of differentiation among the articulating subsystems, there is an increasing flexibility that facilitates the concrete relations coming to be established by relatively specific processes.

Thus, there is, first, a pluralism of economic interests which, if uncontrolled, would tend to destroy the solidarity of the societal community—indeed, it may be suggested that an exaggerated anxiety about this underlies much of the modern socialist dogma that only the central societal collectivity, the state, can be trusted with any interest which seems important to the public welfare. However, there is a second pluralism of "interest groups" in the political context which, though of course linked with the economic pluralism, is by no means the same. The political process, as that leading to collective decision making, is in part a "political struggle" among such interest groups. Thus, it has great potential for disrupting societal solidarity. However, the latter can also not merely contain the struggle but, even more positively, further integrate the disparate groups by virtue of various mechanisms of integrative control. Finally, the more differentiated societal community tends also to be culturally pluralistic. This is particularly conspicuous in the few Western societies which have attained a certain level of religious pluralism. Thus, at the very least, contemporary American society is a multidenominational, Judaeo–Christian society which also *includes* secular humanists who prefer not to affiliate with any explicitly religious association. In one sense, it has "transcended" the historic bases of religious conflict which prevailed in the Western world for centuries. The basis of this is genuine denominational pluralism, not only before the law but also in terms of acceptance in the community.

Very closely associated with this is the pluralism among the intellectual disciplines which has gained institutionalization in modern society, especially in the university system (Parsons 1965). The rise of the sciences was, in the first instance, a profound symptom of this pluralization. But it has now become a major factor in the future development of modern society in a variety of ways. The problem of "ethical" pluralism is analytically more difficult and complex. The trend seems to be away from the special *kind* of moral uniformity which characterizes societies in which mechanical solidarity predominates. The essential point concerns the level of generality at which common moral standards are defined: if a pluralistic society is to integrate its many various kinds of units into a solidary societal community, what counts as moral obligation cannot be defined in terms specific to each kind of unit but must be sufficiently general to apply to the considerable range of differentiated classes of units. Moral*ism* ties morality to the specifics of a subgroup or a particular stage of social development and must be distinguished from concern with maintaining control of action in accord with more generalized moral standards.

Cultural system and political system

The societal community in the present sense is articulated most directly with the cultural and political subsystems of the society. Furthermore, it is in these two relationships that the main connections between organic and mechanical solidarity are lodged.

The cultural (or pattern-maintenance) system centers on the institutionalization of cultural value patterns, which, at the general cultural level, may be regarded as moral. Institutionalized societal values, and their specifications to societal subsystems, comprise only part of the relevance of moral values to action; moral values are also involved, through internalization, in structures of the personality and behavioral organism; and, more generally, they articulate with religion, science, and the arts within the cultural system.

Community in the present sense is never a simple matter of the "acting out" of value commitments. It also involves differentiated acceptance, in valuational terms, of the *conditions* necessary for the functioning of societies and their subsystems. Essentially this latter element draws the line between utopianism—making an imperative of "pure" value actualization—and realistic social idealism. Avoiding the utopian dilemma involves organizing the value system so as to include the positive valuation of social relationships for their own sake, not only as being rigidly instrumental to specific value patterns.

But this is not the whole story. In addition to a general "set" establishing a presumption of legitimacy for the social system as such, there must also be a more flexible set of mechanisms providing for adaptation between the cultural subsystem of the society and the societal community itself. These mechanisms concern the capacity for handling the changing needs and exigencies of various associational relationships in the light of both their developing interrelations and their relations with the value system; the more particularized commitments must be a function of changing conceptions of the imperatives of relationship, as defining the nature of "valued association." The commitment to the societal community is, so far as this interchange develops flexibility, no longer ascriptive but dependent on the need for such commitment and on an evaluation of its compatibility with deeper moral commitments at the cultural level. One aspect of this flexibility is the individual's enhanced moral independence from imperatives of unquestioning obligations to conformity. But the obverse aspect is the "right" of the community to expect appropriate flexibility in the adaptation of moral demands to exigencies of realistic implementation.

The minimum imperatives of specified *common* value commitment define one pole of the structures of the societal system organized with mechanical solidarity. There is a place for organic solidarity in this context so far as such commitments are so firm as *not* to be "negotiable" and so general as to permit the kind of flexibility in adapting to particular "exigencies" which has just been discussed. What I above called moralism is the limiting case where lack of generality (and perhaps firmness of commitment) forecloses such flexibility. The basic rights of members in the societal community constitute, in negative definition, the limits of application of these value commitments. Members' complementary obligations to the societal community constitute the obverse expectations of contribution to the functioning of a social system to which they are committed.

In a sense, the "payoff" on such obligations comes in the relation between the societal community and the political subsystem, since the latter is concerned with collective goal attainment as a function of the total society and, *pari passu*, of each subsystem grounded in communal solidarity. This relation between the societal community and the political subsystem concerns a further step toward mastering exigencies in the interest of the implementation of values. It is a matter not just of establishing particular relationships of solidarity as the "setting" for value implementation but, further, of committing the interests of that community to particular collective goals—which involves dealing with the exigencies of particular environmental conditions. For the individual, then, this concerns not merely his personal commitment to the goal but his obligations as a member of the community. Committing the community implies a solution to the problem of integrating the community with reference to the "policy" in question, whether this involves developing a broad consensus or ruthlessly suppressing minority, or even majority, views. As a somewhat extreme case, entering a war commits the national community, whatever various membership elements think about it, short of their mustering a resistance which would favor the enemy cause.

Here, as in the relation of the national community to the "cultural" subsystem, two importantly different levels are involved. One concerns the general "authority" of differentiated elements in the society to commit or bind the collectivity as a whole in the pursuit of particular goals in particular situations. One extreme in this context would be an absolutist or despotic "government" which presumed to act as it pleased, regardless of consent or opposition in the broader societal community. An opposite extreme would be a community which made any collective action dependent on virtually unanimous and explicit consent.

By differentiating the two levels, modern governmental systems avoid being caught in the above dilemma. They set up procedural rules defining the level of support needed to authorize collective action binding the collectivity as a whole, including minorities that dissent in various contexts. For this to work, the minorities must be committed to the legitimacy of the governmental system, even though they refuse to support particular policy decisions of the moment.

For the individual (or political minority groups), however, such situations may present a moral dilemma. In his role as a responsible member of the societal community, which includes an obligation to support its government (not particular decisions or parties) the member of a minority subgroup is, up to a point, obligated not only to accept but often also to cooperate actively in implementing a policy of which he disapproves. There may, however, be a point beyond which his conscience will not allow this. He will then be driven into various levels of resistance, ranging from withdrawal of active participation, through public protest, conspicuous noncooperation, and militant attempts to prevent or sabotage its implementation, to revolution.

The development of political differentiation and pluralism, including the generalization of the crucial levels of political obligation, tends to broaden the range of individual freedom for dissent and also to draw the lines between politically institutionalized—as distinguished from moral—rights of dissent and opposition and those institutionally defined as illegitimate. The basic independence of the cultural–moral and the socially institutionalized systems, however, precludes *any* social community from being completely immune to the kind of political opposition which can lead to the disruption of its basic solidarity.

The element of mechanical solidarity here concerns the *legitimation* of collective decision-making authorities. Such legitimation must derive from common value commitments to the societal community and, hence, to the kinds of collective action considered legitimate, including the identification of the agencies entitled to take such action. Ob-

versely, this also concerns the rights of membership elements to give or withhold support for particular policies and, more generally, particular claims to leadership status. The appeals for such support, however, must be on grounds of organic rather than mechanical solidarity. The procedural rules become the focus of common commitments, while particular outcomes become matters for legitimate contest.

Solidarity and the economy

At this point, we may recall that Durkheim introduced the concept of organic solidarity in analyzing the division of labor in the economic sense. This was quite logical in the light both of the utilitarian theories to which he was critically orienting himself and of the economy's relative remoteness from the setting of the system of mechanical solidarity as that which was just discussed. Focus on the economic system was the most convenient way to set up a clear conceptual dichotomy.

Nevertheless, it now seems better to approach the problem of the economic system indirectly, through its relations to the other aspects of a social system. We conceive of the economy as the functional subsystem of a society differentiated about producing and allocating fluidly disposable resources within the society. As put in a quite familiar paradigm, it operates through combining the factors of production—e.g., land, labor, capital, and organization—to produce the two primary categories of output: commodities and services. The economic categories are not the physical objects or the physical behavior involved as such, but certain ways of controlling them: in the case of commodities, essentially property rights; in the case of services, the kind of authority or power over the performer we associate with the status of employer.

The actual combinatorial processes, which we call economic production, take place in goal-oriented organizational units that economists call firms. The strictly economic functions concern the management of the boundary relations of these units through what is ordinarily called the market system, and should be distinguished from the technological functions. The economic functions involve procuring control of the factors of production (including determination of requirements for them) and disposing of the outputs of production through marketing. These processes operate by adjusting relations between supply and demand through establishing terms for the transfer of control that equate quantity and price for both parties to the exchange.

Here the primary institutional focus of organic

solidarity is the institution of contract, which is essentially the set of procedural rules regulating transfers of both factors of production and economic outputs. This institutional complex not only regulates the actual settlement of contracts but also defines what types of contract may—and may not—be entered into, how agreements may be arrived at, their bearing on the interests of third parties, and the obligations of parties under various special contingencies, such as the development of unforeseen obstacles to the fulfillment of terms.

The institution of property, then, is the normative system regulating acquisition, disposal, control, and use of physical objects in relation to the contractual system, whether the objects be factors of production or commodity outputs. And the institutional complex we call employment regulates the acquisition and utilization of human services, either as factors of production or as ultimate agents of valued consumption.

Generalized media of interchange

In sufficiently developed and differentiated systems, a central role in economic process is played by money, as both a symbolic medium of exchange and a measure and store of value in the economic sense. Money may be defined as the capacity of a societal unit to command economically valuable resources through the exchange process, i.e., through contractual agreements, without giving commodities or services in return. The payment of money constitutes the transfer of such capacity from one unit to another. In most transactions in a developed economy, entities that have "value in use" figure on only one side of an exchange relationship, being balanced by a monetary "consideration" on the other. To "pay" money is to accept certain economic obligations, defined by a proportionate diminution in one's capacity to command economic "values" in other transactions. To accept money in payment, on the other hand, is to gain the right to an expectation that others will make economically valuable goods and services available at the times and places of one's own choosing, within the limits defined in the market nexus. It has long been a commonplace of economics that only a far-reaching institutionalization of the monetary mechanism can make an extended division of labor possible (see, for example, Adam Smith's classic statement in 1776, book 1, especially chapter 3), though it is known that politically controlled administrative allocation of resources can substitute for the contractual–monetary mechanisms up to a point, as in the "command" economy of the Soviet Union, which reached its highest development in the late Stalinist period (see Gross-

man 1962). Nevertheless, the extent of an economy's "monetization" is undoubtedly the most important single index of the mobilizability of its resources and, hence, the flexibility of their allocation, at all combinatorial stages, from ultimate natural resources and human energies or skills, to finished consumption goods and services.

Money is also important theoretically as the best-understood member of the family of generalized symbolic media of interchange involved in social interaction processes. Political power and influence as used in political leadership processes certainly belong to this family (Parsons 1963a; 1963b).

The economy, as here conceived, articulates with the societal community primarily through the institutional complex of contract, property, and the employment–occupation system. Its solidarity is maintained by keeping its transactions in line with certain integrative imperatives, e.g., by protecting the interests both of parties to contractual relations and of third parties and by providing a basis in solidary relations for effective collective action, especially through making economic resources available to collective units, including particularly the government.

Money, like the other members of the family of media, is a *symbolic* medium which, without being too farfetched, we may call a specialized language. Like all such media, it expresses and communicates messages having meanings with reference to a *code*—that is, a set of rules for the use, transformation, and combination of symbols. (The theory of the operation of such types of messages and codes of rules has been developed in the field of linguistics by, particularly, Jakobson & Halle 1956; Chomsky 1957; 1964). In the case of money, as institutionalized, it is highly important to recognize that the relevant code is part of the *legal* system; this is most clear in societies having a sufficiently high level of differentiation. As we have put it, the institutions of contract, property, and employment, as parts of the legal system, constitute the code in terms of which transformations between money and commodities or services and among different forms of monetary assets operate. Financial transactions, therefore, constitute a certain type of "conversations."

This paradigm is also applicable to relations between the societal community and the other primary functional subsystems of the society. In the case of the polity, the medium which corresponds to money is *power*. This I conceive as the generalized medium of mobilizing capacities for effective collective action, utilizable by members of collectivities to contribute toward binding the collectivity to particular courses of action, either determining or contributing to the implementation of specific policy goals. (This usage of the concept of political power is clearly different from those most common in both sociology and political science; for a discussion of the issues involved in the usage of this concept, see Parsons 1963*b.*) The code within which power as a medium operates centers about the institution of *authority*, which in turn articulates with the patterns of institutionalized leadership and administrative responsibility for maintaining regulatory norms.

In the sphere of articulation with the cultural system, the operative medium is what I call commitments. This concerns the specification of the general value patterns to the levels necessary for their workable combination with the other factors requisite to their implementation in concrete action. Commitment to valued associations of the societal community type is the prototype here (unfortunately, I have not yet been able to develop for publication an analysis of the commitments medium on the same level as I have done for money, power, and influence). The relevant code is the set of institutions which constitutes the underpinning of society's mechanical solidarity—in American society those formulated in the bill of rights, etc., as noted. Within this context, the *civil* component holds precedence, because it formulates the valuational basis of community membership.

Finally, the societal community itself is the focus of operation for a fourth generalized medium, which I have called, in a special technical sense, *influence* (Parsons 1963*a*). Here the relevant code is comprised of the norms underlying organic solidarity, as they relate to the pluralistic structure of differentiated societies. Since their primary context is that of the solidarity of the society, we may consider their major focus to be *justification* for the allocation of loyalties. Here justification must be carefully distinguished from legitimation. Justification is less absolute and operates at a lower level in the cybernetic hierarchy. The *system* may well be legitimated while questions of the justification of certain choices between alternative subsidiary solidarities are still left open where actual or potential dilemmas are posed.

These different code components are more or less adequately integrated in a going societal system, where they constitute its basic normative structure. They should be distinguished from the primary normative components of a pattern-maintenance system, since the latter are made up of value patterns and their specifications, not of differentiated norms. The integratively oriented code

of the societal system must be anchored in a value system if it is to have a basis of legitimation. But its structure is determined not only by value specification but also by adjustment to the exigencies of the other functional subsystems. But in this process of adjustment the integratively oriented code still maintains a certain level of integrity with respect to the value commitment and solidarity of the societal community. In highly differentiated societies, this basic code system is the core of the legal system.

Societies and their environments

We may now return to the problem of the relations of a society as a social system with its environments. The basis of the differentiation between the societal community and the other three primary subsystems of the society should be sought in the basis on which they in turn are differentiated from it and from each other. In general, it can be said that the reason for the existence of these patterned differentiations is that they help the social system to cope with the exigencies imposed on it by its environments.

The organic–physical environment. In dealing with this problem, perhaps we had best begin with the economy, partly because the relevant theoretical analysis is most highly developed there. In the terms of our general paradigm, the intrasocial relation between societal community and economy is paralleled at the level of the general action system by the relation between the social system and the behavioral organism.

First, it should be emphasized that all relations between the social system and the *physical* environment are mediated through the behavioral organism. The perceptual processes of the organism are the source of information about the physical environment, which gains cultural organization from its conceptual and theoretical components. The organism is also the source of the "instinctual" components of the motivation of individuals' personalities.

The relation between the organism and the society's economic subsystem, which is of direct concern here, constitutes the *technological* system. This involves the utilization of empirical knowledge, structured by perceptual feedback through the cultural system, for the design and production of commodities having utility for human social functions. *What* is to be produced, in what quantities relative to alternative uses of the factors of production (cost factors), is economically determined; *how* it is to be produced is a technological problem. Technology involves not only the use of ultimate "natural" resources (analytically a "land" factor) and "equipment" (a benefit from previous production) but also labor—a factor that, sociologically speaking, takes the form of service. This is a particularly important category of the interpenetration of the economy with other parts of the societal system. We conceive of service as an output from the economy which "corresponds" to labor as a factor of production but which should definitely not be identified with labor. Very importantly, however, service is a crucial factor in technological efficiency. This apparently paradoxical conception derives from the fact that technological processes always occur within a framework of *social* organization, never as "purely physical" phenomena. This means that the physical, behavioral operations of persons in technological settings are a function of their commitments, as members of the societal community and its relevant subsystems, to devote their energy and skill to productive uses in the economic sense. This human component is then combined, at the general action system level, with empirical knowledge of standards of socioeconomic utility to produce facilities which can be relatively freely allocated to the various functional needs of societal units. Analyses in these terms can contribute much toward resolving the old controversy about whether the material basis of a complex societal system is "ultimately" economic or technological, or whether the distinction between these categories should be abandoned.

Physical location is a particularly important involvement of technological systems, deriving from the necessity to bring together physical materials, plant, equipment, and organisms as performers of service. Role differentiation between the occupational and residential units tends to involve physical separation of workplaces from places of residence, although the involvement of the same persons in both units sets certain requirements for the physical interrelations of the units' locations. In particular, the modern urban community is very largely built about the relationship between these two sets of locations.

Residence, like occupation, also articulates physical location and the organism into the social system. But it operates in the context of the organic rhythm, such as sleep, nutrition, and sexual activity, to which human beings are bound. Another limiting factor is that the household (which, in spite of many exceptions, remains the usual unit of residence), has at its core kinship units centering on one or more nuclear families. The place of residence is the human individual's residual location, the place where he is likely to be, and is often normatively expected to be, when he is not engaged in such other specific activities as work and special recreation.

Communication and transportation—of both goods and persons—therefore require physical media and must be involved in the physical world, perhaps especially in its spatial aspects. The actual communication of a message from a sender in one physical location to a receiver in another is always problematic, even if the two are engaged in face-to-face conversation in the same room. The same is true of broadcast communication—newspapers must get from the printing plant to the readers, radio and television broadcasts must be transmitted through the "air"—and of the conveyance of persons and goods from place to place.

In certain senses, though, the most fundamental problem here is that the normative orders constitutive of social systems must "apply" to categories of persons and their acts in ways that include specifications of where the persons or acts are located. Very generally, then, the societal community and various of its subsystems "claim jurisdiction" over persons and their acts with reference to particular territorial areas. A most important reason for the prominence of territoriality is that normative obligations, if taken sufficiently seriously, must on occasion be somehow enforced, and this involves resort at some point to physical negative sanctions, which can only be applied to the noncompliant individual where he is. This, in turn, obviously includes enforcing claims to the jurisdiction over, and the utilization of resources within, an area and, hence, a readiness to enforce respect for such control upon outsiders, i.e., the function of defense (Parsons 1960*b*).

Thus, spatial location is involved in all the functions of social systems. Its articulation with social processes is what we ordinarily call the ecological aspect of the system—the distribution of its various activities in physical space and their orientation to spatial considerations. In principle, all other analytically distinguishable aspects of physical systems are comparably involved with social interaction, but the foregoing will have to serve for illustration.

The core of the social system, the societal community, relates to the physical environment primarily through two mediating systems: the economy, which is primarily social but which interpenetrates with the technological system, and the technological system, which is primarily organic–physical but which interpenetrates with the economy. Organic–physical factors, then, operate in all the other primary subsystems of the society, each of which has its technological and economic aspects, although they are subordinated to other considerations, such as the political.

The cultural environment.   There is parallel complexity at the other end of the cybernetic hierarchy, in which action and, hence, social systems are involved. A society, or any other type of social system, has a pattern-maintenance subsystem, the units of which (once the system is sufficiently differentiated) have *cultural* primacy. These social system units, then, interpenetrate with both the societal community (and other societal subsystems) and with the cultural system proper. With progressing differentiation, they tend to become distinctively different according to whether their primary concern is cultural or social.

Religion comprises the matrix from which cultural institutions in general have become differentiated and remains the "master system" in the cybernetic sense. But secular intellectual disciplines (science), arts in the expressive–symbolic sense, and normative disciplines (e.g., ethics and law) have gained differentiation from it.

This formulates very briefly the main line of internal differentiation of a cultural system. The pattern-maintenance system, however, is not a cultural system in a strict sense (though for simplification the distinction has not always been made in this article), but the subsystem of the social system articulating most closely with the cultural system. Religion as a *cultural* phenomenon is *not* part of the pattern-maintenance system. Rather, the relevant structure is the collective organization of religious orientations, e.g., in churches or in prophetic movements. Science as a body of knowledge is cultural; universities as collectivities organized about the development of science through research and about its communication through teaching are parts of the society. Pattern-maintenance structures in this connection have cultural primacy only in that their societal functions concern interchange with the cultural system and in that they interpenetrate with the latter. Thus, religious orientations or scientific "systems of knowledge" are constitutive parts of churches and universities, not only "environments" to them.

Just as man has no direct contact with the physical world independent of the organisms (which, however, is itself part of that world), so he has no direct contact with the ultimate nonempirical "grounds" of his existence, what Weber called the world of "ultimate realities." His *objects* in this realm to which he orients himself are not the ultimate entities as such but his representations of them. They are cultural objects—parts of the cultural system in the action sense—and hence interpenetrate with all the other subsystems of action.

As structures of such interpenetration, "theological schools" or "prophetic movements," though quite distinct from religion as a component of the culture, are cultural subsystems of the society that have religious primacy but also interpenetrate with churches or other forms of the social institutionalization of religion. In the same way, law schools, as companies of legal scholars, are cultural subsystems, whereas courts of law are the social-system units in which legal doctrines are applied to social situations. In the more strictly cognitive disciplines, "companies of scholars" constitute cultural subsystems, which often involve "schools" at the level of cultural content, whereas universities and other educational collectivities constitute the articulated social system units.

For certain purposes, we may, as above, legitimately equate the pattern-maintenance subsystem of a society with the cultural system, since its primary function is articulating the social system as such—the system constituted by social interaction —with cultural patterns and norms. This, however, is elliptical. In the first instance, there are the more complex relationships just sketched. But there is also a further complication. Any system of cultural content, particularly a value system, must be specified from the most general relevant levels to levels relevant to the highly particular functions and exigencies of many and various subsystems. For instance, every technological system producing a particular commodity has special exigencies that the general principles of the relevant science cannot handle alone; similarly, every medical case is in some sense unique, and the physician must tailor his general medical knowledge to its specificities.

One set of exigencies of human societies has a special bearing here. It concerns the consequences of the fact that culture is *learned* by the human being; it is not part of his hereditary equipment. If a given society is defined by its institutionalization of certain cultural patterns, then the necessity of internalizing those patterns in the oncoming generation is second in functional importance only to maintenance of the adult levels of that culture. This cultural imperative evidently underlies the functioning of kinship institutions in all known human societies and, at higher levels of differentiation, of many kinds and levels of formal education.

This whole subsystem of institutions, as well as those involved with cultural innovation (e.g., research organizations), should be included in the pattern-maintenance subsystem of a society, characterized by primary interpenetration with the cultural system of action. Kinship, however, having special reference to child care, is the substructure of the pattern-maintenance system that operates at the farthest remove from the considerations of the general culture; at the appropriate level of specification of values, however, it *has* cultural primacy. Furthermore, it also relates quite specially not only to the society but also to the exigencies of both organism and personality, about which a few words must now be said.

The psychological environment. The personality, as analytically distinguished from the organism, constitutes the third primary environment of a social system. It interpenetrates with the individual organism in the obvious and fundamental sense that the storage facilities of learned content must be organic, as must the physical mechanisms of perception and cognition, of the control of learned behavior, and of the bases of motivation.

At the level of this discussion, however, the personality forms a distinct system articulated with social systems through their political subsystems, not simply in the sense of government but of any collective ordering. This is to say that *the primary goal output of social systems is to the personalities of their members.* Although they interpenetrate crucially with social systems, the personalities of individuals are not core constituents of social systems (nor vice versa) but precisely environments of them. Freud, especially in his later work, was quite clear about the obverse relationship: namely, that the individual personality's primary environment consists of the social systems into which it becomes integrated. Freud's famous "reality principle" is the principle of ego adaptation to the *social* environment.

I am treating the personality last among the primary environments of the social system because, of the three, it is the least commonly conceptualized as such. This conceptualization directly counters the long tradition that a society is "composed" or "made up" of "individuals." The latter may be true if the society and the individual are conceived of as concrete entities. Here, however, social system and personality—the concrete term "individual" is avoided in this context—are used as abstractly defined systems which are distinguished analytically, though allowance is made for the crucial relation of interpenetration. The unit of interpenetration between a personality and a social system is not the individual but a *role* or complex of *roles.* The *same* personality may participate in *several* social systems in different roles.

From the viewpoint of the psychology of the personality, the positive outputs from the social system are rewards. Indeed, I would even say that, at the level of cultural symbolization, except for inter-

mediate cases specially involved at the crux of differentiation between organism and personality (notably, erotic pleasure), all rewards are social system outputs. Conversely, outputs from the personality to the social system are personal goal achievements which, from the viewpoint of the receiving social system, are *contributions* to its functioning, insofar as the two systems are integrated with each other.

The focus of such integration is the phenomenon of "identification," through which the personality acquires a motivationally and cognitively meaningful role set and the social system acquires a member who can make meaningful contributions. Malintegration means that this matching relationship has failed in one way or another—"deviance," "alienation," and a variety of other phenomena fit in this category. It is also crucial to allow for personal creativity in relation to the social system. The analytical independence of social system and personality is the basic origin of both the prevalence of deviant behavior and the openings for creativity. The frequent allegation that sociology teaches the necessity of flat "conformity" is a conspicuous case of the fallacy of misplaced concreteness. If our analytical generalizations about social systems "applied" without qualification to all the member personalities, this would be the case. The mutual independence of the two categories of system—though accounting for their interdependence and interpenetration—is the theoretical basis for the fundamental and general phenomenon of the autonomy of the individual, so far as the social system is concerned.

Two important considerations reinforce this assertion of the reality of personal autonomy, the degrees and kinds of which must be seen as varying with different types of social system. First, analytically and apart from its direct relation to the social system, the personality system is the *primary meeting ground* of the cultural system, the behavioral organism, and, secondarily, the physical world. Although there have been serious theoretical difficulties with the "culture and personality" studies of the last generation in behavioral science, they did focus upon a crucial relationship here, as did the "behavioristic" traditions of psychology in studying the interrelations of personality and organism. Hence, it can be said not only that the personality is autonomous *as* a distinct subsystem of action, but also that this autonomy is importantly grounded in the personality's interchanges with the cultural and organic levels of the organization of action. These three sets of considerations (plus the uniqueness of the genetic constitution of practically every human organism) go far in explaining the *irreducibility* of the distinctiveness of all human personalities, as well as their autonomy.

The second consideration derives from an internal feature of social systems that is generally called "role pluralism." That is, not only do individuals have plural role involvements, but also different individuals' *combinations* of role participations vary widely. Such variance includes complexes of differing roles which are often categorized together for limited purposes. Thus, one "middle-class suburban mother" may have one child, another three, and another five, and the assortments of the children by age and sex may vary, so that even "being a mother" is not an identical thing for each member of that category, even sociologically. To this we can add differences in occupation of husbands, religion, ethnicity, participation in community affairs, etc.

When so many mutually independent—though also interdependent—factors are operating, anyone familiar with the logic of combinatorial variability should find it difficult to maintain that a modern, highly differentiated society is incompatible with individuality. Of course, there are also matters of the *specific kinds* of autonomy and individuality which are at stake. However, the arguments alleging that modern societies are repressive of all autonomy and stifling of all individuality are frequently so overgeneralized that they appear to deny altogether the combinatorial argument just outlined. Furthermore, a strong case can be made that the trend of *modern* society, because it has become so highly differentiated and pluralistic, is positively to favor individuality rather than to suppress it in favor of conformism.

We have confined our attention here to human-level social systems and have emphasized the importance of the symbolic systems, which we call cultural, that become constitutive of them through being involved in action and interpenetrating with social systems. Perhaps the most general matrix of these symbolic systems is language. On various levels, there is great familiarity with the concept of symbolic systems, e.g., of "ideas" having a predominantly cognitive focus and of "expressive symbols" in the arts and in ritual.

The media of interchange revisited

In conclusion, we may carry a little further the discussion, introduced above, of another category of symbolic systems that emerges into great prominence in highly differentiated social systems: the media of interchange. Attention was called above to money as the medium of exchange in economic transactions. Though the science of economics has gone far in understanding the vastly complex phenomena of monetary systems, they have generally been considered as unique. I have suggested that money is not unique in either of two senses.

First, it can be considered a special case of a very general phenomenon: language. It is in fact a very highly specialized language. Crucial here is the recognition that it operates at the *symbolic* level and that its primary function is communication, though of a special, normative sort. The "monetary system" is a *code*, in the grammatical–syntactical sense. The circulation of money is the "sending" of messages which give the recipient capacity to command goods and services through market channels. The recipient gains the *expectation* that he can "request," by virtue of his holding money, access to goods and services of a given value. There is an institutionalized obligation on those receiving such requests—if they are "in business"—to comply. But the process of money circulation involves literally nothing except communicated messages. A check is only a filled-in form letter to the bank on which it is drawn.

Second, money is not the only specialized language of this sort operating in social systems. Political power is certainly another. It centers on the use of discretionary authority in collective organizations to make decisions which, as binding on the collectivity, require performances of those who are obligated to further their implementation. Not only executive decisions constitute uses of power in this sense, but also the exercise of franchises in many connections, from voting in governmental elections to voting as a member of a small committee.

A third generalized symbolic medium is influence. By this I mean, quite technically, the capacity to achieve "consensus" with other members of an associated group through persuasion, without having to give fully adequate reasons (an adequate reason, in this sense, would be one that gave the recipient sufficient information for making a rational decision himself, or one that was at least fully understandable to him). Thus, a physician, as a technical specialist, may persuade a patient to follow his advice even when it is out of the question that the patient is competent to understand its technical grounds. The patient must, as members of the profession often put it, have "confidence" in his physician.

Fourth is the medium of generalized *commitments* to the implementation of cultural values, at the level of the social system as such. It is the most difficult to conceptualize, and the least can be said about it.

The need for generalized media of interchange is a function of the differentiatedness of social structures; in this sense they are all partly integrative mechanisms. The relations between markets and money and the division of labor are well known, but similar considerations apply in the other cases.

In the political case, the necessity for the mechanism of power stems from the social "status distance" between the loci of decision making and the loci of the performances necessary for the implementation of the decisions. In complex organizations, it is not realistically possible for decision makers to consult in detail with every person upon whose compliance effective implementation of their decisions depends. This may involve reasons of time and urgency, technical considerations, access to special information, or various exigencies of coordination. Thus, elections must lead to a concentration of power in the hands of the candidates elected. There cannot, however, be a simple consensus between all the members of the electorate and the preferred candidate—this would be incompatible with the voter's freedom of choice. Hence, the individual voter must agree to make a binding decision that he prefers candidate X over Y. If enough voters do likewise, X will be elected. The electoral authorities are obligated to comply with the aggregate of decisions of the voters.

In the case of influence, the functional need involves bridging certain gaps between the bases of accepting "advice" (in the sense of attempts to persuade without either situational inducements or threats of coercive sanctions) and the intrinsically cogent "reasons" for such acceptance. Complex communities cannot wait for fully rational demonstrations of the advisability of all commitments. Therefore, they must rely on influence or, as we sometimes say, prestige, as utilized by persons in responsible roles. The user of influence creates a *presumption* for the reasonableness of his case, so that the object of his attempts at persuasion feels, in the integrated case, reasonably sure in trusting him.

Similarly, commitments are given to others when an individual enters into a situation (i.e., makes or, more appropriately, gives a commitment) without in fact being fully able to ensure that the process of action implementation will be carried out in a manner conducive to preserving or enhancing the integrity of his values. Thus, in a sense different from that of the influence context, he has either to trust others or to sacrifice the prospect of successful implementation. In turn, others must trust him to gain fulfillment of *their* commit-

ments. It is in this sense that commitments may be considered a "circulating" medium.

These media appear in generalized and differentiated form only when relatively high levels of differentiation in the relevant spheres have been attained. Primitive societies never have money and market systems, and many archaic societies have them only rudimentarily, if at all. What Weber called "patriarchal" political structures do not have power as a *generalized* medium, and "patrimonial" regimes show only its first emergence.

Other generalized media seem to operate in the zones of interpenetration between the social system and the other primary subsystems of action. As already noted, what Freud called erotic pleasure is at the same time both organic (i.e., a component of the personality) and, because of its involvement with interpersonal relations, a component of certain elementary social systems. What psychoanalytic and other social psychologists have called *affect* is probably another such mechanism, operating among persons in the interchange between the personality and social systems rather than in direct relation to the organism. The two famous "wishes" for recognition and for response discussed by W. I. Thomas perhaps designate still another medium which, however, may be a subdivision of the more general mechanism of affect. In the organic–physical set of relations, technological "know-how" and skill are probably well regarded in this way.

Another set of media operate in the zone of interpenetration between the social and cultural systems. Ideology is a conspicuous example. The concept *conscience*, as used in Puritan traditions especially, seems to belong in this category. *Reputation*, as that term is used in discussing the social structure of scientific communities, is probably another case. The concept *faith*, as used in Christian tradition, especially Protestantism, probably refers to a generalized mechanism peculiar to the cultural level of action organization.

The relative salience of the various generalized media of interchange (and of particular cases within them) *for* specific structures is a useful guide to the structural arrangements among and within the subsytems of more generalized social systems, notably societies. We have also claimed that the core of a society is the societal community, which, functionally regarded, is the integrative subsystem. It interpenetrates and interchanges directly with each of the other primary subsystems: the pattern-maintenance or cultural-primary subsystems; the goal-attainment subsystem, or polity; and the adaptive subsystem, or economy. The medium focal to the societal community is influence, which is interchangeable for power, money, and value commitments.

Each of the other three subsystems constitutes a zone of primary interpenetration and interchange between the social system and one of its intra-action environments. The economy interchanges with the organic–physical environment; and money, in a sufficiently differentiated economy, can be used in exchange for the factors of production, which are then also technologically combined. Though a modern economy is structured primarily about financial institutions and market systems, these latter interpenetrate, in turn, with the technological organization of production.

The polity interpenetrates, in the first instance, with the personality. Power, as the medium having political primacy, can be used to acquire both human services and the demands for collective action which justify leadership initiative. Underlying these two forms of "mobile" human resources are the processes that generate and stabilize them. Here the interpenetration between social system and personality leads toward both the psychological "depths" of the personality and the relational contexts articulating the basic integration of social systems. Above all, family and kinship, as well as neighborhood and education, fit this context but so do complexes such as recreation. These operate, however, at a level quite different from the direct interchanges between personality and polity. For *macrosocial* purposes, therefore, they should be treated as pattern-maintenance processes.

Finally, the interpenetration between social and cultural systems concerns, most saliently, the place of religion in relation to social structure. Indeed, the primary structures of the most primitive societies fall almost entirely into the two basic categories of kinship and religion. With further differentiation, however, religion becomes more and more clearly distinguished from political organization. It also tends to become distinguished from economic structuring, while the latter remains ascribed to both kinship and, above all, to the polity (in the broad, analytical sense).

In relatively advanced societies, the cultural system itself begins to differentiate, particularly through the appearance of secular cultural disciplines. Thus, law, in close relation to ethical philosophy; the arts, as something other than direct handmaidens of religion; and, generally last, science have become independent cultural realms—though they are always *also* interdependent and interpenetrating with each other and with the social system. Value commitments constitute the principal *societal* medium operating in this realm, though various others are involved secondarily. A modern society, then, contains a considerable number of structural units having cultural primacy. Religious collectivities need hardly be mentioned, so conspicuous are they from any comparative point of view. Increasingly, modern societies have universities, which institutionalize the intellectual disciplines that are in some sense sciences, various organizations focusing upon the arts, and the very crucial institutions of highly generalized law, with their articulations to ethics.

The social system is, thus, a very complex entity. As an organization of human interests, activities, and commitments, it must be viewed as a system and in functional perspective. This is the key to its lines of organization, its modes of differentiation, and its integration. Such a system may be considered as *both* structure and process, in different aspects and for different scientific purposes. Structurally, we have suggested that there is a double basis for systematizing differentiation and variation: that internal to the primary social system itself and that involved in its relations to its primary environments, as analyzed with reference to the general system of action. Processually, the categories of analysis must follow from and integrate with those of structure. I suggest that, given the central position of language as definitive of human society, the more differentiated and specialized symbolic media of interchange constitute the master scheme for the systematic analysis of social system processes.

TALCOTT PARSONS

[*See also* LINGUISTICS; SOCIAL INSTITUTIONS; SOCIAL STRUCTURE; SOCIETY; STATE; *and the biographies of* COOLEY; DURKHEIM; MEAD; PARETO; THOMAS; WEBER, MAX; WHITEHEAD.]

BIBLIOGRAPHY

AYER, A. J. 1956 *The Problem of Knowledge.* New York: St. Martins. → A paperback edition was published in 1962 by Penguin.

CHOMSKY, NOAM 1957 *Syntactic Structures.* The Hague: Mouton.

CHOMSKY, NOAM 1964 *Current Issues in Linguistic Theory.* The Hague: Mouton.

GROSSMAN, GREGORY 1962 The Structure and Organization of the Soviet Economy. *Slavic Review* 21:203–222.

JAKOBSON, ROMAN; and HALLE, MORRIS 1956 *Fundamentals of Language.* The Hague: Mouton.

MARSHALL, T. H. (1949) 1964 Citizenship and Social Class. Pages 65–122 in T. H. Marshall, *Class, Citizenship, and Social Development: Essays.* Garden City, N.Y.: Doubleday. → The essay is based on the Marshall lecture delivered at Cambridge in 1949. The collection of essays was first published in England in 1963 as *Sociology at the Crossroads*.

MEAD, GEORGE H. 1938 *The Philosophy of the Act*. Univ. of Chicago Press. → Published posthumously.

PARSONS, TALCOTT 1960a Durkheim's Contribution to the Theory of Integration of Social Systems. Pages 118–153 in Kurt Wolff (editor), *Émile Durkheim, 1858–1917: A Collection of Essays With Translations and a Bibliography*. Columbus: Ohio State Univ. Press.

PARSONS, TALCOTT 1960b The Principal Structures of Community. Pages 250–279 in Talcott Parsons, *Structure and Process in Modern Societies*. Glencoe, Ill.: Free Press.

PARSONS, TALCOTT 1963a On the Concept of Influence. *Public Opinion Quarterly* 27:37–62. → A comment by J. S. Coleman appears on pages 63–82; a communication by R. A. Bauer, on pages 83–86; and a rejoinder by Talcott Parsons, on pages 87–92.

PARSONS, TALCOTT 1963b On the Concept of Political Power. American Philosophical Society, *Proceedings* 107:232–262.

PARSONS, TALCOTT 1965 Unity and Diversity in the Modern Intellectual Disciplines: The Role of the Social Sciences. *Dædalus* 94:39–65.

SMITH, ADAM (1776) 1952 *An Inquiry Into the Nature and Causes of the Wealth of Nations*. Chicago: Encyclopaedia Britannica. → A two-volume paperback edition was published in 1963 by Irwin.

WHITEHEAD, ALFRED N. (1929) 1957 *Process and Reality: An Essay in Cosmology*. New York: Humanities.

III

POLITICAL SYSTEMS

Political systems analysis attempts to delineate the fields of political science and political action, to give them coherence and order, to define their properties and guide research, as well as to integrate relevant findings. It seeks to isolate the arena of politics as an independent system from the remainder of society. In one sense this has been done by students of politics from the very beginning of political thought. The current efforts are distinguished by a more self-conscious approach and by the more refined technical tools that are available.

From the systems perspective, societies and other social groups tend to be seen as relatively persistent entities functioning within larger environments. These entities qualify as systems because they are considered sets of *interdependent* elements or variables, which can be identified and measured. Systems have distinguishable boundaries setting them off from their environments, and each has a tendency toward a state of equilibrium, i.e., the system tends to maintain itself through various processes whenever it is disturbed, either from within or without its boundaries. Each system tends to be structured in accordance with certain invariant problems characteristic of all social systems. Internal differentiation takes place, with specific structures and processes being developed to handle

specific kinds of problems, and, as a result, various subsystems will evolve, such as the economic system, the political system, social stratification, etc. In the case of political systems, the major task and function, or contribution to society, is that of selecting societal goals, mobilizing resources for their attainment, and making societal decisions.

Precursors and sources. The concept of systems has come to political science only recently. In adopting it, political scientists have drawn upon the work of other social scientists, as well as biologists, physical scientists, and engineers. The physiologist Cannon, in *The Wisdom of the Body* (1932), influenced social scientists and particularly gave currency to the use of the term "homeostasis" to describe a crucial property of biological systems and a highly suggestive one in the study of social systems. The writings of Bertalanffy on biology and general systems analysis (1949; 1950) have been of considerable importance. Few political scientists have turned to these writings directly, but there have been important linkages through the more widely known work of some sociologists, such as Parsons (1951; 1958), Homans (1950), and Roethlisberger and Dickson (1939). Parsons, especially, has developed the technical idea of a social system, and it has been through his work that several political scientists have come to employ the approach in the study of politics. Almond (1956; 1966), Easton (1957; 1965a; 1965b), and Mitchell (1962) have based much of their conception of the political system on Parsons' own expositions in the realm of politics (1960).

Although the idea of a system of economic behavior or action has been prominent in economics almost from the very beginning of that science (in the work of Quesnay and the physiocrats, later of the neoclassicists, as well as that of mathematical economists such as Walras, Pareto, and Cournot, in which the notion of system was honed to the precision and elegance of the calculus), economists have not exerted the most direct influence on political science. For one thing, political scientists have usually lacked the necessary mathematical sophistication, and for another, few political scientists have been exposed to homologous social processes or action. The conception that political behavior could be specified in terms of a sharply delimited number of quantitatively linear variables has found only gradual acceptance in political science. However, since the 1950s the application of economic conceptions and models has been rigorously attempted (Arrow 1951; Downs 1957; Black 1958; Buchanan & Tullock 1962; Riker 1962).

Finally, one must note the contribution of certain students of organizations, especially Chester I. Barnard (1938) and Herbert A. Simon (1947). The historical closeness of public administration to political science made these men's work familiar to many political scientists and thereby prepared the ground for viewing politics in terms of organizations or, more broadly, social systems: inputs, outputs, equilibrium, resources, support, etc. From all these sources have come elements of the current developments in systems analysis as it applies to politics.

The political system

Structure of the system.   The most traditional and conventional problem of political science has been that of describing and accounting for the internal structure of political systems. The term "structure" is generally applied to those patterns of power and authority which characterize relationships between rulers and ruled—relationships which are more or less enduring and therefore more or less predictable.

The unit of analysis for these power relationships is usually "role," a concept developed primarily in social psychology and widely used in sociology. While the concept has a variety of meanings, basically it refers to those norms which prescribe and proscribe behavior in specific settings, relationships, and functions. Power and authority roles pertain to the acquisition, maintenance, and employment of power and thereby constitute the building blocks from which the polity is constructed. Political roles are concerned with the making of decisions in the name of society and the performance of actions which achieve or implement these decisions and allocate scarce values and costs. The set of these roles and the behavior which stems from them make up the political system.

In analyzing the internal structure of a polity, the political scientist describes these roles and the persons taking them as they engage in interaction. The content of the roles, their origins, changes, influences on behavior, etc., have been questions of interest for political scientists. Likewise, political scientists have analyzed the outcomes of various types of structures, such as the allocation of values and costs, the effective achievement of collective goals, and the maintenance of peace and order.

In order to characterize structures and distinguish them, political scientists have employed a variety of concepts and tools. Traditionally, the chief basis of classification has been the *distribution* of power among the members of the system.

This single base line has not proved adequate for descriptions of political systems, and even valid and reliable statements about the distribution of power are an insufficient basis upon which to compare political systems. Many crucial similarities are missed when analysis proceeds on a single dimension. Systems analysts have therefore devised more inclusive sets of variables and at the same time insisted that they be measurable. Parsons has advanced a set of concepts called the "pattern-variables" (1951), to make possible more complete analysis of social and, accordingly, political structures. Similarly, Almond (1956; 1966) has suggested a classification scheme of structures that is based on the following basic dimensions of the political system: (1) the degree of differentiation; (2) the extent to which the system is "manifest," or "visible"; (3) the stability of the functions of various roles; and (4) the distribution of power. A fifth possibility concerns the "substitutability of roles."

The list of these properties of political systems is likely to be extended and refined, and many actual political systems will be reclassified. Some of the recent research efforts are tending in the direction of "classifying" according to numerical scales of the cardinal type, which allow much more accurate placement of various systems within larger classification schemes. Political scientists will probably be interested in exact measures of specific properties, rather than the simple presence or absence of a property. They will not be concerned just with identifying a particular norm or institution but will want to achieve accurate measurements of its specificity, explicitness, flexibility, universality, and mode of operation. Political systems will no longer be thought of as unique congeries of attributes but will be regarded as systems which have more or less of some set of properties. Profiles of systems will be constructed, allowing comparison which will be theoretically more complex and empirically closer to reality.

Boundaries.   A system is generally thought of as being distinct from its environment or as being self-contained and therefore having observable boundaries. Analysis seeks to determine both the members of the system—if they are concrete individuals—and the analytically distinct units of action which characterize the system. In the former instance we speak of those who actually are regarded as formal members, or citizens. In the second case, we speak of the actions that go into making up the political system of behavior, not in terms of concrete individuals but of the segments of their behavior which are politically relevant. In doing so, we arbitrarily assign boundaries to the political system. We then consider certain activities as political and temporarily ignore all others.

Boundary exchanges—inputs and outputs. Once the existence of bounded systems and subsystems is postulated, analysis must also account for the relationships that are to be found between systems. Common sense suggests that few, if any, actual social systems are either completely isolated or closed to specific kinds of external influences. As a consequence, systems analysis must be concerned with detecting relationships across boundaries—the problem of "inputs" and "outputs." No firm agreement yet exists among political scientists as to the appropriate labels or concepts to be used in designating such matters. Easton (1957; 1965*a*), for example, sees the inputs from society and its various subsystems to the polity as consisting of "demands" and "support," while Almond and Coleman (1960) further divide and specify the inputs to the polity: "political socialization," "recruitment," "interest articulation," "interest aggregation," and "political communication." Easton calls the output of the polity "decisions" concerning the authoritative allocation of values. Almond and Coleman, on the other hand, describe these outputs as "rule making," "rule application," and "rule adjudication." Mitchell (1962) uses the terms "expectations and demands," "resources," and "support" to specify inputs; and "system goals," "values and costs," and "controls" to describe the political outputs.

While these several concepts vary, they are quite similar in the connotation of what is being exchanged across the boundaries of the polity and other subsystems. When Easton, Almond, and Mitchell speak of demands and of interest articulation and aggregation, they are referring to empirical phenomena concerning who demands what, from whom, how, when, and with what consequences for the participants and the system. These are all operational problems of research which can and have been treated empirically and even quantitatively. Put another way, systems analysts expect to measure inputs and outputs, so that comparisons can be made between political systems throughout the world. The objective is to establish minimal ratios of these exchanges, as a basis for predicting stability of systems and their capacity to achieve goals and to provide minimal levels of civic satisfaction for their members.

System processes. The "ultimate" concern is not simply to describe structures but to describe and account for the internal functioning of systems. At present we know far more about institutions than we do about political behavior, both in its in-

dividual and aggregate forms. Systematic information about the basic means or processes by which inputs in various systems become transformed or converted into political outputs is scant. For the most part, the major problem of inquiry seems to have been how politics allocate scarce values, but the formulation was not put in quite these terms until Easton's work appeared (1953). Others also contributed: Dahl and Lindblom (1953), for example, elaborated four basic sociopolitical processes by which societies rationally calculate and control their collective actions: the price system, hierarchy, polyarchy, and bargaining. These four processes—not all purely political—are presumably found in varying combinations in all societies. Because they are found in different combinations and environments, they produce different results, all of which can be evaluated.

Other, more purely theoretical and mathematical attempts to handle the allocation problem are being made by the application of game theory and notions derived from welfare economics. Among these efforts is Anthony Downs's attempt (1957) to use economic theory to account for the behavior of citizen and politician in a democracy. As yet these formulations have not been widely used by political scientists as theories of actual allocation outcomes in large-scale political systems.

In addition to the primary interest in allocative problems, political scientists, influenced by systems analysis, have been increasingly concerned with matters affecting the stability of systems and, more especially, with political socialization and other support inputs. A number of studies deal with the means whereby societies and polities assure loyalty and stimulate public participation. These studies are stimulated not only by theoretical developments in political science but also by problems in the real world of politics, such as the dramatic and often cruel means of control used in twentieth-century totalitarian states and the difficulties of establishing stable regimes in the newly developing states.

Other problems of the polity provide focal points for still other political processes and research endeavors. They include the means by which polities achieve collective goals from diverse individual demands and integrate their memberships. Much traditional work on leadership, power, bureaucracy, and control is relevant here. But the processes have not been well incorporated into the systems frame of reference.

The polity, as a system, can be assumed to have set functional problems, or exigencies, which are similar to those of all other social systems. It, too, tends to develop an internally differentiated set of substructures and processes to cope with each of its problems. In this view, first formulated by Parsons (1951; Parsons & Smelser 1956) and adapted by Mitchell to an interpretation of the American polity (1962), the internal processes of the polity are analogous to those of the larger social system, namely: goal attainment, adaptation, system maintenance and tension management, and integration. To these may be added the problem of the allocation of roles, resources, and values and costs. Identified as political processes, then, are the actions which members of a polity take with respect to the meeting or handling of each of these universal situations. A major task of empirical political science will be to clarify these processes; a major task of normative politics will be to improve the performances.

Empirical applications

While much of the writing employing systems concepts, ideas, and hypotheses has been programmatic and theoretical, a growing number of empirical applications may be noted. These applications range from full-scale efforts at systems analysis to partial studies of very restricted forms of behavior and tests of but small segments of the more general scheme. They range in subject matter from international politics to intranational affairs. The international studies have been directly concerned with the structure of systems. Kaplan (1957) and Kaplan and Katzenbach (1961), for example, deal with the structure of international systems and norms in such systems. Likewise, Liska deals (1957) with the structure of international politics, equilibrium, and (1962) with coalitions or alliances within what must be described as an implicit systems framework. And Rosecrance (1963) considers nine distinct historical international systems within an explicit systems framework.

Investigations of national politics and cross-national or comparative political units are concerned with data on the inputs, especially those of demands and support within nation-states. Among the more notable studies are those of Almond and Coleman (1960) which, based on the previous theoretical work of Almond and of Easton, explored the political life of Asia, Africa, the Middle East, and Latin America. Works on single nation-states include Apter's studies of Ghana (1955) and Uganda (1961). On the Soviet Union there is the volume of Bauer, Inkeles, and Kluckhohn (1956), which is explicitly based on the theory of social systems. Although these works place varying emphases on input–output categories, all are premised on the general idea of the polity as a boundary-maintaining, interdependent, and equilibrated system. An explicit attempt to use the input–output categories on a nation-state is Mitchell's study of the United States (1962). The work of Karl Deutsch (1963) also indicates a concern for the kind of data that are required by comparative systems analysis. His data inventories relate mainly to the support input, resources for goal attainment, and the problems of integration. Many other such inventories will be needed before reliable generalizations about large numbers of nation-states can be made (see Russett et al. 1964).

At the level of specific institutions and behavior within single nation-states, systems analysis has been applied primarily to American data, with a special emphasis upon legislatures. Young's work on Congress (1958) seems to have been influenced by systems notions. The case study by Freeman (1955) of congressional–administrative bureau relations is explicitly based on systems concepts. The major study to date on legislatures is that of Wahlke and his associates (1962). In this study of four American state legislatures, systems notions are employed with rigor and sophistication. For the most part, the study is one of role structures and orientations of the memberships rather than of system processes or the outputs. However, a variety of intersystem relationships, such as those of legislators with their constituencies, as well as with interest groups, are considered. Generally, however, the analysis is static. Typical of a more limited inquiry into legislatures is Fenno's article (1962) and book (1966) on the Appropriations Committee of Congress as a small system. The focus of the inquiry is integration, its processes and outcomes with regard to that crucial committee.

Still other systems-based investigations and studies are Parsons' own interpretation of elections within the systems framework (1959) and Eulau's study of elections as a system process (1962). Easton's work on political socialization and the support input (Easton & Hess 1961) grows directly out of his earlier development of the systems approach to politics. These various studies are all indicative of a growing trend in political science to cast its theoretical and empirical work in terms of the system framework. Even so, not all political scientists observe the trend with equanimity, for there are some consequential problems involving theoretical and research points that require answers.

Theoretical and research difficulties

The critique of systems analysis, regardless of the source, is really three-pronged: some maintain that it has certain crucial methodological weaknesses; others claim that it is not suitable for empirical research; and still others suggest that it betrays and perpetuates a conservative bias.

The methodological criticisms are the most serious and the least likely to be resolved. For they do not raise problems subject to empirical test but, rather, question postulates about reality. Some maintain that systems analysis is misleading when it assumes that reality "really" consists of systems. In this view societies consist of far more individual and isolated events than systems analysis is capable of handling. In other words, not all variables in the supposed system are immediately affected by the disturbance of one element. Because there may be no "reciprocity," there can be no maintenance of the system. The extent to which the elements of a society or polity are interdependent is questioned; interdependencies are matters, it is said, for empirical investigation, not for axiomatic treatment.

A second misgiving or criticism of the systems approach concerns the "boundaries" of the system. The point of the critics is that one cannot speak of systems unless one can identify boundaries or state the variables that constitute the system. The defense is that a system is an abstraction and can be specified in an arbitrary decision. There has been some clarification and refinement, so that boundaries may be empirically described and located. Thus, one may speak of different types of boundaries in terms of their permeability. Schoeffler (1955), for instance, has characterized economic systems as (1) mechanically closed; (2) stochastically closed; (3) semiclosed (mechanically and stochastically); (4) conditionally closed; or (5) essentially open. All of these types are based on a scale of probabilities concerning the possibilities of outside influences, ranging from no influence to complete and continuous influence of outside variables. While these more or less logically derived system boundaries help to clarify the situation considerably, they do not easily lend themselves to operational definitions and empirical research. The most convenient and conventional specification of system boundaries in research is in terms of the membership, such as that of a formal association or organization. But this convenience, although often used, skirts many methodological and theoretical difficulties.

A third criticism has to do with the concept of equilibrium. There is more critical literature on this aspect of systems analysis than on any other single point. In brief, the claim is made that the concept "equilibrium" cannot be operationally defined, except perhaps in the context of economic behavior. This criticism follows logically either from the belief that systems do not in fact exist in society or from the assumption that the variables which constitute them are not linear and therefore cannot be expressed so that a state of equilibrium could be calculated or even identified. As the notion of equilibrium has not been used, in other than a very crude sense, as an analogy or metaphor in political science, criticism has not been marked. David Easton, the only political scientist who has devoted serious attention to the matter, is critical, even though his own formulation of the political system lends itself to the use of equilibrium treatment with respect to the exchanges of inputs and outputs with other segments of society. It is likely that as systems analysis is more frequently employed in political science, there will be increasing concern with the utility and shortcomings of the concept of "equilibrium."

A fourth difficulty with systems analysis concerns the problems of boundary exchanges, or the various sets of inputs and outputs between a system and its environment or between subsystems of a larger system. So far, the use of such inputs and outputs in political science and sociology has been minimal. These elements of systems analysis can be fairly readily identified and measured, but this has seldom been done in actual research. Nevertheless, it can be pointed out that identifying these multiple exchanges is by no means a purely scientific procedure, nor are many of these presumed exchanges readily susceptible to empirical testing. What is exchanged in physical and organic systems appears to be considerably simpler to identify and measure and certainly more plausible to the conventional modes of thought.

Systems analysis is likely to be used for a long time to come, but the exact forms in which it will be cast are less certain. At present, two distinct variations may be detected: The first is the "structural–functional" approach, found mostly in sociology and comparative political studies of nation-states, which stems from organic analogies used in biology; the second—at once more mechanical and more mathematical—is found in economics and international relations analyses. The former school has tended to present a more complex and empirical picture of political systems, whereas the second variant has tended to develop abstract models of very delimited numbers of variables, which deal with a more restricted set of problems, generally centered about conflict. There are important differences in the style, methods, and data of the two approaches. But improved techniques of research will undoubtedly permit a gradual integration (Deutsch 1963), inspired perhaps by the historical example of the gradual unification of biology and physics.

WILLIAM C. MITCHELL

[*See also* POLITICAL BEHAVIOR; POLITICAL SCIENCE.]

BIBLIOGRAPHY

ALMOND, GABRIEL A. 1956 Comparative Political Systems. *Journal of Politics* 18:391–409.

ALMOND, GABRIEL A.; and COLEMAN, JAMES S. (editors) 1960 *The Politics of the Developing Areas.* Princeton Univ. Press.

ALMOND, GABRIEL A.; and POWELL, G. BINGHAM JR. 1966 *Comparative Politics: A Developmental Approach.* Boston: Little.

APTER, DAVID E. (1955) 1963 *Ghana in Transition.* Rev. ed. New York: Atheneum. → First published as *The Gold Coast in Transition.*

APTER, DAVID E. 1961 *The Political Kingdom of Uganda: A Study in Bureaucratic Nationalism.* Princeton Univ. Press.

ARROW, KENNETH J. 1951 *Social Choice and Individual Values.* New York: Wiley.

BARNARD, CHESTER I. (1938) 1962 *The Functions of the Executive.* Cambridge, Mass.: Harvard Univ. Press.

BAUER, RAYMOND; INKELES, ALEX; and KLUCKHOHN, CLYDE 1956 *How the Soviet System Works: Cultural, Psychological, and Social Themes.* Russian Research Center Studies, No. 24. Cambridge, Mass.: Harvard Univ. Press. → A paperback edition was published in 1961 by Random House.

BERTALANFFY, LUDWIG VON (1949) 1960 *Problems of Life: An Evaluation of Modern Biological Thought.* New York: Harper. → First published as Volume 1 of *Das biologische Weltbild.*

BERTALANFFY, LUDWIG VON 1950 An Outline of General System Theory. *British Journal for the Philosophy of Science* 1:134–165.

BLACK, DUNCAN 1958 *The Theory of Committees and Elections.* Cambridge Univ. Press.

BUCHANAN, JAMES M.; and TULLOCK, GORDON 1962 *The Calculus of Consent: Logical Foundations of Constitutional Democracy.* Ann Arbor: Univ. of Michigan Press.

CANNON, WALTER B. (1932) 1963 *The Wisdom of the Body.* Rev. & enl. ed. New York: Norton.

DAHL, ROBERT A.; and LINDBLOM, CHARLES E. 1953 *Politics, Economics, and Welfare: Planning and Politico-Economic Systems Resolved Into Basic Social Processes.* New York: Harper. → A paperback edition was published in 1963.

DEUTSCH, KARL W. 1963 *The Nerves of Government: Models of Political Communication and Control.* New York: Free Press.

DOWNS, ANTHONY 1957 *An Economic Theory of Democracy.* New York: Harper.

EASTON, DAVID 1953 *The Political System: An Inquiry Into the State of Political Science.* New York: Knopf.

EASTON, DAVID 1957 An Approach to the Analysis of Political Systems. *World Politics* 9:383–400.

EASTON, DAVID 1965a *A Framework for Political Analysis.* Englewood Cliffs, N.J.: Prentice-Hall.

EASTON, DAVID 1965b *A Systems Analysis of Political Life.* New York: Wiley.

EASTON, DAVID; and HESS, ROBERT D. 1961 Youth and the Political System. Pages 226–251 in Seymour M. Lipset and Leo Lowenthal (editors), *Culture and So-cial Character: The Work of David Riesman Reviewed.* New York: Free Press.

EISENSTADT, SHMUEL N. 1963 *The Political Systems of Empires.* New York: Free Press.

EULAU, HEINZ 1962 *Class and Party in the Eisenhower Years: Class Roles and Perspectives in the 1952 and 1956 Elections.* New York: Free Press.

FENNO, RICHARD F. 1962 The House Appropriations Committee as a Political System: The Problem of Integration. *American Political Science Review* 56:310–324.

FENNO, RICHARD F. 1966 *The Power of the Purse: Appropriations Politics in Congress.* Boston: Little.

FREEMAN, J. LEIPER 1955 *The Political Process: Executive Bureau–Legislative Committee Relations.* New York: Doubleday.

HOMANS, GEORGE C. 1950 *The Human Group.* New York: Harcourt.

KAPLAN, MORTON A. 1957 *System and Process in International Politics.* New York: Wiley.

KAPLAN, MORTON A.; and KATZENBACH, NICHOLAS DEB. 1961 *The Political Foundations of International Law.* New York: Wiley.

LISKA, GEORGE 1957 *International Equilibrium: A Theoretical Essay on the Politics and Organization of Security.* Cambridge, Mass.: Harvard Univ. Press.

LISKA, GEORGE 1962 *Nations in Alliance: The Limits of Interdependence.* Baltimore: Johns Hopkins Press.

McCLELLAND, CHARLES A. (1955) 1961 Applications of General Systems Theory in International Relations. Pages 412–420 in James N. Rosenau (editor), *International Politics and Foreign Policy: A Reader in Research and Theory.* New York: Free Press. → First published in Volume 12 of *Main Currents in Modern Thought.*

MITCHELL, WILLIAM C. 1962 *The American Polity: A Social and Cultural Interpretation.* New York: Free Press.

PARSONS, TALCOTT 1951 *The Social System.* Glencoe, Ill.: Free Press.

PARSONS, TALCOTT 1958 Some Highlights of the General Theory of Action. Pages 282–301 in Roland A. Young (editor), *Approaches to the Study of Politics.* Evanston, Ill.: Northwestern Univ. Press.

PARSONS, TALCOTT 1959 *Voting* and the Equilibrium of the American Political System. Pages 80–120 in Eugene Burdick and Arthur J. Brodbeck (editors), *American Voting Behavior.* Glencoe, Ill.: Free Press.

PARSONS, TALCOTT 1960 *Structure and Process in Modern Societies.* Glencoe, Ill.: Free Press.

PARSONS, TALCOTT; and SMELSER, NEIL J. 1956 *Economy and Society: A Study in the Integration of Economic and Social Theory.* Glencoe, Ill.: Free Press.

RIKER, WILLIAM H. 1962 *The Theory of Political Coalitions.* New Haven: Yale Univ. Press.

ROETHLISBERGER, FRITZ J.; and DICKSON, WILLIAM J. (1939) 1961 *Management and the Worker: An Account of a Research Program Conducted by the Western Electric Company, Hawthorne Works, Chicago.* Cambridge, Mass.: Harvard Univ. Press. → A paperback edition was published in 1964 by Wiley.

ROSECRANCE, RICHARD N. 1963 *Action and Reaction in World Politics: International Systems in Perspective.* Boston: Little.

RUSSETT, BRUCE M. et al. 1964 *World Handbook of Political and Social Indicators.* New Haven: Yale Univ. Press.

SCHOEFFLER, SIDNEY 1955 *The Failure of Economics: A*

Diagnostic Study. Cambridge, Mass.: Harvard Univ. Press.

SIMON, HERBERT A. (1947) 1961 *Administrative Behavior: A Study of Decision-making Processes in Administrative Organization.* New York: Macmillan.

WAHLKE, JOHN et al. 1962 *The Legislative System: Explorations in Legislative Behavior.* New York: Wiley.

YOUNG, ROLAND A. 1958 *The American Congress.* New York: Harper.

IV
INTERNATIONAL SYSTEMS

The modern use of the concept of system as a distinctive method of analysis has the following characteristics: (1) the system to be investigated is explicitly distinguished from its environment; (2) the internal elements of the system are explicitly stated; (3) there are relationships between the elements of the system and between the system and its environment that are explicitly stated; (4) where these relationships involve deductions, the canons of logical or of mathematical reasoning are employed; and (5) assertions concerning the relationships between the system and the real world are confirmed according to the canons of scientific method (see Ashby 1952).

The application of the systems concept to nonmechanical systems—and all social systems are nonmechanical—involves special problems. Whereas the independently measurable equalities of mechanical systems may provide highly general explanatory frameworks, nonmechanical systems require theoretical explanations adjusted to the special features of the system. Indeed, the use of the systems approach in the social sciences directs attention to differences in the subjects studied and in the explanatory theories that are employed to account for them. This last consideration will constitute the criterion for distinguishing between kinds of systems. Where the explanations of the behavior of two systems are derived from the same theory, the systems will be treated as being of the same kind; where the explanations are derived from different theories, the systems will be considered to be of different kinds. A new theory might, of course, produce different distinctions.

To illustrate, it will later be shown how the "balance of power" theory, which predicts rapid shifts of alliances and limited wars, can be used as at least a partial explanation of the rigid alliances and the almost unlimited nature of World War I. The pre-1870 and the post-1871 systems are considered to be similar kinds of systems operating under different circumstances. However, the loose bipolar system of the post-1945 period is regarded as different, because its behavior cannot be deduced from the assumptions employed in the "balance of power" theory, and indeed there are also different structural elements in the system.

In some cases, however, it may be possible to account for actual historical behavior by adjusting the parameters of either of two theoretical systems. And it may not be clear which adjustment gives greater explanatory power or which theoretical system comes closer to serving as an analogue for the historical situation. In such a twilight zone, individual judgment and utility are the decisive criteria.

The use of the concept of system means that attention is directed toward a specified group of interacting variables. The system, therefore, can be distinguished from its environment, and it can be compared for explicit features with other similar systems; in addition, the behavior of the system can be explained by a distinctive theory that in turn can be used to explain more complex historical situations.

The theory

The concept of an international system was first explicated in 1957 in Kaplan's *System and Process in International Politics*; by 1961, the term "international system" had become sufficiently common to serve as the title of a special issue of *World Politics*.

Types of international systems. Kaplan specified six types of international systems: the "balance of power" system, the loose bipolar system, the tight bipolar system, the universal system, the hierarchical system, and the unit veto system. (These types are not exhaustive but are intended to permit useful comparative analysis.) The systems have the following characteristics in common: they contain sets of essential rules, they share other internal elements (for example, types of actors, capabilities of actor, information factors, and transformation rules), and they all have boundary conditions. The systems also include specifications of conditions for three types of equilibrium: First, the essential rules are in equilibrium in the sense that a change in one rule will produce a change in at least one other rule. Second, a change in the set of rules will produce a change in other system characteristics and vice versa. Third, the system is also in equilibrium with its environment; changes in the system will change the environment and vice versa.

"Balance of power" system. In the "balance of power" system the only essential actors are nation states with very large military and economic capabilities. It is a system without role differentiation, and unless there are at least five essential national actors it is likely to prove unstable. If there are

five or more such nations, then they are more interested in preventing the elimination of other nations as essential factors, in order to preserve them as future potential allies, than they are in dividing up their capabilities and resuming the competition within the system with a smaller number of actors. They do have an interest in acquiring a margin of security, by gaining more than an equal share of the capabilities of the system, and will therefore form alliances and go to war. But the wars will be limited and the alliances will shift rapidly and will tend to break up when the war is won, particularly if one of the victorious actors tries to eliminate one of the defeated foes. For similar reasons coalitions will tend to form that are directed against actors who threaten to predominate or who have organizational or ideological advantages that might produce dominance. Any essential national actor will be an acceptable role partner, for only thus can a national actor optimize the probability that he will be in a winning coalition or that he will not suffer too severe a defeat if he is in a losing coalition. This system is quite stable. [*See* BALANCE OF POWER.]

Loose bipolar system. The loose bipolar system is role differentiated, having different kinds of actors, such as nations, blocs of nations, bloc leaders, bloc members, nonbloc members, and universal organizations. Here stability is increased if the leaders of the blocs possess nuclear-weapons systems and if they are the only actors who possess them. Alliances in this system tend to be based on long-term interests, even where immediate interests might at times argue for independent action. Wars would tend to be total rather than limited were it not for the destructiveness of nuclear weapons and the mediation efforts of nonbloc members and universal actors. This system tends to be less stable than the "balance of power" system.

Unit veto system. The unit veto system is a system of national actors or of bloc actors in which each actor possesses an extensive nuclear-weapons system. The unit veto system does not tend to produce alliances. It tends to keep low the probability of war but to give rise to tensions that might make for relative instability. It is less stable than the loose bipolar system.

The "balance of power" and loose bipolar systems models have had empirical counterparts. The unit veto system could develop out of the existing international system largely as a consequence of the diffusion of effective second-strike nuclear-weapons systems. The following three models rest upon more extensive changes from past international systems, and one of the models, the tight

bipolar system, would require conditions running counter to existing developments.

Tight bipolar system. The tight bipolar system would have many features in common with the loose bipolar system except that the role of the uncommitted nation would wither away and the role of the universal organization would largely be atrophied. It would be a system of very high tension.

Universal system. The universal system would arise if a number of important political powers were transferred to a universal organization, perhaps as a consequence of the nuclear arms race or because the actors fear the dangers of the escalation of disputes. This system would require a reorientation on the part of the member actors, giving high priority to collective and international values. The universal organization would also require capabilities greater than those of any one member actor.

Hierarchical system. The hierarchical system might arise as a consequence of changes in scale in international organization, or as a consequence of the very successful functioning of a universal system, or as a consequence of conquest or dominance by a single actor. In the first two cases the resulting system would probably be a federal and democratic one. In the last case it would probably be an authoritarian system.

Other possible systems. Roger Masters (1961) has constructed a model for a system of nuclear blocs. He concluded that the characteristics of such a bloc system would probably resemble in many ways those of the "balance of power" system.

Other variations of international systems in the nuclear age have also been discussed. In one system catalytic war was a possibility (Burns 1959), and in another possession of nuclear-weapons systems by many states was consistent with international stability (Burns 1960). The latter study was based on the assumption that if one state suffered a surprise nuclear attack its retaliatory strike would make the aggressor extremely vulnerable to attack by still a third nuclear state. Thus, in effect, the decision to attack would disarm a state if it still had to face other nuclear enemies. The symmetry of this situation would seem likely to produce peace.

Although the six main systems described above were analyzed in terms of their equilibrium conditions, it is not assumed that equilibrium is either more likely than disequilibrium or even inherently desirable. It is assumed that under equilibrium conditions actors are motivated to maintain the equilibrium.

The systems can, however, undergo certain transformations, and some examples of these follow. A "balance of power" system, for instance, might be transformed into a unit veto system if most of the major states acquire sufficiently large second-strike nuclear systems. In such a case a technological change at the system's boundary would produce changes in its essential rules. If, on the contrary, scale factors restrict viable nuclear establishments to two national actors, and particularly if one of them possesses national institutions capable of international extension, the blocs of a bipolar system might arise. Other requirements in the system might then produce a universal organization, such as the United Nations, having a differentiated role function in the system. The "balance of power" system would then have been transformed into a loose bipolar system.

Prediction and explanation

International systems can be viewed normatively; that is, their essential rules can be regarded as optimal rules of statecraft under the conditions specified for the system and the assumptions concerning the motivation of actors. Alternatively, they can be viewed as making predictions concerning actor behavior if the conditions specified by the theory hold and if the decision makers for the actors are rational, informed, and free to act on the basis of external considerations alone. Systems can also be used as aids in predicting what might happen if the conditions specified by the theory do not hold or if decision makers (statesmen) act contrary to the essential rules of the system.

If one uses the theory either to predict or to explain, then factors not included in the central theory must be taken into account. This is the problem of engineering the theory (see Knorr & Verba 1961, pp. 6–24). As this engineering occurs, the system is brought closer to the complex reality, but it loses generality.

Two examples will show how a theory can be used for purposes of explanation. The "balance of power" theory, for instance, predicts that alliances will be short-lived, based on immediate interest, and neglectful of existing or previous alliance status. It is not predictive of which actors would be in which alliance. Nicolson's historical study of the Congress of Vienna (1946) shows the many accidental features that produced the individual alliances during the congress. Yet the series of shifting alliances as a whole is congruent with the theory.

The rigid alliance systems of the European great nations between 1871 and 1914 and the relatively unlimited nature of World War I seem, superficially at least, inconsistent with the prescriptions of the "balance of power" theory. If one recognizes, however, that Prussia's seizure of Alsace–Lorraine created in France a public opinion that was ineluctably revanchist (as Bismarck probably foresaw that it would), then this parameter change is seen to be consistent with the developments that followed. As long as Germany was unwilling to return Alsace–Lorraine to France, France would be Germany's enemy. Thus, France and Germany became in time the poles of rigidly opposed alliances and would not enter the same coalition, regardless of other, common interests. The chief motivation for limitation upon conflict in the theoretical "balance of power" system is the need to maintain the existence of other essential actors as potential future allies. However, since neither France nor Germany perceived the other as even a potential ally, neither had any incentive to limit its war aims against the other.

Rigor of systems theory. International systems theory is heuristic. It contains formulations that so far can be related to empirical systems only with great difficulty, primarily because appropriate empirical information has not yet been collected but also because the criteria for confirmation are inadequately developed. However, the theory directs research to some important questions; for instance, is the kind of shifting of alliances called for by the "balance of power" theory actually found in historical "balance of power" systems? Is a minimum of five essential actors really required for stability in such systems?

The international systems theory is also nonrigorous in that the conclusions are derived from the premises in a fashion that is no more than plausible. The internal mechanics of the systems are not completely understood, and some of the more important questions have not been analyzed. For instance, what difference does it make in a "balance of power" system to move from five to six, or from six to seven, essential actors? Does it make any difference if one, or more than one, of the essential actors is motivated by hegemonic ambitions? To answer such questions, one must use techniques that were not available in the late 1950s, when the theory was developed. Instead, insights from game theory were applied to broader questions concerning the general stability of the system.

Applications and related approaches

Theories of the "balance of power" and the loose bipolar systems have been applied to international law. Kaplan and Katzenbach hypothesized (1959; 1961) that wars would tend to be more limited under the "balance of power" system than under the loose bipolar system and that the laws of war would tend to be more closely observed. The rule of nonintervention in the internal affairs of other sovereign states would be more closely adhered to in the "balance of power" system. In the loose bipolar system recognition of states would require more political qualifications and would be less likely to be decided according to neutral rules of law. The rise of bipolarity has also been related, by hypothesis, to the functional transfer of sovereignty from the state to supranational organizations. Hoffmann has also related systematic changes in international law to changes in international political systems (Knorr & Verba 1961, pp. 205–237).

The "balance of power" and loose bipolar systems have also been related to problems of foreign policy. In applying the "balance of power" model it has often been found possible to ignore the role of internal characteristics of states in the formation of alliances, except where there are important deviant actors. In applications of the loose bipolar model, however, problems of bloc cohesion and identification may make it necessary to consider the domestic features of the actors' regimes (Kaplan 1962).

These derived applications of the theory involve additional variables and less rigorous reasoning than the central propositions of systems theory. Thus, their conclusions are even more tentative.

Size and stability in "balance" systems. Scholars tend to agree that a lower bound of five essential actors is necessary for stability in a "balance of power" system. Below this bound the value of maintaining a defeated state is not plausible enough to counterbalance alternative motivations. However, there is some disagreement about the effects of increasing the number of actors above five. A. L. Burns (1957) regards five as the point of greatest stability, whereas Kaplan (1957) believes that stability increases as the number of actors increases to an upper bound, unspecified as yet. Burns believes that there is an inherent tendency to decrease the number of actors and no tendency to increase the number. Kaplan believes there is an inherent tendency to maintain the number and some tendency to increase it.

Burns's analysis, based on a set of explicit propositions, gave rise to two important concepts: balancing and deterrence. The propositions are based on the concepts of pressure, interaction opportunities, security, military effectiveness, and allocation of attention. Normally, nonnuclear weapons en-

courage balancing and nuclear weapons make for deterrence.

Multipolar power systems have also been analyzed from the standpoint of mathematical models (Deutsch & Singer 1964). The analysis explicitly takes arms races into account, as well as interaction opportunities and allocation of attention. This study also concludes that five is a minimal bound for stability in a "balance of power" system and that such a system may be stable for several hundred years at least. But the authors note that no historic "balance of power" system has in fact lasted longer than several hundred years. Thus, they say, such systems, although more stable than bipolar ones, are inherently unstable. On the basis of chance alone, a four-to-one rather than a three-to-two coalition is likely to occur at some point, and such overwhelming strength in one coalition is likely to lead to the destruction of the system.

In assuming that a four-to-one coalition will be destructive of the system the authors overlook the instability of the victorious coalition, a factor that tends to assure the maintenance of the system (Kaplan et al. 1960). In the machine model discussed below, several series of four-to-one wars have occurred in which the system remained stable. These runs were continued through several hundred war cycles and were discontinued only when it became clear that further runs would not affect the results.

Instability could be produced, of course, if one programmed the machine to behave as if it lacked information or were irrational. However, other hypotheses could also be employed to achieve this end. For instance, changes could occur in the scale of activity, or political movements that cut across national boundaries could develop. It is at least plausible that such factors—and not coalition dominance—operated in the real world to produce instability in some historic "balance of power" systems and therefore that external, rather than internal, factors were responsible for the collapse of some historic "balance of power" systems.

Does the presence or the absence of the arms race from some models lead to significant differences between them? Possibly, but the incentive for war and for the spoils of war as it operates in the "balance of power" system is likely to produce most of the consequences of the arms race and will do so under the condition ordinarily assumed to maximize instability—that is, military conflict. In any event, this problem can be resolved on the basis of tests.

Parameter-oriented systems. A number of writers treat international systems more from the standpoint of the parameter or boundary conditions that influence them than from the standpoint of system structure and functions. Quite often these writers do not make this distinction explicitly.

George Modelski (see Knorr & Verba 1961, pp. 205–237) distinguishes international systems according to whether they are based on agrarian or on industrial systems. Wars in agrarian systems, he finds, tend to be less destructive than wars in industrial ones. To some extent the reasoning behind this is compelling. The technologies of industrial systems permit more destructiveness and greater social control. They also provide more resources that can be made available to the state for the purpose of fighting or otherwise pursuing its objectives. Thus, Modelski's position is reasonable as a statement of a tendency, although inaccurate with respect to many historical systems. His proposition, however, is not integrated into a theory or used to suggest modifications of the behavior of one or more types of international system.

In his analysis of communism as an international system, Modelski (1960) stresses structural and behavioral features of the system and is thus able to investigate how ideological and organizational factors specific to communism affect the relationships of communist states in a larger world system.

Quincy Wright (1955), drawing on Talcott Parsons' work, has established a number of analytic fields, covering values and capabilities. After states are located in these fields, it might be possible to make a number of statements concerning trends in their behavior, but problems of measurement are enormous here, as are problems of relating the variables covered by the fields. This work does not distinguish systems so much as it aspires to measure state characteristics; thus, it is not of the same genre as international systems theories.

Kenneth Boulding (1959) has attempted to define national images and to relate them systematically to other characteristics of international systems. National images, he states, are impregnated with valuational distortions that produce national responses inconsistent with peaceful equilibrium. This view of images could perhaps be assimilated to the informational factor in Kaplan's systems, and these systems could then be tested under various conditions of misinformation.

Boulding (1962) has also formulated a theory of conflict and defense, based on Hotelling models, in which strength diminishes with distance and in which equilibrium occurs where strengths are equal. These systems models do not take into account the fact that diminishing strength is neither linear with distance, nor continuous, nor transferable between weapons systems. Boulding's theory does distinguish between conventional and nuclear weapons. In his nuclear systems, strengths do not diminish with distance, although most empirical studies show that they do (Wohlstetter et al. 1954). This also holds true for strategic nuclear missiles and for strategic bomber forces.

Methods for studying international systems

A number of difficult methodological questions arise in the study of international systems. These questions concern both the theories of the systems and the relationships between theories and empirical reality. To help overcome some of these problems, games and machines have recently been used to simulate both theories and reality, and some comparative analyses of historical systems have been attempted.

Simulations of reality. Harold Guetzkow and his associates (1963) have conducted simulation experiments in which they adapted the small-group methods of organization specialists and social psychologists to the simulation of international systems. In these simulations, individuals are used to represent the executive branch, the Congress, the United Nations, foreign countries, the press, and so forth. They interact within a specified framework. This technique is useful in suggesting hypotheses, and it might possibly replicate some important aspects of reality. The experiment, however, is probably too complex for complete analysis, and some of the variables, including the calculations made by the individual role players, cannot easily be related to international factors. Moreover, the representation of the domestic political process as an intervening variable in the international process is much oversimplified.

Still another method of simulating international politics has been attempted by Clark Abt (see Abt & Jaros 1961). He employs an extremely complex computer model that includes great and small nations, budgetary decision processes, complicated military postures, and so forth, as well as Kaplan's essential rules. His model is so complex that it becomes *ad hoc*. Very small changes in some of his parameters might produce quite different results. All, or at least most, of the important variables have been included in the simulation, but it is difficult to know whether the computer problem has any real empirical referent despite its explicit empirical orientation.

Simulations of theories. In order to represent important aspects of the "balance of power" theory rather than to simulate reality, a table-stakes game was designed (Kaplan et al. 1960). It used players who tried to optimize particular kinds of counters. The game was designed to minimize the influence of the players' images about international politics. And the game, indeed, can be played without any reference to international politics. It was thus hoped to use the players' minds as a computer for the strictly strategic elements of play in lieu of programming a computer to play the game. Even so, it was by no means clear what produced the results, and they were, therefore, suggestive at best.

Some of the difficulties in using a computer to test the theory have, however, been overcome. A simple model of the "balance of power" system has been placed on a computer which in the initial phase makes decisions for five players, but the program is being generalized for three to seven players. The players, representing essential national actors, are assigned sizes, military potentials, attitudes toward risk, attitudes toward foreign imbalance, subjective estimates of military strengths (which may differ from the objective strengths), and a factor representing eagerness to form coalitions. The machine then makes decisions for the players on the basis of recursive optimization procedures, which take into account the results over one war cycle.

According to the early runs, if the players have a small distaste for foreign imbalance—that is, if they behave like the postulated "balance of power" players—there is a series of limited wars that do not eliminate any of the players. Increasing the distaste for foreign imbalance produces peace. Decreasing it produces an unstable series of wars in which players are eliminated. If one of the players likes foreign imbalance, it is necessary to increase the distaste of the other players to produce stability. Stability might also be maintained by employing a counter-deviancy factor (analogous to rule four of Kaplan's "balance of power" system) that calls for coalitions against deviant players that strive for hegemony within the system. In the absence of such a counter-deviancy factor, if one of the players likes imbalance and if the distaste for imbalance of the other players is not increased, one or more of the players will be eliminated. The deviant player who likes imbalance will not be among the eliminated players and thus will have a selective advantage. It would therefore seem to be advantageous, even for the players with a distaste for foreign imbalance, to play as if they liked it. But in this case the system would become unstable. And having—or acting as if one had—a liking for imbalance would then create no selective advantage; but security would be lower than if all players acted as if they had a distaste for imbalance.

Alternative formulas for figuring imbalance in the system are employed to guard against the possibility that the results are artifacts of the formulas. Two methods have been found that increase the ratio of three-to-two wars: changes in the battle ratios and side-payments for latecomers to coalitions.

No effort has yet been made in the project to put more complicated international systems (for instance, systems similar to the loose bipolar one) on the computer. It is not yet known how to program for the complicated features of this system, and more sophisticated computers with more powerful memory systems may well be required. Furthermore, although an attempt had been made (Kaplan 1957) to relate a number of internal political processes and structural political elements to the theory and to indicate how these would modify it, the computer was programmed only for the simplest features of national or bloc decision making. Once it is known how the models operate in the absence of internal politics, *ad hoc* adjustments can be made. [*See* SIMULATION, *article on* POLITICAL PROCESSES.]

Systematic empirical research. Although one can show how theories of international systems can be used to explain real political events, it is less easy to test these theories systematically. One could attempt to test individual propositions derived from the theory—the usual method in the physical sciences, where circumstances permit. It has been suggested that both patterns of historical activity and frequency of interaction processes should be investigated (Kaplan 1957). It now appears that the frequency of interactions plays a less important role than was originally anticipated. Since the number of cases is too small, different variables assume importance in different cases, and in many cases events have no simple meanings that are discoverable apart from contextual analysis. Thus, the investigation of historical patterns of activity now appears to assume even greater importance than was originally anticipated.

Little systematic historical analysis, however, has been carried out. Richard Rosecrance's work (1963), although interesting, is not directly useful for testing hypotheses stemming from theory, because his evidence is not collected according to a systematic set of questions. At the Ford Workshop at the University of Chicago, efforts are being made to study empirical international systems—such as the Italian city-state system and the Chinese-warlord system. These studies use a systematic theory of international politics and are therefore oriented toward a systematic set of questions.

Such historical studies should probably investigate interactions between those variables included in the theory and other important variables that affect the behavior of the specific system under investigation. In the Italian city-state system, for example, the use of mercenaries by the city-states helped maintain the equilibrium conditions specified by the theory. The mercenaries themselves had an incentive to behave consistently with the essential rules of the system, for instability would have undercut their own role in the system. In this case the explanation offered by the theory holds in general, but the particular way in which the equilibrium is maintained requires, among other things, an analysis of the interaction of the mercenary system with the city-state system.

This problem suggests the way in which empirical research and computer analysis could be combined to test, evaluate, and, if necessary, reformulate the propositions of international systems theory.

The mercenary system might have been an element that increased the stability of the historic system but that was not strictly necessary for stability. If so, one would not desire to change the theory, for a change in the theory would narrow its range of useful application. However, if investigation seemed to show that historic "balance of power" systems are stable only when some additional factor is operating, the system might be modified to include it. This factor might then be built into the computer model, and if the model is stable without it, one might investigate what other changes in the model would be needed—conceivably, the addition of motivation or information elements—to make such a factor necessary for stability. Alternatively, the computer runs could show that the specific elements in the historical systems not included in the theoretical system merely maintain the parameters of the systems at their theoretical equilibrium or merely move them from equilibrium under specific conditions.

There may—and ideally should—be a continual process of learning that relates historical studies, systems theories, and computer models. Although this methodology will not provide the kind of assurance that the "hard" sciences aspire to, it will introduce more rigor and scientific method into the study of international politics.

MORTON A. KAPLAN

[*See also* ALLIANCES; BALANCE OF POWER; COMMUNISM, *article on* THE INTERNATIONAL SYSTEM; DIPLOMACY; POWER TRANSITION. *Also relevant are the entries* INTERNATIONAL POLITICS; INTERNATIONAL RELATIONS.]

BIBLIOGRAPHY

ABT, CLARK C.; and JAROS, WALTER F. 1961 *Design for a Strategic Model.* No. BR 1354A. Bedford, Mass.: Raytheon Company, Missile and Space Division.

ARON, RAYMOND (1962) 1967 *Peace and War: A Theory of International Relations.* Garden City, N.Y.: Doubleday. → First published as *Paix et guerre entre les nations.*

ASHBY, W. ROSS (1952) 1960 *Design for a Brain: The Origin of Adaptive Behavior.* 2d ed., rev. New York: Wiley.

BOULDING, KENNETH E. (1959) 1961 National Images and International Systems. Pages 391–398 in James N. Rosenau (editor), *International Politics and Foreign Policy: A Reader in Research and Theory.* New York: Free Press.

BOULDING, KENNETH E. 1962 *Conflict and Defense: A General Theory.* New York: Harper.

BURNS, ARTHUR L. 1957 From Balance to Deterrence: A Theoretical Analysis. *World Politics* 9:494–529.

BURNS, ARTHUR L. 1959 *The Rationale of Catalytic War.* Research Monograph No. 3. Princeton Univ., Center of International Studies.

BURNS, ARTHUR L. 1960 *Power Politics and the Growing Nuclear Club.* Policy Memorandum No. 20. Princeton Univ., Center of International Studies.

DEUTSCH, KARL W.; and SINGER, J. DAVID 1964 Multipolar Power Systems and International Stability. *World Politics* 16:390–406.

GUETZKOW, HAROLD S. et al. 1963 *Simulation in International Relations: Developments for Research and Teaching.* Englewood Cliffs, N.J.: Prentice-Hall.

KAPLAN, MORTON A. 1957 *System and Process in International Politics.* New York: Wiley.

KAPLAN, MORTON A. (editor) 1962 *The Revolution in World Politics.* New York: Wiley.

KAPLAN, MORTON A.; BURNS, ARTHUR L.; and QUANDT, RICHARD E. 1960 Theoretical Analysis of the "Balance of Power." *Behavioral Science* 5:240–252.

KAPLAN, MORTON A.; and KATZENBACH, NICHOLAS DEB. 1959 The Patterns of International Politics and of International Law. *American Political Science Review* 53:693–712.

KAPLAN, MORTON A.; and KATZENBACH, NICHOLAS DEB. 1961 *The Political Foundations of International Law.* New York: Wiley.

KNORR, KLAUS E.; and VERBA, SIDNEY (editors) 1961 *The International System: Theoretical Essays.* Princeton Univ. Press. → See especially pages 6–24, "Problems of Theory Confirmation in International Politics," by Morton A. Kaplan; pages 118–143, "Agraria and Industria: Two Models of the International System," by George A. Modelski; and pages 205–237, "International Systems and International Law," by Stanley Hoffmann.

MASTERS, ROGER D. 1961 A Multi-bloc Model of the International System. *American Political Science Review* 55:780–798.

MODELSKI, GEORGE A. 1960 *The Communist International System.* Princeton University, Center of International Studies, Research Monograph No. 9. Princeton Univ. Press.

NICOLSON, HAROLD (1946) 1961 *The Congress of Vienna: A Study in Allied Unity, 1812–1822.* New York: Viking.

ROSECRANCE, RICHARD N. 1963 *Action and Reaction in World Politics: International Systems in Perspective.* Boston: Little.

WOHLSTETTER, ALBERT A. et al. 1954 *Selection and Use of Strategic Air Bases.* Santa Monica, Calif.: RAND Corp.

WRIGHT, QUINCY 1955 *The Study of International Relations.* New York: Appleton.

V

PSYCHOLOGICAL SYSTEMS

Systems, or systemic, analysis in contemporary psychology is an attempt to relate behavior to the *organizational* aspects of its underlying structure. It is a way of conceptualizing the phenomena that mediate between a stimulus—or environmental event—and the behaving organism's response to it. This article will briefly describe some considerations of general systems theory and will continue with discussions of important systemic variables in psychological analyses, some representative usage of systems analysis by psychologists, including its potential for the area of mental ability and retardation, and an evaluation.

It must be pointed out clearly that there is an alternate use of the phrase "systems analysis" in psychology. The language, concepts, and theoretical propositions devised to understand, integrate, and explain behavioral phenomena may themselves constitute systems. These systems have been subject to thorough and critical evaluation and analysis (e.g., Koch 1959). Such analyses, which *treat of* and *transcend* psychological phenomena, are *not* the concern of this article, which deals, rather, with systems *involved in* and *part of* psychological phenomena.

Definition and general considerations

The problems of defining and identifying systems are discussed at length in the other articles on systems analysis. It is sufficient here to quote Miller (1955): "Systems are bounded regions in space-time, involving energy interchange among their parts, which are associated in functional relationships, and with their environment. . . ." A system is also considered to be a group of events that have a higher interchange of energy or a higher rate of communication among themselves than with other events (see Scott 1962, p. 97). The generality of this definition allows the several sciences the opportunity to select various types and levels of events to be treated as systems. Even so, within individual disciplines there are diverse conceptions of systems.

In psychology the assumptions made about the nature of behavioral phenomena are reflected in the conceptions of the systems that govern these events. Allport very carefully, and with considerable breadth and perspective, describes four levels of "openness" in psychological systems (1960). The lowest level of openness is exhibited by those systems whose relations with their environment consist merely of engaging in intake and output of matter and energy. Perhaps this is the lowest common denominator of all organic systems. The traditional psychophysics of Wundt and the classical and instrumental learning models of Pavlov, Watson, and Skinner consider behavioral events in such terms: behavior is primarily reflexive, stimulus-generated, and unmediated. The relationship between the behaving organism and its environment is unilateral and mechanical.

A second level of openness is attained when, in addition, systems achieve and maintain homeostasis. Hullian learning theory and Freudian psychoanalysis view behavioral systems at this level. The importance of the internal state of the system is fully appreciated. Behavior is considered to be adjustive and represents some form of mediation of stimuli by internal mechanisms. [*See* HOMEOSTASIS.]

With the addition of increasing organization among the internal components of the system, a third level of openness is reached. Gestalt theories of perception and of insight learning, stressing the tendencies to organize, to restructure, and to improve upon present status, and personality theories, such as Jung's and those of the ego psychologists, that emphasize growth and development of the self in addition to immediate adjustment, conceive of psychological systems at this level. Behavior is not viewed as merely a mediation of the external by the internal to achieve some adjustive, tension-free state but includes, as well, natural growth and development of the mediating agency, apart from and not necessarily contingent upon external events.

Finally, at the fourth and highest level of openness, Allport places those conceptualizations of behavioral events which provide for their engaging in transaction with their environment. Allport is less explicit at this level, but he implies that the system itself is capable of acting upon its environment with appreciable autonomy and is not restricted to mere responding or reacting. Allport is careful to point out that such acts must nonetheless be viewed and understood with proper consideration of the environment in which they occur.

Needless to say, the Western philosophical heritage, which encourages an "integumented" view of personality as well as a dichotomous view of man and his social world, has prevented a full appreciation of the extent of this transaction.

Allport's use of the term "openness" is somewhat at variance with the usage of others, but his emphasis on the need to consider human behavior as a reflection of systems that are more open rather than less open (or quasi closed) can be readily appreciated. And his discussion is an interesting general exposition of various systemic analyses: ways of relating behavior to its organizational aspects. [See PERSONALITY: CONTEMPORARY VIEWPOINTS, *article on* A UNIQUE AND OPEN SYSTEM.]

Structural and functional dimensions. The most important structural concept in systems analysis is the *boundary* (see, for example, Parsons 1959, p. 645). A boundary (of a system or subsystem) is often difficult to demonstrate, depending for the most part on relatively different frequencies and intensities of interchange between events. Where one set of events demonstrates greater interchange within itself than with other events or sets of events, a boundary is said to exist around it, and the set of events is considered a bounded region.

Psychologists who employ a systemic framework are primarily concerned with the nature and relationships of bounded regions within—and, to a lesser extent, with the boundaries between—systems. Boundaries can be considered in terms of the frequency with which they occur within a system; in other words, the number of parts of which the system is constructed, the dimension of *differentiation*.

Boundaries can be considered, in addition, in terms of the extent to which they permit interchange between regions of a system and between a system and its environment: the dimension of *interdependence*. (When interchange occurs with equal frequency and intensity within and between regions, by definition no boundary exists.)

The dimension of *openness* refers to the degree of interchange across the outer boundary of the system itself; in other words, the degree of interchange with the system's environment.

Differentiation, interdependence, and openness are basic structural attributes. "Structural" may be a misnomer, however, in the case of openness, since openness implies some activity or response on the part of the organism and thus has functional import. Indeed, the very essence of systems analysis is its appreciation of the close relationship between structure and function.

One way of separating these two levels of dis-

course is to think of structure as involving a spatial dimension and of function as involving a temporal one. Even so, in systems where there is increasing organization over time, the structures themselves will become functions.

Still, one can think of function as implying the continued existence of the system over time, the perpetuation of its outer boundary, and the maintenance and growth of its inner regions.

Representative major uses

Three representative uses of systems analysis in psychology will be considered. For each, the universe of events treated as a system will be outlined, along with a discussion of differentiation, interdependence, openness, and their implications. The first two sections especially refer to works that provide considerable breadth, depth, and detail, and their treatment here is not meant to be synoptic but selective. In addition, the implications of systems analysis for mental ability and retardation will be discussed.

Open and closed minds. Rokeach and his associates, in an attempt to integrate findings in areas such as authoritarianism, conformity, yielding, resistance to acculturation, ethnocentrism, and prejudice, have devoted considerable attention to the belief–disbelief system (Rokeach 1960). Each person, in the course of his development, acquires an "organization of verbal and nonverbal, implicit and explicit beliefs, sets, or expectancies" about the world in which he lives (p. 32). He has beliefs about the physical world, about the past, about the future, about the supernatural, and about the social world. The simple statement "Table salt is made up of sodium and chlorine" is in actuality a belief; it may well be prefaced by "I believe."

In addition to the set of beliefs and expectancies that the person accepts as true, he also has a set of beliefs that he rejects as false. These involve the same kinds of events or objects—the supernatural, physicality, etc.—as do the accepted beliefs. Together, the set of beliefs accepted as true and the set rejected as false—disbeliefs—constitute the belief–disbelief system. The disbelief system itself comprises a series of disbelief subsystems, each reflecting a different degree of rejection. The term "system" implies that there is an organization of parts and that the nature of this organization has implications for the behavior and functioning of the system.

Differentiation. Rokeach's concern with differentiation is manifested in his assertion that belief–disbelief systems vary in their "degrees of differentiation or articulation or richness of detail"

(1960, pp. 37–38). The amount of knowledge a person has about things he believes or disbelieves is one indication of the degree to which the belief–disbelief system or either part of it is differentiated. Differentiation within the disbelief system can be measured by the degree to which two disbelief subsystems are perceived as different. The Hearst press concept "communazi" implies no differentiation between disbeliefs, while an individual's distinction between communism and national socialism indicates that they are differentiated by him, even though they may each be a disbelief. It is further assumed that there is generally greater differentiation in the belief system than in the disbelief system.

Rokeach is also theoretically concerned with the total number—or the range of—disbelief subsystems represented in a belief–disbelief system. While he calls this comprehensiveness or narrowness, it is essentially differentiation.

Isolation.   Rokeach's concern with interdependence is reflected in the assertion that the belief–disbelief system can vary in the extent to which a person sees his beliefs as being connected or related in some way. When two intrinsically related beliefs are seen as being in no way related, Rokeach terms them isolated. One indication of isolation is the coexistence of logically contradictory beliefs within the belief system. As examples, Rokeach points to the person who believes in democracy and who advocates, at the same time, that a government should be run by the intellectually elite. Another indication is the accentuation of differences and the minimization of similarities between belief and disbelief systems, as when, for example, a staunch advocate of psychoanalysis claims that it has nothing in common with behaviorism. Other indications of isolation are a disproportionate tendency to perceive events as irrelevant to one's beliefs and a tendency to deny that events contradict one's beliefs. When logically related beliefs are perceived as being related, then communication exists between them; communication is identical with the concept of interdependence.

Openness, closedness, and structure.   A major goal for Rokeach and his associates is relating structural, organizational variables, such as differentiation and isolation (interdependence), to a dimension called openness–closedness. In any behavioral situation, a person's response can be appropriate to the relevant characteristics of the situation or determined primarily by factors not related to the real demands of the situation. It is necessary, then, for people to be able to distinguish and evaluate relevant and irrelevant cues. A basic, defining characteristic of "open" minds is the ability to "receive, evaluate, and act on relevant information received from the outside on its own intrinsic merits, unencumbered by irrelevant factors in the situation arising from within the person or from the outside . . ." (Rokeach 1960, p. 57). Such irrelevant internal pressures are unrelated habits, irrational motives, a need to allay anxiety; irrelevant external pressures include rewards and punishments from external authorities.

It is explicitly suggested that all communication has a dual character: it contains information about a *source*, as well as information about an *event* or set of events. Of major importance are the relative strengths of two powerful and opposing motives served by all belief–disbelief systems: "the need for a cognitive framework to know and to understand and the need to ward off threatening aspects of reality" (Rokeach 1960, p. 67). When the need to know is dominant and the need to ward off threat is minimal, irrelevant pressures and drives are pushed aside and information is objectively evaluated; when the need to ward off threat is stronger, the need to know becomes weaker and source and substance are not properly separated.

Threat arises from experiences that make man feel alone, isolated and helpless, and anxious about his future. Accordingly, under threat, when a man cannot appreciate the duality between source and substance, he accepts a belief on the basis of irrelevant factors rather than on its inherent merits, and the relation between his beliefs will reflect this irrelevance: there will be no necessary logical consistency; his beliefs will exist in isolation from one another. Where the dual nature of communication is understood and properly evaluated, beliefs are more readily accepted for their coherence and logical consistency; there will be less isolation (greater interdependence) between them.

In addition, if a person is able to distinguish between source and substance, he will be more ready to seek information about beliefs he rejects from the sources that advocate them. The more he is unable to distinguish source from substance, the more readily he will depend on the sources that advocate his own beliefs for information about the disbelief system. The closed mind, consequently, will become even more rejecting of its disbeliefs and will know much less about them.

In this way the open mind is considered to represent a structural organization generally having greater differentiation within its disbelief system and greater communication within and between belief and disbelief systems (interdependence), while the closed mind is characterized by less differentiation within its disbelief system and greater isolation within and between belief and disbelief systems.

Methodology.   From the above theoretical considerations Rokeach and his associates developed the Dogmatism Scale, to measure the degree of openness or closedness of belief–disbelief systems. The Dogmatism Scale contains items specifically related to differentiation and isolation, as well as items deemed relevant to other related characteristics, including the degree to which a person feels isolated, uncertain, and inadequate: the experiences of threat, from which arise closed systems. The Opinionation Scale, designed to assess the degree to which a person's acceptance or rejection of others is based on how similar their beliefs are to his own, was also developed. Both of these scales were designed to eliminate the effects of specific belief contents and to stress instead the structure of the belief system.

Results and implications.   A discussion of all the subtle and varied relations between performances on the above scales and aspects of behavior is precluded. However, it was demonstrated that closed systems exhibit greater difficulty than open systems in forming totally new belief systems but exhibit no differences in overcoming individual old beliefs (Rokeach & Vidulich 1960). This poorer ability to synthesize leads to greater difficulty in certain kinds of problem-solving tasks, where synthesis is crucial. Also, closed minds persist in trying to handle insoluble problems with a belief system that had formerly proved useful. They do not defect from their belief systems as readily as do open minds. This strange, seemingly maladaptive loyalty is considered to be an indication of lack of communication across boundaries within the belief system (Rokeach et al. 1960*a*). Closed minds seem to perform less adequately in perceptual synthesis, or the restructuring of the perceptual field (Levy & Rokeach 1960), to be less receptive to "new music" (Mikol 1960), and to exhibit more compliance than open minds in accepting new beliefs when these are presented all at once rather than gradually (Rokeach et al. 1960*b*). It is pointed out that closed minds are not always resistant to change and will, in fact, change more readily than open minds when new belief systems are offered to them all at once and arbitrarily.

To the extent that circumstances demand synthesis—the ability to integrate and accept a series of new beliefs in place of old ones ("beliefs" broadly defined)—the open-minded person, i.e., the person whose belief–disbelief system comprises differentiated parts that are in communication with each other, will have an advantage over the closed-minded person.

Furthermore, Rokeach has demonstrated that authoritarians of both left and right political orientations have belief systems that are structurally similar. Both groups score relatively high on the Dogmatism and Opinionation scales. This represents an advance over the widely used California *F* and *E* scales, which are attuned primarily to a fascistic and ethnocentric authoritarianism and do not reveal the dogmatism and authoritarianism of the communist, who to as great an extent is closed-minded and dependent on limited authoritarian sources and whose belief system may be reflecting the same defenses against anxiety attributed to the traditional conception of authoritarianism. And it is consistent with the concept of implied greater rejection of disbeliefs that the closed mind is found to be more opinionated and prejudiced than the open mind.

Concrete and abstract conceptual systems.   Harvey, Hunt, and Schroder present another attempt to integrate many areas of interest to psychologists and other social scientists: child development, attitude change, personality measurement, motivation, and psychopathology. Of prime concern to their work are concepts, or conceptual systems. Concepts refer to ". . . the individual's standardized evaluative predilections toward differentiated aspects of his external world. . . . A concept is a system of ordering that serves as the mediating linkage between the input side (stimuli) and the output side (response)" (1961, p. 1). Of basic interest is the structural nature of these concepts: *how* the person is related to objects in his world, rather than the nature and content of these objects.

It is assumed that a single concept probably never functions independently of others; accordingly, it makes more sense to discuss groupings of concepts, or conceptual systems. The totality of all of a person's conceptual systems is termed the self system. Regardless of the size of the conceptual system, the same types of structural analyses are appropriate.

Concreteness–abstractness.   The most important functional dimension of a conceptual system is the degree to which it is concrete or abstract. "Concreteness" implies that the relation between the person and an object is determined primarily by the physical attributes of that object. "Abstractness" connotes that the relation between a person and an object is determined to a considerably lesser degree by the physical nature of the object and to a much greater degree by mediating factors that result from the individual's experiences and activities.

Among other things, abstractness involves being able to detach oneself from immediate inner and outer experiences, to switch mental sets, to grasp essential aspects of a given whole and be able to analyze its parts, and to plan ahead ideationally, all of which represent a minimal amount of stimulus determination (Harvey et al. 1961, p. 25).

Although concreteness–abstractness is called a structural attribute, the relative nature of the terms "structure" and "function" is recognized (pp. 19–20). Accordingly, in the terminology of this article concreteness–abstractness is considered a functional aspect of systems, to be related to the system's structural aspects.

Harvey, Hunt, and Schroder consider development to represent increasing abstractness, and learning is considered to be the acquisition of concepts. Learning occurs through a process of differentiation and integration, wherein the child breaks down or analyzes his perceived environment into parts that are relevant to him and then relates these parts to each other and to his entire conceptual system (p. 4). Abstractness reflects the degree to which the processes of differentiation and integration have occurred within conceptual systems.

Structural attributes. The processes of differentiation and integration result in several important structural attributes, among them clarity–ambiguity, compartmentalization–interrelatedness, and openness–closedness. Clarity–ambiguity refers to the degree to which the concept, or relation between the person and an object or event, is composed of articulate, differentiated parts. The greater the number of these differentiated parts, the greater is the concept's clarity. Thus, clarity–ambiguity within a concept or within a conceptual system is identical to the dimension of differentiation treated in this discussion. Compartmentalization–interrelatedness refers to the degree to which differentiated concepts within a system are connected and is identical to interdependence. Openness–closedness represents the receptivity or sensitivity of the system, much as it has been defined in this article.

Harvey, Hunt, and Schroder proceed to relate concreteness–abstractness to these structural components. Concrete functioning is assumed to reflect conceptual systems that are unarticulated, highly compartmentalized, and inaccessible to impinging events, whereas abstract functioning is an attribute of conceptual systems that are highly articulated, highly interrelated, and sensitive to impinging events.

The developmental process. Considerable detail is provided (Harvey, Hunt & Schroder 1961, chap-

ters 4, 5) as to how training and experiential conditions influence development and shape the emergence of a high level of abstract functioning. Normally, at the very earliest stage of development, when differentiation has not yet taken place, the child's concepts are poorly articulated, relatively ambiguous. Accordingly, his behavior is determined by the absolute (to him) physical nature of objects in the world around him: external criteria control him; rules and their goals are not distinguished; and rules have an absolutistic quality. As development proceeds, the child becomes aware of the limits of such absolutes: through the occurrence of gross differentiation, the external attributes of objects are distinguished from the internal wishes and needs of the child. At this point internal needs develop a compelling force on the child's behavior, in much the same absolute way that external attributes categorically controlled him before. And there is considerable resistance to and hostility toward external control. It is only through increased differentiation and integration of his concepts both of external and of internal events that the young person can become aware of an increasing number of facets of his environment and thus take these into account in his behavior, giving him a basis for more abstract functioning.

For example, the child's earliest concept of an understood parental demand or request is largely undifferentiated. It is categorical, to be complied with unquestioningly. As differentiation progresses and the parent himself is perceived as being psychologically distinct from the child, the child comes to differentiate his own needs and wishes from each other and from those of the parent, and the concept of the parental demand comes to represent these articulated components. After some initial conflict between the external and the internal requirements, the internal requirements will become ascendant for a while, and the child's behavior will be determined by them. However, as the process of integration emerges, there will develop some synthesis of juxtaposed external and internal demands, and the concept of the parental command will contain an evaluation of its positive and negative effects on the child, as well as the positive and negative implications of the child's acceptance or rejection of the command. Consequently, the child's response will reflect greater mediation and more abstractness. He has "multiple alternatives" to consider as bases for his behavior.

Psychopathology. It is also pointed out that various psychopathological "syndromes" can be related to the structural organization of conceptual systems. When a person encounters experiences or events that refute his conceptual system, he experiences *threat*. When concepts are relatively unarticulated, as they are in early childhood, threat is likely to occur when experiences deny the absoluteness of rules or the absolute validity of a concept. Schizophrenia is seen to be an extreme means of warding off threat in the earliest, unarticulated, concretistic system. When internal and external aspects have been grossly differentiated, threat is produced by pressures toward dependency on the external. The psychopathic personality is seen as an extreme reaction to threat in the conceptual system that has grossly differentiated internal and external events and is negatively dependent on the external. Other forms of extreme reactions to threat are systematically considered, as are the abnormal behaviors reflecting less extreme reactions to threat.

The structural attribute of openness–closedness is relevant here. Where differentiation and integration either have not occurred or have occurred in limited measure, where concepts are poorly articulated, too many events in the environment are potentially refuting. Where concepts represent categoricals, any experiences that cast doubt on their "oughtness" are refutive. Consequently, to preserve the existing conceptual structure, the person avoids coming into contact with the threatening experiences, fails to perceive them, denies they exist, or misinterprets them. On the other hand, more abstract conceptual systems are threatened by experiences that deny the validity of "multiple alternatives" and that employ categorical evaluations and emphasize authoritarian submission. These systems are considerably more open in general and react much differently to such threats. For example, the possible validity of two different viewpoints may be asserted, or the person may engage in information-seeking behavior.

Cognitive tuning. Zajonc (1960) has provided a systematic attempt at experimentally manipulating aspects of cognitive systems. Defining a cognitive structure as "an organized subset of the given cognitive universe in terms of which the individual identifies and discriminates a particular object or event" (p. 159), Zajonc suggests the importance of the structural properties of differentiation, complexity, unity, and organization in determining the behavior of the cognitive structure.

Structural attributes. Differentiation is reflected in the number of attributes that can be utilized in identifying and discriminating objects. Unity reflects the degree to which the differentiated attributes depend on each other, theoretically identical to interdependence. Unity is mathematically and behaviorally represented by the degree to which a change in one attribute is reflected in changes in other attributes. Complexity is a more advanced treatment of differentiation and represents the number of different *categories* of discriminanda that are represented in the number of discriminated attributes. Organization reflects the grouping of parts and the degree to which any part or grouping dominates the whole; basically it is an aspect of unity.

Experimental findings and implications. Zajonc's study consisted of experimentally varying situational demands and measuring the ensuing differences in the structural aspects of cognitive systems. It was predicted that when subjects Ss anticipated they would be *receiving* information, they would exhibit cognitive systems qualitatively different from those exhibited when they anticipated they would be *transmitting* information.

Experimental Ss were all given copies of a letter from a job applicant to a potential employer and were told to imagine what kind of person the applicant was. After reading the letter, Ss in the transmitter group were told that they would be responsible for communicating the information obtained about the letter writer to another group of persons but that before they proceeded, they were to write down what they had learned from the letter. Ss in the receiver group were told that another group of persons had detailed information about the letter writer and would communicate this to them but that before this was done, Ss were to write down what they had learned from the letter. Special forms were distributed for writing down the information. The number of characteristics attributed to the letter writer was used as a measure of differentiation; the number of groupings into which Ss were then able to arrange these characteristics was used as a measure of complexity; measures of unity and organization were based on asking Ss to list all of the other characteristics that would change if characteristic X were changed.

"Receivers" demonstrated significantly less differentiation, complexity, unity, and organization than did "transmitters." The nature of the task, it seems, is an important determinant of the structural aspects of cognitive systems. When it is necessary to anticipate admitting all types of information to the system, fewer specifically differentiated attributes are required than when specific information must be transmitted. And the existing attributes had better represent broad, inclusive classes of differentiated attributes, rather than many, clearly distinguishable classes.

In a second, related experiment, Zajonc demonstrated that when Ss deal with incongruent information, the major differences between receivers and transmitters decrease. Transmitters exhibit somewhat less differentiation; receivers, somewhat more differentiation and significantly more unity, when dealing with incongruent, rather than congruent, information. According to Zajonc,

Susceptibility and resistance to change may be thought of in terms of the strength of forces necessary to induce changes in a given cognitive structure. In order to change a highly unified structure a strong force is necessary because the components of the structure depend on one another to a great degree. Thus a change in one attribute should result in changes in other attributes. In order to change a single attribute of a highly unified cognitive structure, a force must be applied which is capable of overcoming the resistance of not only the given attribute, but of all the other attributes on which it depends. To produce a similar change in an un-unified structure, a force is required that is capable of overcoming the resistance of the given component alone.   (1960, p. 163)

In this way interdependence is seen as a barrier against change that is inconsistent with the subject's existing cognitive structure.

Mental ability and retardation. As far back as 1935 Lewin ascribed feeble-mindedness to a relative lack of differentiation and interdependence in cognitive systems (Lewin 1935). Kounin (1941) supported Lewin's contention with experimental demonstrations that perseveration and stereotyped responses in the feeble-minded were reflections of such cognitive variables. [*See* MENTAL RETARDATION *for a discussion somewhat at variance with this view.*]

Gochman (1962; 1966) has extended the systemic approach to show that adaptive and flexible problem-solving behavior represents differentiated perceptual–cognitive systems in children at all levels of IQ and that differentiation is a more reliable predictor of problem-solving ability than IQ scores for fifth-grade and sixth-grade youngsters with low and average IQs (56–113). The results led to the interpretation that the person whose perceptual–cognitive system is poorly differentiated may, in fact, not even be aware of a problem which confronts him or may not be aware of a sufficient number of facets of the problem to permit him to solve it efficiently or of multiple alternatives of solution. These parts of his physical world have not become parts of his perceptual–cognitive system; less of his world has relevance for him.

On the other hand, greater differentiation of the perceptual–cognitive system increases the likelihood that the aspects of the world relevant to coping with problems will become part of the individual's own awareness. To the extent that these aspects exist in his awareness, he will be more likely to benefit from them in his dealings with the world. Accordingly, there is support for the view that mental retardation is a reflection of lack of differentiation, and normal mental ability a reflection of the acquisition of a differentiated perceptual–cognitive system. Furthermore, differentiation of perceptual–cognitive systems appears ultimately to provide a theoretical underpinning for the nontheoretically based IQ.

Evaluation

Certain comparisons are warranted of the three major works discussed. Rokeach's and Harvey, Hunt, and Schroder's broad perspectives on the day-to-day normal functions of the human personality are considerably different from, and strongly contrast with, Zajonc's unique and ingenious experimental manipulation in a laboratory setting, but the value of both approaches is appreciable. The differences between Rokeach and Harvey, Hunt, and Schroder are primarily those of emphasis: Harvey, Hunt, and Schroder are considerably more concerned with development, with the effects of parental training, and with psychopathology. Rokeach is more concerned with underlying similarities in specific diverse attitude contents, with the development of a definitive technique for assessing these structural determinants, and with the application of this technique in logically derived series of studies. Yet, the phenomenon that Rokeach calls a belief or a disbelief is nearly identical to what Harvey, Hunt, and Schroder call a concept; and there is considerable agreement about relevant systemic attributes.

Some substantive differences should be noted, particularly the asymmetry of Rokeach's belief–disbelief system. While it is important to realize that some asymmetry is warranted, i.e., that the disbeliefs are not merely the opposites of the beliefs, the disbelief system is treated as an organized set of subsystems, while the belief system is not treated in this way. It is possible that future research might conceptualize the belief system as a *set of subsystems*. It would make sense within the systemic framework and would be as consistent with observations of real behavior: people do not have one set of beliefs; they have many sets of beliefs, each set focused on one of many different objects or classes of objects, and each of these sets can be considered a separate subsystem, subject to analysis in terms of the same dimensions that subsystems of the disbelief subsystem are. One could then enumerate the number of different things a person believed *in* as one way of measuring differentiation within the belief system; it makes for a considerable difference in behavior whether there is a limited or a wide range of different contents that are held to be valid.

Methodology. While the attempt at integrating a wide variety of phenomena must be appreciated and respected, there is room for some comment on the methods generally employed in systemic approaches.

There is no highly developed, widely validated, generally accepted technique or set of techniques for assessing systemic attributes. The Dogmatism Scale represents a major step toward attaining such an instrument. Harvey and his colleagues have begun to develop the Personal Opinion Scale, as well as a sentence-completion test called This I Believe. These are designed primarily to assess the abstractness or concreteness of conceptual functioning. It remains for future systematic investigations to relate these scales specifically to structural attributes and to devise scales to assess these structural attributes specifically.

One might question the general tendency of researchers to use the existence of seemingly contradictory beliefs within the same belief system as an indication of isolation or compartmentalization. This assumption is often made in cognitive investigations within the systemic framework. The contradiction may not actually exist: in the subject's thinking there may be actual communication, and thus logical connection, between the beliefs. Furthermore, beliefs are maintained with varying degrees of strength and universality. There is considerable difference between beliefs which are implicitly prefaced by "It is universally true in every case and under all circumstances that . . ." and beliefs which are prefaced with "In most cases, it is generally true by and large that . . . ." A belief of this second type can exist in the same system with others that may appear superficially to contradict it, but the contradiction is illusory and the inferred isolation of beliefs is debatable.

An attempt has been made to isolate component systemic variables in a study of school children (Gochman 1962; 1966). Differentiation and interdependence were each measured in several different ways. Differentiation was found to be a homogeneous attribute; interdependence was not. Since the process of integration and ensuing interdependence is presumed to occur later than differentiation, quite probably the fifth graders and sixth graders studied in this research were too young to manifest interdependent perceptual–cognitive sys-

tems. This approach has the further limitation that the perceptual–cognitive systems studied were devoid of content reflecting personal and social experiences.

Zajonc's study has—within its restricted scope—the merit of successfully isolating structural variables and measuring them with considerable ingenuity.

Scott (1963) presents a detailed and comprehensive discussion of methodological problems confronting the systemic approach. He treats both the general problems of assessing cognitive behaviors and problems specific to the assessment of properties such as differentiation and interdependence, with analyses and evaluations of different research strategies employed in each case.

Validity and scope. The merits of a systemic approach are primarily integrative: many different behavioral phenomena can be understood as manifestations of variations in systemic structural variables. Whether the systemic approach has greater validity than other general theoretical orientations is difficult to assess. It has not been subjected to wide-scale experimental tests that contrast it with other theories, but this rarely occurs in contemporary psychology.

Background for the systemic models is found in the pioneer work of Köhler (1929) and Sherif (1936) dealing with perception as a reflection of both internal and external events.

Systemic models have been used with biological phenomena by Weiss (1939, p. 111) and with physical phenomena by Bertalanffy (1950). They have proved very useful in the less tangible area of personality, as Lewin's work exemplified (1926–1933; 1939–1947). Campbell (1958) has applied some gestalt dimensions to social phenomena in an attempt to demonstrate the presence of social systems. Scott (1962) provides an analysis of systemic properties of cognitive and social structures and a discussion of their mutual implications. Newcomb (1961) has demonstrated the effectiveness of a systemic approach in interpersonal relations. Carlson (1956), Rosenberg (1956), and Scott (1958; 1959) have employed the concept of interdependence in their work on attitude structure, consistency, and change. An attitude that is "consistent," i.e., that reflects communication between other cognitive components, is more stable, particularly in the face of nonrational pressures for change.

Tuckman (1966) has used the developmental process outlined by Harvey, Hunt, and Schroder as a basis for the exploring and predicting of probing and self-disclosure behaviors. His study revealed that subjects at the highest level of development, i.e., those with the most complex conceptual systems, tended to be less revealing of information about themselves generally and more apt to probe information from a friend (as opposed to an acquaintance) than were subjects at lower developmental levels.

Cognitive theories of symmetry, balance, and dissonance (e.g., Festinger 1957; Heider 1958) also reflect concern with interdependence in their assertions that there are tendencies for parts of a structure to achieve relative harmony with one another and that the existence of unharmonious components is a source of tension with behavioral implications: the tension must be reduced and harmony restored.

Such a conception of tension and tension reduction provides a way of extending systemic analysis to emotional reactions, one of the most complex and least understood behavioral phenomena. A study by Price, Harburg, and Newcomb (1966) demonstrates how, with some modification, balance theories might provide a model for understanding affective processes.

While the systemic approach at present is particularly relevant to studying beliefs, attitudes, attitude change, intelligence, adaptability, and other cognitive behaviors, its potential applicability to other areas of behavior opens a broad research horizon. The development of future research in systemic analysis is dependent upon isolating component variables, measuring them by a variety of operations, and making specific predictions about their relations to behavior. Essentially, progress will reflect how well psychologists themselves have differentiated and made interdependent their conceptions of the phenomena with which they deal.

DAVID S. GOCHMAN

[*Other relevant material may be found in* ATTITUDES; CONCEPT FORMATION; GESTALT THEORY; PERSONALITY, POLITICAL; THINKING, *article on* COGNITIVE ORGANIZATION AND PROCESSES; VALUES.]

BIBLIOGRAPHY

ALLPORT, GORDON W. 1960 The Open System in Personality Theory. *Journal of Abnormal and Social Psychology* 61:301–310.

BERTALANFFY, LUDWIG VON 1950 The Theory of Open Systems in Physics and Biology. *Science* 111:23–29.

CAMPBELL, DONALD T. 1958 Common Fate, Similarity, and Other Indices of the Status of Aggregates of Persons as Social Entities. *Behavioral Science* 3:14–25.

CARLSON, EARL R. 1956 Attitude Change Through Modification of Attitude Structure. *Journal of Abnormal and Social Psychology* 52:256–261.

FESTINGER, LEON 1957 *A Theory of Cognitive Dissonance.* Evanston, Ill.: Row, Peterson.

GOCHMAN, DAVID S. 1962 System Theory and Adaptability. Ph.D. dissertation, Univ. of Colorado.

GOCHMAN, DAVID S. 1966 A Systemic Approach to Adaptability. *Perceptual and Motor Skills* 23:759–769.

HARVEY, O. J.; HUNT, D. E.; and SCHRODER, H. M. 1961 *Conceptual Systems and Personality Organization.* New York: Wiley.

HEIDER, FRITZ 1958 *The Psychology of Interpersonal Relations.* New York: Wiley.

KOCH, SIGMUND (editor) 1959 *Psychology: A Study of a Science.* Volume 2. New York: McGraw-Hill.

KÖHLER, WOLFGANG 1929 *Gestalt Psychology.* New York: Liveright. → A paperback edition was published in 1947 by New American Library.

KOUNIN, JACOB S. 1941 Experimental Studies of Rigidity. Parts 1–2. *Character and Personality* 9:251–282. → Part 1: "The Measurement of Rigidity in Normal and Feeble-minded Persons." Part 2: "The Explanatory Power of the Concept of Rigidity as Applied to Feeble-mindedness."

LEVY, JACQUES M.; and ROKEACH, MILTON 1960 The Formation of New Perceptual Systems. Pages 257–269 in Milton Rokeach, *The Open and Closed Mind.* New York: Basic Books.

LEWIN, KURT (1926–1933) 1935 *A Dynamic Theory of Personality: Selected Papers.* New York: McGraw-Hill.

LEWIN, KURT (1939–1947) 1963 *Field Theory in Social Science: Selected Theoretical Papers.* Edited by Dorwin Cartwright. London: Tavistock.

MIKOL, BERNARD 1960 The Enjoyment of New Musical Systems. Pages 270–284 in Milton Rokeach, *The Open and Closed Mind.* New York: Basic Books.

MILLER, JAMES G. 1955 Toward a General Theory for the Behavioral Sciences. *American Psychologist* 10:513–531.

NEWCOMB, THEODORE M. 1961 *The Acquaintance Process.* New York: Holt.

PARSONS, TALCOTT 1959 An Approach to Psychological Theory in Terms of the Theory of Action. Volume 3, pages 612–711 in Sigmund Koch (editor), *Psychology: A Study of a Science.* New York: McGraw-Hill.

PRICE, KENDALL O.; HARBURG, ERNEST; and NEWCOMB, THEODORE M. 1966 Psychological Balance in Situations of Negative Interpersonal Attitudes. *Journal of Personality and Social Psychology* 3:265–270.

ROKEACH, MILTON 1960 *The Open and Closed Mind: Investigations Into the Nature of Belief Systems and Personality Systems.* New York: Basic Books.

ROKEACH, MILTON; and VIDULICH, ROBERT N. 1960 The Formation of New Belief Systems: The Roles of Memory and the Capacity to Entertain. Pages 196–214 in Milton Rokeach, *The Open and Closed Mind.* New York: Basic Books.

ROKEACH, MILTON et al. 1960a On Loyalty to and Defection From a Belief System: An Experimental Analogy. Pages 243–256 in Milton Rokeach, *The Open and Closed Mind.* New York: Basic Books.

ROKEACH, MILTON et al. 1960b On Party-line Thinking: An Experimental Analogy. Pages 225–242 in Milton Rokeach, *The Open and Closed Mind.* New York: Basic Books.

ROSENBERG, MILTON J. 1956 Cognitive Structure and Attitudinal Affect. *Journal of Abnormal and Social Psychology* 53:367–372.

SCOTT, WILLIAM A. 1958 Rationality and Non-rationality of International Attitudes. *Journal of Conflict Resolution* 2:7–16.

SCOTT, WILLIAM A. 1959 Cognitive Consistency, Response Reinforcement, and Attitude Change. *Sociometry* 22:219–229.

SCOTT, WILLIAM A. 1962 Cognitive Structure and Social Structure: Some Concepts and Relationships. Volume 1, pages 86–118 in *Decisions, Values and Groups.* Edited by D. Willner. New York: Pergamon.

SCOTT, WILLIAM A. 1963 Conceptualizing and Measuring Structural Properties of Cognition. Pages 266–288 in O. J. Harvey (editor), *Motivation and Social Interaction.* New York: Ronald.

SHERIF, MUZAFER (1936) 1965 *The Psychology of Social Norms.* New York: Octagon.

TUCKMAN, BRUCE W. 1966 Interpersonal Probing and Revealing and Systems of Integrative Complexity. *Journal of Personality and Social Psychology* 3:655–664.

WEISS, PAUL 1939 *Principles of Development.* New York: Holt.

ZAJONC, ROBERT B. 1960 The Process of Cognitive Tuning in Communication. *Journal of Abnormal and Social Psychology* 61:159–167.

T

TABOO
See INCEST; POLLUTION.

TABULAR PRESENTATION

Statistical tables are the most common form of documentation used by the quantitative social scientist, and he should cultivate skill in table construction just as the historian learns to evaluate and cite documents or the geographer learns cartography. Table making is an art (as is table reading), and one should never forget that a table is a form of communication—a way to convey information to a reader. The principles of table making involve matters of taste, convention, typography, aesthetics, and honesty, in addition to the principles of quantification.

It is useful to distinguish between raw data tables and analytic tables, although the line between them is somewhat arbitrary. Raw data tables, for example, in census reports, serve a library function: they arrange and explain the figures in such a way as to make it easier for the user to find what he wants. Here principles of accuracy, completeness, and editorial style are important. The reader can find full treatment of these topics in a number of standard sources (see, for example, U.S. Bureau of the Census 1949). It will be sufficient here to stress the importance of showing raw data whenever this is possible. In a research report, basic data can sometimes be presented in appendix tables, and sometimes they can be presented graphically. Sometimes basic data can be deposited with the American Documentation Institute or a similar organization to facilitate public access. As a last, and obviously least satisfactory, resort, a statement that basic data may be obtained from the author should be appended to a research report.

In analytic tables, on the other hand, the data are organized to support some assertion of the author of the research report. Since numbers do not speak for themselves, analytic tables require careful planning and oblige the table maker to steer a course between art and artifice. Without art, he may fail to convey his evidence to the reader, but technique can also be used to deceive. Thus, the most important rule of table making is this: Arrange the table so the reader may both *see* and *test* the inferences drawn in the text.

Among analytic tables, the most common in many of the social sciences are percentage tables. The percentage is an extremely useful statistic in that it is familiar and meaningful to even relatively naive readers; it is highly analogous to the slightly more technical statistical concept of probability; and it is close enough to the raw data so that they can (if the denominator upon which the percentage is based is given) be reconstructed by a critical reader. Percentage tables thus meet the fundamental criterion: the reader may easily see and test the inferences of the author. Percentage tables, however, suffer from the drawback that they become cluttered and confusing unless they are well constructed. Occasionally a very large percentage table is required to present data that might better be summarized by two or three descriptive coefficients. Accordingly, it is important to make a considered decision between the use of percentage tables and the use of descriptive coefficients. If percentage tables (particularly large and complicated ones) are used, consideration must be given to the main principles and strategies for constructing them.

This article deals primarily with percentage

tables. Most of the principles described, however, are also applicable to other analytic tables, in which the entries may be means, medians, sums of money, descriptive indexes, and so on. In particular, when dealing with these other sorts of tables, as well as when dealing with percentage tables, one should be sensitive to the importance of using clear, meaningful, and consistent units, of including an informative title and indication of the source of the data, and of making some arrangement to indicate the accuracy of the figures.

Most of these principles apply also to the presentation of tables of empirical distributions by absolute or relative frequencies; in these cases, decisions must be made on such matters as the width of class intervals and the location of class marks. [*See* STATISTICAL ANALYSIS, SPECIAL PROBLEMS OF, *article on* GROUPED OBSERVATIONS; STATISTICS, DESCRIPTIVE, *article on* LOCATION AND DISPERSION; *see also* Wallis & Roberts 1956, chapter 6; Yule & Kendall [1911] 1950, chapter 4.]

Basic principles

The simplest percentage table is one that presents the distribution of answers to a single question or observations on a single variable. Table 1 is a typical, although hypothetical, example that serves to illustrate a number of basic principles.

Table 1 — Attitudes toward job*

	Per cent
I like it very much	58%
I like it somewhat	40
I dislike it	2
	100%
Number of respondents (N) =	2,834
No answer =	8
Not applicable (housewife or unemployed) =	314
Total	3,156

* Hypothetical responses to the question "In general, how do you feel about your job?"

Very few people read a research report word by word from beginning to end. Many are interested in a particular chapter or sections; others are looking for one or two specific tables to answer some limited questions. Since it is a nuisance for these readers to have to read many pages of text in order to understand a table, each table presented should provide sufficient information to be meaningful by itself. This information should, of course, include the source or sources of the data presented in the table, if they originate elsewhere than in the present research.

Headings and footnotes. A table should usually have both a title (caption) and a number; the latter should consistently be used for reference, and in a lengthy monograph, it is convenient to articulate it with the chapter number (for example, Table 3.2 refers to the second table in chapter 3) or even with the page (for example, Table 277a refers to the first table on page 277).

The main title should be short and concrete; subtitles or footnotes should indicate clearly what the table describes. Table 1, for example, gives the wording of the question that was asked. If the data in a table are based upon an index, it should be described, usually in a footnote. Well-known indexes or scales need only be described by their names—for example, "Scores on the Stanford–Binet Intelligence Test, Form B."

If the same items appear in a series of tables, the full information need not be given each time, although if an item reappears after a long gap, there should be a reference to the table containing the full explanation.

Some items, like the dichotomy male–female, are virtually unambiguous. Most questions, however, do have variant forms. Age may be reported to the last birthday or the next birthday, and educational attainment may be in terms of degrees acquired, years of schooling completed, and so on.

Percentages. The figures that appear in percentage tables are of two kinds: the percentages themselves and certain absolute numbers indicating frequencies (N's). It is generally crucial to include both kinds of figures; it is also crucial to avoid confusion between the two. Many of the problems in interpreting percentage tables stem from a failure of the author to make this distinction clear. The following practices should be followed in presenting percentages in tables.

Per cent signs. A per cent sign (%) should be placed after the first percentage in a column of percentages that adds to 100 per cent, as shown in Table 1. This is literally redundant, since the column is labeled "per cent," but in this situation redundancy serves the purpose of reminding the reader that he is examining percentages.

Totals. If the total of the percentages in an additive column is not exactly 100 per cent because of rounding, it is good practice to point this out in a footnote. (If the rounding produces a deviation of more than 1 per cent from 100, the arithmetic should be rechecked. By the same token, the last percentage in a column should be obtained by calculation rather than by subtraction; otherwise, a valuable check on the calculations will be destroyed.)

Multiple responses. If a percentage table presents responses to a question to which multiple responses are permitted (for example, "What brands of coffee did you purchase in the past year?"), the percentages should not be presented as if they were additive. The frequently found notation that "percentages add to more than 100 per cent because of multiple answers" is misleading. Rather, each percentage is better treated as half a dichotomous response (for example, 40 per cent of the sample purchased a particular brand of coffee in the past year, and 60 per cent did not). If there are only a few possible responses, the percentages of respondents falling in the various patterns of response may be of interest.

Decimals. The number of decimals to retain in presenting percentages (should 38 per cent, 37.8 per cent, or 37.8342 per cent be reported?) must be determined after careful thought. The case for the use of several decimals is based upon the following arguments: (1) a reader who wants to recalculate the data himself can be more accurate if more decimals are given, and (2) one's own check will be more precise. The case against the use of several decimals is that they often give a spurious air of precision (69.231 per cent of 13 cases means simply nine cases), and that they usually add little information, since only in extraordinarily large samples do differences of 1 per cent or less have any meaning. The policy for retaining decimals should, in most cases, remain the same for all of the entries within an individual table, and usually the same within an entire report, except that relatively raw data tables in an appendix are usually more useful if the data are given to more decimals than they are in analytic tables in the body of the report.

Rounding. Rounding should be to the nearest number. If one decimal place is to be retained, and the original calculation is 76.42 per cent, 76.4 per cent should be used in the table; if the original calculation is 76.48 per cent, 76.5 per cent should be reported. If the original calculation is 76.45000 . . . per cent, an arbitrary convention must be established to guide the rounding. The usual convention is to always round to the *even* possibility. That is, 76.45000 . . . per cent becomes 76.4 per cent, and 76.750000 . . . per cent becomes 76.8 per cent. (See Croxton, Cowden & Klein [1939] 1967, for a discussion of rounding procedures.)

In some investigations, it is desirable to distinguish between a true zero (no observations or responses in a category) and a per cent rounded down to zero (for example, if only one decimal place is being retained, 0.04 per cent will be presented as 0.0 per cent). One convention is to use 0.0e if a true (e = exact) zero is intended. In other cases, the difference may not be important, especially if sampling fluctuation could easily change a true zero to some small nonzero per cent.

Sampling variability. If the data reported in a table are derived from a probability sample, it is usually very desirable to indicate the extent of sampling variability. Sometimes this is done by adding an indication of standard deviation (for example, 76.5 ± 3.2), but this tends to clutter tables and has the danger of creating misunderstandings. (Is 3.2 the estimated standard deviation, the half length of a 95 per cent confidence interval, or what?) A device favored by the U.S. Bureau of the Census is to give approximate confidence interval widths for per cents in various brackets in a footnote or in a small auxiliary table. (In a particular case, for example, such a footnote might indicate that if a per cent lies between 40 and 60, its 95 per cent confidence interval half width is about 5.) If the tables come from a sample that is not based upon probability sampling, the basic problem of sampling fluctuation becomes much more difficult [see SAMPLE SURVEYS, *article on* NONPROBABILITY SAMPLING]. Errors other than sampling ones are often very important but are typically discussed in the text rather than in a table [see ERRORS, *article on* NONSAMPLING ERRORS]. Of course, if there exists a bias whose magnitude might seriously affect a table's interpretation, it is good practice to refer to the relevant text discussion in a footnote to the table.

Frequencies. The absolute frequencies that appear in a percentage table are of three kinds: (1) the total number of individuals or cases in the study, (2) the total number of individuals or cases upon which percentages are based (often called N, or base N), and (3) the cases that are excluded from the percentaging for one reason or another.

Some important reasons for excluding cases are inapplicability (for example, in Table 1, an unemployed person cannot have an opinion about his present employment), the refusal of the respondent to answer the question (or the failure of the interviewer to ask or to record it), the inability of the interviewer to locate the respondent (the persistent not-at-homes), and the inconsistency of a response. Cases of this type are often thrown together into a single No Answer or Not Applicable category, but for some purposes (for example, in considering the magnitudes of possible biases) it is important to separate the reasons. The following practices are recommended in reporting Totals, N's, No Answers, and Not Applicables.

Totals. Unless all cases are accounted for in every table in a series, the total number of cases in the study should be reported in every table. This enables the reader to detect (and perhaps the analyst to avoid) the all-too-common situation in which a result that appears to apply to the entire population studied is really based upon a small fraction of the total. It also forces the analyst to maintain a careful accounting of his cases.

N's or base N's. The number of cases upon which percentages are based should also appear in every table. This is necessary so that the reader may evaluate the reliability of the percentages and, if he desires, reconstruct the original frequencies from the percentages that are presented.

Discrepancies beween Totals and N's. Any discrepancies between Totals and N's should be accounted for by specifying the number of No Answer and Not Applicable cases, as at the bottom of Table 1. It is poor practice to obtain No Answer figures by subtracting the N from the Total, since this destroys a practical check upon the calculations.

The percentaging of No Answers. Some survey analysts include No Answers as a category to be percentaged. This seems inadvisable, since it introduces a logically separate dimension into the classification. The proportion of No Answers depends more strongly on the research procedure than it does on the population being studied. It should be noted that in opinion research the category No Opinion is not the same as No Answer. Respondents who have neither a positive nor a negative opinion on an issue should usually be included in a category to be percentaged, since, for example, differences over time or between subgroups in the proportion of people with no opinion on an issue constitute substantive findings. [*For a discussion of the dangers of a large number of No Opinions and of the effects of No Answers, see* ERRORS, *article on* NON-SAMPLING ERRORS.]

Although few analysts follow the convention, in the analysis of sample surveys, a case can be made for including in the No Answer category respondents who were selected for the sample but never interviewed because of refusals, absences from home, and the like. This practice would provide a fairer picture of the coverage of the data than the standard procedure, which is to describe the completed interviews as the Total and to count as No Answers only instances of skipped questions, illegible answers, refusals to answer a question, and so forth.

The reporting of frequencies. As a general rule it is inadvisable to present the absolute frequencies

Table 2 — Usually wrong!

Category	Per cent	N
High	65%	49
Medium	11	8
Low	24	18
Total	100%	75

Table 3 — Right!

Category	Per cent
High	65%
Medium	11
Low	24
Total	100%

$N = 75$

for the various categories being percentaged unless there is some compelling reason to do so (for example, if the frequencies are the basic data for a statistical test that will be discussed). In general, frequencies should be reported only if they represent 100 per cent (tables 2 and 3).

There are two reasons for preferring Table 3 over Table 2. First, an absolute frequency that is not presented cannot be confused with a percentage (for example, it is not difficult to read 49 per cent instead of 65 per cent for the top line of Table 2, and the confusion is even more likely to arise if the table is more complicated). Second, no additional information is provided by the individual N's, since the interested reader can calculate the individual N's if he is given the base N and the percentages.

Two-variable tables

Two-variable tables present a number of choices for arrangement and layout that do not appear in one-variable tables; Table 4 is a typical example. The following practices are suggested for constructing tables of this type.

Table 4 — Age and cumulative grade-point averages*

Cumulative grade-point average (grouped)	AGE	
	20 or under	Over 20
High	21%	17%
Medium	42	33
Low	37	50
Totals	100%	100%

$N = 2,705 + 3,110 = 5,815$

No answer on:	
Grades only	75
Age only	3
Both	2
	80
Total	5,895

* Hypothetical data.

Arrangement and layout. There is no consistent opinion on the question of whether percentages should run down the columns (as in Table 4) or across the rows. The former is generally preferable, both because it is consistent with the normal pattern of columns of additive figures and because it places the independent variable (the so-called "causal" variable) at the head of the table and the dependent variable (the variable the analyst is seeking to explain) at the side of the table. (See Zeisel [1947] 1957, pp. 24–41, for a discussion of this preference.)

Which way to percentage. The construction of a two-variable table requires a decision as to which way the percentages are to be computed. For example, in constructing a table from the data used in constructing Table 4, should the table present the distribution of grade scores by age (as in Table 4), or the distribution by age of students in the various grade-point groups, or the distribution of the entire sample by the six age by grade-point groups?

A number of considerations enter into the decision. If, for example, the two samples of students (of differing ages) were drawn according to separate sampling plans, that is, if they were considered as separate populations for sampling purposes, then ordinarily one would compute percentages separately for each age group.

Under the assumption that this sampling issue does not arise, the choice of method of presentation depends on which is most useful for the purposes of the analysis. If the analyst is primarily concerned with the question of how grade-point averages differ between younger and older students, then the method used in Table 4 is most appropriate. If, on the other hand, interest is centered on the age distributions of separate grade-point groups (as might be the case, for example, if the age composition of projected remedial classes is of interest), then percentages should be computed the other way.

Thus no general rule can be given, and indeed it is often desirable to compute the percentages both ways. (A detailed discussion of the issue is given in Zeisel [1947] 1957, pp. 24–41.) Consistency within a report is often a consideration. For example, in analysis of political party preferences, it might be better always to use "per cent Democratic," that is, to let party preference always be the dependent variable, rather than to shift back and forth.

Ordering and placing categories. If the independent variable has no intrinsic order among its categories, the results will typically be clearer if

Table 5 — Early consideration of graduate study, by field

Field of graduate study	Percentage of graduate students reporting having considered graduate study in field before junior year in college	N*
Geology	77%	107
Chemistry	75	317
Physics	74	289
Botany	61	53
English	58	273
History	47	305
Clinical psychology	41	153
Sociology	26	85
Total N		1,582

* NA not presented here, because data are part of a larger tabulation in the original.

Source: National Opinion Research Center 1962, p. 222.

the entries are arranged according to increasing or decreasing values of the dependent variable. Table 5 demonstrates this point; an alternate plan would be to group the fields of study by category (physical sciences, social sciences, humanities) and then order the fields within categories by the frequency of the percentages reporting the dependent variable. Although alphabetical ordering is sometimes desirable, it is the least efficient method in a table containing as few groups as Table 5.

Dichotomous dependent variables. When a dependent variable is dichotomous, as in Table 5, a decision has to be made as to whether to present both percentages. The style of Table 5 is generally preferable; the percentage of students who reported that they had *not* considered graduate study in the field is not presented, on the grounds that it is easily computable by the reader through subtraction, and its inclusion would have cluttered the table with unnecessary information. As a general rule, a table should contain as few numbers as possible without excluding vital information.

Per cent signs. It is important that the use of per cent signs in tables be consistent throughout a report. Conventions differ widely, but it is recommended that if a two-variable table reports only one half a dichotomy, a per cent sign should be placed after each percentage if there are only a few (as in Table 6) or after the first percentage in the column if there are many (as in Table 5). If there are many columns or rows, it may be best to eliminate per cent signs altogether, provided that the caption of the table or the headings on the columns or rows indicate clearly that the numbers in the table are percentages. An important consideration is whether or not actual numbers of cases (or amounts such as dollars) should also appear in the table; if they do, per cent signs serve an

Table 6 — Percentage of students expecting professional employment after graduation, by field of study*

Field of study	Percentage expecting employment	N
Chemistry	45%	650
English	46%	375
Astrophysics	100%	1

* Hypothetical data.

important role in preventing confusion. In any event, every total percentage should have a per cent sign.

Reporting N's. A two-variable table distributed by one variable contains more than a single base N (as in Table 6), and it may contain a large number of N's (as in Table 5). It is essential that an N be presented for each row or column of additive percentages; in extremely complex tables, these may be provided in footnotes.

A special problem arises if some of the percentages in a table are based upon a large number of cases while one or more are based upon very few. Table 6 illustrates the problem.

The "100 per cent" figure for astrophysics in Table 6 is unreliable because it is based on only one case, and the unwary reader who does not read the N's upon which percentages are based may mistakenly conclude that a strong difference has been found. One is tempted to protect the reader against this sort of error by omitting categories for which the data are unreliable. If information on one or more categories is excluded from a table, however, the reader is unable to regroup the results and make his own calculations. Furthermore, some readers with a strong interest in a particular category would prefer that any available data be presented, on the grounds that some information is preferable to none at all.

How should this problem be handled? A frequent procedure is to select a value of N below which results are considered unreliable. The value selected is, of course, arbitrary: 10 seems to be the lowest that is ever used, and 20 is much more common. There is one good argument for using at least 20; this is the lowest value at which a single case would make no more than a 5 per cent difference. Beyond selecting a value of 20 or more, three styles of presentation are possible: (1) percentages based upon lower values of N can be reported but placed in brackets (with a footnote explaining their meaning); (2) the N can be reported but the percentage replaced by a dash (again with an explanatory footnote); and (3) procedure (2) can be followed, but in addition to a dash

signifying an unreliable percentage, the actual number of cases that would have been the numerator of the percentage can be given adjacent to the N, properly labeled. Each style has advantages and disadvantages; the use of brackets is probably the best compromise. (Note that if the data are from a probability sample, and if confidence intervals are reported for each percentage, the great width of the confidence interval when N is small serves as a warning of this problem.)

Reporting No Answers. In a cross tabulation of two variables there are three types of No Answers to consider: (1) No Answers on the dependent variable, (2) No Answers on the independent variable, and (3) No Answers on both variables. As a check on calculations, it is necessary to *count* all three types to determine that the totals for each variable are correct. Whether to *report* the No Answers separately or collectively is a matter of individual taste. Two rules of thumb are (1) a total of 10 per cent or more of No Answers of all types is large enough to raise questions in the mind of a critical reader, and (2) No Answers should often be reported separately if one variable contributes a disproportionate share of the total. Table 4 illustrates how No Answers may be reported separately; it also shows that while the total proportion of No Answers is less than 10 per cent, the dependent variable (grade-point average) is the major contributor.

Three-variable tables

Many analyses of survey data require the introduction of a second independent variable, usually an "intervening" variable that specifies or elaborates the relationship between the independent and the dependent variable. Table 7 is a typical example.

If Table 7 is read across the rows, it shows the relationship between combat experience and anxiety at any particular educational level; if it is read

Table 7 — Percentage of soldiers with critical scores on the anxiety index, by educational level and combat experience*

EDUCATIONAL ATTAINMENT	COMBAT EXPERIENCE		
	None	Under fire	Actual combat
Grade school or less	40% (81)	47% (111)	57% (213)
Attended high school	34% (152)	42% (178)	47% (351)
High school graduate	20% (246)	29% (355)	36% (500)

N = 2,187

* Numbers in parentheses are base N's for the percentages.

Source: Adapted from Stouffer et al. 1949, p. 447.

down the columns, it shows the relationship between educational level and anxiety at any particular level of combat experience. (One could also look at the row and column totals—these are discussed below.) Since a frequent problem in survey research is to ascertain the relative influence of traits (educational achievement) and exposure to experience (combat), tables having the format of Table 7 are frequently necessary. (See the tables in Kendall & Lazarsfeld 1950; Berelson et al. 1954; Sills 1957; Hyman 1955; Stouffer [1935–1960] 1962; Lazarsfeld & Thielens 1958; Davis 1964.)

Dichotomizing the dependent variable. The most important principle underlying the construction of tables with two or more independent variables is that in spite of the fact that these tables are mathematically three-, four-, or five-dimensional, they must somehow be presented on two-dimensional paper. (The classic presentation of this idea is in Zeisel [1947] 1957, pp. 67–90.) This can always be done clearly, provided that one of the variables is dependent and that it can be expressed as a dichotomy.

Many variables used in survey research are natural dichotomies, such as voted–did not vote and employed–not employed. Ordered classes, such as low–medium–high, level of education, and military rank can always be dichotomized by combining categories. Items that consist of true qualitative (unordered) categories (such as religious affiliation, field of study, ethnic origin) present difficult problems that are discussed below.

When categories are combined, considerable information is necessarily lost. The analyst who constructs a table is thus placed in a dilemma. If he does not dichotomize the dependent variable, the table may become so complicated that the reader cannot follow it; if he does dichotomize it, the reader may be unable to determine the full relationship between the independent and the dependent variables. Indeed, thoughtless dichotomization may conceal important nonmonotonic relationships—more precisely known as nonisotropic relationships (see Yule & Kendall [1911] 1958, pp. 57–59).

There is no clear-cut resolution of the problem of dichotomization, although a few general guidelines can be set down. First, the analyst should inspect the raw data tables; if he is satisfied that the relationship is *essentially* monotonic, the percentage table should present the dependent variable as a dichotomy. Second, if a more complex form of relationship is found, the data are probably better presented by a graph or by a coefficient of some kind. Third, in cases of doubt, a reference should be made to the raw data tables in the appendix,

so that the reader may draw his own conclusions about the wisdom of the dichotomization. The analyst should remember, however, that rather large samples are required to detect complex relationships reliably and that all the little "jiggles and bounces" in the data are not grounds for excitement.

Ordered classes should be dichotomized as closely as possible to the median (the cutting point that splits the sample into two groups of equal size). This rule is useful, but it has exceptions. For example, if a study concerns the political participation of young people, the age variable should probably be dichotomized at age 21 (or whatever is the local legal age for voting), even if it is not the median, because it provides a particularly meaningful cutting point. Cutting points that leave only a handful of cases in one group should be avoided (for example, it would usually be foolish to dichotomize economic status into "millionaires" and "all others").

Arrangement and symbols. In presenting three-variable tables, the data should be arranged so that the most important comparisons are those between adjacent numbers, because such comparisons are easier for the reader to make than are comparisons between nonadjacent numbers (see the first part of Table 8). Thus, in planning a complex percentage table, it is often useful to place the base N's in parentheses, below and to the right of the percentages. Table 8 presents the preferred and two less preferable ways of presenting base N's. In the second example in Table 8, the base N (745) intervenes between the two comparisons in the first column; in the third example it intervenes between the two comparisons in the first row; in the first example, neither comparison is obstructed. Furthermore, the reader interested in examining the raw numbers can, if the first example is followed, compute the correlation between the two independent variables by comparing bases that are adjacent to each other in rows and columns. For example, the base N's given in Table 7 make it possible to com-

Table 8 — Examples of preferred and nonpreferred methods of displaying base N's

Preferred	56%		88%	
		(745)		(635)
	17%		54%	
		(849)		(586)
Not preferred	56%		88%	
	(745)		(635)	
	17%		54%	
	(849)		(586)	
Not preferred	56% (745)		88% (635)	
	17% (849)		54% (586)	

pute the raw-data (marginal) association between educational level and combat experience.

In general, one independent variable should be displayed in the columns and the other in the rows (see Table 7). This makes for fewer intervening numbers than an all-column or all-row arrangement.

In three-variable tables, it is recommended that a per cent sign be placed adjacent to every percentage in the table. If no per cent signs are used, confusion with the base N's can result; if only the top row of percentages has per cent signs, the non-additive nature of the percentages may not be apparent.

The use of separate tables.   Table 7 presents two partial relationships (between education and anxiety, controlling for combat experience; and between combat experience and anxiety, controlling for education). It does not, however, present the zero-order (two-variable) relationships between the independent and the dependent variables. It is tempting to include these by adding a Totals column giving anxiety percentages by educational level, regardless of combat experience, and a Totals row giving anxiety percentages by amount of combat experience, regardless of educational attainment.

The resulting table would be compact, but it would have drawbacks. First, it would present two mathematically distinct statistical relationships (zero-order and partial relationships) without making a clear visual distinction between them. Second, the natural way of reporting a research finding is to begin with zero-order relationships and then discuss the partials. If Total columns and rows are included, the reader is, in effect, asked to read them while ignoring the partials in the interior of the table.

For these reasons it is generally preferable to present a series of discrete tables. In the present instance, the following sequence is suggested:

Table a—Education and anxiety; Table b—Combat experience and anxiety; Table c—Education and combat experience; Table d—Table 7. This procedure would be space-consuming, but each table would tell a simple and distinct story. In fact, if this sequence is used, the text almost writes itself:

There is an association between education and anxiety (Table a). But combat experience is also associated with anxiety (Table b), and the less-educated soldiers are a little more likely to have been in actual combat (Table c). However, the educational difference is not a spurious effect of differentials in combat, for when combat experience is controlled, the educational difference remains (Table 7).

In practice, one would provide a fuller description of the tables, explaining the variables and the relationships in more detail, but these four tables provide the basic skeleton for a verbal description of the findings.

It should be remembered that even highly educated people are often poor readers of tables. Accordingly, important tables should be inserted in the text, not at the end of a report or in an appendix; furthermore, only essential tables should appear at all.

Dependent variables that cannot be dichotomized.   There remains the problem of how to present in tabular form dependent variables that are true trichotomies, as well as other qualitative classifications that cannot reasonably be dichotomized. If the style of the dichotomy table (for example, Table 8) is followed, the result would be in the form of Table 9, in which major field of study is the dependent variable.

A table format such as that of Table 9 means that column comparisons have a large number of "intervening" figures, and if one is concerned with the effect of variable A as well as of variable B, the table is hard to read. Although more space is consumed, it is often better to break the table down

Table 9 — Three-variable table with a trichotomized dependent variable

		INDEPENDENT VARIABLE B			
		Yes		No	
	Yes	Natural sciences	%	Natural sciences	%
		Social sciences	%	Social sciences	%
		Humanities	%	Humanities	%
			100%		100%
INDEPENDENT VARIABLE A			(N)		(N)
	No	Natural sciences	%	Natural sciences	%
		Social sciences	%	Social sciences	%
		Humanities	%	Humanities	%
			100%		100%
			(N)		(N)

Table 10 — Showing a trichotomized dependent variable with subtables

		PERCENTAGE MAJORING IN THE NATURAL SCIENCES		PERCENTAGE MAJORING IN THE SOCIAL SCIENCES		PERCENTAGE MAJORING IN THE HUMANITIES	
		Independent variable B		Independent variable B		Independent variable B	
		Yes	No	Yes	No	Yes	No
	Yes	%	%	%	%	%	%
		(N)	(N)	(N)	(N)	(N)	(N)
Independent variable A							
	No	%	%	%	%	%	%
		(N)	(N)	(N)	(N)	(N)	(N)

into subtables, one for each category of the dependent variables, particularly if the nature of the difference varies between the categories of the dependent variable (for example, social science majors vary with *A*, natural science majors vary with *B*, and humanities majors vary with neither). Table 10 shows the format of a table of this kind.

Finally, a trichotomized dependent variable can be presented in two dimensions, without collapsing, by the use of triangular coordinate graph paper (see Coleman 1961, p. 29; Davis 1964, especially pp. 95–97). This is a very useful procedure, but it must be carefully explained to readers. Other graphical devices have been suggested; for example, see Anderson 1957.

Four-or-more variable tables

If there are four, five, or six independent variables in one table, no new problems arise, but the old ones become intensified. Such tables have more headings, and they usually have smaller case bases and greater problems of dichotomization.

Reading a four-variable table is a difficult task. To assist the reader, a number of subtables should

be used (as in Table 10). Also, the analyst must be sure to explain the table and the findings it presents very carefully in the text. The technique of "talking through" a table should be employed, as in this example (referring to Table 11):

Beginning in the upper left-hand cell of the table, observe the entry 58 per cent, which is the percentage employed among fathers under 27 years of age attending private schools. Following across that row, the percentages increase from 58 to 69. A similar trend is found in each row, which means that when family role and type of school attended are held constant, the likelihood of employment increases with age. Turning now to the effect of family role. . . .

Note that the above hypothetical text matter is not an interpretation of the results but, rather, a translation of them from percentages into words. Such a description may justifiably run to several hundred words. (An extreme example is Davis 1964, which consists entirely of the discussion of a single table that cross tabulates nine variables.)

Focusing on one independent variable. One variable among the three or more independent variables is often singled out for attention. Given the

Table 11 — Percentage of students employed full-time, by age, family role, and type of school*

			AGE	
			Under 27	27 or older
		Private school	58%	69%
			(40)	(226)
	Father			
		Other school	12%	21%
			(104)	(321)
FAMILY ROLE				
		Private school	20%	35%
			(340)	(315)
	Other			
		Other school	4%	9%
			(889)	(544)

Number of respondents (N) = 2,779
No answer = 63
Total = 2,842

* Numbers in parentheses are base N's for the percentages.

Source: Adapted from National Opinion Research Center 1962, p. 222.

fact that variables *A*, *B*, and *C* are all correlated with variable *D*, the real interest may be in whether *C* is still correlated with *D* when *A* and *B* are held constant rather than in the independent effects of *A* and *B*. Accordingly, if the analyst wants to focus attention on one of the independent variables, he should present it alone in the columns of the table and use the rows for combinations of the other variables, as in Table 11.

Each row in Table 11 shows an age contrast, controlling for family role and type of school. In order to examine other effects, the reader must shift his eyes between the columns and rows.

The percentage-difference table. An extension of the above presentational strategy is the *percentage difference table*, which presents the effects of a given variable for various combinations of control variables. This table consists of rows and columns laid out according to the control variables, with the entries consisting of the percentage difference in the dependent variable produced by the test variable. Table 12 is an example.

Table 12 — Percentage differences in full-time employment for the age dichotomy in Table 11*

| | | TYPE OF SCHOOL | |
		Private	Other
FAMILY ROLE	Father	+11%	+9%
	Other	+15%	+5%

* Percentage employed among those students who are 27 or older minus the percentage employed among those under 27.

Table 12 demonstrates that age has a positive effect on each of the four control categories. In practice, one would probably not present a percentage difference in a situation where there are so few control categories, but when there are many categories, a difference table can make clear what otherwise appears to be an obscure pattern. In particular, a difference table can reveal complex patterns of interactions. Table 13 is a hypothetical example.

Table 13 summarizes the following complex relationship: "Cramming the night before an examination is associated with better final grades only among the students with high IQs who had done fairly well at midterm; the relationship is the same for men and women." A complicated pattern such as this might well have been lost if a standard five-variable table format had been used.

The passive role played by sex in Table 13 raises the question of whether or not data should be presented when there are neither effects nor interactions. In general the answer is No, since these no-effect variables add to the complexity of multivariable tables without adding to their content. In particular, one should avoid the not uncommon practice of maintaining a variable throughout a report simply because it was introduced at an early stage in the analysis and there is reluctance to take the time to recalculate the data. This will avoid the fallacy of pseudo rigor, a tendency to make research appear more meticulous than it is by controlling for irrelevant variables. Nevertheless, there are situations when it is interesting and important to present negative results in tabular form. By presenting such results, the analyst may answer questions that may be in the reader's mind and may prevent others from making unnecessary calculations. In the case of Table 13, for example, it might be argued that there is substantial evidence from other research about sex differences in academic achievement and, accordingly, that it is worthwhile to show that this finding holds for both men and women.

Two important limitations of percentage-difference tables stem from the inherent properties of percentages. First, these tables are appropriate only if both the dependent variable and the independent variable are dichotomized (the range in percentages of the dependent variable produced by variation of the independent variable over multiple levels is not an acceptable measure). Second, the absolute values of the difference must be interpreted with extreme care. When the two percentages are either very large or very small, a slight difference between them may represent as strong an effect as a larger difference when they both are of medium size. Thus, for example, if one calculates the coefficient of association Q for the data in Table 12, one finds that the Q value associated

Table 13 — Percentage differences between crammers and moviegoers in final course grades*

| | | MIDTERM GRADES | | | | | |
| | | High | | Medium | | Low | |
		Men	Women	Men	Women	Men	Women
IQ	High	+19%	+21%	+20%	+18%	0%	0%
	Medium	+16%	+15%	+19%	+20%	−1%	+1%
	Low	−2%	−1%	0%	+1%	+1%	−1%

* Hypothetical data showing percentage receiving high grades among those who crammed the night before the examination minus the percentage among those who went to the movies.

Table 14 — Percentage of respondents scored positively on a dependent variable, by age, sex, and education*

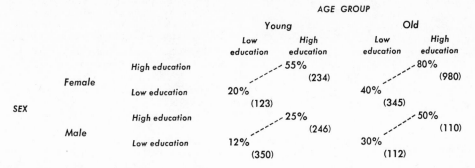

* Numbers in parentheses are base N's for the percentages.

Source: Personal communication from Peter Rossi.

with the 5 per cent in the lower right-hand corner ($Q = .40$) is a little higher than for the 15 per cent in the lower left-hand corner ($Q = .36$). The reason for this difference is that the former is based on two small percentages (9 per cent and 4 per cent), while the latter is based on moderate percentages (35 per cent and 20 per cent). If the size of the effects is important, it is better to use other coefficients of association than the percentage difference. [*See* STATISTICS, DESCRIPTIVE, *article on* ASSOCIATION.]

Comparisons between independent variables. A different situation obtains when the purpose of a table is to show that each of several independent variables makes a difference in the dependent variable, a situation in survey analysis that is somewhat akin to multiple correlation.

The Rossi stratagem. Given the limitations of geometry, as more comparisons are desired, it becomes increasingly difficult to present all the relevant comparisons adjacent to each other. Peter H. Rossi has developed a way to do this for three independent variables (Table 14). The table has an unorthodox appearance, but it has several advantages over any other form of presentation. First, each vertical comparison involves a sex difference, controlling for the other two variables. Second, each horizontal comparison involves an age difference, controlling for the other two variables. Third, each diagonal comparison (represented by broken lines) involves an educational difference, controlling for the other two variables. Fourth, there are no intervening percentages between any two percentages that are to be compared.

Weaker effects "inside" stronger ones. When there are four or more independent variables, even the stratagem developed by Rossi and illustrated in Table 14 breaks down. In such instances, it is impossible to place percentages that are to be compared adjacent to each other. When the variables differ considerably and consistently in their per-

centage effects, the weaker effects should be placed "inside" the stronger effects.

An example using hypothetical data will make the idea clear. Consider four dichotomous independent variables, A, B, C, and D, that produce the following consistent percentage differences in dependent variable E:

$$A = 5\% \; ; B = 5\% \; ; C = 25\% \; ; D = 25\% \; .$$

It is desired to construct a table showing the simultaneous effects of the four independent variables upon the dependent variable, E. Following the rule of placing the weaker effects "inside" the stronger effects, A and C are paired, as are B and D. The table is then designed so that variable A is nearer the cell entries than variable C, and variable B is "inside" variable D (Table 15, where $\bar{A}$, for example, means "not A.")

Table 15 — Percentage of respondents scored positively on variable E, by variables A, B, C, and D*

		$\bar{C}$		C	
		$\bar{A}$	A	$\bar{A}$	A
D	B	30%	35%	55%	60%
		(N)	(N)	(N)	(N)
	$\bar{B}$	25%	30%	50%	55%
		(N)	(N)	(N)	(N)
$\bar{D}$	B	5%	10%	30%	35%
		(N)	(N)	(N)	(N)
	$\bar{B}$	0%	5%	25%	30%
		(N)	(N)	(N)	(N)

* Hypothetical data.

The meaning of Table 15 is clear at a glance. The percentages increase steadily up each column and across each row. Therefore, it is apparent that each independent variable adds to the percentage scoring positively on dependent variable, E. Suppose, however, that the rule for the placing of variables was violated, and the weaker effects were

Table 16 — Percentage of respondents scored positively on variable E, by variables A, B, C, and D*

		$\bar{A}$		A	
		$\bar{C}$	C	$\bar{C}$	C
B	D	30% (N)	55% (N)	35% (N)	60% (N)
	$\bar{D}$	5% (N)	30% (N)	10% (N)	35% (N)
$\bar{B}$	D	25% (N)	50% (N)	30% (N)	55% (N)
	$\bar{D}$	0% (N)	25% (N)	5% (N)	30% (N)

* Hypothetical data.

placed "outside" and the stronger effects "inside" (Table 16).

Tables 15 and 16 present identical information, but the meaning of the data as they are displayed in Table 16 is not at all clear at a glance. The reader must take the time to make his own specific percentage comparisons if he wishes to verify the statements made in the text of the report.

With actual data the percentage effects are seldom as consistent as those in Table 15, and such a perfect progression cannot always be displayed. However, if there are four or more variables whose independent effects are to be shown, it is always worth the time to seek the most lucid arrangement of the variables. Note that even in Table 11 the control variables are displayed so that there is a smooth progression up and down the columns, a style that adds considerably to ease of comprehension.

There is no method of tabular presentation that will make small differences any larger or trivial findings of substantive importance. Nevertheless, the presentation of percentage data in a form that will enable the reader to read them and test them is an important aspect of communicating the findings of survey research.

JAMES A. DAVIS AND ANN M. JACOBS

[See also GRAPHIC PRESENTATION.]

BIBLIOGRAPHY

AMERICAN PSYCHOLOGICAL ASSOCIATION (1952) 1957 *Publication Manual of the American Psychological Association.* Rev. ed. Washington: The Association. → A style manual giving instructions chiefly for the journals of the American Psychological Association, but containing much generally useful material. Tabular presentation is described on pages 30–40.

ANDERSON, EDGAR 1957 A Semigraphical Method for the Analysis of Complex Problems. National Academy of Sciences *Proceedings* 43:923–927.

BERELSON, BERNARD; LAZARSFELD, PAUL F.; and McPHEE, WILLIAM N. 1954 *Voting: A Study of Opinion Formation in a Presidential Campaign.* Univ. of Chicago Press.

CHAUNDY, THEODOR W.; BARRETT, P. R.; and BATEY, CHARLES 1954 *The Printing of Mathematics: Aids for Authors and Editors and Rules for Compositors and Readers at the University Press.* Oxford Univ. Press. → Described by the authors as the successor to G. H. Hardy's pamphlet, *Notes on the Preparation of Mathematical Papers,* published in 1932. Deals chiefly with the setting of equations; pages 68–69 treat tables. Good exposition of mechanics of typesetting for statistical and technical authors.

CHICAGO, UNIVERSITY OF, PRESS (1906) 1956 *A Manual of Style.* 11th ed. Univ. of Chicago Press. → A standard manual of typographic and editorial practice. The chapter on tables, pages 158–172, gives a variety of examples from scholarly disciplines.

COLEMAN, JAMES S. 1961 *The Adolescent Society: The Social Life of the Teenager and Its Impact on Education.* New York: Free Press. → See especially pages 29 ff. for examples of trichotomous data laid out on triangular coordinate graph paper.

CROXTON, FREDERICK E.; COWDEN, DUDLEY J.; and KLEIN, SIDNEY (1939) 1967 *Applied General Statistics.* 3d ed. Englewood Cliffs, N.J.: Prentice-Hall. → A standard text. Pages 45–59 of the 1967 edition cover table construction for the presentation of classified statistical data. Earlier editions were by Croxton and Cowden.

DAVIS, JAMES A. 1964 *Great Aspirations: The Graduate School Plans of America's College Seniors.* Chicago: Aldine. → See especially pages 53 ff. for examples of trichotomous data laid out on triangular coordinate graph paper and two-, three-, and four-variable tables of the kind discussed in this article.

DAVIS, JAMES A. et al. 1961 *Great Books and Small Groups.* New York: Free Press.

DIEXEL, KARL 1936 Normung statistischer Tabellen. Institut International de Statistique, *Revue* 4:232–237.

HALL, RAY O. (1943) 1946 *Handbook of Tabular Presentation; How to Design and Edit Statistical Tables: A Style Manual and Case Book.* New York: Ronald Press.

HYMAN, HERBERT H. 1955 *Survey Design and Analysis: Principles, Cases, and Procedures.* Glencoe, Ill.: Free Press.

KENDALL, PATRICIA L.; and LAZARSFELD, PAUL F. 1950 Problems of Survey Analysis. Pages 133–196 in Robert K. Merton and Paul F. Lazarsfeld (editors), *Continuities in Social Research: Studies in the Scope and Method of The American Soldier.* Glencoe, Ill.: Free Press.

LAZARSFELD, PAUL F.; and THIELENS, WAGNER JR. 1958 *The Academic Mind: Social Scientists in a Time of Crisis.* A report of the Bureau of Applied Social Research, Columbia University. Glencoe, Ill.: Free Press.

MYERS, JOHN H. 1950 *Statistical Presentation.* Ames, Iowa: Littlefield.

NATIONAL OPINION RESEARCH CENTER 1958 Survey of Graduate Students. Unpublished manuscript.

NATIONAL OPINION RESEARCH CENTER 1962 *Stipends and Spouses: The Finances of American Arts and Science Graduate Students,* by James A. Davis et al. Univ. of Chicago Press.

SILLS, DAVID L. 1957 *The Volunteers: Means and Ends in a National Organization.* Glencoe, Ill.: Free Press.

STOUFFER, SAMUEL A. (1935–1960) 1962 *Social Research to Test Ideas: Selected Writings.* New York: Free Press.

STOUFFER, SAMUEL A. et al. 1949 *The American Soldier.* Volume 2: Combat and Its Aftermath. Studies in Social Psychology in World War II, Vol. 2. Princeton Univ. Press.

U.S. BUREAU OF AGRICULTURAL ECONOMICS (1937) 1942 *The Preparation of Statistical Tables: A Handbook.* Washington: Government Printing Office.

U.S. BUREAU OF THE BUDGET, OFFICE OF STATISTICAL STANDARDS 1963 *Statistical Services of the United States Government.* Rev. ed. Washington: Government Printing Office. → See especially "Presentation of the Data."

U.S. BUREAU OF THE CENSUS 1949 *Manual of Tabular Presentation: An Outline of Theory and Practice,* by Bruce L. Jenkinson. Washington: Government Printing Office. → See the review by Hall in the June 1950 issue of the *Journal of the American Statistical Association.*

WALKER, HELEN M.; and BUROST, WALTER N. 1936 *Statistical Tables: Their Structure and Use.* New York: Columbia Univ. Press.

WALLIS, W. ALLEN; and ROBERTS, HARRY V. 1956 *Statistics: A New Approach.* Glencoe, Ill.: Free Press.

WATKINS, GEORGE P. 1915 Theory of Statistical Tabulation. *Journal of the American Statistical Association* 14:742–757.

YULE, G. UDNY; and KENDALL, MAURICE G. (1911) 1958 *An Introduction to the Theory of Statistics.* 14th ed., rev. & enl. London: Griffin. → Kendall has been a joint author since the eleventh edition (1937). The 1958 edition was revised by him.

ZEISEL, HANS (1947) 1957 *Say It With Figures.* 4th ed., rev. New York: Harper. → Designed to initiate the nonstatistical reader into survey analysis. Covers (*inter alia*) multidimensional tables, indexes, analysis of data by cross-tabulation. Copiously illustrated with tables and charts.

TARDE, GABRIEL

Gabriel Tarde (1843–1904) was one of the four leading nineteenth-century French sociologists. He was more concerned than Comte with the empirical validation of ideas, more systematic than Le Play in his theories, and more interested than Durkheim in the relationships of individuals and small groups to the broader society.

Tarde has had fewer disciples than any of the others, although his verbal brilliance was impressive and his ideas were remarkably fresh. His relative obscurity was partly a result of the fact that he spent most of his life outside of Paris and the French university system. Also, his reputation suffered because his work was out of harmony with the dominant intellectual temper of the time: Tarde was only mildly religious in an age of militant Catholic and anti-Catholic sentiment; he was politically uninvolved in an age of *engagement*; he

was neither a true positivist nor an antipositivist when most intellectuals were one or the other.

Within France, Tarde is best known for his criminological work and his criticism of Durkheim. Abroad, his greatest influence was on Edward A. Ross and on Robert Park and Edward Burgess and their University of Chicago colleagues who are associated with the theories of social interaction and cultural diffusion. But, far too frequently, present-day sociologists know Tarde only as Durkheim's whipping boy. His work deserves closer scrutiny.

Tarde was born in Sarlat, a small and rather isolated town about one hundred miles east of Bordeaux. He was descended from a noble family that had lived in the region since the Middle Ages. An only child, Tarde was raised by a sensitive and tender mother, his father, a judge in Sarlat, having died when Tarde was seven. He received a rigid classical education at the local Jesuit school and later maintained that a common classical education was a valuable mechanism for producing social integration among the elite groups of a country.

He obtained a secondary degree in the humanities and at first intended to pursue science and mathematics at the École Polytechnique. An eye disease made him change his plans. Following the family example, he prepared for a career in law, first at the University of Toulouse, and for his last year, at Paris. On completing his studies, he returned to Sarlat as a magistrate. From 1869 to 1894 he held a series of regional court posts in and around Sarlat, refusing to leave his mother or his native region and thereby forgoing the possibility of a more attractive position in Paris. His provincial legal career did provide adequate financial support and a good deal of free time, and Tarde devoted his energy to developing a system of social theory. The outlines of his system—influenced mainly by Leibniz, Hegel, Cournot, and Spencer—were completed by 1875, but he did not publish them for some time.

Between 1883 and 1890 he published *La criminalité comparée* and *La philosophie pénale*, as well as dozens of shorter articles on criminology and penology; these works won him a reputation as one of France's outstanding criminologists. After his mother's death in 1894 Tarde became director of the criminal statistics section of the Ministry of Justice in Paris, a position he held until his death in 1904. Although he continued to participate in French and international advisory boards, councils, and congresses as a criminologist and served from 1893 as codirector of the *Archives d'Anthropologie Criminelle,* after 1890 the bulk of his work was sociological and philosophical. The three works central to his system, *Les lois d'imitation, La logique sociale,* and *L'opposition universelle,* were published in 1890, 1895, and 1897, respectively. After 1896 Tarde taught a course every other year at the École Libre des Sciences Politiques and gave numerous lectures and courses at the Collège Libre des Sciences Sociales. In 1900 he was appointed to the chair of modern philosophy at the Collège de France and was elected to the Académie des Sciences Morales et Politiques.

The general theory

As magistrate and judge Tarde dealt constantly with repeated similar crimes, and this experience influenced both his choice of criminology as a topic for study and his development of a theory in which imitation plays a central role. For the most part he dealt with individuals rather than groups or large organizations. His emphasis on the individual put him in conflict with Durkheim, and the debates between the two men lasted for over a decade. But to label Tarde's work "psychologism" (that is, psychological reductionism) is no more enlightening than to speak of Durkheim's work as "sociologism," although both men gave grounds for such oversimplifications of their positions.

Tarde's point of departure was the process of social interaction, or as he termed it, "intermental activity." He felt that human personalities evolve through the interaction of two psychic raw materials, beliefs and desires. At the core of his theory were three fundamental processes—invention, imitation, and opposition.

Invention. All human innovation and progress stem from creative associations originating in individual minds. Invention is a social form of the "adaptation" process described by Darwin: it is a pattern of activity devised by man to help him adjust to the changing environment. Man's biological make-up, however, places a ceiling on his inventiveness. Citing Galton's work *Men of Genius,* Tarde suggested that the innovative capability of a people at a given time is limited by the range of abilities of its individual members. If all other factors are constant, the more numerous the population and hence the more numerous the interactions among its members, the more likely it is that original combinations of ideas will arise.

Imitation. Thousands of inventions are made, but only a small number are adopted and disseminated; Tarde described the processes that make an invention successful in his analysis of the laws of imitation (see 1890*a*).

One general principle is that inventions exhibit a general tendency toward a regular, unending, geometric progression. Represented graphically,

imitations spread from their geometric center in concentric waves, like the ripples from the point where a rock splashes in a pond. And, just as light or sound waves are influenced by the material through which they travel, so imitations are "refracted" by the environment. Physical and biological factors influence the progress of imitations, but Tarde considered them less important than social variables.

Tarde distinguished logical and extralogical social factors affecting imitation. Inventions disseminate most effectively when they are logically consistent with the rational aspects of a culture. Thus, to be successful, a technical innovation should be at approximately the same level as a society's existing technology: neither inventions that are too simple nor those that are too advanced will be adopted.

Tarde discussed three extralogical factors affecting the diffusion of innovations. First, imitation proceeds from "the internal to the external"; affect precedes cognition, which precedes behavior. Ideas may be transmitted before the words used to express them, doctrines before rites, ends before means. Second, the prestige hierarchy structures the paths of imitation: innovations introduced by social superiors are more likely to be imitated than those introduced by social inferiors. Third, in the same social system, receptivity to different kinds of innovations fluctuates: at times, what is old, traditional, and proved is the most likely to be accepted; at other times, it is the exotic and avant-garde that is most in favor. These shifts in perspective apply to all institutional areas of a society—language, religion, government, the economy, morality, and the arts. Tarde's third extralogical principle parallels his principle cited above concerning the level of rational development: both predict that cultural innovations are most likely to be adopted when they resemble other institutionalized elements within the culture.

Opposition. With the publication in 1897 of his *L'opposition universelle,* Tarde added to his first two general processes the concept of opposition, or conflict. He examined physical conflict and its effects on the movement and energy of masses; he underlined the importance of biological conflict in contributing to the evolution of the species; and he asserted that psychological conflict—the clash of opposing ideas and motivations within the individual mind—may result in environmentally adaptive inventions. As for social conflict, he believed that it tends to occur when proponents of contrasting inventions come into contact with one another. The amount and intensity of resulting conflict varies with the institutional realm: as one moves from moral to economic to political matters, the generality of the issues about which conflict takes place tends to diminish, while the intensity of the conflict increases. This apparent anomaly is explained by the extent of the social adjustments required for innovation to occur in the domains of morality, economics, and politics. Morality is largely a personal matter, and a change does not necessitate major readjustments by the rest of society. Economic decisions for the most part involve only subsectors of a total society, but they have a broader impact than decisions of morality. Political matters, and especially international political matters, tend to have the broadest social consequences of all and therefore generate the most violent disagreements.

Operationalization and measurement

Unlike most system-building theorists, Tarde was continually seeking empirical indicators and, ideally, quantifiable ones, by which he might test his broader generalizations.

He felt it was almost impossible to examine scientifically the psychological variables involved in the process of invention. However, he considered it feasible to study, principally by means of archeological techniques, the societies and historical periods in which various inventions were first made.

Imitation and opposition are better studied with large-scale statistics. Tarde's systemic orientation led him to prefer the analysis of time series to static breakdowns by geographical region, sex, age, occupation, and so forth. The spread of an invention through homogeneous social surroundings, with no opposition in the form of conflicting inventions, may be represented by a geometric progression. Deviations from a fixed progression indicate the extent of "refraction" or opposition to which a given invention is subject.

Tarde deplored the inadequacy of most governmental statistics for social-scientific purposes: although figures on population movements, industrial and commercial matters, and crime were relatively abundant, there were very few quantitative measures of basic values, religious activity, scientific output, or linguistic change, let alone of the emotional and cognitive attributes of individuals. Tarde stated in *The Laws of Imitation*: "Psychological statistics alone, recording the rise and fall of an individual's particular beliefs and desires, . . . would give, if they were practically possible, the deeper meanings behind figures provided by ordinary statistics" (1890a, p. 115).

Since he was writing more than a quarter century before public opinion studies were developed, much of the quantitative support that Tarde needed for his generalizations was lacking; still, he was a skillful analyst of the materials that were available to him, particularly criminal statistics, and he suggested measures by which more complete information could be collected.

To measure the effects of mass communications, for example, Tarde wanted more precise techniques for studying individual and public opinion. He argued that shifts in opinion might be gauged crudely, however, by behavioristic indicators, such as the number of persons attending church, the size of religious donations, the sale of books on different subjects, the circulation of newspapers of different political hues, and voting patterns. He also foresaw the need for a device that could quantitatively evaluate the psychic raw materials—beliefs and desires—and that would provide in aggregate form a measure of public opinion, thus anticipating the outlines of a program of attitude surveys.

Substantive contributions

The bulk of Tarde's substantive writings falls under four headings—mass communications and personal influence, political sociology, the social psychology of economics, and criminology and penology.

Communication and personal influence. Tarde examined the social impact of such technological developments as the telegraph, the telephone, mass-produced books, even printed invitations and announcements, and most important of all, the mass-circulation newspaper. Since the very existence of the modern newspaper depends on innovations in transportation and communication, which are found only in industrialized societies, it is difficult to isolate the influence of newspapers from that of a variety of other aspects of industrialization. Nevertheless, newspapers were important for Tarde, first, as agents of integration and social control, which expand loyalties from narrow communal and corporate groupings to national and even international alliances, and second, as a civilizing and rationalizing force.

Before the development of the printing press, communication, integration, and social control took place largely within more or less fixed traditional social groups—the family, the occupational group, the village. Newspapers led to the emergence of "publics"—aggregates of separate persons who, exposed to the same communications, develop a certain degree of self-consciousness. Through publics, newspapers were a major force in the creation of secondary groupings, such as political parties, national occupational organizations, and religious bodies.

The implications of these extended loyalties are twofold: Tarde noted (as did Simmel) that as the size of a group increases, so does the freedom of its individual members; moreover, overlapping memberships permit groups to shift ideological perspectives and form coalitions and alliances with greater ease and flexibility.

But impersonal communication is not effective by itself. Tarde remarked in *L'opinion et la foule*: "If people did not talk, it would be futile to publish newspapers . . . they would exercise no durable or profound influence, they would be like a vibrating string without a sounding board" (1901, p. 83). Tarde's formulation is close to what has come to be known as "the two-step flow of communication": mass communications exercise influence largely through being "humanized" and adapted to the circumstances of individuals by "opinion leaders" (see Katz & Lazarsfeld 1955).

The idea of opinion leaders meshes with Tarde's general theory: new ideas (inventions), initiated through impersonal communication, are diffused throughout society by the process of imitation. The principle of imitation most relevant in the area of personal influence is that imitation proceeds from social superior to social inferior.

Political sociology. In *Les transformations du pouvoir* (1899) Tarde viewed the political system as for the most part dependent on the same structures and subject to the same processes as those that operate within the total society. Interaction leads to the development of common norms that in turn provide the basis for power.

Innovations in any realm—economic, religious, military—can influence the political system through the persuasive pressure of a numerous and powerful group of supporters.

An elite group with specialized knowledge and performing specialized functions is essential for political change, as indeed for all innovation. Most political innovations are originally diffused through the economic, military, religious, and aesthetic elites and then spread throughout society. In accordance with Tarde's general laws, diffusion tends to flow from capitals to smaller cities and rural areas and from powerful and prestigious nations to less advantaged ones: in this way the ideas of the eighteenth-century democratic theorists spread from France and England to the rest of the world.

In the political sphere, as in any other, imitation and adaptation often produce opposition and conflict. Diffusion of innovations is likely to meet less resistance, however, as improved transportation and mass communication stimulate the growth of large, overlapping publics, such as the modern political party.

The social psychology of economics. Tarde's writings on the economic system, contained chiefly in his two-volume *Psychologie économique* (1902), deal with a number of the social conditions necessary for a viable economy. For instance, price setting, the functioning of markets, and investment decisions require a set of society-wide agreements on certain fundamental values. In order that such agreements be made, there must be sufficient leisure time, for it is leisure that permits informal social interaction, which in turn generates a system of shared values.

Leisure is also a prerequisite of economic innovation, which depends, like all social progress, on a creative elite with more leisure time than the rest of the population. Equalization of leisure would therefore impair the vigor and inventiveness of a nation (although Tarde cited the United States as a partial exception to this rule).

Tarde saw the rise of trade unions as part of the expansion of publics. While, especially in the short run, the rise of large unions might lead to an increase in conflict between labor and industry, Tarde felt that ultimately, as more and more numerous publics came to include workers, managers, and other members of society, there would be social harmony.

Criminology and penology. Tarde's writings on criminology and penology predate the full-scale elaboration of his sociological theory and hence are less directly related than any of his other substantive work to his comprehensive system. In *La criminalité comparée* (1886) and *La philosophie pénale* (1890b), as well as in a variety of articles, Tarde presented what was then probably the most forceful criticism of the biological theories of the origin of crime developed by Lombroso and the Italian school. Although, especially in his earlier writings, he did give some credence to racial characteristics as predisposing factors in criminal behavior, he argued that crime is essentially a social phenomenon, explicable according to general social laws.

As director of the criminal statistics section of the Ministry of Justice, Tarde was aware of the over-all statistical trends in the crime rate. It disturbed him deeply that almost every type of crime had increased continually since the early nineteenth century, when crime statistics were first systematically collected. Tarde considered this increase to be a demonstration of his general ideas on geometrical progression followed by imitation.

Although he believed in the social origin of crime, Tarde rejected Durkheim's view that crime is a "normal" phenomenon, on the grounds that this view is morally irresponsible. Responsibility for criminal acts, Tarde affirmed, must remain with the individual perpetrator.

At an early stage of his work in criminology Tarde favored capital punishment and the expulsion of criminals to penal colonies, but he changed his mind upon finding virtually no statistical relationship between the rate of criminal activity and the severity of penal laws.

Assessment

The objections of most earlier critics to Tarde's work were largely ontological. He was criticized chiefly for his assumption that society is simply an aggregate of individuals and not, as Durkheim liked to say, a reality *sui generis*. When Tarde wrote, the majority of social scientists, especially in France, were occupied more with these ontological questions than with constructing a science of human behavior.

Today we are more inclined to examine Tarde's actual sociological work than his philosophy of social science. From this perspective, a major weakness of his work lies in his tendency to explain away embarrassing data by tenuous interpretation in terms of his own theory (his facile literary style assisted him here); he was seldom moved to question the adequacy of his own formulations. Like so many of his contemporaries, Tarde accepted without criticism two concepts of his day—evolutionism and race. Tarde's "transformationism" was a refined and qualified evolutionary theory, and near the end of his life he was willing to admit that he had resorted too frequently to biological explanations in earlier work.

As for method, Tarde consistently preferred the historical approach to comparative study, a preference reflecting his system's emphasis on the dynamic and its disregard for collective factors. A greater comparative emphasis might have forced him to become more aware of certain systemic inadequacies.

Tarde's enduring contributions fall into three categories—criminology, social interaction theory, and diffusion processes. His criminological writings have perhaps been subject to more continuing attention than any other part of his work; they still serve as a source of hypotheses for contemporary criminologists (e.g., Davidovitch 1963).

At a time when psychologists expressed an antisociological view of man and sociologists an antipsychological one, Tarde's formulations on social interaction and its influence on individuals, groups, and society as a whole provided essential foundations for the emerging discipline of social psychology. E. A. Ross, for example, credited Tarde with many of the basic ideas presented in his *Social Psychology*.

An astute observer of the complex ways in which innovations of all sorts are diffused throughout different types of social systems, Tarde developed a number of principles that are still useful to contemporary students of diffusion processes (e.g., Rogers 1962). For specialists in any area of the social sciences reading Tarde continues to be an instructive experience: his writings exhibit the versatility of what the French call an athletic mind.

TERRY N. CLARK

[*See also* CONFLICT, *article on* SOCIAL ASPECTS; CRIMINOLOGY; DIFFUSION; IMITATION; SOCIOLOGY, *article on* THE EARLY HISTORY OF SOCIAL RESEARCH; SUICIDE, *article on* SOCIAL ASPECTS; *and the biographies of* BURGESS; COMTE; DURKHEIM; GALTON; LE PLAY; PARK; ROSS.]

WORKS BY TARDE

(1886) 1902 *La criminalité comparée.* 5th ed. Paris: Alcan.
(1890a) 1903 *The Laws of Imitation.* New York: Holt. → Translated from the second French edition of 1895.
(1890b) 1912 *Penal Philosophy.* Boston: Little. → First published as *La philosophie pénale.*
(1893) 1922 *Les transformations du droit.* 8th ed. Paris: Alcan.
(1895a) 1898 *La logique sociale.* 2d ed. Paris: Alcan.
1895b *Essais et mélanges sociologiques.* Paris: Masson.
1897 *L'opposition universelle.* Paris: Alcan.
1898a *Études de psychologie sociale.* Paris: Giard & Brière.
(1898b) 1899 *Social Laws.* Translated by Howard C. Warren, with a preface by James Mark Baldwin. New York: Macmillan. → First published in French.
1899 *Les transformations du pouvoir.* Paris: Alcan.
1901 *L'opinion et la foule.* Paris: Alcan. → See especially Chapter 2. The translation of the extract in the text was provided by Terry N. Clark.
1902 *Psychologie économique.* 2 vols. Paris: Alcan.
(1904) 1905 *Underground Men.* With a preface by H. G. Wells. London: Duckworth. → First published as *Fragment d'histoire future.*
Gabriel Tarde: Introduction et pages choisies par ses fils. Paris: Michaud, 1909. → Contains a biographical introduction and selections from his writings.

SUPPLEMENTARY BIBLIOGRAPHY

BARNES, HARRY E. 1919 The Philosophy of the State in the Writings of Gabriel Tarde. *Philosophical Review* 28:248–279.
BOUDON, RAYMOND 1964 La "statistique psychologique" de Tarde. *Annales internationales de criminologie* [1964]:342–357.
BOUGLÉ, C. 1905 Une sociologie individualiste, Gabriel Tarde. *Revue de Paris* 3:294–316.
CLARK, TERRY N. 1966 Empirical Social Research in France, 1850–1914. Ph.D. dissertation, Columbia Univ.
DAGAN, HENRI 1901 Les sociologues contemporains: M. Gabriel Tarde. *Grande revue* 1:141–157.
DAVIDOVITCH, A. 1963 Remarques sur la criminologie de G. Tarde. Seminaire d'Histoire de la Sociologie Empirique en France. Document No. 6. Unpublished manuscript, Univ. of Paris.

DAVIS, MICHAEL M. JR. 1906 Gabriel Tarde: An Essay in Sociological Theory. Ph.D. thesis, Columbia Univ.

DAVIS, MICHAEL M. JR. 1909 *Psychological Interpretations of Society.* Columbia University Studies in History, Economics and Public Law. New York: Longmans.

ESPINAS, ALFRED 1910 Notice sur la vie et les oeuvres de M. Gabriel de Tarde. Académie des Sciences Morales et Politiques, *Séances et travaux* 174:309–422.

GEISERT, M. 1935 *Le système criminaliste de Tarde.* Paris: Éditions Domat-Montchrestien.

HUGHES, EVERETT C. 1961 Tarde's *Psychologie économique*: An Unknown Classic by a Forgotten Sociologist. *American Journal of Sociology* 66:553–559.

KATZ, ELIHU; and LAZARSFELD, PAUL F. 1955 *Personal Influence: The Part Played by People in the Flow of Mass Communications.* Glencoe, Ill.: Free Press.

MAHAIM, E. 1903 L'économie politique de M. Tarde. *Revue d'économie politique* 17:1–34.

MATAGRIN, AMÉDÉE 1910 La psychologie sociale *de Gabriel Tarde.* Paris: Alcan.

ROCHE-AGUSSOL, MAURICE 1926 Tarde et l'économie psychologique. *Revue d'histoire économique et sociale* 14: 68–114, 273–319.

ROGERS, EVERETT M. 1962 *Diffusion of Innovations.* New York: Free Press.

TOSTI, GUSTAVO 1897 The Sociological Theories of Gabriel Tarde. *Political Science Quarterly* 12:490–511.

VIERKANDT, A. 1899 Gabriel Tarde und die Bestrebungen der Sociologie. *Zeitschrift für Social-wissenschaft* 2:557–577.

WARD, LESTER F. 1900 [A Book Review of] Tarde's *Social Laws. Science* New Series 11:260–263.

TARIFFS

See under INTERNATIONAL TRADE CONTROLS; *see also* INTERNATIONAL INTEGRATION, *article on* ECONOMIC UNIONS.

TASTE AND SMELL

The topics of taste and smell are frequently combined for discussion because the nature of the stimulus in each case is defined in chemical terms. Except for this general similarity, the two modalities appear to represent quite distinct phenomena, and it should not be assumed that they are slightly different manifestations of the same basic mechanism. For purposes of scientific discussion, taste refers to those sensations arising from stimulation of specialized receptors in the mouth, primarily on the tongue, while smell refers to those sensations arising from the stimulation of receptors in the upper portion of the nasal cavity. In everyday experience they are typically so intermingled that a large part of sensations commonly called taste are actually olfactory sensations arising from odorous molecules from ingested material in the mouth reaching the olfactory epithelium by way of the posterior nares. The absence of these sensations is recognized during periods of nasal congestion that result in the so-called flat taste of foods.

Among the senses, taste and smell have been relatively neglected as areas of research. Man regulates his behavior only to a small extent by differential sensory input over either of these two routes. In the case of many other animals, however, a different situation prevails. This difference is especially notable for smell, which provides detailed information for the highly specific responses of many species. Instead of being an occasionally useful but primarily affective distance sense, as in man, it serves in a capacity comparable to the other principal distance senses, vision and audition. The male gypsy moth, for instance, responds to the scent of a female one-quarter of a mile upwind. Similarly, the ability of many mammals to track their prey by means of odorous cues is well known.

Both taste and smell participate in the regulation of feeding activities of animals, including man. Although normal caged rats maintain their caloric intake in the absence of taste and smell sensations, rats with dietary deficiencies or with reduced hunger and thirst induced by brain lesions are highly dependent on these sensations for regulation of intake. Dietary deficiencies in man may result in changes in food preferences without affecting taste thresholds. Highly preferred tastes may cause us to overeat to the point of discomfort, and almost everyone has experienced the arousal of appetite by the smell of desirable food as well as the analogous loss of appetite produced by objectionable odors.

The major topics of concern in studying sensation are (1) the qualitative classes into which the sensations can be divided; (2) the quantitative sensitivity of the modality, expressed as threshold measurements; and (3) the nature of the adequate stimulus and the basic mechanism of excitation. Methods of study include both psychophysical and electrophysiological procedures. Detailed coverage and bibliographies can be found in Adey (1959), Geldard (1953, pp. 270–323), Michels et al. (1962), Pfaffmann (1959), Taylor (1937), and the bibliography published by Airkem (1952). Recent research findings are presented in the symposium edited by Zotterman (1963).

Taste

Receptors and neural transmission. The receptor cells for taste are known as taste buds and, in mammals, are distributed throughout the oral cavity, including the larynx and pharynx, with the major concentration on the papillae of the upper and lateral surfaces of the tongue. Man has about 9,000 taste buds. The life of an individual taste cell may be as short as one week, which raises some provocative questions concerning the neural organization of a continuously shifting population that provides constant patterns of information. Three cranial nerves (the seventh, ninth, and tenth) are involved in the transmission of nerve impulses from the taste cells to the brain. The fifth cranial nerve subserves the cutaneous sensations associated with ingestion of sapid substances. There is no area in the cerebral cortex uniquely associated with taste; rather, the incoming impulses are represented along with the sensory and motor mechanisms of the face area.

Taste thresholds and stimulus attributes. The primary qualities of taste are sour, sweet, salty, and bitter. Sensitivity to these qualities is distributed differentially, with the tip of the tongue most sensitive to sweet, the back to bitter, the posterior portion of the sides to sour; the salty taste is perceived equally well in all receptive areas. Table 1 presents some absolute thresholds for representatives of the different qualities.

Table 1 — Absolute thresholds for taste

Substance	Per cent concentration (Approx.)	Molar concentration
Sugar (sucrose)	0.7	0.02
Sodium chloride	0.2	0.035
Hydrochloric acid	0.007	0.002
Saccharin (crystallose)	0.0005	0.00002
Quinine sulfate	0.00003	0.0000004

Source: Geldard 1953, p. 306.

Changes in the temperature of a substance appear to affect its threshold, but the exact nature of this relationship for each quality is not clear at present. In general, absolute thresholds increase with age. Estimates of differential sensitivity, the percentage of change in intensity that can be just perceived, vary from 10 per cent to 100 per cent and are dependent upon such parameters as the qualitative dimension being studied, the level of intensity of stimuli, the size of the area being stimulated, the psychophysical method employed, etc. The measurements so far suggest that differential sensitivity to the salty taste is slightly greater than that to sweet and sour, and sensitivity to bitter is slightly less. More intense stimuli are judged more pleasant in the case of sweet but less pleasant in the case of the other qualities. Two subjective intensity scales have been devised for taste (Geldard 1953, pp. 308–311). Specific ageusias (absences of taste) have been discovered in man;

one of them, to phenyl thiocarbimide (PTC), is especially interesting to geneticists, for it is inherited as a simple Mendelian recessive and can be used as an aid in classifying ethnic groups.

The problem of how the molecules of the stimulating substance affect the receptor cell so that a nerve impulse is produced in the associated afferent neuron is still unsolved. The substance must first of all be soluble in water, i.e., saliva. The critical event might be an enzymatic mechanism. Beidler (1961) has suggested that the adsorption of the stimulus onto the surface of the taste cell may result in a change in the membrane potential of the cell such that a nervous impulse can be generated. Inasmuch as all taste receptors appear to be responsive to stimuli of more than one quality, the mechanism underlying the distinctiveness of the different qualities must be sought in some aspect of the patterning of the afferent neural signals.

The specific stimulus characteristics that are responsible for the initiation of neural patterns that permit qualitative discrimination have not been completely identified. Stimulus substances possessing hydrogen ions taste sour, although hydrogen-ion concentration is not the only determining factor. The salty taste is associated with both the anion and cation of soluble salts. Bitter and sweet tastes occur for representatives of many chemical classes whose essential characteristics are not yet recognized.

Smell

Receptors and neural transmission. The receptors for smell are unique among the special senses, for they are simply rod-shaped endings of the olfactory nerve fibers rather than specialized cells. The nerve endings project into the epithelium of the olfactory clefts, 2.5 square centimeter areas at the upper rear of each nostril. The olfactory, or first cranial, nerve is similarly unique in that its fibers pass directly from the olfactory mucosa into the cerebral cortex, i.e., the olfactory bulb, without a thalamic relay. The cortical projection zone for smell lies on the lower surface of the frontal lobe. From there, the pathway ramifies diffusely to many other cortical and thalamic areas as a complex inherited from man's phylogenetic ancestors, who made more use of smell than does man.

Olfactory thresholds and stimulus attributes. The adequate stimulus for olfaction must be volatile, presumably water-soluble, and possibly lipoid-soluble as well. As yet, no one has succeeded in identifying the primary smell qualities, although many ingenious suggestions have been made. The difficulties arise from the paucity of good electro-physiological data and the subjective complexity of most odors. The latest attempt at identification (Amoore et al. 1964) is based on a new hypothesis concerning the nature of the adequate stimulus and not on a direct analysis of sensory data. Amoore has proposed that the olfactory process is a stereochemical phenomenon, with all odor-producing molecules represented by seven basic shapes. He assumes, in addition, that the olfactory membrane is composed of receptor sites with configurations corresponding to the basic molecular shapes. The surface of the olfactory epithelium is known to have strong adsorptive qualities. The olfactory process, therefore, would be initiated when the molecular shape and the receptor site correspond to some critical degree. Amoore identifies these seven basic shapes with the odor qualities of ethereal, camphoraceous, musky, floral, pepperminty, pungent, and putrid. Although detailed validation of this proposal remains to be provided, there is no satisfactory alternative at present.

Olfactory sensitivity varies widely with the stimulating substance, but it can be so acute as to enable detection of the odor of vanillin at a concentration of 2×10^{-7} milligram per cubic centimeter of air. Even with such a low concentration, the number of odorous molecules actually entering the nose is probably of the order of billions. What proportion reaches the olfactory receptors is difficult to state precisely because they can be reached only by variable air currents, which divert the molecules to the olfactory membrane and away from the main airway. Some olfactometric techniques have been devised that attempt to control this factor. No one has any direct estimates of stimulus concentration at the olfactory area, however. Differential sensitivity seems poor, with estimates ranging from 20 per cent to 100 per cent. A notable characteristic of olfaction is the rapidity with which adaptation occurs, so that repeated threshold measurements must be widely separated. Different degrees of anosmia (absence of smell) occur in human beings, but anosmia is not well understood. Sex hormones influence olfactory sensitivity to certain substances, such as one of the synthetic musks, which is a strong odor for women but a very weak one for men.

BERNICE M. WENZEL

[*Other relevant material may be found in* NERVOUS SYSTEM *and* SENSES.]

BIBLIOGRAPHY

ADEY, W. R. 1959 The Sense of Smell. Volume 1, pages 535–548 in *Handbook of Physiology.* Section 1: Neuro-physiology. Washington: American Physiological Society.

AIRKEM, INC. 1952 *Odors and the Sense of Smell: A Bibliography, 320 B.C.–1947.* New York: Airkem.

AMOORE, JOHN E.; JOHNSTON, JAMES W. JR.; and RUBIN, MARTIN 1964 The Stereochemical Theory of Odor. *Scientific American* 210, Feb.: 42–49.

BEIDLER, LLOYD M. 1961 Biophysical Approaches to Taste. *American Scientist* 49:421–431.

GELDARD, FRANK A. 1953 *The Human Senses.* New York: Wiley.

MICHELS, K. M. et al. 1962 Odor and Olfaction: A Bibliography, 1948–1960. *Perceptual and Motor Skills* 15:475–529.

PFAFFMANN, CARL 1959 The Sense of Taste. Volume 1, pages 507–534 in *Handbook of Physiology.* Section 1: Neurophysiology. Washington: American Physiological Society.

TAYLOR, NORMAN B. (1937) 1961 The Senses of Taste and Smell: Common Chemical Senses. Pages 1458–1469 in Charles H. Best and Norman B. Taylor, *The Physiological Basis of Medical Practice.* 7th ed. Baltimore: Williams & Wilkins.

ZOTTERMAN, YNGVE (editor) 1963 *Olfaction and Taste: Proceedings of the First International Symposium Held at the Wenner–Gren Center, Stockholm, September, 1962.* Oxford: Pergamon Press.

TAUSSIG, FRANK W.

Frank William Taussig (1859–1940), one of the foremost American economists of his age, was born in St. Louis, Missouri. His father had emigrated from Prague to the United States in 1846 and had an unusual career even for nineteenth-century America. He started in wholesale trade, then became successively a medical practitioner, mayor of his community, judge, federal tax collector, banker, and eventually president of a successful railroad. Taussig's mother was the daughter of a Protestant teacher from the Rhineland who had come to the United States in 1848. Taussig entered Harvard as a sophomore in 1876, graduating in 1879 with "highest honors." After a year in Europe, where he traveled extensively and studied Roman law and political economy for a semester in Berlin, he enrolled in the Harvard Law School, soon switched to economics, became secretary to President Eliot of Harvard, and took his PH.D. in economics in 1883 and his LL.B. in 1886. He advanced quickly from instructor in 1885 to full professor of economics in 1892, a position which he held until his retirement in 1935. From 1876 until his death Taussig lived in the academic community of Cambridge, Massachusetts, except for two years in Europe, from 1901 to 1903, for reasons of health, and two years' service in Washington, from 1917 to 1919. There he was the first chairman of the new U.S. Tariff Commission, a close adviser of

President Woodrow Wilson, especially on commercial policy measures, and a member of the Price Fixing Committee. Under his leadership the Tariff Commission acquired an excellent staff and published several reports (especially *Reciprocity and Commercial Treaties* 1919) of lasting value and influence, which helped to shape the liberal turn in American tariff policies in later years. In 1919 he spent several months at the peace conference in Paris as economic adviser and intimate counselor to President Wilson.

Taussig belonged to the same group of American "neoclassical" economists as John Bates Clark, Irving Fisher, and Frank A. Fetter, but he was more deeply rooted in the classical tradition than the others. Schumpeter reported that Taussig once told him that he regarded Ricardo as the greatest economist of all time and considered Böhm-Bawerk the only possible rival (Schumpeter et al. [1941] 1951, p. 199). As a refined and elegant theorist and the inventor and user of mathematical methods, Fisher was unsurpassed among his American contemporaries. But Taussig was foremost in the field of applied economic theory. His work was remarkable for its historical perspective and his intuitive sense both for orders of magnitude of economic variables and for the political feasibility of proposed economic measures.

Through his numerous students and disciples and through his *Principles of Economics* (1911), the leading economic text for a long time, Taussig had a stronger influence than any other American economist of his time on several generations of academic economists as well as on many leading economic civil servants—an influence which can still be clearly felt in many quarters. For 40 years, from 1896 to 1936, Taussig was the editor of the *Quarterly Journal of Economics*. Through his editorial policy, which was discriminating and firm as well as liberal and tolerant, he made a significant contribution to American economics.

His principal field of interest was the theory, history, and practice of international trade and trade policy. In Viner's words, Taussig's work in the field of theory of international trade can be characterized as "a restatement and an elaboration of the analysis of the English classical school." His specific contributions were:

(1) his synthesis of the scattered and unorganized classical materials into a unified and coordinated general theory of international trade; (2) his revision of the classical doctrine of comparative costs dealing especially with problems arising from the existence of different types of labor ("non-competing groups") and of interest costs, which always were a stumbling block

for the labor theory of value; (3) his analysis of the mechanism of international trade under nonmetallic monetary standards; and (4) his use of the theory of international trade in the interpretation of the industrial development of the United States.   (Viner 1936, p. 5)

The theory is treated in the relevant chapters of Taussig's *Principles of Economics* and in greater detail in his later book, *International Trade* (1927), with elaborate attempts at historical and statistical "verifications" so characteristic of all his work.

Taussig's discussion of the balance-of-payments mechanism is contained in numerous articles (see especially 1917) and in Parts II and III of his *International Trade*. In this work he used extensively the results of the studies of particular countries, which had been made at his suggestion and partly under his guidance by his students, notably, James W. Angell and Frank Dunstone Graham (who studied the United States), Norman J. Silberling (Great Britain), Jacob Viner (Canada), John H. Williams (Argentina).

Taussig devoted a great many articles and two important monographs, *The Tariff History of the United States* (1888) and *Some Aspects of the Tariff Question* (1915a), to tariff history and commercial policy. The latter volume has separate chapters on important American industries, such as sugar, iron and steel, silk, cotton, and wool manufacturing, and is an important contribution to general American economic history. Taussig was a moderate free trader, believing that such benefits as accrue from a system of free trade are secured only if that system is maintained for a long time and that, conversely, the greatest evil is a *changing* tariff system. In principle he accepted the validity of the infant industry argument for protection, although he was skeptical of its actual application. In his empirical–historical researches he paid special attention to discovering the extent to which tariffs had contributed to the rise of particular industries; he did not find that protection had made a large contribution to American economic development.

Taussig's main contribution to the field of general economic theory is his book *Wages and Capital* (1896) and the relevant chapters of the *Principles*. His treatment of the theory of distribution of income was systematic, but as Schumpeter put it, he "allowed his exposition to grow out of contemporary American discussion—as shaped primarily by Walker—on a particular point—the wages fund doctrine" (Schumpeter 1936, p. 219). Taussig's own theory can perhaps be described as a blend of Ricardo and Böhm-Bawerk. Like Marshall, whom he knew well and with whom he had extensive correspondence, he did not accept the then prevalent view that there was a sharp break or contrast between the old classical theory of Ricardo, Nassau Senior, and J. S. Mill on the one hand and the modern marginal analysis on the other. On the contrary, he saw a continuous process of improvement, elaboration, and refinement of essentially one body of economic theory, spanning the classical and what we now call the neoclassical epoch. In this belief he was perhaps more modern, by present standards, than most of his contemporaries, although he himself did not use, was not able to use, and even had a certain disdain for refined mathematical methods of economic analysis.

GOTTFRIED HABERLER

[For the historical context of Taussig's work, see the biographies of Böhm-Bawerk; Ricardo; Walker; for discussion of the subsequent development of his ideas, see International trade; International trade controls, article on Tariffs and protectionism.]

WORKS BY TAUSSIG

(1883) 1886   *Protection to Young Industries as Applied in the United States: A Study in Economic History.* 2d ed. New York: Putnam.

(1888) 1931   *The Tariff History of the United States.* 8th ed., rev. New York: Putnam.

(1892–1919) 1920   *Free Trade, the Tariff and Reciprocity.* New York: Macmillan. → Collected essays.

(1896) 1932   *Wages and Capital: An Examination of the Wages Fund Doctrine.* London School of Economics and Political Science.

1905   The Present Position of the Doctrine of Free Trade. (Presidential Address.) American Economic Association, *Publications* Third Series 6:29–65.

1906   Wages and Prices in Relation to International Trade. *Quarterly Journal of Economics* 20:497–522.

1908   Capital, Interest, and Diminishing Returns. *Quarterly Journal of Economics* 22:333–363.

(1911) 1939   *Principles of Economics.* 2 vols., 4th ed. New York: Macmillan.

(1915a) 1931   *Some Aspects of the Tariff Question: An Examination of the Development of American Industries Under Protection.* 3d ed., enl. Harvard Economic Studies, Vol. 12. Cambridge, Mass.: Harvard Univ. Press.

(1915b) 1930   *Inventors and Money-makers: Lectures on Some Relations Between Economics and Psychology Delivered at Brown University in Connection with the Celebration of the 150th Anniversary of the Foundation of the University.* New York: Macmillan.

1917   International Trade Under Depreciated Paper: A Contribution to Theory. *Quarterly Journal of Economics* 31:380–403.

1919   Price-fixing as Seen by a Price-fixer. *Quarterly Journal of Economics* 33:205–241.

1921   Is Market Price Determinate? *Quarterly Journal of Economics* 35:394–411.

1927   *International Trade.* New York: Macmillan.

1932   Taussig, Frank W.; and Joslyn, Carl S. *American Business Leaders: A Study in Social Origins and Social Stratification.* New York: Macmillan.

SUPPLEMENTARY BIBLIOGRAPHY

Explorations in Economics: Notes and Essays Contributed in Honor of F. W. Taussig. 1936   New York: McGraw-Hill. → Contains a bibliography of Taussig's writings.

Opie, Redvers 1941   Frank William Taussig (1859–1940). *Economic Journal* 51:347–368.

Schumpeter, Joseph A. 1936   Professor Taussig on Wages and Capital. Pages 213–222 in *Explorations in Economics: Notes and Essays Contributed in Honor of F. W. Taussig.* New York: McGraw-Hill.

Schumpeter, Joseph A.; Cole, A. H.; and Mason, E. S. (1941) 1951   Frank William Taussig. Pages 191–221 in Joseph A. Schumpeter, *Ten Great Economists From Marx to Keynes.* New York: Oxford Univ. Press. → First published in Volume 55 of the *Quarterly Journal of Economics.*

U.S. Tariff Commission 1919   *Reciprocity and Commercial Treaties.* Washington: Government Printing Office.

Viner, Jacob 1936   Introduction: Professor Taussig's Contribution to the Theory of International Trade. Pages 3–12 in *Explorations in Economics: Notes and Essays Contributed in Honor of F. W. Taussig.* New York: McGraw-Hill.

TAWNEY, R. H.

R. H. Tawney (1880–1962), English social and economic historian, was the son of a distinguished Sanskrit scholar who was principal of the Presidency College in Calcutta. He was educated at Rugby, where he acquired a grounding in the classics and the Old Testament which profoundly affected his prose style, and where he struck up one of the most important friendships of his life—with William Temple, future archbishop of Canterbury. From Rugby he went to Balliol College, Oxford, where he came under the influence of the great tutor and master of Balliol, A. L. Smith, and also of Bishop Gore, whose theological and social doctrines provided the inspiration of his career. In 1903 he obtained a Second in Greats. "I grant you his mind was chaotic," remarked the master of Balliol, "but his examiners ought to have seen that it was the chaos of a great mind."

After graduating, Tawney worked first in the University Settlement in the east end of London, where he saw something of the horrors of slum landlordism, and then for the newly founded Workers' Educational Association, which was to remain one of the chief interests of his career. Given the glaring inequalities of the existing educational system, this was work of the first importance, bringing an opportunity to men and women of lower-class origin to develop their latent intellectual interests. (One of Tawney's first pupils was a future editor of the *Manchester Guardian*, A. P. Wadsworth.) In 1913 Tawney was appointed director of the Ratan Tata Foundation for the study of poverty at the London School of Economics, but two years later he enlisted in the infantry, characteristically in the ranks rather than as an officer, and was very severely wounded in 1916. One result of this terrible experience was a notable contribution to the literature of war called *The Attack* (1953).

In 1918 Tawney was elected fellow of Balliol, but within a year he moved to a readership in economic history at the London School of Economics. The next decade was the most fruitful of his career, as he threw himself into left-wing politics, educational propaganda, teaching, and research. He was involved in the general strike of 1926; he set out his passionate social and political convictions in two brilliant and immediately successful books, *The Acquisitive Society* (1920) and *Equality* (1931); he was joint editor of the newly founded *Economic History Review* for its first crucial seven years; and his output of scholarly works was at its height. From 1931 to 1949 he held the title of professor at the London School of Economics, where he instructed generation after generation of honors students in the social and economic history of Tudor and early Stuart England.

With the outbreak of World War II, Tawney's services were enlisted as labor attaché at the British embassy in Washington, but he was unhappy in this safe administrative backwater and soon returned to the perils and hardships of London. Between 1943 and 1948 he was an influential figure on the University Grants Committee at a time when it had a major role to play in the expansion of higher education.

Writings. The period from 1540 to 1640 is now familiarly known as "Tawney's century," a tribute paid by both friends and enemies to his towering position in English historiography. In 1912 he published *The Agrarian Problem in the Sixteenth Century* in which he tackled the problem of land use in an underdeveloped economy where old social and economic relationships were giving way under the impact of a price revolution and a demographic explosion. His ethical presuppositions may have made him too ready to see all landlords as the rapacious predators they often were, his solution to the problem—to turn customary tenures into freeholds—may have been an oversimplification, but the book opened a new era in historical studies in England and has formed the starting point for a huge amount of subsequent research. A year later

he made a pioneer study (1913) of why the landed classes tried to regulate wages and of the practical results of their efforts. In 1924 the three volumes of *Tudor Economic Documents* were published, edited in collaboration with Eileen Power, which at once made the sixteenth century the best-documented period in the economic history of England. The next year Tawney wrote a long introduction to an edition of an Elizabethan tract, Thomas Wilson's *Discourse Upon Usury*. It contains a brilliant analysis of the foreign exchange and internal credit problems of an under-capitalized economy dependent on precious metals for its circulating medium, a vivid description of the new monied classes ruthlessly exploiting their opportunities, and an account of the shifts of official policy towards usury in the light of changing economic circumstances and ideological theories.

In 1926 Tawney published his most popular work, *Religion and the Rise of Capitalism*, in which he used his great knowledge of early seventeenth-century English Puritan literature to reformulate a thesis previously put forward by Max Weber. Tawney argued that it was not so much Calvinist theological doctrines that, directly or indirectly, created the spirit of capitalism as it was individualism and the concomitant ethic of thrift and hard work that created an efficient labor force and a rational organization of industrial activity. The hypothesis was, and remains, controversial, but it has stimulated generations of students to think about the relationship between religion and economics.

The thirties were a fallow period in Tawney's historical output: his only historical publication (1934) was an analysis of a unique occupational census for Gloucestershire in 1608. He was working on a comprehensive study of the sixteenth-century and early seventeenth-century social scene which in the end was never published, although the skeleton of the work was presented in his Ford lectures at Oxford in 1936.

In the meantime he traveled to China, and the result of his visit was a remarkable pioneer work (1932) on the problems of a country struggling to leap from the fifteenth century to the twentieth, and some concrete proposals for a democratic solution to those problems. Tawney applied to modern China his twenty years of study of preindustrial European societies, using this knowledge to illuminate and give depth to his analysis.

War had already broken out when Tawney published in two famous articles (1941*a*; 1941*b*) his interpretation of the relationship between the political events of the 1640s and changes in the English social structure. He argued that in the century before the Civil War various factors, notably different capacities to adjust landed income to the price revolution and different habits of expenditure, caused a shift in the balance of property from the magnates to the medium-sized landlords, labeled respectively "peers" and "gentry"; and that, as James Harrington had pointed out at the time, it was this shift that caused the collapse of the *ancien régime* in 1640 and so opened the way to Civil War and the subsequent abolition of monarchy, aristocracy, and episcopacy. [*See* HARRINGTON.] Tawney saw the war in terms of a clash between the progressive, capitalist forces and the decaying semifeudal elements in the society. This thesis has since come under bitter criticism, and the truth of the concept of the rise of the gentry remains an open question (H. R. Trevor-Roper 1953; J. H. Hexter 1961). What Tawney certainly achieved, however, was to stimulate interest in the long-term sociological antecedents of the Civil War, and in doing so he provoked a mass of detailed research.

Finally in 1958 he published a study of Lionel Cranfield, the Jacobean cloth exporter and government speculator turned crown economic adviser, who eventually became lord treasurer of England. In this work Tawney once again broke new ground by forcing attention away from the parliamentary opposition, where it had rested for decades, and back to the deficiencies of the central government itself. Since he was a moralist as well as an economic historian, the corrosion of an aristocratic society under the acid of London finance capital was a theme admirably suited to his pen.

Assessment as a historian. The driving impulses of Tawney's life were his individual brand of radical Christianity, his burning hatred of social injustice, and his profound suspicion of money. He was not merely indifferent to money, he actively disliked it. All his historical writings are deeply affected by these ethical and religious preoccupations. He was always, and unashamedly, concerned with making the world a better place to live in, as well as with advancing the frontiers of knowledge. As a professional scholar his technical equipment was far from ideal. His references were not always accurate; his grasp of statistical method was sometimes imperfect; his appreciation of impersonal economic forces like demographic growth and monetary inflation was obscured by his anxiety to identify personal or class responsibility for the ills of the world. Although he could be a dazzlingly brilliant stylist, there were times when his jewelled sentences tended to collapse under their own weight.

What, then, is Tawney's claim to greatness? Historiography does not proceed in a smooth line but by a series of sudden jerks. Every now and then a genius emerges who shifts the emphasis of historical interpretation and directs attention to a new aspect of human affairs until then unnoticed and unappreciated. In English historiography there have been only five such giants—William Stubbs, F. W. Maitland, T. F. Tout, Namier, and Tawney. It is Tawney who directed attention to the close relationship between religious ideologies and ethical codes on the one hand and economic growth and government action on the other; Tawney who demonstrated the importance of economic relationships, such as those between landlord and tenant, employer and worker, in determining the character of a society; Tawney who formulated a sociological interpretation of one of the three great revolutions in modern European history; Tawney who published the documentary tools and generated the enthusiasm which has made his chosen period a standard subject of study in most English secondary schools and one of the most flourishing fields of graduate research in recent years. Tawney's interpretations may ultimately prove to need revision, but it looks as if the problems to which he first drew attention will continue to preoccupy English historians for a long time to come.

LAWRENCE STONE

[*Directly related is the entry* HISTORY, *articles on* ECONOMIC HISTORY *and* SOCIAL HISTORY; *other relevant material may be found in the biography of* WEBER, MAX.]

WORKS BY TAWNEY

(1912) 1963 *The Agrarian Problem in the Sixteenth Century.* New York: Franklin.
1913 The Assessment of Wages in England by the Justices of the Peace. *Vierteljahrsschrift für Sozial- und Wirtschaftsgeschichte* 11:307–337, 533–564.
(1914) 1937 BLAND, ALFRED E.; BROWN, P. A.; and TAWNEY, R. H. (editors) *English Economic History: Select Documents.* London: Bell.
1920 *The Acquisitive Society.* New York: Harcourt. → A paperback edition was published in 1948.
(1924) 1953 TAWNEY, R. H.; and POWER, EILEEN (editors) *Tudor Economic Documents: Being Select Documents Illustrating the Economic and Social History of Tudor England.* 3 vols. New York: Longmans. → Volume 1: *Agriculture and Industry.* Volume 2: *Commerce, Finance and Poor Law.* Volume 3: *Pamphlets, Memoranda and Literary Extracts.*
(1926) 1963 *Religion and the Rise of Capitalism: A Historical Study.* Gloucester, Mass.: Smith.
(1931) 1952 *Equality.* 4th ed., rev. London: Allen & Unwin. → A paperback edition was published in 1961 by Putnam.
(1932) 1964 *Land and Labour in China.* New York: Octagon Books.

1934 TAWNEY, A. J.; and TAWNEY, R. H. An Occupational Census of the Seventeenth Century. *Economic History Review* First Series 5:25–64.

1941*a* Harrington's Interpretation of His Age. British Academy, London, *Proceedings* 27:199–223.

1941*b* The Rise of the Gentry: 1558–1640. *Economic History Review* First Series 11:1–38.

1953 *The Attack, and Other Papers.* London: Allen & Unwin; New York: Harcourt.

1954 The Rise of the Gentry: A Postscript. *Economic History Review* Second Series 7:91–97.

1958*a* *Business and Politics Under James I: Lionel Cranfield as Merchant and Minister.* Cambridge Univ. Press.

1958*b* *Social History and Literature.* Leicester (England) Univ. Press.

SUPPLEMENTARY BIBLIOGRAPHY

ASHTON, THOMAS S. 1962 Richard Henry Tawney, 1880–1962. British Academy, London, *Proceedings* 48:461–482.

HEXTER, J. H. 1961 *Reappraisals in History: New Views on History and Society in Early Modern Europe.* Evanston, Ill.: Northwestern Univ. Press. → A paperback edition was published in 1963 by Harper. See especially the essay "Storm Over the Gentry," first published in 1958 in *Encounter.*

TREVOR-ROPER, H. R. 1953 *The Gentry: 1540–1640.* London: Cambridge Univ. Press.

WILSON, THOMAS (1572) 1925 *A Discourse Upon Usury by Way of Dialogue and Orations . . .* With an historical introduction by R. H. Tawney. London: Bell; New York: Harcourt.

TAXATION

I
GENERAL

Taxation is a general concept for devices used by governments to extract money or other valuable things from people and organizations by the use of law. A tax formula contains at least three elements: the definition of the base, the rate structure, and the identification of the legal taxpayer. The base multiplied by the appropriate rate gives a product, called the tax liability, which is the legal obligation that the taxpayer must meet at specified dates. A tax is identified by the characteristics of its base, such as income in the case of an income tax, the quantity of distilled spirits sold in the case of a liquor tax, and so on. The rate structure may be simple, consisting of one rate applying to the base, such as a specified number of cents per gallon for a tax on gasoline, or complex, for example, varying rates depending upon the size of the base for a tax on personal income.

Taxes may be assessed in money or in kind. The government of Communist China imposes taxes on peasants assessed in units of grain produced, and it requires payment in grain itself. In the American Confederacy, because of the deterioration of the Confederate money during the latter phases of the American Civil War, some taxes were assessed and collected in terms of commodities. In American frontier settlements of the eighteenth and early nineteenth centuries, the local governments formed by the people in the region commonly imposed taxes by requesting that each adult male work a given number of days constructing community facilities such as roads and schools. The modern-day counterpart of this practice is conscription of men for service in the armed forces, although conscription is not generally considered as a tax. The dominant practice, however, in the contemporary world is the assessment of taxes in money and the settlement of the tax liability by the payment of money.

Taxation presupposes private ownership of wealth. If a government owned all wealth in a society, including the wealth embodied in people, it would obtain all income, and there would be nothing to tax. No government has gone to such extremes in concentrating the wealth of a society in its own hands. Even in highly socialized societies, such as the Soviet Union, people are permitted, subject to restrictions, to own themselves, household goods, savings accounts, and money. Taxation therefore becomes feasible. Nevertheless, the more wealth a government itself owns, the less is taxation necessary, because revenue from the management of assets is a substitute for tax receipts. National governments, with the exception of some of the highly socialized countries, typically find themselves on the other side of the ledger, having on balance negative net worths apart from their taxing power. Some local governments in western Europe and the United States have substantial revenues from government-owned facilities such as electric power plants, municipal water facilities, and transport systems. The profits from the management of these facilities are occasionally sufficient to permit a government to dispense with taxation altogether.

Taxes are to be distinguished from prices imposed by a government for goods and services that it provides. A price is a money payment made as a condition of obtaining goods or services. It serves as a rationing device provided that the price is positive and provided that the amount of the goods or services the buyer receives in return depends upon the price. If a government supplies water and charges according to the amount of water taken by the buyer, the device is a price and not a tax. Borderline cases arise in two types of circumstances: (1) when a charge is made as a condition of an all-or-none choice, such as a fee for a license for an automobile as a condition of operating the vehicle on any public highway; or (2) when a government imposes a requirement that the citizen use a service and then charges for the service taken, such as a requirement for a passport for foreign travel accompanied by a charge for the passport. In situations in which the element of government compulsion enters significantly, it is customary as well as reasonable to treat the charge as a tax rather than as a price.

Classification of taxes. Taxes may be classified in various ways. Since a tax is a formula of three ingredients—a base, a rate structure, and identification of the legal taxpayer—a common characteristic of any of these three elements may be employed for grouping. Thus taxes may be classified as personal or business. In such a classification, a tax on beer is a business tax because business organizations are in fact the legal taxpayers. More commonly, taxes are grouped on the basis of similarities of the tax base; for example, commodity taxes refer to all taxes in which the production or sale of commodities becomes the occasion for a government levy. Even though personal income taxes vary widely in their characteristics among countries, the presumed common element of the tax base—personal income—is used for grouping purposes.

Perhaps the single most widely used distinction is between what is called "direct" taxation and what is called "indirect." This is a classification based on certain presumed effects of various taxes. A direct tax in this usage refers to one in which the legal taxpayer cannot shift any of the tax liability to other people, such as customers or suppliers. A clear illustration of a direct tax is a lump-sum charge levied on a person—sometimes called a head tax or poll tax. Income, death, net worth, expenditure, and sometimes property taxes are commonly classified as direct. Indirect taxes refer to those that are thought to be shifted from the legal taxpayer to others. Commonly, taxes on sales of commodities, import duties, and license fees are grouped together as indirect.

By postulating common effects of various taxes, the direct–indirect classification becomes subject to two serious defects. The effects of a particular tax device are not intuitively apparent; their dis-covery entails careful scientific investigation. It is thus awkward to employ a classification that begs these questions in advance. There is the further difficulty that the shifting of a tax by the legal taxpayer to others may occur in various degrees from 0 to 100 per cent. If a particular tax is proved to be shifted to others by the amount of 25 per cent, for example, the direct–indirect classification becomes irrelevant. One should have to say that the tax is 75 per cent direct and 25 per cent indirect. The difficulty arises because an all-or-none test is used when the relevant distinction is one of degree. For these and other reasons, the direct–indirect classification, although widely used in reporting revenue data, is usually avoided in scientific investigations.

Among other possible dichotomous classifications, taxes may be divided into those described as systematic means-test devices and those without this characteristic. Personal income, expenditure, and net worth are examples of means-test taxes: taxes whose base is systematically related to some relevant index of the taxpayer's economic position. Personal income, the money gain a person experiences over a period, may be, and commonly is, looked on as a measure of his economic position. An expenditure tax treats the amount spent for personal living expenses or consumption as the index of relative economic status. Likewise, net worth, the value of assets possessed minus debts owed to others, may be used as such a measure. When the purposes of taxation include large yields and systematic redistribution of economic power, some form of means-test taxation must be employed. Although other taxes can also provide large yields, they are likely to be erratic in their effects on income distribution.

Functions of taxation. Any tax that has a yield extracts money from people or organizations and provides money for a government. As a result of a tax formula, taxpayers find themselves with less money to spend; governments, on the other hand, find themselves with more money. This transfer of money from people to government gives rise to two functions of taxation: a reduction in the spending potential of the private sector and an increase in the spending potential of the public sector.

Revenue. The negative function of reducing the spending potential of people often may be viewed as an unfortunate by-product of taxation. Few city officials, for example, would applaud the fact that as a result of the imposition of local taxes, the local citizenry has less money to spend. For local government units, it is the financial needs of the government that justify taxation. Until recent decades, this view was assumed correct for all levels of government; taxation was believed to arise solely out of the financial needs of governments rather than from a public objective of reducing citizens' spending power.

A sovereign government with an advanced type of financial system controls the money system and, as one feature of this control, can if it wishes provide itself with unlimited quantities of money at negligible cost. This power arises from the use of national monies in the form of bank deposits and currency as opposed to commodities, such as gold and silver, whose quantity cannot be increased by government decree. A national government need no longer levy taxes in order to finance itself.

The discovery of the power of governments to free themselves from internal financial constraints has a long and complicated history. By the time of the Napoleonic Wars, the British government had discovered the convenience of having the Bank of England provide it with funds. In America, the colonies experimented rather freely with the money-issuing power; Massachusetts has the distinction of being the first government in the world to issue paper money. Yet the necessary institutions for the exercise of this power did not exist in the United States at the time of the War of 1812, and the federal government for the first and only time in its history found itself literally bankrupt. World War I was the first occasion when the power to finance government by creating money was freely used by all major belligerents. This financial power was clearly recognized by governments during World War II and was used on a vast scale. In the contemporary world, the possibility of national governments having insufficient money to finance their internal expenditures is no longer a real one. Thus, the amount of revenue to be raised by taxation depends on policy objectives rather than on government financial necessity.

Even though sovereign governments have freed themselves from financial constraints, the revenue function of taxation has not disappeared; this function becomes that of regulating private expenditures so as to stabilize employment and the price level. During periods of insufficient private expenditures, for example during recessions, a national government may allow its revenues to fall automatically and, in addition, may take steps to reduce effective rates of tax in order to increase private expenditures. Similarly, during periods of excessive expenditures, tax rates may be increased as a depressant measure. Even as late as the 1930s, few governments possessed leaders who understood the policy choices available; through fear and desperation they took steps to increase tax rates when effective recovery called for tax reduction. Thanks to the spread of economic intelligence, such serious errors in financial policy are unlikely to be duplicated should a serious world depression ever again develop.

Resource reallocation. In addition to the revenue function of taxation, taxes may alter the product-mix generated within the private sector. In Great Britain, for example, such commodities as automobiles, household appliances, liquor, and tobacco are made more expensive by taxation, whereas such items as milk, vegetables, meat, cider, and household help are made less expensive, in part through subsidies, or negative taxes. As a consequence, the British people use rather more of the latter group of commodities and rather less of the former. The tax-induced change in the product-mix comes about through the effects of taxes on prices and quantities produced. British manufacturers of electric dishwashers, for example, being confronted by a heavy tax on these goods, charge higher prices for them, and so the number these companies can profitably sell is curtailed. The labor and capital services not used to produce dishwashers as a result of the curtailed output of them are devoted instead to the production of other commodities that are lightly taxed or not taxed at all. These other commodities are therefore made more abundant and sell for lower prices. From the point of view of buyers, this alteration of the product-mix benefits those who happen to like the lightly taxed commodities and injures those who prefer the heavily taxed goods. Whether the entire consuming public as a whole can be said to be better off or worse off as a result of the alteration of the product-mix depends on whether an optimum is defined in terms of consumer preferences as expressed in the market or as expressed through political processes. [*See* CONSUMER SOVEREIGNTY.]

Almost all actual tax devices commonly used by governments display some features that may alter the pattern of productive activities in the society. Personal income taxes as found in the Western world define the tax base incompletely, leaving some gains subject to little or no tax. In the administration of net worth taxes in the Scandinavian countries, agricultural land in comparison with other types of assets is appraised lightly for tax purposes. Value-added taxes, as employed in the state of Michigan and in France, completely omit important types of value-adding activities from the tax base. In all such cases, the tax system encourages some activities over others. Although complete neutrality of a tax system can never be achieved in fact, actual tax systems become more neutral as their coverage of economic activities becomes more general.

As tax systems have developed, they have tended to favor activities of a nonmarket character, such as leisure, production of goods for personal use instead of for sale, and "do-it-yourself" projects in general. Governments have difficulty in catching such gainful activities in their tax net and, with occasional exceptions, do not attempt to do so. Consequently, and for political reasons also, tax policies in advanced countries generally favor agricultural over industrial activities.

Income redistribution.   A further main function of taxation is the redistribution of economic power as measured by income or wealth. With respect to money income, a tax system is distributionally neutral if it reduces each person's income in the same proportion. Taxation may be systematically progressive in the sense of taking an increasing proportion of income increases. Technically, a tax system is defined as progressive if the marginal rate of tax with respect to income exceeds the average rate of tax, provided marginal rates do not exceed 100 per cent. Regressive tax structures refer to the opposite case. In this context, "proportional," "progressive," and "regressive" describe the effect of the entire tax system on the distribution of income.

Accompanying the development of democratic political institutions in the Western world, various ethical ideas arose concerning the appropriate criteria for evaluating taxes. The dominant ethical idea that emerged is the "ability-to-pay" doctrine. This rather vague expression is intended to provide a justification for tax systems that are systematically progressive as opposed to those that are proportional, regressive, or merely erratic. Income is usually taken as the appropriate measure of personal ability-to-pay, although net worth and expenditure have also been advocated as appropriate measures. The concept of ability-to-pay implies both equal treatment of people with equal ability, however measured, and a progressive rate structure. The ability-to-pay doctrine has strong affinities to egalitarian social philosophy; both support measures designed to reduce inequalities of wealth and income.

Strict adherence to the test of ability-to-pay, when income is used as the measure of ability, would call for a monolithic tax structure restricted to personal income taxation. Logically, the idea implies systematic negative taxation as well. If a person with a modest income pays zero tax, a person with an even smaller income should pay less than zero tax—that is, receive a subsidy—to achieve appropriate differences in the treatment of people with different tax-paying abilities.

In the development of actual tax systems, only modest success can be claimed for reducing the incomes of the very wealthy by tax measures—even in countries such as the United States, Great Britain, and Australia, all of which use progressive income taxation and have been governed over appreciable periods of time by groups unsympathetic to economic plutocracy. There is little evidence to suggest that in these countries taxes have substantially reduced the wealth of the very wealthy, despite the apparent high rates of tax on large incomes and large estates.

By far the most important government measures used to reduce income inequality have been government welfare programs. Various social services, such as medical care, education, and income maintenance in the form of social security programs, have mitigated the economic hardship of low-income groups in Western countries. These programs directly raise the money incomes of the unemployed, the aged, and the incapacitated; they also potentially raise the consumption of all qualifying groups by providing some services free or at nominal cost. In some Western countries, the programs have virtually eliminated grinding poverty; they have not achieved this goal in the United States.

Shifting and incidence.   A tax is said to be shifted if the legal taxpayer can by some means force others to contribute extra amounts of money to him because of the presence of the tax. Shifting is therefore achieved in degrees ranging from zero, that is, no shifting, to 100 per cent, or complete shifting. To the extent a tax is shifted from the legal taxpayer, such as the proprietor of a retail establishment in the case of a retail sales tax, other people are thereby selected to contribute to the government. Actually, full explanations of tax shifting require the determination of the true amount each person must pay to governments, including the amounts shifted to him, so that at least in principle the investigator can state precisely the amount of money a person or family contributes to government per unit of time. Nothing approaching this precision has yet been achieved in any country. It is a safe generalization that the typical citizen goes through life never knowing, even within wide limits, how much in tax he is actually paying.

The concept of tax incidence, sometimes called tax burden, is closely related to that of tax shifting. If, of the taxes imposed by a government, none are shifted at all, the incidence of a tax is said to fall on those who are the legal taxpayers—those persons who would be sued by the government for failure to pay the amounts specified by the tax formula used. In this event, the incidence of the tax holds few mysteries. The concept does involve difficult issues, however, if a tax is shifted in whole or in part. The concept of tax incidence is concerned with the identification of the persons who "finally" or "ultimately" pay the tax liabilities as opposed to those who, although legally required to pay money to the government, are acting wholly or partly as intermediaries in the tax-collection process. Thus, legislators in voting taxes on such items as liquor or cigarettes do not ordinarily assume that the vendors of these commodities are "really" paying the tax because legislators ordinarily operate on the theory that vendors can pass along the tax to buyers. Granted the validity of the theory, the incidence of the tax falls on these buyers.

Theories of tax shifting and incidence exist in great variety. Insofar as a consensus can be found, it is that means-test taxes (for example, income taxes) either are not shifted at all or are shifted only to a trivial extent and that commodity taxes, including import and export duties, are largely shifted from the legal taxpayers to others. The incidence of the general property tax imposed by local governments in the United States, company (corporation) profits taxes, taxes on the transfer of physical and financial assets, and of many minor levies is analyzed in many different ways; no definite consensus can be found among experts on the subject.

Differences in analysis of various tax devices reflect differences both in the general theoretical framework deemed appropriate to explain economic events and in the precise manner in which the investigator views the device being studied.

Tax theory has developed mainly as a by-product of classical and neoclassical economic theory, as exemplified by the works of such thinkers as Adam Smith, John Stuart Mill, W. Stanley Jevons, and Alfred Marshall. Continental general equilibrium approaches, mainly through their influence on such American thinkers as Irving Fisher, have, after a considerable time lag, become important in the explanation of the effects of various taxes. The Keynesian system of thought has a large and devoted contemporary following; it is widely used to explain the effects of entire fiscal systems. More recent theoretical work has been dominated by model building, often of a highly esoteric kind, constructed with such highly simplifying assumptions that government only rarely gets into the picture at all. Given the variety of approaches to the explanation of economic events, a generally endorsed approach to the explanation of how taxes are shifted and in what amounts cannot be expected.

Real income approach. The question of just what the investigator is attempting to explain in connection with taxation is also approached in different ways. A major disputed issue is the alternative, implicitly or explicitly presupposed, to the tax under investigation. Some students define the problem as the effects of the tax together with some government expenditure assumed to be financed by that tax. Accordingly, the problem of explaining a personal income tax is looked upon as including the effects of certain or all of some government expenditures. This approach is adopted more or less automatically by those who view economics as fundamentally a "real" system, meaning a system in which money is assumed to be absent or in which money is viewed as a purely passive device to effect exchanges, having no distorting effect on price relations among goods and services. In this approach, a tax is viewed as levied in goods and services that the government either uses directly in its affairs or trades with private individuals to obtain the goods and services used in its expenditure programs. Explanation consists of showing how the combination of income taxation and the assumed expenditures changes relative prices, quantities produced, and the amount of leisure taken. The incidence of the tax–expenditure combination is believed to be established by showing what groups experience a decline in real income.

This approach has little appeal to most students of public finance because of its remoteness from reality. (It remains, however, the dominant approach to the analysis of the incidence of import duties in pure international trade theory.) It has the further defect, apart from its restrictive assumptions, of identifying particular taxes with particular government programs, when in fact neither a government nor an individual can generally determine which expenditure is financed from a particular tax or income source. Logically, the approach is inherently incapable of isolating the effects of a tax as such, because a tax apart from expenditures is undefined. Since, in fact, government programs can take on any of a great variety of forms, including negative taxes (subsidies), the approach in principle can only give answers for each of an indefinitely large number of possible combinations.

Money income approach. A relatively recent approach, what may be called the "income theory" of tax incidence, views the basic problem of tax analysis to be the determination of the portion of each person's income diverted to the government by a tax. This approach finds that any tax that provides a government with revenue must simultaneously make the after-tax money income of some people who work or own property smaller by the amount of the revenue. The investigator, accordingly, attempts to identify, for each tax device, those persons whose after-tax incomes are curtailed. In this approach, government expenditure for goods, services, or assets enters as a factor determining demands for current output and as analytically distinct from revenues.

This approach to taxation can be explained by illustration. A tax on cigarettes, for example, is commonly believed to be paid by cigarette smokers. According to the income theory, such a tax reduces the money incomes of certain groups. People, as buyers of services and goods, including cigarettes, are prepared to spend some dollar amount per period. The demand schedule for cigarettes being highly inelastic, a change in price results in little change in the quantity purchased—the tax raises the price of cigarettes by almost the full amount of the tax per unit, and the dollar amount spent on cigarettes increases. Given constraints on total private expenditures, the amount spent on other commodities diminishes. If these "other commodities" consist of all commodities other than cigarettes, all industries find the demands for their products lowered and all will earn lower incomes. If these "other commodities" consist of a narrow class of commodities, such as food, the industries, including agriculture, producing these goods experience reduced prices and reduced income. To only a small extent, because of the low price elasticity of the demand for cigarettes, do tobacco companies and tobacco growers also experience lower profits and wages. The product-mix changes only slightly in this case. If a tax is placed on cornflakes, the pattern of results would be somewhat different. Cornflakes, being one of a great variety of breakfast foods, has a highly elastic demand. The tax would increase the price of cornflakes, greatly reduce the amount bought, and drive resources out of cornflake production. In this case, the companies and workers in the taxed industry would experience lower incomes.

There is no shifting of a general tax on income or net worth; taxpayers experience a lowering of their after-tax income and no incentive is created to reduce further other factor incomes. Commodity taxes, import duties, retail sales taxes, and expenditure taxes are shifted more or less, depending upon the setting where they are used. Property taxes of the American type, where the tax base is mainly the assessed value of real estate, business equipment, and inventories, present complications because of the great diversity in effective rates within and among local jurisdictions and because of the benefit element of local expenditures to owners of taxed property. Property taxes can be shown to reduce property income in general and to be progressive with respect to total income.

The income theory of tax incidence applies in a symmetrical manner to negative taxes, such as subsidies to the production of some food products in Great Britain and to income-maintenance social security programs. The incidence of negative taxes refers to the identification of the ultimate recipient and the amount he receives. As is the case with ordinary taxes, the problem is to identify the private counterpart of the government's financial transactions.

The income theory of tax shifting, as the name implies, treats government income as arising at the expense of private income. Tax revenues are treated as a form of transfer income—as are interest paid to owners of debt instruments, dividends paid by corporations, and pensions and social security payments made by governments.

Role of determinant price systems. In order to arrive at definitive conclusions, all theories of tax shifting need a pricing system that is determinant as opposed to one that is capricious or random. If prices of commodities depend on what executives of corporations eat for breakfast, the incidence of corporation income taxes or commodity taxes cannot be definitively ascertained. Actual price systems in Western countries exhibit capricious elements arising from market power, illustrated by the pricing of some varieties of labor services, government price regulation based on concepts of fair return and historical costs, and many others. Systematic tax theory, like the economic theory of which it is a part, assumes the orderly features of price systems and fails to the extent that the actual world lacks these characteristics. Economists differ widely in their outlook on the degree of orderliness exhibited in contemporary societies; some find that the economic world neatly illustrates the properties of a perfectly competitive pricing system, and, at the opposite pole, others find no system to explain and as a consequence deprecate economic theory.

Taxation and fiscal policy. The main financial weapons of a national government are its expenditures on goods and services, transfers (including negative taxes), taxation, public debt management, and monetary policy. Some or all of these may be manipulated to alter the level of total expenditures by all groups in the economy and at the same time may be used to alter the pattern of these expenditures.

The deliberate manipulation of taxes for the purpose of achieving full employment is subject to both political and economic constraints. The reduction of effective rates of tax, for example, may be irreversible because of political objections to tax rate increases. In addition, taxes have other functions besides revenue, such as resource reallocation and income redistribution, and these functions may be partly defeated by changing the tax structure for purposes of influencing private expenditures. These considerations do not imply that the manipulating of effective rates of tax poses insurmountable difficulties; only that the difficulties must be recognized and, if possible, weighed when making a final decision.

Taxes are interdependent among themselves and also interdependent with other fiscal weapons. A reduction in taxes on company profits leads to increased revenue from a personal income tax because some portion of the increase in after-tax profits will appear as an increase in dividends. Different taxes compete for the income of owners of resources; an increase in the effective rates of one tax reduces the yield of others. In selecting taxes to manipulate in influencing private expenditures, these repercussions on other tax yields must be taken into account if the desired total change in revenues is to be achieved.

Taxes are also interdependent with other fiscal devices. In Western countries, and many others as well, national monetary systems are banking systems characterized by bank creation and destruction of money, fractional reserve requirements, and central bank determination of changes in bank reserves. Treasuries must conduct their finances within this institutional framework. Effective fiscal policy presupposes cooperative central bank policies; otherwise, fiscal measures designed to stimulate the economy may be offset by monetary measures. A main problem in financial administration remains that of effective coordination of fiscal and monetary policies. They are so closely interdependent that some students prefer to speak of national financial policies rather than of two sets of policies, fiscal and monetary.

The use of taxation as a weapon to influence private expenditures becomes feasible to the extent a treasury is free from financial constraints, and freedom from constraint implies access to an unlimited amount of money. Central banks are the institutions that have the power to create money

in any amount. If, then, a government decides, for example, to reduce effective rates of tax as a stimulating measure during a depression, its treasury will initially find itself depleting its cash position or, in the case of European national treasuries, will be increasingly in debt to the central bank. If the treasury department sells public debt or if the central bank does so instead, the cash released to taxpayers is reabsorbed by net sales of public debt. Depending on the circumstances, these combined actions may be perfectly offsetting, or they may on balance be stimulating or depressing with respect to private expenditures on goods and services. If a stimulating combination of measures is to be assured for a given amount of tax reduction, the maximum is achieved if no debt is sold to the public at all. In this event, with a fractional reserve system of banking, bank reserves increase at the rate of the tax cut. Such increases in bank reserves, given the practice of relatively low fractional reserve requirements or customs, would lead to a potential increase in the amount of money so exceedingly large for even modest tax reductions that central bankers would almost certainly feel obliged to offset them in part. Perhaps a more relevant definition of zero offset is a central bank response to a tax-rate change that permits the quantity of demand deposits plus currency in the hands of the public to change by the change in the yield of the tax systems. In actual practice, however, it would be rare to observe such a result. Normally, central banks and treasuries, when tax cuts are made, use debt operations to offset a sizable fraction of the tax change. For this and other reasons, faith in the efficacy of tax changes to influence the economy must be tempered; one must examine what response, in terms of changes in the size of the outstanding debt, may be expected.

World tax structures. In advanced countries, tax revenues range from a high of about 35 per cent of the gross national product in West Germany to a low of about 21 per cent in Japan; the United States government (federal, state, and local) takes an amount equal to about 25 per cent of the gross national product. Such comparisons may, however, be misleading. In advanced European countries, provision for retirement income is usually made through government programs, whereas in the United States various private pension plans supplement in substantial amounts the federal social security programs. Were retirement deductions from the remuneration of employees counted as taxes, the United States would rank closer to such high-tax countries as West Germany, Sweden, and France in effective tax rates.

International comparisons also neglect negative taxes such as family allowances, subsidies, and social security transfers, creating an impression of heavier taxation of the average household than would data showing both the amount taken in tax and the amounts received in the form of government transfers. Net tax data have unfortunately not been systematically compiled for purposes of international comparisons.

The structure of tax systems reflects the political and social characteristics of national groups. France, a country of high taxation, relies heavily on value-added taxation, whereas the United Kingdom, also a high-tax country, relies heavily on income taxes. The United States, being a federal political system with long traditions of local financing of local functions, employs many taxes that can be administered at the state and local levels, resulting in a highly complex combination of taxes, such as federal, state, and even local income taxes, state and local retail sales taxes, and the continuation of the important, though generally criticized, local property tax. A centralized system of taxation as found in France would be alien to the mores of Americans. Tax systems, to be workable, must be in keeping with popular feelings and beliefs. This consideration explains why politicians may succeed when tax experts, especially foreign experts, fail in attempts to redesign a country's tax system.

Of the developing nations, apart from some oil-rich countries, few are in a position to impose taxation at the effective rates found in advanced European and English-speaking countries. Mass poverty, weak public administration, and the concentration of political power in the hands of wealthy groups rule out heavy taxation. Tax systems in these countries ordinarily consist of import duties and, in a few, export duties, transaction and commodity taxes, low-rate income taxes, land taxes, and some form of death tax, usually of the inheritance type. India uses systematic income taxation, although less than 10 per cent of the population is subject to it. As these poor countries develop, their tax systems may be expected to develop as well, and in the direction of higher effective rates of tax.

The outlook generally is for continued high-level taxation where already found and increasingly high effective rates of tax elsewhere, with the possible exception of the communist countries. From a long-run point of view, revenue requirements of government are closely geared to government expenditure and transfer programs. The goods and services that governments provide are looked upon as superior to alternative private commodities, with the consequence that, even apart from military programs, government expenditures exhibit a long-run tendency to rise relative to national income. This tendency is not inevitable and may be reversed. Yet continued urbanization alone, with all that this development implies for government action, may be sufficient to assure relatively expanding government programs. In addition, the welfare state has already demonstrated its political popularity in the Western world, and, despite the lamentations of political conservatives and some economic liberals, government activities appear destined to grow both absolutely and relatively. If so, high taxation can also be expected to be an enduring characteristic of advanced societies.

EARL R. ROLPH

[See also PUBLIC EXPENDITURES.]

BIBLIOGRAPHY

AMERICAN ECONOMIC ASSOCIATION 1959 *Readings in the Economics of Taxation.* Homewood, Ill.: Irwin.

BATOR, FRANCIS M. (1960) 1962 *The Question of Government Spending: Public Needs and Private Wants.* New York: Collier.

BLOUGH, ROY 1952 *The Federal Taxing Process.* Englewood Cliffs, N.J.: Prentice-Hall.

BUTTERS, J. KEITH; and LINTNER, JOHN 1945 *Effect of Federal Taxes on Growing Enterprises.* Cambridge, Mass.: Harvard Univ., Graduate School of Business Administration, Division of Research.

DUE, JOHN F. (1954) 1963 *Government Finance.* 3d ed. Homewood, Ill.: Irwin.

DUE, JOHN F. 1957 *Sales Taxation.* London: Routledge; Urbana: Univ. of Illinois Press.

FABRICANT, SOLOMON 1952 *The Trend of Government Activity in the United States Since 1900.* New York: National Bureau of Economic Research.

HALL, CHALLIS A. 1960 *Fiscal Policy for Stable Growth: A Study in Dynamic Macroeconomics.* New York: Holt.

HANSEN, BENT (1955) 1958 *The Economic Theory of Fiscal Policy.* Cambridge, Mass.: Harvard Univ. Press. → First published as *Finanspolitikens ekonomiska teori.*

HARVARD UNIVERSITY, INTERNATIONAL PROGRAM IN TAXATION 1963 *Taxation in the United States.* Chicago: Commerce Clearing House.

HICKS, J. R.; HICKS, U. K.; and ROSTAS, L. (1941) 1942 *The Taxation of War Wealth.* 2d ed. Oxford: Clarendon.

HOLLAND, DANIEL M. 1958 *The Income Tax Burden on Stockholders.* Princeton Univ. Press.

KALDOR, NICHOLAS 1955 *An Expenditure Tax.* London: Allen & Unwin.

McKEAN, ROLAND N. 1958 *Efficiency in Government Through Systems Analysis: With Emphasis on Water Resources Development.* New York: Wiley.

MUSGRAVE, RICHARD A. 1959 *The Theory of Public Finance: A Study in Public Economy.* New York: McGraw-Hill.

Musgrave, Richard A.; and Peacock, Alan T. (editors) 1958 *Classics in the Theory of Public Finance.* London and New York: Macmillan.

Pigou, A. C. (1928) 1956 *A Study in Public Finance.* 3d ed., rev. New York: St. Martins.

Prest, Alan R. 1960 *Public Finance in Theory and Practice.* Chicago: Quadrangle Books.

Rolph, Earl R. (1954) 1956 *The Theory of Fiscal Economics.* Berkeley: Univ. of California Press.

Rolph, Earl R.; and Break, George F. 1961 *Public Finance.* New York: Ronald Press.

Schultz, William J.; and Harriss, C. Lowell (1931) 1959 *American Public Finance.* 7th ed. Englewood Cliffs, N.J.: Prentice-Hall.

Simons, Henry C. 1938 *Personal Income Taxation: The Definition of Income as a Problem of Fiscal Policy.* Univ. of Chicago Press.

Vickrey, William S. 1947 *Agenda for Progressive Taxation.* New York: Ronald Press.

II
PERSONAL INCOME TAXES

The personal income tax is widely regarded as the fairest method of taxation yet devised. It is the major element of progression in modern tax systems and permits differentiation of tax burdens on the basis of family responsibilities and other personal circumstances of taxpayers. The yield of the tax expands or contracts more rapidly than personal income, thus imparting built-in flexibility to government revenue systems. The income tax is less burdensome on consumption and more burdensome on personal saving than an equal-yield expenditure tax, but the difference in aggregate terms is probably small for taxes of broad coverage. The effect of the income tax on work and investment incentives is unclear. Although personal income taxation has a long history, some of its major features still present numerous unsettled problems.

The first general personal income tax was introduced in 1799 in Great Britain, where it has been in effect continuously since 1842. Despite this early example, other countries were slow in adopting this tax. It was used for a brief period in the United States during and after the Civil War, and it was permanently enacted following the ratification in 1913 of the sixteenth amendment to the constitution. Austria adopted the income tax in 1849 and Italy in 1864; Australia, New Zealand, and Japan followed in the 1880s and Germany and the Netherlands in the 1890s. Elsewhere the income tax is a twentieth-century phenomenon. It spread quickly during and after World War I and became a mass tax in many countries during World War II. Today the personal income tax raises substantial amounts of revenue in all industrialized

countries of the free world and is employed, although to a lesser extent, in most underdeveloped countries.

Equity considerations

Analysis of tax equity has been concerned largely with the distribution of tax burdens among persons in different economic circumstances, i.e., with *vertical* equity. Questions regarding the treatment of persons in essentially the same economic circumstances—the problems of *horizontal* equity—have only received close attention since the 1930s.

Vertical equity. Progressive taxation appeals intuitively to most people as an equitable method of distributing the tax burden by income classes, and economists and political theorists have devoted a great deal of intellectual effort to justify it on logical grounds.

An early theory of taxation that was widely held prior to the mid-nineteenth century was that taxes should be distributed in accordance with benefits received. The benefit theorists supported a minimum of government activity, possibly including defense and police and fire protection, but not much more. The benefits of such government services were assumed to be proportionate to income, and this was regarded as a major rationale for proportional income taxation. This theory of tax distribution proved to be untenable both because of its narrow view of the role of government and the arbitrary assumption it made regarding the distribution of benefits of government services.

In the latter half of the nineteenth century, progressive income taxation was justified by the sacrifice theories that emerged from discussions of "ability to pay." Under this doctrine, ability to pay is assumed to increase as incomes increase, and the objective is to impose taxes on a basis that would involve "equal sacrifice" in some sense. If the marginal utility of income declines more rapidly than income increases, *equal absolute sacrifice* leads to progression, *equal proportionate sacrifice* to still more progression, and *equal marginal sacrifice* to leveling of incomes from the top down until the required revenues are obtained. The assumptions of sacrifice theories—that the relative utility of different incomes is measurable and that the relation between income and utility is approximately the same for all taxpayers—cannot be verified by actual data or experience. Nevertheless, the ability-to-pay idea has been a powerful force in history and has undoubtedly contributed to the widespread acceptance of progressive taxation.

The basic justification for the progressive personal income tax is now probably the socioeconomic objective of reducing great disparities of welfare, opportunity, and economic power arising from the unequal distribution of income. More specifically, the justification is based on two propositions: (*a*) it is appropriate public policy to moderate economic inequality, and (*b*) taxation of personal incomes at progressive rates is an efficient method of promoting this objective, since it does not involve direct intervention in market activities. The acceptable degree of progression varies from time to time and place to place; it depends on the distribution of pre-tax incomes and the post-tax distribution desired by the voters. In practice the redistributive effects of the income tax have been moderate in all countries.

Horizontal equity.   A personal income tax conforming strictly with the "equal treatment" principle would apply to all income from whatever source derived, making allowances only for the taxpayer and his dependents. In accordance with the "accretion" concept, income would be defined as consumption plus (or minus) the net increase (or decrease) in the value of an individual's assets during the taxable period, perhaps modified to exclude gifts and inheritances that are ordinarily subject to separate taxes and, for practical reasons, to include capital gains when realized or when transferred to others through gifts or bequests. In practice most of the income taxes now in existence depart from this standard by a wide margin.

Differentiation of tax liability on the basis of family responsibilities is ordinarily made through a system of personal exemptions for the taxpayer and other members of his family. The personal exemption was originally regarded as a device to avoid taxing individuals and families with incomes that were not adequate to provide minimum levels of subsistence. Today personal exemptions are not high enough to cover a socially acceptable minimum level of subsistence in most countries; they serve primarily to remove low-income recipients from the tax rolls and also contribute to progression in the lower part of the income scale. At higher income levels the purpose of the personal exemption seems to be to moderate the tax burden as family size increases, although the degree of moderation varies greatly among countries. Special exemptions are allowed in some countries for particular groups of taxpayers (e.g., the aged); these exemptions are subsidies that could probably be handled more equitably through direct government outlays.

A second type of differentiation employed in most countries is based on the *source* of income. The provisions include credits for earned income and for dividends, preferential treatment for capital gains, exemptions for transfer payments and amounts set aside for retirement, omission of the rental value of owner-occupied homes, and numerous other special benefits. The earned-income credit is regarded as a convenient method of making rough allowances for depreciation of labor skills and for expenses of earning income from personal effort which are not recognized for tax purposes. The United States abandoned the earned-income credit in 1944 for simplification reasons, but it is still in existence in the United Kingdom, Australia, and other countries. Dividend credits are designed to moderate the so-called "double taxation" of corporate profits. Preferential treatment of capital gains grew out of the English concept of income, which excluded irregular receipts from income. This treatment is now rationalized on incentive grounds and also as a procedure to avoid applying the graduated rates, in the year of realization, to incomes accrued over a period of years. Transfer payments are excluded because they accrue largely to low-income people. Payments by employers into pension plans are not included in employees' taxable income to promote the development of private pension plans. The rental value of owner-occupied homes is untaxed in most places because it is difficult to apply the income tax to nonmoney incomes.

The third type of differentiation is based on the *use* of income. Deductions are required under a "net" income tax for expenditures that are essential to earning income. However, deductions for a wide variety of personal expenditures and for some forms of saving are also permitted. In one country or another, allowances are made for such items as medical expenses, charitable contributions, interest on personal loans and mortgages, state and local taxes, casualty losses, child care in families of working parents, deposits in saving associations, premiums for life, sickness, and accident insurance, and payments into annuity, pension, or other retirement plans.

Personal exemptions are an important element of a progressive income tax, but there is little justification for most of the special exclusions, deductions, and credits based on the source or use of income. Such provisions narrow the tax base and require the use of higher tax rates to raise a given amount of revenue. This puts a premium on earning or spending incomes in forms receiving preferential treatment, interferes with business and investment decisions, and distorts the allocation of resources. Since the deviations from equal treatment tend to be arbitrary, they create dissatisfaction among taxpayers who are subject to discrimination and result in pressures for the enactment of additional special benefits, pressures which legislatures find it difficult to resist. This process has been called "erosion of the tax base" in the United States, where taxable income is at least one-third lower than it would be under a comprehensive income tax. Measures to broaden the base and to use the revenues for rate reduction have been proposed by tax experts, but it is evident from the public and Congressional response that progress along these lines will be slow.

Economic effects

Three major aspects of the personal income tax may be distinguished in appraising its economic effects: first, its automatic response to changes in total personal income; second, its effects on the allocation of personal income between consumption and saving; and, third, its impact on work and investment incentives.

Automatic flexibility. The role of the personal income tax as a built-in stabilizer is one of its most significant features. In the United States, at the rates prevailing in the 1950s and in the 1960s, the personal income tax automatically offset more than ten per cent of the reductions in personal incomes during contractions. The corresponding figure for the United Kingdom was perhaps twice as large, the difference being attributable primarily to the higher starting rate in the United Kingdom. Such changes in tax liability reduce fluctuations in disposable personal income and thus help to stabilize consumption.

Built-in flexibility operates in both the expansion and contraction phases of the business cycle, so that the personal income tax moderates the growth of incomes during a business recovery just as it cushions the fall in income during contractions. This symmetrical response of the income tax (and of other stabilizers) during a business cycle is unavoidable. It should not lead to the abandonment of the stabilizers but rather to the establishment of basic tax–expenditure relationships that would be consistent with a prompt return to high employment following periods of recession. Discretionary changes in tax rates and in expenditures may be needed to implement this objective.

The responsiveness of the income tax to

changes in personal incomes is a useful characteristic for underdeveloped as well as for developed countries. An increasing proportion of the nation's resources must be devoted to public and private investment to increase the rate of economic development. Since voluntary saving is usually inadequate, the bulk of the investment funds must be provided by government. A progressive income tax automatically provides some of the financing as incomes increase. Where development is associated with rising prices, the income tax serves the dual role of moderating inflationary pressures and of increasing the rate of national saving.

Effect on consumption and saving. A personal income tax applies to the income of an individual regardless of the allocation of this income between consumption and saving. By contrast, a general consumption or expenditure tax can be postponed or avoided by delaying or eliminating consumption. It follows that an income tax is less burdensome on consumption than an equal-yielding consumption or expenditure tax which is distributed in the same proportions by income classes. In practice, where the income tax is paid by the large mass of people, much of the tax yield comes from income classes where there is little room in family budgets for reducing consumption in response to tax incentives. Under these circumstances the differential effect of the two types of taxes on total consumption and saving is likely to be relatively small.

Graduated expenditure taxes have been proposed in recent years as a method of avoiding or correcting the effects of income tax erosion, particularly in the top income brackets where exemption or preferential treatment of capital gains permits accumulation of large fortunes without tax payment. Expenditure taxation, it is felt, would discourage lavish living by people with large amounts of property and thus increase saving and risk taking without resorting to regressive taxes. Despite its apparent advantages, the expenditure tax has not been widely used. Rates in excess of 100 per cent would be required to raise significant amounts of revenue from high-income taxpayers. Moreover, the expenditure tax is more difficult to administer than the income tax and also raises much more serious problems of compliance.

Work and investment incentives. It is difficult to evaluate the effect of personal income taxes on work and investment incentives. On the one hand, high tax rates reduce the net rewards of greater effort and risk taking and thus tend to discourage these activities; on the other hand, they may provide a positive stimulus to obtain more income because they cut down on the income left over for spending. These two effects tend to offset one another, and there is no basis for deciding which is more important.

Empirical studies have shed little light on this question. The evidence suggests that income taxation does not have a significant effect on the amount of labor supplied by workers and managers. Work habits are apparently not easily changed, and there is little scope in a modern industrial society for most people to vary the hours of work or the intensity of their efforts in response to changes in tax rates.

A highly graduated income tax applying to *all* property incomes might reduce incentives to take risk somewhat, since it is impossible to reimburse taxpayers for losses at precisely the same rate at which their incomes are taxed. However, the income tax actually applies to a small fraction of property income in all countries. The opportunity to earn income in the form of capital gains—which are either not taxed at all or are taxed at relatively low rates—is a great stimulant to risk taking in the face of high rates on other incomes. Moreover, risk investment is to a large extent undertaken by firms operating in the corporate form; such firms are generally permitted to retain earnings after payment of more moderate tax rates than those applying to investors in the top personal income tax brackets.

Structural problems

The base of the personal income tax is determined by the definition of income, the allowable deductions, and the personal exemptions. Within wide limits, these elements can be combined with various tax rates to produce a given amount of revenue. Many of the difficult issues in most countries are an outgrowth of local problems and developments. Nevertheless, several structural problems in income taxation appear to be common to practically all countries, and these will be discussed briefly in this section.

Tax treatment of the family.   Throughout most of the history of the income tax, differentiation was made among taxpayers with different family responsibilities through the use of personal exemptions. Recently, there has been a trend toward the use of different tax rates to provide additional differentiation, particularly in the middle and higher tax brackets. In the United States, France, and West Germany, this has been accomplished by the adoption of the principle of "income splitting" between husband and wife or among all

family members. Other countries achieve the same objective by applying different rate schedules to taxpayers in different family situations.

In France the income of the family is divided by the number of family units, with the taxpayer and his spouse counting as one unit each and each dependent child as an additional one-half unit. The tax is then calculated as if the income of the family were divided proportionately among the family units. In West Germany and the United States, splitting is extended only to husband and wife. By contrast, the United Kingdom has made the use of joint returns by husband and wife mandatory since the early days of its income tax. Under this system the graduated rates are applied to the couple's combined income after allowance for personal exemptions and other deductions.

Income splitting between two persons doubles the width of the taxable income brackets and thus reduces the progression in tax burdens applying to married couples. The absolute size of the benefit depends entirely on the *rate of graduation*; it bears no relationship to the level of tax rates. For example, if rates increased one percentage point for every $1,000 of taxable income, income splitting would reduce the tax of a married couple with taxable income of $20,000 by $1,000. This would be true whether the starting rate was 1, 10, 20, or 50 per cent.

Income splitting is generally justified on the ground that husbands and wives usually share their combined income equally. For most families the largest portion of the budget goes for consumption, and savings are ordinarily set aside for the children or for the enjoyment of all members of the family. Two conclusions seem to follow if this view is accepted. First, married couples with the same combined income should pay the same tax irrespective of the legal division of income among them; second, the tax liabilities of married couples should be computed as if they were two single persons and their total income were divided equally between them. The first conclusion is now firmly rooted in the tax laws of most countries and seems to be almost universally accepted. It is the second conclusion on which opinions—and practices—still differ.

The case for the sharing argument is applicable to the economic circumstances of taxpayers in the lower income classes, where incomes are used almost entirely for the consumption of the family unit. At the top of the income scale the major rationale of income taxation is the reduction of the economic power of the taxpayer unit, and the use made of income in these levels for family purposes is irrelevant. Obviously, these objectives cannot be reconciled if income splitting is extended to all income brackets.

Aside from reducing progression, the practical effect of income splitting is to produce large differentials in the taxes of single persons and married couples. Differentials by marital status that depend on the rate of graduation are difficult to rationalize. However, it is difficult to justify treating single persons with families more harshly than married persons in similar circumstances. As a remedy for this problem, France grants to a widow or widower the same total number of family units for splitting purposes as if the spouse had survived. The United States permits widows and widowers to split their incomes for two years after the death of the spouse and provides half the advantage of income splitting for single persons who maintain a household for children or other dependents or support their parents in a separate household.

One of the major reasons for the acceptance of income splitting may well be inadequate differentiation provided by the traditional types of personal exemptions among taxpayers in the middle and top brackets. Single people, it is felt, should be taxed more heavily than married couples because they do not bear the costs and responsibilities of raising children. But the allowance of income splitting for husband and wife clearly does not differentiate between taxpayers in this respect since the tax benefit is the same whether or not there are children. Nor does the extension of splitting to children give the correct answer, since the benefits depend on the rate of graduation as well as on family size.

The source of the difficulty in the income-splitting approach is that differentiation of family size is made through the rate structure rather than through the personal exemptions. It would be possible to differentiate among taxpayer units by varying the personal exemptions to take account not only of the number of persons in the unit but also of the size of income, with both a minimum and maximum. If this is unacceptable, the only alternative—other than income splitting which produces anomalous results—is to vary tax rates by marital status and family size, as a number of countries have already done.

Personal deductions. In principle, the use made of a given income should have no bearing on the amount of tax to be paid out of that income. In practice, some allowances are made almost everywhere for selected items of consumption or saving. These deductions may be divided into three major types: (1) those that provide supplement to the personal exemption; (2) those that subsidize particular activities or expenditures; and (3) those that improve coordination of Federal income taxes with state or provincial and local taxes, where they exist.

A strong case can be made for allowing some deductions for large, unusual, and necessary expenditures when the personal exemptions are low. Deductions for medical expenses are the best example of this type of expenditure. They are often involuntary, unpredictable, and may exhaust a large proportion of the taxpayer's income. Expenditures for noninsured losses due to theft, fire, accident, or other casualties are of a similar nature. In keeping with the purpose of this type of deduction, it should be limited to an amount in excess of some percentage of income, which would be high enough to exclude all but extraordinary expenditures for these purposes.

Subsidy-type deductions are most common for contributions to charitable, religious, educational, and other nonprofit organizations. In many countries heavy reliance is placed on philanthropic institutions to supplement governmental activities and in some cases to provide services which governmental units do not perform. It may be argued that private philanthropy should not be encouraged at the expense of government funds. However, few people subscribe to this view because the activities of these organizations, with rare exceptions, are considered desirable and useful.

Subsidy-type deductions are also allowed in some countries for selected items of personal saving. Great Britain has permitted the deduction of a portion of life insurance premiums since the beginning of the income tax. West Germany allows deductions for personal insurance and for deposits in building and savings associations. A number of countries have recently enacted limited deductions for amounts set aside in annuities or retirement plans by self-employed persons and employees not eligible for company pension plans. The major motivation for these deductions appears to be to promote saving, but more particularly to encourage adequate provision for retirement and for catastrophic events that entail large outlays or loss of income. The deductions for personal contributions to retirement plans are also intended to remove the discrimination resulting from the exclusion usually granted to employer contributions to employee pension plans. The growth of allowances for particular types of saving has made substantial inroads into the philosophy of income taxation; in fact, these policies constitute a substantial movement toward the expenditure tax approach.

Suggestions have been made in recent years that the tax laws should permit a deduction for the cost of higher education. These suggestions reflect the importance of higher education for economic growth and the increased costs of a college education. On the one hand, a deduction allowed to parents would give the largest benefits to the highest income classes and would therefore be inequitable. On the other hand, some portion of expenditures for higher education is an investment which is not recognized for tax purposes as an expense of earning income. The appropriate treatment would be to regard the outlay by a parent as a gift to his child and to permit the child to write off a portion of this outlay over his earning career for, say, twenty years. However, there is no basis for estimating the proportion of educational outlays allocatable to investment, and the problems of administration and compliance would be substantial. [See CAPITAL, HUMAN.]

Deductions for income taxes paid to overlapping governmental units are required to prevent confiscation if one or more levels of government employ high rates in the upper end of the income scale. Where the rates are moderate, it is quite appropriate to levy two taxes on the same base without coordination. However, it may be desirable to permit deductions even if the rates are not confiscatory as a device to moderate interstate differentials. For example, with a Federal rate of 70 per cent and without deductibility of state taxes, the combined tax on residents of two states with rates of 5 and 10 per cent would be 75 and 80 per cent, respectively. By permitting taxpayers to deduct the state tax on their Federal returns, the combined rates are reduced to 71.5 and 73 per cent. (If the states also permit a deduction for Federal taxes, the combined rates are further reduced to 70.5 and 71 per cent. This type of mutual deductibility is unnecessary for coordination purposes, since the coordination achieved through single deductibility is quite adequate.)

A deduction for income taxes paid to state and local governments may be a practical necessity in a Federal system, but the same justification does not hold for state and local sales, excise, and property taxes. The latter deductions defeat the purposes of taxes levied to obtain payments from taxpayers for benefits received from state and local governments and reduce the progressivity of the combined tax system.

In the United States, where personal deductions have proliferated more than in any other country except perhaps West Germany, taxpayers are granted a "standard" deduction, in lieu of the itemized deductions, of up to 10 per cent of income (with a maximum of $500 on separate returns of married persons and $1,000 on all other returns). This device was adopted in 1944 for simplification reasons, in recognition of the fact that most personal deductions are small and few taxpayers keep adequate records to support them. To an important degree, the standard deduction violates the rationale of the itemized deduction; it reduces differentiation in tax liabilities while the itemized deductions are intended to introduce such differences for the purposes selected. The existence of both a standard deduction and itemized deductions suggests that there is some ambivalence toward many of the personal deductions in the United States income tax structure.

On balance, equity would be better served by avoiding erosion of the tax base through the use of numerous costly personal deductions. This should not preclude the adoption of a restricted list of deductions for unusually large and extraordinary expenditures to prevent hardships. Subsidy-type deductions are appropriate only if they promote a significant national objective and if the deduction route is the most efficient and equitable method of achieving that objective.

Capital gains and losses. As already indicated, an economic definition of income would include capital gains in full on an accrual basis. This method is impractical for three reasons: (1) valuations of many types of property cannot be estimated with sufficient accuracy to provide a basis for taxation; (2) most people would regard it as inequitable to pay tax unless income has actually been realized; and (3) taxation of accruals might force liquidation of assets to discharge tax liabilities. Thus, where capital gains are taxable, they are included in income only when realized.

Few countries tax the capital gains of individuals, but the United States has done so since the beginning of its income tax. Realized capital gains were originally taxed as ordinary incomes, but they have been subject to preferentially low rates since 1921. The provisions applying to such gains changed frequently during the 1920s and 1930s but were stabilized beginning in 1942. In general, capital gains on assets held for periods longer than six months are subject to half the rates on ordinary income, up to a maximum of 25 per cent.

The treatment of capital gains is likely to be a compromise among conflicting objectives. From the standpoint of equity, it is well established that capital gains should be taken into account in determining personal tax liability. Moreover, low rates or exemption of capital gains encourage the conversion of ordinary income into capital gains by devices that distort patterns of investment and discredit income taxation. On the other hand, the bunching of capital gains in the year of realization requires some provision to moderate the impact of graduation. On economic grounds full taxation of capital gains is resisted because it is believed that it would have a substantial "locking-in" effect on investors and reduce the mobility of capital. It is also argued that preferential treatment of capital gains helps to stimulate a higher rate of economic growth by increasing the attractiveness of investment generally and of risky investments in particular.

The "bunching" problem can be handled by pro-rating capital gains over the length of time the asset was held or by adopting a general averaging system applying to other types of income as well as to capital gains. However, unless the marginal rates were fairly low, the tax might still discourage the transfer of assets. Part of the difficulty is that adherence to the realization principle permits capital gains to be transferred tax-free either as a gift or at death. The solution to this problem is to treat capital gains as if they were constructively realized as a gift or at death, with an averaging provision to spread the gains over a period of years. Great Britain adopted the constructive realization principle when it added a capital gains tax to its tax structure. Under such a system the only advantage taxpayers have from postponing the realization of capital gains is the accumulation of interest on tax postponed. Unless the assets are held for many years, this advantage is small as compared to the advantage of the tax exemption accorded to the gains transferred at death; in any event, the interest on the tax postponed is subject to income tax when the assets are transferred. Under the circumstances, the incentive to hold gains indefinitely for tax considerations alone is very greatly reduced.

Capital losses are no easier to handle than capital gains. In principle, capital losses should be deductible in full either against capital gains or ordinary income. However, when gains and losses are recognized only upon realization, taxpayers can easily time their sales so as to take losses promptly when they occur and to postpone the realization of gains. There is no effective method of avoiding this asymmetry under any system of taxation applying to realized gains and losses. In the United States, capital losses of individuals may be offset against capital gains plus $1,000 of ordi-

nary income in the year of realization and in sub-sequent years for an indefinite time period. This restrictive policy is perhaps most harmful to small investors, who are less likely than those in the higher brackets to have gains against which to offset their losses. The only solution to this problem is a pragmatic one which would be as liberal as possible for the small investor without opening the door to widespread abuse and large revenue losses.

Relation to the corporate income tax. Unless corporate incomes were subject to tax, individuals could avoid the personal tax by accumulating income in corporations. Short of an annual allocation of corporate incomes on a prorata basis—a method which is excellent in theory but not in practice—the equity and revenue potential of the personal income tax can be protected only by a separate tax on corporate incomes. However, the existence of two separate taxes on the same income creates a difficult equity problem. Concern over the "double taxation" of dividends is evident in the various devices used in different countries to alleviate its alleged discriminatory effects.

On the assumption that all or a significant portion of the corporate income tax rests on the stockholder, the effect of double taxation is to impose the heaviest burden on dividends received by stockholders with the lowest incomes. Assume a corporate income tax of 50 per cent and suppose a corporation pays out $50 in dividends. The corporate income before tax from which these dividends were paid amounted to $100. If this $100 had been subject to personal income tax rates only, the nontaxable individual would have paid no tax on it; the additional burden of the corporate income tax in this case is the full $50 corporate tax. By contrast, a stockholder subject to an eighty per cent rate pays a personal income tax of $40 on the dividend, and the total tax burden on the original $100 of corporate earnings is $90. But since he would pay $80 under the personal income tax in any case, the additional burden on him is only $10.

The simplest and most effective method of dealing with this problem would be to permit corporations to deduct all or a portion of their dividends in computing taxable income. This method would apply the regular corporate tax rate to undistributed profits and would reduce or eliminate the corporate tax on distributed earnings. It would also have two additional advantages: first, dividend and interest payments would be treated more nearly alike, thus reducing the discrimination against equity financing by corporations; second, the same proportion of the corporate income tax on distributed income would be eliminated for all taxpayers regardless of their personal income tax status.

Despite these advantages, undistributed profits taxation is not used widely. The United States experimented with it in the 1930s, but the experiment created a great deal of resentment (possibly because the differentiation between distributed and undistributed profits was made by the imposition of a penalty tax on the latter rather than by allowing a deduction for dividends). The major drawback of undistributed profits taxation is that it discourages internal financing by corporations and thus may reduce saving and investment. On the other hand, some believe it is unwise as a matter of policy to permit corporations to avoid the capital markets for financing their investment programs.

If dividend relief is given at the individual level, there are three possibilities. The first is the "withholding" method, under which all or a portion of the corporate tax is regarded as having been paid at the source by the stockholder. The taxpayer includes the tax paid at the source in his income and then receives a tax credit for that amount. This method was used in Great Britain from the enactment of the 1803 income tax until 1965. Tax burdens of shareholders on distributed corporate income are the same as the burdens under the undistributed profits tax approach.

The second alternative is to permit the taxpayer to exclude some or all of his dividends from his tax return, and the third is to permit him to take a credit against his final tax liability computed at a flat percentage of the amount of dividends he receives. The United States exempts the first $100 of dividends; and Canada uses the dividend-credit approach exclusively at a rate of 20 per cent. Great Britain now makes no special allowance for dividends.

Neither the exclusion nor the credit can be regarded as a satisfactory method of removing double taxation, since neither can remove the same proportion of the excess taxation of dividends throughout the income scale. In contrast, the undistributed profits approach and the withholding method remove the same proportion at all income levels.

The desirability of doing something about the double taxation of dividends is still in dispute. First, corporations are viable economic units with characteristics and behavior patterns that have very little relationship to the income and other characteristics of their stockholders. Moreover, stockholders in large, publicly held corporations have only indirect and remote influence on management policies. On these grounds, many experts believe that a modern tax system would be incomplete without a separate tax on corporate enterprises. Second, the argument for moderating or removing the double taxation of dividends assumes that the corporate tax rests on the corporation and, ultimately, the stockholder. If the corporate income tax is shifted forward in the form of higher prices (or backward in the form of lower wages), the case for integration collapses. In the present state of knowledge, the incidence of the corporation income tax is not clear.

If integration of the corporate and personal income taxes were considered appropriate, some solution of the capital gains problem would be an essential first step. Under a system of full taxation of capital gains, including constructive realization at death, generous provision might well be made for alleviating the double tax on distributed profits. Where capital gains are either not taxed at all or are taxed at very low rates, the case for integration is weak. No country has yet resolved all of these problems satisfactorily.

Fluctuating incomes. The use of an annual accounting period combined with progressive rates results in a heavier tax burden on fluctuating incomes than on an equal amount of income distributed evenly over the years. This type of discrimination is hard to defend on equity or economic grounds. Taxpayers do not and cannot arrange their business and personal affairs to conform with the calendar. Annual income fluctuations are frequently beyond the control of the taxpayer, yet he is taxed as if 12 months were a suitable horizon for decision making. In addition, in the absence of averaging, there are great pressures for moderating the impact of the graduated rates on fluctuating incomes by lowering the rates applicable to them. Reduced rates on capital gains are often justified on this basis, although the reductions more than compensate for the absence of averaging.

There may also be a connection between the treatment of fluctuating incomes and incentives to take risk. Even with generous provisions for offsetting losses against gains, business incomes are taxed more heavily than other incomes under a progressive, annual income tax because (*a*) they fluctuate more than other incomes and (*b*) the losses do not come off the top of the taxpayer's income during the loss-offset period and are therefore not credited at the maximum rate. On the assumption that there is a correlation between income variability and risk, a tax system using a one-year accounting period is more burdensome on venturesome than on safe investments and thus is more discouraging to risk taking than a tax system having a longer accounting period.

Experience with general-averaging systems has been disappointing, largely because the methods used have been based on a variant of the moving average. This requires large tax payments when incomes fall below the average and small payments when they rise above it. Taxpayers properly regard such an arrangement as highly inequitable. It is now known that the payment problem may be solved by making the averaging adjustment in the form of a refund. For example, taxpayers might be permitted to average their incomes once every five years and to receive a refund (or credit) for any amount of tax actually paid in excess of 105 or 110 per cent of the tax on the average income during the averaging period. The United States adopted a variant of this method in 1964, allowing individuals to average their incomes over a five-year period where the income in the current year exceeds the average of the four prior years by more than a third and this excess is more than $3,000.

Many averaging systems, varying from cumulative lifetime averaging for every taxpayer to averaging over fairly short periods for specific types of volatile incomes, have been explored in the literature. All averaging proposals would create problems of compliance and administration and might involve substantial revenue losses, particularly if applied to the mass of taxpayers. With the advent of electronic machines, it will be possible to solve most of the administrative problems, but the revenue implications may remain serious.

The personal income tax is still in the process of development. Methods of differentiating tax liabilities of single persons and families of different size are unsatisfactory. There is increasing recognition that capital gains and losses should enter the tax base, but the equity, economic, and administrative objectives of capital gains taxation are difficult to reconcile. The appropriate relationship between the personal and the corporate income tax continues to be disputed. Little progress has been made to alleviate the excessive burden of the income tax on fluctuating income. Finally, the concept of income subject to tax departs considerably in most countries from an economic definition of income, and too many special allowances are made for specific sources and uses of income.

Despite all of these problems, the personal income tax is the best tax yet devised, and it will continue to be an indispensable and significant element of all modern tax systems for the indefinite future.

JOSEPH A. PECHMAN

BIBLIOGRAPHY

BARLOW, ROBIN; BRAZER, HARVEY E.; and MORGAN, JAMES N. 1966 *Economic Behavior of the Affluent.* Washington: Brookings Institution.

BUTTERS, J. KEITH; THOMPSON, L. E.; and BOLLINGER, L. L. 1953 *Effects of Taxation: Investments by Individuals.* Boston: Harvard Univ., Graduate School of Business Admininstration, Division of Research.

CANADA, ROYAL COMMISSION ON TAXATION 1966 *Report.* Ottawa: Queen's Printer.

GOODE, RICHARD B. 1951 *The Corporation Income Tax.* New York: Wiley.

GOODE, RICHARD B. 1964 *The Individual Income Tax.* Washington: Brookings Institution.

GREAT BRITAIN, ROYAL COMMISSION ON THE INCOME TAX 1920 *Report.* Papers by Command, Cmd. 615. London: H.M. Stationery Office.

KAHN, C. HARRY 1960 *Personal Deductions in the Federal Income Tax.* National Bureau of Economic Research, Fiscal Studies, No. 6. Princeton Univ. Press.

KALDOR, NICHOLAS 1955 *An Expenditure Tax.* London: Allen & Unwin.

KALVEN, HARRY; and BLUM, WALTER J. (1952) 1953 *The Uneasy Case for Progressive Taxation.* Univ. of Chicago Press. → First published in Volume 19 of the *University of Chicago Law Review.*

LEWIS, WILFRED 1962 *Federal Fiscal Policy in the Postwar Recessions.* National Committee on Government Finance, Studies in Government Finance. Washington: Brookings Institution.

MUSGRAVE, RICHARD A. 1959 *The Theory of Public Finance: A Study in Public Economy.* New York: McGraw-Hill.

PECHMAN, JOSEPH A. 1957 Erosion of the Individual Income Tax. *National Tax Journal* 10, March: 1–25.

PIGOU, A. C. (1928) 1956 *A Study in Public Finance.* 3d ed., rev. London: Macmillan; New York: St. Martins.

SELIGMAN, EDWIN R. A. (1911) 1921 *The Income Tax: A Study of the History, Theory and Practice of Income Taxation at Home and Abroad.* 2d ed. New York: Macmillan.

SELTZER, LAWRENCE H. 1951 *The Nature and Tax Treatment of Capital Gains and Losses.* National Bureau of Economic Research, Fiscal Studies, No. 3. New York: The Bureau.

SHEHAB, F. 1953 *Progressive Taxation: A Study in the Development of the Progressive Principle in the British Income Tax.* Oxford: Clarendon.

SIMONS, HENRY C. 1938 *Personal Income Taxation: The Definition of Income as a Problem of Fiscal Policy.* Univ. of Chicago Press.

U.S. CONGRESS, HOUSE, COMMITTEE ON WAYS AND MEANS 1959 *Tax Revision Compendium.* 3 vols. Washington: Government Printing Office.

VICKREY, WILLIAM S. 1947 *Agenda for Progressive Taxation.* New York: Ronald Press.

III
CORPORATION INCOME TAXES

The taxation of the income of corporations has come to be one of the major sources of fiscal revenue in most countries. According to the 1965 *Yearbook of National Accounts Statistics* of the United Nations, corporation tax receipts in 1962 equaled or exceeded 2 per cent of the national income in 32 countries, and represented 10 per cent or more of current government receipts in 19 countries. Of the major countries, Japan places the heaviest reliance upon the corporation income tax, receipts from this tax accounting for 22 per cent of current revenues and amounting to 6 per cent of the national income. Australia, Canada, New Zealand, the Republic of South Africa, and the United States all collect more than 15 per cent of their current revenues from this source, the amounts in each case representing more than 5 per cent of national income. In western Europe corporation income taxes typically represent 3–4 per cent of national income and 6–10 per cent of current government revenues. The corporation income tax tends to be less important, relative to national income and government revenues, in the developing countries than in the more advanced economies; but this is due mainly to the fact that the corporate sector itself is less important, rather than to a failure of the developing countries to levy the tax at all or to a tendency on their part to impose the tax at significantly lower rates than those applied by the more advanced countries.

This widespread and heavy reliance on the corporation income tax testifies to its administrative feasibility and political popularity. It is highly feasible administratively because the laws under which corporations are established generally require the maintenance of accounts on a standardized basis; thus the enforcement of the tax reduces to the problem of requiring honest and accurate accounts and of resolving a series of technical issues, such as the determination of which expenditures may be expensed and which must be capitalized, and the setting of allowable rates of depreciation for specific classes of assets. These problems have been handled in most countries by administrative decrees or regulations issued by the tax-collecting authority itself, operating under broad guidelines set out in the tax legislation.

The political appeal of the corporation income tax has two roots. First, the tax obviously conforms to popular conceptions of ability to pay, since the man in the street tends to view corporations as wealthy entities themselves and as being owned predominantly by wealthy stockholders. But second, and in many ways equally important as a source of political appeal, is the fact that the corporation income tax, by definition, cannot be a source of loss to a corporation. Those corporations which have no net income pay no corporation income tax; only "profitable" companies are required to bear this levy. By contrast, other forms of business taxation can themselves be responsible for converting what would otherwise be a net profit situation into one of net loss. Hence, even within the world of business, companies in a marginal or precarious financial situation are likely to prefer the taxation of corporate net income to other forms of business taxation, and the strong opponents of corporate income taxation are likely to be the more profitable companies with the most "ability to pay."

The administrative and political advantages of the corporation income tax do not, however, imply that it is a good tax from the economic point of view. Quite to the contrary, it is readily demonstrable that, of the major revenue sources, this tax is one of the least justifiable on economic grounds. It entails an essentially arbitrary discrimination among industries or activities, it tends to inhibit the growth of the more dynamic sectors of the economy, and it probably causes a reduction in the over-all rate of capital formation.

Efficiency effects

All the discriminatory features of the corporation income tax stem from the fact that corporate net income is the tax base. By the definition of the tax, all unincorporated activities are exempt; and even within the corporate sector of the economy, the tax falls more heavily on activities with low ratios of debt to equity (because interest on debt is a deductible expense). The consequence of these discriminations is a distortion of the economic structure, favoring noncorporate over corporate activities and, within the corporate sector, a distortion favoring those activities which can readily be financed in large measure by debt capital over those which cannot. The tax may also discriminate within the corporate sector against capital-intensive activities and favor labor-intensive activities, but the existence of this effect depends on the incidence of the tax; it may be present but need not be.

The basis for these assertions is the fact that in all economies in the modern world there is a tendency toward the equalization of the rates of return that investors receive on capital in different industries or activities. This tendency can be frustrated by restrictions on the entry of capital into given areas, can be blunted by imperfect information, can be modified by considerations of differential risk or convenience among different invest-ment outlets, and can be obscured by random year-to-year variations in earnings—but it is always present. Stigler (1963, p. 23) found, for example, that whereas the mean rate of return (after taxes) on invested capital in U.S. manufacturing indus-tries averaged 7.6 per cent in 1947–1954, the standard deviation of the rates of return by two-digit industries (about this mean) was only 1.6 per cent. Moreover, he found no significant evi-dence of a risk premium (either positive or nega-tive) when he related observed average rates of return in individual industries to the standard de-viation of each industry's rate of return. Stigler's results accord well with what one would expect a priori from a reasonably well-functioning capital market. If higher-than-average rates of return to capital exist and persist in a given activity, then one would expect investment in that activity to increase and so drive down the rate of return; if lower-than-average rates of return prevail, one would expect investment to fall off, inducing an increase in the rate of return.

The following analysis will, accordingly, be based on a tendency toward equalization of after-tax rates of return to capital in different invest-ment uses. Given this tendency, it is clear that the corporation income tax will produce an equilibrium pattern of net rates of return among industries only through its differential impact's being re-flected in differential gross rates of return. Thus, assuming that the net-of-tax rate of return on equity would, in a given capital-market situation, tend to stabilize at 6 per cent, and assuming that the rate of return to capital in the noncorporate sector and the rate of interest on debt would also tend to stabilize at 6 per cent, we have the follow-ing possible pattern of rates of return on capital, gross of a corporation income tax at a rate of 50 per cent:

Noncorporate Industry	6%
Corporate Industry A: $\frac{2}{3}$ debt	8%
Corporate Industry B: $\frac{1}{3}$ debt	10%
Corporate Industry C: 100% equity	12%

The differentials in gross rates of return on cap-ital induced by the corporation income tax have two kinds of effects: first, they are reflected in product prices and, consequently, in the levels of output of particular activities; second, they con-front the different activities with different relative costs of labor and capital and, hence, induce de-cisions concerning the relative intensity of use of these resources which are uneconomic from the standpoint of the economy as a whole. For exam-

ple, the net annual cost of $100,000 of capital, for a year, to Noncorporate Industry (see above), would be $6,000, while that to Corporate Industry C would be $12,000. If labor of a given class is paid $6,000 per year, Noncorporate Industry is induced to operate at a point where the marginal $100,000 of capital produces a yield equivalent to the mar-ginal product of one man-year of labor, while Cor-porate Industry C will tend to operate at a point where $100,000 of capital will have a yield equiv-alent to the marginal product of two man-years of labor. Clearly, economic efficiency could be im-proved by a tax system which took an equal frac-tion of the income generated by capital in all lines of activity, regardless of whether they were cor-porate in structure or not, and regardless of their degree of access to debt financing.

Effect of other taxation. The foregoing sketch of the efficiency-effects of the corporation income tax implicitly viewed the tax as the only levy in the tax system that affected gross-of-tax rates of return differently in different activities. Actually, there are a variety of taxes and tax provisions in most coun-tries which have such effects, and it is important in any analysis of real-world tax systems to con-sider the combined effect of all such provisions rather than attempt artificially to isolate one tax, such as the corporation income tax, from the over-all structure of which it is a part.

Property taxes, for example, are often levied at different effective rates on real property of different types. More important, property taxes often are levied only on land and buildings. Thus machines, inventories, and such may escape the property tax; and corporate capital, in which machines and in-ventories play a larger role than in noncorporate capital, will then pay relatively less through prop-erty taxation than noncorporate capital. In this way the property tax may tend to offset somewhat the discrimination against the corporate sector that is implicit in the corporation income tax.

Similarly, in countries like the United States, where capital gains are taxed at rates lower than normal personal income tax rates, or in countries with no capital gains taxation at all, the effects of corporate income taxation as such are likely to be offset to some extent by the favored treatment of capital gains. This is so because the earnings of capital in unincorporated enterprises are taxed under the personal income tax as they are earned, at full personal income tax rates, while the per-sonal income tax strikes only that portion of cor-porate earnings paid out in dividends at the full rate. Let D be the proportion of earnings paid out in dividends, t_c be the corporate tax rate, t_p the personal tax rate, and t_g be the effective rate of tax on capital gains. Then \$1 of corporate earnings will pay a total personal-plus-corporate tax bill equal to

$$t_c + (1 - t_c)Dt_p + (1 - t_c)(1 - D)t_g.$$

This can turn out to be lower than t_p, the total income tax paid on \$1 of income of an unincorporated enterprise, provided that the rate of tax applicable to a marginal dollar of personal income is sufficiently higher than the corporate tax rate.

For example, assume that an individual is in the 70 per cent bracket of the personal income tax and is contemplating investing some savings in either a specific corporation, C, or a specific unincorporated enterprise, U. Suppose that both investments are expected to have a gross-of-tax yield of 20 per cent. The net-of-tax return from the investment in U will be 6 per cent, while that from the investment in C will depend on t_c, D, and t_g. Suppose t_c is 40 per cent, D is $33\frac{1}{3}$ per cent, and t_g is 15 per cent. Then, of \$20 of earnings in C, \$8 will be paid in corporation tax, and \$2.80 in personal tax on dividends of \$4. If the corporation's savings of \$8 out of earnings of \$20 ultimately are fully reflected in capital gains, and if these are taxed at an effective rate of 15 per cent, then \$1.20 will be paid in capital gains taxes. The total tax on \$20 of income will be \$12, and the net-of-tax rate of return from the investment in C will be 8 per cent—higher by 2 points than that on the investment in U.

Obviously, the effective rate of corporate-cum-personal tax on an investment will vary from individual to individual (depending on their marginal tax rates) and from corporation to corporation (depending on their dividend policies and on the degree to which their corporate savings are reflected in capital gains). Moreover, the effective rate of tax on capital gains will itself vary from situation to situation, since individuals can postpone realization of capital gains, thus postponing payment of capital gains tax and shrinking the present value of the tax paid on capital gains account. For example, if a share bought for \$100 today rises in value at 8 per cent per year, capital gains tax payable upon sale r years in the future will be $t_g^*[(1.08)^n - 1]$, where t_g^* is the nominal rate of tax on capital gains, but the present value of this tax (evaluated at 8 per cent) will be $t_g^*[1 - (1/1.08)^n]$. This is what was meant above by the effective rate of tax on capital gains. It is clearly, from this example, a decreasing function of the length of time that the stock is held. In the United States, the effective rate of capital gains tax can in fact be zero, since assets held until the death of the owner pass to his heirs, who in turn are taxed only on increases in value that take place after they have inherited the property.

While the property tax and capital gains provisions tend somewhat to offset the distorting effects of the corporation income tax, the traditional treatment of income from owner-occupied housing works to reinforce the distortions implicit in the corporation income tax. Obviously, owner-occupied housing generates income in real terms, but traditionally this income has not been a part of the personal income tax base. As a consequence, this important part of the income generated by capital in the unincorporated sector of the economy pays neither corporate nor personal income tax, while the income generated in the corporate sector is subject to both.

Empirical estimation. Harberger (see Krzyzaniak 1966) has attempted to derive rough estimates of the cost to the U.S. economy of the pattern of distortions created by the differential taxation of capital in different uses. He incorporates into a single model, which distinguishes between the corporate sector and the noncorporate sector, the effects of corporate income taxation, property taxation, capital gains taxation, and the exemption from personal income taxation of the imputed income from owner-occupied housing. Making conservative assumptions about the elasticities of response of the economy to the various distortions involved, Harberger estimates the "efficiency cost" of the U.S. pattern of taxation of income from capital at approximately \$2 billion per year. This estimate concerns *only* the costs associated with the misallocation of a given capital stock, costs which would be zero if all income from capital were to be taxed at a given constant rate. It does not take into account the possible effects of the taxation of income from capital upon the size of the capital stock itself (through the influence of taxation on the rate of saving), nor does it fully incorporate the effects of various special provisions (e.g., percentage depletion) affecting specific industries. Hence, it is a conservative estimate in this respect as well.

Incidence

The incidence of the corporation income tax has long been the subject of debate among economists, a state of affairs which is likely to continue for some time. Underlying this debate are some genuine differences, both analytical (reflecting different assumptions about the behavior of firms) and empirical (reflecting differing views about, for example, the quantitative response of saving to the disturbances engendered by the imposition of the tax). However, expositions of the effects of the corporation income tax at times contain serious conceptual and analytical errors which should long since have been laid to rest.

Perhaps the main source of confusion has been the conception of the incidence of the tax as falling either (*a*) on stockholders, or (*b*) on consumers, or (*c*) on workers, or on some combination of these three. There are three errors involved in this traditional trichotomy. The first has to do with the use of the term "stockholders" rather than "owners of capital"; the second relates to the distinction between consumers and workers; and the third concerns the assumption, which is usually implicit when the trichotomy is stated, that none of the three groups will gain as a consequence of the tax.

The distinction between stockholders and owners of capital. The idea that the burden of the corporation income tax will fall on the stockholders of the affected corporations is a valid one within the confines of standard short-run equilibrium analysis. This is because in the short run, with the capital of each corporation considered as a fixed factor of production, the earnings of equity capital represent the residual share. This residual share is assumed, in traditional short-run models of competitive and of monopolistic behavior, to be maximized by the firm. So long as the demand and cost conditions facing the firm are unchanged— the conventional assumption—the output which generated maximum profit before the tax was imposed will also yield maximum profit in the presence of the tax.

Although the above analysis is correct for the short run, a major change occurs when longer-run adjustments are allowed for. Here the appropriate assumption is that the after-tax rate of return is equalized between the corporate and the noncorporate sectors. Any fall in the rate of return perceived by the owners of shares will therefore also be perceived by the holders of other kinds of titles to capital, and the isolation of *stockholders* as the relevant group when assessing the incidence of the tax is no longer correct. The relevant group becomes *owners of capital*, once attention is focused on the longer-run incidence of the tax.

The distinction between consumers and workers. Once the above is recognized, the error implicit in the distinction between consumers and workers becomes apparent. Since all income-earners in the community are owners of either labor or capital resources or both, the reduction in real income implicit in the tax must reflect the sum of the reductions in the real incomes of these two groups. That is to say, a distribution of the burden of the tax

between people in their role as owners of capital, on the one hand, and people in their role as sellers of labor services, on the other, is exhaustive, leaving no room for an additional burden to be borne by consumers.

This is not to say that, within each group, different individuals will not bear different burdens because of differences in their consumption patterns. In general, those, whether capitalists or workers, who consume a greater-than-average proportion of "corporate" products as against "noncorporate" products will be relatively harder hit as a consequence of the tax than those who have the opposite bias in their consumption pattern. But the extra benefits accruing to those consumers with relatively "noncorporate" consumption patterns must, because of the deviations of these patterns from the average, exactly offset the extra burden borne by those with relatively "corporate" consumption patterns. (This statement is precisely correct if only the first-order effects of the change in tax regime are taken into account. When second-order effects are considered, there emerges an "excess burden" of the tax, deriving from the distortion of consumption patterns and resource allocation which results from the tax. Excess burden, however, is conventionally left out of account in discussions of incidence, for otherwise the sum of all burdens allocated would exceed the yield of the tax; that is, incidence is conventionally defined as dealing only with first-order effects.)

There is, nevertheless, a way in which sense can be made out of a statement like "The tax is wholly passed on to consumers." For if analysis reveals that the real incomes accruing to labor and capital fall by equal percentages as a result of the tax, then it is equally convenient to describe the tax as being borne fully by people in their role as consumers. And if labor's real income falls by 10 per cent as a consequence of the tax, while capital's falls by 20 per cent, it is just as convenient to regard the tax burden as being a 10 per cent reduction of the real income of consumers as such (the percentage point fall common to the two groups), plus an additional 10 per cent reduction falling upon the owners of capital. But if this approach is taken, there is no burden to be allocated to labor in the example just cited, just as there would be none to allocate to capital if its real income fell by 10 per cent and labor's by 20 per cent. Thus the idea of a three-way division of the burden remains illogical even when a plausible device is found for ascribing some of it to consumers.

The "no-gain" fallacy. The third error involved in typical presentations of the trichotomy—the implicit assumption that no group will gain as a consequence of the imposition of a corporation income tax—is perhaps the most serious of all, since it leads to a gross misapprehension of the nature of its incidence. It is not at all true that the share of the total burden of the tax which falls on capital must lie between zero and 100 per cent; a much more plausible range for capital's share runs from a_k to $1/b_c$ (where a_k is the proportion of the national income accruing to capital and b_c is the fraction of the capital stock which is occupied in the corporate sector), though even this range can easily be exceeded.

To demonstrate the plausibility of the suggested range, assume that, with fixed and fully employed stocks of labor and of capital and holding the wage rate constant as the *numéraire*, the net-of-tax return to capital remains unchanged as a consequence of the tax. The nominal income of both labor and capital is therefore unchanged, but the real income of both groups falls because the prices of products of the corporate sector must rise to accommodate the tax. Labor and capital must therefore suffer equiproportionally as a consequence of the tax, capital's fraction of the total burden being a_k, its share in the national income.

The other end of the range is generated when the gross-of-tax rate of return to capital remains unchanged as a consequence of the tax. The net-of-tax rate of return must therefore fall by the percentage rate of the tax imposed. But the equilibrium condition for the capital market assures that if the net-of-tax rate of return falls by this percentage in the corporate sector, it must fall by the same percentage in the noncorporate sector. Since the fall in the return to capital in the corporate sector just reflects the tax paid, the parallel fall in the noncorporate sector reflects that capital is bearing more than the full burden of the tax, the ratio of capital's loss to the full burden of the tax being the ratio of total capital to corporate capital, or $1/b_c$. In this case, therefore, labor gains an amount equal to the reduction in real income per unit of capital times the amount of capital in the noncorporate sector.

The "plausible limits" just outlined can be derived from a two-sector model with homogeneous (of first degree) production functions, on the assumption that the elasticity of substitution between labor and capital is infinite in one sector or the other. If this elasticity is infinite in the untaxed (noncorporate) sector, then so long as some production takes place in that sector in the post-tax equilibrium, the relationship between the return to

a unit of capital and the wage received by a unit of labor must be the same as in the pretax equilibrium. Capital and labor therefore must bear the same percentage losses of real income as a result of the tax. When, on the other hand, the elasticity of substitution between labor and capital is infinite in the corporate sector, the post-tax gross-of-tax return per unit of capital must bear the same relationship to the wage of labor as prevailed before the tax was imposed. Hence the net-of-tax return per unit of capital must fall, in both sectors, relative to the wage of labor, by the percentage of the tax, and capital must accordingly bear $(1/b_c)$ times the full burden of the tax.

Strikingly, these same "plausible limits" come into play when the elasticity of substitution is zero in one of the two sectors and non-zero in the other. When the corporate sector has a zero elasticity of substitution between labor and capital, the reduction in its output resulting from the tax leads to the ejection of labor and capital from that sector in the fixed proportions given by its technical coefficients of production. Suppose that the corporate sector uses labor and capital in the ratio of 1:2; as it contracts, it must therefore eject the factors in these proportions. If, now, the noncorporate sector was, in the pretax equilibrium, using the two factors in just these proportions, it will be able to absorb the "rejects" from the corporate sector without any change in relative factor prices. And since factor prices in the noncorporate sector are already net-of-tax, this means that both factors must suffer in the same proportion as a consequence of the tax, just as in the case of an infinite elasticity of substitution in the noncorporate sector.

The above result occurs when labor and capital were initially used in the same proportions in the two sectors, and it must be modified when the initial proportions differ. If the corporate sector ejects labor and capital in the ratio of 1:2, while the noncorporate sector was initially using them in the ratio 1:1, the noncorporate sector (which is assumed to have a non-zero elasticity of substitution) must alter its factor proportions so as to absorb relatively more capital. Capital's return must therefore fall relative to labor's, in order for equilibrium to be restored; and capital will bear more than the fraction a_k of the total burden of the tax. Conversely, if the noncorporate sector were initially more capital-intensive than the corporate sector, using the factors, say, in the proportions 1:3, the relative price of labor would have to fall so as to enable this sector to absorb the "rejects" from the corporate sector; and capital would end up bearing less than a_k of the total burden of the tax.

Thus, when the elasticity of substitution between labor and capital is zero in the corporate sector, capital will bear the fraction a_k of the total burden if the two sectors have equal factor intensities; will bear more than a_k when the corporate sector is the more capital-intensive of the two; and will bear less than a_k when the corporate sector is the more labor-intensive of the two. Exactly how much more or less than a_k capital will bear depends upon the extent of the difference in factor proportions between the two industries, on the elasticity of substitution between labor and capital in the noncorporate sector (which determines the ease with which it can absorb new factors in proportions different from those initially used), and on the elasticity of substitution on the demand side between corporate products and noncorporate products (the greater this elasticity, the sharper the decline in demand for corporate products as a consequence of the tax, the larger the ejection of resources by this industry, and therefore the greater the shift in relative factor prices required to restore equilibrium).

When, on the other hand, the elasticity of substitution between labor and capital is zero in the untaxed industry and non-zero in the taxed industry, capital tends to bear more than the full burden of the tax. In this case, when the initial factor proportions are the same in both industries, the fixity of proportions in the untaxed industry assures that they will remain the same even after the tax has worked out its full effects. The relative returns to labor and capital, being governed in this case by the proportions in which the factors are used in the taxed industry, will remain the same, gross-of-tax, as they were in the pretax equilibrium. Capital's return net-of-tax will fall by the amount of the tax, but, as in the case of infinite elasticity of substitution in the taxed industry, the reduction will occur for capital used in either industry. The total reduction in capital's earnings will be $(1/b_c)$ times the yield of the tax, reflecting a very substantial "overbearing" of the tax by owners of capital and a corresponding net gain to those whose income accrues principally from the sale of labor services.

The above result (for a zero elasticity of substitution in the untaxed industry) is modified when the initial factor proportions are different in the two sectors. If the corporate sector is initially more labor-intensive than the noncorporate sector, the ejection of capital and labor resources in the pro-

portions in which the latter sector will absorb them will make the corporate sector still more labor-intensive. A readjustment of factor prices against labor and in favor of capital will have to occur, and capital will end up bearing less than $(1/b_c)$ times the observed yield of the tax. Conversely, if the corporate sector is initially more capital-intensive than the noncorporate sector, and has a zero elasticity of substitution, factor proportions will have to alter to make the corporate sector still more capital-intensive, requiring a shift of the gross-of-tax ratio of factor prices against capital. Capital will then bear more than $(1/b_c)$ times the observed yield of the tax.

When capital bears 100 per cent of the burden. Falling well within the "plausible limits" of incidence defined by a_k and $1/b_c$ is the case in which capital bears 100 per cent of the burden of the tax. This result therefore cannot be regarded as being an extreme outcome, as the conventional use of the capital–labor–consumer trichotomy implies. Added insight into the plausibility of capital's bearing the full burden of the tax can be gained from an analysis of the case in which each industry is characterized by a Cobb–Douglas production function and in which the elasticity of substitution in demand between the products of the two sectors is unity. Letting X represent the quantity of the product of the corporate sector, Y the quantity of the product of the noncorporate sector, P_x and P_y their respective prices, and Z the national income, the unit elasticity of substitution between X and Y implies

$$(1) \qquad XP_x = \alpha Z; \qquad YP_y = (1-\alpha)Z,$$

where α is the fraction of Z which is spent on X. Competitive behavior of producers of X and of Y, together with the Cobb–Douglas functions $X = K_x^\beta L_x^{(1-\beta)}$, $Y = K_y^\gamma L_y^{(1-\gamma)}$, where β and γ are constants, lead to the relations

$$(2) \qquad \begin{aligned} K_x P_{kx} &= \beta X P_x; & L_x P_L &= (1-\beta)XP_x, \\ K_y P_k &= \gamma Y P_y; & L_y P_L &= (1-\gamma)YP_y. \end{aligned}$$

Here K_x and K_y represent the amounts of capital used in the X and Y industries, respectively, and L_x and L_y refer to the corresponding amounts of labor. The price of labor is denoted by P_L, this being the same in the two industries. The cost of the services of a unit of capital is denoted by P_{kx} for the corporate sector and by P_k for the noncorporate sector, the former including the corporation income tax and the latter, of course, not including it. If τ is the rate of corporation income tax applied to the earnings of capital in sector X, then $P_k = P_{kx}(1 - \tau)$, since the after-tax *earnings* (as distinct from the before-tax *cost*) of a unit of capital are assumed to be brought to equality in both industries through the workings of the capital market.

It can be seen from relations (1) and (2) that labor will always earn a constant fraction of the national income, regardless of whether a corporation income tax exists or not. This already guarantees that exactly the full burden of the corporation tax must in this case be borne by capital. The precise way in which the burden reaches all units of capital can be seen by analyzing the relations derived from (1) and (2):

$$(3) \qquad K_x P_{kx} = \beta\alpha Z; \qquad K_y P_k = \gamma(1 - \alpha)Z.$$

From these it results that $[(K_x P_{kx})/(K_y P_k)]$ is a constant equal to $\beta\alpha/[\gamma(1 - \alpha)]$. But since $P_k = P_{kx}(1 - \tau)$, this means that $K_x/[K_y(1 - \tau)]$ will also be a constant—that is, the ratio (K_x/K_y) will vary directly with $(1 - \tau)$. If, with no tax at all, there were 150 units of capital in each sector, a tax of 50 per cent will eventually result in there being 100 units of capital in X and 200 in Y. The 200 units of capital in Y will earn the same fraction of national income as was previously earned by the 150 units of capital in Y; hence the net-of-tax return to capital will have been reduced by a quarter, say, from \$1.00 to \$.75 per unit. The 100 units of capital in X will *cost* entrepreneurs \$1.50 per unit and will therefore have the same total cost as the 150 units employed in X at a unit cost of \$1.00 before the tax was imposed. But the after-tax earnings of capital in X will, like those of capital in Y, have fallen from \$1.00 to \$.75 per unit. Overall, capital will have lost \$75, represented by the reduction of \$.25 per unit spread over all 300 units, and this amount will be precisely equal to the yield of the tax to the government.

The result obtained in the above example applies not only to all cases fulfilling relations (1) and (2), which are derived on the basis of unit elasticities of substitution in demand between the two products, and in production between the two factors in each industry. It has been shown elsewhere (see Harberger 1962) that the same result obtains so long as the three critical elasticities of substitution are equal, regardless of their magnitude.

The general-equilibrium, two-sector model. All the cases presented above are special cases of a general-equilibrium, two-sector model of the incidence of taxation, in which the incidence of the corporation income tax is shown to depend in a specific way on the three critical elasticities of substitution and on the relative factor intensities of the two sectors. This model, based on the assumptions that the supplies of capital and labor are not influenced by the presence or absence of the tax, that competition prevails in both the corporate and noncorporate sectors, and that per-unit net-of-tax earnings of each productive factor are equalized between sectors, was first presented by Harberger (1962) and further elaborated by Mieszkowski (1967). They have adapted the model to explore the implications of various possible types of monopolistic and oligopolistic behavior in the corporate sector; the results of the original model have proved quite insensitive to plausible allowances for noncompetitive behavior.

The chief weakness of the model appears, at this writing, to be the assumption that the path of the capital stock through time is independent of the rate of corporate taxation. If, through a tax-induced reduction in the net rate of return on capital and/or through a tax-induced shift in the distribution of disposable income, the rate of saving is affected, the relative supplies of capital and labor will gradually diverge from the path they would have followed in the absence of a corporation income tax, with consequent effects on the distribution of income. The difficulties confronting attempts to resolve this issue are twofold. First, a dynamic rather than a comparative-static approach is required, which, while not a serious obstacle as such, involves additional parameters whose magnitudes are difficult to estimate and requires the specification of the precise nature of the dynamic structure of the economy. A great deal of further work is needed before our understanding of the economy's workings can advance to the point where these dynamic aspects can be treated with a degree of precision comparable to that with which problems of comparative statics are handled today.

The second difficulty is conceptual rather than practical. In a comparative-static approach to incidence, excess-burden being neglected, the sum of the changes in real income of the separate groups of the economy is a global reduction in real income equal to the proceeds of the tax; this is no longer true when a dynamic framework is employed. If the rate of saving is reduced by the corporation income tax, the future incomes accruing to individuals are reduced not only because the tax has to be paid each year, but also because less has been saved in the years since the tax was introduced. But it would be wrong, in estimating the incidence of the tax, to count both (*a*) the full reduction of real income in the year the tax is paid and (*b*) the future reduction in real income stemming from the reduction in savings induced by the tax. If one counts (a), one has already accounted for the present value of the future reduction in real income. To take explicit account of the future effects of changes in the savings pattern, one would properly have to convert the entire calculation of incidence to a consumption rather than an income basis and count (c) the current reduction in consumption resulting from the tax paid today plus (d) the future reduction in consumption occasioned by the reduction in future incomes stemming from the current tax-induced reduction in the rate of saving.

When the above difficulties are considered, it appears that the current-income approach (i.e., counting only (a) as the measure of incidence) is preferable, on grounds of both clarity and convenience, to approaches attempting to introduce dynamic responses into the measurement of incidence. Nevertheless, the dynamic responses in question here are of substantial interest in their own right, even if they are not linked to the analysis of incidence. The study of this aspect of the effects of corporation income taxation has only recently begun, the most important early efforts being those of Krzyzaniak (1966) and Sato (1967).

ARNOLD C. HARBERGER

BIBLIOGRAPHY

GOODE, RICHARD B. 1951 *The Corporation Income Tax.* New York: Wiley.

HARBERGER, ARNOLD C. 1959 The Corporation Income Tax: An Empirical Appraisal. Volume 1, pages 231–250 in U.S. Congress, House, Committee on Ways and Means, *Tax Revision Compendium.* Washington: Government Printing Office.

HARBERGER, ARNOLD C. 1962 The Incidence of the Corporation Income Tax. *Journal of Political Economy* 70:215–240.

HARBERGER, ARNOLD C.; and BAILEY, MARTIN J. (editors) 1968 *The Taxation of Income From Capital.* Washington: Brookings Institution.

KRZYZANIAK, MARIAN (editor) 1966 *Effects of the Corporation Income Tax: Papers Presented at the Symposium on Business Taxation.* Detroit, Mich.: Wayne State Univ. Press. → See pages 107–117, "Efficiency Effects of Taxes on Income From Capital," by Arnold C. Harberger.

MIESZKOWSKI, PETER 1967 On the Theory of Tax Incidence. *Journal of Political Economy* 75:250–262.

MUSGRAVE, RICHARD A. 1959 *The Theory of Public Finance: A Study in Public Economy.* New York: McGraw-Hill.

MUSGRAVE, RICHARD A.; and KRZYZANIAK, MARIAN 1963 *The Shifting of the Corporation Income Tax: An Empirical Study of Its Short-run Effect Upon the Rate of Return.* Baltimore: Johns Hopkins Press.

SATO, KAZUO 1967 Long-run Shifting of the Corporation Income Tax. Unpublished manuscript.

STIGLER, GEORGE J. 1963 *Capital and Rates of Return in Manufacturing Industries.* National Bureau of Economic Research, General Series, No. 78. Princeton Univ. Press.

Yearbook of National Accounts Statistics. → Published by the United Nations since 1958. Contains detailed estimates of national income and related economic measures for some 76 countries.

IV
PROPERTY TAXES

Property taxes are general and recurring taxes on owners or users of property, based on the capital value or the annual rental value of the assets. They are considered distinct forms of taxation, although many other taxes reach some facet of property ownership or use, including taxes on the income from property, taxes on realized appreciation in property values (capital gains), taxes in a number of European countries on net wealth, wealth transfer taxes or succession duties, and taxes on selected types of personal property, such as motor vehicles.

Property taxation is widespread and is typically used by local rather than national governments. It provides the overwhelming bulk of local government tax revenues in the United States, in the other developed English-speaking countries, in the Netherlands, and in a number of the developing countries, especially those exposed to the British tradition. The tax is also important to local governments in Belgium, Denmark, France, Germany, and Japan, countries in which it provides roughly 20 to 30 per cent of local government tax revenues.

Property taxes are most important relative to the over-all fiscal system in the English-speaking countries, where the role of local governments tends to be a large one. In Canada and the United States in recent years, the property tax has accounted for more than 45 per cent of the tax revenues of all subnational governments (including states or provinces), about 16 per cent of the total tax revenues of all governments, and more than 4 per cent of national income. It accounted for more than 13 per cent of Ireland's total taxes; more than 11 per cent of Britain's; and 6 to 8 per cent in Australia, New Zealand, South Africa, Denmark, and Japan.

In most countries, the tax applies to land and/or buildings only, but in the United States, some types of personal property are subject to the property tax in all but four states. Business and farm equipment and inventories are commonly taxed, and account for perhaps 75 per cent of the personal property tax base. Motor vehicles are subject to this tax in more than half the states, and household effects are taxed somewhat more rarely. Intangible personal property—securities, bank deposits, etc.—is infrequently taxed; intangibles have provided only about 2 per cent of property tax revenues recently, and all personal property about 19 per cent. In some Canadian provinces, personal property is taxed, but it provides only 1 per cent of revenues nationally; in Japan, personal property provides nearly 40 per cent of revenues.

The most common basis for taxing real property is its annual rental value, in practice usually gross rents assessed as of some earlier date, with statutory rather than actual allowances for expenses. Real property is taxed on the basis of its capital value mainly in the United States, Canada, South Africa, Germany, Austria, and Denmark. The major difference between the customary annual rental value system, such as the British, and the American–Canadian capital value variant is the treatment of land and vacant improvements. In the British system, the tax is based on the rental value of property in its present, actual use, and vacant properties therefore are not taxed. In the American system, in theory, property is valued at market value or some fraction thereof. Market value is, in an equilibrium situation, the capitalized value of expected net returns from property in its most profitable lawful use, not its present use. The capital value basis therefore tends to favor optimal use of land somewhat more than the customary annual value basis does.

The evolution of European property taxes (and their American descendant) from feudal dues into a general tax on property, and their subsequent narrowing to taxes on land and buildings, has been traced by Seligman (1895). Jensen (1931, chapter 2) gives a similar history of the American property tax. The importance of the property tax in revenue systems has declined over the years, with the growing role of national as compared with local finance. In the United States (and in Canada, as well) the property tax has also been displaced by the adoption of consumption and income taxes by state governments, beginning after 1910 but especially in response to the collapse of property values in the early 1930s. Subventions from state tax revenues increasingly replaced local property taxes, and the property tax as a proportion of total state–local taxes declined from 80 per cent in the 1920s to less than 50 per cent by 1946. However, since 1950, despite very rapid increases in the total scale of state–local finance, the property tax has maintained approximately the same relative importance (U.S. Bureau of the Census 1964).

Experience in the United States. In part, the recent buoyancy of the American property tax is related to the large role of receipts from housing in the tax. Estimates are that in 1957 housing provided about 41 per cent of tax revenues and about 44 per cent in 1962. Real estate taxes on housing amount to an average of one-sixth or more of annual rental receipts, or of cash expenditures for housing in the case of owner-occupants. This is in effect an excise tax at a rate far higher than that on any other broad category of consumer expenditure in the United States. Housing property taxes equal, on the average, about 1.5 per cent of property values (U.S. Bureau of the Census 1963a).

Slightly less than 10 per cent of American property taxes is derived from real and personal farm property. Relative to property values, farm property taxes are lower than those on nonfarm housing or business property—less than 1 per cent in recent years. However, farm property taxes equal nearly 10 per cent of net farm income, and only a slightly smaller fraction of national income originating in agriculture.

Roughly 45 per cent of the tax comes from nonfarm business property. Business property taxes are especially high, however measured, for railroad, pipeline, and other public utility companies. These firms are markedly real-property intensive enterprises and are, furthermore, politically vulnerable to discriminatory taxation. In 1957, estimated property tax payments were equal to 6.3 per cent of net output for railroads and public utilities, 1.4 per cent for manufacturing, and 1.8 per cent for other nonfarm business property.

The American property tax is not a single uniform tax institution but, in reality, thousands of different taxes reflecting differences in the legal coverage of the tax, the economic tax base available, the expenditure requirements to be financed, and the resulting tax rates among the 82,000 governmental units which rely upon the property tax. The tax tends to be of least importance in state–local fiscal systems in the southeastern United States and most important in New England, the Great Lakes states and the northern Plains states. The varying role of state taxes and state aid to local government explains much of this variation, with the property tax more important in those parts of the country where the state government's financial role is smallest.

Because urban government is costly, property tax rates are higher in urban than in rural areas and higher in the more urbanized states, notably in New England and the Middle Atlantic states, where tax rates frequently exceed 2.5 per cent of the market value of taxable property. In contrast, tax rates in most southern and Mountain states average less than 1 per cent (U.S. Advisory Commission . . . 1962, tables 37 and 41). Urbanization does not explain all the differences, however, since property tax rates in large northeastern cities are distinctly higher than in large cities elsewhere, and those in southern cities distinctly lower (U.S. Bureau of the Census 1963a). These large regional differences do not seem to have had major effects on location of industry, however, in view of the relative rates of growth of states with high and low property and other business taxes (Due 1961, p. 171).

Within large urban areas in the United States, tax rate differences are considerable among the great numbers of separate taxing jurisdictions operating in most individual metropolitan areas, and no doubt they do affect locational patterns. In the older parts of the country, per capita taxable property values tend to be lower in central cities than in their suburbs, expenditure requirements higher, and effective tax rates higher. This will tend to spur migration of business and high income residents from central city locations to suburban ones if tax differentials against the central cities are widening, as appears to be the case.

Among suburban taxing jurisdictions, property tax rates are usually lower and the level of public services higher in communities with higher property values per capita—either because they are dormitory suburbs with high-value houses or because they contain heavy concentrations of nonresidential property, a situation which encourages land use planning designed to maximize the fiscal position of individual suburbs (Netzer 1962, p. 193). The results may be both inefficiency in location patterns and, to the extent that racial and other barriers limit intrametropolitan mobility, adverse effects on interpersonal equity. However, these intrametropolitan property tax differentials may be narrowing over time; the evidence is mixed in this regard.

Shifting and incidence. In theory, taxes on the value of sites—bare land—rest on the owners of the sites at the time the tax is initially levied or increased. The tax cannot be shifted forward to other users of the land, since shifting can occur only if supply can be reduced, which is not possible for land. Prospective purchasers of the sites, faced with a new or higher annual tax burden, will reduce their bids, and the higher tax will be capitalized in the form of lower land prices. There are some complications in this analysis, as Simon (1943) points out, but it is generally accepted.

In general, property taxes on improvements and on tangible personal property used in business can be expected to be shifted forward to final consumers of business services and occupants of housing. This is because the taxes will discourage new real investment in these forms, and over time the reduced supply of capital assets will raise their prices. Owner-occupants of housing will themselves bear higher property taxes because there is no way they can be shifted.

This, at any rate, is the theoretical conclusion in partial equilibrium analysis. A general tax on capital could conceivably be shifted backward to owners of capital, in the form of lowered rates of return on the whole stock of capital, provided that the supply of savings is not responsive to interest rates. Another complication is the time lag required to shift taxes on physical capital forward, since the annual increments are usually small fractions of the total stock. In addition, the partial and unequal nature of the property tax limits shifting. Firms competing in national markets are able to shift local property taxes only to the extent that these taxes are common to their competitors or reflect the value of public services financed by these taxes. But, on the whole, most business property taxes are probably shifted forward and much of the remaining portion possibly shifted backward to land owners, by reducing local land values.

Empirical studies of the incidence of the American property tax by income class based on these "shifting" assumptions have generally agreed that the property tax is, on balance, regressive when compared with current money income. Because of the forward shifting of a substantial part of business property taxes, property taxes on nonresidential property are, in part, equivalent to a general consumption tax, regressive through much of the income range. Property taxes on owner-occupied housing and on rented housing appear to be even more regressive than taxes on nonresidential property. This is mainly because housing consumption outlays constitute a larger proportion of lower than of higher current money incomes.

In combination, residential and nonresidential property taxes are markedly regressive for the lowest income groups but only mildly regressive in the middle ranges of the income distribution. If no allowance is made for income tax savings due to the deductibility of property taxes, the latter are progressive for the highest income groups. When measured on the basis of a broader income definition, or one which averages income over a longer time span, the property tax is very nearly proportional in its incidence. The benefits from expenditures financed from the property tax are distinctly progressive in their incidence, notably in connection with education, as Morgan and his colleagues (1962) show.

On balance, therefore, the American property tax is no mean contributor to income redistribution from the richer income groups to the poorer ones, considered in the aggregate. However, in view of the wide dispersion about the means within income classes and of the many geographic differences, the redistributive effects with regard to individual households are highly uneven; the tax contains a substantial element of interpersonal inequity, however progressive or proportional it may be in the aggregate.

Allocative effects. In general, the American property tax (and property taxes in Canada, Britain, Ireland, and other high property tax countries) tends, over time, to shift resources in the aggregate from private construction to education and other public services. This general effect of the tax, like other economic effects, may not be visible in the empirical evidence, since it can readily be overwhelmed by other factors, such as housing subsidies and the like.

Property taxes also discriminate among inputs, encouraging the substitution of other inputs for real property; to the extent that firms and industries are limited in their opportunities to substitute, the property tax is then discriminatory among industries. Railroads are perhaps the best example of this. The competitive decline of the rails in the face of new transport technology was no doubt inevitable, but it was hastened by the property tax. Railroads are inherently real-property intensive and thus are subject to heavier taxes of this type than are their air, water, and road competitors. Rising property tax rates in the postwar years contributed to a rate of increase in rail charges which hardly assisted the carriers in their efforts to compete.

The American property tax tends to discourage housing in general, since it imposes taxes on this use of the consumer's dollar which are markedly higher than those on most other uses. Although property taxes are frequently very high in dormitory suburbs, whether measured by house value or by personal income, the deterrent effect there may be small, since the tax is directly tied to school and other expenditure benefits realized by householders. However, in large cities, the tie to ex-

penditure benefits is tenuous for many housing consumers, and property taxes amounting to large fractions of gross rental receipts—25 per cent or more in large northeastern cities—probably inhibit the construction of new rental housing and the rebuilding of the older cities. In any event, property tax rebates or reductions for selected classes of new housing have proved to be among the most effective stimulants yet devised.

Administration—Assessment problem. The fundamental administrative problem in property taxation is that of valuing or assessing property. In a number of countries, including Britain, valuation is done by a central government agency. In the United States, however, assessment of most classes of property is made (except in Hawaii) by local assessors; according to the U.S. Advisory Commission on Intergovernmental Relations (1963, p. 101), there are probably eighteen thousand assessment districts in the country. The quality of local assessors and assessment varies widely; it has been vigorously criticized by students of the problem since the last quarter of the nineteenth century. Some assessors are elected, part-time amateurs using primitive methods and tools; other assessment organizations are large, professional agencies applying all the technological aids available. In the best-administered jurisdictions in the United States, owners of single-family houses with similar market prices are likely to have assessments which vary by less than 10 to 15 per cent; in the worst the average variation may be far in excess of 50 per cent.

Some observers, such as the Advisory Commission, noting the important revenue role of the property tax, have urged its administrative rehabilitation. This involves limiting the coverage of the tax to classes of property which can be discovered and valued practicably, devising large enough assessment districts so that all can be served by full-time professional staffs, and greatly enlarging the role of the states in the provision of technical assistance to and supervision of local assessment.

Other observers are much more pessimistic. They note the inherent difficulties of valuing widely differing assets, only a few of which are actually sold within a short span of time and some of which—like large industrial plants—are never sold. They regard the standard of "good" assessment—assessments for similarly market-valued properties differing in the aggregate by no more than 20 per cent from the average—as an unacceptably low level of performance as compared with sales and income tax administration. They query whether some of the most glaring disparities in assessment practices—such as discrimination among classes of property within a city—are not in reality accommodations to a level of taxation which, if applied uniformly, would be economically and/or politically intolerable.

Prospect. Despite its inequities, its questionable impact on economic efficiency, and the poor quality of its administration (at least in the United States), the property tax persists and in revenue terms has been holding its own in the past few years in the United States and in a number of other countries. Part of the reason for this is that property tax revenues have risen rapidly in recent years, along with the level of economic activity. The market value of taxable property—the economic base of the tax—has risen almost as rapidly as gross national product in the postwar period, an apparent interruption to a long-term downward trend in capital–output ratios. Burkhead (1963, p. 70) concludes that the property tax is a far more responsive source of local government revenue than its traditional critics have allowed.

Site value tax ("single tax"). Perhaps the most vigorously advocated alternative to the prevalent systems of real property taxation is the site value tax, first propounded as "the single tax" by Henry George in 1879. The equity argument for site value taxation is that bare site values, or location rents, are created by population growth and general community improvements rather than by the actions of individual landowners, and that therefore taxation of this "unearned increment" is highly equitable. The resource allocation argument is that the site value tax applies to a surplus—the differential returns available from conducting an activity at particular sites—and therefore is economically neutral. Taxation does not reduce the supply of sites, but lowers their after-tax capitalized net returns, or price. But this neutrality is in contrast with the existing property tax, which, by applying to improvements as well as to site values, discourages new construction in general. The existing tax, moreover, tends to encourage low intensity uses, or holding of land idle for speculation, since taxes are lower if improvements are minimal. As noted earlier, the British type of property tax has this effect to a marked degree. Shifting to a site value tax would tend to foster improvements in general, and would discourage withholding of land from use, relative to present property tax practices in most places.

Site value tax advocates have tended to claim much more than this for their proposal. Some, for example, argue that site value taxation by itself can cure most of the ills of the large older cities. Opponents have presented three principal arguments against it. The first is the difficulty of separating site values and improvement values in the case of improved property; this appears to be a real difficulty administratively but not conceptually. The second is an equity argument: large windfall losses and gains would stem from a shift from the present system to the site value tax and would be intensified by the fact that many present landowners have not been the recipients of the "unearned increments" but have paid prices reflecting these to previous owners. The third is the problem of revenue adequacy. It has been estimated that to replace the present yield of American taxes on real property with a tax solely on site values would absorb more than the entire (before-tax) rent of land. These arguments suggest that a partial replacement is perhaps the maximum possibility.

Differentially higher taxation of land, or complete exemption of improvements from general ad valorem taxes on real estate, is practiced in the United States only in Pittsburgh and Hawaii but is widespread in Australia, New Zealand, South Africa, and Canada. In Australia and New Zealand, most local taxing units have exempted improvements from taxation, this trend beginning in the 1890s. In South Africa, most local authorities have either differential taxation or complete exemption of improvements. In Canada, differential taxation is widespread in the four western provinces. Because of so many environmental differences other than the property tax, it is difficult to discern whether the advantages claimed for the site value tax have been realized in these places. Most economists, however, agree that the site value tax should have better resource allocation effects than the prevalent property tax institutions.

DICK NETZER

[*See also* LOCAL FINANCE. *Other relevant material may be found in* LAND; PROPERTY; *and the biography of* GEORGE.]

BIBLIOGRAPHY

BURKHEAD, JESSE 1963 *State and Local Taxes for Public Education.* Syracuse Univ. Press.

DUE, JOHN F. 1961 Studies of State–Local Tax Influences on Location of Industry. *National Tax Journal* 14, June: 163–173.

HEILBRUN, JAMES 1966 *Real Estate Taxes and Urban Housing.* New York: Columbia Univ. Press.

JENSEN, JENS P. 1931 *Property Taxation in the United States.* Univ. of Chicago Press.

MORGAN, JAMES N. et al. 1962 Property Taxes and the Benefits of Public Education. Pages 288–308 in Michigan, University of, Survey Research Center, *Income and Welfare in the United States: A Study.* New York: McGraw-Hill.

NETZER, DICK 1962 The Property Tax and Alternatives in Urban Development. Regional Science Association, *Papers and Proceedings* 9:191–200.

NETZER, DICK 1966 *Economics of the Property Tax.* Washington, D.C.: Brookings Institution.

ROBERT SCHALKENBACH FOUNDATION, NEW YORK 1955 *Land-value Taxation Around the World.* Edited by Harry Gunnison Brown et al. New York: The Foundation.

SELIGMAN, EDWIN R. A. (1895) 1928 *Essays in Taxation.* 10th ed., rev. New York: Macmillan. → See especially pages 19–65, "The General Property Tax."

SIMON, HERBERT A. (1943) 1959 The Incidence of a Tax on Urban Real Property. Pages 416–435 in American Economic Association, *Readings in the Economics of Taxation.* Homewood, Ill.: Irwin.

U.S. ADVISORY COMMISSION ON INTERGOVERNMENTAL RELATIONS 1962 *Measures of State and Local Fiscal Capacity and Tax Effort.* Report M-16. Washington: Government Printing Office.

U.S. ADVISORY COMMISSION ON INTERGOVERNMENTAL RELATIONS 1963 *The Role of the States in Strengthening the Property Tax.* 2 vols. Report A-17. Washington: Government Printing Office.

U.S. BUREAU OF THE CENSUS 1963a *Census of Housing: 1960.* Volume 5: Residential Finance. Washington: Government Printing Office. → Contains data on real estate taxes in relation to property value, income, and rental receipts. This census is taken decennially.

U.S. BUREAU OF THE CENSUS 1963b *Census of Governments: 1962.* Volume 2: Taxable Property Values. Washington: Government Printing Office.

U.S. BUREAU OF THE CENSUS 1964 *Census of Governments: 1962.* Volume 4, no. 4: Compendium of Government Finances. Washington: Government Printing Office. → Contains comprehensive data on property tax revenues and all other federal, state, and local government financial data for 1962, by states and counties. This census is taken quinquennially, in years ending in 2 and 7.

V

SALES AND EXCISE TAXES

Taxes on the production or sale of commodities are among the oldest taxes known; they play a significant role in the tax structures of most countries of the world. Despite rapid expansion of income taxation in the last century and widespread acceptance of the argument that by usual standards such taxation is superior, the sales and excise taxes have not only maintained their position but in many countries have increased in importance. Despite the long experience with these taxes, major disputes about them continue—on such questions as shifting and incidence, relative effects on economic welfare through resource reallocation, and effects on economic development and the maintenance of full employment.

Sales and excise taxes have traditionally been classified as forms of indirect taxation, although this term has fallen into disuse because there is no generally accepted delineation between such taxes and those labeled direct. On a somewhat different basis of classification, they are designated as consumption taxes (as distinguished from income, wealth, or other taxes), under the assumption, questioned below, that their burden is distributed in relation to consumer expenditures.

The distinction between excises and sales taxes is based on the scope of coverage. Excises apply to particular commodities or related groups of commodities (such as tobacco products), while sales taxes apply to broad categories of commodities, typically to all commodities other than those specifically exempted. Obviously, a broad system of excises, such as that of Spain, does not differ basically from a sales tax and can have broader coverage than a sales tax limited to certain categories, such as the British purchase tax, or one with widespread exemptions, such as those of the Canadian provinces. However, commodity taxes usually fall clearly into one category or the other, and the distinction is useful for purposes of analysis. The terminology as outlined is not universally employed; for example, excises are sometimes referred to as selective sales taxes, and some proposals for a federal sales tax in the United States have referred to the proposed levy as a general excise tax. But the concepts given are now those most commonly employed.

Historical development. Excises are among the oldest forms of taxation, dating back, in their rudimentary form, to ancient Rome. The first use in England came in 1643. France was a major user, especially under Colbert, in the seventeenth century. Except for a few early attempts, the United States did not employ excises until the Civil War, when an extensive system was introduced for war-financing purposes. Only the liquor and tobacco taxes survived, however. Ultimately, other excises were introduced: during World War I, the depression era, and World War II. Since World War II, the taxes have slowly been reduced, and most of the remaining ones, except those on liquor, tobacco, motor fuel and motor vehicles, and telephone service, were repealed in 1965. The states have confined excises largely to liquor, tobacco, and motor fuel, and these three categories are also the major revenue producers among the federal excises and the excises of other countries. In the newly developing economies excises are typically introduced as supplements to the customs duty system when domestic production of liquor and tobacco products is first undertaken.

Sales taxation dates back to the Spanish *alcabala*, introduced in the fourteenth century. Because this tax was blamed for the commercial decline of Spain, it was not adopted by other countries, and the sales tax did not come into widespread use until the twentieth century. The financial problems during and immediately after World War I led Germany, France, Italy, other Continental countries, and Canada to impose the tax. More countries followed in the depression years and during World War II; among the most recent national sales taxes are those of Sweden and Denmark. The movement in the United States began in the depression years of the 1930s, when the states were squeezed between declining revenues from other taxes and increasing expenditure needs. Following the success of Mississippi with the tax in 1932, some 29 states levied a sales tax prior to World War II, although six subsequently allowed it to expire. In the postwar era the pressures of rising expenditures led additional states to impose the tax. There has also been a trend toward higher rates and broader coverage. The sales tax movement in the provinces of Canada has been similar to that in the United States.

Forms of excise and sales taxes. Excise taxes may be collected at the manufacturing, wholesaling, or retail level; the manufacturing level is by far the most common because the relatively small number of firms facilitates control. Excises may have *specific rates*, applied per unit of the physical product, as, for example, motor fuel taxes; or *ad valorem rates*, applying to the sale price. The former are easier to administer, if the product is highly standardized, but may be regarded as less equitable, since the tax rate does not rise in relation to value, and the yield of the tax is not automatically responsive to price changes. Excise taxes are also often classified in terms of general purpose or philosophy. Those on products such as liquor and tobacco, the use of which the government seeks to penalize as a matter of policy, are known as *sumptuary taxes*. Typically, these are highly productive of revenue. *Luxury excises* are ones designed to distribute tax burden in relation to ability to pay, as measured by purchase of luxury articles. Another group of widely used excises is directly related to motor vehicle use and is designed to distribute the costs of highways on the benefit principle. The United States provides a more direct link between the yield of these taxes and the costs of financing highways than do most countries.

The most significant classification of sales taxes is on the basis of stage of collection. *Multiple-stage* sales taxes are those which apply at two or more stages in the production and distribution channels. The complete turnover tax version applies at all stages in production and distribution: to the sales of materials and parts, as well as to all sales of the finished products—by manufacturers, distributors, and retailers. In practice the turnover taxes in use are not entirely complete or uniform. Lower rates are sometimes applied to sales by wholesalers (e.g., Germany), and retail sales may be excluded (e.g., Belgium). The turnover tax suffers from several major defects: integrated firms are favored over nonintegrated ones, thus encouraging integration; and the over-all tax on a particular product depends upon the number of stages in the production and distribution channels through which it passes.

The *single-stage* taxes are confined to one stage in production and distribution and avoid the disadvantages arising from the multiple application of the turnover tax. There are three major versions. The *manufacturers* sales tax, as used in Canada, applies to the sale by the manufacturer of finished products. The *wholesale* sales tax applies to the last wholesale transaction, that is, the purchase by the retailer. The *retail* sales tax applies to the final sale at retail. Each of these forms of tax will operate satisfactorily. On the whole, the retail tax, while collected from a much larger number of vendors than the others, gives rise to the fewest problems, because it can be applied to the actual selling price in virtually all instances. Avoidance of discrimination among various types of distribution channels is very difficult with the other single-stage taxes, since the taxable price is influenced by the structure of distribution. With a manufacturers tax, a manufacturer selling at retail is subject to a higher tax on a given product than one selling to a wholesale distributor. Attempts to meet this problem lead to serious complications in the tax. Nonretail taxes also tend to pyramid on the way to the final consumer, because of application of percentage markups. The retail tax, however, is not suitable in a country in which most retailing is conducted on a very small-scale, noncommercial basis, through family shops and market stalls.

The most recent version of the sales tax, the *value added* tax, as employed in France and accepted as the ultimate standard form of sales tax for the European Common Market countries, involves the application of tax to each firm in the production and distribution channels but only taxes the value added by the firm (in practice, the tax rate is applied to the firm's gross sales, and from this figure is subtracted the tax paid during the period on goods purchased by the firm). Thus, the evils of the turnover form of tax are avoided, since the type of distribution channel will not affect the amount of tax liability, while the direct impact of the tax is spread out over a much wider range of taxpayers than is the case with the single-stage taxes, and much of the tax is collected from large firms at stages prior to retailing. This form may facilitate exclusion of capital goods from the tax. However, it offers little if any general advantage over the retail sales tax in situations where administration of the latter is feasible.

Present use. It is not feasible to present a detailed survey of existing sales tax structures. Table 1, however, gives a general outline for the major countries. Sales taxes are now employed by all countries of western Europe except Spain (which has an extensive system of excises), although the British purchase tax is of restricted scope. The tax is used by many states in India; by Pakistan, Indonesia, and the Philippines; and by Australia and New Zealand. In Latin America, the tax is used in Brazil by both the national government and the states, and it is a significant revenue source in Chile, Argentina, Uruguay, Ecuador, and Mexico. In Canada the tax is used both by the dominion government (manufacturers sales tax) and by nine provinces (retail taxes). In the United States the retail sales tax is employed in 43 states, but the federal government uses only a limited list of excises. Countries in early stages of economic development find customs duties the most satisfactory form of commodity tax.

Virtually every country of the world uses some form of excise tax, particularly on liquor, tobacco, and motor fuel; others, especially those not using sales taxes, also apply excises to various luxury goods. No simple summary of excise systems is possible.

It is very difficult to make precise comparisons between countries of relative dependence on var-

Table 1 — Sales taxation in major countries, 1967

	Type of tax	Basic percentage rate
Europe:		
France	value added	25
Italy	turnover, to retail	3
Germany	turnover, through retail	4
Belgium	turnover, to retail	6
Netherlands	turnover, to retail	5
Luxembourg	turnover, through retail	2
United Kingdom	wholesale, selected commodity groups	varying
Eire	retail	2.5
Norway	retail	10
Sweden	retail	6
Denmark	wholesale	9
Finland	wholesale and retail	10
Switzerland	wholesale	5.4
Greece	manufacturing	6
Austria	turnover, through retail	5.25
North America:		
United States (43 states)	retail	2 to 5
Canada		
(federal)	manufacturing	11
(9 provinces)	retail	5 to 8
Mexico	turnover	1.8 plus state supplements
South and Central America:		
Argentina	manufacturing	10
Chile	turnover	6
Brazil		
(federal)	manufacturing	varying, 2 to 10
(most states)	turnover	2 to 5
Uruguay	manufacturing	5
Ecuador	turnover	1.5
Honduras	retail	3
Asia:		
Pakistan	wholesale	varying
India (states)	turnover or retail	wide variation
Philippines	retail	varying
Australia	wholesale	varying, 10 to 30
New Zealand	wholesale	20

ious taxes. In the United States, sales taxes generally yield about 25 per cent of the revenues of the states in which they are levied, but in a few states they yield as much as 50 per cent. Excises yield about 11 per cent of federal revenue. The Canadian federal sales tax yields about 18 per cent of total federal tax revenue; the provincial sales taxes, 26 per cent of provincial tax revenue.

The turnover tax provides 42 per cent of the German federal revenues; other figures of sales tax yield include 35 per cent in France, 21 per cent in Italy, 40 per cent in Belgium, 19 per cent in the Netherlands.

Shifting and incidence. Traditionally it has been argued that both excises and sales taxes are typically shifted forward, through price increases, to the consumers of the products and thus are borne in relation to consumer spending on the taxed commodities. In purely competitive markets, with a fixed stock of goods on hand in the market period there will be no initial change in price, and temporarily the burden will be borne by the producers. But output and supply will fall, and the market price will rise. Over a long-run period the exact amount of the tax will shift forward, if the industry is one of constant cost conditions. Under increasing cost conditions, the ultimate increase in price will be less than the amount of the tax and a portion of the burden will be borne by the owners of specialized resources used in the industry, the prices of which decline as the volume of the product sold is reduced because of the higher commodity prices.

In nonpurely competitive markets the pattern of incidence is less clear. Typically—and there is considerable empirical evidence of this—prices will be raised immediately in response to the imposition of the tax, since firms take the initiative in setting their own prices and will likely adjust prices upward when they experience a general increase in costs. As long as the various competing firms follow the same policy, the increase is likely to be profitable. There are certain to be exceptions, however. If some firms fail to increase, the others will find an increase unprofitable. The over-all demand for some products may be so elastic that increases are unprofitable. Over a longer period there will be a greater tendency for price to rise by the amount of the tax, since prices must cover average cost. Here again, however, there will be exceptions. A monopolist or a group of firms following a concerted policy and having obtained, prior to the tax, maximum excess profits for the group will find it profitable in most instances to absorb a portion of the tax, since raising price by the full amount would result in a loss in revenue greater than the reduction in cost due to reduced output. It may be argued that a general sales tax can be shifted more easily than excises, since there is less danger of a loss in sales to untaxed commodities. The common practice (often required by law), under retail sales taxes, of adding the tax to the customer's entire bill, rather than readjusting individual prices, undoubtedly facilitates shifting.

The argument that sales taxes are borne primarily by consumers has been questioned in recent years. Rolph (1952) maintained that a sales tax is borne in the same fashion as a flat-rate income tax, namely, in proportion to factor incomes. Rolph assumed perfectly competitive markets and perfectly inelastic supplies of the factors of production, and he disregarded the use of the revenue received from the tax. Thus, factor demand and factor prices fall. His conclusions, however, have been questioned, particularly in regard to the assumption about the use of the revenues. Buchanan (1960), and Rolph in more recent writings (Rolph & Break 1961, chapter 13), have argued that regardless of the assumption made about the use of the revenue, a sales tax cannot be borne by consumers because a tax rests on consumers only if the general price level increases and general price level increases cannot be attributed to taxes but only to monetary considerations. Musgrave (1959, chapters 10, 15, 16) maintains that the distribution of tax burden depends, not upon the direction of change in prices, but rather upon the relative changes in commodity and factor prices and concludes that a sales tax confined to consumer goods is borne in relation to consumption, whether commodity prices rise and factor prices remain unchanged or factor prices fall while commodity prices remain unchanged. He argues, however, that if the tax applies to both consumption and investment goods, the burden is distributed in the same fashion as that of a proportional income tax, regardless of the direction of change in price levels. Despite this extended theoretical controversy, policy discussions relating to sales taxes generally assume that the tax is, for the most part, shifted to consumers.

The excess burden argument. For a number of years the prime criticism advanced against excise taxes and, to a lesser extent, sales taxes of restricted scope has been that of "excess burden." A tax on a particular commodity shifts purchases to untaxed commodities, thus resulting in a loss in economic welfare without an offsetting gain to the government. The pioneer statements were those of Hotelling (1938) and Joseph (1939). Critics pointed out that the thesis was valid only if the original revenue allocation was an optimum one and the pattern of income distribution the prefererred one. Other critics, such as Wald (1945), argued that income taxes, by affecting the choice between work and leisure and choices among various economic activities, likewise adversely affected economic welfare. But in a recent study of the question, by Harberger (*The Role of Direct and Indirect Taxation in the Federal Revenue System* 1964), the conclusion is reached that, on the basis of reasonable relevant assumptions, it is likely the excess burden of excises is greater than that of income taxes, primarily because of the limited response of work effort to income tax burdens.

General evaluation.   The controversy over the relative desirability of commodity and income taxation has continued for many years with no lessening of intensity. Much of the debate centers on relative economic effects. Supporters of increased reliance on sales and excise taxes argue that income taxes retard economic growth and produce unemployment by discouraging savings, investment in business expansion, and work effort, especially on the part of business executives and professional men. Since sales taxes do not have progressive rates and may be avoided by saving rather than consuming, they do not directly penalize the gains from additional effort or business expansion and give some positive incentive to save more and consume less (except when savings are made for the purchase of goods in the future with the tax still in operation).

The opponents of sales taxation question the seriousness of the adverse effects of the income tax and argue that the greater relative impact of sales taxes on consumption will reduce national income and increase unemployment in situations in which there is some tendency toward unemployment because of inadequate total spending. A sales tax, by concentrating its burden more heavily on persons spending high percentages of their incomes and by providing some limited incentive to save more, may increase the potential rate of capital formation at full employment, but the tax may make it much more difficult to attain full employment and may thus lessen the actual rate of economic growth. Furthermore, to the extent to which the income tax does have adverse effect on the economy, this may be attributed in large measure to the high progressivity of rates and may be eliminated much more simply by changes in the income tax structure than by a shift to a sales tax. The differences attributed to the two forms of taxes are largely a result of the differences in rate structure, rather than in the base of the taxes.

In recent years the emphasis of the discussion has centered on the possibility of the replacement of the corporate income tax by the value added tax. The change has been advocated in large measure on the argument that the foreign exchange position of the country would be improved. Full export rebates would be granted for the value added tax, whereas no rebate is given for the corporate income tax, nor can one be given without violating present GATT (General Agreement on Tariffs and Trade) rules. The argument that the corporate tax places American exporters at a disadvantage, however, has validity only to the extent that the tax is reflected in higher prices of the products. The change proposed would temporarily aid American exports, whether the tax is now shifted or not, but such a change could easily invite retaliatory moves by other countries, especially if the tax is now not shifted.

Increased use of commodity taxation also has equity implications, and much of the opposition to the taxes has always been based on equity grounds. The income tax can be made progressive relative to income and can be adjusted in terms of various circumstances, such as size of family, which are considered to affect taxpaying ability. On the other hand, a sales tax with a broad coverage is regressive relative to income, because the higher-income groups save a greater percentage of their income, on the average, and spend more on nontaxable services. The tax likewise tends to burden large families more heavily, compared with smaller families, at given income levels (Hansen 1962). Food exemption, however, appears to eliminate regressivity (Davies 1961), but it fails to bring the precise adjustment to tax capacity that can be attained with an income tax. Some persons have suggested that the correct basis for comparing burdens is that of permanent income [see CONSUMPTION FUNCTION], rather than actual income (Davies 1961). On this basis, even a broad-based sales tax is not regressive. But it may also be argued that actual year-by-year income is the better basis for measuring tax burdens. The significance of the equity argument is, of course, one of value judgment; to many persons the use of some regressive taxes in a tax structure that is progressive over-all is not objectionable. But in terms of usually accepted standards of equity, major reliance on such taxes is undesirable.

Sales and excise taxes are also justified on administrative grounds—as being easier to enforce than income taxes. With improved income tax administration, this argument has lost most of the merit it once had. Furthermore, since the issue is one of using a sales tax along with, not in lieu of, an income tax, the over-all administrative task is obviously greater with a sales tax than without one.

In countries with a federal government, a final argument for sales taxation is the need of the states for autonomous revenue sources, in light of federal domination of the income tax field.

On the question of the choice between sales and excise taxes, the former are less discriminatory against individuals, in terms of their preferences, than excises and are less likely to distort resource allocation. On the other hand, excises, limited to particular commodities, may be easier to administer, may accomplish certain desired goals in tax policy (such as the placing of special burdens on highway users or consumers of tobacco and liquor), and may provide a more acceptable over-all distribution of burden. But to raise significant revenue, either rates must be relatively high or many commodities of widespread use must be brought within the scope of the tax, and then the excise system comes to resemble a sales tax.

JOHN F. DUE

BIBLIOGRAPHY

BUCHANAN, JAMES M. 1960 *Fiscal Theory and Political Economy.* Chapel Hill: Univ. of North Carolina Press.

DAVIES, DAVID G. 1961 Commodity Taxation and Equity. *Journal of Finance* 16:581–590.

DUE, JOHN F. 1957 *Sales Taxation.* London: Routledge; Urbana: Univ. of Illinois Press.

DUE, JOHN F. 1963a *State Sales Tax Administration.* Chicago: Public Administration Service.

DUE, JOHN F. 1963b Sales Taxation and the Consumer. *American Economic Review* 53:1078–1084.

HANSEN, REED R. 1962 An Empirical Analysis of the Retail Sales Tax With Policy Recommendations. *National Tax Journal* 15, March: 1–13.

HOTELLING, HAROLD 1938 The General Welfare in Relation to Problems of Taxation and of Railway and Utility Rates. *Econometrica* 6:242–269.

JOSEPH, MARGARET F. W. 1939 The Excess Burden of Indirect Taxation. *Review of Economic Studies* 6:226–231.

MORGAN, DANIEL C. 1964 *Retail Sales Tax: An Appraisal of New Issues.* Madison: Univ. of Wisconsin Press.

MUSGRAVE, RICHARD A. 1959 *The Theory of Public Finance: A Study in Public Economy.* New York: McGraw-Hill.

ORGANIZATION FOR EUROPEAN ECONOMIC COOPERATION, EUROPEAN PRODUCTIVITY AGENCY 1958 *The Influence of Sales Taxes on Productivity,* by C. Campet. Paris: The Organization.

The Role of Direct and Indirect Taxation in the Federal Revenue System. 1964 Princeton Univ. Press. →
A conference report of the National Bureau of Economic Research and the Brookings Institution.

ROLPH, EARL R. 1952 A Proposed Revision of Excise-tax Theory. *Journal of Political Economy* 60:102–117.

ROLPH, EARL R.; and BREAK, GEORGE F. 1961 *Public Finance.* New York: Ronald Press.

SULLIVAN, CLARA K. 1965 *The Tax on Value Added.* New York: Columbia Univ. Press.

U.S. CONGRESS, HOUSE, COMMITTEE ON WAYS AND MEANS 1964 *Excise Tax Compendium: Compendium of Papers on Excise Tax Structure. . . .* 6 parts in 2 vols. Washington: Government Printing Office.

WALD, HASKELL P. 1945 The Classical Indictment of Indirect Taxation. *Quarterly Journal of Economics* 59:577–596.

WALKER, DAVID 1955 The Direct–Indirect Tax Problem: Fifteen Years of Controversy. *Public Finance* 10, no. 2:153–176.

VI

DEATH AND GIFT TAXES

Taxes upon the transfer of property at death are known as estate taxes if they are imposed on the value of the decedent's estate as a whole with little or no regard to the status and number of heirs, and as inheritance taxes if they are imposed upon the heirs individually. The estate tax consequently employs a single rate scale applied to the entire estate, while the inheritance tax is calculated separately on the amount received by each heir. The inheritance tax commonly employs a series of rate scales that vary with the degree of relationship of the heir to the decedent.

The tax on gifts made during life (gifts *inter vivos*) can likewise in principle be divided into a tax collected from the donor and a tax collected from the donee. In practice, only the tax on the donor is employed, and even that is used sparingly, most taxing jurisdictions not levying a tax on gifts *inter vivos* at all. Some gift taxes are cumulative, in the sense that a progressive rate scale is applied to the sum of gifts made by a given donor over his lifetime, as is the U.S. federal gift tax (Harvard Law School 1963a, chapter 3). Other gift taxes apply the graduated rate scale only to gifts made during a given year, as is the case in the German Federal Republic (Harvard Law School 1963b, chapter 4).

The death tax and the gift tax could be integrated either as a cumulative tax on all transfers made by a given donor during his lifetime or as a cumulative tax on all accessions to a given donee either through gift or inheritance. The cumulative integrated tax on donors has been proposed from time to time in the United States; as yet no country has employed it. The cumulative donee tax, or accessions tax, was in force for a short time in

Japan—from 1950 to 1953 (Japan, Ministry of Finance 1963, pp. 9, 91), and exists in an incomplete form in Colombia and Italy (Shoup 1966, p. 13).

History. Taxes on the transfer of property at death have a long fiscal history. The Roman *vicesima hereditatum*, "the twentieth penny of inheritances," is mentioned in Adam Smith's *Wealth of Nations* (1776, book 5, chapter 2, appendix to arts. 1 and 2). In the United Kingdom, the tax dates back to 1694, but not until 1779–1780 did it attain something like its modern form (Palgrave [1894–1896] 1963, vol. 1, pp. 490–493). The U.S. federal government levied an inheritance tax during the Civil War and again during the Spanish–American War (Shultz 1926, pp. 151–155). The present U.S. federal estate tax dates from 1916; many of the state death taxes have longer histories (*ibid.*, chapters 8, 9). Virtually all of the industrialized nations now employ some form of death tax, and it is also common in underdeveloped countries (see United Nations 1954).

The death duty predates the modern type of mass income tax and also the modern general sales tax. In many instances it has a longer history even than the more restricted income taxes of the period before World War II. The widespread and early use of the death tax can be explained largely by the fact that property had to be listed and valued in any event—for transfer to the state or to feudal overlords, under prevailing doctrines regarding land tenure; or to members of the family of the deceased possessing certain minimum rights in the property; or to other inheritors. The occasion thus proved a convenient one for computing a tax base and collecting a tax. Valuation remains, however, a vexing problem with respect to much of the transferred property.

Revenue. Although the history of the death tax has been impressive in terms of longevity and spread, its revenue role has been much less so. Today it rarely accounts for more than one per cent of total tax revenues in any country, despite the fairly steep graduation that characterizes most of the rate structures. While the income tax has been transformed in some countries into a tax that strikes almost every family and while social security payroll taxes and the general sales taxes, both inventions of the twentieth century, have added enormously to fiscal revenues, the estate and inheritance taxes have remained confined to only a small percentage of the populace. Most households in most countries have little or no property, at least relative to their incomes. In the more prosperous countries death taxes have high exemptions, and

the starting rates are low. Thus, in the United States in 1961, for example, only some 45,000 out of 1,400,000 adult deaths resulted in estates subject to the federal estate tax (U.S. Department of Health, Education and Welfare 1963, vol. 2, part B, pp. 9–78, table 9–3). No movement has developed in any country to convert the death tax into a mass tax imposed on virtually everyone who dies possessed of property. In any event, conversion to a mass tax would not produce the striking percentage increase in yield that has been experienced under the income tax, since wealth is far more concentrated than income.

Avoidance. Sophisticated avoidance techniques, particularly in the United States and the United Kingdom, restrict the yield of the death tax. Under Anglo-Saxon property law concepts, trusts and life estates can be so set up as to skip one or more generations in the passage of property subject to death duties. In the United Kingdom, where expiration of a life estate gives rise, in principle, to full taxation of the corpus on which the life interest is based, tax has been avoided by several devices, notably the discretionary trust. This can be so formulated that owing to the discretion lodged in the hands of trustees as to who shall receive the life payments, it is not legally certain upon the death of one life tenant that any one of the others obtains any greater interest in the property than he had before (Harvard Law School 1957, chapter 3; Wheatcroft 1965, pp. 68–69, 132–137). In the United States, expiry of a life estate or similar property right does not give rise to inclusion of the corpus in the taxable estate of the decedent. Special statistical studies made by the U.S. Treasury have shown that in the wills of wealthy decedents the life estate that skips at least one generation is common (Shoup 1966, chapter 3; Jantscher 1967, chapters 4–7). These particular avoidance techniques are apparently not available in continental European countries because of the absence of the Anglo-Saxon concept of the trust.

In many countries, including the United Kingdom, gifts made during life (gifts *inter vivos*) are not taxable. In some of these countries, as also in the United States, gifts made within a certain number of years before death, or deemed made in contemplation of death, are included in the taxable estate. Thus, in the United Kingdom gifts made within five years of death are included, in part, in the taxable estate.

Where gifts are subject to a separate gift tax, as in the United States, the lower rate scale of the gift tax and the opportunity for splitting the property into two parts, each of which can obtain the benefit of low brackets (gift tax and estate tax), not to mention certain other technical features, leave a broad avenue for substantial tax reduction by gifts during life. In fact, however, even the most wealthy property holders seem to avail themselves of this possibility far less than a priori reasoning might suggest; the British consequently do not appear to believe that the revenue from their death tax is appreciably imperiled by the absence of a gift tax.

Contributions to charitable, educational, religious, and similar organizations are completely exempt under the U.S. federal estate tax, in contrast to the restricted exemptions, if any, granted in other countries. Once more, the opportunity for complete escape has been utilized rather less than one might expect (Harriss 1949; Shoup 1966, pp. 60–65).

The mobility of elderly wealthy persons is another restraining influence on heavy death taxation. Recently, both the United Kingdom and the United States have altered their death tax laws to include in the tax base real estate located abroad. This change has added pressure on elderly wealth-holders to change their residence and perhaps even citizenship as they reach extreme old age. Again, the number of such decisions will probably prove to be minor compared with the prospective tax saving.

In some respects the death duty offers fewer opportunities for avoidance than does the usual income tax. In the United States, state and local securities are fully subject to inclusion in the decedent's taxable estate even though during his lifetime the interest on such obligations is exempt from the federal income tax. Property values arising from capital gains are fully included for U.S. estate tax purposes and also for the death duties in Britain, while under the income tax they are given preferential treatment. The percentage depletion provisions in the United States that have caused so much comment with respect to the income tax are, of course, not operative for the death tax.

Effect on consumption. Per dollar of revenue, the death tax probably decreases consumption spending less than most other taxes on households. This is so because the decedent-to-be seems unlikely to decrease his standard of living appreciably in order to improve the prospects of his heirs, prospects that have been impaired by the death tax. The future heirs, in turn, seem unlikely to reduce their current standard of living merely because they are aware that they will later receive less than if no death tax were in force. With respect to the

period following transfer of the property at death, it has been cogently argued by Ricardo and others that the heirs tend to look upon the capital that they should preserve as being simply the amount they receive after death tax. They thus feel under no pressure to try to rebuild the estate to a level closer to what it would have been without such a tax (Shoup [1950] 1960, chapters 3, 15). Doctrinal discussion in Anglo-Saxon economic literature over the past century and a half has centered more on the reaction of the decedent-to-be than on the heirs, prospective or actual, and some difference of opinion has developed on this score (Fiekowsky 1959, chapters 1, 3). McCulloch, for example, expressed the opinion that the property owner would attempt to build up his estate somewhat in an effort to recoup for his heirs a part of the value that would be lost by the estate tax. Present-day thought, however, does not follow McCulloch, especially in view of the apparent indifference of wealthy persons as evidenced by their failure to transfer much property during life in order to save tax money for their heirs (Shoup 1966, Appendix F).

On the other hand, it is not at all certain that this failure to take advantage of what appear to be bargain tax rates during life necessarily indicates indifference. The welfare of one's heirs is weighed against other considerations, some more admirable than others. As modern medicine has enhanced the possibility that an elderly person may live to extreme old age, sometimes under very expensive medical and hospital care, the risk that his financial resources may be exhausted before his death has become correspondingly greater. Dread of dependence on his children and loss of flexibility in arranging for his later years, even if expensive medical care is not a problem, are powerful forces in causing a wealthy decedent-to-be to cling to his wealth, particularly when he believes that he has already given enough to his children to start them in life with substantial advantages and conjectures that further wealth would do them more harm than good. To these motives must be added sometimes a desire to retain psychological control over prospective heirs, and sometimes a gradual drift into senility before the individual can be persuaded to think about death and act on his thoughts. Simple inertia explains much, especially on the part of some elderly women who have little interest in property management, and extremely busy men of affairs who do not pause long enough even to sign a will. Family jealousies also play an occasional role in restraining gifts during life.

The transferor or the heir might recoup some

of the death or gift tax by increasing his money-making efforts. The high income tax rates to which this class of persons is commonly subject make this method of capital preservation, as compared with restricting one's consumption, a difficult one.

Effect on distribution. The distribution of wealth and income, as indicated by a Lorenz curve, has probably been made more nearly equal to a modest degree during the past thirty years or so of graduated death taxation in the United States and the United Kingdom, compared with what it would have been if the same revenue had been raised, for example, by an increment to general sales taxes (Fiekowsky 1959, chapter 3). The result seems not to have been as substantial, however, as has been hoped for by proponents of the tax, to whom a chief virtue of death duties is their presumed tendency to limit accumulation of extreme fortunes and to reduce inequality generally. The explanation for this disappointment, if such it is, lies largely in the number of avoidance devices indicated above and partly in the relatively high level of exemption (for the U.S. federal estate tax it is $60,000) and low rates in the initial ranges. No practical support has developed for the Rignano plan or its variants, which would tax especially heavily and eventually confiscate inheritances that came from inheritances, after two or three or four generations. It is instructive to recall that an inventor of one of these variants, Hugh Dalton, made no move to introduce it into the British law while he was chancellor of the exchequer in the late 1940s (Dalton 1923, pp. 114–118 in 1936 edition; p. 232 in 1954 edition).

Death taxes are said to have forced small, closely held family firms to restrict their rate of growth in order to accumulate liquid assets sufficient to pay the tax upon the death of the founder or other large family owner, or alternatively to have induced them to merge with large firms whose stock is actively traded on exchanges so that liquid assets for payment of the tax could be obtained without restricting growth of the business (Somers 1958, pp. 201–210). The extent to which these effects have in fact materialized is not clear. In the United States the law has recently been amended to guarantee the estate the privilege of a ten-year installment payment provision if the company in question meets certain tests. In any case, an extended period of payment can be granted at the discretion of the tax administration.

Present trends. Among the current trends in death and gift taxation, the most noticeable one seems to be a tendency to personalize the estate tax, so that the amount of tax will vary depending particularly upon the relationship of the heir to the decedent. In this way, the estate tax may become more and more like an inheritance tax. The U.S. federal estate tax allows exemption of up to 50 per cent of an estate with respect to transfer to the surviving spouse, and pressure is growing to exempt completely interspousal transfers and to give some tax reduction for transfers to children.

Another trend, this time working toward an increase in revenue, is evidenced in current discussions of methods by which skipping one or more generations can be reduced, through taxing expiry of life estates and inhibiting the use of discretionary trusts. The task is much more difficult than this brief discussion might indicate, because of the intricacies of property law and the consequent opportunities to avoid even the most complex anti-avoidance measures. However, additional legislation on these subjects may be expected in both the United States and the United Kingdom during the next few years. In the view of some, the death and gift tax system should be so constructed that no matter by what route property is transferred to a generation distant in time, the present value of taxes on the transfers would come to the same thing, as under the proposal by Vickrey of a bequeathing power tax (Vickrey 1947, chapter 8). To achieve this end, however, is to relinquish the relationship of heirs to decedent as grounds for differentiation of the tax.

No trend is apparent with respect to the level of exemptions and the rate and type of graduation. Both the exemption and rate structure have shown great stability over time in most countries; in the United States, for example, the present rate scale dates from 1942. Graduation by brackets, as in the income tax, is characteristic of most death taxes, but the British prefer to graduate by a series of effective (average) rates. Such graduation facilitates an equitable division of the tax between the executors of the estate and owners of parcels of property that, although not appearing in the decedent's estate, are nevertheless aggregated with his estate in determining the tax rate applicable to such parcels and to the estate (an example is property that was transferred as a gift *inter vivos* within five years of death).

Jurisdictional problems either among states in a federation or among countries continue to occupy much time and thought of tax lawyers and legislators, but exert little influence on total revenues. In the United States the federal–state issue has been met by allowing up to a certain amount of state death taxes paid to be credited directly against the federal tax, with the consequence that all of the states of the United States, excepting Nevada, impose either the estate or the inheritance tax or both, sometimes indeed rather beyond the limits of the federal credit. The United States has concluded tax conventions with many other countries, chiefly to avoid double taxation of properties of nonresident aliens.

Legal and administrative complications arise through linkages of death and gift taxes with the income tax. In the U.S. federal law, a transfer of property may be an *inter vivos* gift for gift tax purposes but not for income tax purposes; it is not evident, however, that complete uniformity is desirable. Another linkage arises with respect to capital gains. At present, a capital gain accrued at death is not made subject to the income tax, nor is a capital loss recognized. The heirs take over the property with a new basis for computing capital gain or loss on a future sale. This basis is the value of the property in the decedent's estate. Accordingly, a capital gain on property held until death is never subject to the income tax, and a capital loss is never allowed. An attempt by the executive to persuade Congress to eliminate this combination of loophole and hardship in the Tax Reform Bill of 1963 failed. Property given during life, on the other hand, does not have its basis stepped up (or down) in this manner; this fact helps explain the reluctance to pass on appreciated property during life rather than at death.

No taxes have had a better reputation to less effect. Favorable comments on death and gift taxation can be found in the most conservative quarters, but these taxes remain minor and of little concern to politicians and voters. In certain academic circles some doubt is beginning to arise whether many of the aims of the estate and gift taxes could not better be achieved by a low-rate annual tax on individual net wealth, which would not be vulnerable to the devices now being employed to skip generations.

CARL S. SHOUP

BIBLIOGRAPHY

A Critique of Federal Estate and Gift Taxation. 1950 *California Law Review* 38, no. 1 (Special Issue).

DALTON, HUGH (1923) 1954 *Principles of Public Finance*. 4th ed., rev. London: Routledge.

FIEKOWSKY, SEYMOUR 1959 On the Economic Effects of Death Taxation in the United States. Ph.D. dissertation, Harvard Univ.

HARRISS, C. LOWELL 1940 *Gift Taxation in the United States*. Washington: American Council on Public Affairs.

HARRISS, C. LOWELL 1949 Federal Estate Taxes and Philanthropic Bequests. *Journal of Political Economy* 57:337–344.

HARRISS, C. LOWELL 1954 Sources of Injustice in Death Taxation. *National Tax Journal* 7, Sept.: 289–308.

HARVARD LAW SCHOOL, INTERNATIONAL PROGRAM IN TAXATION 1957 *Taxation in the United Kingdom*. Boston: Little.

HARVARD LAW SCHOOL, INTERNATIONAL PROGRAM IN TAXATION 1963a *Taxation in the United States*. Chicago: Commerce Clearing House.

HARVARD LAW SCHOOL, INTERNATIONAL PROGRAM IN TAXATION 1963b *Taxation in the Federal Republic of Germany*. Chicago: Commerce Clearing House.

JANTSCHER, GERALD R. 1967 *Trusts and Estate Taxation*. Washington: Brookings Institution.

JAPAN, MINISTRY OF FINANCE, TAX BUREAU 1963 *An Outline of Japanese Tax: 1963*. Tokyo: The Bureau.

PALGRAVE, ROBERT H. (1894–1896) 1963 Death Duties. Volume 1, pages 490–493 in Robert H. Palgrave, *Palgrave's Dictionary of Political Economy*. Rev. ed. New York: Kelley.

PECHMAN, JOSEPH A. 1950 Analysis of Matched Estate and Gift Tax Returns. *National Tax Journal* 3, June: 153–164.

SHOUP, CARL S. (1950) 1960 *Ricardo on Taxation: An Analysis of the Chapters on Taxation in David Ricardo's* Principles. New York: Columbia Univ. Press.

SHOUP, CARL S. 1966 *Federal Estate and Gift Taxes*. Washington: Brookings Institution.

SHOUP, CARL S. et al. 1949 Taxes on Gifts and Bequests. Volume 2, pages 143–155 in Carl S. Shoup et al., *Report on Japanese Taxation*. Tokyo: Supreme Commander for the Allied Powers.

SHULTZ, WILLIAM J. 1926 *The Taxation of Inheritance*. Boston: Houghton Mifflin.

SHULTZ, WILLIAM J.; and HARRISS, C. LOWELL (1931) 1959 *American Public Finance*. 7th ed. Englewood Cliffs, N.J.: Prentice-Hall. → First published as *American Public Finance and Taxation*, with William J. Shultz as sole author.

SMITH, ADAM (1776) 1952 *An Inquiry Into the Nature and Causes of the Wealth of Nations*. Chicago: Encyclopaedia Britannica. → A 2-volume paperback edition was published in 1963 by Irwin.

SOMERS, HAROLD M. 1958 Estate Taxes and Business Mergers: The Effects of Estate Taxes on Business Structure and Practices in the United States. *Journal of Finance* 13:201–210.

UNITED NATIONS, TECHNICAL ASSISTANCE ADMINISTRATION 1954 *Taxes and Fiscal Policy in Under-developed Countries*. New York: United Nations.

U.S. CONGRESS, JOINT COMMITTEE ON THE ECONOMIC REPORT 1956 *Federal Tax Policy for Economic Growth and Stability*. Hearings Before the Subcommittee on Tax Policy. Washington: Government Printing Office.

U.S. DEPARTMENT OF HEALTH, EDUCATION AND WELFARE 1963 *Vital Statistics of the United States: 1961*. Washington: Government Printing Office. → See especially Volume 2, part B, pages 9–78, Table 9–3.

VICKREY, WILLIAM S. 1947 *Agenda for Progressive Taxation*. New York: Ronald Press.

WHEATCROFT, G. S. A. (1953) 1958 *The Taxation of Gifts and Settlements, by Stamp Duty, Estate Duty, Income Tax and Surtax.* 3d ed. London: Pitman.

WHEATCROFT, G. S. A. 1957 Anti-avoidance Provisions of the Law of Estate Duty in the United Kingdom. *National Tax Journal* 10, March: 46–56.

WHEATCROFT, G. S. A. (editor) 1965 *Estate and Gift Taxation: A Comparative Study.* British Tax Review Guides, No. 3. London: Sweet & Maxwell. → A study of estate and gift taxation in Australia, Canada, Great Britain, and the United States.

TEACHING

A conventional view of teaching holds that it requires no more than Mark Hopkins, a boy, and a log. Common sense tells us we may dispense with the log but that two people, not necessarily man and boy, are essential. Further, there must be an understanding between the two that one knows more about something than the other and should impart it. According to this view, the act of teaching is a simple process: it is to give or impart knowledge.

The conventional view provides us with a plausible model. It suggests popular notions of what may go wrong: poor teaching occurs when teachers have too little knowledge or too little skill to impart the knowledge they have. Yet the model is not satisfying. In referring only to the teacher, it neglects the interaction of teacher and pupil, and it fails to explain the universal, if intermittent, resistance of pupils, the hostility, sometimes alternating with admiration and love, so often directed at teachers.

For there is conflict in teaching; it is a tension-filled, chancy process. Resistance to teaching occurs among pupils who are able and anxious to learn; it occurs when teachers teach well. It is not confined to schools but frequently occurs in the informal teaching situations of everyday life, as everyone knows who has tried to teach a friend to drive a car.

We can approach understanding of one source of the conflict between teacher and pupil if we think of teaching as an attempt to change the pupil by introducing him to new ideas. In this model, teaching is an assault on the self, and resistance to it can be explained as unwillingness to upset one's inner *status quo.* Plausible as it may seem, the model is nevertheless limited in application. It illuminates the rare case: the pupil sufficiently aware of the power of ideas to fear and combat them, the pupil with an eager and persuasive teacher of a subject full of ideas of the kind that open new worlds of understanding of self. It does not explain the much more common case of the forgetful, indifferent pupil who has a dull teacher of a dry subject. But it is probable that there is as much, if not more, conflict between teacher and pupil in the latter case than in the former. We need a model of teaching that fits all types of pupils, teachers, and subjects.

A conflict model of teaching. In every teaching situation, the teacher is, at least temporarily, the superior and his pupil the subordinate, a relationship we may express in propositional form as follows: A (the superior) originates interaction for B (the subordinate), and B responds according to A's wishes; more simply, A gives orders that B obeys (Homans 1950, p. 244). From the superior's standpoint, this statement describes a situation in which his ability to control B's response is unquestioned—an ideal not always attained. When control is uncertain, the ideal takes on the force of obligation: if A does not control B's response, he should; as superior, it is his responsibility.

We can apply this conditional form of Homans' proposition to teaching. As teacher, A originates interaction for B by imparting knowledge or directing him to it. At the same time, A accepts the obligation to see to it that B responds as he (A) wishes. In fulfilling his responsibility, A evaluates the correctness of B's response and controls B's behavior during the interaction sufficiently to make correct response possible. Essentially, A's role is that of command and B's of submission.

While not inevitable, conflict between teacher and pupil is predictable in this model (Waller [1932] 1961, p. 195). The absence, rather than the presence, of resistance requires explanation when one person seeks so much control over another. Teaching, in this model, is *making* the pupil learn; and a teacher's task is one of so managing the conflict his efforts may provoke that submission is temporary and the pupil's spirit unbroken.

Reduction of conflict. Our difficulties with teaching in everyday life suggest that subordination is indeed central to teaching. We feel most at ease when A's status outside the teaching dyad is superior to B's. If not always gladly, young people accept teaching from their elders, and neophytes take it from old hands. Subordination becomes an issue, however, when A is equal or inferior in status to B. In these circumstances, we use a variety of devices to mitigate conflict. Between friends, what is essentially a nonreciprocal relationship can be phrased, "I'll teach you to swim, if you teach me to. . . ." Each takes responsibility for the other in this interaction, but not simultaneously. We depend on the promised reversal of role to sweeten subordination.

In more structured relationships, reciprocity may be impossible. Situations arise in which one of two persons equal in rank knows something the other must know to carry on his work. When this happens, the latter may be induced to ask for help, so that the teacher seems less like a teacher because he does not originate the interaction. The word "teaching" is not used. Instead, one colleague "helps out" another or "lends a hand." The helper may go out of his way to make clear that he considers himself superior in knowledge to his colleague solely on the matter at hand.

Teaching is inappropriate when B has very high status. Captains of ships are not teachable during command, or company presidents on matters of business. In fact, it is folk wisdom not to try to teach anyone his business, whatever his rank. When instruction is needed, high-ranking people employ a consultant on specific problems for which he is asked to furnish solutions to be tried out only after he has gone. Deprived of control over his pupil's learning and of opportunity to evaluate it, the consultant is less threatening to the man who hires him, but he leaves the scene with an uncomfortable sense of unfulfilled responsibility.

Not using the word "teaching" when teaching is being done, inducing the pupil to ask for it, reciprocity of role, and strict limitation of the area of expertise are devices commonly used to avoid the conflict inherent in teaching. Yet uneasiness, if not hostility, remains. Friend, consultant, and helper still feel responsible for their pupil's response and may try to control it. Learners must hide from themselves the knowledge that even in such a truncated relationship they may have revealed themselves incapable of correct response. One can send away the teacher but not before he has taken one's measure.

School and classroom

The devices that mitigate conflict between teacher and pupil in everyday life are seldom used (although they may be play-acted) in the schoolroom. The teacher's status as an adult makes reciprocity of role unthinkable, since he cannot be put in the position of child–pupil. In so-called democratic teaching methods, interaction may seem to originate with the pupil, but all except the youngest sense the teacher's guiding hand and frequently resent the pretense (Seeley et al. 1956, p. 271).

A pupil may take the initiative by asking for help with a problem, so that the teacher becomes a tutor–consultant who acts as if both he and the pupil had to satisfy outside examiners. But this form of interaction is necessarily infrequent; no matter what efforts school and teachers make to teach individuals, much of the day continues in the lockstep the school's economy of time and space requires. The teacher talks to all his pupils as a unit; he assigns lessons and gives examinations to the group. If there are outside examiners, he does his own testing and grading first. It is only at the end of a schooling sequence, when pupils move on to another system, that teacher and class join efforts to pass examinations.

Authority of the teacher.   In everyday teaching situations, we minimize potential conflict by limiting the teacher's power or pretending it does not exist. Schools do the opposite. They support and legitimate his authority in a number of ways. The teacher has the advantage of his own ground—the self-contained unit of the classroom and the enclosing walls of the school building, which cut the pupil off from the rest of his world. The teacher has dependable allies in other teachers, the school administration, and the state. His methods of control and evaluation (discipline and grading) receive institutional support in the record keeping of the administration. While there may be misunderstandings among these allies of the teacher and vulnerability to outside pressures, they have the advantage of being adults dealing with children. They maintain a continuing order in which the pupil is always subject to the authority of a teacher, in a school the law requires him to attend.

The school also bolsters the teacher's authority by legitimating his claims to knowledge. It assures the community that its teachers have academic degrees and experience. Furthermore, the schoolteacher deals with knowledge systems that have an objective character intrinsically separate from the person of both the teacher and the pupil (Simmel 1950, p. 132). Teacher and pupil do not simply agree, as in informal teaching, that the teacher has superior knowledge; it is a matter of public consensus that he does.

With so many allies and so much support of his authority, the teacher's position seems unassailable. If there is to be some form of conflict between him and his pupils, he must surely win. Pupils are not defenseless, however. Their parents may intercede, and the law usually forbids corporal punishment. In the classroom they have the great advantage of being many to the teacher's one. Like any group, pupils can better their condition by acting together to solve common problems, and a united class provides a teacher with a formidable opponent.

In strictly run schools, however, where grades are of primary importance, the teacher often avoids conflict between himself and his pupils by encouraging conflict among the pupils themselves. He prevents pupils from joining in collective action against him by inducing them to compete with each other in classwork. He has each pupil recite to him rather than to the class and upholds the fiction that learning takes place legitimately only within the dyad of teacher and pupil. When a teacher structures interaction in the classroom in this way, pupils are very aware that they offer the same product to a teacher whose chief role is that of evaluator of products. But, as Marshall ([1963] 1965, pp. 181–183) notes, similarity need not divide; competitors often become partners. When they do, a new form of conflict develops, in which pupils unite to bargain with the teacher about the terms of their cooperation with him. In modern egalitarian societies, where teachers often feel uncomfortable in an authoritarian role and deplore competition for grades, bargaining is probably the most frequent form of conflict between teacher and pupils.

Bargaining between teacher and pupils.   The fact that the school's economy requires the teacher to treat his class as a unit in many, if not all, respects undoubtedly facilitates the development of consensus and collective action on the part of pupils or, as it has elsewhere been called, "student culture" (Becker et al. 1961, pp. 435–437). The term designates a subtle use of the businessman's device of limiting the area of the teacher's expertise. This student action is a drive for a modicum of autonomy expressed in bargaining with the teacher about matters he does not conventionally define as teaching but for which he nevertheless feels responsible: control of the pupil's behavior during learning.

By listening carefully to what a teacher says he wants in class and comparing among themselves what grades or comments he gives for what kinds of work, and by "trying things on" (mass shoelace tying, for instance) in the early days of a school term, a class may reach a consensus about its teacher's standards, both academic and disciplinary. It then transforms what the teacher says and does into rules for him to follow. He must not change these rules the class makes for him, and he must apply them to all pupils.

It does not matter much how high a teacher sets standards of quiet, neatness of work, or promptness, although there will be protests if his standards are out of line with those of other teachers. What does matter is consistency of application. In the eyes of his pupils, this is the teacher's part of the bargain. If it is not kept, he can expect trouble. Teachers who fail to understand the basic premise—"We will behave properly, if you behave properly"—find themselves continually engaged in disciplining pupils rather than imparting knowledge.

Some of the rules of the bargain pupils make with a teacher are in that gray area continually subject to negotiation—degrees of neatness or quietness, for example. Other rules are clear-cut: a teacher may not give a test on things not in the text or on matters not covered in class. Rules vary from classroom to classroom and from one school to another, of course, and with the age and sophistication of pupils. But everywhere the largely unspoken bargain his pupils make with him constrains the teacher's behavior whether he knows it or not.

Pupils have effective sanctions which they use to reward and punish teachers who fail to live up to the bargain, sanctions few teachers can withstand. On one day, when a visitor comes, they delight the teacher with exemplary behavior; on the next, they generate an uproar in the classroom that is loud enough to echo in the ears of the principal, the parents, and the entire community. Dependent on his pupils' good will and cooperation, the teacher soon accedes to the bargaining practices of the class, often entering the game on his own behalf. He says, in effect, "If you will be quiet, you may have more time for the test"; by this action he not only recognizes and thus strengthens the collectivity but also tolerates illicit academic practice in order to secure discipline (Blau [1955] 1963, pp. 215–217).

The bargain also defines the teacher's jurisdiction. Pupils agree that in his classroom the teacher may legitimately control the academic (lessons and tests), attempt to control the quasi-academic (note passing and pencil sharpening), and justly refer the nonacademic (dress and morals) to the more encompassing authority of the principal. In pupils' eyes, however, it is always the academic that legitimizes a teacher's control. Hallways, washrooms, and yards are spatially removed from books and study; the teacher controls them as he can.

The teacher is not likely to see the logic of these distinctions. He knows that if he is to control one pupil's academic response in the classroom, control of the whole class is a prerequisite, and that control of the class depends upon the discipline of adjacent rooms and hallways. The school administration, pursuing its bureaucratic course, also finds behavior unrelated to the academic threatening to the smooth functioning of the school and to its reputation. As a consequence, the dress, manners, and morals (sometimes the families of pupils in the case of less privileged groups) become areas of expertise and attempted control. In some schools, teachers and administration rationalize the extension by asserting responsibility, difficult to realize, over the "whole child." It often is in such apparently unimportant matters as proper dress that bargaining between teacher and pupils breaks down, opening the way to various forms of a third form of conflict—revolt.

Whatever its form—competition among pupils that the teacher must carefully perpetuate, bargaining in which he must share, or revolts he must put down—conflict is difficult for the teacher who clings to the conventional idea that his sole function is one of imparting knowledge. If he thinks of himself as a superior controlling the behavior of many unruly subordinates, he may eventually come to enjoy the battle.

Training institutions for teachers

Teachers' colleges and university schools of education supply the school system with employees and share with it the long-range goal of educating the young. In view of this close relationship, we might expect training institutions to prepare teachers for conflict with pupils, but they do not. Instead, they follow the conventional model with which we began: to teach is to impart or offer knowledge. Would-be teachers learn subject matter and techniques of teaching. They take courses in test construction and interpretation, but testing is not recognized as a device for controlling pupils, and discipline (control of a collectivity) is seldom considered a proper subject of instruction. Offhand, such disjunction between the everyday work of an occupation and the training one receives for it seems extraordinary. Yet wherever training is separated from practice (which is to say, wherever there are schools), we find a similar situation. Most schools teach much that is never used and fail to teach what is.

We may explain the disjunction by referring to the situational perspectives (sets of beliefs and actions) of the various groups in the training institution that together make up its culture. People in both the schools and the training institutions for teachers develop ways of acting, goals, and interests in response to the particular problems posed by their situation (Becker et al. 1961, pp. 34–37). Schools and teachers' colleges are both part of the larger hierarchy of educational institutions devoted to a common goal, but their immediate situations differ.

While school people must deal with local politics, neighborhoods (good and bad), parents, and other interest groups, teachers' colleges exist in an academic setting different in situational imperatives and constraints. Theirs is the world of colleges and universities so apt to grant prestige, with all its privileges, largely to the scholarly disciplines. Since the conventional model of teaching emphasizes knowledge, it fits the academic world better than the conflict model with its insistence on social skills. Faculties of education may be "school-bred" —many institutions require professors to have taught in the public schools (Hughes 1963a, p. 152)—but the trend in such faculties over the years is toward a looser tie with the schools. Set apart on his campus with his higher pay and status, the teacher of teachers loses touch with teachers of children. His institution may formally reflect the organization of the school system by its division into special, elementary, and high school programs, and state licensing regulations may set the sequence of students' courses; but these articulating devices tend more to restrict innovation by both training school and student than to bring future teachers closer to the conflict central to teaching.

Recruiting. The disjunction of training and work, which prevents the transmission of usefully exact knowledge of what to expect in an actual teaching situation, undoubtedly helps the school system to recruit young teachers. It is possible to fill teaching jobs even under conditions of shortage, but the schools want to do more than fill them. Like other service institutions and businesses, they want recruits of high ability committed to a lifetime career. In a word, they want professionals.

Unfortunately, students of the highest ability seldom enter training institutions for teachers (Vertein 1961), and not all graduates teach (Osborn & Maul 1961). There are excellent reasons for this. Of the proud old callings, teaching requires the least formal education and consequently the least investment of time, money, and energy. The school of education provides a relatively unspecific college program that can do no harm. To enter training is in no sense a commitment to a career. For would-be athletes, musicians, and artists uncertain of success as performers and for women whose first choice of career is marriage, a degree in education is a form of occupational insurance.

Although teaching is highly visible to children early in their lives, the exposure is not likely to attract them to the occupation. The teacher is too much of a daily antagonist to generate, for example, the charisma of the physician who comes to help the family in time of trouble. For children of manual workers, teaching may carry prestige; but for those of higher social origins, it is more likely to seem a hard life for the reward. As a woman's occupation, it also bears the stigma (for both sexes) of woman's low status in comparison with men; yet it is not feminine enough, except at the nursery level, to attract women strongly.

People who do enter teaching discover that in comparison with other occupations it is startlingly lacking in the auxiliary rewards that facilitate commitment (Becker 1960). Industry and business offer promotion to more responsible positions, while school teaching offers only increases in pay and trivial seniority privileges. Teachers leave the classroom, of course, to become specialists or administrators; but as long they continue to teach, there is little opportunity for the more-than-local influence possible in other professions through publication, lecturing, and consultation.

Although teachers deal with people rather than with things (an ancient status distinction), the people they deal with are minors. They miss the rewards, psychological and political, of serving people of high status and power. Their daily work is often programmed by state departments of education; nonteachers supervise and direct them in ways which make the autonomy prized by traditional professionals and entrepreneurs impossible. Under such conditions, we should not be surprised that the recruiting of committed professionals is difficult.

Career and profession

Once started on a teaching career, the disjunction between their preparation and actuality in the schools often hits teachers hard. Faced as they are each day with hostile children interminably bargaining for greater autonomy, we may wonder why any of them continue. In the absence of research, we can only speculate, but it is probable that many people find themselves committed to teaching because a first-choice career fails them. The desired marriage or acceptance in some world of athletics, literature, or art never materializes. Teachers may also commit themselves unwittingly because the occupation permits other involvements. For a married man, low pay may necessitate moonlighting, and this second job, fitted to a teaching schedule, may become so rewarding that he continues to teach. Married women who find that teaching fits well with household and child-rearing duties may also continue in teaching.

There is, in addition, the security of tenure and, frequently, happiness in inertia. School tasks repeat and repeat; year after year the round is the same. One may become so marked by immersion in the world of a slum school that one feels unfitted for any other (Becker 1952, p. 474). Responsibility to individuals is lessened by the constant turnover of pupils who sit in one's class for a year and are gone. In time, bargaining for control of a class may become enjoyable. Some of the very things about teaching that discourage neophytes may keep veterans at it (Geer 1966).

Teachers as professionals.   More positively, people may commit themselves to teaching because it is, in many respects, a profession. Teachers cannot claim the separate identity given by control of an esoteric body of knowledge (Hughes 1963b, p. 657), but they do have the esoteric skills of the classroom. They do not have professional societies strong enough to protect them from the incursions of the community, parents, and experts on education outside the school system, but it is usually in the interest of the principal to protect them (Becker 1953, pp. 133–139). They are supervised, but there is still something left of the lonely eminence of the classroom. Visibility of performance is low; and few people believe we have learned as yet how to measure teaching ability (Brim 1958).

In the community, teaching seems to retain some of the more unpleasant aspects of a profession. There are remnants of the expectation that teachers should be models of propriety for the young; even adults are sometimes embarrassed in their exacting presence. The public objects to demands for higher pay because teachers live on taxpayers' money. They ought to serve the community gladly.

Teachers themselves display ambiguity about their status by having unions as well as professional societies. The latter have little control (although they increasingly attempt it) over ethics, recruiting, training, or legislation affecting teachers. They have not yet decided whether school administrators and specialists should be included in their associations as "teachers" or kept out as bosses and rivals. Unions help teachers to fight for higher pay and against the encroachments of duties in schoolyards, lunchrooms, and toilets. But they are more apt to lower that prestige so important to a marginal profession than to heighten it.

Teachers feel they have a poor public image and inadequate public appreciation, but for many teaching is a step up in social class and therefore in respect. Large city systems help teachers to get the additional education required for specialization and raises in pay. Opportunity to transfer to the pleasanter working conditions in middle-class schools comes with seniority (Becker 1953). For men, schoolteaching may be a stopgap, if no longer a stepping-stone on the way to more prestigious careers. For women, it can be a satisfying and even creative occupation that intrudes less than others upon a husband and children.

Teachers are not professionals in the usual sense. They do not have clients who choose them, terminate the relationship, or bring to it the immediate need of help that tempers the client's subordination to the physician or lawyer. In a broader sense, they are professionals with the society for client. We cannot do without their transmission, however imperfect, of its heritage. It is even probable that society would be quite different had children no opportunity to engage in conflict with their superior, the teacher, and hence no opportunity to learn early something of the strength that collective action brings to subordinates.

BLANCHE GEER

[See also ADULT EDUCATION; EDUCATION; EDUCATIONAL PSYCHOLOGY; UNIVERSITIES.]

BIBLIOGRAPHY

BARON, GEORGE; and TROPP, ASHER 1961 Teachers in England and America. Pages 545–557 in A. H. Halsey, Jean Floud, and C. Arnold Anderson (editors), Education, Economy, and Society: A Reader in the Sociology of Education. New York: Free Press.

BECKER, HOWARD S. 1952 The Career of the Chicago Public Schoolteacher. American Journal of Sociology 57:470–477.

BECKER, HOWARD S. 1953 The Teacher in the Authority System of the Public School. Journal of Educational Sociology 27:128–141.

BECKER, HOWARD S. 1960 Notes on the Concept of Commitment. American Journal of Sociology 66:32–40.

BECKER, HOWARD S. 1962 The Nature of a Profession. Volume 62, pages 27–46 in National Society for the Study of Education, Yearbook. Part 1: Education for the Professions. Univ. of Chicago Press.

BECKER, HOWARD S. et al. 1961 Boys in White: Student Culture in Medical School. Univ. of Chicago Press.

BLAU, PETER (1955) 1963 The Dynamics of Bureaucracy: A Study of Interpersonal Relations in Two Government Agencies. Rev. ed. Univ. of Chicago Press.

BRIM, ORVILLE G. 1958 Sociology and the Field of Education. New York: Russell Sage Foundation.

FLOUD, JEAN; and SCOTT, W. 1961 Recruitment to Teaching in England and Wales. Pages 527–544 in A. H. Halsey, Jean Floud, and C. Arnold Anderson (editors), Education, Economy, and Society: A Reader in the Sociology of Education. New York: Free Press.

FRIEDENBERG, EDGAR Z. 1965 Coming of Age in America. New York: Random House.

GEER, BLANCHE 1966 Notes on Occupational Commitment. School Review 74, no. 1:31–47.

HOMANS, GEORGE C. 1950 The Human Group. New York: Harcourt.

HUGHES, EVERETT C. 1963a Is Education a Discipline? Pages 147–158 in John Walton and James L. Kuethe (editors), The Discipline of Education. Madison: Univ. of Wisconsin Press.

HUGHES, EVERETT C. 1963b Professions. Dædalus 92: 655–668.

KOB, JANPETER (1958) 1961 Definition of the Teacher's Role. Pages 558–576 in A. H. Halsey, Jean Floud, and C. Arnold Anderson (editors), Education, Economy, and Society: A Reader in the Sociology of Education. New York: Free Press. → This article is abridged and translated from Janpeter Kob's Das soziale Berufsbewusstsein des Lehrers der höheren Schule.

MARSHALL, THOMAS H. (1963) 1964 Class, Citizenship, and Social Development: Essays. Garden City, N.Y.: Doubleday. → Essays first published in book form as Sociology at the Crossroads and Other Essays. A paperback edition was published in 1965.

MASON, WARD S. 1961 The Beginning Teacher; Status and Career Orientations: Final Report on the Survey of New Teachers in the Public Schools 1956–57. U.S. Office of Education, Circular No. 664. Washington: U.S. Office of Education.

OSBORN, W. W.; and MAUL, R. C. 1961 New Emphasis Needed in Teacher Recruitment. Midland Schools 75: 20–21.

PARSONS, TALCOTT (1959) 1961 The School Class as a Social System: Some of Its Functions in American Society. Pages 434–455 in A. H. Halsey, Jean Floud, and C. Arnold Anderson (editors), Education Economy and Society: A Reader in the Sociology of Education. New York: Free Press. → First published in the Harvard Educational Review.

SEELEY, JOHN R. et al. 1956 Crestwood Heights: A Study of the Culture of Suburban Life. New York: Basic Books.

SIMMEL, GEORG The Sociology of Georg Simmel. Edited and translated by Kurt H. Wolff. Glencoe, Ill.: Free Press, 1950. → See especially pages 118–144 on "The Isolated Individual and the Dyad."

SNIDER, G. R.; and LONG, D. 1961 Are Teacher Education Programs Attracting Academically Able Students? Journal of Teacher Education 12:407–411.

STINCHCOMBE, ARTHUR L. 1965 Rebellion in a High School. Chicago: Quadrangle Books.

VERTEIN, LESTER D. 1961 A Study of the Personal–Social and Intellectual Characteristics of a Group of State College Students Preparing to Teach. Journal of Experimental Education 30:159–192.

WALLER, WILLARD W. (1932) 1961 The Sociology of Teaching. New York: Russell.

TEACHING MACHINES

See LEARNING, article on PROGRAMMED LEARNING.

TECHNICAL ASSISTANCE

The diffusion of knowledge and skills is a normal social process that has gone on within and between nations at all times. But since World War II particular effort has been made to stimulate this diffusion. The idea that the prosperous nations might aid the poorer ones through technical assistance has become the basis of large-scale international programs. In December 1946, the United Nations General Assembly instructed the Economic and Social Council to study the problem of furnishing economic, social, and cultural advice to member nations desiring such assistance, and since 1948 the United Nations has allocated a part of its regular budget to technical assistance. The Expanded Program of Technical Assistance under the United Nations and a major program of the United States government followed the 1949 "Point Four" address of President Harry S Truman. In this famous address President Truman said, "Greater production is the key to prosperity and peace. And the key to greater production is a wider and more vigorous application of modern scientific and technical knowledge" ([1949] 1964, p. 115). Confidence that there were reservoirs of scientific and technical knowledge which could bring economic development to the poorer parts of the world was strong at the time and received further expression in the Colombo Plan for Economic Development in south and southeast Asia, which grew out of a meeting of Commonwealth foreign ministers held in January 1950. Programs of technical assistance have since spread widely and have grown substantially both in money expended and in numbers of people involved.

Estimates of the size of technical assistance programs are notoriously subject to international competition and depend, of course, on definitions of what may properly be included. Commonly, technical assistance is taken to include the supplying of expert and professional personnel to the developing countries; the training of nationals of these countries at home and through fellowship aid abroad; and research on scientific and technical problems undertaken by the aiding countries for the developing ones (as in research on tropical diseases or agricultural products). For 1961, expenditures by various nations have been estimated as follows: United States, $185 million; France, $138 million; Great Britain, $79.7 million; Germany, $42.6 million; Belgium, $39.7 million (France . . . 1963, annexe 12, p. 181, table 4). These expenditures typically are parts of aid programs which include substantial expenditures of other sorts. In the French government's program in 1961, for example, about 21 per cent of the expenditures were devoted to "technical cooperation," 61 per cent to capital equipment, and the remaining 18 per cent to other forms of financial aid to development, such as direct subsidies to foreign governments' budgets (*ibid.*, table 3). In U.S. government expenditures on aid, technical assist-

ance has been a considerably smaller part of the total.

Table 1, based on information collected by the Development Assistance Committee of the Organization for European Cooperation and Development (OECD), gives estimates of the total numbers of persons working on technical assistance in the developing countries in 1962. These data yielded an

Table 1 — International technical assistance by supplying country or organization, 1962

	Number of persons
France (including Algeria)	53,887
United Kingdom	17,500
United States	8,529
U.S.S.R. and other Sino–Soviet bloc	8,475
United Nations	4,542
Egypt	3,700
Belgium	3,336
European Economic Community	457
Japan	446
Israel	380
Italy	376
Germany	336
Canada	237
India	234
Yugoslavia	88
Netherlands	74
Sweden	59
Norway	41
Switzerland	29
Denmark	15
Spain	*
Portugal	*

* Not available.

Source: Maddison 1964, p. 186.

estimated world total of over 102,000, of whom about forty thousand were teachers.

Technical assistance through programs that bring students and trainees from developing countries for shorter or longer courses is extensive. An OECD estimate of the minimum number of such student-trainees in all countries in 1962 was 170,000. About a third of the students were on government or United Nations grants; the others were privately supported. Most of the training provided is at the post-secondary school level. In Great Britain, for example, it has been estimated that there were about fifty thousand full-time students and trainees in 1962/1963, and of these, about two-thirds of those helped by technical assistance programs were in universities, technical colleges, or teaching hospitals (Williams 1964, pp. 89–92).

Expenditures on research, consultation, surveys, and equipment are usually included in the total of expenditures on technical assistance, but it is not easy to get reliable comparisons or totals. A suggestion of the scale and character of this form of technical assistance may perhaps be given by noting that the British Department of Technical Cooperation had a total of £2.2 million in its 1963/1964 budget for those purposes, of which about £1.2 million was for expenditure in the developing countries (*ibid.*, p. 101).

Not all of the diffusion of knowledge and skills from prosperous to poorer countries is dependent on official governmental or international programs, and not all of what in actual practice is called technical assistance is the diffusion of knowledge and skills. There is an important body of technical assistance by private organizations, religious and secular, which has a considerably longer history than do governmental programs and which continues on a large scale. The Rockefeller Foundation, for example, pioneered technical assistance in the development of public health programs from the first decades of this century, and missions have played a major role in developing the educational systems and health services of many countries. It is also obvious that private business investment in developing countries provides considerable diffusion of skills and knowledge. Angus Maddison has estimated that there were perhaps 115,000 people brought by religious, philanthropic, and other private organizations to work in developing countries in 1962, and that business organizations brought another 50,000 executives and other highly qualified personnel (1964, pp. 12–14). Only a fraction of the efforts of these people can be regarded as technical assistance, but the numbers are considerable and the total effect may not be far from that achieved by governmental programs.

Whatever the importance of diffusion of knowledge and skills through nongovernmental activities, the character of modern technical assistance is fundamentally shaped by contemporary definitions of the relations of nations. Programs of technical assistance belong to an era that has seen ideas of popular sovereignty, self-determination, and equality extended to all mankind. These ideas have become a part of the accepted pattern of relations between richer and poorer nations. Although it is manifest that some nations are much richer and more powerful than others, these differences in wealth and power are no longer taken as inevitable, or even proper. The right or destiny of all nations ultimately to share in the prosperity displayed by the richer nations is an axiom of modern ideology, and the obligation of the richer to help the poorer is strongly urged and widely accepted. In the contemporary etiquette of international comparisons, one thus speaks of "developed" and "developing" nations, and careful efforts are made to avoid affront to the intrinsic worth of the "developing" nations. Indeed, the titles of governmental aid programs commonly avoid emphasis on "aid" and favor "cooperation"; the United States has had the International Cooperation Administration; France, the Ministry of Cooperation; and Britain, the Department of Technical Cooperation. In particular, references to "civilized" and "backward" nations are avoided, and doctrines of cultural relativity have more than social scientific currency. It is recognized that changes must be wrought in the developing countries to bring them the advantages of the developed countries, but a course is sought which does not obviously affront their cultures or civilizations. If it cannot be assumed that changes will be brought about merely by injections of capital, it can be represented that other importations are essentially *technical*—that is to say, not peculiarly and indelibly a part of the culture from which they are drawn or implying that the receiving culture must become a client of the donor. It is obvious that such a context invites stretching conceptions of what is "technical."

The firm emphasis on the purely technical role of those who provide technical assistance that is found in United Nations doctrine and in other public discussions of the subject arises from other concerns as well. "Experts" are to refrain from political, commercial, and other self-interested activities, and their contributions are to be made on the initiative of the governments of the receiving countries. These requirements derive in part from sensitivity over past domination by colonial powers and fears of exploitation or indoctrination by business or other foreign interests. Colonialism has been, of course, a major vehicle for diffusion of knowledge, skills, and institutions from economically advanced to poorer countries. In the nineteenth century, men like Palmerston, Gladstone, and Livingstone envisaged the spread of trade as a prime vehicle of cultural diffusion, and they explicitly preferred it to the extension of political domination or outright colonialism. Their philosophy of "civilization by trade" had some merits, but it is hardly more popular in the developing countries today than is colonial domination. In important ways contemporary programs of technical assistance are attempts to secure the benefits of older forms of diffusion while avoiding domination and intrusion, and the character of these programs is shaped by reactions against past experiences.

The right of self-determination has, particularly in recent years, gained ascendancy over the notion that countries should meet certain conditions before they are ready for self-government and independence. Particularly in Africa, this has meant that many countries have come to independence before they had sufficient nationals trained to take over the governments, schools, and businesses that had been established in these countries during the colonial era. A notorious case is the former Belgian Congo, which at independence had a sophisticated array of industries and a complex government, but only about a score of Congolese university graduates. If many of these newly independent countries are to maintain existing institutions, continued use of foreign personnel for considerable periods is necessary. Measures to provide these personnel have been a regular feature of British, French, and Belgian policies of colonial devolution; in greater or lesser measure, the former colonial power has paid the costs of these people and has regarded them as part of its technical assistance program.

A notable result of this situation has been that large numbers of the people supplied to developing countries are not directly engaged in the new applications of technical knowledge for increased production which were envisaged in President Truman's Point Four doctrine. They are carrying on as engineers, policemen, tax collectors, doctors, veterinary or agricultural officers, etc., much as they served under the colonial regimes. Many of them do not "advise" or "train counterparts"; they "do the job." Thus, about half of the British government's technical assistance expenditure of £25 million in 1962/1963 was spent on the Overseas Service Assistance Scheme, which pays part of the costs of British personnel employed in regular posts by overseas governments; in east Africa 90 per cent of British technical assistance in 1962/1963 was of this sort. [See PLANNING, ECONOMIC, *article on* DEVELOPMENT PLANNING.]

In actual practice, then, technical assistance programs are neither exclusively concerned with clearly technical matters nor only with teaching and advising. Their effectiveness does, nevertheless, depend on the skills and knowledge that can be transferred or developed, and these skills and knowledge must at some stage be acquired by nationals of the countries being assisted. Two fundamental concerns in technical assistance are thus with the marshaling and increase of relevant knowledge and expertise, and the devising of effective training programs. These subjects are discussed in the two following sections of this article. The possibilities of technical assistance also depend on social and political considerations, some of which derive from the international character of technical assistance, and others from the social

changes that any innovation requires. The final section of this article deals with these questions.

Diffusion and increase of knowledge and skills

The basic assumption of modern technical assistance is that there is a body of technical and scientific knowledge which can be effectively transferred across national boundaries, to the benefit of the receiving countries. An impressive effort to assess the potentials of existing knowledge for development was made at the United Nations Conference on Science and Technology in Development, held at Geneva in 1962; unfortunately, the conference papers were voluminous and no summary report was issued.

The technical assistance programs of various countries have also from time to time organized special investigations of the possibilities scientific knowledge offered for the benefit of particular areas or for the solution of special problems; thus, for example, in 1959 the American aid program financed a committee to seek possible scientific "breakthroughs" that could benefit African development. In general, the result of such assessments has been to point up the need for additional research to bring existing scientific knowledge to bear on the concrete problems of developing countries. Technical breakthroughs which are usable anywhere without significant adaptation—like the recent development of intrauterine devices as cheap and effective contraceptives—are rare. In this sense, the stock of usable scientific knowledge for development is often disappointingly small, and there is scope for technical assistance programs that may increase it.

Because of its overwhelming importance in most of the developing countries, the improvement of agriculture has been a major focus of technical assistance, and it offers an obvious field for the application of scientific and technical knowledge. While it might appear that there would be great reservoirs of immediately applicable knowledge in this field, there is a long history of overconfident and misguided efforts to improve traditional forms of agriculture. Studies like that of Pierre de Schlippe (1956) on the agriculture of the Zande tribe in the northeastern Congo have been needed to make clear that a large amount of valid knowledge on local agricultural possibilities may be accumulated through the empirical methods of nonliterate societies, and that it is often difficult to provide anything better through existing scientific knowledge.

Because of the great variety of climates, soils, and ecological conditions found throughout the world, agricultural technology needs local adaptation. Most modern agricultural science has been developed in the north temperate zones, and the results are usually not directly applicable to the tropical climates, where a great part of the population of the developing countries lives. There are, indeed, many areas for which scientific agriculture has no prescriptions that can significantly increase agricultural productivity without inputs which are clearly beyond the resources of the people.

An appreciation of these facts is essential to understanding that some of the resistance to agricultural innovations which technical assistance programs have encountered is not due to blind traditionalism or apathy. Various recent studies have indicated that the adoption of improved practices is characteristically inhibited by the fact that they involve risks for people who have very low incomes and resources. Losses that would be tolerable at higher levels of income can be disastrous for subsistence cultivators. As long as there is an appreciable probability of such disastrous losses, it must be considered rational behavior for cultivators to proceed cautiously. McKim Marriott (1952) has suggested that one source of resistance to improved varieties is that they may involve the loss of the secondary advantages of the established varieties. In a study on India he found that higher-yielding varieties of wheat were resisted by the peasantry because they had a less usable form of straw as well as other disadvantages, and these secondary uses were important to peasants at such low levels of living. An accumulating body of experience now strongly suggests that new practices in agriculture must give very markedly superior results over established practices if quite rational resistance is to be overcome. It has been suggested, for example, that crop yields which are not less than 50 per cent greater than traditional yields are necessary for rapid adoption of improved but more expensive varieties of seed and for the introduction of fertilizers. Fortunately, research can sometimes meet such severe challenges and produce leaps forward.

The need for agricultural research in tropical conditions has been recognized for a long time and was fostered by the colonial powers through such organizations as the British Colonial Research Council and the French Organisation pour la Recherche Scientifique et Technique d'Outre-Mer (Hailey [1938] 1957, pp. 1600 ff.). Support of research stations at various places throughout the world continues as part of the technical assistance programs of former colonial powers. It has also been prominent in the work of private foundations;

the successes of the Rockefeller Foundation's maize and wheat improvement programs in Latin America have encouraged similar ventures elsewhere, notably in the combined Rockefeller and Ford Foundation support of the International Rice Research Institute in the Philippines.

Agricultural research represents a type of technical assistance in which a relatively small number of highly qualified experts may affect the performance of large numbers of productive units, from peasant holdings to plantations. Lack of trained scientists typically has meant that many of the developing countries are unable to carry out such research for themselves, although in the future they intend to do so, and training programs to this end are normal complements to research programs. Numerous difficult problems exist in devising organizations and career patterns which make possible the attraction of good research talent into technical assistance of this type; organizations that existed under colonial regimes have broken down in the subsequent period of independence because it is impossible to staff them satisfactorily, and it is probable that considerably less technical assistance has been available in this field than is needed.

Research on tropical diseases and public health problems is another classic field in which effective aid to development has had to be based on the accumulation of new knowledge. Technical assistance continues to provide staff and support for medical research organizations, some of them established during the colonial era and others—notably in the field of population control—of more recent origin.

In industrial, as in agricultural, development, the concreteness of effective techniques raises barriers to the easy transfer of knowledge. S. H. Frankel has remarked in his *Economic Impact on Under-developed Societies*: "Technical knowledge, the machine and capital goods in general never exist in the abstract but always only in the relatively fleeting form suited to the momentary situation and to that complex of unique problems to which they have been adapted. . . . That is why they cannot be readily transferred from one situation to another" ([1953] 1959, p. 24). Thus, as with agriculture, the effective growth of industry in developing countries requires extensive study of local conditions and the adaptation of techniques; therefore, feasibility studies—surveys of resources, facilities, and markets—are needed if prudent investments are to occur. It is commonly the case that developing countries lack the specially trained manpower to carry out such investigations. The United Nations Special Fund for Economic Development was established to meet this need, and there are numerous private consulting organizations which have been employed by the technical assistance programs of various countries to perform these functions. They are, indeed, often a necessary preliminary to successful applications for financial aid. Engineers, agronomists, hydrologists, and the like normally dominate the composition of such teams, although economists are increasingly employed. Many of the questions which will affect the success or failure of development projects are essentially sociological, but it is not usual to depend on professional social scientists in assessing such matters.

While technical assistance can unquestionably supply much relevant knowledge for development, either through new research or by drawing on accumulated stores, it is also normal that there are residual uncertainties against which no expertise is infallible. Even in precise technical fields these uncertainties may be significant. They grow very large in many of the subjects on which technical assistance is sought. Development programs commonly call for land reform, settlement schemes, the development of cooperatives, reorganization of taxation systems, and new budgeting or personnel procedures. All of these subjects are ones in which expertise of various sorts exists in various places, and it is rightfully sought and used by technical assistance programs. But it is usually not the sort of expertise that is based on exact scientific knowledge or firmly secure principles. Obviously, a great part of the effective functioning of the developed world rests not on clear deductions from general scientific principles but on an accumulation of experience from pragmatic efforts. Even precise techniques based on exact knowledge depend on much less precise considerations as to what a viable context for their application may be. The ironies that commonly surround the use of the word "expert" thus have abundant justification. But imprecise competence is not incompetence, and that part of the practical planning of technical assistance programs which is concerned with devising selection procedures, orientation, placement, and sufficient lengths of service to maximize the effective transfer of expertise is not futile. The growing literature on the process of technical assistance is providing an accumulation of ideas and case material on these diffuse but vital matters (Bock 1954; Erasmus 1961; Foster 1962).

How effective aid by an expert will be depends on his capacity to make generalized use of his competence. Among the familiar forms of failure in technical assistance are efforts to transfer concrete forms and methods from the expert's home country to a new one. An effective performance must be adapted to the new scene and must in this sense be a creative achievement, broadly comparable in character to the efforts of scientific researchers in technical assistance. An adequate supply of people who are capable of such achievements in the multifarious fields that technical assistance attempts to serve, and who are available for such service, is not easily found. Indeed, the economist I. M. D. Little, in a recent survey of aid to Africa, has concluded that the developed countries are "scraping the bottom of the barrel" (1964, p. 56).

Better recruitment methods and more ample rewards may increase the supply, but even with the best of experts the over-all difficulty and obscurity of the development process remain as barriers and limitations to the possibilities of technical assistance. Technical improvements in special fields are obviously not enough to bring development. Institutions must be built and the whole interdependent system of a society's functioning shaped to sustain higher levels of performance. As long as there is no precise understanding of the total process of growth, there must be limitations on the possible effectiveness of technical assistance. The optimism that has infused the setting up of technical assistance programs must thus be tempered by realization of the evident limitations on what even the most highly developed countries can supply.

Technical assistance in manpower training

Since the aim of the developing countries is not merely development but development executed by their own people under their own control, technical assistance is inherently concerned with education and training. It must not only apply modern knowledge but teach it as well. While technical assistance programs in fact supply large numbers of people in operating posts where they often have no explicit responsibilities for training (or innovation), this is not regarded as a satisfactory situation by either donor or recipient countries. An Asian study group on technical assistance, composed of leading figures from Asian planning organizations and meeting at Bangkok in January 1965, declared that technical assistance had a dual purpose: to develop self-sufficiency in the manpower required for national development and to develop institutions that would accelerate self-sustained growth.

This emphasis on self-sufficiency sometimes leads to conflict with desired standards of achievement and efficiency when experts and technicians are brought into a country to start an institution or execute a development project. David Lilienthal has described the conflict as follows: "If . . . the foreign managers and technicians must . . . place increasing reliance on local people in planning and carrying out the work, it will, *as they see it*, be virtually impossible to make a physical success of the project by any standards of speed, economy, and quality of work they are accustomed to. Too often, therefore, lip service is given to the principle of training, but actual training is ignored. . . ." In accordance with the dominant principles of thinking about technical assistance, Lilienthal denounces this tendency and argues: "If in fact a project cannot be planned and carried out with this kind of local participation and training of human skills without actually jeopardizing the physical work, then it must be seriously questioned whether the project is worth doing at all, worth doing for the country, for the foreign lender, or for the foreign business venturer. . . . This is a bitter lesson to learn, but one that experience is forcing us to learn" (1964, p. 13).

The techniques and processes that a nation can make use of at any given time and the institutions it can effectively operate depend on the state of development of that nation's manpower. Similarly, the pace and character of the future development it can achieve depend on the prospect of improving the competence of its manpower. Although foreign aid agencies, as Lilienthal regrets, sometimes push projects that go beyond the readiness of the country's manpower, inherited institutions and impatient ambition also encourage nations to maintain or develop undertakings before they can be effectively manned by their own people. The need for temporary operational technical assistance is one consequence and may not be repugnant to national pride if its early end is foreseeable. Realistic schedules for the retirement of such operational assistance require that development be planned in accordance with the anticipated growth of trained manpower. Assessment of the manpower sources of a country is now generally regarded as an essential part of national planning and a basis for sound technical assistance programs. India, the United Arab Republic, Tanzania, and various other countries have gone far in the manpower budgeting of development plans, drawing heavily on technical expertise from Western countries, particularly that which grew out of experience in coping with manpower shortages during World War II. The provision of experts in this field has been an important part of the work of the International Labour Organisation, the Ford Foundation, and other technical assistance agencies.

The needs for manpower development of a country can be roughly divided into the need for training and the need for education. Training is here conceived as the preparation for a particular functional role, and it presumably has to be based on some minimal levels of general education and experience. Precisely what levels are satisfactory minimums for profitable training are not easy to determine, and lively controversies over them seem to inhere in the struggles for self-confidence and rapid progress in the developing countries. These controversies are unlikely ever to be resolved by rational argument, although one important function of manpower analysis is to provide guidance on the issues involved. Technical assistance cannot avoid these issues, since it must seek to provide training where it can be effective and must turn to more basic educational preparation where that is deficient.

There is a sense in which the ideal forms of technical assistance are ones that involve a minimum of training. If an innovation brought by an expert is intrinsically valuable and well adapted to the skills of the society, a demonstration or a plan may suffice for large-scale results—a new variety of seed may be widely adopted because of its demonstrated results, or an organizational proposal may be accepted and put into effect. More commonly, however, a substantial measure of training is required. If technical assistance is to be rationally deployed and to have a significant effect on the nation's functioning, this training has to be carefully planned. The number of acceptable foreign experts likely to be available in fields like peasant agriculture is far too limited for them to be the direct agents of innovations that require training. Technical assistance must then turn to "training the trainers," as it often does.

Widespread and significant effects may also be achieved through the training of those who determine policy or give executive direction to organizations. This sort of training may sometimes be carried out in specially arranged courses, but there are obvious advantages in relevance and directness if it can be done on the job. Where an expert is brought in to set up or direct an organization or institution, it is normally the desire of both the supplying agency and the recipient country that the replacement of this expert by an identified national be foreseen. Hence the pattern of counterpart training, which has been orthodox technical assistance practice. Ideally, the counterpart is taught directly on the job, but if no suitable candidates are immediately available, prospective ones may be identified and given preliminary courses. The difficulties in carrying through this ideal pattern of counterpart training are, however, considerable, and experience has often been discouraging. There seem to be several reasons. In the first place, the selection of suitable counterparts depends on the existence of a reasonably ample supply of people with a basis in education and experience onto which the specific training can be added in a limited time. Where such supplies are thin, as is often the case, mediocre or only partially qualified people have to be taken, or if good people can be obtained, they are likely to shift to other opportunities after a brief time. Some of the most discouraging experiences in technical assistance have occurred when sets of counterparts were repeatedly trained, only to transfer to other jobs. Moreover, it is probably only in the most narrowly specific technical functions that a counterpart can learn to do as the expert did. The expert is operating in a new setting, and even if he makes a creative response and adapts accordingly, the counterpart taking over from him will have to make adjustments simply because he is a member of the society and not a visiting expert. And finally, the difficulties of inserting substantial numbers of experts into the operative functioning of a country (for reasons discussed more fully in the next section) mean that only rather limited amounts of on-the-job counterpart training can be effectively provided. There is, of course, an earnest effort to see that experts are placed at points of strategic consequence, and hence it sometimes occurs that counterpart training has an importance quite out of proportion to the number of people involved.

The difficulty of counterpart training is one of the various difficulties that have been experienced in trying to develop effective organizations · in milieus that are generally short of trained people. Efforts to develop segments of a government (frequently, a plan of organization) or stages in a production system have often been frustrated by the fact that other sectors lacked trained people. This acts as a stimulus for technical assistance programs to be more broadly concerned with the total supply of a nation's manpower and the basic educational attainment on which specialized accomplishment must be built.

The figures given earlier indicate that a large part of technical assistance goes into the provision of university courses for exchange students and that teachers make up the largest category of people supplied to the developing countries. Some of these teachers give instruction in technical subjects, but the largest numbers are engaged in secondary school or university teaching and thus are involved in broader forms of education. In many African countries and a few others this concentration of technical assistance in education is clearly related to the manpower needs of development. Many countries are grossly deficient in the numbers of educated people required to meet the high-level manpower needs of development, and they have lacked sufficient teachers to staff the institutions that might produce qualified people. The large programs of educational assistance provided by the United Nations Special Fund, the U.S. Peace Corps, the French government, and other agencies have their rationale in these considerations, and they are supported by capital programs of the World Bank, the European Common Market, Fonds Européens de Développement pour les Pays et Territoires d'Outre-Mer (FEDOM), the U.S. Agency for International Development (USAID), and other agencies.

The development of education at the appropriate pace and of the right quality to supply the manpower needs of a developing country is one of the most difficult and uncertain tasks of development strategy. Frederick Harbison and Charles H. Myers, W. Arthur Lewis, the various experts associated with the Mediterranean development studies of the OECD, and others have attempted to assess the numbers of educated people needed at various levels of development and to chart courses of growth for individual countries (Harbison & Myers 1964; 1965; France . . . 1963; Lewis 1961; 1965).

But not only is sound strategy difficult to discern; it is also obvious that there are heavy pressures to expand education in the developing countries that arise more from individual ambition than from national need, and that there is a readiness of supplying countries to give educational assistance because it is relatively straightforward, acceptable, and a means of cultural influence, rather than because of its indisputable priority. There is thus some danger that technical assistance to education may be unduly favored, leading to the neglect of more difficult forms of assistance and to the aggravation of the unemployment problems that afflict the developing countries.

Social and political problems

We have seen that what technical assistance can do depends on the knowledge and skills it can bring and on the state of development of the receiving country's manpower. It also depends on what the peoples or governments of supplying and receiving countries are willing and able to accept in obligations and mutual relationships.

Learning and adopting the techniques of the modern world typically involve costs in the abandonment of old ways and in the recognition of superior foreign skills. It has been stressed above that much resistance to innovation is based on reasonable doubts about the superiority of the recommended innovations. But whatever the scope that must be given to the rational calculation of advantage in resistance to change, it is clear that social and cultural patterns pose many obstacles too. A considerable part of technical assistance programs has consisted of the direct attempt to improve the livelihood of people in traditional rural settings, and the complex problems encountered in such efforts have been studied by many social scientists. A large and growing literature displays the detailed meaning of the proposition that technical innovation means social and cultural change (Spicer 1952; Erasmus 1961; Foster 1962).

Particular attention has been given to the problems of introducing new health practices or medical treatments and new methods of economic production. It has been found again and again that innovations of these sorts encounter existing definitions of the situation which they must supersede or with which they must be meaningfully reconciled. Moreover, change affects prestige, leadership, and vested interests. For example, in the Ivory Coast an improved method of extracting palm oil caused a change in the distribution of income between men and women, and was therefore resisted (Boutillier & Dupire 1958, pp. 83–87).

Successful innovation may bring improved living standards and status to some individuals and not to others, who feel they should share the same rewards and status. Charles Erasmus tells how Haitian peasants have feared to change their farming methods or living standards, lest they arouse the envy and jealousy of their neighbors (1961, pp. 80–81).

The difficulties of isolating the benefits and incidental effects of a technical change are particularly pronounced in traditional settings, where economic activities are deeply enmeshed in kinship and community ties. This enmeshing is one important reason why subsistence economies have been more resistant to change than economies where money exchange plays a large role. But although social and cultural patterns pose particularly formidable barriers to change in traditional, rural settings, basically similar resistance occurs in all developing societies. Even in the "modern" sectors of those societies, there are institutionalized patterns and distributions of rewards that are affected by innovation. For example, the improved functioning of a civil service or a system of taxation is normally not a purely technical matter; the effectiveness of new technical procedures is almost invariably tied to new performance standards which may require demotions or dismissals for some and new levels of effort for others. The exaction of these costs and losses must ultimately be the responsibility of nationals of the country; but the costs and losses also pose problems for the foreign technical assistance expert and contribute to the difficulties of maintaining an over-all political context in which technical assistance is possible.

It is evident that programs of technical assistance involve delicate political and psychological relationships between the supplying and the receiving countries. In official doctrine, as described above, the initiative in requests for technical assistance must lie with the governments of receiving countries. The Expanded Program of Technical Assistance of the United Nations has been very literal in its interpretation of this doctrine. Priorities are left to the requesting countries, and broadly scattered assistance has been supplied to many countries. A purely responsive policy of this sort has been criticized on the grounds that it leaves the difficult questions of development policy to governments that, by the very fact that they need technical assistance, are dubiously equipped to analyze the questions. If technical assistance is to be more than a gesture of international good will or a pursuit of short-run political advantage, the suppliers must be concerned with maximizing the effectiveness of their assistance in development. If they act on this concern, they cannot be unselectively responsive to the requests they get.

The obverse situation, in which the receiving country does not dictate what technical assistance will be supplied but passively accepts what is offered, is little recognized in official doctrine but is in fact a significant problem in aid programs. A familiar basis of misgivings about aid programs, and about technical assistance in particular, lies in the fear that poor countries will become permanent wards of richer countries and will not in fact strive for the self-reliant independence they claim. Normally, the suppliers of assistance seek something between supine receptivity to and truculent disregard for their aims and judgment. This is the substantive basis for the theme of "technical cooperation," which indeed is much more than a flattering label for an essentially asymmetrical relationship. If a technical assistance program is to have more than trivial or ephemeral effect in a developing country, it must be based on intimate cooperation. There must be good understanding of the country by the suppliers of assistance and sympathetic appreciation of the aims and competence of the nationals. An admission of the need for technical assistance is in some measure an admission of inadequacy by the receivers, and if this admission is not to generate resentment or irresponsibility, it must be accompanied by a balancing self-confidence and trust that assistance will work toward ultimate autonomy, not subjugation.

The actual practice of technical assistance, of course, shows many departures from the ideal of continuing technical cooperation. The delicacy of the relationships of dependency that are inseparable from technical assistance commonly makes for unrealistic haste and demoralizingly short perspectives. Operational technical assistance is particularly vulnerable to quick termination; its only ready defense is its effectiveness, and effectiveness is hardly as easy to demonstrate as is manifest dependence on foreign competence. Figures cited earlier showed that the largest numbers of people engaged in operational technical assistance in the early 1960s were the French and British in their former colonial dependencies, and most of them had been held over from the colonial era. The policies of France and Britain, like those of their former dependencies, have had to be that this operational assistance should be brought to an end as soon as possible, but not necessarily very rapidly where trained nationals are scarce. In fact, the decline in the number of such personnel has typically been more rapid than was planned or expected or, indeed, than has been optimal for development. It would seem that, despite much optimistic planning and relatively amicable negotiations over independence, it has been difficult to hold to the expected withdrawal schedules for former colonial administrators and professionals.

There is also likely to be imperfect agreement on aims and priorities between the suppliers and the receivers of technical assistance. What is a "felt need" to the receiving country may appear as misguided or even fatuous to the potential supplier. What the suppliers think the country needs and what they are ready to give may be resisted, for good or bad reasons; just as experts frequently have difficulty persuading peasants that they can improve their performance and that they need outside help to do so, so also do the experts meet difficulties in persuading governments that they are failing to do things as well as they could with competent help. While there is an evident convergence of interest between donors and recipients in wanting technical assistance to be effective and significant, the measures that are applied inevitably involve differences. Suppliers are under pressure to show tangible results, and this often leads, particularly among the smaller suppliers, to concentration on limited fields or specific projects that may

not represent an optimal allocation of resources for the country's development. The cynical observation that each supplier "has to have his monument" is frequently justified.

The effort to bring together the multifarious needs of a country with the possibilities of assistance has contributed to the emphasis on national planning that characterizes the developing countries. Under the Kennedy administration, it became the guiding doctrine of the U.S. government's aid program to insist on national plans into which U.S. aid could be fitted. The importance and difficulty of national planning mean that technical assistance agencies favor the assignment of experts to national planning. For example, the 1963 review of French aid policy, known as the Jeanneney Report, recommended: "Outside of teaching, the only French technical assistance personnel who should continue are high level consultants." The report went on to argue that three sorts of assistance were particularly to be recommended: advice in planning, the training of administrative cadres, and the study of industrial programs (France... 1963, pp. 82, 94).

These sorts of technical assistance, favored by other suppliers of technical assistance as well, raise many delicate problems. It is, of course, the common doctrine of technical assistance that policy should be determined by the officials and leaders of the receiving country and that the role of technical assistance should be essentially advisory. Thus, in an economic planning program, foreign economists may be used as technical experts, but decisions on the program are the responsibility of senior civil servants, a political minister, or a ministerial committee. It is, of course, difficult to draw a clear line between technical advice, advice on policy, and the actual determination of policy. As Chester Barnard and others have emphasized, the executive functions of an organization are in fact very extensively diffused, and unless there is reason to be concerned about this fact, it occasions no special notice. It may, however, be a serious point of sensitivity in a developing country. If officials are themselves inexperienced and unsure, they may be uncertain of their own capacity to determine policy. They may in particular find it difficult to take the initiative necessary to direct advisory services. This leaves initiative to the advisor, and great delicacy may be required to avoid the fact or appearance of manipulation. Repetitive emphasis of the principle that the foreign advisor works under the guidance of local people may be seen as an indication of the difficulty of these relationships.

Although the ideology of technical assistance

puts emphasis on its dissociation from aims of political influence, there can hardly be such dissociation in actual practice if programs on a large scale are mounted. In fact, the distribution of aid and technical assistance follows substantially the established patterns of political relationship (French aid concentrating in its former colonies and British in the Commonwealth) or current political concern (American aid in countries bordering the communist world). Even if technical assistance personnel are not improperly attempting political influence, the presence of large numbers from a single country may be seen as lingering colonialism or as a threat of neocolonialism. In Vietnam, for example, concern with such impressions led to a policy of dispersing the American personnel throughout the country (Montgomery 1962, pp. 172 ff).

Suppliers of bilateral technical assistance frankly admit that their concentration on particular countries is dictated by political concerns. Similarly, policies of extending cultural influence through aid to education and exchange programs are openly avowed. Since it seems inevitable that the foreign policy of suppliers of bilateral aid will to some extent affect the direction of their aid, with resulting tension in their relations to the receivers, there has been pressure to put more technical assistance on a multilateral basis, through the United Nations or otherwise. Continued discussion of the relative merits of multilateral and bilateral assistance has left doubt about the wisdom and feasibility of making any sharp changes in practice. Where a concern with particular developing countries exists on the part of a developed power, it is open to question whether the costs of dependency are more serious than the sacrifices in reduced assistance that exclusive recourse to multilateral sources might entail. Policies are currently in flux and it is not easy to see how they may evolve, but it seems likely that the political acceptability of assistance programs, both in the supplying and in the receiving countries, will be a weightier determinant of the outcome than will the intrinsic advantages of the other policies for aiding development.

FRANCIS X. SUTTON

[*See also* AGRICULTURE, *article on* DEVELOPING COUNTRIES; ECONOMIC GROWTH; FOREIGN AID; MODERNIZATION.]

BIBLIOGRAPHY

ARENSBERG, CONRAD M.; and NIEHOFF, ARTHUR 1964 *Introducing Social Change: A Manual for Americans Overseas.* Chicago: Aldine.

BARNARD, CHESTER I. (1938) 1962 *The Functions of the Executive.* Cambridge, Mass.: Harvard Univ. Press.

BOCK, EDWIN A. 1954 *Fifty Years of Technical Assistance: Some Administrative Experiences of U.S. Voluntary Agencies.* Chicago: Public Administration Clearing House.

DUPIRE, MARGUERITE; and BOUTILLIER, JEAN-LOUIS 1958 *Le pays Adioukrou et sa palmeraie (Basse-Côte-d'Ivoire): Étude socio-économique.* Paris: Office de la Recherche Scientifique et Technique Outre-Mer.

ERASMUS, CHARLES J. 1961 *Man Takes Control: Cultural Development and American Aid.* Minneapolis: Univ. of Minnesota Press.

FOSTER, GEORGE McC. 1962 *Traditional Cultures, and the Impact of Technological Change.* New York: Harper.

FRANCE, MINISTÈRE D'ÉTAT CHARGÉ DE LA RÉFORME ADMINISTRATIVE 1963 *La politique de coopération avec les pays en voie de développement.* 2 vols. Paris: La Documentation Française. → Known as the Jeanneney Report.

FRANKEL, S. HERBERT (1953) 1959 *The Economic Impact on Under-developed Societies: Essays on International Investment and Social Change.* Cambridge, Mass.: Harvard Univ. Press.

GLICK, PHILIP M. 1957 *The Administration of Technical Assistance: Growth in the Americas.* Univ. of Chicago Press.

GOODENOUGH, WARD H. 1963 *Cooperation in Change: An Anthropological Approach to Community Development.* New York: Russell Sage Foundation.

HAILEY, WILLIAM MALCOLM (1938) 1957 *An African Survey: A Study of Problems Arising in Africa South of the Sahara.* Rev. ed. New York: Oxford Univ. Press.

HARBISON, FREDERICK; and MYERS, CHARLES A. 1964 *Education, Manpower, and Economic Growth: Strategies of Human Resource Development.* New York: McGraw-Hill.

HARBISON, FREDERICK; and MYERS, CHARLES A. (editors) 1965 *Manpower and Education: Country Studies in Economic Development.* New York: McGraw-Hill.

LEWIS, W. ARTHUR Priorities for Educational Expansion. In the mimeographed papers of the OECD Policy Conference on Economic Growth and Investment in Education, Washington, D.C., October 1961. Unpublished manuscript.

LEWIS, W. ARTHUR Aspects of Economic Development. Paper for the African Conference on Progress Through Cooperation, Organized by the Council on World Tensions, in Kampala, Uganda, May 1965. Unpublished manuscript.

LILIENTHAL, DAVID E. 1964 The Road to Change. *International Development Review* 6, no. 4:9–14.

LITTLE, I. M. D. 1964 *Aid to Africa: An Appraisal of U.K. Policy for Aid to Africa South of the Sahara.* New York: Macmillan; London: Pergamon.

MADDISON, ANGUS 1963 The Role of Technical Assistance in Economic Development. Organisation for Economic Co-operation and Development, *Observer* 7:20–26.

MADDISON, ANGUS 1964 The Supply of High Level Skills and Training to Developing Countries. Unpublished manuscript, OECD Development Center, Paris.

MADDISON, ANGUS 1965 *Foreign Skills and Technical Assistance in Economic Development.* Paris: Organisation for Economic Co-operation and Development, Development Centre.

MARRIOTT, McKIM 1952 Technological Change in Over-developed Rural Areas. *Economic Development and Cultural Change* 1, no. 4:261–272.

MATHIASEN, KARL 1966 *Multilateral Technical Assistance: The Role for the U.N. in Africa.* Washington: Brookings Institution.

MONTGOMERY, JOHN D. 1962 *The Politics of Foreign Aid: American Experience in Southeast Asia.* Published for the Council on Foreign Relations. New York: Praeger.

MOSHER, ARTHUR T. 1957 *Technical Co-operation in Latin American Agriculture.* Univ. of Chicago Press.

NATIONAL PLANNING ASSOCIATION 1956 *Technical Co-operation in Latin America: Recommendations for the Future.* Washington: The Association.

SCHLIPPE, PIERRE DE 1956 *Shifting Cultivation in Africa: The Zande System of Agriculture.* London: Routledge.

SPICER, EDWARD H. (editor) 1952 *Human Problems in Technological Change: A Casebook.* New York: Russell Sage Foundation.

SPITZ, ALLAN A.; and WEIDNER, EDWARD W. 1963 *Development Administration: An Annotated Bibliography.* Honolulu: East–West Center Press.

TRUMAN, HARRY S 1964 Inaugural Address, January 20, 1949. Pages 112–116 in U.S. President, *Public Papers of the Presidents of the United States: 1949.* Washington: Government Printing Office.

UNITED NATIONS, SECRETARY-GENERAL, *1961—* 1963 *Science and Technology for Development: Report on the United Nations Conference on the Application of Science and Technology for the Benefit of the Less Developed Areas.* Vols. 1–8. New York: United Nations.

U.S. DEPARTMENT OF STATE, AGENCY FOR INTERNATIONAL DEVELOPMENT 1963 *Development Administration and Assistance: An Annotated Bibliography.* Washington: Government Printing Office.

WILLIAMS, PETER 1964 *British Aid-4; Technical Assistance: A Factual Survey of Britain's Aid to Overseas Development Through Technical Assistance.* London: Overseas Development Institute.

TECHNOLOGY

The first article under this heading is devoted to a discussion of the impact of technology upon society and of conditions affecting technological change; the second article focuses upon the impact of technology upon international relations. The relationship of technology to the social sciences is also reviewed in other articles throughout the encyclopedia. Examples of the technology of non-Western societies are found in CRAFTS; CULTURE CHANGE. *The relation of technology to environment is discussed in* DOMESTICATION; ECOLOGY; URBAN REVOLUTION. *Levels of technological–social integration are examined in* AGRICULTURE, *article on* COMPARATIVE TECHNOLOGY; HUNTING AND GATHERING; INDUSTRIALIZATION; PASTORALISM; PEASANTRY. *The economic aspects of technology are discussed in* AGRICULTURE, *article on* PRODUCTIVITY AND TECHNOLOGY; ECONOMIC GROWTH; INNOVATION; PATENTS; PRODUCTION; PRODUCTIVITY; RESEARCH AND DEVELOPMENT; TECHNICAL ASSISTANCE. *Various aspects of the technological revolution brought about by the electronic computer are reviewed in* AUTOMATION; COMPUTATION; CYBERNETICS; INFORMATION STORAGE AND RETRIEVAL; *and in the biographies of* BABBAGE *and* WIENER. *Also of relevance for an understanding of technology are* CREATIVITY; DIFFUSION; ECONOMIC ANTHROPOLOGY; ECONOMY AND SOCIETY; ENGINEERING; SCIENCE; *and the biography of* OGBURN.

I. THE STUDY OF TECHNOLOGY   Robert S. Merrill
II. TECHNOLOGY AND INTERNATIONAL
     RELATIONS   Warner Schilling

I
THE STUDY OF TECHNOLOGY

One of the most persistent themes in the social sciences, history, and the humanities is the impact of technology and technological change on all aspects of social life. Major changes in human life have been associated with major technological changes, such as the "food-producing revolution," the "urban revolution," and the "industrial revolution" and its modern continuations; even the evolution of biologically modern man has been influenced by innovations in tool using.

Given the long history of concern with the social consequences of technology, it is puzzling that technological systems, unlike such similar aspects of culture as political, legal, economic, social, and magico–religious systems, are not the focus of an established specialty in any of the social sciences. The academic institutionalization of the social study of technology does not even approach that recently attained by its sister subject, science. One reason for this discrepancy is that technologies are not thought to be very interesting. They appear to be readily understandable, to present few intellectually challenging or significant problems. On the other hand, controversies about the conditions and consequences of technological change continually recur and seldom seem to be resolved. It has been only in recent years that developments in the social sciences and in technology itself have pointed toward the real possibility of coherent, systematic, and focused study of some of the major socially significant aspects of technology.

Definition. Technology in its broad meaning connotes the practical arts. These arts range from hunting, fishing, gathering, agriculture, animal husbandry, and mining through manufacturing, construction, transportation, provision of food, power, heat, light, etc., to means of communication, medicine, and military technology. Technologies are bodies of skills, knowledge, and procedures for making, using, and doing useful things.

They are techniques, means for accomplishing recognized purposes. But, as Weber recognized long ago ([1922] 1957, p. 161), there are techniques for every conceivable human activity and purpose. The concept of technology centers on processes that are primarily biological and physical rather than on psychological or social processes. Technologies are the cultural traditions developed in human communities for dealing with the physical and biological environment, including the human biological organism. This usage contrasts with others which are rather arbitrarily narrower, such as those which focus only on modern industrial technology, or only on crafts and manufacturing, or on "material culture" (see, e.g., British Association . . . 1954).

Another major distinction is that between the natural sciences and technology; the former emphasize the acquisition of knowledge, while the latter stresses practical purposes. This is a rough distinction with a number of complications, but it provides important guides in the investigation of sociocultural systems (see Polanyi 1958; Merrill 1962). Recently, the impression that modern technology is primarily applied science has led to the use of such phrases as "science," "science policy," and "science and society" to refer to both the sciences and the practical arts. When this undifferentiated usage enters into work on science, it tends to obscure important differences that need study (compare Barber 1952 and Kaplan 1964 with "Science and Engineering" 1961).

Problems of study. In broad perspective, the study of the conditions and consequences of technical change merges into the general study of sociocultural change. Available evidence certainly suggests that all the major features of a society influence what technological changes occur, the ways they are used, and the repercussions of their use. The kind of broad-ranging inquiry which results is evident in the one sociological tradition focused on technology—that stemming from William F. Ogburn (see Gilfillan 1935; Allen et al. 1957)—as well as in work on diffusion of innovations, economic growth, automation, economic and business history, and the technological aspects of international relations.

A different perspective may be obtained by viewing the problem the other way round. One can ask what needs to be known about technology if one is to have a basis for tracing interconnections between technology and the rest of society. What are the significant characteristics of technologies? How can they be empirically studied? These questions focus attention on the direct links between technol-

ogy and society, on the features of technologies which mediate more remote influences in both directions. Adequate analysis and empirical study of technology from this point of view seem essential if technology is to be a well-understood subsystem that can be incorporated into larger systems of analysis.

The first of the two major themes in studies of technology–society relationships concerns the wide variety of social effects linked to technology by its influence on the kinds and amounts of goods and services which can be provided for the support of a wide variety of human activities and purposes. Here the focus is on the role of technology in production. The second theme concerns the ways in which social and other conditions directly influence technology. Here the focus is on technological change.

Technology and production

Relatively explicit arguments dealing with the effects of technology (and physical environment) on the "forms," "types," or "developmental stages" of society are especially prominent in recent discussions of cultural evolution and cultural ecology. Throughout this literature, the central link between technology and society is viewed as the effect of technology in limiting or making possible the supply of various amounts and kinds of important goods and services. For example, it is argued that, by limiting the amount of subsistence goods, particularly food, that *can* be produced, technologies limit population densities and thus affect the social system itself. Or it is argued that advances in technology which make possible greater outputs of subsistence goods per man-hour thereby "free" time from subsistence production and so make possible the support of craft, religious, military, governing, and other specialists. This in turn makes possible larger-scale, more sedentary societies with more complex economic institutions, social stratification, centralized authority, and so on. Concern with these kinds of relationships has led, in anthropology, sociology, and elsewhere, to the use of such concepts as "surplus" or "energy per capita" to characterize the aspect of technologies linked to such social consequences (see Orans 1966).

It is evident that issues concerning technology–output relations have had an essential quantitative as well as a qualitative aspect. This is an extremely significant fact for students of technology; however, most descriptions of technologies do not include quantitative information unless that happens to be an explicit part of the practitioner's traditions —as, for example, in much modern food preparation and in engineering. As the significance of quantitative features of technologies, whether they are culturally explicit or not, has become clearer, there have been increasing efforts to obtain such data by field workers interested in economic anthropology, cultural ecology, nutrition, housing, consumption, and small-scale industry, and by students of the prehistory and history of technology. However, outside economics and economic history, most of these efforts have not been guided by clearly defined notions of just what data are relevant for what purposes. Careful analysis of direct technology–output–society linkages is a precondition for defining and obtaining data on relevant characteristics of technologies.

Although economists have developed systematic formulations of the quantitative aspects of technology–output relations, these ideas are little known among other social scientists. Almost all work in anthropology, as well as much work in sociology and history, shows little awareness, let alone systematic use, of the idea of production functions, of concepts concerned with productivity, and of technical economic theory relevant to the study of specialization. A variety of recent developments in economics, particularly in the areas of activity and process analysis, programming, and input–output analysis, are making this lack of awareness even more acute (see Cowles Commission . . . 1951; Koopmans 1957; Manne & Markowitz 1963; Dorfman et al. 1958; Chenery & Clark 1959). A set of powerful ideas, computational methods, and strategies of empirical research directly applicable to the study of technology–output relations are becoming available. They make possible kinds of systematic study of this aspect of technology which are of the greatest significance.

An empirical strategy. The general strategy suggested by the developments mentioned is simple but essential. This strategy is to study the role of technological and related factors by comparing actual situations with calculations of what would be possible with particular technologies under various alternative assumptions about other relevant variables. Such work has barely begun, but two examples can be given.

The first comes from one of the most active areas of application of modern economic tools to the study of technological, economic, and related changes: the "new economic history" (see Fogel 1964a; 1965). Fogel (1964b), using programming and other methods, examined the economic impact of railroads on the U.S. economy in the nineteenth century by comparing what actually happened with what the economy would have been if only older modes of transportation had been used. In contrast with prevalent interpretations imputing large economic effects to the development of railroads, Fogel's results suggest that the effects were relatively slight. Whether or not this result stands up in the face of further work, it clearly shows that sorting out the effects of technological factors in complex sequences of change requires the use of highly sophisticated methods. The second example is Hopper's study of the use of farming resources in an Indian village (1957; 1961; see Schultz 1964, pp. 44–48, 94–96). Using programming methods, he was able to show that resources were being used efficiently, given the technological and external demand conditions. His results also indicate that additional investments in the usual forms of capital would yield low rates of return. Such conclusions are contrary to inferences made by many students of Indian village institutions, who believe these institutions constitute barriers to efficiency. Moreover, by showing that output and income are actually being limited by resource and technology conditions, a wide variety of issues concerning the roles of these factors and the kinds of changes that would increase income are brought face to face with empirical findings.

Quantitative technology–output relationships. How should technologies be conceived and characterized if we are to study their relations to output possibilities? The classic concept in economics is the idea of a "production function." From the standpoint of output possibilities, a particular technology is characterized by (1) the *kinds* of inputs used; (2) the *kinds* of output (or output mix) produced; and (3) the quantitative relations between *amounts* of inputs used and *maximum quantities* of output that can be physically produced. If a technology can produce several outputs in variable proportions, production functions can be used to derive an output-possibility, or efficiency, frontier. The frontier will consist, for any given set of inputs, of those combinations of outputs which cannot be exceeded in the following sense: no output within any efficient combination can be increased without decreasing some other output in that combination. All sets of outputs physically producible with the technology from a given set of inputs will then lie on or within the output-possibility frontier corresponding to that set of inputs. In addition to the qualitative kinds of inputs and outputs involved, it is the *quantitative input–output relations* made possible by a technology which must be known if their implications for production possibilities are to be studied.

Generally, in economics, production functions

have been derived only for firms, industries, or other sizable production entities. Moreover, economists usually use price weights to aggregate physical inputs and outputs and use such economic data to estimate input–output relations. This has meant that, in actual use, the production function concept has been institution-bound because only in price-market systems are the requisite economic data available and meaningful. It has also meant that the work has usually been so remote from physical technology that its relevance for students of technology was not evident. Input–output analysis, though phrased in terms of physical technology, also is usually used with economic (aggregated price-weighted) data. However, there has been some interest in seeing whether input–output coefficients or more general production functions could be determined from engineering or other data closer to physical technology rather than from more general economic statistics. In this way, technology and economics are being brought closer together (see Research Project . . . 1953; Vajda 1958; Manne & Markowitz 1963).

The conceptual innovation central to the new programming methods is deceptively simple: instead of conceiving of production functions as characteristics of establishments, firms, or other large-scale institutional systems, these methods consider input–output relations at the level of the component steps, stages, or processes ("activities") which make up each particular technology. In other words, the quantitative framework is brought into more direct relation to technologies known and used by practitioners. However, if one thinks of a factory, a peasant household, or a group of hunters and gatherers, let alone larger regions or societies, it becomes clear that the number of inputs, the number of activities or processes, and the number of outputs are usually very large. This is where mathematical advances and digital computers are useful. Methods are continually being extended and improved for making calculations of points on production-possibility frontiers for systems of hundreds of input–output equations. It is the availability of these computational methods that gives empirical importance to the conceptual framework.

By working closer to physical technology, programming methods make it possible to study more explicitly the relations between the details of technological processes and the economically significant characteristics of production-possibility frontiers based on them. Moreover, such frontiers may be estimated in situations where older economic techniques can be used only with great difficulty or not at all. Finally, by explicitly focusing on com-

ponent processes, the programming framework brings out into the open two major links between physical technology and output possibilities that have generally been obscured by the older production function framework.

The first link may be discovered by asking whether, given data on input availabilities and on the input–output characteristics of the known technological processes, we can then directly determine output possibilities. Are there any other intervening links? Suppose a potter carries out all the steps of pottery making, from gathering clay and other materials to final firing and finishing. Is her rate of output determined or limited solely by her skills, the time she spends, her equipment, and the physical characteristics and locations of her sources of firewood, clay, temper, etc.? There is at least one other major factor that will influence what she can produce: how she arranges her work, in the sense of where she does various things and how she schedules her activities. This will affect, for example, the amount of moving and carrying she does, the extent to which she can economize time by carrying out activities such as forming pots while others are drying or being fired, how close she can come to carrying out processes on the most efficient "batch" scale, etc. Thus, even within a simple production unit, there are major problems of what Koopmans (1957, pp. 69–70) has called *physical maximization* or *physical planning* which will influence outputs obtainable from given inputs and a given technology. These problems were almost completely obscured by the older production function framework.

Where do such work routines fit into our picture of technology? One answer would be that they are additional, essential parts of technological traditions. This would imply that our potter, for example, thought her particular schedule to be just as necessary for the successful making of pots as mixing clay and temper in the right proportions. However, accounts taken from a variety of societies indicate that, though some rigid constraints on production routines may be found, such routines have an appreciable amount of flexibility, in the sense that they are altered or adjusted to varying circumstances. It is highly probable that separable sociocultural factors and processes influence production scheduling. Therefore, we have isolated a major link between technology and output possibilities that needs careful study. Instead of gathering data, say, on the most usual pottery-making routine, the researcher has to ask himself what data are needed to determine the routine that would be most efficient within the culturally defined technological constraints. How do the routines and their variations compare with calculated "efficient" routines for the varying circumstances? Only then will he be able to say to what extent technology and resources are actually limiting output. And then he will also be in a position to assess the production effects of the sociocultural factors which generate the production routines actually followed.

That these issues are not trivial may be seen by reference to an old and important line of argument: the importance of division of labor (specialization) as a way in which outputs can be increased with a given technology and resources. The idea is that if persons with given initial skills and capacities are able to specialize their performance to a greater degree, then their total production will be greater. Similar arguments are applied to the use of different kinds of soils and other resources. Here, again, there is a vast body of incidental evidence that patterns of specialization, even in highly traditional societies, are flexible rather than completely rigid. Therefore, one must explore the magnitude of the consequences of alternative patterns of specialization for production, taking into account such additional activities as transportation. Only then can one really determine how outputs are limited by technology–resource factors or by sociocultural factors related to specialization. Most assertions about technological limits on outputs under given conditions are not only rough guesses; they are guesses made on the basis of relatively little examination of what might be possible if *only* technological and resource constraints were operative. Thus, programming and related methods open up the possibility of making calculations of the magnitude of the production effects of what we might call alternative production arrangements. [*For examples of special problems in dealing with locational interdependencies and with various economies or diseconomies of scale and locational agglomeration, see* CENTRAL PLACE; PROGRAMMING; SPATIAL ECONOMICS.]

A second major implication of the programming framework is that one can compute output possibilities for alternative arrangements of physical production (i.e., persons, facilities, activities, and movements of goods and persons) apart from the sociocultural institutions that "lead to," "bring about," or "generate" any particular pattern of conduct and events. We thus have a clear distinction between these two very different kinds of problems. It becomes apparent that many analyses have ignored this distinction, moving directly from technology to institutions. This results in confusion,

especially of theoretical frameworks, controversy, and failure to study the variety of issues involved.

Technology–resource–output linkages.   Output possibilities depend not only on technology but also on resources or inputs. The links here are more complex than is usually realized, and they involve technology in ways that are only beginning to be studied seriously. If we take the simplest case, natural resources, it is an old idea in anthropology that only culturally known natural features can be resources. Despite this recognition, careful attention to a society's knowledge of resource locations and characteristics and ways of finding new sources of supply is relatively rare. Knowledge of this complex part of technology (which we might call *resource technology*) and quantitative information about the resources actually known are both critical to the study of resource–technology–output relationships. Similarly, outside economics there is a curious tendency to neglect the systematic study of the quantitative role of another major type of resource: *physical capital*, in the sense of durable, man-made improvements, equipment, structures, and inventories. This is especially odd because the stock of physical capital, like population, clearly depends on past social and other processes. The importance of capital formation processes as a link between technology and output possibilities can be assessed by determining how output possibilities vary with assumed changes in the amounts of various kinds of capital goods available. A similar strategy can be used to deal with the complex linkages between population density, labor resources, and output possibilities. One can examine not only the effects of alternative population densities but also the effects of alternative assumptions about culturally or biologically defined "subsistence levels" on production possibilities when they are so constrained.

Other recent work in economics, stimulated by a search for sources of economic growth in modern industrial societies and by the economic problems of nonindustrial societies, has uncovered two additional links between resources, technology, and output possibilities. The first is the fact that many of the production effects of a technology depend on the extent to which it has been physically "embodied" in capital goods (see Salter 1960; Green 1966). Similarly, the second development stresses the importance of *human capital*, in the sense of the technologically relevant knowledge and capacities actually "embodied" in a society's population [*see* CAPITAL, HUMAN]. So far, studies of these linkages between technology and resources have been concerned only with their over-all economic significance and thus have used highly aggregated economic data. More detailed work is crucial for students of technology.

These linkages bring out the important fact that describing a society's technology requires much more than listing the technologies "known," in some unspecified sense, to some members of the society. They also call attention to critical socioeconomic processes influencing technology–output relationships.

Production arrangements. There is another line of argument, intertwined with the one we have been considering, which we may now examine. Instead of being concerned with what outputs can be produced with a given technology, these arguments assume that certain levels of output of certain goods or services are needed or desired. They then argue that certain production activities and arrangements are "required" if these levels of output are to be obtained with a given technology under given conditions. In this way, various societal features have been interpreted as technologically "necessary": the kind of division of labor; household size and composition; local group size, geographic distribution, and spatial movement; daily, seasonal, annual, and other cycles of productive activity and movement; various economic and political institutions, etc. Many plausible, but largely qualitative, arguments of this sort have been made (for older reviews, see Forde 1934; Mead 1937; for a comparative study of task groups, see Udy 1959; for an important comparative case study, see Hill 1963). The framework previously outlined for the study of alternative production arrangements provides a way of assessing the magnitude of their effects on production. Some of the issues that need examination may be indicated by reviewing a few raised by the vast literature concerning the effects of modern industrial technology on factory and firm organization and on work life.

First, we may note that industrial technology is not all of a piece but varies markedly from industry to industry; the implications of such differences for work organization and work life are just beginning to be studied (see Blauner 1964). Second, as the discussion of physical planning indicated, it is not to be assumed that the particular patterns of factory size, task composition and subdivison, grouping of tasks into jobs, and work group arrangements involved in production are a direct consequence of the requirements of physical technology. There is evidence that the patterns of task organization developed by production and indus-

trial engineers are strongly affected by implicit sociopsychological theories, without much exploration of the efficiency of alternative arrangements (see March & Simon 1958, chapter 2; Walker 1962, part 2).

Third, assumptions that particular institutional arrangements are necessary for effective performance need questioning. For example, a widespread theory argues that functionally specific, universalistic criteria of recruitment, advancement, and releasing of personnel must be used if industrial technology is to operate effectively. This reasoning assumes that knowledge and skills have a critical effect on performance (see Levy 1952). Largely on this basis, Abegglen (1958) interprets paternalistic arrangements in Japanese factories as dysfunctional. However, it is probable that performance is significantly affected by what has recently been called "commitment," as well as by knowledge and skills. The net effect of Japanese social institutions, which promote a high degree of organizational commitment, may, in the Japanese setting, promote efficiency rather than inefficiency. [*See* PATERNALISM.]

Finally, and perhaps most important, consideration of the nature of modern industrial economies indicates that the organizational tasks confronting production units are as much a consequence of the *changing* technical and socioeconomic milieus in which they operate as of the units' production technology. This can be seen if one imagines a particular industrial technology being used in a completely "stationary" economy with constant demand, supply, price, technology, and population conditions. (For a vivid picture of some of the implications of stationary "circular flow," see Schumpeter 1912; 1939.) Production could then be an almost completely routinized, even traditionalized, process. This would obviously have very far-reaching implications for the roles of authority and for the kinds of coordination possible (e.g., informational signaling rather than use of commands). It very well may be that many of the organizational and other effects attributed to industrial technology are more consequences of rates of change than they are of particular technologies per se.

Conclusions. It seems clear that tools are now available for making a major empirical attack on many issues concerning technology–output–society relationships. This would require a large-scale effort. However, it is also likely that technology, by itself, will not turn out to be such a powerfully influential factor as some social scientists have thought. Nevertheless, social phenomena are so complex that being able empirically to "factor out" the influence of a major subset of variables is critically important in improving our ability to understand all the others. This strategy is now available in the study of technology.

Technological change

We now turn to the study of factors influencing technologies themselves. Technologies are important not only because they affect social life but also because they constitute a major body of cultural phenomena in their own right. These phenomena pose numerous problems whose study may shed light on a wide range of issues in the social sciences.

Viewed in broad perspective, the practical arts align themselves with many other sets of traditions and customs which are pre-eminently cultural, in the sense that they exhibit historically specific origins, development, and distribution. In this respect they differ from those aspects of social organization which frequently exhibit similar forms in historically unrelated societies. Therefore, prehistory, history, and ethnography are especially important in understanding the course of human technology over space and time. The history of technology has begun to establish itself as a discipline with the publication of two major collaborative histories (Singer et al. 1954–1958; Daumas 1962) and the establishment of a professional society and the journal *Technology and Culture*. However, in scholarly apparatus and in the use of interpretive analyses the history of technology is in its early stages (see [Review Issue] . . . 1960). The "discipline" has several rather independent subdivisions, such as prehistory, ethnography (see Bordaz 1959a; 1959b; Hodges 1964; British Association . . . 1954; Matson 1965), agricultural history, and the history of medicine (see Sigerist 1951–1961; Underwood 1953; Zimmerman & Veith 1961).

The task of understanding technological phenomena and formulating theories of technological change is clearly an enormous and difficult one. This is especially true because our general understanding of historically specific cultural change might best be described as meager and unsatisfactory. Nonetheless, one can find in the rapidly expanding body of recent work a number of clues which point toward major possibilities of systematic study. This brief review will be divided into three sections: recent technological change in modern Western societies; the development of Western technology; and past and present nonindustrial technologies.

Technological change in the modern West. The complexity of modern technology makes it seem an odd place to start, but two other factors make it suitable. First, deliberate technological change has been institutionalized in Western societies for some time. Most modern technologies include not only traditions for making and doing things but also traditions for "advancing the state of the art," for producing new knowledge, processes, and products. Modern technologies are culture-producing as well as culture-using sociocultural systems. Such cultural change seems easier to understand than less institutionalized change. Moreover, when seen in this light, these technologies are similar to such other culture-producing traditions as science, law, art, literature, music, philosophy, history, and journalism. These similarities suggest that what can be learned about each such culture-producing culture may shed light on the others.

Second, events during and immediately after World War II have jolted economists into taking a hard look at technological change in the West (see Universities–National Bureau . . . 1962; Ohio State University . . . 1965). Their work is modifying the common conception that technology grows in an autonomous, cumulative, accelerating fashion, little affected by outside influences. (Such a theory probably has never been held literally by those social scientists who are referred to as supporting it—see, e.g., Ogburn 1922; Leslie White 1949; 1959; Hart 1959—but the idea is nonetheless widespread.) Recent work indicates that in the various private sectors of modern economies, the amount of effort devoted to technological changes, and the magnitude of the changes themselves, are strongly influenced by economic demand and profitability.

This accentuates the importance of distinguishing major steps in the process of technological change which differ in their dependence on physical facilities and other resources and in their relationship to economic costs and rewards. The first step is *invention* or applied research, by which is meant the processes of getting new ideas and bringing them to the point of *technical* feasibility demonstrated through small-scale testing. This is different from the later steps: *development* of workable full-scale plans; *innovation*, which means putting plans into actual, full-scale practical use; and *imitation* or *diffusion* of innovations to additional producers and users. In addition, minor processes of *improvement* may occur in any of these phases. Finally, the spread of technology, even within one society, let alone between societies, is not just a matter of literal imitation but usually involves significant processes of *technological adaptation* to the local habitat and to local economic and other conditions (Merrill 1964). In anthropology and sociology, invention and innovation are terms often used for all of the first three steps, while *acceptance* distinguishes intrasociety spread from diffusion between societies.

There has also been a burgeoning of studies of institutional and social factors which influence the pressures and rewards leading technologists and users of technology to focus attention and resources on changes in certain directions rather than others. These include studies of the social characteristics of business firms, the organizational characteristics of research and development laboratories in industry and government, governmental support and policy, weapons development organization (e.g., Peck & Scherer 1962; Scherer 1964), institutional factors in medicine, and social factors in the diffusion of innovations. In some cases, economic and social analyses appear to conflict, although it is more likely that the interpretations are complementary.

Problem-solving capabilities are as crucial as incentives in determining the directions taken by inventive activity and technological change. The most direct determinants of problem-solving capacities are the technological traditions themselves—the states of the arts. Changes *within* technology, as well as outside it, obviously have something to do with the very recent large expansion of resources devoted to research and development (R & D); with the rapid increase in organized R & D efforts as compared with those of independent inventors; with the expanding role of professional scientists and postgraduate engineers in R & D; with the increasingly radical nature of the technical advances being achieved, particularly in military technology; and with the remarkably wide differences in R & D efforts and accomplishments between industries and technological fields [*see* RESEARCH AND DEVELOPMENT].

So far, it has proved difficult to gain a more precise understanding of the role of technological and related scientific knowledge in technological change. There are indications that technological change is not a simple function of its "cultural base" in the sense of the number of elements available for combination (Ogburn 1922; Hart 1959). Similarly, the idea that recent trends are due to the rise and development of "science-based" industries and technologies (e.g., Maclaurin 1954; Brozen 1965) has been foundering on the difficulty of specifying just what a science base is. Advances in fundamental science do not directly trigger technological changes as frequently as is usually as-

sumed (compare Meier 1951 with Nelson 1962 and Schmookler 1966). General economic–technological histories of particular industries provide helpful information but usually do not make clear the factors involved in technological change (e.g., Bright 1949; Haber 1958; Maclaurin 1949; Passer 1953).

The most revealing information is found in case studies which enable the reader to see situations from the "inside," as technologists see them—to see the problems involved, the tools available and the ways they are used, and the results achieved. (In varying degrees and ways such views may be found in such works as Cohen 1948; Condit 1960; 1961; Enos 1962; Klein 1962; 1965; Killeffer 1948; Marschak 1962; Marshall & Meckling 1962; Merrill 1965; Nelson 1962; *Development of Aircraft...* 1950; Straub 1949; Wright & Wright 1951.) Several extremely important points emerge from the examination of such cases. First, while it is essential to know the body of "results" which are part of a technology in order to understand the way it changes, one also must know the methods and techniques, the approaches and procedures, the tactics and strategies (Conant 1951) which are used to tackle new problems. To study a sequence of technological changes without knowledge of the technological traditions used in producing them is to be confronted with extremely enigmatic phenomena. Second, technologies and technological problems are incredibly diverse. Any attempt to generalize too quickly and too broadly is likely to obscure rather than clarify the ways technological change comes about. Third, each technology, and even each significant technological problem, is an intricate world of its own. Adequate understanding requires intensive study of a kind still relatively rare in work on technology.

Such intensive study, to be useful, requires a clear focus on determining how technologies work. In addition to historical studies, basic sociological research on technology is required. We know surprisingly little about the occupational and professional groups, organizations, institutions, and institutionalized roles which play a part in the use and development of the practical arts (see Merrill 1961). Furthermore, there is a widespread notion in the social sciences that the cognitive structure of technologies is equivalent to that of the empirical sciences, with the minor modification that if–then statements are converted to rules of practice (e.g., Parsons 1937; 1951; Barber 1952). There is good evidence that this conception is drastically askew, but the only major counterformulation (Polanyi 1958) has not been developed. Nor has much use yet been made of developments in engineering which have led to more explicit conceptualizations of what is involved in engineering design, development, and systems engineering (see Asimow 1962; Alger & Hays 1964; Starr 1963; Goode & Machol 1957; A. D. Hall 1962).

The development of Western technology. One of the most fascinating problems of technological change is the rise and continuing development of Western "industrial" technology, and it has attracted a corresponding amount of attention. Here only a very few themes closely linked to technology itself will be discussed, with emphasis on the question of relations between science and technology. Clearly, one major possibility is that the special development of technology in the West was linked to another unique Western development: the development of those cultural traditions we now group together under the label "science." Accumulating historical work has pushed back the sources of both the "scientific revolution" and the "industrial revolution" well into the Middle Ages (see, e.g., Gille 1962; Lynn White 1962*a*; Crombie 1952; Hodgen 1952; Taton 1957–1964, vol. 1; Singer et al. 1954–1958, vol. 2). Moreover, a relatively continuous series of technological changes links the medieval developments with the conventional late eighteenth-century beginning of the "industrial revolution" (see, e.g., Singer et al. 1954–1958, vol. 3; Nef 1932; 1950; 1964). Despite such formal parallelism, the evidence suggests a high degree of independence of changes occurring in the two traditions well into the nineteenth century and beyond. On the other hand, there appear to be an increasing number of less specific influences from the sciences on technology (and vice versa) which are difficult to document and articulate (see "Science and Engineering" 1961). Finally, it is clear that there was great heterogeneity in the patterns of change within each group of traditions. Many of these phenomena are evident in discussions of relations between various craft and learned traditions (e.g., Crombie 1961; A. R. Hall 1952; 1959; Smith 1960).

The historical study of technologies whose traditions are largely unwritten presents extremely difficult problems. Even when evidence from artifacts and from pictorial and other representations is used to supplement documents, and all are interpreted with great sophistication by an author intimately acquainted with the practice and theory of the art he is studying, findings are often extremely uneven and much remains puzzling (e.g., Smith 1960). The source of difficulty appears to be one we have encountered before: the difficulty of interpreting a sequence of technical changes without intimate knowledge of the cultural traditions and contexts from which they emerged (see Lynn White 1962*b*; A. R. Hall 1962).

Past and present nonindustrial technologies. A second major result of recent work bearing on the history of Western technology is the increasing accumulation of evidence, much of it still hotly debated, that a significant fraction of medieval, early modern, and even some later Western technological changes were, or grew out of, diffusions from Asian societies, particularly China.

Studies of the technologies of Asian (especially Needham 1954–1965; Lynn White 1960), early Near Eastern, classical (Forbes 1955–1964), and New World civilizations seem to have one increasingly important implication: Instead of making matters more intelligible, the more detailed evidence adds many more puzzles than it provides even tentative solutions. This may seem very discouraging, but it may have a positive effect. It may eliminate the tendency to think that technological phenomena provide no really significant intellectual problems worthy of concentrated scholarly attention.

Nonetheless, the presence of important problems, however fascinating, does not stimulate scholarly effort unless there are ways of making some headway toward their solution. If a major cause of the historical and prehistorical puzzles is the scarcity of data on unwritten or incompletely recorded technological traditions, what can be done about it? There is one important kind of evidence that could be brought to bear: data provided by really intimate studies of the great variety of nonindustrial technologies still being practiced in various parts of the world. The connections between these present-day technologies and earlier ones are known with varying degrees of precision. In any case, studies of these nonindustrial technologies provide an opportunity to understand the nature and varieties of technological traditions outside the modern Western tradition and the ways such traditions change.

Existing nonindustrial technologies are not so much "unstudied" as they are studied from points of view which do not yield the kinds of data that seem crucial for the interpretation of technological change. Most detailed studies by cultural anthropologists, ethnologists, and students of folk life have been strongly historically oriented and museum-oriented, describing characteristics of technological practices and artifacts which are useful for tracing historical connections among technologies and among the peoples practicing them. As a consequence, there has been a tendency to think of technologies as fixed sequences of standardized acts yielding standardized results. Descriptions of technologies made from a craftsman's or technologist's point of view (e.g., Guthe 1925; O'Neale 1932; Conklin 1957; Shepard 1956) and incidental observations in other studies strongly indicate that this conception is very misleading. Desired technical results are not obtained automatically. Materials vary, circumstances differ, and manipulations are hard to control. Accidents, poor results, or failures occur and are always a possibility. Even "primitive" technologies have a variety of procedures for adapting actions to circumstances, detecting difficulties, and making corrections. A more adequate conception of a technology is that it is a flexible repertoire of skills, knowledge, and methods for attaining desired results and avoiding failures under varying circumstances (Merrill 1958; 1959).

Such a "functional" view of technologies themselves (as against their relations to other things) is surprisingly rare in the social sciences, despite the widespread use of functional ideas. Malinowski recognized the possibilities of this approach only after he returned from the field (1935, vol. 1, appendix 2). Ford's systematic formulation (1937) approximated it but was not followed up. The one major context in which functional problems of technologies have received considerable attention is in studies of magic. Although Malinowski's ideas about magic and technology were not completely developed (Leach 1957; Nadel 1957), little explicit research on this subject has been done, except for Firth's evidence (1939) that magic can inhibit technological change. Even this idea has not been pursued, although the thesis that magic is a major traditionalizing force is central to much of Max Weber's work and is important in Sombart's analysis of the development of technical rationality. Instead, social anthropologists working in this area have focused largely on the social and symbolic interpretation of witchcraft, sorcery, and magic, though all of these impinge on technology through their role in the interpretation of illness, technical accidents, and abnormal successes.

Despite this neglect, ethnographic accounts contain numerous incidental observations which indicate that deeper study of nonindustrial technologies will shed a great deal of light on processes of technological change. Careful analysis of a few relatively well described pottery technologies has already shown that the flexible procedures used to deal with day-to-day problems may operate as sources of significant technological changes under particular circumstances (Merrill 1959). Almost every society has techniques for producing nonstandardized products, such as houses, storage facilities, trails and roads, vessels, settlement or field layouts, and water-supply and drainage arrangements. These have to be "designed" to fit particular local conditions, special uses, or availability of materials. Such designing requires a set of adaptive procedures which may be closely linked to technological change just as the little-studied bodies of knowledge used in routine engineering design play a significant role in modern technological change (Merrill 1961; 1965). Flexible procedures are especially evident in agriculture, where one also finds surprisingly frequent indications of the deliberate use of "trial and error" even in nonliterate societies (see, e.g., Richards 1939; Schlippe 1956; Allan 1965; Conklin 1957).

This evidence suggests that technological traditions are far more complex than usually realized and that they contain numerous features of the greatest significance for understanding the possibilities and processes of technological change. Even "accident," that unpredictable source of change, is well known to depend on a "prepared mind" (see Usher 1955), and preparation has major cultural components. It also appears that the study of the relatively minor, but more frequent and therefore more observable, technical changes involved in various kinds of routine technological adaptation is likely to clarify our understanding of the relations between cultural traditions and cultural change and to provide an essential basis for interpreting more radical "creative" innovations (see Merrill 1959; compare Barnett 1953).

A number of theoretical developments in ethnography have clarified the distinction between cultural traditions as the conceptions that guide action and the behavior, artifacts, or other results brought about by their use (Goodenough 1957). Using this idea and techniques from descriptive linguistics, a series of procedures is being developed for the precise identification of the conceptual categories, taxonomies, and distinctions that participants in a culture use in structuring their world and their actions. Usually called ethnoscience, this work might better be called ethnotechnology. There have been studies of disease diagnosis, color distinctions, plant classifications, curers, firewood, cultural ecology, etc., which have clear technological implications. So far, little has been done to extend this approach to the study of these numerous "inarticulate" or "tacit" (Polanyi 1958, pp. 100–102) aspects of actually making and using things which performers cannot describe or explain in words even when questioned systematically. Harris

(1964) has sketched some ways an observer could detect and formulate interconnected regularities in actual sequences of behavior which could be applied to this problem. He believes that his observer-oriented approach is superior to and incompatible with the ethnosemantic approaches which focus on actors' frames of reference. However, the basic ideas appear to complement rather than contradict one another. Another approach which appears widely applicable is to search for implicit feedback control systems guiding skilled performance (Merrill 1958; 1959).

Because of its focus on conceptual systems, work on ethnoscience (ethnosemantics) may be usefully related to work in psychology on perception and cognitive theory [see COGNITIVE THEORY; PERCEPTION, *article on* SOCIAL PERCEPTION; *see also* French 1963]. Cognitive theory, in turn, provides a link to work on creative thinking and creativity significant for the study of technological change. So far, the most relevant psychological work has been on scientific creativity (see, e.g., McKellar 1957; Taylor & Barron 1963), but work on technological creativity is beginning (e.g., MacKinnon 1962).

It thus appears that there are foundations for the more systematic study of technological change and some of the direct links between technology and social life. It remains to be seen whether these potentialities will be realized through the development of technology as a coherent discipline in the social sciences.

ROBERT S. MERRILL

BIBLIOGRAPHY

ABEGGLEN, JAMES C. 1958 *The Japanese Factory: Aspects of Its Social Organization.* Glencoe, Ill.: Free Press.

ALGER, JOHN R. M.; and HAYS, CARL V. 1964 *Creative Synthesis in Design.* Englewood Cliffs, N.J.: Prentice-Hall.

ALLAN, W. 1965 *The African Husbandman.* New York: Barnes & Noble.

ALLEN, FRANCIS R. et al. 1957 *Technology and Social Change.* New York: Appleton.

ASIMOW, MORRIS 1962 *Introduction to Design.* Englewood Cliffs, N.J.: Prentice-Hall.

BARBER, BERNARD 1952 *Science and the Social Order.* Glencoe, Ill.: Free Press. → A paperback edition was published in 1962.

BARNETT, HOMER, G. 1953 *Innovation: The Basis of Cultural Change.* New York: McGraw-Hill.

BLAUNER, ROBERT 1964 *Alienation and Freedom: The Factory Worker and His Industry.* Univ. of Chicago Press.

BORDAZ, JACQUES 1959a First Tools of Mankind. Part 1. *Natural History Magazine* 68:36–51.

BORDAZ, JACQUES 1959b The New Stone Age. Part 2. *Natural History Magazine* 68:93–103.

BRIGHT, ARTHUR A. 1949 *The Electric-lamp Industry: Technological Change and Economic Development From 1800 to 1947.* New York: Macmillan.

BRITISH ASSOCIATION FOR THE ADVANCEMENT OF SCIENCE 1954 *Notes and Queries on Anthropology.* 6th ed., rev. London: Routledge. → The first edition was published in 1874.

BROZEN, YALE 1965 R & D Differences Among Industries. Pages 83–100 in Ohio State University, Conference on Economics of Research and Development, Columbus, 1962, *Economics of Research and Development.* Edited by Richard A. Tybout. Columbus: Ohio State Univ. Press.

CHENERY, HOLLIS B.; and CLARK, PAUL G. 1959 *Interindustry Economics.* New York: Wiley.

COHEN, I. BERNARD (1948) 1952 *Science, Servant of Man: A Layman's Primer for the Age of Science.* Boston: Little.

CONANT, JAMES B. 1951 *Science and Common Sense.* New Haven: Yale Univ. Press.

CONDIT, CARL W. 1960 *American Building Art: The Nineteenth Century.* New York: Oxford Univ. Press.

CONDIT, CARL W. 1961 *American Building Art: The Twentieth Century.* New York: Oxford Univ. Press.

CONKLIN, HAROLD C. 1957 *Hanunóo Agriculture: A Report on an Integral System of Shifting Cultivation in the Philippines.* Rome: Food and Agriculture Organization.

COWLES COMMISSION FOR RESEARCH IN ECONOMICS 1951 *Activity Analysis of Production and Allocation: Proceedings of a Conference.* Edited by Tjalling C. Koopmans. New York: Wiley.

CROMBIE, ALISTAIR C. (1952) 1959 *Medieval and Early Modern Science.* 2d rev. ed. 2 vols. Garden City, N.Y.: Doubleday.

CROMBIE, ALISTAIR C. 1961 Quantification in Medieval Physics. *Isis* 52:143–160.

DAUMAS, MAURICE (editor) 1962 *Les origines de la civilisation technique.* Paris: Presses Universitaires de France.

Development of Aircraft Engines [by Robert Schlaifer] and *Development of Aviation Fuels* [by S. D. Heron]: *Two Studies of Relations Between Government and Business.* 1950 Boston: Harvard Univ., Graduate School of Business Administration, Division of Research.

DORFMAN, ROBERT; SAMUELSON, PAUL A.; and SOLOW, ROBERT M. 1958 *Linear Programming and Economic Analysis.* New York: McGraw-Hill.

ENOS, JOHN L. 1962 *Petroleum Progress and Profits: A History of Process Innovation.* Cambridge, Mass.: M.I.T. Press.

FIRTH, RAYMOND W. (1939) 1965 *Primitive Polynesian Economy.* 2d ed. Hamden, Conn.: Shoe String Press.

FIRTH, RAYMOND W. (editor) (1957) 1964 *Man and Culture: An Evaluation of the Work of Bronislaw Malinowski.* New York: Harper.

FOGEL, ROBERT W. 1964a Discussion. *American Economic Review,* 54, no. 2:377–389.

FOGEL, ROBERT W. 1964b *Railroads and American Economic Growth: Essays in Econometric History.* Baltimore: Johns Hopkins Press.

FOGEL, ROBERT W. 1965 The Reunification of Economic History With Economic Theory. *American Economic Review,* 55, no. 2:92–98.

FORBES, ROBERT J. 1955–1964 *Studies in Ancient Technology.* 9 vols. Leiden (Netherlands): Brill. → A second edition of volumes 1–4 was published in 1964–1965.

FORD, C. S. 1937 A Sample Comparative Analysis of Material Culture. Pages 225–246 in George P. Murdock (editor), *Studies in the Science of Society: Presented to Albert Galloway Keller*. New Haven: Yale Univ. Press.

FORDE, C. DARYLL (1934) 1952 *Habitat, Economy and Society: A Geographical Introduction to Ethnology*. London: Methuen.

FRENCH, DAVID 1963 The Relationship of Anthropology to Studies in Perception and Cognition. Volume 6, pages 388–428 in Sigmund Koch (editor), *Psychology: A Study of a Science*. New York: McGraw-Hill.

GILFILLAN, S. COLUM 1935 *The Sociology of Invention: An Essay in the Social Causes of Technic Invention and Some of Its Social Results*. Chicago: Follet.

GILLE, BERTRAND 1962 Le moyen âge en occident (Ve siècle–1350). Volume 1, pages 425–598 in Maurice Daumas (editor), *Les origines de la civilisation technique*. Paris: Presses Universitaires de France.

GOODE, HARRY H.; and MACHOL, ROBERT E. 1957 *System Engineering: An Introduction to the Design of Large-scale Systems*. New York: McGraw-Hill.

GOODENOUGH, WARD H. (1957) 1964 Cultural Anthropology and Linguistics. Pages 36–39 in Dell H. Hymes (editor), *Language in Culture and Society: A Reader in Linguistics and Anthropology*. New York: Harper.

GREEN, H. A. JOHN 1966 Embodied Progress, Investment, and Growth. *American Economic Review* 56: 138–151.

GUTHE, CARL E. 1925 *Pueblo Pottery Making: A Study at the Village of San Ildefonso*. New Haven: Yale Univ. Press.

HABER, LUDWIG F. 1958 *The Chemical Industry During the Nineteenth Century: A Study of the Economic Aspects of Applied Chemistry in Europe and North America*. Oxford: Clarendon.

HALL, A. D. 1962 *A Methodology for Systems Engineering*. Princeton, N.J.: Van Nostrand.

HALL, A. RUPERT 1952 *Ballistics in the Seventeenth Century: A Study in the Relations of Science and War With Reference Principally to England*. Cambridge Univ. Press.

HALL, A. RUPERT 1959 The Scholar and the Craftsman in the Scientific Revolution. Pages 3–23 in Institute for the History of Science, University of Wisconsin, 1957, *Critical Problems in the History of Science*. Edited by Marshall Clagett. Madison: Univ. of Wisconsin Press.

HALL, A. RUPERT 1962 The Changing Technical Act. *Technology and Culture* 3:501–515.

HARRIS, MARVIN 1964 *The Nature of Cultural Things*. New York: Random House.

HART, HORNELL 1959 Social Theory and Social Change. Pages 196–238 in Llewellyn Gross (editor), *Symposium on Sociological Theory*. New York: Harper.

HILL, POLLY 1963 *The Migrant Cocoa-farmers of Southern Ghana: A Study in Rural Capitalism*. Cambridge Univ. Press.

HODGEN, MARGARET T. 1952 *Change and History: A Study of the Dated Distributions of Technological Innovations in England*. Viking Fund Publications in Anthropology, No. 18. New York: Wenner–Gren Foundation for Anthropological Research.

HODGES, HENRY 1964 *Artifacts: An Introduction to Primitive Technology*. New York: Praeger.

HOPPER, WILLIAM D. 1957 The Economic Organization of a Village in North-central India. Ph.D. dissertation, Cornell Univ.

HOPPER, WILLIAM D. 1961 Resource Allocation on a Sample of Indian Farms. Unpublished manuscript, Univ. of Chicago.

KAPLAN, NORMAN 1964 Sociology of Science. Pages 852–881 in Robert E. L. Faris (editor), *Handbook of Modern Sociology*. Chicago: Rand McNally.

KILLEFFER, DAVID H. 1948 *The Genius of Industrial Research*. New York: Reinhold.

KLEIN, BURTON H. 1962 The Decision Making Problem in Development. Pages 477–497 in Universities–National Bureau Committee for Economic Research, *The Rate and Direction of Inventive Activity: Economic and Social Factors*. Princeton Univ. Press.

KLEIN, BURTON H. 1965 Policy Issues Involved in the Conduct of Military Development Programs. Pages 309–326 in Ohio State University, Conference on Economics of Research and Development, Columbus, 1962, *Economics of Research and Development*. Edited by Richard A. Tybout. Columbus: Ohio State Univ. Press.

KOOPMANS, TJALLING C. 1957 *Three Essays on the State of Economic Science*. New York: McGraw-Hill.

LEACH, EDMUND R. (1957) 1964 The Epistemological Background to Malinowski's Empiricisms. Pages 119–137 in Raymond W. Firth (editor), *Man and Culture: An Evaluation of the Work of Bronislaw Malinowski*. New York: Harper.

LEVY, MARION J. JR. 1952 *The Structure of Society*. Princeton Univ. Press.

McKELLAR, PETER 1957 *Imagination and Thinking: A Psychological Analysis*. London: Cohen & West.

MacKINNON, DONALD W. 1962 Intellect and Motive in Scientific Inventors: Implications for Supply. Pages 361–384 in Universities–National Bureau Committee for Economic Research, *The Rate and Direction of Inventive Activity: Economic and Social Factors*. Princeton Univ. Press.

MACLAURIN, W. RUPERT 1949 *Invention and Innovation in the Radio Industry*. New York: Macmillan.

MACLAURIN, W. RUPERT 1954 Technological Progress in Some American Industries. *American Economic Review*, 44, no. 2:178-189.

MALINOWSKI, BRONISLAW (1935) 1965 *Coral Gardens and Their Magic*. 2 vols. Bloomington: Indiana Univ. Press.

MANNE, ALAN S.; and MARKOWITZ, HARRY M. (editors) 1963 *Studies in Process Analysis: Economy-wide Production Capabilities*. New York: Wiley.

MARCH, JAMES G.; and SIMON, HERBERT A. 1958 *Organizations*. New York: Wiley.

MARSCHAK, THOMAS A. 1962 Strategy and Organization in a System Development Project. Pages 509–548 in Universities–National Bureau Committee for Economic Research, *The Rate and Direction of Inventive Activity: Economic and Social Factors*. Princeton Univ. Press.

MARSHALL, ANDREW W.; and MECKLING, WILLIAM H. 1962 Predictability of the Costs, Time and Success of Development. Pages 461–475 in Universities–National Bureau Committee for Economic Research, *The Rate and Direction of Inventive Activity: Economic and Social Factors*. Princeton Univ. Press.

MATSON, FREDERICK R. (editor) 1965 *Ceramics and Man*. Viking Fund Publications in Anthropology, No. 41. New York: The Fund.

MEAD, MARGARET (editor) 1937 *Cooperation and Competition Among Primitive Peoples.* New York: McGraw-Hill. → A paperback edition was published in 1961 by Beacon.

MEIER, ROBERT L. 1951 Research as a Social Process: Social Status, Specialism, and Technological Advance in Great Britain. *British Journal of Sociology* 2:91–104.

MERRILL, ROBERT S. 1958 The Cultures of Technologies. Unpublished manuscript.

MERRILL, ROBERT S. 1959 Routine Innovation. Ph.D. dissertation, Univ. of Chicago.

MERRILL, ROBERT S. 1961 Advances in Routine Engineering Design and Their Economic Significance. Unpublished manuscript.

MERRILL, ROBERT S. 1962 Some Society-wide Research and Development Institutions. Pages 409–434 in Universities–National Bureau Committee for Economic Research, *The Rate and Direction of Inventive Activity: Economic and Social Factors.* Princeton Univ. Press.

MERRILL, ROBERT S. 1964 Scientific Communities and Technological Adaptation. Pages 15–20 in *The Diffusion of Technical Knowledge as an Instrument of Economic Development.* National Institute of Social and Behavioral Science, Symposia Studies Series, No. 13. Washington: The Institute.

MERRILL, ROBERT S. 1965 Engineering and Productivity Change: Suspension Bridge Stiffening Trusses. Pages 101–127 in Ohio State University, Conference on Economics of Research and Development, Columbus, 1962, *Economics of Research and Development.* Edited by Richard A. Tybout. Columbus: Ohio State Univ. Press.

NADEL, S. F. (1957) 1960 Malinowski on Magic and Religion. Pages 189–208 in Raymond W. Firth (editor), *Man and Culture: An Evaluation of the Work of Bronislaw Malinowski.* New York: Harper.

NEEDHAM, JOSEPH 1954–1965 *Science and Civilisation in China.* 4 vols. Cambridge Univ. Press.

NEF, JOHN U. 1932 *The Rise of the British Coal Industry.* 2 vols. London: Routledge.

NEF, JOHN U. 1950 *War and Human Progress: An Essay on the Rise of Industrial Civilization.* Cambridge, Mass.: Harvard Univ. Press. → A paperback edition was published in 1963 by Harper as *Western Civilization Since the Renaissance.*

NEF, JOHN U. 1964 *The Conquest of the Material World.* Univ. of Chicago Press.

NELSON, RICHARD R. 1962 The Link Between Science and Invention: The Case of the Transistor. Pages 549–583 in Universities–National Bureau Committee for Economic Research, *The Rate and Direction of Inventive Activity: Economic and Social Factors.* Princeton Univ. Press.

OGBURN, WILLIAM F. (1922) 1950 *Social Change, With Respect to Culture and Original Nature.* New edition with supplementary chapter. New York: Viking.

OHIO STATE UNIVERSITY, CONFERENCE ON ECONOMICS OF RESEARCH AND DEVELOPMENT, COLUMBUS, 1962 1965 *Economics of Research and Development.* Edited by Richard A. Tybout. Columbus: Ohio State Univ. Press.

O'NEALE, LILA M. 1932 *Yurok–Karok Basket Weavers.* University of California Publications in American Archaeology and Ethnology, Vol. 32, No. 1. Berkeley: Univ. of California Press.

ORANS, MARTIN 1966 Surplus. *Human Organization* 25:24–32.

PARSONS, TALCOTT (1937) 1949 *The Structure of Social Action: A Study in Social Theory With Special Reference to a Group of Recent European Writers.* Glencoe, Ill.: Free Press.

PARSONS, TALCOTT 1951 *The Social System.* Glencoe, Ill.: Free Press.

PASSER, HAROLD 1953 *The Electrical Manufacturers, 1875–1900: A Study in Competition, Entrepreneurship, Technical Change, and Economic Growth.* Cambridge, Mass.: Harvard Univ. Press.

PECK, MERTON J.; and SCHERER, FREDERICK M. 1962 *The Weapons Acquisition Process: An Economic Analysis.* Boston: Harvard Univ., Graduate School of Business Administration, Division of Research.

POLANYI, MICHAEL 1958 *Personal Knowledge: Towards a Post-critical Philosophy.* Univ. of Chicago Press.

RESEARCH PROJECT ON THE STRUCTURE OF THE AMERICAN ECONOMY 1953 *Studies in the Structure of the American Economy: Theoretical and Empirical Explorations in Input–Output Analysis,* by Wassily Leontief et al. New York: Oxford Univ. Press.

[Review Issue of] *A History of Technology,* by Charles Singer et al. 1960 *Technology and Culture* 1, no. 4.

RICHARDS, AUDREY I. (1939) 1961 *Land, Labour and Diet in Northern Rhodesia: An Economic Study of the Bemba Tribe.* Oxford Univ. Press.

SALTER, W. E. G. 1960 *Productivity and Technical Change.* Cambridge Univ. Press.

SCHERER, FREDERIC M. 1964 *The Weapons Acquisition Process: Economic Incentives.* Boston: Harvard Univ., Graduate School of Business, Division of Research.

SCHLIPPE, PIERRE DE 1956 *Shifting Cultivation in Africa: The Zande System of Agriculture.* London: Routledge.

SCHMOOKLER, JACOB 1966 *Invention and Economic Growth.* Cambridge, Mass.: Harvard Univ. Press.

SCHULTZ, THEODORE W. 1964 *Transforming Traditional Agriculture.* New Haven: Yale Univ. Press.

SCHUMPETER, JOSEPH A. (1912) 1934 *The Theory of Economic Development: An Inquiry Into Profits, Capital, Credit, Interest, and the Business Cycle.* Harvard Economic Studies, Vol. 46. Cambridge, Mass.: Harvard Univ. Press. → First published as *Theorie der wirtschaftlichen Entwicklung.*

SCHUMPETER, JOSEPH A. 1939 *Business Cycles: A Theoretical, Historical, and Statistical Analysis of the Capitalist Process.* 2 vols. New York and London: McGraw-Hill. → An abridged version was published in 1964.

Science and Engineering. 1961 *Technology and Culture* 2, no. 4.

SHEPARD, ANNA O. 1956 *Ceramics for the Archaeologist.* Carnegie Institution of Washington, Publication No. 609. Washington: The Institution.

SIGERIST, HENRY E. 1951–1961 *A History of Medicine.* 2 vols. New York: Oxford Univ. Press.

SINGER, CHARLES J. et al. (editors) 1954–1958 *A History of Technology.* 5 vols. Oxford: Clarendon.

SMITH, CYRIL S. 1960 *A History of Metallography: The Development of Ideas on the Structure of Metals Before 1890.* Univ. of Chicago Press.

STARR, MARTIN K. 1963 *Product Design and Decision Theory.* Englewood Cliffs, N.J.: Prentice-Hall.

STRAUB, HANS (1949) 1952 *A History of Civil Engineering: An Outline From Ancient to Modern Times.* London: Hill. → First published in German.

TATON, RENÉ (editor) (1957–1964) 1964–1965 *A History of Science.* 3 vols. New York: Basic Books. →

First published in French. Vol. 1: *Ancient and Medieval Science.* Vol. 2: *The Beginnings of Modern Science.* Vol. 3: *Science in the Nineteenth Century.*

TAYLOR, CALVIN W.; and BARRON, FRANK (editors) 1963 *Scientific Creativity: Its Recognition and Development.* New York: Wiley.

Technology and Culture. → Published since 1959 by the Wayne State University Press for the Society for the History of Technology.

UDY, STANLEY H. JR. 1959 *Organization of Work: A Comparative Analysis of Production Among Non-industrial Peoples.* New Haven: Human Relations Area Files Press.

UNDERWOOD, E. ASHWORTH (editor) 1953 *Science, Medicine, and History: Essays on the Evolution of Scientific Thought and Medical Practice, Written in Honor of Charles Singer.* 2 vols. New York: Oxford Univ. Press.

UNIVERSITIES–NATIONAL BUREAU COMMITTEE FOR ECONOMIC RESEARCH 1962 *The Rate and Direction of Inventive Activity: Economic and Social Factors.* National Bureau of Economic Research, Special Conference Series, No. 13. Princeton Univ. Press.

USHER, ALBERT P. 1955 Technical Change and Capital Formation. Pages 523–550 in Universities–National Bureau Committee for Economic Research, *Capital Formation and Economic Growth: A Conference.* Princeton Univ. Press.

VAJDA, S. 1958 *Readings in Linear Programming.* New York: Wiley.

WALKER, CHARLES R. 1962 *Modern Technology and Civilization: An Introduction to Human Problems in the Machine Age.* New York: McGraw-Hill.

WEBER, MAX (1922) 1957 *The Theory of Social and Economic Organization.* Edited by Talcott Parsons. Glencoe, Ill.: Free Press. → First published as Part 1 of *Wirtschaft und Gesellschaft.*

WHITE, LESLIE A. 1949 *The Science of Culture: A Study of Man and Civilization.* New York: Farrar, Strauss. → A paperback edition was published in 1958 by Grove.

WHITE, LESLIE A. 1959 *The Evolution of Culture: The Development of Civilization to the Fall of Rome.* New York: McGraw-Hill.

WHITE, LYNN JR. 1960 Tibet, India and Malaya as Sources of Western Medieval Technology. *American Historical Review* 65:515–526.

WHITE, LYNN JR. 1962a *Medieval Technology and Social Change.* Oxford: Clarendon.

WHITE, LYNN JR. 1962b The Act of Invention: Causes, Contexts, Continuities and Consequences. *Technology and Culture* 3:486–500.

WRIGHT, ORVILLE; and WRIGHT, WILBUR *Miracle at Kitty Hawk: The Letters of Wilbur and Orville Wright.* New York: Farrar, 1951.

ZIMMERMAN, LEO M.; and VEITH, ILZA 1961 *Great Ideas in the History of Surgery.* Baltimore: Williams & Wilkins.

II

TECHNOLOGY AND INTERNATIONAL RELATIONS

Technology can be generally conceived of as encompassing man's methods and tools for manipulating material things and physical forces. The relationship between technology and international relations has been continuous and intimate. From the time of man's most primitive polities, the foreign-policy problems and opportunities of states have been influenced by the nature of their technology for transport, communication, warfare, and economic production. The glory of Athens rested on silver mines, and the might of Sparta on a process for making steel; the Romans ruled through roads, and the Assyrians overran Babylon and Egypt with the chariot. The contemporary effects of hydrogen bombs and intercontinental missiles dramatize a relationship between technology and power and between power and policy that goes back in time through the steam engine and gunpowder to the ox, hoe, and sword and into prehistoric time.

The relationship between technology and foreign policy is neither a new nor a neglected subject among students of world politics. Political geographers have long sought to explore the influence of geographic environment on the foreign policies of states, and in doing this they have had to take account of the manner in which technology has enabled man to adapt to and alter the conditions imposed by his environment. Scholars engaged in the effort to develop quantitative means for measuring and comparing national power have made extensive use of a variety of technological indices such as steel or energy production. Students of nationalism and international organization have been interested in the part played by developments in transportation and communication in the formation of modern states and in the contribution that technology may make toward the establishing of regional or international arrangements among those states. Most recently, stimulated by the events of the last two world wars and the advent of nuclear weapons, scholars have given considerable attention to the interrelationships among weapons technology, military strategy, and foreign policy.

Research in all these areas has had to contend both with the familiar problem of how to make general observations about the effects of a single variable and with the additional problem that the consequences of technological change have become increasingly difficult to analyze. Taken in their aggregate, the technological developments of the past three centuries have had an extensive and accumulative effect on international relations. But the more complex man's technology has become, the more it has served to multiply his choice of actions, and in consequence, considered individually, technological innovations have become increasingly less determinative in their effect.

A survey of past influence

The dominant technological development of the past three centuries has been the large-scale and increasing substitution of inanimate for animate energy as the motive force for man's machines. This substitution had its beginning in the use of gunpowder and wind and water power, but it was only when man discovered how to convert the heat from the burning of fossil fuels into mechanical energy, and how to convert mechanical into electrical energy and back again, that inanimate energy became both plentiful and transportable. It is this energy base that has made possible the whole complex of technological developments that constitutes modern industrial civilization.

None of the key elements in the international political process has been untouched by the industrial revolution. The structure of the state system and of states themselves, the purposes and expectations moving state policy, and the means available to states for achieving their purposes have all been significantly altered.

Consider the changes in the structure of the state system, that is, in the number, location, and relative power of its members. As the industrial revolution transformed the bases of military power and increased its mobility, international relations became global, rather than regional, in scope, and the relations among the members of this global system became continuous, rather than episodic. The hegemony of Europe over the other continents, which began with such rudimentary energy advantages as the sail and cannon, became virtually complete with the advent of the steamship and improved ordnance. The fate of the technically inferior polities was well summed up in the couplet of Hilaire Belloc, "Whatever happens we have got/The Maxim gun and they have not"; and until the industrialization of the United States and Japan, world politics was essentially European politics.

The structure of the European state system itself was no less affected by the new technology. The disparity in power between large and small states was greatly increased (contrast the vulnerability of the Lowlands in 1914 and 1940 with their military exploits against Spain in the sixteenth century and against England in the seventeenth century), and the enhanced opportunities for union, voluntary or involuntary, saw the number of states in Europe reduced from some four hundred at the time of the Treaty of Westphalia to less than one hundred by 1815 and to a mere thirty in 1878. Drastic changes also occurred in the distribution of power among the Great Powers, most notably as a result of the early industrialization of England and the later displacement of France by Germany as the dominant power on the Continent.

These changes in the number, relative power, and location of the states making up the international system have had great consequence both for the stability of the system and for the character of the strategies pursued by individual states within it. Two world wars testify to the instabilities introduced by the rise of German and Japanese power. Similarly, the whole character of American foreign policy changed when the United States moved from a power position where its continued survival depended upon the commitment of European power and interest elsewhere to a position where American military potential exceeded that of the major European powers combined.

The effect of technology on the internal political structure of states has been equally striking. Just as gunpowder brought an end to castles and made it more feasible to establish effective national governments, so the later technology of mass transportation and communication enormously increased the ability of governments to mobilize the time and energy of their citizens. The development of the urban–industrial state has created both new political elites and new political relationships between elites and masses, most notably in the development of mass democratic and mass totalitarian states. Although the foreign-policy consequences of these changes are difficult to disentangle from the effects of other variables, the greater command that central governments can now exercise over people has certainly contributed to the ability of such governments to wage more intensive and more sustained warfare. The state's need for popular support has also brought public opinion (with its moods and emotions) into the conduct of foreign policy and has enlarged the foreign audience for state diplomacy to include government-to-people communications as well as government-to-government communications. Finally, the dispersion of political and bureaucratic power that has attended the development of the industrial state has greatly increased the complexity of the process through which foreign policy is made, with the result that the opportunities for confusion, contradiction, indecision, and instability in the conduct of policy have been significantly increased.

The impact of technology on the purposes of state policy has been most marked on the intermediate level of the ends–means chain. States have continually pursued such general goals as "plenty," "glory," and "power," but there has been considerable change in the operational definition of these goals. Among the underdeveloped states today, the effort to secure industrial technology has itself become one of the major preoccupations of foreign policy, and among the industrial states scientific and technological achievements are now prized as symbols of power and prestige. Consider also the changing value that states have assigned to particular territories on the globe. The steamship contributed to the imperialism of the late nineteenth century by opening to commerce areas difficult to reach by sail; the political importance of the Middle East in the twentieth century has been largely the result of European dependence on its oil reserves; and the advent of the missile-firing nuclear submarine has endowed even the geography of the Arctic with strategic significance. As for the contribution of technology to the more "ultimate" purposes of state policy, the present conflict between the Soviet Union and the United States owes much to the fact that each has evolved a different conception of the proper arrangement of things and people in an industrial society and is persuaded that its conception of the good life must and should prevail elsewhere.

The relation of science to foreign policy has been for the most part indirect, since society usually experiences new additions to scientific knowledge in the form of the technical applications of that knowledge. This is not the case, however, with respect to man's general expectations about the course of human events. Here, new knowledge about man and the universe has led directly to a reorientation of such expectations.

The belief of seventeenth-century and eighteenth-century European statesmen in the balance of power as the natural order of state relations reflected in part their appreciation of the picture of measured order and equilibrium that science then presented of the physical world. Similarly, European and American policies at the turn of the nineteenth century were conditioned by a set of expectations about the "natural" struggle of states and the "inevitability" of the victory of the stronger over the weaker that had been stimulated by Charles Darwin's theories about the evolutionary process.

As in the case of state goals, the general means available to states for securing their purposes have remained the same (persuasion, bargaining, and coercion), but the techniques through which states may employ these means have been greatly altered by recent technology. The development of more rapid and more reliable means of transportation and communication has transformed the conduct of diplomacy. The increased speed of communication between states permits choices to be made on the basis of more recent information about the actions and interests of others. The Anglo–American War of 1812 would probably never have occurred if an Atlantic cable had been available to inform Washington that the British were planning to repeal their orders-in-council. The handicaps that the slow transportation of the period imposed on negotiations are exemplified in the odyssey of President Madison's peace commissioners; they left Washington in April 1813, hoping to meet the British in St. Petersburg, but did not catch up with them until August 1814, at Ghent. Today, the words of governments can be spread almost instantaneously around the world, and their agents are only hours away from the most distant foreign capitals. Central governments can also now exercise far greater control over the actions of their ambassadors and military commanders abroad. The initiative and independence that formerly could sometimes be displayed by a distant ambassador (as in the case of the contribution of Britain's Stratford Canning in Istanbul to the coming of the Crimean War) have now been displaced, potentially at least, by the kind of detailed and continuous command and control that President Kennedy exercised over his representatives in the field during the 1962 Cuban missile crisis. [See DIPLOMACY.]

These changes have significantly increased the pace and coherence of international relations, but they have had no effect on the propensity of those relations to turn to violence. The more rapid communication of words and transport of negotiators provide in themselves no promise that conflicts between states will be either less frequent in occurrence or more easily resolved. There is no guarantee that a conversation over the "hot line" will prove any more effective in preventing war than was the 1914 "Willy–Nicky" correspondence over the telegraph, and as in the case of the 1960 summit conference, the jet plane can bring the major figures of the world quickly together for a dialogue that will only drive them further apart. Similarly, while governments can now exercise greater control over their men and machines in the field, they may not always choose to exercise that control, or the men in the field may not heed it (American policy in the Korean War provided some examples); and there are, in any event, no grounds for expecting, just because policy is more coordinated, that it will for that reason be either more belligerent or more pacific.

In assaying the impact of advanced communication and transportation technologies on the conduct of foreign policy, it is important to note that what technology has given with one hand, by increasing the speed of communication and transportation, it has taken with the other, by decreasing the time available for decision. Not even the telegraph was able to offset the pressures placed upon diplomats in 1914 by the mobilization tables of the general staffs, whose own time pressures were the result of the contribution that the railroad had made to the speed with which armies could be assembled and deployed on enemy frontiers. Indeed, it would be a fair hypothesis that successive increases in the volume and speed of action-forcing agents (messages, visits, events) have so accelerated the pace of international relations that, despite increases in the number of people engaged in the conduct of international relations, policy makers have been not only deciding more but thinking less.

The same double-edged effect can also be seen in the result of advances in technology for military command and control. Today's technology permits strategic choices to be made on the basis of more complete and more rapidly processed information and to be executed with greater precision than in the past, but contemporary military technology has also increased the complexity of strategic problems and made strategic choices far more irreversible in their consequence. As a result, it is doubtful whether contemporary strategic nuclear forces—with their radar, teletypewriters, electronic locks, and computers—are any more "manageable" as instruments of policy, in a meaningful political sense, than were the armies and navies of World War I, with the telegraph and radio, or the armed forces of Napoleon, with the horse and semaphore.

Since the conduct of international relations is ever oriented toward the prospect of war, the relationship between technology and foreign policy is nowhere more evident than in the consequences of changes in the means available to states for coercion. Developments in the means of warfare have affected all the elements in the international political process previously discussed. Note has already been taken of the changes in the structure of the state system that resulted from the near synonymity of great military power and great industrial power. Similarly, the development of governmental structures capable of controlling every sphere of human activity, and the conduct of diplomacy for its impact on domestic as well as foreign audiences, have reflected the state's need for mass armies and the military importance of the civilian labor force. And nowhere has the reciprocal relation between ends and means been better demonstrated than by the advent of twentieth-century total war. As improvements in technology increased the number and the destructive scope of weapons of war, thereby increasing the costs in treasure and blood entailed in their production and use, compensation was sought through

enlarging the purposes of war, and this, in turn, served to stimulate the belligerents to still greater destructive efforts.

The destruction that attended the last two world wars has also left its mark on some of the general expectations about Western civilization, most notably that concerning its inevitable progress. The development of ever more destructive weapons has been accompanied by the disappearance of the few limitations (such as the discrimination between civilians and soldiers) that were formerly thought desirable or at least expedient during the exercise of violence in the name of state policy. The very value structure of science and technology, by emphasizing a pragmatic rather than an absolutist approach to problems, may have contributed to the dominance of military expediency over previously accepted humanitarian norms. At all events, the increasing destructiveness of weapons, coupled with the expectation that future warfare will be governed by the rule of "anything goes," has served to call into question one of the fundamental premises of Western culture: the belief that advances in science and technology will result in man's ultimate benefit.

One of the most striking demonstrations of the effect of changes in military technology on international relations has been that afforded by the development of nuclear weapons. Like the railroad and the steamship before them, nuclear weapons have revolutionized the character of war and the power relationships among states. The new weapons have widened the disparity between large and medium powers, increased the influence of scientific and military elites (and hence their policy perspectives) in state structures, and elevated new goals, such as deterrence and arms control, into the higher ranks of state purposes. The destructive character of nuclear weapons has also led to a dramatic change in expectations about the suitability of general war as an instrument of foreign policy. Thus, their unwillingness to contemplate the certainty of nuclear war compelled the Soviets to revise their theories about the inevitability of war with the United States. Similarly, the dominant expectation in Western capitals has been that, since there are no purposes states could achieve by a nuclear war that would be worth the lives that would be lost in its fighting, nuclear weapons will have the effect of making highly unlikely an all-out war between states which possess them.

Whether such a revolutionary consequence for the conduct of foreign policy can be ascribed to the development of nuclear weapons seems at best problematical. Certainly, nuclear weapons have made war against a well-prepared opponent seem irrational. Nevertheless, the expectation that war between nuclear powers will be prevented by their recognition of the costs involved is open to serious question. To begin with, as many students of military policy have pointed out, deterrence is neither technically simple nor politically automatic. All aside from the possibility of irrational acts, there will be many opportunities for statesmen to conclude—accurately or inaccurately—that the capabilities of their opponent make the costs of war bearable or that the intentions of their opponent make the costs of war unavoidable. Even more to the point, the argument that the loss of life which would attend a nuclear war makes such wars unlikely ignores the fact that the objects for which statesmen contend are rarely weighed in human lives. There are few instances in history of statesmen deciding to go to war after having made a deliberate calculation that their objects would be worth the loss of x lives (but not $x + n$ lives). More frequently, the decisions that have led to war have taken the form of statesmen calculating only that their objects were worth the risk of war.

For these reasons, the consequences of nuclear weapons for the conduct of foreign policy may not prove as revolutionary as many believe. The level of destruction that would attend a nuclear war becomes less relevant if the critical choices should be made through reference to relative, rather than absolute, costs (better World War III now than later). The absolute level of destruction is also less relevant if the choice involved is only to *risk* the costs of war, not to incur them. The diplomacy of nuclear powers since World War II would indicate that, while they have been unwilling to incur the costs of nuclear war, they have been neither willing (nor seen themselves able) to forgo policies which entail the risk of such costs. Yet, as the diplomacy that preceded World War I and World War II amply illustrates, a political process in which states are willing to risk the costs of war can share many of the features, and conceivably the results, of a process where states are willing to incur the costs of war. [*See* NUCLEAR WAR.]

Characteristics and trends

The preceding survey has shown how technological developments of the past three centuries have effected significant changes in every element in the international political process (actors, ends, expectations, means, and system). Attention can now be directed to some of the general characteristics of and trends in the relationship between technology and international relations.

Characteristics. (1) The political changes effected by technology have normally been the result of multiple, rather than single, technological developments. The European colonization of the world was dependent upon the development of the clock, the compass, and gunpowder, as well as improvements in the design of sailing ships. Similarly, the British decision in 1912 that their navy could no longer conduct a close blockade of enemy ports cannot be traced to any single naval innovation. This decision (which led the British to develop procedures for the kind of distant blockade that subsequently strained their relations with neutrals such as the United States during World War I) was the end product of a number of technical developments, most notably steam propulsion, more powerful ordnance, mines, torpedoes, and submarines. The recognition that the effects of technology are best appreciated through reference to some grouping of interrelated individual developments is reflected in the contemporary use of the term "weapons system." The dominant weapons system responsible for the current Soviet–American balance of terror is actually the product of the interaction of three different major technologies: those relating to missiles, electronics, and nuclear energy.

(2) The major political changes associated with technological developments have been the result of a multiplicity of nontechnical, as well as technical, factors. The disappearance of the limitations that characterized European warfare in the eighteenth century can be only partially explained by the technical changes that produced better roads, increased metal production, and improved the efficiency of firearms and artillery. Reference must also be made to critical changes in foreign policy (the displacement of territorial and commercial objectives by the ideological issues of the American and French revolutions); changes in military doctrine (organizational innovations making feasible the direction of larger armies and the development of more aggressive and more sustained campaign tactics); and even changes in the general cultural ethos (a lessened belief in the sinful nature of man, with the consequent loosening of inhibitions against weapons development, and a shift from an interest in production for artistic value to a concern for low-cost quantity production). The complex of technical and nontechnical variables can also be seen in the reasons for the breakup of the European colonial empires after World War II and the consequent doubling of the number of states on the planet. The explanation is to be found partly in technical developments (the global diffusion of European weapons technology, and the contribution of mass com-

munications technology to the growth of a sense of identity among colonial peoples) and partly in political developments (the diffusion of European ideas about nationalism, and the contribution of new theories about racial equality to the weakening of the European determination to maintain colonial rule).

(3) The political problems and opportunities resulting from technological change have been unequally distributed among states, both temporarily and permanently. The American experience with nuclear weapons provides a recent example. The advantages of a short-lived monopoly have been followed by a revolutionary decline in the military security of the United States. Unlike Germany in the first half of this century, the Soviet Union does not have to conquer the Old World before it can command the resources necessary to strike a mortal blow at the American continent. The destructiveness, range, and cheapness of nuclear weapon systems have stripped the United States of her earlier cushion provided by allies, time, and space and have largely canceled out the industrial superiority that meant defeat for her enemies in the last two world wars. The asymmetrical effects of technological change are also evident in the results of the global diffusion, since the end of World War II, of public health techniques innovated in Europe and North America. The application of these techniques in Asia and Latin America reduced death rates in those areas, in a period of a decade, to levels which the Europeans had required centuries to reach. But as a result of their continued high birth rates, the Asians and Latin Americans, unlike the Europeans, must begin their efforts to industrialize under the handicap of an unparalleled expansion in population.

(4) The political consequences of technological change have been largely unanticipated. To begin with, most of the technological developments themselves have come as surprises. A study, sponsored by the United States government in 1937, which endeavored to forecast developments for the next decade failed to anticipate, among other items, atomic energy, jet propulsion, radar, and antibiotics. Even when the general effects of technological developments have been clear, an analysis of their political consequences has not always been forthcoming. As of this writing, the population explosion noted above, one of the major transformations in the world today, has been discussed for over a decade, but its foreign-policy consequences have yet to be delineated beyond the simple Malthusian prophecies of war, plague, and famine. And finally, when efforts have been made to predict the

foreign-policy consequences of new technologies, the score has not been impressive. History is full of confident predictions that this or that development (the hot-air balloon, dynamite) would make war irrational. Similarly, many observers have expected that the advances in transportation and communication technology during the past century would increase international ties and identifications and result in larger states, regional groupings, or even one world. Actually, as a result of the political innovations with which governments met these technical developments (e.g., more effective trade and passport controls, censorship, and more intensive means of political socialization), the world has become, not more "international" since the nineteenth century, but less. History's largest contiguous empire remains that conquered by the Mongols on horseback, and while steam did help to enlarge the European empires created by sail, the main effect of the last century's advances in transportation and communication has been, not to produce larger polities, but to increase the cohesion of existing polities.

Trends. (1) Science now precedes technology. Both the neolithic revolution (the domestication of animals and the development of agriculture) and the industrial revolution took place independently of advances in man's scientific knowledge. Steam engines were built long before their basic laws were formulated. This relationship began to change with the advent of the chemical and electrical industries, and since this century began scientific discovery has increasingly become a necessary preliminary to new technology. Thus, the development of the atomic bomb was dependent on basic research in nuclear physics; and by the end of this century the further development of technology may be almost completely based upon advances in scientific knowledge.

(2) Scientific knowledge and technological innovation are increasing at an exponential rate, at least in the scientifically literate and technically advanced states, for the more technologically complex a society becomes, the more easily it can generate and absorb new information and techniques. It is estimated that 90 per cent of all the scientists who ever lived are alive today, and, as crudely measured by the volume of scientific publication, scientific knowledge is doubling every ten to fifteen years. The change in the rate of technological innovation is equally impressive. In the first three hundred years after the invention of firearms, the improvement in the original product was so slow that Benjamin Franklin gave serious consideration to arming the Continental Army with bows and

arrows. In contrast, only ninety years passed between the first successful steamship and the disappearance of sails from warships, and fifteen years after the first flight of Orville Wright there were 2,600 planes and 300,000 men in the Royal Air Force.

(3) Both the costs of acquiring new scientific knowledge and the costs of product innovation appear to be increasing. One reason American university research budgets have become so dependent on the government for funds is that no other source is rich enough to meet the rising costs of research. The situation in some fields of nuclear physics has been characterized by one scientist's observation that it costs a million dollars just to ask a question. Similarly, the production of a fighter plane required 17,000 engineering hours in 1940, but 1.4 million hours were required by 1955. Finally, as a result of the disappearance of high-grade ores, even the production of basic materials, such as iron, copper, and bauxite, now requires increasing amounts of technical equipment and energy. As a result of these developments, the scientific and technological distance between powers has been steadily widening. At present the United States, the Soviet Union, Europe, and the rest of the world each has one-fourth of the world's supply of scientists and engineers. Even the most technically advanced of the European states are no longer able to compete, on an individual basis, with the United States and the Soviet Union in such technologically intensive fields as nuclear weapons, advanced aircraft, space, and missiles, and the nations which make up the rest of the world are hopelessly outclassed. In 1953, for example, the United States Atomic Energy Commission used six times as much electricity as India produced that year. The point to these developments would seem to be that in the future, not only will the Great Powers alone be able to have great technology but, unless the smaller states pool their efforts, only the Great Powers will have great science.

(4) Scientific research has become increasingly subject to government control and direction. Governments have long sought to foster and exploit technological developments for political, especially military, purposes. (Bessemer began work on his process in order to win a prize that Napoleon III had offered for a cheaper means of producing armor plate, and the governments of several European states took an active part in the construction and location of railroads in order to facilitate the deployment of troops at key frontiers.) But until the advent of the cold war the process of scientific discovery was largely unplanned and random, as far

as government choices were concerned. By the end of the seventeenth century, science had developed into an international and essentially autonomous social institution; during the great ideological conflicts of the early nineteenth century, scientists and their ideas were allowed to pass as freely across political frontiers in time of war as they did in time of peace. Although governments made a primitive effort to put scientists to work on military problems during World War I (the key role of Fritz Haber and other German chemists in the development of poison gas was a harbinger of the part physicists were to play in the development of the atom bomb), it was not until World War II that governments brought the resources of their scientists and engineers fully to bear on the problems of war. The results of this effort (radar, the proximity fuse, the V-2, and the atom bomb) were such as to guarantee that its value would not be forgotten with the war's end.

What has transformed the relationship between science and government has been the previously noted point that the development of technology has become increasingly dependent upon advances in scientific knowledge about the physical world. This trend is especially critical for the United States and the Soviet Union. As these powers throw one weapons systems after another into the effort to maintain at least a balance of terror, neither dares fall behind in either the discovery of new physical relationships or the application of scientific knowledge to military hardware and political–military strategy. It is indicative of the new relationship between science and war that figures and graphs comparing the major powers in number of scientists and engineers have become as familiar as those in the 1930s which compared their output of coal, oil, and steel. Nor is it only in the military field that science has become vital to the course of foreign policy. Science has been harnessed to the advancement of foreign-policy goals in such diverse fields as the exploration of space and oceans, birth and disease control, weather modification, and global communications. [See SCIENCE, article on SCIENCE–GOVERNMENT RELATIONS.]

Prospects

It is a safe prediction that the foreign-policy problems and opportunities of states will continue to be influenced by technological change. Even after the current exponential rates of discovery and invention begin to level off, the pace of discovery and invention will still be far in excess of what man has experienced throughout most of the twentieth century. Moreover, mankind appears to be entering upon an era of technological development commensurate in cultural importance to that of the industrial revolution. Just as the industrial revolution was based on the substitution of inanimate energy for the deficiencies of the human muscular system, so now automation and computers have begun to substitute for the deficiencies of man's brain and central nervous system. In fact, this second development may prove even more revolutionary for man's culture than the first. Man also stands on the threshold of major discoveries in human biology and chemistry. Indeed, the foreign-policy problems posed by nuclear weapons could seem simple compared with those which might result from breakthroughs in the understanding and control of memory, learning, and heredity (the alarm that a state might experience on the discovery of a "gene gap" could easily match the alarm felt by the United States during the "missile gap" scare of the late 1950s). When to these prospects one adds such possibilities as the use of new energy sources and climate control, it would seem evident that the future changes in international relations associated with scientific and technological developments will prove at least as consequential as those of the past.

It is much less certain whether man will be able to improve on his past performance in anticipating and controlling the political consequences of technological change. To date, science and technology have been liberating forces in Western culture. They have served to dispel ignorance and superstition and have given man a sense of control over nature and his destiny. But with the multiplication of knowledge and the increased specialization of disciplines, individuals are becoming ever more ignorant of the workings of the world about them, outside their area of information. Unless this development is balanced by an increased sense of governmental or social control over the course of technology, it could lead to a mounting sense of impotence on the part of technical–urban man. He could begin to display the same kind of fatalism and apathy toward the mysteries of his technical environment that peasant–village man displays toward the mysteries of his natural environment. Should the development of science and technology lead to a perspective of this order, it would mark the final collapse of the eighteenth-century and nineteenth-century ideal of a rational society where man's material environment, no less than his social and political environment, is susceptible to human understanding and control.

In view of the difficulties that attend the problem of prediction, it might seem rash to expect that future discoveries and inventions and their foreign-policy consequences will be better anticipated than has been the case in the past. Nevertheless, the four trends discussed above do provide some grounds for such an expectation. Previous attempts to forecast the development and consequence of technology have been sporadic, informal, and mainly the work of interested but not always appropriately skilled individuals. In the future, as the governments of the major powers play an increasing role in the material support of research and development programs, the mounting costs, together with the multiplication of the possible avenues of inquiry, insure that these governments will become increasingly involved in determining the content and priorities of such programs. The existence of continuous and self-conscious planning efforts of this order, on the part of skilled and concerned government consultants and officials, should have the effect of significantly reducing the degree of "technical surprise" that will attend the results of national research and development programs.

The same trends also point toward a more determined effort by governments to predict the political consequences of their research and development programs. As the opportunities for further research and development in each of a thousand different fields mushroom with the acceleration of scientific knowledge, whatever the government decides to support, it will be deciding *not* to support many more. In consequence, both the government's own interests and the interests of the proponents and opponents of particular programs will combine to place governments under increasing pressure to predict and justify in advance the policy consequences of their choices.

The mere fact that governments will be under pressure to make predictions provides, of course, no guarantee of their accuracy. Still, as with the effort to predict the future course of technology, there is some reason to believe that more determined efforts to predict the consequences of that technology will lead to some improvement over past performance. One reason for the succession of "political surprises" experienced over recent centuries is that predictions have too often taken as their point of departure the alleged identification of a single new "key" discovery or invention. What is clearly needed instead are predictive efforts which take as their point of departure the identification of potential new technological systems. This approach is already employed in the analysis of military research and development options, and there seems no reason why it cannot be extended to other technological fields. [*See* ECONOMICS OF DEFENSE.]

An equally important requirement for more accurate prediction is the necessity to take account of the manner in which political purposes and institutions may shape the consequences of technological change. Man has never been the passive tool of his technology. Important as the scientific discoveries and technical inventions of the past several centuries have been, the history of those years could hardly be written without reference to man's political theories and innovations: nationalism, the Protestant ethic, the balance of power, democratic government, bureaucracy, collective security, or socialism. Consider the current relations between the United States and the Soviet Union. Missiles, electronics, and nuclear weapons have produced a revolutionary change in the two countries' military technology, but the policies which have guided the development and deployment of that technology have been the product of such factors as the "lessons of the 1930s," on one side, and Lenin's reading of nineteenth-century history, on the other.

There is, in short, an "endless frontier" to politics as well as to science, and man's fate will be determined as much by his adventures along the one as along the other. Indeed, the more complex man's technology becomes, the more permissive are its effects on man's action and the more the consequences of technology turn on his political choices. In technologically primitive societies, man's values and social structures are highly conditioned by the nature of his technology. But just as man first used technology to overcome the limitations of his natural environment, so now, in technologically complex societies, man can turn science and technology to the task of overcoming limitations in his technical environment. Increasingly, man's values determine his technology; he can do what he wants.

The result of this development is that in the future, even more than in the past, the task of understanding, predicting, and controlling the impact of scientific and technological developments on international relations will turn not so much on an analysis of the technological possibilities as on an analysis of men's theories about the international political process and their conceptions about the roles that their own and other states should and will play in that process.

WARNER R. SCHILLING

[*Directly related are the entries* COMMUNICATION, POLITICAL; DISARMAMENT; FOREIGN POLICY; GEOGRAPHY, *article on* POLITICAL GEOGRAPHY; INTERNATIONAL POLITICS; MILITARY POWER POTENTIAL; NUCLEAR WAR; STRATEGY. *See also* INTERNATIONAL RELATIONS; WAR; *and the biographies of* DOUHET; MAHAN; RICHARDSON.]

BIBLIOGRAPHY

BERKNER, LLOYD V. 1964 *The Scientific Age: The Impact of Science on Society.* New Haven: Yale Univ. Press.

BORN, MAX 1958 Europe and Science. *Bulletin of the Atomic Scientists* 14:73–79.

BOYKO, HUGO (editor) 1964 *Science and the Future of Mankind.* Bloomington: Indiana Univ. Press.

BRODIE, BERNARD 1941 *Sea Power in the Machine Age.* Princeton Univ. Press.

BRODIE, BERNARD; and BRODIE, FAWN 1962 *From Crossbow To H-Bomb.* New York: Dell.

BROWN, HARRISON; BONNER, JAMES; and WEIR, JOHN 1957 *The Next Hundred Years: Man's Natural and Technological Resources.* New York: Viking.

FOSTER, GEORGE McC. 1962 *Traditional Cultures and the Impact of Technological Change.* New York: Harper.

FULLER, J. F. C. (1945) 1946 *Armament and History: A Study of the Influence of Armament on History From the Dawn of Classical Warfare to the Second World War.* London: Eyre & Spottiswoode.

HASKINS, CARYL P. 1964 *The Scientific Revolution and World Politics.* New York: Harper.

JOHNS HOPKINS UNIVERSITY, WASHINGTON CENTER OF FOREIGN POLICY RESEARCH 1960 *Developments in Military Technology and Their Impact on United States Strategy and Foreign Policy.* U.S. Congress, Senate, Committee on Foreign Relations, U.S. Foreign Policy Study No. 8. Washington: Government Printing Office.

JOHNSON, ELLIS A. 1958 The Crisis in Science and Technology and Its Effect on Military Development. *Operations Research* 6:11–34.

LASSWELL, HAROLD D. 1956 The Political Science of Science: An Inquiry Into the Possible Reconciliation of Mastery and Freedom. *American Political Science Review* 50:961–979.

MUMFORD, LEWIS (1934) 1964 *Technics and Civilization.* New York: Harcourt.

NEF, JOHN U. (1950) 1952 *War and Human Progress.* Cambridge, Mass.: Harvard Univ. Press.

OGBURN, WILLIAM F. (editor) 1949 *Technology and International Relations.* Univ. of Chicago Press.

SCHILLING, WARNER R. 1959 Science, Technology, and Foreign Policy. *Journal of International Affairs* 13:7–18.

SPROUT, HAROLD; and SPROUT, MARGARET 1962 *Foundations of International Politics.* Princeton, N.J.: Van Nostrand. → See especially chapters 7 and 8.

SPROUT, HAROLD; and SPROUT, MARGARET 1965 *The Ecological Perspective on Human Affairs, With Special Reference to International Politics.* Princeton Univ. Press.

STANFORD RESEARCH INSTITUTE 1959 *United States Foreign Policy: Possible Nonmilitary Scientific Developments and Their Potential Impact on Foreign Policy Problems of the United States.* U.S. Congress, Senate, Committee on Foreign Relations, U.S. Foreign Policy Study No. 2. Washington: Government Printing Office.

VLEKKE, B. H. M. 1965 The Development of Modern Science and the New Tasks of Diplomacy. Pages 221–

236 in Karl Braunias and Peter Meraviglia (editors), *Die modernen Wissenschaften und die Aufgaben der Diplomatie.* Graz (Austria): Verlag Styria.

WOHLSTETTER, ALBERT 1964 Technology, Prediction, and Disorder. *Bulletin of the Atomic Scientists* 20, October: 11–15.

WOODWARD, LLEWELLYN 1956 Science and the Relations Between States. *Bulletin of the Atomic Scientists* 12:119–124.

WRIGHT, QUINCY 1955 *The Study of International Relations.* New York: Appleton.

TEGGART, FREDERICK J.

Frederick John Teggart (1870–1946), American historian, is known for his work on the theory of history and for the application of scientific method to historical and social investigation.

Teggart was born in 1870 in Belfast, Ireland. There he attended the Methodist college and, later, Trinity College, Dublin. He came to the United States in 1888 and was graduated from Stanford in 1894. From 1893 to 1916 he was engaged in library administration. He held teaching posts in both history and political science in the University of California at Berkeley but is more widely remembered as the founder in 1919 of the department of social institutions, of which he remained chairman until his retirement in 1940. This department was celebrated on the campus and elsewhere for Teggart's introductory course on the history of the idea of progress. As the first course on this subject ever to be offered in the United States, it influenced many students who later became professors, and it helped to inspire the expansion of the literature on the subject. He was honored by the university in 1935 with an appointment as faculty research lecturer and was awarded the degree of Doctor of Laws in 1943.

Teggart was concerned with the question whether dated or historical material may be utilized for ends other than the composition of narrative. It seemed clear to him that since such data "[constitute] the record of human experience in its broader aspects," it is a matter of highest importance to ascertain whether this dated record, when properly organized, is amenable to the scientific mandate of verification. To his mind, verification turns upon the acceptance of three precepts allying historical investigation with scientific inquiry. He maintained, first, that the aim of the historian who wishes to employ scientific method should be the isolation and investigation of a problem. Second, the problem should have reference to a class of phenomena—in the case of the historian, to a class of datable events. Third, he called upon the investigator to base his procedure, as in all scientific inquiry, upon the elementary technique of comparison—the comparison of classes of dated events at differing periods of time and among differing human groups.

The exposition or exemplification of this proposed type of historical inquiry is presented in two major studies: *The Processes of History* (1918) and *Rome and China* (1939).

The answer to the question "Can scientific method be applied to history?" is affirmative in both books. In the *Processes* it is supported by a program of research stating what is regarded as the most general problem confronting students of mankind and, according to Teggart, its most promising general solution.

Since men, like their animal brethren, are divided into countless groups (usually called cultures), the central problem for all humanists, and one of almost overwhelming magnitude and difficulty, turns upon the question of how man has come to be as he is—culturally different. This ultimate question had confronted the environmentalist, the racialist, and the social evolutionist; no acceptable solution had been reached. How then, asked Teggart, may a new start be made? How may historians with their documentary treasure and the aid of scientific method arrive at a more credible solution?

The first observation Teggart made in the *Processes* in this connection is that human history is not unitary but pluralistic; it is not one dated sequence of happenings but a plurality of sequences associated with a plurality of cultures. The second observation is geographical. Europe and Asia (areas in which dated human histories have been enacted to a marked degree) are geographically indissoluble, and the Eurasian land mass has been the site of plural cultures and plural histories. When scientific method in its elementary aspect of comparison is employed, it promptly reveals not merely a large collection of dated historical series but a collection in which uniformities—political, geographical, and psychological—are observable. It discloses common steps, or similar sequences of events, by which man in Europe and Asia came to be what he is. It reveals (1) that political organization, or the advancement from an earlier system of kindred relationships, has been restricted to certain small areas in geographical pockets on the land mass; (2) that these small politicized or advanced areas have occurred not only in geographical pockets but at the termini of routes of travel or of group migration; and hence, (3) that political organization, civil society, or civilization has arisen at points of human contact, pressure, conflict, or war, followed by the release of at least some measure of individual initiative.

At this point, in order to emphasize the critical importance of using dated materials for ends other than narrative, to convince future students of the practicability and fruitfulness of allying scientific method with the study of dated events, and to obey one of the fundamental injunctions of science, Teggart felt it necessary to verify at least some of the elements of his general solution by presenting at least one test case. This step, so customary in the sciences but so rare in historical studies, was taken in *Rome and China: A Study of Correlations in Historical Events* (1939). Here again the theater of action and investigation was Eurasia, but in conformity with scientific practice, only one phase of the original solution or hypothesis was chosen for immediate confirmation. The phase Teggart selected was that class of recurrent events familiar to all students of history, namely, the barbarian invasions of the Roman Empire during the period from 58 B.C. to A.D. 107. Taking this limited time span, he sought to account for the appearance of a recurrent historical phenomenon, a genus of the larger species of recurrent human migrations discussed in the *Processes*.

After a tireless examination of the barbarian penetrations of the far-flung Roman boundaries, together with their antecedent tribal movements in mid-Asia, the substantiation of this phase of the general hypothesis seemed to be complete. Just as on the larger canvas of the *Processes* the recurrent appearance of civil society was preceded by conditions of contact including war, so, in the more particularized study, every barbarian uprising in Europe followed the outbreak of war either on the eastern frontiers of the Roman Empire or in the western regions of the Chinese Empire.

Thus, the investigation established correlations in historical events, and these correlations, themselves new historical facts, became in turn proper subjects for continued scientific examination and explanation.

The discovery, under conscientious control, that at least some classes of dated events exhibit correlation is a matter of profound importance in historiography and in the history of thought. It demonstrates a type of human historical fact that hitherto has not received attention and suggests the presence of other correlations to be elicited by historical research.

Teggart is known also for his work on other problems in historical and social theory. In the *Prolegomena to History* (1916) and the *Theory of History* (1925) he discussed historiography, the philosophy of history, the history of civilizations, and the theory of social change in its broadest sense. He urged readers to be aware of the historical and naive dependence of the social studies upon the natural sciences and asserted that the refusal of historians, anthropologists, and sociologists to define their assumptions, or to trace the history of their organizing ideas, had left them at the mercy of unexamined, inherited, and antiquated preconceptions. He emphasized the need for close cooperation between history and anthropology —the study of man civilized and primitive, literate and nonliterate—on the basis of a unified set of principles of organization.

MARGARET T. HODGEN

[*See also* ARCHEOLOGY; ETHNOLOGY; HISTORY, *article on* CULTURE HISTORY. *Directly related are the entries* EVOLUTION; HISTORIOGRAPHY; *and the biography of* CHILDE.]

WORKS BY TEGGART

1910 The Circumstance or the Substance of History. *American Historical Review* 15:709–719.

1916 *Prolegomena to History: The Relation of History to Literature, Philosophy, and Science.* University of California Publications in History, Vol. 4, No. 3. Berkeley: Univ. of California Press.

1918 *The Processes of History.* New Haven: Yale Univ. Press.

1919a Anthropology and History. *Journal of Philosophy* 16:691–696.

1919b The Approach to the Study of Man. *Journal of Philosophy* 16:151–156.

1922 Clio. *University of California Chronicle* 24:347–360.

1925 *Theory of History.* New Haven: Yale Univ. Press.

1926a The Humanistic Study of Change in Time. *Journal of Philosophy* 23:309–315.

1926b Turgot's Approach to the Study of Man. *University of California Chronicle* 28:129–142.

(1927–1929) 1930 *Two Essays on History.* Berkeley, Calif.: Privately printed. → Contains "The Responsibility of the Historian," read at the 42d annual meeting of the American Historical Association, 1927; and "Spengler," reprinted from the *Saturday Review of Literature*, Volume 5, 1929, pages 597–599.

1929 Notes on Timeless Sociology. *Social Forces* 7:362–365.

1939 *Rome and China: A Study of Correlations in Historical Events.* Berkeley: Univ. of California Press.

1940 A Problem in the History of Ideas. *Journal of the History of Ideas* 1:494–503.

1941a War and Civilization in the Future. *American Journal of Sociology* 46:582–590.

1941b World History. *Scientia* (Bologna) 69:30–35.

1942 Causation in Historical Events. *Journal of the History of Ideas* 3:3–11.

1947 The Argument of Hesiod's *Works and Days*. *Journal of the History of Ideas* 8:45–77.

TELEKI, PÁL

Pál Teleki (1879–1941) was the founder of economic geography in his native Hungary, one of the leaders of Hungarian science between the two world wars, and a statesman who played a leading part in his country's affairs. Brought up in an aristocratic family with a long tradition of public service, he served his country twice as prime minister and ended his career on a tragic note—rather than accept complete German control of Hungary, he committed suicide as a gesture of protest.

In spite of his political identification with the cause of capitalism, his stature as a scholar is fully recognized by more recent Hungarian Marxist scholars. This is primarily because he did so much for the development of academic geography in Hungary: he founded the first chair in economic geography, in 1921, and occupied it himself until 1939, and he trained an entire generation of geographers who became leaders of the field. He was equally influential in starting research institutes in sociology and political science, and he was also recognized abroad for his contributions to geography.

Teleki's first major work, published in 1909, was *Atlas zur Geschichte der Kartografie der japanischen Inseln* ("Atlas of the History of the Cartography of Japan"), a work honored with the Jomard Prize of the Geographical Society of Paris. Cartography continued to be one of his main interests and led, in 1919, to his preparing an ethnographic map of Hungary, which was presented to the Peace Conference in that year. Instead of the traditional, simplified technique of generalized ethnic–linguistic maps, his "Carte Rouge," as it became known, combined population density and ethnic character, resulting in a more accurate and reliable map that has influenced similar publications ever since.

It was Teleki's interest in mapping the distribution of cultural phenomena that led to his preparing a series of unique maps illustrating the gradual spread of intensive agriculture around the world. Influenced by Thünen's theoretical model of the gradual diminution of intensity in agriculture in a pattern of concentric circles, Teleki and his collaborators prepared a set of four maps. The first showed types of farming throughout the world during the 1850s; the second, during the 1880–1890 period of large-scale development of extra-European farming areas; the third, at the peak of capitalist development in the years immediately preceding World War I; and the fourth, during the 1920s and early 1930s, the period of gradual retrenchment of free trade and the beginnings of the great economic depression. These maps, considered to be his finest contribution to geography, were never published, because of the outbreak of World War II.

Besides his interest in and major contributions to cartography and economic geography, Teleki gave ample evidence in his teaching and in his writings of his concern with a strongly unitarian approach to geography, which he defined as the study of life on earth. Nowhere was this more clearly stated than in his writings on the subject of European unity. Although he was completely committed to nationalism as a prime mover in European affairs, he repeatedly expressed his faith in an eventual emergence of a united Europe. In 1934 he wrote: "Though consisting of many states, and devoid of a single will, Europe nonetheless is an organic unity. There has been developing in Europe a political structure, an economic system, a type of society, a moral polity that no nation, no state, no individual has escaped, or could escape today" ([1934] 1935, p. 133).

GEORGE KISH

[*For the historical context of Teleki's work, see the biography of* THÜNEN. *For discussion of the subsequent development of his ideas, see* CARTOGRAPHY; GEOGRAPHY, *article on* ECONOMIC GEOGRAPHY.]

WORKS BY TELEKI

1909 *Atlas zur Geschichte der Kartografie der japanischen Inseln.* Budapest: Hiersemann.
1917 *A földrajzi gondolat története* (The History of Geographic Thought). Budapest: Privately published.
1920 *Ethnographical Map of Hungary, Based on the Density of Population.* The Hague: Van Stockum.
1923 *The Evolution of Hungary and Its Place in European History.* New York: Macmillan.
(1934) 1935 *Európáról és Magyarországról* (About Europe and Hungary). 2d ed. Budapest: Athenaeum. → Translation of the extract was provided by George Kish.
1936 *A gazdasági élet földrajzi alapjai* (Geographic Bases of Economic Life). 2 vols. Budapest: Centrum.

SUPPLEMENTARY BIBLIOGRAPHY

KISH, GEORGE 1941 Count Paul Teleki. *Geographical Review* 31:514–515.
KOCH, FERENC 1956 Teleki Pál gazdaságföldrajzi munkásságának birálata (Criticism of Pál Teleki's Work in Economic Geography). Magyar Tudományos Akadémia, Budapest, Társadalmi-történeti Tudományok Osztálya, *Közlemények* 7:90–122.

TEMPERAMENT

See EMOTION; PERSONALITY; TRAITS.

TENANCY, AGRICULTURAL

See under LAND TENURE.

TERMAN, LEWIS M.

Lewis Madison Terman (1877–1956) was a pioneer in the American movement of mental testing and was especially interested in the measurement and growth of intelligence.

Quite early, Terman had been convinced that bright children are not queer misfits in society. His doctoral dissertation, written under G. Stanley Hall at Clark University in 1905, had been based on a comparison of seven bright children with seven dull ones, selected by tests of his own devising. The comparison seemed to confirm his thesis.

In 1908 the Binet–Simon scale of intelligence tests appeared, and Edmund B. Huey of Johns Hopkins University advised Terman to take up this French innovation and develop it for use in America. When Terman was called to Stanford University two years later, he adopted Huey's suggestion and undertook to construct a comparable scale in the English language and to calibrate and adjust it. The result was the publication in 1916 of his *The Measurement of Intelligence*, a "guide for the use of the Stanford revision and extension of the Binet–Simon Intelligence Scale." Its use and importance, which would have been great in any case, were enhanced almost immediately by the U.S. Army's undertaking the testing of the intelligence of its recruits in World War I. The army also devised special group tests for assessing mental ability en masse, and Terman was called upon to help with this phase of the work.

Intelligence, as the scale measures it, increases during childhood, at first rapidly and then more slowly, leveling off on the average at an adult maximum a little before the age of 16. The scale is calibrated in terms of mental age, which is the average performance of children of a given chronological age; that is to say, children of 10 should have an average mental age of 10, although some ten-year-olds are much brighter and some much duller. To compare children of different ages, Terman used the intelligence quotient (IQ), a ratio originally suggested by the German psychologist William Stern. The IQ is the percentage that the mental age is of the chronological age. It is obtained by dividing the subject's mental age by his actual age and multiplying the result by 100. A child of 10 with a mental age of 14 has an IQ of 140 and is at the threshold of what Terman was pleased to call "genius." A child of 5 with a mental age of 7 also has an IQ of 140, whereas a retarded child aged 10 with a mental age of 7 has an IQ of only 70. With the assistance of others, Terman

continued to keep the Binet–Stanford scale revised so that it presently became the standard for fixing the IQ's of children and, to a lesser degree, of adults.

If the cultural background of the developing child is constant, as the conventional American background tends to be, the IQ tends to be invariant. This apparent invariance led Terman to believe (1916) that intelligence is fixed in the individual and thus presumably inherited. He weakened a little in this view in the last decades of his life, when scientific opinion had shifted from hereditarianism toward environmentalism. By that time, however, intelligence was being broken up conceptually into component primary abilities or downgraded by being given a more operational label, such as "scholastic aptitude," a conception free of hereditarian implications.

Terman was principally interested in high intelligence—in bright children first and then in the bright adults they became. Four of the five volumes of the *Genetic Studies of Genius* (1925–1959) examine the psychological characteristics of 1,528 very bright schoolchildren. The existence of the Stanford scale made the *Genetic Studies of Genius* possible. In 1911 Terman had used the Binet–Simon scale to select for study 31 children with IQ's in excess of 125, but now he was ready to go ahead on a grand scale. Since it was not practicable to test all of the 160,000 schoolchildren in California, Terman asked schoolteachers to pick out what they thought were the brightest among the youngest children in their classes, and he had these children tested, setting an IQ of 140 as the threshold for further study. His assistants undertook to describe all 1,528 children in terms of medical examinations, anthropological measurements, scholastic achievement, character tests, interests, books read, and games known. The results were reported in 1925, and Terman's faith was confirmed. Allowing for the inevitable exceptions, these "gifted children" constituted a charming, eager band of youth, alert, interesting and interested, socially alive—not misfits, neurotics, or warped daydreamers.

For 35 years they remained to Terman his gifted "children," and he to them a father figure—their spouses were included in the relationship when they married. Follow-up surveys appeared in 1930, 1947, and posthumously in 1959, when the "children" were about 17, 35, and 45 years of age, and the study, begun in 1921, may continue until the year 2010, when the last survivor might be expected to have died. They remained a personable, effective group. Some of the men and a few of the career-minded women attained eminence. The IQ's, on the whole, stood up pretty well, and it turned out that bright young people usually select bright spouses.

The second volume of the *Studies* (1926) was designed as a control for the first. Catherine (Cox) Miles shared the principal authorship with Terman. They studied the biographical records of 300 great men in history, presumptively "geniuses," and estimated their IQ's from the accounts of their youth. These eventually great persons tended, as children, to compare well with Terman's gifted children. The control validated the enterprise. It is interesting to note the magnitude of the assessed IQ's of important leaders in the history of civilization: Goethe was at the top with an estimated IQ of 210, the youthful Descartes was rated at 180, and Darwin at 165, but at 145, Napoleon just barely emerged above Terman's threshold for "genius."

Terman was more of a descriptive scientist than a theorist. He devised measurements, often by inventing and standardizing tests, used the procedures in the problem of his immediate concern, and reported the facts clearly and interestingly but with little theoretical elaboration. He was forced, however, to conclude that Francis Galton's belief that eminence is the mark of genius does not hold universally; women are the most common exceptions, because they may apply their genius to the achievement of private contentment rather than to the attainment of public prestige. Such private success shows that, in addition to intelligence, properly directed motivation is needed to project the gifted person into the pages of history. Gifted people, Terman further suggested, may also have an exceptional capacity for contentment.

At the same time that Terman was working with Maud A. Merrill on a revision of the Stanford revision of the Binet scale (1937), he enlisted the support of Catherine Cox Miles in a study of *Sex and Personality* (1936). They designed a scale of masculinity, which ran from zero to +200, and another of femininity, which ran from zero to −200. The average male was rated +52, and the average female −70. The spread for each sex was enormous, but the overlap of the two sexes was negligible. Women athletes emerged as just a shade more feminine than clergymen. On the average, masculinity increases for males up to about age 16 and then diminishes steadily to zero at age 80. Femininity in women decreases up to the college sophomore level and then increases a little up into old age, but of course at every age the difference between the average male and the average female

is enormous. A little boy is much more masculine than a little girl, and so it is also for both male and female sophomores. This is the sort of factual measured knowledge that delighted Terman.

Terman's other principal adventure into the measurement of important social characteristics was his study of marital happiness (1938). To obtain the requisite data he constructed, with the aid of his assistants, a scale of happiness and applied it to 792 married couples and 109 divorced couples —1,802 persons altogether. Most of the supposed causes of marital happiness and unhappiness turned out to be invalid. Sexual relations mattered much less than Terman had expected, nor were differences in age or education so very important. The general conclusion was that happy persons make up happy pairs. And what makes a person happy? It seems that one important factor that predisposes an individual to happiness is that he or she should have had happy parents. Hereditarian Terman was finding that happiness can be inherited, but not through the genes or in Mendelian fashion. One other finding was that happiness is not necessarily dispensed to pairs, for an unhappy person may have a happy spouse.

Terman was born on a farm in Johnson County, Indiana, on January 15, 1877. He was the twelfth of 14 children; none of the rest ever attained the eminence or intellectual prestige of Lewis or of his son, Frederick E. Terman. Lewis' father, himself a farmer, was the son of a Virginia farmer of Scotch–Irish descent. Lewis never disliked farm work, but he was possessed of an insatiable desire for education, and he loved reading. From the age of ten on he read most of the two hundred books in his father's library, which included an *Encyclopaedia Britannica*. Until he was 13 he attended a one-room rural school with about thirty pupils and one teacher. Then he worked for two years on his father's farm.

When he was 15 his parents satisfied his appetite for education by sending him for two years to the Central Normal College at Danville, Indiana. After that he taught for a year in a one-room rural school to obtain the money to return to Danville to earn a B.S. degree. Again he taught school and then went back to Normal College for a B.PD. Next he borrowed money and kept on for the classical degree, an A.B. Altogether he spent 164 weeks out of six years studying at Danville. He was now 21, and he spent the next three years as principal of a high school in which he taught all the courses to about forty pupils. During this time he married Anna B. Minton, and soon their son Frederick was born. Meanwhile Terman was reading the right kind of books about psychology (at Danville he had had to read William James's *Principles of Psychology* surreptitiously because his instructor disapproved of its literary flavor).

Next, Terman found himself looking to Indiana University, where he could get a better A.B. than at the Normal College and where he could prepare himself to teach pedagogy and psychology. Again he had to borrow money, but education was vital, and he went with his wife's strong support. At Indiana he found three Clark University men, all with PH.D.'s from Stanley Hall: William L. Bryan, who shortly became president of the university and saw little of Terman; John A. Bergström, an experimental psychologist who failed to interest him in the "brass-instrument psychology"; and Ernest H. Lindley, who became his chief mentor. He learned to read German and French well enough so that psychological literature in those languages no longer was closed to him, and in two years he obtained not only the solid A.B. that he sought but also an A.M. Lindley persuaded him to go to Clark to try for a PH.D.

So to Clark he went, already in debt, now head of a family of four, and obliged to borrow more money. Clark turned out to be a wonderful place to this farmer's boy, avid for knowledge. Each of the handful of professors lectured on whatever he pleased three or four times a week. The students went to the lectures they liked. There were no registrations, no class lists, no recitations, and no examinations until the final oral examination for the PH.D. There were, however, incentives for hard work. Hall's seminar became the focus of Terman's endeavor. There, sharp criticism of one's paper was quite devastating to self-esteem. Terman kept pressing his thesis that bright children are not unstable and finally obtained his PH.D. in 1905, when he was 28 years old. For two years he had lived just over the frontier from European psychology, for during that period America looked abroad for learning, and Terman's great psychologists were Binet in France, Galton in England, and, to a lesser extent, the men of the psychological laboratories in Germany.

Just as his new career was about to begin, Terman was struck by tuberculosis. The first attack was in the summer of 1904, after which he rested and then went back to work, guarding his health carefully. In those days Stanley Hall was the leader of the new faith that psychology would revolutionize education, and many of his students went gladly to important posts in high schools or normal schools. Terman looked for an appointment in a southern climate and presently chose one at San Bernardino, California. As he began his work he had another hemorrhage, but after resting briefly he returned to work. At the end of the year he accepted a better post at the Los Angeles State Normal School, where he remained for four years. Other psychologists were there, including two Clark PH.D.'s, Gesell and Huey, and they formed a stimulating group. In 1910 a position at Stanford University became vacant, and Terman was asked to fill it. He began as assistant professor in the department of education and became a full professor in 1916, the year the Stanford revision was published.

Terman spent the last 46 years of his life productively engaged at Stanford. In 1922, on the retirement of Frank Angell from the department of psychology, Terman was asked to become its executive head, and his title was changed to professor of psychology. His contributions to mental testing in World War I were making him well known, and he was elected president of the American Psychological Association in 1923. He had begun the *Genetic Studies of Genius* in the 1920s. In 1928 he was elected to the National Academy of Sciences, an honor which pleased him greatly. The 1930s were an especially productive decade, for they included another volume of the *Genetic Studies*, the studies of sex and personality and of marital happiness. The Stanford Achievement Test, developed with the assistance of T. L. Kelley and G. M. Ruch, a widely used instrument that was standardized on almost 350,000 children, appeared in various revisions in 1919, 1940, and 1953. The revision of the Stanford–Binet scale with Maud Merrill became available in 1937.

The tests brought Terman a comfortable income, but his indefatigability was undiminished. The chief studies mentioned were completed against a background of constant publication which yielded Terman a lifetime bibliography of over 200 items, besides book reviews and introductions to the books of others. There was also his constant correspondence with his gifted children and his interest in their children and grandchildren. The department of psychology at Stanford, with its careful selection of appointees and its subsequent permissive democracy, was becoming famous. Three men from the department were elected to the National Academy of Sciences, and four more became presidents of the American Psychological Association. Terman's department conferred 55 PH.D.'s during his incumbency.

In 1942 Terman retired at the age of 65. He continued his activities on a diminished scale. The fourth volume of the *Genetic Studies* came out, and the fifth was begun. Terman's belief in the inheritance of intelligence was somewhat weakened, yet it was undoubtedly reinforced when in 1946 his son was elected to the National Academy of Sciences. He himself was elected to the American Philosophical Society in 1953, and in 1956 the American Psychological Foundation decided to make the second award of its gold medal to Terman in 1957. Unfortunately, however, the award came too late, for Terman died at Stanford on December 21, 1956.

EDWIN G. BORING

[*For the historical context of Terman's work, see the biographies of* BINET *and* HALL. *For discussion of the later development of his ideas, see* ACHIEVEMENT TESTING; CREATIVITY, *article on* GENIUS AND ABILITY; INTELLIGENCE AND INTELLIGENCE TESTING; PSYCHOMETRICS; *and the biography of* KELLEY.]

WORKS BY TERMAN

1916   *The Measurement of Intelligence: An Explanation of and a Complete Guide For the Use of the Stanford Revision and Extension of the Binet–Simon Intelligence Scale.* Boston: Houghton Mifflin.

1925–1959   *Genetic Studies of Genius.* 5 vols. Stanford Univ. Press. → Volume 1: *Mental and Physical Traits of a Thousand Gifted Children,* 1925, by L. M. Terman et al. Volume 2: *The Early Mental Traits of Three Hundred Geniuses,* 1926, by C. M. Cox et al. Volume 3: *The Promise of Youth: Follow-up Studies of a Thousand Gifted Children,* 1930, by B. S. Burks et al. Volume 4: *The Gifted Child Grows Up,* 1947, by L. M. Terman and M. H. Oden. Volume 5: *The Gifted Group at Mid-life: Thirty-five Years' Follow-up of the Superior Child,* 1959, by L. M. Terman and M. H. Oden.

1932   *Trails to Psychology.* Volume 2, pages 297–331 in *A History of Psychology in Autobiography.* Worcester, Mass.: Clark Univ. Press; Oxford Univ. Press.

1936   TERMAN, LEWIS M.; and MILES, CATHERINE C. *Sex and Personality: Studies in Masculinity and Femininity.* New York: McGraw-Hill.

(1937) 1960   TERMAN, LEWIS M.; and MERRILL, MAUD A. *Measuring Intelligence: A Guide to the Administration of the New Revised Stanford–Binet Tests of Intelligence.* Boston: Houghton Mifflin. → The forms are periodically revised and restandardized.

1938   TERMAN, LEWIS M. et al. *Psychological Factors in Marital Happiness.* New York: McGraw-Hill.

SUPPLEMENTARY BIBLIOGRAPHY

BINET, ALFRED; and SIMON, TH. 1905 Méthodes nouvelles pour le diagnostic du niveau intellectuel des anormaux. *Année psychologique* 11:191–244. → The first revision of this test appeared in 1908.

BORING, EDWIN G. 1959 Lewis Madison Terman: 1877–1956. Volume 33, pages 414–461 in National Academy of Sciences, *Biographical Memoirs.* Washington: Government Printing Office. → Contains a portrait of Terman and a bibliography.

HILGARD, E. R. 1957 Lewis Madison Terman: 1877–1956. *American Journal of Psychology* 70:472–479.

LEWIS, WILLIAM B. 1957 Professor Lewis M. Terman. *British Journal of Statistical Psychology* 10:65–68.

MILES, WALTER R. 1957 Lewis Madison Terman (1877–1956). *Yearbook of the American Philosophical Society* [1957]:165–170.

PSYCHOLOGICAL REGISTER 1932 Terman, Lewis Madison. Volume 3, pages 478–481 in *Psychological Register.* Worcester, Mass.: Clark Univ. Press; London: Oxford Univ. Press. → Contains a bibliography of 99 items, up to 1932.

SEARS, ROBERT R. 1957 L. M. Terman: Pioneer in Mental Measurement. *Science* 125:978–979.

YERKES, ROBERT M. (editor) 1921 Psychological Examining in the United States Army. Volume 15 of National Academy of Sciences, *Memoirs.* Washington: Government Printing Office. → The original military forms of the Army Alpha test can be found in Part 2, chapters 1–4.

TERMS OF TRADE
See under INTERNATIONAL TRADE.

TESTING, PSYCHOLOGICAL
See ACHIEVEMENT TESTING; APTITUDE TESTING; CREATIVITY, *article on* PSYCHOLOGICAL ASPECTS; INTELLIGENCE AND INTELLIGENCE TESTING; PERSONALITY MEASUREMENT; PROJECTIVE METHODS; PSYCHOMETRICS; VOCATIONAL INTEREST TESTING.

TESTING HYPOTHESES
See EXPERIMENTAL DESIGN; HYPOTHESIS TESTING; SIGNIFICANCE, TESTS OF.

THEATER
See DRAMA.

THEMATIC APPERCEPTION TEST (TAT)
See under PROJECTIVE METHODS.

THEOLOGY, PRIMITIVE

The subject matter of theology is the nature of divinities in relation to human experience; thus, as was the ancient classical usage, any discourse on the gods might be called theology. However, it has been significant for anthropological studies of religion that most people have in fact meant something more specific by "theology"—a specialized systematic investigation of the divine, usually undertaken by adherents of particular faiths, in order to deepen and rationalize the understanding of them.

Confessional theology—the logical, historical, and mystical exegesis of an accepted deposit of faith—is quite distinct from the kinds of theology that anthropologists study. But anthropologists have been brought up in societies with pervasive

THEOLOGY, PRIMITIVE *605*

theological teachings, Judaeo–Christian for the most part; and although many have rejected the orthodox interpretation of those teachings, the framework of their investigations into other religions have been formed, often more thoroughly than they have recognized, by the traditions of their own societies. Ethnologists were for a long time drawn into theological debate about the nature and origins of man (see Hodgen 1964). Because Christian theology was part of the background of such prominent anthropological figures as Edward Tylor and James Frazer, the growth of anthropological studies in religion cannot be properly understood without some knowledge of confessional theology.

There are, broadly, three sources from which confessional Christian theology is derived: divine revelation, natural reason, and historical (church) tradition. Many early anthropologists denied, either implicitly or explicitly, the uniqueness of the Christian revelation; however, because of their intellectual background, they could not avoid putting in its place some alternative absolute assessment of religious truth. Using ethnographic evidence, writers like Tylor and Frazer in England and Durkheim in France in effect substituted their own doctrines of the nature of the gods for orthodox doctrine. Frazer showed that beliefs and practices hitherto supposed to be uniquely Christian had parallels among "lowly savages" and therefore represented psychological stages in the evolution of man. Durkheim, by appearing to locate the gods in human social experience only, was also by implication pronouncing on the nature of God. [*See the biographies of* DURKHEIM; FRAZER; TYLOR.]

Christian scholars (Wilhelm Schmidt foremost among them) often tried to accommodate anthropological findings to their own theology. They debated man's original monotheism and the universality of belief in a high god. From a modern standpoint, this discussion attempted to fit ethnographic facts into Christian theological categories.

The Christian acceptance of natural reason as one source of man's knowledge of God provided a model for early anthropological theory. In natural theology it was held that knowledge of God, albeit incomplete, might be arrived at by the exercise of human reason upon natural and moral experience, so that observation of design in nature would lead men to the idea of a designer, God, without supernatural revelation. The theories of many anthropologists followed this line of reasoning; however, belief in natural reason served to replace, not to supplement (as in Christian natural theology), belief in supposedly revealed knowledge. Tylor expressly stated that his idea of *animism*—a belief

in spiritual beings—as constituting the basis of all religion came from treating primitive religious practices as "belonging to theological systems devised by human reason, without supernatural aid or revelation; in other words, as being developments of Natural Religion" ([1871] 1958, vol. 1, p. 427). But this "natural religion" itself and the kind of reason and human psychology it presupposes were themselves more a residue of Christian theology than Tylor seems to have realized. They were not derived from empirical evidence of the behavior and beliefs of peoples ignorant of the Christian revelation but from the remnants of a theology that had first assumed the truth of that revelation.

Durkheim and his followers, almost certainly influenced by the emphasis placed upon the authority of scriptural and historical tradition—the importance of collective solidarity—in their own Hebraic religious upbringing, took a view directly contrary to that of most British scholars. For this French school, religion was not the result of reasoning; it was the foundation of it: "Men owe to it [religion] not only a good part of the substance of their knowledge, but also the form in which this knowledge has been elaborated" (Durkheim [1912] 1954, p. 9). Thus, while the theological bias of what has been called the "English intellectualist" school of interpretation of religion was toward traditional natural theology, that of the French school (composed for the most part of Jewish scholars) was toward the collective experience of the tribe or church as a source of knowledge of the gods.

For both, What really are the gods? and therefore What is God? remained central questions. The answers they gave were often theological, within the universe of discourse set by Judaeo–Christian theological principles. It has only been by finding it possible to avoid this universe of discourse, and thus to pose questions that are not basically theological, that modern studies of specific "primitive" theologies have developed.

Modern studies

The point of departure of modern studies was indicated by Mauss when he said, "A sociological explanation is finished when one has seen *what it is* that people believe and think, and *who are* the people who believe and think that" (quoted in "For a Sociology of India" 1957, p. 13). But, as has been seen, it was by no means easy to begin to approach this limited objective so long as the anthropologist's own theological background was allowed to dictate the selection and arrangement of information, and while, in general, those who made observations were anthropologically untrained and those who formulated theories knew little or nothing of tribal societies at firsthand.

In *The Andaman Islanders* (1922) Radcliffe-Brown, to some extent following Durkheim, tried to escape from the kind of theoretical preoccupations discussed above by presenting the complex of ceremonial behavior, belief, myth, and legend as a systematization of notions and sentiments upon which the organized life of Andaman society depended. Significantly, he deliberately avoided the use of the word "religion," since he could not find a definition of the term that would render it suitable for use in scientific discussions of the beliefs of such primitive peoples as the Andamanese. He argued that when we use the term religion, we inevitably think primarily of what we understand by that term in civilized society. An elaboration of this argument appears in one of the few articles specifically referring to the "theology" of a non-literate people by that term, Evans-Pritchard's "Zande Theology":

In treating of religion . . . we have only to translate primitive religious terms into our own language, and our interpretation of them is already made by the very process of translation. Once we have translated Zande words into such English expressions as "Supreme Being" and "soul," the notions and feelings these words evoke in us already intrude to colour our apprehension of the meaning they possess for Azande. Merely by translating "Mbori" as "Supreme Being" we ascribe to him supremacy, . . . omnipotence, benevolence, and other divine attributes. ([1936] 1963, p. 97)

In this article, Evans-Pritchard's careful examination of the fluidity and imprecision (by Western doctrinal and theological standards) of Zande thought on many religious matters is itself a criticism of the tendency of earlier writers to produce a systematization of foreign beliefs derived not from those beliefs in all the ambiguity of their expression in a foreign language but from literate theological debate.

Nadel's *Nupe Religion* (1954) also exemplified the effort then still required to discard an inappropriate theological language. Nadel (again one of the few writers to discuss "theology" rather than "religion") wrote:

The Nupe deity, then, is something like the *causa causans* of mediaeval philosophy, though the crucial problem of that philosophy, how to reconcile an omnipotent deity with the presence of evil in the world, is not really seen as a problem. Good and evil are both laid into the same creation, as are the various sources of evil—malevolent spirits, disease, witchcraft. Without further speculation about a Free Will, or the weakness of mind and matter, or Satan, the deficiencies of

the world are taken for granted. The only problem in Nupe theology is the actual power of evil, not its origin. And this power is justified, once more without moral speculations, by accepting, simply, the aloofness of the deity. In other words, one does not wonder why God did not create a better world; but one attempts to answer the question—Why does God not better protect Man, who has to live in this world? The answer . . . is that divine concern with the world is limited. (1954, p. 12)

An appreciation of this theological "realism" (if it may be so called to distinguish it from the idealism of much official theology of the universal religions) is to be found in many other writings. Radin's *Primitive Religion* (1937) presents many texts that are to the point. He quoted, for example, from an Eskimo interviewed by Knud Rasmussen:

Why must there be snow and storms and bad weather for hunting, for those who must hunt for our daily food, who seek meat for ourselves and those we love? Why must hunters, after they have slaved all day, return without a catch? Why must the children of my neighbour sit shivering, huddled under a skin-rug, hungry? Why must my old sister suffer pain at the ending of her days? She has done no wrong that we can see but lived her many years and given birth to good strong children.

And with a straightforward appreciation of the ambiguities of life, the Eskimo continues: "Even you cannot answer when we ask you why life is as it is. And so it must be. Our customs all come from life and are directed toward life: we cannot explain, we do not believe in this or that; but the answer lies in what I have just told you. We fear!" (Radin [1937] 1957, p. 54).

When many of the actual sources (native texts) of our knowledge of primitive theology are consulted without foreign theological and philosophical preconceptions, it becomes apparent that earlier theorists were often looking for a precise formulation of belief where none existed or were attempting to fit beliefs into a pattern derived from a type of logical thought that was basically irrelevant to these beliefs. An awareness of this problem underlies Lucien Lévy-Bruhl's idea of "prelogical thought," although unfortunately his work appears to exaggerate the nonlogicality of primitive thought. Certainly the errors of much earlier work on primitive religion may be traced to ignorance of the languages in which it was expressed and an ambition to theorize without an adequate grounding in texts of the kind quoted from the Eskimo above. Notable early exceptions to this tendency are Callaway's *Religious System of the Amazulu* (1868–1870), Hahn's *Tsuni-||Goam: The Supreme Being of the Khoi-Khoi* (1881), and Bleek and Lloyd's *Specimens of Bushman Folklore* (1911).

Modern students have increasingly recognized that theological statements made by members of many preliterate societies may often be confused and self-contradictory if they are simply compared with one another in an effort to elicit a consistent body of doctrine and belief. The same may be true of the statements made by the vast majority of nontheologians in the universal religions. But when beliefs are related to precise human experience, individual and social, and in specific contexts, their real coherence can be grasped. The object of modern studies is therefore not so much an examination of the relationship between a number of theological propositions as it is an examination of their relationship to actual life. By looking at their material this way, anthropologists try to produce what might be called "socio-theologies," which can be regarded as valid both by those who believe in the objective reality of their divinities and those who do not. Moreover, in some modern trends in Christian and comparative theology a similar concern with maintaining a distinction between judgment and understanding may be observed, as, for example, in *The Primal Vision: Christian Presence Amid African Religions* by J. V. Taylor:

We have, then, to ask what is the authentic religious content in the experience of the Muslim, the Hindu, the Buddhist, or whoever he may be. We may, if we have asked humbly and respectfully, still reach the conclusion that our brothers have started from a false premise and reached a faulty conclusion. But we must not arrive at our judgment from outside their religious situation. (1963, pp. 10–11)

In modern anthropological studies, then, the anthropologist's own opinion of the validity of the beliefs he is examining, although it may be expressed, is of marginal relevance. In *Lugbara Religion* (1960), John Middleton, while explicitly disclaiming any intention of presenting the beliefs of this Ugandan people as a system of theology, described the various mystical agents that are believed to cause sickness and death. He stated that he himself assumed that the sequence of events accepted by them is without scientific foundation; however, whether or not this is assumed to be so, his sociological analysis of the way in which a set of beliefs and rituals associated with the ghosts of the dead and spirits is connected with patterns of political authority shows, in a way that a Lugbara himself could accept, what Lugbara religious beliefs imply for this society. Similarly, in *The Work*

of the Gods in Tikopia (1940, vol. 2, p. 376), Raymond Firth expressed the view that the Tikopian gods and spirits are essentially an imaginative and emotional projection of Tikopian social organization, but his detailed exposition of Tikopian ritual and belief is little affected by this judgment of their "true" nature. We may mention here that, as might be expected, people with a highly developed, specialized priesthood like the Maori (see, e.g., Best 1924) or the Dogon (see, e.g., the works of Marcel Griaule and Germaine Dieterlen) produce a more systematic account of their gods, more of a theology in our traditional sense, than those whose priestly institutions are less differentiated from others.

The exploration of the idea of structure in religious belief and ritual—systematic representation of gods as corresponding to structures of thought and experience—distinguishes modern studies from their predecessors. Examples are Evans-Pritchard's study of Nuer religion (1956), in which he examined Nuer spirits as "refractions," in relation to particular situations, of the general concept of spirit; and Lienhardt's *Divinity and Experience: The Religion of the Dinka* (1961), in which Dinka divinities are seen in their relationship to complex combinations of physical, social, and personal experience. In these works, as in many others, the essential ambiguity and ambivalence of divinities as the people understand them—their intrinsic amorality–are recognized. Gods are both creative and destructive, and one figure of God may have both attributes (as in Hinduism). An example of the attempt to resolve what at first sight appear to be contradictory, mutually exclusive interpretations of the nature of a particular god is Dumont's short study entitled "A Structural Definition of a Folk Deity of Tamil Nad: Aiyanar, the Lord" (1953). This god occupies a prominent position in Tamil village religion, yet "his characteristics seem to be chosen at random, so that his nature cannot be grasped through them" ([1953] 1959, p. 75). The central problem of interpretation posed by the god is his "double relation" with the demons on the one hand and the mother goddesses (benign in principle) on the other. Dumont cited earlier authorities with opposed views on the nature of the deity, pointing out their failure to see the double relation as the essential clue to its meaning. He demonstrated that the apparent confusion of characteristics ascribed by the people to Aiyanar ceases to be confusion when he is recognized as a conjunction of theoretically opposed principles: the god is not, for example, *either* a priestly Brahmanic god (as his association at times with "purer" values such as those of vegetarianism suggest) *or* a warrior god commanding demons and thereby associated with impurer habits like meat eating; he is both at the same time. The anthropological study of theologies proceeds as shown in this example, by seeing with as few theological and philosophical presuppositions as possible what "primitive gods" actually do represent—often an expression, rather than a resolution, of the ambiguities of human experience.

GODFREY LIENHARDT

[*For related articles, see the guide under* RELIGION.]

BIBLIOGRAPHY

BEST, ELSDON 1924 *Maori Religion and Mythology.* Wellington (New Zealand): Skinner.

BLEEK, WILHELM H. I.; and LLOYD, LUCY C. 1911 *Specimens of Bushman Folklore.* London: Allen.

CALLAWAY, HENRY (1868–1870) 1885 *The Religious System of the Amazulu.* Folk-lore Society Publication No. 15. London: Trübner.

DUMONT, LOUIS (1953) 1959 A Structural Definition of a Folk Deity of Tamil Nad: Aiyanar, the Lord. *Contributions to Indian Sociology* 3:75–87. → First published as "Définition structurale d'un dieu populaire Tamoul'd" in Volume 241 of the *Journal asiatique.*

DURKHEIM, ÉMILE (1912) 1954 *The Elementary Forms of the Religious Life.* London: Allen & Unwin; New York: Macmillan. → First published as *Les formes élémentaires de la vie religieuse, le système totémique en Australie.* A paperback edition was published in 1961 by Collier.

EVANS-PRITCHARD, E. E. (1936) 1963 Zande Theology. Pages 162–203 in E. E. Evans-Pritchard, *Essays in Social Anthropology.* New York: Free Press. → First published in Volume 19 of *Sudan Notes & Records.*

EVANS-PRITCHARD, E. E. (1956) 1962 *Nuer Religion.* Oxford: Clarendon.

FIRTH, RAYMOND W. 1940 *The Work of the Gods in Tikopia.* 2 vols. London: Humphries.

For a Sociology of India. 1957 *Contributions to Indian Sociology* 1:7–22.

FRANKFORT, HENRI 1948 *Kingship and the Gods: A Study of Ancient Near Eastern Religion as the Integration of Society and Nature.* Univ. of Chicago Press.

HAHN, THEOPHILUS 1881 *Tsuni-IIGoam: The Supreme Being of the Khoi-Khoi.* London: Trübner.

HODGEN, MARGARET T. 1964 *Early Anthropology in the Sixteenth and Seventeenth Centuries.* Philadelphia: Univ. of Pennsylvania Press.

INTERNATIONAL AFRICAN INSTITUTE (1954) 1960 *African Worlds: Studies in the Cosmological Ideas and Social Values of African Peoples.* Edited by Daryll Forde. Oxford Univ. Press.

LÉVY-BRUHL, LUCIEN (1910) 1926 *How Natives Think.* London: Allen & Unwin. → First published as *Les fonctions mentales dans les sociétés primitives.*

LIENHARDT, GODFREY 1961 *Divinity and Experience: The Religion of the Dinka.* Oxford: Clarendon.

MIDDLETON, JOHN 1960 *Lugbara Religion: Ritual and Authority Among an East African People.* Oxford Univ. Press.

NADEL, S. F. 1954 *Nupe Religion.* Glencoe, Ill.: Free Press.

RADCLIFFE-BROWN, A. R. (1922) 1948 *The Andaman Islanders.* Glencoe, Ill.: Free Press.

RADIN, PAUL (1937) 1957 *Primitive Religion: Its Nature and Origin.* New York: Dover.

SUNDKLER, BENGT G. M. (1948) 1964 *Bantu Prophets in South Africa.* 2d ed. Published for the International African Institute. Oxford Univ. Press.

TAYLOR, JOHN V. 1963 *The Primal Vision: Christian Presence Amid African Religions.* Philadelphia: Fortress Press.

TYLOR, EDWARD B. (1871) 1958 *Primitive Culture: Researches Into the Development of Mythology, Philosophy, Religion, Art and Custom.* 2 vols. Gloucester, Mass.: Smith. → Volume 1: *Origins of Culture.* Volume 2: *Religion in Primitive Culture.*

THERAPY

See CLINICAL PSYCHOLOGY; MENTAL DISORDERS, TREATMENT OF; PSYCHOANALYSIS, *article on* THERAPEUTIC METHODS.

THERMONUCLEAR WAR
See NUCLEAR WAR.

THINKING

I. THE FIELD — W. Edgar Vinacke
II. COGNITIVE ORGANIZATION AND PROCESSES — Robert B. Zajonc

I
THE FIELD

Thinking is a subdivision within the broad psychological field that studies cognitive aspects of behavior. In a general sense, thinking pertains to the effects of certain kinds of prior experience upon the current activities of the person. Specifically, it is concerned on the one hand with the covert, symbolic processes that precede and/or accompany observable responses. On the other hand, it refers to a special kind of behavior itself, namely, that which occurs when previously learned responses are organized, or reorganized, in situations differing from the ones in which the original learning took place. We shall endeavor to treat thinking in these terms, although distinctions between the generally recognized categories of cognitive behavior are really a matter of emphasis, rather than of kind. Thus, perception stresses the immediate relations between stimuli and the person's response, whereas thinking emphasizes some meditational process between previous learning and response patterns or response sequences. Learning focuses upon the acquisition of new responses—the changes that take place during exposure to particular kinds of situations, usually with the specification of meeting certain standards of performance. Thinking, in contrast, deals with the later effects of response acquisition, with special attention to the combination and recombination of responses. Memory has to do with the processes of storing and retrieving of learned responses, whereas thinking involves the utilization of the products of memory as the individual copes with internal needs and external environmental demands.

There is, then, no sharp and sustained distinction between the several categories of cognitive behavior, and, in fact, a considerable community of interest exists among psychologists who identify themselves with one or another of these subdivisions. The phenomena assigned to each category depend upon the sorts of questions a researcher asks and upon the kinds of data he wants to collect. Theoretical orientations provide still another means by which to distinguish subinterests within the domain of cognitive processes. We shall touch upon such matters below.

Special human characteristics. First, however, we must point out that thinking, in contrast to other aspects of cognitive behavior, is especially characteristic of human beings. While most psychologists familiar with recent experimental work would probably concede that at least some degree of all the behavioral characteristics of human beings occurs also in animals lower in the evolutionary scale, certain abilities are not only unusually highly developed in man but are also particularly apparent in those processes which we call thinking. These kinds of abilities include the ones described below.

Learning and memory. The human being can acquire great amounts of knowledge that can be stored over long periods of time. Thus, the potentiality of calling upon responses not immediately evoked by the present situation is a distinctive feature of thinking. In this sense it contrasts with all purely reflexive or situation-bound behavior.

Intrinsic symbolic activities. The experience stored in memory can be called upon in rapid and highly efficient fashion without the necessity of reproducing the complete gross motor or sensory responses that occurred during original learning. These implicit responses may continue indefinitely in innumerable combinations, thus permitting the traces of experience widely separated in time to influence the character of ongoing behavior. It also permits the individual to cope with a problem situation at a time long after it is overtly presented —the phenomenon of the *delayed reaction*, which is clearly very highly developed in human beings compared to lower animals.

Concept formation and conceptualization. An especially striking characteristic of symbolic processes is the ability to organize very many discrete impressions into inclusive systems called *concepts;* this ability is not confined to the packaging of information into fixed units, for the individual can, within wide limits, produce new and varied combinations of impressions as they are required. We need, then, to realize that thinking is not a matter alone of utilizing organizations of experience (concepts) but also of continuously organizing experience (conceptualizing) in relation to environmental objects.

Planning, foresight, and control. The foregoing special abilities make possible the establishment of systems by which extensive sequences of responses may be tied together and repeated. Psychological names for such mechanisms include attitudes and sets, values, superego and ego regulative processes, expectancies, cognitive styles, and associative tendencies. An exceedingly important aspect of cognitive control is the ability to anticipate future goals and contingencies by substituting symbolic representations for them. In this way, a person can take into account in the present something that is expected or hoped for in the future. Thus, thinking links the past and the future to the present by attitudinal processes.

Reasoning and imagination. In the tradition, thinking has been divided into the general categories of *reasoning* and *imagination,* with various subdivisions under each heading. Reasoning refers to planful, controlled symbolic processes related to goals and to the utilization of information in prescribed forms according to rules of procedure. Imagination refers to processes determined solely or mainly by intrinsic conditions and connotes the reoccurrence of past experience somewhat at random, or at least without regard to its accuracy, form, or direction. Deductive logic, inductive inference, and problem-solving activities are usually treated as varieties of reasoning. Fantasy and dreams are representative of imagination. It is not easy to place original or creative thinking in either category, since it partakes of reasoning by producing a tangible and orderly product but also resembles imagination because it calls in new and unexpected ways upon the combination of diverse past impressions in response to intrinsic motivational states.

Influence of psychoanalysis. The traditional distinctions have been greatly modified by the influence of psychoanalysis, which from the beginning has seen an intimate relation between organismic conditions and environmental demands. In perhaps oversimplified form we may say that Freud saw internal drives as influencing thinking through the *pleasure principle* (needs and wishes), whereas the environment imposes upon thinking the *reality principle*. In this manner he differentiated between primary-process and secondary-process thinking. Gardner Murphy (1947) has elaborated these ideas by suggesting that the onward course of thinking is a function of the interplay of *autistic* factors (roughly corresponding to primary-process thinking) and of *realistic* forces (corresponding to secondary-process thinking). Cognitive activity is really neither one nor the other but a resultant of both. It is simultaneously a response to intrinsic motivational states and to goal or stimulus conditions. However, the two kinds of forces are not always equal in strength but rather contribute in various proportions to cognitive activity, so that we may formulate a continuum of processes between autistic and realistic poles.

Attitudes and group problem solving. The modern treatment of thinking also places considerable emphasis upon the learning and operation of attitudes—corresponding in large degree to the Freudian concept of ego mechanisms—and to the central place that most behavioristic theories accord to the role of "steering" functions in the motivation system, as exemplified in concepts like "habit" and "expectation." Finally, the past few decades have seen a rapidly mounting interest in group problem solving. Although we shall here omit this area, it must be regarded as an important subdivision within the general topic of thinking.

Methods

The broadly oriented student will find that he cannot become versed in the subject of human thinking without calling upon theory and research from all the social sciences as well as from physiological psychology. There really are no techniques that can properly be assigned specifically to the psychology of thinking in the way that tachistoscopic procedures may be linked with the investigation of perception. Thus, research dealing with the cognitive behavior of children frequently demands the use of semiclinical interviews, like those so productively utilized by Jean Piaget. The examination of the role of the sociocultural context in shaping the character of experience must rely heavily upon cross-cultural methods. The investigation of attitudes and attitude change frequently requires the application of mass survey techniques. Efforts to discover the neural bases of thinking inevitably lead us to the electroencephalogram, the electrical stimulation of the brain, and the effects of drugs.

As in other aspects of experimental psychology, psychometric devices play a large part in facilitating investigation; for example, by providing objective definitions of personality variables, by yielding systematic measures of cognitive performance, and by equating groups of subjects. An excellent illustration is the increasing use of projective tests to assess latent motivational influences in thinking.

Nevertheless, the major research on thinking falls within the experimental tradition of psychology. It is a laboratory discipline, adapting to the special kinds of problems described above all the techniques of inductive verification of hypotheses, the manipulation and control of variables, quantitative analysis, and statistical inference. Most psychologists would maintain that the delay in scientific study of thought processes is more a function of the special difficulties that arise in systematic measurement and observation than in the inherent characteristics of the processes themselves.

Historical development

If we look within the general science of psychology, which became established after the middle of the last century, we can formulate three loosely defined stages in the systematic study of thought processes.

Descriptive phase. At the outset there was an intensive effort to identify the essential characteristics of thinking, building upon the classical categories proposed in Greek philosophy and the logical analyses in which British associationism became so sophisticated. Chiefly instrumental at this stage was the movement called "structuralism," which was founded in Germany by Wilhelm Wundt and transplanted to the United States by Edward B. Titchener of Cornell University. In fact, these psychologists saw the central problem of psychology to be the investigation of conscious mental activities (really including all of the processes which we would now include under the heading of "thinking"). The acquisition of experience, its reappearance as intrinsic activities in various forms and combinations, the effect of environmental stimulation via the phenomenon of attention, distinctions between imaginative and realistic (or logical) mental events —these matters constituted the core of their interests. In keeping with the science of that period, these psychologists sought to identify the basic "elements" of mental activity and to this end proposed sensations, images, and feelings. Thinking was conceived to be primarily a matter of the occurrence of images (the traces of prior experience) and their translation into ideas. It followed from the theories of this school of psychology that one must examine the postulated elements and their interrelations; since the elements are intrinsic, one must look at them inside, so to speak, the boundaries of consciousness. As a consequence the distinctive method of psychology became *introspection,* the careful, controlled, precisely reported scrutiny of the expert psychologist's own mental events.

Another influential description of thought was contributed by William James, who wrote aptly about the "stream of thought." In this doctrine he emphasized the continuous, organized, and dynamic properties of thinking.

Francis Galton added another descriptive dimension in his studies of imagery. By means of questionnaires and interviews he sought to determine individual differences in the incidence and patterning of imagery, in the changes that occur with age, and the like.

The final episode in this early descriptive stage came with the "imageless thought" controversy, associated with the Würzburg School of Oswald Külpe, N. Ach, and others, as well as with names like Robert S. Woodworth and Alfred Binet. These investigators pointed out that cognitive processes may occur in which no evidence of imagery could be secured, for example, in rapid mental arithmetic. Rather, there seemed to be some other efficient mechanism which, once established, served to evoke directly a sequence of cognitive events. Such "determining tendencies" or "sets" were themselves regarded as significant properties of thinking. At the least they had to be included as an additional component of cognition, and at the most they cast basic doubt on the whole concept of a few basic elements. Since that time, sets and attitudes have played an increasing part in the account of thinking.

The end of structuralism was further hastened both by the advocacy of new (and perhaps better) behavioral units, such as stimulus–response bonds, and by an attack against the invocation of units of any kind launched by gestalt psychologists like Max Wertheimer, Wolfgang Köhler, Kurt Koffka, and Kurt Lewin. From a methodological standpoint, exclusive reliance upon introspection drastically receded when the behaviorist John B. Watson and his successors rejected the notion of consciousness as the proper subject matter of psychology, insisting upon the objective definition of variables, the requirement that observation be confined to observable, overt response, and the necessity to emulate the replicability of experiments of the physical sciences.

Laboratory survey of phenomena.   Although the study of thinking has not had nearly as intensive an emphasis (at least in America) as intelligence, learning, and perception—for reasons which are interesting but beyond the scope of this article—nevertheless, throughout the first half of this century there was a steady flow of empirical research dealing with thinking. The salient characteristic of this work has been a sort of one-shot effort to explore phenomena displayed in some relatively circumscribed experimental situation. A good number of these experiments have been influenced by developments in learning theory, intelligence testing, or other aspects of psychology, and many of the concepts frequently employed to describe thought processes have been imported from these areas; an example is "trial-and-error" behavior in problem solving.

The dominant theoretical ideas have come from the dynamic emphasis of American functionalism, the reliance upon situational variables typical of behaviorism, and the organizational principles central to gestalt psychology. Two classes of phenomena have received the most attention, namely, concept formation and problem solving. It is noteworthy that both autistic and creative processes have been infrequent subjects of experimental investigation. It is true that a large body of information has accumulated about behavior in projective-test situations, but the practical clinical applications have vastly overshadowed possible implications for an understanding of thinking itself.

With regard to concept formation, the stage was set by Clark Hull's monograph, published in 1920, and by Piaget's observations of children a few years later. The traditions thus founded have led to a compendium of facts concerning classification and naming behavior, together with a listing of the conditions which influence the efficiency of or changes in this behavior. Virtually all of the experiments have employed one of two basic procedures. In one, subjects have been exposed to a series of stimulus objects with varying properties, with instructions to learn the basis on which groups of those objects can be correctly named. This might be termed an inductive procedure. In the other, subjects have been presented with an array of stimulus objects and asked to sort them into meaningful classes—a procedure with a more deductive character. (Of course, in practice it is quite difficult to preserve the distinction between induction and deduction because subjects readily shift from one approach to the other.)

By these means many phenomena have been reported, but, in general, they point to the fact that concepts are most easily evolved when the stimuli are simple, clearly defined, concrete, and free from competing cues. The work of Piaget and other child psychologists has strikingly revealed the progression from egocentric and prelogical conceptualization during early childhood to the more objective, logical, consistent, and systematic formulations of the adult. The work of L. S. Vigotsky, Kurt Goldstein, and others has helped to clarify differences between concrete and abstract conceptual behavior. In practically all of this research emphasis has been placed upon the objective, or extensional, aspects of concept formation rather than upon idiosyncratic, personal, or intensional aspects.

In the investigation of problem solving, subjects are typically presented with a task which requires the unraveling, as it were, of complex steps to a goal or the organization of available resources (materials for construction, verbal responses, general knowledge, etc.) to discover the correct solution. Popular tasks include mazes, mechanical and arithmetical puzzles, anagrams and word building, and construction problems. A considerable contribution comes from animal experiments, such as Edward L. Thorndike's studies using problem boxes and Wolfgang Köhler's studies of the use of implements by chimpanzees (1917). Other pioneer investigators have been Karl Duncker, Max Wertheimer, Otto Selz, F. C. Bartlett, George Katona, and Norman R. F. Maier. For many years, too, notable contributions emerged from the laboratory at Columbia University under the encouraging influence of Robert S. Woodworth.

All of this research has revealed a wide variety of phenomena, including the manipulative and exploratory characteristics of trial-and-error behavior in tasks such as maze learning, in which the subject must work out a definite but unpredictable sequence of steps to the goal, and the "recentering" (or reorganizing) behavior that follows an understanding of the requirements for attaining a solution, such as in "insight" problems. Other points receiving attention are the formulation and use of hypotheses, the operation of sets (or "direction"), and the transfer of principles discovered in one task to other problems.

Systematic investigation based on theory. The period of sheer phenomenon collecting appears virtually to have ended. Instead, we see now a general attempt to bring the study of thinking into line with other aspects of cognitive behavior. The sophisticated laboratory techniques and hypothesis testing characteristic of research in perception and learning are coming, therefore, to be applied to problem solving and concept formation with, as usual, research in imagination and creative think-

ing lagging behind. It is very likely that the second half of this century will bring quite a new look to our understanding of human thinking. If this perspective is correct, investigators will derive hypotheses from the viable theories of the day and test them in elaborately planned experiments, skillfully building experimental manipulations and controls into them. This strategy is already clearly evident in the investigation of concept formation. It is too early to cite with confidence the names of psychologists to whom the history of this trend will be indebted. Very influential, however, are those individuals, like O. Hobart Mowrer and Ernest R. Hilgard, who are seeking to integrate principles from the various theories of learning and to develop implications for complex aspects of human cognitive processes. On the other hand, students of personality, who take their departure from psychoanalytic, organismic, and Jungian theory and who inevitably locate thinking at a central position in their treatment of behavior, are certain to be equally influential.

Current trends

Following World War II there has been far greater interest in human thought processes than at any other period since the dominance of structuralism. With respect to both theory and experiment, a wide diversity of treatment is apparent. Future historians of the subject may well judge that the several basic fields of psychology have rapidly begun to converge on the investigation of thinking. Perhaps it is not too rash to suggest that symbolic aspects of behavior have once more moved toward the center of the psychological stage. In so brief a survey of these problems we cannot, of course, do more than hint at these developments. Physiological psychology has increasingly moved beyond peripheral and autonomic reactions toward subcortical and cortical functions. In developmental psychology the study of growth, maturation, and intelligence has receded in favor of more attention to concept formation, the establishment of attitudes, and the effects of socialization upon the context of experience. Cognitive theory and conditions of social interaction have played a steadily greater role in the advance of personality–social psychology. Clinical psychologists continue to search actively in many directions for an understanding of the cognitive processes that can account for symptom formation, therapeutic effects, and client–counselor relationships. Educational psychologists are paying steadily more effective attention to the pupil as a problem solver, to the classroom as a medium for the establishment of concepts and attitudes, and to creative thinking. Finally, the loosely defined field of general experimental psychology itself has tried to adapt the techniques painstakingly evolved in the investigation of perception and learning to problem solving, conceptualizing, and even imaginative behavior.

We can perhaps identify briefly six major trends.

Complex learning. The neobehaviorist tradition has sought to extend principles developed in the study of conditioning, verbal rote learning (memorizing), and discrimination learning to the wider area of problem solving. In this respect thinking represents an application in new or modified forms of previously acquired responses, and the solution or outcome of the elaborate sequence of activities evoked thus becomes a part of the subject's response repertory (hence, the phrase "complex learning"). As we have mentioned above, a very active phase of this development has to do with naming and classifying behavior ("concept formation"). Especially significant has been the formulating of broad organizing procedures, or strategies, manifested by the subject. For instance, he may focus upon the successive instances in a series of stimulus objects, or he may look for ways to fit new instances into a general classification.

Numerous investigators are pursuing the stimulus, situational, and personality conditions that influence the adoption of such strategies and that determine the efficiency with which solutions to concept problems are attained.

Factor analysis. The attempt to discover the fundamental categories of human cognitive processes has a long history. A modern approach is the sorting out of correlations among performances in wide varieties of tasks and the subsequent derivation of general factors that account for the common denominators among them. This procedure is especially familiar in the systematic development of intelligence tests. This approach has been applied to a much wider range of behavior than that usually encompassed by tests. Although Charles E. Spearman, L. L. Thurstone, and Raymond B. Cattell have all contributed notably to this method, Joy P. Guilford has been especially influential in its application to thinking. His "model of intellect" is an effort to organize those aspects of cognition, which he calls "operations," "products," and "contents," into a comprehensive system. What effect his theory may have upon research cannot yet be predicted, apart from its contribution to the objective measurement of many sorts of human abilities otherwise insufficiently represented by tests. Nevertheless there can be no doubt that factor analytic

studies will continue to be an active part of the psychology of thinking. [See FACTOR ANALYSIS, article on PSYCHOLOGICAL APPLICATIONS.]

Mediation theory. Recognition that the simple S–R model of behavior is inadequate to account for the more complex aspects of human behavior, especially in thinking, has led to a determined assault on the description of inferred processes that intervene between stimulus and response. The theory of "implicit speech" stated by the behaviorist John B. Watson has been further developed for this purpose in combination with the investigation of the role of language in determining the character and course of thinking. There are now many psychologists who concern themselves with the hypothesis that words act as responses to mediate between stimulus and response and that trains of words constitute much (if not all) of thinking. Research in this approach focuses both upon the properties of emitted words themselves and upon their inferred implicit organization and operation (attitudinal and conceptual mechanisms).

Information theory. The development of electronic computers has stimulated a great deal of interest in their possible analogy to human thinking. Since it has become increasingly evident that computers can be made to perform complex operations involving processes similar to those inferred to characterize the brain, it is natural to scrutinize these operations for clues to the basic properties of thought processes. Thus, the information storage system of the computer resembles "memory," the rules and procedures of a program have affinites with regulating and conceptualizing functions, and feedback devices are not unlike the intrinsic self-propagating circuits of the brain. Most advocates of the computer model of thinking are understandably cautious about equating it with human cognitive processes, preferring to search for parallels between two different kinds of information-processing systems. Nevertheless there can be no doubt that the investigation of computers is leading to fruitful hypotheses to be tested with human subjects. [See INFORMATION THEORY.]

Motivational variables. Although clinical psychology has always made dynamic factors central to its understanding of behavior—perhaps it could not exist otherwise—the rest of the profession has often ignored them to an extraordinary degree or, at best, given them superficial lip service while occupying itself with other matters. Since World War II, however, the conditions which instigate, regulate, and adjust behavior have moved to the forefront of interest. There has been a hardheaded

—often brilliant—attack on theoretical problems with principles derived from psychoanalysis and its successors, organismic psychology, field and biosocial theory, existential philosophy, and Jungian analytic psychology. Lagging only a step or two behind, experimental methodology has forged ahead in many directions to incorporate both intrinsic personality variables and extrinsic situational conditions into an intensive empirical exploration of the factors responsible both for consistency and change in cognitive behavior. The continuum described above between autistic and realistic thinking is inescapably linked at both poles to motivational conditions, on the one hand with internal needs, drives, and motives and on the other hand with goals and other environmental demands. In this fashion the intimate relation between motivation and thought processes is coming increasingly to be understood and, accordingly, to be investigated. It can confidently be predicted that this represents a fundamental trend and one that will vastly influence the future treatment of human thinking. This means that the course of thinking is coming to be viewed in terms of complex interactions among intrinsic properties of the person and the special situational conditions that accompany his problem solving and imaginative activities. [See DRIVES; MOTIVATION.]

Creativity. As our society has steadily placed greater and greater emphasis upon education, technological improvement, and planned cultural change, it has become more crucial to discover talent and to foster its exercise. These requirements have forced psychologists to search for the conditions in the acquisition, organization, and utilization of experience associated with original thinking in all the diverse fields of the arts and sciences. The current period is marked by efforts to investigate these matters in personality development, the classroom, and adult cognitive functioning. We can be sure that this trend will continue.

The six kinds of interest just summarized present a host of profound challenges to psychological scientists. The numerous problems yet to be solved emphasize the empirical infancy of the psychology of thinking. There has been notable progress in moving beyond the maze running of the rat, the rote learning and mechanical puzzles of the college student, and the listing of cognitive oddities characteristic of the psychotic. Now we have a firm recognition that implicit, mediating processes can be treated meaningfully as psychological variables; and we have a concerted endeavor to investigate the relations between cognitive processes and the context of motivational conditions which bring them about.

W. EDGAR VINACKE

[*Directly related are the entries* ATTITUDES; COGNITIVE THEORY; CONCEPT FORMATION; PROBLEM SOLVING; REASONING AND LOGIC. *Other relevant material may be found in* CREATIVITY; DEVELOPMENTAL PSYCHOLOGY, *article on* A THEORY OF DEVELOPMENT; GESTALT THEORY; INTELLIGENCE AND INTELLIGENCE TESTING; LEARNING; PERCEPTION; *and in the biographies of* BARTLETT; BINET; GOLDSTEIN; HULL; JAMES; KOFFKA; KÖHLER; KÜLPE; LEWIN; THORNDIKE; TITCHENER; WATSON; WERTHEIM; WOODWORTH; WUNDT.]

BIBLIOGRAPHY

BARTLETT, FREDERIC C. (1932) 1950 *Remembering: A Study in Experimental and Social Psychology.* Cambridge Univ. Press.

BARTLETT, FREDERIC C. 1958 *Thinking.* London: Allen & Unwin; New York: Basic Books.

BERLYNE, D. E. 1965 *Structure and Direction in Thinking.* New York: Wiley.

BROWN, ROGER W. 1958 *Words and Things.* Glencoe, Ill.: Free Press.

BRUNER, JEROME S.; GOODNOW, J. J.; and AUSTIN, G. A. 1956 *A Study of Thinking.* New York: Wiley.

DUNCKER, KARL 1945 On Problem-solving. *Psychological Monographs* 58, no. 5.

FLAVELL, JOHN H. 1963 *The Developmental Psychology of Jean Piaget.* Princeton, N.J.: Van Nostrand.

HALL, CALVIN S.; and LINDZEY, GARDNER 1957 *Theories of Personality.* New York: Wiley; London: Chapman.

HARVEY, O. J.; HUNT, D. E.; and SCHRODER, H. M. 1961 *Conceptual Systems and Personality Organization.* New York: Wiley.

HAYAKAWA, SAMUEL I. (1949) 1964 *Language in Thought and Action.* 2d ed. New York: Harcourt.

HUMPHREY, GEORGE 1951 *Thinking: An Introduction to Its Experimental Psychology.* London: Methuen; New York: Wiley.

HUNT, EARL B. 1962 *Concept Learning: An Information Processing Problem.* New York: Wiley.

JOHNSON, DONALD McEWEN 1955 *The Psychology of Thought and Judgment.* New York: Harper.

KÖHLER, WOLFGANG (1917) 1956 *The Mentality of Apes.* 2d ed., rev. London: Routledge. → First published in German. A paperback edition was published in 1959 by Random House.

KRECH, DAVID; CRUTCHFIELD, RICHARD S.; and BALLACHEY, E. L. (1948) 1962 *Individual in Society: A Textbook of Social Psychology.* New York: McGraw-Hill. → First published as *Theory and Problems of Social Psychology,* by David Krech and Richard S. Crutchfield.

LEEPER, ROBERT 1951 Cognitive Processes. Pages 730–757 in S. S. Stevens (editor), *Handbook of Experimental Psychology.* New York: Wiley.

MALTZMAN, IRVING 1955 Thinking: From a Behavioristic Point of View. *Psychological Review* 62:275–286.

MOWRER, O. HOBART 1960 *Learning Theory and the Symbolic Processes.* New York: Wiley.

MURPHY, GARDNER 1947 *Personality: A Biosocial Approach to Origins and Structure.* New York: Harper.

NEW YORK ACADEMY OF SCIENCES 1960 *Fundamentals of Psychology: The Psychology of Thinking.* New York Academy of Sciences, Annals, Vol. 91, Article 1. Edited by Ernest Harms. New York: The Academy.

OSGOOD, CHARLES E. (1953) 1959 *Method and Theory in Experimental Psychology.* New York: Oxford Univ. Press. → See especially pages 603–637 on "Problem-solving and Insight," pages 638–679 on "Thinking," and pages 680–727 on "Language Behavior."

OSGOOD, CHARLES E.; SUCI, G. J.; and TANNENBAUM, P. H. (1957) 1961 *The Measurement of Meaning.* Urbana: Univ. of Illinois Press.

PIAGET, JEAN (1927) 1930 *The Child's Conception of Physical Causality.* New York: Harcourt; London: Routledge. → First published as *La causalité physique chez l'enfant.*

RAPAPORT, DAVID (editor and translator) 1956 *Organization and Pathology of Thought: Selected Sources.* Austen Riggs Foundation, Stockbridge, Mass., Monograph No. 1. New York: Columbia Univ. Press.

ROKEACH, MILTON 1960 *The Open and Closed Mind: Investigations Into the Nature of Belief Systems and Personality Systems.* New York: Basic Books.

RUSSELL, DAVID H. 1956 *Children's Thinking.* Boston: Ginn.

VINACKE, W. EDGAR 1952 *The Psychology of Thinking.* New York: McGraw-Hill.

WERTHEIMER, MAX (1945) 1961 *Productive Thinking.* Enl. ed., edited by Michael Wertheimer. London: Tavistock. → Contains a bibliography of Max Wertheimer's publications.

WOODWORTH, ROBERT S.; and SCHLOSBERG, HAROLD (1938) 1960 *Experimental Psychology.* Rev. ed. New York: Holt. → Woodworth was the sole author of the 1938 edition. See especially pages 814–848.

II

COGNITIVE ORGANIZATION AND PROCESSES

In his "Glossary of Some Terms Used in the Objective Science of Behavior" Verplanck took "cognition" as a term that pretends to theoretical status but that is not reducible to empirical terms, "a hypothetical stimulus–stimulus association or perceptual organization postulated to account for expectancies." He believed that "it is not possible as yet to define [it] in other than intuitive terminology, except for trivial cases" (1957, p. 7).

Verplanck's skepticism is less justified today, although there still is some confusion about the meaning of "cognition." The meaning of this term can be clarified, however, if it is used to refer, not to an identifiable psychological *process*, but to a *problem area* with specifiable research focuses. Let us first distinguish between perception, sensation, and cognition as such problem areas.

"Perception" represents the most general area and includes both sensation and cognition. The term refers to those psychological problems in which one seeks to explain the systematic variation of response by relating this response variation to some systematic variation in stimulation. Perception differs from other interest areas in psychology because in it *stimulation* is considered the critical set of antecedents for the explanation of response variation. In other areas—the study of motivation, for example—response variability is accounted for in terms of variation in the states of deprivation and arousal; in the study of learning, in terms of practice and reinforcement.

Both sensation and cognition deal with the relations between response variation and stimulation, but they differ in the way these relations are conceived. The sensory psychologist analyzes perceptual processes, with an emphasis on the transformation of energy. He measures the input in physical terms, and he wishes to know how this physical energy is transformed by the organism into other forms. In the case of vision, he may begin with electromagnetic energy, observe its transformation into biochemical energy at the retina and then into neural energy along the afferent or central pathways, and perhaps trace it to its fate in overt muscular responses. [*See* HEARING; PERCEPTION; SENSES; VISION.]

For the cognitive theorist, the analysis of the relations between response and stimulus variations focuses, not on energy, but on information. He, too, begins with the stimulus, but he is primarily concerned with its properties as a *signal*. Signals are the same physical events which the sensory psychologist calls *stimuli*. However, they are viewed, not in terms of their energy characteristics, but in terms of the information they carry.

The cognitive theorist may be concerned with the acquiring and processing of information, with further cognitive consequences of this process, or with utilization of information. He may be concerned with the way the individual detects signals, distinguishes one from another, or identifies them. But in order for the person to identify signals, he must have a *code*, which is a set of rules for mapping signals into *symbols*. Language, for instance, is such a code, but gestures of humans and songs of birds are others. The analysis may also be concerned with the sequential arrangement of symbols into *messages* and with the extraction of information from these messages and its utilization. In these processes the individual utilizes information acquired in the past, codes, rules of message sequencing (e.g., syntax), and inferential heuristics. The totality of this apparatus has become known as the individual's cognitive organization. [*See*

COMMUNICATION, ANIMAL; INFORMATION THEORY; LANGUAGE; REASONING AND LOGIC.]

Cognitive organization

Theorists dealing with cognitive organization stress different aspects: some are concerned with the components and elements of cognitive organization (Kelley 1955; Peak 1958; Harvey et al. 1961; Zajonc 1960a); others are concerned with the ways these components relate to one another (Asch 1946; Anderson 1962; Heider 1946), or with the consequences they have for attitudes and behavior (Festinger 1957). Abelson and Rosenberg (1958) constructed a theory that stresses the implicative and inferential character of cognition. They considered elements of cognitive organization to be "cognitive representations of 'things,' concrete and abstract," to which individuals can attach verbal labels. Three types of elements were distinguished: *actors* (oneself, other people, groups, etc.), *means* (actions, instrumental responses, etc.), and *ends* (outcomes). These elements relate to each other by four types of relations: positive, negative, null, and ambivalent. Two elements together with the relation between them form units called *basic sentences*. Eight *psycho-logical* rules for the implications among basic sentences are postulated. Where A, B, and C are actors and "things" and p and n are positive and negative relations, respectively, one rule is: AnB and BnC implies ApC. For example:

(1) India (A) opposes (n) U.S. Far Eastern policy (B);
(2) U.S. Far Eastern policy (B) is directed against (n) communism (C);
(3) *Therefore*, India (A) is in favor (p) of communism (C).

Another rule in the Abelson–Rosenberg psycho-logic is the following: ApB and BnC implies AnC. Furthermore, if within the given structure matrix we have the four sentences

(1) AnB; (2) BnC; (3) ApD; (4) DnC,

ApC and AnC are *both* implied. And if this arises, the two contradictory implications are combined into one in which A is connected to C by an *ambivalent* (a) relation. A structure without any ambivalent relations is called *balanced*, and a structure with ambivalent relations, *imbalanced*. Like other writers (Heider 1946; Festinger 1957; Osgood & Tannenbaum 1955), Abelson and Rosenberg assume that balanced states are preferred and sought.

In some cases the conceptualization of cognitive organization has been greatly influenced by the gestalt approach. Asch (1946), for instance, read to one group of subjects the following list of characteristics, descriptive of a fictitious person: intelligent, skillful, industrious, warm, determined, practical, cautious. Another group of subjects received the same list except that "cold" was substituted for "warm." Both groups were then asked to endorse on a checklist of 18 traits (generous, wise, strong, honest, etc.) those characteristics that applied to the fictitious person. For some traits, vast differences were obtained as a function of the warm–cold variable.

Asch argued that total impressions are formed not simply by averaging or adding the array of the characteristics given. Some traits are central—they have a great impact on the over-all impression—while others are peripheral and have relatively little influence. In short, impressions are formed according to gestalt-like principles, and they must be analyzed by an appeal to gestalt-like laws.

Recent results, however, suggest that Asch's findings can be accurately described by a simple averaging model or by a weighted averaging model. In one experiment, for instance, Anderson (1962) asked subjects to rate for "likableness" hypothetical persons described by sets of three adjectives. Anderson's data showed that there was an average correlation of 0.967 between the observed scale value of the over-all impression and the average of the scale values of the three adjectives constituting the set.

But in some cases a simple summation of traits also predicts an over-all impression (e.g., Fishbein & Hunter 1964). It should be noted that the averaging model predicts that the compound can *never* be more extreme than the most extreme of its components. The summation model, on the other hand, predicts that the compound is *always* more extreme than the most extreme of its components. Manis, Gleason, and Dawes (1966) have recently proposed a model that constitutes a compromise between the averaging and the summation models and that seems to fit data rather well.

While averaging, summation, and their combination serve well to describe simple cognitive organizations, more complex instances involve interactions and interrelations of cognitive elements that must be described by more complex concepts. Zajonc (1960a), for instance, defined various morphological properties of complex cognitive structures and demonstrated that they are profoundly affected by the function which the cognitive organization serves. For instance, if the individual is "tuned in" for receiving information, he will exhibit a more flexible structure than when he is tuned in for transmission.

Other studies of cognitive organization are more concerned with its content. Especially interesting are those that attempt to relate cognitive organization to the individual's social environment. It is assumed that because of their extended commerce with the society of which they are part, individuals develop subjective and private "theories" about it. On the subjective level, they form principles about interpersonal relations and about behavior in society. These principles serve an adaptive function because they help the individual to predict, to anticipate, to understand, and to take part in the network of social interrelationships. Recent research began analyzing these subjective theories, called *schemata*, emphasizing primarily schemata of such interpersonal relations as liking, influence, dominance, trust, etc. De Soto and Kuethe (1958; 1959) and De Soto (1960) have shown, for instance, that social schemata characterize the liking relation as symmetrical (i.e., reciprocal) and transitive, while schemata characterize the dominance relation as asymmetrical and transitive.

Cognitive consistency

Recent research and theory have paid considerable attention to the processes of cognitive change. It is commonly assumed today that the central dynamic of cognitive change is a striving for consistency. Three approaches to the study of cognitive consistency will be reviewed: structural balance, congruity, and cognitive dissonance.

Structural balance.   The principle of balance was derived from Heider's work on the perception of causality (1944), which led him to specify a set of conditions underlying unit formation. The basic assumption in this general approach is that cognitive units tend to seek steady states. Basic in determining the state of a unit is the "dynamic character" (positive or negative) of its parts. For example, a unit might consist of a person, p, and of his action, x. Each of these two parts might be evaluated positively or negatively and, hence, have either a positive or negative dynamic character. If parts of a unit have the same dynamic character, steady state (balance) is said to exist. When parts of a unit have different dynamic character, disequilibrium arises, and there will be a tendency to segregate the parts from each other (Heider 1946, p. 107). [*See* HOMEOSTASIS.]

The parts of cognitive units consist of persons ($p, o, q, \cdots$), objects ($x, y, z, \cdots$), and their relations to one another. The relations considered by balance theory are either *sentiment relations*, $+L$ and $-L$ (e.g., Bill likes Joe; Joe dislikes candy; Bill feels neighborly toward Jim), or *unit relations* (e.g., Bill owns a car; Joe reminds Al of an acquaintance; Jim built this bookcase). Steady (balanced) states are defined as follows: "A dyad is balanced if the relations between the two entities are all positive . . . or all negative. . . . Disharmony results when relations of different sign character exist. A triad is balanced when all three of the relations are positive or when two of the relations are negative and one is positive" (Heider 1958, p. 202). When only two relations in the triad are positive, imbalance is said to characterize the structure. While Heider tends to define as imbalanced a triad which has three negative relations, he admits that such structures are ambiguous (1958, p. 203). According to the above definition of balance, the following illustrations represent balanced structures: "Bill admires something he owns"; "Joe likes the bicycle which Jim, his friend, bought"; "Al dislikes Art; Al opposes U.S. policy in Vietnam, while Art endorses it."

When a state of imbalance exists, balance may be attained by changing either sentiment relations or unit relations or both. When incomplete structures exist, new relations will be formed according to the principle of balance. If Bill likes Joe and Al, who don't know one another, he might want to bring them together. If Art likes Ann, he will wish that Ann like him. Incomplete structures are completed according to the principle of *symmetry* in the case of the dyad—that is, the sentiment that exists recruits a sentiment of the same sign. In the triad, completion may often occur according to the principle of *transitivity*—that is, if Jim likes Frank and Frank likes Sam, the relation between Jim and Sam will tend to be positive. But when Jim dislikes Frank and Frank dislikes Sam, then transitivity will not apply. According to Heider, given two negative relations in the triad, "balance can be obtained *either* when the third relation is positive or when it is negative, though there appears to be a preference for the positive alternative" (1958, p. 206).

Using the mathematical theory of directed graphs, Cartwright and Harary (1956) formalized Heider's concept of balance and extended it to cover structures larger than the triad and to distinguish between degrees of balance.

The bulk of evidence bearing on Heider's assumption about an underlying preference for balanced states comes from rating hypothetical situations for their pleasantness. For instance, using Heider's definition of balance, Jordan (1953) showed to his subjects statements of the following kind: "I dislike *O*; I like *X*; *O* has no sort of bond or relationship with *X*." The subject is "instructed to imagine himself in the situation playing the role of 'I' and then to rate it for experienced pleasantness or unpleasantness. . . ." In general, Jordan's results supported Heider's hypothesis, and other studies using the same technique confirmed these early findings (Morrissette 1958; Rodrigues 1966). In some experiments, instead of being asked to rate hypothetical situations for pleasantness, the subject is asked to predict a missing bond (Morrissette 1958) or to indicate which of the relations given he would most like to see changed (Rodrigues 1966). These studies, too, give general support to Heider's hypothesis. Similar evidence comes from experiments in which subjects learn hypothetical balanced and unbalanced structures (Zajonc & Burnstein 1965*a*; 1965*b*).

The principle of congruity. Our attitudes toward persons influence the way we interpret their actions and statements. The process of persuasion is characterized by this tendency, and the principle of congruity developed by Osgood and Tannenbaum (1955) is concerned with these problems. The elements of the theory of congruity are a *source*, a *concept*, and an *assertion* made by the source about the concept. When the subject's attitude toward two of these three elements are known, the principle of congruity can predict how these attitudes will change when a third element is introduced. Commonly, the known elements are attitudes toward the source and toward the concept. Thus, for instance, the subject's attitudes toward the *Chicago Tribune* and "abstract art" are measured, and predictions are made about the changes in his attitudes toward both after he finds out that the *Chicago Tribune* has made a positive (or negative) assertion about abstract art.

A state of equilibrium (congruity) prevails when the person's evaluations of the source and of the concept have the same scale values and when they are associated with each other by a positive assertion. A state of equilibrium also exists when these evaluations are exactly opposite and when the assertion connecting source and concept is negative. All other combinations of the three elements are not maximally congruent. When a configuration is in a state of incongruity, there will be pressures toward increased congruity. Although the principle of congruity is a special case of the principle of balance (Zajonc 1960*b*), it goes further because it is able to accommodate evaluations that vary in magnitude and because it is able to make predictions about the direction and magnitude of change. However, the numerical predictions do not always fit obtained results.

In a study by Tannenbaum (1956), attitudes toward some sources (e.g., labor leaders) and concepts (e.g., legalized gambling) were obtained for 405 college students. Five weeks later the subjects were given stories in which the various source–concept pairs were connected by negative or positive assertions. Afterward, the sources and the concepts were rated again by the subjects. The correlation between obtained and predicted attitude changes was 0.91. This coefficient shows that the basic equations are well able *to order* attitude data, which is no mean feat. But the *numerical* predictions are less accurate. For instance, in a study by Norris (1965), pronounced and significant differences were found between obtained and predicted results. When directional or order criteria, rather than magnitude of score values, are used in testing the theory, the principle of congruity fares better (e.g., Tannenbaum & Gengel 1966).

Cognitive dissonance. The theory of cognitive dissonance (Festinger 1957) has stimulated research in various areas of social psychology. It is stated in less formal terms than either the balance or the congruity theory. Cognitions can stand in a *relevant* or *irrelevant* relation to one another, and relevant cognitions can be either *consonant* or *dissonant* with respect to one another. The state of dissonance implies mutual inconsistency (logical and psychological): ". . . *two elements are in a dissonant relation if, considering these two alone, the obverse of one element would follow from the other*. To state it a bit more formally, *x* and *y* are dissonant if not-*x* follows from *y*" (*ibid.*, p. 13).

The entire theory of cognitive dissonance can be stated in a few propositions:

(1) Cognitive dissonance is a noxious state.

(2) The individual will attempt to reduce cognitive dissonance or to eliminate it, and he will act to avoid events that increase it.

(3) In the case of consonance the individual will act to avoid dissonance-producing events.

(4) The severity or the intensity of cognitive dissonance varies with the importance of the cognitions involved and the relative number of cognitions standing in dissonant relation to one another.

(5) The strength of the tendencies enumerated in (2) and (3) is a direct function of the severity of dissonance.

(6) Cognitive dissonance can be reduced or eliminated only by adding new cognitions or by changing existing ones.

(7) The new cognitions may throw added weight

to one side, decreasing the proportion of cognitions which are dissonant.

(8) The added cognitions may change the importance of the cognitive elements that are in dissonant relation with one another.

(9) Cognitions may change so and may become less important or less contradictory with others.

(10) These processes may recruit other behaviors which have cognitive consequences favoring consonance, such as seeking new information.

Empirical work on dissonance theory can be divided into four areas of interest: postdecisional effects; insufficient justification; disconfirmation of expectancies; and exposure to information.

Postdecisional effects. By definition, every decision is followed by dissonance. Since decision involves a selection of one among alternatives, it necessarily entails forsaking the attractive features of the rejected alternative and accepting the negative features of the chosen alternative. The cognition that the chosen alternative has negative features is dissonant with the cognition that it had been chosen, and the cognition that the rejected alternative has some attractive features is dissonant with the cognition that it had been rejected. Dissonance, however, can be resolved by revoking the decision, reversing the decision, or re-evaluating the attractiveness of the alternatives. Revoking or reversing the decision is often impossible or very costly. Moreover, by revoking it, the individual must return to the state of predecision, which, of course, is itself a state of conflict and, hence, noxious. The third form of resolution is most common.

The typical experiment on postdecisional effects requires the subject to make a choice among a set of alternatives whose attractiveness is measured both before and after his decision. In the pioneering study by Brehm (1956), subjects rated eight products with the knowledge that they would receive one of them for taking part in the experiment. Following the initial preference rating, the subject was given the opportunity to choose between two of the eight products. Half of the subjects had to choose between two alternatives that received similar ratings (high dissonance), and half, between two alternatives that were rated farther apart (low dissonance). A control group was given no choice at all and received a gift chosen by the experimenter and equal in desirability to those in the experimental groups. Since the subjects' decisions could not be revoked or reversed, the only avenue of dissonance reduction was through the re-evaluation of the alternatives. Brehm found rather clear support for the hypotheses derived from dissonance

theory: (*a*) the chosen alternative increased in attractiveness following the choice; (*b*) the rejected alternative decreased in attractiveness following the choice; (*c*) both of these changes were more pronounced when the subjects chose among the products close on the preference-rating scales than among products farther apart; and (*d*) in the control group no changes in attractiveness of the received products occurred. Subsequent research has substantiated these findings, and it has further demonstrated that the extent to which the individual feels free in making the choice and the extent to which he feels responsible for it and committed to it enhance dissonance effects (Brehm & Cohen 1962). [See CONFLICT, *article on* PSYCHOLOGICAL ASPECTS; DECISION MAKING, *article on* PSYCHOLOGICAL ASPECTS.]

The "spreading apart" of choice alternatives which follows decision does not give unequivocal support to dissonance theory, because these effects can also be predicted by a self-actualization theory that assumes that the individual wants to think of himself as an intelligent decision maker and that he will distort the consequences of his decisions accordingly. If dissonance reduction is a significant positive incentive, however, it should be sought even when one's self-esteem is threatened. Thus, if the individual regards himself as a poor decision maker, dissonance theory, unlike self-actualization theory, predicts that instead of spreading apart, choice alternatives will be evaluated more homogeneously; since the individual believes he is unable to make wise decisions, he is also likely to believe that the alternative he has decided upon may be inferior to the ones that he has considered and rejected. These arguments were advanced by the Polish social psychologist Malewski (1962). An experiment similar to the original one by Brehm (1956)—except for the introduction of sociometric measures of self-esteem—confirmed Malewski's expectations. An independent study by Gerard, Blevans, and Malcolm (1964) in which self-esteem was manipulated experimentally provided strong support for Malewski's hypothesis.

In some cases the individual finds out only after having made a choice that the chosen object or course of action has undesirable consequences. A state of dissonance ensues, and processes aimed at its reduction are set in motion. An experiment by Aronson and Mills (1959) illustrates this paradigm. College girls were recruited to join a group discussing the psychology of sex. Joining the group, however, required as one condition a severe initiation process, consisting of an "embarrassment test."

Following the demanding test, the subject was allowed to listen in on the group she was about to join. Played to the subject, however, was a tape of an extremely dull discussion. The findings were consistent with the predictions of dissonance theory. Subjects who underwent a severe initiation evaluated the dull discussion and its participants more favorably than did subjects with mild initiation, a result recently substantiated by Gerard and Mathewson (1966).

Insufficient justification. One of the derivations of dissonance theory holds that when the individual finds himself engaged in behavior which is contrary to his convictions, beliefs, or principles or when he finds himself committed to action which promises no rewards, a state of dissonance will exist and the individual will attempt to reduce it in various ways. This assumption led Festinger and Carlsmith (1959) to design a study in which subjects were offered either $1 or $20 for telling a fellow student that a boring and tedious task they had just performed was quite interesting. When examined for their own judgments about the task the subjects who were offered the smaller reward expressed greater interest in the task than subjects offered the larger reward. The results were interpreted by assuming that $1 is an insufficient reward for the false statement, and hence, dissonance exists between the subject's knowledge that the task he just finished is extremely boring and his knowledge that he is nevertheless expressing great enthusiasm about it. One way to reduce this dissonance is to believe that the task wasn't really that boring.

In other experiments on insufficient justification, subjects are offered rewards for arguing against their convictions. The dissonance which exists between the individual's cognition that he believes one thing and the cognition that he is arguing for another is commonly resolved by changing his beliefs in the direction of the position advocated. It has generally been found that the magnitude of this change is an inverse function of the reward offered (e.g., Brehm & Cohen 1962). These results are the subject of lively controversy at this time (for a more complete review, see Zajonc 1967).

An interesting application of the insufficient-justification paradigm is in the area of aggression. An individual who punishes another when he knows him to be a decent fellow may experience dissonance, especially when there is little justification for the punishment. The general finding in this area is that as dissonance increases, post-aggression attitudes toward the victim become increasingly negative. [*See* Brock & Buss 1964; *see also* AGGRESSION.]

If, in the case of compliance, the individual bolsters justification by coming to accept and favor his actions, there should also be effects on these actions themselves. If a person commits himself, for a clearly insufficient reward or under obviously inadequate threat of punishment, to a boring or tedious task, he will come to like this task (Brehm & Cohen 1959). But if he likes this task, he should expend greater effort on it, perform it faster or better, persist at it longer, etc. These hypotheses, advanced by Weick (1964), are finding substantial support in current research. Weick has shown improvements on a concept-formation task given under conditions of low justification. Ferdinand (1965) found similar strong results on a rote-learning task.

Disconfirmed expectancies. When an individual develops expectancies about a given outcome only to discover that the outcome fails to materialize, a state of dissonance exists. Dissonance is further increased if as a result of these expectancies, the individual made a behavioral or attitudinal "investment" in the future outcome. A special and interesting case of disconfirmed expectancies obtains with respect to the individual's view of himself. Aronson and Carlsmith (1962) theorized that when the individual's expectations about his ability on a given task are in conflict with his actual performance, dissonance exists. If the individual is unable to adjust the evaluation of his own ability, his major means of dissonance reduction lies in distorting the evaluation of his performance or in modifying actual performance. He can distort the level of his performance by finding new standards of comparison, call it an accident, attribute his performance to causes independent of his ability, etc. Or he can adjust the performance itself. Aronson and Carlsmith carried out an experiment in which subjects were allowed to develop expectancies about their ability on an unfamiliar task. During the course of the task, some subjects found themselves performing much better than they expected and others, much poorer. When allowed to repeat that task, subjects adjusted their performances according to their expectancies. That is, those who expected to do well and found themselves doing poorly adjusted their performances upward, and—more important—those who expected to do poorly but found themselves doing exceptionally well, adjusted their performances downward.

Exposure to information. According to dissonance theory, postdecisional dissonance may be resolved by a re-evaluation of alternatives in favor of the chosen one. This re-evaluation can be enhanced if the individual can marshal support for it from his environment. For instance, an individual who purchased a car might seek out people who bought the same car; he might try to persuade his friends who are considering buying a car to make a similar purchase; he might demonstrate and display the attractive features of his newly purchased automobile to his friends; and, in general, he might actively seek out information which is favorable to the car he bought and negative to those he considered but rejected. But dissonance reduction will be impaired if the individual exposes himself to information which is favorable to the rejected alternative or unfavorable to the one he selected. In short, it is predicted that if dissonance exists, the individual will expose himself to information so as to reduce dissonance, and if dissonance does not exist, he will avoid dissonance-producing information.

In comparison with other areas, experimental evidence of the preference for supportive information and avoidance of discrepant information is generally weak. In reviewing this evidence, Freedman and Sears concluded that in "no way can the available evidence be said to support the contention that people seek out supportive information and avoid nonsupportive information" (1965, p. 90). In one of the earliest studies in this area (Brodbeck 1956), it was found that subjects exposed to material opposing their beliefs—and, thus, suffering dissonance—were more likely to seek out information from people sharing their beliefs than were subjects not exposed to counterattitudinal material. But a substantial number of subjects were willing to receive information discrepant with their beliefs. Similarly, Ehrlich, Guttman, Schonbach, and Mills (see Ehrlich et al. 1957) found that readership of advertisements by new-car buyers is greater for the car selected than for the cars considered but rejected. However, contrary to the prediction from dissonance theory, advertisements about cars rejected were read more often than those about cars *not considered at all.* Mills, Aronson, and Robinson (1959) allowed students to decide between two kinds of exams they were to take. Afterward the subjects chose between articles which favored or derogated their decision. When the articles were positive toward the two types of exams, the subjects preferred articles favoring their decision, but no difference was obtained for articles that emphasized negative features of the two types of exams. Rosen (1961) found similar results.

Failure to obtain evidence for the selective-exposure hypothesis is also reported in an area where dissonance experienced by the individual must be quite severe: smoking and its harmful effects on health. By definition, "the knowledge that smoking is conducive to lung cancer is dissonant with continuing to smoke" (Festinger 1957, p. 153). While smokers' attitudes and beliefs about cancer differ from those of nonsmokers and former smokers, the evidence of exposure to critical information by these two groups seems to be negative. Feather (1963) found that smokers do not seek out information which contradicts the relationship between smoking and lung cancer more than nonsmokers nor do they avoid more than nonsmokers information about the dangers of smoking. [*See* SMOKING.]

ROBERT B. ZAJONC

[*Directly related are the entries* ATTITUDES; COGNITIVE THEORY; STIMULATION DRIVES; SYSTEMS ANALYSIS, *article on* PSYCHOLOGICAL SYSTEMS. *Other relevant material may be found in* INFORMATION THEORY; HOMEOSTASIS; PERSUASION.]

BIBLIOGRAPHY

ABELSON, R. P.; and ROSENBERG, M. J. 1958 Symbolic Psycho-logic: A Model of Attitudinal Cognition. *Behavioral Science* 3:1–13.

ANDERSON, NORMAN H. 1962 Application of an Additive Model to Impression Formation. *Science* 138: 817–818.

ARONSON, ELLIOT; and CARLSMITH, J. MERRILL 1962 Performance Expectancy as a Determinant of Actual Performance. *Journal of Abnormal and Social Psychology* 65:178–182.

ARONSON, ELLIOT; and MILLS, JUDSON 1959 The Effect of Severity of Initiation on Liking for a Group. *Journal of Abnormal and Social Psychology* 59:177–181.

ASCH, SOLOMON E. 1946 Forming Impressions of Personality. *Journal of Abnormal and Social Psychology* 41:258–290.

BREHM, JACK W. 1956 Post-decision Changes in the Desirability of Alternatives. *Journal of Abnormal and Social Psychology* 52:384–389.

BREHM, JACK W.; and COHEN, ARTHUR R. 1959 Choice and Chance Relative Deprivation as Determinants of Cognitive Dissonance. *Journal of Abnormal and Social Psychology* 58:383–387.

BREHM, JACK W.; and COHEN, ARTHUR R. 1962 *Explorations in Cognitive Dissonance.* New York: Wiley.

BROCK, TIMOTHY C.; and BUSS, ARNOLD H. 1964 Effects of Justification for Aggression and Communication With the Victim on Post Aggression Dissonance. *Journal of Abnormal and Social Psychology* 68:403–412.

BRODBECK, MAY 1956 The Role of Small Groups in Mediating the Effects of Propaganda. *Journal of Abnormal and Social Psychology* 52:166–170.

CARTWRIGHT, DORWIN; and HARARY, FRANK 1956 Structural Balance: A Generalization of Heider's Theory. *Psychological Review* 63:277–293.

DE SOTO, CLINTON B. 1960 Learning a Social Structure. *Journal of Abnormal and Social Psychology* 60:417–421.

DE SOTO, CLINTON B.; and KUETHE, JAMES L. 1958 Perception of Mathematical Properties of Interpersonal Relations. *Perceptual and Motor Skills* 8:279–286.

DE SOTO, CLINTON B.; and KUETHE, JAMES L. 1959 Subjective Probabilities of Interpersonal Relationships.

Journal of Abnormal and Social Psychology 59:290–294.

EHRLICH, DANUTA et al. 1957 Post Decision Exposure to Relevant Information. *Journal of Abnormal and Social Psychology* 54:98–102.

FEATHER, N. T. 1963 Cognitive Dissonance, Sensitivity, and Evaluation. *Journal of Abnormal and Social Psychology* 66:157–163.

FELDMAN, SHEL (editor) 1966 *Cognitive Consistency: Nonrational Antecedents and Behavioral Consequents.* New York: Academic Press. → Contains articles evaluating the status of consistency theories and their relation to other areas in psychology.

FERDINAND, P. R. 1965 The Effect of Forced Compliance on Recognition. Unpublished manuscript.

FESTINGER, LEON 1957 *A Theory of Cognitive Dissonance.* Evanston, Ill.: Row, Peterson.

FESTINGER, LEON; and CARLSMITH, JAMES M. 1959 Cognitive Consequences of Forced Compliance. *Journal of Abnormal and Social Psychology* 58:203–210.

FISHBEIN, MARTIN; and HUNTER, RONDA 1964 Summation Versus Balance in Attitude Organization and Change. *Journal of Abnormal and Social Psychology* 69:505–510.

FREEDMAN, JONATHAN L.; and SEARS, DAVID O. 1965 Selective Exposure. Volume 2, pages 58–97 in L. Berkowitz (editor), *Advances in Experimental Social Psychology.* New York: Academic Press.

GERARD, HAROLD B.; BLEVANS, STEPHAN A.; and MALCOLM, THOMAS 1964 Self-evaluation and the Evaluation of Choice Alternatives. *Journal of Personality* 32:395–410.

GERARD, HAROLD B.; and MATHEWSON, GROVER C. 1966 The Effects of Severity of Initiation on Liking for a Group: A Replication. *Journal of Experimental Social Psychology* 2:278–287.

HARVEY, O. J.; HUNT, D. E.; and SCHRODER, H. M. 1961 *Conceptual Systems and Personality Organization.* New York: Wiley.

HEIDER, FRITZ 1944 Social Perception and Phenomenal Causality. *Psychological Review* 51:358–374.

HEIDER, FRITZ 1946 Attitudes and Cognitive Organization. *Journal of Psychology* 21:107–112.

HEIDER, FRITZ 1958 *The Psychology of Interpersonal Relations.* New York: Wiley.

JANIS, IRVING L.; and GILMORE, J. BERNARD 1965 The Influence of Incentive Conditions on the Success of Role Playing in Modifying Attitudes. *Journal of Personality and Social Psychology* 1:17–27.

JORDAN, NEHEMIAH 1953 Behavioral Forces That Are a Function of Attitudes and of Cognitive Organization. *Human Relations* 6:273–287.

KELLEY, GEORGE A. 1955 *The Psychology of Personal Constructs.* New York: Norton.

MALEWSKI, ANDRZEJ 1962 The Influence of Positive and Negative Self-evaluation on Post Decisional Dissonance. *Polish Sociological Bulletin* No. 3–4:39–49.

MANIS, MELVIN; GLEASON, TERRY C.; and DAWES, ROBYN M. 1966 The Evaluation of Complex Social Stimuli. *Journal of Personality and Social Psychology* 3:404–419.

MILLS, JUDSON; ARONSON, ELLIOT; and ROBINSON, HAL 1959 Selectivity in Exposure to Information. *Journal of Abnormal and Social Psychology* 59:250–253.

MORRISSETTE, JULIAN 1958 An Experimental Study of the Theory of Structural Balance. *Human Relations* 11:239–254.

NORRIS, ELEANOR L. 1965 Attitude Change as a Function of Open or Close-mindedness. *Journalism Quarterly* 42:571–575.

OSGOOD, CHARLES E.; and TANNENBAUM, PERCY H. 1955 The Principle of Congruity in the Prediction of Attitude Change. *Psychological Review* 62:42–55.

PEAK, HELEN 1958 Psychological Structure and Psychological Activity. *Psychological Review* 65:325–347.

RODRIGUES, A. 1966 The Psycho-logic of Interpersonal Relations. Ph.D. dissertation, Univ. of Michigan.

ROSEN, SIDNEY 1961 Post Decision Affinity for Incompatible Information. *Journal of Abnormal and Social Psychology* 63:188–190.

TANNENBAUM, PERCY H. 1956 Initial Attitude Toward Source and Concept as Factors in Attitude Change Through Communication. *Public Opinion Quarterly* 20:413–425.

TANNENBAUM, PERCY H.; and GENGEL, ROY W. 1966 Generalization of Attitude Change Through Congruity Principle Relationships. *Journal of Personality and Social Psychology* 3:299–304.

VERPLANCK, WILLIAM S. 1957 A Glossary of Some Terms Used in the Objective Science of Behavior. *Psychological Review* 64, no. 6 (Supplement), part 2.

WEICK, KARL E. 1964 Reduction of Cognitive Dissonance Through Task Enhancement and Effort Expenditure. *Journal of Abnormal and Social Psychology* 68:533–539.

ZAJONC, ROBERT B. 1960a The Process of Cognitive Tuning in Communication. *Journal of Abnormal and Social Psychology* 61:159–167.

ZAJONC, ROBERT B. 1960b The Concepts of Balance, Congruity, and Dissonance. *Public Opinion Quarterly* 24:280–296.

ZAJONC, ROBERT B. 1967 Cognitive Theories of Social Behavior. Unpublished manuscript.

ZAJONC, ROBERT B.; and BURNSTEIN, EUGENE 1965a The Learning of Balanced and Unbalanced Social Structures. *Journal of Personality* 33:153–163.

ZAJONC, ROBERT B.; and BURNSTEIN, EUGENE 1965b Structural Balance, Reciprocity, and Positivity as Sources of Cognitive Bias. *Journal of Personality* 33:570–583.